EIGHTH EDITION

1025#1

Business
UNIFORM COMMERCIAL CODE

Law
COMPREHENSIVE VOLUME

RONALD A. ANDERSON

Professor of Law and Government,
Drexel University

Member of the Pennsylvania and Philadelphia Bars

Coauthor of *Business Law Principles and Cases*, Fourth Edition

Author of *Anderson's Uniform Commercial Code;
Anderson's Uniform Commercial Code Legal Forms;
Government and Business*, Third Edition;
*Anderson's Pennsylvania Civil Practice;
Couch's Cyclopedia of Insurance Law* (Second Edition);
Wharton's Criminal Law, Procedure, and Evidence

Consulting Editor of the *Pennsylvania Law Encyclopedia*

WALTER A. KUMPF

Editor in Chief,
South-Western Publishing Company

Coauthor of *Business Law Principles and Cases*, Fourth Edition

SOUTH-WESTERN PUBLISHING CO.

Cincinnati   Chicago   Dallas
   Burlingame, Calif.   New Rochelle, N. Y.

L57

Library of Congress Catalog Card Number: 68-19616

6 H 3 2 1 0

Printed in the United States of America

Preface

The new, improved format of this Eighth Edition of BUSINESS LAW reflects the careful and comprehensive revision of its contents. Such a revision is necessary because the law that governs business transactions has been affected significantly by important changes that have occurred in recent years.

Rapid population growth and technological developments have resulted in a change in the nature of business transactions and in an increase in their number, scope, and speed. In 1960, however, only three states had recognized the need for modernizing several uniform statutes to conform to current business practices. Today the general acceptance of the Uniform Commercial Code has converted a hope into a reality. Not only does the Eighth Edition present a thorough Code treatment of several branches of business law (primarily commercial paper, sales, and secured transactions), but also an Appendix sets forth the complete official 1962 text of the Uniform Commercial Code.

Another important change has been the recognition of the effect of social forces and environmental factors on business law. This Eighth Edition continues to emphasize the social, economic, and moral forces that make the law. To the extent that the student is able to understand the purpose and logic of the law and to analyze law as the product of man striving for justice in society, he will have a greater insight into the law itself, the world in which he lives, the field of business, and the mind of man.

The very nature and structure of our legal system means that changes in the law occur through gradual evolutionary development. The pace of this change in recent years has quickened, however, to the extent that important trends often are not recognized by some treatises and other secondary sources. The materials in this edition incorporate changes that are reported only in recent court decisions.

Purposes

Each edition of BUSINESS LAW has presented a carefully documented treatment of the legal framework of business for beginning students on the collegiate level. The diverse interests of such students dictate a presentation of subject matter that will be meaningful in their lives as citizens, business managers and employees, engineers, doctors, lawyers, farmers, teachers, and public servants. The authors have drawn upon their combined experiences in law, business, and education to develop a text that is clear and concise without sacrificing accuracy.

Organization

BUSINESS LAW, Eighth Edition, consists of 62 chapters organized into 12 parts. Important changes in organization include the following:

(1) A newly organized Part I, Law and Society, consists of five chapters and a Prologue to Business Law, as follows:

Chapter 1—Nature of the Law

Chapter 2—Social Forces and the Law

Chapter 3—The Law of Torts

Chapter 4—Criminal Law

Chapter 5—Enforcement of the Law

Prologue—Business Law, An Introduction

A broader basis for the understanding of business law is made possible by the treatment of torts in Chapter 3 and criminal law in Chapter 4. These subjects, together with contract law, which is the principal concern of the book, constitute the three areas of the law that determine whether conduct is wrongful.

(2) A newly organized Part VII, Security Devices, is treated earlier, immediately following the discussion of sales. As a result, there is no break in the discussion of two closely related areas of subject matter that are based upon the Uniform Commercial Code. This part also includes chapters on guaranty and suretyship and on insurance.

Text

(1) Each chapter presents the basic principles of the subject with quotations from and references to adjudicated cases, the Restatements of the American Law Institute, and the uniform statutes. The Restatements deal with such subjects as contracts, agency, property, security, and torts. The Uniform Commercial Code and other uniform statutes or model acts pertain to such subjects as commercial paper, sales, secured transactions, documents of title, gifts to minors, aeronautics, fraudulent conveyances, partnerships, and business corporations.

(2) The material in this edition has been brought up to date through an examination of all professional publications in the field, of new federal legislation, and of all decisions of the federal courts and of the state supreme and intermediate appellate courts that have been reported since the last edition.

(3) Every statement in the text has been carefully researched and documented. Footnotes have been used wherever they might be helpful.

In the areas governed or affected by the Uniform Commercial Code, the subject matter is footnoted for the convenience of instructors and students who may wish to check the exact wording of the provisions of the Code in the Appendix.

(4) Basic areas of subject matter—such as social foundations, contracts, agency, commercial paper, sales, and property—are emphasized.

(5) Principles and rules of law are made meaningful by numerous illustrations and by examples that are adapted from actual cases. In this edition, there is a substantial increase in the number of case examples, many of which are new. In the 11 chapters of Part II—Contracts, for example, there are 40 percent more case examples than in the Seventh Edition, and more than two out of every three case examples are new.

(6) Unnecessary technicalities are omitted. Important new terms are carefully defined and explained when they are used for the first time.

(7) The materials are organized on a psychological, as well as a logical basis. For example, notes, drafts, and checks are discussed in separate chapters.

(8) The principles are presented in a self-outlining form. The importance of each heading is indicated by its position or indention, by the style of type, and usually by an identifying number or letter.

(9) Related subjects are treated in the same part, such as agency and employment in Part III; personal property and bailments (including carriers) in Part V; real property, leases, and mortgages in Part X.

(10) Illustrations of legal forms are limited to the simpler types of commercial paper. The value of illustrating other legal forms is doubtful because the wording and provisions vary in different states. Those forms in local use are best for instructional purposes in collegiate courses in business law.

Questions and Case Problems

A variety of end-of-chapter materials designed to facilitate the mastery of the text by the student is provided. These materials are of four types, as follows:

(1) A checklist of new legal terms introduced and defined in the chapter. Page numbers are provided for easy reference to the definitions in the text.

(2) A statement of principles of law for which the student is asked to state the specific social objective or objectives involved. In this way provision is made for a continuing student involvement in the application of the 15 specific social objectives of the law as presented in Chapter 2, Social Forces and the Law.

(3) Simple hypothetical problems that test the student's ability on the practical application of principles or rules. Many of these have been adapted from actual cases.

(4) Case problems with citations. More case problems are provided as compared with the Seventh Edition, many of which are new. For example, in Part II—Contracts, 80 percent more case problems are included and 80 percent of them are new. Adaptations of actual cases for use as problems constitute a challenge at a higher level in most instances by presenting unfamiliar sets of facts to which the appropriate principles must be applied.

Glossary

A feature of this Eighth Edition is an extensive glossary. Terms that have been included have been selected on the basis of their helpfulness to the beginning student of business law. The glossary supplements the terms that are defined, explained, and illustrated in the text and which can be located by reference to the index. Code definitions are included in this glossary.

Appendix

The appendix sets forth the complete, official 1962 text of the Uniform Commercial Code for the benefit of those wishing to pursue the subject more intensively.

Student Supplement

A correlating Student Supplement, includes for each of most chapters a one-page study guide, consisting of objective-type questions, and several case problems for which the student is required to state in his own words the principle or rule of law that applies. A number of instructors report improved results through the use of this supplement. A tested procedure is that of making the use of the supplement optional with students. A manual of answers to the objective study-guide questions is available, and copies are free in the quantity needed to supply the number of students involved.

Acknowledgments

Throughout the life of this publication, many instructors of business law have contributed to the production of a textbook that is truly a composite of a variety of teaching experiences. To them, the authors are greatly indebted. For this edition, the authors acknowledge particularly the assistance of Robert E. Kendrick, David Lipscomb College.

R.A.A.
W.A.K.

Contents

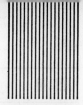

PART XII   GOVERNMENT AND BUSINESS

PART I

Law and Society

Chapter I

Nature of the Law

Law consists of the entire body of principles that govern conduct and the observance of which can be enforced in courts. The expression, "a law," is ordinarily used in connection with a statute enacted by a state legislature or the Congress of the United States, such as an act by the federal Congress to extend the benefits of old-age insurance. All of the principles that make up "law," however, are not "laws" adopted by legislative bodies. Legal principles are also found in national and state constitutions, local ordinances, court decisions, and rules of administrative agencies, such as the National Labor Relations Board.

Law has developed because man and society have wanted relationships between men, and between men and government, to conform to certain standards. Each person has desired to know what conduct he could reasonably expect from others, as well as what conduct others could reasonably expect from him, so that he could make decisions intelligently in terms of his legal rights and obligations. The rules adopted for this purpose have expressed the social, economic, and moral desires, standards, and aspirations of society. As democracy has expanded with the passing centuries, law has more truly expressed these desires of the community.

If there were no man-made law, no doubt many persons would be guided by principles of moral or natural law and choose to live and act much as they do today. Man would conduct himself in accordance with the dictates of his conscience, the precepts of right living that are a part of his religion, and the ethical concepts that are generally accepted in his community. Those who would choose to act otherwise, however, would constitute a serious problem for society. Man-made law is necessary to provide not only rules of conduct but also the machinery and procedures for enforcing right conduct, for punishing wrongful acts, and for settling disputes that arise.

1

An understanding of the law requires a knowledge of its forms, classifications, and sources.

Forms of the Law

Constitutional law includes the constitutions in force in the particular area or territory. In each state, two constitutions are in force—the state and the national constitutions. Federal regulation of business is based primarily on the clause of the Constitution of the United States authorizing Congress to regulate interstate and foreign commerce, and to a lesser extent on the clauses conferring the powers to tax, to borrow money, to adopt bankruptcy laws, to establish and regulate the currency, to fix standards of weights and measures, to operate the post office, to grant patents and copyrights, and to regulate the economy as a step in preparing for, waging, or recovering from the effects of war.[1]

Statutory law includes statutes adopted by the lawmakers. Each state has its own legislature and the United States has the Congress, both of which enact laws. In addition, every city, county, or other subdivision has some power to adopt ordinances which, within their sphere of operation, have the same binding effect as legislative acts.

Of great importance are the *administrative regulations* for business, such as rules of the Securities and Exchange Commission and the National Labor Relations Board. The regulations promulgated by national and state administrative agencies generally have the force of statute and are therefore part of "the law."

Law also includes principles that are expressed for the first time in court decisions. This is *case law*. For example, when a court must decide a new question or problem, its decision becomes a *precedent* and stands as the law for that particular problem in the future. This rule that a court decision becomes a precedent to be followed in similar cases is the *doctrine of stare decisis*.

In England, common or community law developed in the centuries following the Norman Conquest in 1066. This *common law* was a body of unwritten principles that were based on customs and usages of the community. These principles were recognized and enforced by the courts. By the time the colonies were founded in America, the English common law had become a definite, established body of principles and was brought over to the New World to become the basis for the law of the colonies and of virtually all of the states of the United States.

Law also includes treaties made by the United States, and proclamations and orders by the President of the United States or by other public officials.

---

[1] Art. 1, Sec. 8, Cl. 1-5, 7, 8, 11.

Classifications of Law

1 / Classification based upon subject matter. Law is classified for convenience in terms of the subject matter involved. Thus the area of law relating to contracts is contract law, the area relating to corporations is corporation law, and the area relating to rights on the seas is admiralty law.

2 / Substantive and procedural law. Law is sometimes classified in terms of its character as *substantive law,* which defines the substance of legal rights and liabilities, and as *procedural* or *adjective law,* which specifies the procedure that must be followed in enforcing those rights and liabilities.

3 / Classification based upon nature of the law. The great body of our law is *declaratory,* that is, it declares that a person has particular rights; if those rights are violated, the law specifies the procedures by which the injured party can enforce those rights or obtain damages for their breach. Some laws are *mandatory,* requiring the performance of an act, such as labeling drugs with a statement of their chemical composition and directions for use. Other laws are *prohibitive,* such as one prohibiting conspiracies and combinations in restraint of trade. Still other laws are *permissive,* such as a statute that permits proper persons to form a corporation.

4 / Public and private law. Law is classified as *public law* when it deals with the organization of government or with the relation of government to the individual. It includes, for example, *administrative law,* which deals with the mechanics by which government carries out its functions. Law which deals with the rights and liabilities between private individuals, corporations, partnerships, and other organizations is called *private law.*

5 / Law and equity. Law is frequently classified as being "law" or "equity." During the early centuries following the Norman Conquest, it was common for subjects of the English Crown to present to the King petitions requesting particular favors or relief that could not be obtained in the ordinary courts of law. The special relief granted by the chancellor, to whom the King referred such matters, was of such a nature as was dictated by principles of justice and equity. This body of principles was called *equity.* Today the same courts usually administer both "law" and "equity."

6 / Classification based upon historical sources. Law is sometimes classified in terms of its source as the *civil law,* which comes from the Roman civil law, and the *common law,* which is based upon the English common law or the common law that has developed in the states of the United States. The *ecclesiastical law,* which was the law enforced by the church courts, and the *law merchant,* which was the body of principles recognized by early English merchants, have been absorbed to a large extent by the common law.

During the centuries that the common law was developing in England, merchants of different nations, trading in all parts of the world, developed their own sets of rules to govern their business transactions. In many countries local authorities would permit the merchants to set up their own temporary courts to settle disputes. In the course of time the law courts of the various countries of Europe recognized and applied the same principles that the merchants followed. In England these laws of the merchants, constituting what came to be known as the law merchant, were accepted and enforced by the law courts by the end of the Eighteenth Century.

Much of our modern business law relating to commercial paper, insurance, credit transactions, and partnerships originally developed in the law merchant. To the common law we owe most of our business law relating to contracts, agency, property, bailments, carriers, torts, and crimes.

Business Law

Business law is not a separate branch of law but rather it includes the various laws that determine the rights and liabilities of persons taking part in business transactions, whether as individuals or as businessmen. Everyone should have some knowledge of business law. As a member of society and as a voting citizen, he should understand the basic principles of law that govern our economic activities. As a person living in a nation based on free enterprise, he should know the rights and remedies which the community, through law, makes available to those who engage in business transactions.

Everyone should know how to indorse a check, the effect of making an installment purchase, whether a written agreement is required in a given situation, whether he can object if a machine he purchases does not work as he believed it would. On the other hand, there are many points which a person not specially trained in the law should not endeavor to solve for himself. Much of the law is technical and complicated. College business-law training should provide such an understanding of the law that the student will know when a business legal problem is too difficult for him to determine for himself.

How to Find the Law

In order to determine what the law on a particular question or issue is, it may be necessary to examine (1) compilations of constitutions, treaties, statutes, executive orders, proclamations, and administrative regulations; (2) reports of state and federal court decisions; (3) digests of opinions; (4) treatises on the law; and (5) loose-leaf services.

1 / Compilations. In the consideration of a legal problem in business, it is necessary to determine whether the matter is affected or controlled by the

Constitution, national or state; by a national treaty; by an act of Congress or a state legislature, or by a city ordinance; by a decree or proclamation of the President of the United States, a governor, or a mayor; or by a regulation of a federal, state, or local administrative agency.

Each body or person that makes laws, regulations, or ordinances usually will compile and publish at the end of each year or session all of the matter that it has adopted. In addition to the periodical or annual volumes, it is common to compile all the treaties, statutes, regulations, or ordinances in separate volumes.

To illustrate, the federal Anti-Injunction Act may be cited as the Act of March 23, 1932, 47 Stat. 70, 29 U.S.C. Sections 101 et seq. This means that this law was enacted on March 23, 1932, and that this law can be found at page 70 in Volume 47 of the reports that contain all of the statutes adopted by the Congress. The second part of the citation, 29 U.S.C. Sections 101 et seq., means that in the collection of all of the federal statutes, which is known as the United States Code, the full text of the statute can be found in the sections of the 29th volume beginning with Section 101.

2 / Court decisions. For complicated or important legal cases or when an appeal is to be taken, a court will generally write an *opinion,* which explains why the court made the decision. Appellate courts as a rule write opinions. The great majority of these decisions, particularly in the case of the appellate courts, are collected and printed. In order to avoid confusion, the opinions of each court will ordinarily be printed in a separate set of reports, either by official reporters or private publishers.

In the reference "Pennoyer v. Neff, 95 U.S. 714, 24 L.Ed. 565," the first part states the names of the parties. It does not necessarily tell who was the plaintiff and who was the defendant. When an action is begun in a lower court, the first name is that of the plaintiff and the second name that of the defendant. When the case is appealed, generally the name of the person taking the appeal appears on the records of the higher court as the first one and that of the adverse party as the second. Sometimes, therefore, the original order of the names of the parties is reversed.

The balance of the reference consists of two citations. The first citation, 95 U.S. 714, means that the opinion which the court filed in the case of Pennoyer and Neff may be found on page 714 of the 95th volume of a series of books in which are printed officially the opinions of the United States Supreme Court. Sometimes the same opinion is printed in two different sets of volumes. In the example, 24 L.Ed. 565 means that in the 24th volume of another set of books, called *Lawyers' Edition,* of the United States Supreme Court Reports, the same opinion begins on page 565.

In opinions by a state court there are also generally two citations, as in the case of "Morrow v. Corbin, 122 Tex. 553, 62 S.W.2d 641." This means that the opinion in the lawsuit between Morrow and Corbin may be found in the 122d volume of the reports of the highest court of Texas, beginning on page 553; and also in Volume 62 of the *Southwestern Reporter,* Second Series, at page 641.

The West Publishing Company publishes a set of sectional reporters covering the entire United States. They are called sectional because each reporter, instead of being limited to a particular court or a particular state, covers the decisions of the courts of a particular section of the country. Thus the decisions of the courts of Arkansas, Kentucky, Missouri, Tennessee, and Texas are printed by the West Publishing Company as a group in a sectional reporter called the *Southwestern Reporter.*[2] Because of the large number of decisions involved, generally only the opinions of the state appellate courts are printed. A number of states[3] have discontinued publication of the opinions of their courts, and those opinions are now found only in the West reporters.

The reason for the "Second Series" in the Southwestern citation is that when there were 300 volumes in the original series, instead of calling the next volume 301, the publisher called it Volume 1, Second Series. Thus 62 S.W.2d Series really means the 362d volume of the *Southwestern Reporter.* Six to eight volumes appear in a year for each geographic section.

In addition to these state reporters, the West Publishing Company publishes a *Federal Supplement,* which primarily reports the opinions of the Federal District Courts; the *Federal Reporter,* which primarily reports the decisions of the United States Courts of Appeal; and the *Supreme Court Reporter,* which reports the decisions of the United States Supreme Court. The Supreme Court decisions are also reported in a separate set called the *Lawyers' Edition,* published by the Lawyers Co-operative Publishing Company.

The reports published by the West Publishing Company and Lawyers Co-operative Publishing Company are unofficial reports, while those bearing the name or abbreviation of the United States or of a state, such as "95 U.S.

---

[2] The sectional reports are: Atlantic—A. (Connecticut, Delaware, District of Columbia, Maine, Maryland, New Hampshire, New Jersey, Pennsylvania, Rhode Island, Vermont); Northeastern—N.E. (Illinois, Indiana, Massachusetts, New York, Ohio); Northwestern—N.W. (Iowa, Michigan, Minnesota, Nebraska, North Dakota, South Dakota, Wisconsin); Pacific—P. (Alaska, Arizona, California, Colorado, Hawaii, Idaho, Kansas, Montana, Nevada, New Mexico, Oklahoma, Oregon, Utah, Washington, Wyoming); Southeastern—S.E. (Georgia, North Carolina, South Carolina, Virginia, West Virginia); Southwestern—S.W. (Arkansas, Kentucky, Missouri, Tennessee, Texas); and Southern—So. (Alabama, Florida, Louisiana, Mississippi). There is also a special New York State reporter known as the New York Supplement and a special California State reporter known as the California Reporter.

[3] For example, Alaska, Florida, Kentucky, Mississippi, Missouri, North Dakota, Oklahoma, Texas, and Wyoming.

714" or "122 Tex. 553" are official reports. This means that in the case of the latter, the particular court, such as the United States Supreme Court, has officially authorized that its decisions be printed and that by order of statute such official printing is made. In the case of the unofficial reporters, the publisher prints the decisions of a court on its own initiative. Such opinions are part of the public domain and not subject to any copyright restriction.

3 / Digests of opinions. The reports of court decisions are useful only if one has the citation, that is, the name of the book and the page number of the opinion he is seeking. For this reason, digests of the decisions have been prepared. These digests organize the entire field of law under major headings, which are then arranged in alphabetical order. Under each heading, such as "Contracts," the subject is divided into the different questions that can arise with respect to that field. A master outline is thus created on the subject. This outline includes short paragraphs describing what each case holds and giving its citation.

4 / Treatises and restatements. Very helpful in finding a case or a statute are the treatises on the law. These may be special books, each written by an author on a particular subject, such as *Williston on Contracts, Bogert on Trusts, Fletcher on Corporations;* or they may be general encyclopedias, as in the case of *American Jurisprudence, American Jurisprudence Second,* and *Corpus Juris Secundum.*

Another type of treatise is found in the restatements of the law prepared by the American Law Institute. Each restatement consists of one or more volumes devoted to a particular phase of the law, such as the *Restatement of the Law of Contracts, Restatement of the Law of Agency,* and *Restatement of the Law of Property*. In each restatement the American Law Institute, acting through special committees of judges, lawyers, and professors of law, has set forth what the law is; and in many areas where there is no law or the present rule is regarded as unsatisfactory, the restatement specifies what the Institute deems to be the desirable rule.

5 / Loose-leaf services. A number of private publishers, notably Commerce Clearing House and Prentice-Hall, publish loose-leaf books devoted to particular branches of the law. Periodically the publisher sends to the purchaser a number of pages that set forth any decision, regulation, or statute made or adopted since the prior set of pages was prepared. Such services are unofficial.

Uniform Commercial Code

To secure uniformity as far as possible, the National Conference of Commissioners on Uniform State Laws, including representatives from all the states, has drafted statutes on various business subjects for adoption by the states. The uniform laws that had been most widely adopted by the states pertained to commercial paper, warehouse receipts, stock transfers, sales, bills of lading, and partnerships. The law on most of these subjects is now regulated by the Uniform Commercial Code as proposed by the National Conference of Commissioners on Uniform State Laws and the American Law Institute. Specifically the Code regulates the fields of sales of goods; commercial paper, such as checks; secured transactions in personal property; and particular aspects of banking, letters of credit, warehouse receipts, bills of lading, and investment securities.

QUESTIONS AND PROBLEMS

1. Checklist of legal terms:
   (a) constitutional law, statutory law, administrative regulations (page 2)
   (b) case law, precedent, doctrine of stare decisis (2)
   (c) substantive law, procedural law (3)
   (d) declaratory law, mandatory law, prohibitive law, permissive law (3)
   (e) public law, administrative law, private law (3)
   (f) equity (3)
   (g) civil law (3), common law (2,3), ecclesiastical law (3)
   (h) law merchant (3), business law (4)

2. (a) What is law?
   (b) Why has law developed?
   (c) What is the difference between law and a "law"?

3. A state statute provides that no person shall be allowed to work in specified occupations for more than eight hours a day.
   (a) Is this a substantive or procedural law?
   (b) Is this a declaratory, mandatory, permissive, or prohibitive law?

4. Explain each of the following citations:
   (a) Murphy v. Williamson, 180 Iowa 291, 163 N.W. 211.
   (b) New York Central Railroad Company v. White, 243 U.S. 188, 61 L.Ed. 667.
   (c) Rice v. Schmid, 18 Cal.2d 382, 115 P.2d 498.
   (d) United States v. Wm. H. Rorer, Inc., 27 F.S. 671.

5. (a) In what sectional reporter are the opinions of the highest court of your state included?
   (b) Are all the states adjacent to your state covered by the same sectional reporter?

6. (a) What is the function of the National Conference of Commissioners on Uniform State Laws?
   (b) How successfully has the Conference performed this function?

7. What is the Uniform Commercial Code?

Chapter 2

Social Forces and the Law

The purpose of law in its broadest sense is to provide order, stability, and justice. Thus viewed, the law is the crystallization into relatively fixed rules of those patterns of conduct which society believes desirable. That is, according to the social morality of the community, certain conduct is proper and should be allowed or required and certain conduct is improper and should be prohibited. In short, law is a social institution; it is not an end unto itself but is an instrumentality for obtaining social justice.

Law as Social Justice

Many factors and institutions have made their contribution in the molding of concepts of justice. Home and school training, religion, enlightened self-interest, social and business groups, and the various media of modern communication and entertainment all play a part. For example, various organizations, such as chambers of commerce, better business bureaus, informal groups of businessmen, trade groups, and conferences, have emphasized what is ethical in business by stressing fair competition and service to the community. In turn, these organizations and groups have helped to bring about the adoption of statutes that modify the law to reflect the changed business ethics.

It would be a mistake, however, to assume that justice is a universal value which means the same to all people in all ages. Each individual's conception of justice varies in terms of his personality, his training, and his social and economic position. Justice has different meanings to the employer and the employee, to the millionaire and the pauper, to the industrial worker and the farmer, to the retired person and the young married adult, to the progressive and the conservative, or to the professor and the student! For this reason special interest groups attempt to modify the law so that it will be more favorable to the members of those groups. To the extent that such modifications are gained at the expense of the rights of the members of other groups, the law fails in its purpose of achieving justice for all. This is but one evidence of the fact that the law is no better than the human beings who make it, interpret it, and enforce it. Absolute justice is unattainable by human beings, but that is no reason why society should ever relent in its efforts to attain as high a level of substantial justice as is humanly possible.

When we consider a rule of law only as it exists today, it may appear just as arbitrary as the rule that twelve inches make one foot; arbitrary in the sense that there is no reason why it could not be ten inches or fourteen, or any other number. The reason may be that we fail to understand the purpose of the law; or we may not be sufficiently familiar with all sides of the problem to recognize that the rule is just in the sense that it is the best rule that could be devised under the circumstances.

Specific Objectives of the Law

The objectives of the Constitution of the United States are included in the preamble, and important statutes frequently include a statement of their objectives. In many instances, however, the objective of the law is not stated or it is expressed in very general terms. Whether stated or not, each law has an objective; and it is helpful in understanding the nature and purpose of the law to know what the objectives of our various laws are.

In the following enumeration the more important specific objectives of the law are discussed against the background of our understanding of the general objective of creating, maintaining, and restoring order, stability, and justice.

1 / Protection of the state. A number of laws are designed to protect the existing governments, both state and national. Laws condemning treason, sedition, and subversive practices are examples of society taking measures to preserve governmental systems. Less dramatic are the laws that impose taxes to provide for the support of those governments and that provide for compulsory military service to protect them from enemy aliens.

2 / Protection of public health, safety, and morals. The law seeks to protect the public health, safety, and morals in many ways. Laws relating to quarantine, food inspection, and compulsory vaccination are designed to protect the public health. Laws regulating the speed on the highway and those requiring fire escapes or guard devices around moving parts of factory machinery protect safety. Laws prohibiting the sale of liquor to minors and those prohibiting obscenity protect the morals of the public.

3 / Personal protection. At an early date laws were developed to protect the individual from being injured or killed. The field of criminal law is devoted to a large extent to the protection of the person.

Case Example

Facts: Woods was beaten to death in his apartment by his roommates. The next morning, Larrimore, his employer, found his body and notified the police that Woods was either dead or dying. The police entered the apartment without a search warrant, found Woods dead, and took and removed evidence and instruments of the crime. When Patrick was prosecuted for the murder, he objected to the use of this evidence on the ground that it had been obtained without a search warrant.

Decision: The evidence was properly admitted because a search warrant was unnecessary under the circumstances. Here a human life was apparently hanging in the balance when Larrimore called for the police. The public policy in favor of preserving life is superior to the interest of privacy that is protected from search and seizure without a warrant. The entry without a warrant was lawful; and when once inside the apartment it was apparent that a crime had been committed, it was proper to collect relevant evidence. (Patrick v. State, [Del.] 227 A.2d 486)

Under civil law a suit can be brought also to recover damages for the harm done by criminal acts. For example, a grossly negligent driver of a car who injures a pedestrian is subject to a penalty imposed by the state in the form of imprisonment or a fine, or both. He is also liable to the injured person for the payment of damages, which may include not only medical and hospital costs but also loss of time from work and mental anguish. In time, the protection of personal rights has broadened to include protection of reputation and privacy [1] and to protect contracts from malicious interference by outsiders.

4 / Property protection. Just as both criminal and civil laws have been developed to protect the individual's physical well-being, such laws also have been developed to protect one's property from damage, destruction, and other harmful acts. If a thief steals an automobile, he is liable civilly to the owner of the automobile for its value and is criminally responsible to the state for the crime that he has thus committed.

5 / Title protection. Because of the importance of ownership of property, one of the objectives of the law has been to protect the title of an owner to his property so that he remains the owner until it is clearly proved that he has transferred the title to someone else. Thus, if property is stolen, the true owner may recover it from the thief. He may even recover his property from a person who purchased it in good faith from the thief without any knowledge that the goods had been stolen.

6 / Freedom of personal action. In the course of the passing centuries, man became concerned with what he himself could do as well as with protection against what others might do to him or his property. At one time he was increasingly concerned with the restrictions that the monarchs were placing upon his freedom to act. This became particularly pronounced in the era before the American Revolution when the rulers of Europe, acting under the mercantilist theory, regulated the economy to benefit themselves.

---

[1] *Korn* v. *Rennison,* 21 Conn.S. 400, 156 A.2d 476.

In the Anglo-American stream of history, man's desires for freedom from political domination gave rise to the American Revolution, and the desire for freedom from economic domination gave rise to the free-enterprise philosophy. Today we find freedom as the dominant element in the constitutional provisions for the protection of freedom of religion, press, and speech and also in such laws as those against trusts or business combinations in restraint of trade by others.

This right of freedom of personal action, however, cannot be exercised by one person in such a way that it interferes to an unreasonable extent with the rights of others. Freedom of speech, for example, does not mean freedom to speak or write a malicious, false statement about another person's character. In effect, this means that one person's freedom of speech must be balanced with another person's right to be free from defamation of character or reputation.

7 / Freedom of use of property. Closely related to the objective of protection of freedom of action is that of protecting the freedom of the use of property. Freedom in the use of property is protected by prohibiting, restraining, or penalizing acts of others that would hamper the reasonable use of property by its owner.

> **Facts:** The Great Atlantic & Pacific Tea Co. owned a building several hundred feet away from one of the boundaries of the grounds for the New York World's Fair of 1964. On the top of the building, approximately 110 feet above the ground, was a red neon A & P sign approximately 250 feet long with letters 10 feet high. The World's Fair placed artificial trees and shrubbery along the boundary line to hide the electric sign, which the Fair claimed was generally unesthetic and interfered with a fountain and electric light display of the Fair. A & P sued to enjoin the Fair from hiding its sign in this manner.

> **Decision:** Injunction refused. The fact that an occupier's use of his land causes harm to the owner of neighboring land is not controlling. Here the use by the Fair of its land was a reasonable use to protect its exhibits from outside interference. The fact that it was advantageous to A & P that the Fair make no use of its land did not justify the conclusion that the use which the Fair made was unreasonable and subject to injunction as a nuisance. (Great A & P Tea Co. v. New York World's Fair, 42 Misc.2d 855, 249 N.Y.S.2d 256)

Absolute freedom would permit its owner to make any use he chose of his property—even in a way that would harm others, to sell it at any price he desired, or to make any disposition of it that he wished. Such freedom is not recognized today, for everywhere we find some limitation of the right of the owner of property to do as he pleases with it.

The law prohibits an owner from using his property in such a way as to injure another or another's property. Further, zoning laws may limit the use of his land. Building restrictions in a deed may restrict the type of building that the owner may construct on his land. Fire laws and building codes may specify details of construction of his building. Labor laws may require that he equip a business building with safety devices.

8 / Enforcement of intent. The law usually seeks to enforce the expressed intention of a party to a contract. This objective is closely related to the concept that the law seeks to protect the individual's freedom of action. For example, if a person provides by his will for the distribution of his property when he dies, the law will generally allow the property to pass to the persons intended by the deceased owner. The law will likewise seek to carry out the intention of the parties to a business transaction. To illustrate, if you and an electrician agree that he shall rewire your house for $200, the law will ordinarily enforce that contract because that is what was intended by both parties.

The extent to which the intent of one person or of several persons will be carried out has certain limitations. Sometimes the intent is not effective unless it is manifested by a particular formality. For example, a deceased person may have intended that his friend should receive his house, but in most states that intent must be shown by a written will signed by the deceased owner. Likewise, in some cases the intent of the parties may not be carried out because the law regards the purpose of the intent as illegal or otherwise improper.

9 / Protection from exploitation, fraud, and oppression. Many rules of law have developed in the courts and many statutes have been enacted to protect certain groups or individuals from exploitation by others. Thus, the law has developed that a minor (a person under legal age) can set aside his contract, subject to certain exceptions, in order to give the minor an opportunity to avoid a bad bargain.

Persons who buy food that is packed in tin cans are given certain rights against the seller and the manufacturer. Since they cannot see the contents, buyers of such products need special protection against unscrupulous canners who would pack improper foods. The consumer is also protected by laws against adulteration and poisons in foods, drugs, and household products because he would ordinarily be unable to take care of himself. Laws prohibiting unfair competition and discrimination, both economical and social, are also designed to protect from oppression.

For the purpose of brevity "oppression" is here used to include not only conscious wrongdoing by another but also cases of hardship or misfortune where the consequences to the victim may be regarded as extreme or oppressive.[2]

10 / Furtherance of trade. Society may seek to further trade in a variety of ways, as by establishing a currency as a medium of payment; by recognizing and giving legal effect to installment sales; by adopting special rules for checks, notes, and similar instruments so that they can be widely used as credit devices and substitutes for money; or by enacting laws to mitigate the harmful effects of alternating periods of depression and inflation.

Laws that have been considered in connection with other objectives may also serve to further trade. For example, laws protecting against unfair competition have this objective, as well as the objective of protecting certain classes from exploitation by others.

11 / Creditor protection. Society seeks to protect the rights of creditors and to protect them from dishonest or fraudulent acts of debtors. Initially creditors are protected by the law which declares that contracts are binding and which provides the machinery for the enforcement of contracts, and by the provision of the federal Constitution that prohibits states from impairing the obligation of contracts. Further, creditors may compel a debtor to come into bankruptcy in order to settle his debts as far as his property permits. If the debtor has concealed his property or transferred it to a friend in order to hide it from his creditors, the law permits the creditors to claim the property for the payment of the debts due them.

12 / Debtor rehabilitation. Society has come to regard it as unsound that debtors should be ruined forever by the burden of their debts. The passing centuries have seen the debtor's prison abolished. Bankruptcy laws have been adopted to provide the debtor with a means of settling his debts as best he can and then starting upon a new economic life. In times of widespread depression the same objective has been served by special laws that prohibit the foreclosure of mortgages and regulate the amount of the judgments that can be entered against mortgage debtors.

13 / Stability. Stability is particularly important in business transactions. When you buy a house, for example, you not only want to know the exact meaning of the transaction under today's law but you also hope that the transaction will have the same meaning in the future. When the businessman invests money, he desires that the law will remain the same as it was when he acted.

Because of the objective of stability, the courts will ordinarily follow former decisions unless there is some valid reason to depart from them. When

---

[2] *Falcone* v. *Middlesex County Medical Society,* 34 N.J. 582, 170 A.2d 791.

no former case directly bears on the point involved, the desire for stability will influence the courts to reach a decision that is a logical extension of some former decision or which follows a former decision by analogy rather than to strike off on a fresh path and to reach a decision unrelated to the past. Thus stability is achieved through continuity based on the assumption that many problems of today and tomorrow will be basically the same as those that were settled yesterday.

14 / Flexibility. If stability were an absolute objective of the law, the cause of justice would often be thwarted. The reason that originally gave rise to a rule of law may have ceased to exist. The rule then appears unjust because it reflects a concept of justice that is outmoded or obsolete. For example, a rule of law, such as capital punishment, which one age believes just may be condemned by another age as unjust. We must not lose sight of the fact that the rule of law under question was created to further the sense of social justice existing at that time; but our concepts of justice may change.

The law itself may be flexible in that it makes provision for changes in rules to meet situations that cannot be anticipated or for which an explicit set of rules cannot be developed satisfactorily in advance. Our constitutions state the procedures for their amendment. Such changes in constitutional law are purposely made difficult in order to serve the objective of stability, but they are possible when the need for change is generally recognized by the people of the state or nation.

Changes by legislative action in federal and state statutes and local ordinances are relatively easier to make. Furthermore, some statutes recognize the impossibility of laying down in advance a hard-and-fast rule that will do justice in all cases. The typical modern statute, particularly in the field of regulation of business and enterprise, will therefore contain "escape clauses" by which a person can escape from the operation of the statute under certain circumstances. Thus a rent control law may impose a rent ceiling, that is, a maximum above which landlords cannot charge, but it may also authorize a greater charge when special circumstances make it just to allow such exception, as when the landlord has made expensive repairs to the property or when his taxes have increased materially.

The rule of law may be stated in terms of what a reasonable or prudent man would do. Thus, whether you are negligent in driving your automobile is determined in court by whether you exercised the same degree of care that a prudent man would have exercised had he been driving your car under the circumstances in question. This is a vague and variable standard as to how you must drive your car, but it is the only standard that is practical. The alternative would be a detailed motor code specifying how you should drive your car under every possible situation that might arise: a code that obviously could not foresee every possible situation and which certainly would be too long for any driver to know in every detail by memory.

15 / Practical expediency. Frequently the law is influenced by what is practical and expedient in the situation. In some of these situations, the law will strive to make its rules fit the business practices of society. For example, a signature is frequently regarded by the law as including a stamping, printing, or typewriting of a name, in recognition of the business practice of "signing" letters and other instruments by mechanical means. A requirement of a handwritten signature would impose a burden on business that would not be practically expedient.

The concept of practical expediency may also apply when the courts are influenced by the effect upon the courts themselves of the adoption of a particular rule of law. For example, courts will not ordinarily render advisory opinions, that is, give legal advice to people when there is no real lawsuit. It would not be practical for courts to perform that function, for, if they did, the courts would be overburdened with "advice" work.

Conflicting Objectives

As we have seen, the specific objectives of the law sometimes conflict with each other. When this is true, the problem is one of social policy, which in turn means a weighing of social, economic, and moral forces to determine which objective should be furthered. Thus we find a conflict at times between the objectives of the state seeking protection from the conduct of individuals or groups and the objective of freedom of action by those individuals and groups.[8]

Considering more in detail the interplay and conflict of objectives, let us turn to rent control. If we wish to protect the freedom of the use of property, we will then allow the landlord to rent his property in any condition he chooses and at any price he chooses. Underlying this decision will be our belief that if his property is not in good condition, the competition of other landlords will force him to improve his property or to reduce his rent. An examination of the facts, however, may show such a serious housing shortage that property in poor condition can be rented at a high price. Under such circumstances we cannot depend upon the forces of supply and demand to make the landlord improve his property or reduce his rent. Society therefore adopts a law regulating the condition of leased property or specifying the maximum rents which landlords may charge. That is, society seeks to protect the tenant from exploitation by the landlord. By adopting such a control law, society is sacrificing the objective of protecting the free-

---

[8] *United States* v. *Bonanno,* [D.C. S.D. N.Y.] 180 F.S. 71.

dom of the use of property by the landlord to the objective of protecting the tenant from the landlord's exploitation.

As another example, the objective of protecting title may conflict with the objective of furthering trade. Consider again the example of the stolen property that was sold by the thief to one who purchased it for value and in good faith, without reason to know that the goods had been stolen. If we are to further the objective of protecting the title to the property, we will conclude that the owner can recover the property from the innocent purchaser. This rule, however, will discourage trade, for people will be less willing to buy goods if they run the risk that the goods were stolen and may have to be surrendered. If we instead think only of taking steps to encourage buying and selling, we will hold that the buyer takes a good title because he acted in good faith and paid value. If we do this, we then destroy the title of the original owner and obviously abandon our objective of protecting title to property. As a general rule, society has followed the objective of protecting title. In some instances, however, the objective of furthering trade is adopted by statute, and the buyer is given good title as in certain cases of the purchaser of commercial paper (notes, drafts, and checks) or of the purchaser from a regular dealer in other people's goods.

Law as an Evolutionary Process

As of any one minute, or even over a number of years, law appears to be static and, in fact, a number of legal principles have remained the same over the centuries. But many rules of law have changed and are changing.

Facts: Culver was given a life sentence under a habitual criminal statute on the basis that he was a fourth offender. After he had been in prison seven years, it was determined that there were only two prior offenses and that the life sentence was therefore illegal. The court then entered the correct sentence. Culver appealed on the ground that the court had no authority to correct the illegal sentence and therefore he must be allowed to go free.

Decision: In prior centuries when punishments were extreme, law was interpreted with great strictness to enable a defendant to go free. Under this philosophy, the common-law rule was that the court had only one chance to impose the sentence and, if it made a mistake, it could not correct the sentence but was required to free the defendant. In current times, both the treatment of persons accused of crime and the rules of law have been changed to favor the accused so that there is no longer any necessity for leaning over backward to protect the convicted. Hence, a convicted criminal will not be released because of the chance circumstance that the court had imposed an improper sentence. The protection of society requires that the proper sentence be imposed, and the court has the power to do so. (New Jersey v. Culver, 23 N.J. 495, 129 A.2d 715)

The law changes as society seeks to improve its existing rules in order to attain more closely the standards of justice and morality. This change in the law, in turn, may be a reflection of a social and economic change. For example, the law governing relations between landlord and tenant originated in the era of feudalism in which the owner of the land was economically, socially, and politically dominant. The law at that time, therefore, reflected his desires and was designed primarily to protect his interests. In modern society the owner of the land no longer holds that position of dominance; and the law has changed to conform to new concepts of justice and fairness, and greater recognition and protection are given to the rights and interests of the tenant.

Let us consider another example of this type of change. When the economy was patterned on a local community unit in which everyone knew each other and each other's product, the concept of "let the buyer beware" expressed a proper basis on which to conduct business. Much of the early law of the sales of goods was predicated on this philosophy. In today's economy, however, with its emphasis on interstate, national, and even international activities, the buyer has little or no direct contact with the manufacturer or seller, and the packaging of articles makes their presale examination impossible. Under the circumstances the consumer must rely on the integrity of others to an increasing degree. Gradually practices that were tolerated and even approved in an earlier era have been condemned, and the law has changed to protect the buyer by warranties when his own caution can no longer protect him.

Moreover, new principles of law are being developed to meet the new situations that have arisen. Every new invention and every new business practice introduces a number of situations for which there is no satisfactory rule of law. For example, how could there have been a law governing the liability of a food canner to the consumer before canning was invented? How could there have been a law relating to stocks and bonds before those instruments came into existence? How could there have been law with respect to the liability of radio and television broadcasters before such methods of communication were developed? This pattern of change will continue as long as man strives for better ways to achieve his desires.

Law as a Synthesis

Law as a synthesis may be illustrated by the law relating to contracts for the sale of a house. Originally such a contract could be oral, that is, merely spoken words with nothing in writing to prove that there was such a contract. Of course, there was the practical question of proof, that is, whether the jury would believe that there was such a contract, but no rule said that the contract must be in writing. This situation made it possible for a witness in court to swear falsely that Jones had agreed to sell his house for a specified sum. Even though Jones had not made such an agreement, the jury might believe the false witness, and Jones would be required to give up his house on terms to which he had not agreed. To help prevent such a miscarriage of justice, a statute was passed in England in 1677 which declared that contracts for the sale of houses had to be in writing.

This law ended the evil of persons lying that there was an oral agreement for the sale of a house, but was justice finally achieved? Not always, for cases arose in which Jones did in fact make an oral agreement to sell his land to Smith. Smith would take possession of the land and would make valuable improvements at great expense and effort, and then Jones would have Smith thrown off the land. Smith would defend on the ground that Jones had orally agreed to sell the land to him. Jones would then say, "Where is the writing that the statute requires?" To this Smith could only reply that there was no writing. No writing meant no valid agreement and therefore Smith lost the land, leaving Jones with the land and all the improvements that Smith had made, without Smith getting one penny for his trouble. That certainly was not just. What then?

Gradually the law courts developed the rule that in spite of the fact that the statute required a writing, the court would enforce an oral contract for the sale of land when the buyer had gone into possession and made valuable improvements of such a nature that it would be difficult to determine what amount of money would be required to make up the loss if he were to be put off the land.

Thus, the law passed through three stages: (1) The original concept that all land contracts could be oral. Because the perjury evil arose under this rule of law, society swung to (2) the opposite rule that no such contract could be oral. This rule gave rise to the hardship case of the honest buyer under an oral contract who made extensive improvements. The law then swung, not back to the original rule, but to (3) a middle position, combining both (1) and (2), that is combining the element of the written requirement as to the ordinary transaction but allowing oral contracts in the special cases to prevent hardship.

This example is also interesting because it shows the way in which the courts "amend" the law by decision. The flat requirement of the statute was "eroded" by decisions and by exceptions created by the courts in the interest of furthering justice.

A Final Word

As you study the various rules of law in the chapters that follow, consider each rule in relationship to its social, economic, and moral background. Try to determine the particular objective of each important rule. To the extent that you are able to analyze law as the product of man striving for justice in society, you will have a greater insight into the law itself, the world in which you live, the field of business, and the mind of man.

QUESTIONS AND PROBLEMS

1. What is the general purpose of law?
2. What factors and institutions have contributed to the development of concepts of justice?
3. Why is absolute justice unattainable?
4. Give an example or illustration of each of the 15 specific objectives of the law.
5. Of the specific objectives of the law, which do you consider the most important?
6. What is the difference between the objectives of property protection and title protection?
7. (a) Are creditor protection and debtor rehabilitation conflicting specific objectives of the law?
   (b) When specific objectives of the law conflict in a given situation, which objective prevails?
8. What conflicts of specific objectives of the law are illustrated in the following case examples?
   (a) *Patrick* v. *State* (pages 10-11).
   (b) *Great A & P Tea Co.* v. *New York World's Fair* (page 12).
9. (a) How can the law be dynamic if stability is one of the specific objectives of law?
   (b) How do some statutes provide for "built-in" flexibility?
10. Sometimes the development of the law seems to follow a zig-zag course. How can this be explained?

Chapter 3

The Law of Torts

In order to preserve our freedom and to protect the rights that give meaning to that freedom, society, through rules of law and government, imposes certain limitations that apply to everyone. Three areas of the law that determine whether conduct is wrongful are:

(1) Contract law
(2) The law of torts
(3) Criminal law

A claim based upon contract law arises, for example, when an employee sues his employer for failing to pay him his proper wages, or when a homeowner sues the contractor for failing to complete his house in time, or when a beneficiary brings suit on a life insurance policy. Contract law is discussed in Part II. Special types of contracts, such as those for agency and sales, constitute the subject matter of several other parts that follow Part II.

The law of torts is the subject for discussion in this chapter; criminal law, in Chapter 4.

GENERAL PRINCIPLES—TORTS

Definition

A *tort* is a private injury or wrong arising from a breach of a duty created by law. It is often defined as a wrong independent of contract. Most torts, although not all, involve moral wrongs, but not all moral wrongs are torts.

The area of tort law includes harm to the person, as well as to property, caused negligently or intentionally. In some instances, liability is imposed merely because the activity of the wrongdoer is so dangerous that it is deemed proper that he should pay for any harm that has been caused. Torts that affect business security include defamation of reputation (slander and libel); infringement of patents, copyrights, and trademarks; and unfair competition.

1 / Tort and breach of contract distinguished. The wrongs or injuries caused by a breach of contract arise from the violation of an obligation or duty created by consent of the parties. A tort arises from the violation of an obligation or duty created by law. The same act may be both a breach

21

of contract and a tort. To illustrate, when an agent exchanges property instead of selling it as directed by the principal, he is liable for breach of contract and for the tort of conversion. And careless work by a contractor may give rise to liability both for the tort of negligence and for breach of contract.[1]

*2 / **Tort and crime distinguished.*** A *crime* is a wrong arising from a violation of a public duty,[2] whereas a tort is a wrong arising from a violation of a private duty. An act may be both a crime and a tort as in the case of the theft of an automobile.

Although the state recognizes both crimes and torts as wrongs, it attaches different effects to the acts or omissions. In the case of a crime, the state brings the action to enforce a prescribed penalty or punishment. On the other hand, when an act or omission is a tort, the state allows an action for redress by the injured party.

Basis of Tort Liability

The mere fact that a person is hurt or harmed in some way does not mean that he can sue and recover damages from the person causing the harm. There must exist a recognized basis for liability.

*1 / **Voluntary act.*** The defendant must be guilty of a voluntary act or omission.[3] Acts that are committed or omitted by one who is confronted with sudden peril or pressing danger, not of his own making, are considered as having been committed or omitted involuntarily.

*2 / **Intent.*** Whether intent to do an unlawful act or intent to cause harm is required as a basis for tort liability depends upon the nature of the act involved. Liability is imposed for some torts even though the person committing the tort acted in complete ignorance of the nature of his act and without any intent to cause harm. Thus a person entering land or a person cutting trees in a forest is liable for the tort of trespass if the land or trees do not belong to him, unless he has permission from the owner.

In the case of other torts, such as assault, slander, malicious prosecution, or interference with contracts, it is necessary for the plaintiff to show that there was an intent on the part of the defendant to cause harm or at least the intent to do an act which a reasonable man would anticipate as likely to cause harm.

*3 / **Motive.*** As a general rule, motive is immaterial except as it may be evidence to show the existence of intent. In most instances any legal right

---

[1] *Firemen's Mutual Insurance Co.* v. *High Point Sprinkler Co.*, 266 N.C. 134, 146 S.E.2d 53.
[2] *Poston* v. *Home Insurance Co.*, 191 S.C. 314, 4 S.E.2d 261.
[3] Restatement of the Law of Torts, Sec. 2.

may be exercised even with bad motives, and an act that is unlawful is not made legal by good motives.

4 / Negligence. One is entitled to be free from injuries to his person or to his property that are caused by the failure on the part of another to exercise a proper degree of care. One who violates the duty to exercise the required degree of care and causes another harm is guilty of the tort known as *negligence*.

The elements of this tort are a duty on the part of the defendant to exercise care in respect to the plaintiff; a failure to perform that duty; and a resulting injury to the plaintiff that is proximately related to the defendant's act.

(a) DUTY OF CARE. A person is under a duty to act carefully with respect to those persons or things that are likely to be within the area in which they might be affected by his conduct.

At one time the zone of duty to exercise care was narrower when the question involved the negligence of a seller or a manufacturer. For a time it was held that the only person to whom a manufacturer or seller owed any duty was his own purchaser. If the purchaser was injured because of the negligence of the manufacturer or seller in making the product, the purchaser could sue the seller; but if someone else was injured, there was no liability.[4] This rule has gradually been abandoned so that the seller or manufacturer is liable to third persons whom he should have foreseen would be injured.[5]

A person is under a duty of care to other persons whose presence he should reasonably anticipate, but he is not under a duty to anticipate the presence of persons unlawfully on his property. With respect to those persons whom he invites on his property, the landowner must take reasonable measures to insure that the property is safe and must warn the persons of any dangers present. In the case of the trespasser, the owner may ignore him until he knows that he is present.[6] Once he knows that a trespasser is on his property, he cannot take any action which a reasonable man would recognize as exposing the trespasser to unreasonable risk. The owner of the land cannot make his land unsafe for trespassers for the purpose of injuring them, as by setting spring guns.

Facts: Drew sued Lett for damages arising from the death of Drew's eleven-year-old son. Lett was the owner of an abandoned mine. The entrance was open and unguarded. The child entered the mine and was suffocated by poisonous gases.

---

[4] *Huset* v. *J. I. Case Threshing Machine Co.,* [C.A.8th] 120 F. 865.
[5] *MacPherson* v. *Buick Motor Co.,* 217 N.Y. 382, 111 N.E. 1050. See Chapter 38.
[6] *Martinelli* v. *Peters,* 413 Pa. 472, 198 A.2d 530.

Decision: Judgment for Drew. Ordinarily there would be no liability for the injury or death of a trespasser, but many states recognize an exception in favor of children, called the "attractive nuisance" doctrine. Under this theory the owner of property is liable for injury caused to small children who will not realize the danger of harm. The owner must anticipate that children will be children and must take reasonable steps to safeguard them, although he is not required to make his land "accident-proof." (Drew v. Lett, 95 Ind.App. 89, 182 N.E. 547)

(b) DEGREE OF CARE. The degree of care required of a person is that which an ordinarily prudent man would exercise under similar circumstances to avoid reasonably foreseeable harm. The law does not require such a degree of care as would have prevented the harm from occurring, nor is it enough that it is just as much care as everyone else exercises. Nor is it sufficient that one has exercised the degree of care which is customary for persons in the same kind of work or business, or that one has employed the methods customarily used. If one is engaged in services requiring skill, the care, of course, measures up to a higher standard. The degree of care exercised must be commensurate with the danger that would probably result if such care were lacking.[7] In all cases it is the diligence, care, and skill that can be reasonably expected under the circumstances. Whether one has exercised that degree of care is a question which is determined by the jury.

(c) PROOF OF NEGLIGENCE. The plaintiff ordinarily has the burden of proving that the defendant did not exercise reasonable care. In some instances, however, it is sufficient for the plaintiff to prove that the injury was caused by something that is within the control of the defendant. If injury results from such objects only when there is negligence, the proof of these facts is prima facie proof that the defendant was negligent. This is expressed by the maxim *res ipsa loquitur* (the occurrence or thing speaks for itself).

    Facts: Deveny, who was visiting her aunt, went into the cellar to light the hot water heater. The control unit, which was factory sealed, exploded and injured her. She then sued the manufacturer of the hot water heater and its supplier that manufactured the control unit. The defendants raised the defense that no negligence was shown.

Decision: A boiler unit does not ordinarily explode unless someone has been negligent. As the exploding control unit was factory sealed, any negligence necessarily occurred in the course of its manufacture. The principle of res ipsa loquitur therefore applied even though at the time harm was sustained, the defendants no longer had possession of the unit. (Deveny v. Rheem Mfg. Co., [C.A.2d] 319 F.2d 124)

---

[7] *Friese* v. *Boston Consolidated Gas Co.*, 324 Mass. 623, 88 N.E.2d 1.

(d) CONTRIBUTORY NEGLIGENCE. Generally, one cannot recover for injuries caused by another's negligence if his own negligence has contributed to the injury.[8] The plaintiff's negligence, however, must be a proximate cause of the injury, that is, it must contribute to the injury in order to defeat recovery.

In this connection there has developed a doctrine variously called the *doctrine of last clear chance*, the *humanitarian doctrine*, or the *doctrine of discovered peril*. Under this doctrine, although the plaintiff is negligent, the defendant is held liable if he had the last clear chance to avoid the injury.[9] In such a case the theory is that the plaintiff's negligence is not the proximate cause and therefore does not contribute to the injury.

When the plaintiff is guilty of contributory negligence, he is ordinarily denied recovery without regard to whether the defendant was more negligent than he. The common law does not recognize comparative degrees of negligence, nor does it try to apportion the injury to the two parties in terms of the degree of their respective fault.[10] As an exception to these principles, a number of states provide by statute that the negligence of both parties must be compared, and that the plaintiff's negligence does not bar his recovery but merely reduces the amount which he recovers in proportion to the degree or extent of his own negligence.

The burden of proving that the plaintiff was contributorily negligent is upon the defendant.

5 / Proximate cause. In order to fix legal responsibility upon one as a wrongdoer, it is necessary to show that the injury was the proximate result of his voluntary act.[11] Whether an act is the proximate cause of an injury is usually a question of fact for the jury to determine.

6 / Liability without fault. Ordinarily there must be some fault on the defendant's part to impose tort liability for his acts. He must either be negligent or intend harm to result, or he must volitionally do the act which causes the harm, as in a trespass to land, even though he did not intend that result. As an exception to these principles, liability is imposed in some cases, not because of the fault or intent of the defendant, but because the activity in which he has engaged, though lawful, has such a high potential of danger to others that society will make him pay for any harm which results. This is known as the *rule of absolute liability* or *rule of liability without fault.*

This doctrine has been applied to impose liability upon a person keeping vicious, wild animals; a person storing inflammable gases and liquids, and

---

[8] *Farmer* v. *School District*, 171 Wash. 278, 17 P.2d 899.
[9] *Harvey* v. *Burr*, 224 Ark. 62, 271 S.W.2d 777.
[10] *Clark* v. *Foster*, 87 Idaho 134, 391 P.2d 853.
[11] R., Sec. 9; *Amaya* v. *Home Ice, Fuel & Supply Co.*, 59 Cal.2d 295, 379 P.2d 513.

explosives; and persons engaged in blasting [12] or drilling for oil wells. In some states that reject the doctrine, the courts achieve the same result by terming the defendant guilty of a nuisance of such a character that he must pay for the harm done without regard to fault or by applying the rule of res ipsa loquitur. In some states liability without fault is imposed upon railroads for fires caused by locomotives emitting sparks. The basic principle of workmen's compensation statutes is liability without fault. In a number of states statutes have been adopted making the owner or operator of aircraft absolutely liable for any damage caused by the aircraft in the course of its ascent, descent, or flight.[13]

Wrongdoers

In general, all persons are responsible for their torts. In a few instances when a public officer acts for the state, there is no liability on the part of the officer. Ordinarily the state, and generally a city, cannot be sued by an individual except with its consent.

A tort may be caused by several wrongdoers. If they are joint wrongdoers, each is civilly liable for all the harm caused, although the plaintiff can only be paid once for his damages. A *joint wrong* exists when there is concert of action or agreement between the parties although the injury is done by one; a joint wrong is also committed when the parties act independently but produce a single injury. Courts differ as to the extent of the liability of each tort-feasor or wrongdoer in such cases.

Some states allow contribution between joint tort-feasors when they have acted independently without any concert or agreement, or when the conduct of each amounts only to negligence. The trend of decisions has been to widen the exceptions so as to permit contribution in more types of cases. In a number of states this result has been achieved by the adoption of a statute expressly authorizing contribution.[14]

SECURITY FROM BUSINESS TORTS

In business dealings several kinds of torts may occur, such as fraud; slander and libel; infringement of trademarks, patents, and copyrights; and various forms of unfair competition.

Fraud

A person is entitled to be protected from fraud and is entitled to recover damages for the harm caused by fraud.[15] For the purpose of tort law, fraud

---

[12] *McKay* v. *Kelly*, [Tex.Civ.App.] 229 S.W.2d 117.
[13] *Adler's Quality Bakery, Inc.* v. *Gaseteria, Inc.*, 32 N.J. 55, 159 A.2d 97.
[14] *Consolidated Coach Corp.* v. *Burge*, 245 Ky. 631, 54 S.W.2d 16.
[15] *Sawyer* v. *Tildahl*, 275 Minn. 457, 148 N.W.2d 131.

has the same scope and meaning as fraud for the purpose of avoiding a contract,[16] with the important exception that in tort law damages must be sustained by the plaintiff in addition to his reliance on the false statement.

Facts: The seller owned sheets of aluminum, some of which were pitted and corroded. He stacked the sheets so that a good sheet was on top of each bundle of sheets and hid the bad ones. He showed the stacks of aluminum sheets to the buyer without making any comment as to the condition of the sheets. The buyer believed that all of the sheets were in good condition. Because of their size he could not lift the sheets to verify his conclusion. When he learned that they were not all in good condition, he sued the seller.

Decision: The seller was guilty of fraud even though he had not said a misleading word. He had made a fraudulent misrepresentation by arranging the sheets so as to give a wrong impression as to the condition of the stack and so as to make it more difficult to ascertain the truth. (Salzman v. Maldaver, 315 Mich. 403, 24 N.W.2d 161)

Slander

Liability for slander is imposed to provide security of reputation. Reputation is injured by *defamation*, which is a publication tending to cause one to lose the esteem of the community.[17] *Slander* is a form of actionable defamation consisting of the publication or communication to another of false spoken words or gestures.[18]

1 / Damages. Whether the plaintiff must actually prove that he was injured by the slander depends upon the nature of the defamatory matter. Words that charge another with the commission of a crime involving moral turpitude [19] and infamous punishment; that impute a disease at the present time that will exclude one from society; or that have a tendency to injure one in his business, profession, or occupation [20] are regarded by the law as *actionable per se* because from common experience it is known that damages occur as a natural consequence of the publication of such words. If defamatory matter is actionable per se, the plaintiff is not required to prove actual damage sustained in consequence of the slander. Otherwise he must do so and, if he cannot prove injury, he is not entitled to recover damages.

2 / Privilege. Under certain circumstances, no liability arises when false statements are published and cause damage:

---

[16] See p. 113.
[17] R., Sec. 559.
[18] Sec. 568(2); *Jones* v. *Walsh,* 107 N.H. 379, 222 A.2d 830.
[19] *Southwest Drug Stores* v. *Garner,* [Miss.] 195 So.2d 837.
[20] R., Sec. 570.

(a) An *absolute privilege* exists in the case of public officers who, in the performance of their duties, should have no fear of possible liability for damages.[21]

(b) Other circumstances may afford a qualified or *conditional privilege*.[22] A communication made in good faith upon a subject in which the party communicating has an interest, or in reference to which he has a right, is privileged if made to a person having a corresponding interest or right, although it contains criminatory matter which, without this privilege, would be slanderous. Thus a person, in protecting his interests, may in good faith charge another with the theft of his watch. A mercantile agency's credit report is privileged when made to an interested subscriber in good faith in the regular course of its business.[23]

3 / Malice. It is frequently said that there must be "malice" in order to constitute slander. This is not, however, malice in fact, but merely malice in law, which exists when the speaker is not privileged to make his defamatory statements.

Facts: The defendant wrote to the county department of health a letter in which she sharply criticized the plaintiff's performance of her duties as a registered nurse employed by the department. The defendant did not make her complaint in any way to any other person. The plaintiff sued the defendant for defamation and claimed that the letter was malicious.

Decision: As a citizen, the defendant had a right to complain to the government as to the official conduct of one of its employees. This gave the defendant a qualified privilege to make statements that would otherwise be defamatory. While such privilege would have been destroyed if the defendant had acted maliciously, there was nothing to show that there was any malice. The fact that the complaint was not spread among other persons but was made only to the plaintiff's superior indicated that the defendant had acted in good faith and, in the absence of proof to the contrary, was therefore entitled to protection under the privilege. (Nuyen v. Slater, 372 Mich. 654, 127 N.W.2d 369)

Libel

Another wrong against the security of business relations takes the form of written defamation. This is known as *libel*. Although usually in writing, it may be in print, picture, or in any other permanent, visual form.[24] For example, to construct a gallows in front of another's residence is libelous.

---

[21] Secs. 585 et seq.
[22] Secs. 593 to 598.
[23] *Petition of Retailers Commercial Agency, Inc.,* 342 Mass. 515, 174 N.E.2d 376.
[24] R., Sec. 568(1).

The elements necessary to maintain an action for libel are the same as for slander. In the case of libel, however, it is not necessary, as a general rule, to allege and prove damages because damages will be presumed.[25] In other words, all forms of libel are actionable per se.

There is a conflict of authority as to the classification of defamatory statements made over the radio or television. Some courts treat such statements as libelous when read from a written script and slanderous when not. Other courts regard the broadcasting as slander without regard to whether there was a script.

Disparagement of Goods and Slander of Title

In the transaction of business one is entitled to be free from interference by means of malicious false claims or statements in respect to the quality or the title of his property.[26]

Actual damages must be alleged and proved to have proximately resulted from the false communication to a third person. The plaintiff must show that in consequence thereof the third person has refrained from dealing with the plaintiff.

Infringement of Trademarks

A *trademark* is a word, name, device, or symbol, or any combination of these, used by a manufacturer or seller to distinguish his goods from those of other persons. When the trademark of a particular person is used or substantially copied by another, it is said that the trademark is infringed. The owner of the trademark may sue for damages and enjoin its wrongful use.[27]

Geographical and descriptive names cannot ordinarily be adopted as trademarks. To illustrate, "liquid glue" is not a proper trademark. Such names may, however, be used when they do not denote origin, style, or quality. Thus "a geographical name, when not used in a geographical sense, that is, when it does not denote the location of origin, but is used in a fictitious sense merely to indicate ownership and origin independent of location, may be a good trademark. For example, 'Liverpool' for cloth made at Hieddersfield." [28] It is possible, however, through the continued usage of a geographic or descriptive name for a number of years that such a name has acquired a secondary meaning so as to become identified in the mind of the public with a particular product or manufacturer or dealer. In such case the name is protected as a trademark.

---

[25] Sec. 569.
[26] Secs. 624 and 626.
[27] Secs. 744 and 745.
[28] *Drake Medicine Co.* v. *Glessner,* 68 Ohio 337, 67 N.E. 722.

A person who by fraudulent statements obtains the registration of a trademark in the Federal Patent Office is liable for the damages which such false registration causes anyone.

Infringement of Patents

A grant of a *patent* entitles the patentee to prevent others for a period of 17 years from making, using, or selling the particular invention. Anyone doing so without the patentee's permission is guilty of a patent infringement.

An infringement exists, even though all the parts or features of an invention are not copied, if there is a substantial identity of means, operation, and result between the original and new devices. In the case of a process, however, all successive steps or their equivalent must be taken. In the case of a combination of ingredients, the use of the same ingredients with others constitutes an infringement, except when effecting a compound essentially different in nature.

Infringement of Copyrights

A wrong similar to the infringement of a patent is the infringement of a copyright. A *copyright* is the right given by statute to prevent others for a limited time from printing, copying, or publishing a production resulting from intellectual labor. The right exists for a period of 28 years, and it can be renewed for an additional period of 28 years.

Infringement of copyright in general consists of copying the form of expression of ideas or conceptions. There is no copyright in the idea or conception itself, but only in the particular way in which it is expressed. In order to constitute an infringement, the production need not be entirely reproduced or be exact. Substantial reproduction, although paraphrased or otherwise altered, of some part of the original constitutes an infringement. Although appropriation of a word or of a line is insufficient, an appropriation of all of or even a substantial part of the production is unnecessary to amount to an infringement.

One guilty of infringement of copyright is liable to the owner for damages and profits, or only damages, which are to be determined by the court. The owner is also entitled to an injunction to restrain further infringement.

Unfair Competition

Unfair competition is unlawful and the person injured thereby may sue for damages or for an injunction to stop the practice, or he may report the matter to a trade commission or other agency.[29]

A form of unfair competition whereby one is able to fraudulently dispose of his wares is the imitation of signs, store fronts, advertisements, and

[29] See p. 50.

packaging of goods.[30] Thus, when one adopts a box of distinctive size, shape, and color in which to market candy, and another appropriates the same style, form, and dress of the package, the latter may be enjoined from its use and in some cases may be liable for damages.

Wrongful Interference with Business Relations

One of the primary rights of an individual is to earn his living by selling his labor or by engaging in trade or business. A wrongful interference with this liberty is a tort [31] for which damages may be recovered and which, in some cases, may be restrained by an injunction.

The right to conduct one's business is, nevertheless, subject to the rights of others. Hence the injuries suffered by one in business through legitimate competition give no right of redress.[32]

Inducing Breach of Contract

When a person intentionally and without reasonable justification or excuse induces a party to a contract to refuse to perform according to its terms, he is liable to the other party to the contract for the damages which he sustains from the breach of contract.[33] The fact that the person injured by the breach may sue the defaulting party for breaking the contract does not bar suing the person who induced the breach.

Combinations to Divert Trade

Business relations may be disturbed by a combination to keep third persons from dealing with another. Such a combination, resulting in injury, constitutes an actionable wrong known as *conspiracy* if its object is unlawful or if its lawful object is procured by unlawful means.

If the object of a combination is to further lawful interests of the association, no actionable wrong exists so long as lawful means are employed. For example, when employees are united in a strike, they may peacefully persuade others to withhold their patronage from the employer. On the other hand, all combinations to drive or keep away customers or prospective employees by violence, force, threats, or intimidation are actionable wrongs. To illustrate, a combination is usually treated as an unlawful conspiracy for which damages may be recovered when the customers are threatened and for this reason withdraw their patronage.

Labor laws make some combinations unfair labor practices,[34] while other combinations to divert trade are condemned as illegal trusts.[35]

---

[30] R., Sec. 741.
[31] *Harris* v. *Perl*, 41 N.J. 455, 197 A.2d 359.
[32] R., Sec. 708; *Tokuzo Shida* v. *Japan Food Corp.,* [Cal.App.2d] 60 Cal.Reptr. 43.
[33] *Tenta* v. *Guraly*, [Ind.App.] 221 N.E.2d 577.
[34] See Ch. 62, Comprehensive Volume, Ch. 46, Standard Volume.
[35] See Ch. 61, Comprehensive Volume, Ch. 45, Standard Volume.

Nuisance

A *nuisance* (or private nuisance) is an unreasonable use of land that interferes with another person's enjoyment of his land, such as by the maintenance of a dog kennel, or a factory's causing vibration, noise, and air pollution.[36] It contrasts with a *public nuisance*, which is any activity injurious to the public safety, health, or morals,[37] such as operating a gambling resort contrary to law, or double parking on the highway.[38]

Other Torts

Other torts may or may not have a business or commercial background.

1 / Trespass to the person. Trespass to the person consists of any contact with the victim's person to which he has not consented. It thus includes what is technically described as a battery. It likewise includes an assault, in which the victim apprehends the commission of a battery, but he is in fact not touched, and includes false imprisonment.

As a modern extension of the concept of the "person," which is protected from "trespass," there is liability for intentionally causing mental stress that results in physical harm or illness to the victim.[39]

As an aspect of the freedom of the person from unreasonable interference, the law has come to recognize a *right of privacy*. This right is most commonly invaded in one of the following ways: (1) invasion of physical privacy, as by planting a microphone in a person's home; (2) giving unnecessary publicity to personal matters of the plaintiff's life, such as his financial status or his past career; (3) false public association of the plaintiff with some product or principle, such as indicating that he indorses a product or is in favor of a particular law, when such is not the fact; or (4) commercially exploiting the plaintiff's name or picture, as using them in advertising without his permission.

Facts: Korn claimed damages on the ground that through an agreement between Rennison and other defendants, a photograph of Korn, the plaintiff, was published for advertising purposes in the defendant newspaper without the knowledge, consent, or permission of the plaintiff and in violation of her personal liberties and private rights. As a result, the defendants received monetary benefits and advantages while the plaintiff received none and was subjected to ridicule, embarrassment, vexation, and humiliation. The defendant raised the defense that there was no right of privacy at common law or by statute.

---

[36] *Kosich* v. *Poultrymen's Service Corp.*, 136 N.J.Eq. 571, 43 A.2d 15.
[37] *Phoenix* v. *Johnson*, 51 Ariz. 115, 75 P.2d 30.
[38] *Salsbury* v. *United Parcel Service*, 203 Misc. 1008, 120 N.Y.S.2d 33.
[39] *Tate* v. *Canonica*, 180 Cal.App.2d 898, 5 Cal.Rptr. 28.

Decision: Although the right of privacy was not recognized at common law, and even if it is not created by statute, a right of privacy should be recognized. A person needs such protection from unreasonable invasion of his personal interest by advertising media and promotion schemes. (Korn v. Rennison, 21 Conn.S. 400, 156 A.2d 476)

2 / Trespass to land. A *trespass to land* consists of any unpermitted entry below, on, across, or above land. This rule is modified to permit the proper flight of aircraft above the land so long as it does not interfere with a proper use of the land. Many states provide for the recovery of treble damages when the person committing the trespass knows that he is doing wrong and willfully cuts and removes timber.

3 / Trespass to personal property. An illegal invasion of property rights with respect to property other than land constitutes a *trespass to personal property* when done negligently or intentionally. When done in good faith and without negligence, there is no liability, in contrast with the case of trespass to land when good faith is not a defense.

Negligent damage to personal property, as in the case of negligent collision of automobiles, imposes liability for harm done. Intentional damage to personal property will impose liability for the damage done and also may justify exemplary or punitive damages.

Conversion occurs when personal property is taken by the wrongdoer and kept from its true owner or prior possessor. Thus a bank clerk commits conversion when he takes money from the bank. Conversion is thus seen to be the civil side of the crimes relating to stealing. The good faith of the converter, however, is not a defense, and an innocent buyer of stolen goods is liable for damages for converting them.[40]

QUESTIONS AND PROBLEMS

1. Checklist of legal terms:
    (a) tort (21), breach of contract (21), crime (22)
    (b) negligence (23); res ipsa loquitur (24), doctrine of last clear chance (25), rule of absolute liability (25)
    (c) joint wrong (26)
    (d) defamation (27); slander (27), libel (28)
    (e) absolute privilege, conditional privilege (28)
    (f) trademark (29), patent (30), copyright (30)
    (g) inducing breach of contract (31)
    (h) conspiracy (31)
    (i) nuisance, public nuisance (32)
    (j) trespass to person (32), right of privacy (32); trespass to land (33), trespass to personal property (33)
    (k) conversion (33)

---

[40] *McRae* v. *Bandy,* 270 Ala. 12, 115 So.2d 479.

2. State the objective(s) of each of the following rules of law:
   (a) The owner of land cannot make his land unsafe for trespassers for the purpose of injuring them.
   (b) Geographical and descriptive names cannot ordinarily be adopted as trademarks.

3. Miller fell in a Woolworth store. The store employees testified that the place where Miller fell had been swept clean shortly before, using a push broom made of an oil-treated cloth. A third person who happened to be in the store, as well as the employees, testified that there was nothing slippery on the floor. Was Miller entitled to recover from Woolworth? (Miller v. F. W. Woolworth Co., 238 Ark. 709, 384 S.W.2d 947)

4. Giles, a guest at a Pick Hotel, wanted to remove his brief case from the right-hand side of the front seat of his auto. To support himself while so doing, he placed his left hand on the center door pillar of the right-hand side of the car. The hotel bellboy closed the rear door of the car without noticing Giles's hand. One of Giles's fingers was smashed by the closing of the door and thereafter had to be amputated. Giles sued the Pick Hotels Corp. Was he entitled to recover? (Giles v. Pick Hotels Corp., [C.A.6th] 232 F.2d 887)

5. Green was an employee of a contractor who was replacing a roof on the aluminum reduction plant of Reynolds Metal Co. Green fell from the projecting ledge of the roof on which he was working. He had been working on the roof for 13 weeks prior to the accident, and the working conditions were the same throughout this period. There was no guard rail or rope on the section of the roof in question, poisonous gases were emitted from the building in the course of the operations of Reynolds Metal Co. plant, and there was a heavy dust accumulation on the roof. No other person working in the same area as Green had been affected or had fallen. Was Reynolds Metal liable for Green's harm? (Green v. Reynolds Metal Co., [C.A.5th] 328 F.2d 372)

6. Bagwell, who knew that his house was infested with termites, wanted to sell the house. He hired a carpenter to cover up and conceal the termite damage with the result that reasonable inspection would not reveal the true condition of the house. He told Beagle that the house was in good condition and was free of termites. Beagle entered into a contract for the purchase of the house. Later when he learned that there were termites, he sued for damages for fraud. Was he entitled to such damages? (Beagle v. Bagwell, [Fla.] 169 So.2d 43)

7. Knight, a builder, sold a house that he had built to Cantrell. The latter had been a real estate broker for 10 years and had long experience in the building of houses. In the course of negotiations, Cantrell inspected the house and Knight stated it is a "good house," "a well-built house," and "a good constructed house." After Cantrell bought the house, many cracks appeared and he had to spend much money in repairing the house. He sued Knight for damages for fraud. Was he entitled to recover? (Knight v. Cantrell, 154 Colo. 396, 390 P.2d 948)

Chapter 4

Criminal Law

A *crime* is a violation of the law that is punished as an offense against the state or government. The field of criminal law as it affects business security [1] includes obtaining property by false pretenses; using false weights, measures, or labels; swindles and confidence games; using the mails to defraud; forgery; criminal libel; lotteries; larceny, burglary, and robbery; embezzlement; extortion; bribery; and receiving stolen goods.

GENERAL PRINCIPLES—CRIMES

Classifications of Crimes

Crimes may be classified (1) in terms of the source of the law prohibiting them, (2) in terms of their seriousness, or (3) in terms of their nature.

1 / Source of criminal law. Crimes are classified in terms of their origin as common-law and statutory crimes. Some offenses that are defined by statute are merely declaratory of those that existed under the common law. Each state has its own criminal law, although a general pattern among the states may be observed.

2 / Seriousness of offense. Crimes are classified in terms of their seriousness as treason, felonies, and misdemeanors. *Treason* is defined by the Constitution of the United States, which states that "treason against the United States shall consist only in levying war against them, or in adhering to their enemies, giving them aid and comfort." [2]

Felonies include the other more serious crimes, such as arson, homicide, and robbery, which are punishable by confinement in prison or by death.[3] A statute may convert an act, previously a minor offense, into a felony.

Crimes not classified as treason or felonies are *misdemeanors*. Reckless driving, weighing and measuring goods with scales and measuring devices that have not been inspected, and disturbing the peace by illegal picketing are generally classified as misdemeanors. An act may be a felony in one state and a misdemeanor in another.

---

[1] See pp. 39-43.
[2] Art. III, Sec. 3.
[3] *People* v. *Beasley*, 370 Mich. 242, 121 N.W.2d 457.

3 / Nature of misconduct. Crimes are also classified in terms of the nature of the misconduct. *Crimes mala in se* include acts that are inherently vicious or, in other words, that are naturally evil as measured by the standards of a civilized community. *Crimes mala prohibita* include those acts that are wrong merely because they are declared wrong by some statute, such as a law prohibiting parking in certain locations.

Basis of Criminal Liability

A crime generally consists of two elements: (1) an act or omission, and (2) a mental state.[4] In the case of some crimes, such as the illegal operation of a business without a license, it is immaterial whether the act causes harm to others. In other cases, the defendant's act must be the sufficiently direct cause of harm to another in order to impose criminal liability, as in the case of unlawful homicide.[5]

Mental state does not require an awareness or knowledge of guilt. In most crimes it is sufficient that the defendant voluntarily did the act that is criminal, regardless of motive or evil intent. In some instances, a particular mental state is required, such as the necessity that a homicide be with malice aforethought to constitute murder. In some cases, it is the existence of a specific intent that differentiates the crime committed from other offenses, as an assault with intent to kill is distinguished by that intent from an ordinary assault or an assault with intent to rob.

Parties to a Crime

Two or more parties may directly or indirectly contribute to the commission of a crime. At common law participants in the commission of a felony are sometimes known as *principals* and *accessories*. By statute, the distinction has frequently been abolished and all participants are principals.[6] In the case of a misdemeanor, all of the parties, as a general rule, are responsible as principals.

Facts: Friedman, Carolla, and Strada robbed Blaine on the highway. Friedman held a gun in the robbery but did not take any property from Blaine. Friedman was prosecuted for robbery and defended on the ground that he was not guilty of robbery since he did not take any property.

Decision: Friedman was convicted. Since he acted in concert with the person who did commit the robbery and was present at the robbery, he was equally responsible even though he did not take any property. (Missouri v. Friedman, 313 Mo. 88, 280 S.W 1023)

---

[4] *Seattle* v. *Gordon,* 54 Wash.2d 516, 342 P.2d 604.
[5] *Pennsylvania* v. *Root,* 403 Pa. 571, 170 A.2d 310.
[6] *State* v. *Weis,* 92 Ariz. 254, 375 P.2d 735.

*1 / **Principals**.* Principals are divided into two classes: (a) *principals in the first degree* who actually engage in the perpetration of the crime, and (b) *principals in the second degree* who are actually or constructively present and aid and abet in the commission of the act. For example, a person is a principal in the second degree if he assists by words of encouragement, stands ready to assist, or keeps watch to prevent surprise or capture.[7]

*2 / **Accessories**.* Accessories to a crime are also divided into two classes, accessories before the fact and accessories after the fact. An *accessory before the fact* differs from a principal in the second degree only by reason of his absence from the scene of the act.[8] An *accessory after the fact* is a person who knowingly assists one who has committed a felony. Thus a person is an accessory after the fact if, after the commission of the crime and with intent to assist a felon, he gives warning to prevent arrest or shelters or aids in an escape from imprisonment.[9]

Responsibility for Criminal Acts

*1 / **Minors**.* Some states have legislation fixing the age of criminal responsibility of minors. At common law, when a child is under the age of seven years, the law presumes him to be incapable of committing a crime; after the age of fourteen he is presumed to have capacity as though he were over twenty-one; and between the ages of seven and fourteen, no presumption of law arises and it must be shown that the minor has such capacity. The existence of capacity cannot be presumed from the mere commission of the act, and the presumptions noted may be overcome by proof to the contrary.[10]

*2 / **Insane persons**.* An insane person is not criminally responsible for his acts because he cannot form a criminal intent.[11] There is a conflict of opinion as to what constitutes such insanity as to excuse a person from the normal consequence of his acts. All courts, however, agree that intellectual weakness alone is not such insanity.

A test commonly applied is the right-and-wrong test. The responsibility of the defendant is determined in terms of his ability to understand the nature of his act and to distinguish right from wrong in relation to it.

Some courts also use the irresistible-impulse test. The essence of this theory is that, although the defendant may know right from wrong, if he acts under an uncontrollable impulse because of an unsound state of mind caused by disease of any nature, he has not committed a voluntary act and is not criminally responsible.

---

[7] *State* v. *Jones*, 45 Hawaii, 247, 365 P.2d 460.
[8] *State* v. *Bass*, 255 N.C. 42, 120 S.E.2d 580.
[9] *Rudolph* v. *State*, 40 Ala.App. 398, 114 So.2d 299.
[10] *People* v. *Rooks*, 40 Misc.2d 359, 243 N.Y.S.2d 301.
[11] *Brooks* v. *State*, 21 Wis.2d 32, 123 N.W.2d 535.

When insanity takes the form of delusions or hallucinations, the defendant is not legally responsible when the imagined facts, if they were true, would justify the act.

3 / Intoxicated persons. Involuntary intoxication relieves a person from criminal responsibility; voluntary intoxication generally does not. An exception to this rule is made in the case of a crime requiring specific intent when the accused was so intoxicated that he was incapable of forming such intent.[12]

4 / Corporations. The modern tendency is to hold corporations criminally responsible for their acts. A corporation may also be held liable for crimes based upon the failure to act.

Certain crimes, such as perjury, cannot be committed by corporations. It is also usually held that crimes punishable only by imprisonment or corporal punishment cannot be committed by corporate bodies. If the statute imposes a fine in addition to or in lieu of corporal punishment, a corporation may be convicted for the crime. Thus a corporation may be fined for violating the federal antitrust law by conspiring or combining to restrain interstate commerce. A corporation may be fined for committing criminal manslaughter when death has been caused by the corporation's failure to install safety equipment required by statute.

Prevention of Crimes

The usual method employed to prevent crime is punishment. This may take the form of fines, imprisonment, or other penalties. In some states the punishment for a crime is increased if the criminal is a repeating or habitual offender. The legislatures may prescribe any punishment for crime, subject to federal constitutional provisions that prohibit "excessive fines" and "cruel and unusual punishments."

Statutes sometimes require a restitution of property that has been stolen or the payment of damages to the owner upon conviction of larceny. At common law, courts may require a bond to secure the future good behavior of a person who has been convicted of a serious misdemeanor. Statutes sometimes authorize the requirement of a bond for this purpose when a person has been convicted two or more times of violating a specific law.

SECURITY FROM BUSINESS CRIMES

The crimes that affect business are so numerous that it will only be possible to discuss the more common offenses.

---

[12] *People* v. *Reynolds,* 27 Ill.2d 523, 190 N.E.2d 301.

Obtaining Goods by False Pretenses

In almost all of the states, statutes are directed against obtaining money or goods by means of false pretenses.[13] These statutes vary in detail and scope. Sometimes the statutes are directed against particular forms of deception, such as the use of bad checks.[14]

False Weights, Measures, and Labels

Cheating, defrauding, or misleading the public by the use of false, improper, or inadequate weights, measures, and labels is a crime. Numerous federal and state regulations have been adopted on this subject.

Swindles and Confidence Games

The act of a person who, intending to cheat and defraud, obtains money or property by trick, deception, fraud, or other device, is an offense known as a *swindle* [15] or *confidence game*. False or bogus checks and spurious coins are frequently employed in swindling operations directed toward the man engaged in business.

False Coins and Currency

It is a federal crime to make, to possess with intent to pass, or to pass counterfeit coins, bank notes, or obligations or other securities of the United States. Legislation has also been enacted against the passing of counterfeit foreign securities or notes of foreign banks.

The various states also have statutes preventing the making and passing of counterfeit coins and bank notes. These statutes often provide, as does the federal statute, a punishment for the mutilation of bank notes or the lightening or mutilation of coins.

Use of Mails to Promote Fraud

Congress has made it a crime to use the mails to further any scheme or artifice to defraud. To constitute the offense, there must be (1) a contemplated or organized scheme or artifice to defraud or to obtain money or property by false pretenses, and (2) the mailing or the causing of another to mail a letter, writing, or pamphlet for the purpose of executing or attempting to execute such scheme or artifice. Illustrations of schemes or artifices that come within the statute are false statements to secure credit, circulars announcing false cures for sale, false statements to sell stock in a corporation,

---

[13] *Giannetto* v. *General Exchange Insurance Corp.*, 10 App.Div.2d 442, 200 N.Y.S. 2d 238.
[14] *Kauffman* v. *Maryland*, 199 Md. 35, 85 A.2d 446.
[15] *State* v. *Wells*, 265 Minn. 212, 121 N.W.2d 68.

and false statements as to the origin of a fire and the value of the destroyed goods for the purpose of securing indemnity from an insurance company.

Forgery

Forgery consists of the fraudulent making or material altering of an instrument, which apparently creates or changes a legal liability of another.[16] The instrument must have some apparent legal efficacy to constitute forgery.

Ordinarily forgery consists of signing another's name with intent to defraud. It may also consist of the making of an entire instrument or the alteration of an existing one. It may result from signing a fictitious name or the offender's own name with the intent to defraud.

Facts: Phelps & Hines Logging Co. had a bank account in the Lincoln Bank. The signature card filed with the bank required the signing of company checks by both Hines and Benson as agents for the company. Benson, with the intent to defraud, wrote a company check with the name of Hines as a signing agent and then wrote his own name in that capacity. He was convicted of forgery. After conviction he brought review proceedings naming Gladden, the warden, as the adverse party.

Decision: Conviction affirmed. When Benson wrote the signature of Hines, he did so with the intent to defraud. It was forgery to do so even though the intent and effect were not to defraud Hines but rather the company on the account of which the check would not be effective without the signature of Hines and Benson. (Benson v. Gladden, 242 Ore. 132, 407 P.2d 634)

Criminal Libel

A person who falsely defames another without legal excuse or justification may be subject to criminal liability as well as civil liability.[17] *Criminal libel* is based upon its tendency to cause a breach of the peace. Under some statutes, however, the offense appears to be based upon the tendency to injure another.

No publication or communication to third persons is required in the case of criminal libel. The offense is committed when the defendant communicates the libel directly to the person libeled as well as when he makes it known to third persons.

The truth of the statement is now generally a defense, although often limited to cases where the defendant has acted in good faith.

In a number of states, slander generally or particular kinds of slander have been made criminal offenses by statute.

---

[16] *State* v. *Couch*, 250 Iowa 56, 92 N.W.2d 580.
[17] *Commonwealth* v. *Acquaviva*, 187 Pa.Super. 550, 145 A.2d 407.

Lotteries

There are three elements to a *lottery*: (1) a payment of money or something of value for the opportunity to win (2) a prize (3) by lot or chance.[18] If these elements appear, it is immaterial that the transaction appears to be a legitimate form of business or advertising.

Larceny

Larceny is the wrongful or fraudulent taking and carrying away of personal property from another person with the intent to deprive the owner of his property.[19] The offense is committed once the personal property is moved any distance, even though it is not successfully carried off, as in the case where it is chained. The offense is committed without regard to whether the victim is aware that the larceny is being committed. At common law, larceny was divided into grand and petty larceny on the basis of the value of the property taken, but this distinction has been abolished in some states.

Under common-law principles, the "borrowing" of an automobile for a "joy ride" is not larceny on the basis that there is no intent to deprive the owner permanently of the automobile. Statutes in some states, however, declare that this is larceny [20] or make the unpermitted use of the property of another a separate crime. The National Motor Vehicle Theft Act [21] makes it a federal crime to transport a stolen motor vehicle in interstate commerce or to deal therein.

Facts: An automobile was stolen. An hour later, it was found standing. McClanahan was at the driver's seat. The hood and the trunk lid were up. In McClanahan's pocket was a screwdriver and a wire that could be used to open a locked car. The trunk lock had been punched out, and articles had been taken from the trunk and were lying on the ground. The automobile clock had been torn from its position although it was still connected by wires. A jury found McClanahan was guilty of larceny. He appealed.

Decision: Conviction affirmed. The defendant's possession of property that had been recently stolen and the surrounding circumstances justified the jury in deducing that he had stolen the automobile, even though there was no direct evidence of witnesses who had seen the theft. (State v. McClanahan, [Mo.] 419 S.W.2d 20)

Burglary

At common law *burglary* was the unlawful breaking and entering in the nighttime of the dwelling house of another person with intent to commit a

---

18 *State* v. *Bussiere*, 155 Maine 331, 154 A.2d 702.
19 *Iowa* v. *Jackson*, 251 Iowa 537, 101 N.W.2d 731.
20 *New York* v. *Ramistella*, 306 N.Y. 379, 118 N.E.2d 566.
21 18 United States Code, Secs. 2312, 2313.

felony.[22] It was the invasion of the dwelling place which was the crime, and the crime was committed at the moment of the breaking and entering without regard to whether a felony was actually committed thereafter or the wrong-doer was prevented from so doing or even changed his mind. The offense has been changed by statute in many states so as to eliminate the requirement of nighttime and of breaking, and by extending the offense to other places such as warehouses, and telephone booths, and in some instances to any stationary building.[23]

Robbery

Robbery is the unlawful taking of personal property from the person or from the presence of another by means of force or fear exerted upon such person.[24] Statutes commonly make a separate offense of robbery depending upon the means employed, such as armed robbery, or the place of the offense, such as bank robbery. Taking possession by stealth, as by pocket picking, is not robbery as the element of "force or fear" is not satisfied. It is sufficient to constitute robbery that the victim had possession of the property which was taken by the robber, if the victim was either the owner or had the right to possession of the property. The penalty for the crime is designed merely to protect peaceful possession.[25]

Embezzlement

Embezzlement is the fraudulent conversion of property or money owned by another by a person to whom it has been entrusted.[26] It is a statutory crime designed to cover the case of unlawful takings that were not larceny because the wrongdoer did not take the property from the possession of another, and which were not robbery, because there was neither a taking nor the use of force or fear.

It is immaterial whether the defendant received the money or property from the victim or from a third person. Thus an agent commits embezzlement when he receives and keeps payments from third persons which he should remit to his principal, even though the agent is entitled to retain part of such payments as his commissions.[27]

> **Facts:** Tauscher was prosecuted for embezzlement. It was shown that while claiming to act as agent, he, without authority, had drawn a check on his employer's bank account and kept the proceeds of the check for his own use. Was he guilty of embezzlement?

---

[22] *Illinois* v. *Clark*, 30 Ill.2d 216, 195 N.E.2d 631.
[23] *Sanchez* v. *Colorado*, 142 Colo. 58, 349 P.2d 561, 78 A.L.R.2d 775.
[24] *Mason* v. *Virginia*, 200 Va. 253, 105 S.E.2d 149.
[25] *Hawaii* v. *Porkini*, 45 Hawaii 295, 367 P.2d 499, 89 A.L.R.2d 1421.
[26] *New Jersey* v. *Daly*, 38 N.J. 1, 182 A.2d 861.
[27] *Sherman* v. *Mississippi*, 234 Miss. 775, 108 So.2d 205.

Decision: No. Embezzlement can only be committed with respect to tangible property that is physically entrusted to the possession of the defendant. While Tauscher's conduct was fraudulent, it was not "embezzlement." (Oregon v. Tauscher, 227 Ore. 1, 360 P.2d 764, 88 A.L.R.2d 674)

Extortion

Historically *extortion* was the act of a public officer in taking money or property to which he was not entitled and using the color of his authority to force the victim to surrender the money or property. It has been extended by statute to include the obtaining of money or property by anyone by means of force, fear, or threats that induce the victim to "consent" to such payment or transfer of property.[28]

Bribery

Bribery is giving or receiving money or property of value in return for which a public officer agrees to do or refrain from doing some act, contrary to his official duty.[29] By statute it has been extended to nonofficial relations, as the commercial bribery of agents and the bribery of athletes.

Receiving Stolen Goods

The crime of *receiving stolen goods* is generally created by statute, consisting of receiving goods which have been stolen, with knowledge of that fact, and with the intent to deprive the owner of them.[30] In some states, the receiver is treated as an accessory after the fact to the larceny. It is immaterial whether the goods are received from a person who was not the person who stole them,[31] such as another receiver of the goods or an innocent middleman, and it is likewise immaterial that the receiver does not know the owner or the thief.

Facts: Scaggs acquired possession of property that was stolen. He did not know this at the time but learned of it thereafter. Upon so learning, he decided to keep the property for himself. He was prosecuted for receiving stolen goods. He raised the defense that at the time he had "received" the goods he did not know that they were stolen and therefore was not guilty of the offense.

Decision: Scaggs was guilty. The offense of "receiving" is, in effect, a continuing offense including "retaining" possession of stolen goods. When Scaggs retained possession of the goods after knowing that he would thereby deprive the true owner of his property, he committed the offense of "receiving." (California v. Scaggs, 153 Cal.App.2d 339, 314 P.2d 793)

---

[28] *New Jersey* v. *Begyn*, 34 N.J. 35, 167 A.2d 161.
[29] *Louisiana* v. *Bloomenstiel*, 235 La. 860, 106 So.2d 288.
[30] *McCoy* v. *Indiana*, 241 Ind. 104, 170 N.E.2d 43.
[31] *Connecticut* v. *Cohn*, 24 Conn.S. 232, 189 A.2d 508.

QUESTIONS AND PROBLEMS

1. Checklist of legal terms:
   - (a) crime; treason, felony, misdemeanor (35)
   - (b) crimes mala in se, crimes mala prohibita (36)
   - (c) principal, accessory (36)
   - (d) principal in the first degree, principal in the second degree (37)
   - (e) accessory before the fact, accessory after the fact (37)
   - (f) swindle or confidence game (39), forgery (40), criminal libel (40), lottery (41), larceny (41), burglary (41), robbery (42), embezzlement (42), extortion (43), bribery (43), receiving stolen goods (43)

2. What is the objective of the rule that an irresistible impulse to commit a crime does not excuse criminal liability when the mental instability is not the result of disease?

3. Harrison committed an offense for which he was tried, convicted, and sentenced to ten years in the state penitentiary. After being released, he was convicted of committing a felony. At this trial he was sentenced to serve a maximum term in the penintentiary on the ground that he had committed a second felony. Harrison contended that his first offense was a misdemeanor. Was his contention sound?

4. Morse was convicted of forging the name "Hillyard Motors" as the drawer of a check. He appealed on the ground that signing such a name had no legal effect, and that therefore he was not guilty of forgery. Decide. (Washington v. Morse, 38 Wash.2d 927, 234 P.2d 478)

5. Socony Mobil Oil Co. ran a telephone bingo game series. The gasoline station dealers purchased the bingo cards from Socony and gave them free to anyone requesting them, whether a customer or not. It was not possible to play the game without a card. A cash prize was awarded the winner. The State of Texas brought an injunction action against Socony to stop this on the ground that it was a lottery. Socony raised the defense that since no value or consideration was given by the persons participating in the bingo games, it was not a lottery. Decide. (Texas v. Socony Mobil Oil Co., [Tex.Civ.App.] 386 S.W.2d 169)

6. The New York Central and Hudson River Railroad was prosecuted for violating the federal statute prohibiting rebates to shippers. It was claimed that the corporation could not be held criminally responsible because the illegal acts had been done by its agents and because the corporation could not commit a crime as it was not authorized by its charter to act in any way that was not lawful. Were these defenses valid? (New York Central and Hudson River Railroad Co. v. United States, 212 U.S. 481)

Chapter 5

Enforcement of the Law

Legal rights are meaningless unless they can be enforced. The purpose of this chapter is to present the means and methods of such enforcement.

AGENCIES FOR ENFORCEMENT

Government provides a system by which the rights of the parties under the law can be determined and enforced. Generally the instrumentality of government by which this is accomplished is a court; the process involved is an action or a lawsuit. In modern times a suit for a declaratory judgment has been added as an alternative to the traditional type of lawsuit. Administrative agencies have also been created to enforce law and to determine rights within certain areas. At the same time arbitration has developed as an out-of-court method of dispute determination.

Courts

A *court* is a tribunal established by government to hear and decide matters properly brought before it, giving redress to the injured or enforcing punishment against wrongdoers, and to prevent wrongs. A *court of record* is one whose proceedings are preserved in an official record. A *court not of record* has limited judicial powers; its proceedings are not recorded, at least not officially.

Each court has inherent power to establish rules necessary to preserve order in the court or to transact the business of the court. An infraction of these rules or the disobedience to any other lawful order, as well as a willful act contrary to the dignity of the court or tending to pervert or obstruct justice, may be punished as *contempt of court*.

The jurisdiction and organization of courts are regulated by constitutional and statutory provision. The procedure to be followed in a court may be regulated by constitution, statute, case law, or court rule.

Jurisdiction of Courts

Each court is empowered to decide certain types or classes of cases. This power is called *jurisdiction*. A court may have original or appellate jurisdiction, or both. A court with *original jurisdiction* has the authority to hear a

45

controversy when it is first brought into court. A court having *appellate jurisdiction,* on the other hand, has authority to review the judgment of an inferior court.

The jurisdiction of a court may be general as distinguished from limited or special. A court having *general jurisdiction* has power to hear and decide all controversies involving legal rights and duties. A court of *limited* (or special) *jurisdiction* has authority to hear and decide only those cases that fall within a particular class, or only certain cases within a class, such as cases in which the amounts involved are below a specified sum.

Courts are frequently classified in terms of the nature of their jurisdiction. A *criminal court* is one that is established for the trial of cases involving offenses against the public. A *civil court,* on the other hand, is authorized to hear and decide issues involving private rights and duties. In like manner, courts are classified into equity courts, juvenile courts, probate courts, and courts of domestic relations upon the basis of their limited jurisdiction.

Officers of the Court

The *judge* is the primary officer of the court. He is either elected or appointed. *Attorneys* or counselors at law are also officers of the court. They are usually selected by the parties to the controversy—but in some cases by the judge—to present to the court the issues of a case.

The *clerk* of the court is appointed in some of the higher courts, but he is usually elected to office in the lower courts. His principal duties are to enter cases upon the court calendar, to keep an accurate record of the proceedings, to attest the same, and, in some instances, to approve bonds and to compute the amount of costs involved.

The *sheriff* is the chief executive of a county. In addition to the duty of maintaining peace and order within the territorial limits of a county, he has many other duties in connection with the administration of justice in county courts of record. His principal duties consist of summoning witnesses, taking charge of the jury, preserving order in court, serving writs, carrying out judicial sales, and executing judgments. The *marshals* of the United States perform these duties in the federal courts. In county courts not of record, such as the courts of justices of the peace, these duties, when appropriate, are performed by a *constable.* Some of the duties of the sheriff are now performed by persons known as *court criers,* or by deputy sheriffs, known as *bailiffs.*

The Jury

The *jury* is a body of citizens sworn by a court to try to determine by verdict the issues of fact submitted to them. A trial jury consists of not more than twelve persons. The first step in forming a jury is to make a *jury list*. This step consists of the preparation by the proper officers or board of a list of qualified persons from which a jury may be drawn. The statutes usually exempt from jury service persons in certain classes, such as attorneys, doctors, ministers, firemen, and police officers.

A certain number of persons drawn from the jury list constitute the *jury panel*. The number drawn and the procedure are usually prescribed by statutes. Selection of the jury panel is generally made by an impartial means, such as by wheel or by drawing names from a box. A trial jury is selected from members of the panel.

Federal Courts

The federal system of courts includes the following:

1 / Supreme Court of the United States. The Supreme Court is the only federal court expressly established by the Constitution. Congress is authorized by the Constitution to create such other federal courts as are deemed necessary.

The Supreme Court has original jurisdiction in all cases affecting ambassadors, other public ministers, and consuls, and in those cases in which a state is a party. Except as regulated by Congress, it has appellate jurisdiction in all cases that may be brought into the federal courts in accordance with the terms of the Constitution. The Supreme Court also has appellate jurisdiction of certain cases that have been decided by the supreme courts of the states. Over 2,000 cases are filed with this court in a year.

2 / Courts of appeals. The United States, including the District of Columbia, is divided into 11 judicial circuits. Each of the circuits has a court of appeals. These courts are courts of record. (See p. 48.)

A court of appeals has appellate jurisdiction only and is empowered to review the final decisions of the district courts, except in cases that may be taken directly to the Supreme Court. The decisions of the courts of appeal are final in most cases. An appeal may be taken on certain constitutional questions. Otherwise, review depends on the discretion of the Supreme Court and, in some cases, of the court of appeals.

3 / District courts. The United States, including the District of Columbia, is divided into a number of judicial districts. Some states form a single district, whereas others are divided into two or more districts. District courts are also located in the territories.

The district courts have original jurisdiction in practically all cases that may be maintained in the federal courts. They are the trial courts for criminal as well as for civil cases, but the latter are the more numerous.

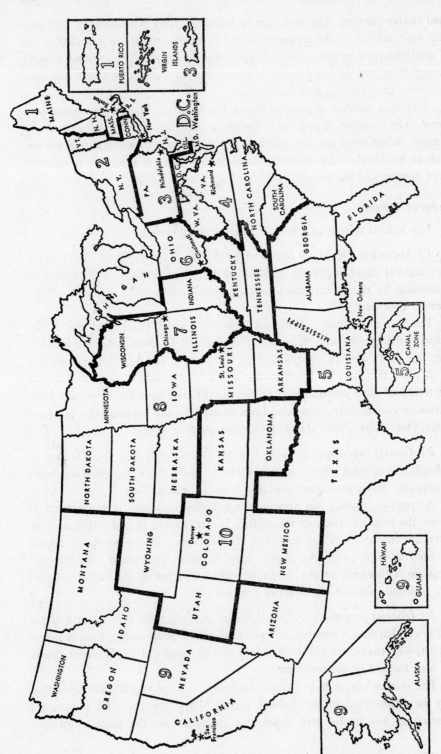

The Eleven Federal Judicial Circuits

The District of Columbia is in the eleventh circuit.

Illustrations of civil cases that may be brought in these courts are (a) civil suits brought by the United States; (b) actions brought by citizens of different states claiming land under grants by different states; (c) proceedings under the bankruptcy, internal revenue, postal, copyright, and patent laws; (d) civil cases of admiralty and maritime jurisdiction; (e) actions against national banking associations; and (f) cases involving $10,000 or more that arise under the federal Constitution, or laws and treaties made thereunder, or between citizens of different states or between citizens of one state and of a foreign state.

In addition to the Supreme Court, the courts of appeals, and the district courts, other courts and tribunals have been created by Congress to determine other matters.

4 / United States Customs Court. This court has the duty of making decisions with respect to the law and facts concerning the classification of imported goods, the rate of duty for each class, and the rules and regulations governing the collection of revenues.

5 / Court of Customs and Patent Appeals. The function of this court of record is to review decisions of the Customs Court on classifications and duties upon imported merchandise, decisions of the Patent Office on patents and trademarks, and legal questions in the findings of the Tariff Commission pertaining to unfair practices in import trade.

6 / Court of Claims. Subject to certain exceptions, this court has jurisdiction over claims of individuals against the United States Government. Its judgments are payable only upon an appropriation by Congress.

7 / Tax Court. The Tax Court of the United States tries controversies that involve deficiencies in or overpayments of federal taxes. Most decisions of the court are subject to review by the appropriate court of appeals.

8 / United States Court of Military Appeals. This is a judicially independent, final appellate tribunal in court-martial convictions.

9 / Territorial courts. These include the district courts for Puerto Rico, the Virgin Islands, the Canal Zone, and Guam.

State Courts

The system of courts in the various states are organized along similar lines, although differing in details, such as the number of courts, their names, and jurisdiction.

1 / State supreme court. The highest court in most states is known as the Supreme Court, although in a few states it may have a different name, as

"Court of Appeals" in New York. The jurisdiction of a supreme court is ordinarily appellate, although in a few instances it is original. In some states the supreme court is required to render an opinion on certain questions that may be referred to it by the legislature or by the chief executive of the state. The decision of the state supreme court is final in all cases not involving the federal Constitution, laws, and treaties.

2 / Intermediate courts. In some states intermediate courts have original jurisdiction in a few cases but, in the main, they have appellate jurisdic-diction of cases removed for review from the county or district courts. They are known as superior, circuit, or district appellate courts. As a general rule their decisions may be reviewed by the highest state court.

3 / County and district courts. These courts of record have appellate jurisdiction of cases tried in the justice and police courts, as well as general original jurisdiction of criminal and civil cases. They also have jurisdiction of testamentary and guardianship matters, except when, as in some states, the jurisdiction of such cases has been given to special orphans', surrogate, or probate courts.

4 / Justice of peace courts. These courts, presided over by justices of the peace, are ordinarily not courts of record. Their jurisdiction extends usually to the preliminary examination of persons accused of felonies and to the trial of misdemeanors and civil cases that involve relatively small amounts of money. In some parts of certain states justice courts have been supplanted by city or municipal courts. There are also courts in almost all cities, called *police courts,* for the trial of misdemeanors.

5 / Small claims courts. In a number of states, chiefly in the larger cities, special courts have been created to handle small claims in the interest of reducing the cost and delay that litigation ordinarily involves. Some states have adopted an alternative of compulsory arbitration of small claims, subject to the right of appeal to a court of law.

6 / Traffic courts. Special courts limited to violations of motor vehicle laws have been created in most metropolitan areas to relieve the regular courts of the great number of such cases that have accompanied the rise in the use of the automobile.

Administrative Agencies

The difficulties of administration by courts of laws regulating business, labor, agriculture, public utilities, and other phases of the economy led Congress and the state legislatures to establish commissions or agencies of experts to make the rules and to pass upon the violation of the rules. Thus we find the Interstate Commerce Commission regulating interstate commerce and passing upon whether conduct of a carrier is a violation of its regulations. The commission is thus a lawmaker, an executive that enforces the law, and a court which interprets and applies the law. This is also true of the Civil Aeronautics Board, the Federal Trade Commission, the Securities and Exchange Commission, the National Labor Relations Board, and many other federal and state administrative agencies.

Generally an appeal may be taken to the courts from the action of such an administrative body. The action of such boards is usually final, however, with respect to questions of fact when there is reasonable or substantial evidence to support the decision, although it may be reversed by the court when the latter disagrees with the board on questions of law.

Arbitration

By the use of *arbitration* a dispute is brought before one or more arbitrators who make a decision which the parties have agreed to accept as final. This procedure first reached an extensive use in the field of commercial contracts.

When a case is tried in court, the members of the jury and the judge frequently are not familiar with the business practices involved. The attorneys find it necessary, therefore, to explain these business practices before presenting the facts of the case. Arbitration enables the parties to present the facts before trained experts because the arbitrators are familiar with the practices that form the background of the dispute.

Parties to a contract which is to be in effect for some time may specify in the contract that any dispute shall be submitted to arbitrators to be selected by the parties. In some instances the contract will name the arbitrators in advance, who will then be a standing board of arbitrators for the duration of the contract. Frequently the parties provide their own remedy against failure to abide by the award of the arbitrators. The parties may execute a mutual indemnity bond by which each agrees to indemnify the other for any loss caused by his failure to carry out the arbitration award.

The growth of arbitration has been greatly aided by the American Arbitration Association not only in the development of standards, procedures, and forms for arbitration, but also by the creation of panels of qualified arbitrators from which the parties to a contract may select those who will settle their dispute.

COURT PROCEDURE

Detailed laws specify how, when, and where a legal dispute can be brought to court. These rules of procedure are necessary in order to achieve an orderly, fair determination of litigation and in order to obtain, as far as humanly possible, the same decisions on the same facts.

Steps in a Lawsuit

1 / Parties. In a lawsuit the person suing is the *plaintiff*, and the person against whom he makes his claim is the *defendant*. There may be more than one plaintiff and more than one defendant. If *A* and *B* jointly own an automobile which is damaged by *C*, both *A* and *B* must join in an action against *C*. It is improper for either *A* or *B* to sue alone since it is "their" and not "his" car.

2 / Proper court. When a person desires to go to court to enforce a right, his attorney must bring the action in the proper court. A decision by the court on a case not within its jurisdiction has no legal effect.

3 / Form of action. The plaintiff's lawyer determines the form of action to bring. Under the old common law this was frequently a difficult problem because there were many forms of action and the plaintiff would lose his case if his attorney selected the wrong form.

A little more than a century ago, many states attempted to overhaul their procedure and reduced the number of forms of action. Accordingly a number of states thus provided that an *ejectment* should be brought for the recovery of all interests in land, a *replevin* for the recovery of any personal property, an *action of assumpsit* for any contract claim, and an *action of trespass* for any tort claim. There were still special actions, such as *mandamus* to compel a public or corporate officer to do certain kinds of acts and *quo warranto* to question the authority of a public or corporate officer to do an act or the authority of a corporation to exercise a particular power. And there were still separate criminal and equity courts. In a number of states a separate court with jurisdiction over wills, decedents' estates, and trusts began to appear.

Other states combined the forms of action and provided that all actions at law should be brought under the name of "a civil action" or "a civil action for damages" without regard to the original common-law name. Most states have abolished the distinction between actions at law and actions in equity so that the "civil action" includes all noncriminal proceedings.

4 / Commencement of action. In the old common-law courts an action was commenced by filing an order with the keeper of the court records to issue a writ to the sheriff. This writ of summons ordered the sheriff to inform the defendant to appear before the court on a particular date. This method of commencing an action is still followed in many states.

By way of contrast, an action in a court of equity was begun when the plaintiff filed with the court a *complaint* in which he stated the facts about which he complained. No writ was issued, but a copy of the complaint was served on the defendant. In many states and in the federal courts, the reform of recent years has extended this equity practice to all legal actions. These actions are today commenced by the filing of the plaintiff's complaint. Some states still preserve the former distinction between law and equity, while others give the plaintiff the option of commencing the action by either method.

5 / Service of process. The defendant must be served with *process* (a writ, notice, or summons; or the complaint itself) to inform him that the action is pending against him and to subject him to the power of the court.

6 / Pleadings. After process has been served on the defendant, the plaintiff is ready to proceed. If he has not filed with the clerk of the court a written statement of his claim or complaint, he will now do so. After the complaint is filed, a copy is served on the defendant. The defendant must make some reply, generally within 15 or 20 days. If he does not, the plaintiff ordinarily wins the case by default and a judgment is entered in his favor.

Before answering the plaintiff's complaint, the defendant may make certain preliminary objections. He may assert, for example, that the action was brought in the wrong court, or that he had not been properly served. If the objection is sustained, the case may be ended, depending upon the nature of the objection, or the plaintiff may be allowed to correct his mistake. The defendant may also raise the objection, sometimes called a *motion to dismiss* or *demurrer*, that even if the plaintiff's complaint is accepted as true, he is still not entitled to any relief.

If the defendant loses on his objection, he must file an *answer,* which either admits or denies some or all of the facts averred by the plaintiff. For example, if the plaintiff declared that the defendant made a contract on a certain date, the defendant may either admit that he made the contract or deny that he did so. The fact that he admits making the contract does not end the case, for the defendant may then plead defenses, for example, that at a later date the plaintiff and the defendant agreed to set it aside.

Without regard to whether he pleads such new matter, the defendant may generally assert a *counterclaim* or *cross complaint* against the plaintiff. Thus he may contend that the plaintiff owes him money or damages and that this liability should be offset against any claim which the plaintiff may have.

After the defendant files his answer, the plaintiff may generally file preliminary objections to the answer. Just as the defendant could raise objections, the plaintiff may, in certain instances, argue that the counterclaim cannot be asserted in the court in which the case is pending, that the answer is fatally defective in form, or that it is not a legally sufficient answer. Again the court must pass upon the preliminary objections. When these are disposed of, the pleading stage is ordinarily over.

Generally, all of the pleadings in an action may raise only a few or perhaps one question of law, or a question of fact, or both. Thus the whole case may depend on whether a letter admittedly written by the defendant amounted to an acceptance of the plaintiff's offer, thereby constituting a contract. If this question of law is answered in favor of the plaintiff, a judgment will be entered for the plaintiff; otherwise, for the defendant. By way of contrast, it may be admitted that a certain letter would be an acceptance if it had been written; but the defendant may deny that he ever wrote it. Here the question is one of fact, and the judgment is entered for the plaintiff if it is determined that the fact happened as he claimed. Otherwise the judgment is entered for the defendant.

If the only questions involved are questions of law, the court will decide the case on the pleadings alone since there is no need for a trial to determine the facts. If questions of fact are involved, then there must be a trial to determine what the facts really were.

7 / Pretrial procedure. Many states and the federal courts have adopted other procedural steps that may be employed before the trial, with the purpose of eliminating the need for a trial, simplifying the issues to be tried, or giving the parties information needed for preparation for trial.

(a) MOTION FOR JUDGMENT ON THE PLEADINGS. After the pleadings are closed, many courts permit either party to move for a *judgment on the pleadings.* When such a motion is made, the court examines the record and may then enter a judgment according to the merits of the case as shown by the record.

(b) MOTION FOR SUMMARY JUDGMENT. In some courts a party may shorten a lawsuit by bringing into court sworn statements and affidavits which show that a claim or defense is false or a sham. This procedure cannot be used when there is substantial dispute of fact concerning the matters to be proved by the use of the affidavits.

(c) PRETRIAL CONFERENCE. In many courts either party may request the court to call a *pretrial conference,* or the court may take the initiative in doing so. This conference is in substance a round-table discussion by a judge of the court and the attorneys in the case. The object of the conference is to eliminate matters that are not in dispute and to determine what issues remain for litigation.

The pretrial conference is not intended as a procedure to compel the parties to settle their case. It not infrequently results, however, that when the attorneys discuss the matter with the court, they recognize that the differences between the conflicting parties are not so great as contemplated or that one side has less merit than was at first believed; in consequence, a settlement of the case is agreed upon.

(d) DISCOVERY. The Federal Rules of Civil Procedure and similar rules in a large number of states now permit one party to inquire of the adverse party and of all witnesses about anything relating to the action. This includes asking the adverse party the names of witnesses; asking the adverse party and the witnesses what they know about the case; examining, inspecting, and photographing books, records, buildings, and machines; and making an examination of the physical or mental condition of a party when it has a bearing on the action. These procedures are classed as *discovery*.

Under the prior practice, except for the relatively unusual situation in which a party could obtain information before trial by filing a bill for discovery in equity, a party never knew what witnesses would appear in court for the adverse party or what they would say, or what documentary evidence would be produced.

(e) DEPOSITIONS. Ordinarily a witness testifies in court at the time of the trial. In some instances it may be necessary or desirable to take his testimony out of court before the time of the trial. It may be that he is aged or infirm or is about to leave the state or country and will not be present when the trial of the action is held. In such a case the interested party is permitted to have the testimony, called a *deposition*, of the witness taken outside of the court.

The taking of the deposition is accomplished by having the witness appear before an officer authorized to administer oaths who places the witness under oath to tell the truth. Questions are then asked the witness as at a regular trial. The answers are recorded, generally by a stenographer, and a transcript is made of the answers. These are ordinarily read by the witness, signed by him, and the questions and answers are sent by the officer to the court in which the action is pending.

8 / Determination of facts.

(a) THE TRIER OF FACTS. If the legal controversy is one which in the common-law days would have been tried by a jury, either party to the action has the constitutional right today to demand that the action be tried before a jury. If all parties agree, however, the case may be tried by the court or judge alone without a jury, and in some instances referred to a master or a referee appointed by the court to hear the matter.

In equity, although there is no constitutional right to a jury trial, the chancellor or equity judge may submit questions to a jury. There is the basic difference that in such cases the verdict or decision of the jury is only advisory to the chancellor; that is, he seeks it for his own information but is free to ignore it if he wants to do so. In contrast, the verdict of a jury in an action at law is binding on the court unless a basic error is present.

When new causes of action are created by statute, such as the right of an employee to obtain workmen's compensation for an injury arising in the course of his employment without regard to whether the employer is negligent, there is no constitutional right to a trial by jury. The trier of facts may accordingly be a judge without a jury, or a special administrative board or agency, such as a Workmen's Compensation Board.

(b) BASIS FOR DECISION. The trier of fact, whether a jury, a judge, a referee, or a board, can only decide questions of fact on the basis of evidence presented before it. Each party offers evidence in support of his claim. The evidence usually consists of the answers of persons to questions in court. Their answers are called *testimony*. The evidence may also include some *real evidence,* that is tangible things, such as papers, books, and records. In some cases, such as a damage action for improper construction of a building, the trier of fact may be taken to view the building so that a better understanding can be obtained.

The witness who testifies in court is usually a person who had some direct contact with the facts in the case, such as a person who saw the events occur or who heard one of the parties say something. In some instances it is also proper to offer the testimony of persons who have no connection with the case when they have expert knowledge and their opinions as experts are desired.

A witness who refuses to appear in court may be ordered to do so by a *subpoena.* He may also be compelled to bring relevant papers with him to court by a *subpoena duces tecum.* If he fails to obey the subpoena, the witness may be arrested for contempt of court. In some states the names of the order upon the witness and the procedure for contempt have been changed, but the substance remains the same.

9 / Conduct of the trial. The conduct of a trial will be discussed in terms of a jury trial. Generally a case is one of several assigned for trial on a certain day or during a certain trial period. When the turn of the case is called, the opposing counsel seat themselves at tables in front of the judge and the jury is drawn. After the jury is sworn, the attorneys usually make *opening addresses* to the jury. Details vary in different jurisdictions, but the general pattern is that each attorney tells the jury what he intends to prove. When this step has been completed, the presentation of the evidence by both sides begins.

The attorney for the plaintiff starts with his first witness and asks him all the questions that he desires and that are proper. This is called the *direct examination* of the witness since it is made by the attorney calling his own witness. After the direct examination has been finished, the opposing counsel asks the same witness such questions as he desires in an effort to disprove his story. This is called *cross-examination*.

After the cross-examination has been completed, the attorney for the plaintiff may ask the same witness other questions to overcome the effect of the cross-examination. This is called *redirect examination*. This step in turn may be followed by further examination by the defendant's attorney, called *recross-examination*.

After the examination of the plaintiff's first witness has been concluded, the plaintiff's second witness takes the witness stand and is subjected to an examination in the same way as the first. This continues until all of the plaintiff's witnesses have been called. Then the plaintiff rests his case, and the defendant calls his first witness. The pattern of examination of witnesses is repeated, except that now the defendant is calling his own witnesses and his attorney conducts the direct and redirect examination, while the questioning by the plaintiff's attorney is cross- or recross-examination.

After the witnesses of both parties have been examined and all the evidence has been presented, each attorney makes another address, a *summation*, to the jury in which he sums up the case and suggests that a verdict be returned for his client.

10 / Charge to the jury and the verdict. The summation by the attorneys is followed by the *charge* of the judge to the jury. This charge is a résumé of what has happened at the trial and an explanation of the applicable law. At its conclusion, the judge instructs the jury to retire and study the case in the light of his charge and then return a *verdict*. By his instructions, the judge leaves to the jury the problem of determining the facts but states the law that they must apply to such facts as they may find. The jury then retires to secret deliberation in the jury room.

11 / Taking the case from the jury and attacking the verdict. At several points during the trial or immediately after, a party may take a step to end the case or to set aside the verdict.

(a) VOLUNTARY NONSUIT. If the plaintiff is dissatisfied with the progress of his case, he may wish to stop the trial and begin again at a later date. In most jurisdictions he can do so by taking a *voluntary nonsuit*.

(b) COMPULSORY NONSUIT. After the plaintiff has presented the testimony of all his witnesses, the defendant may request the court to enter a nonsuit on the ground that the case presented by the plaintiff does not entitle him to recover.

(c) MISTRIAL. When necessary to avoid great injustice, the trial court may declare that there has been a mistrial and thereby terminate the trial and postpone it to a later date. While either party may move the court to enter a mistrial, it is discretionary with the court whether it does so. A mistrial is commonly entered when evidence of a highly prejudicial character has been admitted and the trial judge does not believe that the jury can ignore it even when instructed to do so, or when a juror has been guilty of misconduct.

(d) DIRECTED VERDICT. After the presentation of all the evidence at the trial, either party may request the court to direct the jury to return a verdict in his favor. When the plaintiff would not be entitled to recover even though all the testimony in the plaintiff's favor were believed, the defendant is entitled to have the court direct the jury to return a verdict for the defendant. The plaintiff is entitled to a verdict in his favor when, even if all the evidence on behalf of the defendant were believed, the jury would still be required to find for the plaintiff. In some states the defendant may make such a motion at the close of the plaintiff's proof.

(e) NEW TRIAL. After the verdict has been returned by the jury, a party may move for a new trial if he is not satisfied with the verdict or with the amount of damages that has been awarded. If it is clear that the jury has made a mistake or if material evidence that could not have been discovered sooner is available, the court will award a new trial and the case will be tried again before another jury.

(f) JUDGMENT N.O.V. If the verdict returned by the jury is clearly wrong as a matter of law, the court may set aside the verdict and enter a judgment contrary to the verdict. This in some states is called a *judgment non obstante veredicto,* or as it is abbreviated, a judgment n.o.v.

12 / Judgment and costs. The court enters a judgment conforming to the verdict unless a new trial has been granted, a mistrial declared after the return of the verdict, or a judgment n.o.v. entered. Generally whoever is the winning party will also be awarded costs in the action. In equity actions or those that had their origin in equity, and in certain statutory proceedings, the court has discretion to award costs to the winner, to divide them between the parties, or to have each party bear his own.

Costs ordinarily include the costs of filing papers with the court, the cost of having the sheriff or other officers of the court take official action, the statutory fees paid to the witnesses, the cost of a jury fee, if any, and the cost of printing the record when this is required on appeal. They do not include compensation for the time spent by the party in preparing his case or in being present at the trial, the expense in going to his attorney or to the court, the time lost from work because of the case, or the fee paid by him to his attorney. Sometimes when a special statutory action is brought, the statute authorizes recovery of a small attorney's fee. Thus, a mechanic's lien statute may authorize the recovery of an attorney's fee of 10 percent of the amount recovered, or a "reasonable attorney's fee." As a general rule, the costs that a party recovers represent only a part of the total expenses actually sustained in the litigation.

13 / Appeal. After a judgment has been entered, the party who is aggrieved thereby may appeal. This means that a party who wins the judgment but is not awarded as much as he hoped, as well as a party who loses the case, may take an appeal.

The appellate court does not hear witnesses. It examines the record of the proceedings before the lower court, that is, the file of the case containing all the pleadings, the testimony of witnesses, and the judge's charge, to see if there was error of law. To assist the court, the attorneys for the parties file arguments or briefs and generally make an argument orally before the court.

If the appellate court does not agree with the application of the law made by the lower court, it generally sets aside or modifies the action of the lower court and enters such judgment as it concludes the lower court should have entered. It may set aside the action of the lower court and send the case back to the lower court with directions to hold a new trial or with directions to enter a new judgment in accordance with the opinion that is filed by the appellate court.

14 / Execution. After a judgment has been entered or after an appeal has been decided, the losing party generally will comply with the judgment of the court. If he refuses to do so, the winning party may then take steps to execute or carry out the judgment.

If the judgment is for the payment of a sum of money, the plaintiff may direct the sheriff or other judicial officer to sell as much of the property of the defendant as is necessary to pay the plaintiff's judgment and the costs of the proceedings and of the execution. Acting under this authorization, the sheriff may make a public sale of the defendant's property and apply the proceeds to the payment of the plaintiff's judgment. In most states the defendant is allowed an exemption of several hundred dollars and certain articles, such as personal clothing and tools of his trade.

If the judgment is for the recovery of specific property, the judgment will direct the sheriff to deliver the property to the plaintiff.

If the judgment directs the defendant to do or to refrain from doing an act, it is commonly provided that his failure to obey the order is a contempt of court punishable by fine or imprisonment.

*   *   *   *   *

The foregoing review indicates that a lawsuit may be a long proceeding. Because the winning party does not recover all of his expenses, he may even have less than he would have had if there had been no lawsuit. The losing party has his own expenses and costs to bear, in addition to any judgment for damages that he must pay to the other party. Knowledge of the law before you enter into business transactions, or guidance by one who has that knowledge, therefore, may save you much difficulty and expense.

Declaratory Judgment

In recent years a new procedure for settling disputes, authorized by statute, has made its appearance. This is the *declaratory judgment* procedure. Under it a person, when confronted with the early prospect of an actual controversy, may petition the court to decide the question before loss is actually sustained. A copy of the petition is served on all parties. They may file answers. After all the pleadings have been filed, the court then decides the questions involved just as though a lawsuit had been brought.

The advantage of this procedure is that it enables the court to decide the dispute before any loss is sustained or an act done which causes harm. Since the decision is made in advance of any loss, it is a decision of law and does not involve questions of disputed fact in most cases.

Although the declaratory judgment procedure has these advantages, it cannot always be invoked. Courts have traditionally, with few exceptions, refused to render *advisory opinions*, that is, to give advice in advance of an actual law case. The declaratory judgment tends to become an advisory opinion unless it is clear that there is an actual dispute. Many courts accordingly refuse to allow a petition for a declaratory judgment unless convinced that there are present "the ripening seeds of a controversy."

Attachment and Garnishment of Wages

It is generally provided that a creditor may require a third person who owes money to his debtor to pay such amount to the creditor to satisfy the creditor's claim against the debtor. That is, if *A* has a valid claim for $100 against *B*, and *C* owes *B* $100, *A* can require *C* to pay him $100, which thereby satisfies both *C*'s debt to *B* and *B*'s debt to *A*. The necessary legal procedure, which is frequently regulated in great detail, generally requires the third person to pay the money into court or to the sheriff rather than directly to the original creditor. It is commonly provided that the original creditor may also by this process reach tangible property belonging to his debtor which is in the custody or possession of a third person. This procedure is commonly called *attachment* and the third person is called a *garnishee*.

In most states attachment or garnishment may be used when an employee owes money and his creditor then seeks to compel the employer to pay him the amount of the wages due the employee. It may generally be done after the entry of a judgment against the debtor. When the procedure is allowed, the employee may generally claim an exemption of part of his wages.

QUESTIONS AND PROBLEMS

1. Checklist of legal terms—agencies for enforcement:
   (a) court; court of record, contempt of court (45)
   (b) jurisdiction (45); original jurisdiction (45), appellate jurisdiction (46)
   (c) general jurisdiction, limited jurisdiction (46)
   (d) criminal court, civil court (46)
   (e) judge, attorney, clerk (46)
   (f) sheriff, marshal, constable, court crier, bailiff (46)
   (g) jury (46); jury list (47), jury panel (47)
   (h) administrative agency (50), arbitration (51)

2. A statute granted the Superior Court of Buffalo, New York, jurisdiction of cases involving interests in land located within the limits of that city. The City of Buffalo brought an action in that court to acquire land situated in West Seneca, New York, for use as a park. The action was dismissed by the court. Why?

3. Kent sought to recover damages for breach of contract from Link in a court action. Should such an action be brought in a court of original jurisdiction or in one of appellate jurisdiction? Why?

4. The Missouri River, which forms part of the boundary line between Kansas and Missouri, suddenly changed its course and formed a new channel several miles west of its old bed. The State of Missouri claimed all of the land between the old and the new beds of the river. Could this controversy be tried in the first instance in the Supreme Court of the United States?

5. Jefferson, who lives in California, owes $25,000 to Graf, who lives in Ohio. Is Graf entitled to bring action for this amount against Jefferson in a federal court?

6. Donovan imports some furniture which he claims is over a hundred years old and therefore free from import duties. The customs officer refuses to classify the articles as antiques. Is Donovan entitled to take this controversy to the Court of Claims?

7. The State of Virginia issued certain bonds under a statute which provided that the bonds were receivable for all taxes. A later statute prohibited the receipt of such bonds for taxes. McCullough brought an action against the state, contending that the second statute impaired the obligation of contract and violated a provision of the federal Constitution. The Supreme Court of Virginia upheld the validity of the second statute. Did its decision settle the question conclusively?

8. (a) What is the procedure for settling a dispute by arbitration?
   (b) What are the advantages of this procedure?

9. Checklist of legal terms—court procedure:
   (a) plaintiff, defendant (52)
   (b) ejectment, replevin, action of assumpsit, action of trespass (52)
   (c) mandamus, quo warranto (52)
   (d) complaint, process, motion to dismiss or demurrer, answer, counterclaim or cross complaint (53)
   (e) judgment on the pleadings (54), pretrial conference (54), discovery (55), deposition (55)
   (f) testimony, real evidence, subpoena, subpoena duces tecum (56)
   (g) opening addresses (56), direct examination (57), cross-examination (57), redirect examination (57), recross-examination (57), summation (57)
   (h) verdict (57), voluntary nonsuit (57), directed verdict (58), judgment non obstante veredicto (58)
   (i) appeal, execution (59)
   (j) declaratory judgment, advisory opinion (60)
   (k) attachment, garnishee (61)

10. Bell brought an action against Hopewell Company to recover damages resulting from a breach of contract. No process was served on the defendants, but Bell published notice of the action in the newspaper. Bell secured a judgment against the defendants. Later it was contended that the judgment was not valid. Do you agree?

11. How does each of the following pretrial procedures contribute to the efficiency of a court?
    (a) Discovery
    (b) Motion for judgment on the pleadings
    (c) Motion for summary judgment
    (d) Pretrial conference

12. A witness is willing to testify concerning certain facts in a case, but he lives in another state. How can his testmony be secured for evidence in the trial?

13. Outline briefly the steps in a trial beginning with the opening statements by the attorneys.

14. How is the judgment of the court executed?

Prologue

Business Law—An Introduction

The preceding discussion in Part I has been concerned with the nature of law (Chapter 1), the social forces that determine the law (Chapter 2), the law of torts and crimes (Chapters 3 and 4), and the enforcement of legal rights (Chapter 5). In the parts that follow, an intensive study of the law of business transactions will be undertaken.

Nature of Business Law

This book is devoted to a consideration of the basic or fundamental principles of law that are of the greatest importance to the citizen and the businessman. Business law includes the various branches of law that determine the rights and liabilities of persons taking part in business transactions.

Branches of Business Law

The rise of new ways of social and business life, the development of an industrial society, and the increased use of mechanical devices have led to an increase in the number of laws and of the fields of law.

1 / Contract law. A contract is a binding agreement. The general principles governing contracts are discussed in Part II. Certain types of contracts have developed special principles which govern them, in addition to the general principles applicable to all kinds of contracts. Thus it is necessary to give particular attention to contracts of agency and employment (Part III); the contracts or obligations that arise in connection with commercial paper, such as checks (Part IV); contracts for the sale of goods (Part VI); and secured credit sales and other security devices, such as those used in installment selling, and insurance (Part VII).

2 / Property law. The law governing property is classified in terms of the kind of property involved, and particular transactions relating to it. Some of these principles relate to personal property, the transfer of title to personal property, and bailments of personal property which arise when it is given to another person to store, repair, or transport (Part V). The law of real property, which is ordinarily land and buildings, is discussed both generally, and with respect to the transfer of title, and the renting and mortgaging of real property (Part X).

In a general sense, the chapters on business security (Chapters 3 and 4) may also be regarded as relating to property law, for the security considered is the security of various property rights against harm from various types of misconduct.

3 / Business organizations. Business today is to a very large degree conducted by groups or associations. The law governing the two most common forms of business organizations is set forth in the chapters devoted to partnerships and corporations (Parts VIII and IX).

4 / Estates. Property that belongs to one person often is administered or is nominally owned by another. This situation arises most commonly when property is held by one person in trust for another, when the owner has died and his property is being collected and distributed by his executor or administrator, or when the owner has become bankrupt and his property is being distributed through the bankruptcy court in order to pay his debts (Part XI). Although these situations are not of everyday occurrence, they are of sufficient importance to require an understanding of the basic applicable principles.

5 / Government regulation of business. The law of government regulation of business is considered with respect to the regulation of business enterprises, and the regulation of labor-management relations (Part XII). Although briefly treated because of limitations of space, the importance of the power of government to regulate business and the scope of such regulations must not be minimized.

* * * * * * *

Both as a member of society and as a person whose welfare is affected by the business world, each individual must recognize the importance of the laws that regulate business. The importance of his right to vote and of his duty to exercise that right in an intelligent manner will be appreciated when it is understood that there is little or no protection against unwise regulatory legislation except the vote of the people. The courts will not protect the individual or the economy from unsound business laws. As stated by the United States Supreme Court:

It is not for this Court to reweigh the relevant factors and, perchance, substitute its notion of expediency and fairness for that of Congress. This is so even though the [Act of Congress] may demonstrably be disadvantageous to certain areas or persons. This Court is not a tribunal for relief from the crudities and inequities of complicated experimental economic legislation.[1]

---

[1] *Secretary of Agriculture* v. *Central Roig Refining Company*, 338 U.S. 604.

PART II

Contracts

Chapter 6

Nature and Classes

Almost every personal business activity involves a contract—a membership in a record club; the purchase of an FM radio on credit; the rental of an apartment. Likewise, in each transaction relating to services or to the acquisition of raw materials, their manufacture, and the distribution of the finished products by businesses, a contract defines the relationship and the rights and obligations of the parties.

An essential part of free enterprise in our economic system is that the rights created by contracts are protected. Each party must observe the terms of the contract, and generally government cannot impair the obligations of a contract.

Definition of Contract

In simplest terms a contract is a binding agreement. By one definition, "a *contract* is a promise or a set of promises for the breach of which the law gives a remedy, or the performance of which the law in some way recognizes as a duty." [1] Contracts arise out of agreements; hence a contract is often defined as "an agreement creating an obligation." [2]

Generally a contract is an exchange of promises or assents by two or more persons, resulting in an obligation to do or to refrain from doing a particular act, which obligation is recognized or enforced by law. A contract may also be formed when a promise is made by one person in exchange for the act or the refraining from the doing of an act by another. The substance of the definition of a contract is that by mutual agreement or assent the parties create legally enforceable duties or obligations that did not exist before.

---

[1] Restatement, Contracts, Sec. 1.
[2] *H. Liebes & Co. v. Klengenberg*, [C.A.9th] 23 F.2d 611.

In order to be an enforceable contract, there must be (1) an agreement, (2) between competent parties, (3) based upon the genuine assent of the parties, (4) supported by consideration, (5) made for a lawful object, and (6) in the form required by law, if any. These requirements will be considered in the following chapters.

Nature of Contracts

Contracts arise under a wide variety of circumstances. They may arise from face-to-face conversations or from conversations by telephone, from the exchange of letters or telegrams, or by any other means of communication.

When the contract is part of a common business transaction, a printed form is often used. In such a case, all that is usually necessary to complete the contract is to add the date, the names of the parties, the price, the particular performance or commodity which is the subject matter of the contract, and the signatures of the parties. Familiar types of standard contract forms are insurance policies, leases, and the various forms used for the installment purchase of automobiles, refrigerators, and record players.

Sometimes the contract must comply with certain standards. One law may declare that a particular type of contract shall be in writing. Another

---

THIS AGREEMENT is made on June 2, 1969, between Robert B. Evans, 6468 Oak Street, Albany, New York, the party of the first part, and Clifford R. Gray, 500 Church Street, Albany, New York, the party of the second part.

The party of the first part agrees [here state what he agrees to do; as: to install aluminum triple-track storm windows in the home of the party of the second part at (address) by (date) in accordance with the specifications attached hereto.] In consideration of which the party of the second part agrees [here state what he agrees to do, as: to pay the party of the first part $_____ upon the satisfactory completion of the work.]

Robert B. Evans

Clifford R. Gray

Contract

law may prescribe that certain provisions must be included in the contract. Thus state laws commonly provide that an insurance policy must contain a clause giving the policyholder a 30-day or 31-day period in which to pay overdue premiums before he may be declared in default. The law may state that when a contract calls for the payment of interest, the interest cannot be greater than a specified percent of the amount owed. Certain provisions of contracts may be prohibited entirely by law or may be declared contrary to public policy by the courts.

Subject Matter of Contracts

The subject matter of a contract may relate to the performance of personal services, such as contracts of employment to work on an assembly line in a factory, to work as a secretary in an office, to sing on television, or to build a house. The contract may provide for the transfer of the ownership of property, such as a house (real property) or an automobile (personal property), from one person to another. A contract may also call for a combination of these things. For example, a builder may contract to supply materials and do the work involved in installing the materials, or a person may contract to build a house and then transfer the house and the land to the buyer.

Parties to a Contract

A person who makes a promise is the *promisor,* and the person to whom the promise is made is called the *promisee.* If the promise is binding, it imposes upon the promisor a duty or obligation and he may be called the *obligor.* The promisee who can claim the benefit of the obligation is also called the *obligee.* The parties to a contract are said to stand in privity with each other, and the relationship between them is termed *privity of contract.*

A party to a contract may be an individual, a partnership, a corporation, a government. A person may act for himself, or another person may have authority to act on his behalf. There may be only one person on each side of the contract, or there may be two or more persons on either side.

In written contracts parties may be referred to as "party of the first part" and "party of the second part." Frequently, however, they are given special names that serve better to identify each party. For example, the parties to a contract by which one person agrees that another may occupy his house upon the payment of money are called landlord and tenant, or lessor and lessee, and the contract between them is known as a lease. Other parties have their distinctive names, such as vendor and vendee, for the parties to a sales contract; shipper and carrier, for the parties to a transportation contract; insurer and insured, for the parties to an insurance policy.

In addition to the original parties to the contract, other persons may have rights or duties with respect to it. For example, one party may to some extent assign his rights under the contract to a third person. Again, the contract may have been made for the benefit of a third person, as in a life insurance contract, and the third party is permitted to enforce the contract.

Formal and Simple Contracts

Contracts are classified in terms of their form as (1) contracts under seal, (2) contracts of record, and (3) simple contracts. The first two classes are known as *formal contracts*.[3]

1 / Contracts under seal. A *contract under seal* is executed by affixing a seal or, in other words, by making an impression upon the paper or upon some tenacious substance, such as wax, attached to the instrument. Although at common law an impression was necessary, the courts now treat various signs or marks to be the equivalent of a seal.[4] To illustrate, some states hold that there is a seal if a person's signature or a corporation's name is followed by a scroll or scrawl, the word "seal," or the letters "L. S." [5]

Two or more persons may use the same seal. When one signer affixes a seal, the subsequent signers, if they deliver the instrument, are presumed to have adopted the seal "unless extrinsic circumstances show a contrary intention." [6]

A contract under seal is binding at common law because of its formality. In some states this has been changed by statute. The Uniform Commercial Code abolishes the law of seals for the sale of goods.[7]

2 / Contracts of record. One form of *contract of record* arises when one acknowledges before a proper court that he is obligated to pay a certain sum unless a specified thing is done or not done. For example, a party who has been arrested may be released on his promise to appear in court and may bind himself to pay a certain sum in the event that he fails to do so.[8] An obligation of this kind is known as a *recognizance*.

An obligation imposed by the judgment of a court and entered upon its records is often called a contract of record. It cannot accurately be described as a contract, however, because it is really not based upon an agreement of the parties.

---

[3] R., Sec. 7. The Restatement, Contracts includes in the class of formal contracts commercial paper or negotiable instruments (see Part IV) that are commercial specialties, as distinguished from sealed contracts that are common-law specialties.

[4] R., Sec. 96.

[5] *Stern* v. *Lieberman*, 307 Mass. 77, 29 N.E.2d 839. "L.S." stands for "locus sigilli," the Latin for "the place for the seal."

[6] R., Secs. 98, 99.

[7] Uniform Commercial Code, Sec. 2-203.

[8] *Modern Finance Co.* v. *Martin*, 311 Mass. 509, 42 N.E.2d 533.

3 / Simple contracts. All contracts other than contracts of record and contracts under seal are called *simple contracts* or informal contracts, without regard to whether they are oral or written.[9]

Express and Implied Contracts

Simple contracts may also be classified in terms of the way in which they are created, as express contracts and implied contracts.

1 / Express contracts. An *express contract* is one in which the parties have made oral or written declarations of their intentions and of the terms of the transaction.

2 / Implied contracts. An *implied contract* (or, as sometimes stated, a contract implied in fact) is one in which the evidence of the agreement is not shown by words, written or spoken, but by the acts and conduct of the parties.[10] Such a contract arises, for example, when one person, without being requested to do so, renders services under circumstances indicating that he expects to be paid for them, and the other person, knowing such circumstances, accepts the benefit of those services.[11] An implied contract cannot arise when there is an existing express contract on the same subject.[12] Likewise no contract is implied when the relationship of the parties is such that by a reasonable interpretation the performance of services or the supplying of goods was intended as a gift.

Case Example

Facts: Prior to the death of Emma Center, her nephew's wife, Clara Stewart, rendered various household services to Emma. All of the parties lived in the same house as a family group. During most of the time in question, Clara had a full-time job. After Emma's death, Clara sued Emma's estate for the value of her household services.

Decision: Judgment for the estate. When a member of a family group renders ordinary household services, it is presumed that they are rendered gratuitously unless the claimant can prove that there was an express contract to pay for them or that the services were extraordinary in character. In the absence of such proof, no recovery is allowed. (Stewart v. Brandenburg, [Ky.] 383 S.W.2d 122)

---

[9] R., Sec. 11.

[10] Contracts of this nature may be more accurately described as contracts "expressed" by conduct, as distinguished from contracts expressed in words, for an agreement by conduct differs from an express agreement only in the manner by which its existence is established. It is more common, however, to refer to these contracts as implied.

[11] *DeCaire v. Bishop's Estate,* 330 Mich. 378, 47 N.W.2d 601.

[12] *Moser v. Milner Hotels,* 6 N.J. 278, 78 A.2d 393.

Quasi-Contracts

Under certain conditions the law creates and enforces legal rights and obligations when no real contract, express or implied, exists. Such an obligation is known as a *quasi-contract*. It is an obligation which, in the absence of any agreement, the law creates because one party has received services, money, or property which, in fairness and good conscience, he should pay for or return.[13]

Facts: Dozier and his wife, daughter, and grandson lived in the house Dozier owned. At the request of the daughter and grandson, Paschall made some improvements to the house. Dozier did not authorize these, but he knew that the improvements were being made and did not object to them. Paschall sued Dozier for the reasonable value of the improvements. Dozier defended on the ground that he had not made any contract for such improvements.

Decision: Judgment for Paschall. When a homeowner permits repairs to be made to his home with knowledge that they are being made by a stranger who would expect to be paid for such repairs, there is a quasi-contractual duty to pay for the reasonable value of the improvements to avoid the homeowner's unjust enrichment at the expense of the repairman. (Paschall's v. Dozier, [Tenn.] 407 S.W.2d 150)

Valid and Voidable Contracts and Void Agreements

Another classification of contracts is in terms of their enforceability or validity.

1 / Valid contracts. A *valid contract* is an agreement that is binding and enforceable. It has all the essential requirements mentioned on page 66.

2 / Voidable contracts. A *voidable contract* is an agreement that is otherwise binding and enforceable but, because of the circumstances surrounding its execution or the capacity of one of the parties, it may be rejected at the option of one of the parties.[14] For example, one who has been forced to sign an agreement against his will may in some instances avoid liability on the contract.[15]

3 / Void agreements. A *void agreement* is without legal effect. Thus, an agreement that contemplates the performance of an act prohibited by law is usually incapable of enforcement; hence it is void.[16]

---

[13] *Dass* v. *Epplen*, [Col.] 424 P.2d 779.
[14] R., Sec. 13.
[15] See p. 119.
[16] See p. 138. Although the distinction between a void agreement and a voidable contract is clear in principle, there is frequently confusion because some courts regard a given transaction as void while others regard it as merely voidable.

Executed and Executory Contracts

Contracts may be classified in terms of the extent to which they have been performed, as executed contracts and executory contracts.

1 / Executed contracts. An *executed contract* is one that has been completely performed. In other words, an executed contract is one under the terms of which nothing remains to be done by either party. A contract may be executed at once, as in the case of a cash sale; or it may be executed in the future. In the former instance the transaction is executed at the time the contract is made.

2 / Executory contracts. In an *executory contract* something remains to be done. For example, when a utility company agrees to furnish electricity to another party for a specified period of time at a stipulated price, the contract is wholly executory. If the entire price is paid in advance, the contract is still deemed executory; although, strictly speaking, it is executed on one side and executory on the other.

QUESTIONS AND PROBLEMS

When the concluding question in a problem can be answered yes or no, the principle or rule of law supporting your answer should also be stated.

1. Checklist of legal terms. The following legal terms have been introduced in this chapter:
   (a) contract (65)
   (b) promisor, promisee; obligor, obligee; privity of contract (67)
   (c) formal contract (68), simple contract (69)
   (d) contract under seal, contract of record, recognizance (68)
   (e) express contract (69), implied contract (69); quasi-contract (70)
   (f) valid contract, voidable contract, void agreement (70)
   (g) executed contract, executory contract (71)

2. State the objective(s) of the law (from the list in Chapter 2, pages 10-16) illustrated by each of the following quotations:
   (a) "Economic life would be most uncertain . . . if we did not have the assurance that contracts once made would be binding."
   (b) "A person shall not be allowed to enrich himself unjustly at the expense of another."

3. Classify each of the following as a contract under seal, a contract of record, or a simple contract:
   (a) A purchase of a coat at a department store on a 90-day payment plan
   (b) A recognizance
   (c) A pledge to the United Appeal or Community Chest

4. In each of the following situations which parties have a privity-of-contract relationship?
   (a) *A* contracts to ship *B's* gift to *C*.
   (b) *D* delegates to *E* the job of repairing *F's* television antenna.
   (c) *G* transfers to *H* the right to collect payment from the *J & K* store.
   (d) *L* buys a policy of life insurance naming his wife as beneficiary.

5. Fritts held an Indiana teacher's license. An action was begun by Stone, a county superintendent, to revoke the license. Fritts claimed that his contract rights would be violated if the license were revoked. Was he correct? (Stone v. Fritts, 169 Ind. 361, 82 N.E. 792)

6. McNulty signed a contract with the Medical Service of District of Columbia, Inc. The contract, which was on a printed form prepared by the corporation, concluded with the clause: "In witness whereof, the party of the first part has caused its corporate seal to be hereunto affixed and these presents to be signed by its duly authorized officers and the party of the second part has hereunto set his hand and seal the day and year first above written." The contract had been sent to McNulty, who signed and sealed it, and then returned it to the corporation. The latter signed but did not seal it, and then sent an executed copy of the contract to the plaintiff without referring to the lack of a seal. When McNulty sued on the contract, the corporation claimed that it was an unsealed contract because it had not been sealed by both parties. Was it correct? (McNulty v. Medical Service of District of Columbia, [M.C.App. Dist.Col.] 176 A.2d 783)

7. Martha Parker reared Louis Twiford as a foster son from the time he was 6 or 7 years of age. He lived with her until he was 27 years of age when he married and moved into another house. During the next few years Martha was very ill, and Louis took care of her. She died, and Louis made a claim against Waterfield, her executor, for the reasonable value of the services he had rendered. Was he entitled to recover? (Twiford v. Waterfield, 240 N.C. 582, 83 S.E.2d 548)

8. A state statute required the County Board of Commissioners to advertise their proceedings in a newspaper. The *Greensburg Times* published the notices for the commissioners. The commissioners later refused to pay the newspaper on the ground that they had not executed a written contract with the newspaper on behalf of the county. Decide. (Board of Commissioners v. Greensburg Times, 215 Ind. 471, 19 N.E. 2d 459)

9. Tetrault made a written agreement to sell his land to Bauer. Tetrault died. Bauer claimed that after the agreement for the sale of the land had been made, they had orally agreed that Tetrault would give the land to Bauer for his past services instead of selling it to him. Monroe, who was administering the estate of Tetrault, objected to changing the written contract. A Montana statute provided that a "contract in writing may be altered by a contract in writing or by an executed oral agreement, and not otherwise." Was the oral agreement barred by this statute? (Bauer v. Monroe, 117 Mont. 306, 158 P.2d 485)

Chapter 7

The Agreement—Offer

A contract is a legally binding agreement. This agreement results from an exchange of promises or assents by the parties involved. These assents may be expressed by words or by conduct.

How an Agreement Arises

An agreement arises when one person, the *offeror,* makes an offer and the person to whom the offer is made, the *offeree,* accepts. In every case there must be both an offer and an acceptance. If either is lacking, there is no contract.[1]

An offeror may make an offer to a particular person because he wants only that person to do what he has in mind. On the other hand, he may make the offer to the public at large because he does not care by whom something is done so long as it is done. The latter case arises, for example, when a reward is offered to the public for the return of lost property.

It is frequently said that a meeting of the minds is essential to an agreement or a contract. Modern cases do not stress the meeting of the minds, however, because in some situations the law finds an agreement even though the minds of the parties have not in fact met. For example, an auctioneer may say, "Who will pay $100 for this beautiful vase?" If a person in the crowd raises his hand while looking at the auctioneer, his action is regarded by the law as an offer to pay $100; and, if the auctioneer then brings down his hammer and says, "Sold for $100," there is an acceptance and a binding contract. The man who raised his hand cannot claim that, when he raised it, he did not mean to make an offer but was merely stretching his arm. What he intended is immaterial because it was reasonable for the autioneer to assume that the man's motion was an offer.

The real test, therefore, is not whether the minds of the parties met, but whether under the circumstances one party was reasonably entitled to believe that there was an offer and the other to believe that there was an acceptance.[2]

---

[1] *Milanko* v. *Jensen,* 404 Ill. 261, 88 N.E.2d 857.
[2] Restatement, Contracts. Sec. 20, Comment a; *Markmann* v. *H. A. Bruntjen Co.,* 249 Minn. 281, 81 N.W.2d 858.

Bilateral and Unilateral Contracts

In making an offer, the offeror is in effect extending a promise to do something, such as to pay a sum of money, if the offeree will do what the offeror requests. If the offeror extends a promise and asks for a promise in return and if the offeree accepts the offer by making the promise, the contract is called a *bilateral contract* because one promise is given in exchange for another.

In contrast, the offeror may agree to obligate himself only when something is done by the offeree. Since only one party is obligated to perform after the contract has been made, the contract is called a *unilateral contract*. This is illustrated by the offer of a reward for lost property because the offeror does not care for a mere promise by members of the public that they will try to return the lost property. The offeror wants the property, and he promises to pay anyone who returns the property. When this is done, his offer is accepted, a contract arises, and the offeror is bound by his agreement.[3] The offeree has nothing more to do because he returned the property that was specified by the offer.

> **Facts:** The Weil Furniture Company stated in a newspaper advertisement that each person who sent in an accurate estimate of the number of dots in the ad would receive a credit certificate which could be applied in the purchase of a certain make of television set. Schreiner mailed his estimate and was notified that he had won one of the certificates. The certificate he received stated that it could be used only in the purchase of certain models. The newspaper ad had not contained this restriction. Schreiner objected to this restriction.

> **Decision:** Judgment for Schreiner. The ad constituted an offer which was accepted when Schreiner mailed in an estimate that was a "winner." The contract was based upon the terms of the ad. The limitation found in the certificate was not binding on Schreiner since it was not a term of the contract between the parties. (Schreiner v. Weil Furniture Co., [La.] 68 So.2d 149)

Nature and Requirements of an Offer

An *offer* expresses or appears to express the willingness of the offeror to enter into a contractual agreement regarding a particular subject. It is a promise that is conditional upon an act, a forbearance, or a return promise being given in exchange for the promise or its performance.[4]

A valid offer must meet the tests of (1) contractual intention, (2) definiteness, and (3) communication to the offeree.

---

[3] *Saletic* v. *Stamnes,* 51 Wash.2d 696, 321 P.2d 547.
[4] R., Sec. 24.

*1 / **Contractual intention.*** To constitute an offer, the offeror must intend to create a legal obligation or it must appear that he intends to do so. When there is a lack of such intention on his part, it makes no difference whether the offeree takes any action concerning the offer.

(a) SOCIAL INVITATIONS. Ordinary invitations to social affairs are not "offers" in the eyes of the law. The acceptance of a social invitation, such as an invitation to go to dinner, does not give rise to a legally binding agreement or contract.

(b) OFFERS MADE IN JEST OR EXCITEMENT. If an offer is made in obvious jest, the offeree cannot accept it and then sue the offeror for its breach. Here the offeree, as a reasonable man, should realize that no contract is intended and therefore no contract arises even though the offeror speaks words which, if seriously spoken, could be accepted and result in a contract. Under the same theory an extravagant offer of a reward made in the heat of excitement cannot be acted upon as a valid offer.

It is not always obvious or apparent to the offeree when the offer is made in jest or under excitement. If it is reasonable under the circumstances for the offeree to believe that the offer was made seriously, a contract is formed by the offeree's acceptance.

Facts: Zehmer discussed selling a farm to Lucy. After some discussion of a first draft of a contract, Zehmer and his wife signed a paper stating: "We hereby agree to sell to W. O. Lucy the Ferguson Farm complete for $50,000.00, title satisfactory to buyer." Lucy agreed to purchase the farm on these terms. Thereafter the Zehmers refused to transfer title to Lucy and claimed that they had made the contract for sale as a joke. Lucy brought an action to enforce the contract.

Decision: Judgment for Lucy. It would appear from the circumstances that Zehmer was serious but, even if he were joking, it was apparent that Lucy had believed that he was serious and, as a reasonable man, was entitled to do so under the circumstances. Hence, there was a binding contract. (Lucy v. Zehmer, 196 Va. 493, 84 S.E.2d 516)

(c) INVITATIONS TO NEGOTIATE. The first statement made by one of two persons is not necessarily an offer. In many instances there may be preliminary discussion or an *invitation to negotiate* or talk business by one party to the other. If *A* asks *B*, "Do you want to buy this car?" he is not making an offer but is inviting an offer from *B*. If *B* then says, "I'll pay you $500 for it," he is making an offer that *A* can accept or reject.

On the other hand, after *A's* invitation, *B* may continue the preliminary negotiations by saying, "What do you want for it?" If *A* then replies, "I will sell it to you for $1,000," *A* makes the offer.

Ordinarily, when a seller sends out circulars or catalogs listing prices, he is not regarded as having made an offer to sell at those prices but as merely indicating that he is willing to consider an offer made by a buyer on those terms. The reason for this rule is in part the practical consideration that since a seller does not have an unlimited supply of any commodity, he cannot possibly intend to make a binding contract with everyone who sees his circular. The same principle is applied to merchandise that is displayed with price tags in stores or store windows and to most advertisements.

Facts: The Willis Music Company advertised 16-inch television sets at $22.50 in a Sunday newspaper. Ehrlich ordered a set, but the company refused to deliver on the ground that the price in the newspaper ad was a mistake. Ehrlich sued the company for breach of contract.

Decision: Judgment for the company. Apart from the question of whether there had been a mistake or the effect of a mistake, the newspaper ad was merely an invitation to the public to make offers. It was not an offer that could be accepted by placing an order with the company. (Ehrlich v. Willis Music Co., 93 Ohio App. 246, 113 N.E.2d 252)

The circumstances may be such, however, that even a newspaper advertisement constitutes an offer. Thus it has been held that the seller made an offer when he advertised specific items which would be sold at a clearance sale at the prices listed and added the words "first come, first served." [5]

Quotations of prices, even when sent on request, are likewise not deemed offers in the absence of previous dealings between the parties or the existence of a trade custom which would give the recipient of the quotation reason to believe that an offer was being made to him. Although the businessman is not bound by his quotations and price tags, he will as a matter of goodwill ordinarily make every effort to deliver the merchandise at those prices.[6]

In some instances, it is apparent that an invitation to negotiate and not an offer has been made. When construction work is done for the national government, for a state government, or for a political subdivision, statutes require that a printed statement of the work to be done be published and circulated. Contractors are invited to submit bids on the work, and the statute generally requires that the bid of the lowest responsible bidder be accepted. Such an invitation for bids is clearly an invitation to negotiate, both from its nature and from the fact that it does not specify the price to be paid for the work. The bid of each contractor is an offer, and there is no contract until the government accepts one of these bids. This procedure of

---

[5] *Lefkowitz* v. *Great Minneapolis Surplus Store, Inc.,* 251 Minn. 188, 86 N.W.2d 689.

[6] *Meridian Star* v. *Kay,* 207 Miss. 78, 41 So.2d 746. Statutes prohibiting false or misleading advertising may also require adherence to advertised prices.

advertising for bids is also commonly employed by private persons when a large construction project is involved.

(d) AGREEMENTS TO MAKE A CONTRACT AT A FUTURE DATE. No contract arises when the parties merely agree that at a future date they shall consider making a contract or shall make a contract on terms to be agreed upon at that time.[7] In such case, until the future contract is made, neither party is under any obligation.

(e) DIVISIBLE CONTRACTS. If part of a divisible contract provides for the execution of a future agreement pertaining to certain matters and that part by itself is too vague to be binding, such a provision does not alter the enforceability of other parts of the same contract that are otherwise binding. A *divisible contract* consists of two or more parts and calls for corresponding performances of each part by the parties.

Facts: Fincher was employed by Belk-Sawyer Co. as fashion coordinator for the latter's retail stores. The contract of employment also provided for additional services of Fincher to be thereafter agreed upon in connection with beauty consultation and shopping services to be established at the stores. After Fincher had been employed as fashion coordinator for several months, Belk-Sawyer Co. refused to be bound by the contract on the ground that it was too indefinite.

Decision: Judgment for Fincher. The contract was sufficiently definite as to the present employment, and the intention of the parties to have a present contract on that subject was not to be defeated because they recognized that an additional agreement might be made by them as to other work. (Fincher v. Belk-Sawyer Co., [Fla.App.] 127 So.2d 130)

2 / *Definite offer.* An offer, and the resulting contract, must be definite and certain.[8] If an offer is indefinite or vague or if an essential provision is lacking, it cannot be accepted.[9] The reason is that the courts cannot tell what the parties are to do. Thus an offer to conduct a business for such time as should be profitable is too vague to be considered a valid offer.

Facts: Bonnevier, an employee of the Dairy Cooperative Association, lived in his own home near the employer's plant. The employer wished to expand the plant and decided to purchase Bonnevier's house. Bonnevier was not then working because of an injury. He claimed that an agreement was made to sell the house to the Association in return for which he would be paid $12,000 and would be given "suitable" employment that he "was able to do." The Association did not thereafter employ Bonnevier, who then sued the Association for breach of contract.

---

[7] *Bogert Construction Co.* v. *Lakebrink,* [Mo.App.] 404 S.W.2d 779.

[8] R., Sec. 32. *Southwest Fabricating and Welding Co.* v. *Jones,* [La.App.] 190 So.2d 529.

[9] *Williamson* v. *Miller,* 231 N.C. 722, 58 S.E.2d 743.

Decision: Judgment for the Association. Any agreement as to employment was too vague to be a binding contract because it could not be determined what kind of employment was intended nor what was suitable. (Bonnevier v. Dairy Cooperative Association, 227 Ore. 123, 361 P.2d 262)

Although an offer must be definite and certain, not all of its terms need be expressed. Some of the terms may be implied. For example, an offer "to pay fifty dollars for a watch" does not state the terms of payment. A court would consider that cash payment was to be made upon delivery of the watch.

The offer and contract may also be made definite by reference to another writing, as when the parties agreed that the written lease which was to be executed by them should be the standard form of lease with which both were familiar.[10] Definiteness may also be found by referring to the prior dealings of the parties and trade practices.

As exceptions to the requirement of definiteness, the law has come to recognize certain situations where the practical necessity of doing business makes it desirable to have a "contract," yet the situation is such that it is either impossible or undesirable to adopt definite terms in advance. Thus, the law recognizes binding contracts in the following situations, although at the time that the contract is made there is some element which is not definite:

(a) COST-PLUS CONTRACT. Cost-plus contracts are valid as against the contention that the amount to be paid is not definite when the contract is made. Such contracts protect the contractor by enabling him to enter into a contract without setting up extraordinary reserves against cost contingencies that may arise.[11]

(b) REQUIREMENTS AND OUTPUT CONTRACTS. Contracts by which a supplier agrees in advance to sell its entire future output to a particular buyer or by which a buyer agrees to buy all of its needs or requirements from a particular supplier are valid, as discussed in Chapter 11, although at the time of contracting the amount of goods to be covered by the contract is not known.

(c) SERVICES AS NEEDED. An enterprise may desire to be assured that the services of a given person, customarily a professional man or a specialist, will be available when needed. It is thus becoming valid to make a contract with him to supply such services as in his opinion will be required, although this would appear to be subject to the two evils of not being definite and of giving such person the choice of doing nothing if he so chooses.

---

10 *Emerman* v. *Baldwin,* 186 Pa.Super. 561, 142 A.2d 440.
11 *U. S. Steel Corp.* v. *United States,* [Ct. Claims] 367 F.2d 399.

(d) INDEFINITE DURATION CONTRACTS. Contracts with no specific time limit are valid. The law meets the objection that there is a lack of definiteness by interpreting the contract as being subject to termination at the election of either party. This type of contract is used most commonly in employment and sales transactions.

(e) OPEN-TERM CONTRACTS. Contracts for the sale of goods are valid even though the price or some other term remains open and must be determined at a future date. This is discussed further in Chapter 35.

3 / Communication of offer to the offeree. The offer must be communicated directly to the offeree [12] by the offeror or by another person acting as agent or employee of the offeror or with his consent. Until the offer is made known to the offeree, he does not know that there is something which he can accept. Sometimes, particularly in the case of unilateral contracts, the offeree performs the act called for by the offeror without knowing of the offer's existence. Thus, without knowing that a reward is offered for the arrest of a particular criminal, a person may arrest the criminal. If he learns thereafter that a reward was offered for the arrest, he cannot recover the reward in most states.[13]

Facts: The Fidelity & Deposit Company offered "one hundred dollars reward for the apprehension and conviction of each person burglarizing, robbing, or holding up" any banks that it insured against burglary. One of these banks, located at New Hebron, was burglarized by two persons. Messer and others met an incoming train at Hattiesburg and apprehended the burglars, who were subsequently convicted and sentenced. Messer and the others, however, did not know of the reward at the time of the capture. They brought an action against the company to recover the reward.

Decision: Judgment for Fidelity. The performance of the act called for by the reward was not an acceptance of the reward offer. It was performed without knowledge of the existence of the offer, and the person performing necessarily could not have intended to accept the offer by his conduct. (Fidelity & Deposit Co. v. Messer, 112 Miss. 267, 72 So. 1004)

Termination of Offer

An offer gives the offeree power to bind the offeror by contract. This power does not last forever, and the law specifies that under certain circumstances the power shall be terminated.

---

[12] *Farrell* v. *Neilson,* 43 Wash.2d 647, 263 P.2d 264.
[13] With respect to the offeror, it should not make any difference as a practical matter whether the services were rendered with or without knowledge of the existence of the offer. Only a small number of states have adopted this view, however.

Once the offer is terminated, the offeree cannot revive it. If he attempts to accept the offer after it has been terminated, his act is meaningless,[14] unless the original offeror is willing to regard the "late acceptance" as a new offer which he then accepts.

Methods of Termination of Offer

Offers may be terminated in any one of the following ways: (1) revocation of the offer by the offeror, (2) lapse of time, (3) rejection of offer by offeree, (4) counteroffer by the offeree, (5) death or disability of either party, and (6) subsequent illegality.

1 / Revocation of the offer by the offeror. Ordinarily the offeror can revoke his offer before it is accepted. If he does so, the offeree cannot create a contract by accepting the revoked offer. Thus the bidder at an auction sale may withdraw (revoke) his bid (offer) before it is accepted. The auctioneer cannot thereafter accept the withdrawn bid.

Facts: Maserang made a contract to purchase real estate from the Doerflinger Realty Co. subject to the ability of the realty company to obtain a loan for the buyer at 5 percent. The realty company later informed Maserang that it could only obtain a loan for 5½ percent to 6 percent. The buyer refused to borrow at this higher rate and stopped payment on his deposit check. Three weeks later the realty company informed the buyer that a loan at 5 percent was available and insisted that the buyer take the loan and go through with the purchase contract. The buyer refused to do so and was sued by the realty company.

Decision: Judgment for Maserang. When the realty company had informed the buyer that a loan could not be obtained for 5 percent, the buyer had revoked his offer to take such a loan by stopping payment on the deposit check. The offer could not thereafter be revived by the realty company, the offeree, by making available the loan which the offeror had originally requested. (Doerflinger Realty Co. v. Maserang, [Mo. App.] 311 S.W.2d 123)

An ordinary offer may be revoked at any time before it is accepted,[15] even though the offeror had originally stated that the offer would be good for a stated period which had not yet expired, or he had expressly promised the offeree that he would not revoke the offer before a specified later date.

(a) WHAT CONSTITUTES A REVOCATION? No particular form of words is required to constitute a revocation. Any expression indicating that the offer is revoked or the communication of information inconsistent with a continuation of the offer is sufficient. A notice sent to the offeree that the

---

[14] R., Sec. 35.
[15] *Macy Corp.* v. *Ramey,* 75 Ohio Abs. 334, 144 N.E.2d 698.

property which is the subject of the offer has been sold to a third person is a revocation of the offer. An order for goods by a customer, which is an offer by him to purchase at certain prices, is revoked by a notice to the seller of the cancellation of the order, provided such notice is communicated before the order is accepted.

(b) COMMUNICATION OF REVOCATION. A revocation of an offer is ordinarily effective only when it is made known to the offeree or to his agent or employee. Until it is communicated to him, directly or indirectly, he has reason to believe that there is still an offer which he may accept; and he may rely on this belief.

Except in a few states, a letter or telegram revoking an offer made to a particular offeree is not effective until received by the offeree.[16] It is not a revocation when it is written and signed by the offeror nor even when it is mailed or dispatched. A written revocation is effective, however, when it is delivered to the offeree's agent,[17] or to the offeree's residence or place of business under such circumstances that the offeree would be reasonably expected to be aware of its receipt.

If the offeree accepts an offer before it is effectively revoked, a valid contract is created. Thus there may be a contract when the offeree mails or telegraphs his acceptance without knowing that a letter of revocation has been mailed to him.

When an offer is made to the public, it may usually be revoked in the same manner in which it was made. For example, an offer of a reward that is made to the general public by an advertisement in a newspaper may be revoked in the same manner. A member of the public cannot recover the amount of the reward by thereafter performing the act for which the reward was originally offered. This exception is made to the rule requiring communication of revocation because of the necessities of the situation. The offeror does not know which members of the general public know of his offer so that it would be impossible for him to communicate to every person the fact that he revokes his offer. The public revocation of the public offer is effective even though it is not seen by the person attempting to accept the original offer.

(c) OPTION CONTRACTS. An *option contract* is a binding promise to keep an offer open for a stated period of time or until a specified date. The offeror cannot revoke his offer if he has received consideration, that is, has been paid, for his promise to keep the offer open. If the owner of a house gives a prospective purchaser a sixty-day written option to purchase the

---

[16] *L. & E. Wertheimer* v. *Wehle-Hartford Co.*, 126 Conn. 30, 9 A.2d 279.
[17] *Hogan* v. *Aluminum Lock Shingle Corp.*, 214 Ore. 218, 329 P.2d 271.

property at $15,000 and the customer pays the owner a sum of money, such as $500, the agreement is valid, and the owner cannot revoke the offer within the sixty-day period. Even though he expressly tells the purchaser within that time that the option contract is revoked, the purchaser may exercise the option, that is, he may accept the offer. Under an option contract there is no obligation on the offeree to exercise the option.[18] If the option is exercised, the money paid to obtain the option is ordinarily applied as a down payment on the purchase price. If the option is not exercised, the offeror keeps the money paid him.

If a promise is described by the parties as an "option" but no consideration is given, the promise is subject to revocation as though it were not described as an "option."[19] In those jurisdictions in which the seal retains its common-law force, however, the option contract is binding on the offeror if it is set forth in a sealed writing, even though he does not receive any payment for his agreement.

Frequently an option contract is combined with a lease of real estate or personal property. Thus a tenant may rent a building for a number of years by an agreement which gives him the option of purchasing the building for a specified amount at the end of the lease.

(d) FIRM OFFERS. As another exception to the rule that an offer may be revoked at any time before acceptance, it is provided by statute in some states that an offeror cannot revoke an offer prior to its expiration when he has made a *firm offer*, that is, an offer in writing which states that it is to be irrevocable for a stated period.[20] This doctrine of firm offers applies to a merchant's written offer for the sale of goods for a maximum period of three months.[21]

> **Facts:** Gordon, a contractor, requested bids on structural steel from various suppliers. Coronis submitted an offer by letter. He later withdrew the offer. Gordon sued Coronis for breach of contract on the ground that he could not revoke his offer.

> **Decision:** Judgment for Coronis. The mere making of an offer without an express declaration therein which "gives assurance that it will be held open" does not constitute a firm offer but is merely an ordinary offer which can be revoked at any time. (Coronis Associates v. Gordon Construction Co., 90 N.J.S. 69, 216 A.2d 246)

(e) REVOCATION OF OFFER OF UNILATERAL CONTRACT. Since the offer of a unilateral contract can be accepted only by performing the act

---

[18] *State ex rel.* v. *Howald*, [Mo.] 315 S.W.2d 786.
[19] *McPhail* v. *L. S. Starrett Co.*, [C.A.1st] 257 F.2d 388.
[20] *Jarka Corp.* v. *Hellenic Lines*, [C.A.2d] 182 F.2d 916.
[21] Uniform Commercial Code, Sec. 2-205.

called for, it theoretically follows that there is no acceptance until that act is fully performed by the offeree and that the offeror is free to revoke his offer even though the offeree has partly performed and has expended time and money. To avoid this hardship, a number of courts hold that after the offeree has done some substantial act toward acceptance, the offeror cannot revoke the offer until after the lapse of a reasonable time in which the offeree could have completed performance.

2 / Lapse of time. When the offer states that it is open until a particular date, the offer terminates on that date if it has not been accepted.[22]

If the offer does not specify a time, it will terminate after the lapse of a reasonable time. What constitutes a reasonable time depends upon the circumstances of each case, that is, upon the nature of the subject matter, the nature of the market in which it is sold, the time of the year, and other factors of supply and demand. If the commodity is perishable in nature or fluctuates greatly in value, the reasonable time will be much shorter than if the commodity or subject matter is a staple article. An offer to sell a harvested crop of tomatoes would expire within a very short time.

3 / Rejection of offer by offeree. If the offeree rejects the offer and communicates this rejection to the offeror, his agent, or employee, the offer is terminated, even though the period for which the offeror agreed to keep the offer open has not expired. The offeree thereafter cannot revive the offer by attempting to accept it. It may be that the offeror is willing to renew the offer; but unless he does so, there is no offer for the offeree to accept.[23]

4 / Counteroffer by offeree. Ordinarily if *A* makes an offer, such as to sell a used automobile for $1,000, and *B* makes an offer to buy at $750, the original offer is terminated.[24] *B* is in effect saying, "I refuse your original offer, but in its place I make a different offer." Such an offer by the offeree is known as a *counteroffer*. In substance, the counteroffer presupposes a rejection of the original offer. In some instances, however, it is held that the circumstances showed that both parties knew and intended that the offeree's response was not to be regarded as a definite rejection of the original offer but merely as further discussion or as a request for further information.

Facts: Feaheny offered to sell Quinn her house. She made an offer to sell on an installment payment basis, but also asked Quinn to make a cash offer. Quinn made a cash offer which Feaheny rejected. Quinn then accepted the installment payment basis. Feaheny refused to perform the contract and Quinn sued her.

[22] *Conrad Milwaukee Corp.* v. *Wasilewski*, 30 Wis.2d 481, 141 N.E.2d 240.
[23] *Nabob Oil Co.* v. *Bay State Oil & Gas Co.*, 208 Okla. 296, 255 P.2d 513.
[24] *Goodwin* v. *Eller*, 127 Col. 529, 258 P.2d 493.

Decision: Judgment for Quinn. Under the circumstances the making of the cash
offer was not a counteroffer which rejected the installment plan offer
that the seller had made. When the purchaser accepted that offer after
his cash proposal was rejected, a legal contract was created because
the offer was still in existence and could be accepted. (Quinn v. Feaheny, 252 Mich. 526, 233 N.W. 403)

Counteroffers are not limited to offers that directly contradict the
original offers. Any departure from, or addition to, the original offer is a
counteroffer even though the original offer was silent as to the point added
by the counteroffer. For example, when the offeree stated that he accepted
and added that time was of the essence, the "acceptance" was a counteroffer when the original offer had been silent on that point.[25]

A counteroffer is by definition an offer and, if the original offeror (who
is now the offeree) accepts it, a binding contract results.[26]

5 / Death or disability of either party. If either the offeror or the
offeree dies or becomes insane before the offer is accepted, it is automatically
terminated.

6 / Subsequent illegality. If the performance of the contract becomes
illegal after the offer is made, the offer is terminated. Thus, if an offer is made
to sell alcoholic liquors but a law prohibiting such sales is enacted before the
offer is accepted, the offer is terminated.

QUESTIONS AND PROBLEMS

1. Checklist of legal terms:
   (a) offeror, offeree (73)
   (b) bilateral contract, unilateral contract (74)
   (c) offer (74), invitation to negotiate (75)
   (d) divisible contract (77)
   (e) option contract (81), firm offer (82)
   (f) counteroffer (83)

2. State the objective(s) (from the list in Chapter 2, pages 10-16) of each
   of the following rules of law:
   (a) Certain statements, as well as certain listings or quotations of
       prices, are invitations to negotiate and are not binding as offers.
   (b) An offer is terminated by the lapse of a reasonable time when no
       time has been stated.

3. Rolf offered to convey a tract of land to Burt provided Burt paid Rolf
   $30,000 by the following September 30. Burt paid the money on Sep-
   tember 28. Was the contract created by his payment a bilateral or
   unilateral one? Why?

---

[25] *Cheston L. Eshelman Co.* v. *Friedberg,* 214 Md. 123, 133 A.2d 68.
[26] *V-1 Oil Co.* v. *Anchor Petroleum Co.,* 8 Utah 2d 349, 334 P.2d 760.

4. Mr. and Mrs. John Collins employ a TV star to sing at a party to which a number of their personal and business friends are invited. How does the relationship between the sponsors and their guests differ from that between the sponsors and the singer?

5. Glaser sends an offer to Knox on Wednesday. On Thursday Glaser sends another letter withdrawing his offer. This letter is lost in the mail. Knox accepts the offer on Friday. Has an agreement been formed?

6. Lucas advertised in a newspaper an offer of a reward for the arrest and conviction of the person or persons who set fire to his store. Stone saw the offer and started after the guilty party who, according to rumor, had fled to Mexico. A month later Lucas withdrew his offer by means of an advertisement in the newspaper. Not knowing that the offer had been withdrawn, Stone captured the wrongdoer and brought him back to this country. His prisoner was convicted of setting fire to Lucas' store. Stone now claims the reward. Is he entitled to it?

7. Vance offered to sell his farm for $50,000 to Prickett, who paid Vance $1,000 to keep the offer open for one month. Prickett accepted the offer two weeks later, but he found that Vance had conveyed the property to another person. Was Vance liable to Prickett?

8. Polk mails to Ulmer an offer to sell camping equipment for $100. In his reply Ulmer states that he will pay $85 for the camping equipment. Not hearing from Polk, Ulmer later writes that he accepts Polk's offer to sell the camping equipment at $100. Polk refuses to make delivery, and Ulmer sues for breach of contract.

   (a) Is Ulmer entitled to judgment?

   (b) Under what circumstances is an exception made to the general rule stated in your answer to (a)?

9. Owen wrote to Tunison asking if Tunison would sell his store for $6,000. Tunison replied, "It would not be possible for me to sell unless I received $16,000 cash." Owen replied, "Accept your offer." Tunison denied that there was a contract. Decide. (Owen v. Tunison, 131 Maine 42, 158 A. 926)

10. The Courteen Seed Co. received a telegram from Abraham reading: "I am asking 23 cents per pound for the car of red clover seed from which your sample was taken. Number 1 seed . . . have an offer of 22¾ per pound, f.o.b. Amity." The Courteen Seed Co. replied "Telegram received. We accept your offer. Ship promptly." Abraham refused to ship the seed. Courteen Seed Co. sued him. Decide. (Courteen Seed Co. v. Abraham, 129 Ore. 427, 275 P. 684)

11. High Knob Inc. built houses on land and sold them to Allen and others. The deeds given by High Knob to the buyers prohibited them from opening wells or other water supply on their own land. High Knob agreed that for $200 each purchaser could connect to High Knob's water supply and would receive a "reasonable quantity of water." After supplying water for six months, High Knob cut off the water supply. When the buyers sued High Knob, it claimed that the agreement to supply

water was not binding because it was too indefinite in that it did not state any quantity of water nor any limitation of the time that the water would be supplied. Was the contract binding? (High Knob, Inc. v. Allen, 205 Va. 503, 138 S.E.2d 49)

12. Certain property was leased to Cohen. On or about April 11, 1919, the landlord offered Cohen the right to renew the lease and gave him six months before the end of the lease on December 31, 1922, in which to accept. In January, 1920, the landlord sold the property to a third person. Cohen knew of the sale but gave written notice that he accepted the offer to renew the lease. The purchaser claimed that the attempted renewal of the lease was not effective. Decide. (William Weisman Realty Co. v. Cohen, 157 Minn. 161, 195 N.W. 898)

13. T. E. Gillespie Construction Co. entered into a contract to build a section of highway for the State of Tennessee. Tullahoma Concrete Pipe Co. supplied pipe for use in the highway. Later it sued Gillespie Co. for payment. As one of the aspects of the lawsuit, it was asserted that the disputed amount had been settled by an agreement of the attorneys for the parties for $25,000. It was shown that one attorney had made such an offer of settlement on October 3 and that the other attorney had accepted it on February 20 after attempting to get the first attorney to raise the amount on that date. Was there a binding contract to settle for $25,000? (Tullahoma Concrete Pipe Co. v. T. E. Gillespie Constr. Co., [Tenn.App.] 405 S.W.2d 657)

14. The Brewster Fruit Growers Association did business in Seattle under the name of M. L. Davies Co. On May 23, it sent Coleman a written offer to purchase a carload of 30-pound tins of frozen raspberries at "packer's opening price." This price would be determined for the industry on or about July 15. On August 2, Coleman accepted the offer, signed it, and mailed it to Brewster. Brewster refused to purchase the raspberries. Coleman sued for breach of contract. Was there a contract? (Coleman v. Davies, 39 Wash.2d 312, 235 P.2d 199)

15. Samuel Achenbach owned certain bonds. Kurtz Bros. offered to buy them. Achenbach died without accepting the offer. His administrator accepted the offer and sued Kurtz Bros. for damages when they refused to perform the contract. Decide. (Achenbach v. Kurtz Bros., 306 Pa. 384, 159 A. 718)

Chapter 8

The Agreement—Acceptance

When the offeror has expressed or has appeared to express his willingness to enter into a contractual agreement with the offeree, the latter is in a position to accept the offer. Acceptance by the offeree of the offer made by the offeror is necessary to create an agreement that is essential to the existence of a contract.[1]

Nature of the Acceptance

An *acceptance* is the assent of the offeree to the terms of the offer made by the offeror.

1 / Form of acceptance. No particular form of words or mode of expression is required for an acceptance. Any expression of an intention to agree is sufficient. An acceptance may be indicated, for example, by an informal "O. K.," by a mere affirmative nod of the head, or, in the case of an offer of a unilateral contract, by performing the act called for. A seller's letter stating "Your order of May 27 will be shipped promptly from our nearest branch office" is such an assent to an offer represented by a customer's order. A reply stating merely "Your letter of May 27 is acknowledged" is not an expression of such an assent.

2 / Unqualified acceptance. The acceptance must be absolute and unconditional.[2] It must accept just what was offered. If the offeree changes any term of the offer or adds a new term, he does not accept the offer because he does not agree to what was offered.[3]

Facts: The Park Drug Co. wrote a letter dated May 6, 1932, in which it stated the terms on which it wished to lease office space from the Southern Real Estate & Finance Co. On May 10, 1932, the finance company sent the drug company unsigned forms of leases that contained additional terms not stated in the letter of the drug company. The drug company refused to sign the leases. The finance company sued to recover damages for breach of contract.

---

[1] *Armstrong* v. *James,* [Okla.] 402 P.2d 275.
[2] *Tatsch* v. *Hamilton-Erickson Mfg. Co.,* 76 N.Mex. 729, 418 P.2d 187.
[3] Restatement, Contracts, Secs. 58, 60; *Wycoff Realty Co.* v. *Grover,* [Kan.] 422 P.2d 943.

Decision: Judgment for Park Drug Co. There was no contract which the defendant had broken since there was no acceptance of the plaintiff's offer. The addition of terms in the leases that went beyond the scope of the offer prevented the mailing of the leases from being an acceptance of the drug company's offer. (Southern Real Estate & Finance Co. v. Park Drug Co., 344 Mo. 397, 126 S.W.2d 1169)

An acceptance that merely states what is implied by law, however, does not add a new term within this rule.[4] Thus a provision in an acceptance of an offer to buy that payment must be made in cash will usually not introduce a new term since a cash payment is implied by law in the absence of a contrary provision. Similarly, a provision in an acceptance relating to routine or mechanical details of the execution of a written contract will usually not impair the effect of the acceptance.

Facts: Britt owned real estate which he listed for sale with Carver, a broker. Carver obtained a buyer and notified Britt of the buyer's offer. Britt sent Carver the following telegram: "Your telegram relative sale my property is accepted subject to details to be worked out by you and my attorney. . . ." Thereafter Britt sold and deeded the property to Vallejo, another buyer, for a greater price. Carver sued Britt for his commissions on the theory that he had obtained a buyer and that Britt had entered into a binding contract to sell to that buyer.

Decision: Judgment for Carver. The "additional terms" merely recognized that there would be certain routine details, the disposition of which was necessarily part of the transaction. Reference to them merely expressed what was necessarily implied in the offer and did not amount to adding "new terms" to the acceptance. The acceptance was therefore effective, and there was a binding contract. (Carver v. Britt, 241 N.C. 538, 85 S.E.2d 888)

Likewise, an acceptance otherwise unconditional is not impaired by the fact that an additional matter is requested as a favor rather than being made a condition or term of the acceptance. Accordingly, there is an effective acceptance when the buyer, upon accepting, simply requests additional time in which to complete the transaction.[5]

3 / Who may accept. An offer may be accepted only by the person to whom it is directed. If anyone else attempts to accept it, no agreement or contract with that person arises.

Facts: The Mullaly brothers sent Grieve a signed written statement that "we . . . agree to lease for a period of three years with privilege of one more year (certain specified land) to J. D. Grieve of Davis, Cal."

---

[4] *Rossum* v. *Wick*, 74 S.D. 554, 56 N.W.2d 770.
[5] *Duprey* v. *Donahoe*, 53 Wash.2d 129, 323 P.2d 903.

Grieve sold his rights under this writing to Adams. Adams tendered to the Mullaly brothers a formal lease for them to sign. The lease named Adams as the tenant. The Mullaly brothers refused to sign the lease. Suit was brought against the brothers.

Decision: Judgment for the brothers. Their letter was merely an offer to Grieve. An offer can be accepted only by the offeree, and therefore it could not be accepted by Adams. (Grieve v. Mullaly, 211 Cal. 77, 293 P. 619)

If the offer is directed not to a specified individual but to a particular class, it may be accepted by anyone within that class. If the offer is made to the public at large, it may be accepted by any member of the public at large who has knowledge of the existence of the offer.[6]

4 / Manner of acceptance. The acceptance must conform to any conditions expressed in the offer concerning the manner of acceptance. If the offeror specifies that the acceptance must be written, an oral acceptance is ineffective. If the offeror calls for an acceptance by a specified date, a late acceptance has no effect.[7] An acceptance required by return mail generally must be mailed the same day that the offer is received by the offeree.

If the offer specifies that the acceptance be made by the performance of an act by the offeree, he cannot accept by making a promise to do the act but must actually perform it. Unless the offer is clear that a specified manner of acceptance is exclusive, a manner of acceptance indicated by the offeror will be interpreted as merely a suggestion and the offeree's entering upon the performance of the contract will be an acceptance when the offeror has knowledge that the offeree is doing so.[8] In the absence of any contrary provision, an order or offer to buy goods for prompt or current shipment may be accepted by the seller either by making the shipment or by promptly promising to do so.[9]

5 / Silence as acceptance. In most cases the silence of the offeree and his failure to act cannot be regarded as an acceptance. Ordinarily the offeror cannot frame his offer in such a way as to make the silence and inaction of the offeree operate as an acceptance. When the seller writes to another with whom he has not had any prior dealing that "unless notified to the contrary" he will send that person specified goods to be paid for at specified prices, there is no acceptance if the offeree ignores the offer and does nothing. Such silence was not intended as an acceptance, and the seller as a reasonable man should not have believed that it was so intended. This rule applies to magazines and tickets sent to a person through the mail when he has not ordered

---

[6] R., Sec. 28.
[7] *Swisher v. Clark*, 202 Okla. 25, 209 P.2d 880.
[8] *Allied Steel and Conveyors, Inc. v. Ford Motor Co.*, [C.A.6th] 277 F.2d 907.
[9] Uniform Commercial Code, Sec. 2-206(1)(b).

them and does not use them. The fact that he does not return them does not mean that he accepts them.

In the case of prior dealings between the parties, the offeree may have a duty to reject an offer expressly, and his silence may be regarded as an acceptance.

Facts: Everlith obtained a one-year liability policy of insurance from the insurance company's agent, Phelan. Prior to the expiration of the year, Phelan sent Everlith a renewal policy covering the next year, together with a bill for the renewal premium. The bill stated that the policy should be returned promptly if the renewal was not desired. Everlith did not return the policy or take any other action relating to the insurance. Phelan sued for the renewal premium.

Decision: The silence of Everlith did not constitute an acceptance since there was not a sufficient prior course of conduct between the parties which would lead a reasonable man to believe that the silence indicated an acceptance. The single transaction that had occurred in the past did not establish a course of conduct. (Phelan v. Everlith, 22 Conn.Sup. 377, 173 A.2d 601)

When the parties to the sale of goods are both merchants, the silence of the offeree is in some instances treated as an acceptance of an offer.[10]

6 / Insurer's delay in acting on application. The delay of an insurance company in acting upon an application for insurance generally does not constitute an acceptance.[11] A few cases hold that an acceptance may be implied from the company's failure to reject the application promptly and that there is accordingly a binding contract and the application cannot be rejected, particularly when the applicant has paid the first premium and the insurer fails to return it.[12] Some decisions attain the same practical result by holding the insurer liable for tort if, through its unjustified delay in rejecting the application, the applicant remains unprotected by insurance and then, in the interval, suffers loss that would have been covered by the insurance if it had been issued.[18]

Communication of Acceptance

When communication of the offeree's acceptance is required, the acceptance must be communicated directly to the offeror or his agent. A statement to a third person by the offeree is not effective as an acceptance of the offer.

---

10 UCC Sec. 2-206, Comment 1.
11 *Weaver* v. *West Coast Life Insurance Co.*, 99 Mont. 296, 42 P.2d 729.
12 *Snyder* v. *Redding Motors*, 131 Cal.App.2d 416, 280 P.2d 811.
18 *St. Paul F. & M. Insurance Co.* v. *Creach*, 199 Okla. 372, 186 P.2d 641.

1 / Communication of acceptance in a bilateral contract. If the offer pertains to a bilateral contract, an acceptance is not effective unless communicated to the offeror. Until the offeree makes known that he agrees to perform in the future, there is no way for the offeror to know whether the offeree accepts the offer or not.

2 / Communication of acceptance in a unilateral contract. If the offeror makes an offer of a unilateral contract, communication of acceptance is ordinarily not required.[14] In such a case, the offeror calls for a completed or accomplished act. If that act is performed by the offeree with knowledge of the offer, the offer is accepted without any further action by way of notifying the offeror. As a practical matter there will be a notice to the offeror because the offeree who has performed the act will ask the offeror to carry out his promise.

Facts: Mrs. Hodgkin told her daughter and son-in-law, Brackenbury, that if they would leave their home in Missouri and come to Maine to care for her, they could have the use of her house during her life and that she would will it to them. The daughter and son-in-law moved to Maine and began taking care of the mother. Family quarrels arose and the mother ordered them out of the house. They brought an action in equity to determine their rights. Mrs. Hodgkin defended on the ground that the plaintiffs had not notified her that they would accept her offer.

Decision: Judgment for daughter and son-in-law. The contract offered by the mother was a unilateral contract. She called for the moving to Maine of the plaintiffs and their taking care of her. This they did, and by so doing accepted the offer of the mother. The fact that they did not notify the mother of their acceptance of the offer or did not make a counterpromise to her was immaterial since neither is required in the case of unilateral contracts. (Brackenbury v. Hodgkin, 116 Maine 399, 102 A. 106)

In the sale of goods, if shipment is claimed to constitute an acceptance of the buyer's order, the seller must notify the buyer of such shipment within a reasonable time.[15]

3 / Communication of acceptance in a guaranty contract. The general rule that notification of acceptance is not necessary in cases of an offer requesting the performance of an act is not applied in many states when the offer calls for the extension of credit to a buyer in return for which the offeror promises to pay the debt if it is not paid.[16] To illustrate, an uncle may write to a local merchant that if the merchant allows his nephew to

---

[14] R., Sec. 56.
[15] UCC Sec. 2-206(2).
[16] *Electric Storage Battery Co.* v. *Black,* 27 Wis.2d 366, 134 N.W.2d 481.

purchase goods on credit, the uncle will pay the bill if the nephew does not. The uncle makes an offer of a unilateral contract because he has not asked for a promise by the merchant to extend credit but for the act of extending credit. If the merchant extends the credit, he is doing the act which the uncle calls for by his offer. If the general rule governing acceptances applied, the performance of this act would be a complete acceptance and would create a contract. In the guaranty case, however, another requirement is added, namely, that within a reasonable time after extending credit, the merchant must notify the uncle.

This requirement has a commonsense basis for, unless notified, the uncle might not otherwise know that his offer had been accepted and would not know whether he should set money aside to pay the debt or take steps to see that the nephew does.

Acceptance by Mail or Telegraph

If *E* mails an acceptance, there is a time lag before *R* knows that there has been an acceptance. When does the acceptance take effect? Is the contract made at the time that *E* mails his acceptance or at the time that *R* receives *E*'s acceptance?

1 / Right to use mail or telegraph. Express directions of the offeror, prior dealings between the parties, or custom of the trade may make it clear that only one method of acceptance is proper. For example, in negotiations with respect to property of rapidly fluctuating value, such as wheat or corporation stocks, an acceptance sent by mail may be too slow. When there is no indication that mail or telegraph is not a proper method, an acceptance may be made by either of these instrumentalities.

Facts: The real estate broker for the Millers submitted to Kloepfer Realty Co. in New Mexico a "purchase agreement" signed by the Millers by which they agreed to purchase land in New Mexico owned by the Picketts who lived in Pennsylvania. The purchase agreement stated that the sellers had three days "to complete this purchase agreement." Kloepfer phoned the Picketts. The next day they sent an acceptance by telegram. Later the buyers refused to go through with the sale. They claimed that there was no contract because there was no acceptance of their offer since the purchase agreement had not been signed.

Decision: The offer did not limit acceptance to an actual physical signing of the agreement and, in view of the distance and limited time, acceptance by telegram was a proper means of acceptance and there was a binding contract. (Pickett v. Miller, 76 N.Mex. 105, 412 P.2d 400)

In former years there was authority for the proposition that an offer could only be accepted by the same means by which the offer was communicated. This view is being gradually abandoned. The trend of the modern decisions supports the following provision of the Uniform Commercial Code relating to sales of personal property: "Unless otherwise unambiguously indicated by the language or circumstances, an offer to make a [sales] contract shall be construed as inviting acceptance in any manner and by any medium reasonable in the circumstances." [17]

2 / When acceptance by mail or telegraph is effective. If the offeror specifies that an acceptance shall not be effective until received by him, the law will respect the offeror's wish. If there is no such provision and if acceptance by letter is proper, a mailed acceptance takes effect when the acceptance is properly mailed. The letter must be properly addressed to the offeror, and any other precaution that is ordinarily observed to insure safe transmission must be taken. If it is not mailed in this manner, the acceptance does not take effect until it is received by the offeror.[18]

The rule that a properly mailed acceptance takes effect at the time it is mailed is applied strictly. The rule applies even though the acceptance letter never reaches the offeror.[19]

An acceptance sent by telegraph takes effect at the time that the message is handed to the agent at the telegraph office,[20] unless the offeror specifies otherwise or unless custom or prior dealings indicate that acceptance by telegraph is improper.

3 / Proof of acceptance by mail or telegraph. How can the time of mailing be established, or even the fact of mailing in the case of a destroyed or lost letter? A similar problem arises in the case of a telegraphed acceptance. In either case the problem is not one of law but one of fact, that is, a question of proving the case to the jury. The offeror may testify in court that he never received an acceptance, or he may claim that the acceptance was sent after the offer had been revoked. The offeree or his stenographer may then testify that the letter was mailed at a particular time and place. The offeree's case will be strengthened if he can produce postal receipts for the mailing and delivery of a letter sent to the offeror, although these of course do not establish the contents of the letter. Ultimately the case goes to the jury, or to the judge if a jury trial has been waived, to determine whether the acceptance was made at a certain time and place.

---

[17] UCC Sec. 2-206(1).
[18] R., Sec. 67; *Blake* v. *Hamburg-Bremen Fire Ins. Co.,* 67 Tex. 160, 2 S.W. 368.
[19] Sec. 64; *Western Union Tel. Co.* v. *Wheeler,* 114 Okla. 161, 245 P. 39. By following the procedure prescribed by the United States Post Office Department, the offeree can remove his letter of acceptance from the mail before it reaches the offeror. Even when this is done, the acceptance took effect legally when the letter was mailed.
[20] *State ex rel. Reading* v. *Western Union Tel. Co.,* 336 Mich. 84, 57 N.W.2d 537.

Acceptance by Telephone

Ordinarily acceptance of an offer may be made by telephone unless the circumstances are such that by the intent of the parties or the law of the state no acceptance can be made or contract arise in the absence of a writing. If acceptance by telephone is otherwise proper, the acceptance takes effect at the place where the acceptance is spoken into the phone.[21]

Auction Sales

At an auction sale the statements made by the auctioneer to draw forth bids are merely invitations to negotiate. Each bid is an offer, which is not accepted until the auctioneer indicates that a particular offer or bid is accepted. Usually this is done by the fall of the auctioneer's hammer, indicating that the highest bid made has been accepted.[22] As a bid is merely an offer, the bidder may withdraw his bid at any time before it is accepted by the auctioneer.

Ordinarily the auctioneer may withdraw any article or all of the property from the sale if he is not satisfied with the amounts of the bids that are being made. Once he has accepted a bid, however, he cannot cancel the sale. In addition, if it had been announced that the sale was to be made "without reserve," the goods must be sold to the person making the highest bid regardless of how low that may be.

QUESTIONS AND PROBLEMS

1. What is an acceptance? (87)
2. State the objective(s) of each of the following rules of law:
   (a) No particular form of words or mode of expression is required for an acceptance.
   (b) An acceptance takes effect when it is properly mailed, in the absence of any contrary specification by the offeror.
3. Grover mails an offer to Link to sell him 10 cords of fireplace wood at a specified price per cord. Link answers by stating that he will take 8 cords. Is there an agreement?
4. Kraft mails an offer to buy Mefford's porch glider for $25. The offer makes no mention of method or time of payment. Mefford replies that the offered price is satisfactory but that cash payment must be made at the time of the sale. Is this reply an acceptance of the offer?

---

[21] *Linn* v. *Employers Reinsurance Corporation*, 392 Pa. 58, 139 A.2d 638.

[22] At an auction sale of goods, when a bid is made while the auctioneer's hammer is falling in acceptance of a prior bid, the auctioneer may in his discretion reopen the bidding or declare the goods sold under the bid on which the hammer is falling. UCC Sec. 2-328.

5. Adler offers a reward of $50 to anyone finding and returning his lost dog. Hanna, who knows of the reward, finds and returns the dog. Adler refuses to pay Hanna on the ground that Hanna is a stranger to whom no offer has been made. Is Adler's action justifiable? Why?

6. In offering to sell Applegate 5 tons of steel rails at a given price, Emerson writes, "If you wish to accept, send your reply to my office in Pittsburgh." Applegate mails his acceptance to Emerson at his company's branch office in Columbus. Is there an agreement?

7. Shuford offered to sell a specified machine to the State Machinery Co. The Nutmeg State Machinery Corp. heard of the offer and notified Shuford that it accepted. When Shuford did not deliver the machine, the Nutmeg corporation sued him for breach of contract. Could it recover? (Nutmeg State Machinery Corp. v. Shuford, 129 Conn. 659, 30 A.2d 911)

8. On five occasions Hobbs had sent animal skins to the Massasoit Whip Co., and each time the company had accepted and paid for the skins. Later Hobbs sent additional skins, which were kept by the company for several months and then accidentally destroyed. He sued the company for the price of these skins. The company defended on the ground that there was no contract to pay the purchase price since it had never accepted the offer. Decide. (Hobbs v. Massasoit Whip Co., 158 Mass. 194, 33 N.E. 495)

9. Raysor made an offer to Mallance, Superintendent of the Berkeley County Railway & Lumber Co. Mallance made no reply during the next several months. Raysor brought an action against the Berkeley County Railroad & Lumber Co. in which he claimed that there had been an acceptance because of the failure of Mallance to reject his offer. Do you agree? (Raysor v. Berkeley County Railway & Lumber Co., 26 S.C. 610, 2 S.E. 119)

10. The Great A. & P. Tea Co. rented a store from Geary. On February 25, the company wrote Geary offering to execute a lease for an additional year, commencing on May 1. At 10:30 a.m. on March 7, Geary wrote a letter containing a lease for the additional year and accepting the offer. On the same day at 1:30 p.m. the company mailed Geary a letter stating that it withdrew the offer to execute the new lease. Each party received the other's letter the following day. Was there an effective acceptance of the offer to make a lease? (Geary v. Great A. & P. Tea Co., 366 Ill. 625, 10 N.E.2d 350)

Chapter 9

Capacity of Parties

All persons do not have the same legal capacity to make a contract. In some cases a person's legal capacity has no relation to his actual ability or capacity. A person who is twenty years old, for example, may be just as capable or may have just as much ability to make a contract as an older person. Nevertheless, he may be under a legal incapacity in making a contract. In other cases, such as those involving an insane person, the legal incapacity is based upon his inability to understand the consequences of the particular transaction.[1]

Persons whose legal capacity is or may be restricted include minors, insane persons, intoxicated persons, convicts, and aliens. Such a limitation on married women is now largely historical.[2]

Minors

At common law any person, male or female, under twenty-one years of age is a *minor*. This period of minority usually ends the day before the minor's twenty-first birthday.[3] In some states the common-law definition of minority has been modified. Some statutes may provide that a girl ceases to be a minor upon attaining the age of eighteen or upon being married. In contrast, others provide that a person of either sex attains majority upon marriage. In a few states minority does not end until the twenty-first anniversary of the minor's birth date.

1 / Minor's right to disaffirm contracts. With exceptions that will be noted later in this chapter, a contract made by a minor is voidable at his election.[4]

---

[1] *Conners* v. *Eble*, [Ky.] 269 S.W.2d 716.

[2] The restrictions on the contractual powers of corporations are discussed in Chapter 51 of the Comprehensive Volume.

[3] In determining eligibility for old-age and medicare benefits under the Social Security Act and for double exemption on federal income tax reports, a person is considered as having reached the required age on the day before that birthday. For example, a person whose 65th birthday falls on January 1, 1970 is considered to be 65 years old on December 31, 1969, and is eligible for old-age and medicare benefits for the month beginning December 1, 1969, and for a double exemption on the federal income tax return for 1969.

[4] In some jurisdictions the appointment of an agent or an attorney by a minor is void rather than voidable. There is no reason why this exception should be made, and the courts tend to eliminate it.

Facts: Cattani, age 19, made a contract with Fisher, who operated an employment agency, by which the agency was to obtain a job for her. Fisher's agency obtained a job for Cattani. She agreed to pay a total fee of $146.25 and paid $45 on account. After one month she resigned the job because it was unsatisfactory and promptly notified the agency that she disaffirmed her contract. The agency sued her for $101.25.

Decision: Judgment for Cattani. A minor may disaffirm (avoid) a contract with an employment agency. The fact that employment agencies are subject to statutory regulation to prevent abuse does not destroy the right of minor customers to disaffirm their contracts. (Fisher v. Cattani, 53 Misc.2d 221, 278 N.Y.S.2d 420)

If the minor desires, he may perform his voidable contracts. The adult party to the contract, however, cannot disaffirm the contract on the ground that the minor might avoid the contract. Until the minor does so, the other party is bound by it. If the minor dies, the personal representative of his estate may avoid a contract which the minor could have avoided.

The fact that a minor can avoid his contract explains why stores and dealers will often insist that the parents of a minor sign any contract made with him. A parent or other adult who joins in the contract with the minor is personally bound and must perform even though the minor could or does set it aside as to himself.[5]

2 / Minor's misrepresentation of age. Statutes in some states prevent a minor from avoiding his contract if he has fraudulently misrepresented his age. In the absence of such a statute, however, his fraud generally does not affect his right to avoid the contract when sued for its breach, although there is some authority that in such case he must pay for any damage to, or deterioration of, the property he received under the contract. If the minor is not sued for the breach of the contract but is himself suing to recover what he has paid or given the other party, his fraud in misrepresenting his age generally will bar him from obtaining any relief.[6]

Facts: Approximately 40 days before his twenty-first birthday, Chagnon purchased a new automobile from Keser, a dealer. He notified Keser 64 days after becoming 21 that he disaffirmed the contract, and 10 days later he returned the automobile. Keser claimed that this could not be done because (1) Chagnon had waited too long before disaffirming, (2) Chagnon had stated that he was over 21 at the time of the sale, and (3) the title certificate to the automobile was held by the finance company which refused to surrender it.

---

[5] The fact that a minor's older brother who is over 21 is with the minor when a purchase is made and takes part in the transaction does not affect the right of the minor to avoid the transaction. *Cadigan* v. *Strand Garage,* 351 Mass. 703, 221 N.E.2d 468.

[6] *Carney* v. *Southland Loan Co.,* 92 Ga.App. 559, 88 S.E.2d 805.

Decision: The delay in notifying the dealer of disaffirmance and the slight
additional delay in making the return was not so unreasonable as to
bar the minor's right to disaffirm. The minor's misrepresentation of his
age did not bar disaffirmance but merely entitled the seller to a setoff
or reduction representing the loss in value of the automobile between
the purchase date and the return date. The fact that the title certificate
could not be returned did not bar disaffirmance since the minor was
merely required to return what he had in his possession. Judgment
for Chagnon for the amount of the purchase price of the automobile
less an allowance representing the difference between the reasonable
value of the automobile at the time of its sale and its reasonable value
upon its return by the minor. (Keser v. Chagnon, [Colo.] 410 P.2d
637)

In any case, the other party to the contract may avoid it because of
the minor's fraud. There is a conflict of authority, however, as to whether
the other party may sue the minor for damages because of the minor's fraud.
Recovery is denied in some jurisdictions on the ground that to allow the
other party damages for the minor's misrepresentation of his age would in
effect deny the minor the right to avoid the contract. Elsewhere recovery
is allowed because a minor, although he may avoid his contracts, is liable
for his misconduct.

3 / Time for avoidance. A minor's contract, whether executed or not,
ordinarily can be disaffirmed by the minor at any time during minority or
for a reasonable time after becoming of age. What is a reasonable time is a
question of fact to be determined in the light of all the surrounding circumstances. After the expiration of a reasonable time following the attainment of
majority, it is held that the minor has ratified the contract by his failure to
avoid the contract within that time; but in some states an express affirmance is necessary to make a wholly executory contract binding.

As an exception to the right to disaffirm a contract during minority,
a minor cannot fully avoid a conveyance or transfer of land made by him
until he reaches his majority. Prior to that time, he may partially avoid the
conveyance to the extent that he may retake possession of the land and
enjoy its use or rent it to others, but he cannot set aside the transfer of title
until he is twenty-one.

4 / What constitutes disaffirmance. Disaffirmance or avoidance of a
contract by a minor may be made by any expression of an intention to
repudiate the contract. If the minor performs an act inconsistent with the
continuing validity of the contract, that is deemed a disaffirmance. Thus,
when a minor conveyed property to *A* and later, on reaching majority, made
a conveyance of the same property to *B*, the second conveyance was an
avoidance of the first.

There is authority for the rule that when the contract is executory and the minor has not received any benefits, the contract is not binding upon him unless he ratifies it after attaining the age of twenty-one. Under this rule the minor's silence or inaction is the equivalent of a disaffirmance.[7]

When a minor disaffirms his contract, he must avoid all of it. He cannot keep part of the contract and reject the balance.

5 / Restitution by minor upon avoidance. When a minor avoids his contract, must he return what he has received? What happens if what he received has been spent, used up, damaged, or destroyed? When the minor has in his possession or control the consideration received by him, or any part of it, he must return it or offer to do so before he can require the other party to undo the contract and set things back to their original position, or as it is called, to restore the *status quo ante.* Although the minor must make this restitution if he can, the right to disaffirm his contract is not affected by the fact that he no longer has the money or property to return, or that the property has been damaged. In those states which follow the general rule, the minor can thus refuse to pay for what he has received or he can get back what he has paid or given, even though he himself does not give anything back or returns the property in a damaged condition. There is, however, a trend toward limiting this rule.

> **Facts:** Roy Wilson was an orphan 17 years of age. His aunt retained Porter as attorney to have herself appointed guardian for Roy. Porter later sued Roy to recover $760 as the fee agreed to by Roy for legal services rendered up to the appointment of the guardian. Roy refused to pay the sum on the ground that he was a minor and had disaffirmed the contract.
>
> **Decision:** This was not a complete defense. Although Roy could disaffirm the contract because he was a minor, he was required to make restitution or pay for the reasonable value of the legal services which had been rendered on his behalf, without regard to whether such services were a "necessary." (Porter v. Wilson, 106 N.H. 270, 209 A.2d 730)

If the seller improperly refuses to return the purchase price to the minor, the minor is excused from making the useless gesture of returning the goods, which he knows the seller will not accept; and a minor does not lose the effect of his disaffirmance by the fact that, having become 21, he uses the goods temporarily for 2 months while the lawsuit over his disaffirmance is still pending.[8]

---

[7] In certain states the silence of the minor may be considered in the light of all the other circumstances of the case to determine whether an affirmance may be implied. In some states no distinction is made between an executory and executed contract, and the minor is required to disaffirm both kinds of contracts.

[8] *Adams* v. *Barcomb,* 125 Vt. 380, 216 A.2d 648.

This absolute right to disaffirm is modified in some states where, except as to transactions involving the conveyance of land, a minor must restore what he received or its money equivalent before he can disaffirm the contract. In those states, if he cannot make such restoration, he is denied the right to disaffirm. In a few states this limitation is imposed by statute on minors over a certain age.[9] Many states require the minor to pay for any damage to the returned property if the minor had falsely represented his age when he obtained the property.

When a minor wishes to avoid an insurance contract, he can recover everything that he has paid without regard to whether the insurance company had made any payments to him. The unfairness of this rule has led some jurisdictions to limit the recovery of the minor to the amount of the premiums paid by him in excess of the actual cost of the protection he has enjoyed during the time the policy was in force. In some states the minor is by statute denied the right to avoid a life insurance policy on his own life.

6 / Recovery of property by minor upon avoidance. When the minor avoids his contract, the other contracting party must return all the money or property of the minor that he had received, or the money equivalent of property which he cannot return.[10]

Can a minor who avoids a transaction involving personal property recover that property from a third person to whom the other party to the contract has transferred it? The Uniform Commercial Code[11] makes no provision for protecting the title of the minor under such circumstances. At common law there is authority for the rule that when a minor avoids a transaction as to either real or personal property, he may recover it from the third person, even though that person did not know of the minority and purchased the property for value. In a number of states the common-law rule has been repudiated on the basis of equitable principles apart from statute.

Facts: Wallace, a minor, owned a 1948 automobile. He traded it to Speake for a 1949 car. Wallace went on a three-week trip and found that the 1949 car was not as good as the 1948 car. He asked Speake to return his car but was told that it had been sold to Francis. Wallace then sued Francis for the return of the 1948 car.

Decision: Judgment for Francis. Although Wallace could avoid the sale as against Speake, he could not as against Francis who had acquired the title to the car in good faith and for value. (Wallace v. Francis, 39 Ala.App. 463, 103 So.2d 831)

---

9 *Clark* v. *Stites,* 89 Idaho 191, 404 P.2d 339.
10 *O'Brien* v. *Small,* 101 OhioApp. 408, 122 N.E.2d 701.
11 Uniform Commercial Code, Sec. 2-403(1).

7 / Ratification. A minor's voidable contract becomes binding upon him when he ratifies or approves it. Of necessity, the minor can only ratify a contract when he is no longer a minor. He must have attained his majority or his "ratification" would itself be regarded as voidable in order to protect the minor.[12]

Ratification may consist of any expression that indicates an intention to be bound by the contract. In some states a written ratification or declaration of intention is required. An acknowledgment by the minor that a contract had been made during his minority, without any indication of an intention to be bound thereby, is not a ratification.

Facts: While a minor, Lange executed a mortgage. After she was twenty-one, she stated to the attorney for the holder of the mortgage that she recognized that she would have to pay interest on the mortgage. Later, suit was brought against Lange on the mortgage by the holder of the mortgage, Ruehle. Lange claimed that the mortgage was invalid because it had been executed by her while she was a minor.

Decision: Judgment for Ruehle. Lange, in admitting liability to the attorney for the holder of the mortgage after Lange attained majority, waived the right to avoid the contract that she had made while she was a minor. She had ratified the contract. (Ruehle v. Lange, 223 Mich. 690, 194 N.W. 492)

In addition to ratification based on statements or promises, ratification may be found in the conduct of the minor. If after attaining majority the minor fails to disaffirm an executed contract within a reasonable time, the contract is deemed ratified. If the minor acquired property under his contract and after reaching majority makes a use or disposition of the property inconsistent with disaffirmance, he will also be deemed to have ratified the contract. Thus, if a minor buys an automobile and after attaining twenty-one sells it to a third person, his act of reselling is a ratification.

8 / Contracts for necessaries. A minor is liable for the reasonable value of necessaries that are supplied to him by another person at the minor's request. The minor is not bound by the terms of his contract for necessaries; he is only required to pay the reasonable value of what the seller actually delivers and which the minor receives. This duty of the minor is called a quasi-contractual liability. It is a duty which the law imposes upon the minor rather than one which he has created by the contract.

Originally necessaries were limited to those things absolutely necessary for the sustenance and shelter of the minor. Thus limited, the term would extend only to the most simple foods, clothing, and lodging. In the course of

---

[12] *Dixon National Bank v. Neal,* 5 Ill.2d 328, 125 N.E.2d 463.

time, the rule was relaxed to extend generally to things relating to the health, education, and comfort of the minor. Thus, the rental of a house used by a married minor, his wife, and child, is a necessary. The rule has also been relaxed to hold that whether an item is a necessary in a particular case depends upon the financial and social status, or station in life, of the minor.[13] The rule thus does not treat all minors equally. To illustrate, college education may be regarded as necessary for one minor but not for another, depending upon their stations in life.

Property other than food or clothing acquired by a minor is generally not regarded as a necessary. Although this rule is obviously sound in the case of jewelry and property used for pleasure, the same view is held even though the minor is self-supporting and uses the property in connection with his work, as tools of his trade, or an automobile which he must have to go to and from work. The more recent decisions, however, hold that property used by the minor for his support is a necessary. Thus it has been held that a tractor and farm equipment were necessaries for a married minor who supported his family by farming.[14]

Facts: Bethea, aged 20, purchased an automobile on credit. When sued by Bancredit, Inc. for the purchase price, he raised the defense that he was not liable because he was a minor when he made the contract. Bancredit claimed that the minor was bound by his contract because he used the auto for transportation to and from his place of business.

Decision: The minor was required to pay the reasonable value of the automobile since it was a necessary in the circumstances of the minor's needs and the 20th century patterns of life and work. (Bancredit, Inc. v. Bethea, 65 N.J.S. 538, 168 A.2d 250)

Money loaned to a minor is ordinarily not classified as a necessary, even though the minor thereafter purchases necessaries with the borrowed money. An exception is made to the rule when the lender advances money for that express purpose and makes certain that the minor purchases necessaries with the money. In such a case the minor must pay the lender the amount of the loan.

If the minor is adequately supplied with necessaries [15] or if those purchased by him are excessive in quantity or too expensive, such purchases are not necessary and the contracts are voidable by the minor.

9 / Contracts that minors cannot avoid.

(a) MINOR IN BUSINESS. In order to prevent the minor from using the shield of his minority as a sword to injure others, some states, either by

---

13 *Spaulding* v. *New England Furniture Co.*, 154 Maine 330, 147 A.2d 916.
14 *Williams* v. *Buckler*, [Ky.] 264 S.W.2d 279.
15 *Foster* v. *Adcock*, 161 Tenn. 217, 30 S.W.2d 239.

decision or statute, follow the rule that if a minor engages in a business or employment and operates in the same manner as a person having legal capacity, he will not be permitted to set aside contracts arising from that business or employment.

(b) COURT-APPROVED CONTRACT. In some states permission of the court may be obtained for a minor to execute a contract. When this permission is obtained and the contract is made, it is fully binding upon the minor.[16] In this manner, a minor may execute a binding contract for professional performances on the stage, in the movies, or on television.

(c) CONTRACTS IN PERFORMANCE OF LEGAL DUTY. A minor cannot avoid a contract which the law specifically requires or that provides for the performance of an act which he is legally bound to do. If the law authorizes a minor to make an enlistment contract with a branch of the armed forces, he cannot avoid it on the ground of minority. Many states require that a person file a bond when he brings certain kinds of lawsuits or takes an appeal. If a minor brings such an action and executes the necessary bond, he cannot avoid liability on the bond by claiming that he was a minor.

If property of a father is held in the name of his minor child under an agreement that it is to be conveyed or sold in a particular manner, a conveyance by the son cannot be avoided by him. Here the transaction by the minor is in performance of the duty imposed upon him by his agreement with his father, and the law will not permit the minor to set the contract aside. In this type of case, the minor has no direct interest in the transaction but in a sense is acting as the agent for the father.

(d) VETERANS. In most states statutes permit veterans who are minors to execute valid contracts of certain types, particularly those concerning real property.

(e) BANK ACCOUNTS. By statute in some states a minor may open a bank account in his own name, and all acts of the minor with respect to the account are binding upon him as though he were of full age.

(f) STOCK TRANSFERS. Statutes sometimes provide that when a minor transfers his shares of stock, the transfer shall be as binding as though he were an adult with respect to anyone not knowing that he is a minor.

10 / Liability of parent for minor's contract. Ordinarily a parent is not liable on a contract executed by a minor child. The parent may be liable, however, if the child is acting as the agent of the parent in executing the contract.[17] If the parent has neglected the child, the parent is liable to a

---

[16] *Morgan* v. *Morgan,* 220 Cal.App.2d 665, 34 Cal.Reptr. 82.
[17] See p. 213.

third person for the reasonable value of necessaries supplied by that person to the child.[18] If a parent joins in a contract with a minor, as when the parent acts as a cosigner, the parent is liable on his own undertaking. He then remains bound by his contract even though the minor avoids the contract as to himself.

Insane Persons

If a party to a contract is insane, he lacks capacity and his contract is either void or voidable. In order to constitute insanity within the meaning of this rule, the party must be so deranged mentally that he does not know that he is making a contract or that he does not understand the consequences of what he is doing. If he lacks such understanding, the cause of his mental condition is immaterial. It may be idiocy, senile dementia, lunacy, imbecility,[19] or such excessive use of alcoholic beverages or narcotics as to cause mental impairment.

If at the time the party makes the contract he understands the nature of his action and its consequences, it is immaterial that he has certain delusions or insane intervals, or that he is eccentric. As long as the contract is made in a lucid interval and is not affected by any delusion, it is valid.

1 / Effect of insanity. If a party to a contract is insane, he may generally avoid his contracts in the same manner as a minor. Upon the removal of the disability, that is, upon his becoming sane, he may either ratify or disaffirm the contract. If a proper court has appointed a guardian for the insane person, the contract may be ratified or disaffirmed by the guardian. If the insane person dies, his personal representative or heirs may also affirm or disaffirm the contract made by him.[20]

Facts: Chiara in Texas purchased furniture from Ellard. He sold some to a third person and moved the balance of it to New York. Chiara, who was of unsound mind, later brought an action to set aside the purchase from Ellard. The latter claimed that Chiara must first return all of the property.

Decision: Judgment for Chiara. As to the property resold by him, he was only required to return so much of the proceeds of the sale as he still held. As to the furniture that he still owned, he was required to account for it. This would not require the actual return of the property as it did not have any unique value and its return from New York would be expensive. It was sufficient that he pay the seller the value of the property that he had moved to New York as of the date of the sale. (Ellard v. Chiara, [Tex.Civ.App.] 252 S.W.2d 991)

---

[18] See p. 221.
[19] *Downing* v. *Siddens,* 247 Ky. 311, 57 S.W.2d 1.
[20] *McElroy* v. *Mathews,* [Mo.] 263 S.W.2d 1.

As in the case of minors, the other party to the contract has no right to disaffirm the contract merely because the incompetent has the right to do so.

2 / Exceptions. There are several exceptions to the rule that the contracts of an insane person are voidable:

(a) EXISTENCE OF GUARDIAN. It is commonly provided that when a court has appointed a guardian for the insane person, the latter cannot make any contract whatever and one made by him is therefore void.

(b) NECESSARIES. An insane person has a quasi-contractual liability to pay the reasonable value of necessaries furnished to him, his wife, or his children.

(c) BENEFICIAL CONTRACT. If the contract was fair and reasonable and was advantageous to the incompetent, a substantial number of states hold that he may not avoid the contract when the other party acted without knowledge of the incompetence and in good faith, and it would be impossible to restore the status quo ante.[21]

Intoxicated Persons

The capacity of a party to contract and the validity of his contract are not affected by the fact that he was drunk at the time of making the contract so long as he knew that he was making a contract. The fact that the contract was foolish and that he would not have made it had he been sober does not invalidate the contract unless it can be shown that the other party purposely caused the person to become drunk in order to induce him to execute the contract.

If the degree of intoxication is such that the person does not know at the time that he is executing a contract, there is no valid contract. The situation is the same as though he were so insane at the time that he did not know what he was doing. Upon becoming sober, the person may ratify the contract if he so desires. An unreasonable delay in taking steps to set aside a transaction entered into while intoxicated, however, may bar the intoxicated person from asserting this right.

As in the case of a minor, a drunkard is bound by a contract that carries out an obligation or duty imposed by law. He is also required to pay the reasonable value of necessaries furnished him.

If a person has been adjudicated a habitual drunkard or if a guardian has been appointed for him because of his inability to care for his property, the drunkard is placed under a continuing legal disability to make a contract. The statutes which provide for the appointment of a guardian or the

---

[21] *Manufacturers Trust Co. v. Podvin,* 10 **N.J.** 199, 89 A.2d 672.

adjudication of the status of the drunkard generally specify that after the court has acted, the drunkard has no power to make a contract even when he is sober.

Convicts

The capacity to contract of a person convicted of a major criminal offense, a felony, or treason varies from state to state. In some he may make a valid transfer of his property. In other states such a person has either partial or total disability. When there is a disability, it exists only during the period of imprisonment.

Aliens

An *alien* is a national or subject of a foreign country residing in this country. Originally aliens were subject to many disabilities. These have been removed in most instances by treaty between the United States and the foreign country, under which each nation agrees to give certain rights to the subjects or citizens of the other. Generally the right of the alien to make a contract has been recognized.

If this country is at war with a nation of which an alien is a subject, he is termed an *enemy alien*, without regard to whether he assists his country in the prosecution of the war. An enemy alien is denied the right to make new contracts or to sue on existing ones; but if he is sued, he may defend the action. Contracts made by him, even though made before the war began, will at least be suspended during the war. In some instances, if the contract calls for continuing services or performance, the war terminates the contract.

Married Women

At common law a married woman could not make a binding contract. Her contracts were void, rather than voidable. This disability has almost been abolished by statute in practically all the states.[22] There are still a few restrictions in some jurisdictions, mainly in instances where the wife might be unduly influenced by the husband, as in acting as surety for him, contracting with him, or joining with him in a conveyance of their property to a third person, for in such instances the transaction may be harmful to the wife's best interests.

---

[22] *United States* v. *Yazell*, 382 U.S. 341.

QUESTIONS AND PROBLEMS

1. Checklist of legal terms:
   (a) minor (96)
   (b) disaffirmance (98), ratification (101)
   (c) alien, enemy alien (106)

2. (a) State the objective(s) of the rule of law that when a minor avoids a contract, he usually cannot recover his property if the other party has transferred it to a third person who did not know of the minority and purchased the property for value.
   (b) How is the evolutionary nature of the law illustrated by the changes in the definition of a minor's necessaries?

3. Cobb brought a court action against Fansher. The action was prosecuted on the day before Cobb celebrated his twenty-first birthday. Fansher contended that Cobb was still a minor at the time of the prosecution of the action. Do you agree?

4. A minor and his grandfather sign a contract for the purchase of an automobile to be used by the minor. What is the liability of the minor? of the grandparent?

5. Decker, a minor, conveyed a tract of land to Stacy. While still a minor, Decker sought to avoid the conveyance and to recover the land. Was he entitled to do so?

6. Fullerton lent money to Briggs, a minor, so that Briggs could rent suitable lodging quarters which he needed. Fullerton accompanied Briggs and saw that the money was used for this purpose. Could Briggs avoid repaying the money he borrowed on the ground of being a minor?

7. DeBrue was adjudicated as insane, and the court appointed a guardian for him. Later DeBrue entered into an agreement for the purchase of clothing from a merchant. Was this agreement binding on DeBrue?

8. Ferris purchases a topcoat from Ellratt. Later it is discovered that Ferris was insane at the time of the purchase. Is the agreement binding on Ferris?

9. Austin sues McGee for breach of contract. McGee proves that he was intoxicated when the contract was executed. Under what circumstances would this fact affect the validity of the agreement?

10. Bauer is convicted of a felony and sentenced to imprisonment for twenty years. Does this fact restrict Bauer's capacity to make contracts?

11. During World War II Suzuski, a citizen of Japan, wanted to bring an action on a contract against Baldwin, a citizen of the United States, in a court in this country. Could he do so?

12. Frost brought an action against Lockwood to recover damages arising out of the breach of a contract between them. At the time Lockwood was an enemy alien. Was Lockwood entitled to defend the action?

13. Rich, a minor, borrowed money from Kilgore by having him pay a board bill that Rich had incurred while attending school. Thereafter Kilgore brought an action to recover the money. Decide. (Kilgore v. Rich, 83 Maine 305, 22 A. 176)

14. Stafford was a minor of considerable wealth. A guardian had been appointed to manage his estate and to provide him with clothing and support. A number of merchants sold Stafford clothing on credit, which he would then resell to obtain money that he would squander. He refused to pay for the clothes. One of the dealers, Kline, then sued his guardian, L'Amoreux, for the purchasing price. Could he recover? (Kline v. L'Amoreux, 2 Paige [N.Y.] 419, 22 Am.Dec. 652)

15. Byers was convicted of a felony and sentenced to the penitentiary. While in prison he hired Sheffler, an attorney, to obtain a parole for him. In order to pay the attorney, Byers gave him a promissory note for $1,000. Sheffler transferred the note to the Sun Savings Bank. He obtained the parole. When the bank sought to collect the amount of the note, Byers claimed that he was not bound by the note on the theory that a convict confined in jail had no capacity to make a contract. Decide. (Byers v. Sun Savings Banks, 41 Okla. 728, 139 P. 948)

16. In 1936 Palmer was adjudicated incompetent. In 1942 he was adjudicated competent. In 1952 he purchased policies of fire insurance from the Lititz Mutual Insurance Co. The property insured was destroyed by fire. The company refused to pay on the policies on the ground that Palmer was insane when he applied for and obtained the insurance. Was this a valid defense? (Palmer v. Lititz Mutual Ins. Co.. [W.D. S.C.] 113 F.S. 857)

Chapter 10

Genuineness of Assent

An agreement is the result of an offer and an acceptance by competent parties. The enforceability of a contract based upon an agreement may be affected, however, because a mistake was made by either or both of the parties or because the assent of one of the parties was obtained through fraud, undue influence, or duress. Appropriate remedies are provided when the enforceability of a contract is affected.

Mistakes

The law does not treat all mistakes the same. Some have no effect whatever; others make the agreement voidable or unenforceable.

1 / Unilateral and mutual mistakes. Mistakes may be unilateral or mutual (bilateral).

(a) UNILATERAL MISTAKE. Ordinarily a unilateral mistake regarding a fact does not affect the contract unless the contract states that it shall be void if the fact is not as believed. Enforceability is not affected if the mistake is known to or should be recognized by the other party. A unilateral mistake as to the provisions of a contract, for example, is not an excuse from liability for the party who signed the contract without reading it or who only "half-read" it before signing.[1]

A unilateral mistake of law or as to expectations does not have any effect upon the contract. The law refuses to recognize ignorance of the law as an excuse. If it did, the unscrupulous could avoid their contracts at will by saying that they did not understand the law that applied.

(b) MUTUAL MISTAKE. When both parties make the same mistake of fact, the agreement is void.[2] When the mutual or bilateral mistake is one of law, the contract generally is binding. A few courts have refused to follow this rule, and in several states statutes provide that a mutual mistake of law shall have the same effect as a mutual mistake of fact. A bilateral mistake with respect to expectations ordinarily has no effect on the contract[3] unless

---

[1] *Dunlap* v. *Warmack-Fitts Steel Co.,* [C.A.8th] 370 F.2d 876.
[2] *Murphy* v. *Torstrick,* [Ky.] 309 S.W.2d 767.
[3] *Cook* v. *Kelley,* [Mass.] 227 N.E.2d 330.

the realization of those expectations is made a condition of the contract by the parties.

2 / Mistake as to possibility of performance. An agreement is void if there is a mutual mistake as to the possibility of performing it.[4] Assume that *A* (seller) meets *B* (buyer) downtown and makes an agreement to sell to *B* his automobile, which both believe to be in *A's* garage. Actually the automobile was destroyed by fire an hour before the agreement was made. Since this fact was unknown to both parties, there is a mutual mistake as to the possibility of performance, and the agreement is void.[5]

It is possible to make the contract absolute so that it obligates the seller to perform or to pay damages regardless of whether the goods or the subject matter of the contract existed at the time. The law will not reach such a result, however, unless the contract expressly imposes such absolute liability.

3 / Mistake as to identity of subject matter. An agreement is void if there is a mutual mistake as to the identity of the subject matter of the contract.[6] For example, if a buyer and seller discuss the sale of an electrical transformer, but one is thinking of a one-phase transformer and the other of a three-phase transformer, there is no contract.[7]

4 / Mistake as to identity of parties. When the parties deal face to face, a contract is not affected by the fact that one party may be mistaken as to the identity of the other.[8] When Brown enters Jones' store and purchases on credit from Jones, the contract is not void if Jones wrongly thought that Brown was the local rich man whereas he turns out to be a Brown of low financial standing. Here the mistake does not affect the contract because Jones did contract with the person with whom he intended to contract, that is, the person in front of him. His mistake related only to a matter which induced him to make the contract with that particular person, and it therefore does not affect the contract. When the mistake as to the identity of a party is induced by trick or deception of that party, however, the contract is voidable and may be set aside by the deceived party.

(a) OBJECTIVE VERSUS SUBJECTIVE TEST. A different question arises when the parties do not deal face to face, as when Brown mails an order which Jones accepts, again under the mistaken belief that Brown is the rich man. The courts differ as to the effect of such a mistake, influenced

---

[4] Restatement, Contracts, Sec. 456.
[5] Uniform Commercial Code, Sec. 2-613.
[6] R., Sec. 71.
[7] *Lipschultz* v. *Gregory Electric Co.,* 116 Cal.App.2d 915, 253 P.2d 537. The same result could be obtained by applying the rule that a contract must be certain in all of its material terms. If the agreement does not specify which type of transformer is purchased, an essential term is lacking and there is no contract.
[8] *Ludwinska* v. *John Hancock Mutual Life Ins. Co.,* 317 Pa. 577, 178 A. 28.

by whether they follow the modern objective test of "appearances to a reasonable man" or the old subjective test of the "meeting of the minds." When Jones accepts, Brown has no reason to believe that Jones was acting under a mistaken belief. There is, accordingly, a valid contract under the theory of appearances to a reasonable man. Under the meeting-of-the-minds theory, Jones never intended to deal with the poor Brown; consequently there cannot be a contract.

The objective test is a better one because the seller is always in a position to make a credit examination and, if he makes a mistake, it is his own fault. Furthermore, it is illogical to require a buyer to send an inquiring letter to the seller to check whether the seller really knows who the buyer is and intends to make the contract with him. Thus there is the possibility of a binding contract between an impostor and the person with whom he deals.

(b) CREDIT CARDS. An impostor's conduct may impose a liability on the person he is thought to be and on other third persons. For example, when an impostor steals or finds a credit card and then represents himself to be the lawful owner of the card, the credit-extending agency is liable to the person dealing with the impostor for credit extended to him. Furthermore, the lawful owner of the credit card is, in turn, liable to the credit-extending agency after it has paid the bills incurred by the impostor if the owner failed to report the loss or theft of the card to the agency promptly.

Misrepresentation

Suppose that one party to a contract makes a statement of fact which is false but that he does so innocently without intending to deceive the other party. Can the other party set aside the contract on the grounds that he was misled by the statement? It is often held he cannot. In certain instances, however, the law protects the deceived person by permitting him to avoid the contract.

Equity will permit the rescission of the contract when the innocent misstatement of a material fact induces another to make the contract. If the deceived person is a defendant in an action at law, it is generally held that he cannot use as a defense the fact of innocent deception by the plaintiff. There is a tendency, however, for the law courts to adopt the rule of equity. For example, it may be possible for an insurance company to avoid its policy because of an innocent misstatement of a material fact by the applicant.[9]

Facts: Amity Estates, a seller, informed Sheehan, a buyer, that a tract of land contained 147 acres and had access to a public road. In fact the tract contained 123 acres and did not have access to any road. When

---

[9] See Ch. 43.

the buyer sought to rescind the contract, the seller defended on the ground that he had acted in good faith, that the property had been described as containing 147 acres "more or less," and that the sale had been made "as is."

Decision: Judgment for Sheehan. The misrepresentation, although innocently made, was so material that the buyer could rescind because of it. The "more or less" and "as is" provisions did not serve to call attention of the buyer to the conditions that actually existed and therefore did not affect his right to rescind. (Sheehan v. Amity Estates, 27 App.Div.2d 594, 275 N.Y.S.2d 644)

Contracts between persons standing in confidential relationships, such as those between parent and child or between guardian and ward, can be set aside for the same reason.

Concealment

Generally, one party cannot set aside a contract because the other party failed to volunteer information which the complaining party would desire to know. Ordinarily if *C* does not ask *A* any questions, *A* is not under any duty to make a full statement of material facts.

If *A* and *C* stand in a confidential relationship, such as that of attorney and client, however, *A* has a duty to reveal anything that is material to *C*'s interests, and his silence has the same effect as though he had knowingly made a false statement that there was no material fact to be told *C*. In such a case *C* can avoid the contract.

As an aspect of the growing recognition of the requirement of good faith,[10] a duty to disclose information is recognized in some instances when the party possessing information knows that the other party is walking into a trap because of his lack of such knowledge.

Facts: The City of Salinas entered into a contract with Souza & McCue Construction Co. to construct a sewer. The city officials knew that unusual subsoil conditions, including extensive quicksands, existed, which would make performance of the contract unusually difficult; but it did not make that information known when it advertised for bids. The advertisement for bids directed bidders to "examine carefully the site of the work" and declared that the submission of a bid would constitute "evidence that the bidder has made such examination." Souza & McCue was awarded the contract, but because of the subsoil conditions it could not complete the contract on time and was sued by Salinas for breach of contract. Souza & McCue counterclaimed on the basis that the City had not revealed its information of the subsoil conditions and was liable for the loss caused thereby.

---

[10] UCC Sec. 1-201(19).

Decision: Judgment for contractor as to the counterclaim. An owner is liable if he does not inform the contractor of unusual difficulties known to the owner which the contractor will encounter in the performance of a contract. As the City knew that the contractor would base its bid on the incomplete information, the City had misled the contractor by such concealment and was liable to the contractor for the loss caused thereby. The provision as to the examination of "site of the work" did not alter this conclusion since there was nothing in that provision which would call to the contractor's attention the conditions that would be encountered nor which disclaimed liability for concealed subsoil conditions. (City of Salinas v. Souza & McCue Construction Co., 57 Cal.Rptr. 337, 424 P.2d 921)

Concealment may be more than the passive failure to volunteer information. It may consist of a positive act of hiding information from the other party by physical concealment, or it may consist of furnishing the wrong information. Conduct of such nature is generally classified and treated as fraud.

Fraud

Fraud exists when a person makes a misrepresentation of a material fact, known to him to be untrue or made with reckless indifference as to whether it is true, with the intention of causing the other party to enter into a contract, and the other party is entitled to rely thereon and enters into the contract. When one party to the contract is guilty of fraud, the contract is voidable and may be set aside by the injured party. Conduct that is unethical but which does not satisfy these elements is not fraud.

Facts: On December 1, 1964, Neely, a senior in college, made a contract to play the following year for the Houston Oilers professional football team. It was agreed orally that the making of this contract would be kept secret so that Neely would appear to be eligible for a postseason college game. Neely then received a better offer from the Dallas Cowboys and after college went to play for them. Houston sought an injunction against Neely. Neely claimed that the contract with Houston could not be enforced by Houston because of its fraud in stating that the contract would be binding on January 2, 1965, and then filing of the contract with the League Commissioner before that time in violation of the agreement to keep the execution of the contract secret so as to make him appear eligible for the postseason college football game.

Decision: Judgment in favor of Houston Oilers. Neely had not been deceived and knew that the secrecy was designed to conceal his ineligibility. Although the conduct of the Oilers might be unethical, it was not fraudulent, for the Oilers had not deceived Neely as to the nature and effect of their agreement and there was no duty to make public the fact that they had made any particular contract. (Houston Oilers v. Neely, [C.A. 10th] 361 F.2d 36)

Some elements of fraud are given a liberal interpretation by the courts, and further consideration of them is necessary. For convenience, the following illustrations refer to fraudulent statements, but any kind of communication may be used. The misrepresentation may be made by conduct as well as by words.[11]

Fraud is not easy to define because the law tries to balance its desire to protect the injured person from the act of the wrongdoer and its unwillingness to protect the careless person from the consequences of his own neglect.

1 / Mental state. The speaker must intend to deceive. This means that he must either know or believe that what he is saying is false and must intend to mislead, or that he is recklessly indifferent as to whether what he says is true or not.[12] The deceiver must intend that the injured party rely upon the statement and be deceived. Since it is practically impossible to show this directly, it is sufficient if the surrounding circumstances make it so appear.

2 / Misstatement of past or present fact. A misstatement of a past or present fact may constitute fraud. A statement that a painting is the work of Rembrandt, when the speaker knows that it is the work of an art student in a neighboring school, is such a misstatement.

An intentional misrepresentation of the nature of the transaction between the parties is fraudulent. A person is guilty of fraud, for example, when he falsely makes another believe that the contract about to be signed is not a contract but is a receipt or a release.

3 / Misstatement of intention. A misstatement of intention can constitute fraud when a promise is made by a person who does not intend to keep it.[13] To illustrate, a customer purchases goods from a merchant on credit and agrees to pay for them in sixty days. The merchant sells the goods to the customer because he believes the customer's statement that he will pay in sixty days. Actually, the customer does not intend to pay for the goods, and he does not do so. He is guilty of fraud in misstating his intention. Suppose that the customer had purchased the goods, intending to pay for them, but that he discovered later that he was unable to do so or decided later not to pay for them. In that event, he would not be guilty of fraud. He would be liable, however, for a breach of his contract to pay as promised.

Facts: Janney purchased land, agreeing to pay a certain sum, in reliance on the statements made by the seller that he would make valuable improve-

---

[11] *McGinn* v. *Tobey,* 62 Mich. 252, 28 N.W. 818.
[12] *Shackett* v. *Bickford,* 74 N.H. 57, 65 A. 252.
[13] *Snow* v. *Howard Motors,* 3 Conn.Cir. 702, 223 A.2d 409.

ments to the neighboring lots, thereby enhancing the value of the lot purchased by Janney. These statements were false when made, and there was no intention to make the improvements. Janney was later sued for the purchase price by the Snell National Bank.

Decision: Judgment for Janney. A promise or statement as to a future undertaking is fraudulent, justifying rescission of a contract, when at the time it is made it is false and there is no intention to perform in the future. (Snell National Bank v. Janney, 219 Ala. 396, 122 So. 362)

4 / Misstatement of opinion or value. Ordinarily a misstatement of opinion or value is not regarded as fraudulent,[14] on the theory that the person hearing the statement recognizes or should recognize that it is merely the speaker's personal view and not a statement of fact. When the speaker has expert knowledge or information not available to the other and he should realize that his listener relies upon his expert opinion, however, a misstatement by him of his opinion or of value, if intentionally made, amounts to fraud.[15]

5 / Misstatement of law. A misstatement of law is usually treated in the same manner as a misstatement of opinion or value. Ordinarily the listener is regarded as having an opportunity of knowing what the law is, an opportunity equal to that of his speaker, so that he is not entitled to rely on what the speaker tells him. When the speaker has expert knowledge of the law or represents that he has such knowledge, however, his misstatement can be the basis of fraud.[16]

6 / Materiality of misstatement. Does it make any difference if the misstatement concerns a trivial matter, or must it be something that a reasonable man would regard as material? Generally the misstatement must pertain to a material matter.[17]

7 / Investigation before relying on statement. If the injured person has available the ready means of determining the truth, as by looking at something in front of him, he cannot rely on the false statement.[18] The fact that he relies on the other person, that he is too busy to read the paper, or that he is in a hurry does not protect him. He takes the risk that the paper will state what he thinks it does when he signs it without reading it. When an illiterate person or one physically unable to read signs a paper without

---

[14] *Williams* v. *Lockhart,* 221 Ga. 343, 144 S.E.2d 528.
[15] *Lone Star Olds Cadillac Co.* v. *Vinson,* [Tex.Civ.App.] 168 S.W.2d 673.
[16] R., Sec. 474(a), Comment (d).
[17] The Restatement of the Law of Contracts, however, adopts the view that any statement, whether material or not, constitutes fraud if all the other elements are present. Sec. 471, Comment (i).
[18] *Scocozzo* v. *General Devel. Corp.,* [Fla.] 191 So.2d 572.

having it explained or read to him, he is ordinarily bound by its contents. As a limitation on this rule, however, some courts hold that the negligence of the injured party is not a bar to a claim for damages when the wrong-doer takes active steps to conceal the truth, as by substituting one paper for another and falsely informing the injured party as to the nature of the paper.

If an examination by the injured person does not reveal the defect, or if the injured person cannot be expected to understand what he sees because of its technical nature, or if such a simple examination is not available, the injured person may rely on the statements of the other party and raise the issue of fraud when he learns that they are false. A misrepresentation made to prevent further inquiry also constitutes fraud.[19]

> **Facts:** Swann traded in his old car and purchased a used car from Bob Wilson, Inc. The latter's President, Lenoff, wrote down the terms of the sale on a top sheet and then requested Swann to sign the top sheet and the sheets underneath, stating that they were duplicates. Lenoff thereafter had Swann acknowledge each of the sheets before a notary public and write in the margin of each sheet, "We have read this contract; it is correct and complete." Swann did not read the contract and did not see that the copies had additional interest and charges totaling $613.20, which he was required to pay. He sued the company for overcharging him.

> **Decision:** Judgment for Swann. As Lenoff had deliberately sought to mislead Swann by his conduct, the misconduct of Lenoff should not be excused by the fact that Swann may have prevented the intended harm had he been more careful. (Bob Wilson, Inc. v. Swann, [App.D.C.] 168 A.2d 198)

8 / Reliance and damage. A person can complain of the misrepresentation of another only if he was misled by it and acted in reliance on it. If *A* (owner) says that his house is in good condition when it is infested with termites but *B* (buyer) does not buy the house, *B* cannot complain that *A*'s statement was false since *B* cannot show that he was harmed in any way. Even if *B* purchased the house, he cannot recover from *A* when it can be shown that *B* knew there were termites and purchased the property anyway or that he did not care because he intended to tear down the building and erect a new building on the land.

When a person seeks to avoid a contract for fraud, it is theoretically immaterial whether the defrauded person is damaged in the sense that he can show a definite financial loss as the result of the fraud.[20] As a practical matter, however, the defrauded person would probably not raise the question if he did not suffer some damage. If the injured person wishes to sue

---

[19] *Rummer v. Throop,* 38 Wash.2d 624, 231 P.2d 313.
[20] R., Sec. 476, Comment (c).

the wrongdoer for damages, as distinguished from avoiding the contract, he must show that he has sustained some loss or injury.

9 / *Who may complain.* The wrongdoer is liable only to the person he intended to deceive. Ordinarily a fraudulent statement is made directly by the wrongdoer to his intended victim. Suppose, however, that unknown to the speaker a third person overhears him or looks at a letter containing his false statement. Can that third person complain of the speaker's fraud when he thereafter relies upon it? Since the wrongdoer did not intend to harm the third person, no liability results.

This rule does not require that the speaker make the misrepresentation directly to the intended victim. If the speaker makes a public announcement, any member of the public defrauded can bring an action against him. As an illustration, if *P*, in organizing a corporation, issues a prospectus that falsely describes the corporation and its financial status, any person who purchases the stock in reliance on that false prospectus may sue *P,* the promoter.

When the speaker gives false information to one person, intending that it will be communicated to another whom he hopes to deceive, the latter person may sue for fraud.

Facts: The Baltimore Shoe House falsely informed R. G. Dun Co., a commercial rating agency, that it was solvent. The Ohio Shoe Company consulted publications of Dun which erroneously stated that Baltimore was solvent. On the basis of that statement, the Ohio Shoe Company sold shoes to the Baltimore company. The purchaser then went into bankruptcy, and the Ohio Shoe Company sued the trustee in bankruptcy, Manly, to recover the shoes.

Decision: Judgment for the Ohio Shoe Company. The false report of the purchaser was made to the credit rating agency for the purpose of inducing third persons to rely on it. It was immaterial that a credit agency was an intermediate party between the purchaser and the seller. (Manly v. Ohio Shoe Company, [C.A.4th] 25 F.2d 384)

10 / *Use of assumed name.* The use of an assumed name is not necessarily fraudulent or unlawful. It is such only when the impostor assumes the name of another person or makes up a name for the purpose of concealing his identity from persons to whom he owes money or a duty, or to avoid arrest, or for the purpose of deceiving the person with whom he is dealing, or of imitating the name of a competitor.

Facts: Euge opened a checking account under the assumed name of Horn with the Manchester Bank. He drew a check for an amount greater than his account and was prosecuted for the crime of issuing a bogus check, the prosecution claiming that the check was drawn by a fictitious person on a fictitious account.

Decision: Euge was not guilty as there was an actual account although under the fictitious name he had assumed. The contract with the bank was lawful, and the bank would have been protected had it honored Euge's checks in the assumed name that he used. The account was an existing account under a fictitious name, but this did not constitute the crime charged. (State v. Euge, [Mo.] 400 S.W.2d 119)

In the absence of any intent to evade or deceive by the use of the assumed name, it is lawful for a person to go by any name he chooses, although other persons may refuse to deal with him unless he uses his actual name. If a person makes a contract in an assumed or fictitious name or in a trade name, he will be bound by his contract because that name was in fact intended to identify him.[21]

(a) CHANGE OF NAME. In most states, a person may obtain a decree of court officially changing his name upon filing a petition with the court, setting forth the reason for the desired change and satisfactory proof that there is no fraudulent or criminal purpose in effecting the change. In addition, a person's name may be changed as an incident to being adopted or divorced.

(b) FICTITIOUS NAME REGISTRATION. If a person or a group of persons, other than a corporation, do business under a fictitious name, a statement must generally be filed in a specified government office setting forth the names and addresses of the persons actually owning or operating the business, together with the name, address, and nature of the business. Violation of such a statute is made a crime and, if the statute expressly so declares, prevents the enterprise from bringing suit on a business contract so long as the name is not registered. No violation generally exists, however, when the other contracting party knows the identity of the persons doing business under the unregistered fictitious name.

11 / Fraud as a tort. Apart from its effect upon the validity of the contract, the fraud of one party is a tort or civil wrong upon the injured party. The injured party may bring a tort action, in which he may recover the money damages that he has sustained as the result of the fraudulent statement.

Undue Influence

It is a common experience for an aged parent to entrust all his business affairs to his son; for an invalid to rely on his nurse; for a client to follow implicitly whatever his attorney recommends. The relationship is such that for practical purposes the one person is helpless in the hands of the other.

---

[21] See UCC Sec. 3-401(2) with respect to the signing of commercial paper.

In such cases, the parent, the invalid, or the client is not in fact exercising his free will in making a contract suggested by the son, nurse, or attorney, but is merely following the will of the other person. Such relationships are called *confidential relationships*. Because of the great possibility that the person dominating the other may take advantage of him, the law presumes that the dominating person exerts *undue influence* upon the other person whenever the dominating person obtains any benefit from a contract made by the dominated person. The contract is then voidable and may be set aside by the other person to the contract unless the dominating person can prove that no advantage was taken by him.[22]

The class of confidential relationships is not well defined. It includes the relationships of parent and child, guardian and ward, physician and patient, attorney and client, and any other relationship of trust and confidence in which one party exercises a control or influence over another.

Whether undue influence exists is a difficult question for the court (ordinarily the jury) to determine. The law does not regard every "influence" as undue. Thus a nagging wife may drive a man to make a contract, but that is not ordinarily regarded as undue influence. Persuasion and argument are not in themselves undue influence.

An essential element of undue influence is that the person making the contract does not exercise his own free will in so doing. In the absence of a recognized type of confidential relationship, such as that between parent and child, the courts are likely to take the attitude that the person who claims to have been dominated was merely persuaded and wanted to make the contract.

> **Facts:** Studley and Bentson made a contract by which the latter agreed to transfer to the former certain property in consideration of the promise of Studley to provide a home and take care of Bentson for life. The contract was prepared by a third person, and its effect was explained to Bentson by the president of the bank where he deposited his money. Bentson died, and the administratrix of his estate sued to set aside the contract, claiming undue influence.

> **Decision:** Judgment for Studley. The fact that Studley and Bentson had been friends and that the latter had confidence in the former did not make the relationship a confidential relationship so as to cast on Studley the burden of sustaining the validity of the contract. (Johnson v. Studley, 80 Cal.App. 538, 252 P. 638)

Duress

Assume that *A* threatens to do physical harm to *B* if *B* does not sign a contract and that *B* signs the contract. This contract is executed by *B* under

---

[22] *Swain* v. *Moore*, 31 Del.Ch. 288, 71 A.2d 264.

duress, that is, under pressure of the threat. In such a case, *B* may avoid the contract since it was not voluntarily assented to by him.

What degree or kind of pressure must be applied to amount to duress? A person can claim duress if the threat of violence or other harm would restrain the free choice of a person of similar mentality, physical health, experience, education, and intelligence.[23] The fact that the victim was deprived of his free will is sufficient, but whether other persons would have been similarly affected may influence a jury in determining whether the victim had in fact been deprived of his free will.

The threats may be directed against third persons who are near relatives of the intimidated person making the contract. Thus a threat to injure one's parent, child, husband, wife, brother, aunt, grandchild, or son-in-law may be duress. The threat may be directed at the property of the intimidated person, such as a threat to burn down his house if he does not sign the contract. When the effect is to prevent the intimidated person from exercising his own free will, duress exists.

Generally, a threat of economic loss,[24] such as a threat to prevent a contractor from securing further credit necessary to obtain building materials, is not regarded as duress. Some courts have held it to be duress when so serious a loss threatened the victim, if he did not agree, that he in fact was not exercising a free choice when he made the contract. In any case, in order to prove duress by business or economic compulsion, it is necessary to show that the victim would suffer irreparable loss for which he could not adequately recover, if at all, by suing the wrongdoer.[25]

> **Facts:** Fahn leased a building to Lewis for business purposes. The lease provided for a reduction in the rent while the building was being repaired by Lewis. After Lewis had made expensive remodeling of the building, Fahn demanded payment of the full amount of the rent and threatened to cancel the lease and to sue to evict Lewis. Under protest, Lewis paid the full amount of the rent and later sued Fahn to recover the amount of the reduction that he should have been allowed.

> **Decision:** Judgment for Lewis. The economic pressure placed by Fahn upon Lewis constituted duress. Even though the eviction action against him would be groundless, such action could damage the credit standing of the tenant's business. (Lewis v. Fahn, 113 Cal.App.2d 95, 247 P.2d 831)

A threat to prosecute a person or a member of his family for a crime is usually held to constitute duress without regard to whether the person is

---

[23] *Tallmadge* v. *Robinson*, 158 Ohio 333, 109 N.E.2d 496.
[24] *Grad* v. *Roberts*, 14 N.Y.2d 70, 248 N.Y.S.2d 633.
[25] *Tri-State Roofing Co.* v. *Simon*, 187 Pa.Super. 17, 142 A.2d 333.

guilty of the crime or not.[26] However, a threat to resort to civil litigation made in the belief that there is a right to sue is not duress even though the belief is unfounded.[27] The fact that the person claiming duress had obtained legal advice before making the challenged contract is very strong evidence that there was no duress.[28]

Remedies

Mistake, fraud, undue influence, and duress may make the contract voidable or, in some instances, void. If the contract is voidable, it can be rescinded or set aside by the party who has been injured or of whom advantage has been taken. If he does not elect to avoid it, however, the contract is valid and binding. In no case can the other party, the wrongdoer, set aside the contract and thus profit by his own wrong. If the agreement is void, neither party can enforce it and no act of avoidance is required by either party to set it aside.

If the injured party has the right to rescind a contract, he is entitled to recover anything that he has paid or given the other in performance of the contract. If the injured party has received any money or property from the wrongdoer, he must return it as a condition to rescission. If restoration is not possible, as when the injured party has spent the money or consumed the property that he has received, or has sold the property to a third person, or has received personal services under the contract, the injured party is generally barred from rescinding the contract.

When a contract is voidable, the right to rescind the contract is lost by any conduct that is inconsistent with an intention to avoid it. The right to rescind the contract is lost if the injured party, with full knowledge of the facts, affirms the transaction,[29] or when, with such knowledge, he fails to object to the guilty party within a reasonable time.[30] In determining whether a reasonable time has expired, the court considers whether the delay benefited the injured party, whether a late avoidance of the contract would cause unreasonable harm to the guilty person, and whether avoidance would harm rights of third persons acquired after the original transaction.

If the other party was guilty of a wrong, such as fraud, as distinguished from making an innocent mistake, the injured party may sue him for damages caused by such wrong.

When the contract has resulted in the transfer of property from the guilty person to the victim, the latter also loses the right to rescind if, with

---

[26] *Thrift Credit Union* v. *Moore*, 88 Ga.App. 92, 76 S.E.2d 129.
[27] *Automatic Radio Mfg. Co.* v. *Hazeltine Research*, [C.A.1st] 176 F.2d 799.
[28] *Del Carlo* v. *Sonoma County*, [Cal.App.2d] 53 Cal.Rptr. 771.
[29] R., Sec. 484; *Sutton* v. *Crane*, [Fla.] 101 So.2d 823.
[30] Sec. 483.

knowledge of the true situation, he retains and uses the property, sells it to another, or uses it after the guilty person refuses to take it back.[31]

When the result of a mutual mistake is that a writing does not correctly state the agreement made by the parties, either party can have the court reform the contract to express the intended meaning.[32]

QUESTIONS AND PROBLEMS

1. Checklist of legal terms:

    (a) concealment, fraud (113)
    (b) confidential relationship, undue influence (119)
    (c) duress (120)

2. State the objective(s) of each of the following rules of law:

    (a) One party generally cannot set aside a contract because the other party failed to volunteer information which the complaining party would desire to know.

    (b) In certain close relationships that are regarded as confidential, it is presumed that a contract which benefits the dominating person was obtained by undue influence, and he has the burden of proving the contrary.

3. Davis shows Fuller a watch that he has found. Fuller, thinking that it is worth $75, makes an offer of $35. Davis accepts the offer and delivers the watch to Fuller. Later when Fuller discovers that the watch is worth only $10, he refuses to pay the agreed amount. Davis brings an action for the contract price. Is he entitled to judgment?

4. Ames borrows money from Bailey under an agreement calling for the payment of the highest rate of interest permitted in the state in which they both live. Both men believe that this rate is 6 percent. Bailey learns later that it is 10 percent and brings suit for that amount when Ames refuses to pay more than 6 percent. Ames argues that the agreement is void because there has been a mutual mistake as to the law. Decide.

5. Cole contracted to buy certain merchandise. On the strength of that agreement Cole entered into several other contracts providing for the sale of that merchandise. Later Cole learned that his first contract was not binding because, unknown to the seller and buyer, the goods had been destroyed before the parties made the agreement. Cole now stands to lose on his other contracts. How could he have protected himself from such loss?

6. Evans mailed to Fisher an offer to sell his house at 5617 Ross Avenue in a certain city for $32,000. In accepting the offer, Fisher had in mind

---

[31] Sec. 482.
[32] *Kear* v. *Hausmann*, 152 Neb. 512, 41 N.W.2d 850.

Evans' house located on Ross Circle in the same city. When Fisher refused to carry out the agreement, Evans brought an action to recover damages. Was he entitled to judgment?

7. In dealing with Noble, O'Neal represented himself to be Swartz. For this reason Noble agreed to sell certain furniture to O'Neal on credit. When Noble refused to carry out the agreement, O'Neal brought an action against Noble to recover damages. Was O'Neal entitled to judgment?

8. Porter, without mentioning that his dog barks at children, offers to sell the animal to Russell for $25. Russell accepts. When Russell discovers that the dog barks at children, he returns the dog to Porter and states that he will not pay for it. Porter brings an action for the price. Is he entitled to recover the amount agreed upon?

9. On the representation that the instrument before him was a receipt, Spencer, who could not read English, signed a note. When the note was due, could the holder recover the amount from Spencer?

10. Thacker gave a promissory note to Vogel in connection with the purchase of property in Springfield, Illinois. Vogel had misrepresented the location of Springfield. Thacker knew, however, that Vogel's description of the location of Springfield was incorrect. When Vogel sued Thacker on the note, Thacker claimed fraud by Vogel. Was this claim sound?

11. A ward conveyed certain property to his guardian. The conveyance was later attacked upon the ground of undue influence. What burden did the guardian have in order to sustain the conveyance?

12. Wright conveyed certain land to Young by deed. Later Wright brought suit to avoid the conveyance. He alleged that Young, accompanied by three other members of an unlawful association, came to his home and threatened personal violence if he did not execute the deed. As a result of repeated threats by these men, Wright executed the deed. Was he entitled to avoid the conveyance?

13. Roberts, an educated person, purchased real estate from Morrison. Roberts merely "half-read" the contract which she signed. As a result, she did not notice the provision in the contract with respect to interest on the unpaid portion of the purchase price. She refused to pay the interest specified in the contract. Morrison sued her. Could he recover? (Morrison v. Roberts, 195 Ga. 45, 23 S.E.2d 164)

14. An agent of Thor Food Service Corp. was seeking to sell Makofske a combination refrigerator-freezer and food purchase plan. Makofske was married and had three children. After being informed of the eating habits of Makofske and his family, the agent stated that the cost of the freezer and food would be about $95 to $100 a month. Makofske carefully examined the agent's itemized estimate and made some changes to it. Makofske then signed the contract and purchased the refrigerator-freezer. The cost proved to be greater than the estimated $95 to $100 a month, and Makofske claimed that the contract had been obtained by fraud. Decide. (Thor Food Service Corp. v. Makofske, 28 Misc.2d 872, 218 N.Y.S.2d 93)

Chapter II

Consideration

To constitute a valid contract, the agreement must meet requirements other than genuine mutual assent by competent parties. Ordinarily one of these requirements is consideration.

Definition

Consideration is what a promisor demands and receives as the price for his promise. A promise usually is binding upon a person only when he has received consideration.[1] It must be something to which the promisor is not otherwise entitled, and it must be the very thing that the promisor specifies as the price for his promise.

Although some cases define consideration in terms of benefit to the promisor or detriment to the promisee, it is immaterial whether benefit or detriment is present. The essential element is that the act or thing which is done or promised has been specified by the promisor as the price to be paid in order to obtain his promise.

A promise to make a gift or a promise to do or not to do something without receiving consideration is unenforceable, but an executed gift or a performance without consideration cannot be rescinded for lack of consideration. Likewise a promise to lend property, such as an automobile, to another person is not binding when the promisor does not receive anything in return for his promise. In contrast, if he actually lends the automobile to the promisee, the latter is lawfully entitled to possession until the loan of the car is terminated.

If the contract is bilateral, each party to the contract is a promisor and must receive consideration to make his promise binding. Thus, when *O* (owner) promises to pay *C* (contractor) $500 for painting *O's* house and *C* promises to paint *O's* house for the $500, *O* is a promisor and has received for his promise the undertaking of *C* to paint the house; likewise, *C* is a promisor and has received for his promise the undertaking of *O* to pay for the painting of the house.

A unilateral contract has only one promisor, and the performance of the act which he called for is the consideration for his promise.

---

[1] *Hanson* v. *Central Show Printing Co.*, 256 Iowa 1221, 130 N.W.2d 654.

Consideration is sometimes qualified or described as "valuable considera-tion" to distinguish it from the so-called "good consideration," that is, the love and affection existing between near relatives. In most states good con-sideration is not consideration at all but is merely a matter of inducement in the making of the promise. Moral obligation is likewise not consideration.

Forbearance as Consideration

In most cases consideration consists of the performance of an act or the making of a promise to act. But consideration may also consist of *forbear-ance*, which is refraining from doing an act, or a promise of forbearance.[2] In other words, the promisor may desire to buy the inaction of the other party or his promise not to act. For example, an officer of a corporation may ask a creditor of the corporation to refrain from suing it. When the officer makes a promise to the creditor that he will pay the debt if the corporation does not, the forbearance or promise to forbear by the creditor is considera-tion for the promise of the officer.

The waiving or giving up of any right, legal or equitable, can be con-sideration for the promise of another.[3] Thus the relinquishment of a right in property, of a right to sue for damages, or of homestead rights will support a promise given in return for it.

Facts: Because of erroneous plans and specifications prepared by Los Angeles County, Healy, as general contractor, and Brewster, as earthwork subcontractor, made a mutual mistake as to the condition of the earth to be encountered in building an airstrip for Los Angeles County. Because of this mistake of fact, Brewster was entitled to rescind the subcontract. Healy promised to pay him an additional sum, repre-senting the cost of the extra work required because of the actual conditions, if Brewster would proceed with the subcontract and not rescind. Later Healy refused to make such payment and claimed that his promise to pay was not binding because it was not supported by consideration.

Decision: Judgment for Brewster. The forbearing of his right to rescind for the mutual mistake of fact was consideration for the promise to pay him for the additional work involved because of the actual condition which existed. (Healy v. Brewster, [Cal.App.2d] 59 Cal.Rptr. 752)

The right that is surrendered in return for a promise may be a right against a third person or his property, as well as one against the promisor or his property. There is no consideration when the right is known to be worthless by the person surrendering it.

---

[2] *A & S Distributing Co.* v. *Nall-Tucker, Inc.,* [Okla.] 428 P.2d 254.
[3] **Restatement, Contracts, Sec. 75.**

Present Versus Past Consideration

Since consideration is what the promisor states must be received for his promise, it must be given after the promisor states what he demands for his promise. Past consideration is not valid.

As an illustration, an uncle (*U*) may say to his nephew (*N*), "You have been a good boy during the past year. I promise to give you $100." Although *U* makes the promise because of or "in consideration of" *N's* past conduct, that conduct is not consideration. *N's* conduct is merely the fact or circumstance that induced the making of the promise. *U* did not state to *N* that in order to obtain the promise *N* must do or refrain from doing certain acts. The promise is accordingly not binding on *U,* and he can change his mind without being liable for a breach of contract.

If, however, *U* stated, "I will pay you $100 in exchange for your promise to come home early at night during the coming year," there would be consideration for *U's* promise. Here *U* is saying that he is willing to give a promise but that the price of that promise is a counterpromise by *N* as to his future conduct. *U* is in effect buying the promise of *N* rather than rewarding past conduct.

When one person performs some service for another without the latter's knowledge or without an understanding that compensation is to be paid, a promise made later to pay for such services is not supported by consideration and is unenforceable.

Some courts hold that when benefits are derived by fraud or under circumstances that create a moral obligation, a promise to compensate is supported by consideration. When one promises to pay a debt that was unenforceable because of his minority,[4] or that is barred by the Statute of Limitations,[5] or that has been discharged in bankruptcy,[6] the promise is binding. There must be clear proof, however, that a subsequent promise was in fact made.[7] The better theory is that the new promise is a waiver of the bar or defense to the action and that no consideration is necessary.[8] Some courts regard the new promise as supported by moral consideration to pay the old debt. This is not a satisfactory explanation since ordinarily neither a moral obligation nor a past performance is deemed consideration.

Binding Character of Promise

To constitute consideration, the promise must be binding, that is, it must impose a liability or create a duty. Suppose that a coal company promises

---

[4] R., Sec. 89.
[5] Sec. 86.
[6] Sec. 87.
[7] *Lupinski* v. *Fischer,* 255 Wis. 182, 38 N.W.2d 429.
[8] R., Sec. 85.

to sell to a factory all the coal which it orders at a specified price, and that the factory agrees to pay that price for any coal which it orders from the coal company. The promise of the factory is not consideration because it does not obligate the factory to buy any coal from the coal company.

If, however, the factory promises to purchase all the coal it requires for a specified period and the coal dealer agrees to supply it at a specified price per ton, there is a valid contract according to most courts. It is true that it cannot be known beforehand how much coal will be ordered. The factory may have a strike or a fire and not operate at all during the year, and therefore require no coal. Moreover, the factory might convert to oil. In spite of these possibilities such a contract is usually regarded as valid by the courts.

Although a contract must impose a binding obligation, it may authorize one or either party to terminate or cancel the agreement under certain circumstances or upon giving notice to the other party. The fact that the contract may be terminated in this manner does not make the contract any the less binding prior to such termination.

Facts: Hood agreed with Heins and his associates that Hood would purchase all the milk produced by them as long as Hood did business in the area or until Heins terminated the contract by a 90-day notice. It was later claimed that this contract was not binding because Heins could terminate the contract and Hood could stop requiring milk.

Decision: The contract was binding. It must be recognized that the contract was made by persons intending to stay in business and that every contract is subject to a duty of good faith. It was unlikely that Hood would go out of business purposely to avoid the contract; and even if Heins gave a termination notice, the obligation of the contract would continue for 90 days thereafter. Hence, each party was subject to an obligation. (Hood v. Heins, 124 Vt. 331, 205 A.2d 561)

In some instances where it is manifest that a particular act is impossible to perform, a promise to do that act is not regarded as valid consideration. If there is a possibility that the performance can be made, the consideration is valid.

Promise to Perform Existing Obligations

Ordinarily, a promise to do, or the performance of, what one is already under a legal obligation to do is not consideration. It is immaterial whether the legal obligation is based upon contract, upon the duties pertaining to an office held by the promisor, or upon statute or general principles of law. This rule is based on the theory that in such instances the promisor receives nothing for his promise since he was entitled to the conduct called for without paying anything extra.

Facts: An insurance company offered a reward for the arrest and conviction of a thief who robbed insured premises. The reward was claimed by Davis. He was a salaried, full-time "crime detector" employed by the county and assigned to the office of the prosecuting attorney. Other persons claiming the reward contended that Davis was not eligible to receive the reward.

Decision: Judgment against Davis. As it was the duty of Davis to give the prosecuting attorney any information that he acquired with respect to the commission of crimes, it was contrary to public policy to permit him to accept a reward offer for doing the work which it was his duty to do. (Davis v. Mathews, [C.A.4th] 361 F.2d 899)

If the act requested is over and beyond the call of duty, however, the performance of that act will make the promise binding.[9]

Similarly, a promise to refrain from doing what one has no legal right to do is not consideration.

1 / Completion of contract. When a contractor refuses to complete a building unless the owner promises him a payment or bonus in addition to the sum specified in the original contract, and the owner promises to make that payment, the question arises whether the owner's promise is binding. A few courts hold that the promise is binding on the theory that the first contract was mutually rescinded and that a second contract including the promise to pay the bonus was executed. Some courts hold the promise enforceable on the theory that the contractor has given up his right of election (a) to perform or (b) to abandon the contract and pay damages.[10] Most courts, however, hold that the second promise is without consideration.

Facts: Vinson entered into a contract with Leggett to construct a building. Vinson found that he could not complete the work at the price fixed in the contract. He claimed that when he informed Leggett to that effect, Leggett agreed to pay him whatever loss he would sustain in completing the building. After completing the building, Vinson sued Leggett for the amount of the loss.

Decision: Judgment for Leggett. As the contractor was legally bound to complete the contract at the time the owner made the promise to pay the additional amount, the promise to complete the contract could not be consideration for the promise to pay such amount. The owner did not obtain anything for his promise to which he was not already entitled. (Leggett v. Vinson, 155 Miss. 411, 124 So. 472)

---

9 R., Sec. 84(c); *Kimmons* v. *James,* 243 Miss. 535, 137 So.2d 912.
10 *Swartz* v. *Lieberman,* 323 Mass. 109, 80 N.E.2d 5.

The courts holding that there is no consideration for the second promise make an exception when there are extraordinary circumstances caused by unforeseeable difficulties or mistakes and when the additional amount demanded by the contractor is reasonable for the extra work done by him.[11] They do so usually upon the theory that the first contract was discharged because of an implied condition that the facts would be or would continue to be as supposed by the parties and that the completion of the contract was the consideration for the new promise. Generally, however, unanticipated difficulty or expense, such as a strike or a price increase, does not affect the liabilities of the parties.[12] Such risks one takes in making a contract in the same sense that when you buy a coat or a house, you take the risk that you may not like it as much as you thought you would.

If the promise of the contractor is to do something that is neither expressly nor impliedly a part of the first contract, then the promise of the other party is binding. For example, if a bonus of $1,000 is promised in return for the promise of a contractor to complete the building at a date earlier than that specified in the original agreement, the promise would be binding.

2 / Compromise and release of claims. The rule that doing or promising to do what one is bound to do is not consideration applies to a part payment made in satisfaction of an admitted debt. For example, if one person owes another $100, the promise of the latter to take $50 in full payment is not binding upon him and will not prevent him from demanding the remainder later, because the partial payment by the debtor is not consideration.

This rule has been severely criticized because it seems unfair to permit the creditor to go back on his promise even though the debtor does owe him the money. In some instances it has been changed by statute or by court decision. Some courts treat the transaction as a binding gift of the remainder on the part of the creditor. Other courts seize the slightest opportunity to find some new consideration.

If the debtor pays before the debt is due, there is, of course, consideration since on the day when payment was made the creditor was not entitled to demand any payment. Likewise, if the creditor accepts some article, even of slight value, in addition to the part payment, the agreement is binding.

Facts: Post owed the bank $9,922.20. The bank agreed to reduce the claim to $8,000 if Post would give the bank a mortgage for that amount. The mortgage was given. The bank subsequently sued Post for $9,922.20.

---

[11] *Pittsburgh Testing Laboratory* v. *Farnsworth & Chambers Co.,* [C.A.10th] 251 F.2d 77.
[12] R., Sec. 467.

Decision: Judgment for the bank for only $8,000. The giving of security for an unsecured debt or the changing of security can be consideration when called for by the creditor as the price for his promise to reduce his claim. (Post v. First National Bank, 138 Ill. 559, 28 N.E. 978)

If there is a bona fide dispute as to the amount owed or whether any amount is owed, a payment by the debtor of less than the amount claimed by the creditor is consideration for the latter's agreement to release or settle the claim. It is generally sufficient if the claimant believes in his claim; but if he knows that his claim does not have any merit and he is pressing it to force some payment to buy peace from the annoyance of a lawsuit, the settlement agreement based on the part payment is not binding. A minority of states hold that the claimant must also have a reasonable ground for believing that his claim is valid.

The acceptance of a check for part of a debt releases the entire debt, without regard to the existence of a dispute, if the check bears a notation that it is intended as final or full payment.[13]

3 / Composition of creditors. In a *composition of creditors*, the various creditors of one debtor mutually agree to accept a fractional part of their claims in full satisfaction thereof. Such agreements are binding and are deemed supported by consideration.

Adequacy of Consideration

Ordinarily the law does not weigh the adequacy of consideration.[14] Assume that a farmer owns two farms, one of which is larger, more productive, and obviously more valuable than the other. He makes separate contracts to sell each to a different purchaser. Purchaser *A* promises to pay $20,000 for the better farm, and purchaser *B* promises to pay $20,000 for the poorer. A court will not set aside *B's* promise on the ground that he was getting less than his money's worth since *A* was getting a much better farm for the same money.

In the absence of fraud or other misconduct, the courts usually will not interfere to make sure that each side is getting a fair return. The courts leave each person to his contract and do not seek to reappraise the value that he has placed upon the consideration which he has received. The fact that the consideration given may seem small or trifling to other persons or to a reasonable man does not, in the absence of fraud, affect the validity of the contract.

---

[13] Uniform Commercial Code, Sec. 3-408, Official Comment, point 2. See also Sec. 1-107, generally, and Sec. 2-209(1) as to the sale of goods.
[14] *Roberts v. Clevenger,* [Mo.] 225 S.W.2d 728.

Facts: Upon the death of their mother, the children of James Smith gave their interest in the mother's estate to their father in consideration of his payment of $1 to each and of his promise to leave them the property on his death. The father died without leaving them the property. The children sued their father's second wife to obtain the property in accordance with the agreement.

Decision: Judgment for children. The promises between the father and the children created a binding contract, as against the argument that the contract was not binding because the children got so little from the father, since all they received was the $1 and the chance that when the father died, there would be something in his estate which could be left to them. This argument was rejected as the law will not consider the adequacy or amount of consideration where there is no element of fraud. (Smith v. Smith, 340 Ill. 34, 172 N.E. 32)

1 / Forbearance. If forbearance is called for by the promisor as the price of his promise, it is not material whether the parties agree that the forbearance shall be for a long or a short time. The promisee must forbear for the period called for by the promisor, and the law will not attempt to say whether the period of forbearance is adequate consideration for the promise.

When no specific period of forbearance is stated, the promisee is under a duty to forbear for a reasonable time. If, however, there is no duty to forbear for any period at all, as when the promisee merely agrees to forbear as long as he wishes, there is no consideration since the promisor has not bought anything with his promise.

2 / Exceptions. There are some exceptions to the rule that the courts will not weigh the consideration, as follows:

(a) UNCONSCIONABILITY. An excessively hard bargain obtained by a seller of goods at the expense of a small buyer with weak purchasing power has been held to constitute unconscionability,[15] although such a conclusion is merely another way of stating that the consideration received by the buyer was not adequate.

(b) STATUTORY EXCEPTIONS. In a few states statutes require that the consideration be adequate, or fair or reasonable, in order to make a contract binding.

Adequacy of the consideration may be questioned in computing tax liability. For example, when it is claimed that the taxable balance of a decedent's estate should be reduced by the amount owed a given creditor,

---

[15] *Frostifresh Corp.* v. *Reynoso,* 52 Misc.2d 26, 274 N.Y.S.2d 757; affirmed on this point, [App.Div.2d] 4 U.C.C.R.S. 300 (ordering new trial as to damages). See also *American Home Improvement, Inc.* v. *MacIver,* 105 N.H. 435, 201 A.2d 886.

such debt may be deducted only to the extent that the decedent had received an equivalent value from the creditor. Thus, if the decedent owed the creditor $1,000 for property that was worth $200, only the sum of $200 could be deducted in computing the value of the estate. This determination for tax purposes, however, does not affect the validity of the creditor's contract.

(c) EVIDENCE OF FRAUD. The smallness of the consideration may be evidence of fraud.[16] Suppose that R sells a $10,000 house to E for $100. It might be a perfectly innocent transaction in which R virtually makes a gift in return for the nominal payment. Since R as the owner of his house could give it away, nothing prevents his "selling" it at such a low figure. The transaction, however, may be of a different nature. It may be that E has defrauded R into believing that the property is worthless and R therefore sells it for $100. Or there may be collusion between R and E to transfer the property in order to hide it from creditors of R. The smallness of the consideration does not mean that the transaction is necessarily made in bad faith or for a fraudulent purpose; but if other evidence indicates fraud, the smallness of the consideration corroborates that evidence.

(d) EXCHANGE OF DIFFERENT QUANTITIES OF IDENTICAL UNITS. A promise to pay a particular amount of money or to deliver a particular quantity of goods in exchange for a promise to pay or deliver a greater amount or quantity of the same kind of money or goods at the same time and place is not adequate consideration.[17] If I promise to pay you $50 in exchange for your promise to pay me $100 under such circumstances, my promise is not regarded as adequate consideration for your promise, and your promise therefore is not binding upon you.[18]

If there is a difference between the nature of the units promised by the two parties, the law will find that there is consideration and will not ask whether the consideration is adequate. A promise to pay $60 in return for a promise to pay one penny would not be supported by consideration if both amounts of money are current legal tender. On the other hand, a promise to pay $60 in Revolutionary currency in return for one penny of current money or a promise to pay $60 of current money for a coin collector's penny would be supported by consideration since in each case the units are not equivalent.

Exceptions to Requirement of Consideration

Ordinarily, a promise is not binding unless supported by consideration. Under some statutes there is prima facie presumption of consideration, how-

---

[16] *Woods* v. *Griffin*, 204 Ark. 514, 163 S.W.2d 322.
[17] R., Sec. 76(c).
[18] Note that this is similar to the rule that payment of part of a debt which is due is not consideration for the granting of an extension as to the balance. *Shepherd* v. *Erickson*. [Tex.Civ.App.] 416 S.W.2d 450.

ever, which may be rebutted as between the immediate parties. There are certain other exceptions to this rule.

1 / Voluntary subscriptions. When charitable enterprises are financed by voluntary subscriptions of a number of persons, the promise of each one is generally enforceable. For example, when a number of people make pledges or subscriptions for the construction of a church, for a charitable institution, or for a college, the subscriptions are binding.[19]

The theories for sustaining such promises vary. One view is that the promise of each subscriber is consideration for the promises of the others. This view is not sound because the promises are not given in exchange for each other. Another view is that the promisor cannot revoke his promise because others have incurred obligations in reliance on his promise.[20] Still another view treats a subscription as an offer of a unilateral contract which is accepted by creating liabilities or making expenditures.[21] Under this theory the promise would be revocable until the act is performed. It is also held by some courts that the acceptance of a subscription carries an implied promise creating an obligation to perform in accordance with the offer.[22]

The real answer is that in these cases consideration is lacking according to the technical standards applied in ordinary contract cases. Nevertheless, the courts enforce such promises as a matter of public policy.

2 / Sealed instruments. At common law consideration was not necessary to support a promise under seal. When the seal has its original common-law effect, a gratuitous promise or a promise to make a gift is enforceable when it is set forth in a sealed instrument.

This common-law rule has been abolished or modified in most states. In some states a promise under seal must be supported by consideration, just as though it did not have a seal. Other states take a middle position and hold that the presence of a seal is prima facie proof that there is consideration to support the promise. This means that if nothing more than the existence of the sealed promise is shown, it is deemed supported by consideration. But if the promisor proves that there was no consideration, the promise is not binding upon him.

Even in those states in which the contract under seal is binding, the courts of equity will refuse to grant special relief, such as specifically enforcing the contract, if there is not a fair or reasonable consideration for the promise.[23]

---

[19] *Board of Home Missions v. Manley,* 129 Cal.App. 541, 19 P.2d 21.
[20] *Rochester Civic Theatre v. Ramsay,* [C.A.8th] 368 F.2d 748.
[21] *Cohoes Memorial Hospital v. Mossey,* 25 App.Div.2d 476, 266 N.Y.S.2d 501.
[22] *Presbyterian Board of Foreign Missions v. Smith,* 209 Pa. 361, 58 A. 689.
[23] See p. 208.

3 / Debts of record. No consideration is necessary to support an obligation of record, such as a judgment or recognizance. These obligations are enforceable as a matter of public policy.

4 / Model Written Obligations Act. Under statutes in some states no consideration is necessary in order to make certain written promises binding. The Model Written Obligations Act provides that no release (or promise) hereafter made and signed by the person releasing (or promising) shall be "invalid or unenforceable for lack of consideration, if the writing also contains an express statement, in any form of language, that the signer intends to be legally bound." [24]

5 / Firm offers by merchants—goods. Consideration is not required for (a) a merchant's written firm offer as to goods, stated to be irrevocable for a fixed time not over three months,[25] (b) a written discharge of a claim for an alleged breach of a commercial contract,[26] or (c) an agreement to modify a contract for the sale of goods.[27]

6 / Promissory estoppel. Some courts enforce promises that are not supported by consideration upon the *doctrine of promissory estoppel.* By this doctrine, if a person makes a promise to another and that other person acts upon that promise, the promisor is barred from setting up the absence of consideration in order to avoid his promise.[28] The enforcement of the promise, even though there is no consideration, is deemed proper when the promisor should reasonably expect to induce and does induce action or forbearance of a definite and substantial character on the part of the promisee and when "injustice can be avoided only by enforcement of the promise." [29] The doctrine of promissory estoppel, although conflicting with the basic requirement of consideration, is being given wider recognition as a means of attaining justice.

Facts: Hoffman wanted to acquire a franchise as a Red Owl Grocery Store, Red Owl being a corporation that maintained a system of chain stores. The agent of Red Owl informed Hoffman and his wife that if they would sell their bakery in Wautoma, acquire a certain tract of land in Chilton, another city, and put up a specified amount of money, he would be given a franchise as desired. Hoffman sold his business, acquired the land in Chilton, but was never granted a franchise. He and his wife sued Red Owl, which raised the defense that there had only been an assurance that Hoffman would receive a franchise but no

---

[24] MWOA, Sec. 1. The Act has been adopted in Pennsylvania.
[25] See p. 82.
[26] UCC, Sec. 1-107.
[27] Sec. 2-209(1).
[28] *Metropolitan Convoy Corp.* v. *Chrysler Corp.,* [Del.] 208 A.2d 519.
[29] R., Sec. 90.

promise supported by consideration and therefore no binding contract to give him a franchise.

Decision: Judgment for the Hoffmans. Injustice would result under the circumstances of the case if the Hoffmans were not granted relief because of the failure of Red Owl to keep the promise made by its authorized agent. The plaintiffs had acted in reliance on such promise and would be harmed if the promise were not held binding. (Hoffman v. Red Owl Stores, Inc. 26 Wis. 2d 683, 133 N.W.2d 267)

Promissory estoppel differs from consideration in that the reliance of the promisee is not the bargained for response sought by the promisor. To be consideration, it would be necessary that the promisor specified or requested reliance as the price of his making his promise. In contrast, in the promissory estoppel there is no such specification or request by the promisor; but the promisor, as a reasonable man, should recognize that his action will lead the promisee to rely on the promise and that the promisee will sustain substantial harm if the promise is not performed.[30]

The doctrine of promissory estoppel is not applied when no promise is made and one party merely takes a chance on future developments; nor does it apply when it is made clear that certain conditions must be met before any obligation will arise and the claimant fails to meet those conditions, such as making payment in advance.[31] Likewise, since promissory estoppel is based on the ground that there has been reliance on a promise, there must be a communication of the promise to the promisee, in the same sense that an offer must be communicated to an offeree.[32]

Promissory estoppel is also applied to require an offeror to hold an offer open for a reasonable time although there is no consideration to do so and although the firm offer concept of the Code is not applicable. Thus it is held in some states that when a subcontractor makes a bid to a general contractor and recognizes that the general contractor will rely thereon in making his bid for the construction job, the subcontractor is barred from revoking his offer until a reasonable time has elapsed in which the contractor may accept the offer of the subcontractor.[33]

Legality of Consideration

The law will not permit persons to make contracts that violate the law. Accordingly, a promise to do something which the law prohibits or a promise to refrain from doing something which the law requires is not valid consideration and the contract is illegal.

[30] *Day* v. *Mortgage Ins. Corp.,* [Idaho] 428 P.2d 524.
[31] *Corbit* v. *J. I. Case Co.,* 66 Wash.2d 30, 424 P.2d 290.
[32] *Hilton* v. *Alexander & Baldwin,* [Wash.2d] 400 P.2d 772.
[33] *Drennan* v. *Star Paving Co.,* 51 Cal.2d 409, 333 P.2d 757.

QUESTIONS AND PROBLEMS

1. Checklist of legal terms:
   (a) consideration (124), forbearance (125)
   (b) composition of creditors (130)
   (c) doctrine of promissory estoppel (134)

2. State the objective(s) of each of the following rules of law:
   (a) An executed gift or a performance that has been rendered without consideration cannot be rescinded for lack of consideration.
   (b) In the absence of fraud, the adequacy of consideration is usually immaterial.

3. Wesley promises to perform certain services for Yost in return for 15 shares of a certain corporate stock. The market value of the shares declines in value before Wesley renders those services. Wesley claims that he is not bound. Is his contention sound?

4. Greer borrows $1,000 from Hardy for eight months. A month later, Hardy demands security for the loan. As a favor to Greer and without compensation, Haller gives Hardy a written promise to pay in the event of Greer's default. When Greer defaults, Hardy sues and obtains a judgment against him but is unable to collect. Hardy then sues Haller. Decide.

5. According to the terms of an agreement between the Tri-State Refining Company and Krammer, the company agreed to sell all the oil Krammer would need in his business during the next year at a specified price. When the company failed to perform as agreed, Krammer brought an action to recover damages. Was he entitled to judgment?

6. Miller agreed to construct a split-level house for Ingram for $35,000. When Miller refused to perform, Ingram promised him $40,000 for the construction of a two-story house. Miller built the two-story house, but Ingram refused to pay more than $35,000. Was Miller entitled to $40,000?

7. On April 10 Lindsay accepts $475 in payment of Huston's note for $500 which is due on April 15. Later Lindsay sues Huston for the balance. Lindsay maintains that no consideration was given for his promise to release Huston from his obligation to pay the difference of $25. Is his contention sound?

8. Lane's creditors sign an agreement that they will accept 55 cents on the dollar in satisfaction of their claims. Later one of these creditors sues Lane for the balance of Lane's debt to him. Can he collect?

9. Madden promises to pay $25 to Hurst in return for Hurst's promise to give him a silver dollar. Later Madden refuses to carry out his agreement. Under what circumstances could Hurst recover damages?

10. Nolan was one of many voluntary subscribers to a fund for the construction of a monument to be dedicated to members of the armed

services who had served in Vietnam. When the amount of his subscription became due, Nolan refused to pay his pledge. Was his promise enforceable?

11. When Spilker threatens to strike Townsend, the latter promises to give Spilker $25 if he will not do so. Is Townsend's promise enforceable?

12. Frame gave his wife a written promise agreeing that his estate should pay her $5,000 after his death if she remained with him and took "care of things as she has always done." After his death, his widow sued the husband's estate on this promise. Was she entitled to collect? (Frame v. Frame, 120 Tex. 61, 36 S.W.2d 152)

13. Schmidt and Foster discussed having Foster build and manage an apartment house for Schmidt. They signed an agreement part of which stated that "Foster agrees to serve as manager of the apartment house as long as he is able and his services in that capacity are desired, subject to reasonable vacations and absences." Later he sued Schmidt for breach of the contract to give him the job of manager. The defense was raised that there was no consideration for any promise to employ Foster as manager. Was this a good defense? (Schmidt v. Foster, [Wyo.] 380 P.2d 124)

14. Mangus and Present were both real estate brokers. Mangus was trying to sell certain houses for his customers who had listed the properties with him for sale. Mangus made a contract with Present that if Present produced a purchaser for any of these properties, Mangus and Present would divide the commissions on the sale. Present produced a purchaser and received commissions from his customer but refused to divide them with Mangus. Mangus then sued Present for breach of contract. The latter raised the defense that there was no consideration for the promise to divide the commissions since Mangus did not have the exclusive agency to sell the real estate in question, which therefore could have been sold by the owner or any other agent, in which case Mangus would not have been entitled to any commissions. Decide. (Mangus v. Present, [Fla.] 135 So.2d 417)

15. The Association of Army and Navy Stores gave a price discount to customer members of the association. The association agreed to list Young's Store as a member store, and Young agreed to pay the association a percentage of the sales made at its store to association customer members plus a fixed monthly charge of $2.50. No new customers purchased at Young's Store. He refused to pay the association the monthly charge on the grounds that the consideration for the contract had failed. Decide. (Association of Army and Navy Stores v. Young, 296 Ky. 61, 176 S.W.2d 136)

Chapter 12

Legality of Contract

A contract is illegal when either the formation or the performance of the agreement is a crime or a tort, or is opposed to public policy or interest. Ordinarily an illegal contract is void.[1]

Effect of Illegal Contracts

When a contract is illegal, the parties are usually regarded as being beyond the pale of the courts and not entitled to their aid. If the illegal contract has not been performed, neither party can sue the other to obtain performance or damages. If the contract has been performed, neither party can sue the other for damages or to set the contract aside.[2]

There are the following exceptions to the rule that the court will not aid the parties to an unlawful contract:

(1) When the law which the agreement violates is intended for the protection of one of the parties, that party may seek relief. For example, when in order to protect the public the law forbids the issuance of corporate securities without governmental approval, a person who has purchased them may recover his money or enforce the statutory liability of those promoting the sale.[3]

(2) When the parties are not equally guilty or, as it is said, are not *in pari delicto,* the one less guilty is granted relief when public interest is advanced by so doing.[4] This rule is applied to illegal agreements that are induced by undue influence, duress, or fraud.

(3) Another exception exists in most states when a consideration has been paid for an illegal act that has not been performed.[5] Thus, a person who had placed money with a stakeholder for the purpose of swindling another by a pretended race was allowed to recover when he repudiated the agreement and requested his money from the stakeholder before the race was scheduled to be run.

---

[1] See p. 70.
[2] Restatement, Contracts, Sec. 598; *Vock* v. *Vock,* 365 Ill. 432, 6 N.E.2d 843.
[3] *Maner* v. *Mydland,* [Cal.App.2d] 58 Cal.Reptr. 740.
[4] R., Sec. 604.
[5] Sec. 605.

(4) An exception may also exist when the illegality is collateral or incidental, as when one of the parties has not obtained a government permit or license to perform the contract.

Facts: The Ilice Construction Company made masonry alterations to a building occupied by Caravello as tenant and owned by Rose. A city ordinance required that anyone making such alterations must first obtain a building license. Ilice had not obtained a license. Caravello and Rose refused to pay Ilice for the work. Ilice joined in an action brought by Meissner, another contractor, to enforce a mechanic's lien against the property. No claim was made that the work as done by Ilice did not satisfy the requirements of the building code, and Ilice obtained a permit for the work after the action had been brought on the mechanic's lien.

Decision: Judgment for Ilice. While the law required a permit and imposed penalties for failing to have a permit, the law did not specifically state that a contract made without a permit could not be enforced. As the permit law was primarily concerned with the construction of proper buildings, the statutory objective of requiring a permit was satisfied when a building that was constructed was in fact proper. The fact that the building was proper was shown by the issuance of the permit after it was constructed. (Meissner v. Caravello, 4 Ill.App.2d 428, 124 N.E.2d 615)

Partial Illegality

An agreement may involve the performance of several promises, some of which are illegal and some legal. The legal parts of the agreement may be enforced, provided that they can be separated from the parts which are illegal. The same rule applies when the consideration is illegal in part.[6] The rule is not applied, however, when the illegal act or consideration is said to taint and strike down the entire agreement, when the elimination of the void provision would so unbalance the rights of the parties that they would never have entered into the contract in that modified form, or when it would work a hardship on them to be compelled to accept the revised contract.[7]

Facts: Sturm, an insurance agent, sued Truby to recover premiums due on policies of insurance. Truby defended on the ground that the plaintiff had promised to rebate to him part of the premiums, that a rebate of premiums violated the state insurance law, and that accordingly the plaintiff could not sue for any part of the premiums. The plaintiff contended that only the agreement with respect to the rebate was illegal and that the agreement that the insured should pay premiums was lawful and could be enforced.

---

[6] Sec. 607.
[7] *McGinnis Equipment Co. v. Riggs*, 4 Ariz.App. 556, 422 P.2d 187.

Decision: Judgment for Truby on the ground that the illegal agreement as to the rebate was an integral part of the agreement to pay premiums initially, since the latter agreement would not have been made without the agreement as to rebate. The illegal part thus tainted the entire contract and made it void. (Sturm v. Truby, 245 App.Div. 357, 282 N.Y.S. 433)

When there is an indivisible promise to perform several acts, some of which are illegal, the agreement is void.[8] Also when there is a single promise to do a legal act, supported by several considerations, some of which are illegal, the agreement cannot be enforced.

If a contract is susceptible of two interpretations, one legal and the other illegal, the court will assume that the legal meaning was intended unless the contrary is clearly indicated.[9]

Crimes and Civil Wrongs

An agreement is illegal and therefore void when it calls for the commission of any act that constitutes a crime.[10] To illustrate, one cannot enforce a contract by which the other party agrees to commit an assault, to steal property, to burn a house, to print a libelous article, or to kill a person.

An agreement that calls for the commission of a civil wrong is also illegal and void.[11] Examples are agreements to damage the goods of another, to slander a third person, to defraud another,[12] or to infringe another's patent, trademark, or copyright. Thus, an agreement for *A's* orchestra to use the name of *B*, a skilled musician, is illegal as a fraud upon the public when *B* is not actually to appear with the orchestra. The use of his name would give the impression that the orchestra was conducted by him.

Contracts Injuring Public Service

Any contract that tends to interfere with the proper performance of the duties of a public officer, whether legislative, administrative, or judicial, is contrary to public policy and void.[13] Thus an agreement to procure the award of a public contract by corrupt means is not enforceable. Other examples are agreements to sell public offices, to procure pardons by corrupt means, or to pay a public officer more or less than his legal fees or salary.[14]

One of the most common contracts within this class is the *illegal lobbying contract*. This term is ordinarily used to describe a contract by which one

---

[8] *Kelly* v. *Silver Bow County,* 125 Mont. 272, 233 P.2d 1035.
[9] *American Machine & Metals* v. *De Bothezat Impeller Co.,* [C.A.2d] 180 F.2d 342.
[10] R., Sec. 512.
[11] Secs. 571 to 579.
[12] *Kryl* v. *Frank Holton & Co.,* 217 Wis. 628, 259 N.W. 828.
[13] R., Secs. 559 to 570.
[14] *Allen* v. *City of Lawrence,* 318 Mass. 210, 61 N.E.2d 133.

party agrees to use bribery, threats of a loss to votes, or any other improper means to procure or prevent the adoption of particular legislation by a lawmaking body, such as Congress or a state legislature. Such agreements are clearly contrary to the public interest since they interfere with the workings of the democratic process. They are accordingly illegal and void.

Some courts hold illegal all agreements to influence legislation, regardless of the means contemplated or employed. Other courts adopt the better rule that such agreements are valid in the absence of the use of improper influence or the contemplation of using such influence. According to the latter courts, since an individual has the right to state his case to the lawmaker in the hope of influencing his action, it is perfectly proper for the individual to retain and pay an agent or attorney to present his case to the lawmaker. So long as no improper inducement or threat is to be made to the lawmaker and the agent is to confine himself to stating the facts of the case, leaving it to the free will of the lawmaker to decide for himself, no illegality is present.

Contracts Obstructing Legal Processes

Any agreement intended to obstruct or pervert legal processes is contrary to public interest and therefore void.[15] Contracts that promise to pay money in return for the abandonment of the prosecution of a criminal case, for the suppression of evidence in any legal proceeding, for the stirring up of litigation, or for the perpetration of any fraud upon the court are therefore void.

An agreement to pay an ordinary witness more than the regular witness fee allowed by law or a promise to pay him a greater amount if the promisor wins the lawsuit is void. The danger here is that the witness will lie in order to help his party win the case, resulting in perjury and the miscarriage of justice.

Facts: Burchell, Ledford, and Hubbard were candidates for sheriff. Hubbard was elected, but Burchell had evidence that would invalidate the election. Burchell agreed to give Ledford this evidence in return for Ledford's promise to appoint Burchell deputy sheriff if Ledford was able to oust Hubbard and have himself declared the sheriff. Ledford was successful in having himself declared the lawful sheriff. Burchell then sued Ledford to enforce his agreement.

Decision: Judgment for Ledford. Any agreement making the compensation or reward of a witness or person producing evidence contingent upon the success of a litigant is contrary to public policy and void because of the tendency to induce perjury and the fabrication of evidence. The contract was therefore void and could not be enforced. (Burchell v. Ledford, 226 Ky. 155, 10 S.W.2d 622)

---

[15] R., Secs. 540 to 558.

Contracts providing for the arbitration of disputes are generally recognized as valid.

Usury

A person is guilty of *usury* when he makes a loan of money that is to be paid unconditionally and he specifies a rate of interest which is greater than allowed by statute. In determining whether a transaction is usurious, the court will look through the form of the transaction to determine whether there is in fact a loan on which excessive interest is charged.[16] Consequently, if a lender requires the borrower to take out insurance on his life to protect the lender, the transaction is usurious when the lender has a direct financial interest in the insurance, as agent of the insurer or as the insurer, and the borrower has assets or has given collateral that adequately protects the debt without the need of the insurance.[17]

1 / Interest rates. Most states prohibit by statute the taking of more than a stated annual rate of interest. These statutes provide a *maximum contract rate* of interest—usually 6, 8, or 10 percent—which is the highest annual rate that can be exacted or demanded under the law of a given state. It is usually recoverable only when there is an agreement in writing to pay that amount.

All states provide for a legal rate of interest. When there is an agreement for interest to be paid but no rate is specified or when the law implies a duty to pay interest, as on judgments, the *legal rate* is applied. In most states the legal rate of interest is 6 percent per year. In some states the maximum contract rate is the same as the legal rate of interest.

If the maximum contract rate of interest is specified for a short-term loan (not exceeding a year), the collection of the interest in advance as a discount from the nominal amount of the loan does not constitute usury even though the amount of interest collected represents a rate of interest in excess of that permitted by law. The usury statutes do not apply, either, to contracts that provide for the payment of the annual interest charge at the maximum rate in several installments, such as quarterly or monthly.[18]

Usually state statutes permit small loan associations, pawnbrokers, and similar licensed money lenders to charge a higher rate of interest than is permissible in ordinary business transactions, on the theory that a much greater risk is involved.[19]

---

[16] *Alt* v. *Bailey,* 211 Miss. 547, 52 So.2d 283.
[17] *Equitable Assur. Soc.* v. *Scali,* 75 Ill.App.2d 255, 220 N.E.2d 893.
[18] R., Sec. 534.
[19] Small loan statutes have been adopted in most states. See *Seaboard Finance Co.* v. *Wahlen,* 123 Utah 529, 260 P.2d 556.

Contract and Legal Rates of Interest

STATES AND TERRITORIES	MAXIMUM CONTRACT RATE PERCENT	LEGAL RATE PERCENT	STATES AND TERRITORIES	MAXIMUM CONTRACT RATE PERCENT	LEGAL RATE PERCENT
Alabama	8	6	Montana	10	6
Alaska	8	6	Nebraska	9	6
Arizona	8	6	Nevada	12	7
Arkansas	10	6	New Hampshire	Any rate	6
California	10	7	New Jersey	6	6
Colorado	Any rate [a]	6	New Mexico	10 [b]	6
Connecticut	12	6	New York	6	6
Delaware	6	6	North Carolina	6	6
D. of Columbia	8	6	North Dakota	7	4
Florida	10	6	Ohio	8	6
Georgia	8	7	Oklahoma	10	6
Hawaii	12	6	Oregon	10	6
Idaho	8	6	Pennsylvania	6	6
Illinois	7	5	Puerto Rico	9 [c]	6
Indiana	8	6	Rhode Island	21	6
Iowa	7	5	South Carolina	7	6
Kansas	10	6	South Dakota	8	6
Kentucky	7	6	Tennessee	6	6
Louisiana	8	5	Texas	10	6
Maine	Any rate	6	Utah	10	6
Maryland	6	6	Vermont	6	6
Massachusetts	Any rate	6	Virginia	6	6
Michigan	7	5	Washington	12	6
Minnesota	8	6	West Virginia	6	6
Mississippi	8	6	Wisconsin	12	5
Missouri	8	6	Wyoming	10	7

[a] When any rate is permitted for contracts, there usually is a limit for a small loan of approximately $300 or less, although this limit may be as high as 3 percent a month.
[b] When a loan is not secured by collateral, the contract rate may be 12 percent.
[c] When the amount is more than $3,000, the maximum contract rate is 8 percent.

2 / Effect of usury. The effect of an agreement that violates the usury laws differs in the various states. In some states the entire amount of interest is forfeited.[20] In other states, the recovery of the excess only is denied. In still others, the agreement is held to be void.[21] If the interest has been paid, the states differ as to whether the borrower recovers merely the amount of the interest paid or whether he recovers two or three times that amount as a penalty.

3 / Credit sale price. Usury statutes generally do not apply to sales made on credit, such as installment sales.[22] This rule is based on the narrow definition of usury as the charging of more than the lawful rate of interest on a loan. According to the theory of the law, when goods are sold on

[20] *Service Loan & Finance Corp.* v. *McDaniel,* 115 Ga.App. 548, 154 S.E.2d 823.
[21] *Curtis* v. *Securities Acceptance Corp.,* 166 Neb. 815, 91 N.W.2d 19.
[22] *Nazarian* v. *Lincoln Finance Co.,* 77 R.I. 497, 78 A.2d 7.

credit or on the installment plan, the seller does not lend money to the buyer but agrees that he is to be paid by the buyer later or at stated times rather than at the time of sale. Since no loan is made, the usury law does not apply and the seller is free to sell for cash at one price and on time at a different price that is much higher and which would be usurious if the usury law applied.

> **Facts:** Grannas and his partner purchased heavy equipment from Aggregates Equipment on credit, agreeing to pay in 36 monthly installments including a "credit service charge" of $11,713.44. Aggregates assigned the contract to a finance company, Equipment Finance, which later sued Grannas and his partner when they stopped paying the installments. Grannas and his partner raised the defense that the credit service charge was usurious.

> **Decision:** Judgment for Equipment Finance. The usury laws do not apply in determining how much greater a time sale price may be than a cash sale price. It is therefore immaterial that the seller adds to the price a "credit service charge," which is greater than the maximum interest that would be allowed on a loan of the amount of the cash price. (Equipment Finance, Inc. v. Grannas, 207 Pa.Super. 363, 218 A.2d 81)

This approach of the law ignores the economic reality which, as far as the buyer is concerned, is the same as if the seller made a loan to him of the cash price and then charged him usurious interest on the loan. In recognition of this situation, a few states hold that the time price differential is subject to the usury law [23] or have amended their usury laws or have adopted statutes to regulate the differential between cash and time prices that may be charged by the seller. Such statutes, however, are sometimes limited to sales by retailers to consumers or apply only to sales under a stated dollar maximum. In any case, the price differential credit sale will be held a usurious transaction when it is in fact a loan of money that is disguised as a sale for the purpose of avoiding the usury law.

4 / Corporations and usury. In some states corporations are prohibited from raising the defense of usury. If a loan is nominally made to a corporation, however, in order to bar the defense of usury, it may be shown that the loan was actually made to an individual who may then raise the defense of usury.

Wagers and Lotteries

Largely as a result of the adoption of antigambling statutes, wagers are generally illegal.[24] Lotteries containing the three main elements of prize,

---

[23] *Lloyd* v. *Gutgsell,* 175 Neb. 775, 124 N.W.2d 198.
[24] R., Sec. 520.

chance, and consideration, or similar affairs of chance, also are generally held illegal. Raffles are usually regarded as lotteries.[25] Sales promotion schemes calling for the distribution of property according to chance among the purchasers of goods are held illegal as lotteries, without regard to whether the scheme is called a guessing contest, raffle, or gift.

Facts: Holmes paid $1 for membership in an association and for a 6-months' subscription to its magazine. The subscription was evidenced by a numbered ticket. On a given date one ticket was to be drawn from all the subscription tickets and its owner would receive an automobile. The ticket of Holmes was drawn, but the automobile was not delivered. Holmes sued Saunders and others running the enterprise for the automobile.

Decision: Judgment for Saunders. The claim of the plaintiff was based on winning the automobile in a lottery. As a lottery was illegal, his contract could not be enforced. The fact that he obtained a membership and a magazine in addition to the chance to win the automobile did not affect the result. (Holmes v. Saunders, 114 Cal.App.2d 389, 250 P.2d 269)

Transactions in Futures

A person may contract to deliver in the future goods which he does not own at the time he makes the agreement. The fact that the seller does not have the goods at the time the contract is made, or that he intends to obtain securities by buying them on margin rather than paying cash in full, does not affect the legality of the transaction.[26] If, however, the parties to the sale and purchase intend that delivery shall not be made but merely that one party shall pay the other the difference between the contract price and market price on the date set for delivery, the transaction is a gambling contract or wager upon the future market price and the contract is illegal and void.[27] Generally, an undisclosed intention of either party or both parties that actual delivery should not be made does not affect the validity of the transaction. Furthermore, it is the intent at the time of the making of the contract which governs. Accordingly, a contract is not rendered illegal because after its formation the parties agree that instead of actual delivery a payment representing the market price differential shall be made.

Transactions calling for the future purchase or delivery of commodities such as wheat, corn, and soybeans, through organized commodity exchanges, provide a valuable means by which a dealer or manufacturer can protect himself from future price fluctuations. This is *hedging*. By means of this device the manufacturer or dealer who buys one of these commodities

---

[25] *Horner* v. *United States*, 147 U.S. 449, 37 L.Ed. 237.
[26] *Taylor & Co.'s Estate*, 192 Pa. 304, 43 A. 973.
[27] R., Sec. 523.

(wheat, for example) for the purpose of processing it and selling the product (flour) makes a simultaneous speculative contract to sell the same quantity of the commodity (wheat) at a future date when the processed product (flour) will be ready for sale. Any change in price that will cause a loss on one transaction is offset by a gain on the other transaction.

Sunday Laws

Under the English common law, an agreement or contract could be executed on any day of the week. Today, however, most states have statutes that prohibit to some extent the making or performance of contracts on Sunday.[28] The terms of the statutes vary greatly from state to state. The statutes may expressly declare agreements void if they are made on Sunday or if they call for performance on Sunday, or they may prohibit the sale of merchandise on Sunday. They may prohibit only "servile" or manual labor, prohibit "worldly employment," or prohibit labor or business of one's "ordinary calling." Under a provision of the last type, one could legally enter into an agreement or do work outside of his regular calling.

Sunday laws expressly provide that they do not apply to works of charity or necessity. *Works of charity* include those acts that are involved in religious worship or in aiding persons in distress. In general a *work of necessity* is an act which must be done at the time in order to be effective in saving life, health, or property.

When an offer is made on Sunday but the acceptance is not made until the next day, the agreement is valid because in law it is made on the weekday when it is accepted.[29] If a contract is made on Sunday, some courts hold that it can be ratified on another day. Other courts, however, hold the contrary on the ground that the contract was illegal when made, and an illegal contract or transaction cannot be ratified.[30]

Licensed Callings or Dealings

Statutes frequently require that a person obtain a license, certificate, or diploma before he can practice certain professions, such as law or medicine, or carry on a particular business or trade, such as that of a real-estate broker, peddler, stockbroker, hotelkeeper, or pawnbroker. If the requirement is imposed to protect the public, a contract to engage in such a profession or business without having obtained the necessary license or certificate is void.[31] Thus a contract with an unlicensed physician for services cannot be enforced.

---

[28] *McGowan* v. *Maryland,* 366 U.S. 420.
[29] *Isenberg* v. *Williams,* 306 Mass. 86, 27 N.E.2d 726.
[30] *R.,* Sec. 539; *McNeel Marble Co.* v. *Robinette,* 259 Ala. 66, 65 So.2d 221.
[31] *R.,* Sec. 580.

On the other hand, a license may be imposed solely as a revenue measure by requiring the payment of a fee for the license. In that event an agreement made by one not licensed in violation of the statute is generally held valid. The contract may also sometimes be held valid when it is shown that no harm has resulted from the failure to obtain a permit to do the work contemplated by the particular contract.

It is likewise frequently held that the absence of a license cannot be raised as to transactions between persons who should all be licensed, such as dealers, when the purpose of the license requirement is not to protect such persons as against each other but to protect the public generally against such persons.

Facts: Fomco, Inc. and Joe Maggio, Inc. were both in the business of growing, harvesting, and marketing carrots. Fomco made a contract with Maggio to harvest carrots on Maggio's land, to market them, and to divide the net profits with Maggio. The market price of carrots rose greatly above the contract rate, and Maggio refused to allow Fomco to harvest the full quantity of carrots specified in the contract. Maggio thereby obtained a $30,000 profit for itself by reselling the carrots. When Fomco sued for breach of contract, Maggio raised the defense that Fomco had failed to obtain a license under the state agricultural code, and was thus guilty of misdemeanor, and the contract between the parties was therefore not binding.

Decision: Judgment for Fomco. Both parties were required to obtain a license. The fact that there was no license did not bar suit on the contract since the statute was not designed to protect dealers against each other but to protect members of the public from unlicensed dealers. Hence there was no necessity to extend the operation of the statute to the interdealer situation. (Fomco, Inc. v. Joe Maggio, Inc., 8 Cal.Rep. 459, 356 P.2d 203)

Statutes regulating doing business or requiring a license to engage in a business do not ordinarily apply to a person making an isolated transaction. Thus the owner of a house may generally sell it directly to a buyer even though he does not have a real estate broker's license.

Regulation of Business

Local, state, and national laws regulate a wide variety of business activities and practices. A businessman violating such regulations may under some statutes be subject to a fine or criminal prosecution, or under others to an order to cease and desist entered by an administrative agency or commission.

Whether a contract made in connection with business conducted in violation of the law is binding or void depends upon how strongly opposed the public policy is to the prohibited act. Some courts take the view that the contract is not void unless the statute expressly so specifies.[32] In some instances, as in the case of the failure to register a fictitious name under which the business is done, the statute expressly preserves the validity of the contract by permitting the violator to sue on a contract made while illegally conducting business after his name is registered as required by the statute.

Fraudulent Sales

Statutes commonly regulate the sale of certain commodities. Scales and measures of grocers and other vendors must be checked periodically, and they must be approved and sealed by the proper official. Certain articles must be inspected before they are sold. Others must be labeled in a particular way to show their contents and to warn the public of the presence of any dangerous or poisonous substance. Since the laws are generally designed to protect the public, transactions in violation of such laws are void.

When the purpose of the law is to raise revenue by requiring the payment of a fee, the violation merely makes the wrongdoer liable for the penalty imposed by the law but does not make the transaction void. The fact that a fee must be paid under the statute does not by itself determine that the statute is a mere revenue measure. The fee may be imposed to defray the expenses of administration, in which case the character of the law as designed to protect the public is not affected.

Contracts in Restraint of Trade

A contract that unreasonably restrains trade is illegal and void on the ground that it is contrary to public policy.[33] Such agreements take many forms, such as a combination to create a monopoly or to obtain a corner on the market, or an association of merchants to increase prices.[34] In addition to the illegality of the contract based on general principles of law, statutes frequently declare monopolies illegal and subject the parties to such agreements to various civil and criminal penalties.[35] In some instances, however, the law expressly authorizes combined action.

> **Facts:** Lentz made a contract that he would sell any loganberries raised by him to the Oregon Growers' Co-op. Association. Lentz was about to violate this agreement. The association then sought an injunction to compel him to perform his agreement. He claimed that it was void because it created an illegal monopoly.

---

[32] *Fleetham* v. *Schneekloth,* 52 Wash.2d 176, 324 P.2d 429.
[33] R., Sec. 514.
[34] Sec. 515.
[35] Sherman Antitrust Act, 15 United States Code Annotated (USCA) Secs. 1-7; Clayton Act, 15 USCA Secs. 12-27; Federal Trade Commission Act, 15 USCA Secs. 41 to 58.

Decision: Judgment for the association. Since statutes authorize the creation of farmers' co-operatives, their contracts could not be criticized as monopolistic. Therefore, unless the contract was clearly unreasonable, it would be enforced. The contract in question was a reasonable exclusive marketing contract necessary for the effectiveness of a co-operative and was therefore valid. (Oregon Growers' Co-op. Association v. Lentz, 107 Ore. 561, 212 P. 811)

1 / Agreements not to compete. When a going business is sold, it is commonly stated in the contract that the seller shall not go into the same or a similar business again within a certain geographical area, or for a certain period of time, or both. In early times, such agreements were held void since they deprived the public of the service of the person who agreed not to compete, impaired the latter's means of earning a livelihood, reduced competition, and exposed the public to monopoly.[36] To the modern courts, the question is whether under the circumstances the restriction imposed upon one party is reasonable to protect the other party. If the restriction is reasonable, it is valid.[37]

A similar problem arises when an employee agrees with his employer that he will not compete with the employer should he leave his employment. The courts recognize that business and professional men would be reluctant to employ and instruct assistants unless they could require such employees to refrain from competing with them after learning the details and secrets of their business. Restrictions to prevent such competition are held valid when reasonable and necessary to protect the interest of the employer.[38]

Facts: Pierce worked for the Mutual Loan Company in Sioux City, Iowa, checking up on delinquent customers. By the written contract of employment he agreed not to enter the employ of any competing small loan business in the same town while employed or for one year thereafter. Upon the termination of his employment with Mutual, he went to work for a competing personal loan company. Mutual sought an injunction to prevent him from continuing in such employment.

Decision: Judgment for Pierce. Mutual could not be harmed by Pierce's working for a competitor since Pierce did not possess any secret knowledge gained from Mutual that gave rise to any right of Mutual to keep such knowledge from reaching a competitor. Moreover it was unlikely that Pierce would have made customer friends while working for Mutual who would follow him to his new employer. A restriction on further employment is not valid when it imposes a restraint greater than is needed to protect the employer. As the restriction did not serve to protect Mutual, it was invalid as to Pierce. (Mutual Loan Co. v. Pierce, 245 Iowa 1051, 65 N.W.2d 405)

---

[36] *Alger* v. *Thacher,* 19 Pick. (Mass.) 51.
[37] R., Sec. 516(a); *Baker* v. *Starkey,* [Iowa] 144 N.W.2d 889.
[38] R., Sec. 516(f); *Parker* v. *Smith,* [Tex.Civ.App.] 254 S.W.2d 144.

In the absence of the sale of a business or the making of an employment contract, an agreement not to compete is void as a restraint of trade and a violation of the antitrust law.[39]

When a restriction on competition as agreed to by the parties is held invalid because its scope as to time or geographical area is too great, there is a conflict of authority as to the action to be taken by the court. Some courts apply the "blue pencil" rule and trim the covenant down to a scope which they deem reasonable and require the parties to abide by that revision.[40] Other courts hold that this is rewriting the contract for the parties, which courts ordinarily cannot do, and refuse to revise the covenant, holding that the covenant is totally void and that the contract is to be applied as though it did not contain any restrictive covenant.[41]

2 / *Resale price maintenance agreements.* Under antitrust legislation, an agreement between a manufacturer and distributor or between a distributor and dealer that the latter should not resell below a specified minimum price was void.[42] Congress and many of the states have adopted statutes, called *fair trade acts,* which change this rule and sustain the validity of such agreements when they relate to trademark or brand-name articles.[43]

The theory of such laws is that it is reasonable and desirable to prevent a party from reselling in the course of regular business an established article at too low a price because such sales may harm the reputation or market established by the manufacturer or distributor of the article. If the article is not a trademark or brand-name article, an agreement against price cutting on resale is illegal as a restraint of trade in violation of the antitrust laws.

The federal statute and many state laws apply not only to those who are parties to the price maintenance agreement but also to anyone having knowledge of the agreement who thereafter in the course of regular business resells the article under its trade name or mark.[44]

---

[39] *Hayes* v. *Parklane Hosiery Co.,* 24 Conn.Sup. 218, 189 A.2d 522.
[40] *Extine* v. *Williamson Midwest,* 176 Ohio 403, 200 N.E.2d 297.
[41] *Brown* v. *Devine,* 240 Ark. 838, 402 S.W.2d 669.
[42] *Miles Medical Co.* v. *Park,* 220 U.S. 373.
[43] The state acts apply only to intrastate sales. The federal statute applies to interstate sales and permits resale price maintenance agreements when such agreements are lawful in the state in which the goods are to be resold or into which they are to be sent.
[44] Miller-Tydings Act, 50 Stat. 693, 15 USCA Sec. 1; McGuire Act, 66 Stat. 632, 15 USCA, Sec. 45. It is commonly provided that the parties to such a contract may recover damages from third persons who sell the article below the agreement price or may obtain an injunction to compel the observance of that price. The courts of a number of states have held constitutional the provisions of the state laws binding non-signers. *Olin Mathieson Chemical Corp.* v. *Ontario Store,* 9 Ohio 2d 67, 223 N.E.2d 592. Many other state courts have held such provision invalid. *Olin Mathieson Chemical Corp.* v. *Francis,* 134 Colo. 160, 301 P.2d 139; *Shakespeare Co.* v. *Lippman's Tool Shop Sporting Goods Co.,* 334 Mich. 109, 54 N.W.2d 268. In a majority of states the problem of price cutting is also regulated by statutes prohibiting resale of goods below cost when the purpose is to injure competitors.

Unconscionable and Oppressive Contracts

In a number of instances the law holds that contracts or contract clauses will not be enforced because they are too harsh or oppressive to one of the two parties. This principle is most commonly applied to invalidate a clause providing for the payment by one party of a large penalty if he breaks his contract or, by way of contrast, a provision declaring that a party shall not be liable for the consequences of his negligence. This principle is extended in connection with the sale of goods to provide that "if the court . . . finds the contract or any clause of the contract to have been unconscionable at the time it was made, the court may refuse to enforce the contract, or it may enforce the remainder of the contract without the unconscionable clause, or it may so limit the application of any unconscionable clause as to avoid any unconscionable result." [45]

> **Facts:** The Walker-Thomas Furniture Co. sold furniture on credit under contracts which contained a provision that a customer did not own his purchase as long as any balance on the purchase remained due. It sold goods to Williams. At the time when the balance of her account was $164, Walker-Thomas Furniture Co. sold her a $514 stereo set with knowledge that she was supporting herself and seven children on a government relief check of $218 a month. From 1957 to 1962 Williams had purchased $1,800 worth of goods and made payments of $1,400. When she stopped making payments in 1962, Walker-Thomas sought to take back everything she had purchased since 1957.

> **Decision:** Under the circumstances the contract appeared to create such a one-sided bargain that it should be declared invalid because it was unconscionable. A hearing was therefore directed to pass on that question. (Williams v. Walker-Thomas Furniture Co., [C.A.Dist.Col.] 350 F.2d 445)

Illegality in Performing Contract

When a contract is otherwise legal, the fact that one of the parties in performing his part of the contract commits illegal acts not contemplated by the other party does not ordinarily prevent the wrongdoer from recovering on the contract. In some instances, however, the wrong may be regarded as so serious that the wrongdoer is punished by denying him the right to recover on the contract which he has performed.

> **Facts:** Commonwealth Pictures Corp. agreed to pay McConnell $10,000 and a specified commission if he could persuade Universal Pictures Company to give Commonwealth the distribution rights on its pictures. Without

---

[45] Uniform Commercial Code, Sec. 2-302(1).

the knowledge of either Universal or Commonwealth, McConnell obtained the distribution rights by paying an agent of Universal the $10,000 Commonwealth paid McConnell. McConnell thereafter sued Commonwealth for the agreed commission.

Decision: Judgment for Commonwealth Pictures. Although there was nothing illegal in the contract between the parties, the methods used by the agent in performing were so unethical that it was contrary to public policy to permit him to recover under the contract, even though the result of so deciding is to give the other contracting party, the agent's employer, the desired services or results without making any payment for them. (McConnell v. Commonwealth Pictures Corp., 7 N.Y.2d 465, 199 N.Y.S.2d 483)

Statutory Regulation of Contracts

In order to establish uniformity or to protect one of the parties to a contract, statutes frequently provide that contracts of a given class must follow a statutory model or must contain specified provisions. For example, statutes commonly specify that particular clauses must be included in insurance policies in order to protect the persons insured and their beneficiaries. Others require that contracts executed in connection with credit buying and loans contain particular provisions designed to protect the debtor, as by specifying that he may pay off his debt at an earlier date or buy back within a specified period the property that has been used as security. Motor-vehicle-financing statutes commonly specify that an installment sale contract must contain the cash price, the down payment, the trade-in value if any, the cash balance, the insurance costs, the finance charges, the amount and time of installments, and similar items.[46]

Noncompliance with the statutory requirements may in some instances make the entire contract void; while in others the contract will be enforced as though it did not contain the improper or illegal clauses but did contain the provisions required by the statute.

When the statute imposes a fine or imprisonment for violation, the court should not hold that the contract is void as that would increase the penalty which the legislature had imposed.[47] If a statute prohibits the making of certain kinds of contracts or imposes limitations on the contracts that can be made, the attorney general or other government official may generally be able to obtain an injunction or court order to stop the parties from entering into a prohibited kind of contract.[48]

---

[46] *Roxy Auto Co.* v. *Moore,* 180 Pa.Super. 603, 122 A.2d 87.
[47] *Gladden* v. *Guyer,* [Colo.] 426 P.2d 953.
[48] *People* v. *Arthur Murray,* 238 Cal.App.2d 333, 47 Cal.Rptr. 700.

QUESTIONS AND PROBLEMS

1. Checklist of legal terms:
   - (a) illegal lobbying contract (140)
   - (b) usury, maximum contract rate; legal rate (142)
   - (c) hedging (145)
   - (d) works of charity, works of necessity (146)
   - (e) fair trade acts (150)

2. (a) State the objective(s) of the law that usury statutes generally do not apply to prices charged for sales made on credit.
   (b) What rule of law in this chapter illustrates the evolutionary nature of the law?

3. Vetter purchased wild game in violation of a statute prohibiting such sales. An hour later he returned what he had purchased. Could he expect the aid of a court in obtaining the return of the purchase price from the seller?

4. Piper gives $1,000 for Rice's promise to blackmail Vontz. Piper repents before Rice performs his promise. Is Piper entitled to recover the money he paid Rice?

5. Tomlin agrees to sell Asher an automobile for $800 and a machine gun for $100. A statute prohibits the sale of machine guns. What are Asher's rights if Tomlin refuses to carry out his promise?

6. North Drug Co. sold several drugs to Carpenter. Two of these drugs were sold illegally. Carpenter gave North a note for the total amount of his purchase. Can North enforce payment of the note?

7. Boyd promises to pay $750 to Victor if Victor will destroy evidence that is needed in a criminal action against Boyd. Victor destroys the evidence and sues Boyd for the promised amount when Boyd refuses to pay. Is Victor entitled to judgment?

8. Dudley promises to build a factory for Carr. They also agree that neither shall have a right of action in court on the contract until any dispute had been referred to and settled by arbitrators. Carr claims that Dudley failed to perform and sues him for breach of contract without waiting for a settlement by arbitration. Does Dudley have a valid defense?

9. Stanley buys a farm truck on credit for $3,500, makes a down payment of $500, and agrees to pay the balance of $3,000 in 12 months. The truck has an established cash price of $3,100. The maximum contract rate of interest in that state is 10 percent. Is the transaction usurious?

10. Carey gives Eckert a note for $2,000, with interest, payable one year from date. The interest rate is not stated. In this state the legal rate of interest is 6 percent and the maximum rate is 8 percent. How much is Eckert entitled to collect when the note falls due?

11. On Sunday Fry offers to sell his motorcycle to Andrews for $250. On the following Wednesday Andrews accepts. Does a local statute that makes contracts executed on Sunday illegal apply to this agreement?

12. A statute requires that real estate brokers be licensed. O'Connor, without securing a license, engages in this type of business. He sues Parker to recover a fee for his services as broker. Is O'Connor entitled to judgment?

13. Reeder, Heis, and Canter, partners in an accounting firm with a local practice in Cincinnati, purchase the accounting practice and goodwill of Steele and Tate, a firm with 25 years local experience in Dayton, Ohio, less than 60 miles away. The written contract provides that Steele and Tate, either as individuals or as a firm, are not to engage in accounting practice anywhere in the United States east of the Rocky Mountains for ten years. Steele violates this clause of the agreement. Can Reeder and his partners recover damages?

14. Slater, a retail merchant, agreed with Neff, a manufacturer located in another state, not to sell the latter's brand-name products for less than specified prices. Neff sued Slater for breach of contract. Slater defended on the ground that the agreement was illegal. Was his defense valid?

15. Las Vegas Hacienda, Inc., advertised that it would pay $5,000 to anyone shooting a hole in one on its golf course. Gibson, who paid the fee of 50 cents, made a hole in one. The golf course corporation refused to pay the $5,000. When Gibson sued for breach of contract, the corporation raised the defense that the contract was an illegal gambling contract, and could not be enforced even though gambling as such was legalized in the state. Decide. (Las Vegas Hacienda, Inc. v. Gibson, 77 Nev. 25, 359 P.2d 85)

16. John Licznerski was a member of the armed forces of the United States. His mother was designated as the beneficiary of his national service life insurance. After his death his mother assigned her interest as beneficiary to the minor daughter of John. At that time the federal law prohibited assignment of interests in such policies. Subsequently the federal law was amended to permit an assignment to certain persons including children of the insured. Thereafter the mother and the daughter of the insured each claimed the insurance money. Decide. (Licznerski v. United States, [C.A.3d] 180 F.2d 862)

17. The Rhode Island Grocers Association held an annual exhibition. As an added feature to attract public interest, arrangements were made with the Transocean Air Lines for a drawing of a door prize for a free round trip to Hawaii for two. Any spectator attending the exhibition could participate in the drawing by filling out a card with his name and address. Was this a lottery? (Finch v. Rhode Island Grocers Association, 93 R.I. 323, 175 A.2d 177)

Chapter 13

Formality and Interpretation

As a practical matter, it is desirable to put important contracts in writing. Each party then knows what he is agreeing to when the agreement is written. The writing assures both parties that at a future date there will be less chance of disagreement as to what has been agreed upon. It eliminates the possibility that either party to the contract can effectively deny having made the contract.

General Rule

Generally a contract is valid whether it is written or not. As important exceptions, statutes provide that conveyances of land and commercial paper must be written. In some states, a promise affirming a contract made during minority must be in writing. The most common provisions concerning the form of contracts are to be found in the Statute of Frauds.

Apart from statute, the parties may agree that their oral agreement is not to be binding until a formal written contract is executed.[1] Conversely, they may agree that their oral contract is binding even though a written contract is to be executed. If one of the parties, with the knowledge or approval of the other contracting party, undertakes performance of the contract before it is reduced to writing, it is generally held that the parties intended to be bound from the moment of the making of the oral contract.

Statute of Frauds

In 1677, an English statute[2] aimed at reducing the evil of perjured testimony by providing that certain contracts could not be enforced if they depended upon the testimony of witnesses and were not evidenced by a writing. As stated in the preamble of the statute, its purpose was the "prevention of many fraudulent practices, which are commonly endeavored to be upheld by perjury and subornation of perjury." From this recital, the common name of the statute, *Statute of Frauds* or *Statute of Frauds and Perjuries,* is derived. Its provisions have been closely followed by statutes adopted in the various states of this country.

---

[1] *Pacific Coast Joint Stock Land Bank* v. *Jones,* 14 Cal.2d 8, 92 P.2d 390.
[2] 29 Car. II, Ch. 3.

155

The statute is designed to prevent the use of the courts for the purpose of enforcing certain oral agreements or alleged oral agreements. It does not apply when an oral agreement has been performed by both sides or when the parties voluntarily perform the agreement. Sometimes special statutes apply to particular contracts and take the place of the general Statute of Frauds.

Fourth Section of the Statute of Frauds

The fourth section of the Statute of Frauds provides that "no action shall be brought [on certain agreements] unless the agreement upon which such action shall be brought, or some memorandum or note thereof, shall be in writing, and signed by the party to be charged therewith, or some person thereunto by him lawfully authorized." The section does not apply to quasi-contracts.

The contracts governed by this section of the Statute of Frauds are of two general types: those that will not be performed within a relatively short time and those that deal with specified subjects.

1 / An agreement that cannot be performed within one year after the contract is made. A writing is required when the contract by its terms cannot be performed by both parties within one year after the date of the agreement.[3] In computing the year for this purpose, the day on which the contract was made is excluded. The year begins with the following day and ends at the close of the first anniversary of the day on which the agreement was made.[4]

The Statute of Frauds does not apply if it is possible under the terms of the agreement to perform the contract within one year. Thus, under the statute a writing is not required when no time for performance is specified and the performance will not necessarily take more than a year. In this case it would be possible to perform the contract within a year, and the statute is deemed inapplicable without regard to the time when performance is actually begun or completed. A promise to do an act at or upon or until the death of a person does not require a writing, even though that event may not occur until more than a year from the time the agreement is made.

When the contract calls not for a single act but for continuing services to run indefinitely into the future, the Statute of Frauds is applicable. For example, a business contract to pay an agent a commission for new customers procured by the agent for as long as such customers continue to purchase contemplates acts that may be performed beyond the statutory year and a

---

[3] *Loncope v. Lucerne-in-Maine Community Assn.,* 127 Maine 282, 143 A. 64.
[4] *Nickerson v. Harvard College,* 298 Mass. 484, 11 N.E.2d 444.

writing is therefore required. An oral promise to pay a bonus of a specified percentage of the employer's gross annual sales does not come within the statute nor require a writing although the amount of the bonus cannot be determined until after the year has expired.[5]

In most states a writing is not required if the contract may or must be fully performed within a year by one of the contracting parties. By this view, a loan made today to be repaid in three years does not come within the statute because the performance of the lender necessarily takes place within the year. In a minority of states, the statute is applicable as long as performance by one of the parties may be made after the period of a year.

2 / An agreement to sell or a sale of any interest in real property. All contracts to sell and sales of land, buildings, or interests in land, such as mortgages which are treated as such an interest, must be in writing. The statute applies only to the agreement between the owner and the purchaser, or between their agents. It does not apply to other or collateral agreements, such as those which the purchaser may make in order to raise the money to pay for the property, or to agreements to pay for an examination or search of the title of the property. Similarly, a partnership agreement to deal in real estate is generally not required to be in writing. The statute ordinarily does not apply to a contract between a real estate agent and one of the parties to the sales contract employing him.[6] Special statutes may require a writing in such a case, however.

3 / A promise to answer for the debt or default of another. When *A* promises *C* to pay *B's* debt to *C* if *B* does not do so, *A* is promising to answer for the debt of another. Such a promise must usually be in writing to be enforceable.[7]

The requirement of a writing does not apply when the promisor makes the promise primarily for his own benefit.

Facts: Boeing Airplane Co. contracted with Pittsburgh-Des Moines Steel Co. for the latter to construct a supersonic wind tunnel. R. H. Freitag Mfg. Co. sold material to York-Gillespie Co., which subcontracted to do part of the work. In order to persuade Freitag to keep supplying materials on credit, Boeing and the principal contractor both assured Freitag that he would be paid. Freitag was not paid by the subcontractor and then sued Boeing and the contractor. They defended on the ground that the assurances given Freitag were not written.

---

[5] *White Lighting Co.* v. *Wolfson,* [Cal.2d] 66 Cal.Rptr. 697, 438 P.2d 345.
[6] *Bleakley* v. *Knights of Columbus,* 26 Conn.S. 192, 216 A.2d 643.
[7] Restatement, Contracts, Secs. 180-191; *Marshall* v. *Bellin,* 27 Wis.2d 88, 133 N.W.2d 751; also see Ch. 42.

Decision: Judgment for Freitag. The promise to pay the bills of the subcontractor was made by the defendants primarily for their benefit in order to keep the work progressing so that they, in turn, would not be held liable for failure to complete. Hence, the case came within the primary benefit exception to the written guaranty provision of the Statute of Frauds. (R. H. Freitag Mfg. Co. v. Boeing Airplane Co., 55 Wash.2d 334, 347 P.2d 1074)

No writing is required when the debt incurred is the debt of the person promising to pay, even though a third person designated by the promisor benefits thereby. Thus, if *A* buys on his own credit from *C* and directs that *C* deliver the goods to *B, A* is not promising to pay the debt of *B* but is incurring his own debt.[8]

4 / A promise by the executor or administrator of a decedent's estate to pay a claim against the estate from his personal funds. The executor or administrator has the duty of winding up the affairs of a deceased person, paying the debts from the proceeds of the estate and distributing any balance remaining. The executor or administrator is not personally liable for the claims against the estate of the decedent. If the personal representative promises to pay the decedent's debts, however, the promise cannot be enforced unless it is in a writing that complies with the terms of the statute.

If the personal representative makes a contract on behalf of the estate in the course of administering the estate, a writing is not required since the representative is then contracting on behalf of the estate and not on his own behalf. Thus, if he employs an attorney to settle the estate or makes a burial contract with an undertaker, no writing is required.

5 / A promise made in consideration of marriage. If a person makes a promise to pay a sum of money or to give property to another in consideration of marriage or a promise to marry, the agreement must be in writing. This provision of the Statute of Frauds is not applicable to ordinary mutual promises to marry, and is not affected by the statutes in some states that prohibit the bringing of any action for breach of promise of marriage.

Seventeenth Section of the Statute of Frauds

With respect to the sale of goods (tangible personal property), a special provision was made by the English Statute of Frauds. This separate treatment has been continued.[9] When the total contract price for such a sale is $500 or more, a writing is required unless an oral contract can be proved by receipt and acceptance of the goods or payment by the buyer, as explained in Chapter 35.

---

[8] *Gillhespy* v. *Bolema Lumber and Building Supplies,* 5 Mich.App.2d 351, 146 N.W.2d 666.
[9] See Uniform Commercial Code, Sec. 2-201 and Chapter 35.

Note or Memorandum

The Statute of Frauds requires a writing for those contracts which come within its scope. This writing may be a note or memorandum, as distinguished from a formal contract. It may be in any form because its only purpose is to serve as evidence of the contract.

1 / Contents. Except in the case of a sale of goods, the note or memorandum must contain all the material terms of the contract so that the court can determine just what was agreed.[10] Thus, it is insufficient if the contract is partly oral and partly written.[11] The writing must name or identify the parties to the contract and must reasonably describe any land involved.[12] An ordinary check is not a sufficient memorandum when it bears the notation "payment land" but contains no other details.[13] The subject matter must be identified either within the writing itself or in other writings to which it refers.

Facts: Smith leased certain property to a corporation named Seattle Flower Growers. Following the signatures on the lease, there was the handwritten word "Personal" followed by the signature of John Twohy. He was a director and shareholder of the corporation, but the lease did not make any reference to him in any way. The corporation did not make the payments due on the lease, and Smith sued Twohy claiming that he had guaranteed that the rents would be paid.

Decision: Judgment for Twohy. By the Statute of Frauds any agreement to answer for the debts of the corporation with respect to payments under the lease had to be in writing. The word "Personal" and Twohy's signature did not state that he agreed to answer for the rents to be paid by the corporation; and even if there had been an oral agreement, the court could not have enforced it because of the lack of a writing as required by the Statute of Frauds. (Smith v. Twohy, [Wash.2d] 425 P.2d 12)

The note or memorandum may consist of one writing or instrument or of separate papers, such as letters or telegrams, or of a combination of such papers.[14] The memorandum may be made at the time of the original transaction or at a later date. It must, however, ordinarily exist at the time an action is brought upon the agreement.

2 / Signing. The note or memorandum must be signed by the party sought to be charged or his agent.[15] Some states require that the authorization

---

[10] R., Secs. 207, 209; *Irvine* v. *Haniotis,* 208 Okla. 1, 252 P.2d 470.
[11] *Forsyth* v. *Brillhart,* 216 Md. 437, 140 A.2d 904.
[12] *State* v. *Conway,* 34 Wis.2d 76, 148 N.W.2d 721.
[13] *Lewis* v. *Starlin,* 127 Mont. 474, 267 P.2d 127.
[14] *Vachon* v. *Tomascak,* [Conn.] 230 A.2d 5.
[15] R., Secs. 210, 211.

of an agent to execute a contract coming within the Statute of Frauds must itself be in writing.[16] In the case of an auction, it is the usual practice for the auctioneer to be the agent of both parties for the purpose of signing the memorandum. If the seller himself acts as auctioneer, however, he cannot sign as agent for the buyer. An exception is made in some situations when the contract is between merchants and involves the sale of goods, as explained in Chapter 35.

The signature may be made at any place on the writing, although in some states it is expressly required that the signature appear at the end of the writing. The signature may be an ordinary one or any symbol that is adopted by the party as his signature. It may consist of initials, figures, or a mark. When a signature consists of a mark made by a person who is illiterate or physically incapacitated, it is commonly required that the name of the person be placed upon the writing by someone else, who may be required to sign the instrument as a witness. A person signing a trade or an assumed name is liable to the same extent as though he signed in his own name. In the absence of a local statute that provides otherwise, the signature may be made by pencil, as well as by pen, or by typewriter, by print, or by stamp.

Effect of Noncompliance

The majority of states hold that an agreement which does not comply with the Statute of Frauds is voidable. A small minority of states hold that it is void. In those jurisdictions where it is voidable, the Statute of Frauds is a defense personal to the defendant. This means that an action can be brought to enforce the contract, but the defendant can raise the objection that it is not written. It also means that no one other than the defendant, or his successor in interest, can make the objection. Thus an insurance company cannot refuse to pay on its policy on the ground that the insured did not have any insurable interest in the insured property because he did not have a writing relating to the property that satisfied the Statute of Frauds.[17] Likewise, when a suit is brought for malicious interference with contract rights, it is no defense that the contract was an oral contract for which the Statute of Frauds requires a writing, the absence of a writing not making the contract void.[18]

In some cases, when a writing is not made as required by the statute, the courts will nevertheless enforce the agreement if there has been a sufficient part performance to make it clear that a contract existed.[19] In

---

[16] See p. 215.
[17] *Commercial Union Insurance Co.* v. *Padrick Chevrolet Co.,* [Fla.] 196 So.2d 235.
[18] *Warner Bros.* v. *Simon,* 39 Misc.2d 853, 241 N.Y.S.2d 914.
[19] *Casper* v. *Frey,* 152 Neb. 441, 41 N.W.2d 363.

other instances the court will not enforce the contract but will permit a party to recover the fair value of work and improvements that he has made in reliance upon the contract. This situation commonly arises when a vendee or purchaser of land under an oral agreement enters into possession of the land. If the purchaser has made valuable improvements to the land, the courts will commonly enforce the oral agreement. Ordinarily the performance of personal services does not constitute such part performance as will take the case out of the Statute of Frauds, except in extraordinary cases when the value of the services cannot be measured by money.[20]

Before the court dispenses with the need for a writing, it must find that there has been such reliance upon the existence of the oral contract that it would be grossly unfair to one of the parties to refuse to enforce the contract in his favor.

In most instances, a person who is prevented from enforcing a contract because of the Statute of Frauds is nevertheless entitled to recover from the other party the value of any services or property furnished or money given under the contract. Recovery is based not upon the terms of the contract but upon the quasi-contractual obligation of the other party to restore to the plaintiff what he has received in order to prevent his unjust enrichment at the plaintiff's expense.

There is, however, a division of authority as to whether a real estate broker may recover for the value of his services in procuring a buyer under an oral brokerage agreement in states which require that such agreements be in writing. Recovery is commonly denied [21] on the theory that the real estate broker can be expected to know that his contracts must be in writing and that, as he makes such contracts constantly, it is unlikely that a broker would not appreciate his legal position when he acts under an oral contract. In substance it is held that protecting the public at large from unethical brokers making false claims under alleged oral contracts outweighs the necessity for protecting the occasional broker from oppression at the hands of an unethical customer refusing to recognize an oral contract.

The performance of services for which one is periodically paid is generally regarded as not taking out of the statute an oral contract that cannot be performed in one year. Such performance and payment do not indicate anything more than an agreement to render the services that were rendered and to compensate for them. Furthermore, the person performing the services is in fact paid for what he has done, and therefore he does not sustain any unusual hardship if the alleged oral contract is not enforced.[22]

---

[20] *Crosby* v. *Strahan's Estate,* 78 Wyo. 302, 324 P.2d 492.
[21] *Augustine* v. *Trucco,* 124 Cal.App.2d 229, 268 P.2d 780.
[22] *Rowland* v. *Ewell,* [Fla.] 174 So.2d 78.

Parol Evidence Rule

Can a written contract be contradicted by the testimony of the witnesses? The general rule is that spoken words, that is, *parol evidence,* will not be allowed to modify or contradict the terms of a written contract which is complete on its face unless there is clear proof that because of fraud, accident, or mistake the writing is not in fact a contract or the complete contract.[23] This is called the *parol evidence rule.* It refers to words spoken before or at the time the contract was made.

To illustrate, assume that *L,* the landlord who is the owner of several new stores in the same vicinity, discusses leasing one of them to *T* (tenant). *L* considers giving *T* the exclusive rights to sell soft drinks and stipulating in the leases with the tenants of the other stores that they cannot do so. *L* and *T* then execute a detailed written lease for the store. The lease makes no provision with respect to an exclusive right of *T* to sell soft drinks. Thereafter *L* leases the other stores to *A, B,* and *C* without restricting them as to the sale of soft drinks, which they then begin to sell, causing *T* to lose money. *T* sues *L,* claiming that the latter has broken his contract by which *T* was to have an exclusive right to sell soft drinks. *L* defends on the ground that the lease, which is a contract, contains no such provision. *T* replies that there was a prior oral understanding to that effect. Will the court permit *T* to prove that there was such an oral agreement?

On the facts as stated, if nothing more is shown, the court will not permit such parol evidence to be presented. The operation of this principle can be understood more easily if the actual courtroom procedure is followed. When *T* sues *L,* his first step will be to prove that there is a contract between them. Accordingly, *T* will offer in evidence the written lease between *T* and *L,* or under certain circumstances, a copy of the lease. *T* will then take the witness stand and begin to testify about an oral agreement giving him an exclusive right. At that point *L's* attorney will object to the admission of the oral testimony by *T* as it would modify the terms of the written lease. The court will then look at the lease to see if it appears to be complete; and if the court decides that it is, the court will refuse to allow *T* to offer evidence of an oral agreement. Since *T* will not be allowed to offer proof of the oral agreement, the only evidence before the court will be the written lease. *T* will lose because nothing is in the written lease about an exclusive right to sell soft drinks.

If a written contract appears to be complete, the parol evidence rule prohibits its alteration not only by oral testimony but also by proof of other writings or memorandums made before or at the time the written contract was executed. An exception is made when the written contract refers to and

---

[23] *Ray* v. *Eurice & Bros.,* 201 Md. 115, 93 A.2d 272.

identifies other writings or memorandums and states that they are to be regarded as part of the written contract. In such a case, it is said that the other writings are incorporated by reference.

1 / Reason for the parol evidence rule. The parol evidence rule is based on the theory that either (a) there never was an oral agreement or (b) if there was, the parties purposely abandoned it when they executed their written contract.

2 / When the parol evidence rule does not apply.

(a) INCOMPLETE CONTRACT. At the time that *L's* attorney objected to the oral testimony in the example stated above, *T* could have raised the counterobjection that the lease was not complete. If the court had agreed, he would have been permitted to prove the oral agreement. The parol evidence rule is based on the theory that the written contract sums up or integrates the entire contract. Accordingly, if the written contract is on its face or is admittedly not a complete summation, the parties naturally did not intend to abandon the points upon which they had agreed but which were not noted in the memorandum; and parol evidence is admissible to show the actual transaction or agreement of the parties.[24]

A contract may appear on its face to be complete and yet not include everything the parties agreed upon. It must be remembered that there is no absolute standard by which to determine when a contract is complete. All that the court can consider is whether all essential terms of the contract are present, that is, whether the contract is sufficiently definite to be enforceable, and whether it contains all provisions which would ordinarily be included in a contract of that nature.

(b) FRAUD, ACCIDENT, OR MISTAKE. A contract apparently complete on its face may have omitted a provision which should have been included. This situation may easily arise in modern times when parties tentatively agree to a draft of a contract which is then typewritten or printed. Frequently people will sign the final copy without adequate attention, assuming that it is a true copy of the earlier draft. It may be that the final copy is not a true copy because one of the parties fraudulently deceived the other into believing that it was a complete copy; because a stenographer or printer, in making the final copy, accidentally omitted a provision; or because a similar accident or mistake has occurred. For these reasons, it is important to read a final contract just as carefully as a preliminary draft and to compare the two before signing.

If, however, the final copy is not a true copy in that it omits a provision because of fraud, accident, or mistake, and this fact is proved to the satisfaction of the court, it is proper to show by oral testimony what the terms

---

[24] *Johnson Hill's Press, Inc.* v. *Nasco Industries,* 33 Wis.2d 545, 148 N.W.2d 9.

of the omitted provision were.[25] Thus it may be shown that an agreement to purchase property was intended by the parties to be subject to the condition that the buyer obtain bank financing for the purchase, although the signed writing did not make any mention of such a condition.[26]

(c) AMBIGUITY. If a written contract is not clear in all its provisions, parol evidence may generally be admitted to clarify the meaning. This is particularly true when the contract contains contradictory measurements or descriptions, or when it employs symbols or abbreviations that have no general meaning known to the court. Parol evidence may also be admitted to show that a word used in a contract has a special trade meaning or a meaning in the particular locality that differs from the common meaning of that word.

(d) CONDUCT OF PARTIES. The parol evidence rule does not prevent either party from showing by parol evidence that he was fraudulently induced to execute the contract or that the other party to the contract has not performed his obligations.

3 / Existence or modification of contract. The parol evidence rule prohibits only the contradiction of a complete written contract. It does not prohibit proof that an obligation under the contract never existed because a condition precedent [27] was not satisfied or that the contract was thereafter modified or terminated.

Facts: McCarthy, as owner, made a contract with Harrington to build a home. The contract stated that no changes could be made for work in addition to that called for by the contract unless there was a written order for such extra work specifying the charges to be made. During the course of construction, McCarthy orally requested Harrington to make certain additions to the work. This was done without any written order being executed. When the work was finished, McCarthy refused to pay for the extra work on the ground that there were no written orders for such work.

Decision: Judgment for Harrington. Although the contract required written orders for extra work, the subsequent conduct of the parties with respect to the extra work that was done constituted a modification of the original contract. The fact that the original contract contained a requirement of written work modifications did not prevent proof that the parties had proceeded in disregard of such requirement, and thereby modified the original contract with respect to the work done. The contractor was therefore entitled to recover for the extra work. (Harrington v. McCarthy, [Idaho] 420 P.2d 790)

---

[25] *Snipes Mountain Co.* v. *Benz Bros. & Co.,* 162 Wash. 334, 298 P. 714.
[26] *Fulton* v. *Bailey,* [Mo.] 413 S.W.2d 514.
[27] *Perry* v. *Little,* [Tex.Civ.App.] 377 S.W.2d 765.

To return to the illustration of the lease of the store by *L* and the alleged oral agreement of an exclusive right to sell soft drinks, three situations may arise. It may be claimed that the oral agreement was made (a) before the execution of the final written lease; (b) at the same time, that is, contemporaneously with the execution of the written lease; or (c) subsequent to the execution of the written lease. The parol evidence rule only prohibits the proof of the oral agreement under (a) and (b). It is not applicable to (c), for it can be shown that subsequent to the execution of the contract the parties modified the contract, even though the original contract was in writing and the subsequent modification was oral. Clear proof of the later agreement is required.[28]

When it is claimed that a contract is modified by a later agreement, consideration must support the modifying agreement except in the case of a contract for the sale of goods.[29] In any case, if the parties have performed the part of the contract that is modified, it is immaterial that there was no consideration for the agreement for such modification.[30]

Interpretation of Contracts

The terms of a contract should be clearly stated, and all important terms should be included. If they are not, the parties might interpret the terms differently. When such differences cannot be resolved satisfactorily by the parties and the issue is brought into court, certain principles of construction and interpretation are applied. An understanding of these rules should help contracting parties to avoid many of the difficulties that may arise when a contract is not drafted carefully.

1 / Intention. A contract is to be enforced according to its terms. The court must examine the contract to determine and give effect to what the parties intended, provided that their objective is lawful.[31] It is the intention of the parties as expressed in the contract that must prevail.

Facts: Keyworth was employed by Industrial Sales Co. In the course of employment, he was injured by Israelson. Industrial Sales made a contract with Keyworth to pay him $100 per week until he was able to return to normal work but specified that such payments would be paid back to Industrial Sales from any recovery that Keyworth would obtain in a lawsuit against Israelson, such payments to be made to Industrial Sales upon the "successful conclusion of the case." Keyworth obtained a recovery in the action against Israelson of $16,600 but

[28] *Finocchiaro* v. *D'Amico,* 8 N.J.S. 29, 73 A.2d 260.
[29] UCC Sec. 2-209(1).
[30] *Eluschuk* v. *Chemical Engineers Termite Control,* [Cal.App.2d] 54 Cal.Rptr. 711.
[31] *Winkler* v. *Appalachian Amusement Co.,* 238 N.C. 589, 79 S.E.2d 185.

refused to make any payment to Industrial Sales because he believed there was not a "successful conclusion of the case." Industrial Sales sued Keyworth.

Decision: Judgment for Industrial Sales Co. The fair meaning of the language was that winning the lawsuit was a "successful conclusion of the case." The fact that one of the parties may have a particular belief or intent that it meant winning a particular minimum amount would not be allowed to change the intent of the parties as expressed by the words of the contract. (Keyworth v. Industrial Sales Co., 241 Md. 453, 217 A.2d 253)

A secret intention of one party that is not expressed in the contract has no effect, and a court cannot remake a contract for the parties under the guise of interpreting it. Of course, if the contract is so vague or indefinite that the intended performance cannot be determined, the contract cannot be enforced.

In arriving at the meaning of a contract, a court must endeavor to give meaning to every word. At the same time, no particular form of words is required and any words manifesting the intent of the parties are sufficient.[32] In the absence of proof that a word has a peculiar meaning or that it was employed by the parties with a particular meaning, a common word is given its ordinary meaning and a technical word is given its ordinary technical meaning.[33]

A word will not be given its literal meaning when it is clear that the parties did not intend such a meaning. For example, "and" may be substituted for "or," "may" for "shall," and "void" for "voidable," and vice versa, when it is clear that the parties so intended.

Rules of grammatical construction and punctuation may be employed to throw light on the intention of the parties, but they are ignored when they clearly conflict with the intention of the parties.

(a) DIVISIBLE CONTRACT. When a contract contains a number of provisions or performances to be rendered, the question arises as to whether the parties intended merely a group of separate, divisible contracts or whether it was to be a "package deal" so that complete performance by each party is essential.

Facts: Richard and Ruby Lewis owned separate tracts of land, designated as Section 1 and Section 18, which they leased to Gailey and Sredanovich. The lease specified that the Lewises would convey to the tenants a one-half interest in the land if the tenants developed water on

---

[32] *Shaw* v. *E. I. duPont DeNemours & Company*, [Vt.] 226 A.2d 903.
[33] *Reno Club* v. *Young Investment Co.*, 64 Nev. 312, 182 P.2d 1011.

the land suitable for irrigation. The tenants developed such a water supply on Section 18 but not on Section 1. Arrow Gas Co. acquired the interest of the tenants and claimed that it was entitled to a one-half interest in Section 18. The Lewises contended that Arrow was not entitled to any interest in the land because the tenants had not developed nor made any effort to develop water on Section 1.

Decision: Judgment for Arrow Gas Co. The contract was to be interpreted as making a separate provision for each of the two tracts so that if water was developed as to either one of them, the duty arose to transfer an interest therein even though water was not developed on the other. (Arrow Gas Co. v. Lewis, 71 N.Mex. 232, 377 P.2d 655)

(b) ERRORS AND OMISSIONS. Clerical errors and omissions are ignored and the contract is read as the parties intended, provided that the errors or omissions are not so material or do not raise such a conflict as to make it impossible to determine the intention of the parties.[34]

2 / Whole contract. The provisions of a contract must be construed as a whole. This rule is followed even when the contract is partly written and partly oral, but this principle does not apply when an oral agreement must be excluded according to the parol evidence rule.[35]

When several writings, whether letters, telegrams, and/or memorandums are executed as part of one transaction, either at the same time or at different times, they are all to be construed as a single writing when it can be determined that that was the intent of the parties.[36]

Terms in a printed letterhead or billhead or on the reverse side of a printed contract form are not part of a contract written thereon unless a reasonable man would regard such terms as part of the contract.

3 / Contradictory terms. When a contract is partly printed or typewritten and partly written and the written part conflicts with the printed or typewritten part, the written part prevails. When there is a conflict between a printed part and a typewritten part, the latter prevails. When there is a conflict between an amount or quantity expressed both in words and figures, the amount or quantity expressed in words prevails.

Facts: Integrated, Inc., entered into a contract with the State of California to construct a building. It then subcontracted the electrical work to Alec Fergusson Electrical Contractors. The subcontract was a printed form with blanks filled in by typewriting. The printed payment clause required Integrated to pay Fergusson on the 15th day of the month

---

[34] As to the extent to which parol evidence may be employed to explain the meaning of terms and to show the intent of the parties, see page 163.
[35] See p. 162.
[36] *Charpentier* v. *Welch,* 74 Idaho 242, 259 P.2d 814.

following the submission of invoices by Fergusson. The typewritten part of the contract required Integrated to pay Fergusson "immediately following payment" (by the State) to the general contractor.

Decision: The typed and printed payment clauses were inconsistent. Therefore, the typewritten clause prevailed. The word "immediately" used therein did not require actual "immediate" action, however, but was satisfied by payment within a reasonable time, having regard to the nature of the circumstances of the case, which necessarily included sufficient time in which to process the payment received from the State before making payment therefrom to the subcontractor. (Integrated, Inc. v. Alec Fergusson Electrical Contractors, [Cal.App.2d] 58 Cal.Rptr. 503)

When it is possible to give a contract two interpretations and one is lawful and the other unlawful, it is assumed that the lawful interpretation was intended by the parties. Similarly, an interpretation that is fair is preferred over one that will work an unjust hardship or cause one of the parties to forfeit valuable rights.

A contract is interpreted more strictly against the party who drafted it. Thus printed forms of a contract supplied by one party to the transaction are interpreted against him and in favor of the other party when two interpretations are reasonably possible.[37] This principle of strict construction is applied particularly when there is great inequality of bargaining power between the parties so that a contract is not the result of free bargaining but is entered into on a "take-it-or-leave-it" basis. The law frequently refers to such a contract as an "adhesion contract," which means that the weaker party had only the choice of "adhering" to the prepared contract or of doing without.[38]

4 / Implied terms. Although a contract should be explicit and provide for all reasonably foreseeable events, it is not necessary that every provision be set forth. In some cases a term may be implied in the absence of an express statement to the contrary.

Facts: Standard Oil Co. made a nonexclusive jobbing or wholesale dealership contract with Perkins, which limited him to selling Standard's products and required Perkins to maintain certain minimum prices. Standard Oil had the right to approve or disapprove of Perkins' customers. In order to be able to perform under this contract, Perkins had to make a substantial money investment, and his only income was from the commissions on the sales of Standard's products. Standard Oil made some sales directly to Perkins' customers. When Perkins protested, Standard Oil pointed out that the contract did not contain any provision making his rights exclusive. Perkins sued Standard Oil to compel it to stop dealing with his customers.

---

[37] *Covington* v. *Basich Bros. Constr. Co.,* 72 Ariz. 280, 233 P.2d 837.
[38] *Hamilton* v. *Stockton Unified School District,* [Cal.App.2d] 54 Cal.Rptr. 463.

Decision: Judgment for Perkins. In view of the expenditure required of Perkins in order to operate his business and to perform his part of the contract and of his dependence upon his customers, the interpretation should be made that Standard Oil would not solicit customers of Perkins, even though the contract did not give him an exclusive dealership within the given geographic area. (Perkins v. Standard Oil Co., 235 Ore. 7, 383 P.2d 107)

An obligation to pay a certain sum of money is implied to mean payment in legal tender. Likewise, in a contract to perform work there is an implied promise to use such skill as is necessary for the proper performance of the work.[39] In a "cost-plus" contract there is an implied undertaking that the costs will be reasonable and proper. When a note representing a loan is extended by agreement, an implied promise to pay interest during the extension period arises when nothing about interest is stated by the parties.[40]

A local custom or trade practice, such as that of allowing 30 days' credit to buyers, may form part of the contract when it is clear that the parties intended to be governed by this custom or trade practice or when a reasonable man would believe that they had so intended. Local custom and trade usage may be shown not only to interpret particular words of an existing contract but also to determine whether there was a contract by showing what intent was manifested by the parties, as when it was claimed that the offeree had so acted after receiving the offer that his conduct, when viewed in the light of local custom and usage, showed an intention to accept the offer.[41]

Conflict of Laws

Since we have 50 state court systems and the federal court system, questions sometimes arise as to what law will be applied by a court. *Conflict of laws* is that branch of law which determines which body of law shall apply in these situations.

1 / State courts. It is important to distinguish between the state or states in which the parties are domiciled or have their permanent home, the state in which the contract is made, and the state in which the contract is to be performed. The state in which the contract is made is determined by finding the state in which the last act essential to the formation of the contract was performed. Thus, when an acceptance is mailed in one state to an offeror in another state, the state of formation of the contract is the state in which the acceptance is mailed if the acceptance becomes effective at that time.[42]

---

[39] *Previews, Inc.* v. *Everets,* 326 Mass. 333, 94 N.E.2d 267.
[40] *Hackin* v. *First National Bank,* 101 Ariz. 350, 419 P.2d 529.
[41] *Industrial Electric-Seattle, Inc.,* v. *Bosko,* 67 Wash.2d 783, 410 P.2d 10.
[42] *Emerson Co.* v. *Proctor,* 97 Me. 360, 54 A. 849. As to acceptance by mailing, see page 92.

If an action on a contract made in one state is brought in a court of another state, an initial question is whether that court will lend its aid to the enforcement of a foreign contract. Ordinarily suit may be brought on a foreign cause of action. But if there is a strong contrary local policy, recovery may be denied even though the contract was valid in the state where it was made.[43]

The capacity of a natural person to make a contract is governed by the place of contracting; a corporation's capacity to do so is determined by the law of the state of incorporation. The law of the state where the contract is made determines whether it is valid in substance and satisfies requirements as to form. Matters relating to the performance of the contract, excuse or liability for nonperformance, and the measure of damages for nonperformance are generally governed by the law of the state where the contract is to be performed.[44]

When a lawsuit is brought on a contract, the *law of the forum,* that is, of the court in which the action is brought, determines the procedure and the rules of evidence.[45]

Whether there is any right that can be assigned is determined by the law of the state which determines whether the contract is substantively valid. The formal validity of the assignment is determined by the law of the state in which it is made.

(a) CENTER OF GRAVITY. There is a growing acceptance of the rule that, in place of the rigid or mechanical standards described above, a contract should be governed by the law of the state that has the most significant contacts with the transaction, to which state the contract may be said to gravitate.

Facts: Henry Osborn was a resident of Ohio. Katherine was a resident of Massachusetts. They became engaged to marry and, just before their marriage, they made an agreement with respect to the sharing of their property that neither would make any claim against the estate of the other. Osborn died and the validity of the agreement was disputed. The agreement was invalid if the law of Massachusetts applied, but it was valid if the law of Ohio was applied. It was claimed that the Massachusetts law should apply because Osborn and the widow had consulted a Massachusetts lawyer, had signed the agreement in Massachusetts, and were married there. The widow claimed that the validity of the agreement was to be determined by the law of Ohio and,

---

[43] *Windt* v. *Lindy,* 169 Tenn. 210, 84 S.W.2d 99.

[44] *Scudder* v. *Union Natl. Bank,* 91 U.S. 406.

[45] In contract actions it is generally held that whether a claim is barred by the Statute of Limitations is determined by the law of the forum. There is a division of authority as to whether a Statute of Frauds relates to the substance of the contract, the law of the place of making then governing, or whether it is a question of procedure, the law of the forum then governing.

as it was in fact prepared by an Ohio lawyer, it was the intention of the parties that performance would take place in Ohio, and the Osborns after their marriage had moved to Ohio and remained residents of that State.

Decision: As the State of Ohio had "the most significant contacts with and paramount interest in the parties," questions concerning its validity were to be interpreted by the law of Ohio rather than the law of Massachusetts. (Osborn v. Osborn, 10 Ohio Misc. 171, 226 N.E.2d 814)

(b) SPECIFICATION BY THE PARTIES. It is common for the more important contracts to specify that they shall be governed by the law of a particular state. When this is done, it is generally held that if the contract is lawful in the designated state, it will be enforced in another state and interpreted according to the law of the designated state, even though a contrary result would be reached if governed by the law of the state in which the suit is brought. The Uniform Commercial Code provides that whenever a transaction is governed by the Code, the parties may agree that their rights and duties shall be governed by the law of any state or nation which "bears a reasonable relation" to the transaction.[46]

2 / Federal courts. When the parties to the contract are domiciled in different states and an action is brought on the contract in a federal court because of this diversity of citizenship, the federal court must apply the same rules of conflict of laws that would be applied by the courts of the state in which the federal court is sitting.[47] Thus a federal court in Chicago deciding a case involving parties from Indiana and Wisconsin must apply the same rules of conflict of laws as would be applied by the courts of Illinois. The state law must be followed by the federal court in such a case whether or not the federal court agrees with the state law.[48]

QUESTIONS AND PROBLEMS

1. Checklist of legal terms:
   (a) Statute of Frauds (155)
   (b) parol evidence, parol evidence rule (162)
   (c) conflict of laws, law of the forum (170)

2. State the objective(s) of each of the following rules of law:
   (a) A contract is generally valid whether it is written or not.
   (b) Parol evidence is not admissible for the purpose of modifying a written contract when that evidence relates to an agreement made before or at the time that the written contract was executed.

---

[46] UCC Sec. 1-105(1).
[47] *Erie R.R. Co.* v. *Tompkins,* 304 U.S. 64.
[48] *John Hancock Mutual Life Insurance Co.* v. *Tarrence,* [C.A.6th] 244 F.2d 86.

3. A contract made on March 15 is to be effective for ten months beginning on May 1 of the same year. Does the Statute of Frauds apply?

4. Betz orally agrees to pay Duncan for checking the title to a lot that he plans to buy. Must such an agreement be in writing?

5. In return for Connor's promise to pay for Dutton's purchases, Adler sells certain items of clothing to Dutton. Must Connor's promise be in writing to be enforceable?

6. Bonner was appointed executor for the estate of Clauson whose will cut off Hayden, an heir of the deceased. Hayden threatened to contest the will on the ground of undue influence. Bonner orally promises to pay Hayden $500 in return for Hayden's promise that he will not contest the will. Hayden brings an action to recover the $500. Bonner pleads the Statute of Frauds as a defense. Is Hayden entitled to judgment?

7. Grayson and Kraft made an oral agreement that could not be performed by either party within a year. Later a memorandum of the agreement was drafted and signed by Grayson. When sued by Kraft, Grayson contended that the memorandum was not valid because Kraft was identified only by the title "President of the Coastal National Bank." Was his contention sound?

8. King entered into an oral agreement with Jennings whereby he promised to construct a building for Jennings two years later. As a reminder of the transaction, King sent Jennings a letter in which he set forth the terms of the agreement. When King failed to construct the building, Jennings brought an action to recover damages. King set up the Statute of Frauds as a defense. Was Jennings entitled to judgment?

9. Healy orally agrees to sell his farm to Hutchison. He gives the latter the following memorandum which is dated and signed: "On this date I hereby agree to sell my farm, Black Acre, to George Hutchison for $65,000." Hutchison refuses to carry out the agreement. Can Hutchison defend on the basis of the Statute of Frauds?

10. Ludwig agrees to supply Grote with certain building materials. Their contract states that, if Ludwig does not make delivery by July 1, the agreement shall be "void." Delivery is not made by the specified date. When Grote demands delivery on July 15, Ludwig is in a position to make delivery. Is Ludwig no longer obligated to perform?

11. Mills, who was employed in Hammond, Indiana, assigned his wages to Kroeger in Chicago to pay for clothing. Suit was brought in Illinois by Kroeger against Mill's employer. According to Illinois law, the assignment was valid, but according to Indiana law it was void. Which law governed?

12. Keith sued Heffernan on a contract for the sale of land. Heffernan raised the defense that there was no writing which satisfied the Statute of Frauds. Keith introduced into evidence: (1) a series of letters from the defendant

to the defendant's real estate broker describing the property in question and putting it up for sale with the broker at $10,000; (2) the testimony of the broker that he telephoned to the defendant the offer received by the broker from the plaintiff as to the purchase of the property in question; and (3) a telegram received by the broker in response to his request to the seller for a confirming telegram, which telegram read: "Accept $10,000 net for 5 acres 125th Avenue deal to close by March 9th." Was Keith entitled to enforce the contract? (Heffernan v. Keith, [Fla.] 127 So.2d 903)

13. Holland, doing business as the American Homes Co., sold Sandi Brown a set of kitchenware on the installment plan. When she stated that she did not have the money to make the monthly payments, it was agreed that Holland would put it on the layaway plan for her. Thereafter Holland and American Homes Co. sued her for the purchase price. She claimed that she had not become the owner of the kitchenware by the transaction which, if true, meant that she could not be sued for the purchase price. She offered witnesses who testified that a layaway plan did not make the goods become the property of the customer but merely put them away where they would not be sold to other customers and that the goods did not become the property of a buyer until the buyer claimed and made payment for the goods within a specified time. Holland objected to the admission of this evidence. Decide. (Holland v. Brown, 15 Utah 2d 422, 394 P.2d 77)

14. Blakely Kendall applied for and was issued a policy of life insurance in Missouri by the Metropolitan Life Insurance Co. After his death, his beneficiary, Amos Kendall, sued the insurance company in Arkansas. The insurance company sought to offer in evidence statements made by the insured to his doctors. Amos claimed that by the law of Arkansas such statements could not be admitted in evidence. Was this correct? (Metropolitan Life Ins. Co. v. Kendall, 225 Ark. 731, 284 S.W.2d 863)

15. A Texas statute provides that no action shall be brought "for the recovery of any commission for the sale or purchase of real estate" unless the contract or promise is evidenced by a writing. Barnes, a contractor, made an oral contract with Howard, a real estate agent, promising to pay the agent for furnishing to him names of persons desiring to build houses. Barnes was to pay the agent 5 percent of the amount of any contract which the contractor obtained in that manner. Howard sued Barnes for failing to pay the commissions. He defended on the ground that there was no written contract. Decide. (Barnes v. Howard, [Tex.Civ.App.] 317 S.W.2d 117)

Chapter 14

Nature and Transfer of Contract Rights

Ordinarily one person makes a contract with another person and no question arises as to the nature of the rights created. Rather frequently, however, two or more persons make a contract with one or more other persons. Furthermore, a person who was not a party to the original agreement may acquire rights under that contract. Under these circumstances questions concerning the nature of the rights created arise.

Joint, Several, and Joint and Several Contracts

When two or more persons make a contract with one or more other persons, the contract may be (1) joint, (2) several, or (3) joint and several.

1 / Joint contracts. A *joint contract* is one in which two or more persons jointly promise to perform an obligation or in which two or more persons are jointly entitled to the benefit of the performance by the other party or parties. If *A, B,* and *C* sign a contract stating "we jointly promise" to do a particular act, the obligation is the joint obligation of *A, B,* and *C.* In the absence of an express intent to the contrary, a promise by two or more persons is generally presumed to be joint and not several.[1]

Each of two or more joint promisors is liable for the entire obligation, but an action must be brought against all who are living and within the jurisdiction of the court.[2] When a judgment is obtained against two joint promisors, execution on the judgment may be levied wholly on the property of one promisor or partially on the property of each one. However, if only one (or fewer than all) is sued and if he does not object to the fact that all are not sued, he cannot object after he has lost the action, because the defect is regarded as cured by the entry of a judgment. At common law the entry of the judgment in such a case also barred the plaintiff from subsequently suing the other joint obligors. This rule has been changed by statute in many states so that the plaintiff can bring a later action against those whom he had not sued originally.[3]

---

[1] *Mintz* v. *Tri-County Natural Gas Co.,* 259 Pa. 477, 103 A. 285.
[2] Restatement, Contracts, Sec. 117.
[3] *Isaacson's Estate* v. *Hertz,* 80 Ill.App.2d 109, 225 N.E.2d 106.

If one of the joint promisors dies, the surviving promisors remain bound to perform the contract unless it was personal in character and required the joint action of all the obligors for its performance. If the deceased obligor had received a benefit from the contract, a court of equity will also hold his estate liable for the performance of the contract.[4]

Generally the release by the promisee of one or more of the joint obligors releases all.[5]

These principles apply equally to the rights of joint promisees.[6]

2 / Several contracts. Several contracts arise when two or more persons separately agree to perform the same obligation even though the separate agreements are set forth in the same instrument.[7] At common law these persons were liable individually and could not be sued jointly in one action. This rule has been changed in many jurisdictions by the adoption of statutes, or by rules of courts making procedural reforms, that permit persons liable on related causes of action to be sued at one time.

If *A, B,* and *C* sign a contract stating "we severally promise" or "each of us promises" to do a particular act or to pay a specified sum of money, the three signers are severally bound to perform or to pay, that is, each signer is individually bound.

Upon the death of a several obligor, his liability descends to his estate and not to the surviving parties to the contract. Thus, upon the death of a person making a several contract, the promisee may maintain an action against the personal representative of the deceased obligor.

Since the liability of each obligor to a several contract is by definition separate or distinct, the release of one or more of the obligors by the promisee does not release the others.

The same principles apply when the rights of two or more obligees are several.

3 / Joint and several contracts. A *joint and several contract* is one in which two or more persons are bound both jointly and severally.[8] If *A, B,* and *C* sign a contract stating "we, and each of us, promise" or "I promise" to pay a specified sum of money, they are jointly and severally bound. In such a contract, the obligee may treat the claim either as a joint claim or as a group of separate claims. He may bring a suit against all or against one at a time. Under modern procedural rules and statutes, the plaintiff may sue any number of the severally liable parties instead of suing them either singly or all at one time.

---

[4] *Pickersgill* v. *Lahens,* 82 U.S. 140.
[5] R., Sec. 121.
[6] Secs. 129, 132.
[7] Sec. 113.
[8] Sec. 114.

In some states it is declared by statute that a joint contract is to be interpreted as a joint and several contract.[9]

Third Party Beneficiary Contracts

Ordinarily *A* and *B* will make a contract that concerns only them. They, however, may make a contract by which *B* promises *A* that *B* will make a payment of money to *C*. If *B* fails to perform his promise, *C*, the third party, may enforce it against *B*, the promisor.

Facts: The local labor union made a collective bargaining agreement with the Powder Power Tool Corp. governing the rates of pay for the latter's employees. Springer brought a suit on behalf of certain employees of the corporation who had not received the full pay under the agreement. It was claimed by the corporation that Springer could not bring this action for breach of contract since he was not a party to it.

Decision: Judgment for Springer. Although Springer was not a party to the contract, the contract had been made for the benefit of persons of the class to which he belonged. Accordingly he could sue upon the contract for its breach. (Springer v. Powder Power Tool Corp., 220 Ore. 102, 348 P.2d 1112)

1 / Creditor and donee beneficiaries. The third person may be either a creditor beneficiary or a donee beneficiary.[10] A *creditor beneficiary* is a creditor of the promisee whose obligation will be discharged to the extent that the promisor performs his promise. A *donee beneficiary* is a person to whom no legal duty was owed by the promisee, and as to whom the performance of the promise is a gift.

In some instances the rights of a third party beneficiary cannot be revoked even though the original parties to the contract change their minds. The creation of the contract gave the beneficiary definite rights, and in the absence of an express reservation those rights cannot be destroyed without his consent.[11]

2 / Incidental beneficiaries. Although the right of a third party beneficiary to sue is now generally recognized, not everyone who benefits from the performance of a contract between others is such a beneficiary.[12] If a city makes a contract with a contractor to pave certain streets, property owners living along those streets will naturally receive a benefit from the performance. This fact, however, does not confer upon them the status of third party beneficiaries. Accordingly, the property owners cannot sue the contractor

---

[9] *Thomas* v. *Schapeler,* [Mo.App.] 92 S.W.2d 982.
[10] *Stewart* v. *Sullivan County,* 196 Tenn. 49, 264 S.W.2d 217.
[11] *Fidelity-Philadelphia Trust Co.* v. *Bankers Life Insurance Co.,* 370 Pa. 513, 88 A.2d 710. The Restatement of Contracts to some extent authorizes a contrary conclusion. Secs. 142, 143.
[12] *Lynn* v. *Rainey,* [Okla.] 400 P.2d 805.

if he fails to perform. The courts reason that such beneficiaries are merely incidentally benefited. The city contracted for the building of the streets to further the general public interest, not primarily to benefit individual property owners.[13]

> **Facts:** The Thomas Manufacturing Co. promised its employees that it would furnish free medical attention in case of accident. Brown, one of its employees, was injured and called Dr. Prather. The latter then sued the company to collect his fees.
>
> **Decision:** Judgment for the Thomas Manufacturing Co. The employer had not made a contract with its employees for the benefit of the doctors who would render medical services to the company's employees. A doctor who did so was merely an incidental beneficiary of the contract between the employer and the employees. (Thomas Mfg. Co. v. Prather, 65 Ark. 27, 44 S.W. 218)

3 / Damage claim of third party. Assume that the failure to perform the contract or its negligent performance causes harm to a third person. Can such third person, who is harmed rather than benefited by the performance or nonperformance, bring suit against the party who has broken his contract obligation?

In some states it is held that only the parties to the contract can sue or be sued for its breach, particularly when the harm sustained is merely economic. Thus it has been held that when a surveyor negligently made a property survey for its owner, he cannot be sued for the breach of his duty by the person to whom the owner sold the land, which subsequent purchaser was the person who sustained loss when the survey was shown to be erroneous. Likewise, a motorist who is injured by the failure of a highway contractor to maintain construction warnings required by his contract with the state does not have any right to sue the contractor.[14] Certain exceptions to this rule are recognized, particularly in connection with the obligation of the sellers of goods (product liability) [15] or the liability of persons making contracts with respect to the condition of buildings (premises liability).

Assignments

Under a contract a party may have both rights and duties. Can he transfer or sell his rights to another person? Can he transfer to someone else the task of performing for him? A builder may contract to build a house. He may then find that he needs money which he can only procure by obtaining a loan from a bank. The bank demands security. Can he assign to the bank

---

[13] R., Sec. 147.
[14] *Davis* v. *Nelson-Deppe, Inc.,* [Idaho] 424 P.2d 733.
[15] See Chapter 38.

his right to receive payment from the owner under the contract? The situation may also arise that the contractor is unable to perform the contract and wants to substitute another builder to do the actual building. Can this be done? The problem considered here is whether the contractor can make a voluntary assignment of his rights or a delegation of his duties under the contract.

Generally an *assignment* is a transfer by a party to a contract of some or all of his rights under the contract to a person not a party to the contract. The party making the assignment is the *assignor,* and the person to whom the assignment is made is the *assignee.* An assignee may generally sue in his own name as though he were a party to the original contract.[16]

Facts: Compton owed money to Atwell and three other persons. To save the expenses of litigation, the other three persons assigned their claims to Atwell, who then brought one lawsuit in his own name against Compton to recover on all four claims. The local rule of court required that actions be brought in the name of the real party in interest. Compton claimed that Atwell was not the real party in interest on the assigned claims because it was intended that Atwell should turn over any money recovered to the three assignors.

Decision: Judgment for Atwell. Since the assignee for collection has the power to control and settle the claim or any suit brought on it, he was the real party in interest for the purpose of suing, without regard to the fact that he was required to surrender the proceeds to others once collection had been accomplished. (Compton v. Atwell, [M.C.App. Dist.Col.] 86 A.2d 623)

1 / Form of assignment. Generally any form of an assignment is sufficient.[17] Any acts or any words, whether written or spoken, that show an intention to transfer or assign will be given the effect of an assignment.[18] Statutes may require that certain kinds of assignments be in writing or be executed in a particular form.[19] This requirement is common in respect to statutes limiting the assignment of claims to wages.

An assignment is a completed transfer, not a contract. It is therefore immaterial whether there is any consideration for the assignment. An assignment may be made as a gift, although it is usually part of a business transaction.

In a contract to make an assignment, which is executory as far as the assignor is concerned (as contrasted with an assignment, which is executed), there must be consideration as in any other contract.

---

[16] *Bush* v. *Eastern Uniform Co.,* 356 Pa. 298, 51 A.2d 731.
[17] R., Sec. 157.
[18] *Buck* v. *Illinois National Bank & Trust Co.,* 79 Ill.App.2d 101, 223 N.E.2d 167.
[19] Assignments that do not become legally effective for certain technical reasons, such as failure to record as required by a local statute, may often be enforced in equity. See p. 3.

2 / Assignment of rights to money. A person entitled to receive money, such as payment for the price of goods or for work done under a contract, may generally assign that right to another person.[20] A contractor entitled to receive payment from the owner can assign that right to the bank as security for a loan, or he can assign it to anyone else. The fact that the assigned right represents money not yet due does not prevent the application of this rule so long as the contract itself exists at the time of the assignment. Thus a contractor on January 15 may assign an installment payment that will be due on February 1 by the terms of the contract which was signed on January 10. Similarly a person entitled to receive payments of money under a contract of employment may ordinarily assign his right to future wages.

(a) NONEXISTING CONTRACTS. If the contract is not in existence at the time the assignment is made, the attempt to assign money due on the contract in the future does not have the effect of a legal assignment. If the assignment has been supported by consideration, however, a court of equity will treat the assignment as a promise to assign and will compel the assignor to make a transfer when the money is due.

(b) RESTRICTIONS UPON ASSIGNMENT. There is a division of authority as to the effect of a prohibition in a contract against its assignment. In some jurisdictions, if a right to money is otherwise assignable, the right to transfer cannot be restricted by the parties to the contract. Such a restriction is regarded in those states as contrary to public policy because it places a limitation on the assignor's right of property. In other states such a prohibition is recognized as valid on the theory that the parties to the original contract may include such a provision if they choose to do so.

In some jurisdictions the distinction is made between a clause by which a party promises that he will not assign and a clause declaring that an assignment cannot be made, and only the latter form of clause is held to bar an assignment.

Rights under contracts for the sale of goods may be assigned, "unless otherwise agreed," except when the assignment would materially change the performance of the other party. Unless the circumstances indicate the contrary, a prohibition of the assignment of "the contract" is to be construed only as prohibiting a delegation of performance.[21]

Statutes may validly prohibit the assignment of rights to money. Contractors who build public works are frequently prohibited from assigning money due or money that will become due under the contract. In some states

---

[20] *Adler* v. *Kansas City Springfield and Memphis R.R. Co.,* 92 Mo. 242, 4 S.W. 917.
[21] Uniform Commercial Code, Sec. 2-210(2), (3).

wage earners are prohibited from assigning their future wages, or the law limits the percentage of their wages that can be assigned. In some instances an assignment of wages is lawful, but the assignment must be a separate instrument complete in itself and not included in the body of any other instrument. The purpose of such a provision is to protect employees from signing printed forms containing "hidden" wage assignment clauses.

In some instances a statute prohibiting the assignment of wage claims is regarded as merely prohibiting the assignment of wages for commercial purposes and as not applying to an assignment of wage claims made by an employee as part of a settlement agreement with his estranged wife.[22]

3 / Assignment of right to a performance. When the right of the obligee under the contract is a right to receive a performance by the other party, he may assign his right, provided the performance required of the other party to the contract will not be materially altered or varied by such assignment.[23] If the assignor has the right to buy a certain quantity of a stated article and to take such property from the seller's warehouse, this right to purchase can be assigned. If, however, the sales contract stipulated that the seller should deliver to the buyer's premises and the assignee lived or had his place of business a substantial distance from the assignor's place of business, the assignment would not be given effect. In this case, the seller would be required to give a performance different from that which he contracted to make. Similarly a right to purchase goods on credit cannot be assigned since the seller would be required to accept a new purchaser whom he had not approved as a credit risk.

(a) PERSONAL SATISFACTION. A similar problem arises when the goods to be furnished must be satisfactory to the personal judgment of the buyer. Since the seller only contracted that his performance would stand or fall according to the buyer's judgment, the law will not permit the buyer to substitute the judgment of his assignee.

(b) PERSONAL SERVICES. The foregoing principle also prohibits the assignment of a right to receive or obtain personal services. An employer cannot assign to another the employer's right to have an employee work for him. The relationship of employer and employee is so personal that the right cannot be assigned.[24] The performance contracted for by the employee was to work for a particular employer at a particular place and at a particular job. To permit an assignee to claim the employee's services would be to change the contract that the employee made.

---

[22] *Downs* v. *American Mut. Liability Ins. Co.*, 14 N.Y.2d 266, 251 N.Y.S.2d 19.
[23] R., Sec. 151.
[24] *Folquet* v. *Woodburn Public Schools*, 146 Ore. 339, 29 P.2d 554.

4 / Delegation of duties. A *delegation of duties* is a transfer of duties by a party to a contract to another person who is to perform them in his stead. Under certain circumstances a contracting party may obtain someone else to do work for him. When the performance is standardized and non-personal so that it is not material who performs, the law will permit the delegation of the performance of the contract. In such cases, however, the contracting party remains liable for the default of the person doing the work just as though the contracting party himself had performed or attempted to perform the job.[25] If the contract expressly prohibits delegation, this cannot be done.

If the performance by the promisor requires his personal skill or is a performance in which his credit standing or the other party's confidence in his ability was material in selecting him, delegation of performance is prohibited. A doctor or an artist hired to render a particular service cannot delegate the performance of that duty to another, as it is obvious that the other party to the contract relied upon his personal skill in selecting him. The law will not permit him by means of delegation to remake the other party's contract without that party's consent.

Facts: The Industrial Construction Co. wanted to raise money to construct a canning factory in Wisconsin. Various persons promised to subscribe the needed amount which they agreed to pay when the construction was completed. The construction company assigned its rights under the agreement to Johnson, who then built the cannery. Vickers, one of the subscribers, refused to pay the amount he had subscribed on the ground that the contract could not be assigned.

Decision: Judgment for Vickers. Since the construction of the canning factory called for the skill and experience of the builder and reliance upon him by the subscribers, the performance of the contract was a personal matter which could not be delegated by the builder without the consent of the subscribers. As Vickers had not consented to such assignment, Johnson had no rights by virtue of the attempted assignment and could not sue for the subscription. (Johnson v. Vickers, 139 Wis. 145, 120 N.W. 837)

Whether a contract calls for a performance of such a nature that it cannot be delegated is a matter which may be difficult to determine. There are necessarily many borderline cases where reasonable persons might disagree as to whether a performance is such a routine matter that it can be done by anyone or is a matter which rests upon the skill, judgment, credit, or reliability of the contracting party. Such borderline cases must be decided by the court in the event of a lawsuit.

---

[25] *Brown* v. *Bowers Constr. Co.*, 236 N.C. 462, 73 S.E.2d 147.

(a) INTENTION TO DELEGATE DUTIES. A question of interpretation arises as to whether an assignment of "the contract" is an assignment only of the rights of the assignor or is both an assignment of those rights and a delegation of his duties. The trend of authority is to regard such a general assignment as both a transfer of rights and delegation of duties.[26]

> Facts: Smith, who owned the Avalon Apartments, sold individual apartments under contracts that required each purchaser to pay $15 a month extra for hot and cold water, heat, refrigeration, taxes, and fire insurance. Smith assigned his interest in the apartment house and under the various contracts to Roberts. When Roberts failed to pay the taxes on the building, Radley and other tenants sued Roberts to compel her to do so.

> Decision: Judgment against Roberts. In the absence of a contrary indication, it is presumed that an "assignment" of a contract delegates the performance of the duties as well as transfers the rights. Here there was no indication that a "package" transfer was not intended, and the assignee was therefore obligated to perform in accordance with the contract terms. (Radley v. Smith, 6 Utah 2d 314, 313 P.2d 465)

With respect to contracts for the sale of goods, "an assignment of 'the contract' or of 'all my rights under the contract' or an assignment in similar general terms is an assignment of rights and, unless the language or the circumstances (as in an assignment for security) indicate the contrary, it is a delegation of performance of the duties of the assignor and its acceptance by the assignee constitutes a promise by him to perform the duties. This promise is enforceable by either the assignor or the other party to the original contract." [27]

(b) NOVATION. One who is entitled to receive performance under a contract may agree to release the person who is bound to perform and to permit another person to take his place. When this occurs, it is not a question of simply assigning the liability under the contract but is really one of abandoning the old contract and substituting in its place a new contract. This change of contract is called a *novation*. For example, if *A* and *B* have a contract, they, together with *C,* may agree that *C* shall take *B's* place. If this is done, there is a novation. *B* is then discharged from his contract, and *A* and *C* are bound. It must be shown that a novation was intended.[28]

5 / Partial assignment. Suppose that a contractor is entitled to receive $1,000 from the party for whom he is constructing a garage. Assume further that the contractor wishes to pay the supplier of cement by assigning to him

---

[26] UCC Sec. 2-210(4).
[27] UCC Sec. 2-210(4).
[28] *Chastain* v. *Cooper & Reed,* 152 Tex. 322, 257 S.W.2d 422.

$200 of the $1,000 which the contractor will receive from the owner. If such a partial transfer could be made, the owner might find himself sued by the contractor for $800 and by the materialman for $200. The owner would thus be subjected to the expense and inconvenience of two lawsuits. To avoid this inconvenience and burden to the obligor, all parties must be joined in the action.[29]

6 / Defenses and setoffs. The assignee's rights rise no higher than those of the assignor.[30] If the obligor (the other party to the original contract) could successfully defend against a suit brought by the assignor, he will also prevail against the assignee.

Facts: The Walkers purchased on trial a mechanical water softener from Partin, who represented that the use of the softener would increase the milk production at the Walkers' dairy, and the purchase price could be paid for through such increased production. Partin assigned his contract with the Walkers to Associates Loan Co. When Associates sued the Walkers for the money due under the contract, the Walkers raised the defense that the mechanical water softener did not work as represented.

Decision: Judgment for Walkers. An assignee acquires only such rights as were owned by the assignor and is subject to defenses available to the obligor against the assignor. (Associates Loan Co. v. Walkers, 76 N.Mex. 520, 416 P.2d 529)

When the assignee sues the obligor, he may be successfully met by the defense that there was no consideration or that there was a failure of performance; that the original contract is not in writing as required by the Statute of Frauds; or that the original contract is not enforceable because of fraud or mistake, or because of the incapacity of the parties. The obligor may also assert against the assignee a defense based on a setoff or counterclaim for damages against the assignor or for defective workmanship of the assignor. For example, a roofing contractor may assign his claim for payment against a house-owner; but the latter may assert against the assignee any claim for the damages sustained by the owner because the contractor failed to do a satisfactory job and the owner was compelled to pay a second contractor to correct the defects.

If the obligor does not know of the assignment, it is immaterial whether these defenses, or setoffs and counterclaims, arise before or after the assignment is made. Those defenses, setoffs, and counterclaims which are based on acts of the assignor after the obligor has been informed or has learned of

---

[29] *State Bank of Sheridan* v. *Heider,* 139 Ore. 185, 9 P.2d 117.
[30] R., Sec. 167; *Harrison Mfg. Co.* v. *Philip Rothman & Son,* 336 Mass. 625, 147 N.E.2d 155.

the assignment cannot be asserted by the obligor against the assignee. In such case the obligor did not regard the assignor as the holder of a claim when the defense, setoff, or counterclaim against the assignor arose. It would therefore be unfair to permit the obligor to assert such claim or defense against the assignee.

The fact that the assignee takes the assignment in good faith and pays value and does not know or have any reason to know that the obligor has a defense or counterclaim available against the assignor does not affect the applicability of these rules.[31] The only way in which the assignee can protect himself is to ask the obligor whether he has any defense or setoff or counterclaim against the assignor. If the obligor states that he has none or makes a declaration of no setoff, he is estopped or barred from contradicting his statement and in most cases is not permitted to prove a defense, setoff, or counterclaim based on facts arising prior to the time of his statement to the assignee if he had no knowledge thereof at the time of the transaction.[32]

> **Facts:** The General Distributing Company installed a heating system in the home of Drabish on credit. When the work was completed, Drabish signed a certificate stating that the work had been completed properly. General assigned its claim for the amount due to the United States National Bank, which took the assignment in reliance on the certificate of completion. When the bank sued Drabish, he raised the defense that the work had not been performed satisfactorily.

> **Decision:** Judgment for the bank. Drabish was estopped from raising any defense of unsatisfactory performance against the assignee because he had executed a satisfactory completion certificate on the basis of which the assignee had taken the assignment. (United States National Bank v. Drabish, 187 Pa.Super. 169, 144 A.2d 640)

7 / Notice of assignment. An assignment, if otherwise valid, takes effect the moment it is made. It is not necessary that the assignee or the assignor give notice to the other party to the contract that the assignment has been made.[33] It is highly desirable, however, that the other party be notified as soon as possible after the making of the assignment because, if notice is not given, the assigned right may be impaired or possibly destroyed.

(a) SETOFFS. The setoffs and counterclaims that may be asserted by the obligor against the assignee not only include those acquired by the obligor before the assignment is made but also include those based on contracts made and acts committed up to the time that the obligor receives notice of the assignment. The giving of prompt notice to the obligor there-

---

[31] *Wm. Iselin & Co.* v. *Saunders,* 231 N.C. 642, 58 S.E.2d 614.
[32] *Tremont Savings and Loan Association* v. *Ortiz,* 275 N.Y.S.2d 868.
[33] R., Sec. 167.

fore reduces the period during which such setoffs or counterclaims can be acquired by the obligor.

To illustrate, let us return to the contractor who is erecting the building for the owner. On the first of the month the contractor assigns a payment due under the contract to his bank as security for a loan. The next day, the contractor negligently causes property loss to the owner. This property loss claim can be asserted against the contractor if the contractor sues for payment. The loss claim can also be asserted against the assignee bank. If, however, the assignment were made on the first of the month, the owner given notice of the assignment on the second, and the property loss sustained on the third, the owner could not assert this loss claim as a setoff against the assignee.

(b) DISCHARGE. Until the obligor knows that there has been an assignment, he is legally entitled to pay to or perform for the assignor just as though there were no assignment. Such payment or performance is a complete discharge of his obligation under the contract; but in such a case the assignee could proceed against the assignor to require him to account for what he had received. If the assignee has given the obligor notice of the assignment, however, the obligor cannot discharge his obligation to the assignee by making a payment to or a performance for the assignor.[34]

(c) PRIORITY. It sometimes happens that a person assigns the same right to two different assignees. A contractor entitled to receive only $1,000 under a building contract might make an assignment of the same $1,000 to two different banks. The question then arises as to which assignee has obtained the right to the $1,000 payment. By the American rule, it is held that the assignee taking the first assignment prevails over the subsequent assignees. Some states adopt the English view by which the assignee first giving notice to the obligor is entitled to the payment. Under this rule, however, the first assignee may recover the payment made to the subsequent assignee if the latter knew of the prior assignment when he acquired his rights. This right of the prior assignee under the English rule is restricted to suit against the subsequent assignee and does not give him the right to sue the obligor.

8 / Warranties of assignor. When the assignment is made for a consideration, the assignor is regarded as impliedly warranting that the right he assigns is valid, that he is the owner of the claim which he assigns, and that he will not interfere with the assignee's enforcement of the obligation. He does not warrant that the other party will pay or perform as required by the contract.

---

[34] *Olshan Lumber Co.* v. *Bullard,* [Tex.Civ.App.] 395 S.W.2d 670.

QUESTIONS AND PROBLEMS

1. Checklist of legal terms:
   (a) joint contracts (174), several contracts (175), joint and several contracts (175)
   (b) creditor beneficiary, donee beneficiary; incidental beneficiary (176)
   (c) assignment; assignor, assignee (178)
   (d) delegation of duties (181)
   (e) novation (182)

2. State the objective(s) of each of the following rules of law:
   (a) An incidental beneficiary cannot recover damages for breach of the contract by which he is benefited.
   (b) Contractors who build public works are frequently prohibited by statute from assigning money due or money that will become due under their contracts.

3. George and Hopper enter into a joint contract with Imholte. Upon failure of performance by the joint promisors, Imholte brings an action against George. George maintains that Imholte cannot sue him without joining Hopper as a codefendant. Is his contention sound?

4. Jones transfers certain office equipment to Kuntz. Under the terms of the agreement Kuntz promises to pay a certain sum of money to the Logan Manufacturing Company, to whom Jones owed this amount. Is the Logan Manufacturing Company entitled to enforce the promise of Kuntz?

5. Lester and Myers enter into a written agreement by which Lester promises to name his son after Myers in exchange for Myers' promise to pay Lester's son $1,000. Lester performs his part of the agreement. His son then brings an action to enforce payment by Myers. Is he entitled to do so?

6. Merritt assigns to Harvey his claim for wages due under an employment contract with Guenther. Is Harvey entitled to collect from Guenther?

7. Fredericks agreed to work as a gardener for Eubanks for three years. A year later Eubanks transferred his right to the services of Fredericks to the Dow Nursery. Fredericks refused to work for the nursery. Was he liable for damages?

8. Bates owes Egan $250 auction fees. Egan gives Duvall an order on Bates for one half of this debt. Is Egan entitled to sue Bates for one half of the debt?

9. Weston assigns to her bank certain rentals of certain property from her tenant, York. York, who has not been notified of the assignment, makes a settlement with Weston. Is the bank entitled to collect from York?

10. Van Camp has a claim against Tucker which he assigns to Richey on January 10 and to Pryor on January 15 of the same year. Pryor notifies

Tucker of the assignment on January 20. Richey gives notice of his assignment on January 23. Who is entitled to enforce the claim against Tucker?

11. Rexroad contracted with the City of Assaria to improve certain streets within the city. The contract specified that "the contractor shall be liable for all damages to buildings . . . located outside the construction limits (and shall) make amicable settlement of such damage claims. . . ." Anderson's house was damaged by the construction work. He sued Rexroad for the damages. The latter defended on the ground that Anderson did not have any agreement with him and had not given him any consideration. Decide. (Anderson v. Rexroad, 175 Kan. 676, 266 P.2d 320)

12. Ewin Engineering Corporation owed money to Girod. The latter borrowed money from the Deposit Guaranty Bank & Trust Co. and assigned to it as security for the loan the claim he held against Ewin. The bank immediately notified Ewin of the assignment. Thereafter Ewin paid Girod the balance due him. Ewin then notified the bank that it had paid Girod in full and that it refused to recognize the assignment. The bank sued Ewin. Could it recover? (Ewin Engineering Corp. v. Deposit Guaranty Bank & Trust Co., 216 Miss. 410, 62 So.2d 572)

13. Deal made a contract with the United States to build an ordnance plant. The contract stated that "the constructor shall compensate laborers and mechanics for all hours worked in . . . [over] eight hours in any one calendar day at a rate not less than one and one-half times the basic rate of pay of such laborers and mechanics." Head was employed by Deal and worked more than eight hours a day. Deal refused to pay him overtime, and Head sued Deal. Could he recover? (H. B. Deal & Co. v. Head, 221 Ark. 47, 251 S.W.2d 1017)

14. Hudgens purchased a used car from Mack, a dealer. Mack falsely informed Hudgens that the car was in good condition when, in fact, it needed extensive repairs. Mack also refused to live up to his 30-day guarantee when the car was brought back within a few days after the sale. The day following the sale Mack had assigned the contract to Universal C.I.T. Credit Corp. When Hudgens refused to pay on the contract, he was sued by Universal. Hudgens claimed the right to set aside the contract for fraud. Was he entitled to do so? (Universal C.I.T. Credit Corp. v. Hudgens, 234 Ark. 668, 356 S.W.2d 658)

15. Bailey was a contractor who was financed by Page. They agreed that Page should bid to obtain a government contract for construction at Matagorda. Among other things, the contract specified that Bailey would pay Page from the payments received under the new contract for a prior debt which had resulted from construction work at Port Lavaca. Was this an assignment of the contractor's rights under the contract? (Page v. Bailey, [C.A.5th] 290 F.2d 483)

Chapter 15

Discharge of Contracts

A contract is discharged by the performance of the terms of the agreement, but termination may also occur by later agreement, impossibility of performance, operation of law, or acceptance of breach. The first four methods of discharge are discussed in this chapter. Discharge by acceptance of breach is treated in Chapter 16.

Discharge by Performance

In most cases the parties perform their promises; and the contract is discharged by performance of its terms. If a dispute arises as to whether there has been performance, the party claiming that he has performed has the burden of proving that fact.

1 / Payment. When payment is required by the contract, performance consists of the payment of money or, if accepted by the other party, the delivery of property or the rendering of services in lieu of the payment of money.

Payment by commercial paper, such as a check, is a conditional payment, unless it is expressly specified that it is accepted as absolute payment without regard to whether the parties bound by the instrument pay the amount due on it. The instrument merely suspends the debt until it is presented for payment. If payment of the instrument is made, the debt is discharged; if not paid, suit may be brought on either the debt or the instrument.[1]

2 / Application of payments. If a debtor owes more than one debt to the creditor and pays him money, a question may arise as to which debt has been paid. If the debtor specifies the debt to which his payment is to be applied and the creditor accepts the money, the creditor is bound to apply the money as specified.[2]

If the debtor does not specify the application to be made, the creditor may apply the payment to any one or more of the debts in such manner as he chooses. As between secured and unsecured claims, the creditor is free

---

[1] Uniform Commercial Code, Sec. 3-802(1)(b).
[2] *S.S. Silberblatt, Inc.* v. *United States,* [C.A.5th] 353 F.2d 545.

to apply the payment to the unsecured claim. The creditor, however, must apply the payment to a debt that is due as contrasted with one which is not yet due. He cannot apply a payment to a claim that is illegal or invalid; but he may apply the payment to a claim which cannot be enforced because it is barred by the Statute of Limitations and, according to some authority, to a claim that cannot be enforced for want of a writing required by the Statute of Frauds.

If neither the debtor nor the creditor has made any application of the payment, application will be made by the court. There is a division of authority, however, whether the court is to make such application as will be more favorable to the creditor [3] or the debtor. The courts tend to the latter view when the rights of third persons are involved, such as the rights of those furnishing the money for the payment.[4]

3 / Time of performance. When the date or period of time for performance is stipulated, performance should be made on that date or in that time period. It may usually occur later than the date, however, unless the nature or terms of the contract indicate clearly that time of performance is vital, as in the case of contracts for the purchase or sale of property of a fluctuating value. When time is vital, it is said to be "of the essence." [5]

Facts: The Federal Sign Company installed an outdoor tower and sign for Fort Worth Motors under a contract that included five years' maintenance. It also specified that the sign company would repair the sign, if possible, within 24 normal working hours after notice of any damage to the sign. The sign was blown down in a windstorm. The sign company knew of this the same day but failed to repair the sign. Fort Worth Motors sued the sign company three months later. Two months thereafter, while the suit was pending, the sign company stated that it would replace the sign.

Decision: Judgment for Fort Worth Motors. The obligation to repair the sign within 24 normal working hours, if possible, after notice of damage made time of the essence. Since there was nothing to show that impossibility excused performance, the company had broken its contract by failing to make timely performance. (Federal Sign Co. v. Fort Worth Motors, [Tex.Civ.App.] 314 S.W.2d 878)

In the absence of an express stipulation, performance generally must be made within a reasonable time. Similarly, a continuing contract that does not specify a termination date runs for a reasonable time and is subject to termination by notice of either party.

---

[3] *Winfield Village* v. *Reliance Ins. Co.* 64 Ill.App.2d 253, 212 N.E.2d 10.
[4] As to sureties generally, see Ch. 42.
[5] Restatement, Contracts, Sec. 276; *Roos* v. *Lassiter,* [C.A.1st] 188 F.2d 427.

Facts: In 1904 the Monon Railroad and the New York Central Railroad made an agreement to share the expenses of maintaining a particular railroad station. The contract did not specify any time limit. In 1961, the New York Central notified Monon that it would no longer share the expenses and stopped making use of the station. In 1964 Monon sued New York Central for one half of the expenses between the years 1961 to 1964.

Decision: Judgment for New York Central. A contract that does not have a fixed termination date is terminable at will, as opposed to the contention that it would run perpetually. (Monon RR v. New York Central RR, [Ind.App.] 227 N.E.2d 450)

In some contracts the time of performance is conditional, that is, it depends upon the happening of a particular event, the failure of a certain event to happen, or the existence of a certain fact. If the condition is not fulfilled, the promisor has no obligation to perform. To illustrate, a fire insurance policy does not impose any duty for performance on the insurance company until there is a loss within the coverage of the contract.

4 / Tender of performance. An offer to perform is known as a *tender.* If performance requires the doing of an act, a tender that is refused will discharge the party offering to perform. If performance requires the payment of a debt, however, a tender that is refused does not discharge the obligation.[6] But it stops the running of interest charges and prevents the collection of court costs if the party is sued, providing the tender is kept open and the money is produced in court.

A *valid tender of payment* consists of an unconditional offer of the exact amount due on the date when due or an amount from which the creditor may take what is due without the necessity of making change. It is unnecessary for the debtor to produce the money, however, if the creditor informs him in advance that he will not accept it. The debtor must offer *legal tender* or, in other words, such form of money as the law recognizes as lawful money and declares to be legal tender for the payment of debts. The offer of a check is not a valid tender since a check is not legal tender.

A tender of part of the debt is not a valid tender.[7]

5 / Substantial performance. If the plaintiff in good faith substantially performed the contract, he can sue the other party for payment. He then recovers the contract price subject to a counterclaim for the damages caused the other party by the plaintiff's failure to perform to the letter of the contract.[8]

---

[6] R., Sec. 415.
[7] *Kuhn* v. *Hamilton,* [N.D.] 138 N.W.2d 604.
[8] *Gamble* v. *Woodlea Construction Co.,* 246 Md. 260, 228 A.2d 243.

This rule is most frequently applied in actions upon building contracts. Thus, if a contractor undertakes to erect a building for $10,000 but the work that he does is not exactly according to specifications in certain minor respects, he may still sue for the amount due on the contract. Assume that it would cost the owner $500 to correct the defects in the contractor's work. The contractor could recover $10,000 minus $500. The owner would then have $500 with which to have the defects corrected so that he would have his building at the original contract price of $10,000.

If, however, the defect is of such a nature that it cannot be remedied without rebuilding or materially injuring a substantial part of the building, the measure of damages is the difference between the value of the building as constructed and the value it would have had if it had been built according to the contract.[9]

This *rule of substantial performance* applies only when the departures from the contract or the defects are not made willfully,[10] and provided that the contract is substantially performed.[11] If the contractor intentionally departs from the contract or if the amount of work he has completed is not substantial, he is in default and cannot recover from the other party to the contract.

When the nature of the deviation is not such that it can be measured by the amount required to correct or complete performance or when the amount performed by the contractor is less than substantial, damages are also held to be the difference between the value which the property would have if the contract had been performed completely and its value with the contract partly performed. Furthermore, there is a tendency in the case of large construction contracts when the total value of the partial performance is large compared to the damages sustained through incomplete or imperfect performance to ignore whether the breach was intentional on the part of the contractor.

6 / Satisfaction of promisee or third person. When the agreement requires that the promisor perform an act to the satisfaction, taste, or judgment of the other party to the contract, the courts are divided as to whether the promisor must so perform as to satisfy the promisee or whether it is sufficient that he perform in a way that would satisfy a reasonable man under the circumstances. When personal taste is an important element, the courts generally hold that the performance is not sufficient unless the promisee is actually satisfied,[12] although in some instances it is insisted that the dissatis-

---

9 *Baker Pool Co.* v. *Bennett,* [Ky.] 411 S.W.2d 335.
10 *Lautenbach* v. *Meredith,* 240 Iowa 166, 35 N.W.2d 870.
11 *Sward* v. *Nash,* 230 Minn. 100, 40 N.W.2d 828.
12 *Wolff* v. *Smith,* 303 Ill.App. 413, 25 N.E.2d 399.

faction be shown in good faith and not merely to avoid paying for the work that has been done.[13] The personal satisfaction of the promisee is generally required under this rule when one promises to make clothes, to write a novel, or to paint a portrait to the satisfaction of the other party.

There is a similar division of authority when the subject matter involves the fitness or mechanical utility of the property. With respect to things mechanical and routine performances, however, the courts are more likely to hold that the promisor has satisfactorily performed if a reasonable man should be satisfied with what was done.[14]

> **Facts:** Johnson was operating a school bus for School District #12 under a two-year written contract which specified that Johnson "is to have option for next 3 years if a bus is run and his service has been satisfactory." At the end of the two-year period Johnson notified the School District that he had elected to exercise the option, but the School District refused to renew the contract. Johnson sued the School District for breach of the option provision. It raised the defense that it was not satisfied with his services and therefore there was no option to renew.

> **Decision:** This was not a defense. When a contract requires "satisfactory" performance, it merely requires performance satisfactory to a reasonable man unless it is clear from the terms or circumstances that "personal" satisfaction is required. Here it should be the "reasonable-man" test since there was no evidence to the contrary. (Johnson v. School District #12, 210 Ore. 585, 312 P.2d 591)

When performance is to be approved by a third person, the tendency is to apply the reasonable-man test of satisfaction, especially when the third person has become incapacitated or has wrongfully withheld his approval.

Discharge by Agreement

A contract may be terminated by the operation of one of its provisions or by a subsequent agreement.

1 / Provision of original contract. The contract may provide that it shall terminate upon the happening of a certain event, such as the destruction of a particular building, or upon the existence of a certain fact, even though the intended performance by one party or both parties has not been completed.[15]

A contract may also provide that either party or both parties can terminate it upon giving a particular notice, such as a 30-day notice, as in

---

[13] *Commercial Mortgage & Finance Corp.* v. *Greenwich Savings Bank,* 112 Ga.App. 388, 145 S.E.2d 249.
[14] R., Sec. 265.
[15] Sec. 396.

the case of an employment contract [16] or a sale with an option to return,[17] or that one party may terminate the contract if he is not satisfied with the performance of the other.[18] Notice to terminate must be clear and definite.[19]

2 / Rescission by agreement. The parties to a contract may agree to undo the contract and place each one in his original position by returning any property or money that had been delivered or paid.[20] It is said that they agree to rescind the contract or that there is a *mutual rescission.* Ordinarily no formality is required for rescission, and an oral rescission, or conduct evidencing such an intent may terminate a written contract. An oral rescission is ineffective, however, in the case of a sale of an interest in land; for, in such a case, the purpose of the rescission is to retransfer the interest in land. Accordingly, the retransfer or rescission must satisfy the same formalities of the Statute of Frauds as applied to the original transfer.[21]

Facts: Southwell listed his property for sale with Dowling, a real estate broker. While the broker was negotiating to sell it to Grogan, Southwell notified the broker that he withdrew the property and would not sell it. The broker made no further efforts to sell the property. More than a year later, Southwell sold his property directly to Grogan. Dowling sued Southwell for commissions as provided by the original contract.

Decision: Judgment for Southwell. The fact that no objection was made and that no action was taken by the broker for over a year showed that he had agreed to a rescission of the original contract. He was therefore not entitled to claim commissions on the basis of that contract. (Dowling v. Southwell, 95 Ga.App. 29, 96 S.E.2d 903)

3 / Waiver. A term of a contractual obligation is discharged by *waiver* when one party fails to demand performance by the other party or to object when the other party fails to perform according to the terms of the contract.[22] Unlike rescission, a waiver does not return the parties to their original positions; it leaves the parties where they are at the time.

4 / Substitution. The parties may decide that their contract is not the one they want. They may then replace it with another contract. If they do so, the original contract is discharged by *substitution.*[23]

---

[16] See p. 263.
[17] See p. 424.
[18] *Ard Dr. Pepper Bottling Co.* v. *Dr. Pepper Co.,* [C.A.5th] 202 F.2d 372.
[19] *Shaw* v. *Beall,* 70 Ariz. 4, 215 P.2d 233.
[20] R., Sec. 406.
[21] Sec. 407.
[22] *Nelson* v. *Cross,* 152 Neb. 197, 40 N.W.2d 663.
[23] R., Sec. 418.

It is not necessary that the parties expressly state that they are making a substitution. Whenever they make a new contract that is clearly inconsistent with a former contract, the court will assume that the former contract has been superseded by the latter. Since the new contract must in itself be a binding agreement, it must be supported by consideration.[24]

5 / Novation. In a novation, as explained in Chapter 14, the original contract may be discharged by the new contract.[25]

6 / Accord and satisfaction. In lieu of the performance of an obligation specified by a contract, the parties may agree to a different performance.[26] Such an agreement is called an *accord.* When the accord is performed or executed, there is an *accord and satisfaction,* which by its terms discharges the original obligation. Ordinarily an accord and satisfaction will not take effect until it is executed, that is, until the performance which is agreed to by the accord is actually rendered.[27]

When the performance of one party under the accord and satisfaction consists of paying a sum of money smaller than that claimed by the other party, it is frequently required that there be a bona fide dispute as to the amount due or that the accord and satisfaction be supported by independent consideration. No dispute is required, however, when a check which states that it is in full settlement of a claim is accepted.[28]

Discharge by Impossibility

Except in the four instances that are discussed in the following paragraphs, impossibility that arises subsequent to the making of the contract has no effect; but some courts have attempted to qualify this rule. Acts of God, such as tornadoes, lightning, and sudden floods, usually do not terminate a contract even though they make performance difficult or impossible. Thus weather conditions constitute a risk that is assumed by a contracting party in the absence of a contrary agreement. An agreement by a subcontractor to pay for "damage by the elements" refers to damage by the forces of nature and covers damages resulting from an earthquake.[29] Likewise, strikes, riots, shortages of materials, and similar factors do not excuse the promisor from performing his contract.[30] The fact that it will prove more costly to perform the contract than originally contemplated,[31] or that

---

[24] *Better Taste Popcorn Co.* v. *Peters,* 124 Ind.App. 319, 114 N.E.2d 817.
[25] R., Sec. 425 et seq.; see page 182.
[26] *Mrs. Tucker's Sales Co.* v. *Frosted Foods, Inc.,* [La.] 68 So.2d 219.
[27] *Long* v. *Weiler,* [Mo.App.] 395 S.W.2d 234.
[28] UCC Sec. 3-408. See also Sec. 2-209(1) as to sales of goods, and Sec. 1-107 generally.
[29] *United States* v. *Henry,* [Alaska] 427 P.2d 584.
[30] *Hein* v. *Fox,* 126 Mont. 514, 254 P.2d 1076.
[31] *P & Z Pacific, Inc.* v. *Panorama Apartments, Inc.,* [C.A.9th] 372 F.2d 759.

the obligor has voluntarily gone out of business, does not constitute impossibility which excuses performance.

Facts: The Transatlantic Financing Corp. made a contract with the United States to haul a cargo of wheat from the United States to a safe port in Iran. The normal route lay through the Suez Canal. As the result of the nationalization of the Canal by Egypt and the subsequent international crisis which developed, the Canal was closed and it was necessary for Transatlantic to go around Africa to get to the destination. It then sued for additional compensation because of the longer route on the theory that it had been discharged from its obligation to carry to Iran for the amount named in the contract because of "impossibility."

Decision: Judgment for United States. Although impossibility does not mean literally impossible, it may be apparent from the contract that the risk of performance becoming commercially impracticable was assumed by one of the parties, in which case such impracticality is necessarily not a defense which that party may raise. As no route was specified and everyone was aware of the problems of international shipping, the unqualified contract to deliver the cargo at a specified point must be interpreted as indicating that the carrier assumed the risk that the shorter route through the Suez Canal might not be available; the carrier thus assumed the risk of "impossibility." (Transatlantic Financing Corp. v. United States, [C.A.Dist.Col.] 363 F.2d 312)

1 / Destruction of particular subject matter. When the parties contract expressly for or with reference to a particular subject matter, the contract is discharged if the subject matter is destroyed through no fault of either party.[32] When a contract calls for the sale of the wheat crop growing on a specific parcel of land, the contract is discharged if that crop is destroyed by blight.

On the other hand, if there is merely a contract to sell a given quantity of wheat, the seller is not discharged because his wheat crop is destroyed by blight. In this case, the seller makes an absolute undertaking, not limited or restricted in any way to any particular property. His obligation is to deliver a certain quantity of wheat regardless of where it is obtained.

2 / Change of law. A contract is discharged when its performance is made illegal by a subsequent change in the law of the state or country in which the contract is to be performed.[33] Thus, a contract to construct a nonfireproof building at a particular place is discharged by the adoption of a zoning law prohibiting such construction within that area. Mere incon-

---

[32] R., Sec. 457.
[33] R., Sec. 458; *Cinquegrano* v. *T. A. Clarke Motors,* 69 R.I. 28, 30 A.2d 859.

venience or temporary delay caused by the law, however, does not excuse performance.

Facts: After the United States entered World War I, the Midland Lumber Co. contracted to sell the Washington Mfg. Co. 20 carloads of lumber. By the time 6 carloads had been delivered, the federal government prohibited further shipments of lumber unless a release had been obtained. The seller obtained releases on all orders held by it except the remaining order of the Washington Mfg. Co. The seller made no effort to secure a release for that order, even though the government had stated that it would release all lumber which was not needed by the government and none of the company's lumber had been taken by the government. The lumber company failed to deliver the balance of the carloads. The Washington Mfg. Co. sued it for breach of contract.

Decision: Judgment for Washington Mfg. Co. The government embargo on lumber did not have the effect of making the contract void but merely of excusing the delay caused by the embargo. Here there was no attempt by the seller to obtain a release, which it apparently could have obtained. The seller therefore could not plead the government action as an excuse for its failure to perform. (Washington Mfg. Co. v. Midland Lumber Co., 113 Wash. 593, 194 P. 777)

The entry of a court order or decree that makes performance impossible is a defense to a party to a contract, provided such order or decree is not the result of his own conduct.

3 / Death or disability. When the contract obligates a party to perform an act that requires personal skill or which contemplates a personal relationship with the obligee or some other person, the death or disability of the obligor, obligee, or other person (as the case may be) discharges the contract.[34] If the act called for by the contract can be performed by others or by the promisor's personal representative, however, this rule does not apply.

When the contract calls for the payment of money, the death of either party does not affect the obligation. If the obligor dies, the obligation is a liability of his estate. If the obligee dies, the right to collect the debt is an asset of his estate. The parties to a contract may agree, however, that the death of either the obligee [35] or the obligor shall terminate the debt. In the latter case, the creditor can obtain insurance on the life of the debtor so that while he loses the debt upon the debtor's death, he is paid by the proceeds of the insurance on the debtor's life.

---

[34] R., Sec. 459; *Kowal* v. *Sportswear by Revere*, [Mass.] 222 N.E.2d 778.
[35] *Woods* v. *McQueen*, 195 Kan. 380, 404 P.2d 955.

4 / Act of other party. When the promisee prevents performance or otherwise makes performance impossible, the promisor is discharged from his contract.[36] Thus, a subcontractor is discharged from his obligation when he is unable to do the work because the principal contractor refuses to deliver to him the material, equipment, or money as required by the subcontract. When the default of the other party consists of failing to supply goods or services, the duty may rest upon the party claiming a discharge of the contract to show that he could not have obtained substitute goods or services elsewhere, either because they were not reasonably available or were not acceptable under the terms of the contract.[37]

Facts: Whitt made a contract to sell Godwin an interest in a motel to be constructed. Godwin made a down payment of $12,000, which Whitt then paid to the Federated Mortgagee Co. as a fee to obtain a construction loan in order to build the motel. Federated was not able to obtain the loan. On March 6, 1962, Whitt and Godwin made a contract by letter which declared that Whitt would pay back to Godwin the $12,000. Federated refused to return any part of the loan fee to Whitt unless Godwin signed a release that he had no claim against Federated. Godwin refused to sign any release. He then sued Whitt for the $12,000. Whitt raised the defense that Godwin, by refusing to sign the release, had made it impossible for Whitt to get any money back from Federated and had thereby prevented Whitt from performing his contract. The contract of March 6, 1962, had said nothing about a release from Whitt.

Decision: The refusal to sign a release did not constitute any defense as there was no obligation in the contract to execute such a release. The fact that the execution of such a release would have aided the other party does not create a duty to execute a release. (Whitt v. Godwin, 205 Va. 797, 139 S.E.2d 841)

When the conduct of the other contracting party does not make performance impossible but merely causes delay or renders performance more expensive, the contract is not discharged; but the injured party is entitled to damages for the loss that he incurs.

Facts: The United States made a contract with Luria Brothers for the construction of aircraft facilities. After the excavation had begun, the United States directed Luria to stop until further tests of the subsoil conditions could be made. It thereafter changed the specifications for the building to require additional and deeper supporting columns. For no justifiable reason nearly a year was spent in reaching this conclusion. Luria presented a claim for damages caused by the delay,

---

[36] *Burke* v. *N. P. Clough,* 116 Vt. 448, 78 A.2d 483.
[37] As to the requirement of the mitigating damages generally, see Ch. 16.

representing fixed costs that it had sustained while men and equipment were kept idle waiting for approval by the government.

Decision: Judgment for Luria. As part of a party's obligation to do nothing that will interfere with performance by the other contracting party is the duty to furnish proper building specifications to a contractor and to act promptly in correcting them when they are found to be erroneous. The specifications were wrong, and the government delayed unreasonably in correcting them. It was therefore responsible for the loss which the contractor could show was caused him by such error and delay in correcting the specifications. (Luria Brothers v. United States, [Ct. Claims] 369 F.2d 701)

Discharge by Operation of Law

Under certain circumstances either a contract is discharged or the right to enforce it is destroyed by operation of law.

1 / Alteration. A written contract, whether under seal or not, may be discharged by alteration.[38] To have this effect (a) it must be a *material alteration,* that is, it must change the nature of the obligation; (b) it must be made by a party to the contract, as alterations made by a stranger have no effect; (c) it must be made intentionally, and not through accident or mistake; and (d) it must be made without the consent of the other party to the contract.[39] For example, when one party to an advertising contract, without the consent of the other party, added "at a monthly payment basis," thus making the rate of payment higher, the advertiser was discharged from any duty under the contract.[40]

2 / Merger. In some instances contract rights are merged into or absorbed by a greater right. If an action is brought upon a contract and a judgment is obtained by the plaintiff against the defendant, the contract claim is merged into the judgment.

3 / Bankruptcy. Subject to many specific regulations and some exceptions in the federal statute, any individual or corporate debtor may voluntarily enter into a federal court of bankruptcy or be compelled to do so by creditors. The trustee in bankruptcy then takes possession of the debtor's property and distributes it as far as it will go among his creditors. After this is done, the court grants the debtor a discharge in bankruptcy if it concludes that he had acted honestly and had not attempted to defraud his creditors.

---

[38] The definition and effect of alteration in the case of commercial paper has been modified by statute. See p. 350.
[39] R., Secs. 434-437.
[40] *National Rwys. Adver. Co.* v. *E. L. Bruce Co.,* 143 Ark. 292, 220 S.W. 48.

Even though all creditors have not been paid in full, the discharge in bankruptcy is a bar to the subsequent enforcement of their ordinary contract claims against the debtor. The cause of action or contract claim is not destroyed, but the bankruptcy discharge bars a proceeding to enforce it.[41] Since the obligation is not extinguished, the debtor may waive the defense of discharge in bankruptcy by promising to pay the debt.[42] Such a waiver is governed by state law. In a few states such a waiver must be in writing.

4 / Statute of Limitations. Statutes provide that after a certain number of years have passed, a contract claim is barred. Technically, this is merely a bar of the remedy and does not destroy the right or cause of action. A few states hold that the statute bars the right as well as the remedy and that there is accordingly no contract after the lapse of the statutory period.

The Statute of Limitations begins to run the moment that the cause of action of the plaintiff arises, that is, when he is first entitled to bring suit. When the party entitled to sue is under a disability, such as insanity, at the time the cause of action arises, the period of the statute does not begin to run until the disability is removed. When a condition or act prevents the

Statutes of Limitations †

STATE	OPEN AC- COUNTS	WRITTEN CON- TRACTS	JUDG- MENTS OF RECORD	STATE	OPEN AC- COUNTS	WRITTEN CON- TRACTS	JUDG- MENTS OF RECORD
	YEARS	YEARS	YEARS		YEARS	YEARS	YEARS
Alabama	3	6	20	Missouri	5	10	10
Alaska	6	6	10	Montana	5	8	10
Arizona	3	6	5	Nebraska	4	5	5
Arkansas	3	5	10	Nevada	4	6	6
California	4	4	10	New Hampshire	6	6	20
Colorado	6	6	20	New Jersey	6	6	20
Connecticut	6	6	21	New Mexico	4	6	7
Delaware	3	3 *	No limit	New York	6	6	20
District of				North Carolina	3	3	10
Columbia	3	3	12	North Dakota	6	6	10
Florida	3	5	20	Ohio	6	15	21
Georgia	4	6	7	Oklahoma	3	5	5
Hawaii	6	6	10	Oregon	6	6	10
Idaho	4	5	6	Pennsylvania	6	6	20
Illinois	5	10	20	Rhode Island	6	6	20
Indiana	6	10 *	20	South Carolina	6	6	10
Iowa	5	10	20	South Dakota	6	6	20
Kansas	3	5	5	Tennessee	6	6	10
Kentucky	5	15	15	Texas	2	4	10
Louisiana	3	10	10	Utah	4	6	8
Maine	6	6	20	Vermont	6	6	8
Maryland	3	3	12	Virginia	3	5	20
Massachusetts	6	6	20	Washington	3	6	6
Michigan	6	6	10	West Virginia	5	10	10
Minnesota	6	6	10	Wisconsin	6	6	20
Mississippi	3	6	7	Wyoming	8	10	5

† The Uniform Commercial Code (Sec. 2-725) specifies a four-year period for actions on contracts for sales of goods.
  * Other than money, 20 years; realty, 15 years.

---

[41] *Earl* v. *Liberty Loan Corp.,* [La.] 193 So.2d 280.
[42] See p. 126.

period of the Statute of Limitations from running, it is said to *toll the running of the statute.*

Statutes of limitations do not run against governments as it is contrary to the public policy that the rights of society generally, as represented by the government, should be prejudiced by the failure of the proper governmental officials to take the necessary action to enforce the claims of the government.

The defense of the Statute of Limitations may be waived by the debtor.[43] The waiver must ordinarily be an express promise to pay or such an acknowledgment of the existence of the debt that the law can imply from the acknowledgment a promise to pay the debt. In some states the promise or acknowledgment must be in writing. Part payment of the principal or interest is also regarded as a waiver of the bar of the statute and revives the debt.

Some contracts, particularly insurance contracts, contain a time limitation within which suit may be brought. This is, in effect, a private Statute of Limitations created by the parties.[44]

QUESTIONS AND PROBLEMS

1. Checklist of legal terms:
   (a) tender, valid tender of payment, legal tender (190)
   (b) rule of substantial performance (191)
   (c) mutual rescission, waiver, substitution (193)
   (d) accord, accord and satisfaction (194)
   (e) material alteration (198)
   (f) merger of contract rights (198)
   (g) Statute of Limitations (199), toll the running of the statute (200)

2. State the objective(s) of each of the following rules of law:
   (a) When a contruction contract is substantially performed in good faith, the contractor may recover the contract price less damages caused the other party for shortcomings in his performance.
   (b) Impossibility of performance that arises subsequent to the making of the contract ordinarily does not excuse the promisor from his obligations.

3. Niles owed the Richmond Pharmacy for several purchases made on different dates. On a payment for which Niles gave no instructions, Richmond applied the payment toward a purchase older than the period provided in the local Statute of Limitations. Did Richmond have the right to apply the payment in this manner?

4. The Powers Company employed Smith as a designer for one year at a salary of $100 a week. Later the parties entered into a contract of employment for the same services and for the same period but at a salary

---

[43] R., Sec. 86.
[44] *Proc* v. *Home Ins. Co.,* 17 N.Y.2d 239, 217 N.E.2d 136.

of $125 a week. In an action brought by the company against Smith, it was contended that the first contract had been terminated by the substitution of a new contract. Do you agree?

5. Roller agrees to give Sinclair a television set in satisfaction of a right of action that Sinclair has against Roller. Before Roller delivers the set, Sinclair brings action against him. Roller pleads that Sinclair had agreed to accept the television set as a satisfaction of his right of action. Is this a valid defense?

6. Green entered into an agreement with the United States to construct a levee. Because of a flood, Green was unable to perform the contract as he had agreed. In an action brought by the United States. Green contended that the contract had been discharged by impossibility. Do you agree?

7. Gaines contracted in writing to sell to Jefferson 100 bushels of peaches to be picked from a particular orchard, payment to be made 30 days after delivery. The orchard was destroyed by a windstorm a day before the peaches were to be picked. Jefferson sues Gaines for damages. Decide.

8. Kemper contracted to sell a warehouse to Lee. Before the time for performance the warehouse was struck by lightning and totally destroyed. Was the contract terminated by impossibility?

9. A statute provides that no action shall be brought on debts later than six years after they are due. Seven years after a debt owed by Marshall to Asher is due and payable, Marshall makes a part payment. Six months later Asher sues Marshall for the remainder of the debt. Marshall pleads the Statute of Limitations. Is this a valid defense?

10. Warren and Geraldine Bates, husband and wife, were about to be divorced. They made a written agreement that Warren would pay Geraldine $50 a month until their younger child attained the age of 18 years and that in consideration thereof Geraldine released Warren from all property claims. The agreement did not say that it was binding upon Warren's estate. Upon his death it was claimed by his second wife that the obligation to make the monthly payments terminated with his death. Decide. (Hutchings v. Bates, [Tex.Civ.App.] 393 S.W.2d 338)

11. Greif obtained credit cards from Socony Mobil Oil Co. for himself and his wife. The card specified, "This card is valid unless expired or revoked. Named holder's approval of all purchases is presumed unless written notice of loss or theft is received." Later Greif returned his card to the company, stating that he was canceling it, but that he could not return the card in his wife's possession because they had separated. Subsequently Socony sued Greif for purchases made by the wife on the credit card in her possession. He defended on the ground that he had canceled the contract. The company claimed that the contract was not revoked until both cards were surrendered since otherwise purchases could still be made on the outstanding card. Decide. (Socony Mobil Oil Co. v. Greif, 10 App.Div.2d 119, 197 N.Y.S.2d 522)

Chapter 16

Breach of Contract and Remedies

When termination is the result of a breach of contract by one party, the other party may have a choice of several remedies.

Discharge by Acceptance of Breach

There is a *breach of contract* whenever one or both parties fail to perform the contract. A contract is discharged by breach if, when one party breaks the contract, the other party accepts the contract as ended. When a breach occurs, however, the injured party is not required to treat the contract as discharged. Since the contract bound the defaulting party to perform, the injured party may insist on the observance of the contract and resort to legal remedies.

A breach of a part of a divisible contract is not a breach of the entire contract.

A breach does not support a discharge of a contract when the term broken is not sufficiently important.[1] A term of a contract that does not go to the root of the contract is a *subsidiary term*. When there is a failure to perform such a term, the agreement is not terminated,[2] although the defaulting party may be liable for damages for its breach.

In addition to the effect of a breach as such, the occurrence of a breach also excuses the injured party from his performance if it is conditioned or dependent upon the performance of the defaulter's obligation.

Facts: K & G Construction Co., as contractor, made a subcontract with Harris and Brooks to perform part of the work. The subcontractor was obligated to perform all work "in a workmanlike manner, and in accordance with the best practices." The contractor was required to pay the subcontractor in monthly installments as the work progressed. The subcontractor did his work in such a negligent way that he damaged a wall being constructed by K & G. The latter refused to pay the subcontractor the next monthly payment under the subcontract. The subcontractor then abandoned the work and sued the contractor for breach of the duty to make payments.

---

[1] *C. C. Leonard Lumber Co.* v. *Reed,* 314 Ky. 703, 236 S.W.2d 961.
[2] Restatement, Contracts, Sec. 274.

Decision: Judgment for contractor. The promise of the subcontractor to perform and the promise of the contractor to pay him for performing were mutually dependent. The breach by the subcontractor through negligent performance excused the contractor from making payment, and the subcontractor was therefore not justified in ceasing performance under the subcontract. (K & G Construction Co. v. Harris and Brooks, 223 Md. 305, 164 A.2d 451)

1 / Renunciation. When a party to a contract declares in advance of the time for performance that he will not perform, the other party may (a) ignore this declaration and insist on performance in accordance with the terms of the contract, (b) accept this declaration as an *anticipatory breach* and sue the promisor for damages,[3] or (c) accept the declaration as a breach of the contract and rescind the contract. It is for the injured party to determine what he wishes to do when the other party has made a renunciation.

The same rule applies when one party to the contract insists on a clearly unwarranted interpretation of the contract, since this indicates that he refuses to abide by the contract as it stands.[4]

If the promisee does not elect to rescind the agreement, the contract continues in force; and his remedy is damages for breach either at once or at the time of performance specified by the contract.

Facts: Treat made a contract in July to deliver barrel staves to the Reliance Cooperage Corp. Delivery was to be completed by December 31. In the latter part of August, Treat notified Reliance that he would not make the delivery of any staves under the contract. The price of staves rose steadily during the rest of the year. Reliance sued Treat for breach of contract, claiming damages representing the difference between the contract price and the market price on December 31. The trial judge limited Reliance to damages representing the difference between the contract price and the market price in August.

Decision: The action of the trial judge was improper. When there is a breach by repudiation in advance of the performance date, the injured party is not limited to damages determined as of that date. Instead the damages are determined as of the performance date. Thus the damages are the same whether the defendant merely fails to perform on the specified performance date or declares in advance that he will not so perform. (Reliance Cooperage Corp. v. Treat, [C.A.8th] 195 F.2d 977)

After renunciation, however, the promisee cannot continue to carry out his part of the agreement, thus increasing the damages which he sustains from the failure of the other party to perform.[5]

---

[3] *Lumbermens Mutual Casualty Co.* v. *Klotz,* [C.A.5th] 251 F.2d 499.
[4] *National Life Co.* v. *Wolverton,* [Tex.Civ.App.] 163 S.W.2d 654.
[5] R., Sec. 336 and Comment (d).

2 / Incapacitating self. Another form of anticipatory breach occurs when the promisor makes it impossible for himself to perform his obligation.[6] Under such circumstances, the promiseee is entitled to treat the contract as discharged. For example, when one who is bound by the terms of the contract to turn over specific bonds, stocks, or notes to another transfers them to a third party instead, the promisee may elect to treat the contract as discharged or he may hold the promisor accountable for nonperformance when the time for performance arrives. The same is true when one agrees to sell specific goods to another person and then sells them to a third person in violation of his original contract.

Remedies for Breach

There are three remedies for breach of contract, one or more of which may be available to the injured party: (1) the injured party is always entitled to bring an action for damages; (2) in some instances he may rescind the contract; (3) in some instances he may bring a suit in equity to obtain specific performance.[7]

1 / Damages. Whenever a breach of contract occurs, the injured party is entitled to bring an action for damages to recover such sum of money as will place him in the same position as he would have been in if the contract had been performed.[8]

(a) MITIGATION OF DAMAGES. The injured party is under a duty to *mitigate the damages* if reasonably possible. That is, he must not permit the damages to increase if he can prevent them from doing so by reasonable efforts. He may thus be required to stop performance on his part of the contract when he knows that the other party is in default. To illustrate, when an architect agreed to prepare preliminary drawings and to complete working drawings and specifications but the other party repudiated the contract upon the completion of the preliminary drawings, the architect could not recover for his services after the repudiation in preparing the working drawings and specifications.[9] In the case of the breach of an employment contract by an employer, the employee is required to seek other similar em-

---

6 Sec. 284.

7 As discussed in Chapter 5, local practice must be checked to determine the form of action and the court in which these actions are to be brought. In some states, the action will be an action in assumpsit (upon contract) or an equity action; while in many others it will be merely a civil action. Furthermore, the action in some states is classified as either an action at law or an action in equity; this distinction is not made in those states in which the courts of law and courts of equity have been merged.

8 *White* v. *Metropolitan Merchandise Mart*, 48 Del. 526, 107 A.2d 892.

9 *Wetzel* v. *Rixse*, 93 Okla. 216, 220 P. 607. This principle does not prevent the plaintiff from recovering for the loss of profits that he could reasonably be expected to have made in the performance of the contract; it only limits the extent to which he can recover for expenses incurred in the performance of the contract.

ployment and the wages earned or which could be earned from the other similar employment must be deducted from the amount of damages claimed.

> **Facts:** Sides contracted to pave the driveways in a building development being constructed by Contemporary Homes. The latter prevented Sides from performing his contract. Sides then sued Homes for damages representing the difference between the contract price for the driveways and the cost to Sides of performing the contract. Homes claimed that Sides was not entitled to such damages because he had kept busy all the time on other construction jobs and thereby did not suffer any loss.

> **Decision:** Judgment for Sides. The rule that money earned working for other persons must be deducted from the damages claimed applies only to a contract for personal services. Under a construction contract, the contractor is entitled to recover his lost profits. (Sides v. Contemporary Homes, [Mo.App.] 311 S.W.2d 117)

(b) MEASURES OF DAMAGES. When the injured party does not sustain an actual loss from the breach of the contract, he is entitled to a judgment of a small sum, such as one dollar, known as *nominal damages*. If the plaintiff has sustained actual loss, he is entitled to a sum of money that will, so far as possible, compensate him for that loss; such damages are termed *compensatory damages*.

When the contract is to purchase property, the damages are generally the difference between the contract price and the market price. The theory is that if the market price is greater, the buyer has sustained the loss of the indicated price differential as he must then purchase in the general market instead of obtaining the goods from the defendant. When the contract is to sell property, the loss incurred on resale represents basically the damages for the breach. In business activities and construction contracts, the damages for the contractor are initially the loss of profits; [10] while to the other contracting party, the damages sustained upon breach by the contractor are primarily any extra cost in having someone else render the performance.[11]

As a general rule, damages that are in excess of actual loss for the purpose of punishing or making an example of the defendant cannot be recovered; such damages are known as *punitive damages* or *exemplary damages*.

Damages may not be recovered for loss caused by remote injuries unless the plaintiff, at the time the contract was executed, had informed the defendant of the existence of facts which would give the defendant reason to foresee that his breach of the contract would cause such loss.[12] What

---

[10] *C. C. Hauff Hardware, Inc.* v. *Long Mfg. Co.,* [Iowa] 148 N.W.2d 425.
[11] *Crowe* v. *Holloway Development Corp.,* 114 Ga.App. 856, 152 S.E.2d 913.
[12] *Wilkins* v. *Grays Harbor Community Hospital.* [Wash.2d] 427 P.2d 716.

constitutes remote loss for which there can be no recovery depends largely upon the facts of each case. Recovery is likewise not allowed as to losses that are not clearly related to the defendant's breach.

Facts: Crommelin was a candidate in a primary election seeking ultimate election to the United States Congress. He made a contract for televising two political speeches with the Montgomery Independent Telecasters. The television company refused to allow him to make the scheduled telecasts. He lost the primary election and then sued for breach of contract, claiming damages consisting of the money that he had spent for campaign expenses and the salary which he would have received as a congressman.

Decision: Judgment for Montgomery Independent Telecasters. Whether a person would win a primary and thereafter win the election was too speculative to conclude that the plaintiff had been deprived of the political office by the defendant's breach of contract. Therefore the defendant could not be held responsible for "causing" the plaintiff's harm and the plaintiff could not recover the damages claimed from the telecaster. (Crommelin v. Montgomery Independent Telecasters, 280 Ala. 391, 194 So.2d 548.

(c) LIQUIDATED DAMAGES. The parties may stipulate in their contract that a certain amount shall be paid in case of default. This amount is known as *liquidated damages*. The provision will be enforced if the amount specified is not excessive [13] and if the contract is of such a nature that it would be difficult to determine the actual damages. For example, it is ordinarily very difficult, if not impossible, to determine what loss the owner of a building under construction suffers when the contractor is late in completing the building. It is therefore customary to include a liquidated damages clause in a building contract, specifying that the contractor is required to pay a stated sum for each day of delay. When a liquidated damages clause is held valid, the injured party cannot collect more than the amount specified by the clause and the defaulting party is bound to pay that much damages once the fact is established that he is in default and has no excuse for his default.

Facts: The Better Food Markets made a contract with the American District Telephone Company by which the latter agreed to transmit burglar alarm signals from the store to the police department. The contract stated that damages for breach of the contract could not be determined and, therefore, the parties agreed that $50 should be paid as liquidated damages for any breach of the contract. Better Food Markets sued the telephone company for breach of contract and claimed that the liquidated damage clause was not binding.

---

[13] *Gruschus* v. *C. R. Davis Contracting Co.*, 75 N.Mex. 649, 409 P.2d 500.

Decision: Judgment for the telephone company. The liquidated damage clause was binding since it would be difficult to estimate the damages caused by a breach of the contract. In the event of theft it could not be determined how much of the damages were caused by the breach of the company. (Better Food Markets v. American District Telephone Co., 40 Cal.2d 179, 253 P.2d 10)

(d) LIMITATION OF LIABILITY. A party to a contract generally may include a provision that he shall not be liable for its breach generally, or for a breach that is due to a particular cause. When the provision is extended so as to free the contracting party from liability for his own negligence, the provision is sometimes held void as contrary to public policy. This is particularly likely to be the result when the party in question is a public utility, which is under the duty to render the performance or to provide the service in question in a nonnegligent way.

Facts: Charles Fedor, a minor, went to a summer camp. His father signed an agreement as a condition to his being admitted to the camp that the minor would not make any claim against the camp for any injury. When Charles was injured at the camp, he sued the camp claiming that the injury was caused by the camp's negligence. It raised the defense that the waiver agreement barred the suit.

Decision: The waiver provision was invalid because it was contrary to public policy to require the surrender of such rights for the sake of going to camp. (Fedor v. Mauwehu Council, 21 Conn.Sup. 38, 143 A.2d 466)

2 / Rescission upon breach. The injured party may also have the right to treat the contract as discharged. When he elects to do so, his duty to perform is ended. For example, if a party fails to receive substantially the performance for which he bargained, he may rescind the contract and free himself from any further responsibility under the contract, provided that he returns to the other party whatever he has received or gives him credit for what he cannot return.

If the injured party exercises the right to rescind after he has performed or paid money due under the contract, he may recover the value of the performance rendered or the money paid. He sues, not on the express contract, but on a quasi-contract which the law implies in order to compel the wrongdoer to pay for what he has received and to keep him from profiting by his own wrong.

The rescinding party must restore the other party to his original position as far as circumstances will permit, and he must rescind the entire contract. If he cannot make restoration because of his own acts, he cannot rescind the contract. Thus a buyer who has placed a mortgage on property purchased by him cannot rescind the sales contract because he cannot return the property the way he received it.[14]

The party who takes the initiative in rescinding the contract acts at his risk that he has proper cause to do so. If he does not have proper cause, he is guilty of a breach of the contract.

3 / Specific performance. Under special circumstances, the injured party may seek the equitable remedy of *specific performance* to compel the other party to carry out the terms of his contract. The granting of this relief is discretionary with the court and will be refused (a) when the contract is not definite; (b) when there is an adequate legal remedy; (c) when it works an undue hardship or an injustice on the defaulting party; (d) when the agreement is illegal, fraudulent, or unconscionable,[15] or (e) when the court is unable to supervise the performance of such acts.[16] The right to specific performance is also lost by unreasonable delay in bringing suit.[17]

> **Facts:** Beck agreed in writing to execute a lease of certain land to Bernstein. The lease required Bernstein to pay an annual rent of $5,600 and "to construct upon said property a fire-proof building at a cost of not less than $50,000." Beck refused to execute the lease, and Bernstein sued for specific performance to compel him to do so.

> **Decision:** Judgment for Beck. The contract was indefinite in that it did not specify what kind of a building was to be constructed by the tenant, and a contract will not be specifically enforced if it is indefinite as to any material term. (Beck v. Bernstein, 198 Md. 244, 81 A.2d 608)

As a general rule, contracts for the purchase of land will be specifically enforced[18] on the theory that each parcel of land is unique and the payment of money damages would only enable the injured person to purchase a similar parcel of land but not the land specified in the contract.

Specific performance of a contract to sell personal property generally cannot be obtained. Money damages are deemed adequate on the basis that the plaintiff can purchase identical goods. Specific performance will be granted, however, when the personal property has a unique value to the plaintiff or when the circumstances are such that identical articles cannot be obtained in the market. Thus, specific performance is granted of a contract to sell articles of an unusual age, beauty, unique history, or other distinction, as in the case of heirlooms, original paintings, old editions of books, or relics.[19] Specific performance is also allowed a buyer in the case of a

---

[14] *Bennett* v. *Emerald Service*, 157 Neb. 176, 59 N.W.2d 171.

[15] *Tuckwiller* v. *Tuckwiller*, [Mo.] 413 S.W.2d 274.

[16] R., Secs. 358, 359, 367, 368, 370, 371; *Rachon* v. *McQuitty*, 125 Mont. 1, 229 P.2d 965.

[17] *Sofio* v. *Glissmann*, 156 Neb. 610, 57 N.W.2d 176.

[18] R., Sec. 360.

[19] Sec. 361.

contract to sell shares of stock essential for control of a close corporation, having no fixed or market value, and not being quoted in the commercial reports or sold on the stock exchange.

Ordinarily contracts for the performance of personal services will not be specifically ordered, both because of the difficulty of supervision by the courts and because of the restriction of the Thirteenth Amendment of the Federal Constitution prohibiting involuntary servitude except as criminal punishment. In some instances, equity will issue a negative injunction which prohibits the defendant from rendering a similar service for anyone else. This may indirectly have the effect of compelling the defendant to work for the plaintiff.

QUESTIONS AND PROBLEMS

1. Checklist of legal terms:
   (a) breach of contract (202), subsidiary term (202), anticipatory breach (203)
   (b) mitigate the damages (204)
   (c) nominal damages (205), compensatory damages (205), punitive or exemplary damages (205), liquidated damages (206)
   (d) specific performance (208)

2. State the objective(s) of each of the following rules of law:
   (a) A party injured by a breach of contract is under a duty to mitigate the damages to the extent that is possible by a reasonable effort.
   (b) Specific performance of certain contracts is granted as an equitable remedy.

3. Gray, an accountant, was retained by Hammond to audit his records and to prepare a report that was to be submitted to Ireland, a prospective buyer of Hammond's business. When half of the work had been completed, Gray was hospitalized and could not finish the job in time for the purpose Hammond had in mind.
   (a) Did Hammond have a valid claim against Gray for damages resulting from breach of contract?
   (b) Did Gray have a valid claim against Hammond for his services?

4. Johnson owned 45 percent of the common stock of the Space-Age Corporation. He contracted for the purchase of the shares of stock owned by Leeds, which represented 10 percent of the total. When Johnson offered payment at the price agreed upon, Leeds refused to perform. Can Johnson compel Leeds to perform as he contracted to do?

5. Kuznicki made a contract for the installation of a fire detection system by Security Safety Corp. for $498. The contract was made one night and canceled at 9:00 a.m. the next morning. Security then claimed one third of the purchase price from Kuznicki by virtue of a provision in the contract that "in the event of cancellation of this agreement . . . the owner

agrees to pay 33⅓ percent of the contract price, as liquidated damages."
Was Security Safety entitled to recover the amount claimed? (Security
Safety Corp. v. Kuznicki, 350 Mass. 157, 213 N.E.2d 866)

6. Cardox Corp., which sold blasting cartridges to the Milvale Coal Co.,
failed to inspect them properly. A defective cartridge exploded pre-
maturely and injured one of Milvale's workers. Because of this, Milvale
was required to pay workmen's compensation to the worker. This additional accident covered by compensation placed Milvale in the next risk
bracket, which required it to pay an additional contribution to the state
workmen's compensation insurance fund. In suing Cardox for breach of
contract, Milvale claimed that it was entitled to recover from Cardox
the amount of this additional state fund compensation contribution.
Decide. (Milvale Coal Co. v. Cardox Corp., 157 Ohio 526, 106 N.E.2d
556)

7. Brown made a contract to sell a motel to the Gulf South Capital Corp.
Nothing was said in the contract about paying off any mortgage or other
claims against the land. When Gulf delivered the down payment, the
check specified that all mortgage and other claims against the land above
a stated amount were to be removed or paid off by the seller. Brown
returned this check and contracted to sell the same motel to another
person. Gulf sued Brown for breach of contract. Decide. (Gulf South
Capital Corp. v. Brown, [Miss.] 183 So.2d 802)

8. Brewer, who operated a lounge, contracted to give Roberts the right to
place amusement machines therein. When Brewer sought to exclude the
machines, Roberts sued for specific performance, which Brewer opposed
on the ground that specific performance would require the court to
supervise the lounge to see that the machines were allowed in it. Decide.
(Roberts v. Brewer, [Tex.Civ.App.] 371 S.W.2d 424)

PART III

Agency and Employment

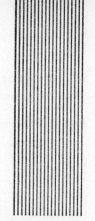

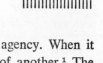

Chapter 17

Nature and Creation of Agency

One of the most common legal relationships is that of agency. When it exists, one person can act for and can stand in the place of another.[1] The law might have held that each man must act for himself and that no one could act through another. This would have greatly handicapped the development of the modern economic world, for it would have limited each man to what he himself could do. Today, by virtue of the agency device, one man can make contracts at a hundred different places at the same time.

NATURE OF THE AGENCY RELATIONSHIP

Agency is a relation based upon an express or implied agreement whereby one person, the *agent,* is authorized to act under the control of and for another, his *principal,* in business transactions with third persons.[2] The acts of the agent obligate the principal to third persons and give the principal rights against the third persons.

Agency is based upon the consent of the parties and, for that reason, it is called a consensual relation.[3] If consideration is present, the relationship is also contractual. The law sometimes imposes an agency relationship, one that is neither consensual nor contractual.

The term "agency" is frequently used with other meanings. It is sometimes used to denote the fact that one has the right to sell certain products, such as when a dealer is said to possess an automobile agency. In other instances, the term is used to mean an exclusive right to sell certain articles within a given territory. In these cases, however, the dealer is not an agent in the sense of representing the manufacturer. The right of the dealer under

---

[1] *King* v. *Young,* [Fla.] 107 So.2d 751.
[2] Restatement, Agency, 2d, Sec. 1; *Rule* v. *Jones,* 256 Wis. 102, 40 N.W.2d 580.
[3] *Valentine Oil Co.* v. *Powers,* 157 Neb. 87, 59 N.W.2d 160.

such arrangements is frequently represented by a *franchise* which he purchases from the manufacturer or supplier.

Agent Distinguished from Employee and Independent Contractor

An agent differs from an employee in that the ordinary employee is not hired to enter into contracts with third persons on behalf of the employer. It is possible, however, for the same person to be both an agent and an employee.[4] For example, the driver of a milk delivery truck is an agent in making contracts between the milk company and its customers, but he is only an employee with respect to the work of delivering the milk.

An agent or employee differs from an *independent contractor* in that the principal or employer has control over and can direct an agent or an employee, but the other party to the contract does not have control over the performance of the work by an independent contractor.[5]

Facts: Nichols contracted for dancing lessons with an Arthur Murray dance studio. When the lessons were never furnished, she sued Arthur Murray, Inc. It defended on the ground that her contract had been made with the local dance studio and that Murray was not liable for the contracts of the local studio as it merely gave the studio a license to use the name and methods of Arthur Murray. The agreement between Arthur Murray, Inc., as licensor, and the local studio stated that all contracts executed by the studio were the latter's obligations and the licensor would not be liable therefor, and that the local studio could not make any contracts in the name of the licensor. It was shown, however, that day-to-day operations of the local studio were controlled by the licensor; including such matters as hiring of employees, the fixing of tuition rates, the financing of student contracts, and the handling of claims for and against the local studio.

Decision: The control exercised by the licensor over the local studio made the latter its agent. Although agency is based on consent, the provision of the agreement with the local studio as to the nonliability of the licensor and the lack of authority of the licensee to make a contract binding the licensor only determined the rights as between the studio and the licensor. It could not determine the rights of third persons who were not parties thereto. As to third persons, the licensor exercised extensive control over the studio, which therefore was its agent, and the licensor was bound by the contract made by the local studio. (Nichols v. Arthur Murray, Inc., [Cal.App.2d] 56 Cal.Rptr. 728)

The fact that the person contracting with a contractor reserves the right to inspect the work or that the owner's architect has the right to require the redoing of work that does not meet contract specifications does not give

---

[4] In business practice, all employed persons, regardless of the nature of the work performed or the services rendered, are considered as employees.

[5] *Jenkins* v. *AAA Heating and Cooling, Inc.*, [Ore.] 421 P.2d 971.

such control over the independent contractor as to make him merely an employee. That is, the reservation of power to determine and ensure compliance with the terms of the contract does not constitute control of how the work is to be done.[6]

Purpose of Agency

Usually an agency may be created to perform any act which the principal himself could lawfully do.[7] The object of the agency may not be criminal, nor may it be contrary to public policy. Thus the courts will not enforce an agency contract by which one person is employed as a marriage broker.[8]

In addition, some acts must be performed by a person himself and cannot be entrusted or delegated to an agent. Voting, swearing to the truth of documents, testifying in court, and making a will are instances where personal action is required. In the preparation of papers, however, it is perfectly proper to employ someone else to prepare the paper which is then signed or sworn to by the employing party.

Who May Be a Principal

Any person, if he is competent to act for himself, may act through an agent. An appointment of an agent by a person lacking capacity is generally regarded as void or voidable to the same extent that a contract made by such person would be.

Groups of persons may also appoint agents to act for them. For example, three men, having formed a partnership, may employ an agent to act for them in the business transactions of the firm. Certain groups of persons, on account of the nature of the organization, must act through agents. Thus a group of persons organized as a corporation can only make a contract through an agent since the corporation is not a living person.[9]

Who May Be an Agent

Since a contract made by an agent is in law the contract of the principal, it is immaterial whether or not the agent has legal capacity to make a contract for himself.[10] It is permissible to employ as agents aliens, minors, and others who are under a natural or legal disability. While ordinarily an agent is one person acting for another, an agent may be a group of persons, such as a partnership or a corporation.

---

[6] *Lipka* v. *United States,* [C.A.2d] 369 F.2d 288.

[7] *Jefferson Standard Life Ins. Co.* v. *Guilford County,* 226 N.C. 441, 38 S.E.2d 519.

[8] *Comm.* v. *Farmers' & Shippers' Tobacco Warehouse Co.,* 107 Ky. 1, 52 S.W.2d 799.

[9] *Kiel* v. *Frank Shoe Mfg. Co.,* 245 Wis. 292, 14 N.W.2d 164.

[10] R. 2d, Sec. 21(1).

In certain instances, the law imposes limitations upon the right to act as an agent. In order to protect the public from loss at the hands of dishonest or untrained "agents," it is common for statutes to provide that a person must obtain a license from an appropriate government agency or bureau before he can act as an auctioneer, a real-estate agent, or a broker.

Classification of Agents

Agents are usually classified in terms of the extent of the business to be transacted by them as (1) special, (2) general, and (3) universal.

1 / Special agents. A *special agent* is authorized by the principal to transact a definite business affair or to do a specific act. One who is authorized by another to purchase a particular house for him is a special agent.

2 / General agents. A *general agent* is authorized by the principal to transact all of his affairs in connection with a particular kind of business or trade, or to transact all of his business at a certain place.[11] To illustrate, a person who is appointed as manager of a store is a general agent.

In some instances, an agent is described as a local agent. It is then necessary to determine whether this describes a general agent whose area of operation is limited to the particular locality,[12] or whether the term refers to an agent with limited authority, such as a soliciting agent of an insurance company.

3 / Universal agents. A *universal agent* is authorized by the principal to do all acts that can be delegated lawfully to representatives. This form of agency arises, for example, when a person in the military service gives another person a "blanket" power of attorney to do anything that has to be done while he is in the service.

Agency Coupled with an Interest

An *agency coupled with an interest* exists when the agent has (1) an interest in the authority granted to him, or (2) an interest in the subject matter of the agency.

1 / Interest in the authority. An agent has an *interest in the authority* when he has given a consideration or has paid for the right to exercise the authority granted to him. To illustrate: when a lender is given as security authority to collect rents due to the borrower and to apply those rents to the payment of the debt owed him, the lender becomes the borrower's agent with an interest in the authority given him to collect the rents.[13]

---

[11] *State* v. *Rooney,* [Mo.] 406 S.W.2d 1.
[12] *Calhoun* v. *Eaves,* 114 Ga.App. 756, 152 S.E.2d 805.
[13] *Halloran-Judge Trust Co.* v. *Heath,* 70 Utah 124, 258 P. 342.

2 / Interest in the subject matter. An agent has an *interest in the subject matter* when for a consideration he is given an interest in the property with which he is dealing. Hence, when the agent is authorized to sell certain property of the principal and is given a lien on such property as security for a debt owed to him by the principal, the agent has an interest in the subject matter.[14]

CREATING THE AGENCY

An agency may be created in any one of the following four ways: authorization by appointment, authorization by principal's conduct, ratification, and operation of law.

Authorization by Appointment

The usual method of creating an agency is by express authorization, that is, a person is appointed to act for and on behalf of another.

No particular form of language is necessary for the appointment of an agent. It is sufficient that the words used indicate that one person wishes another to represent him. The mere fact that a person is described as an "agent," however, does not establish that he is an agent or define the extent of his authority.

In most instances the authorization of the agent may be oral.[15] Some appointments, however, must be made in a particular way. Many states, by statute, require the appointment of an agent to be in writing when the agency is created to acquire or dispose of any interest in land.[16] In a few states the appointment must be in writing when the agent is authorized to make any written contract for the principal. The Statute of Frauds has the effect of requiring that a contract creating the authority of the agent be in writing when the relationship will necessarily exist for a period beyond one year from the date of the contract or is to start later than one year from that date. A written authorization of agency is commonly called a *power of attorney*.

At common law, authority to execute an instrument under seal, such as a bond, could be conferred only by a writing of the same formality.[17] This doctrine is still followed in a number of common-law states.

Authorization by Principal's Conduct

1 / Principal's conduct as to agent. Since agency is created by the consent of the parties, any conduct, including words, that gives the agent

---

[14] *Cleveland* v. *Bateman*, 21 N.Mex. 675, 158 P. 648.

[15] R. 2d, Sec. 26; *Rowan* v. *Hull*, 55 W.Va. 335, 47 S.E. 92.

[16] *Heinrich* v. *Martin*, [N.D.] 134 N.W.2d 786.

[17] R. 2d, Sec. 28(1). The early common-law doctrine that required a sealed authorization for an agent of a corporation has been abandoned by most courts.

reason to believe that the principal consents to his acting as agent is sufficient to create an agency.[18] If one person, knowingly and without objection, permits another to act as his agent, the law will find in his conduct an expression of authorization to the agent, and the principal will not be permitted to deny that the agent was in fact authorized.[19] Thus, if the owner of a hotel allows another person to assume the duties of hotel clerk, that person may infer from the owner's conduct that he has authority to act as the hotel clerk.

2 / Principal's conduct as to third persons. In addition to conduct or dealings with the agent which cause him as a reasonable man to believe that he has authority, the principal may have such dealing with third persons as to cause them to believe that the "agent" has authority.[20] Thus, if the owner of a store places another person in charge, third persons may assume that the person in charge is the agent for the owner in that respect. When this occurs, it is said that the agent has *apparent authority* because he appears to be the agent, and the principal is estopped or prevented from contradicting the appearance that he has created.[21]

> Facts: Walker owned a trailer that he wished to sell. He took it to the business premises of Pacific Mobile Homes. The only person on the premises at that time and several other times when Walker was there was a Stewart who identified himself as a salesman of Pacific and who agreed to take possession of Walker's trailer and to attempt to sell it for him. Stewart made out some forms of Pacific Mobile Homes and thereafter wrote some letters to Walker on the letterhead of Pacific. Walker's trailer was sold, but the salesman disappeared with most of the money. Walker sued Pacific for the proceeds of the sale. It denied liability on the ground that Stewart lacked authority to make any sales agreement and that all salesmen of Pacific were expressly forbidden to take used trailers to try to sell them for their owners.

> Decision: Judgment for Walker. In view of Stewart's frequent presence on the premises and his use of the letterhead of Pacific Mobile Homes, it was reasonable to believe that Stewart had the authority which Walker believed he had. As this was made possible by the conduct of Pacific in allowing Stewart on the premises in the manner described and in allowing him to have access to their letterhead, Pacific was barred from asserting that Stewart lacked the authority which he appeared to have. (Walker v. Pacific Mobile Homes, 68 Wash.2d 347, 413 P.2d 3)

The term "apparent authority" is used only when there is merely the appearance of authority but it in fact does not exist, and it is essential that the

---

18 *Silver* v. *Com. Tr. Co.,* 22 N.J.S. 604, 92 A.2d 152.
19 R. 2d, Sec. 26.
20 *Houtz* v. *General Bonding & Insurance Co.,* [C.A.10th] 235 F.2d 591.
21 *T. S. McShane Co.* v. *Great Lakes Pipe Line Co.,* 156 Neb. 766, 57 N.W.2d 778.

appearance of authority of the agent be due to the acts of the principal.[22] This apparent authority extends to all acts that a person of ordinary prudence, familiar with business usages and the particular business, would be justified in assuming that the agent has authority to perform.[23]

It is also possible for a former agent who has acted in similar transactions to bind his former principal as to third persons who knew him as the agent of the principal if they have not been notified of the termination of the agency.[24]

The mere placing of property in the possession of another person does not give him either actual or apparent authority to sell the property.[25]

Agency by Ratification

An agent may attempt on behalf of the principal to do an act which he has not been authorized to do. Or a person who is not the agent of another may attempt to act as his agent. Ordinarily a person can ratify any unauthorized act done on his behalf which he could have authorized.[26] The effect is the same as though he had authorized the act in the first place.[27]

Initially, ratification is a question of intention. Just as in the case of authorization, where there is the question of whether or not the principal authorized the agent, so there is the question of whether or not the principal intended to approve or ratify the action of the agent. Ratification may thus be found in conduct indicating an intention to ratify, as well as in words.[28]

If the other requirements of ratification are satisfied, a principal ratifies an agent's acts when, with knowledge of the act, he accepts [29] or retains [30] the benefit of the act, or brings an action to enforce legal rights based upon the act or defends an action by asserting the existence of a right based on the unauthorized transaction, or fails to repudiate the agent's act within a reasonable time.[31]

Although ratification may frequently be accompanied by reliance by the third party, it is not necessary that there be such reliance to constitute ratification.[32]

---

22 *Lumber Mart Co.* v. *Buchanan,* [Wash.2d] 419 P.2d 1002.
23 *Berman* v. *Griggs,* 145 Maine 258, 75 A.2d 365.
24 See p. 252.
25 Although under UCC Sec. 2-403, if the entrustee deals in goods of that kind, he has the power but not the right to transfer title to a person buying in good faith in the ordinary course of business.
26 R. 2d, Sec. 84.
27 *Davison* v. *Farr,* [Mo.] 273 S.W.2d 500; *Justheim Petroleum Co.* v. *Hammond,* [C.A.10th] 227 F.2d 629.
28 R. 2d, Sec. 93.
29 *Ashland* v. *Lapiner Motor Co.,* 247 Iowa 596, 75 N.W.2d 357.
30 R. 2d, Sec. 99.
31 R. 2d, Sec. 94.
32 Ratification is a question of manifestation of intent of the principal rather than of estoppel because of the reliance by the third person. *Gillihan* v. *Morguelan,* 299 Ky. 671, 186 S.W.2d 807.

1 / Form of ratification. A ratification must generally meet the same requirements of form as a prior authorization. Ratification may accordingly be oral in most instances. If a writing is not required, ratification may be by conduct; and under certain circumstances it may even consist of failure to repudiate the contract when informed of it.[33] The receipt, acceptance, and deposit of a check by the principal with knowledge that it arises from an unauthorized transaction is a common illustration of ratification by conduct of the unauthorized transaction.[34]

2 / Conditions for ratification. In addition to the necessity of an intent to ratify, expressed in some instances with certain formality, the following conditions must be satisfied in order that the intention take effect as a ratification.

(a) The agent must have purported to act on behalf of the principal.[35] If the person without authority informed the other person that he was acting as agent for the principal, this requirement is satisfied. The requirement that the agent purport to act for the principal does not require, however, that he expressly say that he has authority to so act.[36]

(b) The principal must have been capable of authorizing the act both at the time of the act and at the time when he ratified.[37]

(c) A principal must ratify the entire act of the agent.

Facts: Carolina Equipment and Parts Co. sold a bulldozer and a tractor trailer to Anders under one contract. Anders wanted to return the bulldozer because it was not working properly. Manuel, the collection agent for Carolina, made an agreement with Anders to separate the contract so that the bulldozer could be returned and Anders would continue to pay for the tractor trailer, Anders giving a check payable to Carolina as part of this agreement in the amount of $496.02, "for (3) payments on truck and trailer." The amount of one payment under the original contract was $496. Stephenson, who was the home office man of Carolina above Manuel, refused to agree to the plan, but nevertheless had the check deposited in Carolina's account. Carolina then sued Anders for breach of the original contract, claiming that it was not bound by the substitute contract because Manuel had no authority to make such a contract.

Decision: Judgment for Anders. While Manuel lacked authority, the circumstances were such that a jury could reasonably find that Carolina, through Manuel's superior, had ratified the substitute contract. The check clearly indicated a condition to the submission of the check because

---

[33] When a writing or a sealed instrument is required for an authorization, the ratification must observe the same formality.

[34] *Timber Structures* v. *Chateau Royale Corp.,* 49 Ill.App.2d 343, 199 N.E.2d 623.

[35] *State ex rel. Olsen* v. *Sundling,* 128 Mont. 596, 281 P.2d 499.

[36] *Slater* v. *Berlin,* [Mun.App. Dist.Col.] 94 A.2d 38.

[37] R. 2d, Secs. 84, 86.

both the notation on the check and the amount pointed to the existence of a substitute contract. As the check was part of the substitute contract plan, the principal could not accept the check and reject the balance of the substitute contract plan since a principal must ratify all or reject all of an unauthorized contract. (Carolina Equipment and Parts Co. v. Anders, 265 N.C. 393, 144 S.E.2d 252)

(d) The principal must ratify the act before the third person withdraws.[38] If the third person brings an action against the agent because of lack of authority to make the contract, the bringing of the action is equivalent to a withdrawal that prevents the principal from thereafter ratifying the contract.[39]

(e) The act to be ratified must generally be legal.[40]

(f) The principal must have full knowledge of all material facts.[41] If the agent conceals a material fact, the ratification of the principal made in ignorance of such fact is not binding. Of course, there can be no ratification when the principal does not know of the making of the contract by his agent.

Facts: Kirk Reid Co. made a contract to install an air conditioning and heating system in a building owned by Fine. Construction work was under the "general supervision" of Oliver and Smith, architects, and Hart, an independent engineer. The contract of Fine with the architects and engineer expressly stated that they were to supervise construction and could only authorize minor changes in the construction contract. Because of difficulties encountered in the performance of the contract, they agreed with Kirk to certain major changes in the construction plans which increased the cost of performance. When Kirk demanded payment from Fine of this additional amount, Fine refused to pay on the ground that as no one had authority to modify the original contract, Kirk was not entitled to any additional payment.

Decision: Fine was not liable for the additional expense. He had not authorized the major contract changes which necessitated the additional expense and, as he did not have any knowledge of the changes that had been made, he could not be deemed to have ratified them. (Kirk Reid Co. v. Fine, 205 Va. 778, 139 S.E.2d 829)

It is not always necessary, however, to show that the principal had actual knowledge; for knowledge will be imputed to him if he knows of such other facts as would put a prudent man on inquiry, or if that knowledge will be inferred from the knowledge of other facts or from a course of business.[42] Knowledge is likewise not an essential factor when the principal

---

[38] *LaSalle National Bank* v. *Brodsky,* 51 Ill.App.2d 260, 201 N.E.2d 208.
[39] R. 2d, Sec. 88, Comment (a) and Illustration (4).
[40] Sec. 86.
[41] *Pacific Trading Co.* v. *Sun Ins. Office,* 140 Ore. 314, 13 P.2d 616.
[42] *Van Tassell* v. *Lewis,* 118 Utah 356, 222 P.2d 350.

has indicated that he does not care to know the details and is willing to be bound by the contract regardless of his absence of knowledge.[43]

3 / Circumstances not affecting ratification. Ratification is not affected by the fact (a) that the third person has not agreed again to the transaction after it has been ratified; (b) that the principal first repudiated but then changed his mind and ratified the transaction, provided the third party had not withdrawn prior to the ratification; (c) that the agent would be liable to the third person for breach of warranty of his authority or misrepresentation if the principal were not bound; (d) that the agent or the third person knew the agent was unauthorized; (e) that the agent died or lost capacity prior to the ratification; or (f) that the principal did not communicate his ratifying intent to anyone.[44]

Although communication by the principal of his ratification is not essential, it may as a practical matter be necessary; for in the absence of some communication there may not be any evidence from which it can be found that the principal did have the intent to ratify.

4 / Effect of unratified contract. If an unauthorized contract is not or cannot be ratified, there is no contract between the principal and the third party. In some instances the fact that a contract made by an unauthorized agent and a third person cannot be ratified will not prevent the principal from enforcing the contract. Thus, in some instances the "agent" may assign his contract rights with the third person to the principal even though the principal might not be able to ratify the contract at that time.

Agency by Operation of Law

In certain instances the courts, influenced by necessity or social desirability, create or find an agency when there is none. For example, a wife may purchase necessaries and charge them to her husband's account when he does not supply them. Here the social policy is the furtherance of the welfare of the neglected wife.

Facts: Amplo sued Joseph Di Mauro for the cost of necessaries supplied by her to Joseph's wife. Joseph defended on the ground that he and his wife had separated and that he had published a notice in a newspaper that he would not be responsible for her debts.

Decision: Judgment for Amplo. A husband is liable for necessaries for his wife and cannot avoid this liability or prevent her from obtaining them on his credit by publishing a disclaimer of responsibility in a newspaper. (Amplo v. Di Mauro, 52 Misc.2d 810, 276 N.Y.S.2d 817)

---

[43] *City National Bank & Trust Co.* v. *Finch*, 205 Okla. 340, 237 P.2d 869.
[44] R. 2d, Sec. 92.

No agency relationship arises by virtue of marriage,[45] nor does it arise by virtue of the co-ownership of property of husband and wife.

As another example of agency by operation of law, a minor may purchase necessaries upon the credit of his father when the latter fails to supply them.

Facts: Watkins was divorced and custody of his young daughter was granted to him. Watkins sent her to a dentist, Dr. Burrell. On days on which the child was visiting her mother, the mother sent her to another dentist, Dr. Fuller. The latter's bill was not paid, and he assigned it to the Medical & Dental Finance Bureau, which then sued the father for the dentist bill, on the ground that it was a necessary.

Decision: Judgment for Watkins. The fact that the dentistry work was a necessary did not impose liability on the father unless he had neglected to provide for such work. As he had so provided and the mother had chosen to have a different dentist, the situation was not that of an abandoning father and an agency would not arise by operation of law. (Watkins v. Medical & Dental Finance Bureau, 101 Ariz. 580, 422 P.2d 696)

An emergency power of an agent to act under unusual circumstances not covered by his authority is recognized when the agent is unable to communicate with the principal and failure to act will cause the principal substantial loss.[46]

Proving the Agency Relationship

The burden of proving the existence of an agency relationship rests upon the person who seeks to benefit by such proof.[47] In the absence of sufficient proof, the jury must find that there is no agency. If the principal sues the third person, the principal must show that the one who dealt with the third person was in law the agent of the principal. If the third person sues the principal on a contract which the former negotiated with the agent, the third person must establish the agency relationship. If a defendant, when sued for the nonpayment of a debt, defends on the ground that he paid another person who was the agent of the plaintiff to receive payment, the defendant must prove the existence of the agency.

The existence of an agency cannot be established by the statements or admissions of the alleged agent alone.[48] The fact that the latter told the third person that such relationship existed cannot be shown in evidence to establish that the person so stating was the agent of the principal.[49] The person purporting to act as agent, however, may testify that on a certain day the

---

[45] *Morgart's Estate*, 27 App.Div.2d 856, 279 N.Y.S.2d 546.
[46] R. 2d, Sec. 47.
[47] *Cue Oil Co.* v. *Fornea Oil Co.*, 208 Miss. 810, 45 So.2d 597.
[48] *Aerovias Panama* v. *Air Carrier Engine Service*, [Fla.] 195 So.2d 230.
[49] *Holbeck* v. *Illinois Bankers Life Assurance Co.*, 318 Ill.App. 296, 47 N.E.2d 721.

principal gave him certain instructions and that in following those instructions he made a contract with a third person. This is testifying to the facts from which the court may conclude there was an authorization.[50]

QUESTIONS AND PROBLEMS

1. Checklist of legal terms:
   (a) agency (211); agent (211), principal (211)
   (b) independent contractor (212)
   (c) special agent, general agent, universal agent (214)
   (d) agency coupled with an interest (214); interest in the authority (214), interest in the subject matter (215)
   (e) power of attorney (215)
   (f) apparent authority (216)

2. State the objective(s) of each of the following rules of law:
   (a) A person is bound by the acts of one who has apparent authority to act as his agent.
   (b) The burden of proving the existence of an agency relationship rests upon the person who seeks to benefit by such proof.

3. Knox, a dealer in farm equipment, identifies his business as the "Holmes Farm Machinery Agency" on his letterhead. Does this mean that Knox is an agent of the manufacturer of Holmes tractors?

4. The Scott Coal Company shipped several carloads of coal to its agent, Vogel. Thornton was employed by Vogel to unload the cars. Was Thornton an agent?

5. O'Hara falsely represented himself to be the agent of Purdy for the purpose of selling a set of golf clubs. Rust agreed with O'Hara to purchase the clubs. Purdy knew about the transaction but did not object at the time. Later Purdy refused to sell. When sued by Rust for breach of contract, Purdy contended that he was not bound by the agreement because O'Hara had no authority to act as his agent. Do you agree?

6. Wingate, without authority, purchases an oriental rug for Zanders because he thinks Zanders would like to own it. Some time later Zanders learns of the transaction. What are Zanders' rights and liabilities?

7. On August 7 Foley ratifies an unauthorized oral agreement made by De Roo as his agent. The contract was made by De Roo on February 7 and called for the delivery of construction material on April 15 of the following year. Foley sues for breach of contract. The defense is that the agreement is not in writing as required by law in the case of agreements not to be performed within a year. Is Foley entitled to recover?

8. Armstrong agreed to make a purchase for himself from Barlow. Later Armstrong told Corey that he would be unable to carry out his agree-

---

[50] *Benham* v. *Selected Inv. Corp.*, [Okla.] 313 P.2d 489.

ment with Barlow. Corey informed Barlow that he ratified the act of Armstrong. Now Corey seeks to enforce the agreement. What are his rights?

9. Meade, without authority, sells farm produce as the agent of Levenson and warrants that the produce that he delivers is fresh. Levenson wishes to ratify the sale but not the warranty. May he do so?

10. Klotter, who sold a musical instrument to Minter, sues for the purchase price. Minter claims that he paid Long, the agent of Klotter. Who must prove the agency?

11. Hart sues Gleason on a contract. It is alleged that the agreement was executed by Justice. To prove the agency, a statement made by Justice that he was an agent of Gleason is introduced. Is his statement admissible?

12. Fishbaugh employed Scheibenberger to run a farm for him. Scheibenberger was authorized to rent the farm, to collect the rent, to superintend and direct repairs, and to allow the tenant to sell corn for the payment of taxes and fencing. The agent leased the farm to Hinsley, who sold certain crops to Spunaugle. Fishbaugh sued Spunaugle for the value of these crops. The decision turned on whether Scheibenberger was a general agent. What is your opinion? (Fishbaugh v. Spunaugle, 118 Iowa 337, 92 N.W. 58)

13. Markley sued the Western Union Telegraph Company for damages for delay in delivering a telegram. The company defended on the ground that the plaintiff had not given the company notice within the period of time required by the contract to send the telegraph message. The plaintiff claimed that he had given such notice to Clement who was in charge of the Western Union Telegraph Office. The company objected that there was no proof that Clement was the agent of the company authorized to receive such notice. Decide. (Markley v. Western Union Telegraph Co., 144 Iowa 105, 122 N.W. 136)

14. Barta executed a contract with the Manning-Winthrop Corp., a general contractor, for the construction of a house on a cost plus basis. The contractor sublet the installation of glass work to Goldberg. The contractor did not pay the subcontractor who then sued Barta, claiming that the contractor was Barta's agent. Decide. (Goldberg v. Barta, [Mun. Ct.App. D.C.] 109 A.2d 779)

Chapter 18

Principal and Agent

The agency relationship raises certain basic questions. What authority does the agent have? What are the duties and liabilities of the principal and agent to each other?

AGENT'S AUTHORITY

Scope of Agent's Authority

The authority of an agent includes that which is (1) expressly given by the principal; (2) incidental to the authority that is expressly given by the principal; and (3) customary for such an agent to exercise. In addition, an agent may have (4) apparent authority.

1 / Express authority. If the principal tells the agent to perform a certain act, the agent has *express authority* to do so. Express authority can be indicated by conduct as well as by words.[1] Accordingly, when the agent informs the principal of the intended plans but the principal makes no objection to them, authorization may be implied from such silence.[2]

2 / Incidental authority. In addition to his express authority,[3] an agent has *incidental authority* to perform any act reasonably necessary to execute the express authority given to him.[4] To illustrate, if the principal authorizes the agent to purchase goods without furnishing funds to the agent to pay for them, the agent has implied incidental authority to purchase the goods on credit.

3 / Customary authority. An agent has *customary authority* to do any act which, according to the custom of the community, usually accompanies the transaction for which he is authorized to act as agent.[5] For example, an agent who has authority to receive payments from third persons has authority to give a receipt, since it is customary to give a receipt when payment is made.[6]

---

[1] Compare the classification of contracts into express and implied. See p. 69.
[2] *Boise Payette Lumber Co.* v. *Larsen,* [C.A.9th] 214 F.2d 373.
[3] Incidental and customary authority are forms of implied authority.
[4] Restatement, Agency, 2d, Sec. 35.
[5] R. 2d, Sec. 36.
[6] *Degen* v. *Acme Brick Co.,* 228 Ark. 1054, 312 S.W.2d 194.

An agent with authority to receive checks in payment does not have implied authority to cash them.[7] Authorization to a lawyer to settle a client's claim does not authorize the lawyer to indorse the client's name on a check given in settlement of the claim.[8]

An agent does not have customary or incidental power to release debts owed his principal or to settle disputed amounts of debts for smaller sums, even though he is designated as the "field representative" of the principal. Thus a bank is not bound by an agreement made by its field representative with the owner of a financed automobile that if the owner surrenders the automobile to the representative, the balance of the owner's debt to the bank will be forgiven.[9]

4 / Apparent authority. As already noted,[10] a person has apparent authority as an agent when the principal by his words or conduct reasonably leads a third party to believe that such a person has that authority.

Duty to Ascertain Extent of Agent's Authority

A third person who deals with a person claiming to be an agent cannot rely on the statements made by the agent concerning the extent of his authority. If the agent is not authorized to perform the act involved or is not even the agent of the principal, the transaction between the alleged agent and the third person will have no legal effect between the principal and the third person.

Facts: Laird received an advertisement from an insurance company and mailed the enclosed reply postcard to the company. Whatley then called at Laird's home with the reply card and took Laird's application for insurance with the company. Whatley agreed that the policy would cover all hospital bills without limit. Laird later received the policy but did not read it. The policy contained a maximum limitation on the hospital bills covered. Laird later sued the company for hospital bills in excess of the maximum on the basis that its agent had agreed that the policy was not limited.

Decision: Judgment for the company. Whatley was an agent merely to take the application of Laird. Laird had no reason to believe that the agent had any greater authority than to take his application; that is, the agent was not clothed with authority to make a contract or agreement as to the terms of the insurance coverage. Accordingly, the insurer was not bound by the oral agreement between the agent and Laird. (American National Insurance Co. v. Laird, 228 Ark. 812, 311 S.W.2d 313)

---

[7] *Merchants' & Manufacturers' Assn.* v. *First National Bank,* 40 Ariz. 531, 14 P.2d 717.

[8] *Zidek* v. *Forbes National Bank,* 159 Pa.Super. 442, 48 A.2d 103.

[9] *Peoples First National Bank & Trust Co.* v. *Gaudelli,* 177 Pa.Super. 212, 110 A.2d 900.

[10] See p. 216.

The only certain way that the third person can protect himself is to inquire of the principal whether the agent is in fact the agent of the principal and has the necessary authority. If the principal states that the agent has the authority, the principal cannot later deny this authorization unless the subject matter is such that an authorization must be in writing in order to be binding.[11]

1 / Authority dependent on an event. If the authority of an agent is contingent upon the happening of some event, one may not ordinarily rely upon the statement of the agent as to the happening of that event. Thus, when an agent is authorized to sell for his principal a given quantity of oranges only in the event of the arrival of a specified ship, one dealing with the agent should ascertain for himself whether the ship has arrived and should not rely on the agent's statement that it has.

An exception to this rule is made in cases in which the happening of the event is peculiarly within the knowledge of the agent and cannot easily, if at all, be ascertained by the party dealing with the agent. As an illustration, if the agent of a railroad issues a bill of lading for goods without actually receiving the goods, the principal is held liable to one who accepts the bill in good faith and for value. This exception [12] is justified because, although the authority of the agent to issue bills of lading is dependent upon receiving the goods, persons taking bills of lading have no way of ascertaining whether the agent did receive the goods.

2 / Agent's acts adverse to principal. The third party who deals with an agent is also required to take notice of any acts that are clearly adverse to the interest of the principal. Thus, if the agent is obviously making use of funds of the principal for his own benefit, the person dealing with the agent acts at his own peril.[13]

Limitations on Agent's Authority

A person who has knowledge of a limitation on an agent's authority cannot disregard such limitation. If the authority of the agent is based on a writing and the third person knows that there is such a writing, he is charged with knowledge of the limitations contained in it.

If the principal has clothed his agent with authority to perform certain acts but the principal has given him secret instructions which limit his authority, the third person is allowed to take the authority of the agent at its face value and is not bound by the secret limitations of which he has no knowledge.

---

[11] *Litchfield* v. *Green,* 43 Ariz. 509, 33 P.2d 290.
[12] Uniform Commercial Code Sec. 7-301.
[13] *Central West Casualty Co.* v. *Stewart,* 248 Ky. 137, 58 S.W.2d 366.

Delegation of Authority by Agent

As a general rule, an agent cannot delegate his authority to another.[14] In other words, unless the principal expressly or impliedly consents, an agent cannot appoint *subagents* to carry out his duties.[15] The reason for this rule is that since an agent is usually selected in reliance upon some personal qualifications, it would be unfair and possibly injurious to the principal if the authority to act could be shifted by the agent to another. This is particularly true when the agent was originally appointed for the performance of a task requiring discretion or judgment. For example, an agent who is appointed to adjust claims against an insurance company cannot delegate the performance of his duties to another.

An agent, however, may authorize another to perform his work for him in the following instances:

(1) When the acts to be done involve only mechanical or ministerial duties. Thus, an agent to make application for hail insurance on wheat may delegate to another the clerical act of writing the application.

(2) When a well-known custom justifies such appointment. To illustrate, if one is authorized to buy or sell a grain elevator, he may do so through a broker when that is the customary method.

(3) When the appointment is justified by necessity or sudden emergency and it is impractical to communicate with the principal, and such appointment of a subagent is reasonably necessary for the protection of the interests of the principal entrusted to the agent.[16] For instance, an agent to collect tolls, who is in charge of a bridge, may appoint another to collect tolls in his place when he is required to be on the bridge making repairs.[17]

(4) When it was contemplated by the parties that subagents would be employed. For example, a bank may now generally use subagents to receive payment of notes that have been left for collection since the parties contemplated that this would be done.

DUTIES AND LIABILITIES OF PRINCIPAL AND AGENT

The creation of the principal-agent relationship gives rise not only to powers but also to duties.

Duties and Liabilities of Agent to Principal

The agent owes to the principal the duties of (1) loyalty, (2) obedience and performance, (3) reasonable care, (4) accounting, and (5) information.

---

[14] R. 2d, Sec. 18; *Knudsen* v. *Torrington Co.,* [C.A.2d] 254 F.2d 283.
[15] *Bourg* v. *Hebert,* 224 La. 535, 70 So.2d 116.
[16] *Magenau* v. *Aetna Freight Lines,* [C.A.3d] 257 F.2d 445.
[17] *Ada-Konawa Bridge Co.* v. *Cargo,* 163 Okla. 122, 21 P.2d 1.

1 / Loyalty. An agent must be loyal or faithful to his principal. He must not obtain any secret profit or advantage from his relationship.[18] To illustrate, if an agent knows that his employer is negotiating for a lease and secretly obtains the lease for himself, the court will compel the agent to surrender the lease to the principal.

Similarly, if a broker is retained to purchase certain property, the broker cannot purchase the property for himself either in his own name or in the name of his wife.[19] Likewise, an agent cannot purchase property of the principal, which the agent was hired to sell, without the principal's express consent.[20] Similarly, an agent's wife cannot purchase in her own name property of the principal which the agent was hired to sell.

If the agent owns property, he cannot purchase it from himself on behalf of his principal without disclosing to the principal his interest in the transaction. If he fails to disclose his interest, the principal may avoid the transaction even if he was not financially harmed by the agent's conduct. Or the principal can approve the transaction and sue the agent for any profit realized by the agent.

An agent cannot act as agent for both parties to a transaction unless both know of the dual capacity and agree to it. If he does so act without the consent of both parties, the transaction is voidable at the election of any principal who did not know of the agent's status.

An agent must not accept secret gifts or commissions from third persons in connection with his activities as agent. If he does, the principal may sue him for those gifts or commissions. Such practices are condemned because the judgment of the agent may be influenced by the receipt of gifts or commissions. A principal may also recover from his agent any secret profit that the latter has made in violation of his duty of loyalty to his principal. If an agent makes a false report to the principal in order to conceal the agent's interest, the principal is entitled to recover not only the secret profit made and property acquired by the agent but may also be awarded punitive damages by way of punishing and discouraging such wrongdoing.[21]

Facts: Kribbs owned real estate that had been rented through his agent, Jackson, at a monthly rental of $275. When this lease terminated, Jackson and a third person, Solomon, made an agreement that if the latter obtained a new tenant for a rental of $500 a month, Jackson would pay Solomon $100 a month. The latter obtained a new tenant who paid a monthly rental of $550. Jackson continued to send Kribbs $275 a month, less his commissions and janitor and utility costs; paid Solomon $100 a month; and kept the balance of the rental for himself.

---

18 *Doner* v. *Phoenix Joint Stock Land Bank,* 381 Ill. 106, 45 N.E.2d 20.
19 *Gerhardt* v. *Weiss,* [Cal.App.2d] 55 Cal.Rptr. 425.
20 *Kellett* v. *Boynton,* 87 Ga.App. 692, 75 S.E.2d 292.
21 *Bate* v. *Marsteller,* 232 Cal.App.2d 605, 43 Cal.Rptr. 149.

When Kribbs learned of these facts three years later, he sued Jackson for the money he had kept for himself and that which he had paid Solomon.

Decision: Judgment for Kribbs. An agent must account to his principal for all profits he has secretly made in an agency transaction and for all sums of money he improperly permitted third persons to receive in connection with such transactions. (Kribbs v. Jackson, 387 Pa. 611, 129 A.2d 490)

An agent is, of course, prohibited from aiding the competitors of his principal or disclosing to them information relating to the business of the principal.

2 / Obedience and performance. An agent is obligated to obey all lawful instructions given to him. He is required to perform the services specified for the period and in the way specified.[22] If he does not, he is liable to the principal for any harm caused him.[23] For example, if an agent, without authority to do so, releases one who is in debt under circumstances that the release is binding upon the principal, the agent is liable to the principal for the loss.

If an agent is instructed to take cash payments only but accepts a check in payment, he is liable for any loss caused by his act, such as that which arises when the check accepted by him is not collectible because it is forged.

If the agent violates his instructions, it is immaterial that he acts in good faith or intends to benefit the principal. It is the fact that he violates the instructions and thereby causes his principal a loss which imposes a liability on him. In determining whether the agent has obeyed his instructions, they must be interpreted in the way that a reasonable man would interpret them.[24]

3 / Reasonable care. It is the duty of an agent to act with the care that a reasonable man would exercise under the circumstances. In addition, if the agent possesses a special skill, as in the case of a broker or an attorney, he must exercise that skill.

Facts: Roumel, who owned an apartment house, employed Robbins as manager to live in the building and among other things to collect rent from the tenants. Although banking facilities were available nearby for day and night deposits, Robbins kept rental money in an unlocked desk in her apartment in the building, to which desk tenants and workmen had frequent access. Rent money amounting to $200 collected by Robbins was left in her desk and was apparently stolen from it sometime between the 6th and the 22nd of the month. Roumel sued Robbins for $200.

---

[22] R. 2d, Sec. 383.
[23] *Missouri ex rel. Algiere* v. *Russell,* 359 Mo. 800, 223 S.W.2d 481.
[24] *Smith* v. *Union Savings & Loan Assn.,* 97 Col. 440, 50 P.2d 538.

Decision: Judgment for Roumel. The fact that the money was apparently stolen was not a defense because the agent had not exercised reasonable care. When banking facilities are reasonably available, an agent must deposit the principal's money in a bank. It was negligent to leave the money for an extended period in an unlocked desk, particularly when third persons had ready access to the desk. (Robbins v. Roumel, [Mun. C.A.Dist.Col.] 138 A.2d 922)

4 / Accounting. An agent must account to his principal for all property or money belonging to his principal that comes into the agent's possession.[25] The agent should, within a reasonable time, give notice of collections made and render an accurate account of all receipts and expenditures. The agency agreement may state, of course, at what intervals or on what dates accountings are to be made.

An agent should keep his principal's property and money separate and distinct from his own. If an agent mingles his property with the property of his principal so that the two cannot be identified or separated, the principal may claim all of the commingled mass. Furthermore, when funds of the principal and of the agent are mixed, any loss that occurs must be borne by the agent. For example, when the agent deposits the funds of the principal in a bank account in his own name, he is liable for the amount if the bank should fail.

5 / Information. It is the duty of an agent to keep the principal informed of all facts pertinent to the agency that may enable the principal to protect his interests.[26] In consequence, a principal's promise to pay a bonus to his agent for information secured by the agent in the performance of his duties is unenforceable on the ground that the principal was entitled to the information anyway. The promise is therefore not supported by consideration.

Duties and Liabilities of Principal to Agent

The principal is under certain duties to the agent. He must perform the contract, compensate the agent for his services, reimburse him for proper expenditures, and indemnify him for loss under certain circumstances.

1 / Employment for term of contract. The principal is under the duty to perform the agreement with his agent. This duty requires the principal to permit the agent to continue to act as such for the period, if any, provided by the contract of agency.

2 / Compensation. The principal must pay the agent the compensation agreed upon.

---

[25] R. 2d, Sec. 382.
[26] R. 2d, Sec. 381; *Spritz* v. *Brockton Sav. Bank,* 305 Mass. 170, 25 N.E.2d 155.

Facts: Hyland made a contract with the Oregon Hassam Paving Co. by which he was to receive a commission of 3 percent of all paving contracts awarded the company and in return for which he was to "at all times do everything in his power" to further the business of the company. Hyland sued the company for the commission on contracts awarded.

Decision: Judgment for the company. The court interpreted the contract as contemplating illegal as well as legal activity by Hyland. As such, the contract was contrary to public policy and the compensation could not be recovered. (Hyland v. Oregon Hassam Paving Co., 74 Ore. 1, 144 P. 1160)

If the parties have not fixed the amount of the compensation by their agreement but intended that the agent should be paid, the agent may recover the customary compensation for such services. If there is no established compensation, he may recover the reasonable value of his services.

When one requests another to perform services under circumstances that reasonably justify the expectation of being paid, a duty to make payment arises.[27] For example, when one requests an agent, as a broker or an attorney, to act in his professional capacity, it is implied that compensation is to be given.

When the agent is employed on the contingency that he is to be compensated only if he obtains or produces a specified result, the agent is not entitled to compensation or reimbursement if he does not achieve the desired result, regardless of how much time or money he has spent in the effort.[28] Likewise an agent is not entitled to compensation with respect to transactions canceled by third persons as long as the principal was not at fault. In any case an agent may agree to work without compensation; for it is authorization to act, and not compensation for acting, that is the test of agency.[29]

When agents are paid on a commission basis, it is commonly provided that they may draw up to a stated maximum per week or month as an advance against commissions. The question then arises as to the agent's obligation to return any of such advances when, as events develop, it is found that the advances exceed the commissions earned. Here it is held that the advances are to be treated as wages and that in the absence of an agreement so providing, there is no obligation to refund the "excess" to the principal.[30] In case of doubt, the contract is interpreted against the employer on the theory that it is unfair to make the agent bear all of the risk of loss when the principal stands to gain by the agent's activity if he is successful.

---

[27] R. 2d, Sec. 441.
[28] The agent is entitled to the compensation, however, when it was the act of the principal that prevented him from performing. See p. 197.
[29] *Leidy* v. *Taliaferro*, [Mo.] 260 S.W.2d 504.
[30] *Valoco Building Products* v. *Chafee*, 4 Conn.Cir. 322, 231 A.2d 101.

Facts: Badger was a salesman for Nu-Tone Products Co. The employment contract authorized Nu-Tone to deduct $10 a week from commissions paid Badger in order to maintain a $300 reserve fund against which could be charged advances of commissions in excess of actual commissions earned. The employment contract further provided that advance commissions "shall be a charge or setoff against any commissions due, or thereafter to become due," that they could be charged against the reserve fund and "shall be an obligation of [Badger to Nu-Tone] and shall in any event become due and payable within 90 days from the date of the advancement." Badger received advances in excess of earned commissions. Nu-Tone demanded the repayment of such excess.

Decision: Judgment for Badger. The fact that the agreement spoke of the excess as a "charge" or "setoff" indicated that a personal liability of Badger was not intended, which was confirmed by the fact that the contract provided a particular fund for its repayment. In view of the fact that any uncertainty is to be resolved in favor of the agent, the provision that the excess should be "an obligation" of the agent and "become due and payable" was to be interpreted as meaning that at the end of the 90 days it could be charged against the reserve fund in order to satisfy the obligation of the agent, but not as meaning that he was personally liable for repayment of the excess advances. (Badger v. Nu-Tone Products Co., [Colo.] 425 P.2d 698)

3 / Reimbursement. The principal is under a duty to reimburse the agent for all disbursements made at the request of the principal and for all expenses necessarily incurred in the lawful discharge of the agency for the benefit of the principal.[31] The agent cannot recover, however, for expenses caused by his own misconduct or negligence. By way of illustration, if the agent transfers title to the wrong person, he cannot recover from the principal the amount of expense incurred in correcting the error.

4 / Indemnity. It is the duty of the principal to indemnify the agent for any losses or damages suffered without his fault but occurring on account of the agency.[32] For example, when an agent was compelled by law to pay his own money because under the direction of his principal he, without knowing that they belonged to the third person rather than to the principal, had sold certain goods owned by a third person, he was entitled to recover the amount of such payment from his principal.

When the loss sustained is not the result of obedience to the principal's instructions but of the agent's misconduct, or of an obviously illegal act, the principal is not liable for indemnification.

---

[31] R. 2d, Sec. 439 (a), (b); *Differential Steel Car Co.* v. *MacDonald,* [C.A.6th] 180 F.2d 260.
[32] R. 2d, Sec. 439 (c), (d).

QUESTIONS AND PROBLEMS

1. Checklist of legal terms:

    (a) express authority, incidental authority, customary authority (224)
    (b) subagent (227)

2. State the objective(s) of each of the following rules of law:

    (a) A third person who deals with a person claiming to be an agent cannot rely on the statements made by the agent concerning the extent of his authority.
    (b) If the parties have not fixed the amount of the compensation by their agreement but have intended that the agent should be paid, the agent may recover the customary compensation for his services.

3. Kearns is authorized by Loth to purchase 50 head of cattle from McMillan. As no means of public transportation is available, Kearns hires an automobile to visit McMillan's ranch for the purpose of making the purchase. Loth refuses to pay the owner of the automobile for its use. Is he liable?

4. Graham, who is authorized to sell LaRosa's organ, makes a sale on credit to McCoy. LaRosa refuses to deliver the organ on the ground that Graham did not have authority to sell on credit. McCoy brings action for breach of contract against LaRosa and offers evidence to prove that sales on credit are in accordance with the recognized usages of the trade. Should this kind of evidence be admitted?

5. Maybury, claiming to be Addison's agent, was negotiating the sale of Addison's meat-cutting machine to Cooper. Cooper telephoned Addison who assured him that Maybury was Addison's agent. What other information should Cooper have before he enters into an agreement to purchase the machine?

6. Carnes is authorized to collect debts that are due Drew. Ferris pays Carnes an account due Drew after Carnes tells him that he plans to abscond with his collections. Drew sues Ferris for the amount of the debt. Is he entitled to judgment?

7. Edwards instructs his agent, Fox, to sell a table for $75, if possible, but for not less than $65. Fox agrees to sell the table to Greenwald for $70 in spite of the fact that Ingram was willing to pay $75 for it. When Edwards refuses to deliver the table, Greenwald brings an action for damages against Edwards. Is he entitled to judgment?

8. Hull gives his agent, Ewald, $25,000 to invest in bonds. Ewald purchases common stock instead of bonds. Hull sues Ewald for the money. Is the latter liable for this amount?

9. Garrett employed Jordon, a real estate broker, to sell certain property. Jordon sold the property at a price that Garrett believed to be too low. Garrett sued for damages. Jordon's defense was that he exercised the

care, skill, and diligence that is ordinarily exercised by a prudent man. Was this a valid defense?

10. As an agent for Kistner, McDonald received $500 from the sale of certain merchandise. He deposited this amount in his personal bank account. The bank failed, and Kistner sued McDonald for $500. What is your decision?

11. Hackett is authorized to sell Bolton's land for $300 an acre. While seeking a buyer, Hackett learns that the straightening of a main highway has enhanced the value of the land to $350 an acre. Without disclosing this fact to Bolton, Hackett sells the land for $300 an acre. Bolton sues Hackett for damages. Is he entitled to judgment?

12. Forrester, a real estate broker, is authorized to sell a house and lot for Dexter. Nothing is said about compensation. Forrester makes a charge of 10 percent of the sale price. The customary commission in that community is 6 percent. Is Dexter required to pay the amount charged by Forrester?

13. Hihn and Eastland, doing business in California, were authorized to sell certain land in Texas. They in turn employed Maney, of Texas, to sell the land. He made the sale and then sued them for the commissions due him on the sale. Did Hihn and Eastland have authority to employ Maney to make the sale? (Eastland v. Maney, 36 Tex.Civ.App. 147, 81 S.W. 574)

14. Regional Broadcasters of Michigan, Inc. owned and operated radio station WTRU. Moreschini supplied advertising material to WTRU under contract made with the station manager. When Moreschini sued Regional Broadcasters, it raised the defense that the manager had been instructed not to make any contracts on behalf of the station. Was Regional bound? (Moreschini v. Regional Broadcasters, 373 Mich. 496, 129 N.W.2d 859)

15. McKinney requested E. M. Christmas, a real estate broker, to sell McKinney's property. A sale to a purchaser was effected with the contract calling for monthly installment payments by the purchaser, which payments were to be collected by the broker. When the purchaser stopped making the payments, McKinney was not notified of that fact but one of the broker's employees bought out the purchaser's contract. The broker continued making payments to McKinney as though they were being made by the purchaser. Later Christmas, the broker, resold the land to another buyer at a substantial profit. McKinney sued Christmas for this profit. Decide. (McKinney v. Christmas, 143 Colo. 361, 353 P.2d 373)

Chapter 19

Third Persons

In agency transactions the third party has certain rights and liabilities as a result of the relationship with the agent with whom he deals directly and with the principal with whom he deals indirectly. The following discussion is organized in terms of the liabilities of the agent to the third party, the liabilities of the third party to the agent, the liabilities of the principal to the third party, and the liabilities of the third party to the principal. The liabilities of one party, of course, are the rights of the other.

Liabilities of Agent to Third Party

If an agent makes a contract with a third person on behalf of a disclosed principal and has proper authority to do so, and if the contract is executed properly, the agent has no personal liability on the contract. Whether the principal performs the contract or not, the agent cannot be held liable.[1] If the agent lacks authority, however, or if certain other circumstances exist, he may be liable.

1 / Unauthorized action. If a person purports to act as an agent for another but lacks authority to do so, the contract that he makes is not binding on the principal. His act may cause loss to the third person, however. The agent generally is responsible for this loss. When he purported to act as agent for the principal, he made an implied warranty that he had authority to do so.[2] Under this implied warranty it is immaterial that the agent acted in good faith or misunderstood the scope of his authority. The fact that he was not authorized imposes liability upon him,[3] unless the third person knew that the agent exceeded his authority.

An agent with a written authorization may protect himself from liability on the implied warranty of authority by showing the written authorization to the third person and permitting the third person to determine for himself the scope of the agent's authority. When the third person wrongly decides that the agent has certain authority, the agent has no liability.[4]

---

[1] Restatement, Agency, 2d, Sec. 320.
[2] *Darr Equipment Co.* v. *Owens*, [Tex.Civ.App.] 408 S.W.2d 566.
[3] *Moser* v. *Kyle Corp.*, 255 Wis. 634, 39 N.W.2d 587.
[4] *Fuller* v. *Melko*, 5 N.J. 554, 76 A.2d 683.

2 / No principal with capacity. When a person acts as an agent, he impliedly warrants that he has a principal and that the principal has legal capacity. If there is no principal or if the principal lacks legal authority, the agent is liable for any loss to the third person.

Facts: Bagen and others were planning to organize a corporation to operate a new restaurant by the name of Old Colony Inn. Bagen purchased restaurant equipment from Brown-Wright Hotel Supply Corp. and informed it to bill the Old Colony Inn and "the corporation operating Old Colony Inn." When the bill for this equipment was not paid, Brown-Wright sued Bagen.

Decision: Judgment for Brown-Wright. A person who assumes to act as agent for a nonexisting principal or one lacking legal capacity is personally liable on contracts made on behalf of such principal. The corporation was not in existence, and therefore Bagen did not have any existing principal. (Brown-Wright Hotel Supply Corp. v. Bagen, 112 Ga.App. 300, 145 S.E.2d 294)

3 / Undisclosed and partially disclosed principals. An agent becomes liable as a party to the contract, just as though he were acting for himself, when the third person is not told or does not know that the agent is acting for a principal, that is, when there is an *undisclosed principal.* The agent is also liable on the contract when the third person is told or knows only that the agent is acting as an agent but the identity of the principal is not known or stated, that is, when the principal is only partially disclosed.[5]

Facts: Brazilian & Colombian Co. ordered 40 barrels of olives from Mawer-Gulden-Annis, Inc., but did not disclose that it was acting for its principal, Pantry Queen, although this later become known. Mawer billed and later sued Brazilian for the payment of the contract price.

Decision: Judgment for Mawer. The purchaser, Brazilian, was liable on the purchase contract as it did not disclose (1) the fact that it was acting as an agent and (2) the identity of its principal. This conclusion is not altered by the circumstance that after the contract was made, such information was acquired by the third person. (Mawer-Gulden-Annis, Inc. v. Brazilian & Colombian Coffee Co., 49 Ill.App.2d 400, 199 N.E.2d 222)

4 / Wrongful receipt of money. If an agent obtains a payment of money from the third person by the use of illegal methods, the agent is liable to the third person.[6]

If the third person makes an overpayment to the agent or a payment when none is due, the agent is also usually liable to the third person for the

---

[5] *Special Sections, Inc.* v. *Rappaport,* 25 App.Div.2d 896, 269 N.Y.S.2d 319.
[6] R. 2d, Sec. 343.

amount of such overpayment or payment. If the agent has acted in good faith and does not know that the payment is improperly made, however, he is liable to the third person only so long as he still has the payment in his possession or control. If in such a case he has remitted the payment to the principal before the time the third person makes a demand upon him for its return, the agent is not liable.[7] In the latter case, the third person's right of action, if he has one, is only against the principal. But payment to the principal does not relieve the agent of liability when the agent knows that the payment was not proper.[8]

5 / Assumption of liability. An agent may intentionally make himself liable upon the contract with the third person. This situation frequently occurs when the agent is a well-established local brokerage house or other agency and the principal is located out of town and is not known locally.

6 / Execution of contract. If an agent executes a specialty (that is, a commercial paper, or a sealed instrument in those states in which a seal retains its common-law force) and does so in such a way that he appears to be a party to the instrument, he is bound and he cannot show that the parties did not intend this result. Because of the formal character of the writing, the liability of the parties is determined from the face of the instrument alone and it cannot be modified or contradicted by proof of intention or other matters not set forth in the writing.

If the contract is not a specialty, the parties may prove by other evidence that a different result than that apparent on the face of the writing was intended. Thus a simple contract that would appear to be the contract of the agent can by oral testimony, if believed, be shown to have been intended as a contract between the principal and the third party. If the intention is established, it will be permitted to contradict the face of the written contract, and the contract as thus modified will be enforced.

To avoid any question of interpretation, an agent should execute an instrument by signing either *"A. S. Simms, by William Orr,"* that is, "Principal, by Agent" or *"A. S. Simms, per William Orr,"* that is, "Principal, per Agent." Such a signing is in law a signing by *Simms,* and the agent is therefore not a party to the contract. The signing of the principal's name by an authorized agent without indicating the agent's name or identity is likewise in law the signature of the principal.

7 / Torts. An agent is liable for harm caused the third person by the agent's fraudulent, malicious, or negligent acts. The fact that he is acting

---

[7] *United States National Bank* v. *Stonebrink,* 200 Ore. 176, 265 P.2d 238.
[8] *Hirning* v. *Federal Reserve Bank,* [C.A.8th] 52 F.2d 382.

as an agent at the time or that he is acting in good faith under the directions of his principal does not relieve him of liability if his conduct would impose liability upon him if he were acting for himself.[9] The fact that he is following instructions does not shield him from liability any more than he would be excused from criminal liability if he committed a crime because the principal told him to do so.

> **Facts:** Stickney gave the Ogden and Clarkson Corp. full control of the sale, leasing, and management of a certain house and directed the corporation to make necessary repairs. It failed to do so and Mollino, passing on the street, was injured by the falling of a portion of the roof. He sued the corporation.

> **Decision:** Judgment for Mollino. When an agent is placed in control of property, he is liable to third persons who are injured under such circumstances that the agent would be liable if he had been the owner of the property. As the accident resulted from the negligence with respect to the management of the property, the corporation was liable whether it was an agent or not. (Mollino v. Ogden & Clarkson Corp., 243 N.Y. 450, 154 N.E. 307)

Liabilities of Third Party to Agent

Ordinarily the third party is not liable to the agent for a breach of a contract that the agent has made with the third person on behalf of a disclosed principal.[10] In certain instances, however, the third party may be liable to the agent.

1 / Undisclosed and partially disclosed principal. If the agent executed the contract without informing the third person or without the third party's knowing both of the existence of the agency and the identity of the principal, the agent may sue the third party for breach of contract.[11]

In such instances, if the contract was a simple contract, the principal may also sue the third person even though the third person thought that he was contracting only with the agent. The right of the principal to sue the third person is, of course, superior to the right of the agent to do so. If the contract was a specialty, the undisclosed principal, not appearing on the instrument as a party, could not bring an action to enforce the contract.

> **Facts:** Camp, acting as agent for an undisclosed principal, the Orange County Telephone Co., made a contract with Barber for running a telephone line over his land. Barber later violated his contract and was sued by Camp. Barber raised the defense that Camp could not sue in his own name.

---

[9] R. 2d, Sec. 343; *Dr. Salsbury's Laboratories* v. *Bell*, [Tex.Civ.App.] 386 S.W.2d 341.

[10] R. 2d, Sec. 363.

[11] Sec. 364; *Eppenauer* v. *Davis*, [Tex.Civ.App.] 272 S.W.2d 934.

Decision: Judgment for Camp. As the agent who does not disclose the fact of his
agency is necessarily the other party to the contract, he has the right
to sue on the contract, even though he is acting for the benefit of the
undisclosed principal. (Camp v. Barber, 87 Vt. 235, 88 A. 812)

2 / Agent intending to be bound. If the third person knew that the
agent was acting as an agent but nevertheless the parties intended that the
agent should be personally bound by the contract, the agent may sue the third
person for breach of contract. This is true, also, when by custom it is recognized that the agent should have the right to sue the third person.

3 / Execution of contract. The principles that determine when an agent
is liable to the third person because of the way in which he has executed a
written contract apply equally in determining when the third person is liable
to the agent because of the way in which the contract is executed. If the
agent could be sued by the third person, the third person can be sued by the
agent. Thus, if the agent executes a sealed instrument in his own name, he
alone can sue the third person on that instrument.

4 / Agent as transferee. The agent may sue the third person for breach
of the latter's obligation to the principal when the principal has assigned or
otherwise transferred his claim or right to the agent, whether absolutely for
the agent's own benefit or for the purpose of collecting the money and
remitting it to the principal.[12]

5 / Torts. The third party is liable in tort for fraudulent or other wrongful acts causing injury to the agent.[13] If the third party by slander or other
means wrongfully causes the principal to discharge the agent, the latter may
recover damages. The agent may also bring an action in tort against the
third person for wrongful injuries to his person or property. If the agent has
possession of the principal's property, he may sue any third person whose
acts injure that property.

Liabilities of Principal to Third Party

The principal is liable to the third person for the properly authorized and
executed contracts of his agent and, in certain circumstances, for his agent's
unauthorized contracts and torts as well.

1 / Agent's contracts. When there is a principal with contractual capacity who had authorized or ratified the agent's action and when the agent
properly executed the contract, a contract exists between the principal and
the third person on which each usually can be sued by the other in the event

---

[12] R. 2d, Sec. 365.
[13] Sec. 374.

of a breach. If the contract is a simple contract, the third person may sue the principal whether or not the principal had been disclosed.

> **Facts:** Fishbaugh, acting as agent for his father, made a contract to sell to Menveg land belonging to the father. Fishbaugh did not disclose his agency. Later the father refused to perform the contract made by the son. Menveg, learning of the father's identity as principal, sued him for specific performance.

> **Decision:** Judgment for Menveg. When an agent makes an authorized, simple contract on behalf of an undisclosed principal, the third person may sue the principal when he learns of his existence. (Menveg v. Fishbaugh, 123 Cal.App. 460, 11 P.2d 438)

The right to sue the undisclosed principal on a simple contract is subject to two limitations. First, the third person cannot sue the principal if in good faith the principal has settled his account with the agent with respect to the contract. In some states this exception is limited to those instances in which the conduct of the third person reasonably leads the principal to believe that the account between the agent and third person has been settled.[14]

As a second limitation, the third person cannot sue the principal if the third person has elected to hold the agent and not the principal.[15] In those jurisdictions which permit the third person to join the principal and agent as codefendants, the third party, although he may sue both in one action, must make his election at the end of the trial.[16]

This rule as to election does not apply when the principal is partially disclosed, for in that case the right of the third person is not to be regarded as alternatively against either the agent or the principal but as concurrent—that is, a right against both—and therefore the third person may recover a judgment against either without discharging the other.[17]

When the third person makes his payment to an authorized agent, such payment is deemed as made to the principal. The result is that the principal must give the third person full credit for such payment, even though in fact the agent never remits or delivers the payment to the principal, if the third person made the payment in good faith and had no reason to know that the agent would be guilty of such misconduct.[18]

---

[14] Sec. 208.

[15] R. 2d, Sec. 210(1); *Murphy* v. *Hutchinson*, 93 Miss. 643, 48 So. 178.

[16] R. 2d, Sec. 210A; *Hospelhorn* v. *Poe*, 174 Md. 242, 198 A. 582.

[17] R. 2d, Sec. 184. An exception would arise when the contract makes the obligation the joint obligation of the partially disclosed principal and the agent. In such case, under principles of contract law, a judgment against the one would discharge the liability of the other.

[18] This general rule of law is restated in some states by Sec. 2 of the Uniform Fiduciaries Act, which is expressly extended by Sec. 1 thereof to agents, partners, and corporate officers. Similar statutory provisions are found in a number of other states.

2 / Agent's statements. A principal is bound by a statement made by his agent while transacting business within the scope of his authority.[19] This means that the principal cannot thereafter contradict the statement of his agent and show that it is not true. Statements or declarations of an agent, in order to bind the principal, must be made at the time of performing the act to which they relate or shortly thereafter.

3 / Agent's knowledge. The principal is bound by knowledge or notice of any fact that is acquired by his agent while acting withing the scope of his authority.[20] Thus, an offer is effectively revoked when the fact of revocation is communicated by the offeror to the agent of the offeree having authority to act in connection with the transaction.[21] Conversely, if the subject matter is outside the scope of the agent's authority, the agent is under no duty to inform the principal of knowledge acquired by him. For example, when an agent is authorized and employed only to collect rents, his knowledge of the unsatisfactory condition of the premises is not imputed to the landlord-principal, since the reporting of such information is not part of the agent's collection duties.

The rule that the agent's knowledge is imputed to the principal is extended in some cases to knowledge gained prior to the creation of the agency relationship. The notice and knowledge must appear to be based on reliable information. Thus, when the agent hears only rumors of acts or facts, the principal is not charged with notice.[22]

The principal is not responsible for the knowledge of his agent, that is, he is not charged with having knowledge of what is known by his agent, under the following circumstances: (a) when the agent is under a duty to another principal to conceal his knowledge; (b) when the agent is acting adversely to his principal's interest; or (c) when the third party acts in collusion with the agent for the purpose of cheating the principal. In such cases it is not likely that the agent would communicate his knowledge to the principal. The latter is therefore not bound by the knowledge of the former.[23]

4 / Agent's torts. The principal is liable to third persons for the wrongful acts of his agent committed while acting within the scope of the agent's employment.[24] These acts are usually acts of negligence, but the principal is sometimes liable for the willful acts of the agent. He is always liable for the fraudulent acts or the misrepresentations of the agent made within the scope

---

[19] R. 2d, Sec. 284.
[20] R. 2d, Sec. 272; *Capron* v. *State*, [Cal.App.2d] 55 Cal.Reptr. 330.
[21] *Hogan* v. *Aluminum Lock Shingle Corp.*, 214 Ore. 218, 329 P.2d 271.
[22] *Stanley* v. *Schwalby*, 162 U.S. 255.
[23] *Melgard* v. *Moscow Idaho Seed Co.*, 73 Idaho 265, 251 P.2d 546.
[24] *Oman* v. *United States*, [C.A.10th] 179 F.2d 738.

of his authority. To illustrate, when an agent in the routine of his authorized agency issues false stock certificates, the principal is liable.[25]

When the activity of the agent is not directly employment-related, the fact that one of the motives of the agent is to find customers for the principal's product does not in itself bring the agent's activity within the scope of his agency so as to impose vicarious liability upon the principal for the tort of the agent.

> **Facts:** Graham was a salesman for Collier County Motors. He was required to work on the premises of the employer for two days out of the week. The balance of the time he was free to go as he pleased in the hope that he would find customers. About 75 percent of his sales were obtained by this off-premises solicitation. The only restriction on such activity was that Graham was required to make a weekly report to Collier of the number of contacts made of potential customers. On a day in which he worked the full day on the premises, Graham left work about 5:00 p.m., and about 11:30 p.m. he drove with a friend to a bowling alley to bowl and to make any possible contacts that might be found. On the way to the bowling alley, Graham ran into and killed Morgan. Suit was brought by Morgan's estate against Collier County Motors.

> **Decision:** Judgment for Collier. When a salesman goes driving to engage in a social activity, he is not acting within the scope of his agency and his principal is not liable for the agent's negligence. This conclusion is not altered by the fact that the agent hopes he might meet someone who will be a customer, when the agent in fact does not have any specific person in mind. (Morgan v. Collier County Motors, [Fla.] 193 So.2d 35)

In determining whether the principal is liable for the wrongful actions of his agent, it is immaterial that the principal did not personally benefit by those acts.

Ordinarily the principal is liable only for compensatory damages for the tort of the agent. If, however, the agent's act is of so offensive or extreme a character that the agent would be liable for punitive or exemplary damages, such damages may be recovered from the principal.[26]

When the tort is committed by a person while driving an automobile, some states expand the liability of the supplier of the automobile so as to impose liability for the act of the driver as though the driver were his agent or employee. This has the same effect as imposing agency liability by operation of law and arises in some states in the case of (1) the license-sponsor rule or (2) the family-purpose doctrine.

---

[25] In some states the principal is not liable when he did not authorize or know of the fraud of the agent at the time of the agent's fraudulent statement or misrepresentation. *Littler* v. *Dunbar*, 365 Pa. 277, 74 A.2d 650.

[26] *State ex rel.* v. *Hartford Accident & Ind. Co.*, 44 Tenn.App. 405, 314 S.W.2d 161.

(a) LICENSE-SPONSOR RULE. In a number of states, when a minor under a specified age applies for an automobile operator's license, his parent, or a person standing in the position of his parent, is required to sign his license application as a sponsor. Such a sponsor is by some statutes made jointly and severally liable with the minor for the latter's negligence in driving, although some statutes relieve the sponsor of liability if either he or the minor has filed proof of financial responsibility.

(b) FAMILY-PURPOSE DOCTRINE. In about half of the states, a person who owns or supplies an automobile that he permits to be used by members of his family for their own purposes is vicariously liable for harm caused by the negligent operation of the vehicle by any such member of the family. The family-purpose doctrine is repudiated in nearly half of the states as illogical and contrary to the general principles of agency law. Even when recognized, the doctrine is not applicable if the use of the vehicle is not with the permission of the owner or if the use is outside of the scope of that contemplated.

The family-purpose doctrine is not limited to cases involving minors nor to the children of the providing parent. That is, a person may be liable for providing an automobile to an adult; and the person so provided may be any family member, however related to the person providing the car. In some jurisdictions the person supplied the car may even be one who is not related to the provider, as long as he is a bona fide member of the household of the provider, such as a servant who is provided with or allowed to use the car for his own benefit.

Under the family-purpose doctrine, it is not essential that the provider of the car be the owner of it. The essential element is that he is the one who has control of it and has the power to grant or deny permission to use it so that its use at any particular time is with his permission. Hence, the doctrine, when recognized, is applicable to impose liability upon the father who has control of the use of the car that the child has purchased but which is used by the family when and to the extent that the father permits.

Facts: The father, who was the head of the family, allowed his minor son to keep for himself money which the son had earned raising a tobacco crop. The son purchased an automobile, but the seller would not accept the son as a credit buyer because he was a minor. The father accordingly signed the conditional sales contract, and the automobile was registered in the father's name. The automobile was also insured in the name of the father, with the son named as the principal driver. The registration card for the automobile was kept at all times by the father. The son paid the insurance premiums and drove and maintained the car in all respects as though he were the sole owner, for his own purposes, and without asking permission from his father. When he was involved in a collision, the father was sued. Was the father liable (1) generally or (2) under the family-purpose doctrine?

Decision: The father was not liable merely because he was the father and his son was driving the car since the son was not his agent or employee. The family-purpose doctrine was not applicable, because the car had not been furnished and was not maintained by his father. It was the son who had purchased the automobile with his money and he had purchased it for himself. The fact that the father had made this possible through (1) allowing the son to keep his wages and (2) signing the credit contract, which in effect was merely extending credit as an accommodation maker, did not make it a car that was furnished or maintained by the father. (Smith v. Simpson, 260 N.C. 601, 133 S.E.2d 474)

5 / Agent's crimes. The principal is liable for the crimes of the agent committed at the principal's direction.[27] When not authorized, however, the principal is ordinarily not liable for the crime of his agent merely because it was committed while otherwise acting within the scope of the latter's authority or employment.

Some states impose liability on the principal when the agent has in the course of his employment violated liquor sales laws, pure food laws, and laws regulating prices or prohibiting false weights. Thus, a principal may be held criminally responsible for the sale by his agent or employee of liquor to a minor in violation of the liquor law, even though the sale was not known to the principal and violated his instructions to his agent.

Liabilities of Third Party to Principal

The third party may be liable to the principal either in contract or in tort, or he may be required to make restitution of property of the principal.

1 / Third person's contracts. If the principal is bound by a contract to the third person, the third person is usually bound to the principal. The third person is accordingly liable to the principal on a properly authorized contract that is properly executed as a principal-third party contract. The third person is likewise liable on an unauthorized contract that the principal has ratified. He is also liable to the principal even though the principal was not disclosed, except when the agent has made a sealed contract or commercial paper, in which case only the parties to the instrument can sue or be sued on it. In the case of a commercial paper, however, the undisclosed principal may sue on the contract out of which the instrument arose.

Although the third person is liable to the principal on the contract made by the agent without disclosing any agency, the third person, when sued by

---

[27] *Miller v. Com.*, 240 Ky. 346, 42 S.W.2d 518.

the principal, is entitled to assert against the principal any defense that he could have asserted against the agent.[28]

2 / Torts of third person. The third party is liable to the principal for injuries due to wrongful acts against the interests or property in the care of the agent.[29] He is also responsible to the principal in some cases for causing the agent to fail in the performance of his agreement.[30] Thus, when an agent is willfully persuaded and induced to leave an employment to which he is bound by contract for a fixed term, the principal may bring an action for damages against the party causing the contract to be violated. So, also, one who colludes with an agent to defraud his principal is liable to the principal for damages.[31]

3 / Restitution of property. When property of the principal has been transferred to a third person by an agent lacking authority to do so, the principal may ordinarily recover the property from the third person.

QUESTIONS AND PROBLEMS

1. Checklist of legal terms:
   (a) undisclosed principal (236)
   (b) license-sponsor rule, family-purpose doctrine (243)

2. State the objective(s) of each of the following rules of law:
   (a) The principal is bound by knowledge or notice of any fact that is acquired by his agent while acting within the scope of his authority.
   (b) When property of the principal has been transferred to a third person by an agent lacking authority to do so, the principal may ordinarily recover the property from the third person.

3. Adrian, as agent for Bolte, sells an electric freezer to Craig. When Bolte refuses to deliver, Craig sues Adrian for breach of contract. Is he entitled to recover damages from Adrian?

4. Elder, without authority, acts in behalf of Farmer in executing a contract with Gibbons. When Farmer refuses to carry out the contract, Gibbons sues Elder to recover damages. Is Elder liable to Gibbons?

5. Hurley falsely represents certain facts to Jansen for the purpose of inducing the latter to enter into a contract. Upon discovering the fraud after the contract was made, Jansen brings an action in tort for deceit against Hurley. Hurley's defense is that he is not responsible because he was acting as an agent for Kenton. Is this a valid defense?

---

[28] *Huntsberry's* v. *Du Bonnet Shoe Co.,* [Mun.C.A. Dist.Col.] 143 A.2d 92.
[29] R. 2d, Secs. 314, 315.
[30] Sec. 312.
[31] *Leimkuehler* v. *Wessendorf,* 323 Mo. 64, 18 S.W.2d 445.

6. When Meeker enters into a contract with Kidd, Meeker does not know that the latter is an agent for Habel.
   (a) If Meeker fails to perform, is he liable to Kidd?
   (b) Is he liable to Habel?

7. Compare the second case example on page 236 (Mawer-Gulden-Annis, Inc. v. Brazilian & Colombian Coffee Co.) with the case example on page 240 (Menveg v. Fishbaugh).
   (a) What facts in the two cases are similar?
   (b) What facts in the two cases differ?

8. Landrum is authorized to sell Norton's turkeys. He agrees to furnish May with 100 turkeys. When Landrum fails to deliver, May sues Norton who denies that Landrum represented him in the transaction. May offers to prove that Landrum stated at the time that he was acting for Norton. Is this evidence admissible?

9. Walden, who is authorized to sell securities for Nelson, sells 50 shares of ABC stock to Otto by fraudulent representation. Otto sues Nelson for damages. Is he entitled to judgment?

10. Nixon, without authority, makes a contract for Pittman with Tudor. When Pittman learns of the transaction, he expresses his approval to Tudor. Is Pittman entitled to enforce the contract?

11. Padgett is authorized to buy a tape recorder for Richmond. After making the purchase and while Padgett is delivering the tape recorder to Richmond, Tyler deliberately damages the property. Is Richmond entitled to bring an action in tort against Tyler for damages?

12. Burrows owed money to the principal of Sherin. Burrows arranged for Shepard to pay the debt to Sherin. Shepard by mistake paid more than was due. Sherin turned the entire payment over to his principal. Shepard sued Sherin for the overpayment. Was he entitled to recover? (Shepard v. Sherin, 43 Minn. 382, 45 N.W. 718)

13. Buchanan was a candidate for a political office. His campaign treasurer made a false report of the expenses of the campaign. A statute required the filing of such reports and made it a criminal offense to make a false report. Buchanan was prosecuted for the false report made by his campaign treasurer. Was he guilty of a statutory criminal offense? (Florida v. Buchanan, [Fla.] 189 So.2d 270)

14. Arnold Israel, acting as authorized agent of Unified Consultants, made an authorized contract on their behalf with Tabloid Lithographers. Unified did not perform its part of the contract, and Tabloid sued both Israel and Unified. Tabloid obtained a judgment in the action against Unified, whereupon Israel claimed that he was released from any liability. Was this correct? (Tabloid Lithographers v. Israel, 87 N.J.S. 358, 209 A.2d 364)

Chapter 20

Termination of Agency

An agency may be terminated by the act of one or both of the parties to the agency agreement, or by operation of law. The methods of termination will be discussed as they apply, first to the ordinary agencies, and then to agencies coupled with an interest.

Termination of Ordinary Agency by Act of Parties

An ordinary agency may be terminated by act of the parties in the following ways: (1) expiration of contract, (2) agreement, (3) option of a party, (4) revocation by principal, and (5) renunciation by agent.

1 / Expiration of agency contract. The ordinary agency may expire by the terms of the contract. Thus the contract may provide that it shall last for a stated period, as five years, or until a particular date arrives, or until the happening of a particular event, such as the sale of certain property. In such a case, the agency is automatically terminated when the specified date arrives or the event on which it is to end occurs.[1] When one appoints another to represent him in his business affairs while he is in Europe, the relation ends upon the return of the principal from abroad.

When it is provided that the agency shall last for a stated period of time, it terminates upon the expiration of that period without regard to whether the acts contemplated by the creation of the agency have been performed.[2] If no period is stated, the agency continues for a reasonable time, but it may be terminated at the will of either party.[3]

2 / Agreement. Since the agency relation is based upon consent, it can be terminated by the consent of the principal and agent.[4]

3 / Option of a party. An agency agreement may provide that upon the giving of notice or the payment of a specified sum of money, one party may terminate the relationship.

4 / Revocation by principal. The relationship between principal and agent is terminated whenever the principal discharges the agent. If the

---

[1] Restatement, Agency, 2d, Secs. 105, 106, 107.
[2] R. 2d, Sec. 105.
[3] *Seneca Falls Machine Co.* v. *McBeth,* [C.A.3d] 368 F.2d 915.
[4] R. 2d, Sec. 117.

agency was not created for a specified time but was to exist only at will, or if the agent has been guilty of misconduct, the principal may discharge the agent without liability to him.[5]

Facts: Williams held a promissory note executed by Duckett. He assigned the note to Tinney, an attorney, as agent to collect the note. Tinney began a lawsuit against Duckett, but nothing more was done. After two years, Williams went to Tinney's office, obtained the note from Tinney's associate, and said that "he was taking it to someone else." Williams then had a second suit brought against Duckett, and this fact was known to Tinney. Subsequently, Tinney took action in the lawsuit that he had brought against Duckett, who then raised the defense that Tinney's authority to sue had been revoked.

Decision: Judgment for Duckett. No particular act is required to constitute a revocation of the agent's authority. Either the act of taking back the note or the act of bringing a second action on it manifested to Tinney that his authority had been terminated. (Tinney v. Duckett, [Mun.C.A. Dist.Col.] 141 A.2d 192)

When the agency is based upon a contract to employ the agent for a specified period of time, the principal is liable to the agent for damages if the principal wrongfully discharges the agent. The fact that the principal is liable for damages does not, however, prevent the principal from terminating the agency by discharging the agent. In such a case it is said that the principal has the power to terminate the agency by discharging the agent but he does not have the right to do so.

5 / Renunciation by agent. The agency relationship is terminated if the agent refuses to continue to act as agent,[6] or when he abandons the object of the agency and acts for himself in committing a fraud upon his principal.[7] Ordinarily the principal cannot prevent the agent from stopping even though the agent's action amounts to a breach of contract.

If the relationship is an agency at will, the agent has the right as well as the power to renounce or abandon the agency at any time. In addition, he has the right of renunciation of the relationship in any case if the principal is guilty of making wrongful demands upon him or of other misconduct.

If, however, the agency is based upon a contract calling for the continuation of the relationship for a specified or determinable period, that is, until a particular date arrives or a certain event occurs, the agent has no right to abandon or renounce the relationship when the principal is not guilty of wrong.

[5] *Seattle Times Co.* v. *Murphy*, 172 Wash. 474, 20 P.2d 858.
[6] R. 2d, Sec. 118.
[7] *New York Cas. Co.* v. *Sazenski*, 240 Minn. 202, 60 N.W.2d 368.

When the renunciation by the agent is wrongful, the agent is liable to the principal for the damages that the principal sustains.[8] In some states the agent also forfeits his right to receive any compensation for the services rendered but not due prior to the renunciation. In other states he may recover the reasonable value of such services, but not in excess of the contract price minus the damages sustained by the principal. In all states the agent may recover any salary or commission that had become due prior to the renunciation. This remedy is subject, however, to the opposing claim of the principal for damages.

In a few instances the court will allow an injunction for the purpose of preventing the agent from violating his contract with the principal. This special relief is granted only when the principal can prove that the services of the agent are so unique or extraordinary that money damages will not adequately compensate the principal for the agent's breach of contract.

Termination of Ordinary Agency by Operation of Law

Under certain conditions it becomes impossible or socially undesirable for the agency to continue. The law accordingly provides that the agency shall be deemed terminated by the operation of law in the following ways: (1) death, (2) insanity, (3) bankruptcy, (4) impossibility, (5) war, and (6) unusual event or change in circumstances.

1 / Death. The death of either the principal [9] or agent ordinarily terminates the authority of an agent automatically,[10] even though the death is unknown to the other. In some states statutes have been adopted providing that the death of the principal is not a revocation until the agent has notice nor as to third persons who deal with the agent in good faith and are ignorant of the death. Generally, however, these statutes are limited to principals who are members of the armed forces.

Facts: Julius Stalting had a notary public prepare two deeds, but he left blank the name of the person to receive the property. He executed the deeds but did not fill in the blanks and then left the deeds with the notary public. Subsequently Stalting died. After his death the notary public inserted the names of grandchildren of Stalting. The sons of Stalting brought an action to have the two deeds set aside.

Decision: Judgment for the sons. The notary public, in filling in the deeds, was attempting to act as the agent for Stalting. As the latter was dead when the notary public filled in the blanks, the notary public's act was void. The death of Stalting terminated any agency powers that the notary public had. (Stalting v. Stalting, 52 S.D. 318, 217 N.W. 390)

---

[8] R. 2d, Sec. 400.
[9] *Julian* v. *Lawton*, 240 N.C. 436, 82 S.E.2d 210.
[10] *Commercial Nursery Co.* v. *Ivey*, 164 Tenn. 502, 51 S.W.2d 238.

The fact that a contract of agency is terminated by death does not impose any liability for damages even though the contract has not been completed.[11] In an attorney-client relationship the death of the client does not terminate the agency if the client had expressly agreed that the attorney should conduct the proceeding to its conclusion.[12]

2 / Insanity. The insanity of either the principal or agent ordinarily terminates the agent's authority.[13]

In spite of the termination of the authority, the agent can still bind the principal with respect to a third person who acts in good faith and without knowledge of the insanity if it would work an injustice on the third party to hold that authority had terminated because of the insanity. If the insanity of the principal or agent has been judicially declared by a court, all persons are deemed to know of the status of the incompetent and accordingly they cannot come within this exception.

If the incapacity of the principal is only temporary, the agent's authority may be merely suspended rather than terminated.

3 / Bankruptcy. Bankruptcy of the principal [14] or agent usually terminates the relationship. It is generally held, however, that the bankruptcy of an agent does not terminate his power to deal with goods of the principal that are in his possession.

Insolvency, as distinguished from a formal adjudication of bankruptcy, usually does not terminate the agency. In some states it is accordingly held that the authority of an agent is not terminated by the appointment of a receiver for the principal's financial affairs.[15]

4 / Impossibility. The authority of an agent is terminated when it is impossible to perform the agency for any reason, such as the destruction of the subject matter of the agency, the death or loss of capacity of the third person with whom the agent is to contract, or a change in law that makes it impossible to perform the agency lawfully.[16]

5 / War. When the country of the principal and that of the agent are at war, the authority of the agent is usually terminated or at least suspended until peace is restored. When the war has the effect of making performance impossible, the agency is, of course, terminated. For example, the authority of an agent who is a nonresident enemy alien to sue is terminated because such an alien is not permitted to sue.[17]

---

[11] R. 2d, Sec. 450, Comment (b).
[12] *Jones* v. *Miller,* [C.A.3rd] 203 F.2d 131.
[13] R. 2d, Sec. 122; *Sellers' Estate,* 154 Ohio 483, 96 N.E.2d 595.
[14] *Du Bois* v. *U. S. F. & G. Co.,* 341 Pa. 85, 18 A.2d 802.
[15] *Chilletti* v. *Missouri, Kansas & Texas Rwy. Co.,* 102 Kan. 297, 171 P. 14.
[16] R. 2d, Secs. 116, 124.
[17] *Johnson* v. *Eisentrager,* 339 U.S. 763.

6 / Unusual events or change of circumstances. The view is also held
that the authority of an agent is terminated by the occurrence of an unusual
event or a change in value or business conditions of such a nature that the
agent should reasonably infer that the principal would not desire the agent
to continue to act under the changed circumstances.[18] For example, an agent
employed to sell land at a specified price should regard his authority to sell
at that price as terminated when the value of the land increases greatly
because of the discovery of oil on the land.

Termination of Agency Coupled with an Interest

An ordinary agency may be terminated by act of the principal or agent
and is terminated by the death, insanity, or bankruptcy of either party. If
the agency is coupled with an interest, however, this rule does not have full
application.

The extent to which an agency with an interest may be terminated varies
with the nature of the interest. If the agency is coupled with an interest in the
authority, the agency cannot be terminated by the act of the principal. The
Restatement of the Law of Agency adopts the rule that the principal's death
does not terminate such an agency.[19] In some states, however, it is held to be
terminated by his death.[20]

An agency coupled with an interest in the authority is not revoked by
the death of the agent.[21] Thus, when the agent would have the right to
receive periodic commissions under a continuing contract between the principal and the third person, the agent's estate, if the agency is coupled with
an interest in the authority, may receive the commissions accruing after the
agent's death. If not so coupled, the right to receive commissions terminates
with the agent's death.[22]

When the agency is coupled with an interest in the subject matter, the
principal cannot terminate the agency nor is it terminated or affected by the
death or insanity of either the principal or the agent.

Effect of Termination of Authority

When the authority of an agent is terminated, the agent loses all right
to act for the principal.

If the agency is revoked by the principal, the authority to act for the
principal is not terminated until notice of revocation is given to or received
by the agent. As between the principal and agent, the right of the agent

---

[18] R. 2d, Secs. 108, 109.
[19] Sec. 139(1).
[20] *Weaver* v. *Richards*, 144 Mich. 395, 108 N.W. 382.
[21] R. 2d, Sec. 139(1).
[22] *Mills* v. *Union Cent. Life Ins. Co.*, 77 Miss. 327, 28 So. 954.

to bind his principal to third persons generally ends immediately upon the termination of his authority. Such termination is effective without the giving of notice to third persons.

When the agency is terminated by the act of the principal, notice must be given to third persons. If such notice is not given, the agent may have the power to make contracts that will bind the principal and third persons. This rule is predicated on the theory that a known agent will have the appearance of still being the agent unless notice is given to the contrary.

Facts: Record owned a farm that was operated by his agent, Berry, who lived on the farm. The latter hired Wagner to bale the hay in 1953 and told him to bill Record for this work. Wagner did so and was paid by Record. By the summer of 1954, the agency had been terminated by Record but Berry remained in possession as tenant of the farm and nothing appeared changed. In 1954 Berry asked Wagner to bale the hay the same as in the prior year and bill Record for the work. He did so, but Record refused to pay on the ground that Berry was not then his agent. Wagner sued him.

Decision: Judgment for Wagner. As the agency of Berry had been terminated by the voluntary action of the principal, it was necessary that notice of termination be given to third persons who had dealt with the agent. Since this had not been done, the agent continued to appear to have authority to bind the principal, and he therefore could do so in spite of the actual termination of the authority. (Record v. Wagner, 100 N.H. 419, 128 A.2d 921)

When the law requires the giving of notice in order to end the power of the agent to bind the principal, individual notice must be given or mailed to all persons who had prior dealings with the agent or the principal. Notice to the general public can be given by publishing a statement that the agency has been terminated in a newspaper of general circulation in the affected area. If a notice is actually received, the power of the agent is terminated without regard to whether the method of giving notice had been proper. Conversely, if proper notice is given, it is immaterial that it did not actually come to the attention of the party notified. Thus a member of the general public cannot claim that the principal is bound to him on the ground that the third person did not see the newspaper notice stating that the agent's authority had been terminated.

QUESTIONS AND PROBLEMS

1. Review the definitions of an agency coupled with an interest and the two kinds of interest in such agencies.
2. State the objective(s) of each of the following rules of law:
   (a) The agency relationship is terminated when the principal discharges the agent with or without cause.

(b) If the principal fails to notify third persons when he terminates the agency, the agent may continue to make contracts that are binding on the principal.

3. Getz employed Homer for two months to sell the goods that Getz had purchased from a bankrupt. At the end of that time when Homer had disposed of only part of the merchandise, he accepted another position. Getz brought an action against Homer for breach of contract on the ground that the agency did not terminate until all of the goods had been sold. Was Getz entitled to judgment?

4. Hull employs Imholte to sell goods in Tennessee for one year. At the end of two months Hull transfers Imholte to Alabama. In protest, Imholte leaves Hull's employment and accepts another position. Hull sues for breach of contract. Decide.

5. Kemp is employed as agent for Laird for a year at a salary of $700 a month. Kemp wrongfully abandons his agency in the middle of the seventh month. At that time his salary for the sixth month has not been paid. What are Kemp's rights to compensation?

6. Malone borrows $50 from Ledford. As security for the loan, Malone gives Ledford his watch with authority to sell it if the loan is not repaid. May Malone revoke Ledford's authority to sell the watch?

7. The McGuire Company discharged Ahlers, its purchasing agent. Later Ahlers agreed with Dodson to purchase certain goods for the McGuire Company. At that time Dodson had no knowledge of the termination of Ahlers' authority. Could Dodson hold the company on the contract?

8. Cohen employed Dean to sell merchandise for him for two years. At the end of the first year the agency relationship was terminated by agreement. Cohen published a notice in a local newspaper of general circulation that Dean was no longer his agent. After that, Dean executed an agreement for Cohen to sell merchandise to Fossitt. Fossitt had no previous dealings with Dean. Cohen refused to deliver the merchandise, and Fossitt brought an action for damages against Cohen. Was he entitled to judgment?

9. Wilson authorized Reams to sell some land for $1,400 and, as compensation, authorized him to keep anything in excess of that price. Unknown to Reams, Wilson then sold the property to a purchaser for $1,350. Reams later sold the property to another purchaser for $1,500. When he learned that Wilson had sold the property, he sued for $100 as lost compensation. Decide. (Reams v. Wilson, 147 N.C. 304, 60 S.E. 1124)

10. In December, Shumaker authorized Hazen to act as agent to effect a sale of his shares of stock in the Utex Exploration Co. The power of attorney provided that it should be "irrevocable" for one year. In April of the next calendar year, Shumaker notified Hazen that the power of attorney was terminated. Could Shumaker terminate the agency? (Shumaker v. Hazen, [Okla.] 372 P.2d 873)

Chapter 21

Employment

To a large extent, the law of employment is the same as that of agency. There are material differences, however, and the relationship has become subject to regulation by a large body of statutes generally described as labor legislation.

THE EMPLOYMENT RELATION

The relation of an employer and an employee exists when, pursuant to an express or implied agreement of the parties, one person, the *employee,* undertakes to perform services or to do work under the direction and control of another, the *employer.* In the older cases, this was described as the master-servant relationship.

As already discussed,[1] an employee is hired only to work under the control of the employer, as contrasted with (1) an agent who is to make contracts with third persons on behalf of and under control of the principal, and (2) an independent contractor who is to perform a contract independent of, or free from, control by the other party.

Creation of the Employment Relation

The contract upon which the relationship is based is subject to all the principles applicable to contracts generally. The relation of the employer and employee can be created only by consent of both parties. A person cannot be required to work against his will, nor can he become an employee without the consent of the employer.[2]

The contract of employment may be implied, as when the employer accepts services which, as a reasonable man, he knows are rendered with the expectation of receiving compensation. Thus it has been held that when a minor worked with his father under the supervision of the company's agent, the company impliedly assented to the relationship of employer and employee, even though the minor's name was not on the payroll.[3]

---

[1] See p. 212.

[2] *Taylor* v. *Baltimore etc. R.R. Co.,* 108 Va. 817, 62 S.E. 798.

[3] *Tennessee Coal etc. R.R. Co.* v. *Hayes,* 97 Ala. 201, 12 So. 98.

254

As a result of the rise of labor unions, large segments of industrial life are now covered by *union contracts*. This means that the union and the employer agree upon a basic pattern or set of terms of employment. For example, a union contract will state that all workers performing a specified class of work shall receive a certain hourly wage.

Facts: Eversole was employed by La Combe. The employee was a member of a union with which the employer each year signed a written contract specifying the minimum wages to be paid employees. Each year La Combe paid Eversole less than the minimum. Eversole sued La Combe for the unpaid balance. La Combe defended on the ground that a representative of the union had agreed with him that he could pay Eversole less than the minimum wage.

Decision: Judgment for Eversole. Once the contract was made between the employer and the union, the employee had a right to receive the rate of specified pay and that right could not be surrendered by an officer of the union without the employee's consent. (Eversole v. La Combe, 125 Mont. 87, 231 P.2d 945)

Terms of Employment

Basically the parties are free to make an employment contract on any terms they wish. The employment contemplated must, of course, be lawful; and by statute it is subject to certain limitations. Thus persons under a certain age and women cannot be employed at certain kinds of labor. Statutes commonly specify minimum wages and maximum hours which the employer must observe, and they require employers to provide many safety devices. A state may also require employers to pay employees for the time that they are away from work while voting.[4]

Historically, wages constituted the sole reward of labor. Today, in many fields of employment additional benefits are conferred upon the worker, either by virtue of the contract of employment or by statutory provision.[5]

Duties and Rights of the Employee

The duties and rights of an employee are determined primarily by the contract of employment. As to points not expressly covered by the contract of employment, the law implies certain provisions.

1 / Services. The employee is under a duty to perform or hold himself in readiness to perform such services as may be required by the contract of employment. If the employee holds himself in readiness to comply with his employer's directions, he has discharged his obligation and he will not

---

[4] *State* v. *International Harvester Co.*, 241 Minn. 367, 63 N.W.2d 547.
[5] Various statutory regulations of labor relate to fair labor standards, hours of service, fair employment practices, and labor-management relations.

forfeit his right to compensation because the employer has withheld directions and has thus kept him idle.

The employee impliedly agrees to serve his employer honestly and faithfully. He also impliedly agrees to serve him exclusively during his hours of employment. The employee may do other work, however, if the time and nature of the employment are not inconsistent with his duties to the first employer and the contract of employment does not contain any contrary provision.

The employee impliedly purports that, in performing his duties, he will exercise due care and ordinary diligence in view of the nature of the work. When skill is required, the employee need exercise only ordinary skill, unless the employee had held himself out as possessing a special skill required by the work.

2 / Trade secrets. An employee is frequently given confidential trade secrets by his employer. He is under a duty not to disclose such knowledge. It is immaterial that the contract of employment did not stipulate against such disclosures. If he violates this obligation, the employer may enjoin the use of such information.

Facts: Woltmann was employed by the New England Overall Co. as sales manager. Through the course of the years he acquired much information about suppliers of material and the credit standing and requirements of the company's customers. The company was a small family corporation, and Woltmann was the first outsider to have a position that gave access to such information. Before he had been hired, he agreed that he would never use or divulge such information nor permit it to be used by anyone. After a number of years, Woltmann and one of the salesmen who had made a similar promise set up a business which competed with New England Overall. Later they left their jobs with New England, taking a customers list with them, and then procured clothing articles from the company's suppliers that were almost identical to the company's stock which they sought to sell to the company's customers at lower prices. The company sued to compel Woltmann and the salesman to stop this competition within the area in which the company operated and to return the list of customers.

Decision: Judgment for New England Overall Co. The nature of the business was so highly competitive that the information in dispute was very important to the welfare of the existing enterprise. Hence, this pirating was enjoined even though the information did not relate to secret inventions and processes. (New England Overall Co. v. Woltmann, 343 Mass. 69, 176 N.E.2d 193)

The employee is under no duty to refrain from divulging general information of the particular business in which he is employed. Nor is he under a

duty not to divulge the information of the particular business when the relation between employer and employee is not considered confidential. Mere
knowledge and skill obtained through experience are not in themselves "trade
secrets," and employees may make use of the fruits of their experience in
later employment or in working for themselves.

3 / Inventions. In the absence of an express or implied agreement to
the contrary, the inventions of an employee belong to him, even though he
used the time and property of the employer in their discovery, provided that
he was not employed for the express purpose of inventing the things or the
processes which he has discovered.

Facts: Bandag, Inc. was in the business of recapping used automobile tires.
Morenings was employed as its chief chemist. In the course of his
work he discovered a new process for bonding treads to tires that were
being recapped. He was not employed to discover such a process, and
no agreement had ever been made with Bandag as to the ownership
of any discoveries made by Morenings. Bandag sued Morenings, claiming that, as employer, it was entitled to the ownership of the process
which had been developed in the course of Morenings' employment.

Decision: Judgment for Morenings. The employer has the burden of proving that
he is entitled to the invention or process discovered by an employee
in the course of employment. As Morenings was not employed for the
purpose of discovering the process that he discovered and as there was
no provision in the contract of employment giving the employer the
right to such discovery, the employer had no right to it. (Bandag, Inc.
v. Morenings, [Iowa] 146 N.W.2d 916)

If the invention is discovered during working hours and with the employer's materials and equipment, the employer has the right to use the
invention without charge in the operation of his business. If the employee
has obtained a patent for the invention, he must grant the employer a nonexclusive license to use the invention without the payment of royalty. This
shop right of the employer does not give him the right to make and sell
machines that embody the employee's invention; it only entitles him to use
the invention in the operation of his plant.

When the employee is employed in order to secure certain results from
experiments to be conducted by him, the courts hold that the inventions
equitably belong to the employer on the ground either that there is a trust
relation or that there is an implied agreement by the employee to make an
assignment.[6]

In any case an employee may expressly agree that his inventions made
during his employment will be the property of the employer. If such contracts

---

[6] *United States* v. *Dubilier Condenser Corp.,* 289 U.S. 178.

are not clear and specific, the courts are inclined to rule against the employer. The employee may also agree to assign to the employer inventions made after the term of employment.

4 / Compensation. The rights of an employee with respect to compensation are governed in general by the same principles that apply to the compensation of an agent.

In the absence of an agreement to the contrary, when an employee is discharged, whether for cause or not, the employer must pay him his wages down to the expiration of the last pay period. The express terms of employment or union contracts, or custom, frequently provide for payment of wages for fractional terminal periods, however, and they may even require a severance pay equal to the compensation for a full period.

5 / Employee's lien or preference. At common law an employee was usually given no lien or claim against the employer's property for his wages. Most states today, however, protect an employee's claim for compensation. The statutes vary widely in their terms. Some apply only to persons constructing or improving buildings. Some statutes only apply when the employer is insolvent. These statutes are usually called *laborers'* or *mechanics' lien laws.* Sometimes the statutes limit the privilege to the workmen of a particular class, such as plasterers, bricklayers, or stonemasons. Compensation for the use of materials or machinery is not protected.

EMPLOYER'S LIABILITY FOR EMPLOYEE'S INJURIES

For most kinds of employment workmen's compensation statutes govern. They provide that the injured employee is entitled to compensation as long as the accident occurred in the course of his employment from a risk involved in that employment.

In some employment situations common-law principles apply. Under them the employer is not an insurer of the employee's safety.[7] It is necessary, therefore, to consider the duties and defenses of an employer apart from statute.

Common-Law Status of Employer

1 / Duties. The employer is under the duty to furnish an employee with a reasonably safe place in which to work,[8] reasonably safe tools and appliances, and a sufficient number of competent fellow employees for the work

---

[7] Workmen's compensation statutes by their terms generally do not apply to agricultural, domestic, or casual employment. In addition, in some states the plan of workmen's compensation is optional with the employer or the employee.

[8] *Phillips Oil Co.* v. *Linn,* [C.A.5th] 194 F.2d 903.

involved; and to warn the employee of any unusual dangers peculiar to the employer's business.[9]

Facts: McLarty was employed by Miss Georgia Dairies, Inc. as a milk truck loader. Dry ice was not used on these trucks. One day, he was required to help other employees pack bulk ice cream in dry ice in cardboard boxes for shipment. He did not have any prior experience with dry ice and was not provided with gloves or tongs nor given any warning or instructions as to how to handle the dry ice. In picking it up with his bare hands, a piece of dry ice adhered to his right hand and caused severe injuries. He sued for damages for such injuries.

Decision: Judgment for McLarty. The employer was under the duty to provide safe working equipment and to warn of the dangers involved in the handling of dry ice. The possibility that it would adhere to bare hands and cause intense burns could not be regarded as such a part of the general knowledge that the employer was freed from the responsibility of warning McLarty or that the employee could be deemed to have assumed the risk. (Miss Georgia Dairies, Inc. v. McLarty, 114 Ga.App. 259, 150 S.E.2d 725)

2 / Defenses. The employer at common law is not liable to an injured employee, regardless of the employer's negligence, if the employee was guilty of contributory negligence, or if he was harmed by the act of a fellow employee [10] or if he was harmed by an ordinary hazard of the work, as he is deemed to assume such risks.

Statutory Changes

The rising incidence of industrial accidents, due to the increasing use of more powerful machinery and the growth of the industrial labor population, led to a demand for statutory modification of the common-law rules relating to the liability of employers for industrial accidents.

1 / Modification of common-law defenses. One type of change was to modify by statute the defenses which an employer could assert when sued by an employee for damages. Under such statutes as the Federal Employers' Liability Act and the Federal Safety Appliance Act, which apply to common carriers engaged in interstate commerce, the plaintiff must still bring an action in a court and prove the negligence of the employer or of his employees,[11] but the burden of proving his case is made lighter by limitations on the employer's defenses.

In many states the common-law defenses of employers whose employees are engaged in hazardous types of work have also been modified by statute.

---

[9] Restatement, Agency, 2d, Sec. 510.
[10] R. 2d, Sec. 475.
[11] *Moore* v. *Chesapeake & Ohio Rwy.*, 340 U.S. 573.

2 / Workmen's compensation. A more sweeping development has been made by the adoption of workmen's compensation statutes in every state. With respect to certain industries or businesses, these statutes provide that an employee, or certain relatives of a deceased employee, are entitled to recover damages for the injury or death of the employee whenever the injury arose within the course of the employee's work from a risk involved in that work. In such a case compensation is paid without regard to whether the employer or the employee was negligent, but generally no compensation is allowed for a willfully self-inflicted injury or one sustained while intoxicated.

There has been a gradual widening of the workmen's compensation statutes, either by amendment or by the adoption of special statutes, so that compensation today is generally recoverable for accident-inflicted injuries and occupational diseases.[12] In some states compensation for occupational diseases is limited to those specified in the statute by name, such as silicosis, lead poisoning, or injury to health from radioactivity. In other states any disease arising from the occupation is compensable.

Workmen's compensation proceedings differ from the common-law action for damages or an action for damages under an employer's liability statute in that the latter actions are brought in a court of law, whereas workmen's compensation proceedings are brought before a special administrative agency or workmen's compensation board.

Workmen's compensation statutes do not bar an employee from suing another employee for the injury caused him.

LIABILITY FOR INJURIES OF THIRD PERSONS

Employee's Liability for Injuries of Third Person

Whenever the employee injures another person, whether another employee or an outsider, the liability of the employee for such injuries to the third person is determined by the same principles that would apply if the employee were not employed.

Employer's Liability for Injuries to Third Persons

An employer is liable to third persons for the harm done them by the acts of his employee (1) when the employer expressly directed the act; (2) when the harm was due to the employer's fault in not having competent employees, or in failing to give them proper instructions, or a similar fault; (3) when the act by the employee was within the course of his employment;[13] or (4) when the act was done by the employee without authority but the employer ratified or assented to it.

---

12 *Webb* v. *New Mexico Pub. Co.*, 47 N.M. 279, 141 P.2d 333.
13 *Bryce* v. *Jackson Diners*, 80 R.I. 327, 96 A.2d 637.

The employer is liable under the *doctrine of respondeat superior* for the torts of his employee when committed within the scope of his employment.[14] If the act by the employee is not within the scope of his employment, the employer is not liable under this doctrine.[15]

> **Facts:** Moore was an electronics engineer employed by the United States. While traveling under a work assignment from one air base to another, he ran into and injured Romitti who then sued the United States under the Federal Tort Claims Act. The United States raised the defense that Moore was not acting within the course of his employment while driving to the new job assignment.

> **Decision:** Judgment for Romitti. Under the circumstances, the action of Moore in traveling to the base was part of his work and the government was therefore liable on the basis of respondeat superior. (United States v. Romitti, [C.A.9th] 363 F.2d 662)

An act does not cease to be within the course of employment merely because it was not expressly authorized nor even because it was committed in violation of instructions. Wanton and malicious injury is sometimes within the scope of employment when the employee inflicts such harm in the belief that he is furthering the employer's interest.[16]

There is a tendency toward widening the employer's liability for the tort of his employee, but there is great conflict among the decisions. There is a conflict of authority as to the liability of an employer for the use of force by an employee employed to guard property or in the protection of the employer's interest, with the weight of authority probably in favor of imposing liability.[17] When the employee is employed to recapture or retake property of the principal, as the employee of a finance company employed to repossess automobiles on which installments have not been paid, the courts will generally impose liability on the employer for the unlawful force of the employee used in retaking the property or in committing an assault upon the buyer, but there is some authority to the contrary. In contrast, the majority of decisions do not impose liability on an employer for an assault committed by his bill collector upon the debtor. There is a conflict of authority as to whether the employer is liable for the assault of his employee committed during a dispute over a traffic accident in which the employee has been involved while driving the employer's truck or vehicle.

---

[14] The Restatement, Agency, 2d, declares acts within the scope of the servant's employment to be acts of the kind that the employee was employed to perform; occurring substantially within the authorized time and space limits; and actuated, at least in part, by a purpose to serve the employer; and, if force is intentionally used against another, that its use was not unexpectable. Sec. 228(1).

[15] *Parry* v. *Davison-Paxon Co.*, 87 Ga.App. 51, 73 S.E.2d 59.

[16] R. 2d, Sec. 231. Some courts follow the older rule that the employer is never liable for a willful or malicious act by his employee regardless of its purpose.

[17] *Prince* v. *Brickell*, 87 Ga.App. 697, 75 S.E.2d 288.

The fact that the employer is insured does not determine liability, as the insurer's liability is the same as the employer's.

Liability of Independent Contractor

If work is done by an independent contractor rather than by an employee, the employer or owner is not liable for harm caused by the contractor to third persons or their property. There is, however, a trend toward imposing liability on the employer or owner even in such case when the work undertaken is especially hazardous in nature.

1 / Direct liability of owner. The fact that the owner contracts with an independent contractor does not protect the owner from liability for harm that may be traced directly to the owner's negligence or misconduct. For example, the owner is liable if he has not exercised reasonable care in the selection of a qualified and competent contractor. If the owner negligently supplies plans, materials, or equipment to the contractor that are defective, the owner is liable to a third person injured as the consequence of such negligence. To illustrate, the existence of the independent contractor relationship does not insulate the owner from liability for his own negligence in supplying the contractor with ropes for scaffolding which the owner as a reasonable man would have perceived were defective, and the scaffolding thereafter fell and injured a passerby in the street because the defective rope broke.

2 / Dangerous activity. The owner may undertake an activity which is of such a highly dangerous character that there is an intrinsic element of danger which will remain even though due care is exercised, as in the case of blasting. Or again, the work may be merely of such a nature that there is a high element of risk unless special precautions are taken, although the taking of such precautions will eliminate the hazard. In the demolition of a building, for example, the circumstances are such that the construction of a wooden overhead shelter will protect the passerby from falling debris. In such cases as these, the fact that the owner retains an independent contractor does not shield him from the absolute liability to which he would otherwise be subject in these situations.

3 / Employee of independent contractor. The employee of an independent contractor is not an employee of the owner or person entering into the contract with the independent contractor. In order for the employee of the independent contractor to recover from the owner for injuries sustained by him in the course of the work, it is therefore necessary for the employee to establish the owner's negligence in some manner as in any other suit. An exception arises under the dangerous instrument or *dangerous work doctrine,* under which the owner is liable to the independent contractor's employee when it is likely that the performance of the contract will expose the contractor's employee to harm unless proper precautions be taken and the contractor failed to take them. For example, an electric company hiring an independent contractor to construct and energize high voltage transmission lines provides for a dangerous instrumentality. Hence, the electric company is liable to an employee of the contractor who is injured when the transmission line is energized by the contractor without taking adequate precautions to protect the employees.

Enforcement of Claim by Third Person

When a third person is injured by an employee, he may have a cause of action or enforceable claim against both the employee and the employer. In most states, and in the federal courts, the injured person may now sue either or both in one action. If the injured person sues both, he may obtain judgment against both of them, although he can only collect the full amount of the judgment once.

If the employee was at fault and if his wrongful conduct was not in obedience to his employer's directions, the employer may recover indemnity from the employee for the loss that the employer sustained when he was required to make payment to the third person. This situation arises when an employee acting at the direction of his employer uproots shrubbery on what the employer erroneously believes is the employer's side of the boundary line but which in fact is on the neighboring land. In such a case, if the neighbor recovers from the employee for trespass, the employee is entitled to be indemnified by his employer to the extent that the employee pays the judgment obtained by the third person.

TERMINATION OF EMPLOYMENT CONTRACT

A contract of employment may, in general, be terminated in the same manner as contracts of any other kind.

Death of the employee or his inability to perform his duties will terminate the relation. The same rule is applied upon the death of the employer except when the contract of employment is of such nature that it can be carried out by the personal representative of the deceased employer.

A stipulation in the original agreement may give one or either of the parties the right to terminate the relation upon the happening of a certain contingency. For example, when the employee is hired as the manager of a branch store owned by the employer, the contract may stipulate that the employment is to terminate if the branch store is permanently closed by the employer for any reason. In such a case the closing of the branch is a condition subsequent which discharges the contract of employment.

The employment contract frequently stipulates that the employer may terminate the relation if he is not satisfied with the services of the employee. In such cases the employer is generally considered the sole judge of his reason provided that he acts in good faith.

Justifiable Discharge by Employer

In the absence of a contract or statutory provision to the contrary, an employer may discharge an employee for any reason or for no reason if the employment is at will.[18] If the employment may not be terminated at will, the employer will be liable for damages if he discharges the employee without justification. The employer is justified in discharging an employee because of the employee's (1) nonperformance of duties, (2) misrepresentation or fraud in obtaining the employment, (3) disobedience to proper directions,[19] (4) disloyalty, (5) wrongful misconduct, and (6) incompetency.

Remedies of Employee Wrongfully Discharged

An employee who has been wrongfully discharged may bring against the employer an action for (1) wages, (2) breach of contract,[20] or (3) value of services already rendered. In certain instances, he may also bring (4) an action that results in performance of the employment contract, or (5) a proceeding under a federal or state labor relations statute.

Justifiable Abandonment by Employee

The employee cannot, as a general rule, be compelled to perform his contract of employment. Hence he can at any time end the relation by a refusal to perform the services for which he was engaged. If the contract is not terminable at will, his refusal to carry out his part of the contract may or may not make him liable for damages, depending upon the ground for leaving his employment.

The employment relationship may be abandoned by the employee for (1) nonpayment of wages, (2) wrongful assault by the employer, (3) requirement of services not contemplated, (4) services required but not permitted by employer, and (5) injurious conditions of employment.

Remedies of the Employer for Wrongful Abandonment

When an employee has wrongfully abandoned his employment, the employer may bring (1) an action for breach of contract; and in certain circumstances he may also bring (2) an action against a third person

---

[18] *Odell* v. *Humble Oil & Refining Co.,* [C.A.10th] 201 F.2d 123.
[19] *N.L.R.B.* v. *American Thread Co.,* [C.A.5th] 210 F.2d 381.
[20] *Olsen* v. *Arabian American Oil Co.,* [C.A.2d] 194 F.2d 477.

maliciously inducing the breach of the contract,[21] (3) an action that results in performance of the employment contract, or (4) a proceeding under a federal or state labor relations statute.

Facts: The plumbers' union requested Padden, a master plumber, to use lead bends instead of iron bends in plumbing installations. He claimed that iron bends were lawful and that the union's only interest was that more time was required to install lead bends and employment would be thus increased. In order to force Padden to agree, the union induced his employees to quit and did not allow him to hire any journeymen plumbers to work for him. Padden sued the union for damages.

Decision: Judgment for Padden. The purpose of the union was not justified; therefore, interfering with Padden's employment of plumbers and preventing him from hiring others was a malicious interference with his contract rights, which imposed liability on the union. (Padden v. Local 90 United Assn. of Journeymen Plumbers, 168 Pa.Super. 611, 82 A.2d 327)

QUESTIONS AND PROBLEMS

1. Checklist of legal terms:
   (a) employee, employer (254)
   (b) union contract (255)
   (c) shop right (257)
   (d) laborers' or mechanics' lien laws (258)
   (e) doctrine of respondeat superior (261)
   (f) dangerous work doctrine (262)

2. State the objective(s) of each of the following rules of law:
   (a) An employer is justified in discharging an employee for willful disobedience of a proper order.
   (b) An employer may recover damages from a third person who maliciously induces an employee to leave his employment.

3. Ambrose hires a crew of ten men to move a house. Without comment to Ambrose, Barker joins the crew and works with them daily under the supervision of Ambrose. When Barker is injured, he maintains that he is entitled to the protection of an employee. Is his contention sound?

4. Biddle was employed by the Emerson Company which was engaged in the business of storing meats. During his spare time Biddle worked for the Dutton Company which was engaged in marketing refrigerator equipment. Was Biddle guilty of a breach of duty owed to the Emerson Company?

5. Casper employs Egan as a machinist. Later Casper complains of Egan's work on the ground that it is not performed with the skill exercised by

---

[21] See Chapter 3.

Ervin who is reputed to be one of the best machinists in the city. What degree of skill has Casper a right to expect of Egan?

6. Faulkner works for Newhall, a photographer. Newhall has a special formula for solutions used in the development of photographic negatives. Faulkner discloses this formula to a competitor for $1,000. Can the latter be enjoined from using this information?

7. Van Camp was employed as a salesman in an electric supply shop. At odd times during the day he would experiment with materials belonging to his employer. Eventually he invented a new type of motor. Who was entitled to the invention?

8. Temple is employed by the Reed Company to devise an automatic parachute by which a disabled helicopter can be landed safely. After completing the device, Temple claims the invention. Decide.

9. Six men were employed by Patterson to do a certain job. One man was injured when two others were temporarily called away from the task by Patterson. The injured employee brought an action to recover damages. It was admitted that all the employees were competent and that six constituted an adequate number. Was the employee entitled to judgment?

10. Payton, a patron of a tavern, accused a waitress who was not serving him of shortchanging several of his friends on earlier occasions. Angered by this accusation, the waitress struck Payton. The blow caused Payton, who was seated on a counter stool, to fall over backwards and suffer a broken leg. Payton brought suit against the owner of the tavern for damages resulting from his injury. Was he entitled to recover?

11. Nadler employs Page to drive a truck and expressly instructs him to drive slowly and carefully. While making some deliveries, Page drives through a stop light and damages Rowe's automobile without any fault on Rowe's part. Is Rowe entitled to recover damages from Nadler?

12. The Standard Fertilizer Co. insured its barn against wind damage with the Ohio Farmers' Insurance Co. Under the policy the insurance company had the option of repairing or rebuilding damaged property. During a windstorm some shingles were blown from the barn. The insurance company told the insured to repair the shingles and send the bill to the company. The insured told Borden, one of its employees who did general carpentry work, to fix the roof. In doing so, he fell from the roof and was injured. He brought a workmen's compensation proceeding against the insurance company on the ground that he was working for the insurance company in repairing the roof. Decide. (Ohio Farmers' Ins. Co. v. Borden, 122 Ind.App. 45, 98 N.E.2d 684)

PART IV

Commercial Paper

Chapter 22

Nature, Kinds, and Parties

Under the law of contracts a promise, when supported by consideration, creates certain legal rights that may be assigned to another person. Even before these common-law rules relating to contracts were developing, another body of law, the law merchant, was creating principles relating to another type of obligation and the transfers of rights arising therefrom. In the course of time this other obligation became the bill of exchange, which today we also know as a draft, a trade acceptance, or, with certain modifications, a check. In time another type of instrument, the promissory note, appeared. Drafts and promissory notes may have the quality of negotiability that distinguishes them from ordinary contracts. As a group, they are known today as commercial paper or negotiable instruments.

Nature and Functions

Commercial paper includes written promises or orders to pay money that may be transferred by the process of negotiation. Much of the importance of commercial paper lies in the fact that it is more readily transferred than ordinary contract rights and that the transferee of commercial paper may acquire greater rights than would an ordinary assignee. A person who acquires a commercial paper may therefore be subject to less risk.

Commercial paper often serves as a substitute for money. When a person pays a debt by check, he is using a commercial paper. He might have paid in cash, but for convenience and possibly for safety, he used commercial paper. Of course, such payment is usually conditional upon the instrument being paid.[1]

Commercial paper may create credit. If a debtor gives his creditor a promissory note by which he agrees to pay him in sixty days, that is the same

[1] Uniform Commercial Code (UCC) Sec. 3-802(1); *Makel Textiles* v. *Dolly Originals*, [N.Y.S.2d] 4 UCCRS 95.

267

as an agreement that the creditor will not attempt to collect the claim until sixty days later.

Development of the Law of Commercial Paper

The use of various kinds of commercial paper developed as a result of the efforts of early merchants to avoid the dangers of transporting money to pay for purchases in distant lands. In England the principles relating to these instruments first became a part of the law merchant,[2] which was enforced by special merchants' courts. Later these principles were incorporated in the common law.

In the United States, first the common law and later various state statutes governed the use of negotiable instruments. The subject was then codified by the Uniform Negotiable Instruments Act, which was drafted in 1896. The Uniform Commercial Code was drafted in the middle of the present century. Article 3 of the Code governs commercial paper.

Kinds of Commercial Paper

Commercial paper falls into four categories: (1) promissory notes, (2) drafts or bills of exchange, (3) checks, and (4) certificates of deposit.

1 / Promissory notes. A *negotiable promissory note* is an unconditional promise in writing made by one person to another, signed by the maker, engaging to pay on demand or at a definite time a sum certain in money to order or to bearer.[3] It may be described simply as a written promise by one person, the *maker,* to pay money to another, the *payee.*

If the promissory note is payable "on demand," that is, immediately, it may be used as a substitute for money. If it is not payable until a future

| $500 00 | HARRISBURG, PA. | March 14, 1969 |
| Six months | after date I promise to pay to |
| the order of Harry L. Stone |
| Five hundred and 00/100 — Dollars |
| Payable at First National Bank |
| with interest at 5%. |
| No. 22 Due Sept. 14, 1969 | Allan B. Elliot |

Promissory Note

Parties: maker (buyer, borrower, or debtor)—Allan B. Elliot;
payee (seller, lender, or creditor)—Harry L. Stone.

---

[2] See page 3.
[3] UCC Sec. 3-104(1).

time, the payee in effect extends credit to the maker of the note for the period of time until payment is due.

Special types of promissory notes may or may not be negotiable, depending upon their form.

(a) SECURED NOTES. A mortgage note is secured by a mortgage on property that can be foreclosed if the note is not paid when due. A collateral note is accompanied by collateral security given to the payee by the borrower. Thus a person borrowing money might give the lender certain property, such as stocks or bonds, to hold as security for the payment of the note.

(b) JUDGMENT NOTE. A judgment note contains a clause which gives the holder the right to enter a judgment against the maker if the note is not paid when due. This power to confess judgment for the maker means that the delay and expense of a lawsuit are avoided should the promisor default on his note. Only a few of the states recognize judgment notes, which are also known as cognovit notes. Other states either prohibit or limit their use.

2 / Drafts. A *draft* or *bill of exchange* is an unconditional order in writing addressed by one person to another, signed by the person giving it, requiring the person to whom it is addressed to pay on demand or at a definite time a sum certain in money to order or to bearer.[4] In effect,

Draft (Bill of Exchange)

Drawer (seller or creditor)—Reeder; drawee (buyer or debtor)—Brown; payee (seller's or creditor's bank)—Citizens National Bank.

then, it is an order by one person upon a second person to pay a sum of money to a third person. The person who gives the order is called the *drawer* and is said to draw the bill. The person on whom the order to pay is drawn is the *drawee*. The person to whom payment is to be made is the payee. The drawer may designate himself as the payee.

---

[4] Sec. 3-104(1).

The drawee who is ordered to pay the money is not bound to do so unless he accepts the order. After he accepts, he may be identified as the *acceptor*. From the practice of "accepting" a bill of exchange, the term "acceptance" is sometimes applied to these instruments.

(a) SIGHT AND TIME DRAFTS. A *sight draft* is one that is payable on sight or when the holder presents it to the drawee for payment. A *time draft* is payable at a stated time after sight, such as "30 days after sight" or "30 days after acceptance," or at a stated time after a certain date, such as "30 days after date" (of instrument).

(b) DOMESTIC AND INTERNATIONAL BILLS. If a draft is drawn and payable in the same state, or is drawn in one state and payable in another, it is a *domestic bill*. If it appears on the face of the instrument that it was drawn in one nation and payable in another, it is an *international bill of exchange* or a foreign draft.

(c) TRADE ACCEPTANCES. A draft may be sent by a seller of goods to a purchaser, as the drawee, with the understanding that if he approves of the goods sent him, the drawee will accept the instrument immediately. This type of draft is a *trade acceptance*.

Check [5]

Drawer (depositor and buyer or debtor)—Kline; drawee (depositor's bank)—Liberty National Bank; payee (seller or creditor)—Ace Cleaners.

3 / Checks. A *check* is a bill of exchange drawn on a bank payable on demand.[6] It is an order by a depositor, the drawer, upon his bank, the

---

[5] In many areas checks are sorted by banks by electronic machines. Checks used in these areas carry at the bottom the number and district of the bank and the depositor's account number printed in metallic ink. Through the cooperation of the American Bankers Association, the printers of checks, and business machines manufacturers, a set of numbers has been developed, the peculiar shape of the numbers being chosen in order to give each number a particular metallic weight that can be distinguished from other numbers by the electronic machines.

[6] UCC Sec. 3-104(2)(b).

drawee, to pay a sum of money to the order of another person, the payee. A check is always drawn upon a bank as drawee and is always payable upon demand.

(a) CASHIER'S CHECK. A cashier's check is drawn by a bank on itself, ordering itself to pay the stated sum of money to the depositor or to the person designated by him. The depositor requests his bank to issue a cashier's check for a given amount, which amount either the depositor pays the bank or the bank charges against the depositor's account. The depositor then forwards the cashier's check, instead of his own, to the seller or creditor.

(b) BANK DRAFT. A bank draft is in effect a check drawn by one bank upon another bank in which the first bank has money on deposit, in the same way that a depositor draws a check upon his own bank. It is commonly used for the same purpose as a cashier's check.

4 / Certificates of deposit. A *certificate of deposit* is an instrument issued by a bank that acknowledges the deposit of a specific sum of money and promises to pay the holder of the certificate that amount, usually with interest, when the certificate is surrendered.[7]

Parties to Commercial Paper

A note has two original parties—the maker and the payee; and a draft or a check has three original parties—the drawer, the drawee, and the payee. In addition to these original parties, a commercial paper may have one or more of the following parties:

1 / Indorser.[8] A person who owns a commercial paper may transfer it to another person by signing his name on the back of the instrument and delivering it to the other person. When he does so, he is an *indorser.* Thus, if a check is made payable to the order of *P* to pay a bill owed to him, *P* may indorse it to *E* to pay a debt that *P* owes *E.* In such a case *P,* who was the payee of the check since it was originally made payable to him, is now also an indorser.

2 / Indorsee. The person to whom an indorsement is made is called an *indorsee.* He in turn may indorse the instrument; in that case he is also an indorser.

3 / Bearer. The person in physical possession of a commercial paper which is payable to bearer is called a *bearer.*

---

[7] A certificate of deposit "is an acknowledgment by a bank of receipt of money with an engagement to repay it," as distinguished from a note, which "is a promise other than a certificate of deposit." UCC Sec. 3-104(2)(c), (d).

[8] The form *endorse* is commonly used in business. The form *indorse* is used in the UCC.

4 / Holder. A *holder* is a person in possession of a commercial paper which is payable at that time either to him, as payee or indorsee, or to bearer. A holder may be (a) a holder for value, (b) a holder in due course, or (c) a holder through a holder in due course.

(a) HOLDER FOR VALUE. Ordinarily a commercial paper is given to a person in the course of business in return for or in payment for something. If the holder gives consideration for the instrument or takes it in payment of a debt, he is a *holder for value.* Thus, if an employee is paid wages by check, he is a holder for value of the check since he received it in payment of wages earned and due. If he indorses the check to his landlord to pay the rent, the landlord becomes the holder for value.

A person may receive a commercial paper without giving anything for it. Thus, when an uncle gives his nephew a check for $100 as a Christmas present, the nephew becomes the owner or holder, but he has not given anything for the check and he does not become a holder for value.

(b) HOLDER IN DUE COURSE. A person who becomes a holder of the paper under certain circumstances is given a favored standing and is immune from certain defenses. He is termed a *holder in due course.*[9] A person becoming the holder of an instrument after it was once held by a holder in due course is ordinarily given the same special rights as a holder in due course.[10]

5 / Accommodation party. A person who becomes a party to a commercial paper in order to add the strength of his name to the paper is called an *accommodation party.* If he is a maker, he is called an accommodation maker; if an indorser, an accommodation indorser. For example, *M* applies to a bank for a loan and is willing to give the bank a promissory note naming it as payee. The bank may be unwilling to lend money to *M* on the strength of his own promise. It may be that *C,* who has a satisfactory credit standing, will sign the note as a comaker with *M.* If *C* does this without receiving any value from the payee but only for the purpose of bolstering *M's* credit, it is said that he signs for accommodation and is an accommodation maker.

It is immaterial whether the accommodation party signs the paper merely as a friend or because he is paid for doing so.[11] When the paper is taken for value before it is due, the accommodation party is liable in the capacity in which he signed, even though the holder knows of his accommodation character.[12]

---

[9] See p. 331.
[10] See p. 335.
[11] UCC Sec. 3-415(1).
[12] *Seaboard Finance Co.* v. *Dorman,* 4 Conn.Cir. 154, 227 A.2d 441.

The accommodation party (*C*) is not liable to the party accommodated (*M*).[13] If the accommodation party is required to pay the instrument, however, he may recover the amount of the payment from the person accommodated.

Facts: Bilderbeck, Inc., borrowed money from a bank. As part of the transaction, it signed a promissory note for the amount of the loan, which note was signed by Simson as an accommodation maker. When the note was due, Bilderbeck failed to make payment. The note was paid by Simson, who then sued Bilderbeck for reimbursement for the amount that he paid.

Decision: Judgment for Simson. When an accommodation party pays the holder of the paper, the paper is not discharged by such payment. The accommodation party acquires the rights of a transferee and may proceed against the accommodated party. (Simson v. Bilderbeck, Inc., 76 N.Mex. 667, 417 P.2d 803)

The accommodation party may not assert defenses not available to the accommodated party. Hence an individual as an accommodation party for a corporation cannot raise the defense of usury when under the law the accommodated corporation is barred from raising that defense.[14] Nor can the accommodation party raise any defenses personal to the party accommodated. To illustrate, the fact that the accommodated maker has been declared bankrupt does not relieve an accommodator who signs as comaker as he has a primary liability to the holder.[15]

6 / Guarantor. A *guarantor* is a person who signs a commercial paper and adds a statement that he will pay the instrument under certain circumstances. Ordinarily this is done by merely adding "payment guaranteed" or "collection guaranteed" to the signature of the guarantor on the paper.

The addition of "payment guaranteed" or similar words means that the guarantor will pay the instrument when due even though the holder of the paper has not sought payment from any other party. "Collection guaranteed" or similar words means that the guarantor will not pay the paper until after the holder has sought to collect payment from the maker or acceptor and has been unable to do so. In such a case the holder must first obtain a judgment against the maker or acceptor, which judgment remains unpaid because the sheriff cannot find sufficient property of the debtor in question to pay it, or the debtor must be insolvent.[16]

---

[13] *United Refrigerator Co.* v. *Applebaum,* 410 Pa. 210, 189 A.2d 253.
[14] *Raby* v. *Commercial Banking Corp.,* 208 Pa.Super. 52, 220 A.2d 659.
[15] *Delbrook Associates* v. *Law,* [N.Y.S.2d] 4 UCCRS 88.
[16] UCC Sec. 3-416(1)(2). If the meaning of the guaranty is not clear, it is construed as a guaranty of payment. Sec. 3-416(3). The guaranty written on the commercial paper is binding without regard to whether it may not satisfy the requirements of a local Statute of Frauds. Sec. 3-416(6).

Liability of Parties

A person who by the terms of the instrument is absolutely required to pay is primarily liable. For a note, the maker is primarily liable; for a draft, the acceptor, or drawee who has accepted, is primarily liable. A guarantor of payment is primarily liable in any case. Other parties are either secondarily liable or not liable in any capacity. A person who transfers the paper but does not sign it is not liable for its payment.[17]

QUESTIONS AND PROBLEMS

1. Checklist of legal terms:
   - (a) commercial paper (267)
   - (b) negotiable promissory note; maker, payee (268)
   - (c) draft or bill of exchange (269); drawer (269), drawee (269), acceptor (270)
   - (d) sight draft, time draft; domestic bill, international bill of exchange; trade acceptance (270)
   - (e) check (270)
   - (f) certificate of deposit (271)
   - (g) indorser, indorsee (271)
   - (h) bearer (271); holder (272), holder for value (272), holder in due course (272)
   - (i) accommodation party (272), guarantor (273)

2. State the objective(s) of each of the following rules of law:
   - (a) The transferee of a commercial paper may acquire greater rights than would an ordinary assignee.
   - (b) A holder for value may recover from an accommodation party even though the holder knew of his character as such.

3. Cortner and Wood, in payment for certain sheep, executed and delivered an instrument whereby they promised to pay $2,000 to the order of W. C. Thomas. Thomas signed his name on the back and delivered the note to Fox, at the latter's bank in Lewisburg, Tennessee. Who of the foregoing parties, if any, are properly described as (a) payee, (b) maker, (c) drawer, (d) indorser, (e) acceptor, (f) drawee, and (g) indorsee? (Fox v. Cortner, 145 Tenn. 482, 239 S.W. 1069)

4. Herdlicka and Thieda executed a promissory note as makers. The latter was, in fact, an accommodation party. Subsequently Kratovil, the holder of the note, agreed with Herdlicka to extend the time for paying the note and to reduce the monthly payments that were to be made. When the note was not paid in full, Kratovil sued Thieda who claimed that he was released by the fact that the obligation of Herdlicka had been changed by the extension of time, which was made without Thieda's consent. Decide. (Kratovil v. Thieda, 62 Ill.App.2d 234, 210 N.E.2d 819)

---

[17] Sec. 3-401(1). Such a person, however, may be bound by certain warranties that bind the person transferring commercial paper. See p. 297.

Chapter 23

Negotiability

In order to be negotiable, an instrument must be (1) in writing (2) signed by the maker or drawer; it must contain (3) a promise or order (4) of an unconditional character (5) to pay in money (6) a sum certain; (7) it must be payable on demand or at a definite time; and (8) it must be payable to order or to bearer.[1] (9) If one of the parties is a drawee, he must be identified with reasonable certainty.

In addition to these formal requirements, the instrument usually must be delivered or issued by the maker or drawer to the payee or the latter's agent with the intent that it be effective and create a legal obligation.

If the foregoing requirements are satisfied, the instrument is negotiable and remains so regardless of what happens to it thereafter. If an instrument is not negotiable, it is governed by the law of contracts.[2]

Requirements of Negotiability

1 / Writing. A commercial paper must be in writing. Writing includes typing, printing, engraving, and any other method of setting words down.

The instrument may be written in ink or pencil, but the use of pencil is not wise because such writing is not as durable as ink and the instrument may be more easily altered. A commercial paper may be written partly in ink and partly in pencil, or it may be partly printed and partly typewritten with a handwritten signature. The latter combination is common today through the use of printed forms that are filled out by the parties.

As the commercial paper is in writing, the parol evidence rule applies. This rule prohibits modifying the instrument by proving the existence of a conflicting oral agreement alleged to have been made before or at the time of the execution of the commercial paper. Thus an instrument payable on a certain date cannot be shown by parol evidence to be payable at a later date, nor can parol evidence be introduced to prove the existence of an option to renew the instrument.

---

[1] Uniform Commercial Code, Sec. 3-104(1).

[2] *Business Aircraft Corp.* v. *Electronic Communications,* [Tex.Civ.App.] 391 S.W. 2d 70. Note, however, that if the nonnegotiability results from the fact that the instrument is not payable to order or bearer, it is governed by Article 3 of the Code with the limitation that there cannot be a holder in due course of such paper. UCC Sec. 3-805.

Likewise parol evidence is not admissible to contradict the unconditional promise of a note by showing that repayment was to be made only from the profits of a particular enterprise.[3]

A carbon copy of an instrument is not admissible as evidence until the loss or destruction of the original has been shown.

2 / Signature. The instrument must be signed by the maker or drawer. His signature usually appears at the lower right-hand corner of the face of the instrument. It is immaterial, however, where the signature is placed. If the signature is placed on the instrument in such a manner that it does not in itself clearly indicate that the signer was the maker, drawer, or acceptor, however, he is held to be only an indorser.

The signature itself may consist of the full name or of any symbol adopted for that purpose. It may consist of initials, figures, or a mark.[4] A person signing a trade or an assumed name is liable to the same extent as though he signed his own name.[5]

In the absence of a local statute that provides otherwise, the signature may be made by pencil, by typewriter, by print, or by stamp, as well as by pen.

Facts: Katz sued the Timms Jewelry Company and Sidney Teicher on a promissory note that stated ". . . we promise to pay . . ." and was signed with a rubber stamp of the company name under which was the handwritten signature of Teicher. The company claimed that it was not bound because the rubber stamp was not a sufficient signature.

Decision: Judgment for Katz. A signature may be made by a stamp or by any other process. (Katz v. Teicher, 98 Ga.App. 842, 107 S.E.2d 250)

(a) AGENT. A signature may be made for a person by his authorized agent.[6] No particular form of authorization to an agent to execute or sign a commercial paper is required, and the existence of his authority is established as in other cases.

An agent signing should indicate that he acts in a representative capacity, and he should disclose his principal. When he does both, the agent is not liable if he has acted within the scope of his authority.[7] The representative capacity of an officer of an organization is sufficiently shown when he signs

[3] *Venuto* v. *Strauss,* [Tex.Civ.App.] 415 S.W.2d 543.
[4] When a signature consists of a mark made by a person who is illiterate or physically incapacitated, it is commonly required that the name of the person be placed upon the instrument by someone else, who may be required to sign the instrument as a witness. Any form of signature is sufficient in consequence of the definition of "signed" as including any symbol executed or adopted by a party with the present intention to authenticate a writing. UCC Sec. 1-201(39).
[5] Sec. 3-401(2).
[6] Sec. 3-403(1).
[7] UCC Sec. 3-403; *Childs* v. *Hampton,* 80 Ga.App. 748, 57 S.E.2d 291.

his name and the title of his office either before or after the organization name.[8]

(b) NONDISCLOSURE OF AGENCY. If a person who signs a commercial paper in a representative capacity, such as an agent or officer of a corporation, executes the instrument in such a way as to make it appear that it is his own act, he is personally bound with respect to subsequent holders, regardless of whether he intended it to be his own act or his act in a representative capacity. In such a case, parol evidence is not admissible to show that it was not intended that the agent or representative be bound or to show that it was intended to bind the undisclosed principal. Such evidence is admissible, however, against the person with whom the agent or officer had dealt.

(c) PARTIAL DISCLOSURE OF AGENCY. The instrument may read or the agent may sign in a way that either his principal is identified or the agent's representative capacity is disclosed. In such a case, the agent is personally liable on the instrument to third persons acquiring the instrument; but if sued by the person with whom he dealt, he may prove that it was intended that the principal should be bound.[9]

3 / Promise or order to pay. If the instrument is a promissory note, it must contain a promise to pay money.[10] No particular form of promise is required; the intention as gathered from the face of the instrument controls. If the maker uses such phrases as "I certify to pay" or "the maker obliges himself to pay," a promise is implied even though the word "promise" is not used.

A mere acknowledgment of a debt, such as a writing stating "I.O.U.," is not a commercial paper. It is not a promise to pay, and a promise is not implied from the fact that the existence of the debt is admitted.

Facts: An officer of the Cassone Realty Co. wrote and signed a paper reading, "The Cassone Realty Company owes . . . Anne Schout ten thousand dollars and should be paid to her as soon as possible." Was this a commercial paper?

Decision: No. A mere acknowledgement of an obligation is not an unconditional promise, even though it is coupled with a statement that it should be paid as soon as possible. (Schout v. Cassone Realty Co., [Pa.] 31 Lehigh County 126)

If the instrument is a draft or a check, it must contain an order or command to pay money.[11] As in the case of a promise in a note, no particular form of order or command is required.

---

[8] UCC Sec. 3-403(3).
[9] Sec. 3-403(2)(b).
[10] Sec. 3-104(1)(b).
[11] Sec. 3-104(1)(b).

4 / Unconditional. The promise or order to pay must be unconditional. For example, when an instrument makes the duty to pay dependent upon the completion of the construction of a building or upon its placement in a particular location, the promise is conditional and the instrument is non-negotiable. A promise to pay "when able" is generally interpreted as being conditional, but a minority of states regard it as requiring payment within a reasonable time and as therefore being an absolute promise.[12]

The use of a term of politeness, such as "please," before an otherwise unconditional order to pay does not destroy the effect of the order within the meaning of the requirements for negotiability. But if the effect of the provision is merely a request to pay money or to request it if certain facts are true, the "order" to pay is conditional and the instrument is nonnegotiable.

Whether a promise or an order to pay is conditional or unconditional is determined from an examination of the instrument itself. An unconditional or absolute promise in an instrument cannot be shown to be conditional by a provision found in a separate written agreement or as part of an oral agreement.

An order for the payment of money out of a particular fund, such as ten dollars from next week's salary, is conditional.[13] If, however, the instrument is based upon the general credit of the drawer and the reference to a particular fund is merely to indicate a source of reimbursement for the drawee, such as "charge my expense account," the order is considered to be absolute.[14]

Facts: Wilkes, the agent of the Cow Creek Sheep Co., drew a company check on the First National Bank payable to Brown. On the check was the notation "For Wilkes." Before Brown cashed the check, the company told the bank not to pay the check. When the bank refused to make payment, Brown sued the company. The company defended on the ground that there was no consideration for the promise and that consideration was necessary because the check was nonnegotiable since it did not contain an unconditional order to pay.

Decision: Judgment for Brown. Paper is not made nonnegotiable because it contains a recital of the purpose for which it is drawn or the account to be charged with its payment. (Brown v. Cow Creek Sheep Co., 21 Wyo. 1, 126 P. 886)

A promise or order that is otherwise unconditional is not made conditional by the fact that it "is limited to payment out of a particular fund or the proceeds of a particular source, if the instrument is issued by a government or governmental agency or unit; or is limited to payment out of the

---

12 *Mock v. First Baptist Church,* 252 Ky. 243, 67 S.W.2d 9.
13 UCC Sec. 3-105(2)(b).
14 Sec. 3-105(1)(f); *Rubio Savings Bank v. Acme Farm Products Co.,* 240 Iowa 547, 37 N.W.2d 16.

entire assets of a partnership, unincorporated association, trust, or estate by or on behalf of which the instrument is issued." [15]

5 / Payment in money. A commercial paper must call for payment in *money,* that is, any circulating medium of exchange which is legal tender at the place of payment. It is immaterial, as far as negotiability is concerned, whether it calls for payment in a particular kind of current money. If the order or promise is not for money, the instrument is not negotiable. For example, an instrument which requires the holder to take merchandise in lieu of money is nonnegotiable.

An instrument is also nonnegotiable when the promise or order to pay money is coupled with an agreement by the maker or drawee to do something else, unless that agreement will make it easier for the holder of the instrument to collect the money due on the instrument. A provision of the latter type is deemed not to impair negotiability because the effect of its inclusion is to make the paper more attractive to a purchaser and thus it encourages the exchange or transfer of the commercial paper.

6 / Sum certain. The instrument must not only call for payment in money but also for a sum certain. Unless the instrument is definite on its face as to how much is to be paid, there is no way of determining how much the instrument is worth.

When there is a discrepancy between the amount of money as written in words and the amount as set forth in figures on the face of the instrument, the former is the sum to be paid. If the words that indicate the amount are ambiguous or uncertain, reference may be made to the amount in figures to determine the amount intended.[16] When there is an uncertainty of this type in connection with a check, it is common practice for a bank officer or teller to telephone the drawer in order to learn just what amount was intended before payment is made on the instrument.

The fact that the instrument may require certain payments in addition to the amount specified as due does not make the instrument nonnegotiable when such additional amounts come within any of the following categories:

(a) INTEREST. A provision for the payment of interest does not affect the certainty of the sum, even though the interest rate changes upon default.[17]

Facts: Ingel made a contract with Allied Aluminum Associates for the installation of aluminum siding on his home. He signed a promissory note

---

[15] UCC Sec. 3-105(1)(g), (h).
[16] Sec. 3-118(c).
[17] Sec. 3-106(1)(b).

which stated that group credit life insurance would be obtained by the holder of the note without additional charge to the customer. Later the note was transferred to a finance company, Universal C.I.T. Credit Corp. When it brought suit against Ingel, he claimed that the note was nonnegotiable because of the above insurance provision and also because the note provided for the payment of "interest after maturity at the highest lawful rate."

Decision: Judgment for Universal. The note was negotiable. The obligation to procure insurance was an obligation resting on the holder and not on the maker of the note. The provision for the addition of interest upon the maturity of the note did not violate the requirement of stating a sum certain as its effect was the same as though it had read payable "with interest." (Universal C.I.T. Credit Corp. v. Ingel, 347 Mass. 119, 196 N.E.2d 847)

(b) INSTALLMENTS. A provision for payment in installments does not affect certainty. Nor is certainty affected when the installment provision is coupled with a provision for acceleration of the date of payment for the total amount upon default in any payment.

(c) EXCHANGE. A provision for the addition of exchange charges does not affect the certainty of the sum payable since its object is in effect to preserve the constancy of the value involved. In this connection, the fact that the money due on the instrument is stated in a foreign currency does not make the instrument nonnegotiable.[18]

(d) COLLECTION COSTS AND ATTORNEY'S FEES. The certainty of the sum is not affected by a provision adding collection costs and attorney's fees to the amount due, although general principles of law may place a limit upon the amount that can be recovered for such items.

(e) DISCOUNT AND ADDITION. The certainty of the sum and the negotiability of the instrument are not affected by a provision that allows a discount if earlier payment is made or which increases the amount due if late payment is made.[19]

7 / Time of payment. A commercial paper must be payable on demand or at a definite time. If it is payable "when convenient," the instrument is nonnegotiable because the day of payment may never arrive. An instrument payable only upon the happening of a particular event that may never happen is not negotiable. For example, a provision to pay when a person marries is

---

[18] Sec. 3-107(2). The Code follows banking practice in stating that an instrument payable in a foreign currency calls for the payment of a sum certain of money which, in the absence of contrary provision, is the number of dollars that the foreign currency will purchase at the buying sight rate on the due date or demand date of the instrument.
[19] UCC Sec. 3-106(1)(c).

not payable at a definite time since that particular event may never occur. It is immaterial whether the contingency in fact has happened, because from an examination of the instrument alone it still appears to be subject to a condition that may never happen.

(a) DEMAND. An instrument is payable on demand when it is expressly specified to be payable "on demand;" or at sight or upon presentation, that is, whenever the holder tenders the instrument to the party required to pay and demands payment; or when no time for payment is specified.[20] To illustrate the last point, when a note is completely executed except that the time for payment and the lines indicating payment by installments are left blank, the full amount of the note is payable on demand, as opposed to the contention that no amount is payable.[21]

(b) DEFINITE TIME. The time of payment is definite if it can be determined from the face of the instrument.

An instrument satisfies the requirement of providing for payment at a definite time when it is payable (1) on or before a stated date, (2) at a fixed period after a stated date, (3) at a fixed period after sight, (4) at a definite time subject to any acceleration, (5) at a definite time subject to extension at the option of the holder, (6) at a definite time subject to extension to a further definite date at the option of the maker or acceptor, or (7) at a definite time subject to an extension to a further definite date automatically upon or after the occurrence of a specified act or event.[22]

Facts: Ferri made a note payable to the order of Sylvia "within ten years after date." Within less than that time Sylvia sued for the money due, claiming that the note was uncertain and therefore parol evidence could be admitted to show that it had been agreed that she could have the money any time she needed it.

Decision: Judgment for Ferri. A commercial paper payable "within" a stated period does not mature until the time fixed arrives, which in this instance was ten years after the date of the note. Since the time for payment was certain and complete on the face of the instrument, parol evidence could not be admitted to show that there was a different oral agreement regarding the date of maturity. (Ferri v. Sylvia, [R.I.] 214 A.2d 470)

An instrument payable in relation to an event which though certain to happen will happen on an uncertain date, such as a specified time after death, is not negotiable.[23]

---

[20] Sec. 3-108.
[21] *Master Homecraft Co.* v. *Zimmerman,* 208 Pa.Super. 401, 222 A.2d 440.
[22] UCC Sec. 3-109(1).
[23] Sec. 3-109(2).

8 / Order or bearer. A commercial paper must be payable to order or bearer.[24] This requirement is met by such expressions as "Pay to the order of John Jones," "Pay to John Jones or order," "Pay to bearer," and "Pay to John Jones or bearer." The use of the phrase "to the order of John Jones" or "to John Jones or order" is important in showing that the person executing the instrument is indicating that he does not intend to restrict payment of the instrument to John Jones and that he does not object to paying anyone to whom John Jones orders the paper to be paid. Similarly, if the person executing the instrument originally states that it will be paid "to bearer" or "to John Jones or bearer," he is not restricting the payment of the instrument to the original payee. If the instrument is payable "to John Jones" or "to bearer, John Jones," however, the instrument is not negotiable.

It is not necessary that the instrument actually use the words "order" or "bearer." Any other words indicating the same intention are sufficient. It has been held that the words "pay to holder" could be used in place of "order" or "bearer" without affecting the negotiability of the instrument.

(a) ORDER PAPER. An instrument is *payable to order* when by its terms it is payable to the order or assignees of any person specified therein with reasonable certainty (Pay to the order of H. F. Rousch), or to such a person or his order (Pay to H. F. Rousch or his order).[25]

(b) BEARER PAPER. An instrument is *payable to bearer* when by its terms it is payable (1) to bearer or the order of bearer, (2) to a specified person or bearer, or (3) to "cash," or "the order of cash," or any other indication that does not purport to designate a specified person.[26]

An instrument payable to order and indorsed in blank becomes payable to bearer and may be negotiated by delivery alone until specially indorsed.[27]

9 / Drawee. In the case of a draft or check, the drawee must be named or described in the instrument with reasonable certainty.[28] This requirement, which is based upon practical expediency, is designed to enable the holder of the instrument to know to whom he must go for payment.

When there are two or more drawees, they may be either joint drawees (*A* and *B*) or alternative drawees (*A* or *B*).[29]

---

[24] While an instrument not payable to order or bearer is not commercial paper, it is nevertheless governed by Article 3 of the Code, except that there cannot be a holder in due course. UCC Sec. 3-805.

[25] An instrument is also payable to order when it is conspicuously designated on its face as "exchange" or the like, and names a payee. UCC Sec. 3-110(1).

[26] UCC Sec. 3-111.

[27] Sec. 3-204(2).

[28] Sec. 3-102(1)(b).

[29] Sec. 3-102(1)(b). The instrument is nonnegotiable if there are successive drawees. Successive drawees exist when, if one drawee fails to pay, the holder is required to go to the next drawee for payment rather than proceed at once against secondary parties.

Effect on Negotiability of Provisions for Additional Powers or Benefits to Holder of Instrument

Certain provisions in an instrument that give the holder certain additional powers and benefits may or may not affect negotiability.[30]

1 / Collateral. The inclusion of a power to sell collateral security upon default does not impair negotiability. An instrument secured by collateral contains as absolute a promise or order as an unsecured instrument. Negotiability is not affected by a promise or power to maintain or protect collateral or to give additional collateral,[31] or to make the entire debt due, if the additional collateral is not supplied.

2 / Acceleration. A power to accelerate the due date of an instrument upon a default in the payment of interest or of any installment of the principal, or upon the failure to maintain or provide collateral does not affect the negotiability of an instrument. However, a power to accelerate "at will" or when a person "deems himself insecure" must be exercised in good faith.[32]

Facts: Bellino was a maker of a promissory note payable in installments which contained the provision that upon default in the payment of any installment the holder had the option of declaring the entire balance "due and payable on demand." The note was negotiated to Cassiani, who sued Bellino for the full debt when there was a default on an installment. Bellino raised the defense that no notice of acceleration had been given to her prior to the suit.

Decision: Judgment for Cassiani. An acceleration clause is valid and there is no requirement of notifying the party liable as, having signed the note, he knows of the presence of such a clause and he knows the accelerating fact, his default. (Cassiani v. Bellino, 338 Mass. 765, 157 N.E.2d 409)

3 / Confession of judgment. Negotiability is not affected by a provision authorizing the entry of a judgment by confession upon a default. In a judgment note the confession of judgment saves the holder the expense and delay of a lawsuit. If the holder of the instrument is authorized to confess judgment at any time, whether before maturity or not, however, the instrument is generally nonnegotiable.[33]

4 / Waiver of statutory benefit. State statutes commonly provide that when a person is sued for a debt, a certain amount or kind of his property is exempt from the claim. If the party who executes a commercial paper promises to waive his rights under such a statute in order that it will be a

---

[30] UCC Sec. 3-112.
[31] Sec. 3-112(1)(c).
[32] Sec. 1-208.
[33] *Bittner* v. *McGrath*, 186 Pa.Super. 477, 142 A.2d 323. See p. 269.

little easier to collect the amount due, negotiability is ordinarily not affected. A waiver of this kind is void in some states, however.

5 / Requirement of another act. A provision authorizing the holder to require an act other than the payment of money, such as the delivery of goods, makes the instrument nonnegotiable.[34]

Additional Documents

The fact that a separate document is executed that gives the creditor additional protection, as by a lien on goods or the right to repossess property sold to the maker of the instrument, does not impair its negotiability.

Immaterial Provisions

The addition or omission of certain other provisions has no effect upon the negotiability of an otherwise negotiable instrument.

A commercial paper is not affected by the omission of the date. In such case it is regarded as carrying the date of the day on which it was executed and delivered to the payee. If the date is essential to the operation of the instrument, such as when the instrument is payable a stated number of days or months "after date," any holder who knows the true date may insert that date.

When a commercial paper is dated, the date is deemed prima facie to be the true date, whether the date was originally inserted or was thereafter added.[35] If the wrong date is inserted, the true date can be proved unless the holder is a holder in due course or a holder through a holder in due course, in which case the date, even though wrong, cannot be contradicted.

A commercial paper may be antedated or postdated, provided that is not done to defraud anyone. The holder acquires title as of the date of delivery without regard to whether this is the date stated in the instrument.

It is immaterial, so far as negotiability is concerned (1) whether an instrument bears a seal; (2) whether it calls for payment in a particular kind of current money; (3) whether it fails to state that value has been given; or (4) whether it recites the giving of value without stating its nature or amount.

Although these provisions are not required in order to make the instrument negotiable, local law may require such a recital.

Some forms of checks provide a special space in which the drawer can note the purpose for which the check is given or set forth the items discharged by the check. Statutes may require that some instruments state the purpose for which they are given in order to help avoid certain types of

[34] UCC Sec. 3-112, Official Comment.
[35] Sec. 3-114(3).

fraud. The Code does not repeal any statute requiring the nature of the consideration to be stated in the instrument.[36] The fact that a trade acceptance recites that "the transaction which gives rise to this instrument is the purchase of goods by the acceptor from the drawer" does not affect its negotiability.[37]

Negotiability is not affected by a provision that by indorsing or cashing the instrument, the person receiving it takes it in full settlement of a specified claim or of all claims against the drawer.[38]

QUESTIONS AND PROBLEMS

1. Checklist of legal terms:
   (a) money (279)
   (b) payable to order (282)
   (c) payable to bearer (282)

2. State the objective(s) of each of the following rules of law:
   (a) A signature on a commercial paper may be made by pencil, by typewriter, by print, or by rubber stamp, as well as by pen.
   (b) An instrument is negotiable even though it contains a clause authorizing acceleration when the holder deems himself insecure.

3. Abner writes an instrument that reads as follows: "October 7, 1968. Thirty days from date I, Harold B. Abner, promise to pay James A. Black or order, sixty dollars." Does this instrument satisfy the requirement that it be signed by the maker or drawer?

4. The Chase Company contends that it is not liable on a series of notes that it has issued because the signature of the treasurer of that company was merely a printed signature. Do you agree with this contention?

5. Crocket, a farmer, mails a promissory note and a letter to Darnell. In the letter Crocket states that the promise is made upon the condition that the rainfall for the year is normal. Does this condition affect the negotiability of the note?

6. Ellis executed an instrument by which he ordered Fitzpatrick to pay to the order of Owens $5,000 out of the proceeds of the sale of the contents of a certain Penn Central freight car. When an action was brought by the holder of the instrument, Ellis contended that it was not negotiable. Do you agree?

7. Parsons orders Kraft to "Pay to Shay or order $1,000 and charge the amount to my business account." Is this instrument negotiable?

8. Is an instrument that reads as follows negotiable? "January 23, 1969. Ninety days from date I promise to pay Robert Rolf or order 500 bushels of soybeans. (Signed) Thomas A. Riley."

---

[36] Compare Sec. 3-112(1)(a), (2).
[37] *Federal Factors Inv.* v. *Wellbanks*, 241 Ark. 44, 406 S.W.2d 712.
[38] UCC Sec. 3-112(1)(f).

9. A promissory note contains a provision for adding collection costs and attorney's fees in case of nonpayment at maturity. Does this provision affect the negotiability of the instrument?

10. The amount of a check appears in figures as "$150.00" and in words as "One hundred five and no/100 . . . Dollars." How much is the holder of the check entitled to collect?

11. Pogue sold a car of melons to Sherman. Pogue drew a draft on Sherman to pay the purchase price to the order of the First National Bank. The draft was payable thirty days after the arrival of the car of melons at its destination. Was the instrument negotiable?

12. Barry Thompson executed and delivered to his sister, Jane Thompson, a note for $5,000. The note was payable one day after Barry Thompson's death. When the instrument was presented as a claim against Thompson's estate, it was contended that the instrument was not negotiable because of its time of payment. Do you agree?

13. Cortis contracted to buy storm windows and gave the seller a promissory note in payment. The note promised to pay $3,400 in installments as set forth in the schedule of payments stated in the note. The schedule of payments, however, was left blank. Was the note void because no definite time for payment was stated? (Liberty Aluminum Products Co. v. Cortis, [Pa.] 14 D.&C.2d 624, 38 Wash.Co. 223)

14. Max Melsheimer and John H. Anderson were doing business as Melsheimer & Co. Anderson executed a promissory note on behalf of the firm payable to Hommel. He signed the note "Max Melsheimer & Co. John H. Anderson." When Hommel sued on the note, the defense was raised that the note as signed did not constitute an obligation of the firm. Decide. (Melsheimer v. Hommel, 15 Col. 475, 24 P. 1079)

15. R. Rice executed a promissory note payable to the order of O. Rice, promising to pay the sum of $1,500 when O. Rice became twenty-one. The note was not paid at that time, and a suit was brought to enforce the note. It was claimed that the note was nonnegotiable. Do you agree? (Rice v. Rice, 43 App.Div. 458, 60 N.Y.S. 97)

Chapter 24

Transfer of Commercial Paper

Commercial paper may be transferred by negotiation or assignment. When a commercial paper is transferred by a negotiation, the rights of the transferee may rise higher than those of the transferor. When the transfer is made by assignment, the assignee has only those rights which the assignor possessed and the assignee is subject to all defenses existing against the assignor prior to notice of the assignment.

INDORSEMENTS

The person to whom an instrument is payable on its face or by special indorsement or the person in possession of bearer paper may indorse it for the purpose of negotiating it by merely signing his name on it or he may add certain words or statements as part of his indorsement. By definition, an indorsement is properly written on the back of the instrument.

Kinds of Indorsements

The four principal kinds of indorsements are (1) blank, (2) special, (3) qualified, and (4) restrictive.

1 / Blank indorsement. When the indorser signs only his name, the indorsement is called a *blank indorsement* since it does not indicate the person to whom the instrument is to be paid, that is, the indorsee. This is the most common form of indorsement because it is the simplest and the easiest to write. It may be a dangerous form of indorsement since it has the effect of making the instrument payable to bearer and it can be negotiated by delivery by anyone, even a finder or a thief. Such an indorsement usually may be made with safety on a check when the holder is in a bank where he intends to deposit or cash the check.

Facts: Schroeder, the payee of a note, indorsed the instrument in blank and delivered it to Enyart, Van Camp and Feil, Inc. That corporation changed its name and then merged with the First Securities Co. The cashier of the Enyart company delivered its securities, including the Schroeder note, to the office of the new company. When this company sued Schroeder, he claimed that there was no proof that it was the owner of the note.

Decision: Judgment for First Securities Co. The instrument was bearer paper because the last indorsement was blank. As such, it was negotiated by the physical delivery of the instrument. (First Securities Co. v. Schroeder, 351 Ill.App. 173, 114 N.E.2d 426)

The holder of an instrument on which the last indorsement is blank may protect himself by writing above the signature of the last indorser a statement that the instrument is made payable to him.[1] This is called "completing" the indorsement or "converting" the blank indorsement to a special indorsement by specifying the identity of the indorsee. This has the same effect as though the indorser had named the holder as indorsee.

Negotiation by a blank indorsement does three things: (a) it passes the ownership of the instrument; (b) it makes certain warranties;[2] and (c) it imposes upon the indorser a liability to pay the amount of the instrument if the maker or drawee fails to do so and certain conditions are then satisfied by the holder.

2 / Special indorsement. A *special indorsement* consists of the signature of the indorser and words specifying the person to whom the indorser makes the instrument payable, that is, the indorsee. Common forms of this type of indorsement are "Pay to the order of Robert Hicks, E. S. Flynn" and "Pay to Robert Hicks or order, E. S. Flynn." It is not necessary that the indorsement contain the words "order" or "bearer." Thus a commercial paper indorsed in the form "Pay to Robert Hicks, E. S. Flynn" continues to be negotiable and may be negotiated further. In contrast, an instrument which on its face reads "Pay to E. S. Flynn" is not negotiable.

When the last indorsement on the instrument is special, an indorsement and delivery by or on behalf of the last indorsee is required for further negotiation.[3]

As in the case of the blank indorsement, a special indorsement transfers title to the instrument and results in the making of certain warranties[4] and in imposing a liability upon the indorser to pay the amount of the instrument under certain conditions.

3 / Qualified indorsement. A *qualified indorsement* is one that qualifies the effect of a blank or a special indorsement by destroying the liability of the indorser to answer for the default of the maker or drawee. This may be done by including the words "without recourse" in the body of the indorsement, or by using any other words that indicate an intention to destroy the indorser's secondary liability for the default of the maker or drawee.[5]

---

[1] Uniform Commercial Code, Sec. 3-204(3).
[2] See p. 296.
[3] UCC Sec. 3-204(1).
[4] See p. 297.
[5] UCC Sec. 3-414(1).

The qualifying of an indorsement does not affect the passage of title or the negotiable character of the instrument. It merely limits the indorser's liability to the extent of the qualification.

Facts: Brown executed and delivered a promissory note to E. E. Cressler, who negotiated the note to C. W. Cressler by indorsement without recourse. When C. W. Cressler sued to enforce the note, Brown claimed that there was a lack of consideration. E. E. Cressler knew that consideration was lacking, but he claimed that this did not impose liability on him because he had indorsed the note without recourse.

Decision: Judgment against E. E. Cressler. The indorsement "without recourse" only freed him from liability for the face of the paper. It did not free him from liability based on warranties arising from indorsement without any limitation of warranties. As an element of his warranty liability, he warranted that he had no knowledge of any defense which would be good against him, which warranty was broken because he knew that there was the defense of lack of consideration. (Cressler v. Brown, 79 Okla. 170, 192 P. 417)

This form of indorsement is most commonly used when the qualified indorser is admittedly a person who has no personal interest in the transaction, as in the case of an attorney or an agent who is merely indorsing to his client or principal a check made payable to him by a third person. Here the transferee recognizes that the transferor is not a party to the transaction and therefore is not in a position where he should be asked to guarantee the paper.

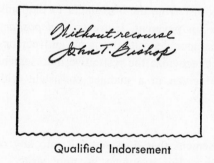

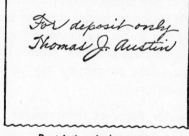

Qualified Indorsement   Restrictive Indorsement

4 / Restrictive indorsements. A *restrictive indorsement* specifies the purpose of the indorsement or the use to be made of the paper. Restrictive indorsements may be of the following types:

(a) INDORSEMENT FOR DEPOSIT. This indorsement indicates an intent that the instrument be deposited, such as "For deposit only," "For deposit only to the account of John Sacuto" and "Pay to the Springfield National Bank for deposit only." [6]

---

[6] Sec. 3-205(c).

(b) INDORSEMENT FOR COLLECTION. This indorsement indicates an intention that the instrument be received by the indorsee for the purpose of effecting the collection of the instrument, such as "For collection only," or "Pay to any bank or banker." [7]

(c) INDORSEMENT PROHIBITING FURTHER NEGOTIATION. The indorsement, "Pay to Harold Singer only," indicates an intent that no further negotiation should occur and is therefore restrictive.[8]

(d) AGENCY OR TRUST INDORSEMENT. An indorsement that makes the indorsee the agent of the indorser, such as "Pay to (indorsee, agent) on account of (indorser, principal)," or which makes the indorsee the owner subject to a trust for another person, such as "Pay to (indorsee, mother) to hold for use of (third person, son)," are restrictive indorsements in that they state that the indorsement is for the benefit or use of the indorser or another person.[9]

(e) CONDITION AS A PART OF THE INDORSEMENT. An indorsement which indicates that it is to become effective only upon the satisfaction of a particular condition, such as "Pay to Calvin Nash upon completion of Contract #83," is a restrictive indorsement.[10]

A restrictive indorsement does not have the effect of prohibiting further negotiation even though it expressly attempts to do so.[11] In all cases the transferee may therefore be a holder, just as is true under a nonrestrictive indorsement. A bank may ignore and is not affected by the restrictive indorsement of any person except the holder transferring the instrument to the bank or the person presenting it to the bank for payment. However, a *depositary bank,* that is, the one in which the customer deposits the item, and persons not in the bank collection process must recognize the restrictive indorsement to the extent of applying any value [12] given in a manner consistent with the indorsement.[13]

Irregular Form of Indorsement

The indorser may make an indorsement that does not fall into any of the standard categories of indorsements. For example, he may write, "I hereby assign all my right, title, and interest in the within note," and then sign his name. The signature in such a case is effective as an indorsement in spite of the added words, on the theory that the indorser actually intended to

---

[7] Sec. 3-205(c).
[8] Sec. 3-205(b).
[9] Sec. 3-205(d).
[10] Sec. 3-205(a).
[11] Sec. 3-206(1).
[12] See p. 331.
[13] UCC Sec. 3-206(2). Additional limitations are imposed in the case of collection and conditional indorsements, Sec. 3-206(3), and trust indorsements, Sec. 3-206(4).

indorse and was merely attempting to make certain that he transferred his interest.[14]

Irregular Indorser

Sometimes the capacity in which a particular party has signed a commercial paper cannot be determined by looking at the instrument. For example, a note may be indorsed by A to the order of B, and then by B to the order of C, and by C to the order of D. Assume that on the back of the note there also appears the signature of M. How does M enter into the history of the instrument? It may be that when A was about to indorse the note to B, B would not accept the note unless M signed it also as an accommodation party. This fact, however, cannot be determined just by looking at the back of the note; and it appears that the indorsement of M is irregular. An *irregular indorser*, then, is a person who signs his name as an indorser before delivery but who is otherwise not a party to the instrument.

An indorsement which is not in the chain of title, that is, which is irregular, thereby gives notice of its accommodation character.[15] In any case, the accommodation party is liable to the holder for value according to the capacity in which he has signed.[16]

Correction of Name by Indorsement

Sometimes the name of the payee or indorsee to a commercial paper is improperly spelled. Thus H. A. Price may receive a paycheck which improperly is payable to the order of "H. O. Price." If this was a clerical error and the check was intended for H. A. Price, the employee may ask his employer to write a new check payable to him in his proper name.

The payee or indorsee whose name is misspelled may indorse the wrong name, his correct name, or both. A person giving or paying value for the instrument may require both.[17]

This correction of name by indorsement may only be used when it was intended that the instrument should be payable to the person making the corrective indorsement. If there were in fact two employees, one named H. A. Price and the other H. O. Price, it would be illegal as a forgery for one to take the check intended for the other and by indorsing it obtain for himself the benefit or proceeds of the check.

The fact that an irregularity in the name of a party has not been corrected does not destroy the validity of the negotiation, and irregularities in the names are to be ignored unless it is shown that different persons were in

---

[14] Sec. 3-202(4).
[15] Sec. 3-415(4).
[16] Sec. 3-415(1), (2).
[17] Sec. 3-203.

fact identified by the different names, as contrasted with the different names merely standing for the one person. Thus, it has been held that a note had been properly negotiated when it was indorsed "Greenlaw & Sons by George M. Greenlaw," although made payable to "Greenlaw & Sons Roofing & Siding Co.," and there was nothing to show that the two enterprises were not the same firm.[18]

Bank Indorsements

In order to simplify the transfer of commercial paper from one bank to another in the process of collecting items, "any agreed method which identifies the transferor bank is sufficient for the item's further transfer to another bank."[19]

Likewise, when a customer has deposited an instrument with a bank but has failed to indorse it, the bank may make an indorsement for him unless the instrument expressly requires the payee's personal indorsement. Furthermore the mere stamping or marking on the item of any notation showing that it was deposited by the customer or credited to his account is as effective as an indorsement by the customer would have been.[20] In this way the annoyance and loss of time of returning the instrument to the customer for his indorsement are eliminated. The exception to the requirement of a "personal indorsement" is commonly applicable in the case of paychecks issued by governments and some corporations.

NEGOTIATION

The method of negotiating an instrument depends upon the terms of the instrument or its indorsement. If it is order paper, it can be negotiated only by indorsement and delivery. If it is bearer paper, it may be negotiated by transfer of possession alone.

Methods of Negotiation

1 / Negotiation of order paper. An instrument payable to order may be negotiated only by the indorsement of the person to whom it is payable at the time and delivery by him or with his authorization.

> Facts: Coppersmith executed and delivered negotiable notes to Elliott. The payee indorsed the notes to Whitehurst but kept the notes in her possession because she wanted to collect the interest during her life and wanted the indorsee to have the notes upon her death. After

---

[18] *Watertown Federal Savings & Loan Ass'n.* v. *Spanks,* 346 Mass. 398, 193 N.E. 2d 333.
[19] UCC Sec. 4-206.
[20] Sec. 4-205(1).

Elliott's death, her executor, Cartwright, found the notes. Both Cartwright and Whitehurst sought to enforce the notes against Coppersmith.

Decision: Judgment for Cartwright. An indorsement alone does not effect a transfer. As the paper was order paper, both indorsement and delivery by Elliott were required to negotiate the instrument. (Cartwright v. Coppersmith, 222 N.C. 573, 24 S.E.2d 246)

The indorsement must be written on the instrument itself [21] or, if necessary, on a paper attached to it, called an *allonge*. The indorsement must be placed on the instrument by the person to whom it is then payable, unless the indorsement is made for accommodation. The indorsement ordinarily must be genuine or authorized in order to make negotiation of the instrument effective.

(a) MULTIPLE PAYEES AND INDORSERS. Ordinarily one person is named as payee by the instrument, but two or more payees may be named. In that case, the instrument may specify that it is payable to any one or more of them or that it is payable to all jointly. If nothing is specified, the instrument is payable to all of the payees [22] and they are *joint payees*. For example, if the instrument is made payable "to the order of *A* and *B*," the two persons named are joint payees. The importance of this kind of designation is that it requires the indorsement of both *A* and *B* to negotiate the instrument further. This protects *A* against the action of *B*, and vice versa. Each knows that the other cannot secretly negotiate the instrument and pocket the proceeds. This rule does not apply, however, when the payees are partners or when one person is authorized to act for all and he indorses for all.

Joint payees or joint indorsees who indorse are deemed to indorse jointly and severally.[23] If the instrument is payable to *alternate payees* or if it has been negotiated to alternate indorsees, as *A or B*, it may be indorsed and delivered by either of them.

(b) AGENT OR OFFICER AS PAYEE. The instrument may be made payable to the order of an officeholder. For example, a check may read, "Pay to the order of the Receiver of Taxes." Such a check may be received and negotiated by the person who at the time is the Receiver of Taxes. This is a matter of convenience since the person writing the instrument is not required to find out the name of the Receiver of Taxes at that time.

---

[21] Sec. 3-202(2). If there is no more space on the instrument itself, the indorsement may be written on another piece of paper provided it is so firmly attached to the instrument that it becomes part of it. The indorsement cannot be on a piece of paper that is merely clipped to the note. *Talcott* v. *Ratowsky*, [Pa.] 38 D.&C.2d 624, 84 Dauph. County 258.

[22] UCC Sec. 3-116.

[23] Sec. 3-118(e).

If the instrument is drawn in favor of a person as "Cashier" or some other fiscal officer of a bank or corporation, it is payable to the bank or corporation of which he is such an officer, and may be negotiated by the indorsement of either the bank or corporation, or of the named officer.[24]

(c) PARTIAL NEGOTIATION. A negotiation of part of the amount cannot be made.[25] The entire instrument must be negotiated to one person or to the same persons. If the instrument has been partly paid, however, the unpaid balance may be transferred by indorsement. This is proper since the amount then due, although it is only a portion of the original amount due, is being transferred.

(d) MISSING INDORSEMENT. Although order paper cannot be negotiated without indorsement, it can be assigned to another without indorsement. In such a case, the transferee has the same right as the transferor; and if he gave value for the paper, he also has the right to require that the transferor indorse the instrument to him for the purpose of effecting a negotiation of the instrument.

2 / Negotiation of bearer paper. Any commercial paper payable to bearer may be negotiated by merely transferring possession, that is, by handing it over to another person.[26] This is true not only when the instrument expressly states that it is payable to bearer, but also when the law interprets it as being payable to bearer, as in the case of a check payable to the order of "Cash."

Although bearer paper may be negotiated by such transfer, the one to whom it is delivered may insist that the bearer indorse the paper so as to impose upon the transferor the liability of an indorser. This situation most commonly arises when a check payable to "Cash" is presented to a bank for payment.

Because bearer paper can be negotiated by a transfer alone, a thief, a finder, or an unauthorized agent can pass title as though he owned or had the right to negotiate the instrument. This means that the use of bearer paper should be avoided whenever possible.

3 / Time for determining character of paper. The character of the paper is determined as of the time when the negotiation is about to take place, without regard to what it was originally or at any intermediate time. Accordingly, when the last indorsement is special, the paper is order paper without regard to whether it was bearer paper originally or at any intermediate time, and the holder cannot ignore or strike out intervening indorse-

---

[24] Sec. 3-117(a).
[25] Sec. 3-202(3). The partial negotiation is not a nullity but is given the effect of a partial assignment.
[26] UCC Sec. 3-202(1).

ments, or otherwise treat it as bearer paper because it had once been bearer paper.

Forged and Unauthorized Indorsements

A forged or unauthorized indorsement is by definition no indorsement of the person by whom it appears to have been made and, accordingly, the possessor of the paper is not the holder when the indorsement of that person was necessary for effective negotiation of the paper to the possessor.

As an exception, the "forgery" of the payee's name is effective as if the payee had made or authorized the "signature" when the case comes within one of the three impostor situations.

An indorsement in the name of a named payee is effective if (1) an impostor has induced the maker or drawer to issue the instrument to him or a confederate in the name of the payee; (2) the person signing as, or on behalf of, the drawer intends that the named payee shall have no interest in the paper; or (3) an agent or employee of the drawer has given the drawer the name used as the payee intending that the latter should not have any interest in the paper. The last situation is illustrated by the case of the employee who fraudulently causes his employer to sign a check made to a customer or other existing person, but the employee does not intend to send the check to that person but rather intends to forge the latter's indorsement, to cash the check, and to keep the money for himself.

These impostor case provisions are based upon the social desire to place the loss upon the party who could have prevented it through the exercise of greater care to protect subsequent holders of an instrument who have no reason to know of any wrongdoing.

Even when the impostor's indorsement is effective, he is subject to civil or criminal liability for making such an indorsement.[27]

> **Facts:** Edmund Jezemski and Paula Jezemski were husband and wife but were separated. Paula and another man who impersonated Edmund borrowed money. The loan check drawn by the Philadephia Title Insurance Company was payable to the order of Edmund Jezemski and Paula Jezemski. The check was then indorsed and Edmund's signature was forged. The check was paid by the Fidelity-Philadelphia Trust Company on which it was drawn. When the forgery was discovered, the Philadelphia Title Insurance Company claimed that the Fidelity-Philadelphia Trust Company was liable for the amount of the check because the latter company had made payment on a forged indorsement.
>
> **Decision:** Judgment for Fidelity-Philadelphia. The check had been made payable to an impersonator who in consequence of the impersonation was de-

---

[27] Sec. 3-405. The rule stated in the text likewise applies to promissory notes although ordinarily the situation arises in connection with checks.

scribed in the check as Edmund Jezemski. The signing of that name on the check by any person was effective as an authorized signature; and the bank, claiming through that signature, was a holder, as against the claim that the payee's name had been forged. (Philadelphia Title Insurance Co. v. Fidelity-Philadelphia Trust Co., 419 Pa. 78, 212 A.2d 222)

Effect of Incapacity or Misconduct on Negotiation

A negotiation is effective even though (a) it is made by a minor or any other person lacking capacity; (b) it is an act beyond the powers of a corporation; (c) it is obtained by fraud, duress, or mistake of any kind; (d) or the negotiation is part of an illegal transaction or was made in breach of duty. Under general principles of law apart from the Code, the transferor in such cases may be able to set aside the negotiation or to obtain some other form of legal relief. If, however, the instrument has in the meantime been acquired by a holder in due course, the negotiation can no longer be set aside.[28]

Assignment of Commercial Paper

In addition to transfer by negotiation, a commercial paper may be transferred by assignment.

1 / Assignment by act of the parties. A commercial paper is regarded as assigned when a person whose indorsement is required on the instrument transfers it without indorsing it. In such a case the transferee has only the rights of an assignee, and he is subject to all defenses existing against the assignor prior to notice of the assignment. He is entitled, however, to require that the transferor indorse the instrument.[29] If the indorsement is obtained, then the transferee is deemed a holder but only as of the time when the indorsement is made.

2 / Assignment by operation of law. An assignment by operation of law occurs when by virtue of the law the title of one person is vested in another. If the holder of a commercial paper becomes a bankrupt or dies, the title to the instrument vests automatically in the trustee in bankruptcy or in the personal representative of the estate.

WARRANTIES OF TRANSFEROR

The transferor, by the act of making the transfer, warrants the existence of certain facts. The warranties of the transferor are not always the same but vary according to the nature of the indorsement he makes or whether he transfers the instrument without indorsement. A distinction is also made

---

[28] UCC Sec. 3-207.
[29] Sec. 3-201(3).

between warranties arising in connection with acceptance or payment [30] and those arising in connection with transfer. In the case of transfer by indorsement the warranty may run to a subsequent holder but in the case of transfer by delivery only to the immediate transferee.

Warranties of Unqualified Indorser

When the holder negotiates it by an unqualified indorsement, and receives consideration, several warranties are implied. The transferor warrants that:

(1) He has a good title, which includes the genuineness of all indorsements necessary to his title to the instrument, or that he is authorized to act for one who has such good title.[31]

(2) His act of transferring the instrument is rightful, independent of the question of his title or authority to act.[32]

(3) The signatures on the instrument are genuine or executed by authorized agents.[33]

(4) The instrument has not been materially altered.[34]

(5) He has no knowledge of the existence or commencement of any insolvency proceeding against the maker or acceptor of the instrument, or against the drawer of an unaccepted bill of exchange.[35]

(6) No defense of any party is good as against him.[36]

These warranties made by the unqualified indorser pass to his transferee and to any subsequent holder who acquires the instrument in good faith.[37]

Warranties of Other Parties

1 / Warranties of qualified indorser. The qualified indorser makes the same warranties as an unqualified indorser except that the warranty as to "no defenses" is limited to a warranty that the indorser does not have knowledge of any defense, rather than that no such defense exists.[38] The warranties of a qualified indorser run to the same persons as those of an unqualified indorser.

2 / Warranties of transferor by delivery. The warranties made by one who transfers a commercial paper by delivery are the same as those made by an unqualified indorser except that they run only to the immediate transferee and then only if he had given consideration for the transfer.[39]

---

[30] See p. 311.
[31] UCC Sec. 3-417(2)(a).
[32] Sec. 3-417(2)(a).
[33] Sec. 3-417(2)(b).
[34] Sec. 3-417(2)(c).
[35] Sec. 3-417(2)(e).
[36] Sec. 3-417(2)(d).
[37] Sec. 3-417(2).
[38] Sec. 3-417(3). The qualified indorsement does not exclude other warranties unless it is specified to be "without warranties."
[39] UCC Sec. 3-417(2).

Subsequent holders cannot enforce such warranties against this prior trans-feror by delivery regardless of the status or character of such holders.

3 / Warranties of selling agent or broker. A selling agent or broker who discloses the fact that he is acting as such only warrants his good faith and authority to act. If he does not disclose such capacity, he is subject to the warranties of an ordinary transferor who transfers in the manner employed by him.[40]

QUESTIONS AND PROBLEMS

1. Checklist of legal terms:
   (a) blank indorsement (287), special indorsement (288), qualified indorsement (288), restrictive indorsement (289)
   (b) depositary bank (290)
   (c) irregular indorser (291)
   (d) allonge (293)
   (e) joint payees, alternate payees (293)

2. State the objective(s) of each of the following rules of law:
   (a) Bearer paper may be negotiated by transferring possession of the instrument without an indorsement.
   (b) The holder of an instrument under a blank indorsement may protect himself from theft or loss of the instrument by writing above the signature of the blank indorser a statement that the instrument is made payable to the holder.

3. Bond negotiates a check to Glenn Craig by blank indorsement. Craig writes the following words above Bond's indorsement: "Pay to the order of Glenn Craig." What is the effect of Craig's act?

4. Curtis, the payee of a note, indorses the instrument without recourse to Dawson. Does this instrument impair the negotiability of the note?

5. In making a deposit at his bank, Ewald uses in the indorsement the words "For deposit only" on a check drawn on another bank. What is the effect of this indorsement on subsequent indorsements on this check?

6. Wilbur O. Bryan receives a check payable to the order of W. O. Byron.
   (a) Under what circumstances can this person correct his name by indorsement?
   (b) How is such a correction made?

7. Fields executed and delivered a draft payable to Norman, Penny, and Shaw. Penny indorsed the draft to Brooks. Was the instrument properly negotiated?

8. A draft was indorsed by the payees, Roberts and Tudor, to Lipton. If the drawee fails to pay the instrument when it is due, can Lipton recover from Tudor?

---

[40] Sec. 3-417(4).

9. Ulmer is the payee of a note for $1,000. He indorses the note to Vickers to the extent of $500. Can Vickers collect $500 from the maker of the note?

10. Wiseman was the holder of a draft payable to his order. Later he delivered the instrument for value without indorsement to Zwick. Can Zwick require Wiseman to indorse the draft?

11. George executed and delivered a note payable to "Walter Haller or bearer." Haller, without indorsing the note, delivered it to Jones. When Jones brought an action to recover on the note, George contended that the instrument had not been negotiated. Was his contention sound?

12. Gorman, who holds Jansen's check payable to bearer, indorses it "to Edward Huston or order." Huston, without indorsing the check, transfers it to Laird. Was this transfer a proper negotiation?

13. Kimble executed and delivered a promissory note payable "to the order of William Ledford." Ledford transferred the note without indorsement for value to his wife. Did this transfer constitute negotiation?

14. When Manning, the payee of a note, died, the executor of his estate indorsed and delivered the instrument to Lacey. Was this a proper transfer?

15. Benton, as agent for Savidge, received an insurance settlement check from the Metropolitan Life Insurance Co. He indorsed it "For deposit" and deposited it in the Bryn Mawr Trust Company in the account of Savidge. What was the nature and effect of this indorsement? (Savidge v. Metropolian Life Insurance Co., 380 Pa. 205, 110 A.2d 730)

16. Mobilla indorsed a negotiable instrument "without recourse." He was later sued by the Union Bank as holder of the instrument for breach of his warranty as a transferor of the instrument. He claimed that he was not liable. Decide. (Union Bank v. Mobilla, [Pa.] 43 Erie Co.L.J. 45)

17. Humphrey drew a check for $100. It was stolen and the payee's name forged as an indorser. The check was then negotiated to Miller who had no knowledge of these facts. Miller indorsed the check to the Citizens Bank. Payment of the check was voided on the ground of the forgery. The Citizens Bank then sued Miller as indorser. Decide. (Citizens Bank of Hattiesburg v. Miller, 194 Miss. 557, 11 So.2d 457)

Chapter 25

Notes and Presentment for Payment

A promissory note is a two-party commercial paper, which means that originally only the maker and payee are involved. The maker is liable for payment on the due date specified in the note or on demand if the note is a demand instrument. If the maker dishonors the note when it is presented to him for payment, the payee and indorser, if any, may become secondarily liable for payment.

The procedures for presenting a promissory note for payment and for giving notice of dishonor, which are explained in this chapter, apply to all types of commercial paper.

Liability of Maker

The liability of a maker of a promissory note is primary. This means that payment may be demanded of him and that he may be sued by the holder as soon as the debt is due. The maker is under the duty to pay the note at the time and at the place named, if any place is specified by the note, unless he can set up a defense that is valid against the holder.

By the very act of signing the promissory note, the maker deprives himself of two possible defenses. He admits (1) the existence of the payee named in the instrument and (2) the payee's capacity at that time to indorse the paper.[1] Consequently, when the payee of a note is a minor or a bankrupt, the maker cannot deny the validity of the title of a subsequent holder of the instrument on the ground that the payee lacked capacity to transfer title.

When a note is issued in payment of a debt, the original obligation is suspended until the instrument is due or until presentment for payment in the case of demand paper. If the note is dishonored for nonpayment, the holder may sue either on the note or on the underlying obligation.[2]

In addition to the liability of the maker on the note, other persons may be liable for the underlying debt or obligation as a matter of general contract law. This occurs when one person borrows money and gives the lender the promissory note of another person as security.

---

[1] Uniform Commercial Code, Sec. 3-413(3).
[2] UCC Sec. 3-802(1)(b).

Facts: Huntington was the general manager of the Eton Furniture Co. From time to time he borrowed money from the bank on behalf of Eton but would give his individual note to the bank and sometimes would pledge his own automobile as security. When Eton's checking account in the bank would have on deposit an amount greater than the loan to, Eton, the bank would deduct the amount of the loan with interest from Eton's account. Eton was declared a bankrupt, and the trustee in bankruptcy demanded that the bank return the amounts which it had deducted from Eton's account.

Decision: Judgment for bank. The loans were in fact loans to Eton; and the mere fact that Huntington had signed the notes did not mean that the loans were made to him, for the circumstances were such that his notes to the bank were security for the loans by the bank to Eton. It was therefore proper for the bank to deduct the loan payments from Eton's bank account. (In re Eton Furniture Company, [C.A.3d] 286 F.2d 93)

Need for Presentment for Payment

The holder of a promissory note need not present the instrument to the maker for payment in order to hold the latter liable on the note.[3] If the note is payable at a definite time, the maker is under a duty to pay the holder the amount due on the instrument as soon as that date is reached. The liability of the maker continues until barred by the Statute of Limitations.

If the note is demand paper, no special demand for payment is required. The holder may even begin a lawsuit against the maker without first making a demand for payment since the act of bringing suit is regarded as the making of a demand. If the note is payable at a definite time, the holder may bring suit on or after the due date without making a prior demand upon the maker.

An unqualified indorser is secondarily liable for the payment of the instrument, which means that he must pay the amount of the instrument to the holder under certain circumstances. Generally this duty arises only if (1) the instrument was presented for payment to the primary party on the due date or at maturity, (2) the primary party defaulted by failing to pay the amount of the instrument to the holder, and (3) the secondary party in question was given proper notice of the primary party's default.

A qualified indorser or a former holder of bearer paper who negotiates the instrument without indorsing it is not liable for payment. Such parties, as well as an unqualified indorser, who does have a secondary liability, may be liable for a breach of warranty, however.

---

[3] Sec. 3-501(1). If timely presentment of a note payable at a bank is not made, the maker is discharged to the extent that he has lost money on deposit in the bank because the bank has failed during the delay. See p. 328. Paper payable at a bank is described as "domiciled" paper.

Presentment for Payment

The following rules apply to the manner of presentment for payment:

1 / Person making presentment. Presentment for payment must be made by the holder of the instrument or by one authorized to act and receive payment for him.

2 / Manner of presentment. Demand for payment in any manner is sufficient. The party to whom the demand is made may require, however, that greater formality be observed, such as by requiring (a) reasonable identification of the person making presentment and evidence of his authority if he acts for another; (b) production of the instrument for payment at a place specified in it or, if there be none, at any place reasonable in the circumstances; and (c) a signed receipt on the instrument for any partial or full payment and its surrender upon full payment. If the party presenting the instrument does not comply with such a request at the time of making presentment, he is allowed a reasonable time within which to do so; but if he does not so comply, the presentment has no effect.[4]

In addition to a presentment for payment made directly between the parties, presentment may be made by sending the paper through the mail to the debtor, or by sending it through a clearing house.[5] A collecting bank may also make presentment for payment by sending merely a notice to the nonbank party to whom the demand for payment is made.[6] If the party so notified fails to act within a specified time, his inaction is treated as a dishonor of the note.[7]

3 / On whom presentment is made. Presentment for payment must be made to the party primarily liable, that is, the maker of the promissory note, or to a person who has authority to make or refuse payment on his behalf.[8] In the case of two or more makers, presentment may be made upon any one.[9] If the instrument is payable at a bank, it must be presented to a proper person in the bank who is authorized to pay the note.[10]

4 / Place of making presentment. Presentment for payment is properly made at the place specified in the instrument. When a place of payment is not specified, presentment is to be made at the place of business or the residence of the person from whom payment is to be demanded.[11]

---

[4] UCC Sec. 3-505.

[5] Sec. 3-504(2)(a),(b).

[6] Sec. 4-210(1). This provision is not applicable if the paper is payable by, through, or at a bank.

[7] UCC Sec. 4-210(2).

[8] Sec. 3-504(3).

[9] Sec. 3-504(3)(a).

[10] Sec. 3-504(4).

[11] Sec. 3-504(2)(c).

5 / Time of making presentment. A note payable at a stated date must be presented for payment on that date.[12] If the balance due on the note has been accelerated, payment must be made within a reasonable time after acceleration.[13] When the question is the secondary liability of any party, presentment for payment must be made within a reasonable time after such person became liable on the instrument.[14]

With respect to the hour of the day, presentment must be made at a reasonable time and, if made at a bank, must be made during its banking day.[15]

(a) COMPUTATION OF TIME. In determining the date of maturity of an instrument, the starting day is excluded and the day of payment is included. Thus an instrument dated July 3 and payable 30 days from date is due on August 2.[16]

(b) INSTRUMENT DUE ON LEGAL OR BUSINESS HOLIDAY. When the presentment of the paper is due on a day that is not a full business day, presentment is due on the next following full business day. This rule is applied whether the due day is not a full business day because it is a legal holiday or merely because the person who is required to make payment or the bank, as a matter of its business practice, is closed all day or for a half day.[17]

This rule is also applied when the due date is a business holiday for either party, that is, if either the person required to present the instrument or the person who is required to pay upon presentment is not open for a full business day on the due date. The date for presentment is extended to the first day that is a full business day for both of them.[18]

(c) EXCUSE FOR DELAY IN MAKING PRESENTMENT. Failure to present an instrument for payment at the proper time will be excused when the delay is caused by circumstances beyond the control of the holder. It must not, however, be caused by his conduct, negligence, or fault. Mere inconvenience is not a valid excuse for delay. When the circumstances that excuse the delay are removed, presentment must be made within a reasonable time.[19]

---

[12] Sec. 3-503(1)(c).

[13] Sec. 3-503(1)(d).

[14] Sec. 3-503(1)(e).

[15] Sec. 3-503(4).

[16] In business practice, when the time is expressed in terms of months rather than days, such as 1 month after date, the date of maturity is the same date in the month of maturity.

[17] UCC Sec. 3-503(3).

[18] Sec. 3-503(3).

[19] Sec. 3-511(1). Delay is also excused when the holder does not know that the instrument is due, UCC Sec. 3-511(1), as could occur if the date had been accelerated by a prior holder.

(d) EFFECT OF DELAY. An unexcused delay in presentment for payment discharges an indorser. If the note is *domiciled*, that is, payable at a bank, the delay may also operate to discharge the maker. The Code provides as to such paper that "any . . . maker of a note payable at a bank who because the . . . payor bank becomes insolvent during the delay is deprived of funds maintained with the . . . payor bank to cover the instrument may discharge his liability by written assignment to the holder of his rights against the . . . payor bank in respect of such funds, but such . . . maker is not otherwise discharged." [20]

When Presentment for Payment Is Excused or Unnecessary

Presentment of a note for payment is not required in order to charge secondary parties under certain circumstances.

1 / Waiver. Presentment is not required if it has been waived by the express or implied agreement of the secondary party in question.[21] A waiver of presentment is binding upon all parties if it appears on the face of the original note. If the waiver is part of an indorsement, however, it binds only that indorser.[22]

2 / Inability. Presentment is not required if it cannot be made in spite of the exercise of due diligence, as when presentment is attempted at the place where payment is to be made but neither the person who is to make payment nor anyone authorized to act for him can be found at that place.[23]

Facts: Samuel and Annie Jacobson executed a promissory note payable to Frank and Angelo Sarandrea. The payees indorsed the note to Cuddy. The makers of the note had moved, leaving no address, and presentment for payment was therefore not made. Notice of dishonor, however, was given to the indorsers. When Cuddy sued the Sarandreas, the defense was raised that Cuddy was not excused from making presentment on the Jacobsons and that the holder was negligent because he failed to ask the payee for the address of the maker.

Decision: There is no duty to ask the payee where the primary parties live. Therefor the defendants were liable. (Cuddy v. Sarandrea, 52 R.I. 465, 161 A. 297)

3 / Death or insolvency. Presentment for payment is not required if the maker of the note has died or if he has gone into insolvency proceedings after he had issued the note.[24]

---

20 UCC Sec. 3-502(1)(b).
21 Sec. 3-511(2)(a).
22 Sec. 3-511(6); *Gerrity Co.* v. *Padalino,* 51 Misc.2d 928, 273 N.Y.S.2d 994.
23 UCC Secs. 3-504(2), 3-511(2)(c).
24 Sec. 3-511(3)(a). Insolvency proceedings are defined by Sec. 1-201(22).

4 / Refusal to pay. The holder is not required to make presentment upon the maker if he has already refused to pay the note for no reason, or for any reason other than an objection that proper presentment was not made.[25]

5 / Belief or conduct of secondary party. The secondary party cannot demand that presentment be made if he has no reason to expect that the instrument would be paid and no right to require that payment be made.[26] This situation could arise when the maker executed the note for the benefit of the secondary party but the latter has breached the agreement with the maker and therefore has no right to expect or require that the maker perform his agreement by paying the note.[27]

Dishonor of Note

If the maker fails or refuses to pay the note when it is properly presented to him, he has dishonored the instrument by nonpayment. The fact that the maker does not make immediate payment of the note when it is presented to him does not dishonor the note. He has the right to withhold making payment until he has made a reasonable examination to determine that the note is properly payable to the holder. He cannot, however, delay payment beyond the close of business on the day of presentment.[28]

1 / Notice of dishonor. If commercial paper is dishonored by nonpayment, any secondary party who is not given proper notice thereof is released from liability, unless the giving of notice is excused.[29] It is only necessary that a party be given notice once, because a notice operates for the benefit of all parties who have rights on the instrument against the party notified.[30]

(a) WHO MAY GIVE NOTICE. The notice of dishonor is ordinarily given by the holder who has been refused payment or by his agent. If the agent made the presentment for payment, he of course may give notice of the dishonor to his principal who in turn may give it to the secondary party in question. When any person who is liable on the paper receives notice of its dishonor, he may in turn give notice to other secondary parties.[31]

---

[25] Sec. 3-511(3)(b).
[26] Sec. 3-511(2)(b).
[27] Sec. 3-511, Official Comment, point 4.
[28] Sec. 3-506(2).
[29] Sec. 3-501(2)(a). In the case of a "domiciled" note payable at a bank, the maker must be given notice that the note was not paid when presented at the bank and, if notice is not so given, the maker is released to the same extent already noted in connection with the effect of failure to present at the bank. UCC Sec. 3-501(2)(b). See p. 304.
[30] Sec. 3-508(8).
[31] Sec. 3-508(1).

(b) PERSON NOTIFIED. The notice of dishonor may be given to any party who is liable on the instrument. Notice to one partner is notice to each, even though the firm has been dissolved. When the party to be notified is dead or incompetent, notice may be sent to his last-known address or be given to his personal representative. If insolvency proceedings were begun against a party after the note was issued, the notice may be given to him or to the representative of his estate.[32]

(c) FORM OF NOTICE. Notice may be given in any reasonable manner. It may be oral or written, and it may be sent by mail. It may have any terms as long as it identifies the instrument and states that it has been dishonored. A misdescription that does not mislead the party notified does not nullify or vitiate the notice. Notice may be effected by sending the instrument itself, with a stamp, ticket, or writing attached thereto, stating that payment has been refused or by sending a notice of debit with respect to the paper.[33] Although not required, it is a sound precaution to give a signed, dated, written notice, and to keep a copy.

(d) PLACE OF NOTICE. The Code does not specify a place to which notice is to be given, but it provides that notice generally shall be deemed given whenever such steps have been taken as may be reasonably required to inform the other person, whether or not he actually comes to know of it. Furthermore, a person is deemed to receive notice or notification whenever the matter comes to his attention, or when the notice is delivered at the place of business through which the contract was made or at any other place held out by him as the place for the receipt of such communications.[34]

Facts: The Century L. & W. Co. gave a note to Merrill, who indorsed it to another person who indorsed it to the Bank of America Nat. T. & S. Association. When Century defaulted in payment of the note, the bank notified both indorsers. The notice sent to Merrill did not reach him because it was sent to an old address shown in the bank's files and not to the address shown in the current city directory. The bank used that directory to obtain the address of the other indorser, who received the notice sent him. Merrill defended on the ground that he had not been notified.

Decision: Judgment for Merrill. The holder had not used due diligence in giving Merrill notice, as established by the fact that the holder had not made use of the same current directory which it used with respect to the other indorser. Merrill was therefore not liable upon his indorsement. (Bank of America Nat. T. & S. Association v. Century L. &. W. Co., 19 Cal.App.2d 197, 65 P.2d 110)

---

[32] Sec. 3-508(1), (5), (6), (7).
[33] Sec. 3-508(3).
[34] Sec. 1-201(26).

(e) TIME OF NOTICE. Notice must be given before midnight of the third business day after dishonor. If the notice is given following the receipt of notice of dishonor from another party, it must be given before the midnight of the third business day after receiving such notice. When required of a bank, notice of dishonor must be given before midnight of the banking day following the banking day on which the note is dishonored or the bank receives notice of such dishonor.[35] A written notice of dishonor is effective when sent. Hence a notice sent by mail is sufficient even though it was never received, provided it was properly addressed, bore the necessary postage, and was properly mailed.[36]

Facts: Browne made a promissory note which was indorsed by Siegel. On the default of Browne, the holder of the note, Durkin, gave notice to Siegel by certified mail, return receipt requested. The notice was returned unopened and undelivered, marked refused, and with the blank form of post office receipt unsigned. When sued later, Siegel defended on the ground that he had not been given proper notice, that ordinary first-class mail could have been forwarded, and that he had been in Canada at the time the notice was sent.

Decision: Judgment for Durkin. Since only the "giving" of notice is required, a proper mailing is sufficient. A mailing is proper when the correct addresses of the addressee and the sender are on the envelope, and the proper postage is attached. The fact that certified mail is used does not impair the sufficiency of the notice, for such mail is safer even though it is not forwarded to a new address. (Durkin v. Siegel, 340 Mass. 445, 165 N.E.2d 81)

2 / Excuse for delay or absence of notice of dishonor. Delay in giving notice of dishonor is excused under the same circumstances as delay in making presentment for payment.[37]

The absence of any notice of dishonor is excused for three of the reasons considered as excusing the absence of presentment; namely (a) waiver, (b) inability to give notice in spite of due diligence, and (c) the fact that the party not notified did not have any reason to believe that the instrument would be paid nor any right to require payment.[38] When an indorser has such knowledge or so participates in the affairs of the primary party that the indorser knows the commercial paper will not be honored by the primary party, it is not required that the holder go through the useless gesture of making a presentment and of notifying the secondary party in order to hold him liable.[39]

[35] Secs. 3-508(2), 4-104(1)(h).
[36] Sec. 3-508(4).
[37] Sec. 3-511.
[38] Sec. 3-511(2). See p. 303.
[39] *Makel Textiles* v. *Dolly Originals,* [N.Y.S.2d] 4 UCCRS 95.

The requirements as to notice of dishonor are not applicable in determining the rights of co-obligors as between themselves. For example, when two indorsers are jointly liable and one pays the full amount, he is entitled to recover one half of such payment by way of contribution from his co-indorser without regard to whether the holder had given the co-indorser proper notice of dishonor.

Facts: Brown executed a promissory note payable to the order of Greenwald and Weinberg at the Peoples City Bank, McKeesport, Pennsylvania. The note was not paid at maturity. The holder mailed notices of dishonor to the payees, as indorsers, in separate enclosures but sent both notices to the address of Greenwald, who paid the amount of the note to the holder. In a suit for contribution brought by Greenwald against Weinberg, the latter disclaimed liability because of lack of notice of dishonor.

Decision: Judgment for Greenwald. Notice is required only as between a holder and a secondary party. There is no requirement of notice as between one secondary party seeking to require another secondary party to pay him his share of the amount paid the holder so that the burden of the payment, for which they were equally liable, will be equally borne by them. (Greenwald v. Weinberg, 102 Pa.Super. 485, 157 A. 351)

Proof of Dishonor

Since the liability of the secondary party depends upon whether certain steps were taken within the proper time, it is important for the holder to be able to prove that he has complied with the requirements of the law. In order to aid him in proving such essential facts, certain documents and records are admissible as evidence of dishonor and of any notice recited therein. The trier of fact must accept such evidence in the absence of proof to the contrary.[40] These documents and records include (1) protests, (2) bank stamps and memorandums, and (3) bank records.

1 / Protests. A *protest* is a memorandum or certificate executed by a notary public, or certain other public officers, upon information satisfactory to him, which sets forth that the particular identified instrument has been dishonored. It may also recite that notice of dishonor was given to all parties or to specified parties.[41]

2 / Banks stamps and memorandums. If the stamp put on the paper by a bank or the memorandum attached to the note by the bank is consistent with a dishonor, it is evidence of that fact. For example, a notation "Not sufficient funds" or "Payment stopped" indicates a dishonor or nonpayment

---

[40] UCC Secs. 3-510, 1-201(31).
[41] Secs. 3-509, 3-510(a).

of the instrument and therefore comes within this rule. On the other hand, a notation of "Indorsement missing" is not consistent with dishonor and is therefore not admissible as evidence of a dishonor.[42]

3 / Bank records. Bank records kept in the usual course of business are admissible as evidence of dishonor even though it cannot be shown who made the entry in the books.[43]

QUESTIONS AND PROBLEMS

1. Checklist of legal terms:
   (a) domiciled (304)
   (b) protest (308)

2. State the objective(s) of each of the following rules of law:
   (a) If a waiver of presentment for payment appears on the face of the instrument, it binds the party making it and all subsequent parties to the instrument.
   (b) If a commercial paper is dishonored by nonpayment, due notice of the dishonor, unless waived, must be given to a secondary party in order to hold him liable for the default.

3. Green, the indorsee of a note, brings an action on the instrument against Jennings, the maker. Jennings claims that Green does not have a valid title because Hobbs, the payee who negotiated the instrument to Green, is a minor. Is this contention sound?

4. Lang executed a note payable to the order of the Marshall Supply Company. Morton indorsed the note for the accommodation of Lang before the instrument was delivered to the company. On the maturity date of the note the Marshall Supply Company made a demand for payment by telephone. Lang was unable to pay. If the proper procedure was followed in all other respects, could the Marshall Supply Company recover from Morton?

5. Lewis, the payee of a note signed by Maxwell, Lambert, and Jefferson, negotiated the instrument to Hight. At the maturity of the note Hight presented it to Lambert who refused to make payment. Was this presentment sufficient?

6. McBride places his home address below his signature on a note payable to Wheaton. Wheaton indorses the note to Van Camp. When the instrument matures, will Van Camp make a proper presentment for payment if he presents it at McBride's place of business and finds no one there?

7. A three-months' note falls due on a Saturday.
   (a) On what day should the note be presented for payment?
   (b) At what time of the day should presentment be made?

---

[42] Sec. 3-510(b), Official Comment, point 2.
[43] Sec. 3-510(c).

8. Eyles was the holder of a note payable two years from date. He transferred the note by blank indorsement to Meyer. The note was not paid at maturity. What must Meyer do in order to hold Eyles liable as indorser?

9. When a note was dishonored, the holder gave notice of the dishonor by telephone to Padgett, an indorser. Was the notice of dishonor properly given?

10. Simpson, the holder of a promissory note, wishes to send a notice of dishonor to Tanner, an indorser for whom no address appears on the instrument. What is the proper place to which such notice should be sent—his business address, his home address, or his temporary address in another state?

11. Topmiller, an indorser of a note, receives notice of its dishonor from the holder. Topmiller wishes to give notice to several prior indorsers who live in the same city. What are the requirements for his giving due notice to these parties?

12. What is the advantage of using a protest when a note presented for payment is dishonored?

13. In an action brought by Hughes against a corporation that had indorsed a promissory note, the latter claimed that notice of protest had not been properly given. It was shown that the notice had been left at the company's office during business hours after the holder was unable to find any of the officers of the corporation. Was sufficient notice given? (Hughes v. Rankin Realty Co., 108 N.J.L. 485, 158 A. 487)

14. The Marianna Mfg. Co. made a promissory note payable to Burton. The note was indorsed by Burton. A subsequent holder, McCaskell, sued Burton because of the failure of the Marianna Mfg. Co. to pay the note. Burton defended on the ground that he had not been notified in writing of the dishonor of the note although he admitted that McCaskill's agent had told him of the dishonor. Was Burton's defense valid? (Burton v. McCaskill, 79 Fla. 173, 83 So. 919)

Chapter 26

Drafts and Presentment for Acceptance

A draft differs from a promissory note in that it is an order upon a third person to pay, instead of a promise to pay. It is made by a drawer who orders the drawee to pay the payee or his order, or to pay the bearer.

A note and a draft differ in another respect. A note must be presented for payment in order to hold secondary parties liable; under certain circumstances a draft must be presented for acceptance as well as for payment to accomplish that purpose.

If the drawer names himself as drawee, the paper is effective as a promissory note.[1] In such a case, the drawer is the primary party and procedures peculiar to drafts, such as presentment for acceptance, are eliminated.

LIABILITIES OF PARTIES TO A DRAFT

Liability of Drawee

1 / Before acceptance. An *acceptance* is the written assent of the drawee to the order of the drawer. Before a drawee accepts a draft, he is not liable for its payment. In the absence of a prior contract to accept the draft, the drawee is not under any duty to do so. His act of refusing to accept the draft does not give the holder any right to sue him on the instrument, even though he may thereby break a contract with the drawer or some other party that he would accept the bill. Neither does the draft operate as an assignment of any money, even though the drawee has in his possession funds of the drawer.[2]

2 / After acceptance. When the drawee accepts a draft, he is an acceptor and becomes primarily liable for its payment.[3] By the acceptance he also admits (a) the existence of the payee and (b) the payee's capacity at the time to indorse the draft.[4]

If the drawee pays the instrument to a person who claims it through a forged indorsement, the drawee must bear the loss of such payment.

---

[1] Uniform Commercial Code, Sec. 3-118(a).
[2] UCC Sec. 3-409(1); *Aiken Bag Corp.* v. *McLeod*, 89 Ga.App. 737, 81 S.E.2d 215.
[3] *Legal Discount Corp.* v. *Martin Hardware Co.*, 199 Wash. 476, 91 P.2d 1010.
[4] UCC Sec. 3-413(3).

Liability of Drawer

The drawer has a secondary liability. By executing the draft, he undertakes to pay the amount of the draft to the holder if, when the instrument is presented to the drawee for acceptance or payment, it is dishonored and proper proceedings are taken by the holder.

> **Facts:** Gill sold his airplane to Hobson for $8,000. The purchase price was paid by delivering to Gill a draft drawn by Yoes on the Phoenix Savings & Loan Company to the order of Gill. Yoes had no money in the savings and loan association but had applied to it for a loan. The loan application was rejected, and when the draft was presented on the association, it refused to pay it. Gill then sued Yoes on the draft. Yoes raised the defense that she had nothing to do with the purchase of the airplane and that she did not need one.

> **Decision:** Judgment for Gill. As Yoes has signed the draft as a drawer, she became secondarily liable as a drawer without regard to whether she had any interest in any transaction in which the draft was used as payment. (Gill v. Yoes, [Okla.] 360 P.2d 506)

The drawer, however, may insert in the draft a provision to exclude or limit his own liability to the holder.[5]

The drawer, as in the case of the maker of a promissory note, admits two things by the act of drawing the draft. He admits (1) the existence of the payee, and (2) the payee's capacity at the time to transfer the instrument. The effect of these statutory admissions is the same as in the case of the maker of a promissory note.[6]

When the drawer executes and delivers to the payee a draft in payment of a debt, the original obligation is suspended until the draft is due, or until presentment for payment if it is demand paper. If the paper is dishonored, the holder may sue either on the paper or on the underlying obligation.[7]

Liability of Indorser

The liability of an unqualified indorser of a draft is broader than that of an unqualified indorser of a promissory note. Initially, any unqualified indorser is under a secondary liability for the nonpayment of the instrument when due. In addition the unqualified indorser of a draft is under a secondary liability for the refusal of the drawee to accept the instrument when it is thereafter presented to him for acceptance.

In order to charge the unqualified indorser of the draft for either non-acceptance or nonpayment, it is necessary to prove that a presentment to

---

[5] Sec. 3-413(2).
[6] See p. 300.
[7] UCC Sec. 3-802(1)(b). Special provisions apply when a bank is the drawer. Sec. 3-802(1)(a).

the drawee had been properly made and due notice given to the indorser of the drawee's failure to accept or pay.

PRESENTMENT OF DRAFT FOR ACCEPTANCE

The best way for the holder to find out whether the drawee will pay the draft is to present it to the drawee for acceptance. If the drawee is not willing to pay the instrument according to its terms, he will reject it, that is, dishonor it by nonacceptance. If he is willing to pay the draft, he will do so immediately in the case of demand paper or paper that has become due by that time. If the paper is not due but he is willing to pay it when it becomes due, he will accept it.[8]

Necessity of Presentment for Acceptance

A draft may always be presented to the drawee for acceptance so that the holder can determine the intentions of the drawee. On the other hand, a presentment for acceptance must be made when (1) it is necessary in order to fix the date of maturity of the draft, such as when the instrument is payable a specified number of days after sight; (2) the draft expressly states that it must be presented for acceptance; or (3) the draft is made payable elsewhere than at the residence or place of business of the drawee.[9]

Manner of Presenting for Acceptance

Presentment of a draft for acceptance is made in the same manner as the presentment of a note for payment,[10] with the obvious difference that the presentment is made upon the drawee rather than upon the maker.

1 / Time for presentment for acceptance. Unless a different time is specified in the draft, presentment for acceptance must be made on or before the date on which the instrument is payable by its express provisions. If it is payable after sight, it must be presented for acceptance or negotiated within a reasonable time after its date or issue, whichever is later. With respect to the liability of any secondary party on any other form of instrument, presentment for acceptance must be made within a reasonable time after that party became liable for it.[11]

The time for presentment of a draft for acceptance with respect to the hour and day or the effect of holidays is the same as in the case of presentment of a note for payment.[12]

---

[8] Sec. 3-410(1).
[9] Sec. 3-501(1)(a).
[10] Sec. 3-504.
[11] Sec. 3-503(1)(a),(b),(e).
[12] See p. 303.

2 / Delay or absence of presentment for acceptance. Delay in a necessary presentment of a draft for acceptance and the failure to make any presentment are excused under the same circumstances as in the case of the presentment of a note for payment.[13]

An unexcused delay in making presentment for acceptance discharges all indorsers.[14] If the draft is domiciled, that is, payable at a bank, the drawer or acceptor is discharged under the circumstances that discharge the maker of a note for dishonor by nonpayment.[15]

3 / Time allowed for acceptance. It is not necessary that the drawee accept or dishonor the draft immediately upon its presentment to him. In order to afford him an opportunity of determining from his records whether he should accept, he may postpone making a decision, without thereby dis- honoring the draft, until the close of the next business day, following the presentment of the draft. Likewise the holder may allow the postponement of acceptance for an additional business day when he acts in good faith in the hope that he will be able to obtain an acceptance. If the holder agrees to such additional postponement, the liability of the secondary parties is not affected and the draft is not thereby dishonored.[16]

Kinds of Acceptances

1 / General acceptance. A *general acceptance* (or simply an "accep- tance") is one in which the acceptor agrees without qualification to pay according to the order of the drawer.

2 / Draft-varying acceptance. A *draft-varying acceptance* is one in which the acceptor agrees to pay but not exactly in conformity with the order of the draft.[17] An acceptance varies the draft when it changes the time or place of payment, when it agrees to pay only a part of the amount of the draft, or when it sets up a condition that must be satisfied before the acceptance is effective.

An acceptance to pay at a particular bank or place in the United States is a general acceptance, unless it expressly states that the draft is to be paid there only and not elsewhere. In the latter case the acceptance varies the draft.[18]

---

[13] UCC Sec. 3-511(1),(2),(3),(6). A minor qualification must be made in that in the case of a draft, it is the death or insolvency proceedings relating to the acceptor or drawee which is material, rather than the death or insolvency of a maker. See also Sec. 3-511(3)(a).
[14] Sec. 3-502(1).
[15] Sec. 3-502(1)(b). See p. 304.
[16] Sec. 3-506.
[17] Sec. 3-412(1).
[18] Sec. 3-412(2).

If the holder does not wish to take the varying acceptance, he may reject it and treat the draft as dishonored by nonacceptance. After giving due notice, he can proceed at once against secondary parties.

If the holder assents to the draft-varying acceptance, however, he in effect consents to the execution of a new instrument; and each drawer and indorser is released from liability unless he affirmatively assents to such acceptance. The fact that a secondary party fails to object is not sufficient to prevent his release from liability.

Form of Acceptance

An acceptance is the drawee's notation on the draft itself that he will make payment as directed thereby. It may be merely his signature, but customarily it will be the word "Accepted," and his signature, and generally the date. In any case, however, the acceptance must be written on the draft itself.[19] Usually it is written across the face of the instrument.

> Facts: Temple was the drawee of a draft of which Lawless was payee. When the draft was presented to Temple for acceptance, he merely wrote his name on its face. Later, when he was sued by Lawless, he denied that he had accepted the draft.
>
> Decision: Judgment for Lawless. A drawee is charged as an acceptor when he merely writes his name on the draft, although it is customary to add the word "Accepted." When a blank acceptance is made, any holder can write "Accepted" above the signature of the acceptor. (Lawless v. Temple, 254 Mass. 395, 150 N.E. 176)

An acceptance cannot be oral, nor can it be contained in some other writing. The fact that the drawee is not liable on the draft because he has not accepted it does not necessarily prevent his being liable because of other obligations or principles of law.

> Facts: Schenk's Motor Sales had a checking account in the Home Savings Bank. Schenk drew a check to the order of the General Finance Corp. The bank certified the check in reliance on the oral promise of the General Finance Corp. to accept a draft drawn on General by Schenk that had just been deposited in Schenk's account. The certified check was paid by the bank, but General refused to pay the draft on the ground that its oral acceptance was not binding. The bank sued General for the amount of the certified check.
>
> Decision: Judgment for the bank because the bank certified and paid the check only because of the oral promise of General Finance to accept the draft. General Finance, having received the benefit of the check, would be unjustly enriched if it could keep that benefit while at the same

---

[19] Sec. 3-410(1).

time refusing to live up to its oral acceptance. To prevent this, General Finance must be required to return the benefit received. (Home Savings Bank v. General Finance Corp., 10 Wis.2d 417, 103 N.W.2d 117)

There can be no acceptance by misconduct. The refusal to return the draft or its destruction by the drawee does not constitute an "acceptance." If the drawee retains the draft and refuses to return it, he is guilty of conversion.[20] The measure of damages is the face amount of the instrument.[21]

Dishonor by Nonacceptance

When a draft that is presented for acceptance is not accepted within the allowed time, the person presenting it must treat the draft as dishonored by nonacceptance.[22] If he fails to do so, the secondary parties are released from liability.   *Time Limit - 3 Business Days*

When a draft is dishonored by nonacceptance, the holder must give the same notice of dishonor as in the case of dishonor of a note by nonpayment. If the draft on its face appears to be drawn or payable outside of the United States, its territories, and the District of Columbia, it is also necessary to protest the dishonor in order to charge the drawer and the indorsers.[23]

PRESENTMENT OF DRAFT FOR PAYMENT

The requirements and limitations upon the necessity of presentment of a draft for payment are the same as in the case of a promissory note, with the circumstances excusing delays in or failure to make presentment of a note likewise excusing delay or failure to make presentment of a draft for payment. The failure to present for payment is likewise excused with respect to a party who has countermanded payment of the draft.[24]

Furthermore, when a draft has been dishonored by nonacceptance, a later presentment for payment is excused unless the instrument has been since accepted.[25]

The provisions governing notice of dishonor of a draft by nonpayment are the same as those for a note.[26]

PROTEST OF DISHONOR

A protest of dishonor of a draft by nonacceptance or nonpayment is not necessary unless the draft appears on its face to be drawn or payable

---

[20] Sec. 3-419(1)(a).
[21] Sec. 3-419(2).
[22] Sec. 3-507(1)(a).
[23] Sec. 3-501(3). As to protest of dishonor, see pp. 308 and 317.
[24] UCC Sec. 3-511(1),(2),(3).
[25] Sec. 3-511(4).
[26] Sec. 3-501(2), 3-508. See p. 305.

outside of the United States, its territories, and the District of Columbia. The holder, however, may protest the dishonor of any instrument.[27] Delay in protesting dishonor or the absence of a protest are excused under the same circumstances that apply in the case of a note dishonored by nonpayment.[28]

A *waiver of protest* is effective to excuse the absence of an otherwise required protest. Protest is commonly waived, particularly in the case of out-of-town instruments, because protesting does involve an additional cost and some inconvenience. Frequently, therefore, the instrument will contain a clause stating that protest is waived, or it may be stamped with the words, "Protest waived" or "No Protest." A waiver of protest is a waiver of the requirement of presentment and notice of dishonor as well as of the protest itself even though protest is not required.[29]

When words of guaranty, such as "payment guaranteed" or "collection guaranteed," are used, presentment, notice of dishonor, and protest are not necessary to charge the person using such language.[30]

QUESTIONS AND PROBLEMS

1. Checklist of legal terms:
   (a) acceptance (311); general acceptance (314), draft-varying acceptance (314)
   (b) waiver of protest (317)
2. State the objective(s) of each of the following rules of law:
   (a) The failure of a drawee to accept a draft by the close of the business day following its presentment constitutes a dishonor of the instrument.
   (b) There can only be an acceptance of a draft by a writing on the instrument itself.
3. Olden draws a draft on Sweeny in favor of Van Atta. Under what circumstances can Sweeny be held liable on this instrument?
4. Rhodes, to whom a draft has been negotiated by the payee, sues the drawer. The latter claims that Rhodes does not have a valid title because the payee is a minor. Is Rhodes entitled to judgment?
5. On April 1, Roller drew a draft on Trapp payable on June 15 of the same year to the order of Upton. Must this instrument be presented for acceptance?
6. Best draws a draft payable sixty days after sight to Dexter. When Dexter presents the instrument for acceptance four months later, it is dishonored. Is Dexter entitled to judgment in an action against Best?
7. Accepting a draft drawn by Cox, Incorporated, Dillon wrote on the instrument as follows: "Accepted for payment as per Falls contract for

[27] UCC Sec. 3-501(3).
[28] Sec. 3-511(1), (2).
[29] Sec. 3-511(5).
[30] Sec. 3-416(5).

amount and date shown thereon." Was this a general or a draft-varying acceptance?

8. Chaney, the holder of a draft, presented it to Edwards, the drawee, for acceptance. Edwards accepted for one half the amount specified in the draft. Edwards failed to pay the instrument when it matured.
   (a) Why cannot Chaney recover on the draft from the drawer?
   (b) How could Chaney have held the drawer liable on the instrument?

9. When a draft was presented to Fritz for acceptance, he wrote his name and the date on the face of the instrument. Did such a writing constitute an acceptance?

10. In the second example on page 315 (Home Savings Bank v. General Finance Corp.), what principle of law governed the decision?

11. Garrett, the holder of a draft, presented it for acceptance to Hill, the drawee. Hill refused to accept the draft or to return it. Garrett immediately notified the drawer of what had happened. Later Garrett brought an action to recover on the draft from the drawer. Was Garrett entitled to judgment?

12. Keeler, the holder of a draft drawn by McCoy, presents it for acceptance to the drawee who is located in the same city. The instrument is dishonored by nonacceptance. Four days later when Keeler demands payment from McCoy, the latter refuses to pay. Is Keeler entitled to judgment in an action on the instrument against McCoy?

13. Slack drew a draft on the Clayton Drug Co. payable to the Clayton Town-Site Co. The draft was accepted orally by the drawee. The Clayton Town-Site Co. sued the Clayton Drug Co. when the former refused payment. Could it recover? (Clayton Town-Site Co. v. Clayton Drug Co., 20 N.Mex. 185, 147 P. 460)

14. Wetmore was the general agent and manager of the New York Iron Mine, a corporation carrying on mining operations near Marquette, Michigan. He executed a draft payable at sight drawn on Tilden, president and treasurer of the corporation, at New York City. The draft was postdated, being drawn on June 16 and dated July 5. The draft was discounted at the Citizens' Bank in Marquette. Was it necessary for the bank to present the draft to the drawee for acceptance? (New York Iron Mine v. Citizens' Bank, 44 Mich. 344, 6 N.W. 823)

15. Rogers, Brown & Co., of New York City and other cities in the United States, sold iron to Soehne, iron merchants doing business in Vienna, Austria. They shipped the iron from Birmingham, Alabama, to the buyers in Austria, and drew in New York City a demand on the buyers for the amount of the purchase price of the iron. The bill, payable to the order of the drawers, was indorsed to G. Amsinck & Co. On February 21, payment was demanded and refused. When suit was brought upon the bill, the defendant drawers claimed that the holder had failed to protest the bill for nonpayment. Decide. (Amsinck v. Rogers, 103 App.Div. 428, 93 N.Y.S. 87)

Chapter 27

Checks and Bank Collections

Of the various types of commercial paper in use today, by far the most common is the check. By means of checks it is possible to make payment safely and conveniently without the need of safeguarding a shipment of money. The checkbook stub and the canceled check make a written record which may be used at a later date to show that a payment was made. The more common aspects of checks and of their payment and collection are considered in this chapter.

Nature of a Check

A check is a particular kind of bill of exchange. The following features of a check distinguish it from other drafts or bills of exchange: [1]

(1) The drawee of a check is always a bank.

(2) As a practical matter, the check is drawn on the assumption that the bank has on deposit in the drawer's account an amount sufficient to pay the check. In the case of a draft there is no assumption that the drawee has any of the drawer's money with which to pay the instrument. Actually, the rights of the parties are not affected by the fact that the depositor does not have funds on deposit with the bank sufficient to pay the check.

If a draft is dishonored, the drawer is civilly liable; but if a check is drawn with intent to defraud the person to whom it is delivered, the drawer is also subject to criminal prosecution [2] in most states under what are known as *bad check laws*. Most states provide that if the check is not made good within a stated period, such as ten days, it will be presumed that the check was originally issued with the intent to defraud.

(3) A check is demand paper. A draft may be payable either on demand or at a future date. The standard form of check does not specify when it is payable, and it is therefore automatically payable on demand. This eliminates the need for an acceptance since the holder of the check will merely present it for payment.

One exception arises when a check is postdated, that is, when the check shows a date later than the actual date of execution and delivery. Here the

---

[1] Checks are governed by both Article 3 of the Uniform Commercial Code relating to commercial paper and Article 4 governing bank deposits and collections.
[2] *State* v. *De Nicola*, 163 Ohio 140, 126 N.E.2d 62.

319

check is not payable until that date arrives. This, in effect, changes the check to time paper without expressly stating so.

Facts: Kelinson was president of the Barkel Meat Packing Co., a wholesale meat packer. On February 2, a shipment of meat was delivered to the company. Kelinson gave the driver a check in payment for the full amount but dated it February 4. Approximately thirty checks given in payment of prior shipments had also been postdated. All prior checks had been paid, but the check of February 2 was not paid. Kelinson was prosecuted for the offenses of passing a worthless check and of obtaining money by false pretenses.

Decision: Kelinson was not guilty. The fact that the check was postdated was a warning that there was not then sufficient funds on deposit to pay the check. Consequently, it was not a bad check but rather a draft that would be due on the date of the check. Likewise, as there was no false representation in such a promise, it was not a "false pretense." (Commonwealth v. Kelinson, 199 Pa.Super. 135, 184 A.2d 374)

The delivery of the check is not regarded as an assignment of the money on deposit. It therefore does not automatically transfer the rights of the depositor against his bank to the holder of the check, and there is no duty on the part of the drawee bank to pay the holder the amount of the check.[3]

Indication of Purpose

Although not required by law, a notation on a check of the purpose for which it is delivered is desirable. It serves to identify the payment in case the purpose is questioned later. Customary notations are "Payment of invoice No. 3924," "Painting house, 1968," or "Fees, drafting of will." If a payee cashes a check bearing such a notation, he is estopped from denying that the payment was made and received for the purpose stated.

A common form of notation is the statement "In full payment (or settlement) of the claim of. . . ." When a check with such a notation is accepted by the payee, the claim referred to is discharged without regard to whether the amount of the check was the full amount of the claim or only a part, and without regard to whether there was any dispute as to the actual amount due.[4]

A special form of check, known as a *voucher check,* is used by some businesses. This form is larger than an ordinary check. The additional space is used for stating the purpose of the check or for listing the items of an invoice for which the check is issued in payment. When the payee receives a voucher check, he detaches the voucher portion of the form and keeps it in his files as a record of the payment that he has received.

---

[3] Uniform Commercial Code, Sec. 3-409(1).
[4] See pp. 130, 194.

Liability of Drawer

If the check is presented for payment and paid, no liability of the drawer arises. If the bank refuses to make payment, the drawer is then subject to a liability similar to that in the case of the nonpayment of an ordinary draft. If proper notice of dishonor is not given the drawer of the check, he may be discharged from liability to the same extent as a drawer of an ordinary draft.

Rights of Drawer

It is necessary to distinguish between the rights of the drawer with respect to his check and his relationships with his bank on the contract of deposit. With respect to the latter, the bank owes its customer, the depositor-drawer, the duty of maintaining secrecy concerning information which the bank acquires in connection with the depositor-bank relationship.

Facts: Peterson, a depositor in the First National Bank, sued the bank for disclosing to his employer without Peterson's consent details relating to Peterson's checking account with the bank and his financial condition.

Decision: Judgment for Peterson. As an implied incident of the contract between a bank and its customers, the bank has the duty to refrain from disclosing to third persons any information relating to its customer's account. (Peterson v. Idaho First National Bank, 83 Idaho 578, 367 P.2d 284)

1 / Refusal of bank to pay. The bank is under a general contractual duty to its depositor to pay on demand [5] all of his checks to the extent of the funds deposited to his credit. When the bank breaches this contract, it is liable to the drawer for damages.[6] In the case of a draft, there is ordinarily no duty on the drawee to accept it, or to make payment if he has not accepted it.

Although the drawee bank is liable for improperly refusing to pay a check, this liability runs in favor of the drawer alone. Even though the holder of the check or the payee may be harmed when the bank refuses to pay the check, the holder or payee has no right to sue the bank. The holder or payee is limited to proceeding against the secondary parties on the instrument. He may also proceed, however, on the original obligation against the person from whom he received the check.[7]

A bank acting in good faith may pay a check presented more than six months after its date (commonly known as a *stale check*) but, unless the check is certified, it is not required to do so.[8]

---

[5] *Petition of Leon Keyser,* 98 N.H. 198, 96 A.2d 551.
[6] *Collins* v. *City Nat. Bank & Trust Co.,* 131 Conn. 167, 38 A.2d 582.
[7] UCC Sec. 3-802(1)(b).
[8] Sec. 4-404.

2 / Stopping payment. The drawer has the power of stopping payment of a check. After the check is issued, he can notify the drawee bank not to pay it when it is presented for payment. This is a useful device when a check is lost or mislaid. A duplicate check can be written and, to make sure that the payee does not receive payment twice or that an improper person does not receive payment on the first check, payment on the first check can be stopped. Likewise, if payment is made by check and then the payee defaults on his contract so that the drawer would have a claim against him, payment on the check can be stopped, assuming that the payee has not cashed it.

The *stop-payment order* may be either oral or written. If oral, however, it is only binding on the bank for 14 calendar days unless confirmed in writing within that time. A written order is not effective after 6 months unless renewed in writing.[9]

If the bank makes payment of a check after it has been properly notified to stop payment, it is liable to the depositor for the loss he sustains, in the absence of a valid limitation of the bank's liability. The burden of establishing the loss resulting in such case rests upon the depositor.[10]

Facts: Cicci drew a check on his bank, Lincoln National Bank and Trust Co., payable to the order of Santo. He thereafter notified the bank to stop payment. The bank ignored the stop-payment order and made payment of the check. Cicci then sued Lincoln National Bank for the amount of the check. The bank raised the defense that Cicci had not shown that he was damaged by the payment of the check.

Decision: The defense was valid. Although the bank violates its duty to its depositor by failing to obey the stop-payment order, the bank does not thereby become automatically liable for the amount of the check. It is only liable to the extent that it is shown that the payment has caused loss to the depositor through the making of a payment on a claim which the depositor was not legally obligated to pay. (Cicci v. Lincoln National Bank and Trust Co., 46 Misc.2d 465, 260 N.Y.S.2d 100)

The act of stopping payment may in some cases make the depositor liable to the holder of the instrument. If the depositor has no proper ground for stopping payment, he is liable to the payee to whom he has delivered the check. In any case, he is liable for stopping payment with respect to any holder in due course or other party having the rights of a holder in due course, unless he stops payment for a reason that may be asserted against such holder as a defense.[11] The fact that the bank refuses to make payment because of the drawer's instruction does not make the case any different from any other instance in which the drawee refuses to pay.

[9] Sec. 4-403(2).
[10] Sec. 4-403(3).
[11] See p. 339.

Generally payment is stopped only when the drawer has good cause with respect to the payee. For example, the purchaser of goods may give the seller a check in advance payment for the goods. The seller may then declare that he is not going to deliver the goods. The purchaser is within his lawful rights if he stops payment on the check since the seller has no right to the check if he does not perform his part of the sales contract. Thus the payee could not sue the drawer-purchaser for stopping payment on the check. If the check has been negotiated to a subsequent holder who is a holder in due course, the purchaser cannot assert this defense. Accordingly, such a favored holder may hold the drawer liable on the dishonored check.

It is to the advantage of the seller to require either a certified check [12] of the buyer or a cashier's check from the buyer's bank payable to the order of the seller, for with respect to either check neither the buyer nor the buyer's bank can stop payment to the seller.[13]

Time of Presentment of Check for Payment

In the case of demand paper generally, presentment for payment must be made on any secondary party to the instrument within a reasonable time after such party becomes liable on it. Reasonable time is determined by the nature of the instrument, by any existing commercial usage, and by the facts of the particular case.[14]

Failure to make such timely presentment discharges all prior indorsers of the instrument. It also discharges the drawer, if the draft is payable at a bank, to the extent that he has lost, through the bank's failure, money which he had on deposit at the bank to meet the payment of the instrument.[15]

As a modification to the foregoing principles, the Code establishes two presumptions as to what is a reasonable time in which to present a check for payment.[16] If the check is not certified and is both drawn and payable within the United States, it is presumed as to the drawer that 30 days after the date of the check or the date of its issuance, whichever is later, is the reasonable period in which to make presentment for payment. In the case of an indorser it is presumed to be 7 days after his indorsement.[17]

Dishonor of Check

When a check is dishonored by nonpayment, the holder must follow the same procedure of notice to each of the secondary parties as in the case of a

---

[12] See p. 327.
[13] *Malphrus* v. *Home Savings Bank,* 44 Misc.2d 705, 254 N.Y.S.2d 980.
[14] UCC Sec. 3-503(1)(e), (2).
[15] Sec. 3-502(1).
[16] A presumption means that the trier of fact is bound by the presumption in the absence of evidence that supports a contrary conclusion. UCC Sec. 1-201(31).
[17] Sec. 3-503(2).

draft or bill of exchange if he wishes to hold them liable for payment. As in the case of any drawer of a draft or bill of exchange who countermands payment, notice of dishonor need not be given to the drawer who has stopped payment on a check. Notice is also excused under any circumstances that would excuse notice in the case of a promissory note. For example, no notice need be given a drawer or an indorser who knows that sufficient funds to cover the check are not on deposit, since such party has no reason to expect that the check will be paid by the bank.[18]

A check that is dishonored by nonpayment may be presented to the drawee bank at a later time in the hope that by the later date there will be sufficient funds in the account of the drawer so that the drawee bank will be able to make payment. Although there is this right to make a subsequent presentation for payment, it is essential that notice be given secondary parties after the dishonor of the instrument upon the first presentation. If they are not duly notified at that time, they are discharged and no new rights can be acquired against them by making a subsequent presentment and then notifying the secondary parties of the second dishonor.

When a check is sent in the course of the collection process to the bank on which it is drawn, that bank must either pay or promptly return the check as unpaid, or send notice of its dishonor, as by returning the check unpaid for "insufficient funds." If the drawee bank does not act before the midnight of the business day on which it received the check, it automatically becomes liable for the face of the instrument.[19]

Liability of Bank for Improper Payment of Check

As pointed out earlier, a bank that honors a check after the depositor has stopped payment is liable to the depositor for the loss he sustains. In addition, the bank is generally liable if it makes an improper payment under the following circumstances:

1 / Payment on forged signature of drawer. The bank is liable to the depositor if it pays a check on which his signature has been forged since a forgery ordinarily has no effect as a signature.[20] A *forgery* of the signature occurs when the name of the depositor has been signed by another person without authority to do so and with the intent to defraud by making it appear that the check was signed by the depositor.[21] The burden of knowing the signatures of all its depositors is thus placed on the bank. Accordingly, upon

---

[18] Sec. 3-511(2)(b).
[19] Sec. 4-302.
[20] Sec. 3-404(1).
[21] A forgery as thus defined is to be distinguished from a changing of the instrument as originally executed, which constitutes an alteration when done by a party to the instrument and a spoliation when done by a stranger to the instrument. See p. 341.

opening an account in a bank, the depositor is required to sign a card in the way in which he will sign his checks. This signature card remains on file in the bank and is used to make a comparison to determine whether checks presented to the bank for payment have been signed by the depositor.

Although the bank has no right to pay a check on which the drawer's signature is forged, the drawer may be barred from objecting that his signature was a forgery. If the drawer's negligence contributed substantially to the forging of his signature, he cannot assert that it was forged when the drawee bank makes payment of the check while acting in good faith and conforming to reasonable commercial standards.[22] For example, if the drawer signs his checks with a mechanical writer, he must exercise reasonable care to prevent unauthorized persons from making use of it to forge or "sign" his name with such a device. If the depositor's negligence enables a third person to make such improper use of it, the depositor is barred from objecting to the payment of the check by the bank.

When the depositor fails to examine his bank statement and canceled checks with reasonable care and promptness and to notify the bank promptly of any forgery, the depositor cannot hold the bank responsible if, in making payment on the forged instrument, it had used ordinary care. Even when the bank failed to exercise care, the depositor cannot object to the forgery of his signature unless he acts within one year.[23]

When a check is presented to the drawee bank for payment, it alone is responsible for determining whether the signature of the drawer, its customer, is a forgery. Hence, the prior indorsers do not warrant that the signature of the drawer is genuine; and, if the bank pays money or gives a cashier's check in payment of the depositor's check, it cannot thereafter recover the money paid or defend against payment on the cashier's check on the ground that the drawer's signature had been forged.[24]

2 / Payment on forged indorsement. A bank that pays a check on a forged indorsement may be liable for conversion.[25] However, a bank that has dealt with an instrument or the proceeds of it on behalf of one who was not the true owner is not liable to the true owner when the bank acted in good faith and in accordance with the reasonable commercial standards applicable to a bank. In the latter case, the liability of the bank is limited to surrendering the instrument or the proceeds of it to the true owner if the bank still has either in its possession.[26]

---

[22] UCC Secs. 3-404(1), 4-406.
[23] Sec. 4-406.
[24] *Citizens Bank of Booneville* v. *National Bank of Commerce,* [C.A.10th] 334 F.2d 257.
[25] UCC Sec. 3-419(1)(c).
[26] Sec. 3-419(3).

Facts: Arena Auto Auction drew a check on the Park State Bank to the order of Plunkett Auto Sales, which was located in Alabama. By mistake the check was mailed to an enterprise of the same name in Rockford, Illinois. The check was indorsed and cashed by the latter. Thereafter, Arena Auto Auction notified the bank to stop payment. Arena claimed that the bank was liable as it had made payment to a person who was not the holder and who had committed forgery by indorsing the payee's name.

Decision: It was the negligence of the drawer in sending the check to the wrong person that made possible the forgery and cashing by the wrong person. The negligence of the drawer was further indicated by its delay in giving notice to the bank to stop payment. The drawer, accordingly, could not object to the cashing of the check by the wrong person. (Park State Bank v. Arena Auto Auction, 59 Ill.App.2d 235, 207 N.E.2d 158)

3 / Payment on missing indorsement. A drawee bank is liable for the loss when it pays a check that lacks an essential indorsement. In such a case, the instrument has not been properly presented and by definition the person presenting the check for payment is not the holder of the instrument and is not entitled to demand or receive payment. It is a defense to the bank, however, that although the person to whom payment was made was not the holder of the instrument, he was in fact the person whom the drawer or the last holder of the check intended should be paid.

When a person deposits a check in his bank but neglects to indorse it, the bank may make an indorsement for him unless the check contains a statement that it must be signed personally by that person. Even if the bank does not indorse, there is an effective negotiation from the customer to his bank when the check is stamped by the bank to indicate that it was deposited by the customer or was credited to his account.[27]

4 / Payment on nonfiduciary indorsement. The bank is not liable when it makes payment on a nonfiduciary indorsement to a person to whom the instrument has been made payable in a fiduciary capacity. Thus the bank is protected when it pays on an indorsement of "D. A. Jones" although the check was drawn to the order of "D. A. Jones, Trustee."

5 / Alteration of check. If the face of the check has been altered so that the amount to be paid has been increased, the bank is liable to the drawer for the amount of the increase when it makes payment for the greater amount. The bank has the opportunity of examining the check when it is presented for payment and, if it fails to detect the alteration, it is responsible for the loss.

---

[27] Sec. 4-205(1).

The drawer may be barred from claiming that there was an alteration by virtue of his conduct with respect to writing the check and his conduct after receiving the canceled check from the bank. As to the former, he is barred if in writing the check he was negligent and that negligence substantially contributed to the making of the material alteration and the bank honored the check in good faith and observed reasonable commercial standards in so doing.[28] For example, the drawer is barred when he leaves blank spaces on his check so that it is readily possible to change "four" to "four hundred," and the drawee bank pays out the latter sum without any cause to know of the alteration. The careful person will therefore write figures and words close together and run a line through or cross out any blank spaces.

To avoid possible mistake or confusion, a check that is incorrectly drawn should be rewritten and the first check destroyed or canceled by writing "Void" across its face. If a correction on the original check is attempted, it is likely that the bank will question whether the change was made by the drawer prior to delivery and this may delay the payment of the check.

The drawer of the check may also be barred from objecting to the alteration by his failure to inform the bank after receiving his canceled checks and bank statement. In such a case he is barred under the same conditions as determine when he is barred from objecting to the drawee bank that his signature on the check is a forgery.[29]

6 / Payment after depositor's death. The effectiveness of a check ordinarily ceases with the death of a drawer. The death of the drawer, however, does not revoke the agency of the bank until it has knowledge of the death and has had reasonable opportunity to act. Even with such knowledge, the bank may continue for ten days to pay or certify checks drawn by the drawer unless ordered to stop payment by a person claiming an interest in the account.[30]

Certified Checks

The drawee bank may certify a check drawn on it, which has the same legal consequence as the acceptance of a draft.[31] The effect of the certification is to set aside in a special account maintained by the bank as much of the depositor's account as is needed to pay the amount of the certified check. With respect to the holder of the check, the certification is an undertaking by the bank that when the check is presented for payment, it will make payment according to the terms of the check without regard to the standing of the depositor's account at that time.

---

[28] Sec. 3-406.
[29] See p. 324.
[30] UCC Sec. 4-405.
[31] Sec. 3-411(1).

The use of a certified check is frequently required for payments made at sheriffs' sales and as filing fees sent to government agencies for various purposes. They are also commonly used when property is sold to a buyer who is not well known or who is deemed an unsatisfactory credit risk.

As in the case of an acceptance, any writing showing an intention to certify a check is sufficient. Ordinarily a certification is made by stamping or printing on the check the word "Certified," the name of the bank, the signature and title of the officer making the certification, and the date.

A check may be certified by a bank upon the request of the drawer or the holder. In the latter case all prior indorsers and the drawer are automatically released from liability.[32] Since the holder could have received payment, as the bank was willing to certify the check, and since the holder did not take the payment but chose to take the promise of certification, the prior secondary parties are released from liability. When the certification is obtained by the drawer, there is no release of the secondary parties.

While, as a practical matter, the certification of a check by a bank makes it "as good as money," it must be remembered that the check is still a check, and that even a certified check is not money.[33]

Agency Status of Collecting Bank

When a person deposits a commercial paper at a bank, he is ordinarily making it his agent to collect or obtain the payment of the instrument. Unless the contrary intent clearly appears, a bank receiving an item is deemed to take it as agent for the depositor rather than as becoming the purchaser of the paper from him. This presumption is not affected by the form of the indorsement nor by the absence of any indorsement. The bank is also regarded as being merely an agent even though the depositor has the right to make immediate withdrawals against the deposited item.[34] In consequence of the agency status, the depositor remains the owner of the item and is therefore subject to the risks of ownership involved in its collection, in the absence of fault on the part of any collecting bank.[35]

QUESTIONS AND PROBLEMS

1. Checklist of legal terms:
    (a) bad check laws (319)
    (b) voucher check (320)
    (c) stop-payment order (322)
    (d) forgery (324)

---

[32] Sec. 3-411(1).
[33] *Olin* v. *Weintraub*, [N.Y.S.2d] 2 UCCRS 623.
[34] UCC Sec. 4-201(1).
[35] Sec. 4-202.

2. State the objective(s) of each of the following rules of law:
   (a) A bad check that is not made good within a stated period will be presumed to have been issued with the intent to defraud.
   (b) The drawer has the power to stop payment of his check.

3. A check was dishonored on June 20 because Fairbanks, the drawer, did not have sufficient funds on deposit in his bank account. On July 1, Fairbanks had not made the check good by paying the holder. Of what wrongs is Fairbanks guilty?

4. Kenton, thinking that a check which he has drawn in favor of MacDonald has been lost, stops payment on the check and issues a duplicate check. Kenton's bank, after receiving the stop-payment notice, pays both checks. Is Kenton entitled to judgment in an action against his bank?

5. Mayer draws and delivers a check to Kane as an advance payment on merchandise that he has contracted to buy. Shortly thereafter Mayer learns that Kane will be unable to fulfill his contract. Mayer stops payment on the check. Is Kane entitled to judgment in an action against Mayer for stopping payment?

6. Leon drew a check for $5.63. Because of the manner in which he wrote the check, an indorsee was able to change the amount in figures and words to $65.63. Leon's bank honors the check for the larger amount. Who must bear the loss?

7. When McGuire, the holder of a certified check, presented the instrument for payment, the drawee bank refused to pay. Against whom should McGuire bring an action?

8. Langhorst draws a check and has it certified by his bank before he delivers it to Minter, the payee, on the morning of November 10. When Minter attempts to cash the check in the afternoon of that same day, he finds that the bank has closed its doors at noon because of financial difficulties. Langhorst contends that he has no liability because the check had been certified. Is his contention sound?

9. Pflaum mailed a check for $5,000 to the Laura Baker School and stated in the accompanying letter that it was a gift to the school which it could use for any purpose. Before the check was presented to the bank for payment, Pflaum stopped payment on it. The school then sued on the check. Decide. (Laura Baker School v. Pflaum, 225 Minn. 181, 30 N.W. 2d 290)

10. The Virginia Salvage Co. drew a check on the National Mechanics Bank and had the bank certify the check. The check was indorsed by the payee, and a subsequent holder, Schmelz National Bank, demanded payment of the check from the National Mechanics Bank. The latter defended on the ground that the salvage company by that time owed the bank more than the amount of the certified check. Was this a valid defense? (National Mechanics Bank v. Schmelz National Bank, 136 Va. 33, 116 S.E. 380)

Chapter 28

Rights of Holders and Defenses

When a contract right is assigned, the assignee's right is subject to any defenses existing between the original parties prior to the notice of the assignment. For example, when the seller assigns his right to collect the purchase price, the buyer may assert against the seller's assignee the defense that the buyer never received the goods. It is immaterial through how many successive assignees the right has been transferred and whether or not the assignees acted in good faith, in ignorance of the original defenses, and gave value for their assignments. Such a principle of law should make a prospective assignee of a contract right extremely cautious. He should make inquiry as to the existence of defenses, particularly those of the original obligor.

If the holder of a commercial paper were required to conduct such an investigation in every instance in order to protect himself, the utility of commercial paper would be greatly impaired. First the law merchant, then the Negotiable Instrument Law, and now the Uniform Commercial Code have met this problem by giving certain holders of commercial paper a preferred standing by protecting them from the operation of certain defenses. Such a favored holder may be either a holder in due course or a holder through a holder in due course. If the holder is not one of these favored holders, he has only the same standing as an ordinary assignee and is subject to all defenses to which an ordinary assignee would be subject.[1]

RIGHTS OF HOLDERS

A holder, whether favored or not, is the only person who has the right to demand payment or to sue on the instrument.[2] Whether he recovers depends upon whether the person sued is liable to him and whether there is any defense that may be asserted against him.

Ordinarily a holder may sue any one or more prior parties on the paper without regard to the order of their liability as between the indorsers themselves.

---

[1] See p. 183. The fact that the holder cannot recover from the defendant in a given case because of a defense raised by the latter does not necessarily mean that the holder has no remedy, for in some instances he may be able to sue a prior party for breach of warranty.

[2] Uniform Commercial Code Sec. 3-301.

The holder is the only one who may grant a discharge of or cancel the liability of another party on the instrument.

Holder in Due Course

In order to be a holder in due course, the person must first be a holder. This means that he must be in possession of bearer paper, or in possession of order paper made or issued to him or properly indorsed to him.

1 / Necessary elements. In addition to being a holder, the holder in due course must meet certain conditions that pertain to (a) value, (b) good faith, (c) ignorance of paper overdue or dishonored, and (d) ignorance of defenses and adverse claims.[3]

(a) VALUE. Since the law of commercial paper is fundamentally a merchant's or businessman's law, it favors only the holders who have given value for the paper. For example, since a legatee under a will does not give value, a person receiving bonds as a legacy is not a holder in due course.[4]

The courts do not measure or appraise the value given. The fact that the value given is less than the face of the instrument does not affect the status of the holder as a holder in due course, unless the value is so slight that it may be evidence of fraud.

A person has taken an instrument for value (1) when he has performed the act for which the instrument was given, such as delivering the goods for which the check is sent in payment; (2) when he has acquired a security interest in the paper, such as when it has been pledged with him as security for another obligation; or (3) when he has taken the instrument in payment or as security for a debt.[5]

Facts: Southern New England Distributing Corporation held two notes of Supreme Radio and indorsed them to Korzenik, an attorney, and his partner "as a retainer for services to be performed." When Korzenik sued Supreme Radio on the notes, it raised the defense of fraud in the procurement. Korzenik claimed that he was a holder in due course.

Decision: He was not a holder in due course because he had not acquired the paper for value. He acquired it in consideration for future services to be performed. The promise to render services in the future is not deemed value. (Korzenik v. Supreme Radio, 347 Mass. 309, 197 N.E.2d 702)

---

[3] UCC Sec. 3-302(1).

[4] *Wyatt* v. *Mount Airy Cemetery,* 209 Pa.Super. 250, 224 A.2d 787.

[5] UCC Sec. 3-303. It is also provided that there is a taking for value when another commercial paper is given in exchange or when the taker makes an irrevocable commitment to a third person as by providing a letter of credit. Sec. 3-303(c).

When an instrument is deposited with a bank, the latter does not become a holder for value by the mere fact that it credits the customer's account with the amount of the deposit when the customer has not yet drawn upon the credit. It is at the latter time that the bank becomes a holder of the commercial paper for value.[6]

(b) GOOD FAITH. The element of good faith requires that the taker of commercial paper has acted honestly in the acquisition of the instrument.[7] Bad faith may sometimes be indicated by the small value given. This does not mean that the transferee must give full value, but that a gross inadequacy of consideration may be evidence of bad faith. Bad faith is established by proof that the transferee had knowledge of such facts as rendered it improper for him to acquire the instrument under the circumstances.

If the transferee takes the instrument in good faith, it is immaterial whether his transferor acted in good faith.

(c) IGNORANCE OF PAPER OVERDUE OR DISHONORED. Commercial paper may be negotiated even though (1) it has been dishonored, whether by nonacceptance or nonpayment; or (2) the paper is overdue, whether because of lapse of time or the acceleration of the due date; or (3) demand paper has been outstanding more than a reasonable time. In other words, ownership may still be transferred. Nevertheless the fact that the paper is circulating at a late date or after it has been dishonored is a suspicious circumstance that is deemed to put the person acquiring the paper on notice that there is some adverse claim or defense. A person who acquires title to the paper under such circumstances therefore cannot be a holder in due course.

If the fact that the paper is overdue or has been dishonored is not apparent from the paper itself, it is immaterial whether it was in fact overdue or dishonored. The new holder is not affected thereby unless he had knowledge or notice that it was overdue or dishonored.[8] Consequently, when the due date of a note is altered so that it appears to be due in 45 days instead of 5 days, a person may be a holder in due course when he takes it after the expiration of the 5 days but before the expiration of the 45 days if the alteration of the note is not apparent, for the holder then takes it without notice of the fact that the note was overdue.[9]

The purchaser of a commercial paper has notice that the instrument is overdue if he has reasonable grounds to believe "(a) that any part of the

---

[6] See p. 328.

[7] *Norman* v. *World Wide Distributors, Inc.*, 202 Pa.Super. 53, 195 A.2d 115.

[8] Notice, as here used, means that the new holder "from all the facts and circumstances known to him at the time in question . . . has reason to know" that the instrument was overdue or dishonored. UCC Sec. 1-201(25)(c).

[9] *Unadilla National Bank* v. *McQueer*, 27 App.Div.2d 778, 277 N.Y.S.2d 221.

principal amount is overdue or that there is an uncured default in payment of another instrument of the same series; or (b) that acceleration of the instrument has been made; or (c) that he is taking a demand instrument after demand has been made or more than a reasonable length of time after its issue. A reasonable time for a check drawn and payable within the states and territories of the United States and the District of Columbia is presumed to be thirty days." [10]

(d) IGNORANCE OF DEFENSES AND ADVERSE CLAIMS. Prior parties on the paper may have defenses which they could raise if sued by the person with whom they had dealt. For example, the drawer of a check, if sued by the payee of the check, might have the defense that the merchandise delivered by the payee was defective. In addition to defenses, third persons, whether prior parties or not, may be able to assert that the instrument belongs to them and not to the holder or to his transferor. A person cannot be a holder in due course if he acquires the commercial paper with notice or knowledge that any party might have a defense or that there is any adverse claim to the ownership of the instrument. Thus he cannot be a holder in due course when he has knowledge of a failure of consideration in an earlier transaction involving the instrument.

When the transferee makes payment for the transfer of the paper in installments and learns of a defense after he has paid in part, he can be a holder in due course as to the payments made before, but not as to payments made after, learning of the existence of the defense.

(e) WHAT CONSTITUTES NOTICE OF A CLAIM OR DEFENSE. Knowledge of certain facts constitutes notice to the person acquiring a commercial paper that there is a defense or an adverse claim. The holder or purchaser of the paper is deemed to have notice of a defense (1) if the instrument is so incomplete, bears such visible evidence of forgery or alteration, or is otherwise so irregular as to call into question its validity, terms, or ownership, or to create an ambiguity as to the party who is required to pay; or (2) if the purchaser has notice that the obligation of any party is voidable in whole or in part, or that all parties to the paper have been discharged. For example, if the subsequent holder knows that a note given for home improvement work in fact covers both the improvements and a loan and that the transaction is usurious because excessive costs were charged to conceal the usurious interest, the subsequent holder is not a holder in due course.[11]

In general, a holder is deemed to have notice when he had knowledge of facts which would put a reasonable man upon inquiry, that is, which would

---

[10] UCC Sec. 3-304(3).
[11] *Mutual Home Dealers Corp.* v. *Alves,* 23 App.Div.2d 791, 258 N.Y.S.2d 786.

make him curious to investigate further, which investigation, if made, would reveal the existence of the defenses.[12]

(f) WHAT DOES NOT CONSTITUTE NOTICE OF A CLAIM OR DEFENSE. A holder does not have notice or knowledge of a defense or adverse claim merely because he knows (1) that the instrument is antedated or postdated; (2) that it was issued or negotiated in return for an executory promise or accompanied by a separate agreement, unless the purchaser has notice that a defense or claim has arisen from the terms thereof; (3) that any party has signed for accommodation; (4) that an incomplete instrument has been completed, unless the purchaser has notice of any improper completion; (5) that any person negotiating the instrument is or was a fiduciary; or (6) that there has been a default in payment of interest on the instrument or in payment of any other instrument, except one of the same series. The fact that a document related to the instrument has been filed or recorded does not constitute notice which will prevent a person from being a holder in due course.[13]

The fact that a holder knows that the payee had a fluctuating financial record does not prevent his becoming a holder in due course.[14] The fact that the payee negotiates a large volume of commercial paper, such as the notes received in the course of the week, does not put the indorsee on notice of any defect or defense.[15]

2 / Who may be a holder in due course. Any person may be a holder in due course. This includes the payee of the instrument provided he satisfies the necessary elements. Ordinarily the payee deals directly with the drawer and therefore would have knowledge of any defense that the latter might raise. But the payee becomes a holder in due course when he acts through an intermediary so that in fact he did not deal with the drawer but acquired the paper from the intermediary, even though the paper was made payable to his order. The net result is the same as though the drawer had made the check payable to the intermediary who in turn indorsed it to the payee.

Facts: Shulman purchased equipment from Sayve on conditional sale. The contract specified that the seller could transfer the contract to James Talcott, Inc. The contract was thereafter assigned and the buyer's note indorsed to Talcott. The latter was an industrial finance company, which had executed a blanket discounting agreement with Sayve and had supplied it with printed forms bearing Talcott's name. In a suit between the parties, Shulman claimed that the finance company was not a holder in due course because of the blanket discounting agreement and the supplying of forms.

---

[12] *Anderson* v. *Lee*, 103 Cal.App.2d 24, 228 P.2d 613.
[13] UCC Sec. 3-304(4), (5).
[14] *Texico State Bank* v. *Hullinger*, 75 Ill.App.2d 212, 220 N.E.2d 248.
[15] *Pugatch* v. *David's Jewelers*, 53 Misc.2d 327, 278 N.Y.S.2d 759.

Decision: Judgment against the buyer. The fact that there was a standing business relationship between the parties and that, to facilitate such relationship, the finance company had supplied printed forms bearing its name did not show that it was not a holder in due course. (Talcott v. Shulman, 82 N.J.S. 438, 198 A.2d 98)

There is a growing tendency, however, to hold that a finance company which takes an active part in arranging the details of a sale is not to be regarded as a holder in due course of a note given by the buyer to the seller and negotiated by the seller to the finance company. In such a case the finance company is regarded as a party to the original transaction and therefore an ordinary holder.

Certain types of purchases of commercial paper do not make the purchaser a holder in due course although he otherwise satisfies all the elements here considered. Such sales are not of an ordinary commercial nature, and therefore the buyer need not be given the protection afforded a holder in due course. Thus a person is not a holder in due course when he acquires the paper by means of a judicial sale, a sale of the assets of an estate, or a bulk sale not in the regular course of business of the transferor.[16]

3 / Proof of status as holder in due course. The status of the holder does not become important until a person sued by the holder raises a defense that can be asserted against an ordinary holder but not against a holder in due course or a holder through a holder in due course.[17] Initially the plaintiff in the action is entitled to recover as soon as the commercial paper is put in evidence and the signatures on it are admitted to be genuine. If the genuine character of any signature is specifically denied, the burden is then on the plaintiff to prove that the signature is genuine.[18] Once the signatures are admitted or established, the plaintiff-holder is entitled to recover [19] unless the defendant establishes a defense. In the latter situation, the plaintiff has the burden of establishing that he is a holder in due course, or a holder through a holder in due course, in order to avoid such defense.[20]

Holder Through a Holder in Due Course

Those persons who become holders of the instrument after a holder in due course are given the same protection as the holder in due course provided they are not parties to any fraud or illegality that would affect the instrument.[21]

---

[16] UCC Sec. 3-302(3).

[17] *Persson* v. *McCormick,* [Okla.] 412 P.2d 619.

[18] UCC Sec. 3-307(1). The plaintiff is aided by a presumption that the signature is genuine or authorized except where the action is to enforce the obligation of a signer who has died or become incompetent. Sec. 3-307(1)(b).

[19] *Altex Aluminum Supply Co.* v. *Asay,* 72 N.J.S. 582, 178 A.2d 636.

[20] UCC Sec. 3-307(3). If the defense is one that may be asserted against any holder, it is immaterial whether the plaintiff is a holder in due course.

[21] UCC Sec. 3-201(1).

This means that if an instrument is indorsed from *A* to *B* to *C* to *D* and that if *B* is a holder in due course, both *C* and *D* will enjoy the same rights as *B*. If *C* received the instrument as a gift or with knowledge of failure of consideration or other defense, or if *D* took the instrument after maturity, they could not themselves be holders in due course. Nevertheless, they are given the same protection as a holder in due course because they took the instrument through such a holder, namely, *B*. It is not only *C*, the person taking directly from *B*, but also *D*, who takes indirectly through *B*, who is given this extra protection.

DEFENSES

The importance of being a holder in due course or a holder through a holder in due course is that those holders are not subject to certain defenses when they demand payment or bring suit upon a commercial paper. These may be described as *limited defenses*. Another class of defenses, *universal defenses*, may be asserted against any holder without regard to whether he is an ordinary holder, a holder in due course, or a holder through a holder in due course. A holder who is neither a holder in due course nor a holder through a holder in due course is subject to every defense just as though the instrument were not negotiable.

The defenses that cannot be raised against a holder in due course are likewise barred with respect to any instrument which is executed to renew or extend the original instrument.

Defenses Available Against an Ordinary Holder

When suit is brought by the original payee, he is subject to every defense that the defendant may possess, unless he qualifies as a holder in due course.[22]

The fact that a person cannot recover on a commercial paper does not necessarily mean that he is not entitled to recover in another action or against another party. He may be able to recover on a contract that was part of the transaction in which the instrument was given. It is also possible that he may be able to hold a party to the instrument liable for breach of an implied warranty or to recover from a person expressly guaranteeing payment of the instrument.

Limited Defenses—Not Available Against a Holder in Due Course

Neither a holder in due course nor one having the rights of such a holder is subject to any of the following defenses:[23]

---

[22] See p. 335.
[23] UCC Sec. 3-305.

1 / Simple contract defenses. In general terms, the defenses that could be raised against a suit on a simple contract cannot be raised against the holder in due course.[24] Accordingly the defendant cannot assert against the holder in due course the defense of lack, failure,[25] or illegality of consideration with respect to the transaction between the defendant and the person with whom he dealt.

2 / Incapacity of defendant. The incapacity of the defendant, with the exception of minority,[26] may not be raised against a holder in due course unless by general principles of law that incapacity makes the instrument a nullity.[27]

3 / Fraud in the inducement. When a person knows that he is executing a commercial paper and knows its essential terms but is persuaded or induced to execute it because of false statements or representations, he cannot defend against a holder in due course or a holder through a holder in due course on the ground of such fraud.[28] As an illustration, *M* is persuaded to purchase an automobile because of *P's* statement concerning its condition. *M* gives *P* a note, which is negotiated until it reaches *H,* who is a holder in due course. *M* meanwhile learns that the car is not as represented and that *P's* statements were fraudulent. When *H* demands payment of the note, *M* cannot refuse to pay him on the ground of *P's* fraud. He must pay the instrument and then recover his loss from *P.*

Facts: Holler sold stolen goods to the Star Provision Company which paid by check, believing that Holler was the owner. The check was subsequently negotiated to Sears, Roebuck & Company, which was a holder in due course. When Sears sued Star for nonpayment of the check, Star raised the defense that the goods had been stolen.

Decision: Judgment for Sears. The fact that the goods were stolen constituted fraud in the inducement and therefore could not be raised against Sears, a holder in due course. (Star Provision Company v. Sears, Roebuck & Co., 93 Ga.App. 799, 92 S.E.2d 835)

4 / Prior payment or cancellation. When a commercial paper is paid before maturity, the person making the payment should demand the surrender of the instrument. If he fails to obtain the instrument, it is possible for the holder to continue to negotiate it. Another person may thus become the holder of the instrument. When the new holder demands payment of the instrument, the defense cannot be raised that payment had been made to a

---

[24] *Wyatt* v. *Mount Airy Cemetery,* 209 Pa.Super. 250, 224 A.2d 787.
[25] *Federal Factors, Inc.* v. *Wellbanks,* 241 Ark. 44, 406 S.W.2d 712.
[26] See p. 96.
[27] UCC Sec. 3-305(2)(b).
[28] *Meadow Brook National Bank* v. *Rogers,* 44 Misc.2d 250, 253 N.Y.S.2d 501.

former holder, if the new holder is a holder in due course. The fact that the person making the payment obtained a receipt from the former holder does not affect the application of this principle.

When the holder and the party primarily liable have agreed to cancel the instrument but the face of the instrument does not show any sign of cancellation, the defense of cancellation cannot be asserted against a holder in due course. Similarly, an order to stop payment of a check cannot be raised as a defense by the drawer of a check against a holder in due course.[29]

5 / Nondelivery of an instrument. A person may make out a commercial paper or indorse an instrument and leave it on his desk for future delivery. At that moment the instrument or the indorsement is not effective because there has been no delivery.

Assume that through the negligence of an employee or through the theft of the instrument, it comes into the hands of another person. If the instrumentment is in such form that it can be negotiated, as when it is payable to bearer, a subsequent receiver of the instrument may be a holder in due course or a holder through a holder in due course. As against him, the person who made out the instrument or indorsed it cannot defend on the ground that he did not deliver it.[30]

6 / Conditional or specified purpose delivery. As against a favored holder, a person who would be liable on the instrument cannot show that the instrument which is absolute on its face was in fact delivered subject to a condition that had not been performed, or that it was delivered for a particular purpose but was not so used. Assume *A* makes out a check to the order of *B* and hands it to *C* with the understanding that *C* shall not deliver the check to *B* until *B* delivers certain merchandise. If *C* should deliver the check to *B* before the condition is satisfied and *B* then negotiates the check, a holder in due course or a holder through a holder in due course may enforce the instrument.

Similarly, if the instrument is itself restrictively indorsed to subject it to a condition, the defendant may not raise against the holder in due course the defense that payment to him would be inconsistent with the restriction.

Somewhat similar to the defense of a conditional delivery is the defense that delivery was made subject to a particular oral agreement or understanding. As against a holder in due course, a defendant-indorser cannot assert that he has negotiated the instrument to his indorsee under an oral agreement that the negotiation should be without recourse as to him.

---

[29] See p. 322.

[30] No distinction is made between a nondelivered instrument that was complete and one which had not been completed by the person executing it. In either case, the defense of nondelivery cannot be raised against the holder in due course.

7 / Duress. The defense that a person signed or executed a commercial paper under threats of harm or violence may not be raised as a defense against a holder in due course when the effect of such duress is merely to make the contract voidable at the election of the victim of the duress.

Facts: Lenchner was purchasing the stock of a company. Smith demanded a high price for his shares and threatened to "kill the deal" if he was not paid his price. Lenchner later gave Smith a promissory note for the purchase price which Smith demanded. In a subsequent suit Lenchner claimed that the note was not binding because made under duress.

Decision: A threat to interfere with a business deal does not constitute duress when there is no threat of actual physical harm or of criminal prosecution and no evidence of any incapacity of the party claiming duress, and when that party dealt at arm's length with the other party and was free to consult an attorney. (Smith v. Lenchner, 204 Pa.Super. 500, 205 A.2d 626)

8 / Unauthorized completion. If a maker or drawer signs a commercial paper and leaves blank the name of the payee, or the amount, or any other term, and then hands the instrument to another to be completed, the defense of an improper completion cannot be raised when payment is demanded or suit brought by a subsequent holder in due course or a holder through a holder in due course. That is, he may enforce the instrument as completed.[31]

This situation arises when an employer gives a signed blank check to an employee with instructions to make certain purchases and to fill in the name of the seller and the amount when these are determined. If the employee fills in the name of a friend and a large amount and then the employee and the friend negotiate the instrument, the employer cannot defend against a subsequent holder in due course or a holder through a holder in due course on the ground that the completion had been without the authority of the employer.

9 / Theft. As a matter of definition, a holder in due course will not have acquired the paper through theft and any defense of theft therefore must relate to the conduct of a prior party. Assuming that the theft of the paper does not result in a defect in the chain of necessary indorsements, the defense that the instrument had been stolen cannot be asserted against a holder in due course.[32]

Universal Defenses—Available Against All Holders

Certain defenses are regarded as so basic that the social interest in preserving them outweighs the social interest of giving commercial paper the

---

[31] UCC Sec. 3-407(3).
[32] Sec. 3-305(1).

free-passing qualities of money. Accordingly, such defenses are given universal effect and may be raised against all holders, whether ordinary holders, holders in due course, or holders through a holder in due course.

1 / Fraud as to the nature or essential terms of the instrument. If a person signs a commercial paper because he has been fraudulently deceived as to its nature or essential terms, he has a defense available against all holders. This is the situation when an experienced businessman induces an illiterate person to sign a note by falsely representing that it is a contract for repairs. This defense, however, cannot be raised when it is the negligence of the defending party that prevented him from learning the true nature and terms of the instrument.[33]

2 / Forgery or lack of authority. The defense that a signature was forged or signed without authority may be raised against any holder unless the person whose name was signed ratified it or is estopped by his conduct or negligence from denying it.[34]

Facts: The United States mailed a tax refund to a taxpayer. Another person who had the same name as the taxpayer obtained possession of the check, indorsed it with his name, and cashed it at the Fulton National Bank. The bank collected the amount of the check from the United States Treasury. The United States then sued the bank for the return of this payment.

Decision: Judgment for the United States. Although the person who indorsed the check used his own name, which also happened to be the name of the payee, the indorsement was forged or made without authority because it had not been made or authorized by the person whom the drawer intended to designate as the payee. Accordingly, the Fulton National Bank never became the holder of the check and had no right to receive or retain the payment which it had received. (Fulton Nat. Bank v. United States, [C.A.5th] 197 F.2d 763)

3 / Duress depriving control. When a person executes or indorses a commercial paper in response to a force of such a nature that under general principles of law there is duress which makes the transaction a nullity, rather than merely voidable, such duress may be raised as a defense against any holder.[35]

4 / Incapacity. The fact that the defendant is a minor who under general principles of contract law may avoid his obligation is a matter that may be raised against any kind of holder. Other kinds of incapacity may only be

---

[33] *Burchett* v. *Allied Concord Financial Corp.,* 74 N.Mex. 575, 396 P.2d 186.
[34] UCC Sec. 3-404(1); *Cohen* v. *Lincoln Savings Bank,* 275 N.Y. 399, 10 N.E.2d 457.
[35] UCC Sec. 3-305(2)(b).

raised as a defense if the effect of the incapacity is to make the instrument a nullity.[36]

5 / Illegality. If the law declares that an instrument is void when executed in connection with certain conduct, such as gambling or usury, or when issued by foreign corporations not authorized to do business within the state, that defense may be raised against any holder. If the law merely makes the transaction illegal but does not make the instrument void, the defense cannot be asserted against a holder in due course or a holder through a holder in due course.[37]

6 / Alteration. The fact that an instrument has been altered may be raised against any holder. Unlike other defenses, however, it is only a partial defense as against a holder in due course. That is, the latter holder may enforce the instrument according to its original terms prior to its alteration.[38] Moreover, if the person sued by the holder in due course has substantially contributed by his negligence to making the alteration possible, that defendant is precluded from asserting the defense of alteration.[39]

An alteration does not have any effect unless it is both material and is fraudulently made. An alteration is material when it changes the contract of any party in any way, as by changing the date, place of payment, rate of interest, or any other term. It also includes any modification that changes the number or the relationship of the parties to the paper, by adding new terms, or by cutting off a part of the paper itself.[40]

Facts: A promissory note was made and delivered to Du Pont, who indorsed it to the First National Bank. Baumer, the receiver of the bank, demanded payment from the maker of the note. When this payment was refused by the maker, due notice of this fact was given Du Pont and suit was later brought against him as indorser. Du Pont showed that, without his consent and at the request of the receiver of the bank, the maker had added a seal after his name.

Decision: Judgment for Du Pont. The addition of a seal had materially changed the obligation by extending the time in which suit could be brought from 6 years to 20 years. As a material change, its effect was to avoid the instrument except with respect to those authorizing or assenting to the alteration and to persons who became parties to the papers subsequent to the alteration. (Baumer v. Du Pont, 338 Pa. 193, 12 A.2d 566)

---

[36] Sec. 3-305(2)(b).

[37] Sec. 3-305(2)(b).

[38] Sec. 3-407(3).

[39] Sec. 3-406. This estoppel may also arise in favor of a drawee or other payor who pays the instrument as altered in good faith, when acting in accord with the reasonable commercial standards of his business.

[40] UCC Sec. 3-407(1).

Conversely, the adding or crossing out of words on the instrument which do not affect the contract of any party is not material. Likewise, there is no "alteration" because there is no fraud when a pencil line is run through the amount of the note after part payment has been made and the current balance is written in pencil, or when a red line is drawn across the face of the note to indicate that the bank examiner had examined the note.[41] Similarly, there is no alteration when the final payment due on a note is changed from $41,000 to $42,000 if the balance of the note showed that this was the correct amount and that the changed figure ($41,000) had been a mistake.[42]

An alteration must be made to the instrument itself. An oral or a collateral written agreement between the holder and one of the parties that modifies the obligation of the party is not an "alteration" within the sense just discussed, even though the obligation of the party is changed or altered thereby.

By definition an alteration is a change made by a party to the instrument. A change of the instrument made by a stranger has no effect, and recovery on the instrument is the same as though the change had not been made provided it can be proved what the instrument had been in its original form.

Adverse Claims to the Instrument

Distinct from a defense which a defendant may raise against a plaintiff as a reason why he should not be required to pay the instrument is a claim of a third person that he and not the plaintiff is the holder or owner of the commercial paper. Assume that a check was made to the order of *A*, that thereafter blank indorsements are made by *B, C,* and *D,* and that *E* in possession of the check appears to be the holder. *B* might then claim and show, if such be the case, that he indorsed the check because he was fraudulently deceived by *C*; that he avoids his indorsement because of such fraud; and that accordingly the check still belongs to him. *B* in such case is making an adverse claim to the instrument.

A holder in due course holds commercial paper free and clear from all adverse claims of any other person to the paper, including both equitable and legal interests of third persons, and the right of a former holder to rescind his negotiation.[43] In contrast, such adverse claims may be asserted against a holder who is not a holder in due course,[44] which means that the adverse claimant may bring such action against the holder since the law generally provides for the recovery of property by the owner from anyone else.

Ordinarily a defendant when sued by a holder cannot raise against the holder the defense that the holder's ownership is subject to an adverse claim.

---

[41] *Bank of New Mexico* v. *Rice,* 78 N.Mex. 170, 429 P.2d 368.
[42] *National State Bank* v. *Kleinberg,* [N.Y.S.2d] 4 UCCRS 100.
[43] UCC Secs. 3-305(1), 3-207.
[44] Sec. 3-306(a), (d).

This may be done only when the adverse claimant has also become a party to the action or is defending the action on behalf of the defendant.[45] Otherwise it would be unfair to the adverse claimant to pass upon the merits of his claim in his absence, as well as being undesirable in opening the door to perjury by giving any defendant the opportunity of beclouding the issues by raising a false claim that a third person has an adverse interest.

QUESTIONS AND PROBLEMS

1. Checklist of legal terms:
   (a) holder through a holder in due course (335)
   (b) limited defense, universal defense (336)

2. State the objective(s) of each of the following rules of law:
   (a) A person cannot be a holder in due course of a check that he has received as a gift.
   (b) Certain defenses can be raised against a holder in due course.

3. The last indorsement on a draft reads as follows: "Pay to the order of the Clifton National Bank for collection, L. K. Britton." When the bank presents the draft for collection to Grey, the acceptor, Grey refuses to pay stating that he will pay it only to Vance, the payee of the draft. Who is entitled to demand payment on this draft?

4. Ballard is induced by fraud to execute a note for $5,000 payable to Huntington. Kern purchases the instrument for $4,750. When Kern sues on the note, Ballard contends that Kern is not entitled to recover because he did not give full value for the instrument. Is Ballard's contention sound?

5. Lindsey obtains a $500 note from Gibson by fraud and sells the instrument to Hanna on terms of $200 cash and $100 a month for three months. After Hanna learns of the fraud, he pays the first installment of $100. What are Hanna's rights on the note against Gibson?

6. Gorman executed a $20,000 note payable to his own order and indorsed the instrument to the Hurst Company. Long, President of the Hurst Company, indorsed the note to Magee in payment of Long's personal obligation. Was Magee entitled to judgment in an action to recover on the instrument from Gorman?

7. The Kuhl Hardware Store executed a note for $500 payable to the order of the Widman Manufacturing Company. Before maturity the note was indorsed to the Gentry Security Company. At the time of this negotiation the note apparently had been altered because certain printed portions had been marked out and other words written in the instrument. When the Gentry Security Company brought an action against the Kuhl Hardware Store, the latter set up as a defense fraud on the part of an agent of the payee. Was the plaintiff entitled to judgment?

---

[45] Sec. 3-306(d).

8. When a draft executed by Drew was transferred by the payee to a bank, it contained an obvious alteration. After maturity of the instrument, the draft was transferred by the bank to Bolton. Could either the bank or Bolton hold the acceptor for the draft as originally executed?

9. Distinguish between the defense of fraud in the inducement and the defense of fraud as to the nature or terms of the commercial paper. Classify each of these defenses as limited or universal.

10. Distinguish between the defense of a threat of harm or violence that would make a contract voidable and the defense of duress that would make a contract void. Classify each defense as limited or universal.

11. Classify each of the following as a limited or universal defense:
    (a) forgery (not involving negligence)
    (b) minority
    (c) nondelivery of instrument
    (d) theft
    (e) voluntary intoxication

12. Vanella sold his automobile to Blackburn Motors by falsely representing that there were no liens on the car. Blackburn paid Vanella with a check that was cashed by the Marine Midland Trust Co. When Blackburn learned of Vanella's fraud, it stopped payment on the check. Midland then sued Blackburn to enforce its secondary liability as drawer. Blackburn raised the defense of Vanella's fraud. Was this defense available to it? (Marine Midland Trust Co. v. Blackburn, 50 Misc.2d 954, 271 N.Y.S.2d 388)

13. In an action on a promissory note it was claimed that there had been a material change of the note. Was this a sufficient defense? (Mandel v. Sedrish, [N.Y.S.2d] 3 UCCRS 524)

14. Wilkins was fraudulently induced to execute a note for $300 payable one day after date to Tilley. The next day Tilley indorsed the note to Usher in payment of a debt of $117. When the note was not paid, Usher sued Wilkins. The latter claimed that Usher was subject to the defense of fraud because he was not a holder in due course since he (a) took the note after maturity, and (b) did not give value for it. Decide. (Wilkins v. Usher, 123 Ky. 696, 97 S.W. 37)

Chapter 29

Discharge of Commercial Paper

A party to a commercial paper who would otherwise be liable on it may be discharged either individually or by some act that has discharged all parties to the paper at one time.

DISCHARGE OF INDIVIDUAL PARTIES

A party to a commercial paper, like a party to an ordinary contract, is usually discharged from liability by making payment to the proper person; but the discharge from liability may be effected in a number of other ways.

Simple Contract Discharge

A party is discharged from liability to any other party (1) with whom he enters into an agreement for his discharge, or (2) with whom he enters into a transaction which under the law of contracts is effective to discharge liability for a simple contract for the payment of money.[1] Accordingly, there may be a discharge by accord and satisfaction, a novation, a covenant not to sue, rescission, or the substitution of another instrument. The liability may also be barred by operation of law as in the case of a discharge in bankruptcy, the operation of the Statute of Limitations, or by the merger of liability into a judgment in favor of the holder when an action has been brought on the instrument.

Discharge by Payment

The obligation of a particular party on commercial paper is discharged when he pays the amount of the instrument to the holder[2] or to his authorized agent. Payment to anyone else, even though in physical possession of the instrument, is not effective. If the holder consents, however, payment may also be made by a third person, even a total stranger to the paper; and surrender of the paper to such a person gives him the rights of a transferee of the instrument.[3]

---

[1] Uniform Commercial Code, Sec. 3-601(2); *Reagan* v. *National Bank of Commerce,* [Tex.Civ.App.] 418 S.W.2d 593.
[2] UCC Sec. 3-603(1).
[3] Sec. 3-603(2).

Facts: Gorman executed and delivered a promissory note to the First National Bank. After several payments, the note was stolen from the bank. Subsequently, Gorman paid the remainder to one representing himself to be Richardson, who previously had been connected with the payee bank. In an action brought by the bank to collect the remainder of the note from Gorman, the latter pleaded payment and produced the note marked paid by the impostor.

Decision: Judgment for First National Bank. Payment of commercial paper is not a discharge when made to a person who is not the holder. This conclusion is not altered by the fact that the person receiving payment of order paper had possession of the paper at the time. (First National Bank v. Gorman, 45 Wyo. 519, 21 P.2d 549)

By definition, a commercial paper provides for the payment of a sum of money. Any party liable on the instrument and the holder thereof may, however, agree that the transfer or delivery of other kinds of property shall operate as payment. Sometimes a new instrument may be executed or delivered to the holder of the original instrument. In the absence of proof of an agreement to the contrary, a delivery of a subsequent instrument, without the destruction or other act to discharge the first, is merely the giving of additional security for the payment of the original instrument but is not in itself a payment or discharge of the first.

Facts: Yowell borrowed money from the First National Bank and gave it a promissory note. When the note was due, he gave the bank a renewal note and the original note was stamped "Paid." When the renewal note was not paid, the bank sued Yowell upon the renewal note; but recovery was denied on the ground that the renewal note had been materially altered by raising the interest rate without the consent of the maker. The bank then sued Yowell upon the first note. He claimed that it had been paid by the giving of the second note.

Decision: Judgment for Yowell. In the absence of proof it is held that the giving of a renewal or a new note is not a discharge of the original note but is additional security for its payment. If the original note is stamped, "Paid," however, it can be inferred that the parties intended that the original note should be discharged unless it is shown that such stamping was the result of a mistake. As that was not shown in this case, the original obligation was discharged. (First National Bank v. Yowell, 155 Tenn. 430, 294 S.W. 1101)

1 / Knowledge of adverse claim to the paper. When the payment of the amount of the paper is made to the holder, the party making payment may know that some other person claims an interest in or ownership of the paper. The knowledge that there is an adverse claimant does not prevent making a payment to the holder, and such payment is still a discharge of the obligation of the party making payment. Specifically, the existence of the adverse claim to the paper may thus be disregarded unless the adverse claimant furnishes the payor with a bond or other indemnity to protect him in the event that he does not pay and the adverse claim proves to be worthless or unless the adverse claimant obtains a court injunction against making payment to the holder.[4]

The purpose of this provision is to give commercial paper greater acceptance since the person writing such paper knows that he will be able to discharge the instrument by making payment in the ordinary case to the holder without the risk of deciding whether an adverse claim is valid.

2 / Satisfaction. The principles governing payment apply to a satisfaction entered into with the holder of the instrument.[5] Instead of paying the holder in full in money, a payment of less than all is accepted as full payment, or some service is rendered or property is given by the party discharged.

3 / Tender of payment. A party who is liable may offer to the holder the full amount when or after the instrument is due. If the holder refuses such payment, the party making the tender of payment is not discharged from his liability for the amount then due; but the holder cannot hold him liable for any interest that accrues after that date. Likewise, in the event that the holder sues the person making the tender, the holder cannot recover legal costs from him nor attorney's fees, as is commonly authorized by commercial paper.[6]

If the holder refuses a proper tender, his refusal may discharge third persons even though it does not affect the liability of the person making the tender. Specifically, any party to the paper who would have a right, if he made payment, to recover that amount from the person making the tender is discharged if the tender is not accepted.[7] For example, if the paper is negotiated through the unqualified indorsers *A, B,* and *C,* to the holder *D,* and if *B* or *C* is required to pay *D,* he would have the right to sue *A,* the prior indorser, to recover from him the amount paid the holder *D.* In such a case, if *A* makes a proper tender of payment which *D* refuses, *B* and *C* are discharged from any liability to *D.*

Cancellation

The holder of an instrument, with or without consideration, may discharge the liability of a particular party by cancellation, by a notation on the

---

[4] Sec. 3-603(1). Certain exceptions are made to this rule when payment is made in bad faith on a stolen instrument or when the instrument is restrictively indorsed. Sec. 3-603(1)(a), (b).
[5] Sec. 3-601(1).
[6] Sec. 3-604(1).
[7] Sec. 3-604(2).

paper which makes that intent apparent, or by destroying, mutilating, or striking out the party's signature on the paper. The fact that by effecting such cancellation an indorsement necessary to the chain of title of the holder is destroyed does not affect his title to the paper,[8] since the fact remains that the paper had been properly negotiated to the holder.

Facts: Sicklick, who was president of the New York & Eastern Realty Company, with its authority made its promissory note to his order for $750 due in four months from date. He indorsed and discounted the instrument with the Broad & Market National Bank. The note was reduced to $700 and paid by another note for that amount. When this note was aue, Sicklick gave his check on the holder bank in payment and received the note stamped or punched "Paid." His check, although charged to his account, was not paid in part because a check for $550 drawn on a bank in Bangor, Pa., was uncollected. In an action brought by the Broad & Market National Bank against the New York & Eastern Realty Company to collect the amount of the note, the maker contended that the note had been discharged.

Decision: The stamping of the note as "paid" upon receipt of the check canceled or discharged the note, even though the check was not itself honored. The holder should have waited until the check was paid before canceling the note. Since he did not do so, he was limited to suing upon the unpaid check. (Broad & Market National Bank v. New York & E. Realty Co., 102 Misc. 82, 168 N.Y.S. 149)

A cancellation is not effective if it is made by a person who is not the holder or who is not acting by his authority or when the physical destruction of the instrument is made by accident or mistake. The party who claims that an apparent cancellation should not take effect has the burden of proof.

Renunciation

The holder of an instrument, with or without consideration, may discharge the liability of a particular party by renunciation. This is effected either (1) by surrendering the instrument to the party to be discharged, or (2) by executing a signed written renunciation which is then delivered to the party to be discharged.[9] If the holder surrenders the instrument in effecting the renunciation, he ceases to be the holder and thereafter cannot hold any party liable on the paper, although such other parties are not themselves discharged with respect to the person to whom the paper was surrendered or any other subsequent holder thereof.

Facts: White System sued Lehmann on a promissory note which he had executed as maker. Lehmann defended on the ground that the holder had

---

[8] Sec. 3-605.
[9] Sec. 3-605.

renounced or canceled the obligation when, after Lehmann's default, it carried the note in its profit and loss account as a loss.

Decision: Judgment for White. The manner in which a holder treats a commercial paper for his accounting purposes is immaterial, since a discharge can only be effected in the manner designated by the statute. (White System v. Lehmann, [La.] 144 So.2d 122)

Impairment of Right of Recourse

In most instances there is at least one party to commercial paper who, if required to pay, will have a right of recourse, or a right to obtain indemnity, from some other party. For example, in the least complicated situation, the payee of a note has indorsed it without qualification to the present holder. If the holder obtains payment from the indorsing payee, the latter has a right of recourse against the maker of the note. If the holder, without the indorser's consent, discharges the liability of the maker, extends the time for payment, or agrees not to sue him, the indorser is also discharged unless he consented thereto, on the theory that his right of recourse has been impaired.[10]

Impairment of Collateral

When commercial paper is executed, the maker or any other party liable on the instrument may give the holder property, such as stocks or bonds, to hold as security for the payment of the instrument. This collateral security benefits all parties who might be liable on the paper because to the extent that payment is obtained from the security, they are not required to make payment. Conversely, if the collateral security is impaired or harmed in any way that reduces its value, the parties who are liable are harmed since the possibility that they will be required to pay increases. Accordingly, a particular party is discharged if the holder unjustifiably impairs collateral security provided by that party or by any person against whom such party has a right of recourse.[11]

Alteration

When an instrument is materially and fraudulently altered by the holder,[12] any party whose obligation on the paper is changed thereby is discharged, unless he had assented to the alteration or is barred by his conduct from asserting that he is discharged.[13] The effect of the discharge by alteration is limited, however; for, if the altered instrument is held by a holder in due course, he may enforce it according to its original terms.[14]

---

[10] Sec. 3-606(1)(a).
[11] Sec. 3-606(1).
[12] See p. 341.
[13] UCC Sec. 3-407(2)(a).
[14] Sec. 3-407(3). See p. 341.

Discharge for Miscellaneous Causes

In addition to the discharge of a party as discussed in the preceding sections, the conduct of certain parties with respect to the commercial paper or the enforcement of rights thereunder may release some of the parties to the paper. This occurs (1) when a check has been certified on the application of the holder;[15] (2) when the holder accepts an acceptance that varies the terms of the draft;[16] and (3) when a presentment, notice of dishonor, or protest, when required, is delayed beyond the time permitted or is absent and such delay or absence is not excused.[17]

In addition, federal or local statutes may provide for the discharge of a party by bankruptcy proceedings or by local laws declaring certain obligations not enforceable because they violate particular statutes.[18]

DISCHARGE OF ALL PARTIES

Discharge of Party Primarily Liable

The primary party on an instrument, that is, the maker of a note or the acceptor of a draft,[19] has no right of recourse against any party on the paper. Conversely, every other party who may be held liable on the paper has a right of recourse against persons primarily liable. If the holder discharges a party who is primarily liable in any way, all parties to the instrument are discharged, since the discharge of the primary party discharges the persons who had a right of recourse against him.[20]

Primary Party's Reacquisition of Paper

When a party primarily liable on the paper reacquires it in his own right at any time, whether before or after it is due, the instrument is then held by one who has no right to sue any other party on the paper. Such reacquisition therefore discharges the liability of all intervening parties to the instrument.[21] Moreover, as reacquisition requires a lawful transfer, it necessarily involves the negotiation or surrender by the person who was then the holder of the right against that party, and no party thereafter remains liable on the paper. The reacquisition by the party who has no right of action or recourse against anyone else on the paper therefore discharges the liability of all parties on it.[22]

---

[15] See p. 328.
[16] See p. 314.
[17] See p. 304.
[18] UCC Sec. 3-601, Official Comment, point 1.
[19] An accommodated payee is in effect also a primary party since the accommodating party, if required to pay an indorsee, has a right of recourse against such payee.
[20] UCC Sec. 3-601(3). In some instances this rule is modified by Sec. 3-606.
[21] Sec. 3-208.
[22] Sec. 3-601(3)(a).

EFFECT OF DISCHARGE ON HOLDER IN DUE COURSE

Discharge of Individual Party

The fact that a party has been discharged of liability, and even that a new holder of the paper knows of it, does not prevent the new holder from being a holder in due course as to any party remaining liable on the paper.[23] If the holder in due course does not have notice or knowledge of a discharge of a party obtained before he acquired the paper, he is not bound by the discharge and may enforce the obligation of the discharged party as though he had never been discharged.[24] In order to protect himself, a party securing his own discharge should have a notation of it made on the paper so that any subsequent party would necessarily have notice of that fact.

Discharge of All Parties

The fact that the liabilities of all parties to a negotiable instrument have been discharged does not destroy the negotiable character nor the existence of the commercial paper. If it should thereafter be negotiated to a person who qualifies as a holder in due course, the latter may enforce the liability of any party on the paper, although otherwise discharged, of whose discharge the holder in due course had no notice or knowledge.[25]

QUESTIONS AND PROBLEMS

1. Review the terms defined in the preceding chapters of Part IV.

2. State the objective(s) of the rule of law that payment does not discharge an instrument payable to order when it is not made to the holder of the instrument or to his authorized agent, even though payment is made to a person, not the holder, who was in possession of the instrument.

3. When Livingston's $1,000 note in favor of Howard became due, Livingston, with Howard's consent, paid $500 cash and issued a new note for $500. The first note was marked paid. When Livingston failed to pay the new note, Howard brought an action against Livingston; but the action failed because the note had been materially altered by changing the term from one year to six months. Howard then brought an action against Livingston on the first note. Livingston contended that that note had been paid. Do you agree?

4. Kirk is the holder of Marvin's note which is due and unpaid. When the two meet on the street, Kirk says, in the presence of Leopold, "I release

---

[23] Sec. 3-305(2)(e).

[24] Sec. 3-602. As an exception to this rule, the holder in due course is bound by a prior discharge in insolvency proceedings, such as bankruptcy, whether he had notice thereof or not. Sec. 3-305(2)(d).

[25] Sec. 3-601, Official Comment, point 3.

all claim that I have against you on your note which is in my safe." Can Kirk collect later in an action against Marvin on the note?

5. Mansfield writes Lacey that he releases all claims against Lacey on a note that is not yet due.
   (a) Can Mansfield collect on the note?
   (b) If Mansfield later negotiated the instrument to Kestner, a holder in due course, could Kestner collect on the note from Lacey?

6. When Ambrose announces that he intends to cancel Berry's note, Chatman tears up the note and throws it in the fire. Under what circumstances would Chatman's action constitute a cancellation?

7. Forbes, who is the holder of a check drawn on the First National Bank, changes the word "First" to "Second" because he knows that the drawer does most of his business at the latter bank. When the drawer of the check is sued, he pleads that the instrument was discharged by alteration. Do you agree?

8. A note executed by Eyles is overdue. Seeing the instrument on the desk of the holder, Eyles appropriates the note. Does this action discharge the note?

9. Henry and Herbert Mordecai were partners doing business under the name of the Southern Cigar Co. They indorsed a promissory note executed by the firm to Henry Mordecai and delivered it to the District National Bank. They also delivered as security a certificate for certain stock in the Monumental Cigar Co. After maturity of the note, the indorsers made an assignment of a claim against the United States to the bank, which accepted it in satisfaction of its rights on the note. Was the note discharged? (District National Bank v. Mordecai, 133 Md. 419, 105 A. 586)

10. The Citizens State Bank issued a cashier's check payable to the order of Donovan. He indorsed it to Denny, who did business as the Houston Aircraft Co., and included in the indorsement a recital that it was "in full [payment of] any and all claims of any character whatever." Denny crossed out this quoted phrase and wrote Donovan and the bank that he had done so. The Houston Aircraft Co. sued the Citizens National Bank on the check. Was the bank liable? (Houston Aircraft Co. v. Citizens State Bank, [Tex.Civ.App.] 184 S.W.2d 335)

11. Twombly, who owned negotiable bonds of the Muskogee Electric Traction Co., was advised by her financial agent, the State Street Trust Co., that the bonds had no value. Acting on this belief, Twombly burned the bonds. Some years later it was found that the bonds had some value, and the trust company, on behalf of Twombly, demanded payment on the bonds. Was it entitled to payment? (State Street Trust Co. v. Muskogee Electric Traction Co., [C.A.10th] 204 F.2d 920)

PART V

Personal Property and Bailments

Chapter 30

Personal Property—Nature and Classes

At one time trade and commerce were concerned only with movables, such as jewelry, fabrics, and furs. In the course of time immovables, such as land and houses, became articles of commerce.

PROPERTY IN GENERAL

Property means the rights and interests which one has in anything subject to ownership, whether that thing be movable or immovable, tangible or intangible, visible or invisible. A right in a thing is property, without regard to whether such right is absolute or conditional, perfect or imperfect, legal or equitable.

Property includes the rights of any person to possess, use, enjoy, and dispose of a thing. It is not necessary that all of these rights be held by the same person at one time.

The term "ownership" is used synonymously with rights in property. Thus one is said to be the owner of a certain property, meaning that he has certain interests in the designated thing. Although the term "ownership" is often used to indicate that one has the highest rights possible to possess, it may be used when one does not have all of the rights in a thing. Thus we say that a person is the owner of a house even though he has rented it to a tenant who has exclusive use of the house during the term of the lease.

The term "property" is also commonly used to designate the thing itself in which one has rights or interests.

Classifications of Property

1 / Real and personal property. Real property means the rights and interests of a certain nature that one has in land and things closely pertaining to land. Technically *real property* is an interest of indeterminate or

353

unfixed duration in things real. Personal property includes all property that is not real property. Technically *personal property* means any interest of determinate or fixed duration in things real and any interest in all other things that we know as things personal.

2 / Private and public property. The term *private property* designates things in which one or more persons have exclusive rights. Such things remain private property if owned by individuals or corporations, even though they are used for or by the public. For example, the equipment of a transportation company owned by individuals is private property although there exists an obligation which requires the use of the equipment for or by the public.

The term *public property* designates things that are owned by a government, such as a state or municipality. To illustrate, state institutions and city parks, which are both created and maintained with public funds for the public benefit, are classed as public property.

Banks, fuel yards, hydro-electric power plants and railroads, when owned by a government, whether national, state, or local, are also public property. The fact that the publicly owned property is not available for use by the general public, or that it is available only upon payment of charges or fees set by the government, does not change the "public" character of the property.

Limitations on Ownership

When one has all possible existing rights in and over a thing, he is said to have *absolute ownership*. The term "absolute," however, is somewhat misleading, for one's rights in respect to the use, enjoyment, and disposal of a thing are subject to certain restrictions, such as the following:

1 / Rights of government. All property is subject to the right of the government to compel the owner to give up a part for public purposes. This *power to tax* is an inherent right of sovereign states. By another power, called the *police power*, the government can pass reasonable rules and regulations in respect to the use and enjoyment of property for the protection of the safety, health, morals, and general welfare of the community. This police power is in substance the power to govern for the common good. Zoning laws that restrict the use of property within specified areas may be adopted under this power.

> **Facts:** Miller owned a hotel in Bakersfield. He was notified that the building did not conform to the fire prevention requirements of the newly-adopted building code. He refused to comply on the grounds that the hotel was a lawful structure when built, and he could not be required to expend money to make it conform to the new code.

Decision: Judgment for the city. When a building is a fire hazard, it has no vested right to continue as such merely because it was created prior to the law which recognizes it as a fire hazard. (Bakersfield v. Miller, 34 Cal.2d 93, 48 Cal.Rptr. 889, 410 P.2d 393)

Private property is also subject to the right of the government to take it for public purposes.[1] This right of *eminent domain* may also be exercised by certain corporations, such as railroads and public utilities. Constitutional provisions require that fair compensation be paid the owner when property is taken by eminent domain.[2] Such provisions do not apply when there is merely a loss of value caused by the use of the police power.

2 / Rights of creditors. Property is subject to the rights of one's creditors. It may be taken by judicial proceedings to satisfy just claims against the owner or his estate. A person cannot dispose of his property in any way so as to defeat the rights of his creditors.

3 / Rights of others. The law restricts the use and enjoyment of property in that the owner is not allowed to use it unreasonably in a way that will injure other members of society.[3] What is reasonable or unreasonable use of property by the owner depends upon the circumstances in a particular situation.

Facts: Shearing was a homeowner in Rochester. The city burned trash on a nearby tract of land. The burning was conducted on the open ground and not in an incinerator. Fires were burning and smoked continuously, at times within 800 yards of the plaintiff's house. The smoke and dirt from the fires settled on the house of the plaintiff and of other persons in the area. The plaintiff sued to stop the continuance of such burning and to recover the damages for the harm done to his house.

Decision: The conduct of the city constituted a nuisance and was stopped by injunction, and damages were awarded to the plaintiff. The fact that the defendant was a city did not exempt it from the operation of the prohibition against using property so as to harm others. (Shearing v. Rochester, 51 Misc.2d 436, 273 N.Y.S.2d 464)

Forms of Ownership

All interests in a particular object of property may be held by one person alone. It may occur, however, that several persons have concurrent interests in the same object.

A further distinction may be made in terms of the relative interests of co-owners as between themselves. For example, when the owner of a bank

---

[1] *Rabinoff* v. *District Court,* 145 Colo. 225, 360 P.2d 114.
[2] *Board of Commissioners* v. *Gardner,* 57 N.Mex. 478, 260 P.2d 682.
[3] *Reynolds* v. *W. Hinman Co.,* 145 Maine 343, 75 A.2d 802.

account causes the bank to add the name of another person to the account so that either may draw checks on the account, both the original and the new owner are co-owners of the account as far as the bank is concerned. As between themselves, however, they may in fact be co-owners or the one whose name is added may merely be an agent for the other. In the latter case, while the agent "owner" has the right to withdraw money, he cannot keep the money for himself.

The forms of ownership include: (1) severalty, (2) tenancy in common, (3) joint tenancy, (4) tenancy by entirety, (5) community property, (6) condominium, and (7) tenancy in partnership.

1 / Severalty. When property is owned by one person, it is said to be held in *severalty*. Ownership in severalty also exists when title is held in the form of "*A* or *B*," for the use of the word "or" is inconsistent with co-ownership.[4]

2 / Tenancy in common. A *tenancy in common* is a form of ownership by two or more persons. The interest of a tenant in common may be transferred or inherited, in which case the taker becomes a tenant in common with the others. This tenancy is terminated only when there is a partition, giving each a specific portion, or when one person acquires all of the interests of the co-owners.

3 / Joint tenancy. A *joint tenancy* is another form of ownership by two or more persons. A joint tenant may transfer his interest to a third party, but this destroys the joint tenancy. In such a case the remaining joint tenant becomes a tenant in common with the third person who has acquired the interest of the other joint tenant.

Upon the death of a joint tenant, the remaining tenants take the share of the deceased, and finally the last surviving joint tenant takes the property as a holder in severalty.[5]

Facts: Frank Stamets opened a savings account in the First National Bank. The account stood in the name of "Frank Stamets or Lena Stamets," Lena being his sister. The signature card, which was signed by Frank only, stated that the account was owned by Frank and Lena as joint tenants with the right of survivorship. All the money deposited was Frank's money. The signature card was never signed by Lena. On Frank's death, Lena claimed the bank account. The estate of Frank claimed it on the ground that Lena had never signed the signature card.

Decision: Judgment for Lena. When Frank deposited the money and signed the signature card, he created a joint tenancy in the fund with his sister.

---

[4] *Jenkins* v. *Meyer*, [Mo.] 380 S.W.2d 315.
[5] *Clausen* v. *Warner*, 118 Ind.App. 340, 78 N.E.2d 551.

The fact that she did not sign the card did not affect his intent nor its consequences. (Stamets' Estate, [Iowa] 148 N.W.2d 468)

A statute may require that the words "or to the survivor of them" be used to create a joint tenancy, with the result that a certificate of deposit only in the name of "*A* or *B*" does not create a joint tenancy because it does not refer to survivorship.[6]

Courts do not favor this form of ownership and will construe a transfer of property to several persons to be a tenancy in common whenever possible. Statutes in many states have abolished or modified joint tenancy, especially as to survivorship.

4 / Tenancy by entirety. At common law a *tenancy by entirety* (or tenancy by the entireties) was created when property was transferred to husband and wife in such a manner that it would create a joint tenancy if transferred to other persons, not husband and wife.[7] It differs from joint tenancy, however, in that the right of survivorship cannot be extinguished and one tenant alone cannot convey his interest to a third person, although in some jurisdictions he may transfer his right to share the possession and the profits. This form of property holding is popular because creditors of one of the spouses cannot reach the property. Only a creditor of both the husband and the wife under the same obligation can obtain execution against the property. Moreover, the tenancy by entirety is in effect a substitute for a will since the surviving spouse acquires the complete property interest upon the death of the other. There may be other reasons, however, why each spouse should make a will.

Generally a tenancy by the entirety is created by the mere fact that property is transferred to two persons who are husband and wife, even though it is not expressly stated that such a tenancy is thereby created, unless, of course, it is expressly stated that a different tenancy is created. This type of tenancy may also be created by either husband or wife. Thus, when a husband opens a bank account in the name of himself and his wife, or the survivor of them, and either the husband or wife may make withdrawals, a tenancy by the entirety is created as to any money that is deposited in the account, even though all deposits are made by the husband.

In some jurisdictions the statutes giving a married woman the capacity to contract and to own her own property are not regarded as affecting or modifying a tenancy by entirety.[8] In other jurisdictions it is held that by virtue of such statutes a creditor of either spouse may issue execution upon the chance or right of survivorship of the debtor spouse, with the result that

---

[6] *Dalton* v. *Eyestone,* 240 Ark. 1032, 403 S.W.2d 730.
[7] *Hoffman* v. *Nerwell,* 249 Ky. 270, 60 S.W.2d 607.
[8] *Whitlock* v. *Public Service Co.,* 239 Ind. 680, 159 N.E.2d 280.

if the debtor is the surviving spouse, who otherwise would acquire the property, the purchaser at the execution sale acquires the property.

5 / Community property. In some states property acquired during the period of marriage is the *community property* of the husband and wife. Some statutes provide for the right of survivorship; others provide that half of the property of the deceased husband or wife shall go to the heirs, or permit such half to be disposed of by will. It is commonly provided that property acquired by either spouse during the marriage is prima facie community property, even though title is taken in the spouse's individual name, unless it can be shown that it was obtained with property possessed by that spouse prior to the marriage.[9]

6 / Condominium. A *condominium* is a combination of co-ownership and ownership in severalty. For example, persons owning an office building or an apartment house by condominium are co-owners of the land and of the halls, lobby, elevators, and other areas used in common, but each individually owns his own apartment or office in the building.

7 / Tenancy in partnership. In states that have adopted the Uniform Partnership Act, a special form of joint tenancy known as a "tenancy in partnership" exists as to property owned by the firm.

PERSONAL PROPERTY

Personal property rights are also known as chattel interests. The term "chattel" is more comprehensive than the word "goods," which is ordinarily confined to movable things.

Classes of Personal Property

Personal property consists of (1) things which are tangible and movable, such as furniture and books; and (2) claims and debts, which are called *choses in action.* Common forms of choses in action are insurance policies, stock certificates, bills of lading, and evidences of indebtedness, such as notes, bonds, and drafts. Choses in action ordinarily also include rights of action, whether arising *ex contractu,* that is, out of the breach of a contract, or *ex delicto,* based upon the infliction of a tort.

Fixtures

Movable chattels may lose their nature as personal property by being annexed or affixed to the land or to a building. They are then known as *fixtures.* The parties may agree that chattels affixed to land are or are not

---

[9] *Lovelady* v. *Loughridge,* 204 Okla. 186, 228 P.2d 358.

to retain their character as personal property. The customs of the community may be significant in determining whether personal property is to be deemed a fixture.

The decision that certain property is a fixture has the effect of changing its classification from personal to real property. This is important for the purpose of tax laws because the fixture is subject to a real estate tax but not a personal property tax. If held to be real estate, it belongs to the land and whoever is entitled to the land or becomes its owner is entitled to the fixture. This is true even to the extent that the owner of personal property loses his ownership when he attaches it in such a way as to become a fixture on the land of another person, the latter person thereby becoming the owner.

The distinction is also important with respect to a sale of the fixture, for as real estate it may be subject to or free from certain restrictions and taxes, whereas such would not be the case if it were still personal property. Likewise the seller of personal property makes certain guarantees or warranties by the mere act of selling, whereas the seller of real estate, including a fixture, makes only those warranties that are included in the deed to the land.

In the absence of an agreement, the courts apply three tests [10] to determine whether the personal property has become a fixture:

1 / Annexation to the realty. Generally the personal property becomes a fixture if it is so attached to the realty that it cannot be removed without materially damaging the realty or destroying the personal property itself. If the property is so affixed as to lose its specific identity, as bricks in a wall, it becomes part of the realty.

2 / Adaptation to or usefulness of the personal property for the purpose for which the realty is used. Personal property especially adapted or suited to the building may constitute a fixture. By the *institutional* or *industrial plant doctrine,* machinery reasonably necessary for the operation of an industrial plant usually becomes part of the realty when installed, without regard to whether it is physically attached or not.[11] This principle does not apply to office equipment and trucks used in the operation of the enterprise.

3 / Intention of the person affixing the property at the time it was affixed. This is the true test; but in the absence of direct proof, it is necessary to resort to the nature of the property, the method of its attachment, and all the surrounding circumstances to determine what the intent was. Generally, when a tenant installs equipment for the operation of a store

---

[10] *Merchants & Mechanics Federal Savings & Loan Ass'n* v. *Herald,* 120 Ohio App. 115, 201 N.E.2d 237.

[11] *United Laundries, Inc.* v. *Board of Property Assessment,* 359 Pa. 195, 58 A.2d 833.

or business, the equipment is regarded as personal property or *trade fixtures* which the tenant may remove when he leaves the rented premises. As against third persons, the mere intention to make personal property a part of the realty may be insufficient when the property has not been attached or is not adapted in such a way as to indicate that it is part of the realty.

Facts: Aegen constructed a new apartment house. The building was concrete with a thin layer of rough plywood on the floors. In order to make the building tenantable, padding was stapled to the plywood and on top of it carpeting was firmly attached from wall to wall. The 112 apartments in the building used 6,500 yards of carpeting. Aegen then raised money by selling the carpeting to Exchange Leasing Corp. and leasing it back from the Exchange. Later Exchange sought to remove the carpeting.

Decision: Judgment against Exchange. The carpeting had become part of the real estate and could not be removed. It was a fixture because removal would probably have destroyed it, the carpeting having been cut to size, and the carpeting was necessary to make the building usable as an apartment house. The owner had installed the carpeting so that the public would rent, which distinguishes the case from one in which the tenant puts carpeting on the floor, and the landlord claims that he has acquired title to the carpeting. (Exchange Leasing Corp. v. Aegen, 7 Ohio App.2d 11, 218 N.E.2d 633)

Severed Realty

Property may be changed from real property to personal property by *severance*. If part of a building is removed or if stones are taken out of the earth, the property thus severed becomes personal property.

In some instances there may be a *constructive severance*. Thus, as soon as a contract for the sale and severance of standing timber is made, the timber is deemed personal property even though it has not been severed.[12]

QUESTIONS AND PROBLEMS

1. Checklist of legal terms:
   (a) property (353); real property (354), personal property (354)
   (b) private property, public property (354)
   (c) absolute ownership (354); power to tax (354), police power (354), eminent domain (355)
   (d) severalty (356), tenancy in common (356), joint tenancy (356), tenancy by entirety (357), community property (358), condominium (358)
   (e) choses in action; ex contractu, ex delicto (358)
   (f) fixtures (358), industrial plant doctrine (359), trade fixtures (360)
   (g) severance, constructive severance (360)

---

[12] Uniform Commercial Code Sec. 2-107(1) is applicable when the seller is to sever.

2. State the objective(s) of each of the following rules of law:
   (a) An owner is not allowed to use his property unreasonably in such a way as to injure other members of society.
   (b) As soon as a contract for the sale and severance of standing timber is made, the timber is deemed personal even though it has not been severed.

3. Which of the following own an interest in property?
   (a) A person who rents a town house
   (b) A water works that has the exclusive privilege of using streets and alleys for the operation of its business
   (c) One who borrows a picnic table
   (d) A person who has offered to pay $2,000 for a used station wagon
   (e) A buyer of a color TV on the installment plan

4. Higgins plans to construct a building for the manufacture of a fertilizer on the rear of his lot in a residential district. Can Kessler, whose home is on the adjoining lot, prevent Higgins from making such use of his property?

5. Harmon wishes to evade payment of his debts by disposing of his property by a gift to his son. May he do so?

6. Andrews owns a summer cottage next door to the one owned by Meredith. Together they own a boat and outboard motor. What form of ownership exists with respect to—
   (a) Each summer cottage?
   (b) The boat and outboard motor?

7. Jerry and Mary Lach owned as joint tenants certain real estate. When Mary Lach died, she left a will by which she bequeathed to Kemp $1,000 to be paid out of her interest in that real estate. After her death, however, Jerry Lach sold the property. Kemp contended that the property was subject to the payment of the sum left to him. Do you agree?

8. Leon's employer owed him $300 as unpaid wages. In an action brought by Arnold, Leon's creditor, to subject the wages due Leon to the satisfaction of Arnold's claim, Leon contended that his claim for wages came under a statute which exempted real and personal property up to $500 from creditors. Was his contention sound?

9. After Downing builds an outdoor fireplace, he has several bricks left which he stores in his garage. Are the bricks used in the fireplace and the surplus bricks real property or personal property?

10. Eastman leases certain land and buildings to be used for manufacturing purposes. He moves upon the premises several large machines which must be set in cement imbedded in the soil. When his lease expires, the owner of the land refuses to allow him to remove the machines. Had the machines become a part of the realty?

11. Flynn sells a farm to Chase but reserves the right to the timber on the land. Is the timber real property?

12. The Belmar Drive-In Theatre Co. brought an action against the Illinois State Toll Highway Commission because the bright lights of the toll road station interfered with the showing of motion pictures at the drive-in. Decide. (Belmar Drive-In Theatre Co. v. Illinois State Toll Highway Com., 34 Ill.2d 544, 216 N.E.2d 788)

13. A zoning ordinance of the city of Dallas, Texas, prohibited the use of property in a residential district for gasoline filling stations. Lombardo brought an action against the city to test the validity of the ordinance. He contended that the ordinance violated the rights of the owners of property in such districts. Do you agree with this contention? (Lombardo v. City of Dallas, 124 Tex. 1, 73 S.W.2d 475)

14. Janet Mandelbaum and Seymour Weiss were engaged to be married. Engagement gifts were given to them with gift cards stating "to Janet and Seymour." Later the engagement was broken and Seymour kept the gifts. Janet sued him for the return of all the gifts. Decide. (Mandelbaum v. Weiss, 11 N.J.S. 27, 77 A.2d 493)

15. Cattie leased a building to Joseph P. Cattie & Brothers, Inc. In order to conduct its manufacturing business in the building, the corporation installed a crane track and a tram track that were embedded in a concrete foundation on the floor or supported by crossbeams embedded in walls of the building. When the lease was about to end, the corporation removed these tracks. This required cutting them with acetylene torches and removing them piece by piece. The equipment was thereby destroyed and, instead of having its original value of approximately $70,000, had a scrap metal value of approximately $10,000 for which it was sold by the corporation. Cattie then sued the corporation for $70,000 on the theory that the tenant had no right to remove the fixtures in question. Was the landlord entitled to the value of the fixtures? (Cattie v. Joseph P. Cattie & Brothers, Inc., 403 Pa. 161, 168 A.2d 313)

16. Epsten sold Clifford a tract of land that had been used as a motor trailer court. At the time of the sale there was on the land a trailer which was used as the office and home of the manager of the trailer court. Clifford claimed that this trailer was a fixture and that he therefore acquired title to it when he purchased the land. Decide. (Clifford v. Epsten, 106 Cal. App.2d 221, 234 P.2d 687)

Chapter 31

Acquiring Title to Personal Property

Title to personal property may be acquired in several different ways. In this chapter the following methods will be discussed: copyrights and patents, accession, confusion, gifts, lost property, occupation, and judgments. Personal property may also be transferred by sale, marriage, bankruptcy, execution, and testate and intestate succession.

Copyrights and Patents

Under its constitutional authority Congress has adopted copyright and patent right laws to further the arts and sciences by granting artists and inventors exclusive rights in the product of their mental labors.

1 / Copyrights. A *copyright* is a grant to authors giving them the exclusive right to possess, make, publish, and sell copies of their intellectual productions, or to authorize others to do so, for a period of 28 years, with the privilege of a renewal and an extension for an additional term of 28 years. A copyright may be secured for lists of addresses, books, maps, musical compositions, motion pictures, and similar productions, provided the work is an original expression of an idea.

Works of domestic origin exported to foreign countries that have ratified the Universal Copyright Convention may use the internationally accepted copyright symbol © in place of or in addition to the word "Copyright" or its abbreviation. Note the form of the copyright notice on the back of the title page of this book.

The right to intellectual publication exists in respect to expressed ideas whether or not they are entirely original, new, or meritorious, as long as they are the result of independent and mental labor. Independently of statute, the author or artist who creates a literary or artistic work has an absolute and perpetual property right in his production as long as it remains unpublished.

Facts: Hotchner wrote a book about Ernest Hemingway. The book dealt primarily with adventures shared and conversations between Hotchner and Hemingway during the last 13 years of Hemingway's life. Hemingway's estate and his widow sued Random House, as publisher, and Hotchner, as author, claiming that Hemingway had a property right in his statements which prevented Hotchner's use of them in his book.

363

Decision: A party to a conversation has the right to use it in a later book. The other party to the conversation, or someone on his behalf, cannot claim that he has a "common-law copyright" protecting his part of the conversation. Thus either party to a conversation may make literary use of it. (Hemingway's Estate v. Random House, 53 Misc.2d 462, 279 N.Y.S.2d 51)

2 / Patents. A *patent* is a grant to one who has given physical expression to an idea, giving him the exclusive right to make, use, and sell, and to authorize others to make, use, and sell the invention for a period of 17 years. A patent is not renewable. The invention must be a new and useful art, machine, or composition of matter not previously known and used.

Accession

Property may be acquired by *accession,* that is, by means of an addition to or an increase of the thing that is owned, as in the case of produce of land or the young of animals. As a general rule, repairs become a part of the article that is repaired.[1] Likewise, when materials are furnished to another to be manufactured into an article, title to the finished article is in the owner of the materials. If the manufacturer, however, adds a large proportion of the materials, title will then usually vest in him.

A more difficult problem arises when a change in property is made against the wishes or at least without the consent of the owner. In such a case, the gaining of property by accession depends upon whether the act was done intentionally and willfully, or unintentionally and innocently.

Facts: Grunwell's automobile, which he insured with the Farm Bureau Mutual Auto Insurance Co., was stolen. The insurance company paid Grunwell under the policy. The car was thereafter found in the possession of Moseley who had purchased it from a used car dealer. The identity of the thief was never established, but both Moseley and the used car dealer had acted in good faith. A new engine had apparently been placed in the car by the thief. Moseley had also made additions to the car. The insurance company sued Moseley to recover the automobile.

Decision: The insurer, representing the true owner, was entitled to recover the automobile because title was not affected by the theft of the automobile. The insurance company was also entitled to the engine put into the car by the thief, since it had become part of the car by accession. Moseley, however, was entitled to keep the additions that he had made (a sun visor, seat covers, and a gas tank) since he had added these in good faith and therefore did not lose title to them by the principle of accession. (Farm Bureau Mutual Automobile Insurance Co. v. Moseley, 47 Del. 256, 90 A.2d 485)

---

[1] *Bozeman Mortuary Ass'n* v. *Fairchild,* 253 Ky. 74, 68 S.W.2d 756.

In other instances the courts determine whether title has passed by accession on the basis of whether or not the labor and materials of the trespasser have changed the property into a different specie. Another rule frequently used is that title does not change by accession when the former value of the goods has been changed, so long as there is no loss of identity. Under this rule the owner of the original material may follow it and seize it in its new shape or form, regardless of the alteration which it has undergone, so long as he can prove the identity of the original material. The factor that influences the courts in applying one or the other rule is the desire to attain as fair a result as possible under the circumstances.

These rules merely relate to the right of the original owner to obtain the return of the property taken from him. They do not relate to his right to sue the person taking the property. Under other rules of property and tort law, the person taking the owner's property from him, however innocently, is liable for money damages representing the value of the property. If the taking is not innocently done, punitive damages may also be recovered by the owner.

Confusion

Personal property may be acquired when the property of two persons becomes intermingled under such circumstances that one owner forfeits his right in his goods. Under this *doctrine of confusion of goods,* if a person willfully and wrongfully mixes his own goods with those of another so as to render them indistinguishable, he loses his part of the property and the innocent party acquires title to the total mass.

The doctrine of confusion does not apply when (1) the mixture is by consent of the parties; (2) the mixture is made without fraudulent intent, as by accident or mistake; or (3) the goods that have been mixed are of equal kind and grade, and thus not capable of being distinguished, as in the case of oil, tea, and wheat. In these three cases each owner is entitled to his proportionate share of the mixture.

Gift

Title to personal property may be transferred by the voluntary act of the owner without receiving anything in exchange, that is, by *gift.* The person making the gift, the *donor,* may do so because of things which the recipient of the gift, the *donee,* has done in the past or which he is expected to do in the future, but such matters of inducement are not deemed consideration so as to alter the "free" character of the gift.

Personal property may be given either absolutely or subject to a condition. The most common type of conditional gift is the *escrow delivery of a gift* by which the donor delivers the item of personal property to a third person who is not to give physical control to the donee until the latter has performed a specified condition.

A donor may make a gift of a fractional interest in property, as when he purchases stock and has it registered in the name of himself and of the donee.[2]

1 / Inter vivos gifts. The ordinary gift that is made between two living persons is an *inter vivos gift.* For practical purposes the rule is that the gift takes effect upon the donor's expressing an intention to make a gift and making delivery, subject to the right of the donee to divest himself of title by disclaiming the gift within a reasonable time after learning that it has been made.[3] Since there is no consideration for a gift, an intended donor cannot be sued for breach of contract, and the courts will not compel the donor to complete the gift.

The intent "to make" a gift requires an intent to transfer title at that time. In contrast, an intent to confer a benefit at a future date is not a sufficient intent to create any right in the intended donee. A gift may be made subject to a condition, such as graduation, but the condition must be expressed.

The delivery of a gift may be a *symbolic delivery,* as by the delivery of means of control of the property, such as keys to a padlock or ignition keys to an engine, or by the delivery of papers that are essential to or closely associated with ownership of the property, such as documents of title or ship's papers. The delivery of a symbol is effective as a gift if the intent to make a gift is established; as contrasted with merely giving the recipient of the token temporary access to property, as for example, until the deliveror comes back from the hospital.[4]

Facts: Juanita Hardy bought ten tickets for a lottery on a Buick car run by St. Matthew's Community Center. On one of the ticket stubs she wrote the name of her niece, Dixie Lee Williams, a minor, and returned the stub to the Center. She later phoned the niece's mother and told her that she had bought a chance for Dixie. The chance with Dixie's name won. Juanita sued the Community Center, claiming that the Buick belonged to her. Dixie filed a claim to the car.

Decision: Judgment for Dixie. The writing of Dixie's name on the lottery ticket and its return to the operator of the lottery showed an intention to make a gift, which intent was confirmed by the declaration to Dixie's mother. (Hardy v. St. Matthew's Community Center, [Ky.] 267 S.W.2d 725)

2 / Gifts causa mortis. A *gift causa mortis* is made when the donor, contemplating his imminent and impending death, delivers personal property

---

[2] *Bunt* v. *Fairbanks,* 81 S.D. 255, 134 N.W.2d 1.
[3] *Canova* v. *Florida National Bank,* [Fla.] 60 So.2d 627.
[4] *Schilling* v. *Waller,* 243 Md. 271, 220 A.2d 580.

to the donee with the intent that the donee shall own it if the donor dies. This is a conditional gift, and the donor is entitled to take the property back (a) if he survives the contemplated death; (b) if he revokes it before he dies; or (c) if the donee dies before the donor does. Such a gift is made only when the donor contemplates immediate death because of an existing illness or an impending peril.

3 / United States Government savings bonds. United States Government savings bonds are issued under a Treasury regulation which specifies that they are payable only to the registered owner and may be transferred only in the manner authorized by the regulation.

4 / Uniform Gifts to Minors Act. Most states have adopted the Uniform Gifts to Minors Act,[5] which provides an additional method for making gifts to minors of money and of registered and unregistered securities. Under the Act, a gift of money may be made to a minor by depositing it with a broker or a bank in an account in the name of the donor or an adult person or trust company "as custodian for [name of minor] under the [name of state] Uniform Gifts to Minors Act." If the gift is a registered security, the donor registers the security in a similar manner. If the gift is an unregistered security, it must be delivered by the donor to an adult person or trust company accompanied by a written statement signed by the donor and the custodian, in which the donor sets forth that he delivers the described property to the custodian as custodian for the minor under the uniform act and in which the custodian acknowledges receipt of the security.[6]

Under the uniform act, the custodian is in effect a guardian of the property for the minor, but he may use it more freely and is not subject to the many restrictions applicable to a true guardianship. The gift is final and irrevocable for tax and other purposes upon complying with the procedure of the act. The property can be transferred by the custodian to a third person free from the possibility that the minor might avoid the transfer.

Lost Property

Personal property is *lost property* when the owner does not know where it is located but intends to retain title or ownership to it. The person finding lost property does not acquire title by his act of taking possession of it. Ordinarily the finder is entitled to possession as against everyone except the true owner.[7]

---

[5] This Act has been adopted with varying minor modifications in substantially all states and for the District of Columbia. The nonconforming states have special statutes on the subject. A 1965 Revised Uniform Gifts to Minors Act has been adopted in New York.

[6] Uniform Gifts to Minors Act (UGMA), Sec. 2.

[7] *Toledo Tr. Co.* v. *Simmons,* 52 Ohio App. 373, 3 N.E.2d 661.

In some states statutes have been adopted permitting the finder to sell the property if the owner does not appear within a stated period. In such a case, the finder is required to give notice, as by newspaper publication, in order to attempt to reach the owner.

The finder of lost property is not entitled to a reward or to compensation for his services in the absence of a statute so providing or a contract with the owner.

If property is found in a public place, such as the public part of a hotel, under such circumstances that to a reasonable man it would appear that the property had been intentionally placed there by the owner and that he is likely to recall where he left it and return for it, the finder is not entitled to possession of the property but must give it to the proprietor or manager of the public place to keep for the owner.[8]

Transfer by Nonowner

Ordinarily a sale or other transfer by one who does not own the property will pass no title. Accordingly, no title is acquired by theft. The thief acquires possession only, and if he makes a sale or gift of the property to a third person, the latter only acquires the possession of the property. The true owner may reclaim the property from the thief or from his transferee, or he may sue them for the conversion of his property and recover the value of the stolen property.

In some states this rule is fortified by statutes which declare that the title to an automobile cannot be transferred, even by the actual owner, without a delivery of a properly-indorsed title certificate. The states that follow the common law do not make the holding of a title certificate essential to the ownership of an automobile, although as a matter of police regulation the owner must obtain such a certificate.

As an exception to the rule that a nonowner cannot transfer title, an agent, who does not own the property but who is authorized to sell it, may transfer the title of his principal. Likewise certain relations create a power to sell and transfer title, such as a pledge or pawn of property. An owner of property may also be barred or estopped from claiming that he is still the owner when he had done such acts as deceive an innocent buyer into believing that someone else was the owner or had authority to sell the property.

Occupation

Title to personal property may be acquired under certain circumstances by *occupation,* that is, by taking and holding possession of property of which no one has title. For example, in the absence of restrictions imposed by game

---

[8] *Jackson* v. *Steinberg,* 186 Ore. 129, 200 P.2d 376.

laws, the person who acquires dominion or control over a wild animal becomes its owner.

Title to abandoned personal property may be acquired by the first person who reduces it to his possession and control.[9] Personal property is deemed *abandoned property* when the owner relinquishes possession of it with the intention to disclaim title to it.

> **Facts:** Menzel fled from Europe upon the approach of enemy armies in World War II, leaving in his apartment certain paintings that were seized by the enemy. After World War II, the paintings were discovered in an art gallery owned by List. Menzel sued List for the paintings. List defended on the ground that Menzel had abandoned the paintings; and therefore title had passed to the person taking possession of them and from such possessor had been transferred lawfully to List.
>
> **Decision:** Judgment for Menzel. There is an abandonment, so as to permit the first occupant to acquire title, only when the act of abandoning is voluntary. When property is left in order to escape from a danger, there is not a voluntary act of abandoning the property and the ownership of the original owner is not lost or affected. (Menzel v. List, 49 Misc.2d 300, 267 N.Y.S.2d 804)

Judgments

The entry of a judgment ordinarily has no effect upon the title to personal property owned by the judgment debtor. Exceptions arise when (1) the purpose is to determine title to the property as against the whole world, or (2) the action is brought to recover the value of converted personal property. In the latter case the payment of the judgment entered against the converter for the value of the goods transfers title to him as though there had been a voluntary sale.

QUESTIONS AND PROBLEMS

1. Checklist of legal terms:
   (a) copyright (363), patent (364)
   (b) accession (364)
   (c) doctrine of confusion of goods (365)
   (d) gift; donor, donee (365)
   (e) escrow delivery of a gift (365)
   (f) inter vivos gift, symbolic delivery; gift causa mortis (366)
   (g) lost property (367); occupation (368), abandoned property (369)

2. State the objective(s) of each of the following rules of law:
   (a) A patent gives an inventor the exclusive right to make, use, and sell the invention for a period of 17 years.
   (b) The owner of stolen property may sue not only the thief but also a transferee of the thief for conversion of the property.

---

[9] *Rodgers* v. *Crum,* 168 Kan. 668, 215 P.2d 190.

3. A small painting in water colors, entitled "Holly, Mistletoe, and Spruce," consists of a representation of small branches or sprigs of the flowers of holly, mistletoe, and spruce, arranged in the form of an open cluster, having substantially the outline of a square. Is the painting a proper subject of a copyright?

4. Abner had $250 on deposit in the Second National Bank. Intending to make a gift of this amount to Cleary, Abner delivered to Cleary the bank passbook. Was the gift invalid for want of delivery?

5. Collins, being critically ill and thinking that he was about to die, gave his watch to Dunville. While convalescing from his illness, Collins was accidentally killed in an airplane accident. His executor claimed the watch, but Dunville refused to give it up. Was Dunville entitled to keep the watch?

6. Barnett and his family stopped in a forest preserve for a picnic supper. While there Barnett changed a tire on his automobile. In doing so, he forgot to pick up a wrench that he had placed on the ground. Daniel found the tool and claimed it as his own. Was he entitled to it?

7. Anne Nichols was the author of a play, "Abie's Irish Rose," which was based upon the religious prejudices of the parents of a young man and a young woman who desired to marry. The ideas upon which the play was based were utilized in a photoplay, "The Cohens and The Kellys." In an action brought by Anne Nichols against the Universal Pictures Corp., a question arose whether the property of a playwright by virtue of copyright extends to ideas. What is your opinion? (Nichols v. Universal Pictures Corp., [C.A.2d] 45 F.2d 119)

8. Brogden acquired a biblical manuscript in 1945. In 1952 he told his sister Lucy that he wanted Texas A. & M. College to have this manuscript. He dictated a note so stating and placed it with the manuscript. He made some effort to have an officer of the college come for the manuscript. In 1956 he delivered the manuscript to his sister, stating that he was afraid that someone would steal it. Later in the year he told a third person that he was going to give the manuscript to the college. In 1957 he was declared incompetent. In 1959 the sister delivered the manuscript to the college. In April, 1960, Brogden died and his heirs, Bailey and others, sued Harrington and other officers of the college to have the title to the manuscript determined. Decide. (Harrington v. Bailey, [Tex.Civ.App.] 351 S.W.2d 946)

9. Timber on a reservation owned by the United States was unlawfully cut by two persons. The timber was worth about $60 at the place where it was cut. These persons then transported the timber some distance where it had a value of $850. The timber was purchased from them in good faith by the Boles Wooden Ware Company. The United States sued this company for $850. Could it recover? (Boles Wooden Ware Co. v. United States, 106 U.S. 432)

Chapter 32

Bailments—Nature and Termination

Many instances arise in which the owner of personal property entrusts it to another. A person checks his coat at a restaurant or loans his car to a friend. He delivers a watch to a jeweler for repairs, takes furniture to a warehouse for storage, or delivers goods to a railroad for shipment. The delivery of property under such circumstances is a bailment.

Definition

A *bailment* is the legal relation that arises whenever one person delivers possession of personal property to another person under an agreement or contract by which the latter is under a duty to return the identical property to the former or to deliver it or dispose of it as agreed.[1] The person who turns over the possession of the property is the *bailor*. The person to whom he gives the possession is the *bailee*.

1 / Agreement. The bailment is based upon an agreement.[2] Technically the bailment is the act of delivering the property to the bailee and the relationship existing thereafter. The agreement that precedes this delivery is an agreement to make a bailment rather than the actual bailment. Generally this agreement will contain all the elements of a contract so that the bailment transaction in fact consists of (a) a contract to bail and (b) the actual bailing of the property.

Ordinarily there is no requirement that the agreement of bailment be in writing. In some states, however, a writing or recording of the bailment agreement may be necessary to protect the interest of the bailor. Thus a statute may provide that if the bailor does not record his title to the bailed property, creditors of the bailee may treat it as the bailee's property when the bailment has lasted more than five years.

2 / Personal property. The subject of a bailment may be any personal property of which possession may be given. Real property cannot be bailed.

3 / Bailor's interest. The bailor is usually the owner of the property, but ownership by him is not required. It is sufficient that the bailor have

---

[1] *Sullivant* v. *Penn. Fire Insurance Co.*, 223 Ark. 721, 268 S.W.2d 372.
[2] *Greenberg* v. *Shoppers' Garage, Inc.*, 329 Mass. 31, 105 N.E.2d 839.

371

physical possession. Thus an employee may be a bailor in leaving his employer's truck at a garage. Whether possession is lawful or not is immaterial. A thief, for example, may be a bailor.

4 / Delivery and acceptance. The bailment does not arise until, pursuant to the agreement of the parties, the property is delivered to the bailee and accepted by him as subject to the bailment agreement.

Facts: Theobald went to the beauty parlor operated by Satterthwaite. When it was her turn, she left her coat on a hook on the wall and went into the back room for her treatment. There was no one in the outer room when she left. Nothing had been stolen from the outer room in its 20 years of operation. When Theobald returned to the outer room, her coat was not there. She sued Satterthwaite claiming that the latter was liable as a negligent bailee.

Decision: Judgment for Satterthwaite. She was not a bailee and therefore was not liable as a negligent bailee. A bailment cannot arise unless the personal property is delivered into the possession of the bailee. The fact that it was left on the premises did not give rise to a bailment. (Theobald v. Satterthwaite, 30 Wash.2d 92, 190 P.2d 714)

Delivery may be actual, as when the bailor physically hands a book to the bailee. Or it may be a *constructive delivery,* as when the bailor points out a package to the bailee who then takes possession of it.

3 / Specific property. A bailment places a duty upon the bailee to return the specific property that was bailed or to deliver or dispose of it in the manner directed by the bailor. If a bailee has an option of paying money or of returning property other than that which was delivered to him, there is generally no bailment. Thus, when a farmer delivers grain to a warehouse which gives him a receipt and promises to return either the grain or a certain amount of money upon presentation of the receipt, the relationship is not a bailment. The importance of this distinction lies in the fact that when the relationship is not a bailment but another relationship, such as a sale, the risk of loss if the property is damaged or destroyed will ordinarily be on the warehouse; whereas if it is a bailment, the bailor would ordinarily bear the loss.

In a number of states a rental of property coupled with an option to purchase is classified as a bailment.[3]

Classifications of Bailments

Bailments are classified as ordinary and extraordinary. *Extraordinary bailments* are those in which the bailee is given unusual duties and liabilities

---

[3] If the parties have agreed on a sale at the beginning and a bailment lease is executed merely for the protection of the seller, the transaction is governed by the Uniform Commercial Code, Article 9—Secured Transactions.

by law, as in the case of bailments in which a hotel or a common carrier is the bailee. *Ordinary bailments* include all other bailments.

Bailments may or may not provide for compensation to the bailee. Upon that basis they may be classified as *contract bailments* and *gratuitous bailments*.

Bailments may also be classified as for the (1) sole benefit of the bailor, as when a farmer gratuitously transports another's produce to the city; (2) sole benefit of the bailee, as when a person borrows the automobile of a friend; or (3) benefit of both parties (mutual-benefit bailment), as when one rents an automobile.

Constructive Bailments

When one person comes into possession of personal property of another without the owner's consent, the law treats the possessor as though he were a bailee. Sometimes this relationship is called a *constructive bailment*. It is thus held that the finder of lost property must treat the property as a bailee.

A police officer taking possession of stolen goods is deemed a bailee for the true owner. A seller who has not yet delivered the goods to his buyer is treated as the bailee of the goods if title has passed to the buyer. Similarly, a buyer who is in possession of goods, the title to which has not passed to him, is a bailee.

Bailment of Contents of Container

It is a question of the intention of the parties, as that appears to a reasonable man, whether the bailing of a container also constitutes a bailment of articles contained in it; that is, whether a bailment of a truck is a bailment of articles in the truck, whether a bailment of a coat is a bailment of articles in the pockets of the coat, and so on. When the contained articles are of a nature that are reasonable or normal to be found within the container, they are regarded as bailed in the absence of an express disclaimer. If the articles are not of such a nature and their presence in the container is unknown to the bailee, there is no bailment of such articles.

Facts: Cerreta parked his automobile with the Kinney Corporation parking lot. On the back seat were valuable drawings and sporting equipment. These were not visible from the outside of the car. When the car was returned to Cerreta, these articles were missing. He sued the Kinney Corporation as bailee.

Decision: Judgment for Kinney Corporation. The articles were not of such a nature that their presence in the automobile was reasonably expectable, and their presence was in fact not known. There was accordingly no bailment of these articles in the absence of an express agreement of bailment concerning them. (Cerreta v. Kinney Corp., 50 N.J.S. 514, 142 A.2d 917)

Bailee's Interest

Title to the property does not pass to the bailee, and he cannot sell the property to a third person unless the bailee is also an agent to make such a sale. If he attempts to do so, his act only transfers possession and the owner may recover the property from the third person.[4]

The bailor may cause third persons to believe that the bailee is the owner of the bailed property. If he does so, he may be estopped to deny that the bailee is the owner as against persons who have relied on the bailor's representations.

1 / Bailee's right to possession. If the bailment is at will, the bailor may retake possession whenever he chooses. If the bailment is for a set term, the bailor under ordinary circumstances is not entitled to take back the property before the expiration of the term. If he should do so, the bailee may treat him as though he were a third person unlawfully trying to take the property. Moreover, if the bailee has a lien on the property for services performed by him, as a repairman, public warehouseman, or carrier, the bailor is not entitled to the return of the property until he has paid the amount due.

The bailee is usually entitled to retain possession as against third persons. If a thief takes the bailed property from the bailee or if a third person damages the bailed property, the possessory interest of the bailee is harmed and he may therefore sue the thief or third person for damages. Either the bailor or the bailee may sue the third person in such instances, although suit against the third person for the total damage to the property brought by either the bailor or the bailee bars a second action against the third person by the other. It has also been held that the bailee is entitled to the protection of a statute specifically designed for the protection of "owners."

As an exception to this right of possession as against third persons, the bailee must usually surrender the bailed property to one who establishes that he is the true owner and that he is entitled to immediate possession as against the bailor.

2 / Interpleader. Ordinarily a bailee is not permitted to question whether the bailor is the true owner but must surrender the property to the bailor when the bailment ends. He cannot refuse to do so on the ground that a third person owns the property. A legal procedure called *interpleader* has been devised by which a bailee may require the bailor and a third person who claims to be the owner to litigate their rival claims so that the bailee will know to whom the property should be delivered. This procedural device is given to the bailee because, although he is under a duty to recognize the

---

[4] *Owen v. Allen,* 169 Okla. 351, 36 P.2d 277.

bailor, he also runs the danger that if the third person claiming ownership is in fact the owner, that third person may sue the bailee for damages as a converter of the property.

Termination of Bailment

A bailment may be terminated by (1) agreement, (2) acceptance of breach, (3) destruction of subject matter, (4) act of the bailor, and (5) operation of law.

1 / Agreement. Since a bailment is based upon an agreement or contract, it may be terminated in accordance with its own terms or by a subsequent agreement.[5]

Facts: Adair contracted to haul certain pipe casings for the Ace Oil Co. from one well site to another. A month or more after he had unloaded all the pipe at the second site, it was taken unlawfully by Roberts. Adair sued Roberts for this conversion on the ground that Adair was the bailee of the pipe for the Ace Oil Co. Roberts defended on the ground that Adair was not the bailee at the time when the pipe was taken and therefore had no right to sue him.

Decision: Adair was not a bailee when the loss occurred. The bailment had terminated when he had given up the possession of the property as directed by the bailment contract. (Adair v. Roberts, [Tex.Civ.App.] 276 S.W.2d 565)

2 / Acceptance of breach. If either party materially violates his obligations under the bailment, the other party has the option of treating the bailment at an end. Accordingly, the bailor may accept the bailee's breach of his duties as a termination of the bailment. Thus, if the bailee unlawfully sells the property to a third person, the bailor may treat the relationship as ended.[6]

If the bailor elects not to treat the bailment as terminated when the bailee makes an improper or unauthorized use of the property, the bailee remains liable for any harm caused thereby.[7]

3 / Destruction of subject matter. There is an implied condition in a bailment that the bailed property be in existence and that it be in either the same condition or form as when bailed or in a condition or form which is suitable for the purpose of the bailment. Consequently the bailment ends if the property is destroyed by a third person or by an act of God, or if it deteriorates so that it is unfit for use for the purpose of the bailment.

---

[5] *Hargis* v. *Spencer,* 254 Ky. 297, 71 S.W.2d 666.
[6] *Aetna Casualty & Surety Co.* v. *Higbee Co.,* 80 Ohio App. 437, 76 N.E.2d 404.
[7] See p. 382.

If the property has been damaged through the bailee's fault, the bailment is not terminated automatically but there is a breach of the agreement which the bailor may treat as terminating the bailment.

4 / Act of bailor. If the bailment is terminable at the will of the bailor, either because expressly made so or because no consideration has been given to keep the bailment in existence for a specified fixed period, the bailor may terminate the bailment at any time by demanding the return of the property, by retaking the property, or by doing any other act which indicates that he has exercised his will to terminate the bailment.

5 / Operation of law. Death, insanity, or bankruptcy of a party to the bailment will terminate the bailment when it is thereafter impossible for the bailee to perform his duties, or when the bailment is for the sole benefit of the bailee who has died, or when the bailment is terminable at will. If the bailment is for a fixed period and is based upon a binding contract, however, the death or incapacity of a party to the bailment does not terminate it and the rights of the deceased party pass to his estate.

QUESTIONS AND PROBLEMS

1. Checklist of legal terms:

   (a) bailment; bailor, bailee (371)
   (b) constructive delivery (372)
   (c) extraordinary bailment, ordinary bailment (373)
   (d) contract bailment, gratuitous bailment (373)
   (e) constructive bailment (373)
   (f) interpleader (374)

2. State the objective(s) of each of the following rules of law:

   (a) In a bailment, title to the property does not pass to the bailee and ordinarily he cannot sell the property to a third person.
   (b) A bailment is not terminated by the death of the bailor when it is based upon a contract providing for a bailment for a fixed period.

3. Cohen, a druggist, secured a bottle of 100 half-grain thyroid tablets from a neighboring druggist in order to fill a prescription. He agreed to return an equal number of the tablets the next day. Was a bailment created?

4. Duncan leases a farm from Friedmann. Is Duncan the bailee of the property?

5. Newman's launch was damaged while being repaired by the Tyler Company in its shops. Was the company the bailee of the launch?

6. Foley leaves a traveling bag that he has stolen at the checkroom in a hotel. When he calls for it, the bag cannot be located. Is Foley entitled to the rights of a bailor?

7. Hackett arranged to borrow Keller's automobile. Hackett did not drive the car away until an hour after he had received the keys from Keller. When was the bailment completed?

8. Classify each of the following bailments:

   (a) Kreuger, a dry cleaner, leaves his delivery truck at a garage for repairs.

   (b) Kreuger permits another businessman to borrow his truck for certain deliveries without compensation.

   (c) Kreuger rents a second truck during a rush season.

9. While hurrying to catch a bus, Leonard loses his billfold. Shortly after that, Wynn finds the billfold and places it in his pocket. Kinsey, who observes Wynn's act, informs Leonard of the situation. Leonard brings an action to hold Wynn liable as a bailee of the goods. Was Wynn a bailee of the billfold?

10. Walden borrows Yeager's electric paint sprayer. After using the sprayer, Walden sells it to Alexander. Can Yeager recover possession from Alexander?

11. Booth examines a watch that Cline has borrowed from Emmett. Booth refuses to return the watch to Cline because he believes that it belongs to Findley. Can Cline recover possession from Booth?

12. Mrs. Mushkatin placed her mink jacket in the unattended cloakroom of the Commodore Hotel. She did not inform the hotel or any employee that she was doing so. When she returned for the jacket, it could not be found. Her insurance company, the National Fire Insurance Co., paid the loss and then sued the hotel on the ground that it was a bailee. Was it a bailee? (National Fire Insurance Co. v. Commodore Hotel, Inc., 259 Minn. 349, 107 N.W.2d 708)

13. Taylor parked his automobile in a garage operated by the Philadelphia Parking Authority and paid a regular monthly charge therefor. There was a written agreement between them which provided: "The Authority shall have the right to move the applicant's automobile to such location as it may deem necessary in order to facilitate the most effective use of the parking space on the roof. Ignition keys must be left in the automobile at all times." It was thereafter agreed between the parties that the plaintiff could retain the ignition key at all times and lock the auto in order to protect the valuable merchandise which Taylor carried in his car. Taylor brought the car into the garage, locked it, and left with the keys. The car was missing when he returned. He sued the parking Authority on the theory that it had breached a duty as bailee. The Authority claimed that it was not a bailee. Was the Authority correct? (Taylor v. Philadelphia Parking Authority, 398 Pa. 9, 156 A.2d 525)

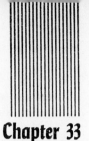

Chapter 33

Ordinary Bailments

A bailment creates certain rights and imposes certain duties and liabilities upon each party. These may generally be increased or modified by statute or custom, or by the express agreement or contract of the parties to the bailment.

Rights of the Bailee

1 / Right to use the property for the bailment purpose. It is a question of intention whether the bailee may use the property for his benefit. If none is expressed, the intention of the parties must be determined from the surrounding circumstances, including the nature of the property and the nature and purpose of the bailment.

In a bailment for the sole benefit of the bailee, the right of the bailee to use the property is strictly limited to the use contemplated by the bailor when he agreed to the relation. If a person borrows property to use in one city, for example, he cannot use it in another. When the bailment is for the sole benefit of the bailor, the bailee may not use or handle the property except to the extent necessary to protect it. If the bailed property is an animal, it may be necessary to use or exercise the animal to keep it in good condition, but the bailee cannot use the animal for his own purpose.

In a mutual-benefit bailment the bailee has the right to use the property in accordance with the terms of the contract. In the case of renting an automobile or equipment, the relationship is commonly called a "lease," although it is basically a bailment. When a mutual-benefit bailment is for storage only, the right to use the property does not exist unless some use is necessary to preserve and protect it. Thus a bailee who is merely a custodian of an automobile has no right to use it without permission from the bailor.

2 / Right to insure the property. The bailee has an insurable interest in the property bailed and may take out insurance on the property. Generally he is not required to do so, although in some instances the bailee may be required by custom, agreement, or statute to insure the property. A commercial bailee, such as a warehouseman, may do so voluntarily in order to make his service more attractive to the public.

3 / Right to compensation for services. Whether the bailee is entitled to compensation for what he does depends upon the agreement. In the absence of an agreement to the contrary, courts assume that the bailor intended to pay the reasonable value of services rendered, unless the circumstances are such that reasonable men in the position of the parties would have realized that the services were rendered without the intention to charge or the expectation to pay.

In a mutual-benefit bailment the bailee is ordinarily entitled to compensation provided he has fully performed according to the terms of the contract. When the bailee is to perform services upon goods furnished by the bailor and the goods are lost, stolen, or destroyed without fault of the bailee, the latter is usually entitled to payment for the work done. Custom or the terms of the contract may, however, place the loss on the bailee. For example, if the bailee is to perform services on goods under an agreement which provides for payment "only after delivery in good order to our store," he assumes the risk that he will not be paid if he fails to make such delivery, whether or not he was at fault.

In a bailment for the sole benefit of the bailee, the bailee is not entitled to compensation for services rendered. If *A* borrows *B's* automobile for his own use, *A* cannot charge *B* a fee for the care he takes of the automobile during the period of the bailment.

4 / Bailee's lien. A bailee who according to agreement performs services that enhance the value of the property has a specific common-law lien on the goods. Other ordinary bailees for hire are not entitled to a lien, but the parties can expressly provide for such a lien in their contract.

Statutes in many states have changed to a considerable extent the common law in regard to the liens of bailees. In some instances the bailee has the right of lien even though his services do not bestow value upon the subject matter of the bailment. Statutes commonly require a public sale of the property subject to the lien, and in some instances they provide for the recording of the lien.

Statutes commonly provide that a lien is retained even though the property is returned to the bailor. In the absence of statute, however, the lien merely confers the right to retain possession and is lost if the lienholder voluntarily parts with possession.

No lien arises when the work is done on credit. When a repairman retains possession of the bailed article for the purpose of asserting a lien on it, he cannot at the same time charge storage for the time that he retains the property.[1]

5 / Action against third persons. The bailee has a possessory right in the goods bailed. This qualified property right entitles him to bring an action

---

[1] *Owens* v. *Pyeatt,* [Cal.App.2d] 57 Cal.Rptr. 100.

against third persons for interfering with his possession or for injury to or destruction of the goods. The bailee can then recover damages for his loss or for his and the bailor's loss.

Duties and Liabilities of the Bailee

1 / Performance. If the bailment is based upon a contract, the bailee must perform his part of the contract and is liable to the bailor for any loss arising out of his failure to do so. If the bailment is for repair, the bailee is under the duty to make the repairs properly. The fact that the bailee uses due care does not excuse him for failing to perform according to his contract.

> **Facts:** Welge owned a sofa and chair which Baena Brothers agreed to reupholster and to reduce the size of the arms. The work was not done according to the agreement, and the furniture when finished had no value to Welge and was not accepted by him. Baena then sued him for the contract price. Welge counterclaimed for the value of the furniture.
>
> **Decision:** Judgment on the counterclaim for Welge. When Baena Brothers made a contract with respect to the furniture, they were required to perform that contract according to ordinary principles of contract law. The concept of due care, which would protect them if the goods were damaged by a third person, act of God, or accident, does not apply when the question is whether the bailee has performed his contract. As there was a failure to perform their contract, Baena Brothers were liable for damages for such breach. (Baena Brothers v. Welge, 3 Conn. Cir. 67, 207 A.2d 749)

2 / Care of the property. The bailee is under a duty to care for the property entrusted to him. If the property is damaged or destroyed, the bailee is liable for the loss (a) if the harm was caused in whole or in part by the bailee's failure to use reasonable care under the circumstances, or (b) if the harm was sustained during unauthorized use of the property by the bailee. Otherwise the bailor bears the loss. Thus, if the bailee was exercising due care and was making an authorized use of the property, the bailor must bear the loss of or damage to the property caused by an act of a third person, whether willful or negligent, by an accident or occurrence for which no one is at fault, or by an act of God. In this connection the term *act of God* means a natural phenomenon that it is not reasonably foreseeable, such as a sudden flood or lightning.

(a) STANDARD OF CARE. The standard for ordinary bailments is reasonable care under the circumstances, that is, the degree of care which a reasonable man would exercise in the situation in order to prevent the realization of reasonably foreseeable harm. In some types of bailments the bailor may reasonably expect or demand that the bailee use greater care than in others. The significant factors in determining what constitutes reasonable care in a bailment are the time and place of making the bailment, the facilities for taking care of the bailed property, the nature of the bailed property, the bailee's knowledge of its nature, and the extent of the bailee's skill and experience in taking care of goods of that kind. Whether due care has been exercised under the circumstances is a question for the jury to decide.

The bailor has the burden of proving that the bailee was guilty of a breach of duty. The bailee has the burden of presenting evidence to explain how the loss occurred; it is not sufficient for him merely to point to a mystery for which he has no explanation.[2]

Facts: Middleton took her auto to Fox Chevrolet Sales for repairs. The shop was located in the industrial section of the city and was bounded on two sides by extensive railroad yards. At night the rear of the shop building was out of the sight and hearing of persons passing by the shop. The two rear doors were locked by padlocks on hasps nailed to the wood. Because there had been breaking of windows of the shop by vandals and the stealing of equipment, a night watchman was employed but he often failed to report for duty. On one of the nights when the watchman failed to report, a thief broke the lock on the two rear doors of the shop and stole Middleton's car. It was later found in a damaged condition. Middleton sued Fox for damages.

Decision: The question was properly submitted to a jury which found in favor of Middleton for the reason that under the surrounding circumstances, Fox had not exercised due care in protecting the car from foreseeable harm. When a bailee fails to exercise such care, it is liable for the harm that follows, even though the harm is a willful act, as theft by a third person. (Fox Chevrolet Sales v. Middleton, 203 Md. 158, 99 A.2d 731)

In any case, however, the jury must decide in favor of the bailee if it is not convinced by a preponderance of the evidence that he has violated his duties. If the jury believes the bailee's testimony that he took proper care of the goods, the bailee is not liable for the loss even though he cannot explain or show what happened.

The bailee is not an insurer of the safety of the property, even though he assures the bailor that he will take good care of the property;[3] and he is not liable when there is no proof of his negligence as a cause of the harm nor of his unauthorized use of the property.

(b) CONTRACT MODIFICATION OF LIABILITY. A bailee's liability may be expanded by contract. A provision that he assumes absolute liability for

---

[2] *National Dairy Products Corp.* v. *Lawrence American Field Warehousing Corp.,* 22 App.Div.2d 420, 255 N.Y.S.2d 788.
[3] *Peacock Motor Co.* v. *Eubanks,* [Fla.] 145 So.2d 498.

the property is binding, but there is a difference of opinion as to whether a stipulation to return the property "in good condition" or "in as good condition as received" has the effect of imposing such absolute liability. An ordinary bailee may limit his liability, except for his willful conduct, by contract. Modern cases hold that a specialized commercial bailee, such as an auto parking garage, cannot limit liability for either its willful or negligent conduct.

Facts: Chas. H. Lilly Co. rented a Scoopmobile from Air-Mac, Inc. on a month-to-month basis. The agreement required Lilly to return the machine in good mechanical condition, except for usual wear and depreciation such as might be caused by reasonable use. Four months later the machine was destroyed by fire. Air-Mac collected the amount of its loss from its insurance company, the St. Paul Fire & Marine Insurance Co., and then assigned to it the claim against Lilly. The insurance company then sued Lilly.

Decision: Judgment for Lilly. The return clause merely gave express statement to the duty of a bailee and was not intended to make the bailee an insurer of the car. The latter view is not in harmony with what reasonable persons would understand by the words they used, particularly since the intent to make the bailee an insurer could be readily expressed in a few words if the parties had so intended. (St. Paul Fire & Marine Insurance Co. v. Chas. H. Lilly Co., 48 Wash.2d 528, 295 P.2d 299)

The parties may also provide that neither will hold the other liable for any claim when the bailee (lessee) obtains insurance or pays for insurance procured by the bailor. The situation is typical of a car or equipment-renting bailment.

3 / Unauthorized use. The bailee is liable if he uses the property without authority or uses it in any manner to which the bailor had not agreed. The bailee is liable for conversion, just as though he stole the property. Ordinarily he will be required to pay compensatory damages, although punitive damages may be inflicted when the improper use was deliberate and the bailee was recklessly indifferent to the effect of his use upon the property.

4 / Return. The bailee is under a duty to return the identical property which is the subject of the bailment or to deliver it as directed. The redelivery to the bailor or delivery to a third person must be made in accordance with the terms of the contract as to time, place, and manner. When the agreement does not control these matters, the customs and usages of the community govern.

The bailee is excused from delivery when the goods are lost, stolen, or destroyed without his fault. If his fault or neglect has caused or contributed to the loss, however, he is liable. To illustrate, certain goods are destroyed by a flood while in the possession of the bailee. If the bailee could have protected the goods from the flood by taking reasonable precautions, the bailee is liable for the loss.

The bailee is excused from the duty to return the goods when they have been taken from him under process of law. To illustrate, if the police seize the property as stolen goods, the bailee is no longer under a duty to return the goods to the bailor.

If the bailee has a lien on the property, he is entitled to keep possession of the property until he has been paid the claim on which the lien is based.

Rights of the Bailor

The rights of the bailor vary with the nature of the bailment.

1 / Compensation. The bailor is entitled to the compensation agreed upon in the bailment contract. If the agreement is silent as to compensation, the bailee must pay the reasonable rental value when the circumstances are such that, as reasonable men, the parties would have expected that there would be compensation.

If the bailee loses possession or use of the goods through no fault of his own, the bailor is entitled to compensation only during the period of use, unless their agreement stipulates otherwise. For example, the bailee is not liable for compensation during a period when he cannot use the property because it is being repaired for a defect for which the bailor is liable. The same rule is applied when the goods are stolen or destroyed, or when they are retaken by the bailor through no fault of the bailee.

The right of the bailor to compensation may be absolute or may depend upon the bailor's performing services, such as keeping the bailed property in repair.

> Facts: Bryant rented a typewriter from Royal McBee Co. The lease stated that the lessor would keep the typewriter in good working condition. The typewriter did not work, and Royal was not able to put it in working condition. Royal sued Bryant for the rental payment.

> Decision: Bryant was not liable because the maintenance of the typewriter in good condition was a condition precedent to Bryant's duty to pay. As Royal had not satisfied this condition, Bryant never became liable to pay. (Royal McBee Corp. v. Bryant, [C.A.Dist.Col.] 217 A.2d 603)

2 / Rights against the bailee. The bailor may sue the bailee for breach of contract if the goods are not redelivered to the bailor or delivered to a third person as specified by the bailment agreement. He may also maintain actions for negligence, willful destruction, and unlawful retention or conversion of the goods when the bailee is guilty of such conduct. Actions for unlawful retention or conversion can only be brought when the bailor is entitled to possession.

3 / Rights against third persons. The bailor may sue third persons damaging or taking the bailed property from the bailee's possession, even though the bailment is for a fixed period that has not expired. In such a case the bailor is said to recover damages for injury to his *reversionary interest,* that is, the right which he has to regain the property upon the expiration of the period of the bailment.

Duties and Liabilities of the Bailor

Duties and liabilities of the bailor arise from the bailment relationship, although they may be modified by statute or by the contract of the parties.

1 / Condition of the property. In a mutual-benefit bailment for hire, the bailor is under a duty to furnish goods reasonably fit for the purpose contemplated by the parties. If the bailee is injured or if his property is damaged because of the defective condition of the bailed property, the bailor may be liable. If the bailment is for the sole benefit of the bailee, the bailor is under a duty to inform the bailee of those defects of which he is actually aware, but he is not under any duty to look for defects. If the bailee is harmed by a defect that was known to the bailor, the bailor is liable for damages. If the bailor receives a benefit from the bailment, he must not only inform the bailee of known defects, but he must also make a reasonable investigation to discover defects. The bailor is liable for the harm resulting from defects which would have been disclosed had he made such an examination, in addition to those which were known to him.

When harm is caused a bailee's employee because of the negligence of the bailor, the latter is liable to the employee of the bailee, although the employee did not have any direct dealings or contractual relationship with the bailor.

If the defect would not have been revealed by a reasonable examination, the bailor, regardless of the classification of the bailment, is not liable for harm which results.

In any case the bailee, if he knows of the defective condition of the bailed property, is barred by his contributory negligence or assumption of risk if, in spite of that knowledge, he makes use of the property and sustains injury because of its condition.

In many cases the duty of the bailor is described as an implied warranty that the goods will be reasonably fit for their intended use. Apart from an implied warranty, the bailor may expressly warrant the condition of the property, in which event he will be liable for the breach of the warranty to the same extent as though he had made a sale rather than a bailment of the property.[4]

---

[4] See Ch. 38 as to sales warranties.

With the modern rise of car and equipment renting, there is beginning to appear a new trend in cases that extends to the bailee and third person the benefit of an implied warranty by the bailor that the article is fit for its intended use and will remain so, as distinguished from merely that it was reasonably fit, or that it was fit at the beginning of the bailment, or that the property was free from defects known to the bailor or which reasonable investigation would disclose.

Facts: Contract Packers rented a truck from Hertz Truck Leasing. Packers' employee, Cintrone, was injured while riding in the truck, being driven by his helper, when the brakes of the truck did not function properly and the truck crashed. Cintrone sued Hertz.

Decision: Judgment for Cintrone. As Hertz was in the business of renting trucks, it should foresee that persons renting them would rely on it to have the trucks in safe condition and they would not be making the inspection and repair that an owner could be expected to make of his own car. Hence, there was an implied warranty or guaranty by Hertz that the truck was fit for normal use. That warranty continued for the duration of the truck rental, and the right to sue for its breach ran in favor of third persons, such as employees of the customer of Hertz, and conversely was not limited to suit by the customer. (Cintrone v. Hertz Truck Leasing & Rental Service, 45 N.J. 434, 212 A.2d 769)

2 / Repair of the property. Under a rental contract the bailor has no duty to make repairs that are ordinary and incidental to the use of the goods bailed. The bailee must bear the expense of such repairs, in the absence of a contrary contract provision. If, however, the repairs required are of an unusual nature or if the bailment is for a short period of time, the bailor is required to make the repairs unless they were caused by the negligence or fault of the bailee.

3 / Reimbursement for payments by bailee. The bailor must reimburse the bailee for any payments made by the bailee that should have been made by the bailor. If the bailee makes repairs that should have been made by the bailor, the bailee may recover the amount so paid. If the bailee is sued by a third person who demands the bailed property on the ground that the bailor did not own it, the bailee is entitled to reimbursement for expenses incurred in the litigation. If the expense is incurred by reason of the bailee's negligence, misconduct, or misuse of the property, however, the bailor is not required to reimburse him.

4 / Performance of contract by bailor. The bailor is, of course, under a duty to perform his part of the contract of bailment. If he violates its provisions, he is answerable to the bailee for damages. Thus, if a person hires another's automobile but the bailor retakes possession without cause before the expiration of the bailment, the bailee may sue him for breach of his duties.

Liability to Third Persons

When the bailee injures a third person with the bailed property, as when a bailee runs into a third person while he is driving a rented automobile, the bailee is liable to the third person to the same extent as though the bailee were the owner of the property. When the bailee repairs bailed property, he is liable to third persons who are injured in consequence of the negligent way in which he has made the repair. Conversely, the bailee is not liable to a third person who is injured by a thief who steals the bailed property from the bailee even though the theft was possible because the bailee was negligent.

The bailor is ordinarily not liable to a third person. Unless the bailee is acting as the employee or agent of the bailor, a fault or negligence of the bailee is not imputed to the bailor.

Facts: Guidry gave his employee, Good, permission to use a truck for Good's own purposes. While so doing, Good negligently ran into and injured Asher. Asher sued Guidry.

Decision: Judgment for Guidry. As Good was admittedly not acting within the course of his employment at the time, the liability of Guidry could only be based on his status as a bailor. But a bailor is not liable for the negligence of his bailee unless the bailor had or should have knowledge that the bailee was physically or mentally unfit to drive. No such claim was made by Asher, and Guidry was therefore not liable. (Asher v. Good, [La.] 198 So.2d 434)

The bailor is liable, however, to the injured third person: (1) if the bailor has entrusted a dangerous instrumentality to one whom he knew was ignorant of its dangerous character; (2) if the bailor has entrusted an instrumentality such as an automobile to one whom he knows to be so incompetent or reckless that injury of third persons is a foreseeable consequence; or (3) if the bailor has entrusted property with a defect that causes harm to the third person when the circumstances are such that bailor would be liable to the bailee if the latter were injured because of the defect.

Facts: Anders was interested in purchasing a used car from Glover Motors. He was trying out one of the cars when, in consequence of a defect in the brakes, he collided with the car driven by Wilcox. The latter sued Glover Motors, claiming that there was liability because Glover Motors knew or should have known that the brakes were defective.

Decision: As the motor vehicle law imposes upon every owner the duty of exercising due care in maintaining the brakes of his automobile in good condition, Glover, as bailor, would be liable to Wilcox for violation of that duty. It was for the jury to determine whether Glover knew or had reason to know that the brakes were defective when it entrusted the car into the possession of Anders. (Wilcox v. Glover Motors, 269 N.C. 473, 153 S.E.2d 76)

Some statutes provide that the bailor of an automobile is liable for the negligence of any person using the car with the owner's permission.[5]

QUESTIONS AND PROBLEMS

1. Checklist of legal terms:
   (a) act of God (380)
   (b) reversionary interest (384)
2. State the objective(s) of each of the following rules of law:
   (a) By virtue of statute, a bailee may retain his lien for work done on the bailed article even though he has surrendered possession.
   (b) The bailee is liable for any harm that befalls the bailed article when he makes an unauthorized use of the property, even though he was acting carefully.
3. At the owner's request, Conrad agreed to keep, free of charge, Ford's pedigreed dog while Ford was on his vacation. During that time Conrad entered the dog in a race. When Ford learned how Conrad had used the animal, he brought an action for damages against Conrad. Was he entitled to judgment?
4. Sanders agrees to refinish several chairs for Van Ness for $75. After the work has been completed, but before the chairs are returned to Van Ness, Sanders' building is totally destroyed by fire without fault on his part. Is Sanders entitled to the $75?
5. For $5 Shay agrees to keep Tate's valuables while the latter is on a business trip for two weeks. When Tate returns, he demands his valuables without offering to pay Shay. Shay refuses to deliver the valuables. Can Tate recover possession of the valuables without paying Shay?
6. Sherwood borrowed Powell's automobile for use until five o'clock in the afternoon for the purpose of making a trip to a neighboring town. On his way back Sherwood stopped at several other places to transact various items of business. About nine o'clock that evening Sherwood, while driving at a legal speed hit a hole in the road and lost control of the car which was damaged when it ran into a ditch. Powell brought an action against Sherwood to recover damages. Was he entitled to judgment?
7. The O'Connor Company stored household goods with Reeves. When the O'Connor Company demanded the return of the goods, Reeves was unable to do so because he had turned the goods over to Albert without the permission of the O'Connor Company. Was the O'Connor Company entitled to judgment in an action against Reeves to recover damages for a refusal to redeliver the goods?

---

[5] *Mordecai* v. *Hollis,* 50 Misc.2d 248, 269 N.Y.S.2d 863. In some of these states, the statute is restricted to cases in which the bailee is under a specified age.

8. Fields hires the Daley Storage Company to keep a grand piano during the summer months. In August the piano is taken from the Daley Storage Company under a writ of execution to satisfy an unpaid judgment which Padgett had secured against Fields. At the end of the summer when Fields discovers that the Daley Storage Company cannot return the piano, he brings an action for damages against the company. Is he entitled to judgment?

9. Carlton borrows a power tool from Darnell to make certain repairs in his store. Because of a defective part in the tool, Carlton is injured. Carlton contends that Darnell is liable because the tool was not reasonably fit for the purpose contemplated. Is his contention sound?

10. When Dexter attempts to collect for Farmer's use of a machine, Farmer sets up a counterclaim for the cost of certain minor repairs that he made on the machine. Is he entitled to deduct the amount of these repairs from the rental that he agreed to pay for the use of the machine?

11. Osell held a private pilot's license. He rented an airplane from Hall. While attempting to land the plane, he flew through a cloud formation, although he could have avoided doing so. In turning out of the clouds he struck a hillside and wrecked the plane. Flying through clouds under these circumstances was a violation of the federal Civil Air Regulations. Hall sued Osell for the destruction of the plane. Decide. (Hall v. Osell, 102 Cal.App.2d 849, 228 P.2d 293)

12. Miller took his auto to the Hand Ford Sales, Inc. to be repaired. Because there was a holiday and the repairs could not be done immediately, he decided to leave his auto at the repair garage. He then asked Hand Ford if he could be supplied with a temporarily loaned automobile. Hand Ford supplied him with an auto. Unknown to Hand Ford, a metal strip that was not noticeable to an occupant in the front seat projected from the underside of the car radio. In sliding across the front seat, Miller was cut by the strip. He sued Hand Ford on the theory that there was a mutual benefit bailment of the loaned automobile and that Hand Ford therefore had the duty to inspect the auto to determine that it was reasonably safe for use; and since it had not done so, it was liable for the harm caused by the strip which such investigation would have disclosed. Was he correct? (Miller v. Hand Ford Sales, Inc., 216 Ore. 567, 340 P.2d 181)

13. Nutrodynamics delivered a quantity of loose pills that it manufactured to Ivers-Lee for the latter to place them in foil packages and then in shipping containers suitable for delivery to customers of Nutrodynamics. Approximately 193 cartons of packaged pills were finished and in Ivers-Lee's possession when Beck brought a suit against Nutrodynamics and directed the sheriff to attach the pills in the possession of Ivers-Lee. Ivers-Lee had not been paid for its work in packaging. It claimed the right to keep the goods until paid but nevertheless surrendered them to the sheriff. Was it entitled to any claim on the goods in the hands of the sheriff? (Beck v. Nutrodynamics, Inc., 77 N.J.S. 448, 186 A.2d 715)

Chapter 34

Special Bailments

In some instances, a hotelkeeper may have a bailee's liability. In addition, a special bailment relation arises when goods are stored in a warehouse, or delivered to a merchant to sell for the owner, or delivered to a carrier to be transported.

HOTELKEEPERS

A *hotelkeeper* is regularly engaged in the business of offering living accommodations to all transient persons. In the early law he was called an innkeeper or a tavernkeeper.

Who Are Guests

A hotelkeeper owes a duty as such only when the patron of the hotel is a guest. The essential element in the definition of *guest* is that he is a transient. He need not be a traveler nor come from a distance. A person living within a short distance of the hotel who engages a room at the hotel and remains there overnight is a guest.

The relationship of guest and hotelkeeper does not begin until a person is received as a guest by the hotelkeeper.[1] The relationship terminates when the guest leaves or when he ceases to be a transient, as when he arranges for a more or less permanent residence at the hotel. The transition from the status of guest to the status of boarder or lodger must be clearly indicated. It is not established by the mere fact that one remains at the hotel for a long period, even though it runs into months.

Discrimination

Since a hotel is by definition an enterprise holding itself out to serve the public, it follows that members of the public, otherwise fit, must be accepted as guests. If the hotel refuses accommodations for an improper reason, it is liable for damages, including exemplary damages. In addition, it may be liable under a civil rights or similar statutory provision, and it may also be guilty of a crime. By virtue of the Federal Civil Rights Act of 1964, neither a

[1] *Langford* v. *Vandaveer*, [Ky.] 254 S.W.2d 498.

hotel nor its concessionaire can discriminate against patrons nor segregate them on the basis of race, color, religion, or national origin. The federal Act is limited to discrimination for the stated reasons and does not in any way interfere with the right of the hotel to exclude those who are unfit persons to admit because they are drunk or criminally violent, nor persons who are not dressed in the manner required by reasonable hotel regulations applied to all persons. When there has been improper discrimination or segregation or it is reasonably believed that such action may occur, the federal Act authorizes the institution of proceedings in the federal courts for an order to stop such prohibited practices.

Liability of Hotelkeeper

In the absence of a valid limitation, the hotelkeeper is generally an insurer of the safety of goods entrusted to his care.[2] As exceptions to the general rule, the hotelkeeper is not liable for loss caused by an act of God, a public enemy, act of public authority, the inherent nature of the property, or the fault of the guest.

In most states statutes limit or provide a method for limiting the liability of a hotelkeeper.[3] The statutes may limit the extent of liability, reduce the liability of the hotelkeeper to that of an ordinary bailee, or permit him to limit his liability by contract or by posting a notice of the limitation.[4] Some statutes relieve the hotelkeeper from liability when directions for depositing valuables with the hotelkeeper are posted on the doors of the rooms occupied and the guest fails to comply with the directions. In any case, the hotel is not liable for more than the value of the property to the exclusion of consequential harm that may flow from the loss of the property.

> **Facts:** Morse, a jewelry salesman, was a guest in the Piedmont Hotel. He entrusted a sample case to a bellboy of the hotel to place on the airport bus of an independent taxicab company. At some point between the hotel and the airport the sample case disappeared. The guest's employer was paid for the loss by his insurer, but the insurer then canceled the policy as to Morse and Morse was fired by the employer. No other insurance company would cover him as a jewelry salesman with the result that he was unable to get another job as such, although he had been a jewelry salesman for 40 years. This shock induced a heart attack that confined him at home for several months. Morse then sued the hotel for the earnings that he had lost, claiming $100,000; and damages for pain and suffering, claiming $25,000.
>
> **Decision:** Judgment for the hotel. While the hotel was liable for the loss of the guest's property, this did not make it liable for every consequence that

---

[2] *Zurich Fire Insurance Co.* v. *Weil,* [Ky.] 259 S.W.2d 54.
[3] *Kelly* v. *Milner Hotels,* 176 Pa.Super. 316, 106 A.2d 636.
[4] *Goodwin* v. *Georgian Hotel Co.,* 197 Wash. 173, 84 P.2d 681.

flowed therefrom. Consequently, there was no liability for the items of damage claimed by Morse as these were indirect damages which would not be anticipated as the probable and natural consequences of the loss of property. Accordingly no recovery could be allowed. (Morse v. Piedmont Hotel Co., 110 Ga.App. 509, 139 S.E.2d 133)

Lien of Hotelkeeper

The hotelkeeper is given a lien on the baggage of his guests for the agreed charges or, if no express agreement was made, the reasonable value of the accommodations furnished. Statutes permit the hotelkeeper to enforce his lien by selling the goods at public sale. The lien of the hotelkeeper is terminated by (a) the guest's payment of the hotel's charges, (b) any conversion of the goods by the hotelkeeper, and (c) surrender of the goods to the guest, except when they are given to him for temporary use.

Boarders or Lodgers

To those persons who are permanent boarders or lodgers, rather than transient guests, the hotelkeeper owes only the duty of an ordinary bailee of their personal property under a mutual-benefit bailment.

A hotelkeeper has no common-law right of lien on property of his boarders or lodgers, as distinguished from his guests, in the absence of an express agreement between the parties. In a number of states, however, legislation giving a lien to a boardinghouse or a lodginghouse keeper has been enacted.

WAREHOUSEMEN

A person engaged in the business of storing the goods of others for compensation is a *warehouseman*. A *public warehouseman* holds himself out generally to serve the public without discrimination.

Rights and Duties of Warehousemen

The common-law rights and duties of a warehouseman, in the absence of modification by statute, are in the main the same as those of a bailee in an ordinary mutual-benefit bailment.[5]

Facts: Motor Freight Lines delivered a shipment of frozen waffles to the Liberty Ice & Cold Storage Co. to hold for a few days awaiting reshipment. The only space available for storage was a compartment already partly filled with frozen lobsters and fish. Motor Freight was not informed of this fact nor of the danger that the waffle cartons

---

[5] Uniform Commercial Code, Sec. 7-204; *Belland* v. *American Auto Insurance Co.,* [C.A.Dist.Col.] 101 A.2d 517. The Uniform Commercial Code does not change the prior rule that when loss by fire is shown, the burden is upon the warehouseman to disprove negligence. *Canty* v. *Wyatt Storage Corp.,* 208 Va. 161, 156 S.E.2d 582.

would pick up the smell of seafood. The cartons of the waffles became so contaminated that it was necessary to repack them. Motor Freight sued Liberty for this expense.

Decision: Judgment for Motor Freight. When the waffles were given to the warehouse for storage, the warehouse was under the duty to exercise due care which included warning the customer of any danger that the storage might cause. (Motor Freight Lines v. Liberty Ice & Cold Storage Co., [La.App.] 85 So.2d 708)

The public warehouseman has a lien against the goods for reasonable charges.[6] It is a specific lien in that it attaches only to the property with respect to which the charges arose and cannot be asserted against other property of the same owner in the possession of the warehouseman. The warehouseman, however, may make a lien carry over to other goods by noting on the receipt for one lot of goods that a lien is also claimed thereon for charges as to other goods.[7] The warehouseman's lien for storage charges may be enforced by sale after due notice has been given to all persons who claim any interest in the property stored.

Most states have passed warehouse acts defining the rights and duties of the warehouseman and prescribing regulations as to charges and liens, bonds for the protection of patrons, the maintenance of storage facilities in a suitable and safe condition, inspections, and general methods of transacting business.

Warehouse Receipts

A *warehouse receipt* is a written acknowledgment by a warehouseman that the property of a named person has been received for storage. It also sets forth the terms of the contract of storage. The warehouse receipt is a document of title because the person lawfully holding the receipt is entitled to the goods or property represented by the receipt. The Code specifies certain details describing the transaction which must be included, but beyond this it does not require any particular form for a warehouse receipt.

The receipt can be issued only if goods have actually been received by the warehouseman. If a receipt is issued without the goods having been so received, the warehouseman is liable to a good-faith purchaser of the receipt for the loss he sustains thereby. The issuance of a receipt when goods have not been received by the warehouseman is also a crime in many states.

Rights of Holders of Warehouse Receipts

A warehouse receipt in which it is stated that the goods received will be delivered to the depositor, or to any other specified person, is a *nonnegotiable*

---

[6] UCC Sec. 7-209 (1).
[7] Sec. 7-209 (1).

warehouse receipt; but a receipt in which it is stated that the goods received will be delivered to the bearer, or to the order of any person named in such receipt, is a *negotiable warehouse receipt.*[8]

The transfer of negotiable warehouse receipts is made by delivery or by indorsement and delivery.[9] It is the duty of the warehouseman to deliver the goods to the holder of a negotiable receipt and to cancel such receipt before making delivery of the goods. The surrender of a nonnegotiable receipt is not required.

If the person who deposited the goods with the warehouse did not own the goods or did not have the power to transfer title to them, the holder of the warehouse receipt is subject to the title of the true owner.[10]

The transferee of a warehouse receipt is also given the protection of certain warranties from his immediate transferor; namely, that the instrument is genuine, that its transfer is rightful and effective, and that the transferor has no knowledge of any facts that impair the validity or worth of the receipt.[11]

Field Warehousing

Ordinarily, stored goods are placed in a warehouse belonging to the warehouseman. The owner of goods, such as a manufacturer, may keep the goods in his own storage room or building, however, and have a warehouse company take control of the room or building. When the warehouseman takes exclusive control of the property, it may issue a warehouse receipt for the goods even though they are still on the premises of the owner. Such a transaction has the same legal effect with respect to other persons and purchasers of the warehouse receipt as though the property were in the warehouse of the warehouseman. This practice is called *field warehousing* since the goods are not taken to the warehouse but remain "in the field."

The purpose of this device is to create warehouse receipts which the owner of the goods is able to pledge as security for loans.[12] The owner could, of course, have done this by actually placing the goods in a warehouse, but this would have involved the expense of transportation and storage.

FACTORS

A *factor* is a special type of bailee who sells goods consigned to him as though he were the owner of the goods. In modern usage the device of entrusting a person with the possession of property for the purpose of sale is

---

[8] Sec. 7-104.
[9] See Chapter 24.
[10] UCC Sec. 7-503 (1).
[11] Sec. 7-507. These warranties are in addition to any that may arise between the parties by virtue of the fact that the transferor is selling the goods represented by the receipt to the transferee. See Chapter 38 as to sellers' warranties.
[12] *Heffron* v. *Bank of America,* [C.C.A.9th] 113 F.2d 239.

commonly called *selling on consignment*. The owner who sends or consigns the goods for sale is the *consignor*. The person or agent to whom they are consigned is the *consignee*; he may also be known as a commission merchant. His compensation is known as a *commission* or *factorage*. The property remains the property of the owner, and the consignee acts as his agent to pass title to the buyer.

Factor as Agent

The relation of principal and factor is a form of agency [13] as well as a special bailment.[14] The main difference between an agent and a factor is that the agent need not have possession of the principal's property, while the factor must have actual or constructive possession of it. The chief difference between a factor and an ordinary bailee is that the former receives goods to sell to purchasers, but the bailee receives them to be returned to the bailor or delivered in accordance with the bailment agreement.

Ordinarily an agent does not guarantee in any way that the third person with whom he makes a contract on behalf of his principal will perform the contract. If a sale is made by the agent on credit, the agent is under the duty to exercise due care in selecting the third person as a credit risk. If he exercises due care, the agent is not responsible when the third person does not pay or perform his part of the contract. In the case of some factors the custom has developed of guaranteeing that the purchaser is solvent and that he will perform the contract. A factor who makes such a guarantee is termed a *del credere factor*.

In some business areas the word "factor" is used to describe a sales broker or agent without regard to whether the possession of the goods is in fact entrusted to him. When possession is not given, the rights and liabilities of the parties are determined by principles of agency law because no element of bailment is present.

Duties and Rights of Factors

The factor must exercise reasonable care in the protection of the goods. The care required is that of a bailee in an ordinary mutual-benefit bailment. Although the factor has power to insure the goods, he is ordinarily under no duty to do so. Such a duty can commonly be found, however, based either upon custom or trade, upon a course of dealings between the parties, or upon express instructions from the owner.

Facts: Mann shipped ten cars of lettuce to Crenshaw to sell as a factor. Without consulting Mann, Crenshaw reshipped four cars of lettuce to other markets and did not order the cars re-iced. This caused the

---

[13] See p. 211.
[14] *Clark* v. *Ashbach & Sons,* 241 Minn. 267, 64 N.W.2d 517.

incurring of liability for additional freight charges, and the lettuce was in a damaged condition on reaching its destination. Mann sued Crenshaw for the loss caused him.

Decision: Judgment for Mann. The factor violated his duty by reshipping the four cars without consulting the principal and was guilty of negligence in reshipping without re-icing. He was accordingly liable to Mann for the loss caused him. (Mann v. W. C. Crenshaw & Co., 158 Va. 193, 163 S.E. 375.

The factor must not mix the goods consigned to him with his own or another's property (1) unless he is authorized to do so by all parties in interest, or (2) unless the goods are fungible [15] in nature.

The factor must maintain accounts or records so that the proceeds to which the consignor is entitled can be accurately determined.

The factor, in making a sale of goods, must act in accordance with the instructions of the consignor. In the absence of express directions, the factor may sell in the manner usually and customarily employed by him. He cannot sell or pledge the goods for his own purposes unless expressly or impliedly authorized to do so by the principal. He has no power to exchange or barter the goods.

The factor has a lien on the goods of the principal in his possession and on the proceeds of sales of such goods for expenses, advances, and compensation. It is a possessory lien and is lost by relinquishment of possession of that property to the principal. It is a general lien in that it may be exercised against any of the principal's goods coming into his possession at any time later. The lien may also be lost by misconduct of the factor.

Statutory Regulation

At common law, if the factor unlawfully transferred the goods, the transferee acquired no title or right against the owner. This rule led to the defrauding of innocent third persons who purchased in good faith from the factor. The Uniform Commercial Code avoids this hardship by providing that when any one entrusts property to a merchant who regularly deals in goods of that kind, the dealer has the power to pass a valid title to a purchaser in the ordinary course of business regardless of whether the goods were entrusted for sale, repair, storage, or any other purpose.[16] Likewise, the creditors of the consignee may reach the entrusted goods as though they were owned by him.[17]

It is constitutional to provide further that the factor who sells in good faith in ignorance of the rights of other persons in the goods he sells is

[15] See p. 425.
[16] UCC Sec. 2-403(2).
[17] See p. 428.

protected from liability and cannot be treated as a converter of the goods,[18] as would be the case in the absence of such a statutory immunity.[19] The fact that a statute licenses factors and requires that they serve the public generally without discrimination does not in itself alter this rule of liability for conversion so as to confer an immunity upon them.[20]

COMMON CARRIERS

A *carrier* is one who undertakes the transportation of goods, regardless of the method of transportation or the distance covered. The *consignor* or shipper is the person who delivers goods to the carrier for shipment. The *consignee* is the person to whom the goods are shipped and to whom the carrier should deliver the goods.

Classification of Carriers

A carrier may be classified as (1) a *common carrier,* which holds itself out as willing to furnish transportation for compensation without discrimination to all members of the public who apply,[21] assuming that the goods to be carried are proper and that facilities of the carrier are available; (2) a *contract carrier,* which transports goods under individual contracts; or (3) a *private carrier,* such as a truck fleet owned and operated by an industrial firm. The common carrier law applies to the first, the bailment law to the second, and the law of employment to the third.

Facts: The J. C. Trucking Co., Inc., was engaged under contracts to transport dress material from New York City to dressmaking establishments in New Haven, Hartford, and Bridgeport, Connecticut and then to transport the finished dresses back to New York City. Dresses that were being carried to Ace-High Dresses, Inc., were stolen from the trucking company. Ace-High Dresses sued the trucking company and claimed that the latter was liable for the loss as a common carrier.

Decision: The trucking company was not a common carrier since it did not hold itself out to carry for the general public. It was a contract carrier as it would only carry if it had a preexisting contract with a shipper to do so. (Ace-High Dresses v. J. C. Trucking Co., 122 Conn. 578, 191 A. 536)

The carriage of goods for hire on a single trip does not constitute the carrier a common carrier so as to make it guilty of violating the law requiring a special permit or license from the state to operate as a common carrier.[22]

---

[18] *Montana Meat Co.* v. *Missoula Livestock Auction Co.,* 125 Mont. 66, 230 P.2d 955.
[19] *Sig Ellingson & Co.* v. *De Vries,* [C.A.8th] 199 F.2d 677.
[20] *Moderie* v. *Schmidt,* 6 Wash.2d 592, 108 P.2d 331.
[21] *P.U.C.* v. *Johnson Motor Transport,* 147 Maine 138, 84 A.2d 142.
[22] *State* v. *Logan,* [Mo.] 411 S.W.2d 86.

Freight Forwarders

A *freight forwarder* accepts freight from shippers who send less-than-carload lots, combines such freight into carloads, and delivers them as carloads to a carrier for shipment to a particlar point where the carload lots are separated and the items carried to their respective destinations. A freight forwarder does not own or operate any of the transportation facilities. By court decision or statute, freight forwarders in some jurisdictions have been declared subject to the same government regulations as common carriers.

Bills of Lading

When the carrier accepts goods for shipment or forwarding, it ordinarily issues to the shipper a *bill of lading* [23] in the case of rail or marine transportation or an *airbill* [24] for air transportation. This instrument is both a receipt for the goods and a contract stating the terms of carriage. Title to the goods may be transferred by a transfer of the bill of lading made with that intention.

With respect to intrastate shipments, bills of lading are governed by the Uniform Commercial Code.[25] Interstate transportation is regulated by the Federal Bills of Lading Act.[26]

A bill of lading is a *negotiable bill of lading* when by its term the goods are to be delivered to bearer or to the order of a named person.[27] Any other bill of lading, such as one that consigns the goods to a specified person, is a nonnegotiable or *straight bill of lading*.[28]

1 / Contents of bill of lading. The form of the bill of lading is regulated in varying degrees by administrative agencies.[29]

As against a bona fide transferee of the bill of lading, a carrier is bound by the recitals in the bill as to the contents, quantity, or weight of goods.[30] This means that the carrier must produce the goods as described, even though they had not existed, or pay damages for failing to do so. This rule is not applied if facts appear on the face of the bill that should keep the transferee from relying on the recital.

---

[23] In order to avoid the delay of waiting for a bill of lading mailed to the destination point from the point where the goods were received by the carrier, UCC Sec. 7-305(1) authorizes the carrier at the request of the consignor to provide for the issuance of the bill at the destination rather than the receipt point.

[24] UCC Sec. 1-201(6).

[25] Article 7.

[26] Title 49, United States Code Sec. 81 et seq.

[27] UCC Sec. 7-104(1)(a).

[28] Sec. 7-104(2). Interstate Commerce Commission regulations applicable to rail shipments require nonnegotiable bills to be printed on white paper and negotiable bills on yellow paper.

[29] The Code contains no provision regulating the form of the bill of lading.

[30] UCC Sec. 7-301(1).

2 / Negotiability. The person to whom a bill of lading has been negotiated acquires the direct obligation of the carrier to hold possession of
the goods for him according to the terms of the bill of lading as fully as if the
carrier had contracted with him, and ordinarily he acquires the title to the
bill and the goods it represents. The rights of the holder of a negotiable bill
are not affected by the fact (a) that the former owner of the bill had been
deprived of it by fraud, accident, mistake, duress, undue influence, loss, theft,
or conversion; or (b) that the goods had already been surrendered by the
carrier or had been stopped in transit.[31]

The rights of the holder of a bill of lading are subject to the title of a
true owner who did not deliver or authorize the delivery of the goods to
the shipper. For example, when a thief steals the goods, delivers them to the
carrier, and then negotiates the bill of lading, the title of the owner prevails
over the claim of the holder of the bill.[32]

3 / Warranties. The transferee for value of either a negotiable or non-
negotiable bill of lading acquires from his transferor, in the absence of any
contrary provision, the benefit of implied warranties that (a) the bill of
lading is genuine, (b) its transfer is rightful and is effective to transfer the
goods represented thereby, and (c) the transferor has no knowledge of any
facts that would impair the validity or worth of the bill of lading.[33]

Rights of Common Carriers

A common carrier of goods has the right to make reasonable and necessary rules for the conduct of its business. It has the right to charge such
rates for its services as yield it a fair return on the property devoted to the
business of transportation, but the exact rates charged are regulated by the
Interstate Commerce Commission in the case of interstate carriers and by
state commissions in the case of intrastate carriers. As an incident of the
right to charge for its services, a carrier may charge *demurrage* for the detention of its cars or equipment for an unreasonable length of time by either
the consignor or consignee.

As security for unpaid transportation and service charges, a common
carrier has a lien on goods that it transports. The carrier's lien also secures
demurrage charges, the costs of preservation of the goods, and the costs of
sale to enforce the lien.[34] The lien of a carrier is a specific, and not a general,

---

[31] Sec. 7-502(2).
[32] Sec. 7-503(1).
[33] UCC Sec. 7-507; Federal Bills of Lading Act (FBLA), 49 USC Secs. 114, 116.
When the transfer of the bill of lading is part of a transaction by which the transferor
sells the goods represented thereby to the transferee, there will also arise the warranties that are found in other sales of goods. See Chapter 38.
[34] UCC Sec. 7-307(1); FBLA, 49 USC Sec. 105.

lien. It attaches only to goods shipped under the particular contract, but includes all of the shipment even though it is sent in installments. Thus, when part of the shipment is delivered, the lien attaches to the portion remaining in possession of the carrier.

Duties of Common Carrier

A common carrier is generally required (1) to receive and carry proper and lawful goods of all persons who offer them for shipment; (2) to furnish facilities that are adequate for the transportation of freight in the usual course of business, and to furnish proper storage facilities for goods awaiting shipment or awaiting delivery after shipment; (3) to follow the directions given by the shipper; (4) to load and unload goods delivered to it for shipment (in less-than-carload lots in the case of railroads), but the shipper or consignee may assume this duty by contract or custom; (5) to deliver the goods to the consignee or his authorized agent, except when custom or special arrangement relieves the carrier of this duty.

Goods must be delivered at the usual place for delivery at the specified destination. When goods are shipped under a negotiable bill of lading, the carrier must not deliver the goods without obtaining possession of the bill properly indorsed. When goods are shipped under a straight bill of lading, the carrier is justified in delivering to the consignee, unless notified by the shipper to deliver to someone else. If the carrier delivers the goods to the wrong person, it is liable for breach of contract and for the tort of conversion.

Liabilities of Common Carriers

When goods are delivered to a common carrier for immediate shipment and while they are in transit, the carrier is absolutely liable for any loss or damage to the goods unless it can prove that it was due solely to one or more of the following excepted causes: (a) act of God, or a natural phenomenon that is not reasonably foreseeable; (b) act of public enemy, such as pirates at sea or the military forces of an opposing government, as distinguished from ordinary robbers; (c) act of public authority, such as a health officer removing goods from the train; (d) act of the shipper, such as fraudulent labeling or defective packing; or (e) inherent nature of the goods, such as those naturally tending to spoil or deteriorate.

> **Facts:** The Ozark White Lime Co. shipped lime from Arkansas by the St. Louis-San Francisco Railway. The shipment was stopped at McBride, Oklahoma, by a landslide which blocked the tracks. The car containing the shipment was placed on a spur line several feet lower than the main tracks. The lime was then destroyed by flood waters from the Grand River. The lime company sued the railroad for the loss. The

lime company showed that the railroad had an engine available to take cars from the spur track up to higher ground and that it had taken other cars beyond the reach of the flood waters. No reason was shown for the failure to remove the car with the plaintiff's shipment.

Decision: Judgment for the lime company. If the carrier relies on an act of God to excuse it from its liability as an insurer, it must show that the act of God was the sole cause of the damage. Here the carrier was negligent in failing to move the shipment to higher ground, which it could have done. (St. Louis-San Francisco Rwy. Co. v. Ozark White Lime Co., 177 Ark. 1018, 9 S.W.2d 17)

1 / Carrier's liability for delay. A carrier is liable for losses caused by its failure to deliver goods within a reasonable time. Thus the carrier is liable for losses arising from a fall in price or a deterioration of the goods caused by their unreasonable delay. The carrier, however, is not liable for every delay. Risks of ordinary delays incidental to the business of transporting goods are assumed by the shipper.

2 / Liability of initial and connecting carriers. When goods are carried over the lines of several carriers, the initial and the final carrier, as well as the carrier on whose line the loss is sustained, may be liable to the shipper or the owner of the goods; but only one payment of the loss may be obtained.

3 / Limiting liability. It is generally held that in the absence of a constitutional or statutory prohibition, a carrier has the right to limit its liability by contract. Generally a clause limiting the liability of the carrier is not enforceable unless consideration is given for it, usually in the form of a reduced rate, and provided further that the shipper is allowed to ship without limitation of liability if he chooses to pay the higher or ordinary rate.[35]

A carrier may by contract relieve itself from liability for losses not arising out of its own negligence. A carrier accepting freight for shipment outside the state cannot require the shipper to agree that the initial carrier will not be liable for losses occurring on the line of a connecting carrier.

A common carrier may make an agreement with the shipper as to the value of the property. If the amount is reasonable, such an agreement will usually bind the shipper whether or not the loss was due to the carrier's fault.

4 / Liability for baggage. A common carrier of passengers is required to receive a reasonable amount of baggage. Its liability in this respect is the same as the liability of a carrier of goods. If the passenger retains custody of his baggage, the carrier is liable only for lack of reasonable care or willful misconduct on the part of its agents and employees. Limitations on baggage

---

[35] UCC Sec. 7-309(2).

liability are commonly authorized by law and are binding upon passengers even though unknown to them.

A passenger in a Pullman car cannot recover for loss of or damage to personal property which he has brought with him unless he can show that the railroad or the employees in the Pullman car failed to exercise reasonable care under the circumstances. A few cases hold the Pullman car employees and the railroad to the standard of care required of hotelkeepers. In the great majority of states this degree of liability applies only to property that is entrusted by the passenger to the Pullman employees for safekeeping.

QUESTIONS AND PROBLEMS

1. Checklist of legal terms—hotelkeepers, warehousemen, factors:
   (a) hotelkeeper, guest (389)
   (b) warehouseman, public warehouseman (391)
   (c) warehouse receipt (392); nonnegotiable warehouse receipt (392), negotiable warehouse receipt (393)
   (d) field warehousing (393)
   (e) selling on consignment, consignor (394)
   (f) commission or factorage (394)
   (g) del credere factor (394)

2. State the objective(s) of each of the following rules of law:
   (a) The owner of stolen goods may recover them from the holder of a negotiable warehouse receipt representing such goods, even though the holder had purchased the receipt for value and in good faith.
   (b) A factor has a general lien for expenses, advances, and compensation, which may be asserted against any property of the principal that comes into the factor's possession at a later time.

3. Polk, who was registered at a hotel, placed two small trunks in charge of the porter. He took one of them with him daily for use in displaying merchandise to businessmen. One day when he failed to bring that trunk back to the hotel, he telephoned the hotelkeeper that he did not intend to pay his bill. The hotelkeeper contended that he had a lien on both trunks for Polk's hotel bill. Was his contention sound?

4. Cassidy stores several rugs at a public warehouse. When he removes them, he is allowed 30 days in which to pay the storage charges. Two weeks later Cassidy stores some furniture in the same warehouse for a month. When the month has elasped, Cassidy pays the storage charges on the furniture. The warehouse refuses to deliver the furniture until Cassidy pays the storage charges on the rugs. Does the warehouseman have a lien on the furniture for these charges?

5. Mears forges a warehouse receipt stating that 10 cartons of books will be delivered to bearer. He sells the receipt to Beech who knows of the forgery. Beech, in turn, transfers the receipt to Ervin. When Ervin

learns that the receipt is a forged instrument, he brings an action against Beech. Is he entitled to judgment?

6. Underhill fails to pay a factor his commission for selling a consignment of goods. Later Underhill consigns a car of wheat to the same factor. The latter claims a lien on the wheat for the commissions due on the earlier transaction. Is he entitled to the lien?

7. Checklist of legal terms—common carriers:
   (a) carrier; consignor, consignee (396)
   (b) common carrier, contract carrier, private carrier (396)
   (c) freight forwarder (397)
   (d) bill of lading, airbill (397)
   (e) negotiable bill of lading, straight bill of lading (397)
   (f) demurrage (398)

8. A carrier issued a bill of lading for a car of 250 boxes of merchandise. The bill was marked to indicate that the shipper had loaded the car and counted the boxes. The bill of lading was transferred to a bona fide purchaser who found that the car contained only 200 boxes. Was the transferee of the bill of lading entitled to judgment in an action against the carrier to recover the value of 50 boxes of the merchandise?

9. A car of Shirmer's melons arrived at the market three days after shipment. Ordinarily transportation of such shipments was completed in two days. As a result of the slower transportation, Shirmer lost money because of a decline in the market price of melons. Shirmer brought an action for damages against the carrier. Under what circumstances would the carrier not be liable?

10. McCarley sued the Foster-Milburn Co., a medical manufacturing company. He claimed that there was jurisdiction to bring the lawsuit because Foster was doing business with the state through an agent, Obergfel. Foster supplied Obergfel with a product called *Westsal,* made by a subsidiary of Foster. Obergfel was to sell this product directly to doctors. He also sold products produced by other medical manufacturers. Obergfel solicited orders from doctors, sold in his own name, incurred all expenses, made all collections, and after deducting his commissions, remitted the balance to Foster. Foster shipped the *Westsal* to Obergfel who warehoused it and then reshipped it to the purchasers. If Obergfel was not an agent of Foster, the suit was not properly brought. Was Obergfel the agent of Foster? (McCarley v. Foster-Milburn Co. [W.D. D.C. N.Y.], 93 F.S. 421)

11. The Utah Public Service Commission granted a permit to the Salt Lake Transportation Company to transport passengers between the Salt Lake airport for four principal airlines and the three leading hotels in the city. The Realty Purchasing Company and various hotels and taxicab companies objected to the granting of the permit on the ground that the company performed a taxicab service and was therefore a common carrier. Decide. (Realty Purchasing Co. v. Public Service Commission, 9 Utah 2d 375, 345 P.2d 606)

PART VI

Sales

Chapter 35

Nature and Form

The most common business transactions are those involving the sale and purchase of goods; that is, items of tangible personal property, such as food, clothing, and books. The law of sales is a fusion of the law merchant, the common law of England, and former statutes as modified and codified by the Uniform Commercial Code (Article 2).

A sale of an interest in real property, such as a house, store, or farm, is governed by different principles.

NATURE AND LEGALITY

A *sale of goods* is a transfer of title to tangible personal property in consideration of a payment of money, an exchange of other property, or the performance of services.[1] The consideration in a sale, regardless of its nature, is known as the *price*. The parties to a sale are the person who owns the property and the person to whom the title is transferred. The transferor is the seller or vendor, and the transferee is the buyer or vendee. If the price is payable wholly or partly in goods, each party is a seller insofar as the goods he is to transfer are concerned.

Sale Distinguished

A sale of goods must be carefully distinguished from related transactions.

1 / Bailment. A sale is an actual present transfer of title. If there is a transfer of a lesser interest than ownership or title, the transaction is not a sale. Thus, a bailment is not a sale because only possession is transferred to the bailee. The bailor remains the owner.

---

[1] *De Mers* v. *O'Leary,* 126 Mont. 528, 254 P.2d 1080; *Com.* v. *Kayfield,* [Pa.] 40 D.&C.2d 689.

2 / Gift. There can be no sale without consideration, or a price. A gift is a gratuitous transfer of the title of property.

3 / Contract to sell. When the parties intend that title to goods will pass at a future time and they make a contract providing for that event, a *contract to sell* is created.[2]

4 / Option to purchase. A sale, a present transfer of title, differs from an *option to purchase.* The latter is neither a transfer of title nor a contract to transfer title but a power to require a sale to be made at a future time.[3]

5 / Conditional sale. A *conditional sale* customarily refers to a "condition precedent" transaction by which title does not vest in the purchaser until he has paid in full for the property purchased. This is the customary type of sale used when personal property is purchased on credit and payment is to be made in installments. This transaction is now classified as a secured transaction under Article 9 of the Code.

6 / Furnishing of labor or services. A contract for personal services is to be distinguished from a sale of goods even when some transfer of personal property is involved in the performing of the services. For example, the contract of a repairman is a contract for services even though in making the repairs he may supply parts necessary to perform his task. The supplying of such parts is not regarded as a sale because it is merely incidental to the primary contract of making repairs, as contrasted with the purchase of goods, such as a television set, with the incidental service of installation.

Similarly, when a surgical pin is inserted in the bone as part of hospitalization, the transaction as to the pin cannot be isolated and treated as a sale but is merely part of a broad contract for services.[4] And an agreement by an artist to make a painting on a television program and donate the painting as part of a charitable drive is an agreement to render services and not a contract for sale of goods.[5]

Facts: Lovett, a patient in the hospital of Emory University, was given a blood transfusion for which a separate charge was made on his hospital bill. He contracted serum hepatitis from the transfusion and died. Suit was brought against the hospital on the ground that there was a breach of implied warranty of fitness of the blood.

Decision: Judgment for the University. The furnishing of blood as part of a blood transfusion is a service and not a sale, and therefore no implied warranty of fitness arises. The fact that a separate charge was made for the blood did not give the blood the character of goods, as the

---

[2] Uniform Commercial Code, Sec. 2-106(1).
[3] *Western Helicopter Operations* v. *Nelson,* 118 Cal.App.2d 359, 257 P.2d 1025.
[4] *Cheshire* v. *Southampton Hospital Association,* 53 Misc.2d 355, 278 N.Y.S.2d 531.
[5] *National Historic Shrines Foundation* v. *Dali,* [N.Y.S.2d] 4 UCCRS 71.

transfusion was still the rendering of a service. (Lovett v. Emory University, 116 Ga.App. 277, 156 S.E.2d 923)

Subject Matter of Sales

The subject matter of a sale is anything that is movable when it is identified as the subject of the transaction.[6]

The subject matter of a sale may not be (1) investment securities, such as stocks and bonds, the sales of which are regulated by Article 8 of the Code; (2) choses in action, since they are assigned or negotiated rather than sold, or which, because of their personal nature, are not transferable in any case;[7] or (3) real estate.

Nonexistent and Future Goods

Generally, a person cannot make a present sale of nonexistent or future goods or goods that he does not own. He can make a contract to sell such goods at a future date; but since he does not have the title, he cannot transfer that title now. For example, an agreement made today that all the fish caught on a fishing trip tomorrow shall belong to a particular person does not make him the owner of those fish.

When the parties purport to effect a present sale of future goods, the agreement operates only as a contract to sell the goods.[8] Thus a farmer purporting to transfer the title today to the future crop would be held subject to a duty to transfer title to the crop when it came into existence. If he did not keep the promise, he could be sued for breach of contract; but the contract would not operate to vest the title in the buyer automatically.

Law of Contracts Applicable

A sale is a voluntary transaction between two persons. Accordingly most of the principles that apply to a contractual agreement are equally applicable to a sale. Modern commercial practices, however, have modified the strict principles of contract law, and this approach to the problem is carried into the Code. Thus it is provided that sales contract can be made in any manner and that it is sufficient that the parties by their conduct recognize the existence of a contract, even though it cannot be determined when the contract was made, and generally even though one or more terms are left open.[9] In some instances the Code treats all buyers and sellers alike. In others, it

---

[6] UCC Sec. 2-105(1). It may also include things which are attached to the land, such as those consisting of (a) timber or minerals or buildings or materials forming part of buildings if they are to be removed or severed by the seller, and (b) other things attached to land to be removed by either party. Sec. 2-107.

[7] See p. 358. As to rights that cannot be transferred because of their personal character, see p. 180.

[8] UCC Sec. 2-105(2).

[9] Sec. 2-204. This provision of the Code is limited by requiring that there be "a reasonably certain basis for giving an appropriate remedy."

treats merchants separately, in contrast with the occasional or casual buyer or seller. Thus the Code recognizes that the merchant is experienced in his field and has a specialized knowledge of the relevant commercial practices.[10]

1 / Offer. Contract law as to offers is applicable to sales except that an offer by a merchant cannot be revoked, even though there is no consideration to keep the offer open, if the offer expresses an intention that it will not be revoked, is made in writing, and is signed by the merchant.[11] The expressed period of irrevocability, however, cannot exceed three months. If nothing is said as to the duration of the offer, this irrevocability continues only for a reasonable time.

2 / Acceptance. The Code redeclares the general principle of contract law that an offer may be accepted in any manner and by any medium which is reasonable under the circumstances, unless a specific manner or medium is clearly indicated by the terms of the offer or the circumstances of the case.[12]

(a) ACCEPTANCE BY SHIPMENT. Unless otherwise clearly indicated, an order or other offer to buy goods that are to be sent out promptly or currently can be accepted either by actually shipping the goods, as though a unilateral contract offer had been made; or by promptly promising to make shipment, as though a bilateral contract, that is, an exchange of promises, had been offered.[13] If acceptance is made by shipping the goods, the seller must notify the buyer within a reasonable time that the offer has been accepted in this manner.[14]

(b) ADDITIONAL TERMS IN ACCEPTANCE. Unless it is expressly specified that an offer must be accepted just as made, the offeree may accept a contract but at the same time propose an additional term. This new term, however, does not become binding unless the offeror thereafter consents to it. Consequently, when the buyer sends an order which the seller acknowledges on his own printed form, any additional material term in the printed form that is not in the order form or which is not implied by custom or prior dealings is merely regarded as an additional offer that may or may not be accepted by the buyer. That is, the order is accepted, but the new term does not become part of the contract until it is accepted by the buyer.

The acceptance by the buyer may be found either in his express statement, orally or in writing, that he accepts the additional term; or it may be deduced from his conduct, as when he accepts the goods with knowledge that the additional term has been made.

---

[10] UCC Sec. 2-104(1).
[11] Sec. 2-205.
[12] Sec. 2-206(1)(a).
[13] Sec. 2-206(1)(b).
[14] Sec. 2-206(2).

In a transaction between merchants, the additional term becomes part of the contract if no objection is made to it and the additional term does not materially alter the terms of the offer.[15] If this additional term in the seller's form or acknowledgment operates solely to his advantage, however, it is a material term which must be accepted by the buyer to be effective.

3 / Determination of price. The price for the goods may be expressly fixed by the contract, or the parties may merely indicate the manner of determining price at a later time.[16] A sales contract is binding even though it calls for a specified price "plus extras" but does not define the extras, which it leaves for future agreement.[17]

Facts: California Lettuce Growers contracted to grow and deliver to Union Sugar Co. 239 acres of sugar beets in a certain year. No price was specified, but Growers knew that it was the custom to make agreements to pay at a later date on the basis of the sugar content of the beets supplied and of the selling price of sugar for the current year. Growers later claimed that the contract was void because the price was not specified in the contract.

Decision: Judgment for Union. Since the parties contracted with the knowledge of the custom as to the method of price determination, the price was to be determined in that manner and the contract was not void because no price was specified in the contract. (California Lettuce Growers v. Union Sugar Co., 45 Cal.2d 474, 289 P.2d 785)

Ordinarily, if nothing is said as to price, the buyer is required to pay the reasonable value of the goods. The reasonable price is generally the market price, but not necessarily, as when the market price is under the control of the seller. When the contract did not fix the price of potatoes, the buyer was obligated to pay the reasonable price for potatoes at the place and time of delivery, and the federal-state market news reports for that city on the day after the potatoes were delivered were evidence of such reasonable price.[18]

In recent years there has been an increase in use of the "cost plus" formula for determining price. Under this form of agreement the buyer pays the seller a sum equal to the cost to the seller of obtaining the goods plus a specified percentage of that cost.

The contract may expressly provide that one of the parties may determine the price, in which case he must act in good faith in so doing.[19] Like-

---

[15] Sec. 2-207; *Application of Doughboy Industries, Inc.*, 17 App.Div. 2d 216, 233 N.Y.S.2d 488.

[16] UCC Sec. 2-305.

[17] *Silver* v. *Sloop Silver Cloud*, [D.C. S.D. N.Y.] 259 F.S. 187.

[18] *Lamberta* v. *Smiling Jim Potato Co.*, [U.S.Dept. of Agriculture] 25 A.D. 1181, 3 UCCRS 981.

[19] Good faith requires that the party in fact act honestly and, in the case of a merchant, also requires that he follow reasonable commercial standards of fair dealing which are recognized in the trade. UCC Secs. 1-201(19), 2-103(b).

wise, the contract may specify that the price shall be determined by some standard or by a third person. If for any reason other than the fault of one of the parties the price cannot be fixed in the manner specified, the buyer is required to pay the reasonable value for the goods unless it is clear that the parties intended that if the price were not determined in the manner specified, there would be no contract. In the latter case, the buyer must return the goods and the seller refund any payment made on account. If the buyer is unable to return such goods as he has received, he must pay their reasonable value at the time of delivery.

4 / Output and requirement contracts. Somewhat related to the open-term concept concerning price is that involved in the output and requirement contracts in which the quantity which is to be sold or purchased is not a specific quantity but is such amount as the seller should produce or the buyer should require. Although this introduces an element of uncertainty, such sales contracts are valid. To prevent oppression, they are subject to two limitations:

(a) The parties must act in good faith.

(b) The quantity offered or demanded must not be unreasonably disproportionate to prior output or requirements or to any estimate stated.[20]

When the sales contract is a continuing contract, as one calling for periodic delivery of fuel, but no time is set for the life of the contract, the contract runs for a reasonable time but may be terminated on notice by either party unless otherwise agreed.[21]

5 / Seals. A seal on a contract or on an offer of sale has no effect. Thus in determining whether there is consideration or if the Statute of Limitations is applicable, the fact that there is a seal on the contract is ignored.[22]

6 / Implied conditions. The field of implied conditions under contract law is broadened to permit the release of a party from his obligation under a sales contract when performance has been made commercially impracticable, as distinguished from impossible: (a) by the occurrence of a contingency, the nonoccurrence of which was a basic assumption on which the contract was made; or (b) by compliance in good faith with any applicable domestic or foreign governmental regulation or order, whether or not it is later held valid by the courts.[23]

---

[20] UCC Sec. 2-306.
[21] Sec. 2-309(2); *Sinkoff Beverage Co.* v. *Schlitz Brewing Co.,* 51 Misc.2d 446, 273 N.Y.S.2d 364.
[22] UCC Sec. 2-203.
[23] Sec. 2-615. If under the circumstances indicated in the text the seller is totally disabled from performing, he is discharged from his contract. If he is able to produce some goods, he must allocate them among customers, but any customer may reject the contract and such fractional offer. Sec. 2-615(b), 2-616.

"A severe shortage of raw materials or of supplies due to a contingency such as war, embargo, local crop failure, unforeseen shutdown of major sources of supply, or the like, which either causes a marked increase in cost or altogether prevents the seller from securing supplies necessary to his performance, is within the contemplation" of this provision of the Code.[24]

7 / Modification of contract. A departure is made from the general principles of contract law in that an agreement to modify the contract for the sale of goods is binding even though the modification is not supported by any consideration.[25]

8 / Parol evidence rule. The parol evidence rule applies to the sale of goods with the slight modification that a writing is not presumed or assumed to represent the entire contract of the parties unless the court so finds. The result is that, in the absence of such a finding, the writing may be supplemented by parol proof of additional terms so long as such terms are not inconsistent with the original terms.[26]

A sales contract, although written, may be modified by an oral agreement except to the extent that a writing is required by the Statute of Frauds. Even when the sales contract specifies that there cannot be an oral modification, the conduct of the parties may be such that there is a waiver of such prohibition and an oral modification is then binding.[27]

9 / Fraud and other defenses. The defenses that may be raised in a suit on a sales contract are in general the same as on any other contract. When one party is defrauded, he may rescind the transaction and recover what he has paid or the goods that he has delivered, together with damages for any loss which he has sustained. If title has passed to the buyer because of a fraud, the title is voidable while the goods are still owned by him and the sale may be set aside if the innocent seller so elects.

If the sales contract or any clause in it was unconscionable when made, a court may refuse to enforce it, as discussed in Chapter 12, page 151.

Illegal Sales

1 / Illegality at common law. At common law a sale is illegal if the subject matter is itself bad, as in the case of an indecent picture. The transaction may also be illegal even though the subject matter of the sale may be unobjectionable in itself, as when the agreement provides that the object of the sale shall be employed for some unlawful purpose or when the seller assists in the unlawful act. To illustrate, when the seller falsely brands goods,

---

[24] UCC Sec. 2-615(1), Official Comment, point 4.
[25] Sec. 2-209(1).
[26] Sec. 2-202; *Hunt Foods and Industries* v. *Doliner,* 49 Misc.2d 246, 267 N.Y.S.2d 364.
[27] *C.I.T. Corp.* v. *Jonnet,* 419 Pa. 435, 214 A.2d 620.

representing them to be imported, to assist the buyer in perpetrating a fraud, the sale is illegal. The mere fact, however, that the seller has knowledge of the buyer's unlawful purpose does not, under the general rule, make the sale illegal unless the purpose is the commission of a serious crime.

2 / Illegality under statutes. Statutes in many states prohibit business transactions, including sales, on Sunday. Practically every state has legislation prohibiting certain sales when they are not conducted according to the requirements of the statutes. Thus a statute may require that a particular class of goods, such as meat, be inspected before a legal sale can be made. In addition to statutes which invalidate the sale, a number of statutes make it criminal or impose a penalty for making a sale under certain circumstances. Statutes commonly regulate sales by establishing standards as to grading, size, weight, and measure, and by prohibiting adulteration.

In addition to the restrictive state statutes, federal legislation regulates the sale of goods in interstate commerce. The Federal Food, Drug, and Cosmetic Act, for example, prohibits the interstate shipment of misbranded or adulterated foods, drugs, cosmetics, and therapeutic devices. Other statutes, such as those designed to regulate competition, further protect the consumer from fraud.

Facts: Sullivan, a druggist, received from a manufacturer in another state a properly labeled container of sulfa tablets. He placed some of these tablets in small pill boxes for resale to the public. These boxes were labeled only "Sulfathiazole." Sullivan was prosecuted for violating the federal law prohibiting the sale of misbranded drugs.

Decision: Sullivan was convicted. The boxes did not carry adequate instructions to the buyers regarding the use of the tablets which, if not taken according to directions, could be harmful. Sullivan therefore violated the federal law. The fact that the tablets had left the channels of interstate commerce did not prevent the federal law from applying since Congress could and had intended "to safeguard the consumer by applying the Act to articles from the moment of their introduction into interstate commerce all the way to the moment of their delivery to the ultimate consumer." (United States v. Sullivan, 332 U.S. 689)

3 / Effect of illegal sale. An illegal sale or contract to sell cannot be enforced. This rule is based on public policy. As a general rule, courts will not aid either party in recovering money or property transferred pursuant to an illegal agreement. Relief is sometimes given, however, to an innocent party to an unlawful agreement. For example, if one party is the victim of a fraudulent transaction, he may recover what he has transferred to the other party even though the agreements between them arose out of some illegal scheme.

Bulk Transfers

Whenever a merchant is about to transfer a major part of his materials, supplies, merchandise, or other inventory, not in the ordinary course of business, advance notice of the transfer must be given to his creditors. If such notice is not given, the creditors may reach the sold property in the hands of the transferee and also in the hands of any subsequent transferee who knew that there had not been compliance with the Code or who did not pay value.[28] This is designed to protect creditors of a merchant from the danger that he may sell all of his inventory, pocket the money, and then disappear, leaving them unpaid. The protection given to creditors by the bulk transfer legislation is in addition to the protection which they have against their debtor for fraudulent transfers or conveyances, and the remedies that can be employed in bankruptcy proceedings.

The fact that there has been noncompliance with Article 6 of the Code regulating bulk transfers, however, does not affect the validity of a bulk sale of goods as between the parties since Article 6 is operative only with respect to the rights of creditors of the seller.[29]

FORMALITY OF THE SALES CONTRACT

In order to protect the parties to a sales contract from false claims, the English Statute of Frauds required, subject to certain exceptions, that all sales of goods above a certain amount must be evidenced by writing. Subsequent statutes and now the Uniform Commercial Code [30] have continued the policy of this statute.

Amount

The Statute of Frauds provision of the Code applies whenever the sales price is $500 or more. If the total contract price equals or exceeds this amount, the Statute of Frauds applies although the contract covers several articles, the individual amounts of which are less than the statutory amount, provided the parties intended to make a single contract rather than a series of separate or divisible contracts. In the latter case, if each contract is for less than the statutory amount, no writing is required.

Nature of the Writing Required

1 / Terms. The writing need only give assurance that there was a transaction. Specifically it need only indicate that a sale or contract to sell has

---

[28] UCC Sec. 6-101 et seq.
[29] *Macy* v. *Oswald*, 198 Pa.Super. 435, 182 A.2d 94.
[30] UCC Sec. 2-201.

been made and state the quantity of goods involved. Any other missing terms may be shown by parol evidence in the event of a dispute.[31]

Facts: Arcuri negotiated with Weiss to purchase his restaurant. He gave him a check bearing the notation, "Tentative deposit on tentative purchase of . . . restaurant, fixtures, equipment, goodwill." Later Arcuri demanded that Weiss return the amount of the check. Weiss refused to do so on the ground there was a binding contract because the notation on the check was a sufficient writing.

Decision: The writing was not sufficient. By the use of the word "tentative" it showed that no transaction had been completed; a writing indicating that "a contract for sale has been made" is required. None of the exceptions to the requirement of a writing applied. (Arcuri v. Weiss, 198 Pa.Super. 506, 608; 184 A.2d 24)

2 / Signature. The writing must be signed by the person who is being sued or his authorized agent. The signature must be placed on the writing with the intention of authenticating the writing. It may consist of initials; or be printed, stamped, or typewritten; as long as made with the necessary intent.

When the transaction is between merchants, an exception is made to the requirement of signing. It provides that the failure of a merchant to repudiate a confirming letter sent him by another merchant binds him just as though he had signed the letter or other writing.[32] This ends the evil of a one-sided writing under which the sender of the letter was bound but the receiver could safely ignore the transaction or could hold the sender as he chose, depending upon which alternative gave him the better financial advantage.

The provision as to merchants makes it necessary for a merchant buyer or merchant seller to watch his mail and to act promptly if he is not to be bound by a contract for sale with respect to which he has signed no writing. It deprives the party who fails to answer the confirmation, by rejecting it, of the defense of the Statute of Frauds.[33]

3 / Time of execution. A writing to satisfy the Statute of Frauds may be made at any time at or after the making of the sale. It may even be made after the contract has been broken or a suit brought on it, since the essential element is the existence of written proof of the transaction when the trial is held. Accordingly, when the buyer writes in reply to the seller, after a 45-day delay, and merely criticizes the quality of some of the goods, the conduct of the buyer is in itself a confirmation.[34]

---

[31] Sec. 2-201(1).

[32] Sec. 2-201(2). The confirming letter must be sent within a reasonable time after the transaction, and the receiving merchant must give written notice of his objection thereto within ten days after receiving the confirming letter.

[33] *Reich* v. *Helen Harper,* [N.Y.S.2d] 3 UCCRS 1048.

[34] *Reich* v. *Helen Harper,* [N.Y.S.2d] 3 UCCRS 1048.

4 / Particular writings. The writing which satisfies the Statute of Frauds may be a single writing or it may be several writings considered as a group. Formal contracts, bills of sale,[35] letters, and telegrams are common forms of writings that satisfy the Statute of Frauds. Purchase orders, cash register receipts, sales tickets, invoices, and similar papers generally do not satisfy the requirements as to a signature and sometimes they do not specify any quantity or commodity.

Effect of Noncompliance

A sales agreement that does not comply with the statute is not enforceable by action, nor can the noncomplying agreement be raised as a defense.[36] The defense that a sales contract does not satisfy the requirements of the Statute of Frauds may be waived, however, and the contract then enforced as though the Statute had been satisfied.

When Proof of Oral Contract Permitted

In some instances the absence of a writing does not bar the proof of a sales contract.

1 / Receipt and acceptance. An oral sales contract may be enforced if it can be shown that the goods were delivered by the seller and were received and accepted by the buyer. Both a receipt and an acceptance by the buyer must be shown. The contract may be enforced only insofar as it relates to those goods received and accepted.[37]

The buyer's receipt of the goods may be symbolic, as in the case of the seller's transfer of a covering bill of lading to the buyer.

2 / Payment. An oral contract may be enforced if the buyer has made full payment on the contract. In the case of part payment, a contract may be enforced only with respect to goods for which payment has been made and accepted.[38] There is some uncertainty under this rule as to the effectiveness of "payment" by check or a promissory note executed by the buyer. Under the law of commercial paper a check or note is conditional payment when delivered, and it does not become absolute until the instrument is paid. The earlier decisions held that the delivery of a negotiable instrument was not such a payment as would make the oral contract enforceable unless it was agreed at that time that the instrument was to be accepted as absolute, and not conditional, payment. A modern contrary view, which is influenced

---

[35] See p. 414.
[36] UCC Sec. 2-201(1). However, the contract itself is not unlawful and may be voluntarily performed by the parties.
[37] UCC Sec. 2-201(3)(c).
[38] Sec. 2-201(3)(c).

by the fact that businessmen ordinarily regard the delivery of a check or note as "payment," holds that the delivery of such an instrument is sufficient to make the oral contract enforceable.[39]

When the buyer has negotiated or assigned to the seller a commercial paper that was executed by a third person and the seller has accepted the instrument, a payment has been made within the meaning of the Statute of Frauds.

A check or promissory note that is tendered as payment but which is refused by the seller does not constitute a payment under the Statute of Frauds.

3 / Judicial admission. No writing is required when the person alleged to have made the contract voluntarily admits in the course of legal proceedings that he has done so.

4 / Nonresellable goods. No writing is required when the goods are specifically made for the buyer and are of such an unusual nature that they are not suitable for sale in the ordinary course of the seller's business. For this exception to apply, however, the seller must have made a substantial beginning in manufacturing the goods or, if he is a middleman, in procuring them, before receiving notice of a repudiation by the buyer.[40]

Bill of Sale

Regardless of the requirement of the Statute of Frauds, the parties may wish to execute a writing as evidence or proof of the sale. Through custom, this writing has become known as a *bill of sale*. It is not a bill or a contract. It is merely a receipt or writing signed by the seller in which he recites that he has transferred the title of the described property to the buyer.[41]

Facts: Stine, a general contractor, owed Forsyth money for repair work. He agreed to pay off his debt by delivering a compressor to Forsyth. He delivered the compressor to Forsyth and later rented it back from Forsyth, and then unknown to Forsyth he sold it to Cramer. When Forsyth sued Cramer for the compressor, the latter claimed that Stine had never sold the compressor to Forsyth since there was no bill of sale.

Decision: Judgment for Forsyth. The transfer and delivery of the compressor to Forsyth in discharge of Stine's debt was a sale, and the absence of a bill of sale was immaterial. (Forsyth Storage & Transfer Inc. v. Cramer, 215 Md.App. 93, 136 A.2d 905)

---

[39] The Restatement of Contracts, Sec. 205, adopts this view. It would appear that the draftsmen of the Uniform Commercial Code are also in favor of this view, for the comment to Sec. 2-201 states that "part payment may be made by money or check, accepted by the seller."

[40] UCC Sec. 2-201(3)(a).

[41] *Bischoff v. Steele,* 75 Idaho 485, 274 P.2d 986.

In many states provision is made for the public recording of bills of sale when goods are left in the seller's possession. In the case of the sale of certain types of property, a bill of sale may be required in order to show that the purchaser is the lawful owner. Thus some states require the production of a bill of sale before the title to an automobile will be registered in the name of the purchaser.

QUESTIONS AND PROBLEMS

1. Checklist of legal terms:
   (a) sale of goods (403), contract to sell (404)
   (b) price (403)
   (c) option to purchase (404)
   (d) conditional sale (404)
   (e) bulk transfer (411)
   (f) bill of sale (414)

2. State the objective(s) of each of the following rules of law:
   (a) A seller who has been defrauded by the buyer may rescind the sale and recover the goods.
   (b) A bill of sale must be produced before the title to an automobile will be registered in some states.

3. When Fossitt moves to another city, he is not certain that he will be permanently located there. Ewald agrees to take Fossitt's furniture and pay for its use until Fossitt returns or sends for it. Does this agreement constitute a sale?

4. On October 4 Varland agreed to sell his truck to Kay on October 14. Without fault of either party, the truck was destroyed by fire on October 11. When Kay refused to pay the agreed price on October 14, Varland brought an action to collect that amount. Varland contends that the transaction on October 4 was a sale. Do you agree?

5. Collins, who holds a $1,000 note executed by Frisby, transfers it to Baynes for $940. Is this transaction a sale?

6. Cherry offers to sell a bookcase. Dennis accepts the offer and takes the bookcase home with him. Nothing is said about price. Later Dennis contends that the transaction was not a sale because no price was stipulated. Is this contention sound?

7. Dorl is induced by Melvin's fraud to purchase certain merchandise, for which he made payment in advance.
   (a) What is Dorl's remedy if he learns of the fraud before the merchandise is delivered?
   (b) What is Dorl's remedy if he learns of the fraud after the merchandise has been delivered?

8. Norman is induced by fraud to purchase a certain article from Rust on credit. After learning of the fraud, Norman sells the article to Sparks. What is the effect of the resale of the article?

9. Stephenson orally agrees to sell a certain quantity of soybeans to Van Horn for $1,000. At the time the agreement is made, Van Horn loads part of the soybeans on his truck and takes them with him. Later he refuses to accept the remainder of the purchase. When Stephenson brings an action for breach of contract, Van Horn's defense is that the agreement is not in writing. Do you consider this to be a valid defense?

10. Pryor orally agrees to pay $6,000 to Raymond for a certain number of bales of cotton. Raymond gives Pryor the bill of lading issued by the carrier that holds the goods. Later Pryor contends that the agreement is unenforceable because he has not received the goods and the agreement is not in writing. Is his contention sound?

11. The Swift Box Company agreed with Ritter to manufacture 25,000 packing cases according to specifications differing from those of the standard cases ordinarily made and kept on hand by the company. The price involved was over the amount specified in the Statute of Frauds provision of the Code. No memorandum of the transaction was made, and no money was given in part payment. When the company failed to perform as agreed, Ritter brought an action to recover damages. Was he entitled to judgment?

12. H. I. Phillips contracted with the Associated Newspapers, a corporation, to furnish daily newspaper articles commenting on the affairs of the day. A dispute arose over the meaning of the contract. A suit was brought in which it was claimed that the contract was for the sale of the articles. Do you agree? (Associated Newspapers v. Phillips, 294 F. 845)

13. The Tober Foreign Motors, Inc., sold an airplane to Skinner on installments. Later it was agreed that the monthly installments should be reduced in half. Thereafter Tober claimed that the reduction agreement was not binding because it was not supported by consideration. Was this claim correct? (Skinner v. Tober Foreign Motors, Inc., 345 Mass. 429, 187 N.E.2d 669)

14. Gallick sold sugar to Castiglione with knowledge that the latter intended to use it in the illegal manufacture of liquor. The buyer did not pay the purchase price. Gallick then sued him for the purchase price. Castiglione defended on the ground that the contract was illegal. Decide. (Gallick v. Castiglione, 2 Cal.App.2d 716, 38 P.2d 858)

15. Members of the Colonial Club purchased beer from outside the state and ordered it sent to the Colonial Club. The club then kept it in the club refrigerator and served the beer to its respective owners upon demand. The club received no compensation or profit from the transaction. The club was indicted for selling liquor unlawfully. Decide. (North Carolina v. Colonial Club, 154 N.C. 177, 69 S.E. 771)

Chapter 36

Title and Risk in Sales Contracts

In the great majority of sales transactions the buyer receives the proper goods, makes payment, and the transaction is thus completed. However, several types of problems may arise. For the most part, these types of problems can be avoided if the parties by their sales contract make express provisions. When the parties have not by their contract specified what results they desire, however, the rules stated in this chapter are applied by the law.

Nature of the Problem

1 / Creditors' claims. Creditors of the seller may seize the goods as belonging to the seller, or the buyer's creditors may seize them on the theory that they belong to the buyer. In such case the question arises whether the creditors are correct as to who owns the goods. The question of ownership is also important in connection with the consequence of a resale by the buyer, or liability for or computation of certain kinds of taxes, and liability under certain registration and criminal statutes.[1]

2 / Insurance. Until the buyer has received the goods and the seller has been paid, both the seller and buyer have an economic interest in the sales transaction.[2] The question arises as to whether either or both have enough interest to entitle them to insure the property involved, that is, whether they have an insurable interest.[3]

3 / Damage to goods. If the goods are damaged or totally destroyed without any fault of either the buyer or the seller, must the seller bear the loss and supply new goods to the buyer; or is it the buyer's loss, so that he must pay the seller the purchase price even though he now has no goods or damaged goods?[4]

---

[1] See Uniform Commercial Code, Sec. 2-401, as to when title passes.

[2] See Sec. 2-501(1)(a), and note also that the seller may have a security interest by virtue of the nature of the shipment or the agreement of the parties. See p. 426 and Chapter 41.

[3] To insure property, a person must have such a right or interest in the property that its damage or destruction would cause him financial loss. When he would be so affected, he is said to have an insurable interest in the property. See Chapter 43. The ownership of personal property for the purpose of insurance is determined by the law of sales. *Motors Ins. Corp.* v. *Safeco Insurance Co.,* [Ky.] 412 S.W.2d 584.

[4] UCC Sec. 2-509.

Nature of the Transaction

The answer to be given to each of the questions noted in the preceding section depends upon the nature of the transaction between the seller and the buyer. Sales transactions may be classified according to (1) the nature of the goods and (2) the terms of the transaction.

1 / Nature of goods. The goods may be *existing goods*, which means that they are physically in existence and are owned by the seller. It is immaterial whether the existing goods are in the condition required by the contract or whether the seller must do some act or complete the manufacture of the goods before they satisfy the terms of the contract.

In addition to existing goods, there are the classifications of identified goods and future goods. The seller and buyer may have agreed which goods are to be received by the buyer, or the seller may have picked out the goods. When such a selection has been made, the goods are described as *identified goods*. If the goods are not both existing and identified at the time of the transaction, they are *future goods*.

2 / Terms of the transaction. The terms of the contract may obligate the seller to deliver the goods at a particular place, for example, to make delivery at destination. In contrast, the contract may only require that the goods be sent or shipped to the buyer, that is, that the seller make shipment. Under the latter contract, the seller's part is performed when he hands over the goods to a carrier for shipment to the buyer; as contrasted with the delivery at a destination provision, under which the seller's part of the contract is not completed until the goods are brought to the destination point and there tendered to the buyer. Ordinarily only delivery to the carrier by the seller is required in the absence of an express requirement of delivery at destination.

Instead of calling for the actual delivery of goods, the transaction may relate to a transfer of the document of title representing the goods. For example, the goods may be stored in a warehouse, the seller and the buyer having no intention of moving the goods, but intending that there should be a sale and a delivery of the warehouse receipt that stands for the goods. Here the obligation of the seller is to produce the proper paper as distinguished from the goods themselves. The same is true when the goods are represented by a bill of lading issued by a carrier or by any other document of title.

As a third type of situation, the goods may be stored with, or held by, a third person who has not issued any document of title for the goods, but the seller and buyer intend that the goods shall remain in that bailee's hands, the transaction being completed without any delivery of the goods themselves or of any document of title.

Transfer of Title, Special Property Interests, and Risk in Particular Transactions

The various kinds of goods and transaction terms may be combined in a number of ways. Only the more common types of transactions will be considered. Keep in mind that the following rules of law apply only in the absence of a contrary agreement by the parties concerning these matters.

1 / Existing goods identified at time of contracting. The title to such goods that are not to be delivered passes to the buyer at the time and place of contracting.

Facts: Hieby sold growing grapefruit to Moffitt. The written contract specified: "All terms of this agreement have been reduced to writing herein." The contract provided for the harvesting of the crop nine weeks later and stated: "Seller agrees that if harvesting is paid by buyer, it is to be charged to seller's account." The crop was damaged by the failure of Hieby to care for and water the orchards after making the sale. Moffitt refused to take the grapefruit.

Decision: Judgment for Hieby. The contract did not impose any duty upon the seller to care for the goods after the sale had been made, and no duty would be implied. Therefore the seller had completed his performance under the contract and was entitled to sue for the breach of the contract by the buyer. (Moffitt v. Hieby, 149 Tex. 161, 229 S.W.2d 1005)

Since the buyer becomes the owner of the goods, he has an insurable interest in them. Conversely, the seller no longer has an insurable interest unless he has reserved a security interest to protect his right to payment.[5]

If the seller is a merchant, the risk of loss passes to the buyer when he receives the goods from the merchant; if a nonmerchant seller, the risk passes when the seller tenders or makes available the goods to the buyer. Thus the risk of loss remains longer on the merchant seller, a distinction which is made on the ground that the merchant seller, being in the business, can more readily protect himself against such continued risk.

The operation of the rule that title is transferred at the time of the transaction applies even though a local statute requires the registration of the transfer of title. Thus the transfer of title of an automobile is complete as between the parties, in the absence of a contrary intention, when the agreement is made to sell or transfer the title to a specific car, even though the delivery of a title certificate as required by law has not been made.[6] For example, where the parties intend a sale of the automobile and unconditional possession of it is given to the buyer, the buyer becomes the owner and the

---

[5] Secured transactions are discussed in Chapters 40 and 41.
[6] *Transportation Equipment Co.* v. *Dabdoub*, [La.] 69 So.2d 640.

Transfer of Title, Special Property Interests, and Risk in Sales Contracts

Problem Fact Situation	Transfer of Title	Transfer of Special Property Interests	Transfer of Risk of Loss
(1) Existing goods identified at time of contracting	Time and place of contracting Sec. 2-401(3)(b)	Time and place of contracting Sec. 2-501(1)(a)	Receipt of goods from merchant seller; tender of goods by nonmerchant seller Sec. 2-509(3)
(2) Delivery of documents of title only	Time and place of delivery of documents Sec. 2-401(3)(a)	Time and place of contracting Sec. 2-501(1)(a)	Receipt of negotiable document of title Sec. 2-509(2)(a)
(3) Acknowledgment by bailee, without documents of title	Time and place of contracting Sec. 2-401(3)(b)	Time and place of contracting Sec. 2-501(1)(a)	Time of bailee's acknowledgment of buyer's right Sec. 2-509(2)(b)
(4) Marking future goods for buyer	No transfer	At time of such act Sec. 2-501(1)(b)	No transfer
(5) Contract for shipment of future goods	Time and place of shipment Sec. 2-401(2)(a)	Time and place of shipment or marking for buyer Sec. 2-501(1)(b)	Delivery to carrier Sec. 2-509(1)(a)
(6) Contract for delivery of future goods at destination	Tender at destination Sec. 2-401(2)(b)	Time and place of shipment Sec. 2-501(1)(b)	Tender at destination Sec. 2-509(1)(b)

car is no longer "owned" or "held for sale" by the seller within the meaning of his insurance policy, even though the title certificate has not been executed.[7] In some states, however, it is expressly declared by statute that no title is transferred in the absence of a delivery of the certificate of title.[8]

The Code does not change a local state rule as to whether a transfer of the document of title is necessary in order to effect a sale of an automobile. Thus it has been held in a state where there is no such requirement that title to an automobile was effectively transferred when the owner gave the keys to the buyer, left the car at the buyer's place of business, and the buyer paid the purchase price, even though the title certificate had not been assigned and transferred to the buyer.[9]

The fact that "title" has not been transferred to a motor vehicle because of a statute making the issuance of a title certificate essential for that purpose does not affect the transfer of the risk of loss as between the seller and buyer.[10]

2 / Negotiable documents representing existing goods identified at time of contracting. Here the buyer has a property interest, but not title, and an insurable interest in the goods at the time and place of contracting; but he does not ordinarily acquire the title nor become subject to the risk of loss until he receives delivery of the documents.[11] Conversely, the seller has an insurable interest and title up to that time.

3 / Existing goods, identified at time of contracting, held by bailee. Here the goods owned by the seller are held by a warehouseman, garageman, repairman, or other bailee, but there is no document of title and the sales contract does not call for a physical delivery of the goods, the parties intending that the goods should remain where they are. In such a case the answers to the various problems are the same as in situation (1), page 419, except that the risk of loss does not pass to the buyer, but remains with the seller, until the bailee acknowledges that he is now holding the goods in question for the buyer.

4 / Seller's marking future goods for buyer. If the buyer sends an order for goods to be manufactured by the seller or to be filled by him from inventory or by purchases from third persons, one step in the process of

---

[7] *Motors Inc. Co.* v. *Safeco Insurance Co.*, [Ky.] 412 S.W.2d 584.
[8] *Schroeder* v. *Zykan*, [Mo.] 255 S.W.2d 105.
[9] *Semple* v. *State Farm Mut. Automobile Ins. Co.*, [D.C. E.D. Pa.] 215 F.S. 645.
[10] *Park County Implement Co.* v. *Craig*, [Wyo.] 397 P.2d 800.
[11] Express provision is made for the case of a nonnegotiable document and other factual variations. UCC Sec. 2-509(2)(c), Sec. 2-503(4). When delivery of documents is to be made, the seller may send the documents through customary banking channels as well as make a tender in person or by an agent. Sec. 2-503(5)(b). Even though the form of the document of title is such that title is retained by the seller for security purposes, the risk of loss nevertheless passes to the buyer.

filling the order is the seller's act of marking, tagging, labeling, or in some way doing an act for the benefit of his shipping department or for himself to indicate that certain goods are the ones to be sent or delivered to the buyer under contract. This act of unilateral identification of the goods is enough to give the buyer a property interest in the goods and gives him the right to insure them.[12] However, neither title nor risk of loss passes to the buyer at that time but remains with the seller [13] who, as the continuing owner, also has an insurable interest in the goods. Thus neither title nor liability passes to the buyer until some other event, such as a shipment or delivery, occurs.

5 / Contract for shipment of future goods. In this situation the buyer has placed an order for goods that will be shipped to him later, and the contract is performed by the seller when he delivers the goods to a carrier for shipment to the buyer. Under such a contract the title and risk of loss pass to the buyer when the goods are delivered to the carrier, that is, at the time and place of shipment. After that happens, the seller has no insurable interest unless he has reserved a security interest in the goods.[14]

Facts: Brown was a local distributor for the Storz Brewing Co. Under the distribution contract, sales were made at prices set by the company "all f.o.b. Storz Brewing Company's plant, from which shipment is made. . . . Distributor agrees . . . to pay all freight and transportation charges from Storz Brewing Company's place of business or to the delivery point designated by the distributor and all delivery expenses." Brown wrote the company to deliver a quantity of beer to a trucker by the name of Steinhaus as soon as the latter would accept the goods. The company delivered the goods to Steinhaus. Snow delayed the transportation and caused the beer to freeze. Brown rejected the beer and was sued by the company for the purchase price.

Decision: Judgment for the company. As the contract called for shipment f.o.b. the seller's plant, the risk of loss passed to the buyer at that time and place. The fact that the goods were damaged thereafter did not affect the buyer's duty to pay for the goods. (Storz Brewing Co. v. Brown, 154 Neb. 204, 47 N.W.2d 407)

Under a shipment contract, "delivery" by the seller is made at the point of delivery to the carrier and not at the destination.[15]

The fact that a shipment of goods is represented by a bill of lading or an airbill issued by the carrier, and that in order to complete the transaction it

---

[12] UCC Sec. 2-501(1)(b). Special provision is made as to crops and unborn young animals. Sec. 2-501(1)(c).
[13] *Silver* v. *Sloop Silver Cloud,* [D.C. S.D. N.Y.] 259 F.S. 187.
[14] The reservation of a security interest by the seller does not affect the transfer of the risk to the buyer.
[15] *Permalum Window & Awning Co.* v. *Permalum Window Mfg. Corp.,* [Ky.] 412 S.W.2d 863.

will be necessary to transfer that bill to the buyer, does not affect these rules or bring the transaction within situation (2), page 421.

6 / Contract for delivery of future goods at destination. When the contract requires the seller to make delivery at a particular destination point, the buyer acquires a property right and an insurable interest in the goods at the time and place they are marked or shipped; but the risk of loss and the title do not pass until the carrier tenders or makes the goods available at the destination point. The seller retains an insurable interest until that time; and if he has a security interest in the goods, he continues to retain that interest until the purchase price has been paid.

Damage or Destruction of Goods

In the absence of a contrary agreement,[16] damage to or the destruction of the goods affects the transaction as follows:

1 / Damage to identified goods before risk of loss passes. When goods that were identified at the time the contract was made suffer some damage or are destroyed without the fault of either party before the risk of loss has passed, the contract is avoided if the loss is total. If the loss is partial or if the goods have so deteriorated that they do not conform to the contract, the buyer has the option, after inspection of the goods, (a) to treat the contract as avoided, or (b) to accept the goods subject to an allowance or deduction from the contract price. In either case, the buyer cannot assert any claim against the seller for breach of contract.[17]

2 / Damage to identified goods after risk of loss passes. If partial damage or total destruction occurs after the risk of loss has passed, it is the buyer's loss. It may be, however, that the buyer will be able to recover the amount of the damages from the person in possession of the goods or from a third person causing the loss. To illustrate, in many instances the risk of loss passes at the time of the transaction even though the seller is to deliver the goods later. During the period from the transfer of the risk of loss to the transfer of possession to the buyer, the seller has the status of a bailee of the goods and is liable to the buyer under the circumstances for which an ordinary bailee would be liable.

3 / Damage to unidentified goods. So long as the goods are unidentified, no risk of loss has passed to the buyer. If any goods are damaged or destroyed during this period, it is the loss of the seller. The buyer is still entitled to receive the goods for which he contracted. If the seller fails to

---

[16] UCC Sec. 2-303.
[17] Sec. 2-613.

deliver the goods, he is liable to the purchaser for the breach of his contract. The only exception arises when the parties have expressly provided in the contract that destruction of the seller's supply shall be deemed a release of the seller's liability or when it is clear that the parties contracted for the purchase and sale of part of the seller's supply to the exclusion of any other possible source of such goods.

4 / Reservation of title or possession. When the seller reserves title or possession solely as security to make certain that he will be paid, the risk of loss is borne by the buyer if the circumstances are such that he would bear the loss in the absence of such reservation.

Sales on Approval and with Right to Return

A sales transaction may give the buyer the privilege of returning the goods. In a *sale on approval,* the sale is not complete until the buyer approves. A *sale or return* is a completed sale with the right of the buyer to return the goods and thereby set aside the sale. The agreement of the parties determines whether the sale is on approval or with return; but if they have failed to indicate their intention, it is deemed a sale on approval if the goods are purchased for use, that is, by a consumer, and a sale or return, if purchased for resale, that is, by a merchant.[18]

1 / Consequence of sale on approval. In the absence of a contrary agreement, title and risk of loss remain with the seller under a sale on approval. Use of the goods by the buyer consistent with the purpose of trial is not an election or approval by him. There is an approval, however, if he acts in a manner that is not consistent with a reasonable trial, or if he fails to express his choice within the time specified or within a reasonable time if no time is specified. If the goods are returned, the seller bears the risk and the expense involved.[19] Since the buyer is not the "owner" of the goods while they are on approval, his creditors cannot reach them.[20]

2 / Consequence of sale or return. In a sale or return, title and risk of loss pass to the buyer as in the case of an ordinary or absolute sale. In the absence of a contrary agreement, the buyer under a sale or return may return all of the goods or any commercial unit thereof. A *commercial unit* is any article, group of articles, or quantity which commercially is regarded as a separate unit or item, as a particular machine, a suite of furniture, or a carload lot.[21] The goods must still be in substantially their original condition,

---

[18] Sec. 2-326(1). An "or return" provision is treated as a sales contract for the purpose of applying the Statute of Frauds, and cannot be established by parol evidence when it would contradict a sales contract indicating an absolute sale. Sec. 2-326(4).

[19] Sec. 2-327(1).

[20] Sec. 2-326(2).

[21] Sec. 2-105(6).

and the option to return must be exercised within the time specified by the contract or within a reasonable time if none is specified. The return under such a contract is at the buyer's risk and expense.[22] As long as the goods are in the buyer's possession under a sale or return contract, his creditors may treat the goods as belonging to him.[23]

3 / Other transactions. A consignment is not a sale on approval or a sale with right to return. In the absence of any contrary provision, it is merely an agency and denotes that property is committed to the consignee for sale. In the absence of some restriction, the consignor may revoke the agency at will and retake possession of his property by any lawful means.[24] Whether goods are sent to a person as buyer or on consignment to sell for the seller is a question of the intention of the parties.[25]

Sale of Fungible Goods

Fungible goods are goods of a homogeneous nature that may be sold by weight or measure. They are goods of which any unit is from its nature or by commercial usage treated as the equivalent of any other unit.[26] Wheat, oil, coal, and similar bulk commodities are fungible goods since, given a mass of the same grade or uniformity, any one bushel or other unit of the mass will be exactly the same as any other bushel or similar unit.

Title to an undivided share or quantity of an identified mass of fungible goods may pass to the buyer at the time of the transaction, making the buyer an owner in common with the seller.[27] For example, when a person sells to another 600 bushels of wheat from his bin which contains 1,000 bushels, title to 600 bushels passes to the buyer at the time of the transaction, giving him a 6/10ths undivided interest in the mass as an owner in common. The courts in some states, however, have held that the title does not pass until a separation has been made.

Sale of Undivided Shares

The problem of the passage of title to a part of a larger mass of fungible goods is distinct from the problem of the passage of title when the sale is made of a fractional interest without any intention to make a later separation. In the former case the buyer is to become the exclusive owner of a separated portion. In the latter case he is to become a co-owner of the entire mass. Thus there may be a sale of a part interest in a radio, an automobile, or a

---

[22] Sec. 2-327(2).
[23] Sec. 2-326(2); *Guardian Discount Co.* v. *Settles,* 114 Ga.App. 418, 151 S.E.2d 530.
[24] *Parks* v. *Atlanta News Agency,* 115 Ga.App. 842, 156 S.E.2d 137.
[25] *Donich* v. *U.S.F.&G. Co.,* [Mont.] 423 P.2d 298.
[26] UCC Sec. 1-201(17).
[27] Sec. 2-105(4).

flock of sheep. The right to make a sale of a fractional interest is recognized by statute.[28]

Auction Sales

When goods are sold at an auction in separate lots, each lot is a separate transaction, and title to each passes independently of the other lots.[29] Title to each lot passes when the auctioneer announces by the fall of the hammer or in any other customary manner that the auction is completed as to that lot.[30]

Reservation of a Security Interest

The seller may fear that the buyer will not pay for the goods. The seller could protect himself by insisting that the buyer pay cash immediately. This may not be practical for geographic or business reasons. The seller may then give credit but protect himself by retaining a security interest in the goods.[31]

1 / Bill of lading. The seller may retain varying degrees of control over the goods by the method of shipment. Thus he may send the goods to himself, the seller, in the buyer's city, receiving from the carrier the bill of lading for the goods.[32] In such a case, the buyer cannot obtain the goods from the carrier since the shipment is not directed to him, as in the case of a straight bill of lading, or because he does not hold the bill of lading, if it is a negotiable or order bill. Conversely, the seller's agent in the buyer's city can arrange for or obtain payment from the buyer and then give him the documents necessary to obtain the goods from the carrier.

If the goods are sent by carrier under a negotiable bill of lading to the order of the buyer or his agent, the seller may also retain the right of possession of the goods by keeping possession of the bill of lading until he receives payment.[33]

2 / C.O.D. shipment. In the absence of an extension of credit a seller has the right to keep the goods until paid, but he loses his right if he delivers possession of the goods to anyone for the buyer. However, where the goods are delivered to a carrier, the seller may preserve his right to possession by making the shipment C.O.D., or by the addition of any other terms indicating an intention that the carrier should not surrender the goods to the buyer until

---

[28] Sec. 2-403(1).
[29] Sec. 2-328(1).
[30] Sec. 2-328(2).
[31] As to the security transactions under the Code, see Chapters 40 and 41. As to other security devices, see Chapters 42-44.
[32] UCC Sec. 2-505.
[33] Sec. 2-505(1)(a).

the buyer has made payment. Such a provision has no effect other than to keep the buyer from obtaining possession until he has made payment. The C.O.D. provision does not affect the problem of determining whether title or risk of loss has passed.

Effect of Sale on Title

As a general rule, a person can sell only such interest or title in goods as he possesses. If the property is subject to a bailment, a sale by the bailor is subject to the bailment. Similarly, the bailee can only transfer his right under the bailment, assuming that the bailment agreement permits his right to be assigned or transferred. The fact that the bailee is in possession does not give him the right to transfer the bailor's title.

Moreover, a thief or finder generally cannot transfer the title to property since he can only pass that which he has, namely the possession but not the title.[34] In fact, the purchaser from the thief not only fails to obtain title but also becomes liable to the owner as a converter of the property even though he made the purchase in good faith.

Facts: Owen told Snyder that he wished to buy Snyder's auto. He drove the car for about ten minutes, returned to Snyder, stated that he wanted to take the auto to show it to his wife, and then left with the auto but never returned. Later Owen sold the auto in another state to Pearson and gave him a bill of sale. Pearson showed the bill of sale to Lincoln, falsely told him the certificate of title for the auto was held by a bank as security for the financing of the auto, and then sold the auto to Lincoln. Snyder sued Lincoln to recover the automobile.

Decision: Judgment for Snyder. Owen had been guilty of larceny in obtaining the automobile, and no title had passed to him. The automobile could therefore be recovered even though the ultimate purchaser gave value and acted in good faith. (Snyder v. Lincoln, 150 Neb. 581, 35 N.W.2d 483)

There are certain instances, however, when either because of the conduct of the owner or the desire of society to protect the bona fide purchaser for value, the law permits a greater title to be transferred than the seller possessed.

1 / Sale by entrustee. If the owner entrusts his goods to a merchant who deals in goods of that kind, the latter has the power to transfer the entruster's title to anyone who buys from him in the ordinary course of business.

Facts: Al's Auto Sales sold and delivered a used car to Cross Motor Co. on December 18, the title certificate to be delivered when payment was made. Cross gave Al a bank draft for the amount of the purchase price

---

[34] *Coomes* v. *Drinkwalter,* 181 Neb. 450, 149 N.W.2d 60.

on the same day. On December 23, Cross resold the car to Moskowitz. Al attached the certificate of title of the car to Cross' draft and sent it through another bank for payment on January 4. The draft was dishonored and returned to Al together with the certificate of title. Al then learned that the car had been resold to Moskowitz and sued him to recover the car.

Decision: Judgment against Al. By sending the certificate, Al had made it appear that Cross Motor had the authority to sell, and title could pass. Having done so, Al was estopped to deny the right of Cross to transfer title. (Al's Auto Sales v. Moskowitz, 203 Okla. 611, 224 P.2d 588)

It is immaterial why the goods were entrusted to the merchant. Hence the leaving of a watch for repairs with a jeweler who sells new and second-hand watches would give the jeweler the power to pass the title to a buyer in the ordinary course of business.[35] The entrustee is, of course, liable to the owner for damages caused by his sale of the goods and is guilty of some form of statutory offense or embezzlement.

If the entrustee is not a merchant, but merely a prospective customer trying out an automobile, there is no transfer of title when a buyer of the car from the entrustee who paid $300, leaving a balance of $600 due, then resells the car for $1,200.[36]

2 / Consignment sales. A manufacturer or distributor may send goods to a dealer for sale to the public with the understanding that the manufacturer or distributor is to remain the owner and the dealer in effect is to act as his agent. When the dealer maintains a place of business at which he deals in goods of the kind in question under a name other than that of the consigning manufacturer or distributor, the creditors of the dealer may reach the goods as though they were owned by him.[37]

3 / Estoppel. The owner of property may estop himself from asserting that he is the owner and denying the right of another person to sell the property. A person may purchase a product and have the bill of sale made out in the name of a friend to whom he then gives possession of the product and the bill of sale. He might do so in order to deceive his own creditors or to keep other persons from knowing that he made the purchase. If the friend should sell the product to a bona fide purchaser who relies on the bill of sale as showing that the friend was the owner, the true owner is estopped or barred from denying the friend's apparent ownership or his authority to sell.

---

[35] UCC Sec. 2-403(2), (3).

[36] *Atlas Auto Rental Corp.* v. *Weisberg,* 54 Misc.2d 168, 281 N.Y.S.2d 400.

[37] UCC Sec. 2-326(3). The manufacturer or dealer may protect himself from this result by entering into a secured transaction agreement and making a proper filing under Article 9 of the Code, or by complying with any local statute that protects him in such case.

4 / Powers. In certain circumstances, persons in possession of someone else's property may sell the property. This arises in the case of pledgees,[38] lienholders, and, in some instances, finders who, by statute, may have authority to sell the property to enforce their claim or when the owner cannot be found.

5 / Documents of title. By statute, certain documents of title, such as bills of lading and warehouse receipts, have been clothed with a degree of negotiability when executed in proper form.[39] By virtue of such provisions, the holder of a negotiable document of title directing delivery of the goods to him or his order, or to bearer, may transfer to a purchaser for value acting in good faith such title as was possessed by the person leaving the property with the issuer of the document. In such cases it is immaterial that the holder had not acquired the documents in a lawful manner.

6 / Recording and filing statutes. In order to protect subsequent purchasers and creditors, statutes may require that certain transactions be recorded or filed and may provide that if that is not done, the transaction has no effect against a purchaser who thereafter buys the goods in good faith from the person who appears to be the owner or against the execution creditors of such an apparent owner. Thus, if a seller retains a security interest in the goods sold to the buyer but fails to file a financing statement in the manner required by the Code, the purchaser appears to be the owner of the goods free from any security interest and subsequent bona fide purchasers or creditors of the buyer can acquire title from him free of the seller's security interest.[40]

7 / Voidable title. If the buyer has a voidable title, as when he obtained the goods by fraud, the seller can rescind the sale while the buyer is still the owner. If, however, the buyer resells the property to a bona fide purchaser before the seller has rescinded the transaction, the subsequent purchaser acquires valid title.[41] It is immaterial whether the buyer having the voidable title had obtained title by fraud as to his identity, or by larceny by trick, or that he had paid for the goods with a bad check, or that the transaction was a cash sale and the purchase price has not been paid.[42]

8 / Goods retained by the seller. When the seller after making the sale is permitted to retain possession of the goods, he has the power to transfer the title to a buyer in the ordinary course of business. Such permitted retention is an entrusting within the sale by entrustee rule described in (1), page

---

[38] See p. 489.
[39] UCC Sec. 7-502(2).
[40] See p. 426.
[41] UCC Sec. 2-403(1).
[42] Sec. 2-403(1)(a) to (d).

427. The purpose of this provision is to protect the second purchaser, on the ground that he had the right to rely on the apparent ownership of his seller.

(a) PROTECTION OF THE SELLER. As will be discussed in connection with the remedies of the parties, a seller who is lawfully in possession of property that he has sold may resell it to a second purchaser if the first purchaser is in default in the payment of the purchase price. Here the object of the statute is not to protect the second purchaser but to enable the seller to remedy the situation created by the first purchaser's default.

(b) PROTECTION OF CREDITORS OF THE SELLER. The continued possession of goods by the seller after their sale is generally deemed evidence that the sale was a fraud upon creditors, that is, that the sale was not a bona fide actual transfer of title but was merely a device to place the title out of the reach of the creditors of the seller. When the sale is fraudulent by local law, the Code provides that creditors of the seller may treat the sale as void and may have the property put up for sale on execution as though the property still belonged to the seller. However, the retention of possession by a merchant seller is declared not fraudulent when made in good faith in the current course of business and when it does not exceed a period of time which is commercially reasonable.[43] For example, the fact that the merchant retains possession until transportation of the goods is arranged is not fraudulent as to creditors.

QUESTIONS AND PROBLEMS

1. Checklist of legal terms:
   (a) existing goods, identified goods; future goods (418)
   (b) sale on approval, sale or return (424)
   (c) commercial unit (424)
   (d) fungible goods (425)

2. State the objective(s) of each of the following rules of law:
   (a) In the absence of any statement to the contrary, title to existing goods identified at the time of contracting and not involving documents passes to the buyer at the time and place of contracting.
   (b) Although a buyer is guilty of fraud in obtaining the sale to him, the seller cannot recover the property from the buyer's purchaser who has bought in good faith and for value.

3. Budd enters into a contract to buy 25 sheep out of Cobb's flock. The next day Budd learns that the entire flock has been sold and delivered to Fields. Budd sues Cobb for conversion of the 25 sheep which he alleges belong to him. Is he entitled to judgment on this or any other basis?

---

[43] Sec. 2-402(2).

4. Baker agrees to purchase a certain quantity of cotton that Freeman, the seller, agrees to bale. The cotton is destroyed before it is baled. Upon whom does the loss fall in each of the following situations?

   (a) Freeman is an ordinary seller.
   (b) Freeman is a merchant seller.

5. Rice directs Huntington to send him 1,000 bushels of corn by railroad freight. When does title to the goods pass?

6. When Selby ships merchandise purchased by O'Brien, Selby makes out the bill of lading to his (Selby's) agent. Who bears the risk of loss during the shipment?

7. Trimble orders goods from Simes on trial for 15 days. The goods are destroyed during this period. The seller brings an action for the price contending that Trimble has title to the goods during this period subject to his right to revest the title in Simes by returning the goods. Do you agree?

8. A manufacturer sells five vending machines of a new type to a dealer. The terms of the agreement provide that the buyer can return the machines within 60 days if he does not succeed in selling them. Twenty days later the machines are destroyed by fire. Upon whom does the loss fall?

9. Dow, who has 30 tons of coal in a bin, sells 10 tons of it to Bowring. Before Bowring calls for his coal, who has title to the coal in the bin?

10. Coleman orders a specified number of sacks of cement mix from Newman who, according to agreement, marks the goods C.O.D. and delivers them to the carrier. The goods are lost in transit. Who must suffer the loss?

11. Eastern Supply Co. purchased lawn mowers from the Turf Man Sales Corp. The purchase order stated on its face "Ship direct to 30th & Harcum Way, Pitts., Pa." Turf Man delivered the goods to Helm's Express, Inc. for shipment and delivery to Eastern at the address in question. Did title pass on delivery of the goods to Helm or upon their arrival at the specified address? (In Re Eastern Supply Co., [D.C. W.D. Pa.], F.S. [Pa.], 21 D.&C.2d 128, 107 Pitts.Leg.J. 451, affirmed [C.A.3d] 331 F.2d 852)

12. Burke fraudulently induced Cavanaugh Bros. to sell him a horse. Three months later Burke sold the horse to Porell, a bona fide purchaser. Cavanaugh sued Porell to obtain the horse on the theory that because of Burke's fraud he never obtained title and Cavanaugh Bros. still owned the horse. Decide. (Porell v. Cavanaugh Bros., 69 N.H. 364, 41 A. 860)

Chapter 37

Obligations of Parties and Performance

The parties to a sales contract are bound to perform according to its terms. Each is likewise under the duty to exercise good faith in its performance [1] and to do nothing that would impair the expectation of the other party that the contract will be duly performed.[2]

Conditions Precedent to Performance

In most sales contracts the duties of the seller and buyer are concurrent. Each one has the right to demand that the other perform at the same time. That is, as the seller hands over the goods, the buyer theoretically must hand over the purchase money. If either party refuses to act, the other party has the right to withhold his performance.[3]

The duty of a party to a sales contract to perform his part of the contract may be subject to a *condition precedent*, that is, by the terms of the contract he is not required to perform until some event occurs or until some act is performed. Quite commonly the condition precedent is performance by the other party. Thus a contract may provide that the seller shall deliver merchandise but that the buyer must first pay for it in full. Under this contract the duty of the seller to deliver the merchandise is subject to the condition precedent of payment in full by the buyer. If the buyer never performs his part of the contract, the duty of the seller never arises.

> **Facts:** Frankart agreed to buy Bultman's piano for $575. It was agreed by the parties that the contract should be "no good" until a down payment of $200 was made. Frankart never made the down payment. Bultman sued him for breach of contract.
>
> **Decision:** Judgment for Frankart. When the parties specify that a contract is not to have any effect until a condition is satisfied or a contingency occurs, there is no contract until that term is met, and neither party can sue the other before that time. (Bultman v. Frankart, 194 Wis. 296, 215 N.W. 432)

---

[1] Uniform Commercial Code, Sec. 1-203. In the case of a merchant, good faith means honesty in fact and the observance of reasonable commercial standards of fair dealing in the trade. UCC Sec. 2-103(1)(b).

[2] Sec. 2-609(1). As to demand for assurance of performance, see p. 439.

[3] Secs. 2-507, 2-511.

In the event that a condition precedent to the obligation of one party is not fulfilled, he may either repudiate the transaction or waive nonfulfillment of the condition and hold the other party to his promise. If there is a promise that the condition shall happen or be performed, the promisee may treat nonperformance as a breach of contract and claim damages of the other party for failing to bring about the fulfillment of the condition.

Seller's Duty to Deliver

It is the seller's duty to make "delivery," [4] which does not refer to a physical delivery but merely means that the seller must permit the transfer of possession of the goods to the buyer. The delivery must be made in accordance with the terms of the sale or contract to sell. [5]

1 / Place, time, and manner of delivery. The terms of the contract determine whether the seller is to send the goods or the buyer is to call for them, or whether the transaction is to be completed by the delivery of documents without the movement of the goods. In the absence of a provision in the contract or usage of trade, the place of delivery is the seller's place of business, if he has one; otherwise, it is his residence. If, however, the subject matter of the contract consists of identified goods that are known by the parties to be in some other place, that place is the place of delivery. Documents of title may be delivered through customary banking channels. [6]

If the seller is required to send the goods but the agreement does not provide for the time of sending them, he must send the goods within a reasonable time. An effectual tender or offer of delivery by the seller must be made at a reasonable hour. [7] The same rule applies to a demand for possession of the goods by the buyer. What constitutes a reasonable hour is a question of fact to be determined in view of the circumstances of each case.

2 / Quantity delivered. The buyer has the right to insist that all the goods be delivered at one time. If the seller delivers a smaller quantity than that stipulated in the contract, the buyer may refuse to accept the goods. If the buyer accepts or retains part of the goods with knowledge of the seller's intention to deliver no more, he must pay the full contract price, unless the contract is divisible so that it is possible to apportion the contract price, in which case the buyer need only pay the proportionate price representing the items or units which he has received. If the goods are used or

---

[4] *Permalum Window & Awning Mfg. Co.* v. *Permalum Mfg. Co.,* [Ky.] 412 S.W.2d 863.

[5] UCC Sec. 2-301.

[6] Sec. 2-308.

[7] Sec. 2-503(1)(a).

disposed of by the buyer before he learns of the seller's intention, the buyer is only required to pay the fair value of the goods he has received.

3 / Delivery in installments. The buyer is under no obligation or duty to accept delivery of goods by installments unless the contract contemplates such deliveries [8] or unless the circumstances are such as to give rise to the right to make delivery in lots.[9]

When the contract provides for delivery and payment by installments, a difficult problem is presented when the seller fails to make a proper delivery or when the buyer fails to pay for one or more installments. For example, *A* agrees to sell 6,000 tons of coal to *B* to be delivered in three equal monthly installments. During one month *A* delivers only 150 tons. The courts in some states hold that the buyer must accept the remaining installments, although he is entitled to damages for the deficiency in the short delivery. Other states take the view that time is of the essence of such contracts and that a failure to deliver or to pay a particular installment goes to the root of the contract, entitling the other party to rescind the entire transaction.

There is a breach of the entire contract whenever the seller's default as to one or more installments substantially impairs the value of the whole contract.[10] Whether the breach of contract is so material that it justifies the injured party in refusing to carry out the remaining terms of the contract and suing for damages for breach of the entire contract, or whether the breach applies only to the defective or missing installments so that the buyer is only entitled to damages as to them, depends on the terms of the contract and the circumstances of the case.

> **Facts:** The Continental Grain Co., a grain dealer, made a contract with the Simpson Feed Co., a grain elevator company, to purchase approximately five carloads of soybeans, delivery to be made from October 1 to November 30 at seller's option, with the buyer to furnish the seller shipping instructions as each of the cars was loaded. On October 30, the first car was loaded and shipping instructions given by the buyer the same day. The next day a second car was loaded, but instructions were not given until after 48 hours. The seller refused to accept such delayed instructions and canceled the contract. The buyer then purchased four carloads of soybeans in the market and brought suit for the difference between the market and the contract price.

---

[8] Sec. 2-307.

[9] Sec. 2-307. This situation would arise whenever it is physically impossible because of the buyer's limited facilities or commercially impractical for any reason for the seller to make complete delivery.

[10] UCC Sec. 2-612(3). The buyer, however, may waive the breach and he is deemed to reinstate the contract if he accepts a nonconforming installment without seasonably notifying the seller that he cancels the contract, or if he sues with respect only to past installments, or if he demands the delivery of future installments.

Decision: Judgment for buyer. Time was not of the essence. The buyer's delay in giving instructions was not any indication of an inability or unwillingness on the part of the buyer to pay for the goods. The cancellation by the seller was therefore unreasonable and constituted a breach of the contract for which he was liable to the buyer. (Continental Grain Co. v. Simpson Feed Co., [D.C. E.D. Ark.] 102 F.S. 354, affirmed 199 F.2d 284 [C.A.8th])

According to the Restatement of the Law of Contracts, if payment is to be made for each installment, the delivery of each installment and the payment for each installment are conditions precedent to the respective duties of the buyer to accept and of the seller to deliver subsequent installments.[11]

4 / Delivery to carrier. When the seller is required to or may send the goods to the buyer but the contract does not require him to make a delivery at a particular destination, the seller, in the absence of a contrary agreement, must put the goods in the possession of a proper carrier and make such contract for their transportation as is reasonable in view of the nature of the goods and other circumstances of the case. The seller must also obtain and promptly deliver or tender in properly indorsed form any document, such as a bill of lading, which is required by the buyer in order to obtain possession of the goods. The seller must likewise promptly notify the buyer of the shipment.[12] If the seller fails to notify the buyer or to make a proper contract of carriage, the buyer may reject the goods when material delay or loss is caused by such breach.[13]

5 / Delivery at destination. If the contract requires the seller to make delivery at a destination point, the duty of the seller is the same as though he were dealing with the buyer face to face, rather than placing the goods in the possession of a carrier. In addition, however, if any documents are issued by the carrier that are necessary to obtain possession of the goods, the seller must also tender such documents.[14]

6 / Cure of defective tender. The seller or vendor has the right to make a second tender or delivery after the first is properly rejected by the buyer because it does not conform to the contract. If the time for making delivery under the contract has not expired, the seller need only give the buyer seasonable (timely) notice of his intention to make a proper delivery within the time allowed by the contract, and he may then do so. If the time for making the delivery has expired, the seller is given an additional reasonable time in which to make a substitute conforming tender if he so notifies

---

[11] Restatement of Contracts, Sec. 272, Illus. 1.
[12] UCC Sec. 2-504.
[13] Sec. 2-504.
[14] Sec. 2-503(3).

the buyer and if he had acted reasonably in making the original tender, believing that it would be acceptable.[15]

Buyer's Duty to Accept Goods

It is the duty of the buyer to accept the delivery of proper goods.

1 / Right to examine goods. Unless otherwise agreed, the buyer, when tender of the goods is made, has the right before payment for or acceptance of the goods to inspect them at any reasonable place or time and in any reasonable manner to determine whether they meet the requirements of the contract.[16] A C.O.D. term, however, bars inspection before payment unless there is an agreement to the contrary.[17]

2 / What constitutes acceptance. Acceptance ordinarily is an express statement by the buyer that he accepts or approves the goods. It may also consist of conduct which expresses such an intent, such as the failure to object within a reasonable period of time or the use of the goods in such a way as would be inconsistent with a rejection of them by the buyer.[18]

Facts: The J. Bartel Company ordered coats from Knobel to be shipped from the seller's factory in New York to the buyer's store in Wisconsin. When the goods were received, some of the coats were damaged; but all were given the regular store tags by the buyer and hung up in the store. The buyer also attempted by a steaming process to remedy the defect. Later the buyer offered to pay the seller in full for those coats that were in good condition but not for the defective coats. The seller then sued for the total contract price. The buyer defended on the ground that it had not accepted the coats.

Decision: Judgment for seller. The buyer had accepted the goods through his conduct, which was inconsistent with continued ownership by the seller. The buyer also had lost any right he might have had by unreasonably delaying in giving notice of refusal to accept. (Knobel v. J. Bartel Co., 176 Wis. 393, 187 N.W. 188)

A buyer accepts an automobile when he signs a contract stating that he accepts it "in good order" and drives it to his home.[19] A buyer, of course, accepts the goods when he modifies them, because such action is inconsistent with the continued ownership of the goods by the seller. Consequently, when the purchaser of a truck installed a hoist and dump bed on it, such action was inconsistent with ownership by the seller and the buyer therefore became liable for the contract price of the truck.[20]

---

[15] Sec. 2-508.
[16] Sec. 2-513(1).
[17] Sec. 2-513(3)(a). See p. 439 for a similar provision for c.i.f. shipments.
[18] Sec. 2-606.
[19] *Razmus* v. *Thompson's Lincoln-Mercury Co.,* 209 Pa.Super. 120, 224 A.2d 782.
[20] *Park County Implement Co.* v. *Craig,* [Wyo.] 397 P.2d 800.

3 / Effect of acceptance on breach. Acceptance of the goods by the buyer does not discharge the seller from liability in damages or other legal remedy for breach of any promise or warranty in the contract to sell or the sale. But the seller is not liable if, after acceptance of the goods, the buyer fails to give notice of the breach of any promise or warranty within a reasonable time after the buyer knows or ought to know of the breach.[21]

Buyer's Duty to Pay

The buyer is under a duty to pay for the goods at the contract rate for any goods accepted.[22] In the absence of a contrary provision, payment must be made in cash and must be made concurrently with receipt of the goods; and, conversely, payment cannot be required before that time.[23]

A buyer is not required to pay for partial or installment deliveries unless the contract so requires. As a qualification to the foregoing, if delivery by lots is proper and the price can be apportioned, the buyer must pay for each lot as delivered.[24]

The seller may accept a commercial paper, such as a check, in payment of the purchase price. This form of payment, unless the parties expressly agree otherwise, is merely a conditional payment, that is, conditional upon the instrument's being honored and paid. If the instrument is not paid, it ceases to be payment of the purchase price and the seller is then an unpaid seller.[25] Refusal of payment by check does not affect the rights of the parties under the sales contract as long as the seller gives the buyer a reasonable time in which to procure the legal tender with which to make payment.[26]

The parties may agree to a sale on credit. This may be done for each sale individually or for sales generally, as in the case of a charge account in a department store. When a sale is made on credit, the parties may include special provisions to protect the seller.

Tender of the purchase price has the same effect as actual payment in imposing upon the seller the duty to make delivery. If the seller fails to make delivery when a proper tender or offer of payment is made, he is in default under the contract.

It must also be remembered that if the seller is in default, the buyer may rescind the contract; in which case, after making the rescission, he is no longer under a duty to maintain the tender.

---

[21] UCC Sec. 2-607(2), (3). This section rejects the view that acceptance of the goods is a waiver of any claim for damages.

[22] Secs. 2-301, 2-607(1).

[23] Sec. 2-310(a). If delivery under the contract is to be made by a delivery of document of title, payment is due at the time and place at which the buyer is to receive the document regardless of where the goods are to be received. Sec. 2-310(c).

[24] Sec. 2-307.

[25] Sec. 2-511.

[26] *Silver* v. *Sloop Silver Cloud,* [D.C. S.D. N.Y.] 259 F.S. 187.

Duties under Particular Terms

A sale may be as simple as a face-to-face exchange of money and goods, but it frequently involves a more complicated pattern, with some element of transportation, generally by a common carrier. This, in turn, generally results in the addition of certain special terms to the sales transaction.

1 / F.O.B. The term "f.o.b.," or "free on board," may be used with reference to the seller's city, or the buyer's city, or an intermediate city, as in the case of a transshipment. It may also be used with reference to a named carrier, such as f.o.b. a specified vessel, car, or other vehicle. In general, an f.o.b. term is to be construed as requiring delivery to be made at the f.o.b. point, as contrasted with merely a shipment to that point,[27] and as imposing upon the seller the risk and expense involved in getting the goods to the designated place or on board the specified carrier.[28]

> **Facts:** Custom Built Homes purchased unassembled prefabricated houses from Page-Hill in Minnesota to be delivered by the seller "f.o.b. building site . . . Kansas." The seller brought the houses to the building site by tractor-trailer, where he would unhitch the trailer and unload the shipment. Kansas taxed Custom Built on the sale on the theory that the sale was made in Kansas.

> **Decision:** Judgment for Tax Commission. Under the terms of the contract the seller was required to deliver the goods to the buyer at the building site in Kansas without charge for transportation to that point. As no contrary intention appeared from the contract, the title to the goods passed at the building site. The sale therefore took place in Kansas and was subject to tax there. (Custom Built Homes Co. v. Kansas State Commission of Revenue, 184 Kan. 31, 334 P.2d 808)

2 / C.I.F. The term "c.i.f." indicates that the payment by the buyer covers the cost (the selling price of the goods), insurance on them, and freight to the specified destination of the goods. The c.i.f. term imposes upon the seller the obligation of putting the goods in the possession of a proper carrier, of loading and paying for the freight, of procuring the proper insurance, and of preparing an invoice of the goods and any other document needed for shipment, and of forwarding all documents to the buyer with commercial promptness.[29]

---

[27] See p. 435. When a port is selected as the f.o.b. point for an imported article, the price is frequently described as the price "p.o.e." or "port of entry."

[28] UCC Sec. 2-319(1).

[29] Sec. 2-320(1), (2). The term "c. & f." or "c.f." imposes the same obligations and risks as a c.i.f. term with the exception of the obligation as to insurance. Under a c. & f. contract, the seller completes his performance by delivery of the goods to the carrier and by proper payment of the freight charges on the shipment, whereupon title and risk of loss pass to the buyer. *Amco Transworld Inc.* v. *M/V Bambi*, [D.C. S.D. Tex.] 257 F.S. 215.

Under a c.i.f. contract the buyer bears the risk of loss after the goods have been delivered to the carrier.[30] He must pay for the goods when proper documents representing them are tendered to him, which in turn means that he is not entitled to inspect the goods before paying for them, unless the contract expressly provides for payment on or after the arrival of the goods.[31]

3 / Ex-ship. If the contract provides for delivery ex-ship, the seller bears the risk of loss until the goods have left the ship's tackle or have otherwise been properly unloaded. He must discharge all liens arising from the transportation of the goods and must furnish the buyer with such documents or instructions as enables him to obtain the goods from the carrier.[32]

4 / No arrival, no sale. When goods are sent under such a term, the seller bears the risk of loss during transportation; but if the goods do not arrive, he is not subject to that liability for in such case there is no sale. The buyer is protected in that he is only required to pay for the goods if they arrive.

The "no arrival, no sale" contract requires the seller to ship proper conforming goods and to tender them on their arrival if they do arrive. He must, of course, refrain from interfering in any way with the arrival of the goods.[33]

Adequate Assurance of Performance

Whenever a party to the sales transaction has reason to believe that the other party may not perform his part of the contract, he may make a written demand upon the other party for adequate assurance that he will in fact perform his contract. For example, when goods are to be delivered at a future date or in installments over a period of time, the buyer may become fearful that the seller will not be able to make the future deliveries required. The buyer may in such case require assurance from the seller that the contract will be performed.[34]

1 / Form of assurance. The person upon whom demand for assurance is made must give "such assurance of due performance as is adequate under the circumstances of the particular case." [35] The Code does not specify the exact form of assurance. If the party on whom demand is made has an estab-

---

[30] UCC Sec. 2-320(2)(a). The c.i.f. and c. & f. contracts may be modified to place the risk of deterioration during shipment on the seller by specifying that the price shall be based on the arrival or "out turn" quality, or by having the seller warrant the condition or quality of the goods on their arrival. Sec. 2-321(2).

[31] Sec. 2-320(4), 2-321(3).

[32] Sec. 2-322(2).

[33] Sec. 2-324(a).

[34] Sec. 2-609(1). Between merchants the reasonableness of the grounds for insecurity is determined according to commercial standards. Sec. 2-609(2).

[35] Sec. 2-609(4).

lished reputation, his reaffirmance of his contract obligation and a statement that he will perform may be sufficient to assure a reasonable man that it will be performed. In contrast, the person's reputation or economic position at the time may be such that there is no assurance that there will be a proper performance in the absence of a guarantee by a third person or the furnishing of security by way of a pledge or other device to protect the demanding party against default.[36]

2 / Failure to give assurance. The party on whom demand is made may state he will not perform; that is, he repudiates the contract. In contrast with a flat repudiation, the party upon whom demand is made may fail to reply or may give only a feeble answer that is not sufficient to assure a reasonable man that performance will be made. The failure to provide adequate assurance within thirty days after receiving the demand, or a lesser time when thirty days would be unreasonable, constitutes a repudiation of the contract.[37]

QUESTIONS AND PROBLEMS

1. Checklist of legal terms:
   (a) condition precedent (432)
   (b) f.o.b. (438), c.i.f. (438), ex-ship (439)

2. State the objective(s) of each of the following rules of law:
   (a) Ordinarily the place of delivery of goods is the seller's place of business.
   (b) In the absence of a contrary provision, a seller cannot require payment before delivery of the goods.

3. Hansen agreed to buy from Darnell a table that was known by both parties to be stored in Brown's Warehouse. Later Hansen refused to pay on the ground that Darnell failed to deliver the table to Hansen's residence. Is Darnell entitled to judgment in an action against Hansen for damages?

4. Eich agreed to sell Chaney 100 pieces of cloth of 60 yards to the piece at a specified price per yard. The cloth that Eich delivered measured 50 to 53 yards to the piece. When Chaney refused to accept and pay for the goods, Eich brought an action to recover damages for a breach of contract. Was Eich entitled to judgment?

5. Caldwell orders certain merchandise from Berling and specifies that it be shipped by insured parcel post. Berling ships the merchandise by parcel post but does not insure the merchandise. In case of damage to the goods, what are Caldwell's rights?

---

[36] Between merchants the adequacy of any assurance is determined according to commercial standards. UCC Sec. 2-609(2).

[37] Sec. 2-609(4). This enables the adverse party to take steps at an earlier date to protect himself against the default of the other party, as by making substitute contracts to replace the repudiated contracts.

6. Blaine orders certain goods from Feldman. After checking Blaine's credit, Feldman decides to ship the merchandise C.O.D. When the goods arrive, Blaine insists upon inspecting the goods before making payment. Does he have this right?

7. Dykes delivers 100 barrels of syrup over and above the amount ordered by Garrison. Garrison accepts the entire quantity but refuses to pay more than the market price for the extra 100 barrels. Is Dykes entitled to judgment in an action to recover payment for the extra quantity at the higher contract price?

8. Holbrook sells and delivers certain goods to Kearns. In an action by Holbrook to recover the price of the goods, Kearns proves that he made a valid tender of the agreed amount, which Holbrook refused. Is Holbrook entitled to judgment?

9. Pastor, in Detroit, sells merchandise to Otto, in Joliet, Illinois. The goods are to be sent f.o.b. Chicago. When does title pass?

10. Upon Stevens' order, Post ships certain merchandise to Stevens under a c.i.f. contract.

    (a) When does risk of loss pass?
    (b) In the absence in the contract of a provision for payment, when must Stevens pay for the goods?

11. Fleet purchased an ice cream freezer and compressor unit from Lang. Thereafter Fleet disconnected the compressor and used it to operate an air conditioner. When sued for the purchase price of the freezer and compressor unit, Fleet claimed that he had not accepted the goods. Was he correct? (Lang v. Fleet, 193 Pa.Super. 365, 165 A.2d 258)

12. Weinstein contracted to sell International Minerals and Metals Corporation scrap metal to be delivered within 30 days. Later the seller informed the buyer that it could not make delivery within that time. The buyer agreed to an extension of time, but no limiting date was set. Within what time must the seller perform? (International Minerals and Metals Corp. v. Weinstein, 236 N.C. 558, 73 S.E.2d 472)

13. The Tri-Bullion Smelting & Development Co. agreed to sell, and Jacobsen to buy, the seller's output of zinc concentrates for a two-year period. A year and a half later, the Tri-Bullion Co. closed its mine and notified Jacobsen that it would make no further deliveries. Jacobsen refused to pay for the last shipment. Jacobsen sued the Tri-Bullion Co. The defendant contended that the plaintiff had breached the contract by failure to pay for the goods delivered. Do you agree? (Tri-Bullion Smelting & Development Co. v. Jacobsen, 147 C.A. 454, 233 F. 646)

Chapter 38

Warranties and Product Liability

The seller may make a guarantee with respect to the goods. If they are not as guaranteed, he may be held liable for the breach of his guarantee. Even when he has not made a guarantee, the law will in some instances hold him responsible as though he had made a guarantee. This type of obligation is called a *warranty*.

Kinds of Warranties

1 / Express warranties. An *express warranty* is a part of the basis for the sale;[1] that is, the buyer has purchased the goods on the reasonable assumption that they were as stated by the seller. Thus a statement by the seller with respect to the quality, capacity, or other characteristic of the goods is an express warranty. To illustrate, the seller may say: "This cloth is all wool," "This paint is for household woodwork," or "This engine can produce 50 horsepower."

(a) FORM OF EXPRESS WARRANTY. No particular form of words is necessary to constitute an express warranty. A seller need not state that he makes a warranty nor even intend to make a warranty.[2] It is sufficient that the seller assert a fact which would naturally induce the buyer to rely and act on the seller's statement. It is not necessary that the seller make an express statement, for the express warranty may be found in his conduct. Accordingly, if the buyer asks for a can of outside house paint and the seller hands him a can of paint, the seller's conduct expresses a warranty that the can is outside house paint.

The seller's statement may be written or printed, as well as oral. The words on the label of a can and in a newspaper ad for "boned chicken" constitute an express warranty that the can contains chicken that is free of bones.[3]

A statement as to the goods may also bind the seller even though it was actually made by the manufacturer, as in the case of a label placed by the latter on a can of household paint. Here the seller is bound by an express

---

[1] Uniform Commercial Code, Sec. 2-313(1).
[2] UCC Sec. 2-313(2).
[3] *Lane* v. *Swanson*, 130 Cal.App.2d 210, 278 P.2d 723.

warranty even though the buyer selected the can of paint from a shelf and without comment paid for it. The seller, by exposing the can to sale with the manufacturer's label appearing on it, has in effect adopted that label as his own statement and it therefore constitutes an express warranty by the seller.

(b) TIME OF MAKING EXPRESS WARRANTY. It is immaterial whether the express warranty is made at the time of or after the sale. No separate consideration is required for the warranty when it is part of a sale. If a warranty is made after the sale, no consideration is required since it is regarded as a modification of the sales contract.[4]

(c) SELLER'S OPINION OR STATEMENT OF VALUE. "An affirmation merely of the value of the goods or a statement purporting to be merely the seller's opinion or commendation of the goods does not create a warranty." [5] A purchaser, as a reasonable man, should not believe such statements implicitly, and therefore he cannot hold the seller to them should they prove false. Thus "sales talk" by a seller that "this is the best piece of cloth in the market" or that glassware "is as good as anyone else's" is merely an opinion which the buyer cannot ordinarily treat as a warranty.

It is probable, however, that the Code will permit an exception to be made, as under the prior law, where the circumstances are such that a reasonable man would rely on such a statement. If the buyer has reason to believe that the seller is possessed of expert knowledge of the conditions of the market and the buyer requests his opinion as an expert, the buyer would be entitled to rely on the seller's statement as to whether a given article was the best obtainable. The criterion is whether a reasonable man would rely on the statement. Thus a statement by a florist that bulbs are of first-grade quality may be relied upon as a warranty.[6]

As another exception to the principle that there is no liability for an opinion, which will probably be recognized under the Code, the seller may be liable when he does not have the belief that he asserts. For example, when the seller knows that a dog is sick and refuses to warrant the animal but states that it is sound as far as he knows, his statement is a warranty as to the absence of his knowledge of any unsoundness.

(d) DUPLICATING WARRANTIES. When it is held that privity is not required and that the buyer may claim the benefits of a warranty made by the manufacturer or former seller, the fact that the warranty of the immediate seller is merely a repetition of the warranty of the remote

---

[4] UCC Sec. 2-313. Official Comment, point 7.
[5] Sec. 2-313(2).
[6] *Diepeveen* v. *Vogt*, 27 N.J.S. 254, 99 A.2d 329.

warrantor does not prevent the immediate seller from being liable for breach of warranty.

Facts: Scovil Motor Co. sold an automobile engine to Chilcoat stating that it was guaranteed for 6,000 miles or 6 months, whichever should occur first. When the engine proved defective, Chilcoat sued Scovil who raised the defense that he was merely repeating the warranty made by the manufacturer.

Decision: Judgment for Chilcoat. When the immediate seller makes the same statements as the manufacturer, he becomes liable on such statements just as though the manufacturer had not made the statements. Thus the warranty liability of a seller is not affected by the circumstance that the warranty he makes is the same as the manufacturer's warranty. (Scovil v. Chilcoat, [Okla.] 424 P.2d 87)

2 / Implied warranties. An *implied warranty* is one that was not made by the seller but which is implied by the law. In certain instances the law implies or reads a warranty into a sale although the seller did not make it. That is, the implied warranty arises automatically from the fact that a sale has been made; as compared with express warranties, which arise because they form part of the basis on which the sale has been made.

The fact that express warranties are made does not exclude implied warranties; and when both express and implied warranties exist, they should be construed as consistent with each other and as cumulative if such construction is reasonable. In case it is unreasonable to construe them as consistent and cumulative, an express warranty prevails over an implied warranty as to the same subject matter, except in the case of an implied warranty of fitness for a particular purpose.[7]

Warranties of All Sellers

A distinction is made between a merchant seller and the casual seller. The Code provides for a greater range of warranties in the case of the merchant seller. The following warranties apply to all sellers:

1 / Warranty of title. Every seller, by the mere act of selling, makes a warranty that his title is good and that the transfer is rightful.[8] A warranty of title may be specifically excluded, or the circumstances may be such as to prevent the warranty from arising. The latter situation is found when the buyer has reason to know that the seller does not claim to hold the title or that he is claiming to sell only such right or title as he or a third person may

---

[7] UCC Sec. 2-317.

[8] Sec. 2-312(1)(a). A warranty of title, as well as a warranty of freedom from encumbrances, which arises when a sale is made, is not classified as an implied warranty by the Code even though it is in the nature of an implied warranty.

have.[9] For example, no warranty of title arises when the seller makes the sale in a representative capacity, such as a sheriff, an auctioneer, or an administrator. Likewise no warranty arises when the seller makes the sale by virtue of a power of sale possessed by him as a pledgee or mortgagee.[10]

2 / Warranty against encumbrances. Every seller by the mere act of selling makes a warranty that the goods shall be delivered free from any security interest or any other lien or encumbrance of which the buyer at the time of the sales transaction had no knowledge.[11] Thus there is a breach of warranty when the automobile sold to the buyer is already subject to an outstanding encumbrance that had been placed on it by the original owner and which was unknown to the buyer at the time of the sale.[12]

This warranty refers to the goods only at the time they are delivered to the buyer and is not concerned with an encumbrance which existed before or at the time the sale was made. For example, a seller may not have paid in full for the goods which he is reselling and the original supplier may have a lien on the goods. The seller may resell the goods while that lien is still on them, and his only duty is to pay off the lien before he delivers the goods to the buyer.

The warranty against encumbrances may be excluded expressly or by the circumstances of the case in the same manner as a warranty of title.[13] By definition, a warranty against encumbrances does not arise if the buyer knows of the existence of the encumbrance in question, although this must be an actual knowledge as contrasted with a constructive notice, which the law deems possessed by everyone by virtue of the fact that an encumbrance is filed or recorded on the public record.

3 / Warranty of conformity to seller's statement or promise. Whenever a statement or promise made by the seller constitutes an express warranty, it is binding on the seller regardless of the type of seller involved.[14]

4 / Warranty of conformity to description, sample, or model. When the contract is based in part on the understanding that the seller will supply goods according to a particular description or that the goods will be the same as the sample or a model, the seller is bound by an express warranty that the goods shall conform to the description, sample, or model.[15] Ordinarily a *sample* is a portion of a whole mass that is the subject of the transaction, while a *model* is a replica of the article in question. The mere fact

---

[9] Sec. 2-312(2).
[10] See Ch. 41.
[11] UCC Sec. 2-312(1)(b).
[12] *Kruger* v. *Bibi*, [N.Y.S.2d] 3 UCCRS 1132.
[13] See preceding topic.
[14] See p. 442.
[15] UCC Sec. 2-313(1)(b), (c).

that a sample is exhibited in the course of negotiations does not make the sale a sale by sample, as there must be an intent manifested that the sample be part of the basis of contracting.[16]

5 / Warranty of fitness for a particular purpose. If the buyer intends to use the goods for a particular or unusual purpose, as contrasted with the ordinary use for which they are customarily sold,[17] the seller makes an implied warranty that the goods will be fit for the purpose when the buyer relies on the seller's skill or judgment to select or furnish suitable goods, and when the seller at the time of contracting knows or has reason to know the buyer's particular purpose and his reliance on the seller's judgment.[18] For example, where a government representative inquired of the seller whether the seller had a tape suitable for use on the government's NCR-304 computer system, there arose an implied warranty, unless otherwise excluded, that the tape furnished by the seller was fit for that purpose.[19]

The fact that the seller did not intend to make a warranty of fitness for a particular purpose is immaterial. Parol evidence is admissible to show that the seller had knowledge of the buyer's intended use.[20]

Additional Warranties of Merchant Seller

In addition to the warranties made by every seller, a merchant seller makes the following additional implied warranties.

1 / Warranty against infringement. Unless otherwise agreed, every seller who is a merchant regularly dealing in goods of the kind which he has sold warrants that the goods shall be delivered free of the rightful claim of any third person by way of patent or trademark infringement or the like.[21]

2 / Warranty of merchantability or fitness for normal use. A merchant seller who makes a sale of goods in which he customarily deals [22] makes an implied warranty of merchantability.[23] The warranty is in fact a group of warranties, the most important of which is that the goods are fit for the ordinary purposes for which they are sold. Consequently, when the

---

[16] *Sylvia Coal Co.* v. *Mercury Coal & Coke Co.*, [W.Va.] 156 S.E.2d 1.
[17] See the topic that follows.
[18] UCC Sec. 2-315. This warranty applies to every seller, but as a matter of fact it will probably always be a merchant seller who has such skill and judgment that the Code provision could be applicable. For example, when a seller of coal has had no experience in the selection of coal for the manufacture of coke, no implied warranty of fitness for that purpose arises. *Sylvia Coal Co.* v. *Mercury Coal & Coke Co.*, [W.Va.] 156 S.E.2d 1.
[19] *Appeals of Reeves Soundcraft Corp.*, [ASBCA] 2 UCCRS 210.
[20] *General Electric Co.'s Appeal,* (U.S.Dept.Interior, Board of Contract Appeals) 73 I.D. 95, 3 UCCRS 510.
[21] UCC Sec. 2-312(3).
[22] This includes the seller of food or drink to be consumed on the premises or to be taken out. UCC Sec. 2-314(1).
[23] Sec. 2-314(1).

seller of ice-making and beverage-vending machines is a merchant of such machines, an implied warranty of fitness for use arises.[24] Also included are implied warranties as to the general or average quality of the goods, and their packaging and labeling.[25]

The implied warranty of merchantability relates to the condition of the goods at the time the seller is to perform under the contract. Once the risk of loss has passed to the buyer,[26] there is no warranty as to the continuing merchantability of the goods unless such subsequent deterioration or condition is proof that the goods were in fact not merchantable when the seller made delivery.

There is no warranty that customers of the buyer will want to buy the goods, that is, "merchantability" does not mean that the buyer will be able to resell the goods.

Warranty of fitness only relates to the fitness of the product that is made or sold. It does not impose upon the manufacturer or seller the duty to employ any particular design or to sell one product rather than another because another might be safer.

Facts: Evans purchased a Chevrolet station wagon made by General Motors. While driving the station wagon, he was struck on the left side by another vehicle. The left side of the station wagon collapsed and inflicted fatal injuries. An action was brought on behalf of his estate against General Motors, claiming that the station wagon had been negligently constructed in that it was built on an X-frame (of two supporting rails crossing diagonally under the body of the car) and that the collapse of the left side would have been avoided if General Motors had added side rails to the X-frame.

Decision: Judgment for General Motors. The requirement that the automobile be fit for its intended purpose did not mean that it must be made accident-proof, particularly in view of the fact that the purpose of the automobile is not engaging in collisions. The fact that some competitors put side rails on the frames, and that some expert stated that this would be safer, did not create liability for failing to do so. (Evans v. General Motors Corp., [C.A.7th] 359 F.2d 822)

Warranties in Particular Sales

Particular types of sales may involve special considerations.

1 / Sale of food or drink. The sale of food or drink, whether to be consumed on or off the seller's premises, is a sale and, when made by a merchant, carries the implied warranty that the food is fit for its ordinary

---

[24] *S.F.C. Acceptance Corp.* v. *Ferree,* [Pa.] 39 D.&C.2d 225.
[25] UCC Sec. 2-314(2). Other implied warranties on the part of a merchant may also arise from a course of dealing or usage of trade. Sec. 2-314(3).
[26] See Ch. 36.

purpose, that is, human consumption.[27] Under the prior law some authorities held that there was no breach of warranty when a harmful object found in the food was natural to the particular kind of food, such as an oyster shell in oysters, a chicken bone in chicken, and so on. Other cases regarded the warranty as breached when the harm-causing substance in the food was such that its presence could not be reasonably expected, without regard to whether the substance was natural, or foreign, as in the case of a nail or piece of glass.

The Code does not end the conflict between courts applying the "foreign-natural" test and those applying the "reasonable-expectation" test. The significance of the two is that in the first test a buyer is barred from recovery as a matter of law where he finds the "natural" substance in the food, as a cherry pit in a cherry pie; whereas under the reasonable expectation test, it is necessary to make a determination of fact, ordinarily by the jury, to determine whether the buyer could reasonably expect the object in the food.[28]

It is, of course, necessary to distinguish the foregoing situations from those in which the preparation of the foods contemplates the continued presence of some element which is not removed, such as prune stones in cooked prunes.

Facts: Webster ordered a bowl of fish chowder in the Blue Ship Tea Room. She was injured by a fish bone in the chowder. She sued the Tea Room for breach of warranty. It was shown that when chowder is made, the entire unboned fish is cooked.

Decision: As the soup was typically made with whole fish, it was apparent that the presence of fish bones in the soup should be foreseen by a reasonable person. Consequently, the warranty of merchantability was not broken. (Webster v. Blue Ship Tea Room, 347 Mass. 421, 198 N.E.2d 309)

2 / Sale of article with patent or trade name. The sale of a patent- or trade-name article is treated with respect to warranties in the same way as any other sale. The fact that the sale is made on the basis of the patent or trade name does not bar the existence of a warranty of fitness for a particular purpose when the circumstances giving rise to such a warranty otherwise exist.[29]

It is a question of fact, however, whether the buyer relied on the seller's skill and judgment when he made the purchase. That is, if the buyer asked for a patent- or trade-name article and insisted on it, it is apparent that he did not rely upon the seller's skill and judgment and therefore the factual basis for an implied warranty of fitness for the particular purpose is lacking.[30]

---

[27] UCC Sec. 2-314(1), (2)(c).
[28] *Hunt* v. *Ferguson-Paulus Enterprises,* 243 Ore. 546, 415 P.2d 13.
[29] See p. 446.
[30] UCC Sec. 2-315, Official Comment, point 5.

If the necessary reliance upon the seller's skill and judgment is shown, however, the warranty arises in that situation.

Facts: Sperry Rand Corp. agreed to convert the recordkeeping system of Industrial Supply Corp. so that it could be maintained by a computer and to sell a computer and nine other items necessary for such a record-keeping system. The computer and the equipment were ordered by identified trade name and number. When the system did not work, Industrial Supply sued Sperry Rand for breach of implied warranty of fitness. Sperry Rand raised the defense that there was no such warranty because the equipment had been ordered by trade name and number.

Decision: The fact that the equipment was ordered by trade name and number did not show that the buyer was purchasing at its risk. The circumstances showed the sale was made in reliance on the seller's skill, and with appreciation of the buyer's problems, and the sale of the particular equipment to the buyer was made as constituting the equipment needed by it. Under such circumstances, a warranty of the fitness of the equipment for such purpose was implied. (Sperry Rand Corp. v. Industrial Supply Corp., [C.A.5th] 337 F.2d 363)

The seller of automobile parts is not liable for breach of the implied warranty of their fitness when the parts were ordered by catalog number for use in a specified vehicle and the seller did not know that the lubrication system of the automobile had been changed so as to make the parts ordered unfit for use.[31]

3 / Sale on buyer's specifications. When the buyer furnishes the seller with exact specifications for the preparation or manufacture of goods, the same warranties arise as in the case of any other sale of such goods by the particular seller. No warranty of fitness for a particular purpose can arise, however, since it is clear that the buyer is purchasing on the basis of his own decision and is not relying on the seller's skill and judgment.

In sales made upon the buyer's specifications, no warranty against infringement is impliedly made by the merchant seller;[32] and conversely, the buyer in substance makes a warranty to protect the seller from liability should the seller be held liable for patent violation by following the specifications of the buyer.[33]

4 / Sale of secondhand or used goods. No warranty arises as to fitness of used property for ordinary use when the sale is made by a casual seller. If made by a merchant seller, such a warranty may sometimes be implied.

---

[31] *Mennella* v. *Schork,* 49 Misc.2d 449, 267 N.Y.S.2d 428.
[32] See p. 446.
[33] UCC Sec. 2-312(3).

Prior to the Code a number of states followed the rule that no warranty arose in connection with used or secondhand goods, particularly automobiles and machinery; [34] whereas some courts found a warranty of fitness for ordinary use in the sale of secondhand goods, particularly airplanes. It is likely that this division of authority will continue under the Code.[35]

Exclusion and Surrender of Warranties

Warranties may be excluded or surrendered by the agreement of the parties, subject to the limitation that such a provision must not be unconscionable.[36] It is proper for the jury to consider the purchase price in determining the scope of the warranty of fitness, as where coal was bought for one-half or less the price of standard coal.[37]

If a warranty of fitness [38] is excluded or surrendered in writing, it must be conspicuous to assure that the buyer will be aware of its presence.[39] If the implied warranty of merchantability is excluded, the exclusion clause must expressly mention the word "merchantability" and must be conspicuous.

1 / Particular provisions. Such a statement as "there are no warranties which extend beyond the description on the face hereof" excludes all implied warranties of fitness.[40] Implied warranties are excluded by the statement of "as is," "with all faults," or other language which in normal common speech calls attention to the warranty exclusion and makes it clear that there is no implied warranty.[41] For example, an implied warranty that a steam heater would work properly in the buyer's dry cleaning plant was effectively excluded by provisions that "the warranties and guarantees herein set forth are made by us and accepted by you in lieu of all statutory or implied warranties or guarantees, other than title. . . . This contract contains all agreements between the parties and there is no agreement, verbal or otherwise, which is not set down herein," and the contract contained only a "one year warranty on labor and material supplied by [seller]." [42]

In order for a disclaimer of warranties to be a binding part of an oral sales contract, the disclaimer must be called to the attention of the buyer.

---

[34] *Kilborn* v. *Henderson,* 37 Ala.App. 173, 65 So.2d 533.
[35] See UCC Sec. 2-314, Official Comment, point 3.
[36] Secs. 2-316(1), 2-302(1). As to unconscionability, see p. 151. A distinction must be made between holding that the circumstances do not give rise to a warranty, thus precluding warranty liability, and holding that the warranty which would otherwise arise has been excluded or surrendered by the contract of the parties. As to the exclusion of the warranties of title and warranty against encumbrances, see pp. 444-445.
[37] *Sylvia Coal Co.* v. *Mercury Coal & Coke Co.,* [W.Va.] 156 S.E.2d 1.
[38] By the letter of the Code, the text statement is applicable to any warranty of fitness, see UCC Sec. 2-316(2), although by the Official Comment to Sec. 2-316, point 4, it would appear to be only the warranty of fitness for a particular purpose.
[39] As to the definition of "conspicuous," see UCC Sec. 1-201(10).
[40] Sec. 2-316(2).
[41] Sec. 2-316(3)(a).
[42] *Thorman* v. *Polytemp,* [N.Y.S.2d] 2 UCCRS 772.

When the contract as made does not disclaim warranties, a disclaimer of warranties that accompanies the goods which are delivered later is not effective because it is a mere unilateral attempt to modify the contract.[43]

2 / Examination. There is no implied warranty with respect to defects in goods that an examination should have revealed when the buyer before making the final contract has examined the goods, or a model or sample, or has refused to make such examination.[44]

3 / Dealings and customs. An implied warranty may be excluded or modified by course of dealings, course of performance, or usage of trade.[45]

Caveat Emptor

In the absence of fraud on the part of the seller or circumstances in which the law finds a warranty, the relationship of the seller and buyer is aptly described by the maxim of *caveat emptor* (let the buyer beware). Courts at common law rigidly applied this rule, requiring the purchaser in the ordinary sale to act in reliance upon his own judgment except when the seller gave him an express warranty. The trend of the earlier statutes, the Uniform Commercial Code, and decisions of modern courts has been to soften the harshness of this rule, primarily by implying warranties for the protection of the buyer. The rule of caveat emptor is still applied, however, when the buyer has full opportunity to make such examination of the goods as would disclose the existence of any defect and the seller is not guilty of fraud.

Product Liability

When harm to person or property results from the use or condition of an article of personal property, the person injured may be entitled to recover damages. This right may be based on the theory that there was a breach of warranty or that the person sued was negligent.

1 / Breach of warranty. At common law the rule was that only the parties to a transaction had any rights relating to it. Accordingly, only the buyer could sue his immediate seller for breach of warranty. The rule was stated in the terms that there could be no suit for breach of warranty unless there was a privity of contract between the plaintiff and the defendant.

In most states an exception to the privity rule developed under which members of the buyer's family and various other remote persons not in privity of contract with the seller or manufacturer can sue for breach of

---

[43] *Admiral Oasis Hotel Corp.* v. *Home Gas Industries, Inc.*, 68 Ill.App.2d 297, 216 N.E.2d 282.
[44] UCC Sec. 2-316(3)(b). *Sylvia Coal Co.* v. *Mercury Coal & Coke Co.*, [W.Va.] 156 S.E.2d 1.
[45] UCC Sec. 2-316(3)(c).

warranty when injured by the harmful condition of food, beverages, or drugs. The right to sue the manufacturer of a bottled or packaged food might be denied where there is evidence that another person has or might have tampered with the item before it reached the buyer or consumer.

The Code expressly abolishes the requirement of privity to a limited extent by permitting a suit for breach of warranty to be brought against the seller by members of the buyer's family, his household, and his guests, with respect to personal injury sustained by them.[46] Apart from the express provision made by the Code, there is a conflict of authority as to whether privity of contract is required in other cases, with the trend being toward the abolition of that requirement. In many states, the doctrine is flatly rejected when suit is brought by a buyer against the manufacturer or a prior seller. In many instances, recovery by the buyer against the remote manufacturer or seller is based on the fact that the defendant had advertised directly to the public and therefore made a warranty to the purchasing consumer of the truth of his advertising. But while advertising by the manufacturer to the consumer is a reason for not requiring privity when the consumer sues the manufacturer, the absence of advertising by the manufacturer does not bar such action by the buyer.[47]

Facts: Hamon purchased Lestoil, a household detergent, from Digliani. She was severely burned by it and sued the seller and its manufacturers, the Lestoil Corporation and the Adell Chemical Company. The manufacturers had extensively promoted the product by television, radio, and newspapers, stating that it could be used safely for household and cleaning tasks and that it was "the all-purpose detergent—for all household cleaning and laundering." The manufacturers defended on the ground that Hamon had not purchased the bottle of Lestoil from them.

Decision: The absence of privity (the fact that the plaintiff had not purchased the product from the defendant) was not a defense. The sale of the product had been promoted by mass media advertising appealing directly to the consumer, and therefore the manufacturer could not raise the defense of lack of privity when the consumer responded to its advertising. (Hamon v. Digliani, 148 Conn. 710, 174 A.2d 294)

Recovery may also be allowed when the consumer mails to the manufacturer a warranty registration card which the manufacturer had packed with the purchased article.

---

[46] Sec. 2-318. Note that this does not cover property loss which the beneficiary might sustain, and that it does not extend to employees of the buyer nor such third persons as pedestrians. The Code expressly leaves open for local state law to determine whether the requirement of privity is abolished further than declared by the Code. A nephew who lives next door to his aunt is a member of her family or household and therefore comes within the scope of UCC Sec. 2-318. *Miller* v. *Preitz*, 422 Pa. 383, 221 A.2d 320.

[47] *Lonzrick v. Republic Steel Corp.*, 6 Ohio 2d 227, 35 O.O.2d 404, 218 N.E.2d 185.

2 / Negligence. Independently of the provisions of the Code, a person injured through the use or condition of personal property may be entitled to sue the manufacturer for the damages which he sustains on the theory that the defendant was negligent in the preparation or manufacture of the article. Historically, such suits were limited by the concept of privity of contract so that only the buyer could sue the seller for the latter's negligence but the buyer could not sue the manufacturer for the latter's negligence. This requirement of privity has generally been abolished. The modern rule is that whenever the manufacturer as a reasonable man should foresee that if he is negligent a particular class of persons will be injured by his product, the manufacturer is liable to an injured member of that class without regard to whether such plaintiff purchased from him or from anyone.

As in the ordinary tort case, there is no liability when harm is not foreseeable. For example, when the law requires that a particular product be used with a safety device, the manufacturer of the product is not negligent when the product is used without the safety device required by law. Thus the manufacturer of grinding wheels had the right to anticipate that the danger of injury from flying fragments of the wheel would be reduced or eliminated by the use of a protective shield as was required by law and was therefore not under any obligation to make the wheels "accident-proof" when used without a protective shield.[48]

3 / Comparison of liability for breach of warranty and for negligence. In many states, an injured plaintiff has the choice of suing for breach of warranty or for damages for negligence. The importance of the distinction between the two remedies lies in the fact that to prove his case for breach of warranty the plaintiff is only required to prove facts of which he has direct knowledge or about which he can readily learn. That is, he need only show that there was a sale and a warranty, that the goods did not conform to the warranty, and that he was injured thereby. In the case of the action for negligence against the manufacturer, the plaintiff figuratively must also go into the defendant's plant or factory and learn how the given article was made and prove in court that there was negligence. Unless the plaintiff is able to show that the design of the manufacturer's product or his general method of manufacture was faulty, it is likely that the plaintiff will be unable to prove that there was negligence. It has been the recognition of this difficulty which, to a large degree, has led the courts to expand the warranty liability under which proof of negligence is not required.

A manufacturer or seller may assume by the terms of his contract a liability broader than would arise from a mere warranty.

---

[48] *Bravo v. Tiebout,* 40 Misc.2d 558, 243 N.Y.S.2d 335.

Facts: Spiegel purchased a jar of skin cream from Saks 34th Street. It had been manufactured by the National Toilet Co. The carton and the jar stated that it was chemically pure and absolutely safe. When Spiegel used the cream, it caused a severe skin rash. She sued Saks and National.

Decision: Judgment for Spiegel. The statements on the carton and the jar constituted an express warranty binding both the seller and the manufacturer. The statement that it was safe was an absolute undertaking that it was safe for everyone; as distinguished from merely an implied warranty of reasonable fitness, which would be subject to an exception of a particular allergy of a plaintiff. (Spiegel v. Saks 34th Street, 43 Misc.2d 1065, 252 N.Y.S.2d 852)

4 / Effect of reprocessing by distributor. Liability of the manufacturer or supplier to the ultimate consumer, whether for warranty or negligence, does not arise when the manufacturer or supplier believes or has reason to believe that the immediate distributor or processor is to complete processing or is to take further steps that will remove an otherwise foreseeable danger.[49] Accordingly, although the supplier of unfinished pork to a retailer should realize that it might contain trichinae and be dangerous to the ultimate consumers, he is not liable to an ultimate consumer who contracts trichinosis when the retailer in purchasing the unfinished pork told the supplier that he would finish processing it, which would destroy any trichinae, and the supplier did not know or have reason to know that the retailer failed to do so.

Identity of Parties

The existence of product liability may be affected by the identity of the claimant or of the defendant.

1 / Third persons. Historically, third persons, meaning persons who were not "buyers" from anyone, such as guests, employees, or total strangers, were denied recovery because of the absence of privity. The Code, however, permits recovery for breach of warranty by the guests of the buyer [50] but makes no provision as to recovery by employees or strangers.

There is a conflict of authority as to whether an employee of the buyer may sue the seller or manufacturer for breach of warranty. In some jurisdictions the employee's right to recover is denied on the ground that he is outside of the distributive chain, not being a buyer. Others allow recovery in such a case.[51] By the latter view, an employee of a construction contractor may recover for breach of the implied warranty of fitness made by the manu-

---

[49] *Schneider* v. *Suhrmann,* 8 Utah 2d 35, 327 P.2d 822.
[50] See p. 452.
[51] *Barfield* v. *Atlantic Coast Line R.R.,* [Fla.] 197 So.2d 545.

facturer of the structural steel which proved defective and, falling, injured the employee.[52]

In some states, the courts have ignored privity of contract when the injured person was not even a subpurchaser but a member of the public or a stranger at large by adopting a doctrine of strict tort liability, which makes a manufacturer liable to anyone who is injured because of a defect in the manufacture of the product when such defect makes the use of the product dangerous to the user or to persons in the vicinity of the product and the person injured or killed is such a user or person in the vicinity.[53] There is also a growing trend to allow recovery by the "stranger" on the theory of breach of warranty. Thus it has been held that a repairman fixing an automobile who is injured because of a defect therein may sue the manufacturer for breach of implied warranty of fitness.[54]

2 / Manufacturer of component part. Many items of goods in today's market place were not made entirely by one manufacturer. Thus the harm caused may result in a given case from a defect in a component part of the finished product. As the manufacturer of the total article was the buyer from the component part manufacturer, it followed that the privity rule barred suit against the component part manufacturer for breach of warranty by anyone injured. In jurisdictions in which privity of contract is not recognized as a bar to recovery, it is not material that the defendant manufactured merely a component part. That is to say, the manufacturer of a component part cannot defend from suit by the ultimate purchaser on the ground of absence of privity. Thus the purchaser of a tractor trailer may recover from the manufacturer of the brake system of the trailer for damages sustained when the brake system failed to work.[55] Likewise, a person injured while on a golf course when an automobile parked on the club parking lot became "unparked" and ran down hill can sue the manufacturer of the defective parking unit.

Nature and Cause of Harm

1 / Nature of harm. The greatest inroad in the concept of privity of contract has been made where the plaintiff has been personally injured as contrasted with economically harmed. Motivated by the social force that places protection of the person of the individual above that of property rights, the law has been more willing to extend the field of liability to aid the

---

[52] *Lonzrick* v. *Republic Steel Corp.,* 6 Ohio 2d 227, 35 O.O. 2d 404, 218 N.E.2d 185.
[53] *Mitchell* v. *Miller,* 26 Conn.Sup. 142, 214 A.2d 694.
[54] *Connolly* v. *Hagi,* 24 Conn.Sup. 198, 188 A.2d 884.
[55] *Suvada* v. *White Motor Co.,* 32 Ill.2d 612, 210 N.E.2d 182.

plaintiff who has been physically injured by a runaway tractor than the plaintiff not able to use the tractor that he purchased and was required to rent another tractor, thereby sustaining an economic rather than a physical loss.

2 / Cause of harm. The harm sustained by the product-liability plaintiff must have been "caused" by the defendant. Here the concepts are the same as in the case of "proximate cause" in tort liability, regardless of whether suit is brought for the negligence of the defendant or on the theory of breach of warranty.

QUESTIONS AND PROBLEMS

1. Checklist of legal terms:
   (a) warranty (442); express warranty (442), implied warranty (444)
   (b) sample, model (445)
   (c) caveat emptor (451)

2. State the objective(s) of each of the following rules of law:
   (a) A statement by a seller may constitute a warranty even though he does not state that he makes a warranty and generally even though he does not intend to make a warranty.
   (b) A manufacturer-seller may in some cases be liable for harm caused by negligence in the manufacture of his product as well as for breach of warranty as to its fitness.

3. A dealer in television sets states to Raye, "This color TV is the finest on the market at the price." Relying on this statement, Raye purchases the set. Upon discovering that the dealer's statement is false, Raye brings an action for breach of warranty. Is he entitled to judgment?

4. While negotiating the sale of a parakeet to Nester, Sherm states, "This bird is healthy, as far as I know." Nester purchases the parakeet in reliance on Sherm's statement. In an action against Sherm, Nester proves that Sherm knew at the time of the sale that the bird was diseased. Is Nester entitled to judgment?

5. Walters sells a set of carpenter tools to Peters. The tools actually belong to Underhill who had possession of them at the time of the sale. Peters brings an action against Walters to recover damages for breach of warranty. Is he entitled to recover?

6. Sands buys a truck at a sale of the personal property of a deceased person. Later the truck is taken from Sands by a finance company which has a security interest in it. Sands brings an action for damages for breach of warranty against the administrator of the estate. Is he entitled to judgment?

7. At Hartlaub's store Skinner asked for a certain type of grass seed. Hartlaub sold Skinner grass seed which was presumably the kind requested.

Skinner sowed the seed; and when it started to grow, he discovered that the grass was of a different kind than he had requested. Was he entitled to judgment in an action brought against Hartlaub for breach of warranty?

8. The Tudor Supply Company sold certain grain by description to Shafer, a retail dealer. Part of the grain delivered by the company was unsalable because it was wet and decayed. Was there a breach of warranty on the part of the seller?

9. Van Dyke orders a certain quantity of a specified grade of leather. He plans to use the material in making luggage. When he discovers that the leather is not suitable for that purpose, he brings an action against the seller for damages arising out of a breach of warranty. Is he entitled to judgment?

10. Distinguish by examples the difference between an implied warranty of fitness for a particular purpose and an implied warranty of merchantability.

11. Wetzel, a dealer, purchased a poultry feed additive called Gro-factor Poultry Supplement from Bingman Laboratories. The public did not buy the supplement. When Bingman sued Wetzel for the purchase price, he claimed that there was a breach of warranty of merchantability because the goods did not sell. Was he correct? (Wetzel v. Bingman Lab., Inc., 39 Ala.App. 506, 104 So.2d 452)

12. Scanlon was a factory employee. At lunch he purchased from a cart vendor, Food Crafts, a hard roll sandwich. It was later shown that the roll was stale and unfit for human consumption. Because of the hardness of the roll, Scanlon broke a tooth. He then sued Food Crafts for the dental bill. Food Crafts denied liability and claimed that the plaintiff's tooth had broken because it was weak. Decide. (Scanlon v. Food Crafts, Inc., 2 Conn.Cir. 3, 193 A.2d 610)

13. Hodge Chile Co. negotiated for the purchase of food cartons from Interstate Folding Box Co. Interstate sent samples of its boxes to Hodge without making any statement as to their qualifications. Hodge subjected the samples to various tests and then placed an order for the boxes with Interstate. Hodge did not pay for the boxes and, when sued for their purchase price, claimed that there was a breach of an implied warranty of fitness of the boxes for use for their intended purpose. It was shown that the defects of which Hodge complained had not been revealed in the tests because the cartons had been filled by hand instead of by machine and the chile that had been put in the boxes was poured at a lower temperature than when poured by machine. Did Hodge have a valid defense? (Interstate Folding Box Co. v. Hodge Chile Co., [Mo.App.] 334 S.W.2d 408)

14. Aegis Productions, Inc. made a contract with Arriflex Corp. for the latter to repair a motion picture camera. The repairs were not properly made. Was Arriflex liable to Aegis for breach of warranty under the Code? (Aegis Productions, Inc. v. Arriflex Corp. 25 App.Div.2d 639, 268 N.Y.S.2d 185)

Chapter 39

Remedies for Breach of Sales Contract

If one of the parties to a sales contract fails to discharge his responsibilities, the other party has several remedies available. In addition, the parties may have included certain provisions pertaining to remedies for breach in their contract.

Remedies of the Seller

1 / Seller's lien. In the absence of a provision for the extension of credit to the purchaser, the seller has a lien on the goods or the right to retain possession of the goods until he is paid for them. Even when the goods are sold on credit, the seller has a lien on the goods if the buyer becomes insolvent or the credit period expires while the goods are in the seller's possession.

The seller's lien is a specific lien, which attaches to the particular goods and only for the purchase price due on them. It cannot be exercised by the seller for the purpose of collecting any other debt or charge owed him by the purchaser.

The seller's lien may be lost by (a) waiver, as by extension of credit, (b) delivery of the goods to a carrier or other bailee for the purpose of delivery to the buyer, without a reservation of title or possession, (c) acquisition of the property by the buyer or his agent by lawful means, (d) payment or tender of the price by the buyer.

Facts: McAuliffe & Burke Co. sold plumbing fixtures to Levine but refused to deliver them unless immediate payment was made in cash. The buyer gave the sellers a worthless check which he assured the sellers was "good as gold." On the basis of this statement, the sellers surrendered the goods to the buyer. Thereafter a creditor of Levine brought an action against him, and the sheriff, Gallagher, seized the goods thus delivered to Levine. The sellers, learning that the check was worthless, claimed that they were entitled to a lien on the goods and sued Gallagher for their return.

Decision: Judgment for the sellers. The lien of the sellers is not lost when possession is unlawfully obtained. Here it had been obtained by the fraudulent representation that the check was "as good as gold," and the sellers could therefore recover the property. (McAuliffe & Burke Co. v. Gallagher, 258 Mass. 215, 154 N.E. 755)

Delivery of part of the goods to the buyer does not bar a lien on the remainder of the goods unless the parties intended that it should have that effect. Moreover, if the buyer is insolvent, the seller may refuse to deliver any further goods unless paid for in cash, not only for those goods but also for any previously supplied under the contract.[1]

2 / Completion or salvage of repudiated contract. It may be that the buyer repudiates or otherwise breaches the contract while the seller has some or all of the goods in his possession in either a finished and ready-to-deliver stage or in a partially manufactured stage. If the seller has in his possession goods that satisfy or conform to the contract with the buyer, he may identify those goods to the contract which the buyer has broken.[2] This will enable the seller to sue the buyer for the purchase price and to make a resale of the goods, holding the buyer responsible for any loss thereon.

If the goods intended for the buyer are in an unfinished state, the seller must exercise reasonable commercial judgment to determine whether (a) to sell them for scrap or salvage or (b) to complete their manufacture, then identify them to the buyer's contract, and resell them.[3] In any case the buyer is liable for the loss sustained by the seller if the latter has acted properly.

3 / Stopping delivery by carrier or bailee. The goods may be in transit on their way to the buyer. They also may be in the hands of a bailee who is to surrender them to the buyer. The seller may stop delivery of the goods to the buyer, without regard to the quantity involved, if the buyer is insolvent.[4] In addition, the seller may stop delivery if the quantity involved is a carload, truckload, or planeload, or more, whenever the buyer has repudiated the contract or failed to make a payment due before delivery or if for any reason the seller would have the right to retain or reclaim the goods.[5]

Except for a carrier's lien for transportation or a bailee's lien for storage charges, the right to stop delivery is superior to other claims. Thus, when the creditors of the buyer attach the goods en route, their claims are subject to the right of the seller.

After the seller regains possession of the goods by stopping delivery, he is in the same legal position as though he had not placed them on the carrier or delivered them to the bailee and may assert against them a seller's lien. When the seller reserves title or the right to possession, the seller need not

---

[1] Uniform Commercial Code, Sec. 2-702(1).
[2] Sec. 2-704(1)(a).
[3] Sec. 2-704(1)(b), (2).
[4] A person is insolvent when he has ceased to pay his debts in the ordinary course of business, or cannot pay his debts as they become due, or is insolvent within the meaning of the Federal Bankruptcy Law. UCC Sec. 1-201(23).
[5] Sec. 2-705(1).

invoke the right to stop delivery since he can withhold the property from the buyer by virtue of such reservation.

(a) EXERCISE OF THE RIGHT. The seller exercises the right to stop delivery by notifying the carrier or bailee that the goods are to be returned to or held for him. If the seller gives the carrier or bailee proper notice in sufficient time so that through the exercise of due diligence it can stop delivery, the carrier or bailee must obey the seller's order. Any additional cost involved must be borne by the seller. If the carrier or bailee fails to act, it is liable to the seller for any loss he sustains.

After proper notice has been given to it, the carrier or bailee must follow the instructions of the seller as to the disposal of the goods. When a negotiable document of title for the goods is in circulation, however, the carrier or bailee is not obliged to deliver the goods until the document is surrendered. The holder of such a document may defeat the seller's right of stopping delivery.[6]

(b) TERMINATION OF RIGHT TO STOP DELIVERY. The seller's right to stop delivery is terminated or lost, even though a proper notification is given, when (1) the goods have been delivered to the buyer, (2) the carrier acknowledges the right of the buyer by reshipping at his direction or by agreeing to hold for him as a warehouseman; (3) the bailee in possession acknowledges that he holds the goods for the buyer, or (4) the seller has negotiated to the buyer a negotiable document of title covering the goods.[7]

4 / Reclamation of goods received by insolvent buyer. The buyer may have obtained goods from the seller on credit when, unknown to the seller, the buyer was insolvent. If the buyer made a false written statement to the seller that he was solvent and received the goods within three months after that time, the seller may at any time demand and reclaim the goods sold to the buyer on credit.[8] If the buyer never made a false written statement of solvency, or if he made it more than three months before he received the goods, the seller, in order to reclaim the goods, must demand the return of the goods within ten days after they are received by the buyer.[9]

5 / Resale. When the buyer has broken the contract by wrongfully rejecting the goods, wrongfully revoking his acceptance, failing to pay, or repudiating the contract, the seller may resell the goods or the balance of them remaining in his possession, or the goods over which he has reacquired possession as by stopping delivery. After the resale, the seller is not liable

---

6 Sec. 2-705(3)(c).
7 Sec. 2-705(2).
8 Sec. 2-702(2).
9 Sec. 2-702(2).

to the original buyer upon the contract or for any profit obtained by him on the resale. On the other hand, if the proceeds are less than the contract price, the seller may recover the loss from the original buyer.[10]

Unless otherwise agreed, the resale may be made either as a public or auction sale or as a private sale, as long as the method followed is commercially reasonable. Certain formalities for the resale are prescribed. A person who purchases in good faith acquires the goods free of all claims of the original buyer, even though the resale was irregular because the seller did not follow the procedure prescribed for such a sale.[11]

Reasonable notice must be given to the original buyer of the intention to make a private sale. Such notice must be given him of a public sale unless the goods are perishable in character or threaten to decline speedily in value. Notice of a public sale must also be given to the general public in such manner as is commercially reasonable under the circumstances.

6 / Cancellation. When the buyer wrongfully rejects the goods, wrongfully revokes an acceptance of the goods, repudiates the contract, or fails to make a payment due on or before delivery, the seller may cancel the contract.[12] Such action puts an end to the contract, discharging all obligations on both sides that are still unperformed, but the seller retains any remedy with respect to the breach by the buyer.[13] Cancellation necessarily revests the seller with title to the goods.

7 / Action for damages. If the buyer wrongfully refuses to accept the goods or if he repudiates the contract, the seller may sue him for the damages that the seller sustains. In the ordinary case the amount of damages is to be measured by the difference between the market price at the time and place of the tender of the goods and the contract price.[14]

If this measure of damages does not place the seller in the position in which he would have been placed by the buyer's performance, recovery may be permitted of lost profits, together with an allowance for overhead.[15] The seller may in any case recover as incidental damages any commercially reasonable charges, expenses, or commissions incurred in enforcing his remedy, such as those sustained in stopping delivery; in the transportation, care, and custody of the goods after the buyer's breach; and in the return or resale of the goods.[16] Such incidental damages are recovered in addition to any other damages that may be recovered by the seller.

---

[10] Sec. 2-706(1), (6).
[11] Sec. 2-706(5).
[12] Sec. 2-703(f).
[13] Sec. 2-106(4).
[14] Sec. 2-708(1); *Iverson* v. *Schnack*, 263 Wis. 266, 57 N.W.2d 400.
[15] UCC 2-708(2).
[16] Sec. 2-710.

8 / Action for the purchase price. The seller may bring an action to recover the purchase price, together with incidental damages as described in connection with the action for damages, if (a) the goods have been accepted and there has not been any rightful revocation of acceptance; (b) conforming goods were damaged or destroyed after the risk of loss passed to the buyer; or (c) the seller has identified proper goods to the contract but after the buyer's breach has been or will be unable to resell them at a reasonable price.[17] In consequence of these limitations, the right to sue for the contract price, as distinguished from a suit for damages for breach of the sales contract, is a remedy that is seldom available to the seller.

Remedies of the Buyer

1 / Rejection of improper delivery. If the goods or the tender made by the seller do not conform to the contract, the buyer has the choice (a) of rejecting the entire quantity tendered, (b) of accepting the entire tender, or (c) of accepting any one or more commercial units and rejecting the rest.[18] Delivery of the goods to a carrier constitutes delivery to the buyer for the purpose of title and risk of loss but is not an "acceptance" of the goods by the buyer, and he may reject them if damaged.[19] The rejection must be made within a reasonable time after the delivery or tender, and the buyer must notify the seller of his action.[20] A two-month delay bars rejection when several times during this interval he visited the building in which the purchased goods were kept and took with him several small articles.[21]

After rejecting the goods, the buyer may not exercise any right of ownership as to the goods but must hold them awaiting instructions from the seller. When the goods are perishable or threaten to decline in value rapidly, the buyer is required to make reasonable efforts to sell the goods if he is a merchant and the seller does not have any agent or place of business in the market of rejection.[22] In any case, if the seller does not furnish the buyer any instructions, the buyer has the option of reshipping the goods to the seller at the seller's expense, or of storing or reselling them for the seller's account.[23]

2 / Revocation of acceptance. The buyer may revoke his acceptance of the goods when they do not conform to the contract to such an extent

---

[17] Sec. 2-709(1).

[18] Sec. 2-601.

[19] *Johnson & Dealaman* v. *Hegarty,* 93 N.J.S. 14, 224 A.2d 510 (recognizing that prior law is continued by the Code).

[20] UCC Sec. 2-602. The failure to specify the particular ground for rejection may bar the buyer from proving it in a subsequent action. Sec. 2-605. As to the right of the seller to cure the default, see Sec. 2-508.

[21] *Campbell* v. *Pollack,* [R.I.] 221 A.2d 615.

[22] UCC Sec. 2-603(1).

[23] Sec. 2-604.

that the defect substantially impairs their value to him,[24] provided (a) he accepted the goods without knowledge of the nonconformity, because it could not be reasonably discovered or because the seller has assured him that the goods were conforming; or (b) he accepted the goods with knowledge of the nonconformity but reasonably believed that the defect would be cured by the seller.[25] Revocation of acceptance may be made not only with respect to the entire quantity of goods but also with respect to any lot or commercial unit that is nonconforming. A buyer who revokes his acceptance stands in the same position as though he had rejected the goods when they had been originally tendered.

The acceptance of goods cannot be revoked unless the buyer gives the seller a notice of revocation. The notice because of nonconformity must specify the nonconformity.[26] This notice must be given within a reasonable time after the buyer discovers that the goods do not conform or after he should have discovered it. But a buyer is not required to notify the seller of his intention to revoke his acceptance until the buyer is reasonably certain that the nonconformity of the goods substantially impairs the value of the goods.[27] Hence a period of three weeks is not unreasonable for a buyer to determine that an airplane does not conform to the contract and that such nonconformity impairs the value of the contract.[28] The notice must also be given before there has been any substantial change in the condition of the goods, apart from the change resulting from their own defective condition.[29]

The requirement of a tender of the goods by the buyer, essential to a rescission of the sales contract, does not apply to a revocation of an acceptance, with respect to which it is sufficient that the buyer seasonably notifies the seller.[30]

3 / Possession of goods on seller's insolvency. The buyer may have paid in advance for the goods that are still in the seller's possession. Assuming that the seller then becomes insolvent, can the buyer claim the goods from the possession of the seller or is he limited to making a general claim for the refund of the amount paid for them? If the goods have been identified to the contract by either or both the buyer and seller, and the seller becomes insolvent within ten days after receipt of the first installment of the price, the buyer is entitled to recover the goods. The buyer who makes a partial payment has a similar right of reclamation if the seller

---

[24] The Code requires "substantial impairment of value" in order to bar revocation of acceptance for trivial matters that may be easily corrected; *Rozmus* v. *Thompson's Lincoln-Mercury Co.*, 209 Pa.Super. 120, 224 A.2d 782.

[25] UCC Sec. 2-608(1).

[26] *Lanners* v. *Whitney*, [Ore.] 428 P.2d 398.

[27] *Lanners* v. *Whitney*, [Ore.] 428 P.2d 398.

[28] *Lanners* v. *Whitney*, [Ore.] 428 P.2d 398.

[29] UCC Sec. 2-608(2).

[30] *Campbell* v. *Pollack*, [R.I.] 221 A.2d 615.

becomes insolvent within ten days after the first payment is made, but he must pay the balance due.[31]

4 / Action for damages for breach of contract. If the seller fails to deliver as required by the contract or repudiates the contract, or if the buyer properly rejects tendered goods or revokes his acceptance as to such goods, the buyer is entitled to sue the seller for damages for breach of contract. The buyer is entitled to recover the difference between the market price at the time the buyer learned of the breach and the contract price.[32]

Within a reasonable time after the seller's breach, the buyer may *cover*, that is, procure the same or similar goods elsewhere. If the buyer acts in good faith, the measure of damages for the seller's nondelivery or repudiation is then the difference between the cost of cover and the contract price.[33] The buyer is not under duty to cover and his right to damages is not affected by his failure to cover.[34]

In any case the buyer is entitled to recover incidental and consequential damages, but he must give the seller credit for expenses saved as a result of the seller's breach.

(a) NOTICE OF BREACH OF CONTRACT AS TO ACCEPTED GOODS. If the buyer has accepted goods that do not conform to the contract or as to which there is a breach of warranty, he must notify the seller of the breach within a reasonable time after he discovers or should have discovered the breach. Otherwise he is not entitled to complain. If the buyer has given the necessary notice of breach, he may recover damages measured by the loss resulting in the normal course of events from the breach.

> **Facts:** Klein sold water softening equipment. His local agent, Schuster, sold a unit to Kopet. After two weeks the unit showed defects about which Kopet complainted to Schuster. After about six months of Schuster's attempting to fix the machine, Kopet notified Klein of the defect. Attempts were made by Klein's repairman to fix the unit. After six more months of attempting to repair the unit, an attorney acting for Kopet wrote Klein that the unit was not operating properly and should be replaced or the purchase price refunded. Klein refused to do either on the ground that Kopet had not given notice within a reasonable time.

> **Decision:** Notice had been given within a reasonable time, although the demand for replacement or refund was not made directly to the defendant and not until a year later. The continuing demands upon the defendant's

---

[31] UCC Sec. 2-502.
[32] Sec. 2-713(1). In the case of anticipatory breach, as when the seller states in advance of the delivery date that he will not perform, the buyer has the option of waiting until the performance date or of treating such repudiation as a breach fixing damages as of that time, unless the buyer effects cover. Sec. 2-610.
[33] Sec. 2-712(2).
[34] Sec. 2-712(3).

local agent and the attempts, first of the agent, and then of the defendant's repairman, to repair the unit, showed that the letter to the defendant was not the first "notice" the defendant had of the defect. (Kopet v. Klein, 275 Minn. 525, 148 N.W.2d 385)

It is not necessary that the buyer give formal "notice of a breach of warranty." It is sufficient that the seller be informed in some manner. Hence, when the buyer sent periodic reports to the seller from which it was apparent that the product was not performing as warranted, the seller had "notice" of the breach.[35] The content of the notice need only let the seller know that a claim has arisen because of a transaction which involves him, and it is not necessary to include a clear statement of all the objections that will be relied upon by the buyer.[36]

(b) WHEN NOTICE NOT REQUIRED. When a buyer sues his seller for product liability based upon tort as distinguished from breach of warranty,[37] or when anyone sues a seller for such tort liability, there is, of course, no requirement that notice be given to the seller. Moreover, when suit is allowed for breach of warranty by a remote buyer or a nonbuyer, that is, when privity of contract is not required, notice is not required for the obvious reason that the person harmed has had no prior opportunity to learn of the defect and probably does not even know the identity of the defendant-seller or manufacturer.

Conversely stated, the requirement of notice of breach of warranty is limited to the single situation where a buyer sues the person from whom he directly made the purchase and sues on the theory of breach of warranty.

(c) MEASURE OF DAMAGES. If suit is brought for breach of warranty, the measure of damages is the difference between the value of the goods as they were when accepted and the value that they would have had if they had been as warranted.

Facts: Holz purchased a Chrysler automobile from the Coates Motor Co. Because of various defects in the car, he sued both Coates and Chrysler for breach of warranty. He claimed that he was entitled to a refund of the purchase price and the financing costs. The defendants showed that the car had been driven between 8,000 to 9,000 miles.

Decision: The fact that the car had been driven a considerable distance showed that it had some value. Therefore, the buyer in the action for money damages for breach of warranty could only recover the difference between the value the car had at the time of the transaction and the value it would have had if it had been as warranted. The buyer

[35] *Babcock Poultry Farm* v. *Shook*, 204 Pa.Super. 141, 203 A.2d 399.
[36] *Nugent* v. *Popular Markets*, [Mass.] 228 N.E.2d 91.
[37] See p. 451.

cannot recover the entire purchase price he has paid if he has made a substantial use of the goods. (Holz v. Coates Motor Co., 206 Va. 894, 147 S.E.2d 152)

In all cases the buyer may recover any incidental or consequential damages sustained.[38] For example, if the merchant seller sells a preservative that he knows will be used by the buyer in the process of preserving other goods, the merchant seller is liable for the destruction of the other goods if the preservative he supplies is not fit for that purpose.

Whenever the buyer would be entitled to recover damages from the seller, he may deduct the amount of them from any balance remaining due on the purchase price provided he notifies the seller that he intends to do so.[39] When the buyer who has accepted the goods is sued for the contract price, he may counterclaim damages for breach of warranty even though the time for revoking the acceptance or rejecting the goods has passed.[40]

(d) NOTICE OF THIRD-PARTY ACTION AGAINST BUYER. The buyer may be sued in consequence of the seller's breach of warranty, as when the buyer's customers sue him because of the condition of the goods which he has resold to them. In such a case it is optional with the buyer whether or not he gives the seller notice of the action against him and requests the seller to defend the action.[41] The buyer may also be sued by a third person because of patent infringement. In this case he must give notice of the action to the seller. Moreover, the seller can demand that the buyer turn over the defense of that action to him.[42]

When the seller is given notice of a suit against the buyer but fails to defend the buyer, the seller cannot dispute the facts shown in that action when he in turn is sued by the buyer.

In any case a buyer has the burden of proving that the goods were not as represented or warranted when he so alleges, whether as a claim in a suit against the seller or as a defense when sued by the seller.

5 / *Cancellation.* The buyer may cancel or rescind the contract if the seller fails to deliver the goods or if he repudiates the contract, or if the buyer has rightfully rejected tendered goods or revoked his acceptance of the goods. The fact that the buyer cancels the contract does not destroy his cause of action against the seller for breach of the contract. The buyer may therefore recover from the seller not only any payment made on the purchase price [48] but, in addition, damages for the breach of the contract. The dam-

---

[38] UCC Sec. 2-714(3).
[39] Sec. 2-717.
[40] *Marbelite Co.* v. *Philadelphia,* 208 Pa.Super. 256, 222 A.2d 443.
[41] UCC Sec. 2-607(5)(a).
[42] Sec. 2-607(3), (5)(b).
[48] *Lanners* v. *Whitney,* [Ore.] 428 P.2d 398.

ages represent the difference between the contract price and the market price, or the difference between the contract price and the cost of cover if the buyer has purchased other goods.[44]

The fact that the goods are returned by the buyer does not in itself establish that there has been a cancellation, since a return of the goods may be merely a revocation of acceptance of the goods with an intent to preserve the contract and receive other goods in exchange.

If the return of the goods to the seller would work a great hardship on the buyer, it may be possible for the buyer to commence an action to obtain a decree of court directing cancellation while retaining the goods until the decree has been entered, rather than putting the buyer to the hardship of doing without such goods.

Facts: Barke was a widow who was not employed. She traded in the house trailer that she used as her home for a new trailer, which was sold to her by Grand Mobile Homes Sales. Because of various defects, she later sued Grand Mobile to rescind the sale. Grand Mobile raised the defense that she could not bring the action without first returning or offering to tender the trailer to Grand Mobile.

Decision: A tender was unnecessary. When a buyer is not claiming to have made a rescission, thereafter suing for a price refund and damages, but is instead bringing an action to have the court set aside the transaction, the buyer is not barred by the fact that the goods had not been returned or tendered to the seller but may await the entry of a court decree directing such return. This rule is followed when it would work a great hardship on the buyer to make an earlier tender. In the present case, a surrender of the trailer prior to the bringing of the action would have made the plaintiff homeless for a number of months. (Barke v. Grand Mobile Homes Sales, 6 Mich.App. 386, 149 N.W.2d 236)

The right of the buyer to cancel or rescind the sales contract may be lost by a delay in exercising that right. A buyer loses the right when he refuses to permit the seller to attempt to make normal adjustments to remedy the defect; with the consequence that when the buyer refused to permit the seller to take the new television set to the shop to determine why the red color was not functioning properly, the buyer was acting unreasonably and lost the right to rescind.[45]

A buyer cannot rescind when with full knowledge of defects in the goods he makes partial payments and performs acts of dominion inconsistent with any intent to rescind.[46]

---

[44] UCC Sec. 2-712(1),(2). In any case, the buyer is entitled to recover incidental and consequential damages as stated on p. 464.

[45] *Wilson* v. *Scampoli,* [C.A.Dist.Col.] 228 A.2d 848.

[46] *Woods* v. *Van Wallis Trailer Sales Co.,* 77 N.Mex. 121, 419 P.2d 964.

6 / Buyer's resale of goods. When the buyer has possession of the goods that he has rightfully rejected or as to which he has revoked his acceptance, he is treated the same as a seller in possession of goods after the default of a buyer. That is, he has a security interest in the goods for his claim against the other party and may resell the goods as though he were a seller.[47] From the proceeds of the sale he is entitled to deduct for himself any payments made on the price and any expenses reasonably incurred in the inspection, receipt, transportation, care and custody, and resale of the goods.[48]

Facts: The Peerless Corporation sold 50 appliances to a dealer, the Hammond Appliance Co. The seller then assigned its contract to Walter E. Heller & Co. When Heller sued Hammond for the purchase price, the latter showed that following the purchase the seller and it had agreed that the goods were defective and had mutually rescinded the contract. In spite of this, the seller never came to pick up the goods even though Hammond repeatedly requested it to do so. After about a year Hammond began repairing the appliances and finally sold 27 of the 50, still having possession of the remaining 23 at the time of the trial. At the trial, in addition to denying liability, Hammond made a counterclaim for the cost of repairing the appliances, the cost of their storage while waiting for the seller to retake them, and the cost of moving the appliances from one store to another in the effort to sell them.

Decision: When a seller refuses without cause to take goods back, the buyer is in the position of an unpaid seller and may charge the seller for storage expenses incurred in holding the goods for instructions and may proceed to sell the goods; but he must hold for the benefit of the seller the proceeds of sale in excess of the amount which the buyer is entitled to for his expenses and for any damages sustained because of the seller's breach of contract. The reasonableness of the amounts to be charged and deducted and the need for a sale by the buyer are questions to be determined by the jury. (Walter E. Heller & Co. v. Hammond Appliance Co., 29 N.J. 589, 151 A.2d 537)

7 / Action for conversion or recovery of goods. When, as a result of the sales agreement, ownership passes to the buyer and the seller wrongfully refuses or neglects to deliver the goods, the buyer may maintain any action allowed by law to the owner of goods wrongfully converted or withheld. Hence, a buyer having the right to immediate possession may bring an action of replevin to recover possession of the goods wrongfully withheld, or he may bring an action to recover the value of the goods on the ground of conversion. Likewise, the buyer may replevy the goods when he satisfies any security interest of the seller in the goods but delivery to the buyer is refused.

---

[47] See p. 460.
[48] UCC Sec. 2-715.

The buyer is also given the right of replevin when the seller has identified the goods to the contract and the circumstances are such that similar goods cannot be reasonably procured by the buyer in the open market.[49] Here it is immaterial whether the title has passed to the buyer, and the action of replevin is in effect an action of specific performance granted to protect the buyer from a harm which would follow from the fact that he is not able to obtain similar goods in the market if he does not obtain them from the seller.

The obligation of the seller to deliver proper goods may be enforced by an order for specific performance when the goods are "unique or in other proper circumstances." [50] This permits the buyer to obtain specific performance, not only when the goods have a peculiar or special quality that makes them unique, but also when it would be a hardship on the buyer to deny him that right. Accordingly, a contract calling for the sale of the seller's output or the supplying of the buyer's requirements may present circumstances where specific performance will be required to permit the buyer to obtain the benefit of his contract.

8 / Remedies for fraud of seller. Independently of the preceding remedies, the buyer has the right to sue the seller for damages for the latter's fraud or to rescind the transaction on that ground.[51] As these remedies for fraud exist independently of the provisions of the Code, the buyer may assert such remedies even when he is barred by the Code from exercising any remedy for a breach of warranty.

Contract Provisions on Remedies

1 / Limitation of damages. The parties may in their sales contract specify that in the event of breach by either party the damages are to be limited to a certain amount. If this amount is unreasonably large, it is void as a penalty. If the amount is reasonable, the injured party is limited to recovering that amount. Whether the limitation is reasonable is determined in the light of the actual harm that would be caused by breach, the difficulty of proving the amount of such loss, and the inconvenience and impracticality of suing for damages or enforcing other remedies for breach.[52]

2 / Down payments and deposits. The buyer may have made a deposit with the seller or an initial or down payment at the time of making the contract. If the contract contains a valid liquidation-of-damages provision, the seller must return any part of the down payment or deposit in excess of the amount specified by the liquidated damages clause. In the absence of

---

[49] Sec. 2-716(3).
[50] Sec. 2-716(1).
[51] Sec. 1-103. As to what constitutes fraud, see Chapter 10. As to the expansion of the damages recoverable, see Sec. 2-721.
[52] Sec. 2-718(1).

such a clause, and in the absence of proof of greater damages sustained by him, the seller's damages are computed as 20 percent of the purchase price or $500, whichever is the smaller. The extent to which the down payment exceeds such amount must be returned to the buyer.[53]

The rule just stated applies to payments made by the buyer in goods as well as in cash as, for example, by making a trade-in. Such goods given in payment are assigned a dollar value for the purpose of determining the payment made by the buyer. If the goods have been resold, their value is the proceeds of the resale; if not, it is the reasonable value of such goods.[54]

3 / Limitation on remedies. The parties may validly limit the remedies. Thus a seller may specify that the only remedy of the buyer for breach of warranty shall be the repair or replacement of the goods, or that the buyer shall be limited to returning the goods and obtaining a refund of the purchase price. How much further the restrictions may go is not clear, but the limitation is not binding if it is unreasonable or unconscionable. The limitation of damages for personal injuries caused by defective goods is prima facie unconscionable, and therefore not binding, when the goods are sold for consumption by the buyer.[55] Moreover, when the seller would be liable to his buyer for a breach of warranty, the seller cannot exclude liability for personal injuries to members of the buyer's family, his household, or his guests.[56]

Statute of Limitations

All actions for breach of a contract of sale must be brought within four years after the breach has occurred.[57] In the case of warranty, the breach occurs when tender of delivery is made although no defect appears and no harm is sustained until a later date.[58]

When a warranty relates to future performance, the Statute of Limitations does not begin to run at the time of the sale but only when the time for the future performance would arise. The result is that when a heating system was installed in midsummer under a warranty that it would heat to a certain degree in subzero weather, the cause of action did not arise until such weather existed. Hence the Statute did not begin to run in the summer at installation but from the later winter when the heating system was found to be inadequate.[59]

---

[53] Sec. 2-718(2).
[54] Sec. 2-718(4). If the seller has notice of the buyer's breach before resale is made, the seller must observe the same standards that apply to the ordinary seller who resells upon breach by the buyer. See p. 460.
[55] UCC Sec. 2-719(3).
[56] Sec. 2-318.
[57] Sec. 2-725(1).
[58] *Wolverine Insurance Co.* v. *Tower Iron Works,* [C.A.1st] [F.2d] 3 UCCRS 1054.
[59] *Perry* v. *Augustine,* [Pa.] 37 D.&C.2d 416.

When product liability is based on the strict tort concept of negligence, the Code Statute of Limitations does not apply but instead the ordinary tort statute applies.[60]

QUESTIONS AND PROBLEMS

1. Define cover (464).

2. State the objective(s) of each of the following rules of law:
   (a) When the seller stops goods in transit, the carrier's lien for transportation is superior to the seller's rights.
   (b) A provision in a sales contract that limits the damages for breach by either party to a certain amount is void if the amount is unreasonably large.

3. Payne sells 100 boxes of paper to Richards. The agreement provides for 15 days' credit. Twenty days later Richards demands the goods. Payne refuses to make delivery until he is paid. Is Richards entitled to judgment in an action to recover the goods?

4. Webb delivers to a carrier certain goods ordered by Haggerty. When Webb learns that Haggerty is insolvent, he notifies the carrier to stop delivery. The following day the bill of lading, which made the goods deliverable to the order of Haggerty, is purchased in good faith for value by Jastram. The carrier delivers the goods to Jastram upon his demand. Is Webb entitled to judgment in an action for damages against the carrier?

5. The Grant Company sold certain goods on credit to White. While the goods were in the warehouse of the carrier at the point of destination awaiting delivery, Yost, a creditor of White, attached the goods to satisfy his claim. In an action brought by the Grant Company, it was contended that the right of the seller to stop the goods in transit had been lost. Do you agree?

6. Holiday sold a vacuum sweeper to Kinney on April 17. Payment was to be made on April 21, and delivery on April 22. When Kinney failed to pay as agreed, Holiday notified Kinney that he rescinded the sale. Later when Kinney tendered payment and Holiday refused to deliver the goods, Kinney brought an action to recover damages. Was Kinney entitled to judgment?

7. When Leeds refuses to accept the goods he has agreed to buy, Hamilton, the seller, brings an action for the price. Leeds contends that he is liable only for damages arising out of the breach of contract. Is his contention sound?

8. Kenton, a dealer, sold a tractor to Laird. Later Laird alleged that there was a breach of warranty. Kenton brought an action to recover the purchase price, contending that Laird had accepted the machine and

---

[60] *Abate* v. *Barkers of Wallingford, Inc.*, 27 Conn.Supp. 46. 229 A.2d 366.

could not rescind the agreement. Assuming that this contention is true, did Laird have any defense to the action?

9. Ogden sold apples to Sternick under an agreement by which the buyer had the option of leaving the apples in the seller's warehouse until the following May. The buyer made a part payment on the purchase price. The apples began to spoil in December, but the buyer refused to remove them at that time. The seller resold the apples to a second buyer and then sued the first buyer for the balance of the purchase price. Decide. (Ogden v. Sternick, 10 N.J.S. 194, 76 A.2d 909)

10. Carta bought from Barker, a dealer, a bicycle that was manufactured by the Union Cycle Co. He took it home for his minor daughter. Sandra, a guest at the Carta home, was injured while using the bicycle. Suit was brought against the Town of Cheshire, claiming that it had defectively maintained the road, and against the manufacturer, claiming that the bicycle was defectively constructed. The manufacturer, Union Cycle, defended on the ground that Sandra had not given it notice of the defect in the bicycle. Decide. (Tomczuk v. Town of Cheshire, 26 Conn. Sup. 219, 217 A.2d 71)

11. Marks contracted with Lehigh Brickface, Inc. to put brickfacing on his house. The brickfacing was not as durable as it was claimed and deteriorated rapidly. Marks notified Lehigh Brickface that it rescinded the contract. Lehigh Brickface defended on the ground that the rescission was not effective because the buyer had not made an offer to return the goods. Was the seller correct? (Marks v. Lehigh Brickface, Inc., [Pa.] 19 D.&C.2d 666, 73 Dau.Co. 244)

12. Braginetz purchased an automobile from the Foreign Motor Sales, Inc. The automobile proved defective, and notice thereof was given promptly by the buyer. The seller made four successive attempts to remedy the defect, each time assuring the buyer that the defect had been remedied. After these unsuccessful attempts, the buyer notified the seller that he revoked the acceptance of the goods. The seller claimed that the buyer had lost the right to revoke acceptance because of his unreasonable delay. Decide. (Braginetz v. Foreign Motor Sales, Inc., [Pa.] 76 Dau.Co. 1)

13. Skopes Rubber Corp. purchased skin-diving suits from the United States Rubber Co. The sale was made on the basis of a sample on which the vinyl coating on the suits had been hand applied and was smooth. The suits that were delivered were wrinkled because the vinyl had been machine applied. In use, the suits split at the wrinkle lines. Skopes returned the first installment of the suits because of this defect. He then sued United States Rubber Co. for breach of warranty. It raised the defense that by returning the first installment, Skopes had rescinded the contract and could not thereafter sue for damages. Was this correct? (Skopes Rubber Corp. v. United States Rubber Co., [C.A.1st] 299 F.2d 584)

PART VII

Security Devices

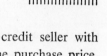

Chapter 40

Secured Consumer Credit Sales

Various devices have been developed to provide the credit seller with protection beyond his general right to sue the buyer for the purchase price. Today such devices, as well as those discussed in Chapter 41, are known as *secured transactions* and are governed by Article 9 of the Uniform Commercial Code.

Nature of a Secured Credit Sale

A *secured credit sale* is a sale in which the possession and the risk of loss pass to the buyer but the seller retains a security interest in the goods until he has been paid in full. In some instances the seller retains the title until paid, but this is not essential. The seller's security interest entitles him to repossess the goods when the buyer fails to make payment as required or when in any other way he commits a breach of the purchase contract. This right of repossession is in addition to the right to sue on the purchase contract for the amount of the purchase price.

Forerunners of this credit device include: (a) a *conditional sale,* where the seller retained title until the condition of payment in full had been satisfied; (2) a *bailment lease,* under which transaction the buyer rented the property and, after the payment of sufficient rentals to equal the purchase price, could elect to take title to the property; and (3) a *chattel mortgage,* by which the buyer, upon taking title from the seller, in turn gave the seller a mortgage on the property for the amount of the purchase price. In these transactions the possession and risk of loss passed to the buyer, but the seller had the right of repossession to protect his interest as well as to sue for breach of contract. The laws pertaining to these three types of transactions have been replaced by the secured transaction provisions of the Code.[1]

---

[1] *Strevell-Patterson Finance Co.* v. *May,* 77 N.Mex. 331, 422 P.2d 366.

The Code, however, has not abolished these transactions nor made them illegal. The parties may still enter into a conditional sale, bailment lease,[2] or chattel mortgage; but if they do, the transaction must satisfy the requirements of the secured transaction under the Code. Thus the Uniform Commercial Code establishes certain minimum requirements applicable to all types of security devices employed by the credit seller.

The Uniform Commercial Code is not designed solely to aid the sellers. The provisions of Article 9 increase the protection given to buyers over that available to them under the former law. Special statutes designed to protect buyers, in addition to the Code, may also be in force within a given state. For example, many states have adopted some form of a retail installment sales act to protect the buyer from improper practices, such as the charging of excessive interest through fictitious charges.[3]

Creation of Security Interest

A security interest for the protection of the seller of goods to a consumer arises as soon as the seller and buyer agree that the buyer shall have property rights in particular goods and that the seller shall have a security interest in them.[4] It is immaterial whether or not the sales agreement provides for the passage of title to the buyer prior to his payment of the goods in full, for the location of title to the property involved, called *collateral,* is immaterial.[5]

1 / Security agreement. The agreement of the seller and buyer that the seller shall have a security interest in the goods must be evidenced by a written [6] *security agreement* which is signed by the buyer and which describes the collateral.[7] This description need only reasonably identify the collateral.[8] It is not necessary that the goods be described specifically, as by serial number or by manufacturer's model.[9] A description is sufficient when it would enable a third person aided by inquiries made to others to determine what goods were involved.[10]

Whether the agreement between the parties is a security agreement depends upon its construction or interpretation. Hence a buyer cannot claim that an outright sale was made to him when the contract is conspicuously

---

[2] *Bloom* v. *Hilty,* 210 Pa.Super. 255, 232 A.2d 126; reversed on other grounds, [Pa.] 234 A.2d 860.
[3] Such laws continue in effect under the Code (Uniform Commercial Code, Secs. 9-201, 9-203(2)) and supplement its provisions.
[4] UCC Sec. 9-204(1).
[5] Sec. 9-202.
[6] *American Card Co.* v. *H.M.H. Co.,* 97 R.I. 159, 196 A.2d 150.
[7] UCC Sec. 9-203(1)(b).
[8] *Cain* v. *Country Club Delicatessen,* 25 Conn.S. 327, 203 A.2d 441.
[9] UCC Sec. 9-110.
[10] The term "accounts receivable" is sufficient to cover future accounts receivable as the quoted words adequately put third persons on notice as to the interest of the creditor in accounts receivable: *In re Platt,* [D.C. E.D. Pa.] 257 F.S. 478.

entitled as a "conditional sales contract" and states that the sale is made "subject to the terms and conditions set forth below and upon the reverse side hereof," when the conditional sale provisions were specified on the reverse side but the buyer apparently neglected to read the reverse side.[11]

2 / Future transactions. The security agreement may contemplate future action by extending to goods not in existence and which are to be acquired and delivered to the buyer at a future date. In general the security interest does not attach to future goods until the buyer has rights in such goods.[12]

Consumer Goods

Consumer goods are those which are used or bought for use primarily for personal, family, or household purposes.[13] It is the intended use rather than the nature of the article which determines its character. An automobile is a consumer good when purchased by the buyer to go to and from work,[14] but a trailer used for a home has been held to be a motor vehicle.[15] Goods purchased by a buyer for resale to ultimate consumers are not consumer goods in the hands of such middleman but constitute a part of his inventory. Equipment used in business is not a consumer good. Hence, a tractor purchased by a construction contractor is not a consumer good.[16] Likewise, a musical instrument used by a nightclub entertainer is equipment.[17]

In this chapter, secured credit sales relating to consumer goods are considered. In Chapter 41, attention will be given to secured credit sales of inventory and equipment, and to secured loan transactions.

RIGHTS OF PARTIES INDEPENDENT OF DEFAULT

In a secured credit sale of consumer goods, both the seller and the buyer have rights independent of default by either party.

Rights of Seller of Consumer Goods Independent of Default

The seller stands in a dual position of being both a seller, having rights under Article 2 of the Code governing sales, and a secured creditor, having rights under Article 9 of the Code regulating secured transactions.[18]

---

[11] *General Motors Acceptance Corp.* v. *Blanco,* 181 Neb. 562, 149 N.W.2d 516.
[12] UCC Sec. 9-204(1)(2).
[13] Sec. 9-109(1).
[14] *Mallicoat* v. *Volunteer Finance & Loan Corp.,* [Tenn.App.] 415 S.W.2d 347.
[15] A filing is required to perfect a security interest therein, as opposed to the contention that it was consumer goods so that a filing was not required for that purpose: *Albany Discount Corp.* v. *Mohawk National Bank,* 54 Misc.2d 238, 282 N.Y.S.2d 401.
[16] *Beam* v. *John Deere Co.,* 240 Ark. 107, 398 S.W.2d 218.
[17] *Strevell-Patterson Finance Co.* v. *May,* 77 N.Mex. 331, 422 P.2d 366.
[18] UCC Sec. 9-113.

The seller may transfer or assign his interest under the sales contract and under the security agreement to a third person, and the assignee acquires all the rights and interest of the seller. The rights of the assignee may rise higher than those of the seller to the extent that there is a defense or claim valid against the seller which is not effective against the assignee because the buyer has waived such a right as against an assignee.[19]

The secured credit seller of consumer goods has rights that are effective not only against the buyer but also against purchasers of the property from the buyer as soon as the security agreement is executed with respect to goods in which the buyer has acquired an interest. From that moment on, the seller's interest is generally effective against third persons [20] and is described as a *perfected security interest*.

1 / Filing not required. In an ordinary case of consumer goods subject to a security interest, no filing is required in order to perfect the secured seller's interest. Such a seller is protected against purchasers from and creditors of the buyer who may acquire the property thereafter.[21]

As an exception to the rule that the seller of such goods has a perfected security interest as soon as the agreement is executed and the buyer has an interest in the property, the seller's security interest is not perfected, and filing is required to perfect it, if the goods purchased are to be attached to buildings or land as a fixture, or if they consist of farm equipment sold for a purchase price of over $2,500. A security interest in a motor vehicle required to be licensed is not perfected unless the vehicle is licensed with a notation of the security interest made in the title certificate, if such is required by law, or if not so required, unless there is a filing under the Code.[22]

2 / Interstate security interests. The Code regulates not only transactions within the state but also the effect to be given security interests in property brought into the state from another state. If the interest of the secured party was perfected in another state, his interest will be regarded as perfected by the state into which the property is brought. Within the second state, however, it is necessary to file within four months in order to keep the security interest continuously protected.

Facts: On July 7, Mulry sold a Ford Thunderbird to Greene in Rhode Island by a conditional sales contract. The contract was never recorded or filed since this was not required in Rhode Island to perfect the interest of Mulry. Unknown to him, Greene took the automobile to Pennsylvania

---

19 See p. 478.
20 UCC Sec. 9-201.
21 Sec. 9-302(1)(d). The Code makes detailed provisions as to the priority of conflicting security interests with respect to fixtures, accessions, and commingled and processed goods. Sec. 9-313 and following.
22 Sec. 9-302(1)(c), (d), (3), (4). As to the requirements of filing generally, see p. 485.

and sold it to Miracle Mile Motors on July 11. The latter obtained a Pennsylvania title certificate to the automobile which stated that it was the owner but bore a notation indicating that the automobile had been brought in from outside of the state. On July 25, Miracle Mile resold the automobile in Pennsylvania to A. C. Lohman, Inc., a New York automobile dealer, who brought the automobile back to New York and sold it in the following May to Churchill Motors, expressly warranting the title. On October 10, Mulry took the automobile from the parking lot of Churchill because he had never been paid by Greene. Churchill then sued Lohman for breach of the warranty of title.

Decision: Judgment for Churchill. When collateral subject to a perfected interest is moved to another state, it remains subject to such security interest for a 4-month period. A purchaser during that time takes the goods subject to the perfected security interest. Even though the perfected interest loses its perfection by failure to refile before the end of the 4-month period, the party who purchased before the end of the period remains subordinated to the security interest; but a good-faith purchaser who would purchase after the expiration of the 4-month period and the loss of perfection would not be subject to the then unperfected security interest. (Churchill Motors, Inc. v. A. C. Lohman, Inc., 16 App.Div. 2d 560, 229 N.Y.S.2d 570)

If the secured party's interest in the goods was unperfected when they were brought into the second state, that interest may be perfected therein.[23]

If title to the property, such as an automobile, is represented by a title certificate, the law of the state which issued the certificate determines whether an interest is perfected. Accordingly, if the law of the certificate-issuing state requires that a security interest be noted on the title certificate in order to be binding, that requirement is the exclusive means of perfecting the interest of the secured creditor.[24]

Rights of the Buyer of Consumer Goods Independent of Default

The buyer under a secured transaction has a double status under the Uniform Commercial Code. By virtue of Article 2 he has certain rights because he is a buyer, and by virtue of Article 9 he has certain rights because he is a debtor under a secured transaction.

1 / Rights as a buyer. The secured credit sale of consumer goods remains fundamentally a sale that is governed by Article 2, and therefore the debtor-buyer has the same rights as an ordinary buyer under that article.[25]

---

[23] UCC Sec. 9-103(3).

[24] Sec. 9-103(4). This provision does not apply to an automobile which was purchased originally in a state that did not provide for the notation of a security interest on the certificate of title, although it was thereafter brought into a state which has such a notation requirement: *First National Bank* v. *Stamper*, 93 N.J.S. 150, 225 A.2d 162.

[25] UCC Sec. 9-206(2).

The buyer has certain rights of ownership in the collateral. It is not material whether technically he is the owner of the title. Whatever interest he owns he may transfer voluntarily, and his creditors may reach it by the process of law as fully as though there were no security agreement.[26] Such third persons generally cannot acquire any greater rights than the buyer, and therefore they hold the property subject to the security interest of the seller.

It is common practice for credit sellers to seek to protect themselves by prohibiting the buyer from reselling the property. Such a provision has no effect and does not prevent an effective resale, even though the security agreement in addition to prohibiting such resale also expressly makes it a default or breach of the contract to make a resale.[27] But the consumer cannot make a sale of the collateral that is clear of the secured creditor's security interest. Thus the purchaser of the collateral, such as an automobile, from the credit buyer is not a buyer in ordinary course from a person in the business of selling goods of that kind; and therefore the purchaser does not take the automobile free of the creditor's security interest.[28]

2 / Rights as a debtor. The secured transaction buyer is a debtor to the extent that there is a balance due on the purchase price. In order for the buyer to know just how much he owes and to check with his own records what the seller claims to be due, the buyer has the right to compel the seller to state what balance is owed and also to specify in what collateral the seller claims a security interest. This is done by the buyer's sending the seller a statement of the amount which he believes to be due, or a statement of the collateral which he believes to be subject to the security agreement, with the request that the seller approve or correct the statement. The seller must so indicate and if he has assigned the contract and the security interest to a third person, he must furnish the buyer with the name and address of such successor in interest.[29]

3 / Waiver of defenses. It is common practice for finance companies that have a standing agreement to purchase sales contracts from a credit seller to provide him with forms to be signed by the buyer. These forms generally specify that the buyer waives, as against the assignee of the sales contract and security agreement, any right that he would have against the seller. In addition to an express agreement waiving his defenses, a buyer who, as part of the purchase transaction, signs both a commercial paper and a security agreement is deemed as a matter of law to waive such defenses, even though nothing is said as to any waiver.

---

[26] Sec. 9-311.
[27] Sec. 9-311. The second buyer is subject to the exceptions noted on **p. 476.**
[28] *First National Bank* v. *Stamper,* 93 N.J.S. 150, 225 A.2d 162.
[29] UCC Sec. 9-208.

Both express and implied waivers are valid and bind the buyer if the assignee takes his assignment for value, in good faith, and without notice or knowledge of any claim or defense of the buyer.[30] The validity of any waiver of defense is subject to two limitations: (a) those defenses which could be raised against the holder in due course of commercial paper cannot be waived; [31] (b) the waiver is not effective if a statute or decision establishes a different rule for buyers of consumer goods.[32]

RIGHTS OF PARTIES AFTER DEFAULT

When the buyer defaults by committing a breach of contract, the secured creditor and the buyer have additional rights.

Secured Seller's Repossession and Resale of Collateral

Upon the buyer's default, the secured party is entitled to take the collateral or purchased property from the buyer. If he can do so without causing a breach of the peace, the seller may repossess the property without legal proceedings. In any case he may use legal proceedings if he desires.[33]

The seller who has repossessed the goods may resell them at a private or public sale at any time and place and on any terms. He must, however, act in good faith and in a manner that is commercially reasonable.[34] The seller must give the buyer reasonable advance notice of a resale unless the goods are perishable, or unless they threaten to decline speedily in value, or unless they are of a type customarily sold on a recognized market.[35] The seller's resale destroys all interest of the buyer in the goods.

If the secured creditor is the highest bidder or the only bidder, it may purchase the collateral sold at a public sale, even though such a sale is conducted in its office.[36]

1 / Repossession. A breach of the peace is defined in terms of the common-law offense as "a disturbance of public order by an act of violence, or by an act likely to produce violence, or which by causing consternation and alarm, disturbs the peace and quiet of the community." Consequently, there is no breach of the peace when the creditor without authorization obtains a duplicate key from a locksmith and enters the debtor's premises to take possession of the collateral upon default.[37]

---

[30] Sec. 9-206(1), (2).
[31] Sec. 9-206(1). See p. 339.
[32] Sec. 9-206(1).
[33] Sec. 9-503.
[34] Sec. 9-504(1)(3).
[35] Sec. 9-504(3).
[36] *American Plan Corp.* v. *Eiseman,* 4 Ohio App.2d 385, 33 O.O.2d 486, 212 N.E.2d 824.
[37] *Cherno* v. *Bank of Babylon,* 54 Misc.2d 277, 282 N.Y.S.2d 114.

When a finance company repossesses its conditionally-sold automobile, its agent does not commit the crime of taking the automobile without the owner's consent, even though he may commit a breach of the peace in so doing. In the latter event the agent is liable for that offense.[38]

2 / Compulsory resale. If the buyer has paid 60 percent or more of the cash price of the consumer goods, the seller must resell them within 90 days after repossession, unless the buyer, after default, has signed a written statement surrendering the right to require the resale. If the seller does not resell within the time specified, the buyer may sue him for conversion of the collateral or proceed under the Code provision applicable to failure to comply with the Code.[39]

3 / Redemption of collateral. If the buyer acts in time, he may redeem or obtain the return to him of the goods by tendering to the secured party the amount that is owed him, including expenses and any legal costs that have been incurred. The right to redeem is destroyed if the seller has made a resale or entered into a binding contract for resale.[40]

4 / Accounting after resale. When the secured party makes a resale of the goods, the proceeds of the sale are applied in the following order to pay (a) reasonable costs of repossession, storage, and resale of the goods; (b) the balance due, including interest and any proper additions such as attorney's fees; and (c) subsequent security interests in the property that are discharged by the sale.[41]

If any balance remains after the payment of these claims, the buyer is entitled to the surplus. Conversely, if the net proceeds of sale are insufficient to pay the costs and the debt due the seller, the buyer is liable to him for such deficiency unless it has been otherwise agreed by the parties.[42]

Secured Seller's Retention of Collateral to Discharge Obligation

If a compulsory disposition of the collateral is not required, the secured party may propose in writing that he keep the collateral in payment of the debt. If the buyer does not object to this proposal, the secured party may do so and the secured obligation is automatically discharged. If written objection to the retention of the collateral by the secured party is made within 30 days, he must then proceed to dispose of it by resale or other reasonable manner.[43] If the objection to retention is not both made in writing and made within

---

[38] *Jerman* v. *Superior Court*, 245 Cal.App.2d 852, 54 Cal.Rptr. 374.
[39] See p. 481.
[40] UCC Sec. 9-506.
[41] Sec. 9-504(1).
[42] Sec. 9-504(2).
[43] Sec. 9-505(2).

the 30-day period, it has no effect and therefore it may be ignored by the seller.

Buyer's Remedies for Violation of Code by Secured Party

The Code authorizes both injunctive and money-damage relief against the secured party who violates the provisions of the Code applicable upon default. The remedies provided by the Code are not exclusive, and the buyer may also invoke any remedies authorized by any other statute applicable to the particular transaction.

When the sales contract is not executed in the manner required by a statute relating to installment sales, the contract is generally voidable at the election of the buyer and the seller is subject to some form of penalty, such as a criminal fine or loss of financing charges.[44]

Facts: Shaw purchased an automobile from Countrywide Motors. The seller financed the purchase, with Shaw executing a contract and a judgment note. Countrywide then sold the contract and note to Alliance Discount Corp. When the installments were not paid on the purchase price, Alliance entered judgment on the note, repossessed the automobile, and sold it at a private sale for a very nominal amount. No notice was given to Shaw of any of the proceedings. He petitioned to open the judgment to permit the true value of the automobile to be shown so that the balance owed on the purchase price could be reduced by the fair value of the automobile. The state Motor Vehicle Sales Finance Act required that this be done and declared that the resale price was not conclusive as to its reasonable value.

Decision: The value of the sold collateral had to be redetermined in the manner specified by the Motor Vehicle Sales Finance Act. That statute was not displaced by the Code, and the remedies afforded by that statute were not abolished nor the debtor limited to those specified by the Code. (Alliance Discount Corp. v. Shaw, 195 Pa.Super. 601, 171 A.2d 548)

The buyer is entitled to recover the damages caused him by the secured party's failure to comply with the Code. In the absence of proof of a greater amount of damages, the buyer is entitled to recover not less than the credit service charge together with 10 percent of the principal amount of the debt or the time price differential plus 10 percent of the cash price.[45]

If a resale has not yet been made nor a binding contract therefor entered into, the buyer may obtain a court order or injunction requiring the seller to comply with the Code provisions.

When the creditor makes a sale of the collateral without giving the debtor notice, the creditor deprives the debtor of his opportunity to bid at the

---

[44] *Keyes* v. *Brown*, [Conn.] 232 A.2d 486.
[45] UCC Sec. 9-507(1`

sale and to retain the property. Consequently, the creditor will not be allowed to recover from the debtor any losses sustained or expenses incurred at such sale.[46]

Facts: The Nides Finance Co. repossessed an automobile purchased on credit by Moody and resold it without giving Moody notice of the sale, although the contract required that such notice be given. A deficiency resulted on the resale, which the finance company then demanded from Moody.

Decision: When the finance company took the car and resold it without giving notice as required to do by the contract, it was regarded as having made an accord and satisfaction that such retention and disposition of the collateral should discharge any balance of the debt remaining due. (Moody v. Nides Finance Co., 115 Ga.App. 859, 156 S.E.2d 310)

QUESTIONS AND PROBLEMS

1. Checklist of legal terms:
   (a) secured transaction (473)
   (b) secured credit sale; conditional sale, bailment lease, chattel mortgage (473)
   (c) collateral (474)
   (d) security agreement (474)
   (e) consumer goods (475)
   (f) perfected security interest (476)

2. State the objective(s) of each of the following rules of law:
   (a) The seller's right of repossession in a secured credit sale is in addition to his right to sue on the contract for the amount of the purchase price.
   (b) A perfected security interest gives the seller of consumer goods rights that are effective against purchasers of the property from the buyer.

3. On September 1 Patterson made a secured credit sale of a television set to Shirmer who paid the first installment of the purchase price at that time. The set was delivered to Shirmer's home and installed on September 10. Identify the law(s) that protect the interests of the two parties.

4. Tanner executes a secured credit sale of an electric stove to Penn.
   (a) What are Tanner's rights in the stove as compared with those of Penn's creditors?
   (b) If Penn, without Tanner's consent, sells the stove to Selby, what are Tanner's rights as compared with those of Selby?

5. Hill, who made a secured credit sale of a record player to Lake, retook possession of the player when Lake had made half of his payments and was not in default. What right, if any, does Lake have against Hill?

---

[46] *Skeels* v. *Universal C.I.T. Credit Corp.*, [D.C. W.D. Pa.] 222 F.S. 696.

6. McCoy sold an air conditioning unit to Hughes on credit, payment to be made in 12 equal installments. When Hughes missed the ninth installment, McCoy took back the television set and then sued Hughes for the balance due. What are Hughes' rights?

7. Sam's Furniture & Appliance Stores sold furniture and home appliances to the public. Sam went bankrupt. At that time, Sam had in his store various items that had been repossessed from customers. Were such goods inventory or consumer goods? (In re Sam's Furniture & Appliance Stores, [D.C. W.D. Pa. Ref.Bankruptcy] 1 UCCRS 422)

8. Cook sold to Martin a new tractor truck for approximately $13,000 with a down payment of approximately $3,000 and the balance to be paid in 30 monthly installments. The sales agreement provided that upon default in any payment Cook could take "immediate possession of the property . . . without notice or demand. For this purpose vendor may enter upon any premises the property may be." Martin failed to pay the installments when due, and Cook notified him that the truck would be repossessed. Martin had the tractor truck, attached to a loaded trailer, locked on the premises of a company in Memphis. Martin intended to drive to the West Coast as soon as the trailer was loaded. When Cook located the tractor truck, no one was around. In order to disconnect the trailer from the truck, as Cook had no right to the trailer, Cook removed the wire screen over a ventilator hole by unscrewing it from the outside with his penknife. He next reached through the ventilator hole with a stick and unlocked the door of the tractor truck. He then disconnected the trailer and had the truck towed away. Martin sued Cook for unlawfully repossessing the truck by committing a breach of the peace. Decide. (Martin v. Cook, 237 Miss. 267, 114 So.2d 669)

9. Hull-Dobbs sold an automobile to Mallicoat and then assigned the sales contract to the Volunteer Finance Co. Later Volunteer repossessed the automobile and sold it. When Volunteer sued Mallicoat for the deficiency between the contract price and the proceeds on resale, Mallicoat raised the defense that he had not been properly notified of the resale. The loan manager of the finance company testified that Mallicoat had been sent a registered letter stating that the car would be sold. He did not state whether the letter merely declared in general terms that the car would be sold or specified a date for its resale. He admitted that the letter never was delivered to Mallicoat and was returned to the finance company "unclaimed." The loan manager also testified that the sale was advertised by posters, but on cross examination he admitted that he was not able to state when or where it was thus advertised. It was shown that Volunteer knew where Mallicoat and his father lived and where Mallicoat was employed. Mallicoat claimed that he had not been properly notified. Volunteer asserted that sufficient notice had been given. Was the notice of the resale sufficient? (Mallicoat v. Volunteer Finance and Loan Corp., [Tenn.App.] 415 S.W.2d 347)

Chapter 41

Other Secured Transactions

Subject to certain exceptions, Article 9 of the Uniform Commercial Code regulates all secured transactions dealing with personal property. The secured transaction relating to consumer goods sold on credit has been discussed in Chapter 40. In this chapter other common forms of secured transactions under the Code are considered.

SECURED CREDIT SALES OF INVENTORY

In contrast with one who buys personal property for his own use, the buyer may be a merchant or dealer who intends to resell the goods. The goods which such a merchant or dealer buys are classified as *inventory*. The financing of the purchase of inventory may involve a third person as creditor rather than the seller. For example, a third person, such as a bank or finance company, may loan the dealer the money with which to make the purchase and to pay the seller in full. In such a case the security interest given by the buyer in the goods he purchases is given to the third person and not to the seller.[1] Accordingly, the terms "creditor" and "secured party" as used in this chapter may refer to both a seller who sells on credit and a third person who finances the purchase of inventory.

In general, the provisions regulating a secured transaction in inventory follow the same pattern as those applicable to the secured credit sale of consumer goods. Variations recognize the differences in the commercial settings of the two transactions.

Use of Property and Extent of Security Interest

A secured transaction relating to inventory will generally give the buyer full freedom to deal with the collateral goods as though he were the absolute owner and the goods were not subject to a security interest. Thus the parties may agree that the buyer-dealer may mingle the goods with his own existing inventory, resell the goods, take goods back and make exchanges, and so on,

---

[1] Prior to the adoption of the Code, security was frequently provided the person financing the purchase of inventory by the device of a trust receipt, under which the purchaser-merchant would declare that he held the inventory in trust for the creditor. This device was regulated by the Uniform Trust Receipts Act (UTRA).

without being required to keep any records of just what became of the goods covered by the security agreement, or to replace the goods sold with other goods, or to account for what is done with the particular goods.[2]

1 / After-acquired property. The security agreement may expressly provide that the security interest of the creditor shall bind after-acquired property, that is, other inventory thereafter acquired by the buyer. The combination of the buyer's freedom to use and dispose of the collateral and the subjecting of after-acquired goods to the interest of the secured creditor permits the latter to have a *floating lien* on a changing or shifting stock of goods of the buyer. Conversely stated, the Code rejects the common-law concept that the security interest was lost if the collateral was not maintained and accounted for separately and that a floating lien upon the buyer's property was void as a fraud against the latter's creditors.

The security interest in inventory covered as after-acquired property has priority over claims of subsequent creditors and third persons, except buyers in the ordinary course of business and sellers to the debtor holding perfected purchase money security interests in the goods sold the debtor.[3]

2 / Proceeds of resale. The security agreement also may expressly cover proceeds resulting from the resale of the goods.[4] If the financing statement covers the proceeds, the secured party's security interest together with any perfection thereof continues in the proceeds obtained by the buyer on the resale of the goods. If the original financing statement does not cover such proceeds, the perfection of the security interest in the original goods continues for only 10 days unless within that time the secured party perfects his interest in the proceeds by filing or by taking possession of the proceeds.[5]

When the creditor has a security interest in a tractor that is traded in and the financing statement for the new purchase covers "proceeds," the creditor has a security interest in the replacement tractor that the buyer obtains by the new purchase.[6]

Filing of Financing Statement

Filing is required to perfect the creditor's interest in inventory or the proceeds therefrom.[7] An exception is made when a statute, such as a motor

---

[2] Uniform Commercial Code, Sec. 9-205.
[3] *Rosenberg* v. *Rudnick*, [D.C.Mass.] 262 F.S. 635.
[4] UCC Sec. 9-203(1)(b); *In re Platt*, [D.C. E.D. Pa.] 257 F.S. 478.
[5] UCC Sec. 9-306(3). Proceeds includes not only money but also checks and other commercial paper, and the account or debt owed by the subpurchaser. Sec. 9-306(1).
[6] *Universal C.I.T. Credit Corp.* v. *Prudential Investment Corp.*, [R.I.] 222 A.2d 571.
[7] A security interest is binding as between the parties although a financing statement has not been filed. *Bloom* v. *Hilty*, 210 Pa.Super. 255, 232 A.2d 26; reversed on other grounds, [Pa.] 234 A.2d 860.

vehicle statute, requires the security interest to be noted on the title certificate issued for the property.[8] An unperfected security interest is likewise valid as against anyone standing in the position of the debtor or whose rights can rise no higher than those of the debtor.

Facts: The Miller Automobile Co. sold an automobile on credit to the Lebanon Woolen Mills Corp. The security agreement was not recorded until four months later on February 23, 1962. Meanwhile in January, 1962, the United States assessed and filed a lien for taxes against Lebanon Mills; and on February 14, 1962, a receiver was appointed for Lebanon. A federal statute provides that when a person owing money or taxes to the United States becomes insolvent, a claim of the United States "shall be first satisfied" from the assets of the debtor. The United States claimed that it was entitled to payment before the Miller Automobile Co., while Miller claimed that it was entitled to rely on the security interest agreement.

Decision: Judgment for Miller Automobile Co. As between Miller and Lebanon, the security agreement was binding although unrecorded. The United States, although entitled to be first paid, could only obtain payment from assets of its debtor Lebanon Mills. As the automobile was subject to the security interest while in the hands of Lebanon, the United States, which stood in the same position as Lebanon, was subject to the interest of Miller. The requirement of filing does not alter this conclusion. (United States v. Lebanon Woolen Mills Corp., [D.C. N.H.] 241 F.S. 393)

1 / Financing statement. The paper that is filed is a financing statement and is distinct from the security agreement which was executed by the parties to give rise to the secured transaction.[9] The *financing statement* must be signed by both the debtor and the secured party, and it must give an address of the secured party from which information concerning the security interest may be obtained and a mailing address of the debtor; and it must contain a statement indicating the types, or describing the items, of collateral.[10]

The Code adopts the system of "notice filing," which requires a filing only of a simple notice which indicates merely that the secured party who has filed may have a security interest in the collateral described.[11] The criterion for the sufficiency of a financing statement is whether anyone searching the records would be misled by the matter of which complaint is made.[12]

---

[8] UCC Sec. 9-302(1), (3), (4). Reference must be made to the Code as adopted in a particular state as to the place of filing, for the Code as submitted for adoption gave the states the option of providing as to certain kinds of property for a system of state-wide-effective filing with the Secretary of State or of requiring a local county filing. See Sec. 9-401.

[9] Sec. 9-402. However, the security agreement may be filed as a financing statement if it contains the required information and is signed by both parties.

[10] UCC Sec. 9-402(1).

[11] *In re Platt,* [D.C. E.D. Pa.] 257 F.S. 478.

[12] *Plemens* v. *Didde-Glaser,* 244 Md. 556, 224 A.2d 464.

2 / Duration and continuation of filing. If the debt is due within less than 5 years, the filing is effective for the entire period until the debt matures and for 60 days thereafter. If the debt is not due within 5 years, a filing is effective only for 5 years. At the expiration of the designated period, the perfection of the security interest terminates unless a continuation statement has been filed prior thereto.[13] The *continuation statement* is merely a written declaration by the secured party which identifies the original filing statement by its file number and declares that it is still effective. The filing of the continuation statement continues the perfection of the security interest for a period of 5 years after the last date on which the original filing was effective. The filing of successive continuation statements will continue the perfection indefinitely.[14]

3 / Termination statement. When the buyer has paid the debt in full, he may make a written demand on the secured party, or the latter's assignee if the security interest has been assigned, to send the buyer a *termination statement* that a security interest is no longer claimed under the specified financing statement. The buyer may then present this statement to the filing officer who marks the record "terminated" and returns to the secured party the various papers which had been filed by him.[15]

4 / Assignments. The secured party may have assigned his interest either before the filing of the financing statement or thereafter. If the assignment was made prior to its filing, the financing statement may include a recital of the assignment and state the name and address of the assignee, or a copy of the assignment may be attached thereto. If the assignment is made subsequent to the filing of the financing statement, a separate written statement of assignment may be filed in the same office.[16]

Protection of Customer of the Buyer

The customer of the buyer takes the goods free from the secured interest of the secured party. That is, one who buys in the ordinary course of business items of property taken from the original buyer's inventory is free of the secured party's interest, even though that interest was perfected and even though such ultimate customer knew of the secured party's interest.[17] And as it is normal for a car rental agency to sell its used cars, a purchaser buying from the agency is to be regarded as a buyer in the ordinary course of

---

[13] UCC Sec. 9-403(2). If the obligation is payable on demand, the filing is effective for five years from filing.
[14] Sec. 9-403(3).
[15] Sec. 9-404.
[16] Sec. 9-405.
[17] Sec. 9-307(1).

business and therefore takes the car clear of the perfected security interest of the bank.[18]

As an exception to this rule, the buyer of consumer goods or of farm equipment not having an original purchase price in excess of $2,500 is subject to the security interest if it had been perfected by filing prior to the ultimate sale. If it had been perfected without filing, the ultimate buyer is also subject to that security interest unless he buys without knowledge of its existence, for value, and for his own personal, family, or household purposes, or his own farming operations.[19]

Rights and Remedies After Default

The rights and remedies of the secured party and the buyer of inventory after a default on the part of the latter are the same as in the case of a secured credit sale of consumer goods.[20] As a partial modification of that pattern, the creditor taking possession of inventory on the buyer's default is not required to make a sale of the goods but may retain them in full discharge of the debt due, unless an objection is made by the buyer to such retention. In the latter case, the creditor must then make a sale.[21]

SECURED CREDIT SALES OF EQUIPMENT

The Code makes a distinction, for the purpose of secured transactions, as to the purpose for which a consumer purchases goods. If the ultimate consumer purchases primarily for his personal, family, or household use, the goods are described as consumer goods.[22] The consumer's purchase, however, is described as *equipment* if used or purchased for use primarily in a business, in farming, or in a profession; or if the goods do not constitute consumer goods, inventory, or farm products.[23]

In general, the equipment secured sale is treated the same as a secured transaction as to inventory, except that the various provisions relating to resale by the buyer and the creditor's rights in proceeds have no practical application because the buyer does not resell the property but makes the purchase with the intention to keep and use or operate it.

Filing is required to perfect a purchase money security interest in equipment, with the exception of farm equipment having a purchase price not in

---

[18] *Hempstead Bank* v. *Andy's Car Rental System, Inc.*, [N.Y.S.2d] 3 UCCRS 962.
[19] UCC Sec. 9-307(2).
[20] See p. 479.
[21] UCC Sec. 9-505(2). In this situation, the secured creditor must give notice not only to his debtor but also to any other party who has a security interest in the goods and who has properly filed a financing statement, or any person known by the secured party to have a security interest in the goods.
[22] As to the secured credit sale of consumer goods, see Chapter 40.
[23] UCC Sec. 9-109(2).

excess of $2,500, and motor vehicles which must be licensed under a specific licensing statute.[24]

Facts: The Park Corrugated Box Co. purchased on credit a machine for making paper boxes from Manufacturers Leasing Corp. In order to protect its interest in the property under the credit sale, Manufacturers filed a financing statement under the Uniform Commercial Code. It filed the statement in the county in which the factory building was located, which was the proper county if the machine was a fixture. When the box company went into bankruptcy, the trustee in bankruptcy claimed that the filing was not proper on the theory that the machine was not a fixture and that the filing should have been made in the office of the Secretary of State.

Decision: The law of the state determined whether the article of property had become a fixture. The machine was not a fixture by the traditional test as it could be removed without damage, and the parties had agreed that the machine should be attached "by removable screws or otherwise, so as to be severable from the realty without material injury to the freehold." Even if regarded as a trade fixture, the machine would not be a fixture at common law nor under the Code, for a trade fixture is by definition removable by the tenant while a fixture which becomes part of the realty is not. The filing was therefore defective; and since the security interest of Manufacturers was not perfected, it was subordinate to the rights of the trustee in bankruptcy of the debtor. (In re Park Corrugated Box Corp., [D.C. N.J.] 249 F.S. 56)

SECURED LOAN TRANSACTIONS

In Chapter 40 and the first part of this chapter, consideration has been given to secured transactions as a means of protecting sellers or third persons financing the purchase of goods. The secured transaction may also be employed to protect one who lends on credit apart from the making of any sale. In the latter case, the secured transaction may be one in which the collateral is delivered to or pledged with the creditor, or it may be one in which the borrower retains possession of the collateral.

Pledge

A *pledge* is a secured transaction in which the lender is given possession of the personal property or collateral in which he has the security interest. More specifically, a pledge is a bailment created as security for the payment of a debt. Under a pledge, specific property is delivered into the possession of a bailee-creditor with the authority, express or implied, that in the event that the debt is not paid, the property may be sold and the proceeds of the sale applied to discharge the debt secured by the pledge. For example, a person

[24] Sec. 9-302(1)(c), (3).

borrowing $1,000 may give his creditor property worth $1,000 or more to hold as security. If the borrower repays the loan, the property is returned to him. If he does not repay the debt, the creditor may sell the property and reduce the debt by the amount of the net proceeds. The notice of the sale must be specific enough to identify the nature of the property to be sold so as to alert persons possibly interested in purchasing.

Facts: Kiamie had pledged stock with the Colonial Trust Co. On default, the company put up the stock for public auction. In the newspaper notice the stock was described as: "5 shs. Sherman Investing Corp. (N.Y.)." The corporation was not generally known, and the stock was not listed on any stock exchange. Kiamie claimed that the sale was defective because the public notice of the sale was inadequate.

Decision: Judgment for Kiamie. Although there is no specific rule as to what the notice of a pledgee's sale must contain, it must identify the property. In the case of unlisted stock of unknown corporations, it is necessary to indicate the nature of the business of the corporation, the assets and liabilities of the corporation, and what part of the outstanding stock was involved. (Kiamie's Estate, 309 N.Y. 325, 130 N.E.2d 745)

Upon default, the pledgee does not become the owner of the pledge but merely has the right to foreclose upon it or expose it to sale.[25] If the pledgee makes a fictitious sale of the property to himself and then resells the property to a third person at a profit, the pledgor is entitled to damages caused thereby.[26]

In general terms, the rights of the debtor (the *pledgor*) and the creditor (the *pledgee*) under a pledge relationship are the same as the rights of a buyer and seller under a secured credit sale of consumer goods.[27] A distinction arises from the fact that the pledgee is given possession from the commencement of the secured transaction, whereas under a secured credit sale the secured party obtains possession only upon default. After a default occurs, the two transactions may be regarded as the same.

1 / Creation and perfection. The pledge relation arises as soon as it is agreed that the pledgee shall have a security interest in the property which is delivered to him and on the basis thereof he gives value, such as lending money.[28] Filing is not required.[29]

2 / Duties of pledgee. Because the secured party or pledgee is in possession of the property or collateral, he must use reasonable care in

---

[25] *Horne* v. *Burress*, [Miss.] 197 So.2d 802.
[26] *Wade* v. *Markwell Co.*, 118 Cal.App.2d 410, 258 P.2d 497, 37 A.L.R.2d 1363.
[27] See Chapter 40.
[28] UCC Sec. 9-204(1).
[29] Secs. 9-302(1)(a), 9-305.

preserving the property and is liable for damage which results from his failure to do so.[30] The pledgee must keep the collateral separate and identified, although fungible goods [31] of the same kind and quality may be commingled.[32] If money, such as dividends, is received by the pledgee by virtue of his holding the collateral, he must apply such money to the reduction of the debt or send it to the debtor.[33]

Pawn

The term *pawn* is often used to indicate a pledge of tangible personal property, rather than documents representing property rights. In such a case the pledgor is called the *pawner,* and the pledgee is called the *pawnee.*

A person engaged in the business of lending money at interest, in which he requires a pawn as security, is known as a *pawnbroker.* In order to avoid usurious loan practices and trafficking in stolen goods, the business of professional pawnbroking is generally regulated by statute.

Securing of Debt Without Change of Possession

This situation is illustrated by the owner of a television set who borrows money from the bank and, to protect the latter, gives the bank a security interest in his property. In general terms, the relation between the lender and the borrower is regulated in the same manner as in the case of a secured credit sale of inventory goods. Filing is required whether or not the collateral constitutes consumer goods.[34] When there is a default in the payment of the debt, the lender has the same choice of remedies under such a secured transaction as the secured credit seller of inventory.

Secured Interest in Goods Being Manufactured

In certain industries, such as the textile industry, the practice developed of advancing money to manufacturers on the security of goods being manufactured or to be sold thereafter. In over half of the states this practice was recognized by statutes providing for a *factor's lien* on the manufacturer's goods when a written agreement therefor was properly filed as a public record. These statutes have been replaced by Article 9 of the Code under which the financing party and the manufacturer execute a security agreement giving the lender a security interest in existing goods and, if desired, in goods to be manufactured thereafter, and the proceeds of all such goods.

---

[30] Sec. 9-207(1), (3). The reasonable expenses of caring for the collateral, including insurance and taxes, are charged to the debtor and are secured by the collateral. Sec. 9-207(2)(a).
[31] See p. 425.
[32] UCC Sec. 9-207(2)(d).
[33] Sec. 9-207(2)(c).
[34] Sec. 9-302(1).

In general this security transaction follows the same pattern as a secured credit sale of inventory.[35]

QUESTIONS AND PROBLEMS

1. Checklist of legal terms:
   (a) inventory (484)
   (b) floating lien (485)
   (c) financing statement (486), continuation statement (487), termination statement (487)
   (d) equipment (488)
   (e) pledge (489); pledgor (490); pledgee (490)
   (f) pawn; pawner, pawnee, pawnbroker (491)
   (g) factor's lien (491)

2. State the objective(s) of each of the following rules of law:
   (a) In a secured credit sale of inventory, the buyer generally can deal with the collateral goods as if he were the absolute owner.
   (b) When the buyer in a secured credit sale of inventory has paid the debt in full, he is entitled to a termination statement from the secured party.

3. In a secured credit sale of inventory, how can the security agreement provide for the seller to have a floating lien on the goods?

4. If the financing statement for a secured transaction relating to the inventory does not cover the proceeds from the resale, what security interest does the seller have in the proceeds?

5. When is filing required to perfect the security interest of the seller—
   (a) In credit sales of inventory? (b) In credit sales of equipment?

6. As security for a loan from the Farmer's National Bank, Westerman, a grocer, executed an instrument stipulating that he gave to the bank a certain automobile owned by him. Westerman retained possession of the car. Aker, a creditor, attached all of Westerman's property including the automobile. During subsequent litigation the bank contended that it had rights in the car as a pledgee. Was this contention sound?

7. Humphrey pledges 100 shares of corporate stock to McMullen as security for a debt. Later McMullen delivers the same stock to Glaser as security for a loan. Is Humphrey entitled to recover damages for the value of the stock?

8. Which of the following statements, if any, is sufficient for a description of the collateral subject to a security interest:
   (a) Passenger and commercial automobiles financed by Girard Trust Corn Exchange Bank?
   (b) Future accounts receivable?
   (c) A description of an automobile that does not contain a serial number?

---

[35] See p. 484.

Chapter 42

Suretyship and Guaranty

The relationship by which one person becomes responsible for the debt or undertaking of another person is used most commonly to insure that a debt will be paid or that a contractor will perform the work called for by his contract.

NATURE AND CREATION

A distinction may be made between two kinds of agreements by which a third person agrees to pay another's debt if the debtor does not. One kind is called a contract or undertaking of *suretyship*, and the third person is called a *surety*. The other kind is called a contract or undertaking of *guaranty*, and the third person is called the *guarantor*. In both cases, the person who owes the money or is under the original obligation to pay is called the *principal*, the principal debtor, or debtor, and the person to whom the debt is owed is known as the *creditor*.[1]

Both suretyship and guaranty undertakings have the common feature of a promise to answer for the debt or default of another; but they have a basic difference. The surety is primarily liable for the debt or obligation of the principal; ordinarily the guarantor is only secondarily liable. This means that the moment the principal is in default, the creditor may demand performance or payment by the surety.[2] He generally cannot do so in the case of the guarantor; he must first attempt to collect from the principal. An exception is an "absolute guaranty" which creates the same obligation as a suretyship. A guaranty of payment creates an absolute guaranty.

There is frequently confusion in the use of the terms suretyship and guaranty, and it becomes a question of construction to determine what the parties really intended by their contract. In some states an undertaking to answer for the debt of another is interpreted as a suretyship agreement in the absence of an express statement to the contrary.

Unless otherwise stated, "surety" as used in the text includes guarantor as well as surety, and "guaranty" is limited to a conditional guaranty.

---

[1] The word "principal" is also used by the law to identify the person who employs an agent. The "principal" in suretyship must be distinguished from the agent's "principal."

[2] *Nichols* v. *Miller*, 91 Ga.App. 99, 84 S.E.2d 841.

493

Indemnity Contract

An *indemnity contract* is an undertaking by one person for a consideration to pay another person a sum of money to indemnify him when he incurs a certain loss.[3] A fire insurance policy is a typical example of an indemnity contract.

Both suretyship and guaranty need to be distinguished from indemnity. In the latter there is no undertaking to answer for the obligation or debt of another. It is important to bear this difference in mind because the modern surety company also writes indemnity bonds. For example, a bank, by paying a premium, may obtain a *fidelity bond* from a surety company by which the latter agrees to indemnify the bank for any loss resulting from embezzlement by the employees of the bank. A fidelity bond therefore is not an ordinary agreement to pay the debt of another.

Creation of the Relation

Suretyship and guaranty are ordinarily based upon contract, express or implied. All of the principles applicable to the formation, validity, and interpretation of contracts are therefore generally applicable to the law of suretyship.[4] The liability of a surety is measured by the terms of his contract, and his obligation is not necessarily as broad as that of his principal.

1 / Offer and acceptance. Generally the ordinary rules of offer and acceptance apply. Notice of the acceptance, however, must sometimes be given by the creditor to the guarantor.[5]

2 / Consideration. A suretyship relation may be created by the contract of the parties either before, after, or at the same time as the principal obligation. Ordinarily there must be consideration for the promise of the surety.

If the suretyship undertaking is entered into before or at the time the principal obligation arises, a separate consideration is not required. If the suretyship promise is made afterwards, it must be supported by a separate consideration since the prior transaction would be "past" consideration.

Facts: Wehle contracted with Rankin for the latter to build a house on Wehle's lot. Baker was considering lending money to Rankin so that he could perform the contract. Wehle wrote Baker that he would make payments under the contract up to a specified amount by checks payable jointly to the contractor and Baker. Baker then loaned Rankin the money, for which Baker later sued Wehle.

---

[3] *Bohannon* v. *Southern Railway Co.*, 97 Ga.App. 849, 104 S.E.2d 603.
[4] *General Phoenix Corp.* v. *Cabot*, 300 N.Y. 87, 89 N.E.2d 238.
[5] See p. 91.

Decision: Judgment for Baker. Wehle had become bound as a guarantor, and it was immaterial that he had not received consideration directly from the creditor. (Wehle v. Baker, 97 Ga.App. 111, 102 S.E.2d 661)

When the surety or guarantor is a party to a commercial paper, he cannot raise the defense of lack of consideration if the instrument is in the hands of a holder in due course or a holder through a holder in due course.

3 / Capacity. Anyone with capacity to contract can be a surety for the obligation of another. In many instances the surety is a corporation organized for the purpose of acting as surety in return for a payment of a premium.

Initially it makes no difference in the eyes of the law whether a surety is a friend of the debtor who wants to help him or whether the surety is a corporation that acts as such because it is being paid to do so. If, however, the contract of suretyship is not clear and two interpretations are possible, the courts are inclined to interpret the contract in favor of a noncorporate surety and strictly against a paid corporate surety.[6]

4 / Form. In most states the Statute of Frauds requires that contracts of guaranty be in writing in order to be enforceable, subject to the exception that no writing is required when the promisor makes the promise primarily for his own benefit.

In the absence of a special statute, no writing is required for contracts of suretyship or indemnity, because they impose primary liability, and not a secondary liability to answer for the debt or default of another. Special statutes or sound business practices, however, commonly require the use of written contracts of suretyship and indemnity.

Special Classes of Surety Contracts

Suretyship or guaranty undertakings are sometimes classified as general or special. If the offer is made to the general public or to anyone who becomes the owner of the debt, it is a *general guaranty*. If the offer is made to a particular person and cannot be accepted by another, it is called a *special guaranty*. This is an application of the principle of contract law that an offer can be accepted only by the person to whom it is made.

The undertaking may be classified in terms of its scope. It is a *continuing guaranty*, for example, when the promisor engages to answer for the payment of as many automobiles as another person desires to purchase or of as many loans as he might make in the future. A *limited guaranty* is restricted to transactions made during a stated period of time or to transactions not exceeding a stated amount. If no restrictions are imposed, an *unlimited guaranty* exists.

---

[6] *Mass. Bonding & Ins. Co.* v. *Feutz,* [C.A.8th] 182 F.2d 752.

RIGHTS OF THE PARTIES

Rights and Duties of the Creditor

1 / Right to demand payment or to sue. In a suretyship and an absolute guaranty the creditor may proceed against the surety immediately upon the default of the principal, without proceeding against the principal. This explains why the surety is regarded as subject to a primary liability, or one in the same degree as the debtor.

Facts: The Bank of New Brockton sued S. M. Rowe as surety for C. J. Rowe's debt. S. M. Rowe defended on the ground that no notice had been given or demand made upon him prior to the commencement of the action.

Decision: Judgment for the bank. "In the absence of a contract to the contrary, the obligation of the surety, who guarantees payment, is the same as that of the principal; the surety may be sued immediately upon default of the principal and before any proceedings are had against the principal, and the bringing of the suit is demand enough." (Rowe v. Bank of New Brockton, 207 Ala. 384, 92 So. 643)

In a guaranty the creditor must first exercise due diligence to obtain payment from the debtor before he can make demand upon or sue the guarantor, unless the debtor is insolvent or bankrupt so that it is obvious that a suit against him would be worthless. This, in turn, explains why the guarantor is regarded as subject to a secondary liability.

A delay on the part of the creditor in bringing his action against the debtor will not ordinarily affect his right against the guarantor. If the delay has prejudiced the guarantor, as when the debtor went bankrupt in the interval, however, the latter is released from liability.

2 / Duty to give notice of default. In the case of strict suretyship or absolute guaranty, the creditor is not required to give the surety or guarantor notice of the default of the principal, unless he is expressly required to do so by the contract.

In a guaranty, notice must be given by the creditor within a reasonable time so that the guarantor can take steps to protect himself. If notice is not given, the guarantor is released from liability to the extent that he can show that he was prejudiced by the creditor's failure to give notice.

3 / Security held by the surety. The surety may be unwilling to act as such unless the debtor transfers property to him as security. If the debtor gives property to the surety as security, the creditor is entitled to satisfy his claim out of such property.

When the right exists for the surety to reach the debtor's property given to the surety as security, the right of the creditor to obtain satisfaction from the security is not lost by virtue of the fact that creditor has lost his right to sue the surety for any reason, such as the running of the Statute of Limitations.

If the surety wrongly spends or misapplies property given as security, the creditor may claim that the property is "a trust fund." He may accordingly trace the property and claim his right against it wherever the property is found unless meanwhile other persons, acting in good faith and in ignorance of his rights, have acquired title to or an interest in the property. In such a case the "equities" of the creditor, that is, his right to reach the property, are deemed to be cut off or destroyed.

Rights of the Surety

The surety has a number of rights to protect him from sustaining loss, to obtain his discharge because of the conduct of others that would be harmful to him, or to recover the money that he has been required to pay because of his contract.

1 / Exoneration. If the surety finds his position threatened with danger, as when the debtor is about to leave the state and take his property with him, the surety may call upon the creditor to take steps to enforce his claim against the debtor while he can still do so. If at that time the creditor could proceed against the debtor and fails to do so, the surety is released or exonerated from liability to the extent that he can show that he has been harmed.[7]

2 / Subrogation. When a surety pays a debt that he is obligated to pay, he acquires the claim and the right of the creditor against the debtor. This right is known as *subrogation.* That is, once the creditor is paid in full, the surety stands in the same position as the creditor and may sue the debtor, or enforce any security that was available to the creditor, in order to recover the amount that he has paid. The effect is the same as if the creditor, on being paid, made an express assignment of all his rights to the surety.

The right of subrogation that arises when a surety on a contractor's labor-and-material bond pays labor and material claimants is not a security interest, and the surety is therefore entitled to recover the payments made although no filing was made under the Code.[8]

3 / Indemnity. A surety who has made payment of a claim for which he was liable as surety is entitled to indemnity from the principal, that is, he is entitled to demand from the principal reimbursement of the amount which he has paid.

---

[7] *Madison County Farmers Ass'n* v. *American Employers Ins. Co.,* [C.A.8th] 209 F.2d 581.
[8] *Jacobs* v. *Northeastern Corp.,* 416 Pa. 417, 206 A.2d 49.

4 / Contribution. If there are two or more sureties, each is liable to the creditor for the full amount of the debt, until the creditor has been paid in full. As between themselves, however, each is only liable for a proportionate share of the debt. Accordingly, if the surety has paid more than his share of the debt, he is entitled to demand that his cosureties contribute to him in order to share the burden which, in the absence of a contrary agreement, must be done equally.

Defenses of the Surety

The surety's defenses include not only those that may be raised by a party to any contract but also the special defenses that are peculiar to the suretyship relation.

1 / Ordinary defenses. Since the relationship of suretyship is based upon a contract, the surety may raise any defense that a party to an ordinary contract may raise, such as lack of capacity of parties, absence of consideration, fraud, mistake, or absence of a required writing.

Fraud and concealment are common defenses. Since the risk of the principal's default is thrown upon the surety, it is unfair for the creditor to conceal from the surety facts that are material to the surety's risk.

Facts: Hugill agreed to deliver shingles to the W. I. Carpenter Lumber Co. He furnished a surety bond to secure the faithful performance of the contract on his part. After a breach of the contract by Hugill, the lumber company brought an action to recover its loss from the surety, the Fidelity & Deposit Co. of Maryland. The surety denied liability on the ground that there was concealment of (1) the price to be paid for the shingles, and (2) the fact that a material advance had been made to the contractor equal to the amount of the profit that he would make by performing he contract.

Decision: Judgment for surety. The concealment of the price of the shingles was not significant in that it would not lead to any loss or prejudice. The advance was prejudicial as it equaled the profit the contractor would make by performing, thereby depriving him of an incentive to complete the contract and depriving the surety of a fund that would be available in case of the contractor's default. (W. I. Carpenter Lumber Co. v. Hugill, 149 Wash. 45, 270 P. 94)

Fraud on the part of the principal that is unknown to the creditor and in which he has not taken part does not ordinarily release the surety.

The creditor is not required to volunteer information to the surety and need not disclose that the principal was insolvent.

2 / Suretyship defenses. The following defenses of the surety are peculiar to the suretyship relation:

(a) Invalidity of original obligation.[9]

(b) Discharge of principal by payment, performance, release,[10] or any other means.

(c) Material modification of the original contract to which the surety does not consent, as by a binding extension of time for performing the contract.

Likewise, when a building contract requires the owner to retain a specified percentage of the amount due the contractor but the owner fails to do so, with the consequence that there is no retained or reserve fund from which to pay claims of labor and materialmen for which the contractor's surety is liable, the surety may sue the owner for the loss caused when the surety is thereafter required to pay the labor and materialmen.[11]

Facts: Tiernan contracted with American Structures to construct a building according to plans and specifications. A bond was obtained from the Equitable Fire & Marine Insurance Co. to protect Tiernan for loss in the event that there was a breach by American Structures. This performance bond specified that no modification could be made to the plans and specifications without the consent of Equitable. Acting without such consent, Tiernan and American Structures agreed to substitute a cheaper air conditioning system for the system specified in the contract. The system proved defective, and Tiernan sued Equitable on the ground that the contract had not been properly performed by American Structures.

Decision: The surety was not liable to the extent that the modification of the contract had caused Tiernan loss. The surety was only bound for the performance of the contract that existed when it undertook to be liable for the performance of the contract. The court recognized that some states would discharge the surety from all liability because of any modification of the contract, while others would require a material modification. The court adopted a third view of discharging the surety to the extent of loss caused it by the contract modification. (Equitable Fire & Marine Ins. Co. v. Tiernan Building Corp., [Fla.] 190 So. 2d 197)

(d) Loss of securities that had been given the creditor to hold as additional security for the performance of the original contract, to the extent that such loss is caused by the misconduct or negligence of the creditor.

---

[9] *Dormeyer* v. *Haffa*, 343 Ill.App. 177, 98 N.E.2d 532.
[10] *Noma Electric Corp.* v. *Fidelity & Deposit Co.*, 201 Md. 407, 94 A.2d 277.
[11] *Southern Gulf Utilities Co.* v. *United Benefit Fire Insurance Co.*, [Fla.] 179 So.2d 618.

QUESTIONS AND PROBLEMS

1. Checklist of legal terms:
   (a) suretyship, guaranty (493)
   (b) surety, guarantor; principal, creditor (493)
   (c) indemnity contract, fidelity bond (494)
   (d) general guaranty, special guaranty (495)
   (e) continuing guaranty; limited guaranty, unlimited guaranty (495)
   (f) subrogation (497)

2. State the objective(s) of each of the following rules of law:
   (a) The courts are inclined to interpret the contract of suretyship in favor of a noncorporate surety and strictly against a paid corporate surety.
   (b) Contribution may be enforced between cosureties even though there is no express provision so authorizing.

3. Baer offers to buy a used car by paying half of the purchase price at the time of sale and the remainder one year later. The seller refuses to accept this offer unless he is given some form of security. Donaldson joins Baer in a promise to pay the balance a year later. Is Donaldson a guarantor or a surety?

4. Morrison Motors sold a truck on credit to Churchhill. The next day the company requested Birkholder to guarantee Churchhill's indebtedness. Birkholder made a written promise to answer for the obligation. When Churchhill failed to pay, the company brought an action to recover from Birkholder after attempting to collect from Churchhill and giving notice of the default to Birkholder. Was the company entitled to judgment?

5. Best told Adamson that if the latter furnished certain merchandise on credit to Stratton, Best would see that the bill was paid. Later Adamson brought an action against Best to recover the amount of Stratton's debt. Was Adamson entitled to judgment?

6. Dameron refuses to sell a saxophone to Foster unless Bolte also promises to pay for it. Bolte makes such a promise. When a suit is brought against Bolte for the price, he proves that Dameron did not attempt to enforce his claim against Foster. Is this a valid defense?

7. Emerson guarantees the collection of a note given by Darnell. When the instrument is not paid at maturity, the creditor immediately brings action against Emerson. Is the creditor entitled to judgment?

8. Bennett guarantees the collectibility of a note. In an action by the creditor against Bennett, it is proved that the creditor's attempt to enforce his claim against the principal was not made within a reasonable time. How does this fact affect Bennett's liability?

9. Ellison guarantees the collection of a draft. Fry, the holder of the instrument, made a reasonably diligent but unsuccessful effort to collect on

the draft but did not give notice of default to Ellison. Could Fry hold Ellison on the guaranty?

10. Page, as guarantor, was compelled to pay an installment on a debt owed by Victor. Page then demanded the securities that Victor had given the creditor to satisfy the debt in case of default. Was Page entitled to the securities?

11. Roller was surety for Olden's debt to Terry. When Olden failed to pay, Terry brought an action against Roller who pleaded infancy as a defense. Was Terry entitled to recover from Roller?

12. Prince became a surety for a debt owed by Shoemaker to Brock. At the time the relationship was created, Brock failed to inform Prince that Shoemaker was insolvent. When Brock brought an action against Prince, the latter set up concealment as a defense. Was Brock entitled to judgment?

13. Beran was surety for a debt that was assigned by the creditor to Glaser for cash. When the principal did not pay the debt, Glaser brought an action against Beran. Do you agree with Beran's contention that he has been discharged from liability?

14. Allen requested Smith & Brand to lend a stated sum of money to his mother and orally promised that he would repay the loan if his mother did not do so. On the basis of that promise, Smith & Brand made a mortgage loan to the mother. The mother then gave Allen a portion of the loan to pay a debt which she had owed him. When the mother failed to pay the loan, Smith & Brand sued Allen. He raised the defense of the Statute of Frauds. Decide. (Allen v. Smith & Brand, 160 Miss. 303, 133 So. 599)

15. In order to induce Herman & Co. to sell goods to Cohen on credit, Williams guaranteed the payment by Cohen of any future debt. Cohen made purchases but failed to pay for them. Herman & Co. then sued Williams. He defended on the ground that Herman & Co. had agreed with Cohen on the amount due and extended the time for payment by accepting from him a promissory note for that amount, payable at a future date. Williams had not been informed of this adjustment and had not consented to it. Decide. (Herman & Co. v. Williams, 36 Fla. 136, 18 So. 351)

16. Hinds Runnels purchased goods from J. R. Watkins Co. He asked A. D. Runnels to sign a paper. This paper was, in fact, an agreement to guarantee that A. D. Runnels would pay for whatever Hinds Runnels would purchase from Watkins. When sued on this promise by Watkins, A. D. Runnels raised the defense that he signed some paper but did not know what he was signing. Was this a valid defense? (J. R. Watkins Co. v. A. D. Runnels, 252 Miss. 87, 172 So.2d 567)

Chapter 43

The Nature of Insurance

At first, insurance was used primarily by merchants as a means of securing themselves against marine or sea loss. In time a new branch of law relating to insurance developed as part of the law merchant. Toward the end of the Eighteenth Century the law of insurance was absorbed by the common law. Gradually, also, the security device of insurance was extended so that today it affords protection against practically every known kind of risk.

Definitions

Insurance is a contract by which a promise is made to pay another a sum of money if the latter sustains a specified loss.[1] Insurance is basically a plan of security against risk by charging losses against a fund created by the *premiums* or payments made by many individuals. The promisor is called the *insurer*, sometimes the underwriter. The person to whom the promise is made is the *insured*, the assured, or the policyholder. The promise of the insurer is generally set forth in a contract called a *policy*.

Sometimes the risk involved is too great for one insurer. Several insurers may then divide the risk among them as *multiple* or *concurrent insurers,* or one insurer may reinsure in other companies against the risk of paying the loss on the policy.

Since the insurance policy is a contract, the general principles of contract law apply to determine what constitutes the agreement between the parties.

Facts: Martell obtained two policies of life insurance from the National Guardian Life Insurance Co. Attached by a paper clip to one of the policies was a specimen value sheet showing that if dividends were left with the company by Martell, the policies would become paid-up endowment policies when he attained the age of 66. When he attained that age, he sued for the combined face value of the two policies, $10,000. National denied that the policies were paid-up endowments, denied that the specimen value sheet was part of its obligation, and offered to pay only the cash surrender value of the policies with dividends and interest.

Decision: Judgment for National Guardian. The policy is the complete contract of insurance in the absence of an express provision incorporating other

---

[1] *Barry's Estate*, 208 Okla. 8, 252 P.2d 437.

documents. The mere physical attachment of a document by a paper clip does not make it part of the insurance contract. The fact that the specimen sheet was described as a "specimen" and that there was only one specimen sheet for the two policies confirmed the conclusion that the parties had not intended to make the specimen sheet part of each contract of insurance. (Martell v. National Guardian Life Insurance Co., 27 Wis.2d 164, 133 N.W.2d 721)

The Parties

As the result of statutory regulation, virtually all insurance policies are today written by corporations, fraternal or benefit societies, and national or state governments.

The insured must have the capacity to make a contract. If a minor procures insurance, the policy is generally voidable by him.[2]

Insurable Interest

The insured must have an insurable interest in the subject matter insured. The nature of the interest varies with the kind of policy.

1 / Insurable interest in property. A person has an insurable interest in property whenever he has any right or interest in the property so that its destruction or damage will cause him a direct pecuniary or money loss.[3] It is immaterial whether the insured is the owner of the legal or equitable title, a lienholder, or a person in possession of the property. A person does not have an insurable interest in property if his only right is based upon an agreement that is unenforceable.

In the case of property insurance the insurable interest must exist at the time the loss occurs. Except when expressly required by statute, it is not necessary that the interest exist at the time when the policy or contract of insurance was made.

Facts: Antell made an offer to purchase a particular house. He then procured a fire insurance policy on the house with the Pearl Assurance Co. Thereafter, his offer to purchase was accepted and title to the house was transferred to him. Some time later his house was damaged by fire. The insurer refused to pay on the ground that Antell did not have an insurable interest when the policy was obtained.

Decision: Judgment for Antell. It is sufficient that the insurable interest exists at the time of the loss. Here the policy had been procured in good faith in the expectation of obtaining an insurable interest, and such interest existed before and at the time of the loss. (Antell v. Pearl Assurance Co., 252 Minn. 118, 89 N.W.2d 726)

---

[2] In an increasing number of states, however, statutes make a minor's contract of insurance binding as though he were an adult, at least when the minor is over a specified age, such as eighteen.

[3] *Closuit* v. *Mitby,* 238 Minn. 274, 56 N.W.2d 428.

A relaxation of the requirement of an insurable interest is made under a personal property or *floater policy*, which covers property owned not only by the insured but also by members of his household or family group.

2 / Insurable interest in life. Every person has an insurable interest in his own life and may therefore insure his own life and name anyone he chooses as beneficiary.

A person has an insurable interest in the life of another if he can expect to receive pecuniary gain from the continued life of the other person and, conversely, would suffer financial loss from the latter's death. Thus it is held that a creditor has an insurable interest in the life of his debtor since the death of the debtor may mean that the creditor will not be paid the amount owed him. The creditor may take out insurance in excess of the amount of the debt, but if the amount of the insurance is unreasonably greater than the debt, the policy will generally be void. In some cases the creditor is limited to recovering from the insurer the amount which is due him by the debtor plus the amount of the premiums paid on the policy and interest on those premiums.

A partnership has an insurable interest in the life of each of the partners, for the death of any one of them will dissolve the firm and cause some degree of loss to the partnership. A business enterprise has an insurable interest in the life of an executive or a key employee because his death would inflict a financial loss upon the business to the extent that he could not be replaced or could not readily be replaced without a period of long training. Otherwise there is no insurable interest whether the employee be employed in an office, factory, or a home.

There is uncertainty as to whether a person has an insurable interest in the life of another merely because of relationship. If there is a relationship of marriage or a close blood relationship, it is generally found that there is an insurable interest. The majority of the cases, however, do not base the decision on the fact of that relationship alone. They hold that in view of the relationship it is proper to conclude that, had the deceased person continued in life, the other person could have expected to receive a pecuniary benefit or gain, of which he is defeated by death. Some recent decisions abandon this presumption of benefit and find an insurable interest solely on the basis of relationship. These courts, however, do not extend this principle to relationships by marriage beyond that of husband and wife.

In the case of life insurance the insurable interest must exist at the time the policy is obtained. It is immaterial that the interest no longer exists when the loss is actually sustained. Thus the fact that the insured husband and wife beneficiary were divorced after the life policy was procured does not affect the validity of the policy.

The Insurance Contract

By statute it is now commonly provided that an insurance policy must be written. In order to avoid deception, many statutes also specify the content of certain policies, in whole or in part, and some even specify the size and style of type to be used in printing them. When a statute sets a standard, provisions in a policy in conflict with the statute are generally void.[4] Most states now require that the forms of policies and endorsements be approved by a state insurance commissioner or other official.

An insurance policy specifies the term or period of time it covers. Often the nature of the risk against which insurance is sought determines the period or life of the policy. If an outdoor athletic event or concert is to be held, it is possible to obtain insurance against loss from rain falling on that day so as to prevent the holding of the scheduled event. Such a policy covers only the term or period of that day. Property insurance policies are usually written for one, three, or five years. A life insurance policy may cover a specified number of years or the balance of the insured's life.

1 / Formation. When a person applies for insurance, he ordinarily makes an offer to the insurance company, which the company may accept or reject. Until the insurance company accepts the offer of the applicant, there is no contract of insurance.[5]

Under some circumstances, the offer of insurance may be made by the insurer, in which case the contract of insurance is binding when the applicant mails his signed application to the insurer.

A contract of insurance to protect against the hazards of a particular trip, as in the case of air travel insurance, is binding when the insured gives the application and premium to the representative of the insurer or places it in the vending machine provided for that purpose.

2 / When the insurance contract is effective. An applicant for insurance may or may not be protected by insurance before a formal written policy is issued to him. Four situations may arise:

(a) When the applicant tells a broker to obtain insurance, the applicant is merely making the broker his agent.[6] If the broker procures a policy, the customer is insured. If the broker fails to do so, the customer does not have any insurance. But the broker may be personally liable to the customer for the loss.

(b) The person seeking insurance and the insurer or its agent may orally agree that the applicant will be protected by insurance during the interval between the time the application is received and the time when the

---

[4] *Herbert L. Farkas Co.* v. *New York Fire Insurance Co.,* 5 N.J. 604, 76 A.2d 895.
[5] As to the effect of delay by the insurer in acting upon an application, see p. 90.
[6] *Gen. Acc. Assurance Co.* v. *Caldwell,* [C.A.9th] 59 F.2d 473.

insurer either rejects the application, or accepts it and issues a written policy. This agreement to protect the applicant by insurance during such an interval is binding even though it is oral. Generally, however, when such a preliminary contract is made, the agent will sign a memorandum stating the essential terms of the policy to be executed. This memorandum is called a *binder*.

If loss occurs during the binder period, the insurer is liable to the insured just as though a formal policy had been issued. If the details of the policy had not been specified in the binder agreement, the binder confers the same rights and is subject to the same limitations as the policy which would have been issued later.[7]

(c) The parties may agree that at a later time a policy will be issued and delivered. In that case the insurance contract is not in effect until the policy is delivered or sent to the applicant. Accordingly, loss sustained after the transaction between the applicant and the insurance agent but before the delivery of the policy is not covered by the policy thereafter delivered. The stipulation that the insurance shall not be binding until the policy is issued is more likely to be found in life insurance because the applicant may be required to pass a physical examination before the insurer will issue a policy.

Regardless of whether the policy has been issued, it may be agreed by the parties that the insurance shall not become effective until the first premium is paid. Generally, however, the agreement of the parties is that the policy shall become effective immediately and the first premium will be paid upon the delivery of the policy.

Most property and liability policies contain no provision with respect to the payment of premiums. These policies become effective according to the agreement of the parties, without regard to whether any premium has been paid.

(d) The parties may agree that a policy of life insurance shall be binding upon the payment of the first premium even though the applicant has not been examined, provided he thereafter passes an examination. Under such an agreement the applicant is ordinarily covered by insurance when he dies before the examination, if it can be shown that he would have passed a fair examination.

3 / Modification of contract form. In order to make changes or corrections to the policy, it may not be necessary to issue a new policy. An *endorsement* on the policy or the execution of a separate *rider* is effective for the purpose of changing the policy.

Facts: Rufus J. Bouler obtained a policy of automobile liability insurance from the Zurich Insurance Co. The policy covered both Rufus and anyone

---

[7] *Altrocchi* v. *Hammond,* 17 Ill.App.2d 192, 149 N.E.2d 646.

using the car with his permission. Thereafter an "endorsement" was attached to the policy which stated, among other things, that "the insurance applies only to the named insured." Thereafter, while the brother of the insured, Harris, was driving the car with the permission of Rufus, he was involved in a collision. Zurich claimed that it was not bound by the policy.

Decision: Judgment for Zurich. The endorsement was clearly inconsistent with the original policy which extended to the named insured, Rufus, and to anyone using the car with his permission, whereas the endorsement limited the coverage to Rufus alone. The inconsistent later endorsement governed and controlled the policy. (Zurich Ins. Co. v. Bouler, [La.] 198 So.2d 129)

Premiums

Statutes commonly prohibit insurance companies from making premium discriminations among members of the same risk class and from making rebates or refunds to particular individuals only.

1 / Method of payment of premiums. Premiums may be paid in legal tender or by check. The latter form of payment is, of course, conditional upon the instrument being properly honored. If the check is not paid, the instrument loses its character as payment. This in itself does not immediately forfeit or terminate the policy of insurance. If the premiums are not paid thereafter, however, the policy will ordinarily lapse because of nonpayment of the premiums, subject to antilapse statutes or provisions.

2 / Return of premiums. After the policy has become binding, the insured cannot ordinarily recover the premiums paid to the insurer. In a few instances, however, the insured may recover them as, for example, when the payments were made under a mistake of fact or when they were induced by fraud on the part of an agent of the insurer. If the insurer wrongfully terminates the policy, most courts allow the insured to recover the premiums paid by him.

3 / Nonforfeiture and antilapse provisions. As to the payment of premiums due on life insurance policies subsequent to the first premium, the policies now in general use provide or a statute may specify that the policy shall not automatically lapse upon the date the next premium is due if payment is not then made. By policy provision or statute, the insured is also allowed a *grace period* of 30 to 31 days, in which to make payment of the premium due. The insurer may be required by statute to issue a paid-up policy in a smaller amount, to provide extended insurance for a period of time, or to pay the cash surrender value of the policy when there is a default in the payment of a premium by the insured.

Defenses of the Insurer

The insurer may raise any defense that would be valid in an action upon a contract. Some defenses that do not apply to an action on an ordinary contract may also be raised.

1 / Violation of statute. Statutes commonly specify that insurance policies shall have certain clauses or must not have certain prohibited clauses. If suit is brought to enforce an illegal provision of the policy, it is generally held that the provision is void because it is contrary to the statute.

Sometimes the violation of the statute is based not on the provisions of the policy but on the way the corporation or insurer does business. Generally it is held that an insurance company cannot profit by its own wrong and therefore cannot claim that it is not liable on its policy because it has conducted its business illegally. Thus a foreign (out-of-state) insurance corporation that violated the law by engaging in business without first obtaining a local license and filing local reports was liable on its policy.

2 / Ultra vires. If a corporation issues a policy of insurance that it has no authority to issue, most states hold that the insurance company cannot raise the defense of ultra vires.[8]

3 / Contrary to public policy. Insurance policies frequently provide that the policy shall not be effective if loss is sustained while the insured is engaged in violating the law.

Life insurance policies commonly provide for payment in the case of death by suicide while "sane or insane." Such a provision generally is held valid, but a local statute may provide otherwise or limit the operation of such a provision.

4 / Lack of insurable interest. If the requirement of an insurable interest is not satisfied, the policy cannot be enforced.

5 / False representations. In addition to rescission for fraud, the insurer may set aside a policy whenever the applicant in giving the insurer necessary information has made a *false representation*, that is, a misstatement, whether oral or written, as to a material fact [9] without regard to whether the applicant intended to deceive.

Facts: Lipsky applied for a policy of hospitalization insurance from the Washington National Insurance Co. covering himself and his family. Later his daughter was hospitalized and the insurer refused to pay for her expenses on the ground that the answer in the application for insurance

---

[8] See p. 591.

[9] *Ransom v. Penn Mutual Life Insurance Co.*, 43 Cal.2d 420, 274 P.2d 633; *Nielsen* **v.** *Mutual Service Casualty Co.*, 243 Minn. 246, 67 N.W.2d 457.

as to whether the daughter had had any prior medical consultation was answered falsely by "no." Lipsky had told the insurer's agent the full medical history, but the agent had concluded that it was not worth mentioning and therefore had answered "no."

Decision: The insurer was liable. Although the answer "no" was false, the insurer could not avoid the policy on that ground that the false answer was in the application because the insurer's agent had put it there after making his own conclusion as to whether there was anything worth reporting. (Lipsky v. Washington Nat. Ins. Co., 7 Mich. 632, 152 N.W.2d 702)

When the insured misstates his age, the amount usually payable "shall be that sum which the premium paid would have provided for had the age been correctly stated."

6 / False warranties. The insurer may generally insist that the applicant agree in the policy that the statements of fact or promises of the applicant shall be warranties so that if the facts prove not to be as stated or if the promise is not fulfilled, the policy can be avoided by the insurer.

A *warranty* differs from a representation in several respects. A warranty is part of the final contract of insurance made between the parties, and its terms therefore appear in the policy itself or are incorporated in it by reference. In contrast, the representation is merely a collateral or separate matter which leads up to or induces the execution of the contract. Thus, the representation is made orally or included in a separate preliminary writing or application by the insured but not made part of the contract.

A breach of a warranty or a false warranty makes the insurance contract voidable without regard to whether the matter is material, while a representation does not affect the contract unless the matter is material. A warranty must be literally true or strictly performed, while a representation need only be substantially true.

Because of these considerations and a general reluctance to enforce forfeiture, the courts will, whenever possible, construe statements as representations rather than warranties; and even when they are held to be warranties, they will be construed strictly against the insurer in order to favor the insured. In addition, a number of states have adopted statutes which abolish the characteristics of warranties and provide that a warranty has no greater effect than a representation and that in the absence of proof of materiality or intention to defraud, a warranty, though broken, does not avoid the policy.

7 / Concealment. When an applicant for insurance withholds or conceals information as to material facts with the intent to deceive the insurer, the policy may ordinarily be avoided by the insurer for fraud.

In marine insurance, withholding material information amounts to concealment even though there is no fraudulent intent.

A fact is deemed material if it significantly increases the risk or loss. It is also held that any fact is material when the insurer specifically inquires about it. If the applicant refuses to answer a specific question or gives an answer that is obviously incomplete, there is no concealment in law.[10]

8 / Breach of condition. Just as in the case of an ordinary contract, a policy of insurance may contain conditions which, if not satisfied, bar recovery on the policy. Thus the failure to give notice to the insurer of a loss within the period specified in the policy discharges the insurer from liability.

Counterdefenses

In some instances the defenses of the insurer may be set aside by counterdefenses that are raised by the insured or the beneficiary.

1 / Waiver. As a general proposition, the insurer may waive any provision in the policy that was intended for its benefit unless the court deems that the waiver is against public policy.

2 / Estoppel. The insurer may be estopped from claiming the benefit of the violation of a provision of the policy by the insured. An estoppel arises whenever the insurer has by its words or acts led the insured to a certain conclusion on which the latter relies and would therefore suffer harm if the insurer were permitted to show that the conclusion was not true. If a company issues a receipt for a premium, for example, it is estopped from later denying that payment was made according to the terms of the insurance contract.

Estoppel may also apply to the insured.

Subrogation

In indemnity insurance, if the loss to the insured has been caused by the wrongful act of a third person, the insured has a right to sue that person for the damages caused him. If meanwhile the insurer has paid the insured for those damages, it would be unjust to permit the insured to recover damages from the wrongdoer also. The law accordingly holds that the insurer has the right to assert the insured's claim and to sue the third person for the damages which he caused the insured.[11]

Ordinarily the principle of subrogation is not applicable to life insurance policies but is limited to those policies which are contracts of indemnity.

---

[10] *Flanagan* v. *Sunshine Mutual Insurance Co.,* 73 S.D. 256, 41 N.W.2d 761.

[11] *Motors Insurance Corp.* v. *Employers' Liability Assurance Corp.,* [La.] 52 So.2d 311.

By statute it is sometimes provided that an employer who is required to make workmen's compensation payments to an injured employee or the survivor of a deceased employee is subrogated to the claim against the third person who injured or killed the employee.

QUESTIONS AND PROBLEMS

1. Checklist of legal terms:
   (a) insurance; insurer, insured (502)
   (b) policy, premiums (502)
   (c) multiple or concurrent insurers (502)
   (d) floater policy (504)
   (e) binder (506)
   (f) endorsement, rider (506)
   (g) grace period (507)
   (h) false representation (508)
   (i) warranty (509)

2. State the objective(s) of each of the following rules of law:
   (a) In the case of property insurance the insured must have an insurable interest at the time of the loss.
   (b) An indemnity insurer paying a property loss claim is subrogated to the claim of the insured against the third person causing the harm.

3. Hickman, who is 19 years old, insures his house against loss by fire. When the house is destroyed by fire, the insurance company refuses to pay the amount of the loss on the ground that the policy was not binding because of Hickman's minority. Hickman brings an action to recover on the policy. Is he entitled to judgment?

4. After Gibson borrows money from Hahn, the latter takes out a policy of insurance on Gibson's life and another against fire on Gibson's home. Later the house is destroyed by fire, and on the following day Gibson dies. Each insurance company contends that Hahn had no insurable interest. Do you agree in either case?

5. On the last day of his grace period Lance gives the agent of his insurance company a check for the amount of the premium due on his life insurance. Two days later the check is returned to the branch office of the insurance company marked "N.S.F." (not sufficient funds). A week later Lance dies. The executor of Lance's estate brings an action against the company to recover on the policy. Is he entitled to judgment?

6. When an insurance company issued a policy of fire insurance on a house owned by Lennie, the company relied on his statement that the building was brick. Actually it was a frame building; but in making his statement to the insurance company, Lennie was momentarily confused because he had recently purchased another house of brick construction. After the house was destroyed by fire, Lennie sued on the policy. Was he entitled to judgment?

7. Godfry insures a store that he owns against loss by fire for one year. The policy contains a warranty that the store will be occupied during that period. Eight months later Godfry's tenant moves, and the premises remain vacant for the remainder of the year. During the twelfth month the building is destroyed. The company seeks to avoid the policy. Godfry contends that the company is not entitled to avoid the policy because he had merely made a promise of future conduct. Is his contention sound?

8. Manning applied for a policy of insurance on his own life. In his application he left one question unanswered. The company accepted the application and issued the policy. After Manning's death, his widow brought an action against the company to recover on the policy. The insurer contended that the policy was not binding because of concealment. Do you agree?

9. At the time that an insurance company delivered a policy of life insurance to Hight, it had knowledge of facts that rendered the policy void at the election of the insurer. After Hight's death, his widow brought an action to recover on the policy. The company sought to avoid liability. Was Mrs. Hight entitled to judgment?

10. Einhorn held warehouse receipts as collateral security for a loan that he had made to the prior holder of the receipts. Einhorn obtained a fire insurance policy from the Firemen's Insurance Co., which insured him against loss of the property by fire to the extent of his interest in the collateral. The property represented by the receipts was destroyed by fire. Einhorn assigned his claim on the policy to Flint Frozen Foods, which then sued the insurer. Was the policy obtained by Einhorn valid? (Flint Frozen Foods v. Firemen's Insurance Co., 8 N.J. 606, 86 A.2d 673)

11. Lisle applied for life insurance with the Federal Life & Casualty Co. Both Lisle and his wife made false, fraudulent statements to the insurer in connection with the application. The insurer's physician examined Lisle twice but did not ascertain anything that revealed the falsity of those statements. After the insured's death about a year later, the insurer denied liability on the ground of fraud. Lisle's widow claimed that the insurer could not raise the question of fraud since it had examined the insured before accepting his application. Was the insurer liable? (Federal Life & Casualty Co. v. Lisle, 140 Ohio 2d 269, 172 N.E.2d 919)

12. Hicks obtained an automobile collision policy from the Alabama Farm Bureau Mutual Casualty Insurance Co. The policy provided that there was no coverage of loss during the period between the expiration of the term of the policy and the date of the actual payment of a renewal premium. Hicks did not pay the renewal premium until several months after the expiration of the policy. During the noncovered period, he was in a collision. When he paid the renewal premium to the agent-manager at the insurer's local office, he informed him of this collision. He then filed a proof of loss for the damage sustained in the collision. The insured sued the insurer. Decide. (Alabama Farm Bureau Mutual Cas. Ins. Co. v. Hicks, 41 Ala.App. 143, 133 So.2d 217)

Chapter 44

Kinds of Insurance

Many different kinds of insurance are available. They tend, however, to group themselves into a few categories in terms of the nature of the interest protected.

FIRE INSURANCE

A *fire insurance policy* is a contract to indemnify the insured for destruction of or damage to property caused by fire. In almost every state the New York standard fire insurance form (1943) has been adopted as the standard policy.

Risk Assumed

There must be an actual flame or burning which is accidental or which has escaped from its proper confines, that is, a *hostile fire*. Damage from heat alone is not covered, but damage from heat or smoke caused by a hostile fire is covered.

> **Facts:** Youse owned a ring that was insured with the Employers Fire Insurance Co. against loss, including "all direct loss or damage by fire." The ring was accidentally thrown by Youse into a trash burner and was damaged when the trash was burned. He sued the insurer.
>
> **Decision:** Judgment for insurer. A fire policy only covers loss caused by a hostile fire. The fire was not hostile in that it burned in the area in which it was intended to burn. (Youse v. Employers Fire Insurance Co., 172 Kan. 111, 238 P.2d 472)

The fire must be the immediate or proximate cause of the loss. When there is a reasonable connection between a fire and the ultimate loss sustained, the insurer is liable for the loss.

In the absence of a stipulation to the contrary, the fire insurance policy also covers various forms of harm that are reasonably foreseeable as incidental to a fire. The policy thus covers loss caused by water used in extinguishing a fire, loss arising from the necessary removal of the property from the scene of the fire, loss due to theft of goods during the fire when the insured was not negligent in protecting them from theft, and loss due to explosions caused by the fire.

513

The New York standard form of fire insurance policy excludes loss or damage caused directly or indirectly by enemy attack by armed forces, invasion, insurrection, rebellion, revolution, civil war, or usurped power, or by order of any civil authority; or by neglect of the insured to use all reasonable means to save and preserve the property at and after a fire or when the property is endangered by fire in neighboring premises; or by theft.

Damage by explosion is also excluded unless fire follows and then the insurer is liable only for that part of the damage caused by the fire. The standard form of fire insurance policy includes protection from lightning damage even though no fire is caused thereby.

Notice and Proof of Loss

Fire insurance policies commonly provide that the insured must give the insurer notice of his loss and file a detailed statement of the loss within a certain period and in a certain manner. If proof of loss is not furnished within the time specified by the statute or policy, the insurer generally is not liable.

Insurer's Liability

Basically the insurer is liable for the actual amount of the loss sustained. This liability is limited, however, by the maximum amount stated in the policy or the amount of damages sustained by total destruction of the property, whichever is less. That is, the recovery can never be greater than the damages which would be sustained in the case of total destruction; and this, in turn, cannot exceed the maximum amount stated in the policy.

The amount of the loss, in the absence of statute or agreement to the contrary, is the actual cash value at the time of the loss. A *total loss* does not necessarily mean that the property has been completely destroyed. The loss is regarded as being total if the unconsumed portion is of no value for the purposes for which the property was utilized at the time of the insurance.

Frequently the insurer will stipulate in the policy that it has the right to replace or restore the property to its former condition in lieu of paying the insured the cash value of the loss.

Assignment of Fire Insurance Policy

Fire insurance is a personal contract, and in the absence of statute or contractual authorization it cannot be assigned without the consent of the insurer before a loss is sustained. In addition, it is commonly provided that the policy shall be voided if an assignment to give a purchaser of the property the protection of the policy is attempted. Such a forfeiture clause does not apply to an equitable assignment or to an assignment of the policy made as collateral to secure a loan by the insured from a third person. Likewise, a mortgagee who assigns his mortgage may assign his rights under a fire insurance policy.

Mortgage Clause

Either or both the mortgagor and mortgagee may take out policies of fire insurance to protect their respective interests in property.[1] In the absence of a contrary stipulation, the policy taken out by either covers only his own interest. When one policy protects both parties as their respective interests may appear, it is generally provided that the insurance of the mortgagee shall not be affected by any act of the mortgagor.

Extended Coverage

In the case of fire insurance policies to protect homes and buildings, it is common to include extended coverage by which the property is insured against hazards in addition to that of fire. The term *extended coverage* generally refers to protection against loss from windstorm, hail, explosions other than those within steam boilers on the premises, riot, civil commotion, aircraft damage, vehicle damage, and smoke damage.

Other Provisions

Fire insurance policies commonly prohibit the insured from doing certain acts that will or may increase the hazard or risk involved and provide that the policy is void if the insured commits the prohibited acts.

It is commonly provided that false statements made by the insured when they are known to be false shall avoid the policy. Under such a provision a fraudulent misstatement of the value of the property avoids the policy.

The insured may take out more than one policy on the same property, in the absence of a provision in any of the policies to the contrary; but in the event of loss he cannot recover more than the total loss he sustains. Such a loss is prorated among the insurers.

An insurer is not liable when the damage or destruction of the property is intentionally caused by the insured. The fact that the insured negligently caused a fire is not a defense to the insurer, even when there is a stipulation that the insured shall not change or increase the hazard insured against.

Cancellation

In the absence of a provision in the fire insurance policy or a statute authorizing the cancellation by the act of one party, the agreement of both

---

[1] *Southwestern Graphite Co.* v. *Fidelity & Guaranty Insurance Corp.,* [C.A.5th] 201 F.2d 553.

parties, the insurer and the insured, is essential. It is common, however, to provide by statute or by the terms of the policy that under certain circumstances the policy may be terminated or canceled by the act of one party alone. When this is done, the provisions of the statute and the policy must be strictly followed in order to make the cancellation effective.[2]

AUTOMOBILE INSURANCE

Commonly, two types of motor vehicle insurance are available. One type compensates the owner or operator for his own loss or damages from fire, theft, and collision or upset, while another type protects the owner from the claims of other persons for damage caused by him to them or their property. The latter type is generally called liability insurance. In addition, many policies include an extended coverage to cover liability for injuries sustained in connection with any kind of accident.

Associations of insurers, such as the National Bureau of Casualty Underwriters and the National Automobile Underwriters Association, have proposed standard forms of policies that have been approved by their members in virtually all the states.

Financial Responsibility Laws

By state law, drivers are required to carry liability insurance in order to obtain or maintain the right to operate an automobile. In practically all states, the law does not apply until the driver is involved in an automobile accident, when he is required to furnish proof of financial responsibility before he can drive again. One of the ways of proving financial responsibility under the statutes is to show that liability insurance in an amount stated by the statute is maintained by the operator. This type of statute is called a *financial responsibility law*. It is open to the criticism that it applies only after a driver has had his first accident,[3] which is little consolation to the victim of the first accident.

Liability Insurance

The owner or operator of a motor vehicle may obtain *liability insurance* to protect himself from claims made by third persons for damage to their property (property damage liability) or person (bodily injury liability) arising from the use or operation of an automobile. When the insurer pays under such a policy, it makes the payment directly to the third person and is liable to pay him the same amount and for the same items as the insured

---

[2] *Mobile Fire & Marine Insurance Co.* v. *Kraft,* 36 Ala.App. 684, 63 So.2d 34.
[3] *Travelers Insurance Co.* v. *Boyd,* 312 Ky.App. 527, 228 S.W.2d 421.

would be required to pay if sued by the third person, although it is not required to pay more than the maximum stated in the policy.

The terms "use" and "operation" are very liberally interpreted to include events in which there is some involvement of the automobile, although not for the purpose of transportation.

Facts: Coleman had an automobile liability insurance policy that was issued by the Employers' Liability Assurance Corp. When she was leaving the supermarket operated by Wrenn & Outlaw, the bagboy employed by the supermarket accidently closed the door of her car on her hand. The insurer claimed that it was not liable for this injury because its policy only covered the "use" of the automobile.

Decision: Judgment against insurer. The use of an automobile includes loading and unloading as an incident to the transportation contemplated or completed. Therefore the action of the bagboy constituted a use of the automobile and the insurance policy was applicable. (Wrenn & Outlaw v. Employers' Liability Assurance Corp., 246 S.C. 97, 142 S.E.2d 741)

If the insurer is liable for the damage caused a third person or his property, it is likewise liable for cost of repairs, destruction of property, loss of services, and other items of damages for which the insured himself would be liable.

The liability of the insured is not affected by the fact that he is insured. The fact that he is legally liable although insured means that if for any reason his policy does not cover the full loss or if the insurance company is not solvent or in business at that time, he is liable for any amount not paid.

1 / Person operating. Liability policies ordinarily protect the owner of the auto from liability when it is operated by another person with the permission of the insured,[4] as in the case of an employee or agent of the owner.

Liability insurance may also protect an insured individual or his spouse against liability incurred while operating another person's automobile. This is referred to as *D.O.C.* (drive-other-car) *coverage.*

2 / Exclusions. In liability insurance the insurer may protect itself by excluding damage claims arising out of certain types of causes. Such policies may exclude claims of employees of the owner or claims under the workmen's compensation laws, or liability for claims when the insured admits to the injured third person that the insured is liable and agrees to pay his claim.

The fact that the owner or operator is violating a speed law does not free the insurer from liability in the absence of an express provision to that effect.

In the case of commercial vehicles the insurer may stipulate that it shall only be bound by the policy "provided: (a) the regular and frequent use of

---

[4] *West* v. *McNamara,* 159 Ohio 187, 111 N.E.2d 909.

the automobile is confined to the area within a fifty mile radius of the limits of the city or town where the automobile is principally garaged . . . , (b) no regular or frequent trips are made by the automobile to any locations beyond such radius." [5]

3 / Notice and cooperation. A liability policy generally provides that the insurer is not liable unless the insured (a) gives the insurer prompt notice of any serious accident or claim or lawsuit brought against him, (b) furnishes the insurance company with all details of the occurrence, and (c) cooperates with the insurer in the preparation of the defense against a lawsuit brought on the policy and participates at the trial. Notice and cooperation under such a policy are conditions precedent to the liability of the insurer.[6]

Collision or Upset Insurance

Liability insurance does not indemnify the owner for damage to his own automobile. In order to obtain this protection, the owner of the auto must obtain property insurance. A policy of collision insurance is not limited to harm arising from colliding with other motor vehicles.

Facts: Ryburn obtained a collision policy from the Washington Fire & Marine Insurance Co. Because of a wet surface on the road, the insured truck careened off the highway and plunged into a ditch filled with water. Ryburn claimed that there was a "collision" with another "object" within the coverage of the policy.

Decision: Judgment for Ryburn. The body of water was an "object" distinct from the road on which the truck was moving, and there was a collision with it. Although there is some conflict, the policy is to be interpreted liberally in favor of the insured to afford indemnity in such a case. (Washington Fire & Marine Ins. Co. v. Ryburn, 228 Ark. 930, 311 S.W.2d 302)

Such a policy commonly provides that the insurer is not liable when the automobile is used by a person engaged in violating the law. It may also be stipulated that liability is avoided if the auto is subject to a lien or encumbrance that has not been disclosed. It is common to exclude damages, resulting from collision, for the loss of the use of the auto, depreciation, or for loss of personal property in the auto.

Automobile collision insurance policies frequently contain a deductible clause and are known, for example, as "$100 deductible" policies. The effect

---

[5] *Bruins* v. *Anderson,* 73 S.D. 620, 47 N.W.2d 493.
[6] *Heimlich* v. *Kees Appliance Co.,* 256 Wis. 356, 41 N.W.2d 359.

of such a clause is that for each accident the insurer is liable only for the loss in excess of the amount stated to be deductible.

As in the case of liability insurance, the auto owner is under a duty to give notice, to inform, and to cooperate with the insurer. He must also give the insurer an opportunity to examine the automobile.

Theft Insurance

The owner of an automobile can secure theft insurance, which will protect him from loss through the theft and from damage to the auto caused by a theft. The standard form of policy covers loss from larceny, robbery, and pilferage as well as theft. In addition, statutes in some states provide that a "theft" occurs within the meaning of a theft policy whenever there is any taking or use of the automobile not authorized by the owner.

It is common to exclude liability for the loss sustained while a passenger auto is used for commercial transportation or is rented to another. Such exclusions are, of course, not found in policies covering vehicles used for commercial purposes or for renting to others.

An automobile theft policy does not necessarily protect against loss of contents. It is common to exclude liability for equipment or personal property taken from the auto, but additional insurance protecting from such theft can be secured.

Fire, Lightning, and Transportation Insurance

In this type of insurance the insurer agrees to pay for any loss arising out of damage to, or the destruction of, a motor vehicle or its equipment caused by fire originating in any manner, by lightning, or by the stranding, sinking, burning, collision, or derailment of any conveyance in or upon which the automobile or the truck is being transported.

This type of policy is commonly combined with a policy against theft and pilferage and is usually subject to the same exclusions.

Comprehensive Insurance

In many automobile insurance policies, comprehensive material damage coverage, which protects the policyholder against virtually all such risks except collision or upset, replaces fire and theft insurance. The exclusions for this kind of insurance include wear and tear, freezing, mechanical breakdown, and loss of personal effects.

LIFE INSURANCE

A contract of *life insurance* requires the insurer to pay a stipulated sum of money upon the death of the insured. It is not a contract of indemnity since the insurer does not undertake to indemnify the beneficiary for the financial loss sustained as the result of the death of the insured.

Kinds of Life Insurance Policies

Life insurance is commonly classified in three groups: (1) ordinary life insurance, (2) group insurance, and (3) industrial insurance. Ordinary life insurance in turn may be subclassified as (a) *straight life insurance,* which requires payments of premiums throughout the life of the insured; (b) *limited payment insurance,* requiring the payment of premiums during a limited period, such as ten, twenty, or thirty years, or until the death of the insured if that should occur before the end of the specified period; (c) *endowment insurance,* under which the insurer undertakes to pay a stipulated sum when the insured reaches a specified age, or upon his death if that occurs earlier; and (d) *term insurance,* under which the insurer undertakes to pay a stipulated sum only in the event of the death of the insured during a specified period, such as one, two, five, or ten years.

Somewhat similar to policies of endowment insurance are *annuity policies* and *retirement income insurance* under which the insured either pays a lump sum to the insurer and thereafter receives fixed annual payments, or pays periodic premiums to the insurer until a certain date and then receives fixed annual payments.

Group life insurance is an insurance of the lives of employees of a particular employer or persons engaged in a particular business or profession. Such policies are usually either term policies or ordinary policies. A medical examination is usually not required.

Industrial insurance is in substance ordinary life insurance written for a small amount, usually from $100 to $500. Premiums are generally paid weekly or monthly and are collected from door to door by the agent of the insured. No physical examination is required for industrial insurance. The industrial policy may be either term, straight life, limited payment, or endowment.

Life insurance policies may provide for *double indemnity* if death is caused by an accident and occurs within ninety days after the accident; for the making of payments to the insured in the event of his total permanent disability; and for reinstatement upon lapse of the policy for nonpayment of premiums.

Disability is usually defined in a life insurance policy as any "incapacity resulting from bodily injury or disease to engage in any occupation for remuneration or profit." The policy generally provides that a disability which has continued for a stated minimum period, such as four to six months, will be regarded as a *total permanent disability.* The policy may also provide that during such a period of disability, the payment of premiums will be waived. The waiver of premium payments during disability may be included in a policy without a provision for payments to the insured for his disability.

The Beneficiary

The person to whom the proceeds of a life insurance policy are payable upon the death of the insured is called the *beneficiary*. He may be a third person, or the beneficiary may be the estate of the insured. There may be more than one beneficiary. When the policy is payable directly to a named beneficiary, the proceeds of the policy are generally not subject to the debts of the insured.[7]

The customary policy provides that the insured reserves the right to change the beneficiary without the latter's consent. When the policy contains such a provision, the beneficiary cannot object to a change that destroys all rights which he had under the policy by naming another beneficiary. The need for a beneficiary change may be met in advance in some instances by designating both a primary and a contingent beneficiary.

The insurance policy will ordinarily prescribe that in order to change the beneficiary, the insurer must be so instructed in writing by the insured and the policy must then be endorsed by the company with the change of the beneficiary. These provisions are generally liberally construed. If the insured has properly notified the insurer but dies before the endorsement of the change is made by the company, the change of beneficiary is effective. If the insured has clearly indicated his intention to change the beneficiary, the consent of the insurer to the change is not required.

> **Facts:** Reeves was insured in the Beneficial Mutual Life Insurance Co. The policy named his wife, Margaret, beneficiary and stated that the beneficiary could be changed by filing at the home office a "written designation of beneficiary." Reeves wrote the company requesting that "the usual procedure be instituted making" his sister, Mary, the beneficiary. The insurance company then mailed him a printed form to change the beneficiary with instructions that he should sign and return the form. Reeves did not sign or return the form and was killed in an accident three months later. His widow, Margaret Reeves, and his sister, Mary Tomaneng, each claimed the proceeds of insurance and brought an action to determine their respective rights.
>
> **Decision:** Judgment for Margaret Reeves. While literal compliance with the procedure specified in a policy for changing a beneficiary is not required, it must be shown that the insured intended to change the beneficiary and that he did everything in his power to make the change. The letter requesting the institution of the usual procedure to change the bene-

---

[7] *Succession of Onorato*, 219 La. 1, 51 So.2d 804.

ficiary was not in itself an unequivocal designation of a change of beneficiary. Since the insured never filled out the form that was sent him, there was accordingly no change of beneficiary. (Tomaneng v. Reeves, [C.A.6th] 180 F.2d 208)

In industrial policies it is also customary for the policy to contain a "facility-of-payment clause" under which the insurer is given the option of selecting from a designated class or group anyone whom the insurer deems equitably entitled to receive payment and to make payment to that person. Such a clause enables the insurer to pay the amount of the insurance proceeds directly to any person who pays the debts of the decedent, such as his funeral bills, rather than to a named beneficiary who has not expended any money on behalf of the decedent or his estate.

Risks Assumed by the Insured

Policies frequently provide that death shall not be within the protection of the policy or that a double indemnity provision shall not be applicable when death is due to or caused by (1) suicide, (2) narcotics, (3) violation of the law, (4) execution for crime, (5) war activities, or (6) operation of aircraft.

It is generally provided by statute or stated by decision that a beneficiary who has feloniously killed the insured is not entitled to receive the proceeds of the policy.[8]

Incontestable Clause

Statutes commonly provide, and many life insurance companies regardless of statutes provide, for the inclusion of an incontestable clause in life insurance policies. Ordinarily this clause states that after the lapse of two years the policy cannot be contested by the insurance company. The insurer is free to contest the validity of the policy at any time during the contestable period; but once that period has expired, it must pay the stipulated sum upon the death of the insured and cannot claim that in obtaining the policy the insured had been guilty of misrepresentation, fraud, or any other conduct that would exempt it from liability.

The incontestable clause does not bar matters of defense that arise subsequent to the sustaining of loss. Generally the incontestable clause is not applicable to double indemnity or disability provisions of the policy.

Assignment by Insured

In the absence of a stipulation in the policy or a provision of a statute to the contrary, a policy of life insurance may be assigned before it matures

---

[8] *Neff* v. *Mass. Mutual Life Insurance Co.*, 158 Ohio 45, 107 N.E.2d 100.

or before the right of the insured becomes vested in it. In itself, an assignment does not change the beneficiary.

The assignment of a life insurance policy is frequently governed by statute. It is commonly provided that the assignment must be in writing, and in some states the right to make an assignment is restricted when the beneficiary is a wife or child of the insured.

Loans and Surrender of Policy

The insured may to a certain extent obtain a loan on a policy from the insurer, or surrender it to the insurer for its cash surrender value or in return for a paid-up policy or one of extended insurance.

1 / Paid-up policy. The insured may, under modern statutes or common forms of policies, request the insurer to issue to him a new policy of paid-up insurance. Instead of losing the reserve value that he has built up by the payment of his premiums, the insured in effect takes out a new paid-up policy of insurance for a smaller amount of protection and pays for that policy through the transfer of the reserve value of the old policy.

In some states it is provided that when a policy lapses for nonpayment of premiums, the insurer must automatically issue a paid-up policy on the basis of the reserve value of the lapsed policy.

2 / Extended insurance. Instead of taking a paid-up policy for a smaller amount, it is generally possible under modern statutes and policies to obtain term insurance giving the same amount of protection. This remains effective until the reserve value of the original policy has been consumed.

Rights of Creditors

If the insured makes the policy payable to his estate, the proceeds become part of the general assets of his estate upon his death and, in the absence of statute, are subject to the claims of his creditors. If the insured makes the policy on his own life payable to another person and if the insured is at all times solvent when he pays the premiums, his creditors cannot reach the policy in any way, and the beneficiary is entitled to the proceeds of the policy.

Between these two extremes are a variety of situations. The insured may have been insolvent during part or all of the life of the policy; or the obtaining of the insurance policy or the assignment of it or the changing of the beneficiary may have been done in fraud of creditors.

If the policy is originally payable to the estate of the insured, an assignment by the insured of his interest when made in fraud of creditors will not defeat the right of the creditors.

If the policy is made payable to a third person as beneficiary but the insured is insolvent, courts differ as to the rights of the insured's creditors.

Facts: Jones had insured his life, making the policy payable to his estate. When he was insolvent, he changed the beneficiaries of the policy to name his sister, Cramer, and his son as beneficiaries. After his death, Davis and Giles, creditors, claimed that the proceeds of the insurance policy should be paid into the decedent's estate on the theory that the change of the beneficiary was a transfer made in fraud of creditors.

Decision: Judgment for creditors in part. The court held that the change had been made in fraud of creditors but that the surrender value of the policies on the date of the change of the beneficiaries was all the creditors were entitled to since that was the only amount over which Jones had control at the time he made the change of beneficiaries. (Davis v. Cramer, 133 Ark. 224, 202 S.W. 239)

QUESTIONS AND PROBLEMS

1. Checklist of legal terms—fire insurance:
    (a) fire insurance policy (513)
    (b) hostile fire (513)
    (c) total loss (514)
    (d) extended coverage (515)

2. State the objective(s) of each of the following rules of law:
    (a) In a policy which insures the interest of the mortgagor and mortgagee as their interests appear, it may be provided that the rights of the mortgagee in the policy will not be affected by the acts of the mortgagor.
    (b) Financial responsibility laws generally do not require that an automobile driver obtain insurance until after he has had an accident.
    (c) A change of beneficiary is effective although all the steps specified by the policy have not been taken, if the insured has done everything within his power to effect the change.

3. A steam radiator in Van Saun's house became intensely heated, damaging the adjacent wall. Van Saun filed a claim against the insurer on his policy of fire insurance. When the company refused to pay, Van Saun brought action on the policy. Was he entitled to judgment?

4. A fire destroyed an apartment building on the lot adjoining Homer's property. During the fire one of the walls of the building fell on Homer's house and damaged the roof. Homer claimed indemnity for this damage under his policy of fire insurance. Was he entitled to recover on the policy?

5. A small fire in Larkin's gift shop caused considerable damage to merchandise and equipment by water. He also suffered loss through the theft of certain merchandise that was removed from the building during the fire. To what extent will Larkin's policy of fire insurance indemnify him for these losses?

6. Walden's policy of fire insurance on his house provides that the insurer will be liable for the maximum amount of the policy in the event of total

loss. A fire consumes all of the building except the four walls. The insurer refuses to pay the maximum amount of the policy on the ground that Walden has not suffered a total loss of the building. Is Walden entitled to judgment in an action on the policy?

7. Ashworth insures his house against loss by fire. Later he conveys the premises to Briggs. Upon the destruction of the house by fire, Briggs demands indemnity from the insurance company. When the company refuses to pay, Briggs brings an action on Ashworth's policy. Is he entitled to judgment?

8. Conrad's business property is valued at $100,000. He secures a fire insurance policy from one company for $50,000 and another from a second company for $30,000. When his building is damaged by fire to the extent of $16,000, how much is he entitled to collect?

9. Marshall Produce Co. insured its milk and egg processing plant against fire with the St. Paul Fire & Marine Insurance Co. Smoke from a fire near its plant was absorbed by its egg powder. Cans of the powder delivered to the United States Government were rejected as contaminated. Marshall Produce sued the insurance company for a total loss. The insurer contended that there had been no fire involving the insured property and no total loss. Decide. (Marshall Produce Co. v. St. Paul Fire & Marine Insurance Co., 256 Minn. 404, 98 N.W.2d 280)

10. Checklist of legal terms—automobile insurance:
    (a) financial responsibility law (516)
    (b) liability insurance (516)
    (c) D.O.C. coverage (517)

11. Curtis took out a policy of property damage liability insurance on his car. One day when he entered his garage, he failed to apply his brakes quickly enough and ran through the rear of his garage causing damage amounting to $100. When the insurer refused to pay for the damage to the garage, Curtis brought an action to recover for breach of contract. Was he entitled to judgment?

12. Pierce's insurance on his automobile covers liability for both bodily injury and property damage. Pierce gives his neighbor, Vogel, permission to drive his car. Vogel negligently runs into Shipley's car, damaging it and causing Shipley to suffer cuts and bruises. Does Pierce's policy cover any liability that he may incur in an accident?

13. Gates' car disappeared from its parking place while he was shopping. The car was recovered by the local police in a few days and returned to Gates. The upholstery had been damaged. Is Gates protected by his policy of automobile theft insurance?

14. A tool kit was stolen from Klotter's automobile while it was parked in front of the home of one of his friends. The insurer refused to pay for the loss under a policy of theft insurance. Was Klotter entitled to judgment in an action against the company to recover on the policy?

15. Sackett insured his automobile with the Farmers Insurance Exchange against loss by accidental means. A gas station attendant improperly fastened the radiator cap with the result that the water boiled out of the radiator and damaged the engine. The Farmers Insurance Exchange claimed that it was not liable because the harm came within the exception of "mechanical breakdown and failure." Was the insurer correct? (Sackett v. Farmers Insurance Exchange, 237 Cal.App.2d 899, 47 Cal. Rep. 350)

16. Checklist of legal terms—life insurance:
    (a) life insurance (520)
    (b) straight life insurance, limited payment insurance, endowment insurance, term insurance (520)
    (c) annuity policy, retirement income insurance (520)
    (d) group life insurance, industrial insurance (520)
    (e) double indemnity (520)
    (f) disability, total permanent disability (520)
    (g) beneficiary (521)

17. Levenson's policy of life insurance was payable to his wife. The policy provided that the insured reserved the right to change the beneficiary. Before Levenson's death, he made Jastram beneficiary of the policy. Upon his death, the proceeds of the policy were collected by Jastram. Mrs. Levenson brought an action against Jastram contending that she was entitled to the proceeds. Do you agree?

18. Lockwood, a factory employee, has an industrial life insurance policy with a facility-of-payment clause. The policy, which was taken out before his marriage, names his mother as beneficiary. Upon Lockwood's death, his widow pays the funeral expenses. Who is entitled to payment on the policy?

19. Monroe's life insurance policy, which provides for double indemnity and disability benefits, contains an incontestable clause. Five years later when Monroe dies, the insurer proves fraud on Monroe's part in securing the policy. What effect, if any, does this proof of fraud have upon the insurer's liability?

20. After Hurley's death, a policy of life insurance is found in his desk. The proceeds of the policy are payable to his estate. After the executor collects payment from the insurer, Hurley's heirs and his creditors both demand the money. Who is entitled to the money?

21. Walker obtained a policy of life insurance from the National Life and Accident Insurance Co. The policy reserved the right to change the beneficiary. Walker named his wife as beneficiary, and she paid the premiums on the policy. Later Walker's wife sued the insurance company and claimed that the insured could not change the beneficiary because she had paid the premiums on the policy. Decide. (National Life and Accident Insurance Co. v. Walker, [Ky.] 246 S.W.2d 139)

PART VIII

Partnerships

Chapter 45

Creation and Termination

The single proprietorship is the most common form of business organization, but many larger businesses have two or more owners. The partnership is a very common form of multiple ownership.

NATURE AND CREATION

Modern partnership law shows traces of Roman law, the law merchant, and the common law of England. A Uniform Partnership Act, formulated by the National Conference of Commissioners on Uniform State Laws for the purpose of bringing about uniformity in this branch of the law, has been adopted in most states.[1]

Definitions

A *partnership* or copartnership is a legal relationship created by the voluntary "association of two or more persons to carry on as co-owners a business for profit."[2] The persons so associated are called *partners* or copartners.

A partnership can be described more realistically in terms of its characteristics:

(1) A partnership is a voluntary contractual relation; it is not imposed by law. Because of the intimate and confidential nature of the partnership relation, courts do not attempt to thrust a partner upon anyone. As between the partners themselves, the relation is formed, governed, and terminated by the agreement.

---

[1] This Act has been adopted in the District of Columbia, Guam, the Virgin Islands, and all states except Alabama, Florida, Georgia, Hawaii, Iowa, Kansas, Louisiana, Maine, Mississippi, and New Hampshire.

[2] Uniform Partnership Act, Sec. 6(1); *Carle v. Carle Tool & Engineering Co.,* 33 N.J.S. 469, 110 A.2d 568.

(2) The relation of partnership usually involves contributions by the members of capital, labor, or skill, or a combination of these.

(3) The parties are associated as co-owners and principals to transact the business of the firm.

(4) A partnership is organized for the pecuniary profit of its members. If profit is not its object, the group will commonly be an unincorporated association.[3]

The trend of the law is to treat a partnership as a separate legal person,[4] although historically and technically it is merely a group of individuals with each partner being the owner of a fractional interest in the common enterprise.

Facts: Loucks and Del Martinez were the members of a partnership that did business under the name of L & M Paint and Body Shop. The partners had a checking account in the firm name in the Albuquerque National Bank. Martinez owed money on his personal note to the Bank. When he became delinquent in payment on his note, the Bank deducted the payments due from the partnership account. This made the partnership account insufficient to meet checks that were drawn on it by the partnership, and the bank dishonored the partnership checks. The two partners sued the bank for damages claimed to have been caused each of them by the wrongful dishonor of the checks.

Decision: The deductions had been improperly made from the partnership bank account, but the partners individually could not sue for damages because the partnership was the depositor and therefore was the "person" entitled to sue for breach of the bank-depositor contract. (Loucks v. Albuquerque National Bank, 76 N.Mex. 735, 418 P.2d 191)

As this type of enterprise is based upon the agreement of the parties, the characteristics and attributes of the partnership relationship are initially a matter of the application of general principles of contract law, upon which principles are superimposed the principles of partnership law.

Purposes of a Partnership

A partnership may be formed for any lawful purpose. It is immaterial whether it relates to the conduct of a business or a profession.

The partnership cannot be formed to carry out immoral or illegal acts, or acts that are contrary to public policy. The effect of an illegal purpose is a denial to the partners of a right to sue on the contracts that involve the illegality. Moreover, in such cases the partners cannot seek the aid of courts to settle their affairs among themselves. In addition, if the conduct of the partnership constitutes a crime, all persons involved in the commission of the crime are subject to punishment.

---

[3] See p. 561.
[4] *Mendonca Dairy* v. *Mauldin*, [Okla.] 420 P.2d 552.

Classification of Partnerships

Ordinary partnerships are classified as general and special partnerships, and as trading and nontrading partnerships.

1 / General and special partnerships. A *general partnership* is created for the general conduct of a particular kind of business, such as a hardware business or a manufacturing business. A *special partnership* is formed for a single transaction, such as the purchase and resale of a certain building.

2 / Trading and nontrading partnerships. A *trading partnership* is organized for the purpose of buying and selling, such as a firm engaged in the retail grocery business. A *nontrading partnership* is one organized for a purpose other than engaging in commerce, such as the practice of law.

Firm Name

In the absence of a statutory requirement it is not necessary that a partnership have a firm name, although it is customary to have one. The partners may, as a general rule, adopt any firm name they desire. They may use a fictitious name or even the name of a stranger. Moreover, a firm may have more than one name; as, for example, a firm that has branch houses or conducts business at two or more places.

There are, however, certain limitations upon the adoption of a firm name:

(1) The name cannot be the same as or deceptively similar to the name of another firm for the purpose of attracting its patrons.

(2) Some states prohibit the use of the words "and company" unless they indicate an additional partner.

(3) Many states require the registration of a fictitious partnership name.

Classification of Partners

(1) A *general partner* is one who publicly and actively engages in the transaction of firm business.

(2) A *nominal partner* holds himself out as a partner or permits others to hold him out as such. He is not in fact a partner since he neither shares in the management nor the profits; but in some instances he may be held liable as a partner.

(3) A *silent partner* is one who, although he may be known to the public as a partner, takes no active part in the business.

(4) A *secret partner* is one who takes an active part in the management of the firm but who is not known to the public as a partner.

(5) A *dormant partner* is one who takes no active part in transacting the business and who remains unknown to the public.

Who May Be Partners

In the absence of statutory provisions to the contrary, persons who are competent to contract may form a partnership. A minor may become a partner, but he may avoid the contract of partnership and withdraw.[5]

In general, the capacity of an insane person to be a partner is similar to that of a minor, except that an adjudication of insanity usually makes subsequent agreements void rather than merely voidable. An enemy alien may not be a partner, but other aliens may enter into the relation. A corporation, unless expressly authorized by statute or its charter, may not be a partner.

Creation of Partnership

A partnership is a voluntary association and exists because the parties agree to be in partnership. If there is no agreement, there is no partnership. If the parties agree that the legal relationship between them shall be such that they in fact operate a business for profit as co-owners, a partnership is created even though the parties may not have labeled their new relationship a "partnership." [6] The law is concerned with the substance of what is done rather than the name.

Conversely, a partnership does not arise if the parties do not agree to the elements of a partnership, even though they call it a partnership.

Articles of Partnership

As a general rule, partnership agreements need not be in writing.[7] A partnership agreement must be in writing, however, if it is within the provision of the Statute of Frauds that a contract which cannot be performed within one year must be in writing. In some situations, the agreement may come under the provision of the statute that requires a transfer of interest in land to be in writing. Generally, however, the agreement need not be written solely because the partnership is formed to engage in the business of buying and selling real estate.

Even when unnecessary, it is always desirable to have the partnership agreement in writing to avoid subsequent controversies as to mutual rights and duties. The formal document that is prepared to evidence the contract of the parties is termed a *partnership agreement, articles of partnership,* or *articles of copartnership.*

Determining Existence of Partnership

Whether a partnership exists is basically a matter of proving the intent of the parties.

---

[5] See p. 96.
[6] *Kaufman-Brown Potato Co.* v. *Long,* [C.A.9th] 182 F.2d 594.
[7] *Love* v. *Pitman Laboratory Sales,* 389 Pa. 224, 132 A.2d 672.

Facts: Forker brought a suit against Butler to recover one half of the loss sustained in the construction of a bridge for the county, the theory being that the plaintiff and the defendant were partners. The existence of a partnership was denied and, as evidence that there was no partnership, it was shown that no partnership books were kept.

Decision: The absence of partnership books is not controlling. Although the Uniform Partnership Act makes provision as to the place of keeping partnership books and the right of the partners to inspect them, the Act does not make the existence of partnership books a condition to the existence of a partnership. Hence, it could be found that there was a partnership although there were no "partnership books." (Butler v. Forker, [Ind.App.] 221 N.E.2d 570)

As in the case of agency, the burden of proving the existence of a partnership is upon the person who claims that one exists.[8]

When the parties have not clearly indicated the nature of their relationship, the law has developed the following guides to aid in determining whether the parties have created a partnership:

1 / Sharing profits and losses. The fact that the parties share profits and losses is strong evidence of a partnership.

2 / Sharing profits. An agreement that does not provide for sharing losses but does provide for sharing profits is evidence that the parties are united in partnership, as it is assumed that they will also share losses.[9] The Uniform Partnership Act provides that sharing profits is prima facie evidence of a partnership, but that a partnership is not to be inferred when profits are received in payment (a) of a debt, (b) of wages, (c) of rent, (d) of an annuity to a deceased partner's widow or representative, (e) of interest, or (f) for the goodwill of the business.[10] If there is no evidence of the reason for receiving the profits, it must be held that a partnership of the parties involved exists.

3 / Gross returns. The sharing of gross returns is of itself very slight, if any, evidence of partnership. To illustrate, in a case in which one party owned a show that was exhibited upon land owned by another under an agreement to divide the gross proceeds, no partnership was proved because there was no co-ownership or community of interest in the business.

4 / Co-ownership. Neither the co-ownership of property nor the sharing of profits or rents from property which two or more persons own creates a partnership.

---

[8] *Jewell* v. *Harper*, 199 Ore. 223, 258 P.2d 115.
[9] *Bengston* v. *Shain*, 42 Wash.2d 404, 255 P.2d 892.
[10] UPA Sec. 7(4).

5 / Contribution of property. The fact that all persons have not contributed property to the enterprise does not establish that the enterprise is not a partnership. A partnership may be formed even though some of its members furnish only skill or labor.[11]

Partners as to Third Persons

In some instances a person who is in fact not a partner or a member of a partnership may be held accountable to third persons as though he were a partner. This liability arises when a person conducts himself in such a manner that third persons are reasonably led to believe that he is a partner and to act in reliance on that belief to their injury.[12] The person who incurs such a liability is termed a nominal partner, a partner by estoppel, or an ostensible partner.

Partnership Property

In general, partnership property consists of all the property contributed by the partners or acquired for the firm or with its funds.[13] There is usually no limitation upon the kind and amount of property that a partnership may acquire.

1 / Title to personal property in firm name. A partnership may hold and transfer the title to personal property in the firm name, whether the name is fictitious or consists of the names of living people. Thus a partnership may hold a mortgage on personal property in the firm name, such as "Keystone Cleaners."

2 / Title to real property in firm name. A majority of states now permit a partnership to hold or transfer the title to real property in the firm name alone, without regard to whether that name is fictitious or not.[14]

3 / Transferees of firm's real property. In order for a transfer of a firm's real property to be technically correct, (a) it must have been made by a partner or agent with the authority to make the transfer and (b) it must have been made in the name of the holder of the title. When both conditions have been satisfied, the transferee has legal title as against the partnership.

If the transfer was authorized but was not made in the name of the title holder, the transferee acquires equitable title to the property and the right to have a proper deed or instrument of conveyance executed. If the transfer

---

[11] *Watson* v. *Watson*, 231 Ind. 385, 108 N.E.2d 893.
[12] UPA Sec. 16(1).
[13] Sec. 8; *All Florida Sand* v. *Lawler Construction Co.*, 209 Ga. 720, 75 S.E.2d 559.
[14] UPA Sec. 8(3), (4).

of the partnership property was not authorized, the firm may recover the property from the transferee if he knew that it was firm property or if he did not purchase it for value. When the title to the firm property is recorded but not in the name of the firm, a person who purchases from the record holder in good faith, for value, and without notice or knowledge of the partnership title, may keep the property.

Tenancy in Partnership

Partners hold firm property by *tenancy in partnership*.[15] The characteristics of such a tenancy are:

(1) In the absence of contrary agreement all partners have equal right to use firm property for partnership purposes.

(2) A partner possesses no interest in any specific portion of the partnership property that he can sell, assign, or mortgage.[16] The partner has no right in any specific property that he can transfer to a third person, although he may transfer his interest in specific property to his sole surviving partner.

(3) In most states the creditors of a partner cannot levy on and sell his interest in specific partnership property.[17]

(4) The interest of a deceased partner in specific firm property vests in the surviving partners, but only for partnership purposes.

(5) A partner's interest in specific property is not subject on his death to any rights of his surviving spouse.

This distinct form of tenure is sometimes confused with joint tenancies and tenancies in common. The ordinary joint tenant has full beneficial ownership upon the death of the cotenant, whereas a surviving partner does not. A cotenant may alienate or transfer his interest, putting another in his place, but a partner cannot do so.

DISSOLUTION AND TERMINATION

Dissolution ends the right of the partnership to exist as a going concern. It is followed by a winding-up period, upon the conclusion of which the partnership's legal existence is terminated.

Methods and Causes of Dissolution

1 / Dissolution by act of parties.

(a) AGREEMENT. A partnership may be dissolved in accordance with the terms of the original agreement of the parties, as by the passing of the

---

[15] UPA Sec. 25(1); *Williams* v. *Dovell*, 202 Md. 646, 96 A.2d 484.
[16] *Cook* v. *Lauten*, 1 Ill.App.2d 255, 117 N.E.2d 414.
[17] UPA Sec. 25(c).

period for which the relation was to continue or by the performance of the object for which it was organized.[18] The relation may also be dissolved by subsequent agreement, as when the partners agree to dissolve the firm before the lapse of the time specified in the articles of partnership or before the attainment of the object for which the firm was created. The sale or assignment by one partner of his interest to the remaining partners does not in itself dissolve the partnership.

(b) WITHDRAWAL. A partner has the power to withdraw at any time; but if his withdrawal violates his agreement, he becomes liable to his co-partners for damages for breach of contract. When the relation is for no definite purpose or time, a partner may withdraw without liability at any time,[19] unless a sudden withdrawal would do irreparable damage to the firm.

(c) EXPULSION. A partnership is dissolved by the expulsion of any partner from the business bona fide in accordance with such a power conferred by the agreement between the partners.

(d) ALIENATION OF INTEREST. Under the Uniform Partnership Act neither a voluntary sale [20] nor an involuntary sale for the benefit of creditors [21] works a dissolution of the partnership. A minority of states follow the contrary rule of the common law under which such sales dissolve the firm.

2 / Dissolution by operation of law.

(a) DEATH. An ordinary partnership is dissolved immediately upon the death of any partner,[22] even when the agreement provides for continuance of the business. Thus, when the executor of a deceased partner carries on the business with the remaining partner, there is legally a new firm.

(b) BANKRUPTCY. Bankruptcy of the firm or of one of the partners causes the dissolution of the firm; insolvency alone does not.

(c) WAR. A firm is ordinarily dissolved when there is war between the governments to which the different partners owe allegiance.

(d) ILLEGALITY. A partnership is dissolved "by any event which makes it unlawful for the business of the partnership to be carried on or for the members to carry it on in partnership." [23] To illustrate, when it is made unlawful by statute for judges to engage in the practice of law, a law firm is dissolved when one of its members becomes a judge.

---

[18] Sec. 31(1)(a).
[19] *Butler* v. *Thomasson*, [Tex.Civ.App.] 256 S.W.2d 936.
[20] UPA Sec. 27.
[21] Sec. 28.
[22] *Hurley* v. *Hurley*, 33 Del.Ch. 231, 91 A.2d 674.
[23] UPA Sec. 31(3).

3 / Dissolution by decree of court. When a partnership is to continue for a certain time, there are several situations in which one partner is permitted to obtain its dissolution through a decree of court. A court will not order the dissolution for trifling causes or temporary grievances that do not involve a permanent harm or injury to the partnership. The causes that enable a partner to ask for a dissolution under the common law have been substantially codified by the Uniform Partnership Act.

(a) INSANITY. A partner may obtain a decree of dissolution when his partner has been judicially declared a lunatic or when it is shown that he is of unsound mind.

(b) INCAPACITY. A decree of dissolution will be granted when one partner becomes in any way incapable of performing the terms of the partnership agreement. For example, a serious injury to one partner making it physically impossible for him to do his part is a cause for dissolution.

(c) MISCONDUCT. A partner may obtain a decree of dissolution when his partner has been guilty of conduct that tends substantially to affect the continuance of the business prejudicially. The habitual drunkenness of a partner is a sufficient cause for judicial dissolution.

(d) IMPRACTICABILITY. A partner may obtain a decree of dissolution when another partner habitually or purposely commits a breach of the partnership contract or so conducts himself in matters relating to the partnership business that it is not reasonably practicable to carry on the business in partnership with him.

(e) LACK OF SUCCESS. A decree of dissolution will be granted when the partnership cannot be continued except at a loss.

(f) EQUITABLE CIRCUMSTANCES. A decree of dissolution will be granted under any other circumstances that equitably call for a dissolution. A situation of this kind, for example, is present when one partner has been induced by fraud to enter into partnership.

Effect of Dissolution

Dissolution involves a change in the relation of the partners but does not end the partnership. "On dissolution the partnership is not terminated, but continues until the winding up of partnership affairs is completed." [24] The vested rights of the partners are not extinguished by dissolving the firm, and the existing liabilities remain. Thus, when the relation is dissolved by the death of a partner, the estate of the deceased member is liable to the same extent as was the deceased partner.

---

[24] Sec. 30.

The dissolution, however, does affect the authority of the partners. From the moment of dissolution the partners lose authority to act for the firm, "except so far as may be necessary to wind up partnership affairs or to complete transactions begun but not then finished." [25]

Notice of Dissolution

The rule that dissolution terminates the authority of the partners to act for the firm requires some modification. Under some circumstances one partner may continue to possess the power to make a binding contract.

1 / Notice to partners. When the firm is dissolved by an act of a partner, notice must be given to the other partners unless his act clearly shows an intent to withdraw from or to dissolve the firm. If he acts without notice to his partners, he is bound as between them upon contracts created for the firm. The Uniform Partnership Act declares that "where the dissolution is caused by the act, death, or bankruptcy of a partner, each partner is liable to his copartners for his share of any liability created by any partner acting for the partnership as if the partnership had not been dissolved unless (a) the dissolution being by act of any partner, the partner acting for the partnership had knowledge of the dissolution, or (b) the dissolution being by the death or bankruptcy of a partner, the partner acting for the partnership had knowledge or notice of the death or bankruptcy." [26]

2 / Notice to third persons. When dissolution is caused by the act of a partner or of the partners, notice must be given to third parties.[27]

Facts: Paul Babich ran a business under the name of "House of Paul." The latter became a partnership between Babich, Dyson, and Schnepp but continued under the same name. The partners arranged for printing of advertising material with Philipp Lithographing Co., making contracts on three separate occasions for such printing. During the course of these dealings the "House of Paul" became a corporation. When the printing bills were not paid in full, Philipp sued the partners as individuals. They claimed they were not liable because the corporation had made the contracts.

Decision: Whether or not the "House of Paul" was a corporation with respect to a particular contract was not important because no notice had been given of its change from a partnership to a corporation. Having done business with the persons originally as a partnership, the plaintiff could hold the firm and the individual persons liable as partners until notice was given to the plaintiff to the contrary. (Philipp Lithographing Co. v. Babich, 27 Wis.2d 645, 135 N.W.2d 343)

---

[25] Sec. 33.
[26] Sec. 34.
[27] *Adkins* v. *Hash,* 190 Va. 86, 56 S.E.2d 60.

Actual notice of dissolution must be given to persons who have dealt with the firm. To persons who know of the relation but have had no dealings with the firm, a publication of the fact is sufficient. Such notice may be by newspaper publication, by posting a placard in a public place, or by any similar method. Failure to give proper notice continues the power of each partner to bind the others in respect to third persons on contracts within the scope of the business.

When dissolution has been caused by operation of law, notice to third persons is not required. As between the partners, however, the Uniform Partnership Act requires knowledge or notice of dissolution by death and bankruptcy.

Winding Up Partnership Affairs

Although the partners after dissolution have no authority to create new obligations, they retain authority for acts necessary to wind up the business. With a few exceptions, all partners have the right to participate in the winding up of the business.[28]

> **Facts:** Ed Cox and his son William were partners. They were performing a highway construction contract when the father died. The son continued the performance of the contract and, to finance it, borrowed a large sum from the Farmers State Bank. The Bank later sued the partnership, bringing the action, as was required by local law, in the name of the State. The defense was raised that after the death of one partner the surviving partner could not enter into a new transaction, such as borrowing money.
>
> **Decision:** The loan was needed by the winding up partner to complete performance under the prior contract. It was therefore not a "new" transaction but merely an incident of winding up the prior or old contract. Hence the loan was a binding obligation of the firm. (State to the use of Farmers State Bank v. Cox, 81 S.D. 165, 132 N.W.2d 282)

When the firm is dissolved by the death of one partner, the partnership property vests in the surviving partners for the purpose of administration. They must collect and preserve the assets, pay the debts, and with reasonable promptness make an accounting to the representative of the deceased partner. In connection with these duties, the law requires the highest degree of integrity. A partner in performing these acts cannot sell to himself any of the partnership property.

Distribution of Assets

Creditors have first claim on the assets of the partnership. Difficulty arises when there is a contest between the creditors of the firm and the creditors

---

[28] UPA Sec. 37.

of the individual partners. The general rule is that firm creditors have first claim on assets of the firm, and the individual creditors share in the remaining assets, if there are any. Conversely, individual creditors have priority in the distribution of individual assets; the claims of the firm creditors may be satisfied only after claims of individual creditors are settled.

After the firm liabilities to nonpartners have been paid, the assets of the partnership are distributed as follows:

(1) Each partner is entitled to a refund of advances made to or for the firm.

(2) Contributions to the capital of the firm are then returned.

(3) The remaining assets, if any, are divided equally as profits among the partners unless there is some other agreement. Likewise, if the partnership has sustained a loss, the partners share it equally in the absence of a contrary agreement.

QUESTIONS AND PROBLEMS

1. Checklist of legal terms:

   (a) partnership, partner (527)
   (b) general partnership, special partnership (529)
   (c) trading partnership, nontrading partnership (529)
   (d) general partner, nominal partner, silent partner, secret partner, dormant partner (529)
   (e) articles of partnership (530)
   (f) tenancy in partnership (533)

2. State the objective(s) of each of the following rules of law:

   (a) A partnership may generally hold property in its own name.
   (b) Dissolution ends the right of the partnership to continue to exist as a partnership but does not terminate its existence.

3. Wiley and Graham form a partnership for the purpose of engaging in fraudulent sales of land. Some time later Wiley refuses to make an accounting of his transactions. Is Graham entitled to recover in an action to compel Wiley to divide the profits?

4. Weaver, Kinley, and Mandel Company is a partnership conducting a restaurant. Weaver actively conducts the business. Kinley, a lawyer, takes no active part in the business, but he is known to be a partner in the firm. Mandel has merely given the partnership permission to use his name. Hackett, a fourth partner, takes no active part in the business and is not known to the public as a partner. Classify each person.

5. Kieth sells his business to Woodruff for a payment of $30,000 in cash for the property and annual payments of 10 percent of the profits for the goodwill of the business. A creditor brings an action against Kieth and Woodruff as partners. Is he entitled to judgment against Kieth?

6. A partnership buys a farm for business purposes. In conveying the property the seller makes out the title to Withdrow and Company, the name of the partnership. Is such a title valid?

7. Ziegler sold his interest in a partnership to his partners. During subsequent litigation it was contended that a partner's interest in firm property was neither that of a tenant in common nor that of a joint tenant. If you agree with this contention, what is the nature of a partner's interest in firm property?

8. Perry and Randolph form a partnership that is to continue for five years. At the end of the fourth year Perry notifies Randolph of his intention to withdraw from the firm. Do you agree with Randolph's contention that Perry cannot dissolve the partnership for another year?

9. Upon the death of a partner, his executor carries on the business with other members of the firm. Pastor sold goods on credit to the firm before the death of the partner, and Strong became a creditor after the partner's death. Are Pastor and Strong creditors of the same firm?

10. Shaw and Taylor form a ten-year partnership to practice surgery. As a result of a serious automobile accident, it is necessary to amputate both of Taylor's arms. Under these circumstances, may Shaw obtain a court decree of dissolution?

11. Williams owned and operated a bakery business. His two sons were employed in the business and from time to time received a share of the profits as a bonus. The father and one of the sons died. The administrator of the son's estate, the First National Bank, then sued against the estate of the father for an accounting, claiming that the father and the two sons were a partnership and that the deceased son's estate was therefore entitled to a one-third share. Decide. (First National Bank v. Williams, 142 Ore. 648, 20 P.2d 222)

12. J. M. Hignite and Nantz were partners under the firm name of Hignite & Nantz. The firm was indebted to J. L. Hignite. The firm was dissolved. Two years later J. M. Hignite executed a promissory note payable to the order of the creditor for the amount of the debt owed by the firm and signed it in the firm name. The creditor knew that the firm had been dissolved. The creditor later sued both partners on the note. Nantz claimed that he was not bound by the note. Decide. (Hignite v. Nantz, 254 Ky. 214, 71 S.W.2d 442)

13. The Weidlich Sterling Spoon Co., a partnership owned by three brothers, was dissolved. By agreement, one of the brothers was designated as liquidating partner. After he completed liquidation, he filed an account which related only to certain legal charges and expenses that had been incurred. Was this a proper accounting? (Weidlich v. Weidlich, 147 Conn. 160, 157 A.2d 910)

Chapter 46

Authority of Partners

Decisions on business matters concerning the partnership are made by the partners, usually by a majority vote. In relationship to third persons, a partner's authority to act for the firm is similar to that of an agent to act for his principal.

Authority of Majority of Partners

When there are more than two partners in a firm, the decision of the majority prevails on matters involving the manner in which the ordinary functions of the business will be conducted.

Facts: Pearce and others formed a partnership to operate a cotton gin. The partners agreed that Pearce was to buy and sell all of the cottonseed handled by the company. A few months later, after a controversy with the manager of the Cotton Plant Oil Co., Pearce began shipping the seed to the Buckeye Cotton Oil Co. As Pearce was preparing to ship a quantity of seed to Buckeye, four of the partners, a majority, authorized two members to sell the seed then in freight cars to the Cotton Plant Oil Co., and this was done. Pearce, however, persuaded the agent of the railroad company to make the bill of lading in the name of Buckeye. Thereupon, the Cotton Plant Oil Co. brought an action against the partners to recover possession of the seed. The Buckeye Cotton Oil Co. intervened, claiming to own the two cars of seed and contending that only Pearce had authority to sell the seed.

Decision: Judgment for Cotton Plant Oil Co. The vote of the majority of the partners was binding upon Pearce. Consequently, the sale made by him was unauthorized and his buyer did not acquire title to the goods. (Cotton Plant Oil Co. v. Buckeye Cotton Oil Co., 92 Ark. 271, 122 S.W. 658)

The act of the majority is not binding if it contravenes the original agreement. For such matters unanimous action is required.[1] Thus the majority of the members cannot change the nature of the business against the protests of the minority.

When there are two or any other even number of partners, there is the possibility of an even division on a matter that requires majority approval.

---

[1] Uniform Partnership Act, Sec. 18(h).

In such a case no action can be taken, and the partnership is deadlocked. If the division is over a basic issue and the partners persist in the deadlock, any one of the partners may petition the court to order the dissolution of the firm since it is impossible for the partnership to function if the deadlock persists. The court will order such a dissolution only when the deadlock issues are so basic as to prevent the profitable continuation of the partnership.[2]

Authority of Individual Partners

An individual partner may have express authority to do certain acts, either because the partnership agreement so declares or because a sufficient number of partners have agreed thereto. In addition, he has authority to do those acts which are customary for a member of such a partnership. As in the case of an agent, the acts of a partner in excess of his authority do not ordinarily bind the partnership.

1 / Customary authority. A partner, by virtue of the fact that he is a comanager of the business, customarily has certain powers necessary and proper to carrying out that business. In the absence of express limitation, the law will therefore imply that he has such powers. The scope of such powers varies with the nature of the partnership and also with the business customs and usages of the area in which the partnership operates.

The following are the more common of the customary or implied powers:

(a) CONTRACTS. A partner may make any contract necessary to the transaction of firm business. He cannot make a contract of guaranty, however, merely because it will induce a third person to purchase from the partnership.

Facts: John Farson and his son, John Farson, Jr., were partners engaged in the business of buying and selling bonds and other securities under the name of Farson, Son & Co. A salesman of the firm sold to the First National Bank of Ann Arbor, Michigan, five bonds of the Eden Irrigation and Land Co. As an inducement to buy the bonds, the bank was given a written guaranty of payment of the principal and interest executed in the firm name and delivered by the cashier of the partnership under the authorization of John Farson, Sr. When the principal and interest were not paid, the bank brought an action on the guaranty against John Farson, Jr., the surviving partner, and another. The defendants contended that John Farson, Sr., had no power to bind the firm on a guaranty.

Decision: Judgment for defendants. The authority to sell does not include the power to guarantee. There was no local usage of trade or custom that

---

[2] *Mayhew v. McGlothlin,* 269 Ky. 184, 106 S.W.2d 643.

would regard a partner as impliedly having such a power. Hence, the guarantee was made without actual or apparent authority and did not bind the partnership or any of the partners. (First National Bank v. Farson, 226 N.Y. 218, 123 N.E. 490)

(b) SALES. A partner may sell the firm's goods in the regular course of business and make the usual warranties incidental to such sales. This authority, however, is limited to the goods kept for sale.

(c) PURCHASES. A partner may purchase any kind of property within the scope of the business, and for this purpose he may pledge the credit of the firm. This authority is not affected by the fact that he subsequently misuses or keeps the goods.

(d) LOANS. A partner in a trading firm may borrow money for partnership purposes. In doing so, he may execute commercial paper in the firm name or give security, such as a mortgage or a pledge of the personal property of the firm. If the third person acts in good faith, the transaction is binding even though the partner misappropriates the money.[3] A partner in a nontrading partnership does not ordinarily possess the power to borrow.

Facts: Wilcomb, Linder, and Darnutzer were partners engaged in a farming and stock-raising business under the name of Trout Creek Land Co. One of the partners executed and delivered four promissory notes, each signed "Trout Creek Land Co., by A. J. Wilcomb." Reid, as receiver of the Bank of Twin Bridges, Montana, a corporation, brought an action against the members of the partnership to recover on the notes. Wilcomb's partners, as a defense, alleged that he had no authority to bind his partners on a firm note, and that he used the money for speculation.

Decision: Judgment for plaintiff. The partnership was a trading partnership since it was engaged in buying and selling. Every partner of a trading partnership has authority to borrow money and to execute promissory notes on the credit of the firm. Consequently, the notes so issued by Wilcomb were binding upon the partnership without regard to the use to which the money procured thereby was put by the borrowing partner. (Reid v. Linder, 77 Mont. 406, 251 P. 157)

(e) INSURANCE. A partner may insure the firm property, cancel a policy of insurance, or make proof and accept settlement for the loss.

(f) EMPLOYMENT. A partner may engage such employees and agents as are necessary to carry out the purpose of the enterprise.

---

[3] *Zander* v. *Larsen,* 41 Wash.2d 503, 250 P.2d 531.

(g) CLAIMS AGAINST FIRM. A partner has the authority to compromise, adjust, and pay bona fide claims against the partnership. He may pay debts out of firm funds, or he may pay them by transferring firm property. Although he has no power to pay his own debts from firm assets, his creditors are protected if they receive such payments in good faith and without knowledge that it comes from firm assets.

(h) CLAIMS OF FIRM. A partner may adjust, receive payment of, and release debts and other claims of the firm. He may take money or commercial paper but, as a rule, cannot accept goods in payment. One who makes a proper payment is protected even though the partner to whom payment is made fails to account to the firm.

(i) ADMISSIONS. A partner may bind the firm by admissions or statements that are adverse to the interests of the partnership if they are made in regard to firm affairs and in the pursuance of firm business.

(j) NOTICE. A partner may receive notice of matters affecting the partnership affairs, and such notice, in the absence of fraud, is binding on the others.[4]

2 / Limitations on authority. The partners may agree to limit the normal powers of each partner. When a partner, contrary to such an agreement, negotiates a contract for the firm with a third person, the firm is bound if the third person was unaware of the agreement. In such a case, the partner violating the agreement is liable to his partners for any loss caused by the breach of his contract. If the third person knew of the limitation, the firm would not be bound.[5]

A third person cannot assume that the partner has all the authority which he purports to have. If there is anything that would put a reasonable man on notice that the partner's customary powers are limited, the third person is bound by the limitation.

The third person must be on the alert for the following situations in particular, as they serve to notify him that the partner with whom he deals either has restricted authority or no authority at all:

(a) NATURE OF BUSINESS. A third person must take notice of limitations arising out of the nature of the business. A partnership may be organized for a particular kind of business, trade, or profession, and third persons are presumed to know the limitations commonly laid upon partners in such an enterprise. Thus an act of a partner that would ordinarily bind a commercial firm, such as the issuance of a note, would not bind a partnership

---

[4] UPA Sec. 12.
[5] Sec. 9(4).

engaged in a profession.[6] A partner in a trading partnership has much greater powers than one in a nontrading firm.[7]

(b) Scope of Business. A third person must recognize and act in accordance with limitations that arise from the scope of the business. A partner cannot bind the firm to a third person in a transaction not within the scope of the firm's business unless he has express authority to do so. Thus, when a partner in a dental firm speculates in land or when a partner in a firm dealing in automobiles buys television sets for resale, the third person, in the absence of estoppel or express authority, cannot hold the other partners on such a contract. The scope of the business is a question of fact to be determined by the jury from the circumstances of each case. In general, it means the activities commonly recognized as a part of a given business at a given place and time. The usual scope, however, may be enlarged by agreement or by conduct.

(c) Termination of Partnership. A third person must watch for the termination of the partnership relation, either when the partnership is terminated under conditions requiring no notice or when notice of the termination has been properly given.

(d) Adverse Interest. A third person must take notice of an act of a partner that is obviously against the interest of the firm. To illustrate, if a partner issues a promissory note in the firm name and delivers it to his creditor in payment of a personal obligation, the latter acts at his peril because such an act may be a fraud upon the firm.

3 / Prohibited transactions. There are certain transactions into which a partner cannot enter on behalf of the partnership unless he is expressly authorized to do so. A third person entering into such a transaction therefore acts at his peril when the partner has not been so authorized. In such a case, the third person should check with the other partners to determine whether the transaction is authorized.

The following are examples of prohibited transactions:

(a) Cessation of Business. A partner cannot bind the firm by a contract that would make it impossible for the firm to conduct its usual business.

(b) Suretyship. A partner has no implied authority to bind the firm by contracts of surety, guaranty, or indemnity for purposes other than the firm business.

---

[6] *Livingston* v. *Roosevelt,* 4 Johns. [N.Y.] 251.
[7] *Marsh* v. *Wheeler,* 77 Conn. 449, 59 A. 410.

(c) ARBITRATION. A partner in most states cannot submit controversies of his firm to arbitration. The Uniform Partnership Act expressly denies this power "unless authorized by the other partners or unless they have abandoned the business." [8]

(d) CONFESSION OF JUDGMENT. A partner cannot confess judgment against the firm upon one of its obligations because all partners should have an opportunity to defend in court. This power is expressly denied by the Uniform Partnership Act, except when the other partners consent or when "they have abandoned the business." [9]

(e) ASSIGNMENT FOR CREDITORS. A partner cannot ordinarily make a general assignment of firm property for the benefit of creditors. Exceptions are usually made in cases of bona fide acts in an emergency. The exceptions appear to be limited by the Uniform Partnership Act, which provides that "unless authorized by the other partners or unless they have abandoned the business, one or more but less than all the partners have no authority to assign the partnership property in trust for creditors or on the assignee's promise to pay the debts of the partnership." [10]

(f) PERSONAL OBLIGATIONS. A partner cannot discharge his personal obligations or claims of the firm by interchanging them in any way.

(g) SEALED INSTRUMENTS. In a minority of the states a partner cannot bind his copartners by an instrument under seal. A majority of states, however, hold that instruments under seal are binding upon the firm when they are made in the usual course of business.

QUESTIONS AND PROBLEMS

1. Review the definitions of legal terms in the checklist on page 538.
2. State the objective(s) of each of the following rules of law:
   (a) A partner in a nontrading partnership does not have authority to borrow money in the firm name.
   (b) A partner cannot ordinarily make a general assignment of firm property for the benefit of creditors.
3. Phillips, Bass, and Rose were partners in a small manufacturing business. Against the wishes of Phillips, Bass and Rose authorized an attorney to prosecute a claim against a trucking company. Was it necessary to have the consent of all the members of the firm to prosecute the action?
4. Regan, Patrick, and Tate form a partnership to sell automobiles. The firm is offered a dealer's contract to sell freezer units for home use.

---

[8] UPA Sec. 9(3)(e).
[9] Sec. 9(3)(d).
[10] Sec. 9(3)(a).

Regan and Patrick agree to enter into the contract over the objections of Tate. Does the agreement bind Tate?

5. The Robinson Company is owned and operated by four partners. On an important question pertaining to their advertising budget two partners favor the proposal and two oppose it.
   (a) What is the effect of this division of authority?
   (b) What solution to this kind of situation is available if the division of authority pertains to a basic issue?

6. A member of a partnership sold the firm's office safe without the consent of his partners. Does a partner have authority to make such a sale?

7. Powell and Seaman are partners in a trading firm. Powell borrows $500 from a bank on a note that he executes in the firm name. If Powell spends the money for his own purposes, may the bank hold the partnership on the note?

8. Ignoring an agreement that Lennie has made with his partners, he purchases certain merchandise for the firm from Malone.
   (a) Under what circumstances is the partnership liable to Malone?
   (b) If the firm suffers a loss as a result of Lennie's contract, does it have any recourse?

9. Calvin and Jackson operate a lumberyard as a partnership. Calvin contracted in the firm name with Howe to construct a house. Later Calvin contended that the contract did not bind the partnership. Do you agree?

10. Milton Smith, Maude Smith, and Warren Ten Brook were partners doing business as "Greenwood Sales & Service." Pretending to act on behalf of the partnership, Ten Brook borrowed $6,000 from Holloway, giving her a note that was signed: "Greenwood Sales & Service, by Warren Ten Brook, Partner." In fact, Ten Brook borrowed the $6,000 so that he could make his capital contribution to the partnership. The check so obtained from Holloway was payable to the order of the partnership and was in fact deposited by Ten Brook in the partnership account. When the note was not paid, Holloway sued all of the partners. The other partners claimed that neither the partnership nor they were bound by Ten Brook's unauthorized act committed for personal gain. Was this defense valid? (Holloway v. Smith, 197 Va. 334, 88 S.E.2d 909)

11. Damsker and Carey, partners, entered into a contract with Goldberg for the construction of a building. The construction contract provided that disputes arising thereunder would be submitted to arbitration. A dispute arose relating to extra work, and Damsker gave notice that arbitration was requested on behalf of the partnership. Goldberg opposed the entry of an order to arbitrate on the ground that the application for arbitration was not made by both partners. Decide. (Application of Damsker, 283 App.Div. 719, 127 N.Y.S.2d 355)

Chapter 47

Partners' Duties, Rights, and Remedies

There is no stronger fiduciary relation than that of a partnership, in which one man's property and property rights are subject to the control of another.

Duties of Partners

In many respects the duties and responsibilities of a partner are the same as those of an agent.

1 / Loyalty and good faith. Each partner owes a duty of loyalty to the firm, which requires him to devote himself to the firm business and bars him from making any secret profit at the expense of the firm,[1] or from using the firm's funds for his personal benefit, or from making a secret gain in connection with business opportunities within the field of the business of the partnership.[2] A partner must always act with strict fidelity to the interests of the firm. He must use his powers and the firm's property for the benefit of the partners and not for his individual gain. His duties to the firm must be observed above the furtherance of his own interests. To illustrate, when one partner in his own name renewed a lease on the premises occupied by the firm, he was compelled to hold the lease for the firm on the ground that his conduct was contrary to the good faith required of partners.

A partner, in the absence of an agreement to the contrary, is required to give his undivided time and energy to the development of the business of the partnership. Even when a partner is not required to give all of his time to the firm's business, he cannot promote a competing business. If he does so, he is liable for damages to the partnership. To illustrate, two persons form a partnership for the purpose of making and selling hats, and one of them, unknown to the other, engages in an individual enterprise of the same nature. The latter, not having given his assent, may compel the former to account for the profits of the competing business.

2 / Obedience. Each partner is under an obligation to do all that is required of him by the partnership agreement. Duties and restrictions are

---

[1] *Baum* v. *McBride,* 152 Neb. 152, 40 N.W.2d 649.
[2] *Stark* v. *Reingold,* 18 N.J. 251, 113 A.2d 379.

frequently imposed upon certain members by the articles of partnership. To illustrate, if a partner agrees to take no part in the business and a loss is suffered because of a violation of the agreement, he must indemnify his partners.

In addition, each partner must observe any limitations imposed by a majority of the partners with respect to the ordinary details of the business. If a majority of the partners have decided that no sales shall be made on credit, a partner who is placed in charge of the store must observe this limitation. If a third person does not know of this limitation of authority, the managing partner will have the power to make a binding sale on credit to the third person. If the third person does not pay the bill and the firm thereby suffers loss, the partner who violated the "no-credit" limitation is liable to the firm for the loss caused by his disobedience.

3 / Reasonable care. A partner must use reasonable care in the transaction of the business of the firm. He is liable for any loss resulting from his failure to do so. He is not liable, however, for honest mistakes or errors of judgment. Nor is he liable when the complaining partner likewise failed in his duty to do or not to do the same act. Thus, when one partner failed to use reasonable care in collecting the debts owed to the firm, the other partner who was equally at fault in not making the collection was not justified in complaining, unless the former, as managing partner, had been entrusted with general control of the partnership affairs.

4 / Information. A partner has the duty to inform the partnership of matters relating to the partnership. He must "render on demand true and full information of all things affecting the partnership to any partner or the legal representative of any deceased partner or partner under legal disability." [3]

5 / Accounting. A partner must make and keep, or turn over to the proper person, correct records of all business that he has transacted for the firm. When the partners are equally at fault in not making and keeping proper records, however, none can complain. Thus, if a firm employs a book-keeper who commits serious errors, one partner cannot complain against another partner unless the latter was in some way responsible for the errors.

One partner may be charged with maintaining the books and accounts of the firm. In such a case he has, of course, the duty to maintain proper records. If it is shown that he has been guilty of improper conduct, he has the burden of proving the accuracy of his records. Any doubt will be resolved against him. That is, if it is not clear whether he has or has not accounted

---

[3] Uniform Partnership Act, Sec. 20.

for a particular item, it will be assumed that he has not and he will be liable to the firm for the item.[4]

Rights of the Partners as Owners

Each partner has the following rights, which stem from the fact that he is a co-owner of the partnership business:

1 / Management. Each partner, in the absence of a contrary agreement, has a right to take an equal part in transacting the business of the firm. To illustrate, three persons enter into a partnership. The first contributes $5,000 in cash; the second, property valued at $3,000; and the third, his skill and labor. All possess equal rights to participate in the conduct of the partnership business.[5] It is immaterial that one partner contributed more than another to the firm.

As an incident of the right to manage the partnership, each partner has the right to possession of the partnership property for the purposes of the partnership.

2 / Inspection of books. In the absence of an agreement to the contrary, all partners are equally entitled to inspect the books of the firm. "The partnership books shall be kept, subject to any agreement between the partners, at the principal place of business of the partnership, and every partner shall at all times have access to and may inspect and copy any of them."[6]

3 / Share of profits. Each partner is entitled to a share of the profits. The partners may provide, if they so wish, that profits shall be shared in unequal proportions. In the absence of such a provision in the partnership agreement, each partner is entitled to an equal share of the profits without regard to the extent of his capital contribution to the partnership or to the extent of his services.

The right to profits is regarded as personal property regardless of the nature of the partnership property. Upon the death of a partner, his right to sue for profits and an accounting passes to his executor or administrator.

Facts: Armstrong and Caldwell formed a partnership and purchased land. Armstrong died, and the beneficiaries under her will brought an action against Caldwell for an accounting.

Decision: Suit for an accounting brought on behalf of a deceased partner must be brought by the personal representative of his estate. Armstrong's interest is personal property, which passes to the personal representative for the purpose of administration and ultimate distribution to the

---

[4] *Wilson* v. *Moline,* 234 Minn. 174, 47 N.W.2d 865.
[5] *Katz* v. *Brewington,* 71 Md. 79, 20 A. 139; UPA Sec. 18(e).
[6] UPA Sec. 19.

deceased partner's creditors and beneficiaries. (Ewing v. Caldwell, 243 N.C. 18, 89 S.E.2d 774)

4 / Compensation. Although one partner performs more duties or renders more valuable services than the other partner, he is not entitled to compensation for these extra services in the absence of an agreement to that effect.[7] To illustrate, when one partner becomes seriously ill and the other partners transact all of the firm's business, they are not entitled to compensation for these services, as the sickness of a partner is considered a risk assumed in the relation.

As an exception, "a surviving partner is entitled to reasonable compensation for his services in winding up the partnership affairs." [8] A minority of states deny compensation even to the surviving partner.

5 / Repayment of loans. A partner is entitled to have returned to him any money advanced to or for the firm. These amounts, however, must be separate and distinct from original or additional contributions to the capital of the firm.

6 / Payment of interest. In the absence of an agreement to the contrary, contributions to capital do not draw interest. The theory is that the profits constitute sufficient compensation. A partner may, therefore, receive interest only on the capital contributed by him from the date when repayment should be made.[9] The partners, of course, may agree to pay interest on the capital contributions.

In earlier decisions courts were reluctant to allow interest on other advances until after an accounting was made, unless interest was provided for by agreement. A majority now treat advances in the form of loans as if they were made by a stranger. The Uniform Partnership Act provides that "a partner, who in aid of the partnership makes any payment or advance beyond the amount of capital which he agrees to contribute, shall be paid interest from the date of the payment or advance." [10]

When one partner embezzles or unlawfully withholds partnership property or money, the other partner may recover interest thereon when he sues for a dissolution of the partnership and the recovery of his proportionate share of the assets embezzled or withheld.[11]

7 / Contribution and indemnity. A partner who pays more than his share of the debts of the firm has a right to contribution from his copartners.

---

[7] *Lewis* v. *Hill*, [Tex.Civ.App.] 409 S.W.2d 946.
[8] UPA Sec. 18(f).
[9] Sec. 18(d).
[10] Sec. 18(c).
[11] *Luchs* v. *Ormsby*, 171 Cal.App.2d 377, 340 P.2d 702.

Under this principle, if any employee of a firm negligently injures a third person while acting within the scope of his employment and the injured party collects damages from one partner, the latter may enforce contribution from the copartners.

The Uniform Partnership Act states that "the partnership must indemnify every partner in respect of payments made and personal liabilities reasonably incurred by him in the ordinary and proper conduct of its business or for the preservation of its business or property." [12] The partner has no right, however, to indemnity or reimbursement when he (a) acts in bad faith, (b) negligently causes the necessity for payment, or (c) has previously agreed to bear the expense alone.

8 / Distribution of capital. Each partner is entitled to receive a share of the firm property upon dissolution after the payment of all creditors and the repayment of loans made to the firm by partners. Unless otherwise stated in the articles of partnership, each partner is entitled to the return of his capital contribution.

After such distribution is made, each partner is the sole owner of the fractional part distributed to him, rather than a co-owner of all the property, as he was during the existence of the partnership.

Remedies of Partners

The remedies available to the members of a firm are, in some instances, limited because of the peculiar relation of the partners and because of the nature of their claims. In the following discussion the distinction between actions at law and actions in equity is preserved, although in many states and in the federal courts there is today only a civil action.[13]

1 / Actions at law. A partner cannot maintain an action at law against the firm upon a claim against the partnership. A partnership cannot bring an action at common law against one of its members on claims that the firm holds against him. In the absence of statute, a partnership cannot maintain an action against another firm when they have partners in common.

One partner cannot maintain an action at common law against another on claims involving partnership transactions. There are two exceptions to this general rule: (a) when the claim has been distinguished from the firm dealings by agreement; and (b) when the firm accounts have been balanced and show the amount to be due.

Partners may sue each other at common law in cases in which there is no necessity of investigating the partnership accounts. Situations of this kind

---

[12] UPA Sec. 18(b).
[13] See p. 52.

exist when a partner dissolves the relation in violation of his agreement, when a partner fails to furnish capital or services agreed, or when a partner wrongfully causes injuries to his copartner, which in no way involve the partnership.

2 / Actions in equity. The proper tribunal to settle all controversies growing out of partnership transactions is a court of equity. For example, an action by a partner to recover his share of profits should be brought in equity. The powers and the procedure of this court are such as to enable it to settle fully problems that arise in winding up the affairs of the firm.

In most instances the aid of the equity court is sought in connection with an accounting and a dissolution of the firm. It was at one time held that an accounting must be accompanied by a dissolution, but this view was later modified so as to permit a separate accounting. The Uniform Partnership Act states that a partner is entitled to an accounting (a) if he is wrongfully excluded from the partnership business or possession of its property by his copartners; (b) if the right exists under the terms of any agreement; (c) if he is a trustee; or, (d) if other circumstances render an accounting just and reasonable.[14]

Partner's Liability as to Particular Acts

Just as a principal is not liable for every act of his agent, so the partnership and the members of the partnership are not liable for every act of each partner. Just as an agent's act binds the principal only when it is within the agent's scope of authority, real or apparent, so a partner's act binds the firm and other partners only when it is within the scope of the partner's authority, real or apparent.

1 / Contracts. All members of the firm are liable on contracts made by a partner for the partnership and in its name if they were made within the scope of his actual or implied powers. This is true even though the partners may be unknown to the third persons. Thus a dormant partner, when discovered, is bound with the others.

When a partner makes a simple contract in his own name, the other members of the firm are liable as undisclosed principals, unless the third person knowing of the existence of the partnership intended to deal exclusively with the partner as an individual. To illustrate, a firm is not liable when a partner borrows money to make his contribution to the partnership capital.

If a partner signs a commercial paper in his own name, the partnership, as undisclosed principal, cannot sue or be sued thereon.[15]

---

[14] UPA Sec. 22.
[15] The signing by the partner in such case is governed by the Uniform Commercial Code, Sec. 3-403. See p. 276.

Facts: William and Woodson Johnson, partners in a dairy, purchased their feed from Edwards Feed Mill. Woodson made a purchase of feed in his own name and executed a promissory note for its payment in his own name. Edwards sued both partners on the note on the theory that William was also liable since the partnership had received the benefit of the purchase.

Decision: Judgment for William. The note was not a partnership note but a personal obligation of Woodson. It was immaterial whether the other partner had in fact received the benefit of the note. (Edwards Feed Mill v. Johnson, [Tex.Civ.App.] 302 S.W.2d 151)

2 / Torts. All partners are liable for torts, such as fraud, trespass, negligence, and deceit, committed by one partner while transacting firm business.[16] The members of a firm are also liable for breach of trust by a partner in respect to goods or money of a third person held by the firm.

3 / Crimes. The partners of a firm and the partnership itself are liable for certain crimes committed by a partner in the course of the business, such as selling goods without obtaining a necessary vendor's license or selling in violation of a statute prohibiting sale. If carrying on the firm business does not necessarily involve the commission of the act constituting a crime, it is generally held that the firm and the partners not participating in the commission of a crime or authorizing its commission are not criminally liable. This exception is not recognized in some cases, such as the making of prohibited sales to minors or sales of adulterated products.

Facts: Maurer & Garst formed a partnership to practice law. Maurer embezzled money belonging to Douglas Reservoirs Water Users Association. Douglas brought suit against the partnership and against Garst to recover damages for the loss.

Decision: Judgment against Douglas. When a partner commits a crime outside of the scope of the partnership business, as was here done, there is no liability of the partnership or of the other partners with respect to such conduct. (Douglas Reservoirs Water Users Association v. Maurer & Garst, [Wyo.] 398 P.2d 74)

As a practical matter, the criminal liability of a partnership is limited to the imposition of a fine because it is not possible to imprison the partnership.

Nature of Partner's Liability

By virtue of local statutes, partners are jointly liable on all firm contracts in some states; they are jointly and severally liable in other states.[17] They

---
[16] UPA Sec. 13.
[17] *Roberts* v. *White*, 117 Vt. 573, 97 A.2d 245.

are jointly and severally liable for all torts committed by an employee or one of the partners in the scope of the partnership business.

Facts: Johnson was injured by a truck driven by Gill and owned by Mattox. Johnson sued Gill and Mattox, claiming that they were liable as partners.

Decision: Judgment for Mattox and against Gill. The existence of a partnership was not shown by the fact that Mattox owned the truck driven by Gill. Regardless of the relationship between Gill and Mattox, Gill was liable to Johnson for the consequence of his own conduct. (Johnson v. Gill, 235 N.C. 40, 68 S.E.2d 788)

When partners are liable for the wrongful injury caused a third person, the latter may sue any number of the members of the firm.

Extent of Partner's Liability

Each member of the firm is individually and unlimitedly liable for the debts of the partnership regardless of his investment or his interest in its management. Moreover, the individual property of a partner, even before the firm property has been exhausted, may be sold in satisfaction of the judgment.

1 / Liability of new partners. At common law a new partner entering an old firm is liable only for obligations arising thereafter. He may, however, expressly or impliedly assume the existing liabilities. Thus, when a new firm takes over the assets of an old firm, courts may infer an agreement to pay existing obligations.

The Uniform Partnership Act states that a "person admitted as a partner into an existing partnership is liable for all the obligations of the partnership arising before his admission as though he had been a partner when such obligations were incurred, except that this liability shall be satisfied only out of partnership property." [18] Thus his liability does not extend to his individual property.

2 / Effect of dissolution on partner's liability. A partner remains liable after dissolution unless the creditors expressly release him or unless the claims against the firm are satisfied. The Uniform Partnership Act states the following rules: "First, the dissolution of the partnership does not of itself discharge the existing liability of any partner. Second, a partner is discharged from any existing liability upon dissolution of the partnership by an agreement to that effect between himself, the partnership creditors, and the person or partnership continuing the business; and such agreement may be inferred from the course of dealing between the creditor having knowledge

---

[18] UPA Sec. 17; also see Secs. 41(1) and (7).

of the dissolution and the person or partnership continuing the business. Third, where a person agrees to assume the existing obligations of a dissolved partnership, the partners whose obligations have been assumed shall be discharged from any liability to any creditor of the partnership who, knowing of the agreement, consents to a material alteration in the nature or time of payment of such obligations." [19]

Enforcement of Partner's Liability

The manner in which the civil liability of a partner may be enforced depends upon the form of the lawsuit brought by the creditor. The firm may have been sued in the name of all the individual partners doing business as the partnership, as "Plaintiff v. *A, B,* and *C,* doing business as the Ajax Warehouse." In such a case those partners named are bound by the judgment against the firm if they have been properly served in the suit. Partners either not named or not served are generally not bound by the judgment.[20]

If the judgment binds an individual partner, the creditor may enforce the judgment against that partner before, at the same time, or after he seeks to enforce the judgment against the firm or other partners who are also bound by the judgment. If a partner is not bound by the judgment, the creditor must bring another lawsuit against the partner in which he establishes that the defendant is a partner in the particular partnership and that a judgment was entered against the partnership for a partnership liability. When this is established, a judgment is entered in favor of the creditor against the particular partner. The creditor may then have execution on this judgment against the property of the partner.

Suit in the Firm Name

At common law a partnership could not sue or be sued in the firm name on the theory that there was no legal person by that name. If the partnership was composed of *A, B,* and *C,* it was necessary for them to sue or be sued as *A, B,* and *C.* If the firm name was "The X Bakery," some states required that they appear in the action as "*A, B,* and *C,* trading as The X Bakery." By statute or court rule this principle of the common law has been abolished in many states, and a partnership may sue or be sued either in the names of the partners or in the firm name.

The identity of the parties to an action is determined by the nature of the obligation on which the action is brought. If the action is brought on a commercial paper held by one partner, the action must be brought in his name, although he could readily change this situation by indorsing the instrument to the firm.

---

[19] Sec. 36.
[20] *Denver National Bank* v. *Grimes,* 97 Colo. 158, 47 P.2d 862.

QUESTIONS AND PROBLEMS

1. Review the definitions of legal terms in the checklist on page 538.

2. State the objective(s) of each of the following rules of law:

   (a) Although each partner is an owner of the business, he must obey any limitations agreed to by a majority of the partners with respect to the ordinary details of the business.

   (b) A partner is unlimitedly liable for the obligations of the partnership.

3. Blaney, Clements, and Tyler form a partnership to manufacture small kitchen utensils. Without the knowledge of his partners, Tyler engages in the manufacture of work gloves. When Tyler's partners learn of this fact, they claim that their partnership has a right to the profits of Tyler's firm. Do you agree?

4. Sinclair and Cassidy are partners in a retail paint business. A claim that the partnership has against a contractor for paint has become unenforceable because of the Statute of Limitations. Cassidy contends that Sinclair is liable to the firm for this loss because Sinclair failed to take steps to collect the debt early enough. Do you agree?

5. Trimble seeks an accounting from his partner, Dillon, for certain important transactions that the latter has completed for the firm. Dillon has not kept a record of these transactions. His defense is that he turned over to the firm's bookkeeper the business forms that were completed in connection with those transactions. Is Dillon liable to Trimble?

6. Chatman and Flint each make a capital contribution of $30,000 to a partnership. In another partnership Bressler contributes $45,000 and Jester, $15,000. Neither partnership agreement specifies how the profits shall be divided. In each case what is each partner's share of the profits?

7. The partnership agreement between Allgood and Barnes made no provision for the payment of compensation to either partner. Allgood contends that he is entitled to a commission on the sale of land that he made for the firm. Is his contention sound?

8. Jennings, a partner, uses the firm's truck after business hours to move his household furniture. While doing so, he negligently damages Theskin's automobile. Theskin compels Jennings to pay for the damages incurred. Can Jennings compel his partners to share his loss?

9. Quinton contributes $40,000 and Jenny $20,000 to their partnership. Their agreement provides that profits shall be distributed in proportion to their capital contributions and that, upon dissolution, the assets of the firm shall be divided in the same manner. Later Jenny makes a loan of $10,000 to the firm. When the partnership is dissolved, $85,000 remains after the firm's creditors have been paid. How will the $85,000 be divided between the partners?

10. A clothing firm lends $500 to Shivler, one of the firm's partners. When Shivler fails to pay the loan when it falls due, the firm brings an action at law to recover the amount. Is it entitled to judgment?

11. Mallory and Jessen organized a partnership to operate a turkey farm. Jessen wrongfully took and withheld possession of certain personal goods belonging to Mallory. Mallory brought an action at law against Jessen to recover damages. It was contended that Mallory was not entitled to bring such an action against his partner. Do you agree?

12. Putnick, who is employed by a partnership to drive a delivery truck, negligently damages several small trees on Thaxton's lawn. Is Thaxton entitled to judgment in an action for damages against one of the members of the firm?

13. Mahaney and Thaley, who were partners, owed the Springfield National Bank $750. Mahaney paid the bank $500 to apply on the debt. The bank brought an action against Mahaney to recover the remaining $250. Can an obligation of the firm be collected from the personal assets of one partner?

14. A partnership purchased certain goods on credit from the Atlas Wholesale House. Later Quill entered this partnership. Could the wholesale company hold Quill liable for its claim against the partnership?

15. Nelson, Kelly, and Bank were partners engaged in the hauling business. Nelson and Kelly excluded Bank from participating in managing the business, paid themselves large salaries, and rented partnership property to themselves as individuals at a very low rental. Bank complained of their conduct. What was the legal basis for his complaint? (Bank v. Nelson, 199 Wash. 631, 92 P.2d 711)

16. The partnership agreement specified that the partners who worked as full-time employees "shall draw a salary for their work in such amounts as may be agreed on from time to time by unanimous consent and agreement of all the partners." In a dispute between Horn, one of the partners, and the partnership, it was claimed by Horn that this agreement entitled him to compensation for the life of the partnership, and could not be terminated by a vote of the other partners. Was he correct? (Horn v. Builders Supply Co., [Tex.Civ.App.] 401 S.W.2d 143)

17. Johnstone and Morris were partners. The firm was dissolved, and Morris bought Johnstone's share and gave him a promissory note for $16,800. Morris paid $4,250. Later Johnstone sued him for the balance of $12,550 due on the note. Morris claimed that he had refused to pay this balance because he had learned that Johnstone and the firm bookkeeper, who was Johnstone's wife, had intentionally kept false records and had misappropriated partnership money. The jury sustained the defense of Morris and entered a verdict in his favor of $12,550 which canceled the amount due on the note. Johnstone then appealed on the ground that the action was governed by equitable principles, and that accordingly there was no right to a trial by jury and the jury's verdict should be set aside. Decide. (Johnstone v. Morris, 210 Cal. 580, 292 P. 970)

Chapter 48

Special Partnerships and Associations

In addition to the general partnership and the ordinary business corporation, discussed in the next chapter, there are a number of hybrid organizations that are neither true partnerships nor corporations but which partake of the characteristics of one or both.

Limited Partnership

A common form of modified partnership is the limited partnership. This form of partnership is solely a creature of statute; that is, it cannot be created in the absence of a statute authorizing it. Most of the states have adopted the Uniform Limited Partnership Act.[1]

In a *limited partnership* certain members can contribute capital without assuming personal liability for firm debts beyond the amount of their investment. These members are known as *special* or *limited partners*. The members who manage the business and assume full personal liability for firm debts are known as *general partners*. A limited partnership can be formed under the Uniform Limited Partnership Act by "one or more general partners and one or more limited partners." [2]

Unlike a general partnership, this special form can be created only by executing and swearing to a certificate setting forth the essential details of the partnership and the relative rights of the partners. The certificate, when executed, must be recorded in the office of the official in charge of public records, such as the Recorder of Deeds, of the county in which the principal place of business of the partnership is located.

The limited partner contributes cash or property, but not services.[3] With certain exceptions, his name cannot appear in the firm name. His rights are limited to receiving his share of the profits and a return of capital upon dissolution; he cannot exercise any control over the business. If improper use is made of his name, giving the public the impression that he is an active partner, or if he exercises a control over the business, he becomes liable as

---

[1] This Act has been adopted in the District of Columbia, the Virgin Islands, and all states except Alabama, Delaware, Kansas, Kentucky, Louisiana, Maine, Oregon, and Wyoming.

[2] Uniform Limited Partnership Act, Sec. 1.

[3] ULPA Sec. 4.

a general partner. In any case, a limited partner cannot withdraw his capital contribution when it is needed to pay creditors.

Facts: The War Assets Administration sold a machine to Consolidated Machine Works, a limited partnership. The partnership was composed of Derrick, as a general partner, and Neal and Nauts, as limited partners. Subsequently the partnership was dissolved and the capital contributions of the limited partners were returned to them. Such repayments made the partnership insolvent and unable to pay the War Assets Administration for the machine. The United States then sued the limited partners for the purchase price.

Decision: Judgment for United States. The withdrawal of capital contributions was improper because it was needed to pay creditors. Therefore the limited partners were liable to creditors of the partnership to the extent that capital was withdrawn. (Neal v. United States, [C.A.5th] 195 F.2d 336)

In many respects the Uniform Limited Partnership Act follows the general pattern of the Uniform Partnership Act.

Joint Venture

A *joint venture*, or joint adventure, is a relationship in which two or more persons combine their labor or property for a single undertaking and share profits and losses equally,[4] or as otherwise agreed.

Facts: Three corporations and two individuals pooled their equipment, services, and assets for the performance of a contract to construct a tunnel. Wheatley brought suit against them and claimed that they were a joint venture.

Decision: The corporations and individuals had formed a joint venture since they had pooled everything and had limited their associating to the performance of the one tunnel construction contract. (Wheatley v. Halvorson, 213 Ore. 228, 323 P.2d 49)

A joint venture is similar in many respects to a partnership, but it differs primarily in that the joint venture relates to the prosecution of a single venture or transaction, although its accomplishment may require several years, while a partnership is generally a continuing business or enterprise. This is not an exact definition because a partnership may be expressly created for a single transaction. Because this distinction is so insubstantial, many courts hold that a joint venture is subject to the same principles of law as partnerships.[5] Thus the duties owed by the joint venturers to each other are

---

[4] *Burbank* v. *Sinclair Prairie Oil Co.*, 304 Ky. 833, 202 S.W.2d 420.
[5] *Shoemaker* v. *Davis*, 146 Kan. 909, 73 P.2d 1043.

the same as in the case of partnerships, with the result that where the joint venturers agree to acquire and develop a certain tract of land but some of the venturers secretly purchase the land in their own names, the other joint venturers are entitled to recover damages for this breach of the duty of loyalty.[6]

An agreement for farming operations that provides for sharing expenses and profits, or an agreement to purchase real estate for development and resale, will often be regarded as a joint venture.

It is essential that there be a community of interest or purpose and that each co-adventurer have an equal right to control the operations or activities of the undertaking. The actual control of the operations may be entrusted to one of the joint adventurers. Thus the fact that one joint adventurer is placed in control of the farming and livestock operations of the undertaking and appears to be the owner of the land does not destroy the joint adventure relationship.[7]

Mining Partnership

A *mining partnership* is an association formed for the purpose of conducting mining operations. In some states it is declared by statute that a mining partnership exists when two or more persons engage in working a mine claim. Apart from statute, the formation of such a partnership is a matter of intention, as in the case of an ordinary partnership, evidenced by words or conduct of the parties. The intent to create a mining partnership must be shown.

In many respects the mining partnership is governed by the same principles as an ordinary partnership. The authority of a mining partner to bind the mining partnership is more limited than in the case of a general partnership. Ordinarily, that authority is limited to matters that are necessary and proper or usual for the purpose of working the mine. Moreover, the interest of a partner is transferable, and his transferee becomes a partner in the firm in his place without regard to the wishes of the other partners. Similarly, there is no dissolution when the interest of a partner passes to another person by operation of law, or when a partner becomes bankrupt or dies. Profits and losses, unless otherwise stipulated, are shared proportionately according to the contributions made or shares held by each partner.

Syndicate

A *syndicate* is generally defined as an association of persons formed to conduct a particular business transaction, generally of a financial nature.

---

[6] *Boyd* v. *Bevilacqua*, [Cal.App.2d] 55 Cal.Rptr. 610.
[7] *McAnelly's Estate*, 127 Mont. 158, 258 P.2d 741.

Thus a syndicate may be formed by which its members agree to contribute sufficient money to purchase the control of a railroad. One of the common types of this form of business is the *underwriting syndicate*, which is an organization of investment banks for the purpose of marketing large issues of stocks or bonds.

A syndicate may be incorporated, in which case it has the attributes of an ordinary corporation. If it is not incorporated, it is treated in many respects the same as a general partnership, although it is held that, as in the case of the mining partnership, the personal factor or relationship between the partners is not important. When this is so held, it also follows that the interest of each member is freely transferable and that his transferee succeeds to his rights and membership in the syndicate.

Unincorporated Association

An *unincorporated association* is a combination of two or more persons for the furtherance of a common nonprofit purpose. No particular form of organization is required, and any conduct or agreement indicating an attempt to associate or work together for a common purpose is sufficient. Social clubs, fraternal associations, and political parties are common examples of unincorporated associations.

Generally the members of an unincorporated association are not liable for the debts or liabilities of the association by the mere fact that they are members. It is generally required to show that they authorized or ratified the act in question. If either authorization or ratification by a particular member can be shown, he is unlimitedly liable as in the case of a general partner.

Except when otherwise provided by statute, an unincorporated association does not have any legal existence, such as has a corporation, apart from the members who compose it.[8] Thus an unincorporated association cannot sue or be sued in its own name.[9]

Cooperative

A *cooperative* consists of a group of two or more independent persons or enterprises which cooperate with respect to a common objective or function. Thus farmers may pool their farm products and sell them as a group. Consumers may likewise pool their orders and purchase goods in bulk.

Initially the cooperative is itself an unincorporated association, and the rights and liabilities of all parties are determined in accordance with the principles governing an ordinary unincorporated association. In a majority of states, however, statutes subject cooperatives to regulation, particularly in

---

[8] *Harker* v. *McKissock*, 12 N.J. 310, 96 A.2d 660.
[9] *Kansas Private Club Association* v. *Londerholm*, 196 Kan. 319, 410 P.2d 429.

the case of farm and dairy cooperatives. Incorporation by a special form of charter is commonly allowed and in some instances is required.

As the agreement by the members of sellers' cooperatives that all products shall be sold at a common price is an agreement to fix prices, the sellers' cooperative is basically an agreement in restraint of trade. The Capper-Volstead Act of 1922 expressly exempts normal selling activities of farmers' and dairymen's cooperatives from the operation of the federal Sherman Antitrust Act as long as they engage in normal cooperative practices and do not conspire with outsiders to fix prices.

Business Trust

A *business, common-law,* or *Massachusetts trust* arises when the owners of property transfer the ownership to one or more persons, called *trustees,* to be managed for business purposes by the trustees for the benefit of the original owners. Although the trustee or trustees, in a sense, are put in charge of the business for the benefit of the original owners, the relationship is more formal than an ordinary employer-employee relationship. In addition to the transfer of the legal title to the trustee or trustees, *trust certificates* or *shares* are issued to the former owners as evidence of their interest, and the profits are divided proportionately among the holders of the certificates.

Like shares in a corporation, shares in a business trust may be transferred. Unlike a corporation, the holders of the shares do not have control of the trustees running the business, as do shareholders over the board of directors of a corporation. Some courts hold that the business trust is merely a trust and the fact that it is designed for business operations, rather than to pay money for the support of certain persons or institutions, does not prevent the ordinary trust relationship law from applying.[10]

Facts: The Greer Investment Co. transferred money to F. H. Greer and others to hold as trustees under a business trust with the name of The Petroleum Royalties Co. The trust was to continue for 20 years. The trust agreement authorized the trustees to convey the property to new trustees when this was deemed judicious. Toward the end of the 20-year period, the trustees, then Catlett and others, decided to continue the business by conveying the assets to a new business trust, Petroleum Royalties, Limited, and to require the shareholders of the old trust to become shareholders of the new trust. To determine the validity of this plan, Catlett and the other trustees brought an action against Hauser and the other shareholders in the original business trust.

Decision: Judgment against the trustees. The trust was lawful but, as the trust was to terminate at the end of 20 years, that intention of the persons creating the trust could not be evaded by the device of transferring

---

[10] See p. 673.

the stock to another trust. (Hauser v. Catlett, 197 Okla. 668, 173 P.2d 728)

Other courts hold that for the purpose of taxation or the regulation of the business, the business trust is to be classified as a corporation.[11]

One of the objectives of the business trust is to achieve a limited liability for the members or holders of trust certificates. In most jurisdictions it is held that the certificate holders are not liable for the debts of the business trust if they have relinquished all control over management to the trustees. The same conclusion is reached if there is a clause in the agreement establishing the trust by which it is stated that the certificate holders shall not be liable, at least with respect to persons dealing with the trust with knowledge or notice of such a limitation. In order to bring knowledge of such a limitation to third persons, it is common for the stationery of the business trust to state that such a limitation exists.

Joint-Stock Company

Joint-stock companies are of common-law origin, although in a number of states they are now regulated by statute. This form of association has features resembling both a partnership and a corporation, or a business trust. Like a corporation, the shares of its members are transferable. The contract of the members provides that any member may transfer his share and that the person to whom the share is transferred shall be accepted as a member. The management of the company is generally delegated to designated persons because as a general rule the membership is much larger than that of an ordinary partnership. The business is usually conducted under an impersonal name.

QUESTIONS AND PROBLEMS

1. Checklist of legal terms:
   (a) limited partnership; special or limited partner, general partner (558)
   (b) joint venture (559)
   (c) mining partnership (560)
   (d) syndicate (560), underwriting syndicate (561)
   (e) unincorporated association (561)
   (f) cooperative (561)
   (g) business trust, trustee, trust certificates (562)

2. State the objective(s) of each of the following rules of law:
   (a) Members of an unincorporated association are ordinarily not liable for debts of the group unless they had authorized, ratified, or in some way participated in creating the debts.

---

[11] *Rubens* v. *Costello*, 75 Ariz. 5, 251 P.2d 306.

(b) Normal selling activities of farmers' and dairymen's cooperatives are exempt from the operation of the federal antitrust act.

3. Kash, Merrill, Pollard, and Reger created a limited partnership with the firm name of Kash and Pollard. Kash contributes cash and services, Merrill contributes property, Pollard contributes his services as sales manager, and Reger contributes his services as treasurer.

(a) Which are general and which are special partners, and why?
(b) To what extent is Kash liable for a debt of the firm to a creditor?
(c) To what extent is Merrill liable for such a debt?

4. Several dealers in securities form an unincorporated underwriting syndicate to market the preferred stock of a large corporation. One of these dealers wishes to transfer his interest. Can he do so without dissolving the syndicate?

5. Engel, Kay, and Hunnicut are members of an unincorporated social club. At a meeting at which it was voted to borrow $500 from a bank for six months, Engel votes no, Kay votes yes, and Hunnicut did not vote because he was absent. What is the liability of each of these members for the debt to the bank?

6. The Farmers' Dairy Co-op enters into an agreement with several retail distributors of dairy products to fix prices. Is such an agreement lawful?

7. Shilling and Ryan consider the possibility of organizing a joint-stock company. Shilling contends that this form of partnership differs from an ordinary partnership chiefly in the fact that in the former the management of the company is delegated to designated persons. Do you agree?

8. Simpson and Saunders each had a used car dealer's license. They made an agreement to run their businesses independently but to share a lot, the building thereon, the furnishings, and the use of a telephone. Bates sued both Simpson and Saunders claiming that they were joint venturers and therefore both were liable for the fraudulent conduct of Simpson. Was Saunders liable? (Bates v. Simpson, 121 Utah 165, 239 P.2d 749)

9. Ettelsohn, Allen, and Levinson formed a limited partnership. The proceedings for the formation of the limited partnership complied with requirements of the statute except that Ettelsohn, the limited partner, contributed goods instead of cash as specified by the statute. In an action brought by Claflin, a creditor of the firm, it was claimed that Ettelsohn was a general partner. Decide. (Claflin v. Sattler, 41 Minn. 430, 43 N.W. 382)

Chapter 49

Nature and Classification

The corporation is one of the most important forms of business organization. To the large-scale enterprise it offers an easier way to finance itself by means of dividing its ownership into many small units that can be sold to a wide economic range of purchasers. In addition to assisting financing operations, the corporate device offers a limited liability to the persons interested in the enterprise and a perpetual succession not affected by the death of any particular owner or by the transfer of his interest. Because of its limited liability, the corporation is also popular with many smaller businesses.

Preliminary Survey

A corporation is formed by obtaining approval of articles of incorporation or a charter from the state or national government. The persons who develop the idea and induce others to join in the enterprise are called *promoters*. The persons who make the application to the government for the charter are called *incorporators*.

A corporation is controlled or managed by three groups of persons. The *board of directors* meets from time to time to determine the main policies of the corporation. This board selects the *officers* of the corporation, such as president, vice-president, treasurer, and secretary, who manage the corporation from day to day. In the ordinary business corporation *shareholders* or stockholders own shares of stock in the corporation and are the owners of the corporation. The shares of some or all of the shareholders are voting shares. Through the election of the directors, the voting shareholders exercise an indirect control over the management of the corporation.

Shareholders have varying rights depending upon the nature of their stock. If the stock has no particular right or priority over any other stock, it

565

is known as *common stock.* If the stock has a priority or preference over other stock, it is called *preferred stock.*

Stock may also be distinguished in terms of whether the share of stock has a value specified in the stock certificate at the time it is issued, called a *par value,* or whether it is a share without any such specified value, in which case it is called *no-par stock.*

When a corporation is created, it is authorized to issue certain amounts and kinds of stock. If stock has been issued, it is said that the shares issued are outstanding. The outstanding stock of a corporation is also referred to as the capital stock of the corporation.

As the shareholders are the owners of the corporation, they are entitled to share in the profits of the business. The profits are distributed to the shareholders in the form of *dividends* when the board of directors deems it advisable. Dividends are ordinarily paid in money, but they may also be paid in property.

When a corporation goes out of business, all creditors are paid if possible. Any balance is distributed among the shareholders.

Definition of a Corporation

A *corporation* is an entity, an artificial legal being, created by government grant and endowed with certain powers. That is, the corporation exists in the eyes of the law as though it were a person, separate and distinct from the people who own the corporation.

> **Facts:** North Gate Corporation leased property to National Food Stores. The lease contained a provision that neither the corporation nor its "beneficiaries" would engage in a competing business within a specified radius. Some shareholders of North Gate Corporation engaged in such a business within the prohibited area. National Food Stores claimed that the restriction on "beneficiaries" applied to "shareholders" of North Gate.

> **Decision:** Judgment against National Food Stores. Restrictive covenants are strictly interpreted so that the covenant would not apply to shareholders when it did not expressly so state. The shareholders are not subject to the limitation imposed on the corporation as they are distinct from the corporation. Likewise "shareholders" are not "beneficiaries" so that they were not embraced by the terms of the covenant. (North Gate Corporation v. National Food Stores, Inc., 30 Wis.2d 317, 140 N.W. 2d 744)

This concept means that property of the corporation is not owned by the persons who own shares in the corporation, but by the corporation.[1]

---

[1] *Wells* v. *Hiskett,* [Tex.Civ.App.] 288 S.W.2d 257.

Debts of the corporation are debts of this artificial person and not of the people running the corporation or owning shares of stock in it. The corporation can sue and be sued in its own name with respect to corporate rights and liabilities, but the shareholders cannot sue or be sued as to those rights and liabilities. Furthermore, a corporation has independent life in the sense that it continues to exist without regard to the death of the individuals involved in its corporate affairs or the transfer by them of their interests in the corporation. Similarly a parent company and its wholly-owned subsidiary are regarded as separate entities.

Facts: Di Re was employed by the Central Livestock Order Buying Co., which was a subsidiary of the Central Livestock Association, Inc. The officers and directors of both corporations were identical. The subsidiary company had been formed because the Federal Packers and Stockyards Act had required the parent company to separate its buying and selling agencies. The subsidiary company notified Di Re that a reduction in staff was necessary and that he was discharged. The parent company then offered him another job. He refused to take the other job and applied for unemployment compensation. The subsidiary objected to the allowance of unemployment compensation on the theory that the two companies constituted a single employer and that Di Re was not unemployed but was merely transferred from one department to another.

Decision: In the absence of fraud or some improper purpose in creating separate corporate entities, the law must recognize the distinct existence of each corporation. Consequently, the parent and the subsidiary corporations were two different employers and Di Re's employment with his original employer had therefore been terminated. (Di Re v. Central Livestock Order Buying Co., 246 Minn. 279, 74 N.W.2d 518)

In some instances the law will look behind the corporate identity to determine who in fact runs the business if the corporate device has been employed to conceal crime or fraud. In other instances this will be done to eliminate the claim that a different enterprise is involved, as when a partnership incorporates and it is then claimed that the corporation is a new legal person, but the court rejects this claim on the ground that it is still the same enterprise only organized differently.

The court will not go behind the corporate identity merely because the corporation has been formed to obtain tax savings or to obtain limited liability for its shareholders. Likewise the corporate entity will not be ignored merely because the corporation does not have sufficient assets to pay the claim against it.[2]

Facts: London owned 98 percent of the stock of a corporation engaged in sports promotion, named Mike London Sports. His mother and wife

---

[2] *Walkovszky* v. *Carlton*, 18 N.Y.2d 414, 276 N.Y.S.2d 585.

each owned one share. London leased in his own name from Bruskas property that was used by the corporation. Bruskas wrongly canceled the lease. London sued him and proved the damages caused to the corporation by the breach.

Decision: It was held that London, as the tenant, could only show the damages caused to him personally by the defendant's breach. The corporation was a distinct person, and the harm caused it was not an injury to London. The corporate identity would not be ignored even though London owned 98 percent of the stock. (London v. Bruskas, 64 N.Mex. 73, 324 P.2d 424)

Power to Create a Corporation

Since by definition a corporation is created by government grant, individuals cannot create a corporation merely by agreeing to do so. The right to be a corporation as evidenced by a *charter* or approval of *articles of incorporation* must be obtained from the proper government.[3]

1 / Federal power. The federal government is not expressly granted power to create corporations, but it may do so whenever appropriate to carry out the powers expressly granted to it. In addition, Congress has the right to authorize the creation of corporations in the District of Columbia and the territories of the United States.

Facts: Maryland enacted a law that imposed a tax on bank notes issued by any bank not chartered by the state legislature. McCulloch, the cashier of the Baltimore branch of the United States Bank, issued bank notes on which this tax had not been paid. Suit was brought by the state of Maryland against McCulloch to recover the statutory penalties imposed for the violation of the law.

Decision: Held that the Congress, as a means of carrying out its express powers, had the implied authority to create a national bank and that such a bank could not be subjected to state taxation. (McCulloch v. Maryland, 4 Wheat [U.S.] 316)

2 / State power. Generally a state by virtue of its police power may create any kind of corporation for any purpose. Some limitations on this power are found in state constitutions, and the power is, of course, subordinate to the federal powers. In many states the constitution provides that the legislature cannot create a corporation by a special act but only in accordance with a general law.

Most states have a *general corporation code* that lists certain requirements, and those groups which satisfy the requirements and which file the necessary papers with the government to prove compliance may automatically

---

[3] *Lloyds of Texas,* [D.C.Tex.] 43 F.2d 383.

become corporations. Many states have several corporation codes, such as a code for the incorporation of business or profit corporations, another code for nonprofit or charitable corporations, and frequently special codes for such specialized corporate institutions as banks, savings and loan associations, insurance companies, and railroads. The American Bar Association has proposed a Model Business Corporation Act which has been adopted or is the basis for the business corporation code in several states.[4] There is no uniform corporation act.[5]

Classifications of Corporations

1 / Public, private, and quasi-public corporations. A *public corporation* is one established for governmental purposes and for the administration of public affairs. A city is a public or municipal corporation acting under authority granted it by the state.

A *private corporation* is one established by private interests, whether for charitable and benevolent purposes or for purposes of finance, industry, and commerce. Private corporations are often called "public" in business circles when their stock is sold to the public.

A *quasi-public corporation*, which is also known as a public service corporation or a public utility, is a private corporation furnishing services upon which the public is particularly dependent. Examples of this class of corporations are those operating railroads, canals, and bridges or those supplying gas, electricity, and water. Such corporations are usually given special franchises and powers, such as the power of eminent domain.

2 / Stock and nonstock corporations. A *stock corporation* is one having its capital stock divided into shares, the rights and liabilities of the members being determined by ownership of such shares.

A *nonstock corporation* is one in which the membership with attending rights and liabilities is acquired by agreement rather than by the acquisition of shares of stock, as in the case of incorporated fraternal organizations.

3 / Nonprofit and profit corporations. A *nonprofit corporation* (or an eleemosynary corporation) is one that is organized for charitable or benevolent purposes, such as certain hospitals, homes, and universities.[6]

---

[4] This Act has been adopted in Alaska, Arkansas, Colorado, Iowa, Mississippi, Nebraska, North Dakota, Oregon, South Carolina, South Dakota, Texas, Utah, Washington, Virginia, Wisconsin, Wyoming, and the District of Columbia.

[5] The Commissioners on Uniform State Laws had proposed a Uniform Business Corporation Act in 1928. This Act was adopted in Idaho, Kentucky, Louisiana, and Washington, and substantially influenced the corporation laws in a number of states. In 1943 the Commissioners designated it a model act, rather than a uniform act, to indicate that it was not believed that uniformity in the various states was essential. In 1957, as the result of the growth of the ABA model act, the Commissioners withdrew their model act.

[6] *Gilbert* v. *McLeod Infirmary*, 219 S.C. 174, 64 S.E.2d 524.

A *profit corporation* (or a business or civil corporation) is one organized for purposes other than charitable or benevolent purposes.

4 / Domestic and foreign corporations. If a corporation has been created under the law of a particular state or nation, it is called a *domestic corporation* with respect to that state or nation. Any other corporation going into that state or nation is called a *foreign corporation.* Thus a corporation holding an Illinois charter is a domestic corporation in Illinois but a foreign corporation in all other states and nations. This distinction becomes important in considering the extent of control that may be exercised by a government over corporations operating within its territorial boundaries. Whether a corporation is domestic is determined without regard to the residence of its shareholders or incorporators, or the state in which it conducts business.[7] A corporation created under the law of one nation is also classified as an *alien corporation* in other nations.

Regulation of Corporations

In addition to determining whether a corporate power exists, it is necessary to consider whether there is any government regulation imposed upon the exercise of that power. Both the federal and state governments, by virtue of their power to create corporations, can exercise a degree of control over corporations. In addition, corporations, as in the case of all other persons, are subject to the law generally. Thus a corporation must pay a real-estate tax on its land and observe zoning and fire regulations just as though it were an individual owner.

1 / Domestic corporations. Domestic corporations are regulated by the provisions of the code or general statutes under which they are organized and also by the tax laws and general laws of the state of their origin. The fact that a corporation goes outside its home state to conduct business does not remove it from all control by the incorporating state, although that control may in fact be very slight.

2 / Foreign corporations. A foreign corporation is also subject to regulation and taxation, except as later noted, in every state in which it does business. Generally a foreign corporation must register to do business within the state, and it may be required to consent to be sued upon causes of action arising within the state.

3 / Constitutional limitations. In regulating a corporation, both state and national governments must observe certain limitations because corporations come within the protection of certain constitutional guarantees.

---

[7] *Omaha National Bank* v. *Jensen,* 157 Neb. 22, 58 N.W.2d 582.

(a) THE CORPORATION AS A PERSON. The Constitution of the United States prohibits the national government and the state governments from depriving any "person" of life, liberty, or property without due process of law. Many state constitutions contain a similar limitation upon their respective state governments. A corporation is regarded as a "person" within the meaning of such provisions.

The federal Constitution prohibits states from denying to any "person" within its jurisdiction the equal protection of the laws. No such limitation is placed upon the federal government, although the due process clause binding the federal government has been liberally interpreted so that it would prohibit substantial inequality of treatment. Again it is held that a corporation enjoys the same equal protection of the laws as a natural person or individual.

(b) THE CORPORATION AS A CITIZEN. For certain purposes, such as determining the right to bring a lawsuit in a federal court, a corporation is today deemed a "citizen" of any state in which it has been incorporated and of the state where it has its principal place of business, without regard to the actual citizenship of the individual persons owning the stock of the corporation. Thus a corporation incorporated in New York is a New York corporation even though its shareholders are citizens of many other states.

The federal Constitution prohibits states from abridging "the privileges or immunities of citizens of the United States." A corporation, however, is not regarded as a "citizen" within this clause. Thus, with one exception, a foreign corporation has no constitutional right to do business in another state if that other state wishes to exclude it. For example, Pennsylvania can deny a New York corporation the right to come into Pennsylvania to do business. As a practical matter, most states do not exclude foreign corporations but seize upon this power as justifying special regulation or taxation. On this basis it is commonly provided that a foreign corporation must register or even take out a domestic charter, file copies of its charter, pay certain taxes, or appoint a resident agent before it can do business within the state. These regulations are sustained on the theory that since the foreign corporation could be excluded completely, it can be admitted on condition or at a price. Once the foreign corporation is admitted, however, the state cannot deny it due process or equal protection of the laws.

As an exception to the power of a state, it cannot exclude a foreign corporation when the latter engages solely in interstate commerce even though it is within the boundaries of the state. A state cannot require a license or registration of a foreign interstate commerce corporation or impose a tax on the right to engage in such a business.

QUESTIONS AND PROBLEMS

1. Checklist of legal terms:

    (a) promoters, incorporators (565)

    (b) board of directors, officers, shareholders (565)

    (c) common stock, preferred stock; par value, no-par stock; dividends (566)

    (d) corporation (566), charter (568); general corporation code (569)

    (e) public corporation, private corporation; quasi-public corporation (569)

    (f) stock corporation, nonstock corporation (569)

    (g) nonprofit corporation, profit corporation (569)

    (h) domestic corporation, foreign corporation, alien corporation (570)

2. State the objective(s) of each of the following rules of law:

    (a) A corporation is created as an independent legal person by the act of the state in granting a charter or in approving articles of incorporation.

    (b) Incorporation is now generally obtained by complying with the requirements of a corporation code, rather than by obtaining a special grant or charter from the legislature.

3. Ewing is the vice-president, Hoffer a shareholder, and Fulford a director in the same corporation. What levels (a) of responsibility and (b) of authority do they represent?

4. "A corporation is an artificial, legal person that has perpetual life." Explain the following terms in this statement: (a) artificial person; (b) legal person; (c) perpetual life.

5. An Illinois corporation does business in that state and in four neighboring states. Is the corporation a domestic or foreign corporation?

6. A state statute established traffic rates for railroads that would not permit the carriers to earn a reasonable return on their property. The corporations operating these railroads protested that the statute violated the Fourteenth Amendment, which declares that no state shall deprive any person of property without due process of law nor deny to any person within its jurisdiction the equal protection of the laws. The state contended that a corporation is not a person within the meaning of this provision. Do you agree?

7. An action was brought by Alabama Tank Lines and other carriers against the Martin Truck Line, claiming that the truck line was operating without the necessary certificate of the state Public Service Commission. It was shown that Martin Truck Line had obtained a certificate at a time when all of its stock was owned by Thornbury, Cook, and Edwards. The stock was thereafter sold to Houghland and Page. No approval of the transfer of stock to them was obtained from the Public Service Commission. Was Martin Truck Line entitled to continue to do business under the certificate that had been originally issued? (Martin Truck Line v. Alabama Tank Lines, 261 Ala. 163, 73 So.2d 756)

Chapter 50

Creation and Termination

A corporation receives its authority from government. Statutory law therefore specifies the requirements that must be met for creating a corporation and the manner in which a corporation can be dissolved or terminated.

CREATION OF THE CORPORATION

All states have general laws governing the creation of corporations by a specified number of persons who comply with the provisions of the statutes.

Requisites to Creation

Persons who wish to incorporate must substantially comply with such requirements as:

1 / Number and qualifications of incorporators. The statutes usually require a certain number of applicants who possess, in addition to the capacity to contract, the qualification of residence or citizenship. The American Bar Association Model Business Corporation Act permits the corporation to be incorporated by natural persons or other corporations.[1]

In most states a minimum of three incorporators is required. About one fourth of the states require that the incorporators be shareholders.

Although many states exclude a corporation from acting as an incorporator, an exception is commonly made when corporations in existence are being consolidated to form a new corporation.

2 / Application for incorporation. The organizers must apply for a charter and file certain documents, such as the proposed articles of incorporation. The application must generally state the following:

(a) NAME OF THE PROPOSED CORPORATION. Subject to certain limitations, the incorporators may select any name for the firm.[2]

(b) OBJECT OF THE PROPOSED CORPORATION. Sometimes the statute enumerates the purposes for which a corporation may be formed. The purpose or object must be lawful. A corporation may be forbidden to do acts

---

[1] American Bar Association Model Business Corporation Act, Sec. 47.
[2] See p. 586.

that would be lawful if done by an individual. To illustrate, persons may be forbidden to incorporate for the purpose of practicing law, medicine, or related arts.[3] A corporation can neither practice one of the learned professions nor employ a licensed practitioner to practice for it.

Facts: The State of Kansas, on the complaint of the attorney general, brought an original action in the Supreme Court of Kansas against the Zale Jewelry Co., a corporation, to order it to stop the practice of optometry and to forfeit its charter for engaging therein. The State claimed that Dr. Marks, who practiced optometry in one part of the store, and the Douglas Optical Co., which also did business in part of the store, were in fact employees of the Zale Co. which, as their employer, was therefore engaging in optometry. Zale defended on the ground that they were not its employees but were tenants to whom Zale had leased space in its store. The leases specified that financial affairs of Marks and Douglas were to be controlled by Zale, and work done on credit was carried on Zale's charge account records; and the area in which Marks and the Douglas Optical Co. operated was marked by a sign "Optical Department."

Decision: The state was correct. Zale exercised such control over the operations and financial affairs of Marks and Optical as to make the latter Zale's employees. The fact that the relationship was described as a lease did not bar the court from determining the true character of the relationship. (State v. Zale Jewelry Company, 179 Kan. 628, 298 P.2d 283)

In some instances an exception is made to the prohibition against a corporation engaging in the practice of law, in order to carry out antipoverty and civil rights advancement programs; but even in such cases there is authority that all persons involved must be lawyers and that the corporation cannot be controlled by nonlawyer sponsors.[4]

Some states also require a statement of the means to be used to attain the object of the corporation. This is particularly common in the case of nonprofit or charitable corporations.

(c) CAPITAL STOCK. The amount of capital stock to be authorized and the number and value of the shares into which it is divided must be specified.

---

[3] In order to permit self-employed professional men to obtain the tax advantages of deferred retirement plans enjoyed by corporate employees, a majority of states have adopted laws permitting the organization of professional corporations or associations. Note, however, that Opinion 303 of the American Bar Association Committee on Professional Ethics expresses "grave doubts" as to the propriety of lawyers forming organizations under such laws.

[4] *Application of Community Action for Legal Services,* 26 App.Div.2d 354, 274 N.Y.S.2d 779. A labor union has a constitutional right to employ a lawyer on a salary basis to provide free legal services for union members. *United Mine Workers* v. *Illinois State Bar Ass'n,* [U.S.] 19 L.Ed.2d 426.

The Model Business Corporation Act also requires that the articles of incorporation state a description of the classes of shares, the number of shares in each class, the relative rights of each class, and that the corporation will not commence business until consideration of the value of at least $1,000 has been received for the issuance of shares.[5] Other statutes have similar requirements.

(d) PLACE OF BUSINESS. The location of the principal office or place of business of the proposed corporation must be stated.

(e) DURATION. The period during which the proposed corporation is to exist must be set forth. Most states permit the incorporators to select perpetual life for the corporation, but some states limit the number of years.

(f) DIRECTORS AND OFFICERS. In half of the states the number of directors or the names and addresses of directors for the first year must be stated. Sometimes additional information regarding the directors is required. In some instances the names and addresses of the officers for the first year must also be stated.

The purpose of requiring the naming of the first board of directors is to provide the corporation with a body to govern or manage the corporation during the interval from the moment that the corporate life begins until the organization meeting of the shareholders is held. In some states that do not require the naming of the first board of directors in this manner, the incorporators have the power of management during this period.

(g) INCORPORATORS. The names and addresses of the incorporators must be given, together with the number of shares subscribed by each. Sometimes the method of payment for those shares must also be stated.

3 / Advertisement. Statutes may require incorporators to give public notice, such as by advertisement in a newspaper, of the intention to form the corporation. It is sometimes required that the name and purpose of the corporation be advertised. In addition to giving the public general knowledge of the incorporation, such notice also gives existing companies an opportunity to object that the name of the proposed corporation is the same as, or deceptively similar to, the name of an existing company. Provision may also be made that any person objecting to the proposed corporation may file a written objection, ordinarily with the officer with whom incorporators are required to file their application. That officer may refuse to allow the incorporation when a sound objection is made; or he may require the incorporators to modify their plans, after which he will grant the charter.

---

[5] ABA MBCA Sec. 48.

The Charter

After the application for a charter or the articles of incorporation are filed, the fee paid, and other conditions precedent fulfilled, usually an administrative official, such as the secretary of state, examines the papers. If the requirements of the law have been met, a certificate of incorporation, license, or charter is issued and recorded or filed, as specified by the terms of the local statute.[6]

Under the Model Business Corporation Act corporate existence begins upon the issuance of the certificate of incorporation by the state official.[7] In some states corporate existence does not begin until an organization meeting is held under the charter to put the corporation in operation, and in others, not until a report on the organization is made. The statute may declare that the charter shall be void if the certificate of organization is not properly filed within the prescribed time.

The charter not only creates the corporation but also confers contractual rights and imposes contractual duties as between the state, the corporation, and the shareholders.[8] In theory it is required that the corporation accept the charter which is given to it; but unless expressly required by statute, it is not necessary for the corporation to inform any state officer that the charter is accepted. The acceptance can be inferred from conduct, such as holding an organization meeting or doing business under the charter.[9]

Since the charter is regarded as a contract, the corporation is protected from subsequent change or modification by the clause of the federal Constitution that prohibits states from impairing the obligation of contracts.[10] This does not mean that in no case can the rights given by a charter be modified. Under many statutes it is expressly provided that the charter granted by the state is subject to the power reserved by the state to change the charter should it desire to do so. Independently of such a reservation, the rule has developed that permits the state, under the exercise of its police power, to modify existing contracts, including corporate charters, to further the public health, safety, morals, or general welfare.

Proper and Defective Incorporations

If the legal procedure for incorporation has been followed, the corporation has a perfect legal right to exist. It is therefore called a *corporation de jure*, meaning that it is a corporation by virtue of law.

---

[6] Sec. 49.
[7] Compare Sec. 50.
[8] *Petition of Collins-Doan Co.*, 3 N.J. 382, 70 A.2d 159.
[9] *Bank of U.S.* v. *Dandridge*, 12 Wheat. [U.S.] 64.
[10] *Dartmouth College Case*, 4 Wheat. [U.S.] 518.

Suppose that after the charter has been issued to a corporation, it is found that the legal procedure was not followed in every detail, that some of the blanks in the application for the charter were not filled in, that the corporation did not have the amount of paid-in capital stated in the application, or that none of the incorporators was qualified under the statute. What effect do such irregularities in the incorporation procedure have upon the corporation?

If the defect in the incorporation is not a material one, the law usually will overlook the defect and hold that the corporation is a corporation de jure. No simple rule can be stated as to when a defect will be overlooked by the courts or will be held so fundamental that it cannot be ignored. Generally the courts attempt to determine which provisions of the law must have been regarded by the legislature as so basic that they must be observed and those that the legislature wished followed but did not deem so vital. As an illustration of the former, it has been held that the failure to set forth the amount of the capital is fatal to an attempted incorporation.

1 / De facto corporation. The defect in the incorporation may be so substantial that the law cannot ignore it and will not accept the corporation as a de jure corporation. Yet there may be sufficient compliance so that the law will recognize that there is a corporation. When this occurs, the association is called a *de facto corporation.* It exists in fact but not by right, and the state may bring proceedings to have the corporate charter revoked because of the defects.[11] If, however, the state does not take proceedings against the defective corporation, the de facto corporation has all the rights and privileges of a regular lawful or de jure corporation, and third persons contracting with it cannot avoid their contracts on the ground that the corporation was merely a de facto corporation. The de facto corporation is, in a sense, like a voidable contract. It can be set aside by the state; but unless the state acts, the corporation is lawful with respect to the entire world. The shareholders of a de facto corporation generally have limited liability.

In nearly all states, statutes provide that the approval of the articles of incorporation by the specified state official or the issuance by him of a certificate of incorporation shall conclusively evidence the incorporation, subject only to dissolution at the suit of the state.

Facts: A municipal corporation, the Bloom Township High School District, was about to issue bonds. Taxpayers brought a suit to stop it from doing so and raised as a ground a claim that the district had not been legally organized and therefore had no right to exist or to issue bonds.

---

[11] *Colonial Investment Co.* v. *Cherrydale Cement Block Co.,* 194 Va. 454, 73 S.E. 2d 419.

Decision: Judgment against the taxpayers. For over 25 years the municipal corporation had functioned as a school district. The question as to whether
it was a de facto or a de jure corporation could not be raised in an
action by taxpayers but could only be raised in an action brought by
the attorney general to revoke the charter. (Fiedler v. Eckfeldt, 335
Ill. 11, 166 N.E. 504)

Although there is conflict among the authorities, most courts hold that
a de facto corporation must meet four tests: (a) there must be a valid law
under which the corporation could have been properly incorporated; (b) the
attempt to organize the corporation must have been made in good faith;
(c) the attempt to organize must result in colorable compliance with the
requirements of the statute; and (d) there must be a use of the corporate
powers.

2 / Partnership v. corporation by estoppel. The defect in incorporation may be so great that the law will not accept the corporation even as a
de facto corporation, let alone as a de jure corporation. In such a case, in
the absence of a statute making the incorporation conclusive, there is no
corporation, and no one is bound to accept it as such. As an illustration,
A, B, and *C* may organize a business for profit and intend to incorporate it.
Assume a basic defect in the incorporation, such as the failure to file an
application for a charter. Assume also that a third person, *T,* is injured by
an employee of the business. *T* sues *A* individually. *A* defends on the ground
that the claim of the plaintiff is against the corporation and not *A,* who is
merely a shareholder in the corporation. The court would hold that the
attempt to create a corporation was so defective that there was no corporation, and that the liabilities of *A, B,* and *C* were therefore the same as if
they had organized a partnership.[12]

The concept that the "shareholders" of the defective corporation are
liable as partners is not applied by most courts to inactive shareholders.
That is, those actively running the defective corporation are treated as partners while the inactive shareholders are clothed with limited liability.

In a minority of states the court will not hold the individuals liable as
partners, but it will hold liable the person who committed the act on behalf
of the business on the theory that he was an agent who acted without
authority and is therefore liable for breach of the implied warranties of the
existence of a proper principal and of proper authorization.[13]

The partnership liability rule is sometimes not applied when the third
person dealt with the business as though it were actually a corporation. In
such instances it is stated that the third person is estopped from denying that

[12] *Doggrell* v. *Great Southern Box Co.,* [C.A.6th] 206 F.2d 671.
[13] See pp. 235-236.

the "corporation" with which he did business has legal existence. The court in effect holds that there is a *corporation by estoppel* with respect to that creditor.

> **Facts:** Namerdy entered into a contract with Generalcar. In the contract the latter was identified as a Belgian corporation. Later when Generalcar sued Namerdy for breach of the agreement, he defended by asserting that Generalcar failed to prove that it was a corporation.

> **Decision:** Namerdy, by entering into a contract that described Generalcar as a Belgian corporation, was estopped from challenging the existence of its corporate character; and it was not necessary for Generalcar to prove that it was a Belgian corporation when it sued on the agreement. (Namerdy v. Generalcar, [C.A. Dist.Col.] 217 A.2d 109)

The doctrine of corporation by estoppel is not always applied, and it is difficult to bring one's case within the rule by showing that the third person dealt with the defective corporation as a corporation. The doctrine is applied when one of the promoters or incorporators attempts to deny that there is a corporation. Here it is held that having attempted to create the corporation or having purported to do so, the promoter or incorporator cannot deny that a corporation was created.

If the incorporators have failed to obtain a charter and have not done business together, neither the corporation by estoppel nor the partnership rule will be applied.

Promoters

The promoters are persons who plan the corporation and sell the idea to others. They may also file the necessary papers with the government to create the corporation. They are independent operators. They are not regarded as agents of the corporation since the corporation is not yet in existence.

A promoter, in the absence of statutory authority, cannot bind the corporation [14] or give it rights by a preincorporation contract even though he purports to act for it. The corporation, upon coming into existence, may become a party to such a contract, however, by assignment or by novation. Moreover, when the corporation knowingly accepts the benefits of the promoter's contract, it becomes liable on that contract.[15]

The promoter is personally liable for all contracts made in behalf of the corporation before its existence unless he is exempted by the terms of the agreement or by the circumstances surrounding it. Even when the promoter

---

[14] *Mankin* v. *Bryant*, 206 Ga. 120, 56 S.E.2d 447.
[15] *Frye & Smith* v. *Foote*, 113 Cal.App.2d 907, 247 P.2d 825.

openly sells his property to the corporation, the latter does not become liable for the unpaid balance due on such property in the absence of an adoption by the corporation of that debt.

A promoter is also liable for all torts that he commits in connection with his activities. Although the corporation is not ordinarily liable for the torts of the promoter, it may become so by its conduct after incorporation. Thus, when a corporation, with actual or implied notice of the fraud of the promoter, assumes responsibility for the promoter's contract, it is liable for the fraud.

A promoter stands in a fiduciary relation to the corporation and to stock subscribers.[16] He cannot make secret profits at their expense. Accordingly, if a promoter makes secret profits on a sale of land to a corporation, he must account to the corporation for those profits, that is, he must surrender the profits to it.

The corporation is not liable in most states for the expenses and services of the promoter unless it subsequently promises to pay for them or unless its charter or a statute imposes such liability upon it.

DISSOLUTION AND TERMINATION

A corporation may be dissolved or terminated by agreement, insolvency, reorganization proceedings, consolidation, merger, or forfeiture of charter. Some statutes provide for the dissolution of small corporations by court decree upon proof of a continuing stalemate between rival factions,[17] similar to the judicial dissolution of partnerships under such circumstances.

Dissolution by Agreement

1 / Expiration of time. If the incorporators have selected a corporate life of a stated number of years, the corporate existence automatically terminates upon the expiration of that period. Some courts hold that the corporation may continue thereafter as a de facto corporation.

2 / Surrender of charter. The shareholders may terminate the corporate existence by surrendering the charter to the state. The surrender is not effective until the state accepts the charter. The state will ordinarily not accept it if any creditors have not been paid, since the state's acceptance of a surrender of the charter ends the corporate existence and generally extinguishes the liability of the corporation for debts.

3 / Repeal of charter. The corporation may be formed with the provision that the legislature may terminate its existence at will or upon the

---

[16] *Arent* v. *Bray,* [C.A.4th] 371 F.2d 571.
[17] *Laskey* v. *L&L Manchester Drive-In,* [Maine] 216 A.2d 310.

happening of a certain contingency. This right may be contained in the provisions of the charter, or in the statute or constitution of the government. In exercising the right of repeal, however, the government cannot impair vested rights, as by taking the assets of the corporation from the shareholders or creditors.

Insolvency

The insolvency of a corporation does not in itself terminate the corporate existence. Statutes in some states, however, provide that when the corporation is insolvent, creditors may commence proceedings to dissolve the corporation. Sometimes the statute merely dissolves the corporation as to creditors. This situation is sometimes called a *de facto* or *quasi dissolution*.

The appointment of a receiver for the corporation does not in itself dissolve the corporation, although the administration of the property by the receiver may result in the practical termination of the corporation. In some states the appointment of liquidators to wind up an insolvent corporation automatically dissolves the corporation.[18] In the absence of statute, a court cannot appoint a receiver for a solvent corporation and order its dissolution.[19]

Reorganization

When a reorganization of a corporation occurs under the federal bankruptcy laws, the corporate existence is not terminated. If the reorganization is successful, the result is the same as though the corporation merely exchanged obligations.

Consolidation

In a *consolidation* of two or more corporations, the separate corporate existences cease; and a new corporation with the property and assets of the old corporations comes into being.[20] When a consolidation is effected, the new corporation ordinarily succeeds to the rights, powers, and immunities of its component parts.[21] Limitations, however, may be prescribed by charter, constitution, or statute. As a general rule, the consolidated corporation is subject to all the liabilities of the constituent corporations.

Merger

Merger differs from consolidation in that, when two corporations merge, one absorbs the other. One corporation preserves its original charter and identity and continues to exist, and the other disappears and its corporate existence terminates.

---

[18] *Brown & Son* v. *Wholesalers, Inc.*, [La.] 52 So.2d 321.
[19] *Hepner* v. *Miller*, 130 Colo. 243, 274 P.2d 818.
[20] *Freeman* v. *Hiznay*, 349 Pa. 89, 36 A.2d 509.
[21] ABA MBCA Sec. 69.

Facts: A labor union made a collective bargaining agreement with Interscience Publishers, Inc. The contract made no provision that it was binding on successors of the contracting parties. Later, for general business reasons and not as an antilabor measure, Interscience merged with and disappeared into another publishing corporation, John Wiley & Sons, Inc. The former's employees, with a few exceptions, worked for Wiley. Thereafter the labor union claimed that Wiley was required to submit to arbitration, in accordance with the terms of the contract with Interscience, certain questions relating to employees who had worked for Interscience but were working for Wiley after the merger. Wiley claimed that it was not bound by the arbitration agreement with Interscience.

Decision: Wiley was bound by the contract. In order to prevent the defeating of the purpose of collective bargaining as a consequence of the reorganization of a corporate employer, the surviving corporation is bound by the bargaining contract of any other enterprise absorbed by it with respect to employees of the disappeared employer when there is a substantial identity of the work done by the surviving and disappearing corporations and the work done by the employees before and after the reorganization. (John Wiley & Sons v. Livingston, 376 U.S. 543, 11 L.Ed.2d 898, 84 S.Ct. 909)

Forfeiture of Charter

The government that granted the charter may forfeit or revoke the charter for good cause. Sometimes the legislature provides in a general statute that the charter of any corporation shall be automatically forfeited when certain acts are committed or omitted.

Common grounds for forfeiture are fraudulent incorporation; *willful nonuser*, that is, failure to exercise powers; or *misuser*, that is, abuse of corporate powers and franchises. When it is claimed that a corporation has abused its privileges, such acts must be willful, serious, and injurious to the public. The action against the corporation to forfeit its charter must be brought by and in the name of the government, meaning ordinarily an action by the attorney general of the state.[22] Forfeiture of a charter is an extreme penalty. Because of its severity, it is rarely used.

QUESTIONS AND PROBLEMS

1. Checklist of legal terms:
    (a) corporation de jure (577), de facto corporation (577), corporation by estoppel (579)
    (b) de facto or quasi dissolution (581)
    (c) consolidation, merger (581)
    (d) willful nonuser, misuser (582)

---

[22] *Petition of Collins-Doan Co.*, 3 N.J. 382, 70 A.2d 159.

2. State the objective(s) of each of the following rules of law:
   (a) When a corporation knowingly accepts the benefits of a promoter's contract, it becomes bound by the contract.
   (b) A corporate charter is subject to revocation for misuse of power by the corporation.

3. A group of incorporators who secured a charter from one state held the organization meeting in another state and passed a resolution accepting the charter. Was the corporation regularly incorporated?

4. The application for incorporation of the Selbert Corporation does not state the amount of the capital stock. The application for incorporation of the McClain Corporation incorrectly states the street address of its home office. In both cases a charter was issued to the corporation. Is either corporation a corporation de jure?

5. An action that was brought to question the right of a certain organization to act as a corporation resulted in a judgment denying the right. Creditors claimed that this judgment rendered the incorporators liable as partners. Do you agree with this contention?

6. Codey had in his possession an electric organ belonging to the De Beck Music Company. Knowing that the company claimed to be a corporation, Codey negotiated for the purchase of the organ. Later the company brought an action against Codey to recover possession of the organ. As a defense, Codey questioned the corporate existence of the company. Was he entitled to do so?

7. Deaton makes a shipment of goods as ordered by an association known as the Lantz Manufacturing Company. Unknown to Deaton, this association pretends to be a corporation. It turns out later that the association is neither a corporation de jure nor a corporation de facto. Deaton brings an action against the members of the association as partners. The defense is that Deaton is estopped to deny the corporate existence of the association. Is Deaton entitled to judgment?

8. Dumas was a promoter of a company incorporated to operate a shoe factory. Before the corporation was created, Dumas agreed to pay Gannon for his time and services in obtaining subscriptions to shares of stock. When Dumas failed to pay Gannon, the latter brought an action against the corporation to recover his compensation. Was he entitled to judgment?

9. A corporation, which was formed to operate a river ferry, became insolvent. When an action was brought in its corporate name on a debt which Murphy owed the company, Murphy's defense was that the corporation was dissolved by its insolvency and that consequently an action could not be brought in its name. Was the corporation entitled to judgment?

10. The creditors of a corporation meet for the purpose of deciding whether they will apply for the appointment of a receiver. Several creditors

object to this proposal on the ground that such an appointment will dissolve the corporation. Is this contention sound?

11. The Franklin Gas Company and the Franklin Electric Company are authorized by the legislature and by the shareholders of the two companies to consolidate. The consolidated company is called the Franklin Gas and Electric Company. At the time of consolidation the Franklin Gas Company is entitled to interest from bonds of a municipal corporation. May the Franklin Gas and Electric Company enforce this claim?

12. The Spurlock Institute of Learning was incorporated for the purpose of establishing and maintaining a correspondence school. It failed to maintain such an institution for ten years during which time its property was exempt from taxation and its buildings were sold. Holmes, the state's attorney, brought an action against the corporation to obtain a forfeiture of its charter. Was the state entitled to judgment?

13. The incorporators of the North Park & Dodd Trust Co. appointed a committee of three to attend to the actual details of incorporation. Reid, as chairman of the committee, did the bulk of the work. After the organization and incorporation were completed, a meeting of shareholders adopted a resolution approving the incorporation and the work of the incorporators and their committee. The new company refused to pay Reid for his services. He then sued the company. Decide. (Reid v. North Park & Dodd Trust Co., 110 N.J.L. 222, 164 A. 280)

14. The Maid of the Mist Steamboat Co. was organized for operating sight-seeing steamships on the Niagara River. It had a 50-year charter which expired in 1942. No one realized that fact until 1947. In that year an application was made under the New York law to renew the charter of the corporation. During the intervening period from 1942 to 1947 the corporation had continued to do business as usual. What kind of corporation was it during that period? (Garzo v. Maid of the Mist Steamboat Co., 303 N.Y. 516, 104 N.E.2d 882)

15. A certificate of incorporation was filed with the Secretary of State, incorporating the Pittsburgh, Fort Wayne, and Chicago Railroad Co. Fifty years later, Lanier and others were running the affairs of the corporation. An action was brought by the state's attorney to question the right of Lanier and others to run the corporation. It was claimed that since they had not been original founders of the corporation, they had no right to run the corporation. Decide. (Illinois v. Wayman, 256 Ill. 151, 99 N.E. 941)

Chapter 51

Corporate Powers

Some of the powers possessed by a corporation are the same as those powers held by a natural person, such as the right to own property. Others are distinct powers not possessed by ordinary persons, such as the power to exist perpetually in those states where this is allowed.[1]

Nature of Corporate Powers

All corporations do not have the same powers. For example, those that operate banks, insurance companies, building and loan associations, and railroads generally have special powers.

Except for limitations by the federal Constitution or the state's own constitution, a state may grant to a corporation any powers that it chooses. In addition, a corporation has certain powers that are incidental to corporate existence. These powers are implied because they are reasonably necessary to carry out and make effective the expressly granted powers. Moreover, in exercising their powers, corporations have a choice of employing any lawful means.[2]

Statutes defining the powers of a corporation are to be interpreted liberally and not as limited to the pattern of commerce or the state of science at the time the statute was adopted.

> **Facts:** A dispute arose as to whether the corporation named John B. Waldbillig, Inc. had the authority to engage in professional engineering and land surveying. The certificate of incorporation of Waldbillig stated that the purposes for which the corporation was formed were: "To engage in the business of building, construction, and contracting generally for public or private corporations or persons in this state or elsewhere, and to do and transact all business incidental thereto, and to own and hold real property, buildings, machinery, equipment, and tools, incidental to said business, and to do all things necessary to carry on the business of building, construction, and contracting generally."

> **Decision:** Judgment against Waldbillig. Although corporate powers are liberally interpreted, a corporation does not have a power merely because it may be advantageous or convenient to possess. It is necessary that powers

---

[1] See p. 586.
[2] *Greenwich Water Co.* v. *Adams,* 145 Conn. 535, 144 A.2d 323.

not expressly granted be directly and immediately appropriate or necessary to the execution of the powers expressly granted. The practice of engineering is not directly or immediately appropriate and necessary to the business of contracting and was therefore beyond the scope of Waldbillig's certificate of incorporation. (Waldbillig v. Gottfried, 43 Misc.2d 664, 251 N.Y.S.2d 991)

1 / Perpetual succession. One of the distinctive features of a corporation is its perpetual succession or continuous life—the power to continue as a unit forever or for a stated period of time regardless of changes in stock ownership. If no period is fixed for its duration, the corporation will exist indefinitely unless it is legally dissolved. When the period is limited, the corporation may in many states extend the period by meeting additional requirements of the statute.

In most states, a corporation has perpetual existence unless a shorter period is specified; while in the other states, the life of the corporation must be limited to a specified number of years.

2 / Corporate name. A corporation must have a name to identify it. As a general rule it may select any name for this purpose. It may not, however, select for its exclusive use a name that all may lawfully use, such as a descriptive name, or one that another firm has the exclusive right to use.

The Model Business Corporation Act prohibits the use of the same or a deceptively similar name of any domestic corporation or any foreign corporation authorized to do business in the state.[3] Even though the practice of imitating another's name is not prohibited by the statutes of a particular state, the imitation may still be prohibited as unfair competition. Under this principle, it was held that the Mount Hope Cemetery Association could prevent a rival corporation from using New Mount Hope Cemetery Association as its corporate name.[4]

Statutes frequently require that the last word of the name be "Corporation" or that the word "Limited" or "Incorporated" be used in conjunction with the name selected. The Model Business Corporation Act requires that the name include "Incorporated" or "Corporation," "Company" or "Limited," or an abbreviation of such words.[5]

A corporation has the same right as an individual to assume a fictitious name under which it conducts business, provided that it complies with the statute relating to the registration of such names.[6]

---

[3] American Bar Association Model Business Corporation Act, Sec. 7.
[4] *Mount Hope Cemetery Association* v. *New Mount Hope Cemetery Association,* 246 Ill. 416, 92 N.E. 912.
[5] ABA MBCA Sec. 7.
[6] *Seattle Ass'n of Credit Men* v. *Green,* 45 Wash.2d 139, 273 P.2d 513.

3 / Corporate seal. A corporate seal was indispensable under early law, which required its use in the making of all but minor contracts of the corporation. At present, however, a corporation need not use a seal in the transaction of business unless it is required by statute to use a seal or unless a natural person in transacting that business would be required to use a seal.

4 / Bylaws. The shareholders of a corporation have inherent power to make bylaws to supplement the charter of the corporation, but the right to do so is commonly expressed by statute or in the charter of the corporation.

Bylaws are adopted by the action of the shareholders, but some statutes provide for the adoption of bylaws by the directors unless otherwise provided by the articles of incorporation. Action by the state or an amendment of the corporation charter is not required to make the bylaws effective. The difference between bylaws and provisions of a charter is a practical consideration. The charter represents provisions that should endure throughout the life of the corporation. The *bylaws* represent provisions for governing the corporation but which might become undesirable in the course of events, and therefore they should not be given the same permanence as the charter. This distinction is not always observed, and there is frequently a tendency to put much detail into the charter. No actual harm is done by so doing, except that it makes the charter unnecessarily long and also makes a change more difficult since state approval is required to amend the charter, while bylaws can be changed by the action of the shareholders alone.

The bylaws are subordinate to the general law of the state, including the statute under which the corporation is formed, as well as to the charter of the corporation. Bylaws that conflict with such superior authority or which are in themselves unreasonable are invalid. Bylaws that are valid are binding upon all shareholders regardless of whether they know of the existence of those bylaws or were among the majority which consented to their adoption. Bylaws are not binding upon third persons, however, unless they have notice or knowledge of them.

5 / Borrowing money. Corporations have the implied power to borrow money in carrying out their authorized business purposes. For example, a fire insurance company may borrow money to pay losses due on policies issued by it. Statutes commonly prohibit corporations from raising the defense of usury.

6 / Execution of commercial paper. The power to issue or indorse commercial paper, or to accept drafts, is implied when the corporation has the power to borrow money and when such means are appropriate and ordinarily used to further the authorized objectives of the corporation.

7 / Bonds. A corporation having the power to borrow money may do so in any form. A corporation accordingly has the implied power to issue various types of bonds.

8 / Transferring property. The corporate property may be leased, assigned for the benefit of creditors, or sold. In many states, however, a solvent corporation may not transfer all of its property except with the consent of all or a substantial majority of its shareholders. In any case, the sale must be for a fair price.

> **Facts:** The board of directors of Pressed Metals of America contracted to sell the assets of the company for approximately 2½ million dollars. The book value of the assets was approximately 5 million dollars. Baron, a minority shareholder of the corporation, brought an action to prevent the sale on the ground that the consideration was grossly inadequate. The directors defended on the ground that they had sought to sell the property over an 11-month period, that they had obtained three offers to purchase, and that the sale price was slightly better than the highest bidder had been initially willing to pay. There was no evidence of fraud or secret profit.

> **Decision:** The sale was proper as it was apparent that every reasonable effort had been made to obtain the best price. Under such circumstances, it was not significant that the price so obtained was less than that shown by the book value. (Baron v. Pressed Metals of America, 35 Del.Ch. 581, 123 A.2d 848)

A corporation, having power to incur debts, may mortgage or pledge its property as security for those debts. This rule does not apply to franchises of public service companies, such as street transit systems and gas and electric companies.

9 / Acquisition of property. Although the power to acquire and hold property is usually given in the charter, a corporation always has the implied power to acquire and hold such property as is reasonably necessary for carrying out its express powers. In some states the power of a corporation to hold property is restricted as to the method of acquiring it, or is limited as to the quantity or the value of the property or the period of time for which it may be held. Restrictions on holding real estate are also imposed upon corporations by the constitutions of some states.[7]

Under modern corporation codes it is generally provided that a corporation may acquire the stock of other corporations. Ordinarily, the stock held by one corporation in another corporation will not be so great as to enable

---

[7] Kentucky 192, Louisiana XIII-1, Missouri XI-5, Oklahoma XXII-2, Pennsylvania XVI-6, and South Dakota XVII-7. *United States Gypsum Co.* v. *State ex rel. Rutherford,* [Okla.] 328 P.2d 431.

the stock-owning corporation to control the operations of the other corporation. It is possible, however, that the stock-owning company may own such a percentage of the stock of the other company that it controls the latter's operations. In such a case the first company is commonly called a *holding company*. Sometimes it is organized solely for the purpose of controlling other companies called *operating* or *subsidiary companies*.

The device of a holding company may be socially desirable or undesirable depending upon the circumstances under which it operates. If it is merely a device to coordinate different phases of an economic activity, the holding company is a proper device. If its object is to eliminate competition between the operating companies whose stock is held, it may be illegal under state or federal antitrust laws.[8] If a holding company that operates in interstate commerce holds stock of electric or gas public utility companies, it may be ordered dissolved when it is found by the Securities and Exchange Commission to serve no economically useful purpose.[9] It is no objection, however, that the subsidiary company engages in a business in which the holding company could not lawfully engage.

Facts: Connecticut General Life Insurance Co. obtained a license to write life insurance policies in New York. It thereafter proposed to acquire 80 percent or more of the common stock of the National Fire Insurance Co. of Hartford, a fire and casualty insurance company licensed to write policies in New York. In a declaratory judgment action, the New York State Superintendent of Insurance claimed that the Connecticut Company was prohibited from writing life policies in New York if it acquired such stock because, through its subsidiary, it would then be writing fire and casualty insurance in New York.

Decision: Judgment for insurer. An insurance company may own stock of other corporations, even to the point that the other corporation becomes a subsidiary of the insurer corporation, and even though the subsidiary engages in a business prohibited to the insurer. This conclusion follows from the fact that in the absence of fraud or illegality the separate identity of the subsidiary corporation and of its shareholders, here the parent corporation, prevents reaching the conclusion that the parent corporation is engaging in the business of the subsidiary corporation. (Connecticut General Life Insurance Co. v. Superintendent of Insurance, 10 N.Y.2d 42, 176 N.E.2d 63)

10 / Acquisition of own stock. Generally a corporation may purchase its own stock, if it is solvent at the time and the purchase is made from surplus so that capital is not impaired. In a few states corporations are denied implied power to purchase their own stock, but are permitted to receive it as a gift, in payment of a debt, or for the security of a debt.

---

[8] *Northern Securities Co.* v. *U.S.*, 193 U.S. 197.
[9] *American Power and Light Co.* v. *S.E.C.*, 329 U.S. 90.

Stock that is reacquired by the corporation that issued it is commonly called *treasury stock*. Ordinarily, the treasury stock is regarded as still being issued or outstanding stock. As such, the shares are not subject to the rule that original shares cannot be issued for less than par. They can be sold by the corporation at any price.[10]

Although treasury stock retains the character of outstanding stock, it has an inactive status while it is held by the corporation. Thus the treasury shares cannot be voted [11] nor can dividends be declared on them.

11 / Business in another state. A corporation has the inherent power and generally is expressly authorized to engage in business in other states. This grant of power by the incorporating state does not exempt the corporation, however, from satisfying the restrictions imposed by the foreign state in which it seeks to do business.[12]

Limitations on Corporate Powers

If a power is expressly prohibited to a corporation, the corporation cannot exercise that power. In addition, certain other powers cannot be implied and therefore cannot be exercised in the absence of express authorization. It is generally held that there is no implied power to lend credit, to enter a partnership,[13] to consolidate, or to merge.

In some jurisdictions a merger must not only satisfy the procedural requirements specified by statute but must also be fair and equitable.[14] In addition to having to satisfy the requirement of state law, a merger, when accompanied by one corporation's acquisition of all or a substantial part of the assets of another corporation, may be prohibited on the ground that it tends to lessen competition in interstate commerce.[15]

Independently of the rights given for the protection of minority shareholders, the circumstances may be such as to give rise to a liability of the majority shareholders for fraud when by false statements and promises they have obtained the consent of the minority; as, for example, when the manager of the corporate radio station was falsely promised that he would keep his job after the merger, and in reliance on such false promise he voted for the merger.[16]

---

[10] *State ex rel. Weede* v. *Bechtel*, 244 Iowa 785, 56 N.W.2d 173.

[11] *Atterbury* v. *Consol. Coppermines Corp.*, 26 Del.Ch. 1, 20 A.2d 743. Likewise a subsidiary corporation holding shares of stock of the parent corporation by which it is controlled cannot vote such shares of the parent corporation. *Italo Petroleum Corp.* v. *Producers' Oil Corp.*, 20 Del.Ch. 283, 174 A. 276.

[12] See p. 570.

[13] *Leventhal* v. *Atlantic Finance Corp.*, 316 Mass. 194, 55 N.E.2d 20.

[14] *Brundage* v. *New Jersey Zinc Co.*, 48 N.J. 450, 226 A.2d 585.

[15] *United States* v. *Continental Can Co.*, 378 U.S. 441.

[16] *Victor Broadcasting Co.* v. *Mahurin*, 236 Ark. 196, 365 S.W.2d 265.

Ultra Vires Acts

Any act that goes beyond the powers which the corporation can lawfully exercise is an *ultra vires act*. Such an act is improper because it is a violation of the obligation of the corporation to the state in that a power not granted has been exercised. It is also improper with respect to shareholders and creditors of the corporation because corporate funds have been diverted to unauthorized uses.

As an illustration of the latter point, assume that a corporation is created and authorized to manufacture television sets. Various persons purchase stock in the corporation, lend it money, or sell to it on credit because of their estimate of the worth of the television business in general and of the corporation as a television manufacturing company in particular. Assume that the corporation has funds that it uses for the ultra vires purpose of lending to persons to buy homes. Many of the shareholders and creditors would probably never have become associated with the corporation if it had been organized for that purpose. The fact that the ultra vires use of the money may be better economically or socially than the authorized use does not alter the fact that the shareholders' and the creditors' money is not used the way they intended.

1 / Ultra vires acts and illegality distinguished. Although it is not lawful for a corporation to perform ultra vires acts, the objection to the commission of such acts is distinct from the objection of illegality.[17] In the case of illegality the act would be wrong regardless of the nature of the person or the association committing it. The fact that an act is ultra vires merely means that this particular corporation does not have permission from the state to do the act. Thus it would ordinarily be beyond the powers of a business corporation, and therefore ultra vires, to engage in a charitable enterprise, such as the building of a church or college. But the activity would hardly be termed illegal.

2 / Effect of ultra vires contracts. There is some conflict in the law as to the effect of an ultra vires act. Under the modern statutory trend, ultra vires cannot be raised to attack the validity of any act, contract, or transfer of property,[18] except as noted under heading (3) on page 592.

In the absence of statute, most courts recognize ultra vires as a defense but refuse to apply it in a particular case if it would be inequitable and work a hardship. The courts also refuse to recognize it as a defense against the holder of a commercial paper on which the corporation has, without authority, been an accommodation party. Likewise, a transfer of real or personal

---

[17] *Healy* v. *Geilfuss,* 37 Del.Ch. 502, 146 A.2d 5.
[18] ABA MBCA Sec. 6; *Inter-Continental Corp.* v. *Moody,* [Tex.App.] 411 S.W.2d 578.

property cannot be set aside on the ground that it is ultra vires. Here the object of the law is to preserve the security of titles even though the result is to permit the wrongful act of the corporation to stand.

In most states, if the ultra vires contract has been completely performed, neither party can rescind the contract on the ground that it was originally ultra vires.[19] Conversely, if neither party to the ultra vires contract has performed his part, the court will neither enforce the contract nor hold either party liable for a breach of the contract.

Facts: The Bank of Campbellsville was practically owned by the men who were its directors and officers. They personally owed a debt to Marshall, one of their depositors, for money they had borrowed to use as funds of the bank. Marshall overdrew his account in the bank and the directors and officers then agreed with him that they would pay the overdraft for Marshall and that their debt to him would be reduced by the amount of such payment. The bank became insolvent, and Webster was appointed to liquidate the bank. He claimed that Marshall was required to pay back to the bank the amount of the overdraft. Marshall brought an action for a declaratory judgment for the purpose of determining his rights.

Decision: Judgment for Marshall. The transaction with respect to the overdraft, having been completed, would not be deemed inoperative; and the bank that had benefited by the transaction would be held liable for the value which it had received. (Marshall v. Webster, 287 Ky. 692, 155 S.W. 2d 13)

3 / Remedies for ultra vires act. In all states (a) a shareholder may obtain an injunction to stop the board of directors or other persons involved from entering into an ultra vires transaction; (b) the corporation or a shareholder acting on behalf of the corporation may sue the persons who made or approved the contract to recover damages for the loss caused the corporation by the ultra vires act; and (c) an action may be brought by the attorney general of the state to revoke the charter on the ground of its serious or repeated violation.

QUESTIONS AND PROBLEMS

1. Checklist of legal terms:
   (a) bylaws (587)
   (b) holding company, operating or subsidiary company (589)
   (c) treasury stock (590)
   (d) ultra vires act (591)

---

[19] *Anderson* v. *Rexroad,* 175 Kan. 676, 266 P.2d 320.

2. State the objective(s) of each of the following rules of law:

   (a) In some states the defense of ultra vires cannot be raised in a suit between the corporation and the person with whom the ultra vires contract was made.

   (b) Corporations are persons within the constitutional protection of the life, liberty, and property of "persons."

3. Blum, Incorporated, employs a general manager, executes a note to its bank as a basis for a loan, and conveys a vacant lot that it does not need to a buyer. For which of these transactions is it necessary for this company to use its corporate seal?

4. The Coates Corporation seeks to escape liability to Blevins under an agreement made by an agent of the corporation with Blevins. Authority for such action was expressly limited to the treasurer by the corporate bylaws. Under what circumstances could Blevins hold the corporation liable?

5. An incorporated savings and loan association borrowed $10,000 on its promissory notes for the purpose of lending the money to others. The charter contained no express authority for issuing such instruments. The state contended that the corporation had acted beyond its powers. Do you agree?

6. A company was incorporated to operate a printing and engraving business. Its charter did not expressly authorize the acquisition and holding of real property. Wishing to expand its business, the company desired to purchase a piece of land and to construct a building on it suitable for its purpose. Did the corporation possess the power to proceed with these plans?

7. A company that operated several motels along the route of a bus company issued bonds for $100,000. To facilitate the marketing of these bonds, the bus company entered into a contract by which it guaranteed interest on the bonds. Was this contract within the powers of the bus company?

8. The Green Corporation, which is authorized to manufacture TV cabinets, embarks upon the manufacture of pinball machines as well. The manufacture and sale of such machines are prohibited by state law. Is the Green Corporation engaging in an illegal or an ultra vires act?

9. A corporation engaged in the manufacture of sewing machines enters into an agreement to execute a promissory note as an accommodation maker for Morrell. When the company refuses to issue the note, Morrell brings an action against it for damages arising out of a breach of contract. Is he entitled to judgment?

10. A corporation formed for the purpose of selling newspapers and magazines purchases a fruit farm from Rathman. Later Rathman demands that the land be reconveyed to him and offers to return the purchase

price. Upon the company's refusal to comply with this demand, Rathman brings an action to recover the property. Is he entitled to judgment?

11. The Warren Corporation has been guilty of serious ultra vires acts. What remedies, if any, do each of the following have:

    (a) A shareholder of the corporation?

    (b) The government of the state in which the business was incorporated?

12. The Central Mutual Auto Insurance Co. was a Michigan corporation. A foreign corporation, the Central Mutual Insurance Co., was granted a license to do business in Michigan. Central Mutual Auto Insurance Co. brought an action to prevent the foreign corporation from doing business within Michigan under that name. Decide. (Central Mutual Auto Insurance Co. v. Central Mutual Insurance Co., 275 Mich. 554, 267 N.W. 733)

13. The Philadelphia Electric Co. was incorporated "for the purpose of supplying heating, lighting, and power by electricity to the public." The company supplied electricity but in addition began to sell electrical appliances. An action was brought by the attorney general against the corporation to forfeit its charter for engaging in ultra vires acts. Decide. (Commonwealth of Pennsylvania ex rel. Baldridge, Attorney General v. Philadelphia Electric Co., 300 Pa. 577, 151 A. 344)

14. A bylaw of the Coleman Realty Co. provided that the corporation could not sell its stock to a person not a shareholder without first offering to sell it at its book value to the corporation or to the remaining shareholders in proportion to their interests. This bylaw was later repealed at a shareholders' meeting by the vote of Mrs. Ludgate who owned a majority of the stock. Bechtold, a minority shareholder, brought an action to declare that the repeal of the bylaw was invalid and had no effect. Was the repeal of the bylaw effective? (Bechtold v. Coleman Realty Co., 367 Pa. 208, 79 A.2d 661)

Chapter 52

Corporate Stock

Membership in a corporation is usually based upon ownership of one or more shares of stock of the corporation. Each share represents a fractional interest in the total property possessed by the corporation. It confers the right to receive the dividends, when declared, and the right to participate in a distribution of capital upon the dissolution of the corporation. The shareholder does not own or have an interest in any specific property of the corporation; the corporation is the owner of all of its property.

Certificate of Stock

A corporation ordinarily issues a *certificate of stock* to show the ownership of the shareholder. The issuance of such certificates is not essential either to the existence of a corporation or to the ownership of its stock, but it is the almost universal practice since it makes transfer of ownership easier. Any form that identifies the interest owned by the person in a particular corporation is sufficient.

The Model Business Corporation Act requires that the certificate include (1) the state of incorporation; (2) the name of the person to whom issued; (3) the number and the class of shares represented and the designation of the series, if any; (4) the par value of each share or a statement that there is no par value; and (5) if there is more than one class of shares, a summary of each class, or a statement that such information will be furnished on demand.[1]

By virtue of statutes,[2] ownership of the certificate is essential to owning an interest in the corporation, and the shareholder's interest cannot be fully transferred without the certificate.

---

[1] American Bar Association Model Business Corporation Act, Sec. 21. The issuance of a certificate before the shares represented by it have been paid in full is prohibited.

[2] The transfer of share certificates is governed by the Uniform Commercial Code (Article 8), formerly by the Uniform Stock Transfer Act. The Code Article is broader in scope than the USTA in that the Code also governs corporate bearer bonds, which were formerly governed by the Uniform Negotiable Instruments Law, and registered bonds and other types of investment paper, which were not covered by any uniform act. A bond in bearer form, which is a commercial paper and governed by Article 3, can be an investment security if it is one of a series and is traded on an exchange. It does not seem that the rights of the parties in a transaction involving this instrument should be markedly different under Article 8 from what they would be under Article 3. *Hutton & Co.* v. *Manufacturers National Bank*, [D.C. E.D. Mich.] 259 F.S. 513.

Kinds of Stock

In the absence of statutory restriction the stock of a corporation may be divided into two or more classes. Certain definite varieties of stock have acquired through usage their particular names, such as common stock and preferred stock. Sometimes a corporation may issue two or more classes of the same kind of stock, such as "preferred stock A" and "preferred stock B," or "first preferred" and "second preferred."

1 / Common stock. Common stock is ordinary stock. Each share usually entitles the holder to one vote and to a share of the profits in the form of dividends, when declared, and to participate in the distribution of capital upon dissolution of the corporation.[3]

2 / Preferred stock. Preferred stock has a priority over common stock. The priority may be with respect to dividends. The shares of "6% preferred stock of $100 per value" means that the holders of such shares are entitled to receive annual dividends of $6 for each share before any dividends are paid to the holders of the common stock. Preferred stock may also have a priority over common stock in the distribution of capital upon dissolution of the corporation. Preferred stock is ordinarily nonvoting.

(a) CUMULATIVE PREFERRED STOCK. Ordinarily the right to receive dividends is contingent upon the declaration of dividends by the board of directors for that particular period of time. If there is no fund from which the dividends may be declared or if the directors do not declare them from an available fund, the shareholder has no right to dividends. The fact that a shareholder, even a preferred shareholder, has not received dividends for the current year does not in itself give him the right to carry over into the next year a claim for those dividends.

If the right to dividends on preferred stock does not accumulate, it is possible for the directors to defeat the rights of preferred shareholders in favor of the common shareholders. To illustrate, assume that in a corporation in which there are equal amounts of outstanding common and preferred stock, a surplus is available in each of five years for the declaration of a 6 percent dividend on the preferred stock of $100 par value but that nothing is available for the common stock. If the board of directors declared no dividends until the fifth year and if the preferred shareholders were not permitted to accumulate their preferences for the prior years, they would receive only 6 percent or $6 a share in the fifth year and the holders of common stock could receive the balance, whereas the common shareholders would

---

[3] *Storrow* v. *Texas Consolidated Compress & Mfg. Association,* [C.A.5th] 87 F. 612.

have received nothing had annual dividends of $6 been declared on the preferred stock.

In the absence of a statement that the right to dividends is noncumulative, it is frequently held that preferred stock has the right to cumulate dividends,[4] particularly with respect to each year in which there was a surplus available for dividend declaration.

Facts: The articles of incorporation of the Arizona Power Co. stated that no dividends could be paid upon the common stock until unpaid dividends for all preceding years had been fully paid to the preferred shareholders. Stuart, the Collector of Internal Revenue (now identified as the Director of Internal Revenue), claimed that the preferred stock was not cumulative because it was not expressly stated so and because the payment of the dividends was not guaranteed by the corporation.

Decision: Judgment against Stuart. It is not necessary to use the word "cumulative" to create that privilege. The charter clearly indicated an intention that the preferred stock should be cumulative even though that word was not used. The fact that dividends were not guaranteed and would vary depending upon whether there were any net profits from which to pay them did not affect the cumulative character of the stock. (Arizona Power Co. v. Stuart, [C.A.9th] 212 F.2d 535)

(b) PARTICIPATING PREFERRED STOCK. Sometimes the preferred stock is given the right of participation. For example, after the common shares receive dividends or a capital distribution equal to that first received by the preferred stock, both kinds share equally in the balance.

Capital and Capital Stock

1 / Capital. Capital refers to the net assets of the corporation. It signifies the actual worth, whether in money or property, of the corporation. It is the aggregate of the sums subscribed and paid in by the shareholders, together with all gains or profits arising from the business, less losses that have been incurred.

2 / Capital stock. Capital stock refers to the declared money value of the outstanding stock of the corporation.[5] Thus in a corporation that has issued 1,000 shares of $100 par value stock, the capital stock of the corporation would be $100,000.

3 / Control of capital and capital stock. Modern corporation codes generally provide for changing the amount of the authorized capital stock. The Model Business Corporation Act provides that the capital stock may be

---

[4] *Hazel Atlas Glass Co.* v. *Van Dyk & Reeves,* [C.A.2d] 8 F.2d 716.
[5] *Burton* v. *Burton,* 161 Cal.App.2d 572, 326 P.2d 855.

reduced by a two-third's vote of the shareholders. Similar provisions govern increases in the capital stock.[6]

The corporation has the same control over its property as would be enjoyed by an individual in like circumstances.[7] Consequently, a corporation's transfer of corporate property in fraud of its creditors may be set aside.[8] Creditors of a corporation cannot assert greater control, however, than could creditors of an individual.

Valuation of Stock

The valuation of stock becomes significant in connection with various types of tax laws and in connection with proceedings for purchasing stock from dissenting shareholders.

1 / Par value. Corporate stock commonly has a specified *par value*. This means that the person subscribing to the stock and acquiring it from the corporation must pay that amount. Shares are frequently issued with no par value. In such a case no amount is stated in the certificate, and the amount that the subscriber pays the corporation is determined by the board of directors. Apart from the legal requirement of paying the par value, a subscriber may find it necessary to pay an additional sum to obtain the stock.

2 / Book value. The statement of the par value of stock or the decision by the board of directors of the value of no-par shares does not mean that the stock will always have that value. Assume that a corporation issued 1,000 shares of $10 par-value stock and had no other stock. Assuming that all the stock was properly paid for, the corporation would at that moment have assets of $10,000. Assume, however, that because of losses the net assets of the corporation dwindled to $5,000. At that time the holder of each of the 1,000 shares would be entitled to a 1/1000 share of those assets. This share would only be $5. The fact that each shareholder owned a certificate stating that his share had a $10 par value would not alter the fact that the share really represented only five dollars' worth of present assets, as shown by the books of the corporation. The value thus determined is the *book value* of the shares.

3 / Market value. In addition to the par value and the book value, stock usually has a *market value*. Assume that the $10 par-value share has a book value of $5. The prospects may be that the corporation will sustain even greater loss in the future. In such a case it is unlikely that anyone would be willing to buy the stock at either the par value of $10 or at the book value of $5. Conversely, if the prospects of the corporation are good, the purchaser

[6] ABA MBCA Sec. 54.
[7] *MacQueen* v. *Dollar Sav. Bank Co.,* 135 Ohio 579, 15 N.E.2d 529.
[8] *Cohen* v. *Sutherland,* [C.A.3d] 257 F.2d 137.

may be willing to pay more than the book value and more than the par value of the stock.

Acquisition of Shares

Shares of stock may be acquired by (1) subscription, either before or after the corporation is organized, or (2) transfer of existing shares from a shareholder or from the corporation.[9]

1 / Subscription. A *stock subscription* is a contract or an agreement to buy a specific number and kind of shares of stock when they are issued. As in the case of any other contract,[10] the agreement to subscribe to shares of a corporation is subject to avoidance for fraud.[11]

(a) FORMALITY. By the great weight of authority, a contract to subscribe for shares of a corporation not yet formed or for unissued shares of stock of an existing corporation is not within the Statute of Frauds and therefore need not be in writing. By way of contrast, a contract for the transfer of existing corporate stock comes within the Statute of Frauds and a writing is required to make the contract binding.[12]

Apart from the Statute of Frauds, no particular formality is ordinarily required for a subscription to stock.[13] Occasionally, however, a special statute requires a writing for a stock subscription, or stipulates that the subscription be accompanied by a cash payment or that the original subscribers sign the articles of incorporation.

(b) SUBSCRIPTION BEFORE ORGANIZATION. Many subscriptions are made prior to incorporation. In most states the corporation must expressly or impliedly accept the subscription before the subscriber is bound. Unless this is done, the subscription is regarded as an offer to the corporation to be formed; and the ordinary rules relating to offers apply. A few states hold that such subscriptions automatically become binding contracts when the organization has been completed.

The Model Business Corporation Act declares that, unless otherwise provided in the subscription agreement, or unless all the subscribers consent thereto, the preorganization subscription shall be irrevocable for the period of six months.[14] As in the case of any contract, there may be a rescission upon proper grounds.

---

[9] ABA MBCA Sec. 16.
[10] See Chapter 10.
[11] *Cumberland Co-op. Bakeries* v. *Lawson*, 91 W.Va. 245, 112 S.E. 568.
[12] Uniform Commercial Code, Sec. 8-319. Compliance with the Statute of Frauds provision, when applicable, is mandatory; *Previti* v. *Rubenstein*, [N.Y.S.2d] 3 UCCRS 882.
[13] *Nickum* v. *Burckhardt*, 30 Ore. 464, 47 P. 788.
[14] ABA MBCA Sec. 16.

Generally a subscriber is not entitled to receive his share certificate until he has paid for the shares it represents.[15]

(c) SUBSCRIPTION AFTER ORGANIZATION. Subscriptions are also made after incorporation. In that event the transaction is like any other contract with the corporation. The offer of the subscription may come from the subscriber or from the corporation, but in either case there must be an acceptance. Upon acceptance the subscriber immediately becomes a shareholder with all the rights, privileges, and liabilities of a shareholder even though the subscriber has not paid any of the purchase price. The transaction, however, may only be a contract for the future transfer of shares rather than a present subscription.

(d) CONDITIONS PRECEDENT. The subscription may provide that it shall be dependent upon the performance of some act or the happening of some contingency. Such a subscription, if made after incorporation, is valid, unless it is contrary to a charter or statutory provision, and the subscriber becomes a shareholder only upon the fulfillment of the condition. A conditional subscription made prior to incorporation is generally held void on the grounds that it is fraudulent as to unqualified subscribers and to creditors.

2 / Transfer of shares. In the absence of restrictions imposed by statute, charter, bylaws, or agreement, a shareholder may transfer his shares to anyone he chooses. Restrictions on the transfer of stock are valid provided they are not unreasonable.[16] It is valid to provide that a shareholder must give the corporation the option of purchasing his shares before he sells it to a third person.

There is a conflict of authority as to the validity of a provision that no transfers may be made of shares without the approval of the directors or the other shareholders. The trend is to sustain such a provision when the shareholders are the owner-tenants of an incorporated cooperative apartment house.[17] In any case a restriction on transfer is interpreted in favor of transferability. For example, a restriction on the transfer by a retiring employee of the corporation was held not applicable to an employee who was discharged, and a restriction on the "sale" of shares was held not to bar a gift inter vivos or a bequest by will.[18]

Facts: Davis, an employee of the Household Finance Corporation, owned 100 shares of stock in the corporation. Davis transferred his shares to Lawson, and indorsed and delivered his stock certificate to him. The stock certificate set forth the provision of the certificate of incorporation

---

[15] *Cornhusker Development & Investment Group* v. *Knecht,* 180 Neb. 873, 146 N.W.2d 567.
[16] *Tracey* v. *Franklin,* 31 Del.Ch. 477, 67 A.2d 56.
[17] *Gale* v. *York Center Community Co-op., Inc.,* 21 Ill.2d 86, 171 N.E.2d 30.
[18] *Stern* v. *Stern,* 79 C.A. Dist.Col. 340, 146 F.2d 870.

and the bylaws of the corporation that the stock could not be sold without giving the corporation first opportunity to purchase it at its fair value to be determined by appraisal. When Lawson presented the purchased certificate to the corporation for cancellation and the issuance to him of a new certificate, the corporation refused to recognize the transfer. Lawson sued to compel it to do so.

Decision: Judgment for the corporation. In order to insure that its employees would have the best interests of the corporation at heart, it was proper for the corporation to sell its stock to its employees and to keep the stock from going into the hands of strangers by insisting that it be given the first right to purchase. In order to make such a provision effective, the corporation could refuse to recognize any transfer made in violation of such a restriction. (Lawson v. Household Finance Corp., 17 Del.Ch. 1, 147 A. 312)

A restriction upon the right to transfer is not valid as against a purchaser of the certificate unless the restriction is conspicuously noted on the certificate or the transferee has actual knowledge of the restriction.[19]

The transfer of shares may be absolute, that is, it may divest all ownership and make the transferee the full owner, or it may be merely for security, as when stock is pledged to secure the repayment of a loan. Since it is an essential element of a pledge transaction that the pledgee be able to sell the pledged property upon default, a pledge of stock requires the delivery to the pledgee of the stock certificate together with a separate assignment of or indorsement on the stock certificate in favor of the pledgee or bearer. When this is done, the pledgee will be able to transfer title to the shares in case of default.

Directors and officers of a corporation may purchase stock held by shareholders of the corporation. It is generally held that in so doing, they purchase at arm's length and are not required to disclose to the shareholders facts known to them by virtue of their position which might affect the value of the shares. Exceptions to this rule are made when special facts are present, such as the concealment by the director of his identity.[20]

(a) MECHANICS OF TRANSFER. The ownership of shares is transferred by the delivery of the certificate of stock indorsed by its owner in blank, or to a specified person, or by the delivery of the certificate by such person accompanied by a separate assignment or power of attorney executed by him.[21] A transfer made in this manner is effective as between the parties even though the corporate charter or bylaws specify that shares cannot be

---

[19] UCC Sec. 8-204.
[20] *Taylor* v. *Wright*, 69 Cal.App.2d 371, 159 P.2d 980.
[21] UCC Sec. 8-309. The second alternative of a delivery of an unindorsed certificate is designed to keep the certificate "clean," as when the transfer is for a temporary or special purpose as in the case of a pledge of the certificate as security for a loan.

transferred until a transfer is made on the books of the corporation or the records of a corporate transfer agent.

Facts: LaVern Millin owned 3,700 shares of stock in the Western Printing & Lithographing Co. He went with his son James to the local bank and told the vice president that he wanted the stock transferred to his son. LaVern signed his name on the transfer form on the back of each certificate, the vice president signed each certificate as a guarantor of LaVern's signature, and the certificates were sent to Western with a covering letter requesting that a new certificate be issued in the name of the son James and sent directly to him. Thereafter it was claimed that the transaction had no effect because the share certificates were not delivered by the father to his son.

Decision: The transaction was effective to constitute a delivery of the stock certificates. A delivery to the transferee personally is not required. Under the circumstances it was clear that the delivery was made to the corporation, as agent, to act for the son in issuing him new shares. (Kintzinger v. Millin, 254 Iowa 173, 117 N.W.2d 68)

A physical transfer of the certificate without a necessary indorsement is effective as between the parties. Thus delivery of a stock certificate as security is effective as between the parties even though the certificate is not indorsed, as indorsement is necessary only to make a transferee a "bona fide" purchaser as against third parties.[22]

In the absence of a delivery of the certificate or an assignment or similar writing, there can be no effective transfer of ownership of the shares. Hence the fact that the decedent indorsed stock certificates in blank did not establish a gift when he died in possession of the certificates apparently without having made any delivery of them.[23]

In general, the transfer agent stands in the same position as the corporation with respect to the stock in question and must make a formal transfer whenever the corporation would itself be required to recognize a transfer.

Possession of the certificate is also essential to an involuntary transfer by execution of judicial process, and no attachment or levy upon shares of stock for which a certificate is outstanding is valid unless the certificate is actually seized by the officer making the attachment or levy.[24]

(b) NEGOTIABILITY. Under the common law the transferee of shares of stock had no greater right than the transferor because the certificate and the shares represented by the certificate were nonnegotiable. By statute, the common-law rule has been changed by imparting negotiability to the cer-

---

[22] *Jorgensen's Estate*, 70 Ill.App.2d 398, 217 N.E.2d 290.
[23] *Donsavage's Estate*, 420 Pa. 587, 218 A.2d 112.
[24] UCC Sec. 8-317.

tificate and giving to the purchaser of the certificate an absolute title to the shares if he pays value for the certificate and acts in good faith.[25]

In addition, just as various defenses cannot be asserted against the holder in due course of a commercial paper it is provided that similar defenses cannot be raised against the person acquiring the certificate in good faith and for value. As against such a person, the defenses cannot be raised that his transferor did not own the shares, that he did not have authority to deliver the certificate, or that the transfer was made in violation of a restriction upon transfer not known to such person and not set forth in the certificate. A former owner cannot object as against a subsequent purchaser for value and in good faith that his transferee obtained the certificate from him by fraud, duress, mistake, or did not give him any consideration.[26] Conversely, if the purchaser of stock knows that his vendor holds the title subject to the claims of other persons, such as a divorced wife claiming an interest therein, the purchaser acquires his interest in the stock subject to the rights of such third persons.[27]

This concept of negotiability is also recognized as against corporate lien claims on the stock. Although modern statutes commonly give the corporation a lien upon stock for a debt owed it by the shareholder, the corporation cannot assert a lien against a purchaser of the shares unless the right of the corporation to the lien is noted conspicuously on the certificate.[28]

(c) TRANSFER AS AFFECTING CORPORATION. Until there is a transfer on the books in accordance with a lawful requirement, the corporation is entitled to treat as the owner the person whose name is on the books.[29] The corporation may properly refuse to recognize the transferee when the corporation is given notice or has knowledge that the transfer is void or in breach of trust. In such case the corporation properly refuses to effect a transfer until the rights of the parties have been determined.[30]

The corporation may also refuse to register the transfer of shares when the outstanding certificate is not surrendered to it, in the absence of satisfactory proof that it had been lost, destroyed, or stolen.

Protection for the Public

1 / Blue-sky laws. In order to protect the public from the sale of securities of nonexistent or worthless corporations, many states have adopted regulations called *blue-sky laws.* The statutes vary greatly in detail. Some impose a criminal penalty for engaging in fraudulent practices, while others

---

[25] Secs. 8-301, 8-315.
[26] Secs. 8-301, 8-311, 8-315.
[27] *Blanton* v. *Austin*, [Tex.Civ.App.] 392 S.W.2d 140.
[28] UCC Sec. 8-103.
[29] Sec. 8-207.
[30] *Holmes* v. *Birtman Electric Co.*, 22 Ill.App.2d 72, 159 N.E.2d 272.

require the licensing of dealers in securities and approval by a government commission before a given security can be sold to the public.

A salesman selling stock as representative of a corporation is deemed a "seller" within the operation of a blue-sky law imposing liability on the "seller" of unregistered securities, as opposed to the contention that the seller subjected to statutory control must be the corporation or owner of the stock.[31]

> **Facts:** Davis purchased in Nebraska shares of stock and securities of the W & M Oil Co., a Nebraska corporation. No license had ever been obtained from the Department of Banking as was required by Nebraska law for making such sales. The shares of stock and securities purchased by Davis proved worthless. He then sued Walker and others, who were the directors and officers of W & M when he made the purchase, to recover the amount of his loss.

> **Decision:** The officers and directors were liable. Because of their position, they knew that no license had been obtained and that the corporation was illegally selling its shares. As they were in control of running the corporation, they should be held liable for loss caused by the corporation although technically the unlawful sale was made by the corporation and not by them. (Davis v. Walker, 170 Neb. 891, 104 N.W.2d 479)

2 / Federal Securities Act. The state blue-sky laws are subject to the very important limitation that they can apply only to intrastate transactions and cannot apply to sales made in interstate commerce. To meet this defect, the Federal Securities Act of 1933 was adopted. This act declares it unlawful for any issuer, underwriter, or dealer in securities to send either the securities or a prospectus for them in interstate commerce or the mails without having first registered the issue with the Securities and Exchange Commission. The effect of registration is to provide a full and adequate disclosure of information of which private investors may then avail themselves. The registration is not an approval of the security by the Commission or by the government, nor any guaranty of the safety of the investment. The act does not apply to the ordinary sale and purchase of stock by private individuals, nor does it apply to security issues of $300,000 or less.

A criminal penalty is imposed for failure to register or for making false statements to the Commission. The Commission may enjoin any practice that violates the act, and persons injured may bring suit for civil damages against the violator.

3 / Federal Securities Exchange Act. In addition to the evils connected with the issuing and floating of securities, a number of evils were due to practices at security exchanges. The Federal Securities Exchange Act of

---

[31] *Spears* v. *Lawrence Securities, Inc.,* 239 Ore. 583, 399 P.2d 348.

1934 declares it unlawful for any broker, dealer, or exchange, directly or indirectly, to make use of the mails or any means of communication for the purpose of using the facilities of an exchange to effect any transaction in a security, unless such exchange is registered as a national securities exchange with the Securities and Exchange Commission or unless it is exempt from registration.

Various practices that were used in market manipulation are declared unlawful and prohibited by the act. Wash sales, matched orders, and circulation of false rumors and tips are made unlawful and prohibited. These devices attempt to create the impression of great trading activity in a particular stock, thus tending to increase the price that the public is willing to pay for it.

Other practices that can be used either for a lawful trading or an unlawful manipulating purpose are not prohibited by the act but are subject to the regulation of the Securities and Exchange Commission so that the Commission may see that they are used for a legitimate purpose. Speculative activity on exchanges is restricted by giving the Board of Governors of the Federal Reserve System power to fix the margin on which trading can be conducted and to restrict the extent to which money can be borrowed to finance stock transactions.

Control of corporations by insiders is checked to some extent by the act by requiring that solicitations for proxies state the identity and interest of the solicitor and what action is to be passed upon at the corporate meeting for which the proxy is solicited. Corporate insiders are also prohibited under certain circumstances from making a profit on the basis of information that they have but that the general public could not have.

4 / Later federal regulations. Later statutes provide for the registration of interstate electric or gas utility holding companies with the Securities and Exchange Commission and authorize the Federal Power Commission to regulate the rates on interstate shipments of natural gas and electric power. In registering, the holding company must file detailed information concerning its corporate structure and financing.

Authority is given to the Securities and Exchange Commission to order the dissolution of holding companies that have been created merely for the purpose of corporate manipulation. If such a holding company does not register as required by law, it is illegal for it to engage in any interstate business transactions. Such a holding company that has registered is subject to various restrictions as to financing and security issues, and the Commission is given supervisory powers over the company's financial records.

QUESTIONS AND PROBLEMS

1. Checklist of legal terms:
   (a) certificate of stock (595)
   (b) common stock, preferred stock (596)
   (c) cumulative preferred stock (596), participating preferred stock (597)
   (d) capital, capital stock (597)
   (e) par value, book value, market value (598)
   (f) stock subscription (599)
   (g) blue-sky laws (604)

2. State the objective(s) of each of the following rules of law:
   (a) A shareholder can be required to give the corporation the option of purchasing his stock before he may sell it to an outsider.
   (b) A transfer of stock is not effective without a transfer of the certificate.

3. The Strothman Company has issued common stock and 6 percent preferred stock. For three successive years the corporation earned 4 percent annually on its outstanding stock. During that time no dividend was declared by the directors. At the end of the fourth year the directors declared a 6 percent dividend on the preferred stock and a 4 percent dividend on the common. Wood, a holder of preferred stock, contends that the directors cannot lawfully declare this dividend on the common shares. Do you agree?

4. The charter of the Winstead Corporation permits the issuance of 10,000 shares of stock with a par value of $50. The corporation has issued 8,000 shares, and its net assets are $400,000. What is the amount of its (a) capital, (b) authorized capital stock, and (c) outstanding capital stock?

5. Zink orally agrees to buy 500 shares of stock in a given corporation and to pay the par value of $10 a share. When the corporation seeks to collect the amount agreed upon, Zink refuses to pay, contending that the agreement is unenforceable because it is not in writing. Is the corporation entitled to judgment in an action to recover the amount of Zink's oral subscription?

6. Salzman subscribes for 100 shares of stock in a corporation that is being organized. About two weeks before incorporation, Salzman informs all of the parties concerned that he is canceling his subscription. After the corporation is formed, it brings an action against Salzman for the amount of his subscription. Is the corporation entitled to judgment?

7. The Jackson Company was authorized by its charter to issue 20,000 shares of stock at a par value of $100 each. Subscriptions were received for all of the shares, and installments of $200,000 on these subscriptions had been paid to the corporation. A state law provided that corporations should pay an annual license fee or franchise tax of one tenth of 1 per-

cent of the amount of its capital stock. The state contended that the company was liable for an annual payment of $2,000. Do you agree?

8. All of the shares of the Rankin Company are owned by five shareholders. The certificates of stock provide that when a shareholder wishes to sell his shares, he must offer them to the other shareholders before offering them for sale to the public. Is such a provision valid?

9. The charter of a corporation provides that its shares of stock shall be transferable on the corporate books in a manner prescribed by the directors. McNay transfers his shares in this company to Osborne who does not have the transfer recorded on the books of the corporation. The company mails a dividend check to McNay. Osborne contends that the corporation is liable to him for the dividend. Do you agree?

10. Chandler owned stock in a corporation. The stock was taxed by the town of New Gloucester as property owned by Chandler. Sweetsir, the proper official, sued Chandler for the taxes due. Chandler defended on the ground that the stock should be taxed as evidence of a debt, the same as a bond, and that the tax as assessed was therefore unlawful. Was his contention valid? (Sweetsir v. Chandler, 98 Me. 145, 56 A. 584)

11. Elizabeth Szabo, who owned stock of the American Telephone & Telegraph Co., was notified by the company that there had been a three-for-one split of the company's stock effective as of April 24, 1959, and that on May 29, 1959, the company would prepare and mail to her an additional stock certificate representing twice the number of shares already held by her. Upon receiving the notice from the company, Szabo indorsed on her certificate a transfer to herself and her son as joint tenants with the right of survivorship. She delivered the indorsed certificate to the stock transfer agent of the corporation but directed him to hold up the transfer of the stock until the new certificate for the split shares was available. The stock transfer agent was also notified to have the new certificate made out to Szabo and her son as joint tenants with the right of survivorship. Three days before the new certificate for the stock split was issued, Szabo died. Her son claimed the original shares of stock from her estate and the new shares issued on the stock split. Was he entitled to both? (Szabo's Estate, 10 N.Y.2d 123, 217 N.Y.S.2d 593, 176 N.E.2d 395)

12. The Skinner Packing Co., which was incorporated under the laws of Maine, was authorized to do business in Nebraska where it had its principal place of business. The company sent an agent to Excelsior Springs, Missouri, where he contracted for the sale of 100 shares of stock in the company to Rhines. Within a year thereafter, Rhines concluded that he had been swindled and brought an action against the company to recover the purchase price of the stock. He based his claim upon a violation of the Missouri Blue-Sky Law. The defendant asserted that the transaction was not governed by the Missouri statute. Do you agree? (Rhines v. Skinner Packing Co., 108 Neb. 105, 187 N.W. 874)

Chapter 53

Shareholders

The control of the shareholders over the corporation is indirect. Periodically, ordinarily once a year, the shareholders elect directors and through this means can control the corporation. At other times, however, the shareholders have no right or power to control the corporate activity so long as it is conducted within lawful channels. An exception to this rule is that frequently holders of a stated percentage of stock can call a special meeting of the shareholders and to that extent take affairs into their own hands.

Rights of Shareholders

1 / Certificate of stock. A shareholder has the right to have issued to him a properly executed certificate as evidence of his ownership of shares.[1] If, on proper demand, the officers wrongfully refuse to issue a certificate, the courts may compel the issuance of a certificate or the payment of damages for refusing to do so.

2 / Transfer of shares. Subject to certain valid restrictions,[2] a shareholder has the right to transfer his shares as he chooses and may sell the shares at any price or transfer them as a gift.[3]

3 / Vote. The right to vote means the right to vote at shareholders' meetings for the election of directors and on such other special matters as must be passed upon by the shareholders.[4] As an illustration of the latter, a proposal to change the capital stock structure of the corporation or a proposal to sell all or substantially all of the assets of the corporation must be approved by the shareholders.[5]

> **Facts:** A meeting of the shareholders of the Spokane Savings and Loan Society voted to dissolve the corporation and to transfer its assets to the Spokane Savings Bank. It was objected that the vote was illegal because certain voters were directors and shareholders of both the loan society and the bank, and that because of their status as directors of

---

[1] *State* ex rel. *Bross* v. *Carpenter,* 51 Ohio 83, 37 N.E. 261.
[2] See p. 600.
[3] See Ch. 31.
[4] See p. 620.
[5] *Good* v. *Lackawanna Leather Co.,* 96 N.J.S. 439, 233 A.2d 201.

the society they could not vote as shareholders of the society for the purpose of transferring the assets to the bank in which they were also directors and shareholders.

Decision: Held that although the directors of the society could not act adversely to the society as directors, they were nevertheless free to vote as shareholders in any way they chose, regardless of the fact that they were directors. A shareholder may always vote as he pleases for the protection of his own interest. (Beutelspacher v. Spokane Savings Bank, 164 Wash. 227, 2 P.2d 729)

(a) WHO MAY VOTE. The articles of incorporation state which classes of shareholders can vote. Ordinarily only those common shareholders in whose names the stock appears on the books of the corporation are entitled to vote. In some instances the owner is not permitted to vote unless his stock has been registered for a specified period of time before the meeting.[6] For example, a transferee of shares of stock may be denied the right to vote for directors unless the transfer was made on the books 10 days prior to the election.

(b) NUMBER OF VOTES. Each shareholder is ordinarily entitled to one vote for each voting share of stock. In some states, however, the number of votes allowed to each shareholder is limited by statute. There is a conflict of authority whether a shareholder may vote a fractional share.[7] Whole shares may only be voted as whole shares and cannot be voted as fractional shares and divided between candidates.[8]

In nearly half of the states cumulative voting in the election of directors may be provided for in the articles or automatically exists when the contrary is not stated in the articles.[9] In nearly half of the states cumulative voting is mandatory, being imposed by either constitution or statute. A few states prohibit cumulative voting.

Under a *cumulative voting* plan each shareholder has as many votes as the number of shares he owns multiplied by the number of directors to be elected, and he can distribute them as he sees fit. To illustrate, if a person owns 30 shares and 10 directors are to be elected, he is entitled to cast 300 votes. He may cast 30 votes for each of 10 nominees, 50 for each of 6, 60 votes for each of 5, 75 for each of 4, 100 for each of 3, 150 for each of 2, or 300 votes for 1.

There is a conflict of authority as to the validity of a provision for the election of the directors by classes, as when directors serve for three years

---

[6] American Bar Association Model Business Corporation Act. Sec. 28.
[7] *Com.* ex rel. *Cartwright* v. *Cartwright,* 350 Pa. 638, 40 A.2d 30.
[8] *Garnier* v. *Garnier,* [Cal.App.2d] 56 Cal.Rptr. 247.
[9] ABA MBCA Sec. 31. This section supplies both a mandatory and a permissive form.

and one third of the directors are elected each year. In some jurisdictions such a provision is held invalid as impairing the right of cumulative voting. In other jurisdictions such a system is valid and cumulative voting is exercised as to the directors within each class to be elected at each election.

(c) VOTING BY PROXY. A shareholder has the right to authorize another to vote for him.[10] This is known as *voting by proxy.* In the absence of restrictions to the contrary, any person, even one who is not a shareholder, may act as a proxy. As in the case of any other agency, unless it is coupled with interest,[11] the authority of a proxy can be revoked at any time. Ordinarily authority to act as a proxy may be conferred by an informal written instrument.[12]

(d) VOTING AGREEMENTS AND TRUSTS. Shareholders, as a general rule, are allowed to enter into an agreement by which they concentrate their voting strength for the purpose of controlling the management, unless their agreement is fraudulent or oppressive as to other members. A *voting trust* exists when by agreement a group of shareholders, or all of the shareholders, transfer their shares in trust to one or more persons, as trustees, who are authorized to vote the stock during the life of the trust agreement.[13]

In general, such agreements have been upheld if their object is lawful.[14] In some states voting trusts are valid only to the extent that they are authorized by and comply with local statutes.[15] In the majority of states there is a specific limitation on the number of years a voting trust may continue and the maximum is most commonly ten years. When the maximum is specified by statute, there is a conflict of authority as to whether a voting trust agreement that specifies a longer period is totally void, or whether it is void only as to the period in excess of the permitted statutory time.

When a corporation owns shares in another corporation, the board of directors of the owning corporation may transfer such shares to voting trustees even though the effect of so doing is to delegate to such trustees the power to vote the shares as they, rather than the directors, see fit. This constitutes an exception to the general rule that directors may not delegate the exercise of their discretion to anyone.[16]

4 / Pre-emptive offer of shares. If the capital stock of a corporation is increased, each shareholder ordinarily has the pre-emptive right to sub-

---

[10] ABA MBCA Sec. 31.
[11] See p. 251.
[12] See, for example, the regulations of the Securities and Exchange Commission, Rule X-14A-4. By statute it has been declared in at least one jurisdiction that "a telegram . . . is a sufficient writing." In a few states an oral proxy is valid.
[13] *Brown* v. *McLanahan,* [C.A.4th] 148 F.2d 703.
[14] ABA MBCA Sec. 32 (ten-year limitation).
[15] *Abercrombie* v. *Davies,* 36 Del.Ch. 371, 130 A.2d 338.
[16] *Adams* v. *Clearance Corp.,* 35 Del.Ch. 459, 121 A.2d 302; see page 623.

scribe to such a percentage of the new shares as his old shares bore to the former total of capital stock. This right is given in order to enable each shareholder to maintain his relative interest in the corporation.[17]

In certain instances, however, the furthering of the interests of the corporate group is more important than the preservation of the position of the individual shareholder. In such cases there is no pre-emptive right.

5 / Inspection of books. A shareholder has the right to be informed about the business of the corporation. He has the right to inspect the books and property of his corporation so that he can keep himself informed about its condition. The shareholder must ask for examination in good faith, for proper motives, and at a reasonable time and place.[18]

Facts: The Peninsular Telephone Co., which owned stock in the Florida Telephone Corporation, requested permission to examine the latter's books in order to learn the names and addresses of the shareholders so that it could seek to buy their stock from them. When the corporation refused to permit this inspection, Peninsular brought an action in the name of the state to compel such inspection.

Decision: Judgment for Peninsular Telephone Co. The reason for the inspection of the records was proper as it enabled a shareholder to protect his interest in the corporation by increasing his ownership and voting power. A contrary decision would be particularly undesirable since it would give management a complete control of such information, which it could use to further its control by proxy solicitation or purchase of outstanding shares. (Florida Telephone Corporation v. Florida ex rel. Peninsular Telephone Co., [Fla.App.] 111 So.2d 677)

Inspection need not be made personally. A shareholder may employ an accountant or an attorney to examine the records for him.

6 / Dividends. A shareholder has the right to receive his proportion of dividends as they are declared, subject to the relative rights of other shareholders to preferences, accumulation of dividends, and participation.[19] However, there is no absolute right to receive dividends.[20]

(a) FUNDS AVAILABLE FOR DECLARATION OF DIVIDENDS. Statutes commonly provide that no dividends may be declared unless there is a "surplus" for their payment. This surplus is generally calculated as the amount of the corporate assets in excess of all outstanding liabilities and outstanding shares of the corporation.[21] Thus, if a corporation owed $10,000 and had

---

[17] *Gord v. Iowana Farms Milk Co.,* 245 Iowa 1, 60 N.W.2d 820.
[18] *Sanders v. Pacific Gamble Robinson Co.,* 250 Minn. 265, 84 N.W.2d 919.
[19] See p. 596.
[20] *Wabash R. Co. v. Barclay,* 280 U.S. 197.
[21] *Randall v. Bailey,* 288 N.Y. 280, 43 N.E.2d 43.

issued capital stock of $20,000, there could not be a fund for the declaration of dividends until the corporate assets were in excess of $30,000. The theory is that there must be preserved intact such a fund as will pay off all creditors of the corporation and return to each shareholder his capital investment before any dividends can be paid.

Cash dividends may be paid from paid-in surplus. This is the amount that is paid for stock in excess of its par value, if it is par-value stock, and of the amount designated by the board of directors as payment for shares having no par value.

A book surplus may be created by decreasing the capital stock or increasing the value of the corporate assets. Some states permit the declaration of a stock dividend,[22] but not of a cash dividend from a surplus based on such an unrealized appreciation of corporate assets. That is, a corporation cannot increase the valuation of its property on its books and then declare a cash dividend from the resulting paper surplus.

Conversely, for the purpose of dividend declaration, a corporation should write down its assets when because of their risk, nature, or depreciation they are in effect overvalued.[23] The effect of these rules is to deny a corporation a right to declare dividends from current net profits if there is a deficit from prior years.

As an exception to these rules, a wasting assets corporation may pay dividends out of current net profits without regard to the preservation of the corporate assets. The category of *wasting assets corporations* includes those enterprises that are designed to exhaust or use up the assets of the corporation, as by extracting oil, coal, iron, and other ores, as compared with a manufacturing plant where the object is to preserve the plant as well as to continue to manufacture. A wasting assets corporation may also be formed for the purpose of purchasing and liquidating a bankrupt's stock of merchandise.

In some of the states, statutes provide that dividends may be declared from current net profits, without regard to the existence of a deficit from former years, or from surplus.

If dividends are about to be declared from an unlawful source, an injunction can be obtained to stop their declaration or payment. If the payment has already been made, the directors responsible for the action may be sued individually and be made to indemnify the corporation for the loss they have caused it by the improper payment; but generally it is necessary to show that the directors acted negligently or in bad faith in declaring the dividends.

---

[22] See p. 613.
[23] *Vogtman* v. *Merchants Mtge & Credit Co.*, 20 Del.Ch. 364, 178 A. 99.

(b) DISCRETION OF DIRECTORS. Assuming that a fund is available for the declaration of dividends, it is then a matter primarily within the discretion of the board of directors whether a dividend shall be declared. The fact that there is a surplus which could be used for dividends does not determine that they must be declared.[24] The directors have the task of running the corporate business. This rule is not affected by the nature of the shares. Thus, the fact that the shareholders hold cumulative preferred shares does not give them any right to demand a declaration of dividends or to interfere with an honest exercise of discretion by the directors.[25]

In general, a court will refuse to substitute its judgment for the judgment of the directors and will interfere only when it is shown that their conduct is harmful to the welfare of the corporation or its shareholders.[26]

The courts, however, will intervene and compel the declaration of a dividend when it is apparent that the directors have amassed a surplus beyond any practical business need.

Once dividends are duly declared, a debtor-creditor relation exists between the corporation and the shareholders as to those dividends. The shareholder may accordingly sue the corporation to recover the amount of his lawfully declared dividends if it fails to pay them, and the corporation cannot recapture them without the shareholder's consent.[27]

(c) FORM OF DIVIDENDS. Customarily, a dividend is paid in the form of money; but it may be paid in property, such as a product manufactured by the corporation, in the shares of other corporations held by the corporation, or in the shares of the corporation itself. In the last case, referred to as a *stock dividend*, the result is the same as though the directors paid a cash dividend and all the shareholders then purchased additional stock in amounts proportionate to their original holdings. The corporation merely capitalizes or transfers to the capital account earnings or earned surplus in an amount equal to the par or stated value of the stock dividend.[28] The result is that the stock dividend does not change the proportionate interest of each shareholder but only the evidence which represents that interest. He now has a greater number of shares, but his total shares represent the same proportionate interest in the corporation as before.[29]

It is necessary to distinguish between stock splits and stock dividends. For example, when a corporation splits its shares in two, the number of outstanding shares is doubled and consequently each share then stands for

---

[24] *Agnew* v. *American Ice Co.*, 2 N.J. 291, 66 A.2d 330.
[25] *Treves* v. *Menzies*, 37 Del.Ch. 330, 142 A.2d 520.
[26] *Gordon* v. *Elliman*, 306 N.Y. 456, 119 N.E.2d 331.
[27] *Crellin's Estate* v. *Com. of Internal Revenue*, [C.A.9th] 203 F.2d 812.
[28] *Fosdick Trust*, 4 N.Y.2d 646, 152 N.E.2d 228.
[29] *Merritt-Chapman and Scott Corp.* v. *N.Y. Trust Co.*, [C.A.2d] 184 F.2d 954

only one half of the interest in the corporation represented by an original share. Although a holder of one share receives an additional share, the additional share is not a "dividend," but merely offsets the 50 percent dilution of the value of his original share of stock resulting from doubling the number of outstanding shares.

(d) EFFECT OF TRANSFER OF SHARES. In determining who is entitled to dividends, it is immaterial when the surplus from which the distribution is made was earned. As between the transferor and the transferee, if the dividend is in cash or property other than the shares of the corporation declaring the dividend, the person who was the owner on the date the dividend was declared is entitled to the dividend. Thus, if a cash dividend is declared before the transfer is made, the transferor is entitled to it. If the transfer was made before the declaration date, the transferee is entitled to it. It is immaterial when distribution of the dividend was made.

The rule that the date of declaration determines the right to a cash dividend is subject to modification by the corporation. The board of directors in declaring the dividend may state that it will be payable to those who will be the holders of record on a later specified date.

If the dividend consists of shares in the corporation declaring the dividend, ownership is determined by the date of distribution. Whichever party is the owner of the shares when the stock dividend is distributed is entitled to the stock dividend. The reason for this variation from the cash dividend rule lies in the fact that the declaration of a stock dividend has the effect of diluting the existing corporate assets among a larger number of shares. The value of the holding represented by each share is accordingly diminished. Unless the person who owns the stock on the date when distribution is made receives a proportionate share of the stock dividends, the net effect will be to lessen his holdings.

The transferor and transferee may enter into any agreement they choose with respect to dividends.

These rules determine the rights to dividends as between transferor and transferee. Regardless of what those rights may be, the corporation is generally entitled to continue to recognize the transferor as a shareholder until it has been notified that a transfer has been made and the corporate records are accordingly changed.[30] If the corporation, believing that the transferor is still the owner of the shares, sends him a dividend to which the transferee is entitled, the transferee cannot sue the corporation. In that case, the remedy of the transferee is to sue the transferor for the money or property that the latter has received.

---

[30] *Davis* v. *Fraser*, 307 N.Y. 433, 121 N.E.2d 406.

7 / Shareholders' actions. When the corporation has the right to sue its directors or officers or third persons for damages caused by them to the corporation or for breach of contract, one or more shareholders may bring such action if the corporation refuses to do so.[31] An action cannot be brought by minority shareholders, however, if the action of the corporate directors or officers has been ratified by a majority of the shareholders acting in good faith and the matter is of such a nature that had such majority originally authorized the acts of the directors or officers there would not have been any wrong.[32]

Shareholders may also intervene or join in an action brought against the corporation when the corporation refuses to defend the action against it or is not doing so in good faith. Otherwise the shareholders may take no part in an action against the corporation.[33]

8 / Capital distribution. Upon the dissolution of the corporation, the shareholders are entitled to receive any balance of the corporate assets that remains after the payment of all creditors. Certain classes of stock may have a preference or priority in this distribution.[34]

Liabilities of Shareholders

1 / Limited liability. The liability of a shareholder in an ordinary corporation is generally limited. This means that he is not personally responsible for the debts and liabilities of the corporation. The capital contributed by the shareholders may be exhausted by the claims of creditors, but he has no greater liability. The risk of the shareholder is thus limited to the original capital invested by him. By way of comparison, if a partnership had debts of $1,000,000, any partner would be liable without limitation for the total amount of the debt.[35] In the case of a corporation owing $1,000,000, no shareholder is personally liable for any part. The explanation for this rule is that the corporation is a distinct, legal person, and it alone owes the debts and is liable for the claims.

It is this feature of limited liability that, to a large degree, explains the great number of small corporations. There are many three-man corporations, small corporations in which a man who runs a business forms a corporation and, in order to have the necessary number of incorporators, lists his wife as the owner of a share of stock in the corporation to be formed, and his brother as the owner of another share, and lists himself as the owner of the remaining shares. After incorporation, he may obtain a transfer to himself

---

[31] See p. 624.
[32] *Claman* v. *Robertson,* 164 Ohio 61, 128 N.E.2d 429.
[33] *Ingalls Iron Works Co.* v. *Ingalls Foundation,* 266 Ala. 656, 98 So.2d 30.
[34] See p. 596.
[35] See p. 554.

of the shares held by his wife and brother so that he then owns all of the shares. The result then is that creditors of the business that is run by the corporation cannot assert their claims against the businessman. He thus insures himself against personal liability for corporate liabilities and losses.

If the court is convinced that a fraud is being perpetrated, it will decide the case as though there were no corporation.[36] In such a case, the court "will pierce the corporate veil." Ordinarily, it will not do this, and the fact that a person owns all or substantially all of the shares of a corporation and that he has incorporated for the express purpose of insulating himself from liability does not constitute such fraud as justifies the court in ignoring the shielding effect of the corporation.

Similarly a parent company and its wholly owned subsidiary are regarded as separate entities.

> **Facts:** A group of persons proposed to build two apartment houses. In order to take advantage of the Federal Housing Act, they formed two separate corporations upon the recommendation of the Federal Housing Administration. Each corporation managed one of the apartment houses and kept a separate set of books. Neither corporation employed sufficient employees to be subject to the Michigan Employment Security Act. It was claimed that the number of employees for the two corporations should be added together, thus bringing them within the act.

> **Decision:** Judgment for the corporations. A corporation is an entity separate from its shareholders. The fact that two corporations have identical shareholders does not justify the court in regarding them as being one enterprise. The Act, therefore, did not apply because neither corporation alone was subject thereto. (Schusterman v. Appeal Bd., 336 Mich. 246, 57 N.W.2d 869)

Statutes sometimes provide that the shareholders shall be unlimitedly liable for the wage claims of corporate employees.

2 / Unpaid subscriptions. Most states prohibit the issuance of par value shares for less than par or except for "money, labor done, or property actually received." Whenever shares issued by a corporation are not fully paid for, the original subscriber receiving the shares or any transferee who does not give value, or who knows that the shares were not fully paid, may be liable for the unpaid balance if the corporation is insolvent and the money is required to pay the debts of creditors.

If the corporation has issued the shares as fully paid, or has given them as a bonus, or has agreed to release the subscriber for the unpaid balance, the corporation cannot recover that balance. The fact that the corporation is thus barred does not prevent the creditors of the corporation from bringing an

---

[36] *Central Fibre Products Co.* v. *Lorenz,* 246 Iowa 384, 66 N.W.2d 30.

action to compel payment of the balance.[37] The same rules are applied when stock is issued as fully paid in return for property or services which are overvalued so that the stock is not actually paid for in full. There is a conflict of authority, however, as to whether the shareholder is liable from the mere fact that the property or service he gave for the shares was in fact overvalued by the directors or whether in addition it must be shown that the directors had acted in bad faith in making the erroneous valuation.

If a statute makes void the shares issued for less than par, they may be canceled upon suit of the corporation.

The common provision that stock shall not be issued except for services performed or money or property actually delivered or paid and prohibiting payment by promissory notes, does not invalidate a note that is given contrary to the statute. The consequence of violating the statute is merely that the stock is deemed unpaid, but the violation of the statute is not a defense to a suit on the note to enforce it.[38]

3 / Unauthorized dividends. If dividends are improperly paid out of capital, it is generally held that the shareholders are liable to creditors to the extent of such depletion of capital.[39] In some states the liability of the shareholder depends on whether the corporation was insolvent at the time, whether the debts were existing at the time, and whether the shareholders had notice of the source of the dividend.

QUESTIONS AND PROBLEMS

1. Checklist of legal terms:
   (a) cumulative voting (609)
   (b) voting by proxy (610)
   (c) voting trust (610)
   (d) wasting assets corporation (612)
   (e) stock dividend (613)

2. State the objective(s) of each of the following rules of law:
   (a) Shareholders may generally vote cumulatively for directors of the corporation.
   (b) The directors have discretion as to whether dividends should be declared from a fund legally available for that purpose.

3. Revis borrows $20,000 from St. Clair. As security, St. Clair receives a pledge of 1,000 shares of stock in a given corporation and the authority to vote the stock. Just prior to a corporation meeting Revis decides to revoke the authority to vote that he has given to St. Clair. Is he entitled to do so?

---

[37] *Strong* v. *Crancer*, 335 Mo. 1209, 76 S.W.2d 383.
[38] *Haselbush* v. *Alsco*, [Colo.] 421 P.2d 113.
[39] This liability is declared by statute in a number of states, but no such provision is made by the ABA MBCA.

4. Three shareholders in the same corporation agree to transfer their stock to Rymer in trust for five years and to authorize him to vote the stock during that period. At the end of three years one of the shareholders wishes to withdraw from the agreement. Is his contention that the agreement is not binding sound?

5. Walsh owned 150 shares of stock in the Riddell Corporation. At a meeting of the shareholders of this company it was decided to increase the amount of its stock. Walsh contended that he was entitled to purchase 30 shares of the new stock which represented his pro rata share of the increase. Was his contention sound?

6. Schmitt, a shareholder, made a demand to inspect the books of the corporation. The demand was refused until the directors saw fit to grant this privilege. Schmitt brought an action against the corporation contending that the decision of the directors was illegal. Do you agree?

7. At the beginning of the current fiscal year the assets of the Simpson Corporation total $50,000. The corporation had outstanding stock of $40,000 and liabilities amounting to $20,000. During the year the corporation earned a net profit of $2,500. How large a dividend could the board of directors declare?

8. The Van Fleet Furnace Company earned $200,000 annually for a period of three years. The board of directors, however, did not declare a dividend during this period. Stevenson, one of the shareholders, brought an action to compel the directors to declare a dividend. Stevenson proved that the earnings of the company were sufficient to pay a $4 dividend each year. Would Stevenson succeed in his action?

9. The fiscal year of the Wadsworth Corporation ends on June 30. On August 1 the board of directors declares a cash dividend to be paid on August 15. Voss, who purchased 10 shares of stock in this corporation from Leach on July 25, did not have the transfer recorded on the books of the corporation until August 31. What rights, if any, does Voss have (a) against the corporation; (b) against Leach?

10. The Nolan Corporation is organized in a state that requires a minimum of three incorporators. This corporation is organized with five incorporators, and all of the stock is sold to them. Is it legal for one of these incorporators to acquire later all of the shares of stock of this corporation?

11. Balinger bought 100 shares of stock at $25 a share when a certain corporation was organized. Longo bought through a broker 100 shares in the same corporation at a cost of $20 a share. Hamblen subscribed for 100 shares of a later stock issue by the corporation at $15 a share, but had paid only $500 on his subscription. To what extent are these shareholders personally liable for the debts of the corporation?

12. The Fraizer Corporation issues 50 shares of stock at a par value of $100 to Horton in exchange for a piece of property that is worth not more than $3,000. When the corporation becomes insolvent, Stein, a creditor, brings

an action to compel Horton to pay the difference between the par value of the stock and the price he paid for it. Is Stein entitled to judgment?

13. Mayer, who owned stock in the Cincinnati Economy Drug Co., requested permission from the company to make a list of its shareholders. The company refused on the ground that Mayer also owned stock in competing drug companies. Was it justified in so doing? (Mayer v. Cincinnati Economy Drug Co., 89 Ohio App. 512, 103 N.E.2d 1)

14. In determining dividends that could be paid, the directors of the Durant Motor Co. deducted from gross income amounts paid for insurance on the corporate property and reserves for depreciation. Objection was made that dividends should be paid on the basis of the gross income prior to such deductions. Decide. (National Newark & Essex Banking Co. v. Durant Motor Co., 124 N.J.Eq. 213, 1 A.2d 316)

15. Carlson and others were in the business of buying up small telephone companies. The Ringgold County Mutual Telephone Co. had 356 shares outstanding. Carlson publicly advertised that his group was willing to purchase such shares at $200 per share, an amount slightly in excess of the book value. In this manner the Carlson group acquired 203 shares. The directors of the company, seeing that they no longer held control of the company, authorized the issuance of 644 shares at $40 a share upon the condition that such shares had to be offered to the company by shareholders before they could be resold. Acting under this resolution the directors sold 225 shares at $40 each, principally to their families, relatives, friends, and employees. On the making of each sale, the purchaser was also required to execute a proxy in favor of the defendant directors. When Carlson learned of the offering of these new shares, he brought suit to claim his pre-emptive right thereto. The company opposed the recognition of pre-emptive rights on the ground that Carlson's purpose was merely to obtain control of the company and then to exploit it to the advantage of his group. Furthermore, a corporate bylaw provided that "transfers of stock shall be made only on approval of the board of directors," and Ringgold took the position that the board of directors refused to approve the transfer of additional shares to Carlson. Was Carlson entitled to shares by virtue of a pre-emptive right? (Carlson v. Ringgold County Mutual Telephone Co., 252 Iowa 748, 108 N.W.2d 478)

16. Thomsen, a shareholder of the Yankee Mariner Corp., brought an action against it and a newly-elected board of directors to determine the validity of the election. It was shown that two of the shareholders, Langs and Napier, had given proxies to Donnelley on March 8 which were irrevocable for 90 days and gave him the right to vote their stock for the purpose of removing the then directors of the corporation and electing new directors. Although they had given their proxies, Langs and Napier appeared at the regular meeting and voted their stock. In the action by Thomsen it was claimed that their voting was illegal since their proxies were still outstanding. Decide. (Thomsen v. Yankee Mariner Corp., 106 Cal.App.2d 454, 235 P.2d 234)

Chapter 54

Management of Corporations

A corporation is managed, directly or indirectly, by its shareholders, board of directors, and officers.

Shareholders

Shareholders do not participate directly in the management of ordinary corporate affairs. Without express authorization by the corporation, a shareholder cannot bind it by contract. It is through the board of directors, the officers, and the employees hired by the corporation that a corporation conducts its business. Since the shareholders have the right to select the directors, they indirectly determine the policies to be followed in the management of the business.

When certain major matters are involved, as distinguished from the ordinary operations of the business, statutes commonly require action by the shareholders. Thus, when a change in the character of the enterprise is contemplated, the consent of all shareholders is required.[1] To illustrate, the unanimous consent of the shareholders is required for a material alteration of a charter to permit an electric lighting company to engage in the operation of a street railway.

Meetings of Shareholders

Action by shareholders must be taken at a regular or special meeting; otherwise, it has no legal effect unless the consent of all shareholders is obtained.

1 / Place of shareholders' meeting. Some courts hold that the first meeting of shareholders must be held in the home state. Statutes, however, generally permit such meetings to be held in any state.[2]

The place of holding stated meetings may be prescribed by the charter or bylaws, or it may be left in the hands of the directors. Unless otherwise

---

[1] The American Bar Association Model Business Corporation Act requires, in the absence of a provision in the articles of incorporation to the contrary, a majority of two thirds of the voting power to alter the articles of incorporation. Sec. 54(c).

[2] The ABA MBCA provides that shareholders' meetings may be held in any state authorized by the bylaws, Sec. 26.

prohibited by statute, a meeting improperly held as to place or time is binding on those who assent to it.

2 / Regular meetings. Meetings of the shareholders may be regular or special. The time and place of regular or stated meetings are usually prescribed by the charter or bylaws. Notice to shareholders of such meetings is ordinarily not required but is usually given as a matter of good business practice. Some statutes, however, require that notice be given of all meetings whether regular or special, and it is generally required that a notice be given specifying the subject matter of the meeting when it is of an unusual character.[3]

3 / Special meetings. Unless otherwise prescribed by charter or bylaws, special meetings are called by the directors; but a call by the president, the secretary, or the chairman of the board of directors is commonly authorized. It is sometimes provided that a special meeting may be called by a certain percentage of the shareholders. The purpose of this alternative is to prevent a board of directors from ruling the corporation with an iron hand. In the absence of express authorization, shareholders, even though they hold a majority of the stock, may not call a special meeting. In such a case the only remedy of the shareholders desiring a meeting is to bring an action, commonly of mandamus, to compel the proper officer to call a special meeting when the circumstances are such that his refusal to do so is improper.[4]

Notice of the day, hour, and the place of a special meeting must be given to all shareholders. The notice must also include a statement of the nature of the business to be transacted, and no other business may be lawfully transacted at such a meeting unless there is a waiver of compliance with such requirement by all shareholders.[5]

If proper notice is not given, the defect may be cured at a properly held meeting by ratification of the action taken by the earlier meeting.

4 / Quorum. A valid meeting requires the presence of a quorum of the voting shareholders. At common law any number of shareholders assembled at a proper meeting constituted a quorum, and action by the majority of such a quorum was binding. The purpose of this rule was to prevent a group of dissenters from blocking action by refusing to be present at a meeting. It is commonly provided by statute, charter, or bylaws, however, that in order to constitute a *quorum,* a specified number of shareholders or a number authorized to vote a stated proportion of the voting stock must attend.[6] Most

---

[3] *Klein* v. *Scranton Life Ins. Co.,* 139 Pa.Super. 369, 11 A.2d 770.
[4] *Auer* v. *Dressel,* 306 N.Y. 427, 118 N.E.2d 590.
[5] *Matter of 74 & 76 West Tremont Ave. Corp.,* 10 Misc.2d 662, 173 N.Y.S.2d 154.
[6] The ABA MBCA provides that, unless otherwise provided in the articles of incorporation, a majority of shares entitled to vote constitute a quorum. Sec. 30.

commonly a simple majority is specified, or such a majority is required by statute unless otherwise provided by the articles or the bylaws.

It is generally held that when a meeting opens with a quorum, the quorum is not thereafter broken if shareholders leave the meeting and those remaining would not have been sufficient to constitute a quorum originally. This principle is designed to prevent obstructionist tactics by groups of dissenting shareholders.

A charter or bylaw provision may lawfully require more than a simple majority vote of shareholders on any issue.[7] But when the business corporation code authorizes action by a simple majority, a bylaw generally cannot require approval by a two-thirds majority.[8]

Directors

The management of a corporation is usually entrusted to a board of directors who are elected by the shareholders. The number of directors to be elected varies, depending upon statute, charter, or bylaw.

1 / Qualifications. Eligibility for membership to a board of directors is determined by statute, charter, or bylaw.[9] In the absence of controlling provisions, any person is eligible for membership, including a nonresident, a minor, or even a person who is not a shareholder. Generally, however, it is required that all or some of the members on the board of directors meet certain requirements.

2 / Meetings of directors. Generally action by directors can only be taken at a proper meeting of the board.[10]

The statutes, charter, or bylaws sometimes require the meeting of directors to be held at a particular place. In the absence of restrictions the meeting of the directors may be held outside the state.[11] Directors who participate without objection in a meeting held at a place or time other than as specified in the bylaws cannot object later.

A director is not allowed to vote by proxy,[12] but a few states permit the articles of incorporation or bylaws to authorize voting by proxy. The theory underlying the general rule is that the director must attend personally to the affairs of the corporation. Similarly the directors as a board cannot delegate their duty to others.[13]

---

[7] *Katcher* v. *Ohsman*, 26 N.J.S. 28, 97 A.2d 180.

[8] *Model, Roland & Co.* v. *Industrial Acoustics Co.*, 16 N.Y.2d 703, 209 N.E.2d 553.

[9] ABA MBCA Sec. 33.

[10] *Dicks* v. *Clarence L. Boyd*, 205 Okla. 383, 238 P.2d 315, unless the directors are the only shareholders of the corporation. *Temple Enterprises* v. *Combs,* 164 Ore. 133, 100 P.2d 613.

[11] ABA MBCA Sec. 39; *Webb* v. *Midway Lumber Co.*, 68 Mo.App. 546.

[12] *Greenberg* v. *Harrison*, 143 Conn. 519, 124 A.2d 216.

[13] *Besseliew* v. *Brown*, 177 N.C. 65, 97 S.E. 743.

A quorum requires the presence of a majority of the directors, unless otherwise provided in the charter, statute, or bylaws.[14] In the determination of whether the requisite number of directors to transact business is present, a director ordinarily cannot be counted if he has a personal interest in the matter before the board. The fact that he has such interest is deemed to disqualify him since, in the eyes of the law, he cannot act impartially.[15]

Facts: Smith was a director and Abbott a director and president of the Indurated Concrete Corp. There were four directors in all. At a meeting at which one director was absent, Smith and Abbott presented claims that they held against the corporation for special services rendered by them. As directors, they voted in favor of paying their claims. The remaining director present voted against the claims. A new board of directors was elected the next year, and the corporation sued Smith and Abbott to recover the money that had been paid on those claims.

Decision: Judgment for corporation. The claims had been improperly allowed. Smith and Abbott were disqualified by their interest from voting on the allowance of their claims. Without the vote of Abbott and Smith, the allowance of the claims was not approved. Hence the voting to approve them, in which they participated, had no effect. (Indurated Concrete Corp. v. Abbott, 195 Md. 496, 74 A.2d 17)

A director who also acts as general manager of the corporation cannot vote at a directors' meeting on a resolution to give him special compensation for his services as manager.[16]

3 / Powers of directors. The board of directors has authority to manage the corporation. The court will not interfere with its discretion in the absence of illegal conduct or fraud harming the rights of creditors, shareholders, or the corporation.[17]

Facts: Before a new corporation, Gateway Life Insurance Co., was formed, an agreement was made between the plaintiff, Wilson, and the defendants, McClenny and others, that the plaintiff should be the president of Gateway and the defendants should be directors and that all should acquire certain amounts of stock. Wilson was hired by the corporation as president in consequence of this agreement but on a yearly contract. When the contract came up for renewal, the directors who had signed this agreement and the other directors voted against renewal of the contract because the plaintiff had a serious drinking problem and had voluntarily committed himself to an institution for inebriates for 21

---

[14] ABA MBCA Sec. 37.

[15] *Garwin* v. *Anderson*, 334 Mich. 287, 54 N.W.2d 667. In contrast, a shareholder who has a personal interest in a matter before a shareholders' meeting may be counted in determining whether a quorum is present and he is not disqualified from voting on the matter.

[16] *J. C. Adams* v. *Mid-West Chevrolet Corp.*, 198 Okla. 461, 179 P.2d 147.

[17] *Greenfield* v. *Harper Ave., Bldg. Corp.*, 351 Ill.App. 375, 115 N.E.2d 357.

days. Wilson sued the defendants in tort because, as directors, they had interfered with his contract by voting against its renewal when, in fact, his drinking had not interfered with the conduct of the business.

Decision: Judgment against Wilson. In determining whether a contract should be renewed, the directors were free to act as they thought best for the corporation and were in fact under the duty to do so. Whether they were correct in the belief that Wilson was unfit was immaterial for at most it would be merely an error in judgment, for which there would be no tort liability. As there was no evidence of malice or an intention to cause Wilson loss, there was no liability to him. (Wilson v. McClenny, 262 N.C. 121, 136 S.E.2d 569)

The board of directors may enter into any contract or transaction necessary to carry out the business for which the corporation was formed. The board may appoint officers and other agents to act for the company or may delegate authority to one or more of its members to do so. For example, it may appoint several of its own members as an executive committee to act for the board between board meetings.

Knowledge of a director of a corporation is knowledge of the corporation when the director acquires such knowledge while acting in the course of his employment and in the scope of his authority. Knowledge learned by a director while acting in his own interest, however, is not imputed to the corporation.[18]

4 / Liability of directors. Directors are fiduciaries entrusted with the management of the corporation. They are not liable for losses resulting from their management when they have acted in good faith and with due diligence, and have exercised reasonable care.[19] For willful or negligent acts, however, they are held strictly accountable, and they are bound by all the rules that the law imposes on those in a fiduciary position.[20] Thus directors are liable to the corporation when they have made a secret profit at the expense of the corporation. They are also liable when they have depleted corporate assets by an improper declaration of dividends. And a director who was a former vice-president and sales manager is obviously prohibited from using confidential information obtained while so employed for his own personal gain.[21]

Actions against directors should be brought by the corporation. If the corporation fails to act, as is the case when the directors who are sued are in control of the corporation, one or more shareholders may bring the action in a representative capacity for the corporation. This is a secondary or derivative action in that the shareholder enforces only the cause of action of

---

[18] *Niman* v. *Pecatonica Livestock Exchange,* 13 Ill.App.2d 144, 141 N.E.2d 327.

[19] ABA MBCA Sec. 43, specifies a number of instances in which directors are liable.

[20] *Guth* v. *Loft,* 23 Del.Ch. 255, 5 A.2d 503.

[21] *Opie Brush Co.* v. *Bland,* [Mo.] 409 S.W.2d 752.

the corporation, and any money recovered is paid into the corporate treasury.[22] Statutes commonly require that the plaintiffs own at least 5 percent of the outstanding stock or furnish security for costs, in order to limit the danger of crank or nuisance suits.

Directors of a corporation are not personally liable for wrongs committed by the corporation merely by virtue of the fact that they are directors. It must be shown that they have authorized or ratified the improper conduct or have in some way participated therein.[23]

Facts: Nottingham was employed by a corporation. The corporation broke this contract by firing him. He claimed that the breach had been caused by the malicious conduct of Wrigley, Jr., the majority shareholder, and other directors of the corporation. Nottingham sued Wrigley, Jr., and other directors for damages for the tort of maliciously inducing the breach of the contract. The defense was raised that as the defendants had acted as directors on behalf of the corporation, the plaintiff could recover, if at all, only from the corporation.

Decision: The defense was not valid. If a corporate officer, director, or employee is guilty of misconduct, he may be sued by the injured person although the facts may be such that the corporation is also liable. (Wrigley v. Nottingham, 111 Ga.App. 404, 141 S.E.2d 859)

When the director has dealt personally with his own corporation, as in the case when he has sold it his property, or when a transaction occurs between corporations with common directors, the burden is on the director or directors to show that the transaction was proper.

Officers

1 / Selection of officers. Sometimes the officers are elected by the shareholders, but usually they are appointed by the board of directors.[24] Ordinarily no particular formality need be observed in making such appointments. Unless prohibited, a director may hold an executive office.

Seldom are particular qualifications required of officers.

Persons outside of the corporation cannot challenge the propriety of the election of persons acting as corporate officers. Hence the sufficiency of a petition to separate land from a park district, which by statute was required to be signed by a specified number of property owners, cannot be challenged on the ground that those signing on behalf of a corporate landowner had no authority to do so, on the theory that they had not been properly elected as officers.[25]

---

[22] *Taormina* v. *Taormina Corp.*, 32 Del.Ch. 18, 78 A.2d 473.
[23] *Lowell Hoit & Co.* v. *Detig*, 320 Ill.App. 179, 50 N.E.2d 602.
[24] ABA MBCA Sec. 44.
[25] *Jack* v. *Oakbrook Terrace Community Park District*, 36 Ill.App.2d 390, 202 N.E.2d 7.

2 / Powers of officers. The officers of a corporation are its agents. Consequently their powers are controlled by the laws of agency, subject to limitations imposed by the charter and bylaws or by the instructions of the board of directors.

(a) PRESIDENT. It is sometimes held that in the absence of some limitation upon his authority, the president of a corporation has, by virtue of his office, authority to act as agent on behalf of the corporation within the scope of the business in which the corporation is empowered to engage.[26] There is authority, however, that the president has such broad powers only when he is the general manager of the corporation and then such powers stem from the office of general manager and not from that of president.[27] In any event, the president does not have authority by virtue of his office to make a contract which because of its unusual character would require action by the board of directors. The president, therefore, cannot make a contract to fix the compensation to be paid a director of the corporation, to make long-term or unusual contracts of employment, to bind the corporation as a guarantor, to release a claim of the corporation, or to promise that the corporation will later repurchase shares which are issued to a subscriber. Where the president of a family corporation owned approximately 80 percent of its stock and dominated the corporation, however, his agreement that an employee would receive retirement benefits was binding on the corporation without regard to the absence of approval or authorization by the board of directors.[28]

(b) OTHER OFFICERS. The authority of other officers, such as secretary or treasurer, is generally limited to the duties of their offices. Their authority may, however, be extended by the conduct of the corporation, in accordance with the general principles governing apparent authority based on the conduct of the principal.[29] An unauthorized act of an officer may, of course, be ratified.

(c) OFFICER AS GENERAL MANAGER. When an officer is placed in the position of a general manager, irrespective of the name given to the office, he has implied power to do such acts as are necessary to carry out the particular business. This power includes authority to employ an attorney to represent the corporation.[30] An officer, however, does not have authority to make contracts of an extraordinary nature, in the absence of proper authorization or ratification of his acts.

---

[26] *Pegram-West* v. *Winston Mutual Life Ins. Co.*, 231 N.C. 277, 56 S.E.2d 607.
[27] *Fletcher Oil Co.* v. *Bay City*, 346 Mich. 411, 78 N.W.2d 205.
[28] *Hessler Inc.* v. *Farrell*, [Del.] 226 A.2d 708.
[29] See p. 216.
[30] *New Mexico Potash & Chemical Co.* v. *Oliver*, 123 Col. 268, 228 P.2d 979.

3 / Liability of officers. The relation of the officers to the corporation, like that of the directors,[31] is a fiduciary relationship. For this reason, the officers are liable for secret profits made at the expense of the corporation.

> **Facts:** Brooks, Kinsel, and Remo were officers and directors of the Missouri Valley Limestone Co. In their corporate capacities they were sent out to locate new quarry lands so that the company could keep in business. They took a lease on land owned by Claar, but took it in their own names. Thereafter Snater, who owned 92 percent of the stock of the corporation, sold his stock to Schildberg Rock Products Co. Schildberg then sued Brooks, Kinsel, and Remo to require them to assign their lease of the Claar land to Schildberg.

> **Decision:** Judgment for Schildberg. The defendants, as officers and directors of the corporation, must be loyal to the corporation and cannot act so as to further their own interests at the expense of those of the corporation. It was to the interest of the corporation to acquire the lease. It desired to and could afford to do so. It was therefore improper for the defendants to take advantage of the lease for themselves. (Schildberg Rock Products Co. v. Brooks, [Iowa] 140 N.W.2d 132)

Officers are also liable for willful or negligent acts that cause a loss to the corporation. On the other hand, they are not liable for mere errors in judgment committed while exercising their discretion, provided they have acted with reasonable prudence and skill.[32]

Statutes commonly impose liability upon directors for commencing business before the statutory amount of capital has been paid in, making improper loans of corporate funds, declaring dividends from an improper source, purchasing shares of the corporation with improper funds, or distributing capital assets without making adequate provision for the payment of creditors. In addition, the directors may be liable for violating the Federal Securities Exchange Act or regulations adopted under the Securities and Exchange Commission, and a number of other federal statutes.

QUESTIONS AND PROBLEMS

1. Define quorum (621).

2. State the objective(s) of each of the following rules of law:

   (a) The action of shareholders at a meeting may ratify the action taken at an earlier meeting and cure the defect of an improper notice or lack of notice of the prior meeting.

   (b) If the corporation fails to sue a corporate officer for loss caused by him, shareholders may bring an action against the officer on behalf of the corporation.

---

[31] See p. 624.
[32] *Warner* v. *E. C. Warner Co.*, 226 Minn. 565, 33 N.W.2d 721.

3. The majority of the shareholders of a corporation approve of a proposal to alter its charter to engage in the manufacture of an entirely different product. Vincent, a shareholder in the corporation, refuses to consent to the change and contends that it cannot be made without his consent. Do you agree?

4. Walls desires to purchase certain land owned by a corporation. After drawing up a contract to sell, he makes his offer to each of the directors at his home and secures the signatures of all of them. Is this contract binding on the corporation?

5. The board of directors of a certain corporation decides to wind up the affairs of the business. Accordingly they enter into a contract to sell all of the corporate property to another company. Did they act within the scope of their authority?

6. Poole, a shareholder, brings an action against two directors of the business who have made a secret profit at the expense of the corporation. Poole is succesful in this action. What are Poole's rights in the money recovered?

7. Wellington receives credit from a corporation by depositing with it securities valued at $5,000. Porter, the treasurer of the corporation, later returns the securities to Wellington and releases him from liability without receiving payment. The corporation brings an action on the debt against Wellington. Is it entitled to judgment?

8. The directors of the American Founders Life Insurance Co. made a contract with the Colorado Management Corp. for certain services. American Founders later sued for the return of the money paid to Colorado on the ground that the contract could be set aside because it had been approved by American Founders at a board of directors' meeting at which only six of the eight directors were present and three of these directors were also directors of Colorado and two of them were also officers of Colorado. The bylaws of American Founders required a majority, which was five, to constitute a quorum for a directors' meeting. Was American Founders entitled to recover? (Colorado Management Corp. v. American Founders Life Insurance Co., 145 Colo. 413, 359 P.2d 665)

9. Cholfin and his wife were two of the three directors of the Allied Freightways Corporation. Cholfin ran the business, and his wife and the other director took no active part in its management. Cholfin unlawfully used $16,587.25 of the corporate funds to pay his own debts and $3,086.39 of the corporate funds to pay those of his wife. Allied Freightways brought suit to recover from the Cholfins the money improperly spent from the corporation. Allied Freightways claimed that each of the defendants was liable for the full amount of all improper expenditures. Was this correct? (Allied Freightways v. Cholfin, 325 Mass. 630, 91 N.E.2d 765)

PART X

Real Property

Chapter 55

Real Property—Deeds

The law of real property to a large extent uses a technical vocabulary drawn from the days of feudalism. Much of the earlier law of real property is no longer of practical importance in the modern business world. The following discussion is therefore a simplified, modern presentation of the subject.

NATURE AND TRANSFER

Definitions

Real property includes (1) land, (2) buildings and fixtures, and (3) rights in the land of another. Real property, like personal property, may have one or more owners.

1 / Land. Land means more than the surface of the earth. It embraces the soil and all things of a permanent nature affixed to the ground, such as herbs, grass, or trees, and other growing, natural products. The term also includes the waters upon the ground and things that are embedded beneath the surface. For example, coal, oil, and marble embedded beneath the surface form part of the land.

Technically, land is considered as extending downward to the earth's center and upward indefinitely. The Uniform Aeronautics Act states that the owner of land owns the space above, subject to the right of flight in aircraft which does not interfere with the use of the land and is not dangerous to persons or property lawfully on the land.[1]

---

[1] The Uniform Aeronautics Act (UAA) has been adopted in Arizona, Delaware, Georgia, Hawaii, Idaho, Indiana, Maryland, Minnesota, Missouri, Montana, Nevada, New Jersey, North Carolina, North Dakota, Pennsylvania, South Carolina, South Dakota, Tennessee, Utah, Vermont, and Wisconsin, but was withdrawn by the Commissioners on Uniform Laws in 1943.

Facts: Duncan owned a ranch. Airplanes of the Southwest Weather Research Inc. flew over the ranch and surrounding territory for the purpose of "seeding" clouds, a program that Research claimed prevented hail storms. Research had a contract with a number of farmers for this purpose. Duncan sued to enjoin such flights over his land on the ground that the seeding had dissipated clouds which, if permitted to remain, would have brought rain to his land.

Decision: Judgment for Duncan. As an owner of the land, Duncan had the right to receive rain from the clouds free from any interference with them. The act of Research was therefore a wrong to Duncan as a property owner, and he could prevent them from doing their wrongful act. (Southwest Weather Research Inc. v. Duncan, [Tex.Civ.App.] 319 S.W.2d 940)

2 / Buildings and fixtures. A *building* includes any structure placed on or beneath the surface of land, without regard to its purpose or use. A *fixture* includes personal property that is attached to the earth or placed in a building in such a way or under such circumstances that it is deemed part of the real property.[2]

3 / Rights in the land of another. These rights include easements, such as the right to cross another's land, and profits, such as the right to take coal from another's land.

Easements

An *easement* is not only a right in the land of another, but it is a right that belongs to the land which is benefited. The benefited land is called the *dominant tenement,* and the subject land is called the *servient tenement.*

An easement may be created by:

(1) Deed.

(2) Implication when one conveys part of this land that has been used as a dominant estate in relation to the part retained.[3] To illustrate, if water or drain pipes run from the part alienated through the part retained, there is an implied right to have such use continued. In order that an easement will be implied in such a case, the use must be apparent, continuous, and necessary. The last requirement is usually construed as meaning reasonably necessary.

(3) Implication when it is necessary to the use of the land alienated. This ordinarily arises when one sells land to which no entry can be made, except over the land retained, or over the land of a stranger. The right to use the land retained for the purpose of going to and from the land is known as a *way of necessity.*

---

[2] See p. 358.
[3] *Carter* v. *Michel,* 403 Ill. 610, 87 N.E.2d 759.

(4) Estoppel, as when the grantor states that the plot conveyed is bounded by a street. If, in such a case, the grantor owns the adjoining plot, he cannot deny the public the right to use the area which he has described as a street.

(5) Prescription by adverse use for a prescribed period.[4]

Duration and Extent of Ownership

The interest held by a person in real property may be defined in terms of the period of time for which he will remain the owner. He may have (1) a fee simple estate or (2) a life estate. These estates are termed *freehold estates.*[5] In addition, either of these estates may be subject to a condition or may expire or terminate upon the happening of a specified contingency. Although a person may own property for a specified number of years, this interest is not regarded as a freehold estate, but is a *leasehold estate* and is subject to different rules of law.[6]

1 / Fee simple estate. An *estate in fee, fee simple,* or a *fee simple absolute,* is the largest estate known to our law. The owner of such fee has the absolute and entire property in the land. The important characteristics of this estate are as follows: (a) it is alienable during life; (b) it is alienable by will; (c) it descends to heirs generally if not devised (transferred by will); (d) it is subject to rights of the owner's surviving spouse; and (e) it is liable for debts of the owner before or after death.

2 / Life estate. A *life estate* (or life tenancy), as its name indicates, lasts only during the life of a person, ordinarily its owner. Upon his death no interest remains to pass to his heirs or by his will.

Transferring Real Property

1 / Deed. The most common form of transfer of title to real property is by the delivery of a deed by the owner.[7]

2 / Public grant or patent. Real property may be acquired directly from the government. The method of transfer in such a case may be made by legislative grant or by patent. The latter method is commonly used by the federal government under the homestead laws.

3 / Dedication. Any person possessing a legal or equitable interest in land may appropriate it to the use of the public. This is known as a *dedication.* The real property must be set apart with the intention to surrender it to

---

[4] See p. 633.
[5] *Hartman* v. *Drake*, 166 Neb. 187, 87 N.W.2d 895.
[6] See p. 643.
[7] See p. 634.

the use of the public.[8] An acceptance is usually necessary on the part of the municipality or the state.

4 /Eminent domain.[9] Two important questions are involved in the transfer of property by eminent domain; namely, whether there is a taking of property and whether the property is intended for public use. In respect to the first, it is not necessary that one be physically deprived of his land. It is sufficient if he is denied the normal use of his property. It is not necessary that the public actually use the land. It is sufficient that it is appropriated for a purpose that is intended for the public benefit.

Facts: The Commonwealth of Pennsylvania proposed to take land by eminent domain in order to widen a highway. The effect of this would be to give better automobile access to the South Gate Shopping Center. The taking by eminent domain was objected to by Washington Park, which was a competing shopping center. Its objection was that the taking by eminent domain was improper because it would benefit private persons, the other shopping center, and not the public.

Decision: Judgment against Washington Park. The fact that there may be an individual or private benefit resulting from eminent domain does not impair the propriety of its exercise. The widening of the road would benefit travel by the public, and eminent domain is not concerned with why the public would want to travel on the road. (In re Legislative Route 62214, 425 Pa. 349, 229 A.2d 1)

5 / Accretion. The owner of land acquires or loses title to land that is added or taken away by the imperceptible action of water upon his property. An increase of land caused by the action of water upon its borders is known as *accretion.* This gain or increase may result from alluvion or dereliction. *Alluvion* occurs when soil or sand is washed up by the water and becomes attached to the land. *Dereliction* occurs when the water recedes, leaving bare land which was formerly a part of its bed. Thus, when the boundary line between two farms is the middle of a stream, gradual changes in the course of the stream add to the land on one side and take away from the land on the other.

6 / Adverse possession. Title to land may be acquired by holding it adversely to the true owner for a certain period of time. In such a case one gains title by *adverse possession.* If such adverse possession is maintained, the possessor automatically becomes the owner of the property even though he admittedly had no lawful claim to the land before.

In order to acquire title in this manner, possession must be (a) actual,[10] (b) visible and notorious so that the owner upon reasonable inspection of

---

[8] *Choals* v. *Plummer,* 353 Mich. 64, 90 N.W.2d 851.
[9] See p. 355.
[10] *Cusick* v. *Cutshaw,* 34 Tenn.App. 283, 237 S.W.2d 563.

the land could discover the presence of someone making an adverse claim, (c) exclusive as to third persons as well as the owner, (d) hostile [11] in the sense that the holding is under a claim inconsistent with the rights of the owner, and (e) continuous for a required period of years.

The period during which land must be held adversely in order to gain title varies in the different states. In many states the statute prescribes twenty or twenty-one years, whereas in others the period is less.

As a special exception to the requirement that adverse possession must be continued for a specific period, it is held that when the owners of neighboring lots have a bona fide dispute as to the location of the boundary line between them and in good faith agree upon and continue to recognize a boundary for a number of years, the boundary line will be deemed fixed where agreed although the time elapsed since the agreement is less than the adverse possession period.[12]

7 / Prescription. The right to use another's land for some purpose, as in the case of an easement, may be acquired by adverse use. This is known as *prescription.* The elements requisite to the acquiring of rights by prescription are practically the same as in adverse possession, except that the use need not be exclusive of others. A modification is also made in that continuous use is not literally required.

8 / Marriage. In most states, if the deceased spouse did not leave a will, the surviving spouse is given absolute ownership of a fractional share of all property owned by the other spouse at the date of death. Provision is generally made for varying the share inversely to the number of children or other heirs, for rejecting the provisions of a will that deprive the surviving spouse of the statutory share,[13] and sometimes for permitting a spouse to claim an interest in property conveyed during the deceased spouse's lifetime without the consent of the surviving spouse.

9 / Abandonment. Unlike personal property,[14] title to real estate generally cannot be lost or transferred by abandonment. However, an easement may be lost in most states by abandonment if such intent is clearly shown by affirmative acts, as distinguished from mere nonuse.[15]

DEEDS

Although many of the technical limitations of the feudal and old common-law days have disappeared, much of the law relating to the modern

---

[11] *Brewer* v. *Porch,* 93 N.J.S. 66, 224 A.2d 697.
[12] *Lake* v. *Crosser,* 202 Okla. 582, 216 P.2d 583.
[13] See Ch. 59.
[14] See p. 369.
[15] *Hatcher* v. *Chesner,* 422 Pa. 138, 221 A.2d 305.

deed originated in those days. For this reason the drawing of a deed to transfer the title to land should be entrusted only to one who knows exactly what must be done.

Definition of Deed

A *deed* is an instrument or writing by which an owner or *grantor* transfers or conveys an interest in land to a new owner called a *grantee* or transferee. In some states that have retained the influence of the common law, the deed must be sealed.[16]

Unlike a contract, no consideration is required to make a deed effective. Real property, as in the case of personal property, may either be sold or given as a gift. Although consideration is not required to make a valid deed or transfer of title by deed, the absence of consideration may be evidence to show that the transfer was made by the owner in fraud of his creditors, who may then be able to set aside the transfer.[17] A deed is necessary to transfer title to land, even though it is a gift.

Classification of Deeds

Deeds may be classified in terms of the interest conveyed as (1) a *quitclaim* deed, which transfers merely whatever interest, if any, the grantor may have in the property, without specifying that interest in any way, and (2) a *warranty deed,* which purports to transfer a specified interest and which warrants or guarantees that such interest is transferred.

A deed may also be classified as (1) a statutory deed or (2) a common-law deed. The *common-law deed* is a long form that sets forth the details of the transaction, such as the names of the parties, the consideration paid, the words of grant which declare that an interest is conveyed, and a description of the property in question; a description of the estate or interest in the property that is conveyed; [18] a description of any interests reserved by the grantor; a recital of any conditions imposed upon the grant and of any covenants made by the grantor or the grantee; and a recital of the execution of the deed by the grantor. The *statutory deed* eliminates much of the detail of the common-law form and in substance merely recites that a named person is making a certain conveyance to a named grantee.

Grantor's Warranties

In the common-law warranty deed the grantor expressly warrants or makes certain guarantees. The statutes authorizing a short form of deed

---

[16] *New Home Building Supply Co.* v. *Nations,* 259 N.C. 681, 131 S.E.2d 425.
[17] *Jones* v. *Seal,* [Tenn.App.] 409 S.W.2d 382.
[18] *Linder* v. *Horne,* 237 N.C. 129, 74 S.E.2d 227.

provide that unless otherwise stated in the deed, the grantor shall be presumed to have made certain warranties.

The more important of the covenants or warranties of title which the grantor may make are: (1) *covenant of seizin,* or guarantee that the grantor owns the exact estate which he has purported to convey; (2) *covenant of right to convey,* or guarantee that the grantor, if he is not the owner, as in the case of an agent, has the right or authority to make the conveyance; (3) *covenant against encumbrances,* or guarantee that the land is not subject to any right or interest of a third person, such as a lien, easement, or dower right; (4) *covenant for quiet enjoyment,* or covenant by the grantor that the grantee's possession of the land shall not be disturbed either by (a) the grantor, in the case of a limited covenant, or (b) the grantor or any person claiming title under him, in the case of a general covenant; and (5) *covenant for further assurances,* or promise by the grantor that he will execute any additional document that may be required to perfect the title of the grantee.

Facts: Johnson and his wife conveyed land to Old Falls, Inc. by a deed that contained a covenant against encumbrances. Unknown to all parties, there existed a public right of way across the land. Old Falls later sued the Johnsons for breach of the covenant because of this road.

Decision: A covenant against encumbrances is not broken by the existence of a public way across the land when the way is so apparent that the grantee must be regarded as accepting the covenant subject to the exception of the visible public way. If such way existed but was not so apparent, however, there is a breach of the covenant against encumbrances. It was therefore necessary for the jury to determine whether the public way was so used as to be apparent to the grantee. (Old Falls, Inc. v. Johnson, 88 N.J.S. 441, 212 A.2d 674)

In the absence of a warranty in the deed, no warranty arises. Unlike sales of personal property, there are no implied warranties in a sale or conveyance of land under the common law.

Execution of Deeds

Ordinarily a deed must be signed, by signature or mark,[19] and sealed by the grantor. In order to have the deed recorded, statutes generally require that two or more witnesses sign the deed and that the grantor then acknowledge his deed before a notary public or other officer. In the interest of legibility, it is frequently required that the signatures of the parties be followed by their printed or typewritten names.

The deed remains binding as between the grantor and his grantee even though it has not been acknowledged or recorded.

---

[19] *Witt* v. *Panek,* 408 Ill. 328, 97 N.E.2d 283.

Delivery

A deed has no effect and title does not pass until the deed has been delivered. Delivery is a matter of intent as shown by both words and conduct; no particular form of ceremony is required. The essential intent in delivering a deed is not merely that the grantor intends to hand over physical control and possession of the paper on which the deed is written, but that he intends to divest himself of ownership of the property described in the deed.[20] That is, he must deliver the deed with the intent that it should take effect as a deed and convey an interest in the property.

A deed is ordinarily made effective by handing it to the grantee with the intention that he should thenceforth be the owner of the property described in the deed. A delivery may also be made by placing the deed, addressed to the grantee, in the mail or by giving it to a third person with directions to hand it to the grantee.

When a deed is delivered to a third person for the purpose of delivery by him to the grantee upon the happening of some event or contingency, the transaction is called a *delivery in escrow*. No title passes until the fulfillment of the condition or the happening of the event or contingency.

Acceptance

Generally there must be an acceptance by the grantee. In the absence of statute no particular mode of acceptance is necessary. Acceptance may be proved by words, formal or informal, or by conduct or acts, such as conveying or mortgaging of the land, retaining the deed instead of returning it to the grantor, or asserting rights with respect to the land, such as cultivating it, which are incidents of ownership and inconsistent with nonownership.

A more practical statement of the rule is that in all cases an acceptance is presumed,[21] but the grantee may disclaim the transfer if he acts within a reasonable time after learning that the transfer has been made.

Cancellation of Deeds

A deed, although delivered, acknowledged, and recorded, may be set aside or canceled by the grantor upon proof of such circumstances as would warrant the setting aside of a contract. For example, when a conveyance is made in consideration of a promise to support the grantor, the failure of the grantee to perform will ordinarily justify cancellation of the deed.

Recording of Deeds

If the owner of the land desires to do so, he may record his deed in the office of a public official sometimes called a recorder or commissioner of

---

[20] *Lambert* v. *Lambert*, 77 R.I. 463, 77 A.2d 325.
[21] *Wilkie* v. *Elmore*, [Mo.] 395 S.W.2d 168.

deeds. The recording is not required to make the deed effective to pass title,[22] but it is done so that the public will know that the grantee is the present owner and thereby prevent the former owner from making any other transaction relating to the property. The recording statutes provide that a person purchasing land from the last holder of record will take title free of any unrecorded claim to the land of which the purchaser does not have notice or knowledge.

The fact that a deed is recorded charges all persons with knowledge of its existence even though they in fact do not know of it because they have neglected to examine the record. The recording of a deed, however, is only such notice if the deed was properly executed. Likewise, the grantee of the land cannot claim any protection by virtue of the recording of a deed when (1) an adverse claim is made by one whose title is superior to that of the owner of record; (2) the grantee had notice or knowledge of the adverse claim when he acquired title; (3) a person acting under a hostile claim was then in possession of the land; (4) the grantee received the land as a gift; or (5) the transfer to the grantee was fraudulent.

Additional Protection of Third Parties

Apart from the protection given to buyers and third persons by the recorded title to property, a buyer may generally also protect himself by procuring title insurance [23] or an *abstract of title,* which is a summarized report of the title to the property as shown by the records, together with a report of all judgments, mortgages, and similar claims against the property that have also been recorded. The buyer relies upon the accuracy with which the abstract has been made and the correctness of the interpretation given to it.

Donees and Purchasers with Notice

Donees or persons who do not give value and persons who have knowledge or notice of outstanding claims always take title to property subject to adverse claims, such as unrecorded deeds and equitable or statutory liens on the land.

Creditors of Grantor

The transfer of title under a deed may be defeated in some instances by creditors of the grantor.

1 / Fraudulent conveyances. Following an English statute,[24] it is held in most states that a conveyance for the purpose of hindering, delaying, or

---

[22] *Malamed* v. *Sedelsky,* 367 Pa. 353, 80 A.2d 853.
[23] *Shaver* v. *Title Guaranty & Trust Co.,* 163 Tenn. 232, 43 S.W.2d 212.
[24] Statute 13, Elizabeth, Ch. 5.

defrauding creditors is voidable as against such creditors. The rule is applicable in the case of subsequent creditors, as well as those existing at the time of the conveyance. For example, when one, just before entering into debt, makes a conveyance that he knows is likely to render him unable to pay his obligations, the subsequent creditor may avoid the conveyance. When the transfer is made to a bona fide purchaser without notice, the title passes under a deed free from the demands or claims of either existing or subsequent creditors. In any case the person who claims that a transfer of title has been made in fraud of creditors has the burden of proving that fact.[25]

Under the Uniform Fraudulent Conveyance Act [26] conveyances in certain situations are classified as being in fraud of creditors. If the claim of a defrauded creditor of the grantor is due, he may have the fraudulent conveyance set aside or he may disregard the conveyance and attach or levy execution upon the property conveyed, subject to whatever consideration has been paid by the grantee. If his claim has not matured, he may have the conveyance set aside or a receiver appointed or obtain such relief as may be appropriate.

2 / Federal Bankruptcy Act. Another situation in which the claims of creditors may defeat the passing of title is that in which the conveyance violates a provision of the Federal Bankruptcy Act. Under the provisions of that statute a conveyance that operates to give a preference to one creditor as against another may be set aside if the conveyance was made within four months prior to the time when the grantor was adjudged a bankrupt. The trustee in bankruptcy is also authorized to avoid any conveyance that is a fraud upon creditors.[27]

Grantee's Covenants

In a deed the grantee may undertake to do or to refrain from doing certain acts. Such an agreement becomes a binding contract between the grantor and the grantee. The grantor may sue the grantee for their breach. When the covenant of the grantee relates directly to the property conveyed, such as an agreement to maintain fences on the property or that the property shall be used only for residential purposes, it is said not only that the covenant is binding between the grantor and the grantee but also that it *runs with the land*. This means that anyone acquiring the grantee's land from the grantee is also bound by the covenant of the grantee, even though this subsequent owner had not made any such agreement with anyone.

[25] *Faiella* v. *Tortolani*, 76 R.I. 488, 72 A.2d 434.
[26] This Act has been adopted in Arizona, California, Delaware, Maryland, Massachusetts, Michigan, Minnesota, Montana, Nevada, New Hampshire, New Jersey, New Mexico, New York, North Dakota, Ohio, Oklahoma, Pennsylvania, South Dakota, Tennessee, Utah, Virgin Islands, Washington, Wisconsin, and Wyoming.
[27] See p. 703.

Similarly the right to enforce the covenant also runs with the land owned by the grantor to whom the promise was made.

A covenant which provides that the grantee shall refrain from certain conduct is termed a *restrictive* (or negative) *covenant*. It runs with the land in the same manner as a covenant that calls for the performance of an act, that is, an *affirmative covenant*. Negative covenants most commonly relate to the type of building that the purchaser will place on the land or the nature of the use to which he will put the land.

As a covenant is a contract, a grantee's covenant may be enforced by the grantor or an adjoining property owner intended to be benefited by the covenant.[28] The grantee's covenant may be enforced in an action at law for damages. In the case of restrictive or negative covenants, the complaining person may also obtain the aid of the equity jurisdiction that will grant an injunction compelling the owner of the land to comply with the terms of the covenant. Equitable relief is generally denied, however, in the case of affirmative covenants.

Relief, whether at law or in equity, will not be afforded when enforcement of the restriction would amount to a discrimination prohibited by the Fourteenth Amendment of the Constitution of the United States,[29] or when the circumstances and neighborhood have so changed that it would be absurd to continue to enforce the restriction. Thus restrictions in deeds delivered sixty years ago stipulating that no private automobile garages could be erected or maintained have frequently been held invalid in recent years because the auto is now so commonplace that its exclusion would be ridiculous and would now make the ownership of the property less valuable. Restrictions requiring that premises be used only for residential purposes may often be ignored when stores and other commercial or industrial enterprises have entered the neighborhood in such a large number that the character of the neighborhood is no longer predominantly residential. However, every change in character does not warrant an abandonment of a restrictive covenant.

Facts: Long owned real estate in what was designated as Block #2 of Harrodsburg, Kentucky. All lots in this block were subject to a restrictive covenant that they could only be used for residential purposes. A state highway was relocated so that it ran through Block #2, and from 400 to 500 motor vehicles passed on the highway per hour. A number of commercial enterprises had been built outside of but near Block #2. Long and others brought an action against Cochran and others owning property in Block #2 to determine whether this change of conditions released their land from the covenant that it be used only for residential purposes.

---

28 *Oak Lane Corp.* v. *Duke*, 196 Md.App. 136, 75 A.2d 80.
29 *Shelley* v. *Kraemer*, 334 U.S. 1; *Barrows* v. *Jackson*, 346 U.S. 249.

Decision: The covenant was binding. The changes were not sufficiently significant to justify the disregarding of the restrictive covenant, particularly since, apart from the highway, the changes that took place were outside of the restricted area. (Cochran v. Long, [Ky.App.] 294 S.W.2d 503)

Likewise the mere fact that the owner can make more money from the use of his property for commercial purposes is not in itself sufficient to justify ignoring the restriction that it be used for residential purposes.[30]

QUESTIONS AND PROBLEMS

1. Checklist of legal terms—nature and transfer of real property:
   (a) real property (629); land (629), building (630), fixture (630)
   (b) easement; dominant tenement, servient tenement; way of necessity (630)
   (c) freehold estate, leasehold estate (631)
   (d) estate in fee, life estate (631)
   (e) dedication (631)
   (f) accretion; alluvion, dereliction (632)
   (g) adverse possession (632), prescription (633)

2. State the objective(s) of each of the following rules of law:
   (a) Acceptance by the government is necessary to make a dedication effective.
   (b) A grantee's covenant relating to the use of the land generally runs with the land so as to bind a subsequent grantee although he made no agreement concerning the matter.

3. Garrison builds his house so that the eaves extend over the land of his neighbor. Has he violated a right of his neighbor?

4. Jeffries purchased a tract of land from Garr. At the time the land was surrounded partly by land belonging to Garr and partly by land belonging to other persons. Later Garr sold his remaining land to Orr who forbade Jeffries and his family to cross the land to reach a public road. Jeffries brought an action to compel Orr to allow him to cross Orr's land for the purpose of reaching the road. Was he entitled to judgment?

5. Orman, a prosperous businessman, wishes to appropriate a large tract of land that he owns to the use of the public as a park. How can he do so?

6. The Defense Department starts a training school in chemical warfare on land adjoining Sheriden's property. The fumes make it impossible for Sheriden to use his land. Is he entitled to compensation for his land?

7. William Martin went into possession of certain land, claiming that he was the owner. After a number of years he gave the land to his son, John, who kept possession of it, claiming that it was his land. Between the two of them, they were in possession of the land for more than

---

[30] *Cowherd Development Co. v. Littick*, 360 Mo. 1001, 238 S.W.2d 346.

twenty years. Some years later Jordan sued the son and claimed ownership of the land. Decide. (Martin v. Jordan, 117 Maine 574, 105 A. 104)

8. The South-West Lumber Co., a private corporation engaged in lumbering and logging, had large contracts with the United States and New Mexico. It wished to obtain land on which to build a spur log railroad line to link its mills with a forest that would furnish about 18 years' supply of lumber. It brought an action to condemn a strip of the land of Threlkeld for a right of way. Was it entitled to acquire the property by eminent domain? (Threlkeld v. Third Judicial District Court, 36 N.Mex. 350, 15 P.2d 671)

9. Checklist of legal terms—deeds:
   (a) deed; grantor, grantee (634)
   (b) quitclaim deed, warranty deed (634)
   (c) common-law deed, statutory deed (634)
   (d) covenant of seizin, covenant of right to convey, covenant against encumbrances, covenant for quiet enjoyment, covenant for further assurances (635)
   (e) delivery in escrow (636)
   (f) abstract of title (637)
   (g) runs with the land (638)
   (h) restrictive covenant, affirmative covenant (639)

10. Walden brought an action against Stamper to settle the title to certain land. Walden's title had been obtained through Horner, who had received a quitclaim deed from Lueders, who was admitted to have been the absolute owner of the property at the time he executed the deed. Walden contended that the grantee under the quitclaim deed from Lueders had become the absolute owner. Do you agree?

11. Howell and his wife conveyed a certain lot to Freeberg. The deed contained a covenant for quiet enjoyment. Later Freeberg was evicted from the land by persons who were mere trespassers having no title to the land and no right to the possession of it. Freeberg brought an action against Howell and his wife, contending that there was a breach of warranty. Do you agree?

12. Lunsford, who executed and acknowledged a deed with the name of the grantee omitted, placed the instrument in his desk. Lunsford's brother, who had a key to the desk, removed the deed and wrote in the name of Hodges as grantee without Lunsford's consent. Hodges conveyed the property to Perry. Perry then brought an action to eject Lunsford from the premises. Was he entitled to judgment?

13. Schott executes a deed to convey a house and lot to Moxley. Moxley refuses to accept the deed. Pratt, who is injured because of the poor condition of the walks in front of this house, brings an action for damages against Moxley. A statute makes the owner of property liable for the care of sidewalks. Is Pratt entitled to judgment against Moxley?

14. Stine conveyed his house and lot by deed to Herzog on August 16. On September 5 of the same year Stine conveyed this property to Curry, who took possession. Herzog brought a suit against Curry for possession of the property. At the trial Herzog proved that his deed had been recorded on August 17. Curry proved that the deed on record had only one witness instead of the two required by law. Was Herzog entitled to judgment?

15. Dial conveyed the minerals underlying certain land to Cutter. Cutter conveyed these minerals to Kahn, who in turn conveyed them to the Merz Iron, Coal, and Coke Company. This last deed was not properly certified and recorded. After making the conveyance to Cutter, Dial conveyed the land to Rahe, who had knowledge of Dial's former transfer. Rahe brought an action against the coal company to quiet title to the minerals. Was he entitled to judgment?

16. After obtaining an abstract of title that disclosed no encumbrances, Rybolt purchased a house and lot from Saunders. Saunders conveyed the property to Rybolt by means of a warranty deed. Under what circumstances would there be a possibility of loss to Rybolt?

17. Abraham, who was in debt to several retail stores, made no effort to pay his obligations. He conveyed certain land without consideration to his wife with the intent to hinder, delay, and defraud his creditors, leaving only a lot worth $2,000 and his earnings as a laborer for the satisfaction of his creditors' claims. His creditors brought a suit to set aside the conveyance to Mrs. Abraham. Were they entitled to judgment?

18. While insolvent, Angelo conveys a vacant lot to Bovard, one of his creditors. The value of the lot equals the amount that Angelo owes Bovard. Two months later Angelo is judicially declared a bankrupt. The trustee in bankruptcy brings a suit to have this deed set aside. Is he entitled to judgment?

19. Castlewood Terrace is a residential district which by the original deed of 1896 could only be used for single-family residences. Paschen wanted to build a high-rise apartment in the area. Paschen brought an action for a declaratory judgment that Pashkow could not do so. Pashkow claimed that the restrictive covenant was no longer binding because a school had been built in the area and that the value of his land would be more than doubled if used for a high-rise apartment than if used for a single-family dwelling. Was the covenant binding? (Paschen v. Pashkow, 63 Ill.App.2d 56, 211 N.E.2d 576)

Chapter 56

Leases

The relation of landlord and tenant exists whenever one person holds possession of the real property of another under an express or implied agreement.

CREATION AND TERMINATION

The person who owns the real property and permits the occupation of the premises is known as the *landlord* or *lessor*. The *tenant* or *lessee* is the one who occupies the property. A *lease* establishes the relationship of landlord and tenant. It is in effect a conveyance of the leasehold estate in land.[1] The term "lease" is also used to designate the paper that is evidence of this transfer of interest and sets forth its terms.

Essential Elements in Relationship

The following elements are necessary in the establishment of the relation of landlord and tenant:

(1) The occupation must be with the express or implied consent of the landlord.

(2) The tenant must occupy the premises in subordination to the rights of the landlord. To illustrate, the relation is not established if the person occupying the land claims ownership of the property.

(3) A reversionary interest in the land must remain in the landlord. That is, the landlord must be entitled to retake the possession of the land upon the expiration of the lease.

(4) The tenant must have an estate in the land of present possession. This means that he must have a right that entitles him to be in possession of the land now.

The requirement that a tenant have possession distinguishes the tenant's interest from the interests of others in the land. A person may receive permission from the owner of land to erect and maintain a billboard on the owner's land. This is merely a *license* and does not create a leasehold interest. Similarly, a person having a right of way, or a right to cross, over his

---

[1] *Tri-Bullion Corp.* v. *American Smelting & Refining Co.*, 58 N.Mex. 787, 277 P.2d 293.

643

neighbor's land is not in possession of that land. He has merely an easement and is not a tenant of the neighbor. A tenant also differs from a *sharecropper*, for the latter is in substance the servant of the landlord who is paid by a share of the crops he raises.

Classifications of Tenancies

Tenancies are divided into four classes in terms of the duration of the estate created:

1 / Tenancy for years. A *tenancy for years* is one under which the tenant has an estate of definite duration. The term "for years" is used to describe such a tenancy even though the duration of the tenancy is for only one year or for less than a year, and even though the lease may be terminated by notice.

The right to terminate the lease upon notice may be made dependent upon the occurrence of a specified event or condition. Thus the lease may provide that when a tenant rents a store in a shopping center, the tenant shall have the right to terminate by notice in the event that a specified supermarket ceases to be a tenant in the development area.[2]

2 / Tenancy from year to year. A *tenancy from year to year* is one under which a tenant, holding an estate in land for an indefinite period of duration, pays an annual rent. A distinguishing feature of this tenancy is the fact that it does not terminate at the end of a year, except upon proper notice.

In almost all states a tenancy from year to year is implied if the tenant holds over after a tenancy for years[3] with the consent of the landlord, as shown by his express statement or by conduct such as continuing to accept rent. The landlord may reject the holding over, however, and the tenant is then a trespasser. The lease will frequently state that a holding over shall give rise to a tenancy from year to year unless written notice to the contrary be given, or will expressly provide for an extension or renewal of the lease.

Facts: Balaco rented property to Wanous for a term of years. The lease gave Wanous the option to purchase the property. The term of the lease expired, but Wanous remained in possession and paid Balaco rent. He later notified Balaco that he exercised the option to purchase the property. Balaco denied that Wanous had any option to purchase the property.

Decision: Judgment for Balaco. The holding over after the expiration of the original tenancy and the payment of rent did not renew the original lease; it created a new tenancy. An option to purchase found in the

---

[2] *Lilac Variety, Inc.* v. *Dallas Texas Co.,* [Tex.Civ.App.] 383 S.W.2d 193.
[3] *Hemberger* v. *Hagemann,* 120 Colo. 431, 210 P.2d 995.

original lease does not carry over into the new tenancy. (Wanous v. Balaco, 412 Ill. 545, 107 N.E.2d 791)

A lease may run from month to month or from week to week in the same manner as a lease from year to year.

3 / Tenancy at will. When land is held for an indefinite period, which may be terminated at any time by the landlord, or by the landlord and the tenant acting together, a *tenancy at will* exists. A person who enters into possession of land for an indefinite period with the owner's permission but without any reservation of rent is a tenant at will.[4] An agreement that a person can move into an empty house and live there until he finds a home to buy creates a tenancy at will.

Statutes in some states and decisions in others require advance notice of the termination of this type of tenancy.

4 / Tenancy by sufferance. When a tenant holds over without permission of the landlord, the latter may treat him as a trespasser or as a tenant. Until he elects to do one or the other, a *tenancy by sufferance* exists.

Creation of the Relation

The relation of landlord and tenant is created by an express or implied contract. An oral lease is valid at common law, but statutes in most states require written leases for certain tenancies. Many statutes follow the English Statute of Frauds, which provides that a lease for a term exceeding three years must be in writing. Statutes in other states require written leases when the term exceeds one year. Some courts apply to leases the provision of the Statute of Frauds which states that an agreement not to be performed within the space of one year from its execution shall be in writing. When a writing is required by the Statute of Frauds for a lease, it is also necessary that there be a sufficient memorandum for a modification of the lease.[5]

Terms of Lease

Ordinarily a lease need not be in any particular form of language, provided it is clear and definite, showing an intention to transfer possession of the premises by lease.

Some obligations of the parties specified in the lease are described as covenants. Thus a promise by the tenant to make repairs is called a *covenant to repair*. Sometimes it is provided that the lease shall be forfeited or terminated upon a breach of a promise, and the provision is then called a *condition* rather than a covenant.

---

[4] *Gretkowski* v. *Wojciechowski*, 26 N.J.S. 245, 97 A.2d 701.
[5] *Gunderson* v. *Friden*, [C.A. 6th] 372 F.2d 303.

Facts: Reno Press Brick Co. leased land to Nevada Food King. The lease stated: "Lessor shall not lease any property owned by it in that general vicinity for operation of a retail grocery, or meat market, nor shall itself operate the same." The lease specifically defined the area covered by the term "general vicinity." Thereafter Reno decided to develop a shopping center in the area, which center would include a food supermarket on the lot adjoining the "general vicinity." Reno Press brought an action for a declaratory judgment to determine its right to do so.

Decision: Judgment for Reno. A restrictive covenant is not to be extended beyond its express terms. The prohibition applied to the defined area so that no restriction existed as to other land owned by Reno that was outside the defined area. As the parties did not make any broader prohibition, the court would not rewrite the lease on the theory that the competition of the neighboring supermarket would be inconsistent with the spirit or the object of the restrictive covenant. (Nevada Food King v. Reno Press Brick Co., 81 Nev. 135, 400 P.2d 140)

Termination of Lease

A lease is generally not terminated by the death, insanity, or bankruptcy of either party, except in the case of a tenancy at will.

1 / Expiration of term in a tenancy for years. When a tenancy for years exists, the relation of landlord and tenant ceases upon the expiration of the agreed term, without any requirement that one party give the other any notice of termination. Express notice to end the term may be required of either or both parties by provisions in the lease, except when a statute prohibits imposing such a requirement.

2 / Notice in a tenancy from year to year. A tenancy from year to year may be terminated at the end of a period by a prior notice to quit by the landlord or a notice of intention to quit by the tenant. In the absence of an agreement or a statute to the contrary, the landlord wishing to end the tenancy from year to year at the end of a period is required to give notice. The tenant is also usually required to give notice of his intention to quit. When either of them fails to give any necessary notice, the other party may elect to continue the relation for another period.

In the absence of an agreement of the parties, notice is now usually governed by statutes. Thirty or sixty days' notice is generally required to end a tenancy from year to year. As to tenancies for periods of less than a year, the provisions of the statute may require only one week.

A notice to quit or the notice of intention to quit must be definite. Statute or lease provision may require that it be written. No particular words are necessary to constitute a sufficient notice, provided the words used clearly indicate the intention of the party.

3 / Release. The relation of landlord and tenant is terminated if the landlord makes a release or conveyance of his interest in the land to the tenant.

4 / Merger. If the tenant acquires the landlord's interest in any manner, as by inheritance or purchase, the leasehold interest is said to disappear by merger into the title to the land now held by the former tenant. The result is the same if the tenant has an estate for years and inherits a life estate in the same premises because a life estate is regarded as a greater interest.

5 / Surrender. A surrender or giving up by the tenant of his estate to the landlord terminates the tenancy if the surrender is accepted by the latter. A surrender may be made expressly or impliedly.

An express surrender must, under the Statute of Frauds, be in writing and signed by the person making the surrender or by his authorized agent.

A surrender by operation of law occurs only when the acts of the parties clearly show that both consider that the premises have been surrendered, as when the premises have been abandoned by the tenant and their return has been accepted by the landlord. An acceptance may be inferred from the conduct of the landlord, but such conduct must clearly indicate an intention to accept. The mere taking of possession and re-entry by the landlord does not in itself prove an acceptance [6] as he has the right to enter for the purpose of protecting or repairing the premises, and an entrance for that purpose or the performance of such work will not convert an abandonment by the tenant into a surrender and an acceptance. The same is true when the landlord leases the property to another tenant, or relets. Whether an acceptance of a surrender is implied in such a case depends on whether the landlord relets on his own or on the tenant's account in order to produce a rent to be applied in reduction of the landlord's claim against the tenant.

6 / Forfeiture. The landlord may terminate the tenancy by forfeiting the relation because of the tenant's misconduct or breach of a condition, if a term of the lease or a statute so provides. In the absence of such a provision the landlord may only make a claim for damages.[7] This method of terminating the relation is not favored by courts, and the terms of a lease providing for a forfeiture are construed strictly against the landlord and limited to the grounds specified in the lease.

7 / Destruction of property. Either by express provision in the lease or by a statute, the destruction of the building releases the tenant from his liability or reduces the amount of rent in proportion to the loss sustained.

---

[6] *Kanter* v. *Safran*, [Fla.] 68 So.2d 553.
[7] *Wehrle* v. *Landsman*, 23 N.J.S. 40, 92 A.2d 525.

Such statutes do not impose upon the landlord any duty to repair or restore the property to its former condition. When the lease covers rooms or an apartment in a building, a destruction of the leased premises terminates the lease.

TENANT AND LANDLORD

The rights and duties of the tenant and landlord relate to such matters as possession and use of the premises, rent, repairs and improvements, taxes and assessments, liability for injury on the premises, and assignment of the lease and subletting.

Rights and Duties

1 / Possession. Possession involves both the right to acquire possession at the beginning of the lease and the right to retain possession until the lease is ended.

(a) TENANT'S RIGHT TO ACQUIRE POSSESSION. By making a lease, the landlord impliedly covenants that he will give possession of the premises to the tenant at the agreed time. If the landlord rents a building which is being constructed, there is an implied covenant that it will be ready for occupancy at the commencement of the term of the lease.[8]

(b) TENANT'S RIGHT TO RETAIN POSSESSION. After the tenant has entered into possession, he has exclusive possession and control of the premises as long as the lease continues and so long as he is not in default under the lease, unless the lease otherwise provides. Thus the tenant can refuse to allow the landlord to enter the property for the purpose of showing it to prospective customers, although today most leases expressly give this right to the landlord.

If the landlord interferes with this possession by evicting the tenant, he commits a wrong for which the tenant is afforded legal redress. An *eviction* exists when the tenant is deprived of the possession, use, and enjoyment of the premises by the interference of the landlord or one acting under him. If the landlord wrongfully deprives the tenant of the use of one room when he is entitled to the use of the whole building, there is a *partial eviction.*

Facts: Hagedorn rented a farm to Dinkel for a three-year term. Before the term had expired, Dinkel acquired a farm in another county, locked up the rented farm, and moved to the new farm. Before the lease on the rented farm expired, Hagedorn moved into the farm. When Dinkel came back within the period of the lease to get his property and stored crops,

---

[8] *Canady* v. *Krueger,* 156 Neb. 287, 56 N.W.2d 123.

Hagedorn did not let him take them. Dinkel sued Hagedorn for eviction. The defense was raised that there was no eviction since Dinkel had voluntarily left the farm.

Decision: Judgment for Dinkel. An eviction does not require an expulsion of the tenant by force. Whenever the landlord enters the premises before the expiration of the lease and holds possession in a manner inconsistent with the rights of the tenant under the lease, there is an eviction. (Dinkel v. Hagedorn, 156 Neb. 419, 56 N.W.2d 464)

Most written leases today contain an express covenant to protect the tenant in the quiet enjoyment of his possession.

(c) Constructive Eviction. An eviction may be actual or constructive. It is a *constructive eviction* when some act or omission of the landlord substantially deprives the tenant of the use and enjoyment of the premises.[9] It is essential in a constructive eviction that the landlord intend to deprive the tenant of the use and enjoyment of the premises. This intent may, however, be inferred from the results of his conduct. The tenant must also abandon the premises in consequence of the landlord's conduct. If he continues to occupy the premises for more than a reasonable time after the acts claimed to constitute a constructive eviction, he is deemed to waive the eviction. He cannot thereafter abandon the premises and claim that he has been evicted.[10]

A landlord commits a constructive eviction when he intentionally drives the tenant out of the property by shutting off the heat, gas, or water supply, or keeps him from entering the property by refusing to operate the elevators.

2 / Use of premises. The lease generally specifies the use to which the tenant may put the property and authorizes the landlord to adopt regulations with respect to the use of the premises that are binding upon the tenant as long as they are reasonable, lawful, and not in conflict with the terms of the lease. In the absence of express or implied restrictions, a tenant is entitled to use the premises for any purpose for which they are adapted or for which they are ordinarily employed, or in a manner contemplated by the parties in executing the lease. He is under an implied duty to use the premises properly even when the lease is silent as to the matter. What constitutes proper use of the premises depends, in the first place, upon the wording of the lease. The tenant is also under an implied duty to use the premises for lawful purposes.

The tenant is under an implied duty to refrain from willful or permissive waste. At common law the tenant of farm land is entitled to cut sufficient

---

[9] *South Falls Corp.* v. *Kalkstein*, [C.A.5th] 349 F.2d 378.
[10] *Abbott* v. *McCoy*, 208 Okla. 224, 254 P.2d 997.

timber for fuel and for repairs to fences, buildings, and farm implements. This rule is extended in many jurisdictions to allow the tenant to clear timber to a reasonable degree so that he may put the land under cultivation. If this would involve any substantial area, it is likely that the lease would define the rights of the parties in this respect.

3 / Rent. The tenant is under a duty to pay rent as compensation to the landlord.[11] In times of emergency, war, and recovery from war, however, government may impose maximum limitations on rents that are charged. When a business is conducted on the leased premises, it is quite common to provide for both a base rent and an additional rent that is computed as a percentage of the sales made by the tenant.

It is generally held that a tenant is not excused from paying the rent because government restrictions prevent him from obtaining the goods which he expected to sell in the rented property.[12]

The time of payment of rent is ordinarily fixed by the lease. When the lease does not control, rent generally is not due until the end of the term. Statutes or custom, however, may require rent to be paid in advance when the agreement of the parties does not regulate the point. Rent that is payable in crops is generally payable at the end of the term.

If the lease is assigned, the assignee is liable to the landlord for the rent. The assignment, however, does not in itself discharge the tenant from his obligations under the lease. The landlord may bring an action for the rent against either the tenant or the assignee, or both, but he is entitled to only one satisfaction. A sublessee ordinarily is not liable to the original lessor for rent, unless he assumes such liability or unless the liability is imposed by statute.

4 / Repairs. In the absence of an agreement to the contrary, the tenant has the duty to make those repairs that are necessary to prevent waste and decay of the premises, and he is liable for *permissive waste* if he fails to do so. When the landlord leases only a portion of the premises, or leases the premises to different tenants, he is under a duty to make repairs in connecting parts, such as halls, basements, elevators, and stairways, which are under his control. Some statutes require that a landlord who leases a building for dwelling purposes must keep it in condition fit for habitation.[13]

Most states deny the landlord the right to enter the leased premises to inspect them except when the right is expressly reserved in the lease.

5 / Improvements. In the absence of special agreement, neither the tenant nor the landlord is under a duty to make improvements. Either may,

---

[11] For the effect of destruction of the premises on the duty to pay rent, see p. 647.
[12] *Wood* v. *Bartolina*, 48 N.Mex. 175, 146 P.2d 883.
[13] *Michaels* v. *Brookchester*, 26 N.J. 379, 140 A.2d 199.

however, make a covenant for improvements, in which case a failure to perform will render him liable in an action for damages for breach of contract brought by the other party. In the absence of an agreement to the contrary, improvements that are attached to the land become part of the realty and belong to the landlord.[14]

6 / Taxes and assessments. In the absence of an agreement to the contrary, the landlord and not the tenant is usually under a duty to pay taxes or assessments. If the tax or assessment, however, is chargeable to improvements made by the tenant that do not become a part of the property, the tenant is liable.[15]

If the tenant pays taxes or assessments to protect his interests, he may recover the amount, including damages, from the landlord, or withhold the amount from the rent.

When the premises are assigned by the tenant, the assignee is bound by any covenants of the tenant to pay taxes and assessments. Such covenants are said to "run with the land." The fact that the assignee is bound by the covenants does not, however, discharge the tenant from liability.

A sublessee is not bound by the covenants of the tenant, but he may expressly assume them. In the latter case, however, the tenant is not discharged from his covenants.

Remedies of Landlord

1 / Landlord's lien. In the absence of an agreement or statute so providing, the landlord does not have a lien upon the personal property or crops of the tenants for money due him for rent. The parties may create by express or implied contract, however, a lien in favor of the landlord for rent, and also for advances, taxes, or damages for failure to make repairs.

2 / Suit for rent. Whether or not the landlord has a lien for unpaid rent, he may sue the tenant on the latter's contract to pay rent as specified in the lease or, if payment of rent is not specified, he may enforce a quasi-contractual obligation to pay.

3 / Distress. The common law has devised a speedy remedy to aid the landlord in collecting his rent. It permits him to seize personal property found on the premises and to hold it until the arrears are paid. This right is known as *distress*. It is not an action against the tenant for rent, but merely a right to retain the property as security until the rent is paid. Statutes have generally either abolished or greatly modified the right of distress, as by giving the landlord the right to sell the distrained property.

---

[14] As to the removal of improvements as trade fixtures, see p. 360.
[15] *Witschger* v. *Kamages*, 275 App.Div. 1053, 92 N.Y.S.2d 846.

4 / Recovery of possession. It is commonly provided in a lease that upon the breach of any of its provisions by the tenant, such as the failure to pay rent, the lease shall terminate or the landlord may, at his option, declare it terminated. When the lease is terminated, the landlord then has the right to evict the tenant and retake possession of the property.

Liabilities for Injuries on Premises

1 / Landlord's liability to tenant. In the absence of a covenant to keep the premises in repair, the landlord is ordinarily not liable to the tenant for the latter's personal injuries caused by the defective condition of the premises that are by the lease placed under the control of the tenant. In other words, the landlord makes no implied warranty as to safeness.[16] He is, however, liable to the tenant for injuries caused by nonapparent defects of which the landlord had knowledge.[17]

Facts: The Golf Club Co. owned an apartment house and leased one of the apartments to Rothstein. In back of the apartment house was a grassy area which dropped off into a ravine. There was no protecting fence or other barrier to prevent someone from falling into the ravine. While playing on the grassy area, Rothstein's child fell down the ravine and was injured. Rothstein sued the Golf Club Co.

Decision: Judgment for Golf Club Co. The condition of the grassy plot and the unguarded ravine was obvious to everyone when Rothstein rented his apartment. (Golf Club Co. v. H. I. Rothstein, 97 Ga.App. 128, 102 S.E.2d 654)

When the landlord has agreed as a term of the lease, or by a subsequent contract, to make repairs, some courts hold that the tenant may recover in a tort action for injuries he receives. Other courts hold that he has only a right of action for breach of contract. Such a covenant, however, does not make the landlord an insurer of the tenant.

When the landlord retains control of part of his building or land that is rented to others, he is liable to a tenant who is injured because of the defective condition of such retained portion if the condition was the result of his failure to exercise the proper degree of care. And when by statute it is made the landlord's duty to remove snow and ice but he is negligent in failing to do so, a tenant injured thereby may recover damages from him, although the lease contained a clause exculpating the landlord, because such a clause is deemed void when the landlord negligently breaches his statutory duty.[18]

---

16 *Luedtke* v. *Phillips,* 190 Va.App. 207, 56 S.E.2d 80.
17 *Hacker* v. *Nitschke,* 310 Mass. 754, 39 N.E.2d 644.
18 *Feldman* v. *Stein Building & Lumber Co.,* 6 Mich.App. 180, 148 N.W.2d 544.

2 / Landlord's liability to third persons. If the landlord retains control over a portion of the premises, he is liable for injuries to third persons caused by his failure to exercise proper care in connection with that part of the premises. Thus a landlord who rents different parts of a building to various tenants and retains control of the stairways, passageways, hallways, or other methods of approach to the several portions of the building for the common use of the tenants, has resting upon him an implied duty to use reasonable care to keep such places in a reasonably safe condition, and he is generally liable for injuries which are sustained by persons lawfully in the building from a breach of such duty. The landlord of an apartment house who reserves control of and operates the elevators in the building is liable for neglect in the maintenance and operation of the elevators to persons lawfully in the building.

The owner may obtain financial protection from such liability by insurance against public liability, including not only liability to the general public but also tenants and their guests.

3 / Tenant's liability to third persons. Liability follows control. A tenant in complete possession has control of the property and is therefore liable when his failure to use due care under the circumstances causes harm to (a) *licensees*, or persons whom he permits on the premises, such as a person allowed to use his telephone, and (b) *invitees*, or persons whom he induces or desires to come on the premises, such as customers entering his store. With respect to both classes of third persons, the liability of the tenant is the same as any owner in possession of his property.[19] It is likewise immaterial whether the property is used for residential, commercial, or manufacturing purposes, provided the tenant has control of the area where the injury occurs.

The liability of the tenant to third persons is not affected by the fact that the landlord may have contracted in the lease to make repairs, which if made would have avoided the injury. The tenant can obtain financial protection, however, in the same manner that the landlord can, by procuring public liability insurance to indemnify him for loss by claims of third persons.

Transfer of Rights

1 / Transfer of reversionary interest. The reversionary interest of the landlord may be transferred voluntarily by his act, or involuntarily by a judicial or execution sale. The tenant then becomes the tenant of the new owner of the reversionary interest, and the new owner is bound by the terms of the lease.[20]

---

[19] *Mitchell* v. *Thomas*, 91 Mont. 370, 8 P.2d 639.
[20] *Bender* v. *Kaelin*, 257 Ky. 783, 79 S.W.2d 250.

2 / Assignment of lease and sublease. An *assignment of a lease* is a transfer by the tenant of his entire interest in the premises to a third person. A tenancy for years may be assigned by the tenant unless he is restricted from doing so by the terms of the lease or by statute.[21]

The lease may contain provisions denying the right to assign or sublet or imposing specified restrictions on the privilege of assigning or subletting. Such restrictions are enforceable in order to enable the landlord to preserve control of his property. A no-assignment clause is strictly construed, but it generally does not apply to a change in business organization of the tenant when there is no actual change of use or identity of the persons using the premises.

Since the provision restricting the right of the tenant to assign the lease or requiring the landlord's written consent thereto is for the benefit of the landlord, it may be waived by him.[22] In the case of commercial leasing when the difference between tenants relates primarily to financial standing rather than the way in which the property will be used, the landlord may be under the duty to waive the no-assignment clause and to accept a financially-sound subtenant in order to reduce his claim against the original tenant for rent.

Facts: Scheinfeld, doing business as Greenleaf Investors, leased a warehouse to Muntz TV, Inc. Thereafter, with Greenleaf's written consent, Muntz sublet the warehouse to Breuer Electric Mfg. Co. It later decided to sublet to Calumet Mfg. Co., but Greenleaf refused to consent thereto. Breuer vacated the premises. Scheinfeld then proceeded against Muntz TV for the full rent. Muntz TV claimed that it was only liable for the difference between the full rent and the rent that Calumet would have paid.

Decision: The tenant was only liable for the differential amount and not for the full rent specified in his lease. When a tenant proposes to sublet commercial property to a third person, the landlord is required to accept such third person as the new tenant if he is commercially acceptable and there is no reasonable ground for rejecting him. If the landlord refuses to do so, he cannot then hold the original tenant liable for the full rental in the original lease but only for the difference between that rental and the amount that the proposed subtenant would pay. (Scheinfeld v. Muntz TV, Inc., 67 Ill.App.2d 8, 214 N.E.2d 506)

A *sublease* is a transfer of the premises by the tenant to a third person, the *sublessee*, for a period less than the term of the lease. The rules governing assignment are also applicable to subletting. In both cases restrictions in the lease are construed liberally in favor of the tenant. An ineffectual

---

[21] *MacFadden-Deauville Hotel* v. *Murrell*, [C.A.5th] 182 F.2d 537.
[22] *R.F.C.* v. *Home Investment Co.*, 221 Ark. 131, 252 S.W.2d 398.

attempt to assign or sublet does not violate a provision prohibiting such acts. This is equally true when another is merely permitted to use the land. As a general rule a transfer of all or part of the premises by operation of law is not a breach of such a provision. The lease, however, may give the landlord the right to avoid the lease in such a case.

As neither the act of subletting nor the landlord's agreement to it releases the original tenant from liability under the terms of the original lease, it is customary and desirable for the tenant to require the sublessee to covenant or promise that he will perform all obligations under the original lease and that he will indemnify the tenant for any loss caused by default of the sublessee. An express covenant or promise by the sublessee is necessary to impose liability upon him. The fact that the sublease is made "subject" to the terms of the original lease merely recognizes the superiority of the original lease, but does not impose any duty upon the sublessee to perform the tenant's obligations under the original lease.[23] If the sublessee promises the tenant that he will assume the obligation of the original lease, the landlord, as a third-party beneficiary, may sue the sublessee for breach of the provisions of the original lease.[24] In contrast with a sublease, when the lease is assigned and the assignee takes possession of the property, he becomes bound by the terms of the lease.

An assignment or a sublease must be in writing when the term transferred or sublet is of such duration that a writing would be required if any original lease were made for that period.

QUESTIONS AND PROBLEMS

1. Checklist of legal terms—creation and termination:
   (a) lease; landlord or lessor, tenant or lessee (643)
   (b) license (643)
   (c) sharecropper (644)
   (d) tenancy for years (644), tenancy from year to year (644), tenancy at will (645), tenancy by sufferance (645)
   (e) covenant to repair, condition (645)

2. State the objective(s) of each of the following rules of law:
   (a) A notice to terminate a tenancy from year to year must be definite.
   (b) The landlord is liable to third persons for injuries due to the condition of those parts of the rented building over which the landlord retains control.

3. Carroll, the owner of a hotel building, leases the premises to Ellison. The terms of the lease prohibit any transfer by the tenant without the consent of the landlord. Carroll consents to an assignment of the lease

---

[23] *Coles Trading Co.* v. *Spiegel*, [C.A.9th] 187 F.2d 989.
[24] *Shearer* v. *United Carbon Co.*, 143 W.Va. 482, 103 S.E.2d 883.

to a partnership composed of Joerger and Karnes. Later Galvin enters the partnership. Galvin now claims that the relation of landlord and tenant exists between Carroll and him. Do you agree?

4. Kato agreed to execute a lease of his property to McKinsey on the first day of the following month. Did this transaction create a relation of landlord and tenant between the parties?

5. For a consideration McMillan gave the Penrod Bill Posting Company the exclusive privilege of erecting and using a signboard to be located on McMillan's land. According to the agreement McMillan reserved the right in the event that he sold the property to cancel all privileges upon returning to the company a pro rata amount of the consideration for the unexpired term of the agreement. In an action brought by McMillan against the company, it was contended that this transaction did not create the relation of landlord and tenant. Do you agree?

6. Penley leases Ruff's house and lot for 12 months. Penley contends that he holds the property under a tenancy for years. Ruff contends that Penley holds the property under a tenancy from year to year. With which party do you agree?

7. Rubin held certain farm land under a tenancy that terminated at the end of the calendar year. Without the permission of Samuelson, the landlord, Rubin remained in possession of the property after December 31 of that year. Samuelson brought an action early in the next year to dispossess Rubin. What tenancy, if any, did Rubin have after December 31?

8. Tatum orally agreed to lease a farm to Sanders for ten years. Later Tatum refused to surrender possession of the farm to Sanders. Was the agreement enforceable?

9. Wells leases Yelton's farm for five years. At the end of this period Wells moves from the farm without giving notice of his intention to quit. Was Wells under a duty to give notice?

10. Tassey and Wallace executed a lease for a house and lot that gave the former a tenancy from month to month. At the end of a given month Tassey suddenly moved from the premises into an apartment house. Wallace brought an action against Tassey to recover rent for the next month. Was he entitled to judgment?

11. Tarvin leased certain business property to the Weiss Company, a corporation operating a department store. Before the end of the term of the lease the corporation abandoned the property and without communicating with Tarvin sent the keys to the building to him. In an action brought by Tarvin against the corporation for the rent, a question arose as to whether there had been a surrender of the lease. What is your opinion?

12. Diatz leased property to the Washington Technical School. The school wanted to abandon the lease and offered to return the key if Diatz would

release the school from further liability. Diatz refused to do so and declared that he would take possession of the property, relet it, and credit the school for any rent received by him from a new tenant. The school refused to give him the key. Thereafter Diatz leased the property to a new tenant and then sued the school for the difference between the rent due under the school lease and the rent received from the new tenant. The school claimed that when Diatz took possession and relet the property, there was a surrender of the school lease and its liability for rent ended. Decide. (Diatz v. Washington Technical School, [Mun.Ct. Dist.Col.] 73 A.2d 718)

13. Clay, who owned a tract of land, permitted Hartney to occupy a cabin on the land. There was no agreement as to the length of time that it could be occupied, and either could terminate the relationship when he chose. There was no provision for rent. Hartney died. The next day Clay closed up the cabin and put Hartney's possessions outside the door. Paddock, who was appointed the executor of Hartney's will, claimed the right to occupy the cabin. Was he entitled to do so? (Paddock v. Clay, 138 Mont. 541, 357 P.2d 1)

14. Boyar leased certain property to Wallenberg. The tenancy was from month to month at an agreed monthly rental, payable on the first of each month in advance. On the 27th of the following month, Wallenberg vacated the premises without giving any due notice of his intention to move. Boyar brought an action against Wallenberg to recover one month's rent. Decide. (Boyar v. Wallenberg, 132 Misc. 116, 228 N.Y.S. 358)

15. Checklist of legal terms—tenant and landlord:
    (a) eviction (648); partial eviction (648), constructive eviction (649)
    (b) permissive waste (650)
    (c) distress (651)
    (d) licensee, invitee (653)
    (e) assignment of a lease; sublease, sublessee (654)

16. Yates, who has been operating a home appliance business in his own building, decides to retire. He agrees to lease his building to Thomas for one year at a rental of $300 a month. Later Yates changes his mind and refuses to surrender possession of the building to Thomas. Thomas sues for damages. How will the amount of damages to which Thomas is entitled be determined?

17. Shortly after Wynne moved to a farm that he had leased from Rink, Sutton took possession of the farm during Wynne's absence. Wynne complained to the landlord, but the latter took no action to remove the trespasser. Wynne brought an action against the landlord for damages. Was he entitled to judgment?

18. A fence on the premises leased by Rigney from Melvin was damaged as the result of heavy rains. Rigney repaired the fence. Was Melvin obligated to reimburse Rigney for these repairs?

19. Zimmer leased Sutherland's house and lot for ten years. During the sixth year Zimmer noticed that the property was listed for sale for unpaid taxes. Zimmer paid the taxes in arrears in order to protect his interest. Was Zimmer entitled to reimbursement from Sutherland?

20. Von Hazel, a guest of Rippey, was injured from a fall caused by a loose board in a hallway of the building in which Rippey leased an apartment from Spreen. Von Hazel brings an action for damages against Spreen. Can he recover?

21. Sumner, who rents his home from Volker, gives Riggs permission to use his telephone. As Riggs leaves the house, he is injured by a fall caused by a loose step that has been in need of repair for some time. Is Sumner liable to Riggs for the latter's injuries?

22. Redmond leased his house and lot to Phillips for one year at a monthly rental of $150 to be paid in advance on the first day of each month. The lease began on May 1. On June 15 Redmond assigned the rent under this contract to Overman. On August 1 Phillips paid Redmond rent for July and August. Overman brought an action against Phillips for the amount the latter had paid to Redmond. Was he entitled to recover?

23. Joy White rented an apartment in an apartment house operated by Ridgleawood, Inc. After some discussion, she gave her apartment over to Allan and took a more expensive apartment in the same apartment house. Ridgleawood accepted rent from both White and Allan for the respective apartments. When Allan damaged his apartment, Ridgleawood sued White on the ground she was liable for the conduct of her assignee. Decide. (Ridgleawood, Inc. v. White, [Tex.Civ.App.] 380 S.W.2d 766)

24. Spears owned a building. On the first floor he rented space to a dry cleaner and a barber shop. The center door, which was at the top of an open stairway leading down into the basement, gave the appearance of a part of a double door leading into the dry cleaner's. There was no warning sign over the center door, and the door was unlocked. Trimble wanted to enter the dry cleaner's as a customer and by mistake opened the center door. Before she could realize her mistake, she fell down the stairs and was injured. When she sued Spears, he denied liability and further claimed that Trimble was guilty of contributory negligence. Decide. (Trimble v. Spears, 182 Kan. 406, 320 P.2d 1029)

Chapter 57

Real Mortgages

A mortgage is a credit and a security device. By means of it, a person or business may borrow money by pledging property as security.

NATURE AND CREATION

An agreement that creates an interest in real property as security for an obligation and which is to cease upon the performance of the obligation is a *real mortgage*. The debtor whose interest in the property is given as security is the *mortgagor*. The creditor who receives the security is the *mortgagee*.

Nature of Mortgage

A mortgage is based upon the agreement of the parties and arises only in connection with some debt or obligation to be secured.[1] If there is no debt, there can be no mortgage.

Facts: Donohoe owed money to Osborne. In order to pay the debt, he conveyed a tract of land to Osborne and the parties agreed that the debt was canceled. The deed contained a clause that Osborne would reconvey the land to Donohoe if the amount of the canceled debt were paid. In a suit against Landoe, Osborne's executor, Donohoe claimed that the deed was merely a mortgage.

Decision: The debt of Donohoe had been canceled when he executed the deed. Since there was no debt, there could be no mortgage. The instrument was therefore a deed. (Donohoe v. Landoe, 126 Mont. 351, 251 P.2d 560)

It is sometimes difficult to determine whether a given transaction creates a mortgage relationship or some other relationship. There are three outstanding characteristics of a mortgage: (1) the termination of the mortgagee's interest upon the performance of the obligation secured by the mortgage; (2) the right of the mortgagee to enforce the mortgage by foreclosure upon the mortgagor's failure to perform; and (3) the mortgagor's right to redeem or regain the property.

---

[1] *Rogers* v. *Snow Bros. Hardware Co.*, 186 Ark. 183, 52 S.W.2d 969.

In any case, however, the intention of the parties determines whether there is a mortgage. If it appears from all circumstances that the parties intended to create a mortgage, the courts will treat the agreement as such. Thus, even when there is an apparent absolute conveyance or sale of property, the transaction will be given the effect of a mortgage if the court or jury is convinced that the parties intended the conveyance to be for security only.[2]

Classification of Mortgages

Under the common law a mortgage of land was an absolute conveyance of the title to the mortgaged property subject to a condition subsequent which divested the title of the mortgagee upon the satisfaction of the condition, namely payment of the debt. Most states have abandoned the title theory of the mortgage and treat it merely as a lien upon the property.[3] Today there is not much practical difference between the two theories because many title theory states regard the mortgage as a lien with respect to third persons, that is, the mortgagor is still the owner of the land with respect to third persons.

The only practical difference today between the two theories is that under the lien theory the mortgagee is limited to foreclosing the lien of the mortgage, while under the title theory the mortgagee is entitled to go into possession upon default and collect the rents and profits as well as foreclose the mortgage. Under either theory the mortgagor may be sued on the mortgage debt.

Property Subject to Mortgage

In general, any form of property that may be sold or conveyed may be mortgaged. It is immaterial whether the right is a present right or a future interest, or merely a right in the land of another. It is not necessary that the mortgagor have complete or absolute ownership in the property. He may mortgage any interest, legal or equitable, divided or undivided, that he owns.

A mortgage binds after-acquired property that does not become part of the freehold only if the mortgage states in an *after-acquired property clause* that such property is bound.[4] If the after-acquired property becomes part of the freehold, it is bound by the mortgage in any case.

Obligations Secured

A mortgage is by definition a right given to secure an obligation. The mortgage may be given to secure the performance of some act or the

---

[2] *Klein* v. *Mangan*, 369 Ill. 645, 17 N.E.2d 958.
[3] *Alpert Industries* v. *Oakland Metal Stamping Co.*, 379 Mich. 272, 150 N.W.2d 765.
[4] *Fox* v. *Pinson*, 180 Ark. 68, 20 S.W.2d 645.

discharge of a present or future, contingent or absolute, liability. When given for a money claim, the amount may be liquidated or unliquidated, that is, for a fixed or for an uncertain amount. Generally the obligation secured includes all extensions or renewals of the original obligation. It does not, however, include any obligation not described in the mortgage. For example, if a mortgage recites that it is given as security for the purchase of goods, it cannot be enforced for other claims against the mortgagor held by the mortgagee.

The obligation itself may be evidenced by a bond, a note, or a series of notes. The mortgagee may sell or assign his rights under the mortgage transaction, in which case an assignment or a negotiation of the bond or note is made, together with the rights in the property subject to the mortgage.

A mortgage may be an *open-end mortgage*, that is, it may expressly declare that it is to cover not only a specified debt but also all advances which may be made at a later date, or all such advances up to a stated maximum. Most courts hold that a mortgage given to secure future advances in whole or in part has the same priority for such advances as if they were made at the time of the giving of the mortgage, when the mortgagee is required to make the later advances. If, however, the making of the future advances is optional with the mortgagee, such advances as are made after the mortgagee has actual knowledge of another encumbrance rank subsequent to that encumbrance.[5]

Facts: Jurist mortgaged certain land to Freeman to secure a debt of $13,000. Jurist subsequently mortgaged the same property to Sutro to secure payment of $5,000 and "future advances." Thereafter, the Northwestern National Bank & Trust Co., believing the property to be mortgaged for only $18,000, extended credit to Jurist from time to time until the indebtedness amounted to more than $41,000. The Freeman mortgage was assigned to Batten, who brought suit against Jurist to foreclose the mortgage. After payment of the Freeman debt, there remained $16,339.76 in the hands of the sheriff. Sutro, who had advanced an additional $15,000 to Jurist, claimed this money. The Northwestern National Bank & Trust Co. contended that Sutro was entitled only to the amount specifically set out in the mortgage, $5,000, and interest.

Decision: Judgment for Sutro. His mortgage was entitled to priority not only with respect to the original loan amount stated in the mortgage but also with respect to the subsequent advance made by him. The protection given a future advance mortgage is not affected by the recording statutes, although it is impossible to determine from the recorded mortgage just how large a debt is covered thereby. (Batten v. Jurist, 306 Pa. 64, 158 A. 557)

_____
[5] *Axel Newman Heating & Plumbing Co.* v. *Sauers,* 234 Minn. 140, 47 N.W.2d 769.

In some states, statutory restrictions have been placed on this kind of mortgage to prevent the incurring of excessive indebtedness.

Form of Mortgage

A mortgage is almost universally required to be in writing. A mortgage upon real property, since it transfers an interest in the property, must be in writing by virtue of the Statute of Frauds. For the same reason, a contract to mortgage land to another must be in writing.

As a general rule, no particular form of language is required, provided the language used clearly expresses the intent of the parties. In title theory states, however, the mortgage must be in the form of a conveyance since it transfers a legal title. This form of mortgage is also usually employed in states following the lien theory. In many states the substance is practically identical to that of a deed with the exception that a mortgage contains a defeasance clause, a description of the obligation secured, and sometimes a covenant to pay or perform the obligation. The *defeasance clause* states that the mortgage shall cease to have any effect when the obligation is performed, as when the debt is paid. In many states statutes provide a form of mortgage that may be used.

Special forms of mortgages have been developed in the case of mortgages securing the payment of corporate bonds and mortgages given to finance real-estate developments.

Parties to the Mortgage

The mortgage must be executed by the persons who are the owners of the property. Thus, when two or more persons are co-owners of the property, all must join as mortgagors. When property is owned solely by the husband or wife, a mortgage executed by the owner should also be signed by the other spouse when necessary to release the marital right of that spouse in the land, except when it is a *purchase-money mortgage*. This is a mortgage that is given by the purchaser of property to the seller of property as settlement for all or part of the purchase price, as distinguished from a mortgage that the owner of property places upon it when he borrows money from another person.

Recording or Filing of Mortgages

An unrecorded mortgage is valid and binding between the parties to it. The heirs, devisees, or donees of a mortgagor cannot defend against the mortgage on the ground that it had not been recorded.[6] Recording statutes in most states, however, provide that purchasers or creditors who give value

---

[6] *Niehaus* v. *Niehaus*, 2 Ill.App.2d 434, 120 N.W.2d 66.

and act in good faith in ignorance of an unrecorded mortgage may enforce their respective rights against the land without regard to the existence of the unrecorded mortgage. Accordingly the purchaser of the land in good faith for value from the mortgagor holds the land free of the unrecorded mortgage, and the mortgagee's only remedy is against the mortgagor on the debt due to him. In such a case the mortgagee has the burden of proving that the transferee of the land did not purchase in good faith, for value, and in ignorance of the unrecorded mortgage.[7]

RIGHTS OF PARTIES BEFORE DEFAULT

The rights and duties of the parties before default pertain to the possession of the property, rents and profits, repairs and improvements, taxes, assessments, insurance, impairment of security, transfer of interests in the property, performance of the obligation, and evidence of discharge of the obligation.

Possession of Property

In most title theory states the mortgagor is entitled to retain possession of the property until he is in default, whereupon the mortgagee is entitled to take possession, either actually or constructively by collecting rents and profits. Under the lien theory of mortgages, the mortgagor remains in possession until there has been a foreclosure sale, or a receiver is appointed by the court.

Even when the mortgagor is entitled to possession, he may agree with the mortgagee that the latter shall have possession. Moreover, those states that deny the mortgagee the right to possession upon default will permit him to remain in possession until the debt is paid or the obligation performed if he has already lawfully obtained possession. In some states "lawfully obtained" possession requires the consent of the mortgagor to the entry by the mortgagee, while in other states it is enough that the mortgagee has acquired possession without committing a breach of the peace.

Rents and Profits

1 / Mortgagor in possession. As long as the mortgagor is in possession, he has sole rights to the rents and profits of the mortgaged property and may dispose of them without regard to the existence of the mortgage on the land unless the rents and profits, by express agreement, are also pledged to secure the obligation. This rule is followed even though the mortgagor is in default on the mortgage.[8]

---

[7] *McCahill* v. *Travis Co.,* [Fla.] 45 So.2d 191.
[8] *Mid-Continent Supply Co.* v. *Hauser,* 176 Kan. 9, 269 P.2d 453.

2 / Mortgagee in possession. If the mortgagee is lawfully in possession, the mortgagor does not have the right to collect the rents and profits or to forfeit a tenant's deposit because of nonpayment of rent, but he does have the right to demand that they be properly expended by the mortgagee and that any surplus be paid to the mortgagor.[9]

The duty of the mortgagee in possession is not merely to account for what he has received but also to use due diligence in keeping the property rented and in collecting the rents, and to use reasonable prudence in management and in the creation of profits. Failure to exercise such diligence or prudence renders him liable to the mortgagor for losses that result from such a cause.

The fact that the mortgagee reduces rents or that the premises are vacant is not alone sufficient to establish liability for losses. For example, the vacancy may be caused by some act on the part of the mortgagor or by general economic conditions.

When the mortgagee is entitled to collect the rents, he is under a duty to pay the taxes on the property from them. If he fails to do so and the property is sold by the government for unpaid taxes, and he then buys the property at the tax sale, he cannot claim the property as his own. Since he would thereby be profiting from his own neglect, he must hold the property in trust for the mortgagor,[10] who may then recover it from him after the mortgage is paid in full.

The mortgagee, receiving the rents and profits, is under a duty, after payment of necessary repairs and taxes, to apply them to the mortgage debt and to turn over any surplus to the mortgagor. When the property has been placed in the hands of a receiver, the mortgagee is also entitled to have the rents and profits applied to the payment of the mortgage debt.

Repairs and Improvements

In the absence of an agreement to the contrary, a mortgagor is under no duty to make improvements or to restore or repair parts of the premises that are destroyed or damaged without negligence on his part.

The mortgagee, when in possession, must make reasonable and necessary repairs in order to preserve the estate. He is entitled to reimbursement for such repairs on the ground that they inure to the benefit of the mortgagor. Ordinarily, however, the mortgagee may not charge to the mortgagor expenditures for valuable or enduring improvements. A mortgagee will not be allowed to improve a mortgagor out of his estate by making it too costly for the mortgagor to redeem.

---

[9] *Miami Gardens* v. *Conway*, [Fla.] 102 So.2d 622.
[10] *Elliott* v. *Moffett*, 365 Pa. 247, 74 A.2d 164.

Taxes, Assessments, and Insurance

The duty to pay taxes and assessments rests upon the mortgagor. However, if the mortgagee is in possession, he is under a duty to pay the taxes and assessments out of the rents and profits.

In the absence of an agreement neither party is under a duty to insure the mortgaged property. Both parties, however, may insure their respective interests. It is common practice for the mortgagor to obtain a single policy of insurance on the property payable to the mortgagee and the mortgagor as their interests may appear.

If the mortgagor fails to perform the duty of paying taxes, assessments, or insurance premiums, the mortgagee is entitled to make such payments and to receive reimbursement. Such payments are generally treated as future advances for the purpose of determining their priority as against subsequent creditors and purchasers. If the mortgagor fails to pay taxes that he is required to pay and then buys the property at the tax sale thereof, he continues to hold the land subject to the mortgage, as otherwise he would profit from his own wrong.

> **Facts:** Dampier mortgaged land to the Federal Land Bank. The mortgage agreement required him to pay the taxes on the land. He failed to do so, and the land was sold by the state for taxes. Dampier purchased the land at the tax sale in 1936 and remained in possession of the land. The mortgage was assigned to Polk who sought to enforce it. Dampier claimed ownership of the land free of the mortgage.

> **Decision:** The mortgage was not discharged by the sale because the sale took place only as the consequence of the mortgagor's failing to perform his obligation to pay taxes. A person will not be allowed to profit by his own wrong, as would occur if the mortgagor could default on his obligation under the mortgage, cause the property thereby to be sold because of his default, and then, by purchasing the property, claim that he held it free of the mortgage. (Dampier v. Polk, 214 Miss. 65, 58 So.2d 44)

Impairment of Security

The mortgagor is liable to the mortgagee for any damage to the property, due to his fault, that impairs the security of the mortgage by materially reducing the value of the property. For example, the mortgagee is entitled to an injunction to restrain the removal of fixtures that tends to impair the security. The impairment of security by fraudulent injury, concealment, sale, or removal on the part of the mortgagor is sometimes made a criminal act.

The mortgagee, whether or not he is in possession, is liable to the mortgagor for injuries to the property due to his fault. Both the mortgagor and the mortgagee have a right of action against a third person who wrongfully injures the property. In some states the mortgagor loses this right after the mortgagee takes possession.

Facts: The mortgagor removed dirt and gravel from his land and sold it to the Berns Construction Co. The mortgagee claimed that he could not do so because that impaired the value of the land. The mortgagor claimed that he could do so because, as mortgagor, he was still the owner and could use the land to make money.

Decision: The mortgagor could not remove anything from the land when it would result in a permanent loss to the land. The earth once removed was gone forever. This constituted waste regardless of what was left or the actual value of what was taken. This contrasts with the growing of things on the land, as such things may be removed by the mortgagor as rents or profit. (Berns Construction Co. v. Highley, [C.A.7th] 332 F.2d 240)

Receivership Before Foreclosure

At the request of the mortgagee, the proper court may appoint a receiver for the mortgaged property prior to foreclosure in order to administer the property to prevent waste. In some states a receiver may be appointed only upon showing that the mortgagor is insolvent and is committing waste and that the mortgaged property is not by itself adequate security for the payment of the mortgage debt. In other states a receiver cannot be appointed for an individual, as distinguished from a corporate debtor.

Transfer of Interest

1 / Transfer by mortgagor. The mortgagor may ordinarily transfer his interest in the land without the consent of the mortgagee. A transfer by the mortgagor does not divest or impair the mortgage, and the grantee of the mortgagor holds the property subject to the mortgage, except the recording statutes may cut off the mortgage when it is not recorded and the mortgagor's grantee purchases in good faith for value, not knowing of the existence of the mortgage.

The transfer by the mortgagor of his interest does not affect the liability of the mortgagor to the mortgagee. Unless the latter has agreed to substitute the mortgagor's grantee for the mortgagor, the latter remains liable as though no transfer had been made. If, however, the mortgagor is required to pay the mortgage, he is subrogated to the rights of the mortgagee against his transferee.

2 / Liability of mortgagor's transferee. The purchaser of mortgaged property does not become personally liable for the debt secured unless he expressly assumes the debt. Even when he does so, the mortgagor continues to be liable unless released by the mortgagee. If the purchaser assumes liability for the debt, the mortgagee, after notice thereof, must treat the mortgagor as a surety to the extent that he must do nothing that will injure the mortgagor's interest.

3 / Transfer by mortgagee. In most states a mortgage may be transferred or assigned by the mortgagee. A few states, following the title theory of a mortgage, hold that a mortgage is nonassignable at law and that the title of the mortgagee can be transferred only by a formal conveyance. The assignability of mortgages, however, has always been recognized by courts of equity. Although an equitable assignment only requires that the intent of the parties be shown, a written assignment is necessary as a general rule in order to pass a legal title. Formal assignment is sometimes required by statute, and it is usually necessary for recording purposes.

Performance of Obligation

The mortgagee is entitled to the performance of the obligation secured by the mortgage according to its terms. When the obligation is a debt, its payment should be made to the mortgagee or to an agent authorized to receive payment when payment is due. A mortgagee need not accept payment from a stranger, but any person succeeding to the rights of the mortgagor or having an interest to protect, such as an executor, heir, or widow of the mortgagor, or a second mortgagee, may pay the debt.

The effect of a mortgagee's rejection of a valid tender or offer of the money due varies in the states. Some courts hold that a tender of the amount due on the due date does not discharge the lien. Most courts hold that the lien is discharged when the tender is arbitrarily or unreasonably refused. In any case, the debt is not discharged.

The courts are also in conflict as to whether a tender after default releases the property from the lien. In order to be a valid tender, the total amount due, including interest, must be tendered. It is insufficient to tender merely the face amount of the mortgage.[11]

If the debt is in any way discharged, the mortgage is also discharged. A discharge of the debtor from personal liability, however, does not release the lien of the mortgage. Thus the discharge of the mortgagor in bankruptcy does not affect the lien of the mortgage.

Evidence of Discharge

The mortgagee, after receiving payment or satisfaction of the debt, is under a duty to give the mortgagor a receipt, certificate, or other evidence that the mortgage has been discharged. This duty may be enforced by various

---

[11] *Decker* v. *State National Bank*, 255 Ala. 373, 51 So.2d 538.

actions in the different states. Statutes usually require the filing of a discharge or an entry of satisfaction of the mortgage in the margin of the record book in which the mortgage has been recorded.

RIGHTS OF PARTIES AFTER DEFAULT

Rights of Mortgagee After Default

Upon the mortgagor's default, the mortgagee in some states is entitled to obtain possession of the property and to collect the rents or to have a receiver appointed for that purpose.[12] In all states he may enforce the mortgage by foreclosure and sue to enforce the mortgage debt.

Generally it is provided that upon any default under the terms of the mortgage agreement, the mortgagee has the right to declare that the entire mortgage debt is due even though the default related only to an installment or to the doing of some act, such as maintaining insurance on the property or producing receipts for taxes.

1 / Foreclosure. In most states, *foreclosure* requires the mortgagee to sell the property under an order of the court or by a sale made by an officer of the court. If sufficient, the proceeds of the sale are used to pay the mortgage debt, interest, and costs of sale. There may also be taxes due on the real estate. If there is a surplus above these liabilities, the mortgagor is entitled to the surplus since it is his property that is being sold.

An exception to this disposition of the surplus arises when there are other liens upon the foreclosed property and those liens are discharged or destroyed by the foreclosure sale. It is generally held that the holders of such destroyed liens are entitled to receive payment from the surplus remaining after the taxes and the mortgagee's claims have been paid. Accordingly, it is only after all such claimants have been paid, as well as the mortgagee, that there is any surplus available for distribution to the mortgagor.

2 / Deficiency judgment. A sale on the foreclosure of the mortgage destroys the mortgage, and the property passes at the sale free of the mortgage. But the extinction of the mortgage by foreclosure does not destroy the debt that was secured by the mortgage. The mortgagor remains liable for any unpaid balance or deficiency. This amount still due is determined by subtracting the net proceeds of the sale from the debt, interest, and costs due at the time of the sale. It is generally provided by statute that if the mortgagee purchases the property at foreclosure, the mortgagor may request that the appraised fair value of the property, rather than the net proceeds of the sale, be credited against the debt.

---

[12] See p. 666.

Facts: The National City Bank, which held a mortgage on property owned by Gelfert, foreclosed the mortgage and purchased the property at the foreclosure sale. At the time that the mortgage had been executed, the law of the state provided that a mortgagee was entitled to a deficiency judgment against the mortgagor for the balance of the mortgage debt remaining unsatisfied after the mortgagor was credited with the net proceeds of the foreclosure sale. At the time that the mortgage was foreclosed, the state law provided that the court in fixing the amount of the deficiency judgment should "determine, upon affidavit or otherwise as it shall direct, the fair and reasonable market value of the mortgaged premises" and should deduct from the amount of the debt the "market value as determined by the court or the sale price of the property whichever shall be higher. . . ." The mortgagee objected to the application of the latter statute in determining the amount of his deficiency judgment on the ground that it impaired the obligation of the mortgage contract.

Decision: The statute did not impair the obligation of the mortgage contract since it did no more than prevent the mortgagee from getting paid more than once. That is, the land acquired by the mortgagee should be regarded as being a payment on account of the mortgage debt so that the debt would be reduced by the value of the land. (Gelfert v. National City Bank, 313 U.S. 221)

Some states limit the period of time within which a deficiency judgment may be enforced against property that is used by the mortgagor as his home. Other states also provide that no deficiency judgment may be entered on a purchase money mortgage.[18]

3 / Action on mortgage debt. In case of default a mortgagee, in the absence of statute or agreement, is not required to foreclose, but he may pursue any other remedy that he possesses. He may therefore bring an action on the debt, recover judgment, and obtain satisfaction of the debt by execution.

Rights of Mortgagor After Default

1 / Stay of foreclosure. In certain cases, authorized by statute, a *stay* (or delay) *of foreclosure* may be obtained by the mortgagor to prevent undue hardship. The Federal Soldiers' and Sailors' Civil Relief Act prohibits the foreclosure of mortgaged property while the "owner" is in military service, if the owner is not able to make the required payments because of such service.

2 / Redemption. The *right of redemption* means the right of the mortgagor to free the property of the mortgage lien after default. By statute in

---

[18] *Brown* v. *Jensen,* 41 Cal.2d 193, 259 P.2d 425.

many states the right may be exercised during a certain time following foreclosure and sale.

In general, redemption may be made only by a person whose interests will be affected by foreclosure. The right to redeem may be exercised by the executor or the heirs of the mortgagor, and in most states by a second mortgagee.

Rights of Third Persons

The fact that a mortgage is in default, and that there are subsequent foreclosure proceedings thereon, does not affect the rights of other persons who have prior mortgage, judgment, or mechanic's liens on the property. Liens that are subsequent or subordinate to the mortgage are generally destroyed by a sale of the land in execution on the mortgage.

QUESTIONS AND PROBLEMS

1. Checklist of legal terms:
   (a) real mortgage; mortgagor, mortgagee (659)
   (b) after-acquired property clause (660), open-end mortgage (661)
   (c) defeasance clause (662)
   (d) purchase-money mortgage (662)
   (e) foreclosure (668)
   (f) stay of foreclosure, right of redemption (669)

2. State the objective(s) of each of the following rules of law:
   (a) A mortgage need not be restricted to a specified debt but may cover advances that may be made at later dates.
   (b) The transfer by the mortgagor of his interest does not affect his liability to the mortgagee.

3. Connor brought an action of ejectment against Deane to recover a water ditch. Connor had an instrument in writing by which a ditch company "granted, bargained, and sold" this particular water ditch to him. By the instrument Connor was authorized "to collect, demand, and receive the rents, issues, profits, and the entire proceeds of the ditch, or sufficient to meet the payments of the installments to the sum of $12,000." The instrument also provided that upon the payment of the installments the conveyance would be void. Deane's defense was that the instrument was a mortgage that did not entitle Connor to possession of the ditch. Do you agree?

4. When Conley died, he was survived by his widow and two children. The widow borrowed $2,000 from Dearborn and executed a mortgage on her undivided share of the land left by the deceased husband. Later Egner purchased the interests of the widow and the children in the land. Could Egner claim title to the land free from Dearborn's mortgage?

5. Fishburn gave to the Comstock Trust Company a mortgage on 160 acres of land to secure payment of two notes "or any indebtedness of whatever sort or nature that may be due from the mortgagor to the mortgagee at the time of foreclosing the mortgage." Gilbert purchased the claim of the bank and took an assignment of the mortgage. When Gilbert foreclosed the mortgage, he did so not only for the debt owed by the mortgagor to the trust company, but also for other debts due Gilbert that arose out of later transactions. Was he entitled to do this?

6. To finance the purchase of a house and lot from Dawson, Courtney executes a mortgage to Dawson for part of the purchase price.
   (a) What type of mortgage is involved in this situation?
   (b) Must Courtney's wife join in the mortgage?

7. Edwards mortgaged to Fitzer certain land to secure the payment of a $5,000 note. Later Edwards mortgaged the same land to De Voe to secure the payment of a $10,000 loan. The mortgage to Fitzer was not recorded, but De Voe knew of its existence when he took the second mortgage. When Fitzer brought an action against Edwards and De Voe to foreclose his mortgage, De Voe contended that he had a superior right under the later mortgage. Was De Voe's contention sound?

8. Giles gave a mortgage on two adjoining farms to Hassett as security for the payment of a note for $20,000. Giles lived on one farm and rented the other to Iser. Hassett contended that he was entitled to the profits from the first farm and to the rent from the other. Do you agree?

9. Agee executed a mortgage to Dallman to secure the payment of several notes. With Agee's consent, Dallman took possession of the property. Dallman spent $800 in clearing brush and timber from the land to prepare it for cultivation. Was Dallman entitled to reimbursement from Agee for this expenditure?

10. Isler remains in possession of property that he mortgages to Jansen. Later, in order to save the property from a tax sale, Jansen pays the back taxes. Is Jansen entitled to reimbursement for this payment?

11. Kanter executed a mortgage on his business property to Layne as security for a note. Later Kanter transferred his interest in the property to Adams, who promised that he would pay the note. Layne brought an action against Kanter to recover on the note. Was Layne entitled to judgment?

12. Markus executed a first mortgage on certain land to Hillman and a second mortgage to the Russell Company. The first mortgage was foreclosed, and the proceeds were more than necessary to pay the debt secured by that mortgage. Siebert, a creditor of Markus, brought an action to subject the surplus money from the foreclosure sale to his claim. The Russell Company contended that the surplus money should be applied first to the payment of the debt covered by the second mortgage. Was Siebert entitled to judgment?

13. Liston executes to Hatfield a mortgage for $15,000 to secure the payment of a note for that amount. When Liston does not pay the mortgage upon maturity, Hatfield forecloses. The amount realized from the foreclosure sale is sufficient to pay only $12,000 of the debt. Is the entire debt discharged?

14. Keppler executed a first mortgage to Lynd and later a second mortgage to Guthrie and still later a third mortgage to Motz. Guthrie foreclosed the second mortgage but did not make the holders of the first and third mortgages parties to the suit. Did the purchaser at the foreclosure sale take the property free from the liens of the first and third mortgages?

15. Crase gave a mortgage of certain land to Kremer. Crase then leased the right to mine part of the land to Rule. Kremer objected to the opening of the mine. Decide. (Kremer v. Rule, 209 Wis. 183, 244 N.W. 596)

16. Bradham and others, trustees of the Mount Olivet Church, brought an action to cancel a mortgage on the church property that had been executed by Davis and others as trustees of the church and given to Robinson as mortgagee. It was found by the court that Davis and the others, who had acted in executing the mortgage, were not lawful trustees of the church and had no authority to execute the mortgage. Furthermore, the court found that the church was not indebted to the mortgagee for any amount. Should the mortgage have been canceled? (Bradham v. Robinson, 236 N.C. 589, 73 S.E.2d 555)

17. Garland and Evans owned a tract of land subject to a mortgage given to the Federal Land Bank. The mortgage authorized the bank to pay taxes on the land if the owners failed to do so and to add such taxes to the mortgage debt. As a disabled war veteran, Garland was entitled to a tax exemption. Through a clerical error the township carried the real estate on its books as belonging to Evans, who did not have a tax exemption, and charged the property for the full amount of the taxes. The owners did not bring any action to correct this mistake, and the Federal Land Bank was never notified of it. At the end of five years the township put up the property for sale for unpaid taxes. The Federal Land Bank was notified of the sale and paid the taxes and interest to prevent the sale. Thereafter, the bank foreclosed the mortgage and added to its claim the taxes and interest it had paid. Garland brought an action to enjoin the bank from foreclosing on the ground that the adding of the taxes was improper because the taxes had been improperly charged as he had a tax exemption. Was Garland entitled to the injunction? (Garland v. Federal Land Bank of Springfield, 101 N.H. 260, 140 A.2d 568)

PART XI

Estates and Bankruptcy

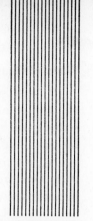

Chapter 58

Trust Estates

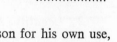

In addition to absolute transfers of property to a person for his own use, the law recognizes transfers made to one person for the use and benefit of another person.

Definitions

A transfer of property to one person with the understanding that he will hold the property for the benefit or use of another person is a *trust* or a trust relationship. It is an express trust because the trust duty arises from the express statement by the original owner who transferred the property in trust.

The owner who creates the trust is the *settlor,* the word being taken from the old legal language of "settling the property in trust." He is sometimes called the donor. The person to whom the property is transferred in trust is the *trustee.* The person for whose benefit the trustee holds the property is the *beneficiary* or *cestui que trust.*

Although an express trust is ordinarily created by a transfer of property, the settlor may retain the property in question and declare that he holds it as trustee for the beneficiary.[1]

Property held in trust is sometimes called the *trust corpus, trust fund, trust estate,* or *trust res.* A distinction is made between the *principal,* or the property in trust, and the *income* which is earned by the principal and distributed by the trustee.

The fact that there is an obligation or duty to make a payment does not create a trust. Thus the duty of a city to make annual contributions to a pension plan is not a trust.[2]

---

[1] Restatement, Law of Trusts 2d, Sec. 17.
[2] *Milwaukee* v. *Firemen's Relief Association,* 34 Wis.2d 350, 149 N.W.2d 589.

Kinds of Trusts

If the trust is created to take effect within the lifetime of the settlor, it is an *inter vivos trust* or a living trust. If the trust is provided for in the settlor's will and is to become effective only when his will takes effect after his death, the trust is called a *testamentary trust*.

A trust created for the benefit of private individuals is termed a *private trust*. One created for the benefit of the public or certain classes of the public is known as a *charitable trust*.

Creation of Trusts

1 / Consideration. Since a trust is a transfer of property, consideration is not required, although the absence of consideration may show that the trust is a voidable transfer in fraud of creditors.

2 / Legality. A trust may be created for any lawful purpose,[3] although in a few states statutes limit the purposes.

A trust is invalid when it is for an unlawful purpose or can be set aside if it is in fraud of creditors. A trust may also be void in whole or in part for violating the *rule against perpetuities*. This rule prohibits a person from creating by any transfer, whether in trust or not, a "floating" interest in property that will not become definite or vested until a date further away than twenty-one years after the death of persons alive at the time the owner of the property attempts to create the interest. For example, the owner of property who has no children cannot create a trust for the children (not yet born) of his own children (not yet born). The law is opposed to tying up property for such long periods of time because no one would know who was the owner of the property until all the grandchildren were born.

In varying degrees some states likewise prevent a settlor from directing that income be accumulated until a special event occurs, instead of paying it to the beneficiaries as it accrues.

3 / Capacity of parties. Anyone having capacity to make an outright transfer of property can transfer it in trust, and any person having capacity to own the property in question may receive that property in trust. The capacity of the beneficiary of the trust to hold property or to contract is immaterial, and many trusts are created because the beneficiary lacks legal or actual capacity to manage the property for himself.

4 / Formality. In creating a trust, it is common practice to execute a writing, called a *trust agreement* or *deed of trust*. No particular form of language is necessary to create a trust so long as the property, the trust purpose, and the beneficiaries are designated. If an inter vivos trust relates

---

[3] R.2d, Sec. 59.

to an interest in land, the Statute of Frauds requires that the trust be evidenced by a writing setting forth the details of the trust. When the trust depends upon a transfer of title to land, there must be a valid transfer of the title to the trustee in addition to a writing establishing the trust. Ordinarily the two will be combined in one instrument so that the deed which transfers title will also specify the trust duties.

If a trust is created by the will of the settlor, there must be a writing which meets the requirements of a will.

5 / Intention. An intention to impose a duty on the trustee with respect to specific property must be expressed. It is not necessary, however, that the word "trust" or "trustee" be used. The settlor will ordinarily name a trustee, but his failure to do so is not fatal to the trust as a trustee can be appointed by a court.

6 / Active duty. A trust does not exist unless an active duty is placed upon the trustee to manage the property in some manner or to exercise discretion or judgment. Thus, when a decedent transferred $500 to a trustee to be held in trust for *A*, it was held that no trust was created. The bare direction to hold the property in trust without any direction as to its use or distribution is not a sufficient duty. The courts further hold that since the trust failed, *A*, the intended beneficiary, is entitled to receive the property outright as though the decedent had not attempted to create a trust.

7 / Identity of beneficiary. Every trust must have a beneficiary. In a private trust the beneficiaries must be identified by name, description, or designation of the class to which the beneficiaries belong. In a charitable trust it is sufficient that the beneficiaries be members of the public at large or a general class of the public.

Trusts for religious masses, for the maintenance of grave monuments, or for the care of particular animals are technically invalid but are nevertheless enforced because of the social interests that are involved.

8 / Acceptance of trust. As the performance of a trust imposes burdens upon the trustee, he cannot be required to serve as trustee against his wishes. He may therefore renounce or reject the trust. A renunciation, however, does not affect the validity of the trust because a court will appoint a substitute trustee if the settlor does not do so.

It is also said that it is necessary that the beneficiary accept the trust, but this is modified by the rule that the beneficiary's consent will be presumed in the absence of disclaimer.

9 / Bond of trustee. Local statutes govern whether a trustee must file a bond for the faithful performance of his duties. Such a bond is generally required of a nonresident, and it may also be required of a resident by the court when it believes that the trustee may be guilty of misconduct that will harm the trust estate. The settlor may ordinarily declare that no bond shall be required of his trustee.

Nature of Beneficiary's Interest

The effect of a transfer in trust is to divide the property so that the legal title is given to the trustee and the beneficial interest or *equitable title* is given to the beneficiary. The beneficiary may ordinarily transfer or assign his interest in the trust, and his creditors may reach his interest in satisfaction of their claims. An exception arises when the settlor has restricted the trust in such a way that the beneficiary cannot assign nor his creditors reach his interest, resulting in what is commonly called a *spendthrift trust.*

Powers of Trustee

A trustee can exercise only those powers that are expressly given to him or those which the court will construe as being impliedly given.[4] Modern trusts commonly give the trustee discretion to make decisions on matters that could not be foreseen by the settlor. For example, the trustee may be authorized to expend principal as well as income when in the trustee's opinion it is necessary for the education or medical care of a beneficiary.

Duties of Trustee

1 / Performance. A trustee is under the duty to carry out the trust according to its terms. When he fails to do so, he is personally liable for any loss sustained unless he can justify his failure. A trustee cannot delegate the performance of his personal duties.[5]

2 / Due care. The trustee is under a duty to use reasonable skill, prudence, and diligence in the performance of his trust duties. More simply stated, he must use due care. He is not an insurer against loss and is not liable if he has exercised the degree of care which a reasonable man would exercise under the circumstances.[6]

Facts: James and Cora Parks created a trust for William Parks and others. James and Cora were the original trustees. Upon their deaths the Seattle First National Bank was made trustee. The trust assets were principally minority holdings of stock in businesses owned by members of the Parks family. These businesses and others owned by the family were actively managed by Harold Parks. Wilson and other beneficiaries

---

[4] *Rosencrans v. Fry*, 12 N.J. 88, 95 A.2d 905.
[5] *Hill v. Irons*, 92 Ohio App. 141, 109 N.E.2d 699.
[6] *Mereto's Estate*, 373 Pa. 308, 96 A.2d 115.

claimed the trustee was negligent because it had not taken adequate steps to see that Harold Parks was not running the businesses in such a way as to prejudice those in which the trust had an interest. Specifically, it was claimed that the trustees were negligent in using spot check audits rather than complete audits of the various enterprises.

Decision: The use of spot check audits was proper since the cost of full audits would have been so great, particularly in view of the fact that the trust had only small holdings in the businesses. Moreover, the spot check was the type of audit commonly used in business and therefore .he trustees could not be regarded as having failed to act as reasonable men. (Parks' Trust, 39 Wash.2d 763, 238 P.2d 1205)

A trustee is protected in making decisions if he has relied on the advice of an attorney, at least when there is no circumstance which would make a reasonable man believe that he should not follow the attorney's advice.

3 / Loyalty. A trustee is not permitted to profit personally from his position as trustee, other than to receive the compensation allowed him by contract or by law.[7] An executive officer of a corporate trustee, though not personally a trustee, must not profit from the trust in any way that would not be proper for a trustee.

4 / Taking possession and preserving trust property. The trustee is under a duty to take possession of trust property and to preserve it from loss or damage. If the property includes accounts receivable or outstanding debts, he is under the duty to collect them.

5 / Defense of trust. The trustee is under a legal duty to defend the trust when its validity is disputed in court. Conversely, he cannot attack its validity.

6 / Production of income. Either by express or implied direction, the trustee is required to invest the money or property in enterprises or transactions that will yield an income to the estate.

Facts: Berry owned a business which he transferred by deed to his sons in trust to operate and to pay the income in a specified manner. Some years later, after the death of Berry and of several of the sons, a suit was brought by some of the beneficiaries to require the trustee to invest $104,000 that had been held in the trust and remained uninvested for 14 years and to compel the trustee to insure the trust property which had not been covered by insurance.

Decision: The trustees must invest the money, as it is the duty of a trustee to make the trust fund productive. Whether there was a duty to insure

---

[7] See p. 679.

could not be determined without additional information as the circumstances might be such that it was proper for the trustee to set aside a fund against loss rather than procure insurance from an insurance company. (Berry v. McCourt, 1 Ohio App.2d 172, 204 N.E.2d 235)

By statute the trustee is generally limited as to the nature of investments that he may make. Most states now permit him to invest in corporate stocks. Court approval is generally required of all transactions relating to real estate held by the trust.

A trustee is generally permitted to invest in bonds of the United States, or of instrumentalities of the United States; bonds of states, cities, and counties, subject to certain restrictions; first mortgages on real estate when the mortgage does not represent more than a specified percentage of the value of the land; and mortgage bonds of certain types of corporations. In a majority of states, investments in corporate stocks are permitted.

Facts: Guggenheim transferred property to the Commercial Trust Co. and George Mason in trust for certain purposes. The trustees invested all the trust funds in tax-exempt, low-income producing government bonds. The beneficiaries of the trust protested on the ground that the trustees were under a duty to diversify the investments.

Decision: Judgment for the trustees. The duty to diversify investments is intended to minimize the risk of large losses by avoiding a disproportionately large holding in any one type or kind of security, the value of which might collapse. As the entire estate was invested in government bonds, the trustees had safe-guarded all the estate and the reason for the requirement of diversification did not exist. (Commercial Trust Co. v. Barnard, 27 N.J. 332, 142 A.2d 865)

The device of the *common trust fund* has been legalized in a number of states. Under this plan the trustee, often a bank which is a trustee for a number of small trusts, pools the assets of all the trusts into a common trust fund. Each trust is given certificates in the fund proportionate to the size of its contribution. The fund is then invested in such investments as mortgages on large buildings and factories, in which the individual trust funds could not have been invested directly because of their small size.

7 / Accounting and information. A trustee must keep accurate records so that it can be determined whether he has properly administered the trust. Upon request by the beneficiary, the trustee must furnish information with respect to the trust. Periodically, or at certain times, as determined by the law in each state, he must file an account in court, at which time the court passes upon his stewardship of the trust.

Compensation of Trustee

A trustee is entitled to compensation. In some states a statute or a court rule prescribes the amount or percentage of compensation. In modern trust instruments it is common to specify that the trustee shall receive specific compensation expressed in terms of percentages of the principal or income amounts administered by him. In the absence of any controlling provision, the court in which the trustee files his account will award him such compensation as the court determines reasonable for the services rendered by him.

Remedies for Breach of Trust

A breach of trust may occur in a variety of ways, which in turn affect the remedies available. These remedies include:

(1) Money judgment against trustee for loss caused by him.

(2) Injunction or order to compel the trustee to do or refrain from doing an act.

(3) Criminal prosecution of the trustee for his misconduct.

(4) Tracing and recovery of trust property which has been converted by the trustee, unless the property has been acquired by a bona fide purchaser who gives value and purchases without notice of the breach of trust.

(5) Judgment against surety on trustee's bond for loss caused the trust by the trustee's default.

(6) Removal of trustee for misconduct.

(7) Suit against third persons who participated in a breach of trust.

Termination of Trust

A trust may be terminated (1) in accordance with its terms; (2) because of the impossibility of attaining the object of the trust; (3) by revocation by the settlor, when allowed by the terms of the trust; [8] (4) by merger of all interests in the same person; and (5) upon the request of all the beneficiaries when there is no express purpose that requires continuation of the trust.

Tentative Trusts

The law has developed a peculiar trust theory to govern a bank deposit made by A of his own money in an account marked "A, in trust for B." If this were a true trust, A could not withdraw the money for his own use or revoke the trust, and the creditors of A could not reach the deposit unless they could show that the creation of the trust was in fraud of them. The law recognizes that many persons make such a deposit without actually intending to create a formal trust. It is therefore held that in the absence of any evidence showing an intention to create a formal trust by this method of

---

[8] *D.A.R.* v. *Washburn College,* 160 Kan. 583, 164 P.2d 129.

deposit, a true trust is not created. Such a deposit is regarded as creating a *tentative trust* in which the depositor and his creditors are permitted to treat the deposit as though there were no trust; but if the depositor dies, any money that remains in the account after creditors are paid belongs to the person named as the beneficiary.[9] Some states refuse to recognize tentative trusts, while others have expressly authorized them by statute.

Charitable Trusts

1 / Purpose. Charitable trusts may be created for any purpose that advances the public welfare. These include trusts to: (a) maintain or propagate religion, religious education, and missionary work; (b) further health and relieve human suffering by establishing institutions or by direct aid of food, clothing, shelter, and medical care to the needy; (c) found or maintain educational institutions, museums, libraries, or aid individual students or teachers; (d) care for and maintain public cemeteries; (e) erect monuments to public men or national heroes; (f) construct and maintain public buildings or improvements, such as an irrigation system or a playground; (g) further patriotism; and (h) prevent cruelty to animals.

Facts: Shields conveyed land to the Catholic Bishop of Chicago to be used "as a Burial Ground for the Catholic people of Joliet in Will County . . . and its vicinity." Murr claimed that this provision of the deed was void.

Decision: The deed was valid. A trust for public burial purposes is valid even though it is limited to persons from a specified geographical area or of a specific religious faith. (Catholic Bishop of Chicago v. Murr, 3 Ill.2d 107, 120 N.E.2d 4)

The mere fact that the purpose of a trust is to give money to others does not make it a charitable trust.

In the absence of a contrary provision in the trust agreement, the law will not permit a charitable trust to end even though the original purpose has been accomplished or can no longer be achieved, or because the beneficiary no longer exists. In such a case the courts apply the *cy-pres doctrine,* an abbreviation of the Norman French words "cy pres comme possible" or "as near as possible." By this doctrine the court directs that the trust fund be held for another purpose that will be as near as possible to that intended by the settlor.

Facts: By his will dated 1870, Joseph How bequeathed his residuary estate in trust to pay the income therefrom to certain persons for their respective lives and upon their deaths to be used by his trustee to found a "home

---

[9] *Bearinger's Estate,* 336 Pa. 253, 9 A.2d 342.

for indigent seamen." Joseph had been the master and the captain of Ellen Stevens, a three-masted sailing vessel. At the time of his death his estate was valued at $1,500. Thereafter certain investments that Joseph had made which were regarded as worthless increased in value to more than $300,000 and income of $100,000 was received by the trustee. A petition was then filed with the court for instructions as to how this fund should be expended under the will.

Decision: The trust was to be held for the benefit of men whose livelihood was gained from the sea whether in fishing or transportation and without regard to the nature of the vessel. The trust was a charitable trust and showed a dominant intent to benefit the toilers of the sea rather than a specific class of sailors. As the trust fund was far in excess of the amount needed to execute the original purposes, the trust purposes would be broadened by applying the cy-pres doctrine to carry out the general charitable intent of the testator. (Pierce's Petition, 153 Maine 180, 136 A.2d 510)

If, however, it is clear that he intended the trust to be performed exactly as he has indicated or not at all, the trust fails when it is not possible to follow his direction. In such a case the cy-pres doctrine will not be applied.

2 / Limitations. In most aspects a charitable trust is the same as a private trust. In some states additional limitations are imposed. Thus a maximum amount may be set on the property that a charitable corporation may own. In some states a decedent is limited as to the amount of his property which he can leave to charity when he is survived by near relatives.

In many states a gift to charity or for a charitable trust is void if the donor dies within a minimum period, such as thirty days, after making the gift. In those states it is also generally provided that a clause in a will making such a gift is void if the decedent dies within thirty days after making the will.

Implied Trusts

In certain instances trusts are implied in order to carry out the presumed intention of the parties [10] or to protect the former owner from the fraud of the present owner. When the court implies a trust to carry out the presumed intent of the parties, the trust is called a *resulting trust*; when it implies a trust to right or to prevent a wrong, it is called a *constructive trust.*

1 / Purchase-money resulting trust. The most common resulting trust arises when a person pays for the purchase of property but title to the property is taken in the name of another person. It is then presumed that the titleholder was intended to hold as trustee for the benefit of the person paying

---

[10] *Kellow* v. *Bumgardner,* 196 Va. 247, 835 S.E.2d 391.

the money. To give effect to this presumption, a resulting trust is generally imposed upon the property and the titleholder. This means that the titleholder cannot use the property as his own but must use it or dispose of it as directed by the person paying the money. This presumption is not conclusive and may be overcome by evidence showing that it was the intention of the person paying the money to lend the money to the person taking title or to make a gift of the property to him. If the person paying the money is the husband or parent of the person taking title, there is a presumption that the payment was made as a gift, in which case a resulting trust does not arise unless the presumption of a gift is overcome by contrary evidence.[11]

2 / Constructive trust of improperly acquired property. When a person has acquired title to property by unlawful or unfair means or in breach of his duty as an agent or trustee, equity will make him hold it as constructive trustee for the person whom he has unjustly deprived of the property. Thus, if an agent purchases for himself in his own name property that he was instructed to purchase for his principal, the latter may hold the agent as constructive trustee.

QUESTIONS AND PROBLEMS

1. Checklist of legal terms:
   - (a) trust; settlor, trustee, beneficiary or cestui que trust (673)
   - (b) trust corpus, trust fund, trust estate, or trust res (673)
   - (c) principal, income (673)
   - (d) inter vivos trust, testamentary trust (674)
   - (e) private trust, charitable trust (674)
   - (f) rule against perpetuities (674)
   - (g) trust agreement or deed of trust (674)
   - (h) equitable title (676)
   - (i) spendthrift trust (676)
   - (j) common trust fund (678)
   - (k) tentative trust (679)
   - (l) cy-pres doctrine (680)
   - (m) resulting trust, constructive trust (681)

2. State the objective(s) of each of the following rules of law:
   - (a) The law recognizes and enforces as a trust a transfer to one person made for the use of another.
   - (b) In the absence of a reserved power the settlor ordinarily has no power to revoke a trust.

3. Five years after his marriage Harvey creates a trust fund that shall be available first for the benefit of his children and then for the benefit of his grandchildren. Under what circumstances is such a trust void?

---

[11] *Hanley v. Hanley*, 14 Ill.2d 566, 152 N.E.2d 879.

4. Simpson transfers to Havlin certain shares of stock that are to be held in trust for the benefit of Simpson's wife.
   (a) Who has the legal title to the property?
   (b) Who has the equitable title?

5. Allan is the beneficiary of a trust.
   (a) Can Allan transfer or assign his interest in the trust property?
   (b) Can Allan's creditors satisfy their claims out of the trust fund?

6. Simmons is the trustee of Homan's trust fund that has been created for Pryor's benefit. Is Simmons obligated to make an accounting to Pryor upon the latter's request?

7. Ward is the beneficiary of the income from a trust fund. At his death the principal is payable to Hatton. If the deed of trust makes no provision for the compensation of Kittle, the trustee, how will he be paid?

8. Warburg opens a bank savings account in the name of "Warburg, in trust for Struke." What are the rights of Warburg, Struke, and Warburg's creditors in this account?

9. William and Walter Asher were trustees under the will of J. M. Asher, deceased. As trustees, they loaned money to themselves at a low rate of interest, without security, and paid commissions to themselves from principal. Morrison, a beneficiary of the trust brought an action to have them removed as trustees. Decide. (Morrison v. Asher, [Mo.App.] 361 S.W.2d 844)

10. Fry was made trustee of approximately 880 acres of oil and gas land. The trust agreement gave him authority to execute "leases" of the land. He executed a lease of 80 acres to McCormick. Later Fry sued to set aside the lease on the ground that he had no authority to lease a portion of the property. Decide. (Fry v. McCormick, 170 Kan. 741, 228 P.2d 727)

11. Symonds bequeathed a legacy to the City of Keene to pay for and maintain a set of chimes on the public library or some other city building. Was this provision valid? (City of Keene v. Martin, 96 N.H. 504, 79 A.2d 13)

12. By her will, Hendricks provided: "I give, devise, and bequeath (the balance of my estate) to the City of Brookfield, Missouri, for the sole purpose of building and equipping and maintaining a city hospital. . . ." The city claimed that this was an absolute gift to the city subject to a condition as to its use. Decide. (Ramsey v. City of Brookfield, 361 Mo. 857, 237 S.W.2d 143)

Chapter 59

Decedents' Estates

After all of the debts of a decedent are paid, distribution is made of the balance of his estate, if any, to those entitled to receive it. If the decedent made a valid will, it determines which persons are entitled to receive the property. If the decedent did not make a valid will, the distribution is determined by the intestate law.

WILLS

Testate distribution describes the distribution that is made when the decedent leaves a valid will. A *will* is ordinarily a writing that provides for a distribution of property upon the death of the writer but which confers no rights prior to that time.[1] A person who makes a will is called a *testator* or, if a woman, a *testatrix*. Prior to his death, the testator may destroy or cancel the will. The person to whom property is left by a will is called the *beneficiary*.

A gift of personal property by will is called a *legacy* or *bequest,* in which case the beneficiary may also be called a *legatee*. A gift of real property by will is a *devise,* in which case the beneficiary may be called a *devisee*.

Requirements of a Will

A will must satisfy requirements as to (1) capacity of parties, (2) intention, (3) formality, and, in some states, (4) witnesses.

1 / Capacity of parties.

(a) TESTATOR. Generally the right to make a will is limited to persons over 21. In some states the age qualification is lowered to 18 years. In a few states a girl of 12 years or over, or a boy of 14 years or over, may make a will disposing of personal property.

The testator must also have *testamentary capacity*. This is not the same as the capacity to make a contract but is apparently a lower standard. The testator must have sufficient mental capacity at the time of executing his will to know the natural objects of his bounty, to understand the kind and extent

---

[1] *Floyd* v. *Christian Church & Orphans' Home,* 296 Ky. 196, 176 S.W.2d 125.

of his property, to understand what he is doing when he makes a will, and to have the ability to dispose of the property according to a plan formed by him.[2] Eccentricities of the decedent or peculiarities of his will do not establish that he lacked mental capacity sufficient to make a will.[3] The fact that he does not have sufficient capacity to conduct business affairs does not mean that he necessarily lacks capacity to make a will.

An insane person lacks capacity to make a will. If the testator is insane but has lucid intervals, his will can be sustained when it is shown that the testator executed the will during a lucid interval. When a person is otherwise sane but suffers from an insane delusion, his will is invalid if it is affected by the insane delusion.

(b) BENEFICIARY. Generally there is no restriction with respect to the capacity of the beneficiary of a will. In some instances, as in the case of charitable corporations, a statute may set a maximum upon the amount of property that it may own. Such a limitation may prevent the corporation from receiving an additional gift by will.

Generally, a beneficiary who murders the testator is not entitled to receive a bequest made in the testator's will to the murderer.

2 / Intention. There cannot be a will unless the testator manifests an intention to make a provision that will be effective only upon his death. This is called a *testamentary intent.*

Facts: Marie Elizabeth Purnell executed a will by which she left her estate to her immediate family and made no provision for more distant relatives. Seven years later she wrote a paper entitled "Last Will and Testament" in which she declared that it was her "last will and testament" and explained therein that she had left nothing to a certain named distant relative and declared that under no circumstances should that relative receive any part of her estate. After Marie's death, the earlier will was admitted to probate but the second writing was not.

Decision: The later writing, although described as a will, was not a will because it did not make any provision effective on her death whether by making or affecting the disposition of her property or by way of appointing an executor or coexecutor. It was merely an explanation of what she had done. It therefore lacked testamentary character or intent and could not be probated as a will. (Delly v. Seaboard Citizens National Bank, 202 Va. 764, 120 S.E.2d 457)

A contract to make a will is not effective as a will, although the estate of the decedent may generally be sued for breach of the contract.

---

[2] *Appelhaus* v. *Jurgenson*, 336 Ill. 427, 168 N.E. 327.
[3] *Wadsworth's Estate*, [Okla.] 273 P.2d 997.

3 / Formality. Generally a will must be written and must be signed by the decedent at the end. As is customary in the law, "writing" includes printing and typewriting. The signing must ordinarily be written by the decedent himself, although merely making an "X" is sufficient when illiteracy or illness makes any other signing impossible. There is a conflict of authority whether the signing must be at the physical or the logical end of the will. There is generally no requirement that a will be dated although some states so require when the will is written completely in the handwriting of the decedent.

4 / Witnesses. In some states no witnesses are required for a will. In others, two or three witnesses are required to subscribe the will under an *attestation clause* stating that they witnessed its execution by the decedent. It is commonly provided that attestation be made by the witnesses in the presence of the testator and of each other. *Publication* is the act of the testator in informing the attesting witnesses that the document which he is signing before them is his will. The law varies between states as to the necessity of publication.

Revocation

1 / Revocation by act of testator. A will is revoked when the testator destroys, burns, or tears the will, or crosses out provisions of the will with the intention to revoke it in whole or in part.

A will is also revoked by the execution of a later will which either expressly declares the prior will revoked or which displaces the prior will by disposing of all the property of the testator. In many states a will may also be revoked by a later writing executed with the same formality as a will which merely declares that the will is revoked.[4] Such a writing is effective although it does not itself make any disposition of the property of the testator. In any case, a revocation that does not comply with the formal requirements of the Statute of Wills is not effective.

Facts: By his original will, Heath bequeathed one third of his estate to Morse. When the will was probated, it was found that the bequest to Morse had been crossed out and at the bottom of the will was a typewritten statement "Under no condition do I wish . . . Morse . . . to be included in this will." Both the will and the final addition were signed by Heath. The will was witnessed and acknowledged, but the addition was not. By the applicable statute, witnessing and acknowledgment were required of a will and a writing revoking a will. There was no evidence as to when or under what circumstances any of the changes had been made to the will. There was no evidence as to where the will had been kept

---

[4] *Harchuck* v. *Campana,* 139 Conn. 549, 95 A.2d 566.

at any time. The Fletcher Trust Co. brought an action against Morse to obtain a declaratory judgment to determine what interest he had under the will.

Decision: The interest of Morse was not affected by the addition to the will. In order to protect from fraud, the formal requirements of wills and documents relating to wills must be satisfied. The addition to the will had no effect because it was not witnessed and acknowledged. Therefore the will as originally written remained in effect. The cancellation of Morse's name had no effect because it was not shown that it had been done by the testator. Furthermore, there was no evidence that the will had been in the possession of the testator, which would have given rise to a presumption that he must have been the one who made the cancellation. (Fletcher Trust Co. v. Morse, 230 Ind. 44, 101 N.E.2d 658)

A testator must have the same degree of mental capacity when he revokes his will as is required when he makes a will.

2 / Revocation by operation of law. In certain instances statutes provide that a change of circumstances shall have the effect of a revocation. Thus it may be provided that when a person marries after executing his will, the will is revoked in whole or in part or is presumed revoked [5] unless it was made in contemplation of marriage or unless it provided for the future spouse. In some states the revocation is not total but only to the extent of allowing the spouse to take such share of the estate as that to which she would have been entitled had there been no will.

It is also commonly provided that the birth or adoption of a child after the execution of a will works a revocation or partial revocation as to that child. In some states both marriage and the birth of a child are necessary to revoke the decedent's will by operation of law.[6]

The divorce of the testator does not in itself work a revocation; but the majority of courts hold that if a property settlement is carried out on the basis of the divorce, a prior will of the testator is revoked, at least to the extent of the legacy given to the divorced spouse.

Modification of Will

A will may be modified by executing a codicil. A *codicil* is a separate writing that amends a will. The will, except as changed by the codicil, remains the same. A codicil must be executed with all the formality of a will.

A will cannot be modified merely by crossing out a clause of the will and writing in what the testator wishes. Such an interlineation is not operative

---

[5] *Kent's Estate*, 4 Ill.2d 81, 122 N.E.2d 283.
[6] *Rankin* v. *McDearmon*, 38 Tenn.App. 160, 270 S.W.2d 660.

unless it is executed with the same formality required of a will, or in some states unless the will is republished in its interlineated form.

Revival

Revival is the act of giving new validity to a will that has been revoked. This may be done by executing a codicil which specifically refers to the revoked will and indicates that it is to be effective. The will may also be revived by the direct procedure of re-executing the will. Beyond these two clear rules, there is great conflict of authority among the states as to whether any other conduct, such as merely republishing but not re-executing a revoked will, can revive it.

Probate and Contest of Will

Probate is the act by which the proper court or official accepts a will and declares that the instrument satisfies the statutory requirements as the will of the testator. Until a will is probated, it has no legal effect.

Any qualified person wishing to object to the probate of the will on the ground that it is not a proper will may appear before the official or court prior to the entry of the decree of probate, or he may petition after probate to have the probate of the will set aside.

The probate of a will may be refused or set aside on the ground that the will is not the free expression of the intention of the testator. It may be attacked on the ground of (1) lack of mental capacity to execute a will, (2) undue influence, duress, fraud, or mistake inducing the execution of the will,[7] or (3) forgery of the testator's signature. With the exception of mental capacity, these concepts mean substantially the same as they do in contract law.

Special Types of Wills

1 / Holographic wills. A *holographic will* is one that is written by the testator entirely in his own handwriting.[8] In many states no distinction is made between a holographic and other wills. In other states the general body of the law of wills applies, but certain variations are established.

2 / Nuncupative wills. A *nuncupative will* is an oral will made and declared by the testator in the presence of witnesses to be his will. Generally it can be made only during the last illness of the testator and can take effect only with respect to personal property.

3 / Soldiers' and seamen's wills. It is generally provided that soldiers and seamen may make an oral or a written will of personal property without

---

[7] *Thompson's Will,* 248 N.C. 588, 104 S.E.2d 280.
[8] *Moody's Estate,* 118 Cal.App.2d 300, 257 P.2d 709.

complying with the formalities required of other wills. Such a will remains in force even though the testator returns to civilian life, and it must be revoked in the same manner as any other will.

4 / Conditional or contingent will. A *conditional* or *contingent will* is one that the testator intends to be effective only upon the occurrence or satisfaction of a condition or contingency specified in the will. For example, a will is conditional if the testator writes, "If I should not return from my trip to Europe, I bequeath my house to John."

Interpretation and Distribution Under the Will

If the decedent dies testate, the last phase of the administration of his estate by his personal representative is the distribution of his property remaining after the payment of all debts and taxes, in accordance with the terms of his will.

There is no particular form that a will must follow, and there can be as many different forms as there are testators. Actually wills tend to follow a common pattern. The testator may bequeath to named persons certain sums of money, called *general legacies* because no particular money is specified; or identified property, called *specific legacies* or *devises*.[9] Thus he may say, "$1,000 to *A*; $1,000 to *B*; my auto to *C*." The first two bequests are general, the third is specific. After he has made such legacies, he may make a bequest of everything remaining, called a *residuary bequest, devise,* or *legacy,* such as "the balance of my estate to *D*." A testator may also make a *demonstrative bequest,* such as "$1,000 to be paid from the money in my office safe."

Persons, typically husband and wife, may make a joint will. This differs from an ordinary will only in that the wishes of the two people are set forth in one writing rather than in two separate writings.

1 / Abatement of legacies. If the estate is insufficient to pay all legacies in full, they *abate* or bear loss in the following order: (a) residuary, (b) general, (c) specific. The law also holds that legatees of the same class abate proportionately. Assume in the preceding example that after all debts are paid, there remains only $1,500 and the auto. What disposition is to be made? In the hypothetical case, *C,* the specific legatee, would receive the auto; *A* and *B,* the general legatees, would each receive $750; and *D,* the residuary legatee, would not receive anything.

A demonstrative bequest is only affected by the insufficiency of the fund from which it is to be paid.

---

[9] *Mellott's Estate*, 162 Ohio 113, 121 N.E.2d 7.

Facts: By his will Henry bequeathed $10,000 to the Park Lake Presbyterian Church and a specified number of shares of named corporations to several legatees. At the time of the decedent's death, he owned shares of stock of the named corporations in amounts equal to or greater than those bequeathed, but his estate was insufficient to pay all claims against it without abating the legacies. The legatees of the stock claimed that Park Lake's general legacy should be first used in the payment of the claims against the estate.

Decision: Judgment for Park Lake. The bequests of shares of stock of specific corporations were general legacies and therefore abated proportionately with the pecuniary legacy to Park Lake. The decedent had not pointed out any particular fund from which the stock legacies were to be distributed. (Park Lake Presbyterian Church v. Henry's Estate, [Fla.] 106 So.2d 215)

2 / Ademption of property. When specifically bequeathed property is sold, given away, or destroyed by the testator before his death, the specific legacy is adeemed and the specific legatee is not entitled to receive any property or money.[10] *Ademption* has the same consequence as though the testator had formally canceled the bequest.[11]

No ademption takes place when specifically bequeathed property has been changed in form but preserves its basic identity. For example, a specific bequest of shares of stock is effective as a bequest of shares given in exchange for those shares in the course of a corporate reorganization, or additional shares issued on a stock split-up.

3 / Death of legatee. If a legatee dies before the testator, the interest given him by the will usually lapses or is inoperative. Assume that in our example, *B,* to whom $1,000 was willed, died before the testator. Ordinarily the bequest to *B* would lapse or would be of no effect.

In a number of states antilapse statutes have been adopted. They provide that when the deceased legatee bears a certain family relationship to the testator, the gift to him shall not lapse but may be claimed by his children. Such statutes are common when the deceased legatee is a descendant of the testator and to a lesser extent when the legatee is a brother or sister of the testator. Thus, in the above case, if *B* came within the provisions of an antilapse statute and had a son, *F,* the $1,000 bequest would not lapse but would be paid to *F.* Such statutes generally apply only in the case of blood relatives (consanguinity).

4 / Election to take against the will. In order to protect the husband or wife of a testator from unfair treatment, it is generally provided that a

---

[10] *Busch v. Plews,* 12 N.J. 352, 96 A.2d 761.
[11] *In re Dittrich's Estate,* 53 Misc.2d 782, 279 N.Y.S.2d 657.

surviving spouse may ignore the provisions of the will and elect to take against the will. In such a case the surviving spouse receives the share of the estate which that spouse would have received had the testator died without leaving a will, or a fractional share specified by statute.

The right to take against the will is generally barred by certain specified kinds of misconduct of the surviving spouse. Thus, if the spouse is guilty of such desertion or nonsupport as would have justified the decedent in obtaining a divorce, it is usually provided that the surviving spouse cannot elect to take against the will.

5 / Intestate distribution. If the will is void for any reason, the decedent's estate is distributed as though there had been no will. When the will fails as to part of the estate, the share passes to the residuary legatee, if there is one.

6 / Disinheritance. With two exceptions,[12] any person may be disinherited or excluded from sharing in the estate of a decedent. A person who would inherit if there were no will is excluded from receiving any part of a decedent's estate if the decedent has left a will by which he gives all of his estate to other persons. It is not necessary that the decedent expressly declare in his will that the disinherited person is to receive nothing, nor is it necessary to bequeath him a nominal sum of money, such as a dollar, although there is a general erroneous belief to the contrary.

7 / Tax liability. A gift made by will may be subject to a state inheritance tax, and state and federal estate taxes. In making distribution, the personal representative must charge such taxes against the proper legatees or funds and if he fails to do so, he will generally be personally liable for the amount of the taxes.

INTESTACY

If the decedent does not effectively dispose of his property by will or if he does not have a will, his property will be distributed by *intestate succession* to certain persons related to him.

Plan of Intestate Distribution

Although wide variations exist among the statutory provisions of the states, they generally provide for distribution to the surviving spouse and children and *lineal* (or blood) *descendants*; and if this does not exhaust the estate, then to parents and to *collateral heirs*. The latter are not descendants

---

[12] The exceptions to this rule are based (a) upon the election of a spouse to take against the will and (b) in certain cases upon the partial revocation of a will by subsequent marriage, birth, or adoption.

of the decedent but are related to him through a common ancestor. Under some statutes a degree of relationship is specified, and no person more remotely related to the decedent is permitted to share in the estate. If the entire estate is not distributed within the permitted degree of relationship, the property that has not been distributed is given to the state government. This right of the state to take the property is the *right of escheat.* Under some statutes the right of escheat arises only when there is no relative of the decedent, however remotely related, to take his property.

It must be remembered that the above outline presents a composite picture. Within a particular state, qualification may be required in terms of homestead, dower and curtesy rights, or a modern statutory equivalent of such rights, in addition to changes in the actual pattern of distribution.

1 / Distribution per capita and per stirpes. The fact that different generations of distributees may be entitled to receive the estate creates a problem of determining the proportions in which distribution is to be made. When all the distributees stand in the same degree of relationship to the decedent, *distribution* is made *per capita,* each receiving the same share. Thus, if the decedent is survived by three sons, *A*, *B*, and *C*, each of them would be entitled to receive one third of the estate.

If the distributees stand in different degrees of relationship, distribution is made in as many equal parts as there are family lines or stirpes represented in the nearest generation. Parents take to the exclusion of their children or subsequent descendants; and when members of the nearest generation have died, descendants of such deceased members take by way of representation. This is called *stirpital distribution* or *distribution per stirpes.* This means that if, in the above illustration, *A* had died before the decedent and was survived by two sons, *D* and *E*; and *B* had died before the decedent and was survived by three sons and one daughter, *F*, *G*, *H*, and *I*; and *C* was living and had two sons, *J* and *K*, at the time of the decedent's death, distribution would be made as follows:

(1) Since there are three family lines, the estate would be divided into three equal parts and each line would receive one part.

(2) *C* would receive a one-third share and since *C* is living, his children *J* and *K* would not receive any part of the estate.

(3) *A* and *B* died before the decedent but are survived by children who would therefore take the shares which their respective parents would have received.

(4) As the children of *A* are in the same degree of relationship and as they are to divide a one-third share between them, *D* and *E* each would receive a one-sixth share.

(5) As the children of *B* are in the same degree of relationship and as they are to divide a one-third share between them, *F*, *G*, *H*, and *I* each would receive a one-twelfth share.

The distribution may be graphically represented as follows:

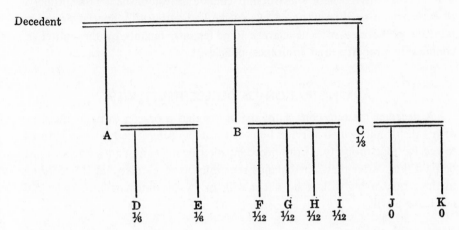

2 / *Nature of relation.* A person not related to the decedent by marriage may inherit only if he has a blood relationship. "In-law" relations do not share under the intestate statutes.

Intestate statutes providing for the distribution of part of the decedent's estate to children, whether of the decedent or of other persons, are interpreted as applying to natural legitimate children. Modern statutes quite commonly extend this definition to include adopted children and treat them the same as natural children. By statute, illegitimate children are treated as legitimate children with respect to inheritance from or through their mother or members of her family, but are ignored in distribution with respect to the father or his family. If the paternity of the illegitimate children has been acknowledged or legally established, however, such children will inherit from the father.

3 / *Murder of decedent.* The trend of intestate legislation is to provide that a person who murders the decedent cannot inherit from him by intestacy. In the absence of such a statute a majority of courts hold that such inheritance cannot be denied, while a minority refuse to allow inheritance under such circumstances.[13]

4 / *Death of distributee after decedent.* The persons entitled to distribution of a decedent's estate are determined as of the date of his death.

---

[13] *Reagan* v. *Brown*, 59 N.Mex. 423, 285 P.2d 789.

If a distributee dies thereafter, his rights are not extinguished but pass to his own estate to be distributed either to his heirs or in accordance with the terms of his will.

5 / Simultaneous death. Under the Uniform Simultaneous Death Act, it is provided that where survivorship cannot be established, "the property of each person shall be disposed of as if he had survived." Special provision is made in the case of beneficiaries, joint tenants, tenants by the entireties, community property, and insurance policies.[14]

ADMINISTRATION OF DECEDENTS' ESTATES

A decedent's estate consists of the assets that a person owns at the time of his death and which survive him. It must be determined who is entitled to receive that property. If the decedent died owing debts, those debts must be paid first. After that, any balance remaining is to be distributed according to the terms of his will, if he left a will, or by the intestate law, if he did not leave a will.

Definitions

The decedent has the privilege of naming in his will the person to administer his estate. If he does so, the person is called an *executor*. If the person so named is a woman, the title is *executrix*. If the decedent failed to name an executor in his will or if he did not leave a will, the law permits another person, usually a close relative, to obtain the appointment of someone to wind up the estate. The latter person is an *administrator* or *administratrix*. Administrators and executors are often referred to generally as *personal representatives* of the decedent since they represent the decedent or stand in his place.

When Administration Is Not Necessary

No administration is required when the decedent did not own any property at the time of his death or when all the property he owned was jointly owned with another person who acquired the decedent's interest by right of survivorship upon his death.

In some states special statutes have been adopted providing for a shortened procedure of administration when the decedent leaves only a small estate, commonly under $1,000. In many states, if all of the parties in interest, creditors and relatives of the decedent, can agree on what shares or amounts each one is to receive, it is possible for a *settlement agreement*

---

[14] This Act has been adopted for the District of Columbia and the Panama Canal Zone and in every state except Arizona, Louisiana, and Ohio.

to be made by which the estate is divided without any formal court proceedings.

Appointment of Personal Representative

An executor or administrator is appointed by a court or officer by granting *letters testamentary,* in the case of an executor, or *letters of administration,* in the case of an administrator. For the appointment of a personal representative, an application or petition is filed with the court or officer setting forth the details of the decedent's death, stating that the decedent, if a resident of the state, lived within the county or, if a nonresident, that property of the decedent is within the county, and reciting the facts which justify the appointment of the personal representative.

1 / Person entitled to act as personal representative. If the decedent has named an executor in his will, that person has the right to act as personal representative or to decline to do so. If he refuses to act, or if no executor has been named, an administrator is appointed. Statutes generally give the right to act as administrator to the surviving spouse or near relatives of the decedent and his creditors, in that order. If there is no one in any of these classes who is willing to serve, provision is made for the appointment of "any fit person" to act as administrator.

Facts: Eli Adkins owed money to his creditors. In order to delay and defraud them, he transferred his property to his wife Nellie. When he died, there was only $300 in his estate. The creditors, who were still unpaid, opposed the granting of letters of administration to Nellie.

Decision: Judgment for Adkins' creditors. Nellie was disqualified from serving as administratrix because her interest was adverse to the creditors of the estate since she was a party to the plan to defraud them and would naturally oppose giving up the property in order that they be paid. (Adkins Estate, 133 Mont. 27, 319 P.2d 512)

2 / Oath and bond. When a personal representative is appointed, he is required to take an oath and file a bond that he will properly administer the estate according to law. In some states an executor is not required to furnish a bond if he is a resident of the state and in sound financial condition or if the testator has expressly directed in his will that no bond be required.

Proof of Claims Against the Estate

1 / Procedure. In very general terms the statutes provide for some form of public notice of the grant of letters, as by advertisement. Creditors are then required to give notice of their claims within a period specified either by statute or a court order, as within six months. In most states the failure to present the claim within the specified time bars the claim. In other states the creditor may assert a late claim with respect to any assets of the estate in the hands of the representative at the time that he asserts his claim.

2 / Nature of claims. Generally any debt or liability of the decedent existing at the time of his death may be asserted against the estate. An exception is made to this rule in the case of those causes of action which are regarded as being so personal that the cause of action dies with the death of a party to it. In addition to those claims that were the personal obligations of the decedent, his estate is also liable for reasonable funeral expenses, the expense of administering his estate, a statutory allowance given to the family to help tide them over the period of adjustment following the death, and estate taxes.

> **Facts:** Haeberle and Barth, undertakers, presented a claim to Weber as executor of the estate of Fredericks for his funeral which had been arranged for by his widow. Weber refused to pay the bill because the funeral had been arranged for by the decedent's widow without consulting the executor.

> **Decision:** Judgment against the estate. The estate of a decedent is liable for reasonable funeral expenses even though contracted by a surviving member of the family without prior consultation with the executor. (Haeberle v. Weber, 56 N.J.S. 556, 153 A.2d 390)

3 / Priority of claims. When the estate of a decedent is insolvent, that is, when it is not sufficiently large to pay all debts and taxes, the law generally provides that certain claims shall be paid first. Although there is great variation of detail, the common pattern of priority provides for the payment of claims against the estate in the following order: (a) funeral expenses; (b) administration expenses; (c) family allowance; (d) claims due the United States; [15] (e) expenses of the last illness; (f) debts due the state, county, and city governments; (g) claims for wages; (h) lien claims; (i) all other debts.

If there are several claimants within a particular class, but not enough money to pay each in full, they share proportionately the balance remaining and creditors in lower priorities receive nothing.

Powers and Duties of Personal Representative

Apart from special powers or duties that a decedent may confer or impose upon his executor, the powers of an executor and administrator are the same. A personal representative is in substance the same as a trustee

---

[15] 31 United States Code, Sec. 191.

with respect to performance of his duties, the use of due care,[16] and the observance of loyalty. His right to compensation and the remedies for the breach of his duties are likewise the same as in the case of a trustee. Statutes also impose upon him various duties peculiar to the winding up of a decedent's estate, such as filing inventories showing the assets of the estate and the payment of estate taxes.

Unlike the trustee whose duty is in general to preserve and manage the trust fund, the personal representative's duty is to distribute the entire estate. He must use reasonable diligence to determine the proper persons to whom distribution is to be made,[17] and to make distribution to them. He must pay the creditors, recognizing their priorities in the case of an insolvent estate, and distribute the balance remaining after the payment of debts to those persons entitled to it. In some states it may be necessary to obtain approval from the court or an official of the distribution to be made.

Termination of Authority of Personal Representative

Ordinarily the authority of a personal representative ends by his being discharged officially upon the completion of his duties. His authority may also be terminated by the revocation of his letters of appointment because they were improperly granted, by his removal because of misconduct, or by his resignation or death.

QUESTIONS AND PROBLEMS

1. Checklist of legal terms—wills:
    (a) testate distribution (684)
    (b) will; testator or testatrix, beneficiary (684)
    (c) legacy or bequest, legatee (684)
    (d) devise, devisee (684)
    (e) testamentary capacity (684)
    (f) testamentary intent (685)
    (g) attestation clause, publication (686)
    (h) codicil (687)
    (i) revival (688)
    (j) probate (688)
    (k) holographic will (688), nuncupative will (688), conditional or contingent will (689)
    (l) general legacy; specific legacy or devise; residuary bequest, devise, or legacy (689)
    (m) demonstrative bequest (689)
    (n) abate (689)
    (o) ademption (690)

---

[16] *In re Stewart*, 145 Ore. 460, 28 P.2d 642.
[17] *Peterson* v. *Peterson*, 173 Kan. 636, 251 P.2d 221.

2. State the objective(s) of each of the following rules of law:
   (a) A testator may have capacity to make a will even though he does not have capacity to make a contract.
   (b) When the estate of a decedent is insolvent and therefore all debts cannot be paid in full, the law generally provides for the payment of claims against the estate in a particular order.

3. Liggett's will names Macke as a legatee. At the time of Liggett's death Macke has been committed to a mental institution. Is Macke disqualified as a beneficiary?

4. Holstead executes a will. Later he revokes this will but makes no provision for the distribution of his estate. After Holstead's death it is established that he was sane at the earlier date but insane at the later one. How will Holstead's estate be distributed?

5. Liberman executes a will providing for the distribution of his entire estate to his brother and two sisters. Later Liberman marries. What effect, if any, does the marriage have upon Liberman's will?

6. Nesbitt's last will revoked an earlier will that is available at the time of probate. Lindberg proves that Nesbitt's last will was executed under undue influence. How will Nesbitt's estate be distributed?

7. James writes his will in longhand. Is this instrument classified as a holographic or nuncupative will?

8. McGrath bequeaths $10,000 to O'Grady, $5,000 to Tussey, and $1,000 to Pacella. He also bequeaths his oil paintings to Robb and names Sagel as residuary legatee. After McGrath's death there is available for distribution $8,000 in cash and the oil paintings. How will McGrath's estate be distributed?

9. Magee, who is named as a legatee of $5,000 in Ogden's will, dies before Ogden does. If Ogden does not revise his will, what distribution will be made of Magee's legacy?

10. Anna Miller wrote a will 11 pages long and enclosed it in an envelope, which she sealed, and then wrote on the envelope, "My last will & testament" and signed her name below this statement. This was the only place where she signed her name on any of the papers. Could this be admitted to probate as her will? (Miller's Executor v. Shannon, [Ky.] 299 S.W.2d 103)

11. Field executed a will. Upon her death the will was found in her safe deposit box, but the part of the will containing the fifth bequest was torn from the will. This torn fragment was also found in the box. There was no evidence that anyone other than Field had ever opened the box. A proceeding was brought to determine whether the will was entitled to be probated. Decide. (Flora v. Hughes, 312 Ky. 478, 228 S.W.2d 27)

12. Checklist of legal terms—intestacy and administration:
    (a) intestate succession; lineal descendant, collateral heirs (691)
    (b) right of escheat (692)
    (c) distribution per capita, stirpital distribution or distribution per stirpes (692)
    (d) executor or executrix, administrator or administratrix, personal representative (694)
    (e) settlement agreement (694)
    (f) letters testamentary, letters of administration (695)

13. Nester bequeaths his estate to his surviving brothers and sisters. Will the distribution of his estate be on a per capita or per stirpes basis?

14. Ong, who dies intestate, is survived by his son, Joseph, and Joseph's three children; and by two other grandchildren who are children of Ong's daughter, Helen, deceased. How will Ong's estate be divided?

15. Paden and his wife own certain property as tenants by the entireties. Paden's policies of life insurance name his wife as beneficiary. If Paden dies intestate, how will his estate be settled?

16. Rahn dies intestate, leaving an estate valued at $20,000. In a state that permits a settlement agreement, what would be the procedure for winding up Rahn's estate in this manner?

17. Poe, who dies intestate, was preceded in death by his wife. He has no surviving relatives. Who may be appointed administrator of Poe's estate?

18. Randall is awarded judgment for $1,000 in an action against Tuttle. Before Randall collects his judgment, Tuttle dies. What recourse, if any, does Randall have?

19. In the administration of Winkler's estate, $1,000 remains for the general creditors after prior claims have been paid. The claims of the general creditors consist of Powers' account for $1,000 dated January 15, Tutt's account for $200 dated July 2, Herrmann's account for $300 dated December 20, and Lanham's account for $500 dated March 31. All of the claims originated in the same calendar year. How much will each of these creditors receive?

20. Turner, the sole proprietor of a successful retail bakery, dies intestate. What is the duty of the administrator of Turner's estate with regard to the bakery?

21. By his will, Joseph Novak bequeathed $500 to his wife's nephew. The nephew died before Joseph. The nephew's daughter, Claire Kortan, claimed that she was entitled to the nephew's share because of a statute providing that a bequest to a relative of a testator shall not fail because of the legatee's death before the testator but should pass to the "issue" of the legatee so dying. Was she entitled to the nephew's share? (Kovar v. Kortan, 3 Ohio Misc. 63, 209 N.E.2d 762)

Chapter 60

Bankruptcy

Under a survival-of-the-fittest system, society could ignore those who become insolvent. However, our society is not willing to do so. It has accordingly provided a system by which the honest debtor can, in substance, pay into court what he has, be relieved of all unpaid debts, and start economic life anew. This is achieved by means of bankruptcy laws in the case of the federal government and insolvency laws in the case of the states.

Historically these laws were not concerned with benefiting the debtor as much as they were with benefiting creditors. In their origin bankruptcy laws were designed to enable creditors to compel a fraudulent debtor to bring his property into court and pay it to his creditors, thus preventing him from concealing his property or from paying it only to some of his creditors. Today, bankruptcy and insolvency proceedings partake of both features as can be seen from the fact that such a proceeding may be started by the debtor himself or by his creditors.

State insolvency laws have only a limited sphere of operation today because the federal bankruptcy laws have superseded them to a large degree, but state statutes relating to voluntary assignments made by a debtor for the benefit of all of his creditors may still be in force.

Bankruptcy proceedings under the federal law are brought in the federal district courts.

Classification of Bankrupts

1 / Voluntary bankrupts. A *voluntary bankrupt* is one who subjects himself to the bankruptcy law. Any person, and in most instances any corporation or an association, may become a voluntary bankrupt. The filing of a voluntary petition automatically operates as an adjudication or determination that the petitioner is bankrupt.

Municipal, railroad, insurance, and banking corporations, and savings and loan associations cannot be voluntary bankrupts.[1] Ordinarily it is unimportant why the debtor chooses to go into bankruptcy so long as the facts exist that bring the debtor within the scope of the bankruptcy act.

---

[1] 11 United States Code, Sec. 22(a).

2 / Involuntary bankrupts. An *involuntary bankrupt* is one who has been subjected to the bankruptcy law upon the petition of his creditors. Under the prescribed circumstances, most natural persons, partnerships, and corporations owing debts that amount to the sum of $1,000 or more may be forced by creditors into bankruptcy. Wage earners [2] and farmers; municipal, railroad, insurance, and banking corporations; and savings and loan associations cannot be adjudicated involuntary bankrupts.[3]

Involuntary Proceedings

If there are twelve or more creditors, three or more of them must join in the petition. If there are less than twelve creditors, it is permissible for one of them to file the petition.[4]

The petitioning creditor or creditors must have provable claims [5] against the debtor totaling $500 or more. The amount of the claims must be in excess of the value of pledged securities held by the creditors.

Facts: Day was a debtor against whom the East Tennessee National Bank filed a petition in bankruptcy. In the petition the bank alleged that it had made a loan to Day which was secured by stock as collateral, that upon default it sold the stock, and that there was a deficiency which it claimed as a creditor. Day objected by stating that a secured creditor cannot establish any claim in bankruptcy proceedings.

Decision: Judgment for the bank. A secured creditor may assert in bankruptcy a claim for the excess of his debt over the security. If the security has been sold and a claim is made for a deficiency, the secured creditor must aver that a proper sale of the security has been made. The bankrupt may then challenge the validity of the sale of the security or the existence of a deficiency. (East Tennessee National Bank v. Day, [D.C. Fla.] 5 F.S. 473)

The debtor against whom the petition is filed may appear and oppose the petition.[6] If the debtor should allege that there are more than eleven creditors when less than three filed the petition, the creditors who have not joined in the petition are given an opportunity to be heard. If the statutory number of creditors do not join in the petition, it will be dismissed.[7]

---

[2] A "wage earner" for this purpose is defined as an individual who works for wages, salary, or hire, and whose compensation does not exceed $1,500 a year. 11 USC Sec. 1(32).

[3] Special statutory provision is made for the reorganization and liquidation of such corporations because of the nature of the enterprise and in order to protect the public.

[4] 11 USC Sec. 95(b).

[5] See p. 704. A claim may be unliquidated as to amount provided that it is not contingent as to liability, although the unliquidated claim may be disqualified if a maximum value cannot be estimated. Sec. 95(b).

[6] 11 USC Sec. 41(b).

[7] Sec. 95(d).

Acts of Bankruptcy

An involuntary petition may not be filed unless the debtor has committed an act of bankruptcy within four months prior to the filing of the petition.[8]

A debtor commits an act of bankruptcy under federal statute (1) by concealing, removing, or permitting to be concealed or removed, any part of his property with intent to hinder, delay, or defraud his creditors, or any of them; (2) by transferring, while insolvent, any portion of his property to one or more of his creditors with intent to prefer such creditor or creditors over his other creditors; (3) by suffering, or permitting, while insolvent, any creditor to obtain a lien upon any of his property through legal proceedings and not having vacated or discharged such lien within thirty days from date thereof or at least five days before the date set for any sale or other disposition of such property; (4) by making a general assignment for the benefit of his creditors; (5) while insolvent, by permitting or being forced to put a receiver or a trustee in charge of his property; or (6) by admitting in writing his inability to pay his debts and his willingness to be adjudged a bankrupt.[9]

Insolvency is a necessary element of the second, third, and fifth acts of bankruptcy, but not of the others. The Bankruptcy Act declares that a person is deemed to be *insolvent* under the provisions of the statute "whenever the aggregate of his property, exclusive of any property which he may have conveyed, transferred, concealed, removed, or permitted to be concealed or removed, with intent to defraud, hinder, or delay his creditors, shall not at a fair valuation be sufficient in amount to pay his debts." [10]

Bankruptcy Officials

The actual bankruptcy proceeding, apart from that which takes place in court, is under the control of certain officials:

1 / Receiver. On the petition of creditors who fear that the assets of the debtor will be lost, a *receiver* may be appointed as custodian to preserve the assets [11] and turn them over to the trustee when appointed.

2 / Trustee. The creditors of the debtor elect—or if they fail to do so, the court appoints—a trustee. The *trustee* has a double role in that he automatically by operation of law becomes the owner of the property of the debtor not otherwise exempt, and he acquires the rights that a most favored creditor would have to set aside past transactions of the debtor that are

---

[8] Sec. 21(b).
[9] The filing of a voluntary petition in bankruptcy is in itself an act of bankruptcy since the debtor admits in writing his inability to pay his debts and his willingness to be adjudged a bankrupt.
[10] 11 USC Sec. 1(19).
[11] Sec. 11(3).

harmful to his creditors. Specifically he is authorized to avoid certain preferences gained by a judgment against the bankrupt or by a transfer of property, of which recording or registering is required, within four months prior to the filing of the petition or after the filing thereof and before adjudication.[12] He is required by the terms of the Bankruptcy Act to recover for the benefit of the creditors any of the bankrupt's property that has been transferred within four months prior to the filing of the petition, with the intent to hinder, delay, or defraud any creditors, or that is in the hands of a person under a transfer that is void by the laws of any state.[13]

Facts: Burbank owed money to Philbrick. The latter went into bankruptcy but by accident failed to list as an asset the debt owed him by Burbank. Philbrick was discharged in bankruptcy. Some time thereafter he sued Burbank for the balance due. Burbank defended on the ground that title to the debt had passed to the trustee who had abandoned the debt by not taking action to collect it, and therefore the claim could not be collected by Philbrick.

Decision: Judgment for Philbrick. There could be no abandonment by the trustee of property that was not listed as an asset of the estate and which was not known to the trustee. Upon the discharge of the bankrupt and the termination of the authority of the trustee in bankruptcy, the title to the unadministered asset is revested in the bankrupt, by whom it could be collected. However, creditors of the bankrupt who had not been paid in full could thereafter claim that the money recovered by the discharged bankrupt should be applied to the payment of their otherwise discharged claims. (Philbrick v. Burbank, 101 N.H. 311, 141 A.2d 888)

3 / Referee. A *referee* is appointed for a six-year term to hear the evidence in bankruptcy cases and to submit his findings to the court. He acts in the nature of a special bankruptcy court.

Administration of the Bankrupt's Estate

1 / Meetings of creditors. At various times in the administration of the bankruptcy, a meeting of the creditors is held, such as the initial meeting to appoint a trustee, subsequent meetings to pass on particular matters authorized by the Bankruptcy Act, and a final meeting when the estate is to be closed.[14]

The creditors pass upon matters submitted to them by a majority in number and in the amount of claims of all creditors and who are present and whose claims have been allowed. Creditors who have priority or security are

---

[12] Sec. 96(b). The mere adjudication in bankruptcy does not automatically avoid or vacate a lien created within the four months period, and the lien remains in force unless avoided by the trustee. *Crystal Laundry & Cleaners, Inc.* v. *Continental Finance & Loan Co.,* 97 Ga.App. 823, 104 S.E.2d 654.
[13] 11 USC Secs. 107(d), 110(e).
[14] Sec. 91(d), (e).

not entitled to vote, nor are their claims counted in computing the number of creditors or the amounts of their claims, unless the amounts of their claims exceed the values of such priorities or securities, and then only for such excess.[15]

2 / Examination of persons. Provision is made for the examination of the bankrupt and other persons as to his property and his conduct relating thereto. The wife of the bankrupt may be examined only in respect to business transacted by her or to which she is a party, and to determine whether she has transacted or has been a party to any business of her husband.[16]

3 / Sale of bankrupt's assets. In order to pay the debts of the bankrupt, it is necessary to convert his assets into cash and the trustee is accordingly authorized to sell his property. The sale in general may be made in any manner that is in the best interests of the estate. Such sales are under the supervision of the bankruptcy court; and if any property is sold for less than 75 percent of its value, confirmation by the court is necessary.

4 / Proof and allowance of claims. Each creditor is required to file a sworn statement setting forth his claim and the basis thereof. These claims are ordinarily passed upon by the referee, although in some instances they may be considered initially by the court. The claim is then allowed or disallowed as in any other lawsuit. A claim must ordinarily be disallowed if not presented until more than six months after the first meeting of creditors.[17] A creditor who received some preferential payment or transfer of property within four months prior to the filing of the petition in bankruptcy cannot prove his claim unless he surrenders such payment or transfer.[18] If the claim of a creditor is secured, he is also barred from proving his claim except as to that part of his claim in excess of the security.

5 / Claims that are provable. Not all claims may be proven, that is, be permitted to share in the distribution of the assets of the bankrupt debtor. The claims that may be proved are: (1) a debt evidenced by a judgment or an instrument in writing, absolutely owing at the time of the filing of the petition by or against the bankrupt, whether then payable or not; (2) a debt due as costs against a bankrupt who was, at the time of the filing of the petition by or against the bankrupt, the plaintiff in an action that would pass to the trustee and that the trustee, upon notice thereof, declines to prosecute; (3) a debt founded upon a claim for costs, incurred in good faith by a

---

[15] Sec. 92(a), (b).
[16] Sec. 44(a).
[17] Sec. 93(n).
[18] Secs. 93(g), 96(b), 107.

creditor before the filing of the petition, in an action to recover a provable debt; (4) a debt based upon an open account, or upon a contract expressed or implied; (5) a debt based upon a provable debt reduced to judgment after the filing of the petition and before the consideration of the bankrupt's application for a discharge, less costs and interest after the filing of the petition; (6) an award of workmen's compensation; (7) a right to damages for negligence; (8) contingent debts and contingent contractual liabilities; and (9) claims for anticipatory breach of contract.[19]

In respect to an *unliquidated claim* of a creditor, that is, a claim for an uncertain or disputed amount, the Bankruptcy Act provides that upon application to the court of bankruptcy, such a claim shall be liquidated or estimated in such a manner as the court shall direct. If possible to liquidate or estimate the claim within a reasonable time, the claim may be allowed against the estate.[20]

6 / Distribution of estate. After all of the bankrupt's debts are determined, the assets that have been collected by the trustee are distributed first to those creditors with priorities; then to the general creditors without priorities; and, should any balance remain after all creditors have been paid, the balance to the bankrupt. These payments, called *dividends,* are made in installments.

The Bankruptcy Act confers a prior right of payment to (a) costs of administration and expenses necessary to preserve the estate, filing fees paid by creditors in involuntary proceedings, expenses of creditors in recovering property transferred or concealed by the bankrupt, and the reasonable expenses of creditors in opposing a composition that is refused or set aside; (b) wages due to workmen, clerks, traveling or city salesmen, or servants, earned within three months preceding the petition, not to exceed $600 to each person; (c) expenses of creditors in opposing an arrangement or a plan for the discharge of a bankrupt, or in convicting a person of violating the bankruptcy law; (d) taxes owed by the bankrupt, except taxes against property over and above the value of the interest of the bankrupt therein; and (e) debts owed persons, including the United States, who by law are entitled to priority.

Facts: A proceeding was pending for the reorganization of the Pacific Oil & Meal Co., a debtor corporation, under the provisions of the Bankruptcy Act. Hart filed a claim for $1,556.81. He contended that he was entitled to priority of payment to the extent of $600 on the ground that such sum was earned as a clerk within three months prior to the commence-

---

[19] Sec. 103(a).
[20] Secs. 93(d), 103(d).

ment of the proceedings. One of the creditors filed an objection to the allowance of the priority of payment on the ground that Hart was the secretary and treasurer of the corporation and was therefore not an employee whose claim for wages was given a priority. Hart claimed that in spite of his title he was and did the work of a clerk, which, if true, would entitle him to a priority.

Decision: Hart was not entitled to a priority. He had been hired as an executive officer and the bulk of his duties were as such. The fact that he performed some services that could be performed by a clerk did not alter the fact that he was an officer. His compensation was indivisible so that it was not possible to allocate any particular part of it to his officer's duties and to his nonofficer's duties. Hence no part of his salary was entitled to a priority on the ground that it was compensation for his clerical activities. (In re Pacific Oil & Meal Co., [D.C. S.D. Cal.] 24 F.S. 767)

Rights and Duties of Bankrupt

The Bankruptcy Act confers certain rights upon and imposes certain duties on the bankrupt.[21] If the debtor fails to cooperate or if he deceives the court as by the concealment of property which he hopes to save for himself, the law provides adequate penalties, in addition to denying the bankrupt the benefits of the statute.

1 / Rights. The debtor has the right to request a discharge in bankruptcy and to object to being declared or adjudicated a bankrupt. He is also protected generally from arrest on civil process while within the court district on matters relating to the bankruptcy proceeding. The debtor is given an immunity from criminal prosecution based on his testimony at meetings other than at the hearing on his discharge and other than in a prosecution for perjury.

2 / Duties. The debtor is required to file statements showing the property he possesses, any claim to an exemption, and the names of his creditors, with detailed information as to their claims. He must also attend meetings of creditors and hearings before the referee and court, and answer all proper questions relating to his estate. He must examine the proofs of claim filed against him to see if he disputes them, and he must obey orders of the bankruptcy court.

Discharge in Bankruptcy

1 / Application for discharge. The adjudication of any individual to be a bankrupt operates automatically as an application for a discharge in

---

[21] Sec. 25.

bankruptcy. A corporation may file an application for a discharge within six months after it is adjudged to be a bankrupt.[22]

The application for discharge will be denied if the bankrupt has: (a) committed certain offenses punishable by imprisonment as provided in the act; (b) unjustifiably destroyed, mutilated, falsified, concealed, or failed to keep books of account or records from which his financial status and business transactions might be ascertained; (c) obtained money or property on credit by a false representation in writing concerning his financial condition; (d) permitted others, within a year previous to the filing of the petition, to remove, transfer, conceal, or destroy any of his property, with the intent to hinder, delay, or defraud creditors, or has been guilty of this himself; (e) been granted a discharge in bankruptcy within six years; (f) refused, during the proceedings, to answer any material question approved by the court, or to obey any lawful order of the court; or (g) failed to explain satisfactorily the loss of any assets, or the deficiency of his assets to pay his debts.[23]

2 / Effect of discharge. A discharge in bankruptcy releases the bankrupt from all his provable debts, except debts that:[24] (a) are due as taxes; (b) are liabilities (1) for obtaining property by false pretenses or false representation, (2) for willful and malicious injuries to the person or the property of another, (3) for alimony for the support of a wife or a child, (4) for seduction of an unmarried female, (5) for breach of promise accompanied by seduction, and (6) for criminal conversation; (c) have not been listed by the bankrupt in time to be proved, unless the creditor had notice or actual knowledge of the proceedings; (d) are created by the bankrupt's fraud, embezzlement, misappropriation, or defalcation while acting as an officer or in any fiduciary position; (e) are wages due to workmen, clerks, salesmen, or servants, which have been earned within three months preceding the petition; or (f) are due for moneys of an employee received or retained by the bankrupt to secure the faithful performance by such employee of the provisions of the contract of employment.

Facts: Schwaner borrowed money from the Seybold Finance Co. He obtained a renewal of the loan on the basis of an application that did not state the total amount of debts owed to third persons. Later Schwaner was discharged in bankruptcy after having properly listed the debt due to the Seybold Finance Co. The finance company claimed that it was not barred by the discharge in bankruptcy because the renewal of its loan had been obtained on the basis of a false application. Schwaner asserted that he had not been told to make a complete statement of all his debts but merely to list some credit references.

[22] Sec. 32(a).
[23] Sec. 32(c).
[24] Sec. 35.

Decision: Judgment for Schwaner. All that was shown was that the application for renewal did not state all the bankrupt's debts. It was not shown that the bankrupt had tried to defraud the finance company, nor that the company had acted in reliance on the false statement. Since the company did not show that there was an obtaining of property by false representations, the discharge in bankruptcy was a bar to its claim. (Seybold Finance Service v. Schwaner, [La.App.] 102 So.2d 317)

Compositions

The National Bankruptcy Act as amended in 1938 provides several plans for debtors that are in the nature of compositions. These plans are known as corporate reorganizations, arrangements, real property arrangements by persons other than corporations, and wage earners' plans.

1 / Corporate reorganizations. The provisions for corporate reorganizations [25] permit a corporation, an indenture trustee, or three or more creditors of the corporation with certain claims amounting in the aggregate to $5,000 or over to file a petition for a reorganization. The petition must show among other things that the corporation is insolvent or is unable to pay its debts as they mature and that relief is necessary under this plan. It may also include the proposed scheme of reorganization. The statute directs the court to confirm a plan of reorganization provided that it is fair, equitable, and feasible; that it has been proposed and accepted in good faith; and that all payments made or promised are approved as reasonable.[26]

2 / Arrangements. The provisions for arrangements [27] permit any debtor who could become a bankrupt to file a petition for the acceptance of a plan for the settlement, satisfaction, or extension of the time of payment of his unsecured debts. The statute directs the court to confirm the plan if it is satisfied that the plan is fair, equitable, and feasible, that the debtor has done no act which would bar a discharge in bankruptcy, and that the proposal and the acceptance are made in good faith.

3 / Real property arrangements. The provisions for real property arrangements [28] permit any debtor who could become a bankrupt, except a corporation, to file a petition for the acceptance of a plan for the alteration or the modification of the rights of creditors holding debts secured by real property or by a chattel real of which the debtor is the legal or equitable owner. The statute stipulates that the court shall confirm a plan that is accepted by the creditors in good faith.

---

[25] 11 USCA, Secs. 501 to 676, inclusive.
[26] *S.E.C.* v. *United States Realty and Improvement Co.*, 310 U.S. 434.
[27] 11 USCA, Secs. 701 to 799, inclusive.
[28] Ch. 12, Secs. 801 to 926, inclusive.

4 / Wage earners' plans. The provisions for wage earners' plans [29] permit an individual who is insolvent or is unable to pay his debts as they mature and whose principal income is derived from salary, wages, or commissions to file a petition for the acceptance of a composition or an extension of time, or both, in view of future earnings or salary. The statute directs the court to confirm a plan that is proposed and accepted by the creditors in good faith.

QUESTIONS AND PROBLEMS

1. Checklist of legal terms:
   - (a) voluntary bankrupt (700), involuntary bankrupt (701)
   - (b) insolvent (702)
   - (c) receiver (702), trustee (702), referee (703)
   - (d) unliquidated claim (705)
   - (e) dividends (705)
   - (f) corporate reorganizations (708), arrangements (708), real property arrangements (708), wage earners' plans (709)

2. State the objective(s) of each of the following rules of law:
   - (a) The filing of a voluntary petition automatically operates as an adjudication that the petitioner is bankrupt.
   - (b) A debtor may obtain court approval of a fair plan of adjustment or arrangement of his debts without going into bankruptcy.

3. McElroy, a farmer, owed $2,000 to several creditors. Were these creditors entitled to subject McElroy to the bankruptcy law when McElroy's debts were due and unpaid?

4. Three creditors filed a petition in bankruptcy against Paine. It was proved that within four months preceding the filing of the petition, Paine had concealed the greater part of his assets with the intent to defraud his creditors. In opposing the petition, it was contended that Paine had not committed an act of bankruptcy because he had not been insolvent at the time of the conveyance of his assets. Do you agree?

5. The Kimble Grocery and Meat Market, a partnership, was indebted to the McDevitt Wholesale Grocery Company and other creditors. Certain of these creditors filed a petition in involuntary bankruptcy against the partnership, charging that, while insolvent, it had paid $500 to the McDevitt Wholesale Grocery Company with the intent to give a preference over other creditors. May the partnership be forced into involuntary bankruptcy by the creditors of the firm?

6. While solvent, O'Neal permitted a creditor to obtain a lien on his property through a legal proceeding. The lien was not discharged by O'Neal within thirty days from the date the lien was obtained. Other creditors of O'Neal filed a petition to have him adjudged a bankrupt.

---

[29] Ch. 13, Secs. 1001 to 1086, inclusive.

O'Neal contended that he had not committed an act of bankruptcy. Was his contention sound?

7. Within four months prior to the filing of a petition in bankruptcy, Kimmell transferred a truck to Plummer, his brother-in-law, for the purpose of defrauding his creditors. The trustee in bankruptcy brought an action to compel Plummer to return the truck or, if the truck had been sold, to pay the trustee the proceeds of the sale. Was the trustee entitled to judgment?

8. At a meeting of creditors certain decisions were made by a majority of one vote. Two of the creditors who voted in favor of these decisions held securities for the amount of their claims. Do you agree with the contention of a creditor that the action on these matters had not been properly taken?

9. At a meeting of creditors the bankrupt's wife was questioned concerning personal transactions that she had made by using money that she had personally inherited. She refused to answer the questions. Was she entitled to do so?

10. Certain property belonging to Shoop, a bankrupt, was ordered sold by a court of bankruptcy. The property was sold at a private sale. Was the sale properly made?

11. Kincaid is one of the creditors of Rogers, a bankrupt. Kincaid has a provable claim of $2,000 for which Rogers had pledged certain securities worth $1,500. What amount of Kincaid's claim will be allowed?

12. The Sherrill Novelty Products Company became a bankrupt. Vogelsang, who had been employed as a traveling salesman by the company, had earned a salary of $1,200 during the two months preceding the filing of the petition. Vogelsang contended that he was entitled to priority in the payment of the bankrupt's debts to the amount of $1,200. Do you agree?

13. Mrs. Putman, as executrix of her husband's estate, obtained a judgment for $10,000 against the Ocean Shore Railway Co. for negligently causing the death of Putman. She and two others filed a petition in bankruptcy against Folger, who had a statutory liability for the debts of the railway corporation. In opposing the petition, he contended that the claim of Mrs. Putman was not a provable debt in bankruptcy. Do you agree? (In re Putman, [D.C. N.D. Cal.] 193 F. 464)

14. De Shazo owed the Household Finance Corporation $349.02. In order to borrow additional money, he submitted a false statement to Household as to the total amount of his debts. Household, relying on this false statement, loaned him $150.98 more and had him sign one note for $500, representing both the unpaid balance of the old loan and the total amount of the new loan. Thereafter De Shazo was discharged in bankruptcy. What effect did the discharge have on the note held by Household Finance and listed in the bankrupt's schedule of indebtedness? (Household Finance Corp. of Seattle v. De Shazo, 57 Wash.2d 771, 359 P.2d 1044)

PART XII

Government and Business

Chapter 61

Government Regulation of Business

The states by virtue of their police power may regulate business in all of its aspects so long as they do not impose an unreasonable burden on interstate commerce or any activity of the federal government. The federal government may impose any regulation upon any phase of business that is required by "the economic needs of the nation." [1]

Neither state nor federal government may impose a regulation that deprives any person of life, liberty, or property without due process of law, nor may it take property except for a public purpose or without paying just compensation. A state may not impair the obligation of contracts nor deprive any person of the equal protection of the laws, nor abridge the privileges and immunities of citizens of the United States. [2]

Regulation of Production, Distribution, and Financing

In order to protect the public from harm, government may establish health and purity standards for food, drugs, and cosmetics, and protect consumers from false advertising and labeling. [3] Without regard to the nature of

---

[1] *American Power & Light Co.* v. *S.E.C.*, 329 U.S. 90.

[2] See generally, Ronald A. Anderson, *Government and Business* (3d ed.; Cincinnati: South-Western Publishing Company, 1966).

[3] Federal legislation is particularly important because of the predominance of interstate business. The Drug Abuse Control Act of 1965 establishes special controls over the production, purchase, and sale of depressant, stimulant, and counterfeit drugs. The Federal Cigarette Labeling Act of 1965 requires the manufacturer of cigarettes to have a conspicuous notation: "Caution: Cigarette Smoking May Be Hazardous to Your Health." Such warning is not required by law in cigarette advertisements, and the power which the Federal Trade Commission would otherwise have to so require has been suspended until July 1, 1969. By amendments to the Food (1958) and Color (1960) Additive Amendments to the Food, Drug, and Cosmetic Act, the addition of cancer-inducing food additives and color additives is prohibited. By the Insecticide, Fungicide, and Rodenticide Acts of 1947, 1954, 1959, and 1964, consumers are provided with various protections from harm through the use of products marketed for such purposes. Additional consumer protection is afforded by the Fair Packaging and Labeling Act of 1966.

711

the product, government may regulate business with respect to what materials may be used, the quantity of a product that may be produced or grown, and the price at which the finished product is to be sold. Government may also engage in competition with private enterprises or own and operate an industry. Ordinarily these powers have only been exercised in case of emergency, as illustrated by the establishment of prices in time of war, or when governmental ownership of the property or enterprise is of great importance to the public, as illustrated by the national ownership of fissionable material.

Under its commerce power the federal government may regulate all methods of interstate transportation and communication, and a like power is exercised by each state as to its intrastate traffic. The financing of business is directly affected by the national government in creating a national currency and in maintaining a federal reserve bank system. State and other national laws may also affect financing by regulating the contracts and documents used in financing, such as bills of lading and commercial paper.

Regulation of Competition

The federal government, and the states in varying degrees, prohibit unfair methods of competition.[4] Frequently a commission is established to determine, subject to review by the courts, whether a given practice comes within the general class of unfair methods of competition. In other instances the statute specifically defines the practice that is condemned.

The Congress has declared "unlawful" all "unfair methods of competition" and has created a Federal Trade Commission to administer the law. The Commission has held that it is unfair to use certain schemes to obtain patronage, such as making gifts to employees for their influence, making gifts to customers, offering so-called "free" articles or services, offering benefits of memberships in a fictitious society or a fictitious membership in a given society, offering pretended guaranties, offering pretended "free trial" offers, offering pretended "valuable" premiums, making offers without intention to supply the goods, making fake demonstrations, securing signatures by trick, and lotteries.

The Commission has also condemned the practice of using harassing tactics, such as coercion by refusing to sell, boycotting, discrimination, disparagement of a competitor or his products, enforcing payment wrongfully, cutting off or restricting the market, securing and using confidential information, spying on competitors, and inducing breach of customer contracts. Another form of unfair competition that has been condemned is misrepresentation by appropriating business or corporate names, simulating trade or

---

[4] Independently of statute, unfair competition may be an actionable tort.

corporate names, appropriating trademarks, simulating the appearance of a competitor's goods, simulating a competitor's advertising, using deceptive brands or labels, and using false and misleading advertising.

Facts: E. Griffiths Hughes, Inc. manufactured and sold Radox Bath Salts, which were falsely advertised as possessing therapeutic qualities. The company was ordered to cease and desist such advertisement by the Federal Trade Commission. The company petitioned for a review of this order.

Decision: Order affirmed. The public is to be protected from false advertising used as a method of unfair competition against other producers of bath salts that make no such claims. (E. Griffiths Hughes, Inc. v. Federal Trade Commission, [C.A.2d] 77 F.2d 886)

In many states, statutes prevent price wars by prohibiting the sale below cost of goods generally or of particular kinds of goods.[5]

Price Discrimination

The federal Clayton Act of 1914, applicable to interstate and foreign commerce, prohibits price discrimination between different buyers of commodities "where the effect of such discrimination may be substantially to lessen competition or tend to create a monopoly in any line of commerce." Discrimination is expressly permitted when it can be justified on the basis of: (1) difference in grade, quality, or quantity involved; (2) the cost of the transportation involved in making the sale; or (3) when the sale is made in good faith in order to meet competition.

The Robinson-Patman Act of 1936 permits price differentials based on differences in the cost of manufacturing, selling, and delivery that are caused by differences in methods or quantities. Price differentials are also permitted because of the deterioration of goods or when the seller in good faith is making a close-out sale of a particular line of goods. The Robinson-Patman Act reaffirms the right of a seller to select his customers and to refuse to deal with anyone he chooses so long as he acts in good faith and not for the purpose of restraining trade.

The federal law prohibits the furnishing of advertising or other services that, when rendered to one purchaser but not another, will have the effect of granting the former a price discrimination or lower rate. It is made illegal for a seller to accept any fee or commission in connection with the sale except for services actually rendered and unless his services are equally available to all on the same terms. The act makes either the giving or the receiving of any illegal price discrimination a criminal offense.

---

[5] *Avella* v. *Almac's*, [R.I.] 211 A.2d 665.

Prevention of Monopolies and Combinations

To protect the public from monopolies and combinations in restraint of trade, almost all of the states have enacted antitrust statutes.

The federal antitrust act, known as the Sherman Act [6] is applicable to both sellers and buyers.

It provides: [Sec. 1] "Every contract, combination in the form of a trust or otherwise, or conspiracy, in restraint of trade or commerce among the several states, or with foreign nations, is declared to be illegal. [Sec. 2] Every person who shall monopolize, or attempt to monopolize, or combine or conspire with any other person or persons to monopolize any part of the trade or commerce among the several states, or with foreign nations, shall be deemed guilty of a misdemeanor." [7]

> Facts: Three California sugar refiners agreed among themselves to pay California sugar-beet farmers a uniform price for their crops. The refined sugar would be sold by the refiners in interstate markets. Mandeville Island Farms, a sugar-beet farmer, sued American Crystal Sugar Co., one of the refiners, for treble damages under the Sherman Act.

> Decision: Judgment for plaintiff. The combination of buyers to pay a fixed price to the sellers was a conspiracy that violated the Sherman Antitrust Act, as against the claim that the Act controlled only sellers. Furthermore, the conspiracy was "within interstate commerce" and therefore subject to the federal statute, because of the effect that the local price-fixing might have on markets in other states in which the refined sugar would be sold. (Mandeville Island Farms v. American Crystal Sugar Co., 334 U.S. 219)

The punishment fixed for the violation of either of these provisions is a fine not exceeding $50,000, or imprisonment not exceeding one year, or both. In addition to this criminal penalty, the law provides for an injunction to stop the unlawful practice and permits the victim of such practices to sue the wrongdoers and recover from them three times the damages that he has sustained.

1 / The rule of reason and industrial giants. The general approach of the Supreme Court of the United States to the trust problem has been that an agreement is not automatically or per se to be condemned as a restraint of interstate commerce merely because it creates a power or a potential to monopolize interstate commerce. It is only when the restraint actually imposed on interstate commerce is unreasonable that the practice is unlawful.

---

[6] This act has been amended by the Clayton Act, the Federal Trade Commission Act, the Shipping Act, and other legislation.
[7] 15 United States Code, Ch. 1, Secs. 1, 2.

Under Section 2 of the Act one man or corporation may violate the law if he or it monopolizes or attempts to monopolize interstate commerce. Some decisions indicated that a single enterprise violated the antitrust law when it held such a position of leadership that by its own act it could change the prices in the industry if it chose. It was apparently indicated that it was illegal to be so big that one could control prices in the industry for an improper purpose if one so desired even though this power had not been exercised. In other words, a giant, even though a sleeping giant, was bad. After seventy odd years of litigation, the question as to whether bigness, unattended by unlawful acts or purposes, is a violation of the antitrust law remains unanswered.

To some extent the question of bigness, at least when it results from merger, has been met by Congress by amending Section 7 of the Clayton Act to provide that a merger of corporations doing interstate business shall be illegal when the effect of the acquisition by one corporation of all or any part of the assets of the other "may be substantially to lessen competition, or to tend to create a monopoly." [8]

2 / Price-fixing. Horizontal price-fixing, that is, agreements between persons performing similar economic functions, such as agreements between manufacturers or between distributors, is illegal under the federal law without regard to whether the price so fixed is reasonable or fair. *Vertical resale price agreements*, that is, agreements made between a manufacturer and his distributor or distributors, a distributor and his dealer or dealers, and so on, are generally valid.[9]

3 / Delivered pricing. In order to meet the problem of maintaining price stability when a geographic distribution of markets is involved, there developed a basing-point system of establishing a fixed price for the goods of all manufacturers within a given line of production. Thus, from 1900 to 1926, the steel industry used the *single basing-point plan* or the "Pittsburgh-Plus Plan" under which the price of steel of any producer to any purchaser anywhere in the United States was quoted as the price of steel at Pittsburgh, plus freight from Pittsburgh to the point of delivery, regardless of the route over which the producer actually shipped the steel. This single basing-point system was later replaced by a *multiple basing-point system* in which, instead of all deliveries being priced at Pittsburgh plus, the country was zoned so that each purchaser would pay the price at a certain city within his zone plus the cost of transportation as though the shipment had come from that city.

Both single and multiple basing-point systems have been condemned by the Supreme Court as illegal whenever they are based upon collusion

---

[8] 15 USC Sec. 18.
[9] See p. 150.

between producers.[10] The exact extent to which they are to be regarded as collusive is not clear. Because of this uncertainty, a number of leading manufacturers have abandoned the basing-point system and have adopted a sales price based on f.o.b. the manufacturer's location.

4 / Stock and director control. The federal Clayton Act prohibits the purchase by a corporation of the stock of another corporation engaged in interstate or foreign commerce when the effect is to lessen competition substantially, or when it restrains commerce or tends to create a monopoly.

Facts: From 1917 to 1919, Du Pont acquired a 23 percent stock interest in General Motors. During the following years, General Motors bought all its automotive finishes and fabrics from Du Pont. In 1949, the United States claimed the effect of the stock acquisition had been to lessen competition in interstate commerce on the theory that the sales to General Motors had not been the result of successful competition but were the result of the stock ownership, and therefore such stock ownership violated the Clayton Act. The United States brought an action against Du Pont, General Motors, and others.

Decision: The ownership of the General Motors stock by the Du Pont company was a violation of the Clayton Act since such stock ownership tended to lessen competition by making it less likely that General Motors would purchase its supplies from an outside supplier. It was immaterial that no unfair advantage had been taken of this power by supplying inferior products. (United States v. E. I. du Pont de Nemours & Company, 353 U.S. 586)

The Clayton Act does not prohibit purchase merely for the purpose of investment or purchase when there is no lessening of competition. It does not prohibit the creation of a subsidiary corporation, nor the acquisition of stock in another company which, though manufacturing or selling the same or a similar article, does not sell within the same price range or within the same geographic market. However, these practices may, in some instances, be condemned as violations of Section 7 of the Clayton Act.

The Clayton Act does not prohibit the holding of stock in competing corporations by the same person. Although it prohibits the director of one corporation from being a director of another competing corporation engaged in commerce if either corporation has assets in excess of $1 million, this prohibition is not effective in checking the monopoly potential of interlocking private shareholding.

5 / Tie-in sales and exclusive dealer agreements. The federal Clayton Act of 1914, applicable to interstate and foreign commerce, prohibits the *tie-in sale* or *tie-in lease* by which the person buying or renting goods agrees

---

[10] *Sugar Institute, Inc.* v. *United States,* 297 U.S. 553.

that he will only use with such goods other material sold or leased by the other party. The Act also prohibits *exclusive dealer agreements* by which a dealer agrees not to handle a competitor's articles. These tie-in and exclusive dealer arrangements are not absolutely prohibited, but only when their effect "may be to substantially lessen competition or tend to create a monopoly in any line of commerce." By virtue of this qualification, a provision that a person leasing machinery shall use only the materials furnished by the lessor is a lawful restriction if the nature of the materials and the machine are such that the machine will not operate with the materials produced or offered by any other person. When the materials furnished by any other competitor would be equally satisfactory, however, the agreement is illegal. Thus an agreement that the lessee of office machinery should use only the paper sold by the lessor for that type of office machine was illegal when it was shown that any other seller could supply paper of suitable quality.

The partial prohibition of the tie-in and the exclusive dealer agreements is limited by the right of a seller to state the terms on which he will deal in bona fide transactions not in restraint of trade. There has also been a judicial trend to approve such agreements when the seller did not hold a dominant position in the market.

6 / Exceptions to the antitrust law. By statute, associations of exporters, marine insurance associations, and farmers' and dairymen's cooperatives are exempt from the Sherman Antitrust Act. By decision, labor unions have been given an exemption. Under certain circumstances a minimum resale price maintenance agreement is also exempt. Congress has also authorized freight pooling and revenue division agreements between railroad carriers, provided the approval of the Interstate Commerce Commission is obtained.

By virtue of statutory exemptions, traffic and trust agreements otherwise prohibited by the antitrust law may be made by ocean carriers, and interstate carriers and telegraph companies may consolidate upon obtaining the approval of the government commission having jurisdiction over them.

Regulation of Employment

Basically the parties are free to make an employment contract on any terms they wish, but by statute employment is subject to certain limitations.[11] Thus persons under a certain age and women cannot be employed at certain kinds of labor. Statutes commonly specify minimum wages and maximum

---

[11] As to workmen's compensation laws, see Ch. 21. As to labor-management relations laws, see Ch. 62.

hours which the employer must observe, and they require employers to provide many safety devices. A state may also require employers to pay employees' wages for the time that they are away from work for the purpose of voting.

1 / Fair Labor Standards Act. By this statute, which is popularly known as the Wage and Hour Act, Congress provides that, subject to certain exceptions, persons working in interstate commerce or in an industry producing goods for interstate commerce must be paid not less than $1.60 an hour; and they cannot be employed for more than 40 hours a week unless they are paid time and a half for overtime. The act prohibits the employment of children under the age of 14 years. It permits the employment of children between the ages of 14 and 16 years in all industries, except mining and manufacturing, under certain prescribed conditions. This act has been followed by a number of states in regulating those phases of industry not within the reach of the federal statute.

2 / Hours of Service Act. Congress provides in this act that no employee of a common carrier engaged in moving trains should work longer than 16 consecutive hours, or within 10 hours thereafter, or within 8 hours after 16 hours of labor within any 24 hours. Employees whose duties are to transmit orders by telephone or telegraph for moving trains are limited to 9 and 13 hours according to the specified circumstances. In case of emergency, however, the hours of work may be extended.

3 / Public Contracts Act. Whenever a contract to manufacture or furnish materials, supplies, and equipment for the United States exceeds $10,000 in amount, the Walsh-Healey Act requires that the contract specify that the contractor shall pay minimum wages and overtime pay, shall not employ child labor, and shall observe standards set by the Act or by the Secretary of Labor of the United States.

4 / Public Works Contracts Act. When a building is constructed for the United States for more than $2,000, the Davis-Bacon Act requires that the contractor agree to pay his laborers and mechanics not less than the prevailing rate of wages as determined by the Department of Labor. By the Copeland Act it is made a federal crime for an employer, or an employee with power to hire and fire, to require any employee on public works construction to return or "kickback" to him any part of the employee's wages.

5 / Fair employment practices acts. With some exceptions, employers are forbidden to discriminate as to compensation and other privileges, and conditions of employment against any person because of race, religious creed, sex, or national origin or because of age.[12] A few states also prohibit discrimination on the basis of age.

The Federal Civil Rights Act of 1964 does not require that every employee be treated the same as every other. It does not prohibit the testing or screening of applicants or employees for the purpose of determining whether a person is qualified to be hired, or promoted, or given a wage increase, or given special training. The Act has no effect upon the employer's right to establish compensation scales, providing for bonus pay and incentive pay, or paying different rates in different geographic areas. The employer may also recognize seniority status, whether voluntarily or as part of a collective bargaining agreement.

The Federal Civil Rights Act expressly declares that an employer is not required to readjust the "balance" of his payroll in order to include any particular percentage of each race, creed, and sex as his employees. When he hires new employees, the only obligation upon him is to refrain from discriminating as to each applicant.

6 / Federal Social Security. The Federal Social Security Act establishes a system of old-age (including health insurance or medicare), survivors, and disability insurance; unemployment compensation insurance; old-age assistance; aid to the needy blind, to dependent children, and to persons permanently and totally disabled; maternal and child-health services; and services for child welfare and crippled children. Only the first of these categories—(OASDHI) the old-age, survivors, disability, and health insurance—is operated directly by the United States government. The balance of the program is operated by the individual states with the national government cooperating and contributing to the cost when the state operates on a plan approved by the national government.

7 / State legislation. The states also have statutory plans of assistance for the unemployed, aged, and disabled. These state plans typically establish an administrative board or agency with which a claim for assistance is filed by a person coming within the category to be benefited by the statute. If the board approves the claim, assistance is given to the applicant in the amount specified by the statute for the number of weeks or other period of time designated by the statute.

State unemployment compensation laws generally deny the payment of benefits when the employee was discharged for good cause; when he abandoned the work without cause, or failed or refused to seek or accept an offer of other suitable employment; or when the unemployment was the result of a labor dispute.

---

[12] Federal Civil Rights Act of 1964. In some states and cities, statutes and ordinances make similar provision.

QUESTIONS AND PROBLEMS

1. Checklist of legal terms:
   (a) horizontal price-fixing, vertical resale price agreements (715)
   (b) single basing-point plan, multiple basing-point system (715)
   (c) tie-in sale (716), exclusive dealer agreement (717)

2. State the objective(s) of each of the following rules of law:
   (a) Horizontal price-fixing is illegal under the federal law without regard to whether the price fixed is fair and reasonable.
   (b) Farmers' and dairymen's co-operatives are exempt by statute from the operation of the Sherman Antitrust Act.

3. McClure is convicted of illegal price discrimination. The discrimination favored Pendery. Can Pendery be prosecuted?

4. A number of master plumbers formed a national organization, the purpose of which was to prevent manufacturers and dealers of plumbing supplies from selling directly to consumers. To accomplish this purpose the members resolved to refuse to patronize any manufacturer or dealer who did not deal exclusively with them. Were these persons guilty of combining to restrain trade and commerce under the terms of federal legislation?

5. What is the legality of—
   (a) horizontal price-fixing?
   (b) vertical price-fixing?

6. (a) When is a single basing-point system of fixing prices illegal?
   (b) When is a multiple basing-point system illegal?

7. (a) Does the Clayton Act prohibit one person from holding stock in two competing corporations?
   (b) Does the act prohibit one person from serving as director of two competing corporations?

8. When are the following arrangements prohibited?
   (a) A tie-in sale?
   (b) An exclusive dealer agreement?

9. To what extent are labor unions subject to the antitrust laws?

10. The Winsted Hosiery Co. labeled mixed wool articles as "natural wool," "Australian wool," and other similar terms that did not indicate the mixed nature of the article. The Federal Trade Commission ordered the company to stop the practice of using a "wool" label to describe a mixed article on the ground that it was an unfair trade practice. The company defended on the ground that all other manufacturers understood that the label was not to be taken as true and that the competitors of the company were not deceived. Was this a valid defense? (Federal Trade Commission v. Winsted Hosiery Company, 258 U.S. 483)

Chapter 62

Labor Law

Labor unions have played an increasingly important role in the relationship of many employees with their employers. The law that has developed as a result of this change in our economic pattern is concerned with labor representation, union security, unfair labor practices, and labor disputes.

Labor Representation

Employees are today generally recognized as having the right to form a union and to require their employer to deal with their union as their bargaining representative.[1]

Although the federal law makes it the duty of both the union and the employer to bargain collectively, there is no duty on either to reach an agreement.

The federal act provides that in the case of industry-wide collective bargaining, the duty to bargain collectively shall also mean that neither party to the contract shall terminate or modify the contract without giving the other party sixty days' notice, and the parties must then meet to negotiate a new contract while both sides continue in operation during the sixty-day period.[2]

1 / Machinery to enforce collective bargaining. To protect the rights of workers to unionize and bargain collectively, the federal government created the National Labor Relations Board. The Board determines the proper collective bargaining unit and who is the representative to bargain on behalf of the workers; and it eliminates unfair practices by which the employer and the unions might interfere with rights of employees.

---

[1] Taft-Hartley Act, Sec. 7. In 1935 the Federal Congress adopted the Wagner Act or National Labor Relations Act. A number of states then adopted similar statutes or "Little Wagner" acts as they were nicknamed. In 1947 the Federal Congress adopted the Taft-Hartley Act or the National Labor Management Relations Act. A number of states then amended their laws to match these changes. The student should therefore bear in mind that wherever it is stated in the text that the federal act of 1935 or 1947 made a particular provision, it is probable that a number of states also copied that provision. In the interest of brevity this observation will not be repeated. In general terms the federal law applies when the employment involved is in interstate commerce or in an industry producing goods for interstate commerce, while a state law applies with respect to local or intrastate production. In addition, the Federal Railway Labor Act contains many provisions similar to the other federal labor relations statutes.

[2] Sec. 8(d).

2 / Equal representation of all employees. Whatever union or person is selected by the majority of the workers within the unit becomes "the exclusive representative(s) of all the employees in such unit for the purposes of collective bargaining in respect to rates of pay, wages, hours of employment, or other conditions of employment." [3] Whether all the workers are members of the representative union or not is immaterial, for in any case this union is the exclusive representative of every employee. [4] It is unlawful for an employee, whether a member of the union or not, to attempt to make a contract with the employer. Except as to grievances, every worker must act through the representative union with respect to his contract of employment. At the same time the union is required to represent all workers fairly, nonmembers as well as members. It is unlawful for the union, in bargaining with the employer, to discriminate in any way against any of the employees. The union cannot use its position as representative of all the workers to further its interests as a union.

Union Security

The *yellow-dog contract* by which the employer specified that an employee would be discharged if he joined any union is now invalid. In addition, the federal law now prohibits a contract by which an employee must belong to a particular union, except to the extent that a union shop is legalized. [5]

1 / Closed and union shops. A *closed shop* in which the employer agrees with a particular union that he will not employ anyone who is not a member of that union was expressly authorized by the 1935 Wagner Act. [6]

A number of statutes and state constitutional amendments were adopted in the late 40's outlawing the closed shop and declaring the right of the nonunion man to work. The Taft-Hartley Act prohibits a closed shop and permits only a *union shop*, when agreed to by the employer and the union. Under this plan the employer is free to hire whomever he pleases but, after a trial period of not more than thirty days, the new employee cannot keep his job unless he joins a union.

It is left to local state law to determine whether an *agency shop* is valid, that is, a union contract provision which requires that nonunion men pay to the union a sum of money equal to union dues in order to retain their employment.

---

[3] Sec. 9(a).
[4] Sec. 9(a).
[5] Sec. 8(a)(3).
[6] Sec. 8(a)(3).

Facts: Higgins and others were nonunion employees of Cardinal Manufacturing Co. Under the union contract with Cardinal, nonunion employees were required to pay to the union an amount equal to the dues and assessments paid to it by the union members. Higgins and the nonunion employees claimed that this agency-shop provision was prohibited by the right-to-work amendment to the Kansas constitution, and brought suit against Cardinal and the union.

Decision: A right-to-work guaranty prohibits an agency-shop agreement. As the right to work is guaranteed, it is improper to subject such right to the condition that the employee make any payment, even though the payment is the same amount that is paid by union members and is sought merely to protect the union from loss of membership that would occur if persons not members could obtain the same benefits as members without paying any dues. (Higgins v. Cardinal Manufacturing Co., 188 Kan. 11, 360 P.2d 456)

2 / Make-work practices. A union may try to make sure that there is enough work for all of its members by refusing to admit new members to the union or by making it very difficult to join, as by a quota system or by the imposition of high initiation fees and dues; by restricting the amount of work which any union man is permitted to do in an hour or a day; by insisting that an employer hire additional or unnecessary men.

At times the policy of one union is in conflict with the policy of another union. This occurs in the case of the *jurisdictional dispute* when two or more unions claim the right to do a particular kind of work. For example, the carpenter's union claims the right to install metal doors because the metal doors replace wooden doors, which were installed by carpenters. The metal worker's union points out that the metal workers and not the carpenters work with metal.

Unfair Labor Practices

The Taft-Hartley Act declares certain practices to be unfair and authorizes the National Labor Relations Board to conduct proceedings to stop such practices.

1 / Unfair employer practices. The federal law declares that it is an unfair labor practice for an employer to interfere with unionization or to discriminate against any employee because of his union activities, or to refuse to bargain collectively.[7]

The Taft-Hartley Act preserves for the parties the right of fair comment. It provides that "the expressing of any views, arguments, or opinion, or the dissemination thereof, whether in written, printed, graphic, or visual form,

---

[7] Sec. 8(a).

shall not constitute or be evidence of an unfair labor practice under any of the provisions of this Act, if such expression contains no threat of reprisal or force or promise of benefit." [8]

2 / Unfair union practices. The federal law declares it to be an unfair labor practice for a union to interfere with employees in forming their unions or refraining from joining a union; to cause an employer to discriminate against an employee because he belongs to another union or no union; to refuse to bargain collectively; and under certain circumstances to stop work or to refuse to work on materials or to persuade others to stop work or refuse to so work.[9]

Although a strike is deemed an unfair labor practice under certain circumstances, the Act does not outlaw strikes generally but provides that "nothing in this Act, except as specifically provided for herein, shall be construed so as either to interfere with or impede or diminish in any way the right to strike, or to affect the limitations or qualifications on that right." [10] This protection is not extended to government employees.[11] It is declared unlawful for them to strike.

The Labor-Management Reporting and Disclosure Act of 1959 expands the definition of unfair labor practices. This Act prohibits and makes criminal picketing conducted to extort money and makes it an unfair labor practice to picket for recognition when a rival union is lawfully recognized and no representation issue can be raised. Agreements between unions and employers that the latter shall not use nonunion materials (hot cargo agreements) are made void and an unfair labor practice, except in the construction and garment industries. Secondary boycotts and the coercion of neutral employers thereby are made unfair labor practices, with exception to some extent of the garment industry.

Neither the limitation of picketing nor the prohibition of secondary boycotts limits the union's right to publicize a labor dispute provided pressure is not exerted thereby on neutral employers nor their employees induced to refuse to work.

3 / Procedure for enforcement. Under the federal act, whenever it is claimed that an unfair labor practice has been committed, the Board issues a complaint. The complaint informs the party of the charges made against him and notifies him to appear at a hearing. The Board makes findings of fact and conclusions of law and either dismisses the complaint or enters an order against the party to stop the unfair labor practice "and to take such

---

[8] Sec. 8(c).
[9] Sec. 8(b).
[10] Sec. 13.
[11] 5 United States Code Sec. 7311, 18 USC Sec. 1918.

affirmative action including reinstatement of employees with or without back pay, as will effectuate the policies of this Act: provided, that where an order directs reinstatement of an employee, back pay may be required of the employer or labor organization, as the case may be, responsible for the discrimination suffered by him. . . ."

Facts: The Phelps Dodge Corp. refused to hire Curtis because he belonged to a labor union. Curtis was unable to find any work for some time. He complained that the Phelps Dodge Corporation was guilty of an unfair labor practice. The National Labor Relations Board ordered the corporation to employ Curtis and to pay him the wages he would have received had he not been improperly denied employment.

Decision: This order was proper. The federal statute authorizes the National Labor Relations Board to award back pay to an employee against whom the employer has discriminated because of union membership when the award of such back pay will "effectuate the policies" of the federal statute. As discrimination in hiring and firing are aspects of the same evil, it follows that back pay may be awarded when it is found that an employer has discriminated against union membership by refusing to hire a job applicant, although from the pay that the rejected applicant would have received had he been hired must be deducted wages which he has in fact received from other employment or from employment that he could have reasonably obtained. (Phelps Dodge Corp., v. N.L.R.B., 313 U.S. 177)

An employee can neither be reinstated nor awarded back pay if he was discharged for cause.[12]

Provision is made for appeals to the court of appeals and for the issuance of court orders to compel obedience by the parties.

Apart from the proceedings under the federal statutes, whenever the unfair labor practice is also a civil wrong or a crime under state law, the wrongdoer may be sued and prosecuted under the state law.

Facts: The United Construction Workers, a labor union, threatened the Laburnum Construction Co. and its employees with violence if the employees did not join the union. The threats were so great that the construction company abandoned all its building projects within the area concerned. The National Labor Relations Board decided that the union was guilty of an unfair labor practice in attempting to coerce the construction company's employees in their choice of a union. The construction company then sued the union in a state court for damages caused by its conduct. The union claimed that the federal statute limited complaining parties to bringing a proceeding before the National Labor Relations Board.

---

[12] Taft-Hartley Act, Sec. 10(c).

Decision: Judgment for the construction company. The creation of a federal
board with power to declare the union's conduct an unfair labor practice does not bar a suit in a state court to recover for damages caused
by an unfair labor practice. (United Construction Workers v. Laburnum
Construction Co., 347 U.S. 656)

Union Organization and Management

In order to insure the honest and democratic administration of unions,
Congress adopted the Labor-Management Reporting and Disclosure Act of
1959 regulating operations in or affecting interstate commerce. Under it,
such unions must adopt constitutions and bylaws, and file copies of them
together with detailed reports on administrative and financial matters. Each
officer and key employee is required to file a report that sets forth any
interest he or a member of his family has which conflicts with his duties to
the union. Reports are required of labor relations consultants, and employers must report payments to union officers. The grounds on which a
national union may exercise control or trusteeship power over a local union
or its funds are specified to prevent abuse of that power.

The Act protects rights of union members within their unions by guaranteeing equality, the right to vote on specified matters, and information
on union matters and contracts, and it protects members from interference
with the enjoyment of these rights. The terms of office and the process of
election are regulated to provide democratic elections by secret ballot by
members in good standing. Communists and persons convicted of major
crimes are barred as officers or employees of unions until a specified period
of time has elapsed since termination of membership or conviction.

Union assets are protected from misappropriation by requiring those
handling them to be bonded, imposing upon them a trustee's duty, making
them criminally liable for theft or embezzlement, giving union members the
right to sue them if the union fails to do so, and providing that the union
cannot agree to release them from liability. Union assets are also protected
by limiting loans to officers or employees and by prohibiting the union from
paying fines imposed on officers or employees.

Labor Disputes

1 / Labor's methods. The most common of the labor techniques are the
strike, the boycott, and picketing. The *strike* is a concerted stopping of work
as distinguished from individual workers deciding to quit. A *boycott* is the
persuasion of others to stop patronizing or working for a particular person.
Picketing is ordinarily placing persons outside a place of employment or
distribution so that by words or banners they can inform others that a labor
dispute is in existence. More recent innovations are the *slowdown,* a con-

certed slowing down of production, and the *sitdown strike,* in which the employees seize the plant and refuse to allow the employer to operate it.

In addition to distinguishing these various techniques, it is also necessary to consider the area of operation. Thus, if employees having a dispute with their employer picket his plant, it is called *primary picketing.* If they picket the plant of another manufacturer who uses the products made by their employer, it is called *secondary picketing.* If the employees picket the stores that sell the finished commodity or the customers who purchase them, it may be called *tertiary picketing,* although commonly any picketing that is not primary is called secondary. The purpose of secondary activity is to bring indirect pressure to bear on the employer and thus force him to agree in the dispute. A boycott is similarly called secondary or tertiary when it affects persons other than the employer.

Labor activity is more likely to be held legal when it relates to hours, wages, or working conditions. Likewise labor activity is more likely to be held lawful when it is engaged in by employees against their own employer with whom they have the dispute.

2 / Employers' methods. The weapons of the employer have been primarily the *lockout* or the closing of the factory, the *blacklist* or the circulation among employers of a list of persons who should not be employed, and the traditional remedies of the injunction and antitrust prosecution.

(a) INJUNCTIONS. The right of the employer to obtain an injunction has been limited by the federal Norris-LaGuardia Act and by many state statutes so that an injunction cannot be obtained in a labor dispute when no physical damage to property is involved. A limited right to obtain an injunction is conferred upon the National Labor Relations Board in order to stop certain unfair labor practices, and an injunction may be obtained upon the direction of the President of the United States to postpone for 80 days a strike in a national industry when national health or safety is threatened.

(b) ANTITRUST LAWS. The Sherman Antitrust law is now not applicable to ordinary activity of labor unions as long as they do not conspire with nonlabor groups. The Taft-Hartley law of 1947, however, subjects unions to a civil suit for damages for certain strikes and secondary boycotts that might in themselves be regarded as illegal conspiracies, and extortion picketing is made a crime by the Labor-Management Reporting and Disclosure Act of 1959.

Settlement of Labor Disputes

A number of special procedures have been devised for the settlement of labor disputes. These include the grievance settlement; conciliation and mediation; arbitration; strike votes; strike notices and cooling off periods; injunctions, under some state laws, against strikes in the case of public utilities, and under the Taft-Hartley law, in the case of a national strike or lockout imperiling national health or safety; and government seizure of a plant in which production has stopped.

Although the procedures have been successful in many instances, there is no certainty that any of them will be effective in a given case. Both the avoidance and the settlement of labor disputes depend upon the ability and willingness of management and labor to find a basis of cooperation.

QUESTIONS AND PROBLEMS

1. Checklist of legal terms:
    (a) yellow-dog contract (722)
    (b) closed shop, union shop, agency shop (722)
    (c) jurisdictional dispute (723)
    (d) strike (726), boycott (726), picketing (726), slowdown (726), sitdown strike (727)
    (e) primary picketing, secondary picketing, tertiary picketing (727)
    (f) lockout, blacklist (727)

2. State the objective(s) of each of the following rules of law:
    (a) Although the federal law makes it the duty of both the union and the employer to bargain collectively, there is no duty on either to reach an agreement.
    (b) The federal Labor Management Relations Act makes it unlawful for government employees to strike while recognizing the right of the employees of private employers to do so.

3. Reiser is not a member of, nor did he vote for, the union that was selected by the employees of the Stropes Company to represent them. He seeks to settle the terms of his employment directly with the employer. Can he do so?

4. Walls filed charges with the National Labor Relations Board against his employer, the Reid Manufacturing Company. For this reason he was discharged. Walls then filed additional charges against the company for violating a provision of the Labor Management Relations Act. Was the employer guilty of the violation of that act?

5. Persons who were not employees of the Babcock & Wilcox Co. began distributing union literature on parking lots that were owned by the company. The plant was located near a small well-settled community where most of the employees of the company lived, and they could be reached by telephone, mail, or door-to-door contact. The company prohibited the distribution of the union literature by the nonemployees. They complained to the N.L.R.B. Decide. (N.L.R.B. v. Babcock & Wilcox Co., 351 U.S. 105)

A

abandon: give up or leave employment; relinquish possession of personal property with intent to disclaim title.

abate: put a stop to a nuisance; reduce or cancel a legacy because the estate of the testator is insufficient to make payment in full.

ab initio: from the beginning.

abrogate: recall or repeal; make void or inoperative.

absolute liability: liability for an act that causes harm even though the actor was not at fault.

absolute privilege: protection from liability for slander or libel given under certain circumstances to statements regardless of the fact that they are false or maliciously made.

abstract of title: history of the transfers of title to a given piece of land, briefly stating the parties to and the effect of all deeds, wills, and judicial proceedings relating to the land.

acceleration clause: provision in a contract or any legal instrument that upon a certain event the time for the performance of specified obligations shall be advanced; for example, a provision making the balance due upon debtor's default.

acceptance: unqualified assent to the act or proposal of another; as the acceptance of a draft (bill of exchange), of an offer to make a contract, of goods delivered by the seller, or of a gift or a deed.

accession: acquisition of title to property by a person by virtue of the fact that it has been attached to property that he already owned or was the offspring of an animal he owned.

accessory after the fact: one who after the commission of a felony knowingly assists the felon.

accessory before the fact: one who is absent at the commission of the crime but who aided and abetted its commission.

accident: an event that occurs even though a reasonable man would not have foreseen its occurrence, because of which the law holds no one legally responsible for the harm caused.

accommodation party: a person who signs a commercial paper to lend credit to another.

accord and satisfaction: an agreement to substitute a different performance for that called for in the contract and the performance of that substitute agreement.

accretion: the acquisition of title to additional land when the owner's land is built up by gradual deposits made by the natural action of water.

acknowledgment: an admission or confirmation, generally of an instrument and usually made before a person authorized to administer oaths, as a notary public; the purpose being to declare that the instrument was executed by the person making the instrument, or that it was his free act, or that he desires that it be recorded.

action: a proceeding brought to enforce any right.

action in personam: an action brought to impose a personal liability upon a person, such as a money judgment.

action in rem: an action brought to declare the status of a thing, such as an action to declare the title to property to be forfeited because of its illegal use.

action of assumpsit: a common-law action brought to recover damages for breach of a contract.

action of ejectment: a common-law action brought to recover the possession of land.

action of mandamus: a common-law action brought to compel the performance of a ministerial or clerical act by an officer.

action of quo warranto: a common-law action brought to challenge the authority of an officer to act or to hold office.

action of replevin: a common-law action brought to recover the possession of personal property.

action of trespass: a common-law action brought to recover damages for a tort.

act of bankruptcy: any of the acts specified by the national bankruptcy law which, when committed by the debtor within the four months preceding the filing of the petition in bankruptcy, is proper ground for declaring the debtor a bankrupt.

act of God: a natural phenomenon that is not reasonably foreseeable.

administrative agency: a governmental commission or board given authority to regulate particular matters.

administrator—administratrix: the person (man—woman) appointed to wind up and settle the estate of a person who has died without a will.

adverse possession: the hostile possession of real estate, which when actual, visible, notorious, exclusive, and continued for the required time, will vest the title to the land in the person in such adverse possession.

advisory opinion: an opinion that may be rendered in a few states when there is no actual controversy before the court and the matter is submitted by private persons, or in some instances by the governor of the state, to obtain the court's opinion.

affidavit: a statement of facts set forth in written form and supported by the oath or affirmation of the person making the statement, setting forth that such facts are true to his knowledge or to his information and belief. The affidavit is executed before a notary public or other person authorized to administer oaths.

affinity: the relationship that exists by virtue of marriage.

affirmative covenant: an express undertaking or promise in a contract or deed to do an act.

agency: the relationship that exists between a person identified as a principal and another by virtue of which the latter may make contracts with third persons on behalf of the principal. (Parties—principal, agent, third person)

agency coupled with an interest in the authority: an agency in which the agent has given a consideration or has paid for the right to exercise the authority granted to him.

agency coupled with an interest in the subject matter: an agency in which for a consideration the agent is given an interest in the property with which he is dealing.

agency shop: a union contract provision requiring that nonunion employees pay to the union the equivalent of union dues in order to retain their employment.

agent: one who is authorized by the principal or by operation of law to make contracts with third persons on behalf of the principal.

allonge: a paper securely fastened to a commercial paper in order to provide additional space for indorsements.

alluvion: the additions made to land by accretion.

alteration: any material change of the terms of a writing fraudulently made by a party thereto.

ambulatory: not effective and there-fore may be changed, as in the case of a will that is not final until the testator has died.

amicable action: an action that all parties agree should be brought and which is begun by the filing of such an agreement, rather than by serving the adverse parties with process. Al-though the parties agree to litigate, the dispute is real, and the decision is not an advisory opinion.

amicus curiae: literally, a friend of the court; one who is appointed by the court to take part in litigation and to assist the court by furnishing his opin-ion in the matter.

annexation: attachment of personal property to realty in such a way as to make it become real property and part of the realty.

annuity: a contract by which the insured pays a lump sum to the insurer and later receives fixed annual payments.

anomalous indorser: a person who signs a commercial paper but is not other-wise a party to the instrument.

anticipatory breach: the repudiation by a promisor of the contract prior to the time he is required to perform when such repudiation is accepted by the promisee as a breach of the contract.

anti-injunction acts: statutes prohibiting the use of injunctions in labor disputes except under exceptional circum-stances; notably the Federal Norris-La Guardia Act of 1932.

Anti-Petrillo Act: a federal statute that makes it a crime to compel a radio broadcasting station to hire musicians not needed, to pay for services not performed, or to refrain from broadcasting music of school children or from foreign countries.

antitrust acts: statutes prohibiting com-binations and contracts in restraint of trade, notably the Federal Sherman Antitrust Act of 1890, now generally inapplicable to labor union activity.

appeal: taking the case to a reviewing court to determine whether the judg-ment of the lower court or adminis-trative agency was correct. (Parties —appellant, appellee)

appellate jurisdiction: the power of a court to hear and decide a given class of cases on appeal from another court or administrative agency.

arbitration: the settlement of disputed questions, whether of law or fact, by one or more arbitrators by whose decision the parties agree to be bound. Increasingly used as a pro-cedure for labor dispute settlement.

assignment: transfer of a right. Gener-ally used in connection with personal property rights, as rights under a con-tract, commercial paper, an insurance policy, a mortgage, or a lease. (Par-ties—assignor, assignee)

assumption of risk: the common-law rule that an employee could not sue the employer for injuries caused by the ordinary risks of employment on the theory that he had assumed such risks by undertaking the work. The rule has been abolished in those areas gov-erned by workmen's compensation laws and most employers' liability statutes.

attachment: the seizure of property of, or a debt owed to, the debtor by the service of process upon a third per-son who is in possession of the prop-erty or who owes a debt to the debtor.

attractive nuisance doctrine: a rule im-posing liability on a landowner for injuries sustained by small children playing on his land when the land-owner permits a condition to exist or maintains equipment that he should realize would attract small children who could not realize the danger. The rule does not apply if an unrea-sonable burden would be imposed on the landowner in taking steps to protect the children.

authenticate: make or establish as genuine, official, or final, as by signing, countersigning, sealing, or any other act indicating approval.

B

bad check laws: laws making it a criminal offense to issue a bad check with intent to defraud.

baggage: such articles of necessity or personal convenience as are usually carried for personal use by passengers of common carriers.

bail: variously used in connection with the release of a person or property from the custody of the law, referring (a) to the act of releasing or bailing (b) to the persons who assume liability in the event that the released person does not appear or it is held that the property should not be released, and (c) to the bond or sum of money that such persons furnish the court or other official as indemnity for nonperformance of the obligation.

bailee's lien: a specific, possessory lien of the bailee on the goods for work done to them. Commonly extended by statute to any bailee's claim for compensation and eliminating the necessity of retention of possession.

bailment: the relation that exists when personal property is delivered into the possession of another under an agreement, express or implied, that the identical property will be returned or will be delivered in accordance with the agreement. (Parties—bailor, bailee)

bankruptcy: a procedure by which one unable to pay his debts may be declared a bankrupt, after which all his assets in excess of his exemption claim are surrendered to the court for administration and distribution to his creditors, and the debtor is given a discharge that releases him from the unpaid balance due on most debts.

bearer: the person in physical possession of commercial paper payable to bearer or of a document of title directing delivery to bearer.

beneficiary: the person to whom the proceeds of a life insurance policy are payable, a person for whose benefit property is held in trust, or a person given property by a will.

bequest: a gift of personal property by will.

bill of exchange (draft): an unconditional order in writing by one person upon another, signed by the person giving it, and ordering the person to whom it is directed to pay or deliver on demand or at a definite time a sum certain in money to order or to bearer.

bill of lading: a document issued by a carrier reciting the receipt of goods and the terms of the contract of transportation. Regulated by the Federal Bills of Lading Act or the Uniform Commercial Code.

bill of sale: a writing signed by the seller reciting that he has sold to the buyer the personal property therein described.

binder: a memorandum delivered to the insured stating the essential terms of a policy to be executed in the future, when it is agreed that the contract of insurance is to be effective before the written policy is executed.

blank indorsement: an indorsement that does not state to whom the instrument is to be paid.

blue-sky laws: state statutes designed to protect the public from the sale of worthless stocks and bonds.

boardinghouse keeper: one regularly engaged in the business of offering living accommodations to permanent lodgers or boarders as distinguished from transient guests.

bona fide: in good faith; without any fraud or deceit.

bond: an obligation or promise in writing and sealed, generally of corporations, personal representatives, trustees; fidelity bonds.

boycott: a combination of two or more persons to cause harm to another by refraining from patronizing or dealing with such other person in any way or inducing others to so refrain; commonly an incident of labor disputes.

bulk sales acts: statutes to protect creditors of a bulk seller by preventing him from obtaining cash for his goods and then leaving the state. Notice must be given creditors, and the bulk sale buyer is liable to the seller's creditors if the statute is not satisfied. Expanded to "bulk transfers" under the Code.

business trust: a form of business organization in which the owners of the property to be devoted to the business transfer the title of the property to trustees with full power to operate the business.

C

cancellation: a crossing out of a part of an instrument or a destruction of all legal effect of the instrument, whether by act of party, upon breach by the other party, or pursuant to agreement or decree of court.

capital: net assets of a corporation.

capital stock: the declared money value of the outstanding stock of the corporation.

cash surrender value: the sum that will be paid the insured if he surrenders his policy to the insurer.

cause of action: the right to damages or other judicial relief when a legally protected right of the plaintiff is violated by an unlawful act of the defendant.

caveat emptor: let the buyer beware. This maxim is subject to modification by warranties.

certificate of protest: a written statement by a notary public setting forth the fact that the holder had presented the commercial paper to the primary party and that the latter had failed to make payment.

cestui que trust: the beneficiary or person for whose benefit the property is held in trust.

charter: the grant of authority from a government to exist as a corporation. Generally replaced today by a certificate approving the articles of incorporation.

chattel mortgage: a security device by which the owner of personal property transfers the title to a creditor as security for the debt owed by the owner to the creditor. Replaced under the Uniform Commercial Code by a secured transaction. (Parties—chattel mortgagor, chattel mortgagee)

chattels personal: tangible personal property.

chattels real: leases of land and buildings.

check: an order by a depositor on his bank to pay a sum of money to a payee; also defined as a bill of exchange drawn on a bank and payable on demand.

chose in action: intangible personal property in the nature of claims against another, such as a claim for accounts receivable or wages.

chose in possession: tangible personal property.

circumstantial evidence: relates to circumstances surrounding the facts in dispute from which the trier of fact may deduce what had happened.

civil action: in many states a simplified form of action combining all or many of the former common-law actions.

civil court: a court with jurisdiction to hear and determine controversies relating to private rights and duties.

closed shop: a place of employment in which only union members may be employed. Now generally prohibited by unfair labor practice statutes.

codicil: a writing by one who has made a will which is executed with all the formality of a will and is treated as an addition to or modification of the will.

coinsurance: a clause requiring the insured to maintain insurance on his property up to a stated amount and providing that to the extent that he fails to do so the insured is to be deemed a coinsurer with the insurer so that the latter is liable only for its proportionate share of the amount of insurance required to be carried.

collateral note: a note accompanied by collateral security.

collective bargaining: the process by which the terms of employment are agreed upon through negotiations between the employer or employers within a given industry or industrial area and the union or the bargaining representative of the employees.

collective bargaining unit: the employment area within which employees are by statute authorized to select a bargaining representative, who is then to represent all the employees in bargaining collectively with the employer.

collusion: an agreement between two or more persons to defraud the government or the courts, as by obtaining a divorce by collusion when no grounds for a divorce exist, or to defraud third persons of their rights.

color of title: circumstances that make a person appear to be the owner when he in fact is not the owner, as the existence of a deed appearing to convey the property to a given person gives him color of title although the deed is worthless because it was executed by one who was not the owner of the property.

commission merchant: a bailee to whom goods are consigned for sale.

common carrier: a carrier that holds out its facilities to serve the general public for compensation without discrimination.

common law: the body of unwritten principles originally based on the usages and customs of the community which were recognized and enforced by the courts.

common stock: stock that has no right or priority over any other stock of the corporation as to dividends or distribution of assets upon dissolution.

common trust fund: a plan by which the assets of small trust estates are pooled into a common fund, each trust being given certificates representing its proportionate ownership of the fund, and the pooled fund is then invested in investments of large size.

community property: the cotenancy held by husband and wife in property acquired during their marriage under the law of some of the states, principally in the southwestern United States.

complaint: the initial pleading filed by the plaintiff in many actions which in many states may be served as original process to acquire jurisdiction over the defendant.

composition of creditors: an agreement among creditors that each shall accept a part payment as full payment in consideration of the other creditors doing the same.

concealment: the failure to volunteer information not requested.

conditional estate: an estate that will come into being upon the satisfaction of a condition precedent or that will be terminated upon the satisfaction of a condition subsequent, provided in the latter case that the grantor or his heirs re-enter and retake possession of the land.

conditional sale: a credit transaction by which the buyer purchases on credit and promises to pay the purchase price in installments, while the seller retains the title to the goods, together with the right of repossession upon default, until the condition of payment in full has been satisfied. The conditional sale is replaced under the Uniform Commercial Code by a secured transaction.

confidential relationship: a relationship in which, because of the legal status of the parties or their respective physical or mental conditions or knowledge, one party places full confidence and trust in the other and relies upon him entirely for guidance.

conflict of laws: the body of law that determines the law of which state is to apply when two or more states are involved in the facts of a given case.

confusion of goods: the mixing of goods of different owners that under certain circumstances results in one of the owners becoming the owner of all the goods.

consanguinity: relationship by blood.

consideration: the promise or performance by the other party that the promisor demands as the price of his promise.

consignment: a bailment made for the purpose of sale by the bailee. (Parties—consignor, consignee)

consolidation of corporations: a combining of two or more corporations in which the corporate existence of each one ceases and a new corporation is created.

constructive: an adjective employed to indicate that the noun which is modified by it does not exist but the law disposes of the matter as though it did; as a constructive bailment or a constructive trust.

contingent beneficiary: the person to whom the proceeds of a life insurance policy are payable in the event that the primary beneficiary dies before the insured.

contract: a binding agreement based upon the genuine assent of the parties, made for a lawful object, between competent parties, in the form re-

quired by law, and generally supported by consideration.

contract carrier: a carrier who transports on the basis of individual contracts that it makes with each shipper.

contract to sell: a contract to make a transfer of title in the future as contrasted with a present sale.

contribution: the right of a cosurety who has paid more than his proportionate share of the loss to demand that the other surety pay him the amount of the excess payment he has made.

contributory negligence: negligence of the plaintiff that contributes to his injury and at common law bars him from recovery from the defendant although the defendant may have been more negligent than the plaintiff.

conveyance: a transfer of an interest in land, ordinarily by the execution and delivery of a deed.

cooling-off period: a procedure designed to avoid strikes by requiring a specified period of delay before the strike may begin during which negotiations for a settlement must continue.

cooperative: a group of two or more persons or enterprises that act through a common agent with respect to a common objective, as buying or selling.

copyright: a grant to an author of an exclusive right to publish and sell his work for a period of 28 years, renewable for a second period of 28 years.

corporation: an artificial legal person or being created by government grant, which for many purposes is treated as a natural person.

cost plus: a method of determining the purchase price or contract price by providing for the payment of an amount equal to the costs of the seller or the contractor to which is added a stated percentage as his profit.

costs: the expenses of suing or being sued, recoverable in some actions by the successful party, and in others, subject to allocation by the court. Ordinarily they do not include attorney's fees or compensation for loss of time.

counterclaim: a claim that the defendant in an action may make against the plaintiff.

covenants of title: covenants of the grantor contained in a deed that guarantee such matters as his right to make the conveyance, his ownership of the property, the freedom of the property from encumbrances, or that the grantee will not be disturbed in the quiet enjoyment of the land.

crime: a violation of the law that is punished as an offense against the state or government.

cross complaint: a claim that the defendant may make against the plaintiff.

cross-examination: the examination made of a witness by the attorney for the adverse party.

cumulative voting: a system of voting for directors in which each stockholder has as many votes as the number of voting shares he owns multiplied by the number of directors to be elected, which votes he can distribute for the various candidates as he desires.

cy-pres doctrine: the rule under which a charitable trust will be carried out as nearly as possible in the way the settlor desired, when for any reason it cannot be carried out exactly in the way or for the purposes he had expressed.

D

damages: a sum of money recovered to redress or make amends for the legal wrong or injury done.

damnum absque injuria: loss or damage without the violation of a legal right, or the mere fact that a person sustains a loss does not mean that his legal rights have been violated or that he is entitled to sue someone.

declaratory judgment: a procedure for obtaining the decision of a court on a question before any action has been taken or loss sustained. It differs from an advisory opinion in that there must be an actual, imminent controversy.

dedication: acquisition by the public or a government of title to land when it is given over by its owner to use by the public and such gift is accepted.

deed: an instrument by which the grantor (owner of land) conveys or transfers the title to a grantee.

de facto: existing in fact as distinguished from as of right, as in the case of an officer or a corporation purporting to act as such without being elected to the office or having been properly incorporated.

deficiency judgment: a personal judgment for the amount still remaining due the mortgagee after foreclosure, which is entered against any person liable on the mortgage bond. Statutes generally require the mortgagee to credit the fair value of the property against the balance due when the mortgagee has purchased the property.

del credere agent: an agent who sells goods for the principal and who guarantees to the principal that the buyer will pay for the goods.

delegation: the transfer of the power to do an act to another.

de minimis non curat lex: a maxim that the law is not concerned with trifles. Not always applied, as in the case of the encroachment of a building over the property line in which case the law will protect the landowner regardless of the extent of the encroachment.

demonstrative evidence: evidence that consists of visible, physical objects, as a sample taken from the wheat in controversy or a photograph of the subject matter involved.

demonstrative legacy: a legacy to be paid or distributed from a specified fund or property.

demurrage: a charge made by the carrier for the unreasonable detention of cars by the consignor or consignee.

demurrer: a pleading that may be filed to attack the sufficiency of the adverse party's pleading as not stating a cause of action or a defense.

dependent relative revocation: the doctrine recognized in some states that if a testator revokes or cancels a will in order to replace it with a later will, the earlier will is to be deemed revived if for any reason the later will does not take effect or no later will is executed.

deposition: the testimony of a witness taken out of court before a person authorized to administer oaths.

devise: a gift of real estate made by will.

directed verdict: a direction by the trial judge to the jury to return a verdict in favor of a specified party to the action.

directors: the persons vested with control of the corporation, subject to the elective power of the shareholders.

discharge in bankruptcy: an order of the bankruptcy court discharging the bankrupt debtor from the unpaid balance of most of the claims against him.

discharge of contract: termination of a contract by performance, agreement, impossibility, acceptance of breach, or operation of law.

discovery: procedures for ascertaining facts prior to the time of trial in order to eliminate the element of surprise in litigation.

dishonor by nonacceptance: the refusal of the drawee to accept a draft (bill of exchange).

dishonor by nonpayment: the refusal to pay a commercial paper when properly presented for payment.

dismiss: a procedure to terminate an action by moving to dismiss on the ground that the plaintiff has not pleaded a cause of action entitling him to relief.

disparagement of goods: the making of malicious, false statements as to the quality of the goods of another.

distress for rent: the common-law right of the lessor to enter the premises when he was not paid the rent and to seize all personal property found on the premises. Statutes have modified or abolished this right in many states.

distributive share: the proportionate part of the estate of the decedent that will be distributed to an heir or legatee, and also as devisee in those jurisdictions in which real estate is administered as part of the decedent's estate.

domestic bill of exchange: a draft drawn in one state and payable in the same or another state.

domestic corporation: a corporation that has been incorporated by the state as opposed to incorporation by another state.

domicile: the home of a person or the state of incorporation of a corporation, to be distinguished from a place where a person lives but which he does not regard as his home, or a state in which a corporation does business but in which it was not incorporated.

dominant tenement: the tract of land that is benefited by an easement to which another tract, or servient tenement, is subject.

double indemnity: a provision for payment of double the amount specified by the insurance contract if death is caused by an accident and occurs under specified circumstances.

D

double jeopardy: the principle that a person who has once been placed in jeopardy by being brought to trial at which the proceedings progressed at least as far as having the jury sworn cannot thereafter be tried a second time for the same offense.

draft: see bill of exchange.

draft-varying acceptance: one in which the acceptor's agreement to pay is not exactly in conformity with the order of the instrument.

due care: the degree of care that a reasonable man would exercise to prevent the realization of harm, which under all the circumstances was reasonably forseeable in the event that such care were not taken.

due process of law: the guarantee by the 5th and 14th amendments of the federal Constitution and of many state constitutions that no person shall be deprived of life, liberty, or property without due process of law. As presently interpreted, this prohibits any law, either state or federal, that sets up an unfair procedure or the substance of which is arbitrary or capricious.

duress: conduct that deprives the victim of his own free will and which generally gives the victim the right to set aside any transaction entered into under such circumstances.

E

easement: a permanent right that one has in the land of another, as the right to cross another's land or easement of way.

eleemosynary corporation: a corporation organized for a charitable or benevolent purpose.

embezzlement: a statutory offense consisting of the unlawful conversion of property entrusted to the wrongdoer with respect to which he owes the owner a fiduciary duty.

eminent domain: the power of a government and certain kinds of corporations to take private property against the objection of the owner, provided the taking is for a public purpose and just compensation is made therefor.

encumbrance: a right held by a third person in or a lien or charge against property, as a mortgage or judgment lien on land.

equity: the body of principles that originally developed because of the inadequacy of the rules then applied by the common-law courts of England.

erosion: the loss of land through a gradual washing away by tides or currents, with the owner losing title to the lost land.

escheat: the transfer to the state of the title to a decedent's property when he dies intestate not survived by anyone capable of taking the property as his heir.

escrow: a conditional delivery of property or of a deed to a custodian or escrow holder, who in turn makes final delivery to the grantee or transferee when a specified condition has been satisfied.

estate: the extent and nature of one's interest in land. Also the assets constituting the decedent's property at the time of his death.

estate in fee simple: the largest estate possible in which the owner has the absolute and entire property in the land.

estoppel: the principle by which a person is barred from pursuing a certain course of action or of disputing the truth of certain matters when his conduct has been such that it would be unjust to permit him to do so.

evidence: that which is presented to the trier of fact as the basis on which the trier is to determine what had happened.

exception: an objection, as an exception to the admission of evidence on the ground that it was hearsay; the exclusion of particular property from the operation of a deed.

ex contractu: a claim or matter that is founded upon or arises out of a contract.

ex delicto: a claim or matter that is founded upon or arises out of a tort.

execution: the carrying out of a judgment of a court, generally directing that property owned by the defendant be sold and the proceeds first used to pay the execution or judgment creditor.

exemplary damages: damages in excess of the amount needed to compensate for the plaintiff's injury, which are awarded in order to punish the defendant for his malicious or wanton conduct so as to make an example of him.

exoneration: an agreement or provision in an agreement that one party shall not be held liable for loss; the right of the surety to demand that those primarily liable pay the claim for which the surety is secondarily liable.

expert witness: one who has acquired special knowledge in a particular field through practical experience, or study, or both, which gives him a superior knowledge so that his opinion is admissible as an aid to the trier of fact.

ex post facto law: a law making criminal an act that was lawful when done or that increases the penalty for an act which was subject to a lesser penalty when done. Such laws are generally prohibited by constitutional provisions.

extraordinary bailment: a bailment in which the bailee is subject to unusual duties and liabilities, as a hotelkeeper or common carrier.

F

facility-of-payment clause: a provision commonly found in an industrial policy permitting the insurer to make payment to any member of a designated class or to any person the insurer believes equitably entitled thereto.

factor: a bailee to whom goods are consigned for sale.

factors' acts: statutes protecting persons who buy in good faith for value from a factor although the goods had not been delivered to the factor with the consent or authorization of their owner.

fair employment practice acts: statutes designed to eliminate discrimination in employment in terms of race, religion, natural origin, or sex.

fair labor standards acts: statutes, particularly the federal statute, designed to prevent excessive hours of employment and low pay, the employment of young children, and other unsound practices.

fair trade acts: statutes that authorize the making of resale price maintenance agreements as to trademark and brand name articles, and generally provide that all persons in the industry are bound by such an agreement whether they have signed it or not.

featherbedding: the exaction of money for services not performed or not to be performed, which is made an unfair labor practice generally and a criminal offense in connection with radio broadcasting.

Federal Securities Act: a statute designed to protect the public from fraudulent securities.

Federal Securities Exchange Act: a statute prohibiting improper practices at and regulating security exchanges.

Federal Trade Commission Act: a statute prohibiting unfair methods of competition in interstate commerce.

fellow-servant rule: a common-law defense of the employer that barred an employee from suing an employer for injuries caused by a fellow employee.

F

felony: a criminal offense that is punishable by confinement in prison or by death, or that is expressly stated by statute to be a felony.

financial responsibility laws: statutes that require a driver involved in an automobile accident to prove his financial responsibility in order to retain his license, which responsibility may be shown by procuring public liability insurance in a specified minimum amount.

financing factor: one who lends money to manufacturers on the security of goods to be manufactured thereafter.

firm offer: an offer stated to be held open for a specified time, which must be so held in some states even in the absence of an option contract, or under the Code, with respect to merchants.

fixture: personal property that has become so attached to or adapted to real estate that it has lost its character as personal property and is part of the real estate.

Food, Drug, and Cosmetic Act: a federal statute prohibiting the interstate shipment of misbranded or adulterated foods, drugs, cosmetics, and therapeutic devices.

forbearance: refraining from doing an act.

foreclosure: procedure for enforcing a mortgage resulting in the public sale of the mortgaged property and less commonly in merely barring the right of the mortgagor to redeem the property from the mortgage.

foreign (international) bill of exchange: a bill of exchange made in one nation and payable in another.

foreign corporation: a corporation incorporated under the laws of another state.

forgery: the fraudulent making or altering of an instrument that apparently creates or alters a legal liability of another.

fraud: the making of a false statement of a past or existing fact with knowledge of its falsity or with reckless indifference as to its truth with the intent to cause another to rely thereon, and he does rely thereon to his injury.

freight forwarder: one who contracts to have goods transported and, in turn, contracts with carriers for such transportation.

fructus industriales: crops that are annually planted and raised.

fructus naturales: fruits from trees, bushes, and grasses growing from perennial roots.

fungible goods: goods of a homogenous nature of which any unit is the equivalent of any other unit or is treated as such by mercantile usage.

future advance mortgage: a mortgage given to secure additional loans to be made in the future as well as an original loan.

G

garnishment: the name given in some states to attachment proceedings.

general creditor: a creditor who has a claim against the debtor but does not have any lien on any of the debtor's property, whether as security for his debt or by way of a judgment or execution upon a judgment.

general damages: damages that in the ordinary course of events follow naturally and probably from the injury caused by the defendant.

general legacy: a legacy to be paid out of the assets generally of the testator without specifying any particular fund or source from which the payment is to be made.

general partnership: a partnership in which the partners conduct as co-owners a business for profit, and each partner has a right to take part in the management of the business and has unlimited liability.

gift causa mortis: a gift made by the donor because he believed he faced immediate and impending death, which gift is revoked or is revocable under certain circumstances.

grace period: a period generally of 30 or 31 days after the due date of a premium of life insurance in which the premium may be paid.

grand jury: a jury not exceeding 23 in number that considers evidence of the commission of crime and prepares indictments to bring offenders to trial before a petty jury.

grant: convey real property; an instrument by which such property has been conveyed, particularly in the case of a government.

gratuitous bailment: a bailment in which the bailee does not receive any compensation or advantage.

grievance settlement: the adjustment of disputes relating to the administration or application of existing contracts as compared with disputes over new terms of employment.

guarantor: one who undertakes the obligation of guaranty.

guaranty: an undertaking to pay the debt of another if the creditor first sues the debtor and is unable to recover the debt from the debtor or principal. (In some instances the liability is primary, in which case it is the same as suretyship.)

H

hearsay evidence: statements made out of court which are offered in court as proof of the information contained in the statements, which, subject to many exceptions, are not admissible in evidence.

hedging: the making of simultaneous contracts to purchase and to sell a particular commodity at a future date with the intention that the loss on one transaction will be offset by the gain on the other.

heirs: those persons specified by statute to receive the estate of a decedent not disposed of by will.

holder: the person in possession of a commercial paper payable to him as payee or indorsee, or the person in possession of a commercial paper payable to bearer.

holder in due course: the holder of a commercial paper under such circumstances that he is treated as favored and is given an immunity from certain defenses.

holder through a holder in due course: a person who is not himself a holder in due course but is a holder of the paper after it was held by some prior party who was a holder in due course, and who is given the same rights as a holder in due course.

holographic will: a will written by the testator in his own hand.

hotelkeeper: one regularly engaged in the business of offering living accommodations to all transient persons.

hung jury: a petty jury that has been unable to agree upon a verdict.

I

ignorantia legis non excusat: ignorance of the law is not an excuse.

implied contract: a contract expressed by conduct or implied or deduced from the facts. Also used to refer to a quasi-contract.

imputed: vicariously attributed to or charged to another, as the knowledge of an agent obtained while acting in the scope of his authority is imputed to his principal.

incidental authority: authority of an agent that is reasonably necessary to execute his express authority.

incontestable clause: a provision that after the lapse of a specified time the insurer cannot dispute the policy on the ground of misrepresentation or fraud of the insured or similar wrongful conduct.

in custodia legis: in the custody of the law.

indemnity: the right of a person secondarily liable to require that a person primarily liable pay him for his loss when the secondary party discharges the obligation which the primary party should have discharged; the right of an agent to be paid the amount of any loss or damage sustained by him without his fault because of his obedience to the principal's instructions; an undertaking by one person for a consideration to pay another person a sum of money to indemnify him when he incurs a specified loss.

independent contractor: a contractor who undertakes to perform a specified task according to the terms of a contract but over whom the other contracting party has no control except as provided for by the contract.

indictment: a formal accusation of crime made by a grand jury which accusation is then tried by a petty or trial jury.

inheritance: the estate which passes from the decedent to his heirs.

injunction: an order of a court of equity to refrain from doing (negative injunction) or to do (affirmative or mandatory injunction) a specified act. Its use in labor disputes has been greatly restricted by statute.

in pari delicto: equally guilty; used in reference to a transaction as to which relief will not be granted to either party because both are equally guilty of wrongdoing.

insolvency: an excess of debts and liabilities over assets.

insurable interest: an interest in the nonoccurrence of the risk insured against, generally because such occurrence would cause financial loss, although sometimes merely because of the close relationship between the insured and the beneficiary.

insurance: a plan of security against risks by charging the loss against a fund created by the payments made by policyholders.

intangible personal property: an interest in an enterprise, such as an interest in a partnership or stock of a corporation, and claims against other persons, whether based on contract or tort.

interlineation: a writing between the lines or adding to the provisions of a document, the effect thereof depending upon the nature of the document.

interlocutory: an intermediate step or proceeding that does not make a final disposition of the action and from which ordinarily no appeal may be taken.

international bill of exchange: an instrument made in one nation and payable in another.

interpleader: a form of action or proceeding by which a person against whom conflicting claims are made may bring the claimants into court to litigate their claims between themselves, as in the case of a bailor when two persons each claim to be the owner of the bailed property, or an insurer when two persons each claim to be the beneficiary of the insurance policy.

inter se: among or between themselves, as the rights of partners inter se or as between themselves.

inter vivos: any transaction which takes place between living persons and creates rights prior to the death of any of them.

intestate: the condition of dying without a will as to any property.

intestate succession: the distribution made as directed by statute of property owned by the decedent of which he did not effectively dispose by will.

ipso facto: by the very act or fact in itself without any further action by any one.

irrebuttable presumption: a presumption which cannot be rebutted by proving that the facts are to the contrary; not a true presumption but merely a rule of law described in terms of a presumption.

irreparable injury to property: an injury that would be of such a nature or inflicted upon such an interest that it would not be reasonably possible to compensate the injured party by the payment of money damages because the property in question could not be purchased in the open market with the money damages which the defendant could be required to pay.

J

joint and several contract: a contract in which two or more persons are jointly and severally obligated or are jointly and severally entitled to recover.

joint contract: a contract in which two or more persons are jointly liable or jointly entitled to performance under the contract.

joint stock company: an association in which the shares of the members are transferable and control is delegated to a group or board.

joint tenancy: the estate held by two or more jointly with the right of survivorship as between them, unless modified by statute.

joint venture: a relationship in which two or more persons combine their labor or property for a single undertaking and share profits and losses equally unless otherwise agreed.

judgment: the final sentence, order, or decision entered into at the conclusion of the action.

judgment note: a promissory note containing a clause authorizing the holder of the note to enter judgment against the maker of the note if it is not paid when due. Also called cognovit note.

judgment n.o.v.: a judgment which may be entered after verdict upon the motion of the losing party on the ground that the verdict is so wrong that a judgment should be entered the opposite of the verdict, or non-obstante veredicto (notwithstanding the verdict).

judgment on the pleadings: a judgment which may be entered after all the pleadings are filed when it is clear from the pleadings that a particular party is entitled to win the action without proceeding any further.

judicial sale: a sale made under order of court by an officer appointed to make the sale or by an officer having such authority as incident to his office. The sale may have the effect of divesting liens on the property.

jurisdiction: the power of a court to hear and determine a given class of cases; the power to act over a particular defendant.

jurisdictional dispute: a dispute between rival labor unions which may take the form of each claiming that particular work should be assigned to it.

justifiable abandonment by employee: the right of an employee to abandon his employment because of nonpayment of wages, wrongful assault, the demand for the performance of services not contemplated, or injurious working conditions.

justifiable discharge of employee: the right of an employer to discharge an employee for nonperformance of duties, fraud, disobedience, disloyalty, or incompetence.

L

laches: the rule that the enforcement of equitable rights will be denied when the party has delayed so long that rights of third persons have intervened or the death or disappearance of witnesses would prejudice any party through the loss of evidence.

J-1

land: earth, including all things imbedded in or attached thereto, whether naturally or by act of man.

last clear chance: the rule that if the defendant had the last clear chance to have avoided injuring the plaintiff, he is liable even though the plaintiff had also been contributorily negligent. In some states also called the humanitarian doctrine.

law of the case: matters decided in the course of litigation which are binding on the parties in the subsequent phases of the litigation.

leading questions: questions which suggest the desired answer to the witness, or assume the existence of a fact which is in dispute.

lease: an agreement between the owner of property and a tenant by which the former agrees to give possession of the property to the latter in consideration of the payment of rent. (Parties—landlord or lessor, tenant or lessee)

leasehold: the estate or interest which the tenant has in land rented to him.

legacy: a gift of personal property made by will.

legal tender: such form of money as the law recognizes as lawful and declares that a tender thereof in the proper amount is a proper tender which the creditor cannot refuse.

letters of administration: the written authorization given to an administrator as evidence of his appointment and authority.

letters testamentary: the written authorization given to an executor as evidence of his appointment and authority.

levy: a seizure of property by an officer of the court in execution of a judgment of the court, although in many states it is sufficient if the officer is physically in the presence of the property and announces the fact that he is "seizing" it, although he then allows the property to remain where he found it.

lex loci: the law of the place where the material facts occurred as governing the rights and liabilities of the parties.

lex loci contractus: the law of the place where the contract was made as governing the rights and liability of the parties to a contract with respect to certain matters.

lex loci fori: the law of the state in which the action is brought as determining the rules of procedure applicable to the action.

lex loci sitae rei: the law of the place where land is located as determining the validity of acts done relating thereto.

libel: the defamation of another without legal justification.

license: a personal privilege to do some act or series of acts upon the land of another not amounting to an easement or a right of possession, as the placing of a sign thereon.

lien: a claim or right against property existing by virtue of the entry of a judgment against its owner or by the entry of a judgment and a levy thereunder on the property, or because of the relationship of the claimant to the particular property, such as an unpaid seller.

life estate: an estate for the duration of a life.

limited jurisdiction: a court with power to hear and determine cases within certain restricted categories.

limited liability: loss of contributed capital as maximum liability.

limited partnership: a partnership in which at least one partner has a liability limited to the loss of the capital contribution that he has made to the partnership, and such a partner neither takes part in the management of the partnership nor appears to the public to be a partner.

lineal consanguinity: the relationship that exists when one person is a direct descendant from the other.

liquidated damages: a provision stipulating the amount of damages to be paid in event of default or breach of contract.

liquidation: the process of converting property into money whether of particular items of property or all the assets of a business.

lis pendens: the doctrine that certain types of pending actions are notice to everyone so that if any right is acquired from a party to that action, the transferee takes that right subject to the outcome of the pending action.

lobbying contract (illegal): a contract by which one party agrees to attempt to influence the action of a legislature or Congress, or any members thereof, by improper means.

lottery: any plan by which a consideration is given for a chance to win a prize.

lucri causa: with the motive of obtaining gain or pecuniary advantage.

M

majority: of age, as contrasted with being a minor; more than half of any group, as a majority of stockholders.

malice in fact: an intention to injure or cause harm.

malice in law: a presumed intention to injure or cause harm when there is no privilege or right to do the act in question, which presumption cannot be contradicted or rebutted.

maliciously inducing breach of contract: the wrong of inducing an employee to break his contract with his employer or inducing the breach of any other kind of contract with knowledge of its existence and without justification.

malum in se: an offense that is criminal because contrary to the fundamental sense of a civilized community, as murder.

malum prohibitum: an offense that is criminal not because inherently wrong but is prohibited for the convenience of society, as overtime parking.

marshalling assets: the distribution of a debtor's assets in such a way as to give the greatest benefit to all of his creditors.

martial law: government exercised by a military commander over property and persons not in the armed forces, as contrasted with military law which governs the military personnel.

mechanics' lien: protection afforded by statute to various types of laborers and persons supplying materials, by giving them a lien on the building and land that has been improved or added to by them.

mens rea: the mental state that must accompany an act to make the act a crime. Sometimes described as the "guilty mind," although appreciation of guilt is not required.

merger by judgment: the discharge of a contract through being merged into a judgment which is entered in a suit on the contract.

merger of corporations: a combining of corporations by which one absorbs the other and continues to exist, preserving its original charter and identity while the other corporation ceases to exist.

mesne: intermediate or intervening, as mesne profits, which are the fruits or income from the land received in between the time that the true owner was wrongfully dispossessed and the time that he recovers the land.

misdemeanor: a criminal offense which is neither treason nor a felony.

misrepresentation: a false statement of fact although made innocently without any intent to deceive.

mobilia sequuntur personam: the maxim that personal property follows the owner and in the eyes of the law is located at the owner's domicile.

M

moratorium: a temporary suspension by statute of the enforcement of debts or the foreclosure of mortgages.

mortgage: an interest in land given by the owner to his creditor as security for the payment to the creditor of a debt, the nature of the interest depending upon the law of the state where the land is located. (Parties—mortgagor, mortgagee)

multiple insurers: insurers who agree to divide a risk so that each is only liable for a specified portion.

N

National Labor Management Relations Act: the federal statute, also known as the Taft-Hartley Act, designed to protect the organizational rights of labor and to prevent unfair labor practices by management or labor.

natural and probable consequences: those ordinary consequences of an act which a reasonable man would foresee.

negative covenant: an undertaking in a deed to refrain from doing an act.

negligence: the failure to exercise due care under the circumstances in consequence of which harm is proximately caused to one to whom the defendant owed a duty to exercise due care.

negligence per se: an action which is regarded as so improper that it is declared by law to be negligent in itself without regard to whether due care was otherwise exercised.

negotiable instruments: drafts, promissory notes, checks, and certificates of deposit in such form that greater rights may be acquired thereunder than by taking an assignment of a contract right.

negotiation: the transfer of a commercial paper by indorsement and delivery by the person to whom then payable in the case of order paper,

and by physical transfer in the case of bearer paper.

nominal damages: a nominal sum awarded the plaintiff in order to establish that his legal rights have been violated although he in fact has not sustained any actual loss or damages.

nominal partner: a person who in fact is not a partner but who holds himself out as a partner or permits others to do so.

Norris-LaGuardia Anti-Injunction Act: a federal statute prohibiting the use of the injunction in labor disputes, except in particular cases.

notice of dishonor: notice given to parties secondarily liable that the primary party to the instrument has refused to accept the instrument or to make payment when it was properly presented for that purpose.

novation: the discharge of a contract between two parties by their agreeing with a third person that such third person shall be substituted for one of the original parties to the contract, who shall thereupon be released.

nudum pactum: a mere promise for which there is no consideration given and which therefore is ordinarily not enforceable.

nuisance: any conduct that harms or prejudices another in the use of his land or which harms or prejudices the public.

nuisance per se: an activity which is in itself a nuisance regardless of the time and place involved.

nuncupative will: an oral will made and declared by the testator in the presence of witnesses to be his will and generally made during the testator's last illness.

O

obiter dictum: that which is said in the opinion of a court in passing or by the way, but which is not necessary to the determination of the case and is therefore not regarded as authoritative as though it were actually involved in the decision.

obliteration: any erasing, writing upon, or crossing out that makes all or part of a will impossible to read, and which has the effect of revoking such part when done by the testator with the intent of effecting a revocation.

occupation: taking and holding possession of property; a method of acquiring title to personal property which has been abandoned.

open-end mortgage: a mortgage given to secure additional loans to be made in the future as well as the original loan.

operation of law: the attaching of certain consequences to certain facts because of legal principles that operate automatically, as contrasted with consequences which arise because of the voluntary action of a party designed to create those consequences.

opinion evidence: evidence not of what the witness himself observed but the conclusion which he draws from what he observed, or in the case of an expert witness, also from what he is asked or what he has heard at the trial.

option contract: a contract to hold an offer to make a contract open for a fixed period of time.

P

paper title: the title of a person evidenced only by deeds or matter appearing of record under the recording statutes.

parol evidence rule: the rule that prohibits the introduction in evidence of oral or written statements made prior to or contemporaneously with the execution of a complete written contract, deed, or instrument, in the absence of clear proof of fraud, accident, or mis-

take causing the omission of the statement in question.

passive trust: a trust that is created without imposing any duty to be performed by the trustee and is therefore treated as an absolute transfer of the title to the trust beneficiary.

past consideration: something that has been performed in the past and which therefore cannot be consideration for a promise made in the present.

patent: the grant to an inventor of an exclusive right to make and sell his invention for a nonrenewable period of 17 years; a deed to land given by a government to a private person.

pawn: a pledge of tangible personal property rather than of documents representing property rights.

pecuniary legacy: a general legacy of a specified amount of money without indicating the source from which payment is to be made.

per autre vie: limitation of an estate. An estate held by *A* during the lifetime of *B*, is an estate of *A* per autre vie.

per curiam opinion: an opinion written "by the court" rather than by a named judge when all the judges of the court are so agreed on the matter that it is not deemed to merit any discussion and may be simply disposed of.

perpetual succession: a phrase describing the continuing life of the corporation unaffected by the death of any stockholder or the transfer by stockholders of their stock.

perpetuities, rule against: a rule of law that prohibits the creation of an interest in property which will not become definite or vested until a date further away than 21 years after the death of persons alive at the time the owner of the property attempts to create the interest.

per se: in, through, or by itself

person: a term that includes both natural persons, or living people, and artificial persons, as corporations which are created by act of government.

personal defenses: limited defenses that cannot be asserted by the defendant against a holder in due course or a holder through a holder in due course. This term is not expressly used in the Uniform Commercial Code.

per stirpes: according to the root or by way of representation. Distribution among heirs related to the decedent in different degrees, the property being divided into lines of descent from the decedent and the share of each line then divided within the line by way of representation.

petty jury: the trial jury of twelve. Also petit jury.

picketing: the placing of persons outside of places of employment or distribution so that by words or banners they may inform the public of the existence of a labor dispute.

pleadings: the papers filed by the parties in an action in order to set forth the facts and frame the issues to be tried, although under some systems, the pleadings merely give notice or a general indication of the nature of the issues.

pledge: a bailment given as security for the payment of a debt or the performance of an obligation owed to the pledgee. (Parties—pledgor, pledgee)

police power: the power to govern; the power to adopt laws for the protection of the public health, welfare, safety, and morals.

policy: the paper evidencing the contract of insurance.

polling the jury: the process of inquiring of each juror individually in open court as to whether the verdict announced by the foreman of the jury was agreed to by him.

possession: exclusive domain and control of property.

possessory lien: a right to retain possession of property of another as security

for some debt or obligation owed the lienor which right continues only as long as possession is retained.

possibility of reverter: the nature of the interest held by the grantor after conveying land outright but subject to a condition or provision that may cause the grantee's interest to become forfeited and the interest to revert to the grantor of his heirs.

postdate: to insert or place a later date on an instrument than the actual date on which it was executed.

power of appointment: a power given to another, commonly a beneficiary of a trust, to designate or appoint who shall be beneficiary or receive the fund upon his death.

power of attorney: a written authorization to an agent by the principal.

precatory words: words indicating merely a desire or a wish that another use property for a particular purpose but which in law will not be enforced in the absence of an express declaration that the property shall be used for the specified purpose.

pre-emptive offer of shares: the right, subject to many exceptions, that each shareholder has that whenever the capital stock of the corporation is increased he will be allowed to subscribe to such a percentage of the new shares as his old shares bore to the former total capital stock.

preferred creditor: a creditor who by some statute is given the right to be paid first or before other creditors.

preferred stock: stock that has a priority or preference as to payment of dividends or upon liquidation, or both.

preponderance of evidence: the degree or quantum of evidence in favor of the existence of a certain fact when from a review of all the evidence it appears more probable that the fact exists than that it does not. The actual number of witnesses involved is not material nor is the fact that the margin of probability is very slight.

prescription: the acquisition of a right to use the land of another, as an easement, through the making of hostile, visible and notorious use of the land, continuing for the period specified by the local law.

presumption: a rule of proof which permits the existence of a fact to be assumed from the proof that another fact exists when there is a logical relationship between the two or when the means of disproving the assumed fact are more readily within the control or knowledge of the adverse party against whom the presumption operates.

presumption of death: the rebuttable presumption which arises that a person has died when he has been continuously absent and unheard of for a period of 7 years.

presumption of innocence: the presumption of fact that a person accused of crime is ·innocent until it is shown that he in fact is guilty of the offense charged.

presumption of payment: a rebuttable presumption that one performing continuing services which would normally be paid periodically, as weekly or monthly, has in fact been paid when a number of years have passed without any objection or demand for payment having been made.

presumptive heir: a person who would be the heir if the ancestor should die at that moment.

pretrial conference: a conference held prior to the trial at which the court and the attorneys seek to simplify the issues in controversy and eliminate matters not in dispute.

price: the consideration for a sale of goods.

prima facie: such evidence as by itself would establish the claim or defense of the party if the evidence were believed.

primary beneficiary: the person designated as the first one to receive the proceeds of a life insurance policy, as distinguished from a contingent beneficiary who will receive the proceeds only if the primary beneficiary dies before the insured.

primary liability: the liability of a person whose act or omission gave rise to the cause of action and who in all fairness should therefore be the one to pay the victim of his wrong, even though others may also be liable for his misconduct.

principal: one who employs an agent to act on his behalf; the person who as between himself and the surety is primarily liable to the third person or creditor.

principal in the first degree: one who actually engages in the commission or perpetration of a crime.

principal in the second degree: one who is actually or constructively present at the commission of the crime and who aids and abets in its commission.

private carrier: a carrier owned by the shipper, such as a company's own fleet of trucks.

privileged communication: information which the witness may refuse to testify to because of the relationship with the person furnishing the information, as husband-wife, attorney-client.

privilege from arrest: the immunity from arrest of parties, witnesses, and attorneys while present within the jurisdiction for the purpose of taking part in other litigation.

privity: a succession or chain of relationship to the same thing or right, as a privity of contract, privity of estate, privity of possession.

probate: the procedure for formally establishing or proving that a given writing is the last will and testament of the person purporting to have signed it.

process: a writ or order of court generally used as a means of acquiring jurisdiction over the person of the defendant by serving him with process.

profit à prendre: the right to take a part of the soil or produce of the land of another, such as to take timber or water.

promissory estoppel: the doctrine that a promise will be enforced although not supported by consideration when the promisor should have reasonably expected that his promise would induce action or forebearance of a definite and substantial character on the part of the promisee, and injustice can only be avoided by enforcement of the promise.

promissory note: an unconditional promise in writing made by one person to another, signed by the maker, engaging to pay on demand, or at a definite time, a sum certain in money to order or to bearer. (Parties—maker, payee)

promissory representation: a representation made by the applicant to the insurer as to what is to occur in the future.

promissory warranty: a representation made by the applicant to the insurer as to what is to occur in the future which the applicant warrants will occur.

promoters: the persons who plan the formation of the corporation and sell or promote the idea to others.

proof: the probative effect of the evidence; the conclusion drawn from the evidence as to the existence of particular facts.

property: the rights and interests one has in anything subject to ownership.

pro rata: proportionately, or divided according to a rate or standard.

protest: the formal certification by a notary public or other authorized person that proper presentment of a commercial paper was made to the primary party and that he defaulted, the certificate commonly also including a recital that notice was given to secondary parties.

proximate cause: the act which is the natural and reasonably foreseeable cause of the harm or event which occurs and injures the plaintiff.

proximate damages: damages which in the ordinary course of events are the natural and reasonably foreseeable result of the defendant's violation of the plaintiff's rights.

proxy: a written authorization by a shareholder to another person to vote the stock owned by the shareholder; the person who is the holder of such a written authorization.

public charge: a person who because of a personal disability or lack of means of support is dependent upon public charity or relief for sustenance.

public domain: public or government owned lands.

public easement: a right of way for use by members of the public at large.

public policy: certain objectives relating to health, morals, and integrity of government that the law seeks to advance by declaring invalid any contract which conflicts with those objectives even though there is no statute expressly declaring such contract illegal.

punitive damages: damages in excess of those required to compensate the plaintiff for the wrong done, which are imposed in order to punish the defendant because of the particularly wanton or willful character of his wrongdoing.

purchase-money mortgage: a mortgage given by the purchaser of land to the seller to secure the seller for the payment of the unpaid balance of the purchase price, which the seller purports to lend the purchaser.

purchaser in good faith: a person who purchases without any notice or knowledge of any defect of title, misconduct, or defense.

Q

qualified acceptance: an acceptance of a draft that varies the order of the bill in some way.

qualified indorsement: an indorsement that includes words such as "without recourse" evidencing the intent of the indorser that he shall not be held liable for the failure of the primary party to pay the instrument.

quantum meruit: an action brought for the value of the services rendered the defendant when there was no express contract as to the payment to be made.

quantum valebant: an action brought for the value of goods sold the defendant when there was no express contract as to the purchase price.

quasi: as if, as though it were, having the characteristics of; a modifier employed to indicate that the subject is to be treated as though it were in fact the noun which follows the word "quasi:" as in quasi contract, quasi corporation, quasi public corporation.

quid pro quo: literally "what for what." An early form of the concept of consideration by which an action for debt could not be brought unless the defendant had obtained something in return for his obligation.

quitclaim deed: a deed by which the grantor purports only to give up whatever right or title he may have in the property without specifying or warranting that he is transferring any particular interest.

quorum: the minimum number of persons, shares represented, or directors who must be present at a meeting in order that business may be lawfully transacted.

R

ratification by minor: the approval of a contract given by a minor after attaining majority.

ratification of agency: the approval of the unauthorized act of an agent or of a person who is not an agent for any purpose after the act has been done, which has the same effect as though the act had been authorized before it was done.

ratio decidendi: the reason or basis for deciding the case in a particular way.

ratio legis: the reason for a principle or rule of law.

real defenses: certain defenses (universal) that are available against any holder of a commercial paper regardless of his character, although this term is not expressly used by the Uniform Commercial Code.

real evidence: tangible objects that are presented in the courtroom for the observation of the trier of fact as proof of the facts in dispute or in support of the theory of a party.

real property: land and all rights in land.

reasonable care: the degree of care that a reasonable man would take under all the circumstances then known.

rebate: a refund made by the seller or the carrier of part of the purchase price or freight bill. Generally illegal as an unfair method of competition.

rebuttable presumption: a presumption which may be overcome or rebutted by proof that the actual facts were different than those presumed.

receiver: an impartial person appointed by a court to take possession of and manage property for the protection of all concerned.

recognizance: an obligation entered into before a court to do some act, such as to appear at a later date for a hearing. Also called a contract of record.

Q -

redemption: the buying back of one's property, which has been sold because of a default, upon paying the amount which had been originally due together with interest and costs.

referee: an impartial person selected by the parties or appointed by a court to determine facts or decide matters in dispute.

referee in bankruptcy: a referee appointed by a bankruptcy court to hear and determine various matters relating to bankruptcy proceedings.

reformation: a remedy by which a written instrument is corrected when it fails to express the actual intent of both parties because of fraud, accident, or mistake.

registration of titles: a system generally known as the Torrens system of permanent registration of title to all land within the state.

reimbursement: the right of one paying money on behalf of another which such other person should have himself paid to recover the amount of the payment from him.

release of liens: an agreement or instrument by which the holder of a lien on property, such as a mortgage lien, releases the property from the lien although the debt itself is not released.

remedy: the action or procedure that is followed in order to enforce a right or to obtain damages for injury to a right.

remote damages: damages which were in fact caused by the defendant's act but the possibility that such damages should occur seemed so improbable and unlikely to a reasonable man that the law does not impose liability for such damages.

renunciation of duty: the repudiation of one's contractual duty in advance of the time for performance, which repudiation may be accepted by the adverse party as an anticipatory breach.

renunciation of right: the surrender of a right or privilege as the right to act as administrator or the right to receive a legacy under the will of a decedent.

reorganization of corporation: procedure devised to restore insolvent corporations to financial stability through readjustment of debt and capital structure either under the supervision of a court of equity or of bankruptcy.

repossession: any taking again of possession although generally used in connection with the act of a secured seller in taking back the property upon the default of the credit buyer.

representations: statements, whether oral or written, made to give the insurer the information which it needs in writing the insurance, and which if false and relating to a material fact will entitle the insurer to avoid the contract.

representative capacity: action taken by one not on his own behalf but on behalf of another, as an executor acting on behalf of the decedent's estate, or action taken both on one's behalf and on behalf of others, as a stockholder bringing a representative action.

resale price maintenance agreement: an agreement that the buyer will not resell a trademark or brand name article below a stated minimum price which agreement, by virtue of fair trade laws, is valid not only as between the contracting parties but may also bind other persons in the trade who know of the agreement although they did not sign it.

rescission upon agreement: the setting aside of a contract by the action of the parties as though the contract had never been made.

rescission upon breach: the action of one party to a contract to set the contract aside when the other party is guilty of a breach of the contract.

reservation: the creation by the grantor of a right that did not exist before, which he reserves or keeps for himself upon making a conveyance of property.

residuary estate: the balance of the testator's estate available for distribution after all administrative expenses, exemptions, debts, taxes, and specific, pecuniary, and demonstrative legacies have been paid.

res inter alios acta: the rule that transactions and declarations between strangers having no connection with the pending action are not admissible in evidence.

res ipsa loquitur: the rebuttable presumption that the thing speaks for itself when the circumstances are such that ordinarily the plaintiff could not have been injured had the defendant not been at fault.

res judicata: the principle that once a final judgment is entered in an action between the parties, it is binding upon them and the matters cannot be litigated again by bringing a second action.

respondeat superior: the doctrine that the principal or employer is vicariously liable for the unauthorized torts committed by his agent or employee while acting with the scope of his agency or the course of his employment, respectively.

restraints on alienation: limitations on the ability of the owner to convey freely as he chooses. Such limitations are generally regarded as invalid.

restrictive covenants: covenants in a deed by which the grantee agrees to refrain from doing specified acts.

restrictive indorsement: an indorsement that prohibits the further transfer, constitutes the indorsee the agent of the indorser, vests the title in the indorsee in trust for or to the use of some other person, is conditional, or is for collection or deposit.

resulting trust: a trust that is created by implication of law when the purpose of the original trust fails or is fully performed and the cy pres doctrine is inapplicable, the effect of the resulting trust being to revert the remaining property to the settlor or his heirs.

retaliatory statute: a statute that provides that when a corporation of another state enters the state it shall be subject to the same taxes and restrictions as would be imposed upon a corporation from the retaliating state if it had entered the other state. Also called reciprocity statutes.

reversible error: an error or defect in court proceedings of so serious a nature that on appeal the appellate court will set aside the proceedings of the lower court.

reversionary interest: the interest that a lessor has in property which is subject to an outstanding lease.

revival of judgment: the taking of appropriate action to preserve a judgment, in most instances to continue the lien of the judgment that would otherwise expire after a specified number of years.

revival of will: the restoration by the testator of a will which he had previously revoked.

rider: a slip of paper executed by the insurer and intended to be attached to the insurance policy for the purpose of changing it in some respect.

riparian rights: the right of a person through whose land runs a natural watercourse to use the water free from unreasonable pollution or diversion by the upper riparian owners and from blocking by lower riparian owners.

risk: the peril or contingency against which the insured is protected by the contract of insurance.

Robinson-Patman Act: a federal statute designed to eliminate price discrimination in interstate commerce.

R

run with the land: the concept that certain covenants in a deed to land are deemed to "run" or pass with the land so that whoever owns the land is bound by or entitled to the benefit of the covenants.

S

sale or return: a sale in which the title to the property passes to the buyer at the time of the transaction but he is given the option of returning the property and restoring the title to the seller.

scienter: knowledge, referring to those wrongs or crimes which require a knowledge of wrong in order to constitute the offense.

scope of employment: the area within which the employee is authorized to act with the consequence that a tort committed while so acting imposes liability upon the employer.

seal: at common law an impression on wax or other tenacious material attached to the instrument. Under modern law, any mark not ordinarily part of the signature is a seal when so intended, including the letters "L. S." and the word "seal," or a pictorial representation of a seal, without regard to whether they had been printed or typed on the instrument before its signing.

sealed verdict: a verdict that is rendered when the jury returns to the courtroom during an adjournment of the court, the verdict then being written down and sealed and later affirmed before the court when the court is in session.

seaman's will: an oral or informal written will made by a seaman to dispose of his personal property.

secondary evidence: copies of original writings or testimony as to the contents of such writings which are admissible when the original cannot be produced and the inability to do so is reasonably explained.

secret partner: a partner who takes an active part in the management of the partnership but is not known to the public as a partner.

secured transaction: a credit sale of goods or a secured loan that provides special protection for the creditor.

settlor: one who settles property in trust or creates a trust estate.

severable contract: a contract the terms of which are such that one part may be separated or severed from the other, so that a default as to one part is not necessarily a default as to the entire contract.

several contracts: separate or independent contracts made by different persons undertaking to perform the same obligation.

severalty: sole ownership of property by one person.

severed realty: real property that has been cut off and made moveable, as by cutting down a tree, and which thereby loses its character as real property and becomes personal property.

shareholder's action: an action brought by one or more shareholders on behalf of the shareholders generally and of the corporation to enforce a cause of action of the corporation against third persons.

sheriff's deed: the deed executed and delivered by the sheriff to the purchaser at a sale conducted by the sheriff in his official capacity.

Sherman Antitrust Act: a federal statute prohibiting combinations and contracts in restraint of interstate trade, now generally inapplicable to labor union activity.

shop right: the right of an employer to use in his business without charge an invention discovered by an employee during working hours and with the employer's material and equipment.

sight draft: a draft or bill of exchange payable on sight or when presented for payment.

silent partner: a partner who takes no active part in the business, without regard to whether he is known to the public as a partner.

sitdown strike: a strike in which the employees remain in the plant and refuse to allow the employer to operate it.

slander: defamation of character by spoken words or gestures.

slander of title: the malicious making of false statements as to a seller's title.

slander per se: certain words deemed slanderous without requiring proof of damages to the victim, as words charging a crime involving moral turpitude and an infamous punishment, a disease which would exclude from society, or which tend to injure the victim in his business, profession, or occupation.

slowdown: a slowing down of production by employees without actual stopping of work.

social security acts: statutes providing for assistance for the aged, blind, unemployed, and similar classes of persons in need.

soldier's will: an oral or informal written will made by a soldier to dispose of his personal estate.

special agent: an agent authorized to transact a specific transaction or to do a specific act.

special damages: damages that do not necessarily result from the injury to the plaintiff but at the same time are not so remote that the defendant should not be held liable therefor provided that the claim for special damages is properly made in the action.

special indorsement: an indorsement that specifies the person to whom the instrument is indorsed.

special jurisdiction: a court with power to hear and determine cases within certain restricted categories.

specific (identified) goods: goods which are so identified to the contract that no other goods may be delivered in performance of the contract.

specific lien: the right of a creditor to hold particular property or assert a lien on any particular property of the debtor because of the creditor's having done work on or having some other association with the property, as distinguished from having a lien generally against the assets of the debtor merely because the debtor is indebted to him.

specific performance: an action brought to compel the adverse party to perform his contract on the theory that merely suing him for damages for its breach will not be an adequate remedy.

spendthrift trust: a trust, which to varying degrees, provides that creditors of the beneficiary shall not be able to reach the principal or income held by the trustee and that the beneficiary shall not be able to assign his interest in the trust.

spoliation: an alteration or change made to a written instrument by a person who has no relationship to or interest in the writing. It has no effect as long as the terms of the instrument can still be ascertained.

stare decisis: the principle that the decision of a court should serve as a guide or precedent and control the decision of a similar case in the future.

status quo: the requirement that before a contract may be rescinded, the status quo must be restored, that is, the parties must be placed in their original positions prior to the making of the contract.

Statute of Frauds: a statute, which in order to prevent fraud through the use of perjured testimony, requires that certain types of transactions be evidenced in writing in order to be binding or enforceable.

S

Statute of Limitations: a statute that restricts the period of time within which an action may be brought.

stoppage in transitu: the right of the unpaid seller to stop goods being shipped to the buyer while they are still in transit and to recover them when the buyer becomes insolvent.

stop payment: an order by a depositor to his bank to refuse to make payment of his check when presented for payment.

sublease: a transfer of the premises by the lessee to a third person, the sub-lessee or subtenant, for a period less than the term of the original lease.

subpoena: a court order directing a person to appear as a witness. In some states also it is the original process that is to be served on the defendant in order to give the court jurisdiction over his person.

subpoena duces tecum: a court order directing a person to appear as a witness and to bring with him specified relevant papers.

subrogation: the right of a party secondarily liable to stand in the place of the creditor after he has made payment to the creditor and to enforce the creditor's right against the party primarily liable in order to obtain indemnity from him.

subsidiary corporation: a corporation that is controlled by another corporation through the ownership by the latter of a controlling amount of the voting stock of the former.

subsidiary term: a provision of a contract that is not fundamental or does not go to the root of the contract.

substantial performance: the equitable doctrine that a contractor substantially performing a contract in good faith is entitled to recover the contract price less damages for noncompletion or defective work.

substantive law: the law that defines rights and liabilities.

substitution: discharge of contracts by substituting another in its place.

subtenant: one who rents the leased premises from the original tenant for a period of time less than the balance of the lease to the original tenant.

sui generis: in a class by itself, or its own kind.

sui juris: legally competent, possessing capacity.

summary judgment: a judgment entered by the court when no substantial dispute of fact is present, the court acting on the basis of affidavits which show that the claim or defense of a party is a sham.

summons: a writ by which an action was commenced under the common law.

superior servant rule: an exception to the fellow-servant rule that is made when the injured servant is under the control of the servant whose conduct caused him injury.

supersedeas: a stay of proceedings pending the taking of an appeal or an order entered for the purpose of effecting such a stay.

surcharge: a money judgment entered against a fiduciary for the amount of loss which his negligence or misconduct has caused the estate under his control.

suretyship: an undertaking to pay the debt or be liable for the default of another.

surrender: the yielding up of the tenant's leasehold estate to the lessor in consequence of which the lease terminates.

survival acts: statutes which provide that causes of action shall not terminate on death but shall survive and may be enforced by or against a decedent's estate.

survivorship: the right by which a surviving joint tenant or tenant by the entireties acquires the interest of the predeceasing tenant automatically upon his death.

symbolic delivery: the delivery of goods by delivery of the means of control, as a key or relevant document of title, as a negotiable bill of lading.

syndicate: an association of individuals formed to conduct a particular business transaction, generally of a financial nature.

T

tacking: the adding together of successive periods of adverse possession of persons in privity with each other in order to constitute a sufficient period of continuous adverse possession to vest title thereby.

Taft-Hartley Act: popular name for the National Labor Management Relations Act of 1947.

tenancy at sufferance: the holding over by a tenant after his lease has expired of the rented land without the permission of the landlord and prior to the time that the landlord has elected to treat him as a trespasser or a tenant.

tenancy at will: the holding of land for an indefinite period that may be terminated at any time by the landlord or by the landlord and tenant acting together.

tenancy for years: a tenancy for a fixed period of time, even though the time is less than a year.

tenancy from year to year: a tenancy which continues indefinitely from year to year until terminated.

tenancy in common: the relation that exists when two or more persons own undivided interests in property.

tenancy in partnership: the ownership relation that exists between partners under the Uniform Partnership Act.

tender of payment: an unconditional offer to pay the exact amount of money due at the time and place specified by the contract.

tender of performance: an unconditional offer to perform at the time and in the manner specified by the contract.

tentative trust: a trust which arises when money is deposited in a bank account in the name of the depositor "in trust for" a named person.

terminable fee: an estate that terminates upon the happening of a contingency without any entry by the grantor or his heirs, as a conveyance for "so long as" the land is used for a specified purpose.

testamentary: designed to take effect at death, as by disposing of property or appointing an executor.

testate: the condition of leaving a will upon death.

testate succession: the distribution of an estate in accordance with the will of the decedent.

testator—testatrix: a man—woman who makes a will.

testimonium clause: a concluding paragraph in a deed, contract, or other instrument, reciting that the instrument has been executed on a specified date by the parties.

testimony: the answers of witnesses under oath to questions given at the time of the trial in the presence of the trier of fact.

theory of the case: the rule that when a case is tried on the basis of one theory, the appellant in taking an appeal cannot argue a different theory to the appellate court.

third-party beneficiary: a third person whom the parties to a contract intend to benefit by the making of the contract and to confer upon him the right to sue for breach of the contract.

tie-in sale: the requirement imposed by the seller that the buyer of particular goods or equipment also purchase certain other goods from the seller in order to obtain the original property desired.

T

time draft: a bill of exchange payable at a stated time after sight or a stated time after a certain date.

title insurance: a form of insurance by which the insurer insures the buyer of real property against the risk of loss should the title acquired from the seller be defective in any way.

toll the statute: stop the running of the period of the Statute of Limitations by the doing of some act by the debtor.

Torrens System: see registration of titles.

tort: a private injury or wrong arising from a breach of a duty created by law.

trade acceptance: a draft or bill of exchange drawn by the seller of goods on the purchaser at the time of sale and accepted by the purchaser.

trade fixtures: articles of personal property which have been attached to the freehold by a tenant and which are used for or are necessary to the carrying on of the tenant's trade.

trademark: a name, device, or symbol used by a manufacturer or seller to distinguish his goods from those of other persons.

trade name: a name under which a business is carried on and, if fictitious, it must be registered.

trade secrets: secrets of any character peculiar and important to the business of the employer that have been communicated to the employee in the course of confidential employment.

treason: an attempt to overthrow or betray the government to which one owes allegiance.

treasury stock: stock of the corporation which the corporation has reacquired.

trier of fact: in most cases a jury, although it may be the judge alone in certain classes of cases, as in equity, or in any case when jury trial is waived, or an administrative agency or commission.

trust: a transfer of property by one person to another with the understanding or declaration that such property be held for the benefit of another, or the holding of property by the owner in trust for another, upon his declaration of trust, without a transfer to another person. (Parties —settlor, trustee, beneficiary.)

trust corpus: the fund or property that is transferred to the trustee as the body or subject matter of the trust.

trust deed: a form of deed which transfers the trust property to the trustee for the purposes therein stated, particularly used as a form of mortgage when the trustee is to hold the title to the mortgagor's land in trust for the benefit of the mortgage bondholders.

trustee de son tort: a person who is not a trustee but who has wrongly intermeddled with property of another and rather than proceed against him for the tort, the law will require him to account for the property as though he were such a trustee.

trustee in bankruptcy: an impartial person elected to administer the bankrupt's estate.

trust receipt: a credit security device under which the wholesale buyer executes a receipt stating that he holds the purchased goods in trust for the person financing the purchase by lending him money. The trust receipt is replaced by the secured transaction under the Uniform Commercial Code.

U

uberrima fides: utmost good faith, a duty to exercise the utmost good faith which arises in certain relationships, as that between an insurer and the applicant for insurance.

ultra vires: an act or contract which the corporation does not have authority to do or make.

underwriter: an insurer.

undisclosed principal: a principal on whose behalf an agent acts without disclosing to the third person the fact that he is an agent nor the identity of the principal.

undue influence: the influence that is asserted upon another person by one who dominates that person.

unfair competition: the wrong of employing competitive methods that have been declared unfair by statute or an administrative agency.

unfair labor practice acts: statutes that prohibit certain labor practices and declare them to be unfair labor practices.

unincorporated association: a combination of two or more persons for the furtherance of a common nonprofit purpose.

union contract: a contract between a labor union and an employer or group of employers prescribing the general terms of employment of workers by the latter.

union shop: under present unfair labor practice statutes, a place of employment where nonunion men may be employed for a trial period of not more than 30 days after which the nonunion worker must join the union or be discharged.

universal agent: an agent authorized by the principal to do all acts that can lawfully be delegated to a representative.

usury: the lending of money at greater than the maximum rate allowed by law.

V

vacation of judgment: the setting aside of a judgment.

valid: legal.

verdict: the decision of the trial or petty jury.

vice-principal rule: the rule that persons performing supervisory functions or acting as vice employers are not to be regarded as fellow servants of those under their authority for the purpose of determining the liability of the employer for the injuries of the employee at common law.

void: of no legal effect and not binding on anyone.

voidable: a transaction that may be set aside by one party thereto because of fraud or similar reason but which is binding on the other party until the injured party elects to avoid the contract.

voidable preference: a preference given by the bankrupt to one of his creditors, but which may be set aside by the trustee in bankruptcy.

voir dire examination: the preliminary examination of a juror or a witness to ascertain that he is qualified to act as such.

volenti non fit injuria: the maxim that the defendant's act cannot constitute a tort if the plaintiff had consented thereto.

voluntary nonsuit: a means of the plaintiff's stopping a trial at any time by moving for a voluntary nonsuit.

voting trust: the transfer by two or more persons of their shares of stock of a corporation to a trustee who is to vote the shares and act for such shareholders.

W

waiver: the release or relinquishment of a known right or objection.

warehouse receipt: a receipt issued by the warehouseman for goods stored with him. Regulated by the Uniform Commercial Code, which clothes the receipt with some degree of negotiability.

warehouseman: a person regularly engaged in the business of storing the goods of others for compensation. If he holds himself out to serve the public without discrimination, he is a public warehouseman.

warranties of indorser of commercial paper: the implied covenants made by an indorser of a commercial paper distinct from any undertaking to pay upon the default of the primary party.

warranties of insured: statements or promises made by the applicant for insurance which he guarantees to be as stated and which if false will entitle the insurer to avoid the contract of insurance in many jurisdictions.

warranties of seller of goods: warranties consisting of express warranties that relate to matters forming part of the basis of the bargain; warranties as to title and right to sell; and the implied warranties which the law adds to a sale depending upon the nature of the transaction.

warranty deed: a deed by which the grantor conveys a specific estate or interest to the grantee and covenants that he has transferred the estate or interest by making one or more of the covenants of title.

warranty of authority: an implied warranty of an agent that he has the authority which he purports to possess.

warranty of principal: an implied warranty of an agent that he is acting for an existing principal who has capacity to contract.

watered stock: stock issued by a corporation as fully paid when in fact it is not.

way: an easement to pass over the land of another.

will: an instrument executed with the formality required by law, by which a person makes a disposition of his property to take effect upon his death or appoints an executor.

willful: intentional as distinguished from accidental or involuntary. In penal statutes, with evil intent or legal malice, or without reasonable ground for believing one's act to be lawful.

witness: a person who has observed the facts to which he testifies or an expert witness who may testify on the basis of observation, the testimony presented in the court, or hypothetical questions put to him by the attorneys in the case.

Wool Products Labeling Act: a federal statute prohibiting the misbranding of woolen fabrics.

workmen's compensation: a system providing for payments to workmen because they have been injured from a risk arising out of the course of their employment while they were employed at their employment or have contracted an occupational disease in that manner, payment being made without consideration of the negligence of any party.

works of charity: in connection with Sunday laws, acts involved in religious worship or aiding persons in distress.

works of necessity: in connection with Sunday laws, acts that must be done at the particular time in order to be effective in saving life, health, or property.

Y

year and a day: the common-law requirement that death result within a year and a day in order to impose criminal liability for homicide.

Z

zoning restrictions: restrictions imposed by government on the use of property for the advancement of the general welfare.

Y-Z

Index

* Page references for definitions are indicated in italic type.

UNIFORM COMMERCIAL CODE

TITLE

An Act

To be known as the Uniform Commercial Code, Relating to Certain Commercial Transactions in or regarding Personal Property and Contracts and other Documents concerning them, including Sales, Commercial Paper, Bank Deposits and Collections, Letters of Credit, Bulk Transfers, Warehouse Receipts, Bills of Lading, other Documents of Title, Investment Securities, and Secured Transactions, including certain Sales of Accounts, Chattel Paper, and Contract Rights; Providing for Public Notice to Third Parties in Certain Circumstances; Regulating Procedure, Evidence and Damages in Certain Court Actions Involving such Transactions, Contracts or Documents; to Make Uniform the Law with Respect Thereto; and Repealing Inconsistent Legislation.

ARTICLE 1

GENERAL PROVISIONS

PART 1

SHORT TITLE, CONSTRUCTION, APPLICATION AND SUBJECT MATTER OF THE ACT

Section 1—101. Short Title.

This Act shall be known and may be cited as Uniform Commercial Code.

Section 1—102. Purposes; Rules of Construction; Variation by Agreement.

(1) This Act shall be liberally construed and applied to promote its underlying purposes and policies.

(2) Underlying purposes and policies of this Act are

   (a) to simplify, clarify and modernize the law governing commercial transactions;

   (b) to permit the continued expansion of commercial practices through custom, usage and agreement of the parties;

   (c) to make uniform the law among the various jurisdictions.

(3) The effect of provisions of this Act may be varied by agreement, except as otherwise provided in this Act and except that the obligations of good faith, diligence, reasonableness and care prescribed by this Act may not be disclaimed by agreement but the parties may by agreement determine the standards by which the performance of such obligations is to be measured if such standards are not manifestly unreasonable.

(4) The presence in certain provisions of this Act of the words "unless otherwise agreed" or words of similar import does not imply that the effect of other provisions may not be varied by agreement under subsection (3).

(5) In this Act unless the context otherwise requires
- (a) words in the singular number include the plural, and in the plural include the singular;
- (b) words of the masculine gender include the feminine and the neuter, and when the sense so indicates words of the neuter gender may refer to any gender.

Section 1—103. Supplementary General Principles of Law Applicable.

Unless displaced by the particular provisions of this Act, the principles of law and equity, including the law merchant and the law relative to capacity to contract, principal and agent, estoppel, fraud, misrepresentation, duress, coercion, mistake, bankruptcy, or other validating or invalidating cause shall supplement its provisions.

Section 1—104. Construction Against Implicit Repeal.

This Act being a general act intended as a unified coverage of its subject matter, no part of it shall be deemed to be impliedly repealed by subsequent legislation if such construction can reasonably be avoided.

Section 1—105. Territorial Application of the Act; Parties' Power to Choose Applicable Law.

(1) Except as provided hereafter in this section, when a transaction bears a reasonable relation to this state and also to another state or nation, the parties may agree that the law either of this state or of such other state or nation shall govern their rights and duties. Failing such agreement this Act applies to transactions bearing an appropriate relation to this state.

(2) Where one of the following provisions of this Act specifies the applicable law, that provision governs and a contrary agreement is effective only to the extent permitted by the law (including the conflict of laws rules) so specified:

Rights of creditors against sold goods. Section 2—402.

Applicability of the Article on Bank Deposits and Collections. Section 4—102.

Bulk transfers subject to the Article on Bulk Transfers. Section 6—102.

Applicability of the Article on Investment Securities. Section 8—106.

Policy and scope of the Article on Secured Transactions. Sections 9—102 and 9—103.

Section 1—106. Remedies to Be Liberally Administered.

(1) The remedies provided by this Act shall be liberally administered to the end that the aggrieved party may be put in as good a position as if the other party had fully performed, but neither consequential or special nor penal damages may be had except as specifically provided in this Act or by other rule of law.

(2) Any right or obligation declared by this Act is enforceable by action unless the provision declaring it specifies a different and limited effect.

Section 1—107. Waiver or Renunciation of Claim or Right After Breach.

Any claim or right arising out of an alleged breach can be discharged in whole or in part without consideration by a written waiver or renunciation signed and delivered by the aggrieved party.

Section 1—108. Severability.

If any provision or clause of this Act or application thereof to any person or circumstances is held invalid, such invalidity shall not affect other provisions or applications of the Act which can be given effect without the invalid provision or application, and to this end the provisions of this Act are declared to be severable.

Section 1—109. Section Captions.

Section captions are parts of this Act.

PART 2

GENERAL DEFINITIONS AND PRINCIPLES
OF INTERPRETATION

Section 1—201. General Definitions.

Subject to additional definitions contained in the subsequent Articles of this Act which are applicable to specific Articles or Parts thereof, and unless the context otherwise requires, in this Act:

(1) "Action" in the sense of a judicial proceeding includes recoupment, counterclaim, set-off, suit in equity and any other proceedings in which rights are determined.

(2) "Aggrieved party" means a party entitled to resort to a remedy.

(3) "Agreement" means the bargain of the parties in fact as found in their language or by implication from other circumstances including course of dealing or usage of trade or course of performance as provided in this Act (Sections 1—205 and 2—208). Whether an agreement has legal consequences is determined by the provisions of this Act, if applicable; otherwise by the law of contracts (Section 1—103). (Compare "Contract".)

(4) "Bank" means any person engaged in the business of banking.

(5) "Bearer" means the person in possession of an instrument, document of title, or security payable to bearer or indorsed in blank.

(6) "Bill of lading" means a document evidencing the receipt of goods for shipment issued by a person engaged in the business of transporting or forwarding goods, and includes an airbill. "Airbill" means a document serving for air transportation as a bill of lading does for marine or rail transportation, and includes an air consignment note or air waybill.

(7) "Branch" includes a separately incorporated foreign branch of a bank.

(8) "Burden of establishing" a fact means the burden of persuading the triers of fact that the existence of the fact is more probable than its nonexistence.

(9) "Buyer in ordinary course of business" means a person who in good faith and without knowledge that the sale to him is in violation of the ownership rights or security interest of a third party in the goods buys in ordinary course from a person in the business of selling goods of that kind but does not include a pawnbroker. "Buying" may be for cash or by exchange of other property or on secured or unsecured credit and includes receiving goods or documents of title under a preexisting contract for sale but does not include a transfer in bulk or as security for or in total or partial satisfaction of a money debt.

(10) "Conspicuous": A term or clause is conspicuous when it is so written that a reasonable person against whom it is to operate ought to have noticed it. A printed heading in capitals (as: NON-NEGOTIABLE BILL OF LADING) is conspicuous. Language in the body of a form is "conspicuous" if it is in larger or other contrasting type or color. But in a telegram any stated term is "conspicuous". Whether a term or clause is "conspicuous" or not is for decision by the court.

(11) "Contract" means the total legal obligation which results from the parties' agreement as affected by this Act and any other applicable rules of law. (Compare "Agreement".)

(12) "Creditor" includes a general creditor, a secured creditor, a lien creditor and any representative of creditors, including an assignee for the benefit of creditors, a trustee in bankruptcy, a receiver in equity and an executor or administrator of an insolvent debtor's or assignor's estate.

(13) "Defendant" includes a person in the position of defendant in a cross-action or counterclaim.

(14) "Delivery" with respect to instruments, documents of title, chattel paper or securities means voluntary transfer of possession.

(15) "Document of title" includes bill of lading, dock warrant, dock receipt,

warehouse receipt or order for the delivery of goods, and also any other document which in the regular course of business or financing is treated as adequately evidencing that the person in possession of it is entitled to receive, hold and dispose of the document and the goods it covers. To be a document of title a document must purport to be issued by or addressed to a bailee and purport to cover goods in the bailee's possession which are either identified or are fungible portions of an identified mass.

(16) "Fault" means wrongful act, omission or breach.

(17) "Fungible" with respect to goods or securities means goods or securities of which any unit is, by nature or usage of trade, the equivalent of any other like unit. Goods which are not fungible shall be deemed fungible for the purposes of this Act to the extent that under a particular agreement or document unlike units are treated as equivalents.

(18) "Genuine" means free of forgery or counterfeiting.

(19) "Good faith" means honesty in fact in the conduct or transaction concerned.

(20) "Holder" means a person who is in possession of a document of title or an instrument or an investment security drawn, issued or indorsed to him or to his order or to bearer or in blank.

(21) To "honor" is to pay or to accept and pay, or where a credit so engages to purchase or discount a draft complying with the terms of the credit.

(22) "Insolvency proceedings" includes any assignment for the benefit of creditors or other proceedings intended to liquidate or rehabilitate the estate of the person involved.

(23) A person is "insolvent" who either has ceased to pay his debts in the ordinary course of business or cannot pay his debts as they become due or is insolvent within the meaning of the federal bankruptcy law.

(24) "Money" means a medium of exchange authorized or adopted by a domestic or foreign government as a part of its currency.

(25) A person has "notice" of a fact when
   (a) he has actual knowledge of it; or
   (b) he has received a notice or notification of it; or
   (c) from all the facts and circumstances known to him at the time in question he has reason to know that it exists.

A person "knows" or has "knowledge" of a fact when he has actual knowledge of it. "Discover" or "learn" or a word or phrase of similar import refers to knowledge rather than to reason to know. The time and circumstances under which a notice or notification may cease to be effective are not determined by this Act.

(26) A person "notifies" or "gives" a notice or notification to another by taking such steps as may be reasonably required to inform the other in ordinary course whether or not such other actually comes to know of it. A person "receives" a notice or notification when
   (a) it comes to his attention; or
   (b) it is duly delivered at the place of business through which the contract was made or at any other place held out by him as the place for receipt of such communications.

(27) Notice, knowledge or a notice or notification received by an organization is effective for a particular transaction from the time when it is brought to the attention of the individual conducting that transaction, and in any event from the time when it would have been brought to his attention if the organization had exercised due diligence. An organization exercises due diligence if it maintains reasonable routines for communicating significant information to the person conducting the transaction and there is reasonable compliance with the routines. Due diligence does not require an individual acting for the organization to communicate information unless such communication is part of his regular duties or unless he has reason to know of the transaction and that the transaction would be materially affected by the information.

(28) "Organization" includes a corporation, government or governmental subdivision or agency, business trust, estate, trust, partnership or association, two or more persons having a joint or common interest, or any other legal or commercial entity.

(29) "Party", as distinct from "third party," means a person who has engaged in a transaction or made an agreement within this Act.

(30) "Person" includes an individual or an organization (See Section 1—102).

(31) "Presumption" or "presumed" means that the trier of fact must find the existence of the fact presumed unless and until evidence is introduced which would support a finding of its nonexistence.

(32) "Purchase" includes taking by sale, discount, negotiation, mortgage, pledge, lien, issue or re-issue, gift or any other voluntary transaction creating an interest in property.

(33) "Purchaser" means a person who takes by purchase.

(34) "Remedy" means any remedial right to which an aggrieved party is entitled with or without resort to a tribunal.

(35) "Representative" includes an agent, an officer of a corporation or association, and a trustee, executor or administrator of an estate, or any other person empowered to act for another.

(36) "Rights" includes remedies.

(37) "Security interest" means an interest in personal property or fixtures which secures payment or performance of an obligation. The retention or reservation of title by a seller of goods notwithstanding shipment or delivery to the buyer (Section 2—401) is limited in effect to a reservation of a "security interest." The term also includes any interest of a buyer of accounts, chattel paper, or contract rights which is subject to Article 9. The special property interest of a buyer of goods on identification of such goods to a contract for sale under Section 2—401 is not a "security interest," but a buyer may also acquire a "security interest" by complying with Article 9. Unless a lease or consignment is intended as security, reservation of title thereunder is not a "security interest" but a consignment is in any event subject to the provisions on consignment sales (Section 2—326). Whether a lease is intended as security is to be determined by the facts of each case; however, (a) the inclusion of an option to purchase does not of itself make the lease one intended for security, and (b) an agreement that upon compliance with the terms of the lease the lessee shall become or has the option to become the owner of the property for no additional consideration or for a nominal consideration does make the lease one intended for security.

(38) "Send" in connection with any writing or notice means to deposit in the mail or deliver for transmission by any other usual means of communication with postage or cost of transmission provided for and properly addressed and in the case of an instrument to an address specified thereon or otherwise agreed, or if there be none to any address reasonable under the circumstances. The receipt of any writing or notice within the time at which it would have arrived if properly sent has the effect of a proper sending.

(39) "Signed" includes any symbol executed or adopted by a party with present intention to authenticate a writing.

(40) "Surety" includes guarantor.

(41) "Telegram" includes a message transmitted by radio, teletype, cable, any mechanical method of transmission, or the like.

(42) "Term" means that portion of an agreement which relates to a particular matter.

(43) "Unauthorized" signature or indorsement means one made without actual, implied or apparent authority and includes a forgery.

(44) "Value." Except as otherwise provided with respect to negotiable instruments and bank collections (Sections 3—303, 4—208 and 4—209) a person gives "value" for rights if he acquires them

    (a) in return for a binding commitment to extend credit or for the extension of immediately available credit whether or not drawn upon and whether or not a charge-back is provided for in the event of difficulties in collection; or

(b) as security for or in total or partial satisfaction of a pre-existing claim; or

(c) by accepting delivery pursuant to a pre-existing contract for purchase; or

(d) generally, in return for any consideration sufficient to support a simple contract.

(45) "Warehouse receipt" means a receipt issued by a person engaged in the business of storing goods for hire.

(46) "Written" or "writing" includes printing, typewriting or any other intentional reduction to tangible form.

Section 1—202. Prima Facie Evidence by Third Party Documents.

A document in due form purporting to be a bill of lading, policy or certificate of insurance, official weigher's or inspector's certificate, consular invoice, or any other document authorized or required by the contract to be issued by a third party shall be prima facie evidence of its own authenticity and genuineness and of the facts stated in the document by the third party.

Section 1—203. Obligation of Good Faith.

Every contract or duty within this Act imposes an obligation of good faith in its performance or enforcement.

Section 1—204. Time; Reasonable Time; "Seasonably."

(1) Whenever this Act requires any action to be taken within a reasonable time, any time which is not manifestly unreasonable may be fixed by agreement.

(2) What is a reasonable time for taking any action depends on the nature, purpose and circumstances of such action.

(3) An action is taken "seasonably" when it is taken at or within the time agreed or if no time is agreed at or within a reasonable time.

Section 1—205. Course of Dealing and Usage of Trade.

(1) A course of dealing is a sequence of previous conduct between the parties to a particular transaction which is fairly to be regarded as establishing a common basis of understanding for interpreting their expressions and other conduct.

(2) A usage of trade is any practice or method of dealing having such regularity of observance in a place, vocation or trade as to justify an expectation that it will be observed with respect to the transaction in question. The existence and scope of such a usage are to be proved as facts. If it is established that such a usage is embodied in a written trade code or similar writing, the interpretation of the writing is for the court.

(3) A course of dealing between parties and any usage of trade in the vocation or trade in which they are engaged or of which they are or should be aware give particular meaning to and supplement or qualify terms of an agreement.

(4) The express terms of an agreement and an applicable course of dealing or usage of trade shall be construed wherever reasonable as consistent with each other; but when such construction is unreasonable, express terms control both course of dealing and usage of trade and course of dealing controls usage of trade.

(5) An applicable usage of trade in the place where any part of performance is to occur shall be used in interpreting the agreement as to that part of the performance.

(6) Evidence of a relevant usage of trade offered by one party is not admissible unless and until he has given the other party such notice as the court finds sufficient to prevent unfair surprise to the latter.

Section 1—206. Statute of Frauds for Kinds of Personal Property Not Otherwise Covered.

(1) Except in the cases described in subsection (2) of this section, a contract for the sale of personal property is not enforceable by way of action or defense beyond five thousand dollars in amount or value of remedy unless there is some writing which indicates that a contract for sale has been made between the parties at a defined or stated price, reasonably identifies the subject matter, and is signed by the party against whom enforcement is sought or by his authorized agent.

(2) Subsection (1) of this section does not apply to contracts for the sale of goods (Section 2—201) nor of securities (Section 8—319) nor to security agreements (Section 9—203).

Section 1—207. Performance or Acceptance Under Reservation of Rights.

A party who with explicit reservation of rights performs or promises performance or assents to performance in a manner demanded or offered by the other party does not thereby prejudice the rights reserved. Such words as "without prejudice", "under protest" or the like are sufficient.

Section 1—208. Option to Accelerate at Will.

A term providing that one party or his successor in interest may accelerate payment or performance or require collateral or additional collateral "at will" or "when he deems himself insecure" or in words of similar import shall be construed to mean that he shall have power to do so only if he in good faith believes that the prospect of payment or performance is impaired. The burden of establishing lack of good faith is on the party against whom the power has been exercised.

ARTICLE 2

SALES

PART 1

SHORT TITLE, GENERAL CONSTRUCTION AND SUBJECT MATTER

Section 2—101. Short Title.

This Article shall be known and may be cited as Uniform Commercial Code—Sales.

Section 2—102. Scope; Certain Security and Other Transactions Excluded from This Article.

Unless the context otherwise requires, this Article applies to transactions in goods; it does not apply to any transaction which although in the form of an unconditional contract to sell or present sale is intended to operate only as a security transaction nor does this Article impair or repeal any statute regulating sales to consumers, farmers or other specified classes of buyers.

Section 2—103. Definitions and Index of Definitions.

(1) In this Article unless the context otherwise requires

    (a) "Buyer" means a person who buys or contracts to buy goods.

    (b) "Good faith" in the case of a merchant means honesty in fact and the observance of reasonable commercial standards of fair dealing in the trade.

    (c) "Receipt" of goods means taking physical possession of them.

    (d) "Seller" means a person who sells or contracts to sell goods.

(2) Other definitions applying to this Article or to specified Parts thereof, and the sections in which they appear are:

"Acceptance". Section 2—606.

"Banker's credit". Section 2—325.

"Between merchants". Section 2–104.

"Cancellation". Section 2–106(4).

"Commercial unit". Section 2–105.

"Confirmed credit". Section 2–325.

"Conforming to contract". Section 2–106.

"Contract for sale". Section 2–106.

"Cover". Section 2–712.

"Entrusting". Section 2–403.

"Financing agency". Section 2–104.

"Future goods". Section 2–105.

"Goods". Section 2–105.

"Identification". Section 2–501.

"Installment contract". Section 2–612.

"Letter of Credit". Section 2–325.

"Lot". Section 2–105.

"Merchant". Section 2–104.

"Overseas". Section 2–323.

"Person in position of seller". Section 2–707.

"Present sale". Section 2–106.

"Sale". Section 2–106.

"Sale on approval". Section 2–326.

"Sale or return". Section 2–326.

"Termination". Section 2–106.

(3) The following definitions in other Articles apply to this Article:

"Check". Section 3–104.

"Consignee". Section 7–102.

"Consignor". Section 7–102.

"Consumer goods". Section 9–109.

"Dishonor". Section 3–507.

"Draft". Section 3–104.

(4) In addition Article 1 contains general definitions and principles of construction and interpretation applicable throughout this Article.

Section 2–104. Definitions: "Merchant"; "Between Merchants"; "Financing Agency".

(1) "Merchant" means a person who deals in goods of the kind or otherwise by his occupation holds himself out as having knowledge or skill peculiar to the practices or goods involved in the transaction or to whom such knowledge or skill may be attributed by his employment of an agent or broker or other intermediary who by his occupation holds himself out as having such knowledge or skill.

(2) "Financing agency" means a bank, finance company or other person who in the ordinary course of business makes advances against goods or documents of title or who by arrangement with either the seller or the buyer intervenes in ordinary course to make or collect payment due or claimed under the contract for sale, as by purchasing or paying the seller's draft or making advances against it or by merely taking it for collection whether or not documents of title accompany the draft. "Financing agency" includes also a bank or other person who similarly intervenes between persons who are in the position of seller and buyer in respect to the goods (Section 2–707).

(3) "Between merchants" means in any transaction with respect to which both parties are chargeable with the knowledge or skill of merchants.

Section 2–105. Definitions: Transferability; "Goods"; "Future" Goods; "Lot"; "Commercial Unit".

(1) "Goods" means all things (including specially manufactured goods) which are movable at the time of identification to the contract for sale other than the money in which the price is to be paid, investment securities (Article 8) and things in action. "Goods" also includes the unborn young of animals and growing crops and other identified things attached to realty as described in the section on goods to be severed from realty (Section 2–107).

(2) Goods must be both existing and identified before any interest in them can pass. Goods which are not both existing and identified are "future" goods. A purported present sale of future goods or of any interest therein operates as a contract to sell.

(3) There may be a sale of a part interest in existing identified goods.

(4) An undivided share in an identified bulk of fungible goods is sufficiently identified to be sold although the quantity of the bulk is not determined. Any agreed proportion of such a bulk or any quantity thereof agreed upon by number, weight or other measure may to the extent of the seller's interest in

the bulk be sold to the buyer who then becomes an owner in common.

(5) "Lot" means a parcel or a single article which is the subject matter of a separate sale or delivery, whether or not it is sufficient to perform the contract.

(6) "Commercial unit" means such a unit of goods as by commercial usage is a single whole for purposes of sale and division of which materially impairs its character or value on the market or in use. A commercial unit may be a single article (as a machine) or a set of articles (as a suite of furniture or an assortment of sizes) or a quantity (as a bale, gross, or carload) or any other unit treated in use or in the relevant market as a single whole.

Section 2—106. Definitions: "Contract"; "Agreement"; "Contract for Sale"; "Sale"; "Present Sale"; "Conforming to Contract; "Termination"; "Cancellation".

(1) In this Article unless the context otherwise requires, "contract" and "agreement" are limited to those relating to the present or future sale of goods. "Contract for sale" includes both a present sale of goods and a contract to sell goods at a future time. A "sale" consists in the passing of title from the seller to the buyer for a price (Section 2—401). A "present sale" means a sale which is accomplished by the making of the contract.

(2) Goods or conduct including any part of a performance are "conforming" or conform to the contract when they are in accordance with the obligations under the contract.

(3) "Termination" occurs when either party pursuant to a power created by agreement or law puts an end to the

contract otherwise than for its breach. On "termination" all obligations which are still executory on both sides are discharged by any right based on prior breach or performance survives.

(4) "Cancellation" occurs when either party puts an end to the contract for breach by the other and its effect is the same as that of "termination" except that the cancelling party also retains any remedy for breach of the whole contract or any unperformed balance.

Section 2—107. Goods to Be Severed from Realty: Recording.

(1) A contract for the sale of timber, minerals or the like or a structure or its materials to be removed from realty is a contract for the sale of goods within this Article if they are to be severed by the seller, but until severance a purported present sale thereof which is not effective as a transfer of an interest in land is effective only as a contract to sell.

(2) A contract for the sale apart from the land of growing crops or other things attached to realty and capable of severance without material harm thereto but not described in subsection (1) is a contract for the sale of goods within this Article whether the subject matter is to be severed by the buyer or by the seller even though it forms part of the realty at the time of contracting, and the parties can by identification effect a present sale before severance.

(3) The provisions of this section are subject to any third party rights provided by the law relating to realty records, and the contract for sale may be executed and recorded as a document transferring an interest in land and shall then constitute notice to third parties of the buyer's rights under the contract for sale.

PART 2

FORM, FORMATION AND READJUSTMENT OF CONTRACT

Section 2—201. Formal Requirements; Statute of Frauds.

(1) Except as otherwise provided in this section, a contract for the sale of goods for the price of $500 or more is

not enforceable by way of action or defense unless there is some writing sufficient to indicate that a contract for sale has been made between the parties and signed by the party against whom enforcement is sought or by his authorized agent or broker. A writing is not insufficient because it omits or incorrectly states a term agreed upon but the contract is not enforceable under this paragraph beyond the quantity of goods shown in such writing.

(2) Between merchants if within a reasonable time a writing in confirmation of the contract and sufficient against the sender is received and the party receiving it has reason to know its contents, it satisfies the requirements of subsection (1) against such party unless written notice of objection to its contents is given within ten days after it is received.

(3) A contract which does not satisfy the requirements of subsection (1) but which is valid in other respects is enforceable

> (a) if the goods are to be specially manufactured for the buyer and are not suitable for sale to others in the ordinary course of the seller's business and the seller, before notice of repudiation is received and under circumstances which reasonably indicate that the goods are for the buyer, has made either a substantial beginning of their manufacture or commitments for their procurement; or
>
> (b) if the party against whom enforcement is sought admits in his pleading, testimony or otherwise in court that a contract for sale was made, but the contract is not enforceable under this provision beyond the quantity of goods admitted; or
>
> (c) with respect to goods for which payment has been made and accepted or which have been received and accepted (Section 2—606).

Section 2—202. Final Written Expression: Parol or Extrinsic Evidence.

Terms with respect to which the confirmatory memoranda of the parties agree or which are otherwise set forth in a writing intended by the parties as a final expression of their agreement with respect to such terms as are included therein may not be contradicted by evidence of any prior agreement or of a contemporaneous oral agreement but may be explained or supplemented

> (a) by course of dealing or usage of trade (Section 1—205) or by course of performance (Section 2—208); and
>
> (b) by evidence of consistent additional terms unless the court finds the writing to have been intended also as a complete and exclusive statement of the terms of the agreement.

Section 2—203. Seals Inoperative.

The affixing of a seal to a writing evidencing a contract for sale or an offer to buy or sell goods does not constitute the writing a sealed instrument, and the law with respect to sealed instruments does not apply to such a contract or offer.

Section 2—204. Formation in General.

(1) A contract for sale of goods may be made in any manner sufficient to show agreement, including conduct by both parties which recognizes the existence of such a contract.

(2) An agreement sufficient to constitute a contract for sale may be found even though the moment of its making is undetermined.

(3) Even though one or more terms are left open, a contract for sale does not fail for indefiniteness if the parties have intended to make a contract and there is a reasonably certain basis for giving an appropriate remedy.

Section 2—205. Firm Offers.

An offer by a merchant to buy or sell goods in a signed writing which by its terms gives assurance that it will be held open is not revocable, for lack of consideration, during the time stated or if no time is stated for a reasonable time, but in no event may such period of irrevocability exceed three months;

but any such term of assurance on a form supplied by the offeree must be separately signed by the offeror.

Section 2—206. Offer and Acceptance in Formation of Contract.

(1) Unless otherwise unambiguously indicated by the language or circumstances

(a) an offer to make a contract shall be construed as inviting acceptance in any manner and by any medium reasonable in the circumstances;

(b) an order or other offer to buy goods for prompt or current shipment shall be construed as inviting acceptance either by a prompt promise to ship or by the prompt or current shipment of conforming or non-conforming goods, but such a shipment of non-conforming goods does not constitute an acceptance if the seller seasonably notifies the buyer that the shipment is offered only as an accommodation to the buyer.

(2) Where the beginning of a requested performance is a reasonable mode of acceptance, an offeror who is not notified of acceptance within a reasonable time may treat the offer as having lapsed before acceptance.

Section 2—207. Additional Terms in Acceptance or Confirmation.

(1) A definite and seasonable expression of acceptance or a written confirmation which is sent within a reasonable time operates as an acceptance even though it states terms additional to or different from those offered or agreed upon, unless acceptance is expressly made conditional on assent to the additional or different terms.

(2) The additional terms are to be construed as proposals for addition to the contract. Between merchants such terms become part of the contract unless:

(a) the offer expressly limits acceptance to the terms of the offer;

(b) they materially alter it; or

(c) notification of objection to them has already been given or is given within a reasonable time after notice of them is received.

(3) Conduct by both parties which recognizes the existence of a contract is sufficient to establish a contract for sale although the writings of the parties do not otherwise establish a contract. In such case the terms of the particular contract consist of those terms on which the writings of the parties agree, together with any supplementary terms incorporated under any other provisions of this Act.

Section 2—208. Course of Performance or Practical Construction.

(1) Where the contract for sale involves repeated occasions for performance by either party with knowledge of the nature of the performance and opportunity for objection to it by the other, any course of performance accepted or acquiesced in without objection shall be relevant to determine the meaning of the agreement.

(2) The express terms of the agreement and any such course of performance, as well as any course of dealing and usage of trade, shall be construed whenever reasonable as consistent with each other; but when such construction is unreasonable, express terms shall control course of performance and course of performance shall control both course of dealing and usage of trade (Section 1—205).

(3) Subject to the provisions of the next section on modification and waiver, such course of performance shall be relevant to show a waiver or modification of any term inconsistent with such course of performance.

Section 2—209. Modification, Rescission and Waiver.

(1) An agreement modifying a contract within this Article needs no consideration to be binding.

(2) A signed agreement which excludes modification or rescission except by a signed writing cannot be otherwise modified or rescinded, but except as between merchants such a requirement

on a form supplied by the merchant must be separately signed by the other party.

(3) The requirements of the statute of frauds section of this Article (Section 2–201) must be satisfied if the contract as modified is within its provisions.

(4) Although an attempt at modification or rescission does not satisfy the requirements of subsection (2) or (3) it can operate as a waiver.

(5) A party who has made a waiver affecting an executory portion of the contract may retract the waiver by reasonable notification received by the other party that strict performance will be required of any term waived, unless the retraction would be unjust in view of a material change of position in reliance on the waiver.

Section 2—210. Delegation of Performance; Assignment of Rights.

(1) A party may perform his duty through a delegate unless otherwise agreed or unless the other party has a substantial interest in having his original promisor perform or control the acts required by the contract. No delegation of performance relieves the party delegating of any duty to perform or any liability for breach.

(2) Unless otherwise agreed all rights of either seller or buyer can be assigned except where the assignment would materially change the duty of the other party, or increase materially the burden or risk imposed on him by his contract, or impair materially his chance of obtaining return performance. A right to damages for breach of the whole contract or a right arising out of the assignor's due performance of his entire obligation can be assigned despite agreement otherwise.

(3) Unless the circumstances indicate the contrary, a prohibition of assignment of "the contract" is to be construed as barring only the delegation to the assignee of the assignor's performance.

(4) An assignment of "the contract" or of "all my rights under the contract" or an assignment in similar general terms is an assignment of rights and unless the language or the circumstances (as in an assignment for security) indicate the contrary, it is a delegation of performance of the duties of the assignor and its acceptance by the assignee constitutes a promise by him to perform those duties. This promise is enforceable by either the assignor or the other party to the original contract.

(5) The other party may treat any assignment which delegates performance as creating reasonable grounds for insecurity and may without prejudice to his rights against the assignor demand assurances from the assignee (Section 2–609).

PART 3

GENERAL OBLIGATION AND CONSTRUCTION OF CONTRACT

Section 2—301. General Obligations of Parties.

The obligation of the seller is to transfer and deliver and that of the buyer is to accept and pay in accordance with the contract.

Section 2—302. Unconscionable Contract or Clause.

(1) If the court as a matter of law finds the contract or any clause of the contract to have been unconscionable at the time it was made, the court may refuse to enforce the contract, or it may enforce the remainder of the contract without the unconscionable clause, or it may so limit the application of any unconscionable clause as to avoid any unconscionable result.

(2) When it is claimed or appears to the court that the contract or any clause thereof may be unconscionable, the parties shall be afforded a reasonable opportunity to present evidence as to its commercial setting, purpose and effect to aid the court in making the determination.

Section 2—303. Allocation or Division of Risks.

Where this Article allocates a risk or a burden as between the parties "unless otherwise agreed", the agreement may not only shift the allocation but may also divide the risk or burden.

Section 2—304. Price Payable in Money, Goods, Realty, or Otherwise.

(1) The price can be made payable in money or otherwise. If it is payable in whole or in part in goods, each party is a seller of the goods which he is to transfer.

(2) Even though all or part of the price is payable in an interest in realty, the transfer of the goods and the seller's obligations with reference to them are subject to this Article, but not the transfer of the interest in realty or the transferor's obligations in connection therewith.

Section 2—305. Open Price Term.

(1) The parties if they so intend can conclude a contract for sale even though the price is not settled. In such a case the price is a reasonable price at the time for delivery if

   (a) nothing is said as to price; or
   (b) the price is left to be agreed by the parties and they fail to agree; or
   (c) the price is to be fixed in terms of some agreed market or other standard as set or recorded by a third person or agency and it is not so set or recorded.

(2) A price to be fixed by the seller or by the buyer means a price for him to fix in good faith.

(3) When a price left to be fixed otherwise than by agreement of the parties fails to be fixed through fault of one party, the other may at his option treat the contract as cancelled or himself fix a reasonable price.

(4) Where, however, the parties intend not to be bound unless the price be fixed or agreed and it is not fixed or agreed, there is no contract. In such a case the buyer must return any goods already received or if unable so to do

must pay their reasonable value at the time of delivery and the seller must return any portion of the price paid on account.

Section 2—306. Output, Requirements and Exclusive Dealings.

(1) A term which measures the quantity by the output of the seller or the requirements of the buyer means such actual output or requirements as may occur in good faith, except that no quantity unreasonably disproportionate to any stated estimate or in the absence of a stated estimate to any normal or otherwise comparable prior output or requirements may be tendered or demanded.

(2) A lawful agreement by either the seller or the buyer for exclusive dealing in the kind of goods concerned imposes unless otherwise agreed an obligation by the seller to use best efforts to supply the goods and by the buyer to use best efforts to promote their sale.

Section 2—307. Delivery in Single Lot or Several Lots.

Unless otherwise agreed all goods called for by a contract for sale must be tendered in a single delivery and payment is due only on such tender, but where the circumstances give either party the right to make or demand delivery in lots the price if it can be apportioned may be demanded for each lot.

Section 2—308. Absence of Specified Place for Delivery.

Unless otherwise agreed

   (a) the place for delivery of goods is the seller's place of business or if he has none his residence; but
   (b) in a contract for sale of identified goods which to the knowledge of the parties at the time of contracting are in some other place, that place is the place for their delivery; and
   (c) documents of title may be delivered through customary banking channels.

Section 2—309. Absence of Specific Time Provisions; Notice of Termination.

(1) The time for shipment or delivery or any other action under a contract if not provided in this Article or agreed upon shall be a reasonable time.

(2) Where the contract provides for successive performances but is indefinite in duration it is valid for a reasonable time but unless otherwise agreed may be terminated at any time by either party.

(3) Termination of a contract by one party except on the happening of an agreed event requires that reasonable notification be received by the other party and an agreement dispensing with notification is invalid if its operation would be unconscionable.

Section 2—310. Open Time for Payment or Running of Credit; Authority to Ship Under Reservation.

Unless otherwise agreed

  (a) payment is due at the time and place at which the buyer is to receive the goods even though the place of shipment is the place of delivery; and

  (b) if the seller is authorized to send the goods he may ship them under reservation, and may tender the documents of title, but the buyer may inspect the goods after their arrival before payment is due unless such inspection is inconsistent with the terms of the contract (Section 2–513); and

  (c) if delivery is authorized and made by way of documents of title otherwise than by subsection (b) then payment is due at the time and place at which the buyer is to receive the documents regardless of where the goods are to be received; and

  (d) where the seller is required or authorized to ship the goods on credit the credit period runs from the time of shipment but post-dating the invoice or de-laying its dispatch will correspondingly delay the starting of the credit period.

Section 2—311. Options and Cooperation Respecting Performance.

(1) An agreement for sale which is otherwise sufficiently definite (subsection (3) of Section 2–204) to be a contract is not made invalid by the fact that it leaves particulars of performance to be specified by one of the parties. Any such specification must be made in good faith and within limits set by commercial reasonableness.

(2) Unless otherwise agreed specifications relating to assortment of the goods are at the buyer's option and except as otherwise provided in subsections (1) (c) and (3) of Section 2–319 specifications or arrangements relating to shipment are at the seller's option.

(3) Where such specification would materially affect the other party's performance but is not seasonably made or where one party's cooperation is necessary to the agreed performance of the other but is not seasonably forthcoming, the other party in addition to all other remedies

  (a) is excused for any resulting delay in his own performance; and

  (b) may also either proceed to perform in any reasonable manner or after the time for a material part of his own performance treat the failure to specify or to cooperate as a breach by failure to deliver or accept the goods.

Section 2—312. Warranty of Title and Against Infringement; Buyer's Obligation Against Infringement.

(1) Subject to subsection (2) there is in a contract for sale a warranty by the seller that

  (a) the title conveyed shall be good, and its transfer rightful; and

  (b) the goods shall be delivered free from any security interest or other lien or encumbrance of which the buyer at the time of contracting has no knowledge.

(2) A warranty under subsection (1) will be excluded or modified only by specific language or by circumstances which give the buyer reason to know that the person selling does not claim title in himself or that he is purporting to sell only such right or title as he or a third person may have.

(3) Unless otherwise agreed a seller who is a merchant regularly dealing in goods of the kind warrants that the goods shall be delivered free of the rightful claim of any third person by way of infringement or the like, but a buyer who furnishes specifications to the seller must hold the seller harmless against any such claim which arises out of compliance with the specifications.

Section 2—313. Express Warranties by Affirmation, Promise, Description, Sample.

(1) Express warranties by the seller are created as follows:

(a) Any affirmation of fact or promise made by the seller to the buyer which relates to the goods and becomes part of the basis of the bargain creates an express warranty that the goods shall conform to the affirmation or promise.

(b) Any description of the goods which is made part of the basis of the bargain creates an express warranty that the goods shall conform to the description.

(c) Any sample or model which is made part of the basis of the bargain creates an express warranty that the whole of the goods shall conform to the sample or model.

(2) It is not necessary to the creation of an express warranty that the seller use formal words such as "warrant" or "guarantee" or that he have a specific intention to make a warranty, but an affirmation merely of the value of the goods or a statement purporting to be merely the seller's opinion or commendation of the goods does not create a warranty.

Section 2—314. Implied Warranty: Merchantability; Usage of Trade.

(1) Unless excluded or modified (Section 2—316), a warranty that the goods shall be merchantable is implied in a contract for their sale if the seller is a merchant with respect to goods of that kind. Under this section the serving for value of food or drink to be consumed either on the premises or elsewhere is a sale.

(2) Goods to be merchantable must be at least such as

(a) pass without objection in the trade under the contract description; and

(b) in the case of fungible goods, are of fair average quality within the description; and

(c) are fit for the ordinary purposes for which such goods are used; and

(d) run, within the variations permitted by the agreement, of even kind, quality and quantity within each unit and among all units involved; and

(e) are adequately contained, packaged, and labeled as the agreement may require; and

(f) conform to the promises or affirmations of fact made on the container or label if any.

(3) Unless excluded or modified (Section 2—316) other implied warranties may arise from course of dealing or usage of trade.

Section 2—315. Implied Warranty: Fitness for Particular Purpose.

Where the seller at the time of contracting has reason to know any particular purpose for which the goods are required and that the buyer is relying on the seller's skill or judgment to select or furnish suitable goods, there is unless excluded or modified under the next section an implied warranty that the goods shall be fit for such purpose.

Section 2—316. Exclusion or Modification of Warranties.

(1) Words or conduct relevant to the creation of an express warranty and words or conduct tending to negate or limit warranty shall be construed wherever reasonable as consistent with each other; but subject to the provisions of this Article on parol or extrinsic evidence (Section 2–202) negation or limitation is inoperative to the extent that such construction is unreasonable.

(2) Subject to subsection (3), to exclude or modify the implied warranty of merchantability or any part of it the language must mention merchantability and in case of a writing must be conspicuous, and to exclude or modify any implied warranty of fitness the exclusion must be by a writing and conspicuous. Language to exclude all implied warranties of fitness is sufficient if it states, for example, that "There are no warranties which extend beyond the description of the face hereof."

(3) Notwithstanding subsection (2)

    (a) unless the circumstances indicate otherwise, all implied warranties are excluded by expressions like "as is", "with all faults" or other language which in common understanding calls the buyer's attention to the exclusion of warranties and makes plain that there is no implied warranty; and

    (b) when the buyer before entering into the contract has examined the goods or the sample or model as fully as he desired or has refused to examine the goods, there is no implied warranty with regard to defects which an examination ought in the circumstances to have revealed to him; and

    (c) an implied warranty can also be excluded or modified by course of dealing or course of performance or usage of trade.

(4) Remedies for breach of warranty can be limited in accordance with the provisions of this Article on liquidation or limitation of damages and on contractual modification of remedy (Sections 2–718 and 2–719).

Section 2—317. Cumulation and Conflict of Warranties Express or Implied.

Warranties whether express or implied shall be construed as consistent with each other and as cumulative, but if such construction is unreasonable the intention of the parties shall determine which warranty is dominant. In ascertaining that intention the following rules apply:

    (a) Exact or technical specifications displace an inconsistent sample or model or general language of description.

    (b) A sample from an existing bulk displaces inconsistent general language of description.

    (c) Express warranties displace inconsistent implied warranties other than an implied warranty of fitness for a particular purpose.

Section 2—318. Third Party Beneficiaries of Warranties Express or Implied.

A seller's warranty whether express or implied extends to any natural person who is in the family or household of his buyer or who is a guest in his home if it is reasonable to expect that such person may use, consume or be affected by the goods and who is injured in person by breach of the warranty. A seller may not exclude or limit the operation of this section.

Section 2—319. F.O.B. and F.A.S. Terms.

(1) Unless otherwise agreed the term F.O.B. (which means "free on board") at a named place, even though used only in connection with the stated price, is a delivery term under which

    (a) when the term is F.O.B. the place of shipment, the seller must at that place ship the goods in the manner provided in this Article (Section 2–504) and bear the expense and risk of putting them into the possession of the carrier; or

(b) when the term is F.O.B. the place of destination, the seller must at his own expense and risk transport the goods to that place and there tender delivery of them in the manner provided in this Article (Section 2–503);

(c) when under either (a) or (b) the term is also F.O.B. vessel, car or other vehicle, the seller must in addition at his own expense and risk load the goods on board. If the term is F.O.B. vessel, the buyer must name the vessel and in an appropriate case the seller must comply with the provisions of this Article on the form of bill of lading (Section 2–323).

(2) Unless otherwise agreed the term F.A.S. vessel (which means "free alongside") at a named port, even though used only in connection with the stated price, is a delivery term under which the seller must

(a) at his own expense and risk deliver the goods alongside the vessel in the manner usual in that port or on a dock designated and provided by the buyer; and

(b) obtain and tender a receipt for the goods in exchange for which the carrier is under a duty to issue a bill of lading.

(3) Unless otherwise agreed in any case falling within subsection (1) (a) or (c) or subsection (2) the buyer must seasonably give any needed instructions for making delivery, including when the term is F.A.S. or F.O.B. the loading berth of the vessel and in an appropriate case its name and sailing date. The seller may treat the failure of needed instructions as a failure of cooperation under this Article (Section 2–311). He may also at his option move the goods in any reasonable manner preparatory to delivery or shipment.

(4) Under the term F.O.B. vessel or F.A.S. unless otherwise agreed the buyer must make payment against tender of the required documents and the seller may not tender nor the buyer demand delivery of the goods in substitution for the documents.

Section 2—320. C.I.F. and C. & F. Terms.

(1) The term C.I.F. means that the price includes in a lump sum the cost of the goods and the insurance and freight to the named destination. The term C. & F. or C.F. means that the price so includes cost and freight to the named destination.

(2) Unless otherwise agreed and even though used only in connection with the stated price and destination, the term C.I.F. destination or its equivalent requires the seller at his own expense and risk to

(a) put the goods into the possession of a carrier at the port for shipment and obtain a negotiable bill or bills of lading covering the entire transportation to the named destination; and

(b) load the goods and obtain a receipt from the carrier (which may be contained in the bill of lading) showing that the freight has been paid or provided for; and

(c) obtain a policy or certificate of insurance, including any war risk insurance, of a kind and on terms then current at the port of shipment in the usual amount, in the currency of the contract, shown to cover the same goods covered by the bill of lading and providing for payment of loss to the order of the buyer or for the account of whom it may concern; but the seller may add to the price the amount of the premium for any such war risk insurance; and

(d) prepare an invoice of the goods and procure any other documents required to effect shipment or to comply with the contract; and

(e) forward and tender with commercial promptness all the documents in due form and with any indorsement necessary to perfect the buyer's rights.

(3) Unless otherwise agreed the term C. & F. or its equivalent has the same effect and imposes upon the seller the same obligations and risks as a C.I.F. term except the obligation as to insurance.

(4) Under the term C.I.F. or C. & F. unless otherwise agreed the buyer must make payment against tender of the required documents and the seller may not tender nor the buyer demand delivery of the goods in substitution for the documents.

Section 2—321. C.I.F. or C. & F.: "Net Landed Weights"; "Payment on Arrival"; Warranty of Condition on Arrival.

Under a contract containing a term C.I.F. or C. & F.

(1) Where the price is based on or is to be adjusted according to "net landed weights", "delivered weights", "out turn" quantity or quality or the like, unless otherwise agreed the seller must reasonably estimate the price. The payment due on tender of the documents called for by the contract is the amount so estimated, but after final adjustment of the price a settlement must be made with commercial promptness.

(2) An agreement described in subsection (1) or any warranty of quality or condition of the goods on arrival places upon the seller the risk of ordinary deterioration, shrinkage and the like in transportation but has no effect on the place or time of identification to the contract for sale or delivery or on the passing of the risk of loss.

(3) Unless otherwise agreed, where the contract provides for payment on or after arrival of the goods, the seller must before payment allow such preliminary inspection as is feasible; but if the goods are lost, delivery of the documents and payment are due when the goods should have arrived.

Section 2—322. Delivery "Ex-Ship".

(1) Unless otherwise agreed a term for delivery of goods "ex-ship" (which

means from the carrying vessel) or in equivalent language is not restricted to a particular ship and requires delivery from a ship which has reached a place at the named port of destination where goods of the kind are usually discharged.

(2) Under such a term unless otherwise agreed

    (a) the seller must discharge all liens arising out of the carriage and furnish the buyer with a direction which puts the carrier under a duty to deliver the goods; and

    (b) the risk of loss does not pass to the buyer until the goods leave the ship's tackle or are otherwise properly unloaded.

Section 2—323. Form of Bill of Lading Required in Overseas Shipment; "Overseas".

(1) Where the contract contemplates overseas shipment and contains a term C.I.F. or C. & F. or F.O.B. vessel, the seller unless otherwise agreed must obtain a negotiable bill of lading stating that the goods have been loaded on board or, in the case of a term C.I.F. or C. & F., received for shipment.

(2) Where in a case within subsection (1) a bill of lading has been issued in a set of parts, unless otherwise agreed if the documents are not to be sent from abroad the buyer may demand tender of the full set; otherwise only one part of the bill of lading need be tendered. Even if the agreement expressly requires a full set

    (a) due tender of a single part is acceptable within the provisions of this Article on cure of improper delivery (subsection (1) of Section 2—508); and

    (b) even though the full set is demanded, if the documents are sent from abroad the person tendering an incomplete set may nevertheless require payment upon furnishing an indemnity which the buyer in good faith deems adequate.

(3) A shipment by water or by air or a contract contemplating such shipment is "overseas" insofar as by usage of

trade or agreement it is subject to the commercial, financing or shipping practices characteristic of international deep water commerce.

Section 2—324. "No Arrival, No Sale" Term.

Under a term "no arrival, no sale" or terms of like meaning, unless otherwise agreed,

    (a) the seller must properly ship conforming goods and if they arrive by any means he must tender them on arrival, but he assumes no obligation that the goods will arrive unless he has caused the non-arrival; and

    (b) where without fault of the seller the goods are in part lost or have so deteriorated as no longer to conform to the contract or arrive after the contract time, the buyer may proceed as if there had been casualty to identified goods (Section 2—613).

Section 2—325. "Letter of Credit" Term; "Confirmed Credit".

(1) Failure of the buyer seasonably to furnish an agreed letter of credit is a breach of the contract for sale.

(2) The delivery to seller of a proper letter of credit suspends the buyer's obligation to pay. If the letter of credit is dishonored, the seller may on seasonable notification to the buyer require payment directly from him.

(3) Unless otherwise agreed the term "letter of credit" or "banker's credit" in a contract for sale means an irrevocable credit issued by a financing agency of good repute and, where the shipment is overseas, of good international repute. The term "confirmed credit" means that the credit must also carry the direct obligation of such an agency which does business in the seller's financial market.

Section 2—326. Sale on Approval and Sale or Return; Consignment Sales and Rights of Creditors.

(1) Unless otherwise agreed, if delivered goods may be returned by the buyer even though they conform to the contract, the transaction is

    (a) a "sale on approval" if the goods are delivered primarily for use, and

    (b) a "sale or return" if the goods are delivered primarily for resale.

(2) Except as provided in subsection (3), goods held on approval are not subject to the claims of the buyer's creditors until acceptance; goods held on sale or return are subject to such claims while in the buyer's possession.

(3) Where goods are delivered to a person for sale and such person maintains a place of business at which he deals in goods of the kind involved, under a name other than the name of the person making delivery, then with respect to claims of creditors of the person conducting the business the goods are deemed to be on sale or return. The provisions of this subsection are applicable even though an agreement purports to reserve title to the person making delivery until payment or resale or uses such words as "on consignment" or "on memorandum". However, this subsection is not applicable if the person making delivery

    (a) complies with an applicable law providing for a consignor's interest or the like to be evidenced by a sign, or

    (b) establishes that the person conducting the business is generally known by his creditors to be substantially engaged in selling the goods of others, or

    (c) complies with the filing provisions of the Article on Secured Transactions (Aritcle 9).

(4) Any "or return" term of a contract for sale is to be treated as a separate contract for sale within the statute of frauds section of this Article (Section 2–201) and as contradicting the sale aspect of the contract within the provisions of this Article on parol or extrinsic evidence (Section 2–202).

Section 2—327. Special Incidents of Sale on Approval and Sale or Return.

(1) Under a sale on approval unless otherwise agreed

(a) although the goods are identified to the contract, the risk of loss and the title do not pass to the buyer until acceptance; and

(b) use of the goods consistent with the purpose of trial is not acceptance but failure seasonably to notify the seller of election to return the goods is acceptance, and if the goods conform to the contract acceptance of any part is acceptance of the whole; and

(c) after due notification of election to return, the return is at the seller's risk and expense but a merchant buyer must follow any reasonable instructions.

(2) Under a sale or return unless otherwise agreed

(a) the option to return extends to the whole or any commercial unit of the goods while in substantially their original condition, but must be exercised seasonably; and

(b) the return is at the buyer's risk and expense.

Section 2—328. Sale by Auction.

(1) In a sale by auction if goods are put up in lots each lot is the subject of a separate sale.

(2) A sale by auction is complete when the auctioneer so announces by the fall of the hammer or in other customary manner. Where a bid is made while the hammer is falling in acceptance of a prior bid, the auctioneer may in his discretion reopen the bidding or declare the goods sold under the bid on which the hammer was falling.

(3) Such a sale is with reserve unless the goods are in explicit terms put up without reserve. In an auction with reserve the auctioneer may withdraw the goods at any time until he announces completion of the sale. In an auction without reserve, after the auctioneer calls for bids on an article or lot, that article or lot cannot be withdrawn unless no bid is made within a reasonable time. In either case a bidder may retract his bid until the auctioneer's announcement of completion of the sale, but a bidder's retraction does not revive any previous bid.

(4) If the auctioneer knowingly receives a bid on the seller's behalf or the seller makes or procures such a bid, and notice has not been given that liberty for such bidding is reserved, the buyer may at his option avoid the sale or take the goods at the price of the last good faith bid prior to the completion of the sale. This subsection shall not apply to any bid at a forced sale.

PART 4

TITLE, CREDITORS AND GOOD FAITH PURCHASERS

Section 2—401. Passing of Title; Reservation for Security; Limited Application of This Section.

Each provision of this Article with regard to the rights, obligations and remedies of the seller, the buyer, purchasers or other third parties applies irrespective of title to the goods except where the provision refers to such title. Insofar as situations are not covered by the other provisions of this Article and matters concerning title become material the following rules apply:

(1) Title to goods cannot pass under a contract for sale prior to their identification to the contract (Section 2–501), and unless otherwise explicitly agreed the buyer acquires by their identification a special property as limited by this Act. Any retention or reservation by the seller of the title (property) in goods shipped or delivered to the buyer is limited in effect to a reservation of a security interest. Subject to these provisions and to the provisions of the Article on Secured Transactions (Article 9), title to goods passes from the seller

to the buyer in any manner and on any conditions explicitly agreed on by the parties.

(2) Unless otherwise explicitly agreed, title passes to the buyer at the time and place at which the seller completes his performance with reference to the physical delivery of the goods, despite any reservation of a security interest and even though a document of title is to be delivered at a different time or place; and in particular and despite any reservation of a security interest by the bill of lading

    (a) if the contract requires or authorizes the seller to send the goods to the buyer but does not require him to deliver them at destination, title passes to the buyer at the time and place of shipment; but

    (b) if the contract requires delivery at destination, title passes on tender there.

(3) Unless otherwise explicitly agreed where delivery is to be made without moving the goods,

    (a) if the seller is to deliver a document of title, title passes at the time when and the place where he delivers such documents; or

    (b) if the goods are at the time of contracting already identified and no documents are to be delivered, title passes at the time and place of contracting.

(4) A rejection or other refusal by the buyer to receive or retain the goods, whether or not justified, or a justified revocation of acceptance revests title to the goods in the seller. Such revesting occurs by operation of law and is not a "sale".

Section 2—402. Rights of Seller's Creditors Against Sold Goods.

(1) Except as provided in subsections (2) and (3), rights of unsecured creditors of the seller with respect to goods which have been identified to a contract for sale are subject to the buyer's rights to recover the goods under this Article (Sections 2—502 and 2—716).

(2) A creditor of the seller may treat a sale or an identification of goods to a

contract for sale as void if as against him a retention of possession by the seller is fraudulent under any rule of law of the state where the goods are situated, except that retention of possession in good faith and current course of trade by a merchant-seller for a commercially reasonable time after a sale or identification is not fraudulent.

(3) Nothing in this Article shall be deemed to impair the rights of creditors of the seller

    (a) under the provisions of the Article on Secured Transactions (Article 9); or

    (b) where identification to the contract or delivery is made not in current course of trade but in satisfaction of or as security for a pre-existing claim for money, security or the like and is made under circumstances which under any rule of law of the state where the goods are situated would apart from this Article constitute the transaction a fraudulent transfer or voidable preference.

Section 2—403. Power to Transfer; Good Faith Purchase of Goods; "Entrusting".

(1) A purchaser of goods acquires all title which his transferor had or had power to transfer except that a purchaser of a limited interest acquires rights only to the extent of the interest purchased. A person with voidable title has power to transfer a good title to a good faith purchaser for value. When goods have been delivered under a transaction of purchase, the purchaser has such power even though

    (a) the transferor was deceived as to the identity of the purchaser, or

    (b) the delivery was in exchange for a check which is later dishonored, or

    (c) it was agreed that the transaction was to be a "cash sale", or

    (d) the delivery was procured through fraud punishable as larcenous under the criminal law.

(2) Any entrusting of possession of goods to a merchant who deals in goods of that kind gives him power to transfer all rights of the entruster to a buyer in ordinary course of business.

(3) "Entrusting" includes any delivery and any acquiescence in retention of possession regardless of any condition expressed between the parties to the delivery or acquiescence and regardless of whether the procurement of the entrusting or the possessor's disposition of the goods have been such as to be larcenous under the criminal law.

(4) The rights of other purchasers of goods and of lien creditors are governed by the Articles on Secured Transactions (Article 9), Bulk Transfers (Article 6) and Documents of Title (Article 7).

PART 5

PERFORMANCE

Section 2—501. Insurable Interest in Goods; Manner of Identification of Goods.

(1) The buyer obtains a special property and an insurable interest in goods by identification of existing goods as goods to which the contract refers even though the goods so identified are non-conforming and he has an option to return or reject them. Such identification can be made at any time and in any manner explicitly agreed to by the parties. In the absence of explicit agreement identification occurs

    (a) when the contract is made if it is for the sale of goods already existing and identified;

    (b) if the contract is for the sale of future goods other than those described in paragraph (c), when goods are shipped, marked or otherwise designated by the seller as goods to which the contract refers;

    (c) when the crops are planted or otherwise become growing crops or the young are conceived if the contract is for the sale of unborn young to be born within twelve months after contracting or for the sale of crops to be harvested within twelve months or the next normal harvest season after contracting whichever is longer.

(2) The seller retains an insurable interest in goods so long as title to or any security interest in the goods remains in him, and where the identification is by the seller alone he may, until default or insolvency or notification to the buyer that the identification is final, substitute other goods for those identified.

(3) Nothing in this section impairs any insurable interest recognized under any other statute or rule of law.

Section 2—502. Buyer's Right to Goods on Seller's Insolvency.

(1) Subject to subsection (2) and even though the goods have not been shipped, a buyer who has paid a part or all of the price of goods in which he has a special property under the provisions of the immediately preceding section may on making and keeping good a tender of any unpaid portion of their price recover them from the seller if the seller becomes insolvent within ten days after receipt of the first installment on their price.

(2) If the identification creating his special property has been made by the buyer, he acquires the right to recover the goods only if they conform to the contract for sale.

Section 2—503. Manner of Seller's Tender of Delivery.

(1) Tender of delivery requires that the seller put and hold conforming goods at the buyer's disposition and give the buyer any notification reasonably necessary to enable him to take delivery. The manner, time and place for tender are determined by the agreement and this Article, and in particular

    (a) tender must be at a reasonable hour, and if it is of goods they must be kept available for the period reasonably necessary to enable the buyer to take posses-sion; but

(b) unless otherwise agreed the buyer must furnish facilities rea-sonably suited to the receipt of the goods.

(2) Where the case is within the next section respecting shipment, tender re-quires that the seller comply with its provisions.

(3) Where the seller is required to deliver at a particular destination, tender requires that he comply with subsection (1) and also in any appropriate case tender documents as described in sub-sections (4) and (5) of this section.

(4) Where goods are in the possession of a bailee and are to be delivered with-out being moved

(a) tender requires that the seller either tender a negotiable docu-ment of title covering such goods or procure acknowledgment by the bailee of the buyer's right to possession of the goods; but

(b) tender to the buyer of a non-negotiable document of title or of a written direction to the bailee to deliver is sufficient tender unless the buyer season-ably objects, and receipt by the bailee of notification of the buyer's rights fixes those rights as against the bailee and all third persons; but risk of loss of the goods and of any failure by the bailee to honor the non-negotiable document of title or to obey the direction remains on the seller until the buyer has had a reasonable time to present the document or direction, and a refusal by the bailee to honor the document or to obey the direction defeats the tender.

(5) Where the contract requires the seller to deliver documents

(a) he must tender all such docu-ments in correct form, except as provided in this Article with respect to bills of lading in a set (subsection (2) of Section 2—323); and

(b) tender through customary bank-ing channels is sufficient and dishonor of a draft accompany-ing the documents constitutes non-acceptance or rejection.

Section 2—504. Shipment by Seller.

Where the seller is required or autho-rized to send the goods to the buyer and the contract does not require him to deliver them at a particular destina-tion, then unless otherwise agreed he must

(a) put the goods in the possession of such a carrier and make such a contract for their transporta-tion as may be reasonable hav-ing regard to the nature of the goods and other circumstances of the case; and

(b) obtain and promptly deliver or tender in due form any docu-ment necessary to enable the buyer to obtain possession of the goods or otherwise required by the agreement or by usage of trade; and

(c) promptly notify the buyer of the shipment.

Failure to notify the buyer under para-graph (c) or to make a proper contract under paragraph (a) is a ground for re-jection only if material delay or loss ensues.

Section 2—505. Seller's Shipment Un-der Reservation.

(1) Where the seller has identified goods to the contract by or before ship-ment:

(a) his procurement of a negotiable bill of lading to his own order or otherwise reserves in him a security interest in the goods. His procurement of the bill to the order of a financing agency or of the buyer indicates in addi-tion only the seller's expectation of transferring that interest to the person named.

(b) a non-negotiable bill of lading to himself or his nominee re-serves possession of the goods as security but except in a case of conditional delivery (subsection (2) of Section 2–507) a non-negotiable bill of lading naming the buyer as consignee reserves no security interest even though the seller retains possession of the bill of lading.

(2) When shipment by the seller with reservation of a security interest is in violation of the contract for sale, it constitutes an improper contract for transportation within the preceding section but impairs neither the rights given to the buyer by shipment and identification of the goods to the contract nor the seller's powers as a holder of a negotiable document.

Section 2—506. Rights of Financing Agency.

(1) A financing agency by paying or purchasing for value a draft which relates to a shipment of goods acquires to the extent of the payment or purchase and in addition to its own rights under the draft and any document of title securing it any rights of the shipper in the goods including the right to stop delivery and the shipper's right to have the draft honored by the buyer.

(2) The right to reimbursement of a financing agency which has in good faith honored or purchased the draft under commitment to or authority from the buyer is not impaired by subsequent discovery of defects with reference to any relevant document which was apparently regular on its face.

Section 2—507. Effect of Seller's Tender; Delivery on Condition.

(1) Tender of delivery is a condition to the buyer's duty to accept the goods and, unless otherwise agreed, to his duty to pay for them. Tender entitles the seller to acceptance of the goods and to payment according to the contract.

(2) Where payment is due and demanded on the delivery to the buyer of goods or documents of title, his right as against the seller to retain or dispose of them is conditional upon his making the payment due.

Section 2—508. Cure by Seller of Improper Tender or Delivery; Replacement.

(1) Where any tender or delivery by the seller is rejected because non-conforming and the time for performance has not yet expired, the seller may seasonably notify the buyer of his intention to cure and may then within the contract time make a conforming delivery.

(2) Where the buyer rejects a non-conforming tender which the seller had reasonable grounds to believe would be acceptable with or without money allowance, the seller may if he seasonably notifies the buyer have a further reasonable time to substitute a conforming tender.

Section 2—509. Risk of Loss in the Absence of Breach.

(1) Where the contract requires or authorizes the seller to ship the goods by carrier

    (a) if it does not require him to deliver them at a particular destination, the risk of loss passes to the buyer when the goods are duly delivered to the carrier even though the shipment is under reservation (Section 2–505); but

    (b) if it does require him to deliver them at a particular destination and the goods are there duly tendered while in the possession of the carrier, the risk of loss passes to the buyer when the goods are there duly so tendered as to enable the buyer to take delivery.

(2) Where the goods are held by a bailee to be delivered without being moved, the risk of loss passes to the buyer

    (a) on his receipt of a negotiable document of title covering the goods; or

    (b) on acknowledgment by the bailee of the buyer's right to possession of the goods; or

(c) after his receipt of a non-negotiable document of title or other written direction to deliver, as provided in subsection (4) (b) of Section 2—503.

(3) In any case not within subsection (1) or (2), the risk of loss passes to the buyer on his receipt of the goods if the seller is a merchant; otherwise the risk passes to the buyer on tender of delivery.

(4) The provisions of this section are subject to contrary agreement of the parties and to the provisions of this Article on sale on approval (Section 2—327) and on effect of breach on risk of loss (Section 2—510).

Section 2—510. Effect of Breach on Risk of Loss.

(1) Where a tender or delivery of goods so fails to conform to the contract as to give a right of rejection, the risk of their loss remains on the seller until cure or acceptance.

(2) Where the buyer rightfully revokes acceptance, he may to the extent of any deficiency in his effective insurance coverage treat the risk of loss as having rested on the seller from the beginning.

(3) Where the buyer as to conforming goods already identified to the contract for sale repudiates or is otherwise in breach before risk of their loss has passed to him, the seller may to the extent of any deficiency in his effective insurance coverage treat the risk of loss as resting on the buyer for a commercially reasonable time.

Section 2—511. Tender of Payment by Buyer; Payment by Check.

(1) Unless otherwise agreed tender of payment is a condition to the seller's duty to tender and complete any delivery.

(2) Tender of payment is sufficient when made by any means or in any manner current in the ordinary course of business unless the seller demands payment in legal tender and gives any extension of time reasonably necessary to procure it.

(3) Subject to the provisions of this Act on the effect of an instrument on an obligation (Section 3—802), payment by check is conditional and is defeated as between the parties by dishonor of the check on due presentment.

Section 2—512. Payment by Buyer Before Inspection.

(1) Where the contract requires payment before inspection, non-conformity of the goods does not excuse the buyer from so making payment unless
   (a) the non-conformity appears without inspection; or
   (b) despite tender of the required documents the circumstances would justify injunction against honor under the provisions of this Act (Section 5—114).

(2) Payment pursuant to subsection (1) does not constitute an acceptance of goods or impair the buyer's right to inspect or any of his remedies.

Section 2—513. Buyer's Right to Inspection of Goods.

(1) Unless otherwise agreed and subject to subsection (3), where goods are tendered or delivered or identified to the contract for sale, the buyer has a right before payment or acceptance to inspect them at any reasonable place and time and in any reasonable manner. When the seller is required or authorized to send the goods to the buyer, the inspection may be after their arrival.

(2) Expenses of inspection must be borne by the buyer but may be recovered from the seller if the goods do not conform and are rejected.

(3) Unless otherwise agreed and subject to the provisions of this Article on C.I.F. contracts (subsection (3) of Section 2—321), the buyer is not entitled to inspect the goods before payment of the price when the contract provides
   (a) for delivery "C.O.D." or on other like terms; or
   (b) for payment against documents of title, except where such payment is due only after the goods are to become available for inspection.

(4) A place or method of inspection fixed by the parties is presumed to be exclusive, but unless otherwise expressly agreed it does not postpone identification or shift the place for delivery or for passing the risk of loss. If compliance becomes impossible, inspection shall be as provided in this section unless the place or method fixed was clearly intended as an indispensable condition failure of which avoids the contract.

Section 2—514. When Documents Deliverable on Acceptance; When on Payment.

Unless otherwise agreed documents against which a draft is drawn are to be delivered to the drawee on acceptance of the draft if it is payable more than three days after presentment; otherwise, only on payment.

Section 2—515. Preserving Evidence of Goods in Dispute.

In furtherance of the adjustment of any claim or dispute
- (a) either party on reasonable notification to the other and for the purpose of ascertaining the facts and preserving evidence has the right to inspect, test and sample the goods including such of them as may be in the possession or control of the other; and
- (b) the parties may agree to a third party inspection or survey to determine the conformity or condition of the goods and may agree that the findings shall be binding upon them in any subsequent litigation or adjustment.

PART 6

BREACH, REPUDIATION AND EXCUSE

Section 2—601. Buyer's Rights on Improper Delivery.

Subject to the provisions of this Article on breach in installment contracts (Section 2–612) and unless otherwise agreed under the sections on contractual limitations of remedy (Sections 2–718 and 2–719), if the goods or the tender of delivery fail in any respect to conform to the contract, the buyer may
- (a) reject the whole; or
- (b) accept the whole; or
- (c) accept any commercial unit or units and reject the rest.

Section 2—602. Manner and Effect of Rightful Rejection.

(1) Rejection of goods must be within a reasonable time after their delivery or tender. It is ineffective unless the buyer seasonably notifies the seller.

(2) Subject to the provisions of the two following sections on rejected goods (Sections 2–603 and 2–604),
- (a) after rejection any exercise of ownership by the buyer with respect to any commercial unit is wrongful as against the seller; and

- (b) if the buyer has before rejection taken physical possession of goods in which he does not have a security interest under the provisions of this Article (subsection (3) of Section 2—711), he is under a duty after rejection to hold them with reasonable care at the seller's disposition for a time sufficient to permit the seller to remove them; but
- (c) the buyer has no further obligations with regard to goods rightfully rejected.

(3) The seller's rights with respect to goods wrongfully rejected are governed by the provisions of this Article on Seller's remedies in general (Section 2–703).

Section 2—603. Merchant Buyer's Duties as to Rightfully Rejected Goods.

(1) Subject to any security interest in the buyer (subsection (3) of Section 2–711), when the seller has no agent or place of business at the market of re-

jection, a merchant buyer is under a duty after rejection of goods in his possession or control to follow any reasonable instructions received from the seller with respect to the goods and in the absence of such instructions to make reasonable efforts to sell them for the seller's account if they are perishable or threaten to decline in value speedily. Instructions are not reasonable if on demand indemnity for expenses is not forthcoming.

(2) When the buyer sells goods under subsection (1), he is entitled to reimbursement from the seller or out of the proceeds for reasonable expenses of caring for and selling them, and if the expenses include no selling commission then to such commission as is usual in the trade or if there is none to a reasonable sum not exceeding ten per cent on the gross proceeds.

(3) In complying with this section the buyer is held only to good faith, and good faith conduct hereunder is neither acceptance nor conversion nor the basis of an action for damages.

Section 2—604. Buyer's Options as to Salvage of Rightfully Rejected Goods.

Subject to the provisions of the immediately preceding section on perishables, if the seller gives no instructions within a reasonable time after notification of rejection, the buyer may store the rejected goods for the seller's account or reship them to him or resell them for the seller's account with reimbursement as provided in the preceding section. Such action is not acceptance or conversion.

Section 2—605. Waiver of Buyer's Objections by Failure to Particularize.

(1) The buyer's failure to state in connection with rejection a particular defect which is ascertainable by reasonable inspection precludes him from relying on the unstated defect to justify rejection or to establish breach

    (a) where the seller could have cured it if stated seasonably; or

    (b) between merchants when the seller has after rejection made request in writing for a full and

final written statement of all defects on which the buyer proposes to rely.

(2) Payment against documents made without reservation of rights precludes recovery of the payment for defects apparent on the face of the documents.

Section 2—606. What Constitutes Acceptance of Goods.

(1) Acceptance of goods occurs when the buyer

    (a) after a reasonable opportunity to inspect the goods signifies to the seller that the goods are conforming or that he will take or retain them in spite of their non-conformity; or

    (b) fails to make an effective rejection (subsection (1) of Section 2—602), but such acceptance does not occur until the buyer has had a reasonable opportunity to inspect them; or

    (c) does any act inconsistent with the seller's ownership; but if such act is wrongful as against the seller it is an acceptance only if ratified by him.

(2) Acceptance of a part of any commercial unit is acceptance of that entire unit.

Section 2—607. Effect of Acceptance; Notice of Breach; Burden of Establishing Breach After Acceptance; Notice of Claim or Litigation to Person Answerable Over.

(1) The buyer must pay at the contract rate for any goods accepted.

(2) Acceptance of goods by the buyer precludes rejection of the goods accepted and, if made with knowledge of a non-conformity, cannot be revoked because of it unless the acceptance was on the reasonable assumption that the non-conformity would be seasonably cured, but acceptance does not of itself impair any other remedy provided by this Article for non-conformity.

(3) Where a tender has been accepted

    (a) the buyer must within a reasonable time after he discovers or should have discovered any breach notify the seller of breach or be barred from any remedy; and

(b) if the claim is one for infringement or the like (subsection (3) of Section 2—312) and the buyer is sued as a result of such a breach, he must so notify the seller within a reasonable time after he receives notice of the litigation or be barred from any remedy over for liability established by the litigation.

(4) The burden is on the buyer to establish any breach with respect to the goods accepted.

(5) Where the buyer is sued for breach of a warranty or other obligation for which his seller is answerable over

(a) he may give his seller written notice of the litigation. If the notice states that the seller may come in and defend and that if the seller does not do so he will be bound in any action against him by his buyer by any determination of fact common to the two litigations, then unless the seller after seasonable receipt of the notice does come in and defend he is so bound.

(b) if the claim is one for infringement or the like (subsection (3) of Section 2—312) the original seller may demand in writing that his buyer turn over to him control of the litigation including settlement or else be barred from any remedy over and if he also agrees to bear all expense and to satisfy any adverse judgment, then unless the buyer after seasonable receipt of the demand does turn over control the buyer is so barred.

(6) The provisions of subsections (3), (4) and (5) apply to any obligation of a buyer to hold the seller harmless against infringement or the like (subsection (3) of Section 2—312).

Section 2—608. Revocation of Acceptance in Whole or in Part.

(1) The buyer may revoke his acceptance of a lot or commercial unit whose non-conformity substantially impairs its value to him if he has accepted it

(a) on the reasonable assumption that its non-conformity would be cured and it has not been seasonably cured; or

(b) without discovery of such non-conformity if his acceptance was reasonably induced either by the difficulty of discovery before acceptance or by the seller's assurances.

(2) Revocation of acceptance must occur within a reasonable time after the buyer discovers or should have discovered the ground for it and before any substantial change in condition of the goods which is not caused by their own defects. It is not effective until the buyer notifies the seller of it.

(3) A buyer who so revokes has the same rights and duties with regard to the goods involved as if he had rejected them.

Section 2—609. Right to Adequate Assurance of Performance.

(1) A contract for sale imposes an obligation on each party that the other's expectation of receiving due performance will not be impaired. When reasonable grounds for insecurity arise with respect to the performance of either party, the other may in writing demand adequate assurance of due performance and until he receives such assurance may if commercially reasonable suspend any performance for which he has not already received the agreed return.

(2) Between merchants the reasonableness of grounds for insecurity and the adequacy of any assurance offered shall be determined according to commercial standards.

(3) Acceptance of any improper delivery or payment does not prejudice the aggrieved party's right to demand adequate assurance of future performance.

(4) After receipt of a justified demand failure to provide within a reasonable time not exceeding thirty days such assurance of due performance as is adequate under the circumstances of the particular case is a repudiation of the contract.

Section 2—610. Anticipatory Repudiation.

When either party repudiates the contract with respect to a performance not yet due the loss of which will substantially impair the value of the contract to the other, the aggrieved party may

(a) for a commercially reasonable time await performance by the repudiating party; or

(b) resort to any remedy for breach (Section 2—703 or Section 2—711), even though he has notified the repudiating party that he would await the latter's performance and has urged retraction; and

(c) in either case suspend his own performance or proceed in accordance with the provisions of this Article on the seller's right to identify goods to the contract notwithstanding breach or to salvage unfinished goods (Section 2—704).

Section 2—611. Retraction of Anticipatory Repudiation.

(1) Until the repudiating party's next performance is due he can retract his repudiation unless the aggrieved party has since the repudiation cancelled or materially changed his position or otherwise indicated that he considers the repudiation final.

(2) Retraction may be by any method which clearly indicates to the aggrieved party that the repudiating party intends to perform, but must include any assurance justifiably demanded under the provisions of this Article (Section 2—609).

(3) Retraction reinstates the repudiating party's rights under the contract with due excuse and allowance to the aggrieved party for any delay occasioned by the repudiation.

Section 2—612. "Installment Contract"; Breach.

(1) An "installment contract" is one which requires or authorizes the delivery of goods in separate lots to be separately accepted, even though the contract contains a clause "each delivery is a separate contract" or its equivalent.

(2) The buyer may reject any installment which is non-conforming if the non-conformity substantially impairs the value of that installment and cannot be cured or if the non-conformity is a defect in the required documents; but if the non-conformity does not fall within subsection (3) and the seller gives adequate assurance of its cure the buyer must accept that installment.

(3) Whenever non-conformity or default with respect to one or more installments substantially impairs the value of the whole contract there is a breach of the whole. But the aggrieved party reinstates the contract if he accepts a non-conforming installment without seasonably notifying of cancellation or if he brings an action with respect only to past installments or demands performance as to future installments.

Section 2—613. Casualty to Identified Goods.

Where the contract requires for its performance goods identified when the contract is made, and the goods suffer casualty without fault of either party before the risk of loss passes to the buyer, or in a proper case under a "no arrival, no sale" term (Section 2—324) then

(a) if the loss is total the contract is avoided; and

(b) if the loss is partial or the goods have so deteriorated as no longer to conform to the contract, the buyer may nevertheless demand inspection and at his option either treat the contract as avoided or accept the goods with due allowance from the contract price for the deterioration or the deficiency in quantity but without further right against the seller.

Section 2—614. Substituted Performance.

(1) Where without fault of either party the agreed berthing, loading, or

unloading facilities fail or an agreed type of carrier becomes unavailable or the agreed manner of delivery otherwise becomes commercially impracticable but a commercially reasonable substitute is available, such substitute performance must be tendered and accepted.

(2) If the agreed means or manner of payment fails because of domestic or foreign governmental regulation, the seller may withhold or stop delivery unless the buyer provides a means or manner of payment which is commercially a substantial equivalent. If delivery has already been taken, payment by the means or in the manner provided by the regulation discharges the buyer's obligation unless the regulation is discriminatory, oppressive or predatory.

Section 2—615. Excuse by Failure of Presupposed Conditions.

Except so far as a seller may have assumed a greater obligation and subject to the preceding section on substituted performance:

  (a) Delay in delivery or non-delivery in whole or in part by a seller who complies with paragraphs (b) and (c) is not a breach of his duty under a contract for sale if performance as agreed has been made impracticable by the occurrence of a contingency the non-occurrence of which was a basic assumption on which the contract was made or by compliance in good faith with any applicable foreign or domestic governmental regulation or order whether or not it later proves to be invalid.

  (b) Where the causes mentioned in paragraph (a) affect only a part of the seller's capacity to perform, he must allocate production and deliveries among his customers but may at his option include regular customers not then under contract as well as his own requirements for further manufacture. He may so allocate in any manner which is fair and reasonable.

  (c) The seller must notify the buyer seasonably that there will be delay or non-delivery and, when allocation is required under paragraph (b), of the estimated quota thus made available for the buyer.

Section 2—616. Procedure on Notice Claiming Excuse.

(1) Where the buyer receives notification of a material or indefinite delay or an allocation justified under the preceding section he may by written notification to the seller as to any delivery concerned, and where the prospective deficiency substantially impairs the value of the whole contract under the provisions of this Article relating to breach of installment contracts (Section 2—612), then also as to the whole,

  (a) terminate and thereby discharge any unexecuted portion of the contract; or

  (b) modify the contract by agreeing to take his available quota in substitution.

(2) If after receipt of such notification from the seller the buyer fails so to modify the contract within a reasonable time not exceeding thirty days, the contract lapses with respect to any deliveries affected.

(3) The provisions of this section may not be negated by agreement except in so far as the seller has assumed a greater obligation under the preceding section.

PART 7

REMEDIES

Section 2—701. Remedies for Breach of Collateral Contracts Not Impaired.

Remedies for breach of any obligation or promise collateral or ancillary to a contract for sale are not impaired by the provisions of this Article.

Section 2—702. Seller's Remedies on Discovery of Buyer's Insolvency.

(1) Where the seller discovers the buyer to be insolvent he may refuse delivery except for cash including payment for all goods theretofore delivered

under the contract, and stop delivery under this Article (Section 2—705).

(2) Where the seller discovers that the buyer has received goods on credit while insolvent he may reclaim the goods upon demand made within ten days after the receipt, but if misrepresentation of solvency has been made to the particular seller in writing within three months before delivery the ten day limitation does not apply. Except as provided in this subsection, the seller may not base a right to reclaim goods on the buyer's fraudulent or innocent misrepresentation of solvency or of intent to pay.

(3) The seller's right to reclaim under subsection (2) is subject to the rights of a buyer in ordinary course or other good faith purchaser or lien creditor under this Article (Section 2—403). Successful reclamation of goods excludes all other remedies with respect to them.

Section 2—703. Seller's Remedies in General.

Where the buyer wrongfully rejects or revokes acceptance of goods or fails to make a payment due on or before delivery or repudiates with respect to a part or the whole, then with respect to any goods directly affected and, if the breach is of the whole contract (Section 2—612), then also with respect to the whole undelivered balance, the aggrieved seller may

    (a) withhold delivery of such goods;

    (b) stop delivery by any bailee as hereafter provided (Section 2—705);

    (c) proceed under the next section respecting goods still unidentified to the contract;

    (d) resell and recover damages as hereafter provided (Section 2—706);

    (e) recover damages for non-acceptance (Section 2—708) or in a proper case the price (Section 2—709);

    (f) cancel.

Section 2—704. Seller's Right to Identify Goods to the Contract Notwithstanding Breach or to Salvage Unfinished Goods.

(1) An aggrieved seller under the preceding section may

    (a) identify to the contract conforming goods not already identified if at the time he learned of the breach they are in his possession or control;

    (b) treat as the subject of resale goods which have demonstrably been intended for the particular contract even though those goods are unfinished.

(2) Where the goods are unfinished an aggrieved seller may in the exercise of reasonable commercial judgment for the purposes of avoiding loss and of effective realization either complete the manufacture and wholly identify the goods to the contract or cease manufacture and resell for scrap or salvage value or proceed in any other reasonable manner.

Section 2—705. Seller's Stoppage of Delivery in Transit or Otherwise.

(1) The seller may stop delivery of goods in the possession of a carrier or other bailee when he discovers the buyer to be insolvent (Section 2—702) and may stop delivery of carload, truckload, planeload or larger shipments of express or freight when the buyer repudiates or fails to make a payment due before delivery or if for any other reason the seller has a right to withhold or reclaim the goods.

(2) As against such buyer the seller may stop delivery until

    (a) receipt of the goods by the buyer; or

    (b) acknowledgment to the buyer by any bailee of the goods except a carrier that the bailee holds the goods for the buyer; or

    (c) such acknowledgment to the buyer by a carrier by reshipment or as warehouseman; or

    (d) negotiation to the buyer of any negotiable document of title covering the goods.

(3) (a) To stop delivery the seller must so notify as to enable the bailee by reasonable diligence to prevent delivery of the goods.

    (b) After such notification the bailee must hold and deliver the goods according to the directions of the seller, but the seller is liable to the bailee for any ensuing charges or damages.

(c) If a negotiable document of title has been issued for goods, the bailee is not obliged to obey a notification to stop until surrender of the document.

(d) A carrier who has issued a nonnegotiable bill of lading is not obliged to obey a notification to stop received from a person other than the consignor.

Section 2—706. Seller's Resale Including Contract for Resale.

(1) Under the conditions stated in Section 2–703 on seller's remedies, the seller may resell the goods concerned or the undelivered balance thereof. Where the resale is made in good faith and in a commercially reasonable manner the seller may recover the difference between the resale price and the contract price together with any incidental damages allowed under the provisions of this Article (Section 2—710), but less expenses saved in consequence of the buyer's breach.

(2) Except as otherwise provided in subsection (3) or unless otherwise agreed, resale may be at public or private sale including sale by way of one or more contracts to sell or of identification to an existing contract of the seller. Sale may be as a unit or in parcels and at any time and place and on any terms but every aspect of the sale including the method, manner, time, place and terms must be commercially reasonable. The resale must be reasonably identified as referring to the broken contract, but it is not necessary that the goods be in existence or that any or all of them have been identified to the contract before the breach.

(3) Where the resale is at private sale the seller must give the buyer reasonable notification of his intention to resell.

(4) Where the resale is at public sale

(a) only identified goods can be sold except where there is a recognized market for a public

sale of futures in goods of the kind; and

(b) it must be made at a usual place or market for public sale if one is reasonably available and except in the case of goods which are perishable or threaten to decline in value speedily the seller must give the buyer reasonable notice of the time and place of the resale; and

(c) if the goods are not to be within the view of those attending the sale, the notification of sale must state the place where the goods are located and provide for their reasonable inspection by prospective bidders; and

(d) the seller may buy.

(5) A purchaser who buys in good faith at a resale takes the goods free of any rights of the original buyer even though the seller fails to comply with one or more of the requirements of this section.

(6) The seller is not accountable to the buyer for any profit made on any resale. A person in the position of a seller (Section 2—707) or a buyer who has rightfully rejected or justifiably revoked acceptance must account for any excess over the amount of his security interest, as hereinafter defined (subsection (3) of Section 2—711).

Section 2—707. "Person in the Position of a Seller".

(1) A "person in the position of a seller" includes as against a principal an agent who has paid or become responsible for the price of goods on behalf of his principal or anyone who otherwise holds a security interest or other right in goods similar to that of a seller.

(2) A person in the position of a seller may as provided in this Article withhold or stop delivery (Section 2—705) and resell (Section 2—706) and recover incidental damages (Section 2—710).

Section 2—708. Seller's Damages for Non-acceptance or Repudiation.

(1) Subject to subsection (2) and to the provisions of this Article with re-

spect to proof of market price (Section 2—723), the measure of damages for non-acceptance or repudiation by the buyer is the difference between the market price at the time and place for tender and the unpaid contract price together with any incidental damages provided in this Article (Section 2—710), but less expenses saved in consequence of the buyer's breach.

(2) If the measure of damages provided in subsection (1) is inadequate to put the seller in as good a position as performance would have done, then the measure of damages is the profit (including reasonable overhead) which the seller would have made from full performance by the buyer, together with any incidental damages provided in this Article (Section 2—710), due allowance for costs reasonably incurred and due credit for payments or proceeds of resale.

Section 2—709. Action for the Price.

(1) When the buyer fails to pay the price as it becomes due the seller may recover, together with any incidental damages under the next section, the price

(a) of goods accepted or of conforming goods lost or damaged within a commercially reasonable time after risk of their loss has passed to the buyer; and

(b) of goods identified to the contract if the seller is unable after reasonable effort to resell them at a reasonable price or the circumstances reasonably indicate that such effort will be unavailing.

(2) Where the seller sues for the price he must hold for the buyer any goods which have been identified to the contract and are still in his control except that if resale becomes possible he may resell them at any time prior to the collection of the judgment. The net proceeds of any such resale must be credited to the buyer and payment of the judgment entitles him to any goods not resold.

(3) After the buyer has wrongfully rejected or revoked acceptance of the

goods or has failed to make a payment due or has repudiated (Section 2—610), a seller who is held not entitled to the price under this section shall nevertheless be awarded damages for non-acceptance under the preceding section.

Section 2—710. Seller's Incidental Damages.

Incidental damages to an aggrieved seller include any commercially reasonable charges, expenses or commissions incurred in stopping delivery, in the transportation, care and custody of goods after the buyer's breach, in connection with return or resale of the goods or otherwise resulting from the breach.

Section 2—711. Buyer's Remedies in General; Buyer's Security Interest in Rejected Goods.

(1) Where the seller fails to make delivery or repudiates or the buyer rightfully rejects or justifiably revokes acceptance then with respect to any goods involved, and with respect to the whole if the breach goes to the whole contract (Section 2—612), the buyer may cancel and whether or not he has done so may in addition to recovering so much of the price as has been paid

(a) "cover" and have damages under the next section as to all the goods affected whether or not they have been identified to the contract; or

(b) recover damages for non-delivery as provided in this Article (Section 2—713).

(2) Where the seller fails to deliver or repudiates the buyer may also

(a) if the goods have been identified recover them as provided in this Article (Section 2—502); or

(b) in a proper case obtain specific performance or replevy the goods as provided in this Article (Section 2—716).

(3) On rightful rejection or justifiable revocation of acceptance a buyer has a security interest in goods in his possession or control for any payments made on their price and any expenses reasonably incurred in their inspection, receipt,

transportation, care and custody and may hold such goods and resell them in like manner as an aggrieved seller (Section 2—706).

Section 2—712. "Cover"; Buyer's Procurement of Substitute Goods.

(1) After a breach within the preceding section the buyer may "cover" by making in good faith and without unreasonable delay any reasonable purchase of or contract to purchase goods in substitution for those due from the seller.

(2) The buyer may recover from the seller as damages the difference between the cost of cover and the contract price together with any incidental or consequential damages as hereinafter defined (Section 2—715), but less expenses saved in consequence of the seller's breach.

(3) Failure of the buyer to effect cover within this section does not bar him from any other remedy.

Section 2—713. Buyer's Damages for Non-Delivery or Repudiation.

(1) Subject to the provisions of this Article with respect to proof of market price (Section 2—723), the measure of damages for non-delivery or repudiation by the seller is the difference between the market price at the time when the buyer learned of the breach and the contract price together with any incidental and consequential damages provided in this Article (Section 2—715), but less expenses saved in consequence of the seller's breach.

' (2) Market price is to be determined as of the place for tender or, in cases of rejection after arrival or revocation of acceptance, as of the place of arrival.

Section 2—714. Buyer's Damages for Breach in Regard to Accepted Goods.

(1) Where the buyer has accepted goods and given notification (subsection (3) of Section 2—607) he may recover as damages for any non-conformity of tender the loss resulting in the ordinary course of events from the seller's breach as determined in any manner which is reasonable.

(2) The measure of damages for breach of warranty is the difference at the time and place of acceptance between the value of the goods accepted and the value they would have had if they had been as warranted, unless special circumstances show proximate damages of a different amount.

(3) In a proper case any incidental and consequential damages under the next section may also be recovered.

Section 2—715. Buyer's Incidental and Consequential Damages.

(1) Incidental damages resulting from the seller's breach include expenses reasonably incurred in inspection, receipt, transportation and care and custody of goods rightfully rejected, any commercially reasonable charges, expenses or commissions in connection with effecting cover and any other reasonable expense incident to the delay or other breach.

(2) Consequential damages resulting from the seller's breach include

   (a) any loss resulting from general or particular requirements and needs of which the seller at the time of contracting had reason to know and which could not reasonably be prevented by cover or otherwise; and

   (b) injury to person or property proximately resulting from any breach of warranty.

Section 2—716. Buyer's Right to Specific Performance or Replevin.

(1) Specific performance may be decreed where the goods are unique or in other proper circumstances.

(2) The decree for specific performance may include such terms and conditions as to payment of the price, damages, or other relief as the court may deem just.

(3) The buyer has a right of replevin for goods identified to the contract if after reasonable effort he is unable to effect cover for such goods or the circumstances reasonably indicate that such effort will be unavailing or if the goods have been shipped under reservation and satisfaction of the security interest in them has been made or tendered.

Section 2—717. Deduction of Damages From the Price.

The buyer on notifying the seller of his intention to do so may deduct all or any part of the damages resulting from any breach of the contract from any part of the price still due under the same contract.

Section 2—718. Liquidation or Limitation of Damages; Deposits.

(1) Damages for breach by either party may be liquidated in the agreement but only at an amount which is reasonable in the light of the anticipated or actual harm caused by the breach, the difficulties of proof of loss, and the inconvenience or non-feasibility of otherwise obtaining an adequate remedy. A term fixing unreasonably large liquidated damages is void as a penalty.

(2) Where the seller justifiably withholds delivery of goods because of the buyer's breach, the buyer is entitled to restitution of any amount by which the sum of his payments exceeds

    (a) the amount to which the seller is entitled by virtue of terms liquidating the seller's damages in accordance with subsection (1), or

    (b) in the absence of such terms, twenty per cent of the value of the total performance for which the buyer is obligated under the contract or $500, whichever is smaller.

(3) The buyer's right to restitution under subsection (2) is subject to offset to the extent that the seller establishes

    (a) a right to recover damages under the provisions of this Article other than subsection (1), and

    (b) the amount or value of any benefits received by the buyer directly or indirectly by reason of the contract.

(4) Where a seller has received payment in goods their reasonable value or the proceeds of their resale shall be treated as payments for the purposes of subsection (2); but if the seller has notice of the buyer's breach before reselling goods received in part performance, his resale is subject to the conditions laid down in this Article on resale by an aggrieved seller (Section 2—706).

Section 2—719. Contractual Modification or Limitation of Remedy.

(1) Subject to the provisions of subsections (2) and (3) of this section and of the preceding section on liquidation and limitation of damages,

    (a) the agreement may provide for remedies in addition to or in substitution for those provided in this Article and may limit or alter the measure of damages recoverable under this Article, as by limiting the buyer's remedies to return of the goods and repayment of the price or to repair and replacement of non-conforming goods or parts; and

    (b) resort to a remedy as provided is optional unless the remedy is expressly agreed to be exclusive, in which case it is the sole remedy.

(2) Where circumstances cause an exclusive or limited remedy to fail of its essential purpose, remedy may be had as provided in this Act.

(3) Consequential damages may be limited or excluded unless the limitation or exclusion is unconscionable. Limitation of consequential damages for injury to the person in the case of consumer goods is prima facie unconscionable, but limitation of damages where the loss is commercial is not.

Section 2—720. Effect of "Cancellation" or "Rescission" on Claims for Antecedent Breach.

Unless the contrary intention clearly appears, expressions of "cancellation" or "rescission" of the contract or the like shall not be construed as a renunciation or discharge of any claim in damages for an antecedent breach.

Section 2—721. Remedies for Fraud.

Remedies for material misrepresentation or fraud include all remedies available under this Article for non-fraudulent breach. Neither rescission or a claim for rescission of the contract for sale nor rejection or return of the goods shall bar or be deemed inconsistent with a claim for damages or other remedy.

Section 2—722. Who Can Sue Third Parties for Injury to Goods.

Where a third party so deals with goods which have been identified to a contract for sale as to cause actionable injury to a party to that contract

- (a) a right of action against the third party is in either party to the contract for sale who has title to or a security interest or a special property or an insurable interest in the goods; and if the goods have been destroyed or converted, a right of action is also in the party who either bore the risk of loss under the contract for sale or has since the injury assumed that risk as against the other;
- (b) if at the time of the injury the party plaintiff did not bear the risk of loss as against the other party to the contract for sale and there is no arrangement between them for disposition of the recovery, his suit or settlement is, subject to his own interest, as a fiduciary for the other party to the contract;
- (c) either party may with the consent of the other sue for the benefit of whom it may concern.

Section 2—723. Proof of Market Price: Time and Place.

(1) If an action based on anticipatory repudiation comes to trial before the time for performance with respect to some or all of the goods, any damages based on market price (Section 2—708 or Section 2—713) shall be determined according to the price of such goods prevailing at the time when the aggrieved party learned of the repudiation.

(2) If evidence of a price prevailing at the times or places described in this Article is not readily available, the price prevailing within any reasonable time before or after the time described or at any other place which in commercial judgment or under usage of trade would serve as a reasonable substitute for the one described may be used, making any proper allowance for the cost of transporting the goods to or from such other place.

(3) Evidence of a relevant price prevailing at a time or place other than the one described in this Article offered by one party is not admissible unless and until he has given the other party such notice as the court finds sufficient to prevent unfair surprise.

Section 2—724. Admissibility of Market Quotations.

Whenever the prevailing price or value of any goods regularly bought and sold in any established commodity market is in issue, reports in official publications or trade journals or in newspapers or periodicals of general circulation published as the reports of such market shall be admissible in evidence. The circumstances of the preparation of such a report may be shown to affect its weight but not its admissibility.

Section 2—725. Statute of Limitations in Contracts for Sale.

(1) An action for breach of any contract for sale must be commenced within four years after the cause of action has accrued. By the original agreement the parties may reduce the period of limitation to not less than one year but may not extend it.

(2) A cause of action accrues when the breach occurs, regardless of the aggrieved party's lack of knowledge of the breach. A breach of warranty occurs when tender of delivery is made, except that where a warranty explicitly extends to future performance of the goods and discovery of the breach must await the time of such performance the cause of action accrues when the breach is or should have been discovered.

(3) Where an action commenced within the time limited by subsection (1) is so terminated as to leave available a remedy by another action for the same

breach, such other action may be commenced after the expiration of the time limited and within six months after the termination of the first action unless the termination resulted from voluntary discontinuance or from dismissal for failure or neglect to prosecute.

(4) This section does not alter the law on tolling of the statute of limitations nor does it apply to causes of action which have accrued before this Act becomes effective.

ARTICLE 3

COMMERCIAL PAPER

PART 1

SHORT TITLE, FORM AND INTERPRETATION

Section 3—101.   Short Title.

This Article shall be known and may be cited as Uniform Commercial Code —Commercial Paper.

Section 3—102.   Definitions and Index of Definitions.

(1) In this Article unless the context otherwise requires

    (a) "Issue" means the first delivery of an instrument to a holder or a remitter.

    (b) An "order" is a direction to pay and must be more than an authorization or request. It must identify the person to pay with reasonable certainty. It may be addressed to one or more such persons jointly or in the alternative but not in succession.

    (c) A "promise" is an undertaking to pay and must be more than an acknowledgment of an obligation.

    (d) "Secondary party" means a drawer or endorser.

    (e) "Instrument" means a negotiable instrument.

(2) Other definitions applying to this Article and the sections in which they appear are:

    "Acceptance". Section 3—410.

"Accommodation party". Section 3—415.

"Alteration". Section 3—407.

"Certificate of deposit". Section 3—104.

"Certification". Section 3—411.

"Check". Section 3—104.

"Definite time". Section 3—109.

"Dishonor". Section 3—507.

"Draft". Section 3—104.

"Holder in due course". Section 3—302.

"Negotiation". Section 3—202.

"Note". Section 3—104.

"Notice of dishonor". Section 3—508.

"On demand". Section 3—108.

"Presentment". Section 3—504.

"Protest". Section 3—509.

"Restrictive Indorsement". Section 3—205.

"Signature". Section 3—401.

(3) The following definitions in other Articles apply to this Article:

"Account". Section 4—104.

"Banking Day". Section 4—104.

"Clearing house". Section 4—104.

"Collecting bank". Section 4—105.

"Customer". Section 4—104.

"Depositary Bank". Section 4—105.

"Documentary Draft". Section 4—104.

"Intermediary Bank". Section 4—105.

"Item". Section 4–104.

"Midnight deadline". Section 4–104.

"Payor bank". Section 4–105.

(4) In addition Article 1 contains general definitions and principles of construction and interpretation applicable throughout this Article.

Section 3—103. Limitations on Scope of Article.

(1) This Article does not apply to money, documents of title or investment securities.

(2) The provisions of this Article are subject to the provisions of the Article on Bank Deposits and Collections (Article 4) and Secured Transactions (Article 9).

Section 3—104. Form of Negotiable Instruments; "Draft"; "Check"; "Certificate of Deposit"; "Note".

(1) Any writing to be a negotiable instrument within this Article must

   (a) be signed by the maker or drawer; and

   (b) contain an unconditional promise or order to pay a sum certain in money and no other promise, order, obligation or power given by the maker or drawer except as authorized by this Article; and

   (c) be payable on demand or at a definite time; and

   (d) be payable to order or to bearer.

(2) A writing which complies with the requirements of this section is

   (a) a "draft" ("bill of exchange") if it is an order;

   (b) a "check" if it is a draft drawn on a bank and payable on demand;

   (c) a "certificate of deposit" if it is an acknowledgment by a bank of receipt of money with an engagement to repay it;

   (d) a "note" if it is a promise other than a certificate of deposit.

(3) As used in other Articles of this Act, and as the context may require, the terms "draft", "check", "certificate of deposit" and "note" may refer to instruments which are not negotiable within this Article as well as to instruments which are so negotiable.

Section 3—105. When Promise or Order Unconditional.

(1) A promise or order otherwise unconditional is not made conditional by the fact that the instrument

   (a) is subject to implied or constructive conditions; or

   (b) states its consideration, whether performed or promised, or the transaction which gave rise to the instrument, or that the promise or order is made or the instrument matures in accordance with or "as per" such transaction; or

   (c) refers to or states that it arises out of a separate agreement or refers to a separate agreement for rights as to prepayment or acceleration; or

   (d) states that it is drawn under a letter of credit; or

   (e) states that it is secured, whether by mortgage, reservation of title or otherwise; or

   (f) indicates a particular account to be debited or any other fund or source from which reimbursement is expected; or

   (g) is limited to payment out of a particular fund or the proceeds of a particular source, if the instrument is issued by a government or governmental agency or unit; or

   (h) is limited to payment out of the entire assets of a partnership, unincorporated association, trust or estate by or on behalf of which the instrument is issued.

(2) A promise or order is not unconditional if the instrument

   (a) states that it is subject to or governed by any other agreement; or

   (b) states that it is to be paid only out of a particular fund or source except as provided in this section.

Section 3—106. Sum Certain.

(1) The sum payable is a sum certain even though it is to be paid
- (a) with stated interest or by stated installments; or
- (b) with stated different rates of interest before and after default or a specified date; or
- (c) with a stated discount or addition if paid before or after the date fixed for payment; or
- (d) with exchange or less exchange, whether at a fixed rate or at the current rate; or
- (e) with costs of collection or an attorney's fee or both upon default.

(2) Nothing in this section shall validate any term which is otherwise illegal.

Section 3—107. Money.

(1) An instrument is payable in money if the medium of exchange in which it is payable is money at the time the instrument is made. An instrument payable in "currency" or "current funds" is payable in money.

(2) A promise or order to pay a sum stated in a foreign currency is for a sum certain in money and, unless a different medium of payment is specified in the instrument, may be satisfied by payment of that number of dollars which the stated foreign currency will purchase at the buying sight rate for that currency on the day on which the instrument is payable or, if payable on demand, on the day of demand. If such an instrument specifies a foreign currency as the medium of payment, the instrument is payable in that currency.

Section 3—108. Payable on Demand.

Instruments payable on demand include those payable at sight or on presentation and those in which no time for payment is stated.

Section 3—109. Definite Time.

(1) An instrument is payable at a definite time if by its terms it is payable
- (a) on or before a stated date or at a fixed period after a stated date; or
- (b) at a fixed period after sight; or
- (c) at a definite time subject to any acceleration; or
- (d) at a definite time subject to extension at the option of the holder, or to extension to a further definite time at the option of the maker or acceptor or automatically upon or after a specified act or event.

(2) An instrument which by its terms is otherwise payable only upon an act or event uncertain as to time of occurrence is not payable at a definite time even though the act or event has occurred.

Section 3—110. Payable to Order.

(1) An instrument is payable to order when by its terms it is payable to the order or assigns of any person therein specified with reasonable certainty, or to him or his order, or when it is conspicuously designed on its face as "exchange" or the like and names a payee. It may be payable to the order of
- (a) the maker or drawer; or
- (b) the drawee; or
- (c) a payee who is not maker, drawer or drawee; or
- (d) two or more payees together or in the alternative; or
- (e) an estate, trust or fund, in which case it is payable to the order of the representative of such estate, trust or fund or his successors; or
- (f) an office, or an officer by his title as such in which case it is payable to the principal, but the incumbent of the office or his successors may act as if he or they were the holder; or
- (g) a partnership or unincorporated association, in which case it is payable to the partnership or association and may be indorsed or transferred by any person thereto authorized.

(2) An instrument not payable to order is not made so payable by such words as "payable upon return of this instrument properly indorsed."

(3) An instrument made payable both to order and to bearer is payable to

order unless the bearer words are handwritten or typewritten.

Section 3—111. Payable to Bearer.

An instrument is payable to bearer when by its terms it is payable to

(a) bearer or the order of bearer; or

(b) a specified person or bearer; or

(c) "cash" or the order of "cash", or any other indication which does not purport to designate a specific payee.

Section 3—112. Terms and Omissions Not Affecting Negotiability.

(1) The negotiability of an instrument is not affected by

(a) the omission of a statement of any consideration or of the place where the instrument is drawn or payable; or

(b) a statement that collateral has been given to secure obligations either on the instrument or otherwise of an obligor on the instrument or that in case of default on those obligations the holder may realize on or dispose of the collateral; or

(c) a promise or power to maintain or protect collateral or to give additional collateral; or

(d) a term authorizing a confession of judgment on the instrument if it is not paid when due; or

(e) a term purporting to waive the benefit of any law intended for the advantage or protection of any obligor; or

(f) a term in a draft providing that the payee by indorsing or cashing it acknowledges full satisfaction of an obligation of the drawer; or

(g) a statement in a draft drawn in a set of parts (Section 3—801) to the effect that the order is effective only if no other part has been honored.

(2) Nothing in this section shall validate any term which is otherwise illegal.

Section 3—113. Seal.

An instrument otherwise negotiable is within this Article even though it is under a seal.

Section 3—114. Date, Antedating, Postdating.

(1) The negotiability of an instrument is not affected by the fact that it is undated, antedated or postdated.

(2) Where an instrument is antedated or postdated the time when it is payable is determined by the stated date if the instrument is payable on demand or at a fixed period after date.

(3) Where the instrument or any signature thereon is dated, the date is presumed to be correct.

Section 3—115. Incomplete Instruments.

(1) When a paper whose contents at the time of signing show that it is intended to become an instrument is signed while still incomplete in any necessary respect, it cannot be enforced until completed, but when it is completed in accordance with authority given it is effective as completed.

(2) If the completion is unauthorized, the rules as to material alteration apply (Section 3—407), even though the paper was not delivered by the maker or drawer; but the burden of establishing that any completion is unauthorized is on the party so asserting.

Section 3—116. Instruments Payable to Two or More Persons.

An instrument payable to the order of two or more persons

(a) if in the alternative is payable to any one of them and may be negotiated, discharged or enforced by any of them who has possession of it;

(b) if not in the alternative is payable to all of them and may be negotiated, discharged or enforced only by all of them.

Section 3—117. Instruments Payable With Words of Description.

An instrument made payable to a named person with the addition of words describing him

(a) as agent or officer of a specified person is payable to his principal, but the agent or officer may act as if he were the holder;

(b) as any other fiduciary for a specified person or purpose is payable to the payee and may be negotiated, discharged or enforced by him;

(c) in any other manner is payable to the payee unconditionally and the additional words are without effect on subsequent parties.

Section 3—118. Ambiguous Terms and Rules of Construction.

The following rules apply to every instrument:

(a) Where there is doubt whether the instrument is a draft or a note the holder may treat it as either. A draft drawn on the drawer is effective as a note.

(b) Handwritten terms control typewritten and printed terms, and typewritten control printed.

(c) Words control figures except that if the words are ambiguous, figures control.

(d) Unless otherwise specified, a provision for interest means interest at the judgment rate at the place of payment from the date of the instrument, or if it is undated from the date of issue.

(e) Unless the instrument otherwise specifies, two or more persons who sign as maker, acceptor or drawer or indorser and as a part of the same transaction are jointly and severally liable even though the instrument contains such words as "I promise to pay."

(f) Unless otherwise specified, consent to extension authorizes a single extension for not longer than the original period. A consent to extension, expressed in the instrument, is binding on secondary parties and accommodation makers. A holder may not exercise his option to extend an instrument over the objection of a maker or acceptor or other party who in accordance with Section 3—604 tenders full pay-

ment when the instrument is due.

Section 3—119. Other Writings Affecting Instrument.

(1) As between the obligor and his immediate obligee or any transferee the terms of an instrument may be modified or affected by any other written agreement executed as a part of the same transaction, except that a holder in due course is not affected by any limitation of his rights arising out of the separate written agreement if he had no notice of the limitation when he took the instrument.

(2) A separate agreement does not affect the negotiability of an instrument.

Section 3—120. Instruments "Payable Through" Bank.

An instrument which states that it is "payable through" a bank or the like designates that bank as a collecting bank to make presentment but does not of itself authorize the bank to pay the instrument.

Section 3—121. Instruments Payable at Bank.

Note: *If this Act is introduced in the Congress of the United States, this section should be omitted.*
(*States to select either alternative*)

Alternative A—

A note or acceptance which states that it is payable at a bank is the equivalent of a draft drawn on the bank payable when it falls due out of any funds of the maker or acceptor in current account or otherwise available for such payment.

Alternative B—

A note or acceptance which states that it is payable at a bank is not of itself an order or authorization to the bank to pay it.

Section 3—122. Accrual of Cause of Action.

(1) A cause of action against a maker or an acceptor accrues

(a) in the case of a time instrument on the day after maturity;

(b) in the case of a demand instrument upon its date or, if no date is stated, on the date of issue.

(2) A cause of action against the obligor of a demand or time certificate of deposit accrues upon demand, but demand on a time certificate may not be made until on or after the date of maturity.

(3) A cause of action against a drawer of a draft or an indorser of any instrument accrues upon demand following dishonor of the instrument. Notice of dishonor is a demand.

(4) Unless an instrument provides otherwise, interest runs at the rate provided by law for a judgment

(a) in the case of a maker, acceptor or other primary obligor of a demand instrument, from the date of demand;

(b) in all other cases from the date of accrual of the cause of action.

PART 2

TRANSFER AND NEGOTIATION

Section 3—201. Transfer: Right to Indorsement.

(1) Transfer of an instrument vests in the transferee such rights as the transferor has therein, except that a transferee who has himself been a party to any fraud or illegality affecting the instrument or who as a prior holder had notice of a defense or claim against it cannot improve his position by taking from a later holder in due course.

(2) A transfer of a security interest in an instrument vests the foregoing rights in the transferee to the extent of the interest transferred.

(3) Unless otherwise agreed, any transfer for value of an instrument not then payable to bearer gives the transferee the specifically enforceable right to have the unqualified indorsement of the transferor. Negotiation takes effect only when the indorsement is made and until that time there is no presumption that the transferee is the owner.

Section 3—202. Negotiation.

(1) Negotiation is the transfer of an instrument in such form that the transferee becomes a holder. If the instrument is payable to order, it is negotiated by delivery with any necessary indorsement; if payable to bearer, it is negotiated by delivery.

(2) An indorsement must be written by or on behalf of the holder and on the instrument or on a paper so firmly affixed thereto as to become a part thereof.

(3) An indorsement is effective for negotiation only when it conveys the entire instrument or any unpaid residue. If it purports to be of less, it operates only as a partial assignment.

(4) Words of assignment, condition, waiver, guaranty, limitation or disclaimer of liability and the like accompanying an indorsement do not affect its character as an indorsement.

Section 3—203. Wrong or Misspelled Name.

Where an instrument is made payable to a person under a misspelled name or one other than his own he may indorse in that name or his own or both; but signature in both names may be required by a person paying or giving value for the instrument.

Section 3—204. Special Indorsement; Blank Indorsement.

(1) A special indorsement specifies the person to whom or to whose order it

makes the instrument payable. Any instrument specially indorsed becomes payable to the order of the special indorsee and may be further negotiated only by his indorsement.

(2) An indorsement in blank specifies no particular indorsee and may consist of a mere signature. An instrument payable to order and indorsed in blank becomes payable to bearer and may be negotiated by delivery alone until specially indorsed.

(3) The holder may convert a blank indorsement into a special indorsement by writing over the signature of the indorser in blank any contract consistent with the character of the indorsement.

Section 3—205. Restrictive Indorsements.

An indorsement is restrictive which either

(a) is conditional; or

(b) purports to prohibit further transfer of the instrument; or

(c) includes the words "for collection", "for deposit", "pay any bank", or like terms signifying a purpose of deposit or collection; or

(d) otherwise states that it is for the benefit or use of the indorser or of another person.

Section 3—206. Effect of Restrictive Indorsement.

(1) No restrictive indorsement prevents further transfer or negotiation of the instrument.

(2) An intermediary bank, or a payor bank which is not the depositary bank, is neither given notice nor otherwise affected by a restrictive indorsement of any person except the bank's immediate transferor or the person presenting for payment.

(3) Except for an intermediary bank, any transferee under an indorsement which is conditional or includes the words "for collection", "for deposit", "pay any bank", or like terms (subpara-

graphs (a) and (c) of Section 3—205) must pay or apply any value given by him for or on the security of the instrument consistently with the indorsement, and to the extent that he does so he becomes a holder for value. In addition such transferee is a holder in due course if he otherwise complies with the requirements of Section 3—302 on what constitutes a holder in due course.

(4) The first taker under an indorsement for the benefit of the indorser or another person (subparagraph (d) of Section 3—205) must pay or apply any value given by him for or on the security of the instrument consistently with the indorsement, and to the extent that he does so he becomes a holder for value. In addition such taker is a holder in due course if he otherwise complies with the requirements of Section 3—302 on what constitutes a holder in due course. A later holder for value is neither given notice nor otherwise affected by such restrictive indorsement unless he has knowledge that a fiduciary or other person has negotiated the instrument in any transaction for his own benefit or otherwise in breach of duty (subsection (2) of Section 3—304).

Section 3—207. Negotiation Effective Although It May Be Rescinded.

(1) Negotiation is effective to transfer the instrument although the negotiation is

(a) made by an infant, a corporation exceeding its powers, or any other person without capacity; or

(b) obtained by fraud, duress or mistake of any kind; or

(c) part of an illegal transaction; or

(d) made in breach of duty.

(2) Except as against a subsequent holder in due course such negotiation is in an appropriate case subject to rescission, the declaration of a constructive trust or any other remedy permitted by law.

Section 3—208. Reacquisition.

Where an instrument is returned to or reacquired by a prior party he may cancel any indorsement which is not necessary to his title and reissue or further negotiate the instrument, but any intervening party is discharged as against the reacquiring party and subsequent holders not in due course and if his indorsement has been cancelled is discharged as against subsequent holders in due course as well.

PART 3

RIGHTS OF A HOLDER

Section 3—301. Rights of a Holder.

The holder of an instrument whether or not he is the owner may transfer or negotiate it and, except as otherwise provided in Section 3—603 on payment or satisfaction, discharge it or enforce payment in his own name.

Section 3—302. Holder in Due Course.

(1) A holder in due course is a holder who takes the instrument

    (a) for value; and

    (b) in good faith; and

    (c) without notice that it is overdue or has been dishonored or of any defense against or claim to it on the part of any person.

(2) A payee may be a holder in due course.

(3) A holder does not become a holder in due course of an instrument:

    (a) by purchase of it at judicial sale or by taking it under legal process; or

    (b) by acquiring it in taking over an estate; or

    (c) by purchasing it as part of a bulk transaction not in regular course of business of the transferor.

(4) A purchaser of a limited interest can be a holder in due course only to the extent of the interest purchased.

Section 3—303. Taking for Value.

A holder takes the instrument for value

    (a) to the extent that the agreed consideration has been performed or that he acquires a security interest in or a lien on the instrument otherwise than by legal process; or

    (b) when he takes the instrument in payment of or as security for an antecedent claim against any person whether or not the claim is due; or

    (c) when he gives a negotiable instrument for it or makes an irrevocable commitment to a third person.

Section 3—304. Notice to Purchaser.

(1) The purchaser has notice of a claim or defense if

    (a) the instrument is so incomplete, bears such visible evidence of forgery or alteration, or is otherwise so irregular as to call into question its validity, terms or ownership or to create an ambiguity as to the party to pay; or

    (b) the purchaser has notice that the obligation of any party is voidable in whole or in part, or that all parties have been discharged.

(2) The purchaser has notice of a claim against the instrument when he has knowledge that a fiduciary has negotiated the instrument in payment of or as security for his own debt or in any transaction for his own benefit or otherwise in breach of duty.

(3) The purchaser has notice that an instrument is overdue if he has reason to know

    (a) that any part of the principal amount is overdue or that there is an uncured default in payment of another instrument of the same series; or

(b) that acceleration of the instrument has been made; or

(c) that he is taking a demand instrument after demand has been made or more than a reasonable length of time after its issue. A reasonable time for a check drawn and payable within the states and territories of the United States and the District of Columbia is presumed to be thirty days.

(4) Knowledge of the following facts does not of itself give the purchaser notice of a defense or claim

(a) that the instrument is antedated or postdated;

(b) that it was issued or negotiated in return for an executory promise or accompanied by a separate agreement, unless the purchaser has notice that a defense or claim has arisen from the terms thereof;

(c) that any party has signed for accommodation;

(d) that an incomplete instrument has been completed, unless the purchaser has notice of any improper completion;

(e) that any person negotiating the instrument is or was a fiduciary;

(f) that there has been default in payment of interest on the instrument or in payment of any other instrument, except one of the same series.

(5) The filing or recording of a document does not of itself constitute notice within the provisions of this Article to a person who would otherwise be a holder in due course.

(6) To be effective notice must be received at such time and in such manner as to give a reasonable opportunity to act on it.

Section 3—305. Rights of a Holder in Due Course.

To the extent that a holder is a holder in due course he takes the instrument free from

(1) all claims to it on the part of any person; and

(2) all defenses of any party to the instrument with whom the holder has not dealt except

(a) infancy, to the extent that it is a defense to a simple contract; and

(b) such other incapacity, or duress, or illegality of the transaction, as renders the obligation of the party a nullity; and

(c) such misrepresentation as has induced the party to sign the instrument with neither knowledge nor reasonable opportunity to obtain knowledge of its character or its essential terms; and

(d) discharge in insolvency proceedings; and

(e) any other discharge of which the holder has notice when he takes the instrument.

Section 3—306. Rights of One Not Holder in Due Course.

Unless he has the rights of a holder in due course, any person takes the instrument subject to

(a) all valid claims to it on the part of any person; and

(b) all defenses of any party which would be available in an action on a simple contract; and

(c) the defenses of want or failure of consideration, nonperformance of any condition precedent, non-delivery, or delivery for a special purpose (Section 3—408); and

(d) the defense that he or a person through whom he holds the instrument acquired it by theft, or that payment or satisfaction to such holder would be inconsistent with the terms of a restrictive indorsement. The claim of any third person to the instrument is not otherwise available as a defense to any party liable thereon unless the third person himself defends the action for such party.

Section 3—307. Burden of Establishing Signatures, Defenses and Due Course.

(1) Unless specifically denied in the pleadings each signature on an instrument is admitted. When the effectiveness of a signature is put in issue

(a) the burden of establishing it is on the party claiming under the signature; but

(b) the signature is presumed to be genuine or authorized except where the action is to enforce the obligation of a purported signer who has died or become incompetent before proof is required.

(2) When signatures are admitted or established, production of the instrument entitles a holder to recover on it unless the defendant establishes a defense.

(3) After it is shown that a defense exists a person claiming the rights of a holder in due course has the burden of establishing that he or some person under whom he claims is in all respects a holder in due course.

PART 4

LIABILITY OF PARTIES

Section 3—401. Signature.

(1) No person is liable on an instrument unless his signature appears thereon.

(2) A signature is made by use of any name, including any trade or assumed name, upon an instrument, or by any word or mark used in lieu of a written signature.

Section 3—402. Signature in Ambiguous Capacity.

Unless the instrument clearly indicates that a signature is made in some other capacity, it is an indorsement.

Section 3—403. Signature by Authorized Representative.

(1) A signature may be made by an agent or other representative, and his authority to make it may be established as in other cases of representation. No particular form of appointment is necessary to establish such authority.

(2) An authorized representative who signs his own name to an instrument

(a) is personally obligated if the instrument neither names the person represented nor shows that the representative signed in a representative capacity;

(b) except as otherwise established between the immediate parties, is personally obligated if the instrument names the person represented but does not show that the representative signed in a representative capacity, or if the instrument does not name the person represented but does show that the representative signed in a representative capacity.

(3) Except as otherwise established, the name of an organization preceded or followed by the name and office of an authorized individual is a signature made in a representative capacity.

Section 3—404. Unauthorized Signatures.

(1) Any unauthorized signature is wholly inoperative as that of the person whose name is signed unless he ratifies it or is precluded from denying it; but it operates as the signature of the unauthorized signer in favor of any person who in good faith pays the instrument or takes it for value.

(2) Any unauthorized signature may be ratified for all purposes of this Article. Such ratification does not of itself affect any rights of the person ratifying against the actual signer.

Section 3—405. Impostors; Signature in Name of Payee.

(1) An indorsement by any person in the name of a named payee is effective if

(a) an impostor by use of the mails or otherwise has induced the maker or drawer to issue the instrument to him or his confederate in the name of the payee; or

(b) a person signing as or on behalf of a maker or drawer intends the payee to have no interest in the instrument; or

(c) an agent or employee of the maker or drawer has supplied him with the name of the payee intending the latter to have no such interest.

(2) Nothing in this section shall affect the criminal or civil liability of the person so indorsing.

Section 3—406. Negligence Contributing to Alteration or Unauthorized Signature.

Any person who by his negligence substantially contributes to a material alteration of the instrument or to the making of an unauthorized signature is precluded from asserting the alteration or lack of authority against a holder in due course or against a drawee or other payor who pays the instrument in good faith and in accordance with the reasonable commercial standards of the drawee's or payor's business.

Section 3—407. Alteration.

(1) Any alteration of an instrument is material which changes the contract of any party thereto in any respect, including any such change in

(a) the number or relations of the parties; or

(b) an incomplete instrument, by completing it otherwise than as authorized; or

(c) the writing as signed, by adding to it or by removing any part of it.

(2) As against any person other than a subsequent holder in due course

(a) alteration by the holder which is both fraudulent and material discharges any party whose contract is thereby changed unless that party assents or is pre-

cluded from asserting the defense;

(b) no other alteration discharges any party and the instrument may be enforced according to its original tenor, or as to incomplete instruments according to the authority given.

(3) A subsequent holder in due course may in all cases enforce the instrument according to its original tenor, and when an incomplete instrument has been completed, he may enforce it as completed.

Section 3—408. Consideration.

Want or failure of consideration is a defense as against any person not having the rights of a holder in due course (Section 3—305), except that no consideration is necessary for an instrument or obligation thereon given in payment of or as security for an antecedent obligation of any kind. Nothing in this section shall be taken to displace any statute outside this Act under which a promise is enforceable notwithstanding lack or failure of consideration. Partial failure of consideration is a defense pro tanto whether or not the failure is in an ascertained or liquidated amount.

Section 3—409. Draft Not an Assignment.

(1) A check or other draft does not of itself operate as an assignment of any funds in the hands of the drawee available for its payment, and the drawee is not liable on the instrument until he accepts it.

(2) Nothing in this section shall affect any liability in contract, tort or otherwise arising from any letter of credit or other obligation or representation which is not an acceptance.

Section 3—410. Definition and Operation of Acceptance.

(1) Acceptance is the drawee's signed engagement to honor the draft as presented. It must be written on the draft and may consist of his signature alone. It becomes operative when completed by delivery or notification.

(2) A draft may be accepted although it has not been signed by the drawer or

is otherwise incomplete or is overdue or has been dishonored.

(3) Where the draft is payable at a fixed period after sight and the acceptor fails to date his acceptance, the holder may complete it by supplying a date in good faith.

Section 3—411. Certification of a Check.

(1) Certification of a check is acceptance. Where a holder procures certification the drawer and all prior indorsers are discharged.

(2) Unless otherwise agreed a bank has no obligation to certify a check.

(3) A bank may certify a check before returning it for lack of proper indorsement. If it does, so the drawer is discharged.

Section 3—412. Acceptance Varying Draft.

(1) Where the drawee's proffered acceptance in any manner varies the draft as presented, the holder may refuse the acceptance and treat the draft as dishonored in which case the drawee is entitled to have his acceptance cancelled.

(2) The terms of the draft are not varied by an acceptance to pay at any particular bank or place in the United States, unless the acceptance states that the draft is to be paid only at such bank or place.

(3) Where the holder assents to an acceptance varying the terms of the draft, each drawer and indorser who does not affirmatively assent is discharged.

Section 3—413. Contract of Maker, Drawer and Acceptor.

(1) The maker or acceptor engages that he will pay the instrument according to its tenor at the time of his engagement or as completed pursuant to Section 3—115 on incomplete instruments.

(2) The drawer engages that upon dishonor of the draft and any necessary notice of dishonor or protest he will pay the amount of the draft to the holder or to any indorser who takes it up. The drawer may disclaim this liability by drawing without recourse.

(3) By making, drawing or accepting the party admits as against all subsequent parties including the drawee the existence of the payee and his then capacity to indorse.

Section 3—414. Contract of Indorser; Order of Liability.

(1) Unless the indorsement otherwise specifies (as by such words as "without recourse") every indorser engages that upon dishonor and any necessary notice of dishonor and protest he will pay the instrument according to its tenor at the time of his indorsement to the holder or to any subsequent indorser who takes it up, even though the indorser who takes it up was not obligated to do so.

(2) Unless they otherwise agree, indorsers are liable to one another in the order in which they indorse, which is presumed to be the order in which their signatures appear on the instrument.

Section 3—415. Contract of Accommodation Party.

(1) An accommodation party is one who signs the instrument in any capacity for the purpose of lending his name to another party to it.

(2) When the instrument has been taken for value before it is due, the accommodation party is liable in the capacity in which he has signed even though the taker knows of the accommodation.

(3) As against a holder in due course and without notice of the accommodation, oral proof of the accommodation is not admissible to give the accommodation party the benefit of discharges dependent on his character as such. In other cases the accommodation character may be shown by oral proof.

(4) An indorsement which shows that it is not in the chain of title is notice of its accommodation character.

(5) An accommodation party is not liable to the party accommodated, and if he pays the instrument has a right of recourse on the instrument against such party.

Section 3—416. Contract of Guarantor.

(1) "Payment guaranteed" or equivalent words added to a signature mean that the signer engages that if the instrument is not paid when due he will pay it according to its tenor without resort by the holder to any other party.

(2) "Collection guaranteed" or equivalent words added to a signature mean that the signer engages that if the instrument is not paid when due he will pay it according to its tenor, but only after the holder has reduced his claim against the maker or acceptor to judgment and execution has been returned unsatisfied, or after the maker or acceptor has become insolvent or it is otherwise apparent that it is useless to proceed against him.

(3) Words of guaranty which do not otherwise specify guarantee payment.

(4) No words of guaranty added to the signature of a sole maker or acceptor affect his liability on the instrument. Such words added to the signature of one of two or more makers or acceptors create a presumption that the signature is for the accommodation of the others.

(5) When words of guaranty are used, presentment, notice of dishonor and protest are not necessary to charge the user.

(6) Any guaranty written on the instrument is enforcible notwithstanding any statute of frauds.

Section 3—417. Warranties on Presentment and Transfer.

(1) Any person who obtains payment or acceptance and any prior transferor warrants to a person who in good faith pays or accepts that

(a) he has a good title to the instrument or is authorized to obtain payment or acceptance on behalf of one who has a good title; and

(b) he has no knowledge that the signature of the maker or drawer is unauthorized, except that this warranty is not given by a holder in due course acting in good faith

(i) to a maker with respect to the maker's own signature; or

(ii) to a drawer with respect to the drawer's own signature, whether or not the drawer is also the drawee; or

(iii) to an acceptor of a draft if the holder in due course took the draft after the acceptance or obtained the acceptance without knowledge that the drawer's signature was unauthorized; and

(c) the instrument has not been materially altered, except that this warranty is not given by a holder in due course acting in good faith

(i) to the maker of a note; or

(ii) to the drawer of a draft whether or not the drawer is also the drawee; or

(iii) to the acceptor of a draft with respect to an alteration made prior to the acceptance if the holder in due course took the draft after the acceptance, even though the acceptance provided "payable as originally drawn" or equivalent terms; or

(iv) to the acceptor of a draft with respect to an alteration made after the acceptance.

(2) Any person who transfers an instrument and receives consideration warrants to his transferee and, if the transfer is by indorsement, to any subsequent holder who takes the instrument in good faith that

(a) he has a good title to the instrument or is authorized to obtain payment or acceptance on behalf of one who has a good title and the transfer is otherwise rightful; and

(b) all signatures are genuine or authorized; and

(c) the instrument has not been materially altered; and

(d) no defense of any party is good against him; and

(e) he has no knowledge of any insolvency proceeding instituted with respect to the maker or acceptor or the drawer of an unaccepted instrument.

(3) By transferring "without recourse" the transferor limits the obligation stated in subsection (2) (d) to a warranty that he has no knowledge of such a defense.

(4) A selling agent or broker who does not disclose the fact that he is acting only as such gives the warranties provided in this section, but if he makes such disclosure warrants only his good faith and authority.

Section 3—418. Finality of Payment or Acceptance.

Except for recovery of bank payments as provided in the Article on Bank Deposits and Collections (Article 4) and except for liability for breach of warranty on presentment under the preceding section, payment or acceptance of any instrument is final in favor of a holder in due course, or a person who has in good faith changed his position in reliance on the payment.

Section 3—419. Conversion of Instrument; Innocent Representative.

(1) An instrument is converted when
  (a) a drawee to whom it is delivered for acceptance refuses to return it on demand; or
  (b) any person to whom it is delivered for payment refuses on demand either to pay or to return it; or
  (c) it is paid on a forged indorsement.

(2) In an action against a drawee under subsection (1) the measure of the drawee's liability is the face amount of the instrument. In any other action under subsection (1) the measure of liability is presumed to be the face amount of the instrument.

(3) Subject to the provisions of this Act concerning restrictive indorsements a representative, including a depositary or collecting bank, who has in good faith and in accordance with the reasonable commercial standards applicable to the business of such representative dealt with an instrument or its proceeds on behalf of one who was not the true owner is not liable in conversion or otherwise to the true owner beyond the amount of any proceeds remaining in his hands.

(4) An intermediary bank or payor bank which is not a depositary bank is not liable in conversion solely by reason of the fact that proceeds of an item indorsed restrictively (Sections 3—205 and 3—206) are not paid or applied consistently with the restrictive indorsement of an indorser other than its immediate transferor.

PART 5

PRESENTMENT, NOTICE OF DISHONOR AND PROTEST

Section 3—501. When Presentment, Notice of Dishonor, and Protest Necessary or Permissible.

(1) Unless excused (Section 3—511) presentment is necessary to charge secondary parties as follows:
  (a) presentment for acceptance is necessary to charge the drawer and indorsers of a draft where the draft so provides, or is payable elsewhere than at the residence or place of business of the drawee, or its date of payment depends upon such presentment. The holder may at his option present for acceptance any other draft payable at a stated date;
  (b) presentment for payment is necessary to charge any indorser;
  (c) in the case of any drawer, the acceptor of a draft payable at a bank or the maker of a note payable at a bank, presentment for payment is necessary, but failure to make presentment discharges such drawer, acceptor or maker only as stated in Section 3—502(1)(b).

(2) Unless excused (Section 3—511)

(a) notice of any dishonor is necessary to charge any indorser;

(b) in the case of any drawer, the acceptor of a draft payable at a bank or the maker of a note payable at a bank, notice of any dishonor is necessary, but failure to give such notice discharges such drawer, acceptor or maker only as stated in Section 3—502(1)(b).

(3) Unless excused (Section 3—511), protest of any dishonor is necessary to charge the drawer and indorsers of any draft which on its face appears to be drawn or payable outside of the states and territories of the United States and the District of Columbia. The holder may at his option make protest of any dishonor of any other instrument and in the case of a foreign draft may on insolvency of the acceptor before maturity make protest for better security.

(4) Notwithstanding any provision of this section, neither presentment nor notice of dishonor nor protest is necessary to charge an indorser who has indorsed an instrument after maturity.

Section 3—502.   Unexcused Delay; Discharge.

(1) Where without excuse any necessary presentment or notice of dishonor is delayed beyond the time when it is due

(a) any indorser is discharged; and

(b) any drawer or the acceptor of a draft payable at a bank or the maker of a note payable at a bank who, because the drawee or payor bank becomes insolvent during the delay, is deprived of funds maintained with the drawee or payor bank to cover the instrument may discharge his liability by written assignment to the holder of his rights against the drawee or payor bank in respect of such funds, but such drawer, acceptor or maker is not otherwise discharged.

(2) Where without excuse a necessary protest is delayed beyond the time when it is due, any drawer or indorser is discharged.

Section 3—503.   Time of Presentment.

(1) Unless a different time is expressed in the instrument, the time for any presentment is determined as follows:

(a) where an instrument is payable at or a fixed period after a stated date, any presentment for acceptance must be made on or before the date it is payable;

(b) where an instrument is payable after sight, it must either be presented for acceptance or negotiated within a reasonable time after date or issue whichever is later;

(c) where an instrument shows the date on which it is payable, presentment for payment is due on that date;

(d) where an instrument is accelerated, presentment for payment is due within a reasonable time after the acceleration;

(e) with respect to the liability of any secondary party presentment for acceptance or payment of any other instrument is due within a reasonable time after such party becomes liable thereon.

(2) A reasonable time for presentment is determined by the nature of the instrument, any usage of banking or trade and the facts of the particular case. In the case of an uncertified check which is drawn and payable within the United States and which is not a draft drawn by a bank the following are presumed to be reasonable periods within which to present for payment or to initiate bank collection:

(a) with respect to the liability of the drawer, thirty days after date or issue whichever is later; and

(b) with respect to the liability of an indorser, seven days after his indorsement.

(3) Where any presentment is due on a day which is not a full business day for either the person making presentment or the party to pay or accept,

presentment is due on the next following day which is a full business day for
both parties.

(4) Presentment to be sufficient must
be made at a reasonable hour, and if at
a bank during its banking day.

Section 3—504. How Presentment Made.

(1) Presentment is a demand for acceptance or payment made upon the
maker, acceptor, drawee or other payor
by or on behalf of the holder.

(2) Presentment may be made

    (a) by mail, in which event the time
of presentment is determined
by the time of receipt of the
mail; or

    (b) through a clearing house; or

    (c) at the place of acceptance of
payment specified in the instrument or if there be none at the
place of business or residence
of the party to accept or pay.
If neither the party to accept
or pay nor anyone authorized
to act for him is present or ac-
cessible at such place, presentment is excused.

(3) It may be made

    (a) to any one of two or more
makers, acceptors, drawees or
other payors; or

    (b) to any person who has authority
to make or refuse the acceptance or payment.

(4) A draft accepted or a note made
payable at a bank in the United States
must be presented at such bank.

(5) In the cases described in Section
4—210 presentment may be made in
the manner and with the result stated
in that section.

Section 3—505. Rights of Party to Whom Presentment Is Made.

(1) The party to whom presentment
is made may without dishonor require

    (a) exhibition of the instrument;
and

    (b) reasonable identification of the
person making presentment and
evidence of his authority to
make it if made for another; and

    (c) that the instrument be produced
for acceptance or payment at a
place specified in it, or if there
be none at any place reasonable
in the circumstances; and

    (d) a signed receipt on the instru-
ment for any partial or full payment and its surrender upon
full payment.

(2) Failure to comply with any such
requirement invalidates the presentment,
but the person presenting has a reasonable time in which to comply and the
time for acceptance or payment runs
from the time of compliance.

Section 3—506. Time Allowed for Acceptance or Payment.

(1) Acceptance may be deferred without dishonor until the close of the next
business day following presentment. The
holder may also in a good faith effort
to obtain acceptance and without either
dishonor of the instrument or discharge
of secondary parties allow postponement
of acceptance for an additional business
day.

(2) Except as a longer time is allowed
in the case of documentary drafts drawn
under a letter of credit, and unless an
earlier time is agreed to by the party
to pay, payment of an instrument may
be deferred without dishonor pending
reasonable examination to determine
whether it is properly payable, but payment must be made in any event before
the close of business on the day of
presentment.

Section 3—507. Dishonor; Holder's Right of Recourse; Term Allowing Re-Presentment.

(1) An instrument is dishonored when

    (a) a necessary or optional present-
ment is duly made and due acceptance or payment is refused
or cannot be obtained within
the prescribed time or in case
of bank collections the instrument is seasonably returned by
the midnight deadline (Section
4—301); or

    (b) presentment is excused and the
instrument is not duly accepted
or paid.

(2) Subject to any necessary notice of dishonor and protest, the holder has upon dishonor an immediate right of recourse against the drawers and indorsers.

(3) Return of an instrument for lack of proper indorsement is not dishonor.

(4) A term in a draft or an indorsement thereof allowing a stated time for re-presentment in the event of any dishonor of the draft by nonacceptance if a time draft or by nonpayment if a sight draft gives the holder as against any secondary party bound by the term an option to waive the dishonor without affecting the liability of the secondary party, and he may present again up to the end of the stated time.

Section 3—508. Notice of Dishonor.

(1) Notice of dishonor may be given to any person who may be liable on the instrument by or on behalf of the holder or any party who has himself received notice, or any other party who can be compelled to pay the instrument. In addition an agent or bank in whose hands the instrument is dishonored may give notice to his principal or customer or to another agent or bank from which the instrument was received.

(2) Any necessary notice must be given by a bank before its midnight deadline and by any other person before midnight of the third business day after dishonor or receipt of notice of dishonor.

(3) Notice may be given in any reasonable manner. It may be oral or written and in any terms which identify the instrument and state that it has been dishonored. A misdescription which does not mislead the party notified does not vitiate the notice. Sending the instrument bearing a stamp, ticket or writing stating that acceptance or payment has been refused or sending a notice of debit with respect to the instrument is sufficient.

(4) Written notice is given when sent although it is not received.

(5) Notice to one partner is notice to each although the firm has been dissolved.

(6) When any party is in insolvency proceedings instituted after the issue of the instrument, notice may be given either to the party or to the representative of his estate.

(7) When any party is dead or incompetent, notice may be sent to his last known address or given to his personal representative.

(8) Notice operates for the benefit of all parties who have rights on the instrument against the party notified.

Section 3—509. Protest; Noting for Protest.

(1) A protest is a certificate of dishonor made under the hand and seal of a United States consul or vice consul or a notary public or other person authorized to certify dishonor by the law of the place where dishonor occurs. It may be made upon information satisfactory to such person.

(2) The protest must identify the instrument and certify either that due presentment has been made or the reason why it is excused and that the instrument has been dishonored by nonacceptance or nonpayment.

(3) The protest may also certify that notice of dishonor has been given to all parties or to specified parties.

(4) Subject to subsection (5) any necessary protest is due by the time that notice of dishonor is due.

(5) If, before protest is due, an instrument has been noted for protest by the officer to make protest, the protest may be made at any time thereafter as of the date of the noting.

Section 3—510. Evidence of Dishonor and Notice of Dishonor.

The following are admissible as evidence and create a presumption of dishonor and of any notice of dishonor therein shown:

(a) a document regular in form as provided in the preceding section which purports to be a protest;

(b) the purported stamp or writing of the drawee, payor bank or presenting bank on the instrument or accompanying it stating that acceptance or payment has been refused for reasons consistent with dishonor;

(c) any book or record of the drawee, payor bank, or any collecting bank kept in the usual course of business which shows dishonor, even though there is no evidence of who made the entry.

Section 3—511. Waived or Excused Presentment, Protest or Notice of Dishonor or Delay Therein.

(1) Delay in presentment, protest or notice of dishonor is excused when the party is without notice that it is due or when the delay is caused by circumstances beyond his control and he exercises reasonable diligence after the cause of the delay ceases to operate.

(2) Presentment or notice or protest as the case may be is entirely excused when

(a) the party to be charged has waived it expressly or by implication either before or after it is due; or

(b) such party has himself dishonored the instrument or has countermanded payment or otherwise has no reason to expect or right to require that the instrument be accepted or paid; or

(c) by reasonable diligence the presentment or protest cannot be made or the notice given.

(3) Presentment is also entirely excused when

(a) the maker, acceptor or drawee of any instrument except a documentary draft is dead or in insolvency proceedings instituted after the issue of the instrument; or

(b) acceptance or payment is refused but not for want of proper presentment.

(4) Where a draft has been dishonored by nonacceptance, a later presentment for payment and any notice of dishonor and protest for nonpayment are excused unless in the meantime the instrument has been accepted.

(5) A waiver of protest is also a waiver of presentment and of notice of dishonor even though protest is not required.

(6) Where a waiver of presentment or notice or protest is embodied in the instrument itself, it is binding upon all parties; but where it is written above the signature of an indorser it binds him only.

PART 6

DISCHARGE

Section 3—601. Discharge of Parties.

(1) The extent of the discharge of any party from liability on an instrument is governed by the sections on

(a) payment or satisfaction (Section 3—603); or

(b) tender of payment (Section 3—604); or

(c) cancellation or renunciation (Section 3—605); or

(d) impairment or right of recourse or of collateral (Section 3—606); or

(e) reacquisition of the instrument by a prior party (Section 3—208); or

(f) fraudulent and material alteration (Section 3—407); or

(g) certification of a check (Section 3—411); or

(h) acceptance varying a draft (Section 3—412); or

(i) unexcused delay in presentment or notice of dishonor or protest (Section 3—502).

(2) Any party is also discharged from his liability on an instrument to another party by any other act or agreement with such party which would discharge his simple contract for the payment of money.

(3) The liability of all parties is discharged when any party who has himself no right of action or recourse on the instrument

(a) reacquires the instrument in his own right; or

(b) is discharged under any provision of this Article, except as otherwise provided with respect to discharge for impairment of recourse or of collateral (Section 3—606).

Section 3—602. Effect of Discharge Against Holder in Due Course.

No discharge of any party provided by this Article is effective against a subsequent holder in due course unless he has notice thereof when he takes the instrument.

Section 3—603. Payment or Satisfaction.

(1) The liability of any party is discharged to the extent of his payment or satisfaction to the holder even though it is made with knowledge of a claim of another person to the instrument unless prior to such payment or satisfaction the person making the claim either supplies indemnity deemed adequate by the party seeking the discharge or enjoins payment or satisfaction by order of a court of competent jurisdiction in an action in which the adverse claimant and the holder are parties. This subsection does not, however, result in the discharge of the liability

    (a) of a party who in bad faith pays or satisfies a holder who acquired the instrument by theft or who (unless having the rights of a holder in due course) holds through one who so acquired it; or

    (b) of a party (other than an intermediary bank or a payor bank which is not a depositary bank) who pays or satisfies the holder of an instrument which has been restrictively indorsed in a manner not consistent with the terms of such restrictive indorsement.

(2) Payment or satisfaction may be made with the consent of the holder by any person including a stranger to the instrument. Surrender of the instrument to such a person gives him the rights of a transferee (Section 3—201).

Section 3—604. Tender of Payment.

(1) Any party making tender of full payment to a holder when or after it is due is discharged to the extent of all subsequent liability for interest, costs and attorney's fees.

(2) The holder's refusal of such tender wholly discharges any party who has a right of recourse against the party making the tender.

(3) Where the maker or acceptor of an instrument payable otherwise than on demand is able and ready to pay at every place of payment specified in the instrument when it is due, it is equivalent to tender.

Section 3—605. Cancellation and Renunciation.

(1) The holder of an instrument may even without consideration discharge any party

    (a) in any manner apparent on the face of the instrument or the indorsement, as by intentionally cancelling the instrument or the party's signature by destruction or mutilation, or by striking out the party's signature; or

    (b) by renouncing his rights by a writing signed and delivered or by surrender of the instrument to the party to be discharged.

(2) Neither cancellation nor renunciation without surrender of the instrument affects the title thereto.

Section 3—606. Impairment of Recourse or of Collateral.

(1) The holder discharges any party to the instrument to the extent that without such party's consent the holder

    (a) without express reservation of rights releases or agrees not to sue any person against whom the party has to the knowledge of the holder a right of recourse or agrees to suspend the right to enforce against such person the instrument or collateral or otherwise discharges such person, except that failure or delay in effecting any required presentment, protest or notice of dishonor with respect to any such person does not discharge any party as to whom presentment, protest or notice of dishonor is effective or unnecessary; or

(b) unjustifiably impairs any collateral for the instrument given by or on behalf of the party or any person against whom he has a right of recourse.

(2) By express reservation of rights against a party with a right of recourse the holder preserves

(a) all his rights against such party as of the time when the instrument was originally due; and

(b) the right of the party to pay the instrument as of that time; and

(c) all rights of such party to recourse against others.

PART 7

ADVICE OF INTERNATIONAL SIGHT DRAFT

Section 3—701. Letter of Advice of International Sight Draft.

(1) A "letter of advice" is a drawer's communication to the drawee that a described draft has been drawn.

(2) Unless otherwise agreed, when a bank receives from another bank a letter of advice of an international sight draft, the drawee bank may immediately debit the drawer's account and stop the running of interest pro tanto. Such a debit and any resulting credit to any account covering outstanding drafts leaves in the drawer full power to stop payment or otherwise dispose of the amount and creates no trust or interest in favor of the holder.

(3) Unless otherwise agreed and except where a draft is drawn under a credit issued by the drawee, the drawee of an international sight draft owes the drawer no duty to pay an unadvised draft but if it does so and the draft is genuine, may appropriately debit the drawer's account.

PART 8

MISCELLANEOUS

Section 3—801. Drafts in a Set.

(1) Where a draft is drawn in a set of parts, each of which is numbered and expressed to be an order only if no other part has been honored, the whole of the parts constitutes one draft, but a taker of any part may become a holder in due course of the draft.

(2) Any person who negotiates, indorses or accepts a single part of a draft drawn in a set thereby becomes liable to any holder in due course of that part as if it were the whole set, but as between different holders in due course to whom different parts have been negotiated the holder whose title first accrues has all rights to the draft and its proceeds.

(3) As against the drawee the first presented part of a draft drawn in a set is the part entitled to payment, or if a time draft to acceptance and payment. Acceptance of any subsequently presented part renders the drawee liable thereon under subsection (2). With respect both to a holder and to the drawer payment of a subsequently presented part of a draft payable at sight has the same effect as payment of a check notwithstanding an effective stop order (Section 4—407).

(4) Except as otherwise provided in this section, where any part of a draft in a set is discharged by payment or otherwise the whole draft is discharged.

Section 3—802. Effect of Instrument on Obligation for Which It Is Given.

(1) Unless otherwise agreed, where an instrument is taken for an underlying obligation

(a) the obligation is pro tanto discharged if a bank is drawer, maker or acceptor of the instrument and there is no recourse on the instrument against the underlying obligor; and

(b) in any other case the obligation is suspended pro tanto until the instrument is due or if it is payable on demand until its presentment. If the instrument is dishonored, action may be maintained on either the instrument or the obligation; discharge of the underlying obligor on the instrument also discharges him on the obligation.

(2) The taking in good faith of a check which is not postdated does not of itself so extend the time on the original obligation as to discharge a surety.

Section 3—803. Notice to Third Party.

Where a defendant is sued for breach of an obligation for which a third person is answerable over under this Article, he may give the third person written notice of the litigation, and the person notified may then give similar notice to any other person who is answerable over to him under this Article. If the notice states that the person notified may come in and defend and that if the person notified does not do so he will in any action against him by the person giving the notice be bound by any determination of fact common to the two litigations, then unless after seasonable receipt of the notice the person notified does come in and defend he is so bound.

Section 3—804. Lost, Destroyed or Stolen Instruments.

The owner of an instrument which is lost, whether by destruction, theft or otherwise, may maintain an action in his own name and recover from any party liable thereon upon due proof of his ownership, the facts which prevent his production of the instrument and its terms. The court may require security indemnifying the defendant against loss by reason of further claims on the instrument.

Section 3—805. Instruments Not Payable to Order or to Bearer.

This Article applies to any instrument whose terms do not preclude transfer and which is otherwise negotiable within this Article but which is not payable to order or to bearer, except that there can be no holder in due course of such an instrument.

ARTICLE 4

BANK DEPOSITS AND COLLECTIONS

PART 1

GENERAL PROVISIONS AND DEFINITIONS

Section 4—101. Short Title.

This Article shall be known and may be cited as Uniform Commercial Code—Bank Deposits and Collections.

Section 4—102. Applicability.

(1) To the extent that items within this Article are also within the scope of Articles 3 and 8, they are subject to the provisions of those Articles. In the event of conflict the provisions of this Article govern those of Article 3, but the provisions of Article 8 govern those of this Article.

(2) The liability of a bank for action or non-action with respect to any item handled by it for purposes of presentment, payment or collection is governed by the law of the place where the bank is located. In the case of action or non-action by or at a branch or separate office of a bank, its liability is governed by the law of the place where the branch or separate office is located.

Section 4—103. Variation by Agreement; Measure of Damages; Certain Action Constituting Ordinary Care.

(1) The effect of the provisions of this Article may be varied by agreement except that no agreement can disclaim a bank's responsibility for its own lack of

good faith or failure to exercise ordinary care or can limit the measure of damages for such lack or failure; but the parties may by agreement determine the standards by which such responsibility is to be measured if such standards are not manifestly unreasonable.

(2) Federal Reserve regulations and operating letters, clearing house rules, and the like, have the effect of agreements under subsection (1), whether or not specifically assented to by all parties interested in items handled.

(3) Action or non-action approved by this Article or pursuant to Federal Reserve regulations or operating letters constitutes the exercise of ordinary care and, in the absence of special instructions, action or non-action consistent with clearing house rules and the like or with a general banking usage not disapproved by this Article, prima facie constitutes the exercise of ordinary care.

(4) The specification or approval of certain procedures by this Article does not constitute disapproval of other procedures which may be reasonable under the circumstances.

(5) The measure of damages for failure to exercise ordinary care in handling an item is the amount of the item reduced by an amount which could not have been realized by the use of ordinary care, and where there is bad faith it includes other damages, if any, suffered by the party as a proximate consequence.

Section 4—104. Definitions and Index of Definitions.

(1) In this Article unless the context otherwise requires

(a) "Account" means any account with a bank and includes a checking, time, interest or savings account;

(b) "Afternoon" means the period of a day between noon and midnight;

(c) "Banking day" means that part of any day on which a bank is open to the public for carrying on substantially all of its banking functions;

(d) "Clearing house" means any association of banks or other payors regularly clearing items;

(e) "Customer" means any person having an account with a bank or for whom a bank has agreed to collect items and includes a bank carrying an account with another bank;

(f) "Documentary draft" means any negotiable or non-negotiable draft with accompanying documents, securities or other papers to be delivered against honor of the draft;

(g) "Item" means any instrument for the payment of money even though it is not negotiable but does not include money;

(h) "Midnight deadline" with respect to a bank is midnight on its next banking day following the banking day on which it receives the relevant item or notice or from which the time for taking action commences to run, whichever is later;

(i) "Properly payable" includes the availability of funds for payment at the time of decision to pay or dishonor;

(j) "Settle" means to pay in cash, by clearing house settlement, in a charge or credit or by remittance, or otherwise as instructed. A settlement may be either provisional or final;

(k) "Suspends payments" with respect to a bank means that it has been closed by order of the supervisory authorities, that a public officer has been appointed to take it over or that it ceases or refuses to make payments in the ordinary course of business.

(2) Other definitions applying to this Article and the sections in which they appear are:

"Collecting bank" Section 4—105.
"Depositary bank" Section 4—105.
"Intermediary bank" Section 4—105.
"Payor bank" Section 4—105.

"Presenting bank" Section 4—105.
"Remitting bank" Section 4—105.
(3) The following definitions in other Articles apply to this Article:
"Acceptance" Section 3—410.
"Certificate of deposit" Section 3—104.
"Certification" Section 3—411.
"Check" Section 3—104.
"Draft" Section 3—104.
"Holder in due course" Section 3—302.
"Notice of dishonor" Section 3—508.
"Presentment" Section 3—504.
"Protest" Section 3—509.
"Secondary party" Section 3—102.
(4) In addition Article 1 contains general definitions and principles of construction and interpretation applicable throughout this Article.

Section 4—105. "Depositary Bank"; "Intermediary Bank"; "Collecting Bank"; "Payor Bank"; "Presenting Bank"; "Remitting Bank".

In this Article unless the context otherwise requires:
  (a) "Depositary bank" means the first bank to which an item is transferred for collection even though it is also the payor bank;
  (b) "Payor bank" means a bank by which an item is payable as drawn or accepted;
  (c) "Intermediary bank" means any bank to which an item is transferred in course of collection except the depositary or payor bank;
  (d) "Collecting bank" means any bank handling the item for collection except the payor bank;
  (e) "Presenting bank" means any bank presenting an item except a payor bank;
  (f) "Remitting bank" means any payor or intermediary bank remitting for an item.

Section 4—106. Separate Office of a Bank.

A branch or separate office of a bank [maintaining its own deposit ledgers] is a separate bank for the purpose of computing the time within which and determining the place at or to which action may be taken or notices or orders shall be given under this Article and under Article 3.
   Note: *The words in brackets are optional.*

Section 4—107. Time of Receipt of Items.

(1) For the purpose of allowing time to process items, prove balances and make the necessary entries on its books to determine its position for the day, a bank may fix an afternoon hour of two P.M. or later as a cut-off hour for the handling of money and items and the making of entries on its books.
(2) Any item or deposit of money received on any day after a cut-off hour so fixed or after the close of the banking day may be treated as being received at the opening of the next banking day.

Section 4—108. Delays.

(1) Unless otherwise instructed, a collecting bank in a good faith effort to secure payment may, in the case of specific items and with or without the approval of any person involved, waive, modify or extend time limits imposed or permitted by this Act for a period not in excess of an additional banking day without discharge of secondary parties and without liability to its transferor or any prior party.
(2) Delay by a collecting bank or payor bank beyond time limits prescribed or permitted by this Act or by instructions is excused if caused by interruption of communication facilities, suspension of payments by another bank, war, emergency conditions or other circumstances beyond the control of the bank provided it exercises such diligence as the circumstances require.

Section 4—109. Process of Posting.

The "process of posting" means the usual procedure followed by a payor bank in determining to pay an item and in recording the payment including one or more of the following or other steps as determined by the bank:

(a) verification of any signature;
(b) ascertaining that sufficient funds are available;
(c) affixing a "paid" or other stamp;

(d) entering a charge or entry to a customer's account;
(e) correcting or reversing an entry or erroneous action with respect to the item.

PART 2

COLLECTION OF ITEMS: DEPOSITARY AND COLLECTING BANKS

Section 4—201. Presumption and Duration of Agency Status of Collecting Banks and Provisional Status of Credits; Applicability of Article; Item Indorsed "Pay Any Bank".

(1) Unless a contrary intent clearly appears and prior to the time that a settlement given by a collecting bank for an item is or becomes final (subsection (3) of Section 4—211 and Sections 4—212 and 4—213) the bank is an agent or sub-agent of the owner of the item and any settlement given for the item is provisional. This provision applies regardless of the form of indorsement or lack of indorsement and even though credit given for the item is subject to immediate withdrawal as of right or is in fact withdrawn; but the continuance of ownership of an item by its owner and any rights of the owner to proceeds of the item are subject to rights of a collecting bank such as those resulting from outstanding advances on the item and valid rights of setoff. When an item is handled by banks for purposes of presentment, payment and collection, the relevant provisions of this Article apply even though action of parties clearly establishes that a particular bank has purchased the item and is the owner of it.

(2) After an item has been indorsed with the words "pay any bank" or the like, only a bank may acquire the rights of a holder

    (a) until the item has been returned to the customer initiating collection; or
    (b) until the item has been specially indorsed by a bank to a person who is not a bank.

Section 4—202. Responsibility for Collection; When Action Seasonable.

(1) A collecting bank must use ordinary care in

    (a) presenting an item or sending it for presentment; and

    (b) sending notice of dishonor or non-payment or returning an item other than a documentary draft to the bank's transferror [or directly to the depositary bank under subsection (2) of Section 4—212] (*see note to Section 4—212*) after learning that the item has not been paid or accepted, as the case may be; and

    (c) settling for an item when the bank receives final settlement; and

    (d) making or providing for any necessary protest; and

    (e) notifying its transferor of any loss or delay in transit within a reasonable time after discovery thereof.

(2) A collecting bank taking proper action before its midnight deadline following receipt of an item, notice or payment acts seasonably; taking proper action within a reasonably longer time may be seasonable but the bank has the burden of so establishing.

(3) Subject to subsection (1) (a), a bank is not liable for the insolvency, neglect, misconduct, mistake or default of another bank or person or for loss or destruction of an item in transit or in the possession of others.

Section 4—203. Effect of Instructions.

Subject to the provisions of Article 3 concerning conversion of instruments (Section 3—419) and the provisions of both Article 3 and this Article concerning restrictive indorsements, only a collecting bank's transferor can give instructions which affect the bank or constitute notice to it and a collecting bank is not liable to prior parties for any action taken pursuant to such instructions or in accordance with any agreement with its transferor.

Section 4—204. Methods of Sending and Presenting; Sending Direct to Payor Bank.

(1) A collecting bank must send items by reasonably prompt method taking into consideration any relevant instructions, the nature of the item, the number of such items on hand, and the cost of collection involved and the method generally used by it or others to present such items.

(2) A collecting bank may send

(a) any item direct to the payor bank;

(b) any item to any non-bank payor if authorized by its transferor; and

(c) any item other than documentary drafts to any non-bank payor, if authorized by Federal Reserve regulation or operating letter, clearing house rule or the like.

(3) Presentment may be made by a presenting bank at a place where the payor bank has requested that presentment be made.

Section 4—205. Supplying Missing Indorsement; No Notice from Prior Indorsement.

(1) A depositary bank which has taken an item for collection may supply any indorsement of the customer which is necessary to title unless the item contains the words "payee's indorsement required" or the like. In the absence of such a requirement a statement placed on the item by the depositary bank to the effect that the item was deposited by a customer or credited to his account is effective as the customer's indorsement.

(2) An intermediary bank, or payor bank which is not a depositary bank, is neither given notice nor otherwise affected by a restrictive indorsement of any person except the bank's immediate transferor.

Section 4—206. Transfer Between Banks.

Any agreed method which identifies the transferor bank is sufficient for the item's further transfer to another bank.

Section 4—207. Warranties of Customer and Collecting Bank on Transfer or Presentment of Items; Time for Claims.

(1) Each customer or collecting bank who obtains payment or acceptance of an item and each prior customer and collecting bank warrants to the payor bank or other payor who in good faith pays or accepts the item that

(a) he has a good title to the item or is authorized to obtain payment or acceptance on behalf of one who has a good title; and

(b) he has no knowledge that the signature of the maker or drawer is unauthorized, except that this warranty is not given by any customer or collecting bank that is a holder in due course and acts in good faith

(i) to a maker with respect to the maker's own signature; or

(ii) to a drawer with respect to the drawer's own signature, whether or not the drawer is also the drawee; or

(iii) to an acceptor of an item if the holder in due course took the item after the acceptance or obtained the acceptance without knowledge that the drawer's signature was unauthorized; and

(c) the item has not been materially altered, except that this warranty is not given by any customer or collecting bank that is a holder in due course and acts in good faith

(i) to the maker of a note; or

(ii) to the drawer of a draft whether or not the drawer is also the drawee; or

(iii) to the acceptor of an item with respect to an alteration made prior to the acceptance if the holder in due course took the item after the acceptance, even though the acceptance provided "payable as originally drawn" or equivalent terms; or

(iv) to the acceptor of an item with respect to an alteration made after the acceptance.

(2) Each customer and collecting bank who transfers an item and receives a settlement or other consideration for it warrants to his transferee and to any subsequent collecting bank who takes the item in good faith that

(a) he has a good title to the item or is authorized to obtain payment or acceptance on behalf of one who has a good title and the transfer is otherwise rightful; and

(b) all signatures are genuine or authorized; and

(c) the item has not been materially altered; and

(d) no defense of any party is good against him; and

(e) he has no knowledge of any insolvency proceeding instituted with respect to the maker or acceptor or the drawer of an unaccepted item.

In addition each customer and collecting bank so transferring an item and receiving a settlement or other consideration engages that upon dishonor and any necessary notice of dishonor and protest he will take up the item.

(3) The warranties and the engagement to honor set forth in the two preceding subsections arise notwithstanding the absence of indorsement or words of guaranty or warranty in the transfer or presentment and a collecting bank remains liable for their breach despite remittance to its transferor. Damages for breach of such warranties or engagement to honor shall not exceed the consideration received by the customer or collecting bank responsible plus finance charges and expenses related to the item, if any.

(4) Unless a claim for breach of warranty under this section is made within a reasonable time after the person claiming learns of the breach, the person liable is discharged to the extent of any loss caused by the delay in making claim.

Section 4—208. Security Interest of Collecting Bank in Items, Accompanying Documents and Proceeds.

(1) A bank has a security interest in an item and any accompanying documents or the proceeds of either

(a) in case of an item deposited in an account to the extent to which credit given for the item has been withdrawn or applied;

(b) in case of an item for which it has given credit available for withdrawal as of right, to the extent of the credit given whether or not the credit is drawn upon and whether or not there is a right of charge-back; or

(c) if it makes an advance on or against the item.

(2) When credit which has been given for several items received at one time or pursuant to a single agreement is withdrawn or applied in part, the security interest remains upon all the items, any accompanying documents or the proceeds of either. For the purpose of this section, credits first given are first withdrawn.

(3) Receipt by a collecting bank of a final settlement for an item is a realization on its security interest in the item, accompanying documents and proceeds. To the extent and so long as the bank does not receive final settlement for the item or give up possession of the item

or accompanying documents for purposes other than collection, the security interest continues and is subject to the provisions of Article 9 except that

    (a) no security agreement is necessary to make the security interest enforceable (subsection (1) (b) of Section 9—203); and

    (b) no filing is required to perfect the security interest; and

    (c) the security interest has priority over conflicting perfected security interests in the item, accompanying documents or proceeds.

Section 4—209. When Bank Gives Value for Purposes of Holder in Due Course.

For purposes of determining its status as a holder in due course, the bank has given value to the extent that it has a security interest in an item provided that the bank otherwise complies with the requirements of Section 3—302 on what constitutes a holder in due course.

Section 4—210. Presentment by Notice of Item Not Payable by, Through or at a Bank; Liability of Secondary Parties.

(1) Unless otherwise instructed, a collecting bank may present an item not payable by, through or at a bank by sending to the party to accept or pay a written notice that the bank holds the item for acceptance or payment. The notice must be sent in time to be received on or before the day when presentment is due and the bank must meet any requirement of the party to accept or pay under Section 3—505 by the close of the bank's next banking day after it knows of the requirement.

(2) Where presentment is made by notice and neither honor nor request for compliance with a requirement under Section 3—505 is received by the close of business on the day after maturity or in the case of demand items by the close of business on the third banking day after notice was sent, the presenting bank may treat the item as dishonored and charge any secondary party by sending him notice of the facts.

Section 4—211. Media of Remittance; Provisional and Final Settlement in Remittance Cases.

(1) A collecting bank may take in settlement of an item

    (a) a check of the remitting bank or of another bank on any bank except the remitting bank; or

    (b) a cashier's check or similar primary obligation of a remitting bank which is a member of or clears through a member of the same clearing house or group as the collecting bank; or

    (c) appropriate authority to charge an account of the remitting bank or of another bank with the collecting bank; or

    (d) if the item is drawn upon or payable by a person other than a bank, a cashier's check, certified check or other bank check or obligation.

(2) If before its midnight deadline the collecting bank properly dishonors a remittance check or authorization to charge on itself or presents or forwards for collection a remittance instrument of or on another bank which is of a kind approved by subsection (1) or has not been authorized by it, the collecting bank is not liable to prior parties in the event of the dishonor of such check, instrument or authorization.

(3) A settlement for an item by means of a remittance instrument or authorization to charge is or becomes a final settlement as to both the person making and the person receiving the settlement

    (a) if the remittance instrument or authorization to charge is of a kind approved by subsection (1) or has not been authorized by the person receiving the settlement and in either case the person receiving the settlement acts seasonably before its midnight deadline in presenting, forwarding for collection or paying the instrument or authorization,—at the time the remittance instrument or authorization is finally paid by the payor by which it is payable;

(b) if the person receiving the settlement has authorized remittance by a non-bank check or obligation or by a cashier's check or similar primary obligation of or a check upon the payor or other remitting bank which is not of a kind approved by subsection (1) (b),—at the time of the receipt of such remittance check or obligation; or

(c) if in a case not covered by subparagraphs (a) or (b) the person receiving the settlement fails to seasonably present, forward for collection, pay or return a remittance instrument or authorization to it to charge before its midnight deadline,—at such midnight deadline.

Section 4—212.   Right of Charge-Back or Refund.

(1) If a collecting bank has made provisional settlement with its customer for an item and itself fails by reason of dishonor, suspension of payments by a bank or otherwise to receive a settlement for the item which is or becomes final, the bank may revoke the settlement given by it, charge back the amount of any credit given for the item to its customer's account or obtain refund from its customer whether or not it is able to return the items if by its midnight deadline or within a longer reasonable time after it learns the facts it returns the item or sends notification of the facts. These rights to revoke, charge-back and obtain refund terminate if and when a settlement for the item received by the bank is or becomes final (subsection (3) of Section 4—211 and subsections (2) and (3) of Section 4—213).

[(2) Within the time and manner prescribed by this section and Section 4—301, an intermediary or payor bank, as the case may be, may return an unpaid item directly to the depositary bank and may send for collection a draft on the depositary bank and obtain reimbursement. In such case, if the depositary bank has received provisional settlement for the item, it must reimburse the bank drawing the draft and any provisional credits for the item between banks shall become and remain final.]

Note: *Direct returns is recognized as an innovation that is not yet established bank practice, and therefore, Paragraph 2 has been bracketed. Some lawyers have doubts whether it should be included in legislation or left to development by agreement.*

(3) A depositary bank which is also the payor may charge-back the amount of an item to its customer's account or obtain refund in accordance with the section governing return of an item received by a payor bank for credit on its books (Section 4—301).

(4) The right to charge-back is not affected by

(a) prior use of the credit given for the item; or

(b) failure by any bank to exercise ordinary care with respect to the item, but any bank so failing remains liable.

(5) A failure to charge-back or claim refund does not affect other rights of the bank against the customer or any other party.

(6) If credit is given in dollars as the equivalent of the value of an item payable in a foreign currency, the dollar amount of any charge-back or refund shall be calculated on the basis of the buying sight rate for the foreign currency prevailing on the day when the person entitled to the charge-back or refund learns that it will not receive payment in ordinary course.

Section 4—213.   Final Payment of Item by Payor Bank; When Provisional Debits and Credits Become Final; When Certain Credits Become Available for Withdrawal.

(1) An item is finally paid by a payor bank when the bank has done any of the following, whichever happens first;

(a) paid the item in cash; or

(b) settled for the item without reserving a right to revoke the settlement and without having such right under statute, clearing house rule or agreement; or

(c) completed the process of posting the item to the indicated account of the drawer, maker or other person to be charged therewith; or

(d) made a provisional settlement for the item and failed to revoke the settlement in the time and manner permitted by statute, clearing house rule or agreement.

Upon a final payment under subparagraphs (b), (c) or (d) the payor bank shall be accountable for the amount of the item.

(2) If provisional settlement for an item between the presenting and payor banks is made through a clearing house or by debits or credits in an account between them, then to the extent that provisional debits or credits for the item are entered in accounts between the presenting and payor banks or between the presenting and successive prior collecting banks seriatim, they become final upon final payment of the item by the payor bank.

(3) If a collecting bank receives a settlement for an item which is or becomes final (subsection (3) of Section 4—211, subsection (2) of Section 4—213) the bank is accountable to its customer for the amount of the item and any provisional credit given for the item in an account with its customer becomes final.

(4) Subject to any right of the bank to apply the credit to an obligation of the customer, credit given by a bank for an item in an account with its customer becomes available for withdrawal as of right

(a) in any case where the bank has received a provisional settlement for the item,—when such settlement becomes final and the bank has had a reasonable time to learn that the settlement is final;

(b) in any case where the bank is both a depositary bank and a payor bank and the item is finally paid,—at the opening of the bank's second banking day following receipt of the item.

(5) A deposit of money in a bank is final when made but, subject to any right of the bank to apply the deposit to an obligation of the customer, the deposit becomes available for withdrawal as of right at the opening of the bank's next banking day following receipt of the deposit.

Section 4—214. Insolvency and Preference.

(1) Any item in or coming into the possession of a payor or collecting bank which suspends payment and which item is not finally paid shall be returned by the receiver, trustee or agent in charge of the closed bank to the presenting bank or the closed bank's customer.

(2) If a payor bank finally pays an item and suspends payments without making a settlement for the item with its customer or the presenting bank which settlement is or becomes final, the owner of the item has a preferred claim against the payor bank.

(3) If a payor bank gives or a collecting bank gives or receives a provisional settlement for an item and thereafter suspends payments, the suspension does not prevent or interfere with the settlement becoming final if such finality occurs automatically upon the lapse of certain time or the happening of certain events (subsection (3) of Section 4—211, subsections (1) (d), (2) and (3) of Section 4—213).

(4) If a collecting bank receives from subsequent parties settlement for an item which settlement is or becomes final and suspends payments without making a settlement for the item with its customer which is or becomes final, the owner of the item has a preferred claim against such collecting bank.

PART 3

COLLECTION OF ITEMS: PAYOR BANKS

Section 4—301. Deferred Posting; Recovery of Payment by Return of Items; Time of Dishonor.

(1) Where an authorized settlement for a demand item (other than a documentary draft) received by a payor bank otherwise than for immediate payment over the counter has been made before midnight of the banking day of receipt, the payor bank may revoke the settlement and recover any payment if before it has made final payment (subsection (1) of Section 4—213) and before its midnight deadline it

(a) returns the item; or

(b) sends written notice of dishonor or nonpayment if the item is held for protest or is otherwise unavailable for return.

(2) If a demand item is received by a payor bank for credit on its books, it may return such item or send notice of dishonor and may revoke any credit given or recover the amount thereof withdrawn by its customer, if it acts within the time limit and in the manner specified in the preceding subsection.

(3) Unless previous notice of dishonor has been sent, an item is dishonored at the time when for purposes of dishonor it is returned or notice sent in accordance with this section.

(4) An item is returned:

(a) as to an item received through a clearing house, when it is delivered to the presenting or last collecting bank or to the clearing house or is sent or delivered in accordance with its rules; or

(b) in all other cases, when it is sent or delivered to the bank's customer or transferor or pursuant to his instructions.

Section 4—302. Payor Bank's Responsibility for Late Return of Item.

In the absence of a valid defense such as breach of a presentment warranty (subsection (1) of Section 4—207), settlement effected or the like, if an item is presented on and received by a payor bank the bank is accountable for the amount of

(a) a demand item other than a documentary draft whether properly payable or not if the bank, in any case where it is not also the depositary bank, retains the item beyond midnight of the banking day of receipt without settling for it or, regardless of whether it is also the depositary bank, does not pay or return the item or send notice of dishonor until after its midnight deadline; or

(b) any other properly payable item unless within the time allowed for acceptance or payment of that item the bank either accepts or pays the item or returns it and accompanying documents.

Section 4—303. When Items Subject to Notice, Stop-Order, Legal Process or Setoff; Order in Which Items May Be Charged or Certified.

(1) Any knowledge, notice or stop-order received by, legal process served upon or setoff exercised by a payor bank, whether or not effective under other rules of law to terminate, suspend or modify the bank's right or duty to pay an item or to charge its customer's account for the item, comes too late to so terminate, suspend or modify such right or duty if the knowledge, notice, stop-order or legal process is received or served and a reasonable time for the bank to act thereon expires or the setoff is exercised after the bank has done any of the following:

(a) accepted or certified the item;

(b) paid the item in cash;

(c) settled for the item without reserving a right to revoke the settlement and without having such right under statute, clearing house rule or agreement;

(d) completed the process of posting the item to the indicated account of the drawer, maker or other person to be charged therewith or otherwise has evidenced by examination of such indicated account and by action its decision to pay the item; or

(e) become accountable for the amount of the item under subsection (1) (d) of Section 4—

213 and Section 4—302 dealing with the payor bank's responsibility for late return of items.

(2) Subject to the provisions of subsection (1) items may be accepted, paid, certified or charged to the indicated account of its customer in any order convenient to the bank.

PART 4

RELATIONSHIP BETWEEN PAYOR BANK AND ITS CUSTOMER

Section 4—401. When Bank May Charge Customer's Account.

(1) As against its customer, a bank may charge against his account any item which is otherwise properly payable from that account even though the charge creates an overdraft.

(2) A bank which in good faith makes payment to a holder may charge the indicated account of its customer according to

(a) the original tenor of his altered item; or

(b) the tenor of his completed item, even though the bank knows the item has been completed unless the bank has notice that the completion was improper.

Section 4—402. Bank's Liability to Customer for Wrongful Dishonor.

A payor bank is liable to its customer for damages proximately caused by the wrongful dishonor of an item. When the dishonor occurs through mistake, liability is limited to actual damages proved. If so proximately caused and proved, damages may include damages for an arrest or prosecution of the customer or other consequential damages. Whether any consequential damages are proximately caused by the wrongful dishonor is a question of fact to be determined in each case.

Section 4—403. Customer's Right to Stop Payment; Burden of Proof of Loss.

(1) A customer may by order to his bank stop payment of any item payable for his account but the order must be

received at such time and in such manner as to afford the bank a reasonable opportunity to act on it prior to any action by the bank with respect to the item described in Section 4—303.

(2) An oral order is binding upon the bank only for fourteen calendar days unless confirmed in writing within that period. A written order is effective for only six months unless renewed in writing.

(3) The burden of establishing the fact and amount of loss resulting from the payment of an item contrary to a binding stop payment order is on the customer.

Section 4—404. Bank Not Obligated to Pay Check More Than Six Months Old.

A bank is under no obligation to a customer having a checking account to pay a check, other than a certified check, which is presented more than six months after its date, but it may charge its customer's account for a payment made thereafter in good faith.

Section 4—405. Death or Incompetence of Customer.

(1) A payor or collecting bank's authority to accept, pay or collect an item or to account for proceeds of its collection if otherwise effective is not rendered ineffective by incompetence of a customer of either bank existing at the time the item is issued or its collection is undertaken if the bank does not know of an adjudication of incompetence. Neither death nor incompetence of a customer revokes such authority

to accept, pay, collect or account until the bank knows of the fact of death or of an adjudication of incompetence and has reasonable opportunity to act on it.

(2) Even with knowledge a bank may for ten days after the date of death pay or certify checks drawn on or prior to that date unless ordered to stop payment by a person claiming an interest in the account.

Section 4—406. Customer's Duty to Discover and Report Unauthorized Signature or Alteration.

(1) When a bank sends to its customer a statement of account accompanied by items paid in good faith in support of the debit entries or holds the statement and items pursuant to a request or instructions of its customer or otherwise in a reasonable manner makes the statement and items available to the customer, the customer must exercise reasonable care and promptness to examine the statement and items to discover his unauthorized signature or any alteration on an item and must notify the bank promptly after discovery thereof.

(2) If the bank establishes that the customer failed with respect to an item to comply with the duties imposed on the customer by subsection (1) the customer is precluded from asserting against the bank

    (a) his unauthorized signature or any alteration on the item if the bank also establishes that it suffered a loss by reason of such failure; and

    (b) an unauthorized signature or alteration by the same wrongdoer on any other item paid in good faith by the bank after the first item and statement was available to the customer for a reasonable period not exceeding fourteen calendar days and before the bank receives notification from the customer of any such unauthorized signature or alteration.

(3) The preclusion under subsection (2) does not apply if the customer estab-

lishes lack of ordinary care on the part of the bank in paying the item(s).

(4) Without regard to care or lack of care of either the customer or the bank, a customer who does not within one year from the time the statement and items are made available to the customer (subsection (1)) discover and report his unauthorized signature or any alteration on the face or back of the item or does not within three years from that time discover and report any unauthorized indorsement is precluded from asserting against the bank such unauthorized signature or indorsement or such alteration.

(5) If under this section a payor bank has a valid defense against a claim of a customer upon or resulting from payment of an item and waives or fails upon request to assert the defense, the bank may not assert against any collecting bank or other prior party presenting or transferring the item a claim based upon the unauthorized signature or alteration giving rise to the customer's claim.

Section 4—407. Payor Bank's Right to Subrogation on Improper Payment.

If a payor bank has paid an item over the stop payment order of the drawer or maker or otherwise under circumstances giving a basis for objection by the drawer or maker, to prevent unjust enrichment and only to the extent necessary to prevent loss to the bank by reason of its payment of the item, the payor bank shall be subrogated to the rights

    (a) of any holder in due course on the item against the drawer or maker; and

    (b) of the payee or any other holder of the item against the drawer or maker either on the item or under the transaction out of which the item arose; and

    (c) of the drawer or maker against the payee or any other holder of the item with respect to the transaction out of which the item arose.

PART 5

COLLECTION OF DOCUMENTARY DRAFTS

Section 4—501. Handling of Documentary Drafts; Duty to Send for Presentment and to Notify Customer of Dishonor.

A bank which takes a documentary draft for collection must present or send the draft and accompanying documents for presentment and upon learning that the draft has not been paid or accepted in due course, must seasonably notify its customer of such fact even though it may have discounted or bought the draft or extended credit available for withdrawal as of right.

Section 4—502. Presentment of "On Arrival" Drafts.

When a draft or the relevant instructions require presentment "on arrival", "when goods arrive" or the like, the collecting bank need not present until in its judgment a reasonable time for arrival of the goods has expired. Refusal to pay or accept because the goods have not arrived is not dishonor; the bank must notify its transferor of such refusal but need not present the draft again until it is instructed to do so or learns of the arrival of the goods.

Section 4—503. Responsibility of Presenting Bank for Documents and Goods; Report of Reasons for Dishonor; Referee in Case of Need.

Unless otherwise instructed and except as provided in Article 5 a bank presenting a documentary draft

(a) must deliver the documents to the drawee on acceptance of the draft if it is payable more than three days after present-

ment; otherwise, only on payment; and

(b) upon dishonor, either in the case of presentment for acceptance or presentment for payment, may seek and follow instructions from any referee in case of need designated in the draft or, if the presenting bank does not choose to utilize his services, it must use diligence and good faith to ascertain the reason for dishonor, must notify its transferor of the dishonor and of the results of its effort to ascertain the reasons therefor and must request instructions.

But the presenting bank is under no obligation with respect to goods represented by the documents except to follow any reasonable instructions seasonably received; it has a right to reimbursement for any expense incurred in following instructions and to prepayment of or indemnity for such expenses.

Section 4—504. Privilege of Presenting Bank to Deal With Goods; Security Interest for Expenses.

(1) A presenting bank which, following the dishonor of a documentary draft, has seasonably requested instructions but does not receive them within a reasonable time may store, sell, or otherwise deal with the goods in any reasonable manner.

(2) For its reasonable expenses incurred by action under subsection (1) the presenting bank has a lien upon the goods or their proceeds, which may be foreclosed in the same manner as an unpaid seller's lien.

ARTICLE 5

LETTERS OF CREDIT

Section 5—101. Short Title.

This Article shall be known and may be cited as Uniform Commercial Code—Letters of Credit.

Section 5—102. Scope.

(1) This Article applies

(a) to a credit issued by a bank if the credit requires a documentary draft or a documentary demand for payment; and

(b) to a credit issued by a person other than a bank if the credit requires that the draft or demand for payment be accompanied by a document of title; and

(c) to a credit issued by a bank or other person if the credit is not within subparagraphs (a) or (b) but conspicuously states that it it a letter of credit or is conspicuously so entitled.

(2) Unless the engagement meets the requirements of subsection (1), this Article does not apply to engagements to make advances or to honor drafts or demands for payment, to authorities to pay or purchase, to guarantees or to general agreements.

(3) This Article deals with some but not all of the rules and concepts of letters of credit as such rules or concepts have developed prior to this act or may hereafter develop. The fact that this Article states a rule does not by itself require, imply or negate application of the same or a converse rule to a situation not provided for or to a person not specified by this Article.

Section 5—103. Definitions.

(1) In this Article unless the context otherwise requires

(a) "Credit" or "letter of credit" means an engagement by a bank or other person made at the request of a customer and of a kind within the scope of this Article (Section 5—102) that the issuer will honor drafts or other demands for payment upon compliance with the conditions specified in the credit. A credit may be either revocable or irrevocable. The engagement may be either an agreement to honor or a statement that the bank or other person is authorized to honor.

(b) A "documentary draft" or a "documentary demand for pay-

ment" is one honor of which is conditioned upon the presentation of a document or documents. "Document" means any paper including document of title, security, invoice, certificate, notice of default and the like.

(c) An "issuer" is a bank or other person issuing a credit.

(d) A "beneficiary" of a credit is a person who is entitled under its terms to draw or demand payment.

(e) An "advising bank" is a bank which gives notification of the issuance of a credit by another bank.

(f) A "confirming bank" is a bank which engages either that it will itself honor a credit already issued by another bank or that such a credit will be honored by the issuer or a third bank.

(g) A "customer" is a buyer or other person who causes an issuer to issue a credit. The term also includes a bank which procures issuance or confirmation on behalf of that bank's customer.

(2) Other definitions applying to this Article and the sections in which they appear are:

"Notation of Credit". Section 5—108.

"Presenter". Section 5—112(3).

(3) Definitions in other Articles applying to this Article and the sections in which they appear are:

"Accept" or "Acceptance". Section 3—410.

"Contract for sale". Section 2—106.

"Draft". Section 3—104.

"Holder in due course". Section 3—302.

"Midnight deadline". Section 4—104.

"Security". Section 8—102.

(4) In addition, Article 1 contains general definitions and principles of construction and interpretation applicable throughout this Article.

Section 5—104. Formal Requirements; Signing.

(1) Except as otherwise required in subsection (1) (c) of Section 5—102 on scope, no particular form of phrasing is required for a credit. A credit must be in writing and signed by the issuer and a confirmation must be in writing and signed by the confirming bank. A modification of the terms of a credit or confirmation must be signed by the issuer or confirming bank.

(2) A telegram may be a sufficient signed writing if it identifies its sender by an authorized authentication. The authentication may be in code and the authorized naming of the issuer in an advice of credit is a sufficient signing.

Section 5—105. Consideration.

No consideration is necessary to establish a credit or to enlarge or otherwise modify its terms.

Section 5—106. Time and Effect of Establishment of Credit.

(1) Unless otherwise agreed a credit is established
    (a) as regards the customer as soon as a letter of credit is sent to him or the letter of credit or an authorized written advice of its issuance is sent to the beneficiary; and
    (b) as regards the beneficiary when he receives a letter of credit or an authorized written advice of its issuance.

(2) Unless otherwise agreed, once an irrevocable credit is established as regards the customer, it can be modified or revoked only with the consent of the customer, and once it is established as regards the beneficiary it can be modified or revoked only with his consent.

(3) Unless otherwise agreed, after a revocable credit is established it may be modified or revoked by the issuer without notice to or consent from the customer or beneficiary.

(4) Notwithstanding any modification or revocation of a revocable credit, any person authorized to honor or negotiate under the terms of the original credit is entitled to reimbursement for or honor of any draft or demand for payment duly honored or negotiated before receipt of notice of the modification or revocation and the issuer in turn is entitled to reimbursement from its customer.

Section 5—107. Advice of Credit; Confirmation; Error in Statement of Terms.

(1) Unless otherwise specified an advising bank by advising a credit issued by another bank does not assume any obligation to honor drafts drawn or demands for payment made under the credit, but it does assume obligation for the accuracy of its own statement.

(2) A confirming bank by confirming a credit becomes directly obligated on the credit to the extent of its confirmation as though it were its issuer and acquires the rights of an issuer.

(3) Even though an advising bank incorrectly advises the terms of a credit it has been authorized to advise, the credit is established as against the issuer to the extent of its original terms.

(4) Unless otherwise specified the customer bears as against the issuer all risks of transmission and reasonable translation or interpretation of any message relating to a credit.

Section 5—108. "Notation Credit"; Exhaustion of Credit.

(1) A credit which specifies that any person purchasing or paying drafts drawn or demands for payment made under it must note the amount of the draft or demand on the letter or advice of credit is a "notation credit".

(2) Under a notation credit
    (a) a person paying the beneficiary or purchasing a draft or demand for payment from him acquires a right to honor only if the appropriate notation is made and, by transferring or forwarding for honor the documents under the credit, such a person warrants to the issuer that the notation has been made; and

(b) unless the credit or a signed statement that an appropriate notation has been made accompanies the draft or demand for payment, the issuer may delay honor until evidence of notation has been procured which is satisfactory to it, but its obligation and that of its customer continue for a reasonable time not exceeding thirty days to obtain such evidence.

(3) If the credit is not a notation credit

    (a) the issuer may honor complying drafts or demands for payment presented to it in the order in which they are presented and is discharged pro tanto by honor of any such draft or demand;

    (b) as between competing good faith purchasers of complying drafts or demands the person first purchasing has priority over a subsequent purchaser even though the later purchased draft or demand has been first honored.

Section 5—109. Issuer's Obligation to Its Customer.

(1) An issuer's obligation to its customer includes good faith and observance of any general banking usage but unless otherwise agreed does not include liability or responsibility

    (a) for performance of the underlying contract for sale or other transaction between the customer and the beneficiary; or

    (b) for any act or omission of any person other than itself or its own branch or for loss or destruction of a draft, demand or document in transit or in the possession of others; or

    (c) based on knowledge or lack of knowledge of any usage of any particular trade.

(2) An issuer must examine documents with care so as to ascertain that on their face they appear to comply with the terms of the credit but unless otherwise agreed assumes no liability or responsibility for the genuineness, falsification or effect of any document which appears on such examination to be regular on its face.

(3) A non-bank issuer is not bound by any banking usage of which it has no knowledge.

Section 5—110. Availability of Credit in Portions; Presenter's Reservation of Lien or Claim.

(1) Unless otherwise specified a credit may be used in portions in the discretion of the beneficiary.

(2) Unless otherwise specified a person by presenting a documentary draft or demand for payment under a credit relinquishes upon its honor all claims to the documents, and a person by transferring such draft or demand or causing such presentment authorizes such relinquishment. An explicit reservation of claim makes the draft or demand non-complying.

Section 5—111. Warranties on Transfer and Presentment.

(1) Unless otherwise agreed the beneficiary by transferring or presenting a documentary draft or demand for payment warrants to all interested parties that the necessary conditions of the credit have been complied with. This is in addition to any warranties arising under Articles 3, 4, 7 and 8.

(2) Unless otherwise agreed a negotiating, advising, confirming, collecting or issuing bank presenting or transferring a draft or demand for payment under a credit warrants only the matters warranted by a collecting bank under Article 4, and any such bank transferring a document warrants only the matters warranted by an intermediary under Articles 7 and 8.

Section 5—112. Time Allowed for Honor or Rejection; Withholding Honor or Rejection by Consent; "Presenter".

(1) A bank to which a documentary draft or demand for payment is presented under a credit may without dishonor of the draft, demand or credit

(a) defer honor until the close of the third banking day following receipt of the documents; and

(b) further defer honor if the presenter has expressly or impliedly consented thereto.

Failure to honor within the time here specified constitutes dishonor of the draft or demand and of the credit [except as otherwise provided in subsection (4) of Section 5—114 on conditional payment].

> Note: *The bracketed language in the last sentence of subsection (1) should be included only if the optional provisions of Section 5—114(4) and (5) are included.*

(2) Upon dishonor the bank may unless otherwise instructed fulfill its duty to return the draft or demand and the documents by holding them at the disposal of the presenter and sending him an advice to that effect.

(3) "Presenter" means any person presenting a draft or demand for payment for honor under a credit even though that person is a confirming bank or other correspondent which is acting under an issuer's authorization.

Section 5—113. Indemnities.

(1) A bank seeking to obtain (whether for itself or another) honor, negotiation or reimbursement under a credit may give an indemnity to induce such honor, negotiation or reimbursement.

(2) An indemnity agreement inducing honor, negotiation or reimbursement

(a) unless otherwise explicitly agreed applies to defects in the documents but not in the goods; and

(b) unless a longer time is explicitly agreed, expires at the end of ten business days following receipt of the documents by the ultimate customer unless notice of objection is sent before such expiration date. The ultimate customer may send notice of objection to the person from whom he received the documents, and any bank receiving such notice is under a duty to send notice

to its transferor before its midnight deadline.

Section 5—114. Issuer's Duty and Privilege to Honor; Right to Reimbursement.

(1) An issuer must honor a draft or demand for payment which complies with the terms of the relevant credit regardless of whether the goods or documents conform to the underlying contract for sale or other contract between the customer and the beneficiary. The issuer is not excused from honor of such a draft or demand by reason of an additional general term that all documents must be satisfactory to the issuer, but an issuer may require that specified documents must be satisfactory to it.

(2) Unless otherwise agreed, when documents appear on their face to comply with the terms of a credit but a required document does not in fact conform to the warranties made on negotiation or transfer of a document of title (Section 7—507) or of a security (Section 8—306) or is forged or fraudulent or there is fraud in the transaction

(a) the issuer must honor the draft or demand for payment if honor is demanded by a negotiating bank or other holder of the draft or demand which has taken the draft or demand under the credit and under circumstances which would make it a holder in due course (Section 3—302) and in an appropriate case would make it a person to whom a document of title has been duly negotiated (Section 7—502) or a bona fide purchaser of a security (Section 8—302); and

(b) in all other cases as against its customer, an issuer acting in good faith may honor the draft or demand for payment despite notification from the customer of fraud, forgery or other defect not apparent on the face of the documents, but a court of appropriate jurisdiction may enjoin such honor.

(3) Unless otherwise agreed an issuer which has duly honored a draft or demand for payment is entitled to immediate reimbursement of any payment made under the credit and to be put in effectively available funds not later than the day before maturity of any acceptance made under the credit.

[(4) When a credit provides for payment by the issuer on receipt of notice that the required documents are in the possession of a correspondent or other agent of the issuer

    (a) any payment made on receipt of such notice is conditional; and

    (b) the issuer may reject documents which do not comply with the credit if it does so within three banking days following its receipt of the documents; and

    (c) in the event of such rejection, the issuer is entitled by charge back or otherwise to return of the payment made.]

[(5) In the case covered by subsection (4) failure to reject documents within the time specified in sub-paragraph (b) constitutes acceptance of the documents and makes the payment final in favor of the beneficiary.]

> Note: *Subsections (4) and (5) are bracketed as optional. If they are included, the bracketed language in the last sentence of Section 5—112 (1) should also be included.*

Section 5—115. Remedy for Improper Dishonor or Anticipatory Repudiation.

(1) When an issuer wrongfully dishonors a draft or demand for payment presented under a credit, the person entitled to honor has with respect to any documents the rights of a person in the position of a seller (Section 2—707) and may recover from the issuer the face amount of the draft or demand together with incidental damages under Section 2—710 on seller's incidental damages and interest but less any amount realized by resale or other use or disposition of the subject matter of the transaction. In the event no resale or other utilization is made the documents, goods or other subject matter involved in the transaction must be turned over to the issuer on payment of judgment.

(2) When an issuer wrongfully cancels or otherwise repudiates a credit before presentment of a draft or demand for payment drawn under it, the beneficiary has the rights of a seller after anticipatory repudiation by the buyer under Section 2—610 if he learns of the repudiation in time reasonably to avoid procurement of the required documents. Otherwise the beneficiary has an immediate right of action for wrongful dishonor.

Section 5—116. Transfer and Assignment.

(1) The right to draw under a credit can be transferred or assigned only when the credit is expressly designated as transferable or assignable.

(2) Even though the credit specifically states that it is nontransferable or nonassignable, the beneficiary may before performance of the conditions of the credit assign his right to proceeds. Such an assignment is an assignment of a contract right under Article 9 on Secured Transactions and is governed by that Article except that

    (a) the assignment is ineffective until the letter of credit or advice of credit is delivered to the assignee which delivery constitutes perfection of the security interest under Article 9; and

    (b) the issuer may honor drafts or demands for payment drawn under the credit until it receives a notification of the assignment signed by the beneficiary which reasonably identifies the credit involved in the assignment and contains a request to pay the assignee; and

    (c) after what reasonably appears to be such a notification has been received the issuer may without dishonor refuse to accept or pay even to a person otherwise entitled to honor until the letter of credit or advice of credit is exhibited to the issuer.

(3) Except where the beneficiary has effectively assigned his right to draw or his right to proceeds, nothing in this section limits his right to transfer or negotiate drafts or demands drawn under the credit.

Section 5—117. Insolvency of Bank Holding Funds for Documentary Credit.

(1) Where an issuer or an advising or confirming bank or a bank which has for a customer procured issuance of a credit by another bank becomes insolvent before final payment under the credit and the credit is one to which this Article is made applicable by paragraphs (a) or (b) of Section 5—102(1) on scope, the receipt or allocation of funds or collateral to secure or meet obligations under the credit shall have the following results:

    (a) to the extent of any funds or collateral turned over after or before the insolvency as indemnity against or specifically for the purpose of payment of drafts or demands for payment drawn under the designated credit, the drafts or demands are entitled to payment in preference over depositors or other general creditors of the issuer or bank; and

    (b) on expiration of the credit or surrender of the beneficiary's rights under it unused, any person who has given such funds or collateral is similarly entitled to return thereof; and

    (c) a change to a general or current account with a bank if specifically consented to for the purpose of indemnity against or payment of drafts or demands for payment drawn under the designated credit falls under the same rules as if the funds had been drawn out in cash and then turned over with specific instructions.

(2) After honor or reimbursement under this section the customer or other person for whose account the insolvent bank has acted is entitled to receive the documents involved.

ARTICLE 6
BULK TRANSFERS

Section 6—101. Short Title.

This Article shall be known and may be cited as Uniform Commercial Code— Bulk Transfers.

Section 6—102. "Bulk Transfers"; Transfers of Equipment; Enterprises Subject to This Article; Bulk Transfers Subject to This Article.

(1) A "bulk transfer" is any transfer in bulk and not in the ordinary course of the transferor's business of a major part of the materials, supplies, merchandise or other inventory (Section 9—109) of an enterprise subject to this Article.

(2) A transfer of a substantial part of the equipment (Section 9—109) of such an enterprise is a bulk transfer if it is made in connection with a bulk transfer of inventory, but not otherwise.

(3) The enterprises subject to this Article are all those whose principal business is the sale of merchandise from stock, including those who manufacture what they sell.

(4) Except as limited by the following section all bulk transfers of goods located within this state are subject to this Article.

Section 6—103. Transfers Excepted from This Article.

The following transfers are not subject to this Article:

(1) Those made to give security for the performance of an obligation;

(2) General assignments for the benefit of all the creditors of the transferor, and subsequent transfers by the assignee thereunder;

(3) Transfers in settlement or realization of a lien or other security interest;

(4) Sales by executors, administrators, receivers, trustees in bankruptcy, or any public officer under judicial process;

(5) Sales made in the course of judicial or administrative proceedings for the dissolution or reorganization of a corporation and of which notice is sent to the creditors of the corporation pursuant to order of the court or administrative agency;

(6) Transfers to a person maintaining a known place of business in this State who becomes bound to pay the debts of the transferor in full and gives public notice of that fact, and who is solvent after becoming so bound;

(7) A transfer to a new business enterprise organized to take over and continue the business, if public notice of the transaction is given and the new enterprise assumes the debts of the transferor and he receives nothing from the transaction except an interest in the new enterprise junior to the claims of creditors;

(8) Transfers of property which is exempt from execution.

Public notice under subsection (6) or subsection (7) may be given by publishing once a week for two consecutive weeks in a newspaper of general circulation where the transferor has its principal place of business in this state an advertisement including the names and addresses of the transferor and transferee and the effective date of the transfer.

Section 6—104. Schedule of Property, List of Creditors.

(1) Except as provided with respect to auction sales (Section 6—108), a bulk transfer subject to this Article is ineffective against any creditor of the transferor unless:

(a) The transferee requires the transferor to furnish a list of his existing creditors prepared as stated in this section; and

(b) The parties prepare a schedule of the property transferred sufficient to identify it; and

(c) The transferee preserves the list and schedule for six months next following the transfer and permits inspection of either or both and copying therefrom at all reasonable hours by any creditor of the transferor, or files the list and schedule in (a public office to be here identified).

(2) The list of creditors must be signed and sworn to or affirmed by the transferor or his agent. It must contain the names and business addresses of all creditors of the transferor, with the amounts when known, and also the names of all persons who are known to the transferor to assert claims against him even though such claims are disputed. If the transferor is the obligor of an outstanding issue of bonds, debentures or the like as to which there is an indenture trustee, the list of creditors need include only the name and address of the indenture trustee and the aggregate outstanding principal amount of the issue.

(3) Responsibility for the completeness and accuracy of the list of creditors rests on the transferor, and the transfer is not rendered ineffective by errors or omissions therein unless the transferee is shown to have had knowledge.

Section 6—105. Notice to Creditors.

In addition to the requirements of the preceding section, any bulk transfer subject to this Article except one made by auction sale (Section 6—108) is ineffective against any creditor of the transferor unless at least ten days before he takes possession of the goods or pays for them, whichever happens first, the transferee gives notice of the transfer in the manner and to the persons hereafter provided (Section 6—107).

Section 6—106. Application of the Proceeds.

In addition to the requirements of the two preceding sections:

(1) Upon every bulk transfer subject to this Article for which new consideration becomes payable, except those made by sale at auction, it is the duty of the transferee to assure that such consideration is applied so far as necessary to pay those debts of the transferor which are either shown on the list furnished by

the transferor (Section 6—104) or filed in writing in the place stated in the notice (Section 6—107) within thirty days after the mailing of such notice. This duty of the transferee runs to all the holders of such debts, and may be enforced by any of them for the benefit of all.

(2) If any of said debts are in dispute, the necessary sum may be withheld from distribution until the dispute is settled or adjudicated.

(3) If the consideration payable is not enough to pay all of the said debts in full, distribution shall be made pro rata.]

Note: *This section is bracketed to indicate division of opinion as to whether or not it is a wise provision, and to suggest that this is a point on which State enactments may differ without serious damage to the principle of uniformity.*

In any State where this section is omitted, the following parts of sections, also bracketed in the text, should also be omitted, namely:

Section 6—107(2)(e).
6—108(3)(c).
6—109(2).

In any State where this section is enacted, these other provisions should be also.

Optional Subsection (4)

[(4) The transferee may within ten days after he takes possession of the goods pay the consideration into the (specify court) in the county where the transferor had its principal place of business in this state and thereafter may discharge his duty under this section by giving notice by registered or certified mail to all the persons to whom the duty runs that the consideration has been paid into that court and that they should file their claims there. On motion of any interested party, the court may order the distribution of the consideration to the persons entitled to it.]

Note: *Optional subsection (4) is recommended for those states which do not have a general statute providing for payment of money into court.*

Section 6—107. The Notice.

(1) The notice to creditors (Section 6—105) shall state:

(a) that a bulk transfer is about to be made; and

(b) the names and business addresses of the transferor and transferee, and all other business names and addresses used by the transferor within three years last past so far as known to the transferee; and

(c) whether or not all the debts of the transferor are to be paid in full as they fall due as a result of the transaction, and if so, the address to which creditors should send their bills.

(2) If the debts of the transferor are not to be paid in full as they fall due or if the transferee is in doubt on that point, then the notice shall state further:

(a) the location and general description of the property to be transferred and the estimated total of the transferor's debts;

(b) the address where the schedule of property and list of creditors (Section 6—104) may be inspected;

(c) whether the transfer is to pay existing debts and if so the amount of such debts and to whom owing;

(d) whether the transfer is for new consideration and if so the amount of such consideration and the time and place of payment; [and]

[(e) if for new consideration the time and place where creditors of the transferor are to file their claims.]

(3) The notice in any case shall be delivered personally or sent by registered or certified mail to all the persons shown on the list of creditors furnished by the transferor (Section 6—104) and to all other persons who are known to the transferee to hold or assert claims against the transferor.

Note: *The words in brackets are optional.*

Section 6—108. Auction Sales; "Auctioneer".

(1) A bulk transfer is subject to this Article even though it is by sale at auction, but only in the manner and with the results stated in this section.

(2) The transferor shall furnish a list of his creditors and assist in the preparation of a schedule of the property to be sold, both prepared as before stated (Section 6—104).

(3) The person or persons other than the transferor who direct, control or are responsible for the auction are collectively called the "auctioneer". The auctioneer shall:

(a) receive and retain the list of creditors and prepare and retain the schedule of property for the period stated in this Article (Section 6—104);

(b) give notice of the auction personally or by registered or certified mail at least ten days before it occurs to all persons shown on the list of creditors and to all other persons who are known to him to hold or assert claims against the transferor; [and]

[(c) assure that the net proceeds of the auction are applied as provided in this Article (Section 6—106).]

(4) Failure of the auctioneer to perform any of these duties does not affect the validity of the sale or the title of the purchasers, but if the auctioneer knows that the auction constitutes a bulk transfer such failure renders the auctioneer liable to the creditors of the transferor as a class for the sums owing to them from the transferor up to but not exceeding the net proceeds of the auction. If the auctioneer consists of several persons, their liability is joint and several.

Note: *The words in brackets are optional.*

Section 6—109. What Creditors Protected; [Credit for Payment to Particular Creditors].

(1) The creditors of the transferor mentioned in this Article are those holding claims based on transactions or events occurring before the bulk transfer, but creditors who become such after notice to creditors is given (Sections 6—105 and 6—107) are not entitled to notice.

[(2) Against the aggregate obligation imposed by the provisions of this Article concerning the application of the proceeds (Section 6—106 and subsection (3) (c) of 6—108) the transferee or auctioneer is entitled to credit for sums paid to particular creditors of the transferor, not exceeding the sums believed in good faith at the time of the payment to be properly payable to such creditors.]

Section 6—110. Subsequent Transfers.

When the title of a transferee to property is subject to a defect by reason of his non-compliance with the requirements of this Article, then:

(1) a purchaser of any of such property from such transferee who pays no value or who takes with notice of such non-compliance takes subject to such defect, but

(2) a purchaser for value in good faith and without such notice takes free of such defect.

Section 6—111. Limitation of Actions and Levies.

No action under this Article shall be brought nor levy made more than six months after the date on which the transferee took possession of the goods unless the transfer has been concealed. If the transfer has been concealed, actions may be brought or levies made within six months after its discovery.

Note to Article 6: *Section 6—106 is bracketed to indicate division of opinion as to whether or not it is a wise provision, and to suggest that this is a point on which State enactments may differ without serious damage to the principle of uniformity.*

In any State where Section 6—106 is not enacted, the following parts of sections, also bracketed in the text, should also be omitted, namely:

Section 6—107(2)(e).
6—108(3)(c).
6—109(2).

In any State where Section 6—106 is enacted, these other provisions should be also.

ARTICLE 7

WAREHOUSE RECEIPTS, BILLS OF LADING AND OTHER DOCUMENTS OF TITLE

PART 1

GENERAL

Section 7—101. Short Title.

This Article shall be known and may be cited as Uniform Commercial Code—Documents of Title.

Section 7—102. Definitions and Index of Definitions.

(1) In this Article, unless the context otherwise requires:

(a) "Bailee" means the person who by a warehouse receipt, bill of lading or other document of title acknowledges possession of goods and contracts to deliver them.

(b) "Consignee" means the person named in a bill to whom or to whose order the bill promises delivery.

(c) "Consignor" means the person named in a bill as the person from whom the goods have been received for shipment.

(d) "Delivery order" means a written order to deliver goods directed to a warehouseman, carrier or other person who in the ordinary course of business issues warehouse receipts or bills of lading.

(e) "Document" means document of title as defined in the general definitions in Article 1 (Section 1—201).

(f) "Goods" means all things which are treated as movable for the purposes of a contract of storage or transportation.

(g) "Issuer" means a bailee who issues a document except that in relation to an unaccepted delivery order it means the person who orders the possessor of goods to deliver. Issuer includes any person for whom an agent or employee purports to act in issuing a document if the agent or employee has real or apparent authority to issue documents, notwithstanding that the issuer received no goods or that the goods were misdescribed or that in any other respect the agent or employee violated his instructions.

(h) "Warehouseman" is a person engaged in the business of storing goods for hire.

(2) Other definitions applying to this Article or to specified Parts thereof, and the sections in which they appear are:

"Duly negotiate". Section 7—501.

"Person entitled under the document". Section 7—403(4).

(3) Definitions in other Articles applying to this Article and the sections in which they appear are:

"Contract for sale". Section 2—106.

"Overseas". Section 2—323.

"Receipt" of goods. Section 2—103.

(4) In addition Article 1 contains general definitions and principles of construction and interpretation applicable throughout this Article.

Section 7—103. Relation of Article to Treaty, Statute, Tariff, Classification or Regulation.

To the extent that any treaty or statute of the United States, regulatory statute of this State or tariff, classification or regulation filed or issued pursuant thereto is applicable, the provisions of this Article are subject thereto.

Section 7—104. Negotiable and Non-Negotiable Warehouse Receipt, Bill of Lading or Other Document of Title.

(1) A warehouse receipt, bill of lading or other document of title is negotiable

    (a) if by its terms the goods are to be delivered to bearer or to the order of a named person; or

    (b) where recognized in overseas trade, if it runs to a named person or assigns.

(2) Any other document is non-negotiable. A bill of lading in which it is stated that the goods are consigned to a named person is not made negotiable by a provision that the goods are to be delivered only against a written order signed by the same or another named person.

Section 7—105. Construction Against Negative Implication.

The omission from either Part 2 or Part 3 of this Article of a provision corresponding to a provision made in the other Part does not imply that a corresponding rule of law is not applicable.

PART 2

WAREHOUSE RECEIPTS: SPECIAL PROVISIONS

Section 7—201. Who May Issue a Warehouse Receipt; Storage Under Government Bond.

(1) A warehouse receipt may be issued by any warehouseman.

(2) Where goods including distilled spirits and agricultural commodities are stored under a statute requiring a bond against withdrawal or a license for the issuance of receipts in the nature of warehouse receipts, a receipt issued for the goods has like effect as a warehouse receipt even though issued by a person who is the owner of the goods and is not a warehouseman.

Section 7—202. Form of Warehouse Receipt; Essential Terms; Optional Terms.

(1) A warehouse receipt need not be in any particular form.

(2) Unless a warehouse receipt embodies within its written or printed terms each of the following, the warehouseman is liable for damages caused by the omission to a person injured thereby:

    (a) the location of the warehouse where the goods are stored;

    (b) the date of issue of the receipt;

    (c) the consecutive number of the receipt;

    (d) a statement whether the goods received will be delivered to the bearer, to a specified person, or to a specified person or his order;

    (e) the rate of storage and handling charges, except that where goods are stored under a field warehousing arrangement a statement of that fact is sufficient on a non-negotiable receipt;

    (f) a description of the goods or of the packages containing them;

    (g) the signature of the warehouseman, which may be made by his authorized agent;

    (h) if the receipt is issued for goods of which the warehouseman is owner, either solely or jointly or in common with others, the fact of such ownership; and

    (i) a statement of the amount of advances made and of liabilities incurred for which the warehouseman claims a lien or security interest (Section 7—209). If the precise amount of such advances made or of such liabilities incurred is, at the time of the issue of the receipt, unknown to the warehouseman or to his agent who issues it, a statement of the fact that advances have been made or liabilities incurred and the purpose thereof is sufficient.

(3) A warehouseman may insert in his receipt any other terms which are not contrary to the provisions of this Act and do not impair his obligation of delivery (Section 7—403) or his duty of

care (Section 7—204). Any contrary provisions shall be ineffective.

Section 7—203. Liability for Non-Receipt or Misdescription.

A party to or purchaser for value in good faith of a document of title other than a bill of lading relying in either case upon the description therein of the goods may recover from the issuer damages caused by the non-receipt or misdescription of the goods, except to the extent that the document conspicuously indicates that the issuer does not know whether any part or all of the goods in fact were received or conform to the description, as where the description is in terms of marks or labels or kind, quantity or condition, or the receipt or description is qualified by "contents, condition and quality unknown", "said to contain" or the like, if such indication be true, or the party or purchaser otherwise has notice.

Section 7—204. Duty of Care; Contractual Limitation of Warehouseman's Liability.

(1) A warehouseman is liable for damages for loss of or injury to the goods caused by his failure to exercise such care in regard to them as a reasonably careful man would exercise under like circumstances but, unless otherwise agreed, he is not liable for damages which could not have been avoided by the exercise of such care.

(2) Damages may be limited by a term in the warehouse receipt or storage agreement limiting the amount of liability in case of loss or damage, and setting forth a specific liability per article or item, or value per unit of weight, beyond which the warehouseman shall not be liable; provided, however, that such liability may on written request of the bailor at the time of signing such storage agreement or within a reasonable time after receipt of the warehouse receipt be increased on part or all of the goods thereunder, in which event increased rates may be charged based on such increased valuation, but that no such increase shall be permitted contrary to a lawful limitation of liability

contained in the warehouseman's tariff, if any. No such limitation is effective with respect to the warehouseman's liability for conversion to his own use.

(3) Reasonable provisions as to the time and manner of presenting claims and instituting actions based on the bailment may be included in the warehouse receipt or tariff.

(4) This section does not impair or repeal . . .

> **Note:** *Insert in subsection (4) a reference to any statute which imposes a higher responsibility upon the warehouseman or invalidates contractual limitations which would be permissible under this Article.*

Section 7—205. Title Under Warehouse Receipt Defeated in Certain Cases.

A buyer in the ordinary course of business of fungible goods sold and delivered by a warehouseman who is also in the business of buying and selling such goods takes free of any claim under a warehouse receipt even though it has been duly negotiated.

Section 7—206. Termination of Storage at Warehouseman's Option.

(1) A warehouseman may on notifying the person on whose account the goods are held and any other person known to claim an interest in the goods require payment of any charges and removal of the goods from the warehouse at the termination of the period of storage fixed by the document, or, if no period is fixed, within a stated period not less than thirty days after the notification. If the goods are not removed before the date specified in the notification, the warehouseman may sell them in accordance with the provisions of the section on enforcement of a warehouseman's lien (Section 7—210).

(2) If a warehouseman in good faith believes that the goods are about to deteriorate or decline in value to less than the amount of his lien within the time prescribed in subsection (1) for notification, advertisement and sale, the warehouseman may specify in the notification any reasonable shorter time for

removal of the goods and in case the goods are not removed, may sell them at public sale held not less than one week after a single advertisement or posting.

(3) If as a result of a quality or condition of the goods of which the warehouseman had no notice at the time of deposit the goods are a hazard to other property or to the warehouse or to persons, the warehouseman may sell the goods at public or private sale without advertisement on reasonable notification to all persons known to claim an interest in the goods. If the warehouseman after a reasonable effort is unable to sell the goods, he may dispose of them in any lawful manner and shall incur no liability by reason of such disposition.

(4) The warehouseman must deliver the goods to any person entitled to them under this Article upon due demand made at any time prior to sale or other disposition under this section.

(5) The warehouseman may satisfy his lien from the proceeds of any sale or disposition under this section but must hold the balance for delivery on the demand of any person to whom he would have been bound to deliver the goods.

Section 7—207. Goods Must Be Kept Separate; Fungible Goods.

(1) Unless the warehouse receipt otherwise provides, a warehouseman must keep separate the goods covered by each receipt so as to permit at all times identification and delivery of those goods except that different lots of fungible goods may be commingled.

(2) Fungible goods so commingled are owned in common by the persons entitled thereto and the warehouseman is severally liable to each owner for that owner's share. Where because of overissue a mass of fungible goods is insufficient to meet all the receipts which the warehouseman has issued against it, the persons entitled include all holders to whom overissued receipts have been duly negotiated.

Section 7—208. Altered Warehouse Receipts.

Where a blank in a negotiable warehouse receipt has been filled in without authority, a purchaser for value and without notice of the want of authority may treat the insertion as authorized. Any other unauthorized alteration leaves any receipt enforceable against the issuer according to its original tenor.

Section 7—209. Lien of Warehouseman.

(1) A warehouseman has a lien against the bailor on the goods covered by a warehouse receipt or on the proceeds thereof in his possession for charges for storage or transportation (including demurrage and terminal charges), insurance, labor, or charges present or future in relation to the goods, and for expenses necessary for preservation of the goods or reasonably incurred in their sale pursuant to law. If the person on whose account the goods are held is liable for like charges or expenses in relation to other goods whenever deposited and it is stated in the receipt that a lien is claimed for charges and expenses in relation to other goods, the warehouseman also has a lien against him for such charges and expenses whether or not the other goods have been delivered by the warehouseman. But against a person to whom a negotiable warehouse receipt is duly negotiated, a warehouseman's lien is limited to charges in an amount or at a rate specified on the receipt or if no charges are so specified then to a reasonable charge for storage of the goods covered by the receipt subsequent to the date of the receipt.

(2) The warehouseman may also reserve a security interest against the bailor for a maximum amount specified on the receipt for charges other than those specified in subsection (1), such as for money advanced and interest. Such a security interest is governed by the Article on Secured Transactions (Article 9).

(3) A warehouseman's lien for charges and expenses under subsection (1) or a security interest under subsection (2) is also effective against any person who so entrusted the bailor with possession of the goods that a pledge of them by him to a good faith purchaser for value would have been valid but is not effective against a person as to whom the document confers no right in the goods covered by it under Section 7—503.

(4) A warehouseman loses his lien on any goods which he voluntarily delivers or which he unjustifiably refuses to deliver.

Section 7—210. Enforcement of Warehouseman's Lien.

(1) Except as provided in subsection (2), a warehouseman's lien may be enforced by public or private sale of the goods in block or in parcels, at any time or place and on any terms which are commercially reasonable, after notifying all persons known to claim an interest in the goods. Such notification must include a statement of the amount due, the nature of the proposed sale and the time and place of any public sale. The fact that a better price could have been obtained by a sale at a different time or in a different method from that selected by the warehouseman is not of itself sufficient to establish that the sale was not made in a commercially reasonable manner. If the warehouseman either sells the goods in the usual manner in any recognized market therefor, or if he sells at the price current in such market at the time of his sale, or if he has otherwise sold in conformity with commercially reasonable practices among dealers in the type of goods sold, he has sold in a commercially reasonable manner. A sale of more goods than apparently necessary to be offered to insure satisfaction of the obligation is not commercially reasonable except in cases covered by the preceding sentence.

(2) A warehouseman's lien on goods other than goods stored by a merchant in the course of his business may be enforced only as follows:

(a) All persons known to claim an interest in the goods must be notified.

(b) The notification must be delivered in person or sent by registered or certified letter to the last known address of any person to be notified.

(c) The notification must include an itemized statement of the claim, a description of the goods subject to the lien, a demand for payment within a specified time not less than ten days after receipt of the notification, and a conspicuous statement that unless the claim is paid within that time the goods will be advertised for sale and sold by auction at a specified time and place.

(d) The sale must conform to the terms of the notification.

(e) The sale must be held at the nearest suitable place to that where the goods are held or stored.

(f) After the expiration of the time given in the notification, an advertisement of the sale must be published once a week for two weeks consecutively in a newspaper of general circulation where the sale is to be held. The advertisement must include a description of the goods, the name of the person on whose account they are being held, and the time and place of the sale. The sale must take place at least fifteen days after the first publication. If there is no newspaper of general circulation where the sale is to be held, the advertisement must be posted at least ten days before the sale in not less than six conspicuous places in the neighborhood of the proposed sale.

(3) Before any sale pursuant to this section any person claiming a right in the goods may pay the amount necessary

to satisfy the lien and the reasonable expenses incurred under this section. In that event the goods must not be sold, but must be retained by the warehouseman subject to the terms of the receipt and this Article.

(4) The warehouseman may buy at any public sale pursuant to this section.

(5) A purchaser in good faith of goods sold to enforce a warehouseman's lien takes the goods free of any rights of persons against whom the lien was valid, despite noncompliance by the warehouseman with the requirements of this section.

(6) The warehouseman may satisfy his lien from the proceeds of any sale pursuant to this section but must hold the balance, if any, for delivery on demand to any person to whom he would have been bound to deliver the goods.

(7) The rights provided by this section shall be in addition to all other rights allowed by law to a creditor against his debtor.

(8) Where a lien is on goods stored by a merchant in the course of his business, the lien may be enforced in accordance with either subsection (1) or (2).

(9) The warehouseman is liable for damages caused by failure to comply with the requirements for sale under this section and in case of willful violation is liable for conversion.

PART 3

BILLS OF LADING: SPECIAL PROVISIONS

Section 7—301. Liability for Non-Receipt or Misdescription; "Said to Contain"; "Shipper's Load and Count"; Improper Handling.

(1) A consignee of a non-negotiable bill who has given value in good faith or a holder to whom a negotiable bill has been duly negotiated relying in either case upon the description therein of the goods, or upon the date therein shown, may recover from the issuer damages caused by the misdating of the bill or the nonreceipt or misdescription of the goods, except to the extent that the document indicates that the issuer does not know whether any part or all of the goods in fact were received or conform to the description, as where the description is in terms of marks or labels or kind, quantity, or condition or the receipt or description is qualified by "contents or conditions of contents of packages unknown", "said to contain", "shipper's weight, load and count" or the like, if such indication be true.

(2) When goods are loaded by an issuer who is a common carrier, the issuer must count the packages of goods if package freight and ascertain the kind and quantity if bulk freight. In such cases "shipper's weight, load and count" or other words indicating that the description was made by the shipper are ineffective except as to freight concealed by packages.

(3) When bulk freight is loaded by a shipper who makes available to the issuer adequate facilities for weighing such freight, an issuer who is a common carrier must ascertain the kind and quantity within a reasonable time after receiving the written request of the shipper to do so. In such cases "shipper's weight" or other words of like purport are ineffective.

(4) The issuer may by inserting in the bill the words "shipper's weight, load and count" or other words of like purport indicate that the goods were loaded by the shipper; and if such statement be true, the issuer shall not be liable for damages caused by the improper loading. But their omission does not imply liability for such damages.

(5) The shipper shall be deemed to have guaranteed to the issuer the accuracy at the time of shipment of the description, marks, labels, number, kind, quantity, condition and weight, as furnished by him; and the shipper shall indemnify the issuer against damage caused by inaccuracies in such particulars. The right of the issuer to such indemnity shall in no way limit his

responsibility and liability under the contract of carriage to any person other than the shipper.

Section 7—302. Through Bills of Lading and Similar Documents.

(1) The issuer of a through bill of lading or other document embodying an undertaking to be performed in part by persons acting as its agents or by connecting carriers is liable to anyone entitled to recover on the document for any breach by such other persons or by a connecting carrier of its obligation under the document, but to the extent that the bill covers an undertaking to be performed overseas or in territory not contiguous to the continental United States or an undertaking including matters other than transportation this liability may be varied by agreement of the parties.

(2) Where goods covered by a through bill of lading or other document embodying an undertaking to be performed in part by persons other than the issuer are received by any such person, he is subject with respect to his own performance while the goods are in his possession to the obligation of the issuer. His obligation is discharged by delivery of the goods to another such person pursuant to the document, and does not include liability for breach by any other such persons or by the issuer.

(3) The issuer of such through bill of lading or other document shall be entitled to recover from the connecting carrier, or such other person in possession of the goods when the breach of the obligation under the document occurred, the amount it may be required to pay to anyone entitled to recover on the document therefore, as may be evidenced by any receipt, judgment, or transcript thereof, and the amount of any expense reasonably incurred by it in defending any action brought by anyone entitled to recover on the document therefor.

Section 7—303. Division; Reconsignment; Change of Instructions.

(1) Unless the bill of lading otherwise provides, the carrier may deliver the goods to a person or destination other than that stated in the bill or may otherwise dispose of the goods on instructions from

    (a) the holder of a negotiable bill; or

    (b) the consignor on a non-negotiable bill notwithstanding contrary instructions from the consignee; or

    (c) the consignee on a non-negotiable bill in the absence of contrary instructions from the consignor, if the goods have arrived at the billed destination or if the consignee is in possession of the bill; or

    (d) the consignee on a non-negotiable bill if he is entitled as against the consignor to dispose of them.

(2) Unless such instructions are noted on a negotiable bill of lading, a person to whom the bill is duly negotiated can hold the bailee according to the original terms.

Section 7—304. Bills of Lading in a Set.

(1) Except where customary in overseas transportation, a bill of lading must not be issued in a set of parts. The issuer is liable for damages caused by violation of this subsection.

(2) Where a bill of lading is lawfully drawn in a set of parts, each of which is numbered and expressed to be valid only if the goods have not been delivered against any other part, the whole of the parts constitute one bill.

(3) Where a bill of lading is lawfully issued in a set of parts and different parts are negotiated to different persons, the title of the holder to whom the first due negotiation is made prevails as to both the document and the goods even though any later holder may have received the goods from the carrier in good faith and discharged the carrier's obligation by surrender of his part.

(4) Any person who negotiates or transfers a single part of a bill of lading drawn in a set is liable to holders of that part as if it were the whole set.

(5) The bailee is obliged to deliver in accordance with Part 4 of this Article against the first presented part of a bill of lading lawfully drawn in a set. Such delivery discharges the bailee's obligation on the whole bill.

Section 7—305. Destination Bills.

(1) Instead of issuing a bill of lading to the consignor at the place of shipment a carrier may at the request of the consignor procure the bill to be issued at destination or at any other place designated in the request.

(2) Upon request of anyone entitled as against the carrier to control the goods while in transit and on surrender of any outstanding bill of lading or other receipt covering such goods, the issuer may procure a substitute bill to be issued at any place designated in the request.

Section 7—306. Altered Bills of Lading.

An unauthorized alteration or filling in of a blank in a bill of lading leaves the bill enforceable according to its original tenor.

Section 7—307. Lien of Carrier.

(1) A carrier has a lien on the goods covered by a bill of lading for charges subsequent to the date of the receipt of the goods for storage or transportation (including demurrage and terminal charges) and for expenses necessary for preservation of the goods incident to their transportation or reasonably incurred in their sale pursuant to law. But against a purchaser for value of a negotiable bill of lading, a carrier's lien is limited to charges stated in the bill or the applicable tariffs, or if no charges are stated then to a reasonable charge.

(2) A lien for charges and expenses under subsection (1) on goods which the carrier was required by law to receive for transportation is effective against the consignor or any person entitled to the goods unless the carrier had notice that the consignor lacked authority to subject the goods to such charges and expenses. Any other lien under subsection (1) is effective against the consignor and any person who permitted the bailor to have control or possession of the goods unless the carrier had notice that the bailor lacked such authority.

(3) A carrier loses his lien on any goods which he voluntarily delivers or which he unjustifiably refuses to deliver.

Section 7—308. Enforcement of Carrier's Lien.

(1) A carrier's lien may be enforced by public or private sale of the goods, in bloc or in parcels, at any time or place and on any terms which are commercially reasonable, after notifying all persons known to claim an interest in the goods. Such notification must include a statement of the amount due, the nature of the proposed sale and the time and place of any public sale. The fact that a better price could have been obtained by a sale at a different time or in a different method from that selected by the carrier is not of itself sufficient to establish that the sale was not made in a commercially reasonable manner. If the carrier either sells the goods in the usual manner in any recognized market therefor or if he sells at the price current in such market at the time of his sale or if he has otherwise sold in conformity with commercially reasonable practices among dealers in the type of goods sold, he has sold in a commercially reasonable manner. A sale of more goods than apparently necessary to be offered to ensure satisfaction of the obligation is not commercially reasonable except in cases covered by the preceding sentence.

(2) Before any sale pursuant to this section any person claiming a right in the goods may pay the amount necessary to satisfy the lien and the reasonable expenses incurred under this section. In that event the goods must not be sold, but must be retained by the carrier subject to the terms of the bill and this Article.

(3) The carrier may buy at any public sale pursuant to this section.

(4) A purchaser in good faith of goods sold to enforce a carrier's lien takes the goods free of any rights of persons against whom the lien was valid, despite

noncompliance by the carrier with the requirements of this section.

(5) The carrier may satisfy his lien from the proceeds of any sale pursuant to this section but must hold the balance, if any, for delivery on demand to any person to whom he would have been bound to deliver the goods.

(6) The rights provided by this section shall be in addition to all other rights allowed by law to a creditor against his debtor.

(7) A carrier's lien may be enforced in accordance with either subsection (1) or the procedure set forth in subsection (2) of Section 7—210.

(8) The carrier is liable for damages caused by failure to comply with the requirements for sale under this section and in case of willful violation is liable for conversion.

Section 7—309. Duty of Care; Contractual Limitation of Carrier's Liability.

(1) A carrier who issues a bill of lading whether negotiable or non-negotiable must exercise the degree of care in relation to the goods which a reasonably careful man would exercise under like circumstances. This subsection does not repeal or change any law or rule of law which imposes liability upon a common carrier for damages not caused by its negligence.

(2) Damages may be limited by a provision that the carrier's liability shall not exceed a value stated in the document if the carrier's rates are dependent upon value and the consignor by the carrier's tariff is afforded an opportunity to declare a higher value or a value as lawfully provided in the tariff, or where no tariff is filed he is otherwise advised of such opportunity; but no such limitation is effective with respect to the carrier's liability for conversion to its own use.

(3) Reasonable provisions as to the time and manner of presenting claims and instituting actions based on the shipment may be included in a bill of lading or tariff.

PART 4

WAREHOUSE RECEIPTS AND BILLS OF LADING: GENERAL OBLIGATIONS

Section 7—401. Irregularities in Issue of Receipt or Bill or Conduct of Issuer.

The obligations imposed by this Article on an issuer apply to a document of title regardless of the fact that

(a) the document may not comply with the requirements of this Article or of any other law or regulation regarding its issue, form or content; or

(b) the issuer may have violated laws regulating the conduct of his business; or

(c) the goods covered by the document were owned by the bailee at the time the document was issued; or

(d) the person issuing the document does not come within the definition of warehouseman if it purports to be a warehouse receipt.

Section 7—402. Duplicate Receipt or Bill; Overissue.

Neither a duplicate nor any other document of title purporting to cover goods already represented by an outstanding document of the same issuer confers any right in the goods, except as provided in the case of bills in a set, overissue of documents for fungible goods and substitutes for lost, stolen or destroyed documents. But the issuer is liable for damages caused by his overissue or failure to identify a duplicate document as such by conspicuous notation on its face.

Section 7—403. Obligation of Warehouseman or Carrier to Deliver; Excuse.

(1) The bailee must deliver the goods to a person entitled under the document

who complies with subsections (2) and (3), unless and to the extent that the bailee establishes any of the following:

  (a) delivery of the goods to a person whose receipt was rightful as against the claimant;

  (b) damage to or delay, loss or destuction of the goods for which the bailee is not liable [, but the burden of establishing negligence in such cases is on the person entitled under the document];

  Note: *The brackets in (1)(b) indicate that State enactments may differ on this point without serious damage to the principle of uniformity.*

  (c) previous sale or other disposition of the goods in lawful enforcement of a lien or on warehouseman's lawful termination of storage;

  (d) the exercise by a seller of his right to stop delivery pursuant to the provisions of the Article on Sales (Section 2—705);

  (e) a diversion, reconsignment or other disposition pursuant to the provisions of this Article (Section 7—303) or tariff regulating such right;

  (f) release, satisfaction or any other fact affording a personal defense against the claimant;

  (g) any other lawful excuse.

(2) A person claiming goods covered by a document of title must satisfy the bailee's lien where the bailee so requests or where the bailee is prohibited by law from delivering the goods until the charges are paid.

(3) Unless the person claiming is one against whom the document confers no right under Sec. 7—503 (1), he must surrender for cancellation or notation of partial deliveries any outstanding negotiable document covering the goods, and the bailee must cancel the document or conspicuously note the partial delivery thereon or be liable to any person to whom the document is duly negotiated.

(4) "Person entitled under the document" means holder in the case of a negotiable document, or the person to whom delivery is to be made by the terms of or pursuant to written instructions under a non-negotiable document.

Section 7—404. No Liability for Good Faith Delivery Pursuant to Receipt or Bill.

A bailee who in good faith including observance of reasonable commercial standards has received goods and delivered or otherwise disposed of them according to the terms of the document of title or pursuant to this Article is not liable therefor. This rule applies even though the person from whom he received the goods had no authority to procure the document or to dispose of the goods and even though the person to whom he delivered the goods had no authority to receive them.

PART 5

WAREHOUSE RECEIPTS AND BILLS OF LADING: NEGOTIATION AND TRANSFER

Section 7—501. Form of Negotiation and Requirements of "Due Negotiation".

(1) A negotiable document of title running to the order of a named person is negotiated by his indorsement and delivery. After his indorsement in blank or to bearer any person can negotiate it by delivery alone.

  (2) (a) A negotiable document of title is also negotiated by delivery alone when by its original terms it runs to bearer.

  (b) When a document running to the order of a named person is delivered to him, the effect is the same as if the document had been negotiated.

(3) Negotiation of a negotiable document of title after it has been indorsed to a specified person requires indorsement by the special indorsee as well as delivery.

(4) A negotiable document of title is "duly negotiated" when it is negotiated in the manner stated in this section to a holder who purchases it in good faith without notice of any defense against or claim to it on the part of any person and for value, unless it is established that the negotiation is not in the regular course of business or financing or involves receiving the document in settlement or payment of a money obligation.

(5) Indorsement of a non-negotiable document neither makes it negotiable nor adds to the transferee's rights.

(6) The naming in a negotiable bill of a person to be notified of the arrival of the goods does not limit the negotiability of the bill nor constitute notice to a purchaser thereof of any interest of such person in the goods.

Section 7—502. Rights Acquired by Due Negotiation.

(1) Subject to the following section and to the provisions of Section 7—205 on fungible goods, a holder to whom a negotiable document of title has been duly negotiated acquires thereby:

(a) title to the document;

(b) title to the goods;

(c) all rights accruing under the law of agency or estoppel, including rights to goods delivered to the bailee after the document was issued; and

(d) the direct obligation of the issuer to hold or deliver the goods according to the terms of the document free of any defense or claim by him except those arising under the terms of the document or under this Article. In the case of a delivery order the bailee's obligation accrues only upon acceptance, and the obligation acquired by the holder is that the issuer and any indorser will procure the acceptance of the bailee.

(2) Subject to the following section, title and rights so acquired are not defeated by any stoppage of the goods represented by the document or by surrender of such goods by the bailee, and are not impaired even though the negotiation or any prior negotiation constituted a breach of duty or even though any person has been deprived of possession of the document by misrepresentation, fraud, accident, mistake, duress, loss, theft or conversion, or even though a previous sale or other transfer of the goods or document has been made to a third person.

Section 7—503. Document of Title to Goods Defeated in Certain Cases.

(1) A document of title confers no right in goods against a person who before issuance of the document had a legal interest or a perfected security interest in them and who neither

(a) delivered or entrusted them or any document of title covering them to the bailor or his nominee with actual or apparent authority to ship, store or sell or with power to obtain delivery under this Article (Section 7—403) or with power of disposition under this Act (Sections 2 —403 and 9—307) or other statute or rule of law; nor

(b) acquiesced in the procurement by the bailor or his nominee of any document of title.

(2) Title to goods based upon an unaccepted delivery order is subject to the rights of anyone to whom a negotiable warehouse receipt or bill of lading covering the goods has been duly negotiated. Such a title may be defeated under the next section to the same extent as the rights of the issuer or a transferee from the issuer.

(3) Title to goods based upon a bill of lading issued to a freight forwarder is subject to the rights of anyone to whom a bill issued by the freight forwarder is duly negotiated; but delivery by the carrier in accordance with Part 4 of this Article pursuant to its own bill of lading discharges the carrier's obligation to deliver.

Section 7—504. Rights Acquired in the Absence of Due Negotiation; Effect of Diversion; Seller's Stoppage of Delivery.

(1) A transferee of a document, whether negotiable or non-negotiable, to whom the document has been delivered but not duly negotiated, acquires the title and rights which his transferor had or had actual authority to convey.

(2) In the case of a non-negotiable document, until but not after the bailee receives notification of the transfer, the rights of the transferee may be defeated

(a) by those creditors of the transferor who could treat the sale as void under Section 2—402; or

(b) by a buyer from the transferor in ordinary course of business if the bailee has delivered the goods to the buyer or received notification of his rights; or

(c) as against the bailee by good faith dealings of the bailee with the transferor.

(3) A diversion or other change of shipping instructions by the consignor in a non-negotiable bill of lading which causes the bailee not to deliver to the consignee defeats the consignee's title to the goods if they have been delivered to a buyer in ordinary course of business and in any event defeats the consignee's rights against the bailee.

(4) Delivery pursuant to a non-negotiable document may be stopped by a seller under Section 2—705, and subject to the requirement of due notification there provided. A bailee honoring the seller's instructions is entitled to be indemnified by the seller against any resulting loss or expense.

Section 7—505. Indorser Not a Guarantor for Other Parties.

The indorsement of a document of title issued by a bailee does not make the indorser liable for any default by the bailee or by previous indorsers.

Section 7—506. Delivery Without Indorsement; Right to Compel Indorsement.

The transferee of a negotiable document of title has a specifically enforceable right to have his transferor supply any necessary indorsement, but the transfer becomes a negotiation only as of the time the indorsement is supplied.

Section 7—507. Warranties on Negotiation or Transfer of Receipt or Bill.

Where a person negotiates or transfers a document of title for value otherwise than as a mere intermediary under the next following section, then unless otherwise agreed he warrants to his immediate purchaser only in addition to any warranty made in selling the goods

(a) that the document is genuine; and

(b) that he has no knowledge of any fact which would impair its validity or worth; and

(c) that his negotiation or transfer is rightful and fully effective with respect to the title to the document and the goods it represents.

Section 7—508. Warranties of Collecting Bank as to Documents.

A collecting bank or other intermediary known to be entrusted with documents on behalf of another or with collection of a draft or other claim against delivery of documents warrants by such delivery of the documents only its own good faith and authority. This rule applies even though the intermediary has purchased or made advances against the claim or draft to be collected.

Section 7—509. Receipt or Bill: When Adequate Compliance With Commercial Contract.

The question whether a document is adequate to fulfill the obligations of a contract for sale or the conditions of a credit is governed by the Articles on Sales (Article 2) and on Letters of Credit (Article 5).

PART 6

WAREHOUSE RECEIPTS AND BILLS OF LADING:
MISCELLANEOUS PROVISIONS

Section 7—601. Lost and Missing Documents.

(1) If a document has been lost, stolen or destroyed, a court may order delivery of the goods or issuance of a substitute document and the bailee may without liability to any person comply with such order. If the document was negotiable, the claimant must post security approved by the court to indemnify any person who may suffer loss as a result of non-surrender of the document. If the document was not negotiable, such security may be required at the discretion of the court. The court may also in its discretion order payment of the bailee's reasonable costs and counsel fees.

(2) A bailee who without court order delivers goods to a person claiming under a missing negotiable document is liable to any person injured thereby, and if the delivery is not in good faith becomes liable for conversion. Delivery in good faith is not conversion if made in accordance with a filed classification or tariff or, where no classification or tariff is filed, if the claimant posts security with the bailee in an amount at least double the value of the goods at the time of posting to indemnify any person injured by the delivery who files a notice of claim within one year after the delivery.

Section 7—602. Attachment of Goods Covered by a Negotiable Document.

Except where the document was originally issued upon delivery of the goods by a person who had no power to dispose of them, no lien attaches by virtue of any judicial process to goods in the possession of a bailee for which a negotiable document of title is outstanding unless the document be first surrendered to the bailee or its negotiation enjoined, and the bailee shall not be compelled to deliver the goods pursuant to process until the document is surrendered to him or impounded by the court. One who purchases the document for value without notice of the process or injunction takes free of the lien imposed by judicial process.

Section 7—603. Conflicting Claims; Interpleader.

If more than one person claims title or possession of the goods, the bailee is excused from delivery until he has had a reasonable time to ascertain the validity of the adverse claims or to bring an action to compel all claimants to interplead and may compel such interpleader, either in defending an action for non-delivery of the goods, or by original action, whichever is appropriate.

ARTICLE 8

INVESTMENT SECURITIES

PART 1

SHORT TITLE AND GENERAL MATTERS

Section 8—101. Short Title.

This Article shall be known and may be cited as Uniform Commercial Code —Investment Securities.

Section 8—102. Definitions and Index of Definitions.

(1) In this Article unless the context otherwise requires
    (a) A "security" is an instrument which

    (i) is issued in bearer or regis-
tered form; and

    (ii) is of a type commonly dealt
in upon securities exchanges
or markets or commonly
recognized in any area in
which it is issued or dealt
in as a medium for investment; and

    (iii) is either one of a class or
series or by its terms is
divisible into a class or
series of instruments; and

    (iv) evidences a share, partici-
pation or other interest in
property or in an enterprise
or evidences an obligation
of the issuer.

(b) A writing which is a security
is governed by this Article and
not by Uniform Commercial
Code-Commercial Paper even
though it also meets the requirements of that Article. This
Article does not apply to money.

(c) A security is in "registered
form" when it specifies a person
entitled to the security or to
the rights it evidences and when
its transfer may be registered
upon books maintained for that
purpose by or on behalf of an
issuer or the security so states.

(d) A security is in "bearer form"
when it runs to bearer according to its terms and not by
reason of any indorsement.

(2) A "subsequent purchaser" is a
person who takes other than by original
issue.

(3) A "clearing corporation" is a corporation all of the capital stock of which
is held by or for a national securities
exchange or association registered under
a statute of the United States such as
the Securities Exchange Act of 1934.

(4) A "custodian bank" is any bank
or trust company which is supervised
and examined by state or federal authority having supervision over banks and
which is acting as custodian for a clearing corporation.

(5) Other definitions applying to this
Article or to specified Parts thereof and
the sections in which they appear are:

"Adverse claim".	Section 8–301.
"Bona fide purchaser".	Section 8–302.
"Broker".	Section 8–303.
"Guarantee of the signature".	Section 8–402.
"Intermediary bank."	Section 4–105.
"Issuer".	Section 8–201.
"Overissue".	Section 8–104.

(6) In addition Article 1 contains
general definitions and principles of construction and interpretation applicable
throughout this Article.

Section 8—103. Issuer's Lien.

A lien upon a security in favor of an
issuer thereof is valid against a purchaser
only if the right of the issuer to such lien
is noted conspicuously on the security.

Section 8—104. Effect of Overissue; "Overissue."

(1) The provisions of this Article
which validate a security or compel its
issue or reissue do not apply to the
extent that validation, issue or reissue
would result in overissue; but

    (a) if an identical security which
does not constitute an overissue
is reasonably available for purchase, the person entitled to
issue or validation may compel
the issuer to purchase and deliver such a security to him
against surrender of the security, if any, which he holds; or

    (b) if a security is not so available
for purchase, the person entitled
to issue or validation may recover from the issuer the price
he or the last purchaser for
value paid for it with interest
from the date of his demand.

(2) "Overissue" means the issue of
securities in excess of the amount which
the issuer has corporate power to issue.

Section 8—105. Securities Negotiable; Presumptions.

(1) Securities governed by this Article
are negotiable instruments.

(2) In any action on a security

    (a) unless specifically denied in the
pleadings, each signature on the
security or in a necessary indorsement is admitted;

(b) when the effectiveness of a signature is put in issue, the burden of establishing it is on the party claiming under the signature but the signature is presumed to be genuine or authorized;

(c) when signatures are admitted or established, production of the instrument entitles a holder to recover on it unless the defendant establishes a defense or a defect going to the validity of the security; and

(d) after it is shown that a defense or defect exists, the plaintiff has the burden of establishing that he or some person under whom he claims is a person against whom the defense or defect is ineffective (Section 8—202).

Section 8—106. Applicability.

The validity of a security and the rights and duties of the issuer with respect to registration of transfer are governed by the law (including the conflict of laws rules) of the jurisdiction of organization of the issuer.

Section 8—107. Securities Deliverable; Action for Price.

(1) Unless otherwise agreed and subject to any applicable law or regulation respecting short sales, a person obligated to deliver securities may deliver any security of the specified issue in bearer form or registered in the name of the transferee or indorsed to him or in blank.

(2) When the buyer fails to pay the price as it comes due under a contract of sale, the seller may recover the price

(a) of securities accepted by the buyer; and

(b) of other securities if efforts at their resale would be unduly burdensome or if there is no readily available market for their resale.

PART 2

ISSUE—ISSUER

Section 8—201. "Issuer."

(1) With respect to obligations on or defenses to a security, "issuer" includes a person who

(a) places or authorizes the placing of his name on a security (otherwise than as authenticating trustee, registrar, transfer agent or the like) to evidence that it represents a share, participation or other interest in his property or in an enterprise or to evidence his duty to perform an obligation evidenced by the security; or

(b) directly or indirectly creates fractional interests in his rights or property which fractional interests are evidenced by securities; or

(c) becomes responsible for or in place of any other person described as an issuer in this section.

(2) With respect to obligations on or defenses to a security, a guarantor is an issuer to the extent of his guaranty whether or not his obligation is noted on the security.

(3) With respect to registration of transfer (Part 4 of this Article) "issuer" means a person on whose behalf transfer books are maintained.

Section 8—202. Issuer's Responsibility and Defenses; Notice of Defect or Defense.

(1) Even against a purchaser for value and without notice, the terms of a security include those stated on the security and those made part of the security by reference to another instrument, indenture or document or to a constitution, statute, ordinance, rule, regulation, order or the like to the extent that the terms so referred to do not conflict with the stated terms. Such a reference does not of itself charge a purchaser for value with notice of a defect going to the

validity of the security even though the security expressly states that a person accepting it admits such notice.

    (2) (a) A security other than one issued by a government or governmental agency or unit, even though issued with a defect going to its validity, is valid in the hands of a purchaser for value and without notice of the particular defect unless the defect involves a violation of constitutional provisions in which case the security is valid in the hands of a subsequent purchaser for value and without notice of the defect.

    (b) The rule of subparagraph (a) applies to an issuer which is a government or governmental agency or unit only if either there has been substantial compliance with the legal requirements governing the issue or the issuer has received a substantial consideration for the issue as a whole or for the particular security and a stated purpose of the issue is one for which the issuer has power to borrow money or issue the security.

(3) Except as otherwise provided in the case of certain unauthorized signatures on issue (Section 8—205), lack of genuineness of a security is a complete defense even against a purchaser for value and without notice.

(4) All other defenses of the issuer including nondelivery and conditional delivery of the security are ineffective against a purchaser for value who has taken without notice of the particular defense.

(5) Nothing in this section shall be construed to affect the right of a party to a "when, as and if issued" or a "when distributed" contract to cancel the contract in the event of a material change in the character of the security which is the subject of the contract or in the plan or arrangement pursuant to which such security is to be issued or distributed.

Section 8—203. Staleness as Notice of Defects or Defenses.

(1) After an act or event which creates a right to immediate performance of the principal obligation evidenced by the security or which sets a date on or after which the security is to be presented or surrendered for redemption or exchange, a purchaser is charged with notice of any defect in its issue or defense of the issuer

    (a) if the act or event is one requiring the payment of money or the delivery of securities or both on presentation or surrender of the security and such funds or securities are available on the date set for payment or exchange and he takes the security more than one year after that date; and

    (b) if the act or event is not covered by paragraph (a) and he takes the security more than two years after the date set for surrender or presentation or the date on which such performance became due.

(2) A call which has been revoked is not within subsection (1).

Section 8—204. Effect of Issuer's Restrictions on Transfer.

Unless noted conspicuously on the security a restriction on transfer imposed by the issuer, even though otherwise lawful, is ineffective except against a person with actual knowledge of it.

Section 8—205. Effect of Unauthorized Signature on Issue.

An unauthorized signature placed on a security prior to or in the course of issue is ineffective except that the signature is effective in favor of a purchaser for value and without notice of the lack of authority if the signing has been done by

    (a) an authenticating trustee, registrar, transfer agent or other person entrusted by the issuer with the signing of the security or of similar securities or their immediate preparation for signing; or

(b) an employee of the issuer or of any of the foregoing entrusted with responsible handling of the security.

Section 8—206. Completion or Alteration of Instrument.

(1) Where a security contains the signatures necessary to its issue or transfer but is incomplete in any other respect

(a) any person may complete it by filling in the blanks as authorized; and

(b) even though the blanks are incorrectly filled in, the security as completed is enforceable by a purchaser who took it for value and without notice of such incorrectness.

(2) A complete security which has been improperly altered even though fraudulently remains enforceable but only according to its original terms.

Section 8—207. Rights of Issuer With Respect to Registered Owners.

(1) Prior to due presentment for registration of transfer of a security in registered form, the issuer or indenture trustee may treat the registered owner as the person exclusively entitled to vote, to receive notifications and otherwise to exercise all the rights and powers of an owner.

(2) Nothing in this Article shall be construed to affect the liability of the registered owner of a security for calls, assessments or the like.

Section 8—208. Effect of Signature of Authenticating Trustee, Registrar or Transfer Agent.

(1) A person placing his signature upon a security as authenticating trustee, registrar, transfer agent or the like warrants to a purchaser for value without notice of the particular defect that

(a) the security is genuine; and

(b) his own participation in the issue of the security is within his capacity and within the scope of the authorization received by him from the issuer; and

(c) he has reasonable grounds to believe that the security is in the form and within the amount the issuer is authorized to issue.

(2) Unless otherwise agreed, a person by so placing his signature does not assume responsibility for the validity of the security in other respects.

PART 3

PURCHASE

Section 8—301. Rights Acquired by Purchaser; "Adverse Claim"; Title Acquired by Bona Fide Purchaser.

(1) Upon delivery of a security the purchaser acquires the rights in the security which his transferor had or had actual authority to convey except that a purchaser who has himself been a party to any fraud or illegality affecting the security or who as a prior holder had notice of an adverse claim cannot improve his position by taking from a later bona fide purchaser. "Adverse claim" includes a claim that a transfer was or would be wrongful or that a particular adverse person is the owner of or has an interest in the security.

(2) A bona fide purchaser in addition to acquiring the rights of a purchaser also acquires the security free of any adverse claim.

(3) A purchaser of a limited interest acquires rights only to the extent of the interest purchased.

Section 8—302. "Bona Fide Purchaser."

A "bona fide purchaser" is a purchaser for value in good faith and without notice of any adverse claim who takes delivery of a security in bearer form or of one in registered form issued to him or indorsed to him or in blank.

Section 8—303. "Broker."

"Broker" means a person engaged for all or part of his time in the business of buying and selling securities, who in the transaction concerned acts for, or buys a security from or sells a security to a customer. Nothing in this Article determines the capacity in which a person acts for purposes of any other statute or rule to which such person is subject.

Section 8—304. Notice to Purchaser of Adverse Claims.

(1) A purchaser (including a broker for the seller or buyer but excluding an intermediary bank) of a security is charged with notice of adverse claims if
  (a) the security whether in bearer or registered form has been indorsed "for collection" or "for surrender" or for some other purpose not involving transfer; or
  (b) the security is in bearer form and has on it an unambiguous statement that it is the property of a person other than the transferor. The mere writing of a name on a security is not such a statement.

(2) The fact that the purchaser (including a broker for the seller or buyer) has notice that the security is held for a third person or is registered in the name of or indorsed by a fiduciary does not create a duty of inquiry into the rightfulness of the transfer or constitute notice of adverse claims. If, however, the purchaser (excluding an intermediary bank) has knowledge that the proceeds are being used or that the transaction is for the individual benefit of the fiduciary or otherwise in breach of duty, the purchaser is charged with notice of adverse claims.

Section 8—305. Staleness as Notice of Adverse Claims.

An act or event which creates a right to immediate performance of the principal obligation evidenced by the security or which sets a date on or after which the security is to be presented or surrendered for redemption or exchange does not of itself constitute any notice of adverse claims except in the case of a purchase

  (a) after one year from any date set for such presentment or surrender for redemption or exchange; or
  (b) after six months from any date set for payment of money against presentation or surrender of the security if funds are available for payment on that date.

Section 8—306. Warranties on Presentment and Transfer.

(1) A person who presents a security for registration of transfer or for payment or exchange warrants to the issuer that he is entitled to the registration, payment or exchange. But a purchaser for value without notice of adverse claims who receives a new, reissued or re-registered security on registration of transfer warrants only that he has no knowledge of any unauthorized signature (Section 8—311) in a necessary indorsement.

(2) A person by transferring a security to a purchaser for value warrants only that
  (a) his transfer is effective and rightful; and
  (b) the security is genuine and has not been materially altered; and
  (c) he knows no fact which might impair the validity of the security.

(3) Where a security is delivered by an intermediary known to be entrusted with delivery of the security on behalf of another or with collection of a draft or other claim against such delivery, the intermediary by such delivery warrants only his own good faith and authority even though he has purchased or made advances against the claim to be collected against the delivery.

(4) A pledgee or other holder for security who redelivers the security received, or after payment and on order of the debtor delivers that security to a third person, makes only the warranties of an intermediary under subsection (3).

(5) A broker gives to his customer and to the issuer and a purchaser the warranties provided in this section and

has the rights and privileges of a purchaser under this section. The warranties of and in favor of the broker acting as an agent are in addition to applicable warranties given by and in favor of his customer.

Section 8—307. Effect of Delivery Without Indorsement; Right to Compel Indorsement.

Where a security in registered form has been delivered to a purchaser without a necessary indorsement, he may become a bona fide purchaser only as of the time the indorsement is supplied, but against the transferor the transfer is complete upon delivery and the purchaser has a specifically enforceable right to have any necessary indorsement supplied.

Section 8—308. Indorsement, How Made; Special Indorsement; Indorser Not a Guarantor; Partial Assignment.

(1) An indorsement of a security in registered form is made when an appropriate person signs on it or on a separate document an assignment or transfer of the security or a power to assign or transfer it or when the signature of such person is written without more upon the back of the security.

(2) An indorsement may be in blank or special. An indorsement in blank includes an indorsement to bearer. A special indorsement specifies the person to whom the security is to be transferred, or who has power to transfer it. A holder may convert a blank indorsement into a special indorsement.

(3) "An appropriate person" in subsection (1) means

   (a) the person specified by the security or by special indorsement to be entitled to the security; or
   (b) where the person so specified is described as a fiduciary but is no longer serving in the described capacity,—either that person or his successor; or
   (c) where the security or indorsement so specifies more than one person as fiduciaries and one or more are no longer serving in

the described capacity,—the remaining fiduciary or fiduciaries, whether or not a successor has been appointed or qualified; or

   (d) where the person so specified is an individual and is without capacity to act by virtue of death, incompetence, infancy or otherwise,—his executor, administrator, guardian or like fiduciary; or
   (e) where the security or indorsement so specifies more than one person as tenants by the entirety or with right of survivorship and by reason of death all cannot sign,—the survivor or survivors; or
   (f) a person having power to sign under applicable law or controlling instrument; or
   (g) to the extent that any of the foregoing persons may act through an agent,—his authorized agent.

(4) Unless otherwise agreed the indorser by his indorsement assumes no obligation that the security will be honored by the issuer.

(5) An indorsement purporting to be only of part of a security representing units intended by the issuer to be separately transferable is effective to the extent of the indorsement.

(6) Whether the person signing is appropriate is determined as of the date of signing and an indorsement by such a person does not become unauthorized for the purposes of this Article by virtue of any subsequent change of circumstances.

(7) Failure of a fiduciary to comply with a controlling instrument or with the law of the state having jurisdiction of the fiduciary relationship, including any law requiring the fiduciary to obtain court approval of the transfer, does not render his indorsement unauthorized for the purpose of this Article.

Section 8—309. Effect of Indorsement Without Delivery.

An indorsement of a security whether special or in blank does not constitute a transfer until delivery of the security on which it appears or, if the indorsement is on a separate document, until delivery of both the document and the security.

Section 8—310. Indorsement of Security in Bearer Form.

An indorsement of a security in bearer form may give notice of adverse claims (Section 8—304) but does not otherwise affect any right to registration the holder may possess.

Section 8—311. Effect of Unauthorized Indorsement.

Unless the owner has ratified an unauthorized indorsement or is otherwise precluded from asserting its ineffectiveness

  (a) he may assert its ineffectiveness against the issuer or any purchaser other than a purchaser for value and without notice of adverse claims who has in good faith received a new, reissued or re-registered security on registration of transfer; or

  (b) an issuer who registers the transfer of a security upon the unauthorized indorsement is subject to liability for improper registration (Section 8—404).

Section 8—312. Effect of Guaranteeing Signature or Indorsement.

(1) Any person guaranteeing a signature of an indorser of a security warrants that at the time of signing

  (a) the signature was genuine; and

  (b) the signer was an appropriate person to indorse (Section 8—308); and

  (c) the signer had legal capacity to sign.

But the guarantor does not otherwise warrant the rightfulness of the particular transfer.

(2) Any person may guarantee an indorsement of a security and by so doing warrants not only the signature (subsection 1) but also the rightfulness of the particular transfer in all respects. But no issuer may require a guarantee

of indorsement as a condition to registration of transfer.

(3) The foregoing warranties are made to any person taking or dealing with the security in reliance on the guarantee and the guarantor is liable to such person for any loss resulting from breach of the warranties.

Section 8—313. When Delivery to the Purchaser Occurs; Purchaser's Broker as Holder.

(1) Delivery to a purchaser occurs when

  (a) he or a person designated by him acquires possession of a security; or

  (b) his broker acquires possession of a security specially indorsed to or issued in the name of the purchaser; or

  (c) his broker sends him confirmation of the purchase and also by book entry or otherwise identifies a specific security in the broker's possession as belonging to the purchaser; or

  (d) with respect to an identified security to be delivered while still in the possession of a third person when that person acknowledges that he holds for the purchaser; or

  (e) appropriate entries on the books of a clearing corporation are made under Section 8—320.

(2) The purchaser is the owner of a security held for him by his broker but is not the holder except as specified in subparagraphs (b), (c) and (e) of subsection (1). Where a security is part of a fungible bulk, the purchaser is the owner of a proportionate property interest in the fungible bulk.

(3) Notice of an adverse claim received by the broker or by the purchaser after the broker takes delivery as a holder for value is not effective either as to the broker or as to the purchaser. However, as between the broker and the purchaser the purchaser may demand delivery of an equivalent security as to which no notice of an adverse claim has been received.

Section 8—314. Duty to Deliver, When Completed.

(1) Unless otherwise agreed, where a sale of a security is made on an exchange or otherwise through brokers

    (a) the selling customer fulfills his duty to deliver when he places such a security in the possession of the selling broker or of a person designated by the broker or if requested causes an acknowledgment to be made to the selling broker that it is held for him; and

    (b) the selling broker including a correspondent broker acting for a selling customer fulfills his duty to deliver by placing the security or a like security in the possession of the buying broker or a person designated by him or by effecting clearance of the sale in accordance with the rules of the exchange on which the transaction took place.

(2) Except as otherwise provided in this section and unless otherwise agreed, a transferor's duty to deliver a security under a contract of purchase is not fulfilled until he places the security in form to be negotiated by the purchaser in the possession of the purchaser or of a person designated by him or at the purchaser's request causes an acknowledgment to be made to the purchaser that it is held for him. Unless made on an exchange a sale to a broker purchasing for his own account is within this subsection and not within subsection (1).

Section 8—315. Action Against Purchaser Based Upon Wrongful Transfer.

(1) Any person against whom the transfer of a security is wrongful for any reason, including his incapacity, may against anyone except a bona fide purchaser reclaim posession of the security or obtain possession of any new security evidencing all or part of the same rights or have damages.

(2) If the transfer is wrongful because of an unauthorized indorsement, the owner may also reclaim or obtain possession of the security or new security even from a bona fide purchaser if the ineffectiveness of the purported indorsement can be asserted against him under the provisions of this Article on unauthorized indorsements (Section 8—311).

(3) The right to obtain or reclaim possession of a security may be specifically enforced and its transfer enjoined and the security impounded pending the litigation.

Section 8—316. Purchaser's Right to Requisites for Registration of Transfer on Books.

Unless otherwise agreed the transferor must on due demand supply his purchaser with any proof of his authority to transfer or with any other requisite which may be necessary to obtain registration of the transfer of the security, but if the transfer is not for value, a transferor need not do so unless the purchaser furnishes the necessary expenses. Failure to comply with a demand made within a reasonable time gives the purchaser the right to reject or rescind the transfer.

Section 8—317. Attachment or Levy upon Security.

(1) No attachment or levy upon a security or any share or other interest evidenced thereby which is outstanding shall be valid until the security is actually seized by the officer making the attachment or levy, but a security which has been surrendered to the issuer may be attached or levied upon at the source.

(2) A creditor whose debtor is the owner of a security shall be entitled to such aid from courts of appropriate jurisdiction, by injunction or otherwise, in reaching such security or in satisfying the claim by means thereof as is allowed at law or in equity in regard to property which cannot readily be attached or levied upon by ordinary legal process.

Section 8—318. No Conversion by Good Faith Delivery.

An agent or bailee who in good faith (including observance of reasonable commercial standards if he is in the business of buying, selling or otherwise dealing with securities) has received securities and sold, pledged or delivered them according to the instructions of his principal is not liable for conversion or for participation in breach of fiduciary duty although the principal had no right to dispose of them.

Section 8—319. Statute of Frauds.

A contract for the sale of securities is not enforceable by way of action or defense unless

(a) there is some writing signed by the party against whom enforcement is sought or by his authorized agent or broker sufficient to indicate that a contract has been made, for sale of a stated quantity of described securities at a defined or stated price; or

(b) delivery of the security has been accepted or payment has been made but the contract is enforceable under this provision only to the extent of such delivery or payment; or

(c) within a reasonable time a writing in confirmation of the sale or purchase and sufficient against the sender under paragraph (a) has been received by the party against whom enforcement is sought and he has failed to send written objection to its contents within ten days after its receipt; or

(d) the party against whom enforcement is sought admits in his pleading, testimony or otherwise in court that a contract was made for sale of a stated quantity of described securities at a defined or stated price.

Section 8—320. Transfer or Pledge within a Central Depository System.

(1) If a security

(a) is in the custody of a clearing corporation or of a custodian bank or a nominee of either subject to the instructions of the clearing corporation; and

(b) is in bearer form or indorsed in blank by an appropriate person or registered in the name of the clearing corporation or custodian bank or a nominee of either; and

(c) is shown on the account of a transferor or pledgor on the books of the clearing corporation;

then, in addition to other methods, a transfer or pledge of the security or any interest therein may be effected by the making of appropriate entries on the books of the clearing corporation reducing the account of the transferor or pledgor and increasing the account of the transferee or pledgee by the amount of the obligation or the number of shares or rights transferred or pledged.

(2) Under this section entries may be with respect to like securities or interests therein as a part of a fungible bulk and may refer merely to a quantity of a particular security without reference to the name of the registered owner, certificate or bond number or the like and, in appropriate cases, may be on a net basis taking into account other transfers or pledges of the same security.

(3) A transfer or pledge under this section has the effect of a delivery of a security in bearer form or duly indorsed in blank (Section 8—301) representing the amount of the obligation or the number of shares or rights transferred or pledged. If a pledge or the creation of a security interest is intended, the making of entries has the effect of a taking of delivery by the pledgee or a secured party (Sections 9—304 and 9—305). A transferee or pledgee under this section is a holder.

(4) A transfer or pledge under this section does not constitute a registration of transfer under Part 4 of this Article.

(5) That entries made on the books of the clearing corporation as provided in subsection (1) are not appropriate does not affect the validity or effect of the entries nor the liabilities or obligations of the clearing corporation to any person adversely affected thereby.

PART 4

REGISTRATION

Section 8—401. Duty of Issuer to Register Transfer.

(1) Where a security in registered form is presented to the issuer with a request to register transfer, the issuer is under a duty to register the transfer as requested if

    (a) the security is indorsed by the appropriate person or persons (Section 8—308); and

    (b) reasonable assurance is given that those indorsements are genuine and effective (Section 8—402); and

    (c) the issuer has no duty to inquire into adverse claims or has discharged any such duty (Section 8—403); and

    (d) any applicable law relating to the collection of taxes has been complied with; and

    (e) the transfer is in fact rightful or is to a bona fide purchaser.

(2) Where an issuer is under a duty to register a transfer of a security, the issuer is also liable to the person presenting it for registration or his principal for loss resulting from any unreasonable delay in registration or from failure or refusal to register the transfer.

Section 8—402. Assurance that Indorsements Are Effective.

(1) The issuer may require the following assurance that each necessary indorsement (Section 8—308) is genuine and effective

    (a) in all cases, a guarantee of the signature (subsection (1) of Section 8—312) of the person indorsing; and

    (b) where the indorsement is by an agent, appropriate assurance of authority to sign;

    (c) where the indorsement is by a fiduciary, appropriate evidence of appointment or incumbency;

    (d) where there is more than one fiduciary, reasonable assurance that all who are required to sign have done so;

    (e) where the indorsement is by a person not covered by any of the foregoing, assurance appropriate to the case corresponding as nearly as may be to the foregoing.

(2) A "guarantee of the signature" in subsection (1) means a guarantee signed by or on behalf of a person reasonably believed by the issuer to be responsible. The issuer may adopt standards with respect to responsibility provided such standards are not manifestly unreasonable.

(3) "Appropriate evidence of appointment or incumbency" in subsection (1) means

    (a) in the case of a fiduciary appointed or qualified by a court, a certificate issued by or under the direction or supervision of that court or an officer thereof and dated within sixty days before the date of presentation for transfer; or

    (b) in any other case, a copy of a document showing the appointment or a certificate issued by or on behalf of a person reasonably believed by the issuer to be responsible or, in the absence of such a document or certificate, other evidence reasonably deemed by the issuer to be appropriate. The issuer may adopt standards with respect to such evidence provided such standards are not manifestly unreasonable. The issuer is not charged with notice of the contents of any document obtained pursuant to this paragraph (b) except to the extent that the contents relate directly to the appointment or incumbency.

(4) The issuer may elect to require reasonable assurance beyond that specified in this section but if it does so and for a purpose other than that specified in subsection 3(b) both requires and

obtains a copy of a will, trust, indenture, articles of co-partnership, by-laws or other controlling instrument, it is charged with notice of all matters contained therein affecting the transfer.

Section 8—403. Limited Duty of Inquiry.

(1) An issuer to whom a security is presented for registration is under a duty to inquire into adverse claims if

(a) a written notification of an adverse claim is received at a time and in a manner which affords the issuer a reasonable opportunity to act on it prior to the issuance of a new, reissued or re-registered security and the notification identifies the claimant, the registered owner and the issue of which the security is a part and provides an address for communications directed to the claimant; or

(b) the issuer is charged with notice of an adverse claim from a controlling instrument which it has elected to require under subsection (4) of Section 8—402.

(2) The issuer may discharge any duty of inquiry by any reasonable means, including notifying an adverse claimant by registered or certified mail at the address furnished by him or if there be no such address at his residence or regular place of business that the security has been presented for registration of transfer by a named person, and that the transfer will be registered unless within thirty days from the date of mailing the notification, either

(a) an appropriate restraining order, injunction or other process issues from a court of competent jurisdiction; or

(b) an indemnity bond sufficient in the issuer's judgment to protect the issuer and any transfer agent, registrar or other agent of the issuer involved, from any loss which it or they may suffer by complying with the adverse claim is filed with the issuer.

(3) Unless an issuer is charged with notice of an adverse claim from a controlling instrument which it has elected to require under subsection (4) of Section 8—402 or receives notification of an adverse claim under subsection (1) of this section, where a security presented for registration is indorsed by the appropriate person or persons the issuer is under no duty to inquire into adverse claims. In particular

(a) an issuer registering a security in the name of a person who is a fiduciary or who is described as a fiduciary is not bound to inquire into the existence, extent, or correct description of the fiduciary relationship; and thereafter the issuer may assume without inquiry that the newly registered owner continues to be the fiduciary until the issuer receives written notice that the fiduciary is no longer acting as such with respect to the particular security;

(b) an issuer registering transfer on an indorsement by a fiduciary is not bound to inquire whether the transfer is made in compliance with a controlling instrument or with the law of the state having jurisdiction of the fiduciary relationship, including any law requiring the fiduciary to obtain court approval of the transfer; and

(c) the issuer is not charged with notice of the contents of any court record or file or other recorded or unrecorded document even though the document is in its possession and even though the transfer is made on the indorsement of a fiduciary to the fiduciary himself or to his nominee.

Section 8—404. Liability and Non-Liability for Registration.

(1) Except as otherwise provided in any law relating to the collection of taxes, the issuer is not liable to the owner or any other person suffering loss as a result of the registration of a transfer of a security if

    (a) there were on or with the security the necessary indorsements (Section 8—308); and

    (b) the issuer had no duty to inquire into adverse claims or has discharged any such duty (Section 8—403).

(2) Where an issuer has registered a transfer of a security to a person not entitled to it, the sisuer on demand must deliver a like security to the true owner unless

    (a) the registration was pursuant to subsection (1); or

    (b) the owner is precluded from asserting any claim for registering the transfer under subsection (1) of the following section; or

    (c) such delivery would result in overissue, in which case the issuer's liability is governed by Section 8—104.

Section 8—405. Lost, Destroyed and Stolen Securities.

(1) Where a security has been lost, apparently destroyed or wrongfully taken and the owner fails to notify the issuer of that fact within a reasonable time after he has notice of it and the issuer registers a transfer of the security before receiving such a notification, the owner is precluded from asserting against the issuer any claim for registering the transfer under the preceding section or any claim to a new security under this section.

(2) Where the owner of a security claims that the security has been lost, destroyed or wrongfully taken, the issuer must issue a new security in place of the original security if the owner

    (a) so requests before the issuer has notice that the security has been acquired by a bona fide purchaser; and

    (b) files with the issuer a sufficient indemnity bond; and

    (c) satisfies any other reasonable requirements imposed by the issuer.

(3) If, after the issue of the new security, a bona fide purchaser of the original security presents it for registration of transfer, the issuer must register the transfer unless registration would result in overissue, in which event the issuer's liability is governed by Section 8—104. In addition to any rights on the indemnity bond, the issuer may recover the new security from the person to whom it was issued or any person taking under him except a bona fide purchaser.

Section 8—406. Duty of Authenticating Trustee, Transfer Agent or Registrar.

(1) Where a person acts as authenticating trustee, transfer agent, registrar, or other agent for an issuer in the registration of transfers of its securities or in the issue of new securities or in the cancellation of surrendered securities

    (a) he is under a duty to the issuer to exercise good faith and due diligence in performing his functions; and

    (b) he has with regard to the particular functions he performs the same obligation to the holder or owner of the security and has the same rights and privileges as the issuer has in regard to those functions.

(2) Notice to an authenticating trustee, transfer agent, registrar or other such agent is notice to the issuer with respect to the functions performed by the agent.

ARTICLE 9

SECURED TRANSACTIONS; SALES OF ACCOUNTS, CONTRACT RIGHTS AND CHATTEL PAPER

PART 1

SHORT TITLE, APPLICABILITY AND DEFINITIONS

Section 9—101.—Short Title.

This Article shall be known and may be cited as Uniform Commercial Code —Secured Transactions.

Section 9—102. Policy and Scope of Article.

(1) Except as otherwise provided in Section 9—103 on multiple state transactions and in Section 9—104 on excluded transactions, this Article applies so far as concerns any personal property and fixtures within the jurisdiction of this state

(a) to any transaction (regardless of its form) which is intended to create a security interest in personal property or fixtures including goods, documents, instruments, general intangibles, chattel papers, accounts or contract rights; and also

(b) to any sale of accounts, contract rights or chattel paper.

(2) This Article applies to security interests created by contract including pledge, assignment, chattel mortgage, chattel trust, trust deed, factor's lien, equipment trust, conditional sale, trust receipt, other lien or title retention contract and lease or consignment intended as security. This Article does not apply to statutory liens except as provided in Section 9—310.

(3) The application of this Article to a security interest in a secured obligation is not affected by the fact that the obligation is itself secured by a transaction or interest to which this Article does not apply.

Note: *The adoption of this Article should be accompanied by the repeal of existing statutes dealing with conditional sales, trust receipts, factor's liens where the factor is given a non-possessory lien, chattel mortgages, crop mortgages, mortgages on railroad equipment, assignment of accounts and generally statutes regulating security interests in personal property.*

Where the state has a retail installment selling act or small loan act, that legislation should be carefully examined to determine what changes in those acts are needed to conform them to this Article. This Article primarily sets out rules defining rights of a secured party against persons dealing with the debtor; it does not prescribe regulations and controls which may be necessary to curb abuses arising in the small loan business or in the financing of consumer purchases on credit. Accordingly there is no intention to repeal existing regulatory acts in those fields. See Section 9—203(2) and the Note thereto.

Section 9—103. Accounts, Contract Rights, General Intangibles and Equipment Relating to Another Jurisdiction; and Incoming Goods Already Subject to a Security Interest.

(1) If the office where the assignor of accounts or contract rights keeps his records concerning them is in this state, the validity and perfection of a security interest therein and the possibility and effect of proper filing is governed by this Article; otherwise by the law (including the conflict of laws rules) of the jurisdiction where such office is located.

(2) If the chief place of business of a debtor is in this state, this Article governs the validity and perfection of a security interest and the possibility and effect of proper filing with regard to general intangibles or with regard to goods of a type which are normally used in more than one jurisdiction (such

as automotive equipment, rolling stock, airplanes, road building equipment, commercial harvesting equipment, construction machinery and the like) if such goods are classified as equipment or classified as inventory by reason of their being leased by the debtor to others. Otherwise, the law (including the conflict of laws rules) of the jurisdiction where such chief place of business is located shall govern. If the chief place of business is located in a jurisdiction which does not provide for perfection of the security interest by filing or recording in that jurisdiction, then the security interest may be perfected by filing in this state. [For the purpose of determining the validity and perfection of a security interest in an airplane, the chief place of business of a debtor who is a foreign air carrier under the Federal Aviation Act of 1958, as amended, is the designated office of the agent upon whom service of process may be made on behalf of the debtor.]

(3) If personal property other than that governed by subsections (1) and (2) is already subject to a security interest when it is brought into this state, the validity of the security interest in this state is to be determined by the law (including the conflict of laws rules) of the jurisdiction where the property was when the security interest attached. However, if the parties to the transaction understood at the time that the security interest attached that the property would be kept in this state and it was brought into this state within 30 days after the security interest attached for purposes other than transportation through this state, then the validity of the security interest in this state is to be determined by the law of this state. If the security interest was already perfected under the law of the jurisdiction where the property was when the security interest attached and before being brought into this state, the security interest continues perfected in this state for four months and also thereafter if within the four month period it is perfected in this state. The security interest may also be perfected in this state after the expiration of the four month period; in such case perfection dates from the time of perfection in this state. If the security interest was not perfected under the law of the jurisdiction where the property was when the security interest attached and before being brought into this state, it may be perfected in this state; in such case perfection dates from the time of perfection in this state.

(4) Notwithstanding subsections (2) and (3), if personal property is covered by a certificate of title issued under a statute of this state or any other jurisdiction which requires indication on a certificate of title of any security interest in the property as a condition of perfection, then the perfection is governed by the law of the jurisdiction which issued the certificate.

[(5) Notwithstanding subsection (1) and Section 9—302, if the office where the assignor of accounts or contract rights keeps his records concerning them is not located in a jurisdiction which is a part of the United States, its territories or possessions, and the accounts or contract rights are within the jurisdiction of this state or the transaction which creates the security interest otherwise bears an appropriate relation to this state, this Article governs the validity and perfection of the security interest and the security interest may only be perfected by notification to the account debtor.]

Note: *The last sentence of subsection (2) and subsection (5) are bracketed to indicate optional enactment. In states engaging in financing of airplanes of foreign carriers and of international open accounts receivable, bracketed language will be of value. In other states not engaging in financing of this type, the bracketed language may not be considered necessary.*

Section 9—104. Transactions Excluded from Article.

This Article does not apply

   (a) to a security interest subject to any statute of the United States such as the Ship Mortgage Act, 1920, to the extent that such statute governs the rights of parties to and third parties affected by transactions in particular types of property; or

(b) to a landlord's lien; or

(c) to a lien given by statute or other rules of law for services or materials except as provided in Section 9—310 on priority of such liens; or

(d) to a transfer of a claim for wages, salary or other compensation of an employee; or

(e) to an equipment trust covering railway rolling stock; or

(f) to a sale of accounts, contract rights or chattel paper as part of a sale of the business out of which they arose, or an assignment of accounts, contract rights or chattel paper which is for the purpose of collection only, or a transfer of a contract right to an assignee who is also to do the performance under the contract; or

(g) to a transfer of an interest or claim in or under any policy of insurance; or

(h) to a right represented by a judgment; or

(i) to any right of set-off; or

(j) except to the extent that provision is made for fixtures in Section 9—313, to the creation or transfer of an interest in or lien on real estate, including a lease or rents thereunder; or

(k) to a transfer in whole or in part of any of the following: any claim arising out of tort; any deposit, savings, passbook or like account maintained with a bank, savings and loan association, credit union or like organization.

Section 9—105. Definitions and Index of Definitions.

(1) In this Article unless the context otherwise requires:

(a) "Account debtor" means the person who is obligated on an account, chattel paper, contract right or general intangible;

(b) "Chattel paper" means a writing or writings which evidence both a monetary obligation and a security interest in or a lease of specific goods. When a transaction is evidenced both by such a security agreement or a lease and by an instrument or a series of instruments, the group of writings taken together constitutes chattel paper;

(c) "Collateral" means the property subject to a security interest, and includes accounts, contract rights and chattel paper which have been sold;

(d) "Debtor" means the person who owes payment or other performance of the obligation secured, whether or not he owns or has rights in the collateral, and includes the seller of accounts, contract rights or chattel paper. Where the debtor and the owner of the collateral are not the same person, the term "debtor" means the owner of the collateral in any provision of the Article dealing with the collateral, the obligor in any provision dealing with the obligation, and may include both where the context so requires;

(e) "Document" means document of title as defined in the general definitions of Article 1 (Section 1—201);

(f) "Goods" includes all things which are movable at the time the security interest attaches or which are fixtures (Section 9—313), but does not include money, documents, instruments, accounts, chattel paper, general intangibles, contract rights and other things in action. "Goods" also include the unborn young of animals and growing crops;

(g) "Instrument" means a negotiable instrument (defined in Section 3—104), or a security (defined in Section 8—102) or any other writing which evidences a right to the payment of money and is not itself a security agreement or lease and is of a type which is in ordinary course of business transferred by delivery with any necessary indorsement or assignment;

(h) "Security agreement" means an agreement which creates or provides for a security interest;

(i) "Secured party" means a lender, seller or other person in whose favor there is a security interest, including a person to whom accounts, contract rights or chattel paper have been sold. When the holders of obligations issued under an indenture of trust, equipment trust agreement or the like are represented by a trustee or other person, the representative is the secured party.

(2) Other definitions applying to this Article and the sections in which they appear are:

"Account". Section 9—106.

"Consumer goods". Section 9—109 (1).

"Contract right". Section 9—106.

"Equipment". Section 9—109(2).

"Farm products". Section 9—109 (3).

"General intangibles". Section 9—106.

"Inventory". Section 9—109(4).

"Lien creditor". Section 9—301(3).

"Proceeds". Section 9—306(1).

"Purchase money security interest". Section 9—107.

(3) The following definitions in other Articles apply to this Article:

"Check". Section 3—104.

"Contract for sale". Section 2—106.

"Holder in due course". Section 3—302.

"Note". Section 3—104.

"Sale". Section 2—106.

(4) In addition Article 1 contains general definitions and principles of construction and interpretation applicable throughout this Article.

Section 9—106. Definitions: "Account"; "Contract Right"; "General Intangibles".

"Account" means any right to payment for goods sold or leased or for services rendered which is not evidenced by an instrument or chattel paper. "Contract right" means any right to payment under a contract not yet earned by performance and not evidenced by an instrument or chattel paper. "General intangibles" means any personal property (including things in action) other than goods, accounts, contract rights, chattel paper, documents and instruments.

Section 9—107. Definitions: "Purchase Money Security Interest".

A security interest is a "purchase money security interest" to the extent that it is

(a) taken or retained by the seller of the collateral to secure all or part of its price; or

(b) taken by a person who by making advances or incurring an obligation gives value to enable the debtor to acquire rights in or the use of collateral if such value is in fact so used.

Section 9—108. When After-Acquired Collateral Not Security for Antecedent Debt.

Where a secured party makes an advance, incurs an obligation, releases a perfected security interest, or otherwise gives new value which is to be secured in whole or in part by after-acquired property, his security interest in the after-acquired collateral shall be deemed to be taken for new value and not as security for an antecedent debt if the debtor acquires his rights in such collateral either in the ordinary course of his business or under a contract of purchase made pursuant to the security agreement within a reasonable time after new value is given.

Section 9—109. Classification of Goods; "Consumer Goods"; "Equipment"; "Farm Products"; "Inventory".

Goods are

(1) "consumer goods" if they are used or bought for use primarily for personal, family or household purposes;

(2) "equipment" if they are used or bought for use primarily in business (including farming or a profession) or by a debtor who is a non-profit organization or a governmental subdivision or agency or if the goods are not included in the definitions of inventory, farm products or consumer goods;

(3) "farm products" if they are crops or livestock or supplies used or produced in farming operations or if they are products of crops or livestock in their unmanufactured states (such as ginned cotton, wool-clip, maple syrup, milk and eggs), and if they are in the possession of a debtor engaged in raising, fattening, grazing or other farming operations. If goods are farm products, they are neither equipment nor inventory;

(4) "inventory" if they are held by a person who holds them for sale or lease or to be furnished under contracts of service or if he has so furnished them, or if they are raw materials, work in process or materials used or consumed in a business. Inventory of a person is not to be classified as his equipment.

Section 9—110. Sufficiency of Description.

For the purposes of this Article any description of personal property or real estate is sufficient whether or not it is specific if it reasonably identifies what is described.

Section 9—111. Applicability of Bulk Transfer Laws.

The creation of a security interest is not a bulk transfer under Article 6 (see Section 6—103).

Section 9—112. Where Collateral Is Not Owned by Debtor.

Unless otherwise agreed, when a secured party knows that collateral is owned by a person who is not the debtor, the owner of the collateral is entitled to receive from the secured party any surplus under Section 9—502(2) or under Section 9—504(1), and is not liable for the debt or for any deficiency after resale, and he has the same right as the debtor

(a) to receive statements under Section 9—208;

(b) to receive notice of and to object to a secured party's proposal to retain the collateral in satisfaction of the indebtedness under Section 9—505;

(c) to redeem the collateral under Section 9—506;

(d) to obtain injunctive or other relief under Section 9—507(1); and

(e) to recover losses caused to him under Section 9—208(2).

Section 9—113. Security Interests Arising Under Article on Sales.

A security interest arising solely under the Article on Sales (Article 2) is subject to the provisions of this Article except that to the extent that and so long as the debtor does not have or does not lawfully obtain possession of the goods

(a) no security agreement is necessary to make the security interest enforceable; and

(b) no filing is required to perfect the security interest; and

(c) the rights of the secured party on default by the debtor are governed by the Article on Sales (Article 2).

PART 2

VALIDITY OF SECURITY AGREEMENT AND RIGHTS
OF PARTIES THERETO

Section 9—201. General Validity of Security Agreement.

Except as otherwise provided by this Act a security agreement is effective according to its terms between the parties, against purchasers of the collateral and against creditors. Nothing in this Article validates any charge or practice illegal under any statute or regulation thereunder governing usury, small loans, retail installment sales, or the like, or extends the application of any such statute or regulation to any transaction not otherwise subject thereto.

Section 9—202. Title to Collateral Immaterial.

Each provision of this Article with regard to rights, obligations and remedies applies whether title to collateral is in the secured party or in the debtor.

Section 9—203. Enforceability of Security Interest; Proceeds, Formal Requisites.

(1) Subject to the provisions of Section 4—208 on the security interest of a collecting bank and Section 9—113 on a security interest arising under the Article on Sales, a security interest is not enforceable against the debtor or third parties unless

  (a) the collateral is in the possession of the secured party; or
  (b) the debtor has signed a security agreement which contains a description of the collateral and in addition, when the security interest covers crops or oil, gas or minerals to be extracted or timber to be cut, a description of the land concerned. In describing collateral, the word "proceeds" is sufficient without further description to cover proceeds of any character.

(2) A transaction, although subject to this Article, is also subject to ....-......*, and in the case of conflict between the provisions of this Article and any such statute, the provisions of such statute control. Failure to comply with any applicable statute has only the effect which is specified therein.

Note: *At * in subsection (2) insert reference to any local statute regulating small loans, retail installment sales and the like.*

The foregoing subsection (2) is designed to make it clear that certain transactions, although subject to this Article, must also comply with other applicable legislation.

This Article is designed to regulate all the "security" aspects of transactions within its scope. There is, however, much regulatory legislation, particularly in the consumer field, which supplements this Article and should not be repealed by its enactment. Examples are small loan acts, retail installment selling acts and the like. Such acts may provide for licensing and rate regulation and may prescribe particular forms of contract. Such provisions should remain in force despite the enactment of this Article. On the other hand if a Retail Installment Selling Act contains provisions on filing, rights on default, etc., such provisions should be repealed as inconsistent with this Article.

Section 9—204. When Security Interest Attaches; After-Acquired Property; Future Advances.

(1) A security interest cannot attach until there is agreement (subsection (3) of Section 1—201) that it attach and value is given and the debtor has rights in the collateral. It attaches as soon as all of the events in the preceding sentence have taken place unless explicit agreement postpones the time of attaching.

(2) For the purposes of this section the debtor has no rights

  (a) in crops until they are planted or otherwise become growing crops, in the young of livestock until they are conceived;

(b) in fish until caught, in oil, gas or minerals until they are extracted, in timber until it is cut;

(c) in a contract right until the contract has been made;

(d) in an account until it comes into existence.

(3) Except as provided in subsection (4) a security agreement may provide that collateral, whenever acquired, shall secure all obligations covered by the security agreement.

(4) No security interest attaches under an after-acquired property clause

(a) to crops which become such more than one year after the security agreement is executed, except that a security interest in crops which is given in conjunction with a lease or a land purchase or improvement transaction evidenced by a contract, mortgage or deed of trust may if so agreed attach to crops to be grown on the land concerned during the period of such real estate transaction;

(b) to consumer goods other than accessions (Section 9—314) when given as additional security unless the debtor acquires rights in them within ten days after the secured party gives value.

(5) Obligations covered by a security agreement may include future advances or other value whether or not the advances or value are given pursuant to commitment.

Section 9—205. Use or Disposition of Collateral Without Accounting Permissible.

A security interest is not invalid or fraudulent against creditors by reason of liberty in the debtor to use, commingle or dispose of all or part of the collateral (including returned or repossessed goods) or to collect or compromise accounts, contract rights or chattel paper, or to accept the return of goods or make repossessions, or to use, commingle or dispose of proceeds, or by

reason of the failure of the secured party to require the debtor to account for proceeds or replace collateral. This section does not relax the requirements of possession where perfection of a security interest depends upon possession of the collateral by the secured party or by a bailee.

Section 9—206. Agreement Not to Assert Defenses Against Assignee; Modification of Sales Warranties Where Security Agreement Exists.

(1) Subject to any statute or decision which establishes a different rule for buyers or lessees of consumer goods, an agreement by a buyer or lessee that he will not assert against an assignee any claim or defense which he may have against the seller or lessor is enforceable by an assignee who takes his assignment for value, in good faith and without notice of a claim or defense, except as to defenses of a type which may be asserted against a holder in due course of a negotiable instrument under the Article on Commercial Paper (Article 3). A buyer who as part of one transaction signs both a negotiable instrument and a security agreement makes such an agreement.

(2) When a seller retains a purchase money security interest in goods, the Article on Sales (Article 2) governs the sale and any disclaimer, limitation or modification of the seller's warranties.

Section 9—207. Rights and Duties When Collateral Is in Secured Party's Possession.

(1) A secured party must use reasonable care in the custody and preservation of collateral in his possession. In the case of an instrument or chattel paper reasonable care includes taking necessary steps to preserve rights against prior parties unless otherwise agreed.

(2) Unless otherwise agreed, when collateral is in the secured party's possession

(a) reasonable expenses (including the cost of any insurance and payment of taxes or other charges) incurred in the custody, preservation, use or operation of the collateral are chargeable to the debtor and are secured by the collateral;

(b) the risk of accidental loss or damage is on the debtor to the extent of any deficiency in any effective insurance coverage;

(c) the secured party may hold as additional security any increase or profits (except money) received from the collateral, but money so received, unless remitted to the debtor, shall be applied in reduction of the secured obligation;

(d) the secured party must keep the collateral identifiable but fungible collateral may be commingled;

(e) the secured party may repledge the collateral upon terms which do not impair the debtor's right to redeem it.

(3) A secured party is liable for any loss caused by his failure to meet any obligation imposed by the preceding subsections but does not lose his security interest.

(4) A secured party may use or operate the collateral for the purpose of preserving the collateral or its value or pursuant to the order of a court of appropriate jurisdiction or, except in the case of consumer goods, in the manner and to the extent provided in the security agreement.

Section 9—208. Request for Statement of Account or List of Collateral.

(1) A debtor may sign a statement indicating what he believes to be the aggregate amount of unpaid indebtedness as of a specified date and may send it to the secured party with a request that the statement be approved or corrected and returned to the debtor. When the security agreement or any other record kept by the secured party identifies the collateral, a debtor may similarly request the secured party to approve or correct a list of the collateral.

(2) The secured party must comply with such a request within two weeks after receipt by sending a written correction or approval. If the secured party claims a security interest in all of a particular type of collateral owned by the debtor, he may indicate that fact in his reply and need not approve or correct an itemized list of such collateral. If the secured party without reasonable excuse fails to comply, he is liable for any loss caused to the debtor thereby; and if the debtor has properly included in his request a good faith statement of the obligation or a list of the collateral or both, the secured party may claim a security interest only as shown in the statement against persons misled by his failure to comply. If he no longer has an interest in the obligation or collateral at the time the request is received, he must disclose the name and address of any successor in interest known to him and he is liable for any loss caused to the debtor as a result of failure to disclose. A successor in interest is not subject to this section until a request is received by him.

(3) A debtor is entitled to such a statement once every six months without charge. The secured party may require payment of a charge not exceeding $10 for each additional statement furnished.

PART 3

RIGHTS OF THIRD PARTIES; PERFECTED AND UNPERFECTED SECURITY INTERESTS; RULES OF PRIORITY

Section 9—301. Persons Who Take Priority Over Unperfected Security Interests; "Lien Creditor".

(1) Except as otherwise provided in subsection (2), an unperfected security interest is subordinate to the rights of

(a) persons entitled to priority under Section 9—312;

(b) a person who becomes a lien creditor without knowledge of the security interest and before it is perfected;

(c) in the case of goods, instruments, documents, and chattel paper, a person who is not a secured party and who is a transferee in bulk or other buyer not in ordinary course of business to the extent that he gives value and receives delivery of the collateral without knowledge of the security interest and before it is perfected;

(d) in the case of accounts, contract rights, and general intangibles, a person who is not a secured party and who is a transferee to the extent that he gives value without knowledge of the security interest and before it is perfected.

(2) If the secured party files with respect to a purchase money security interest before or within ten days after the collateral comes into possession of the debtor, he takes priority over the rights of a transferee in bulk or of a lien creditor which arise between the time the security interest attaches and the time of filing.

(3) A "lien creditor" means a creditor who has acquired a lien on the property involved by attachment, levy or the like and includes an assignee for benefit of creditors from the time of assignment, and a trustee in bankruptcy from the date of the filing of the petition or a receiver in equity from the time of appointment. Unless all the creditors represented had knowledge of the security interest, such a representative of creditors is a lien creditor without knowledge even though he personally has knowledge of the security interest.

Section 9—302. When Filing Is Required to Perfect Security Interest; Security Interests to Which Filing Provisions of This Article Do Not Apply.

(1) A financing statement must be filed to perfect all security interests except the following:

(a) a security interest in collateral in possession of the secured party under Section 9—305;

(b) a security interest temporarily perfected in instruments or documents without delivery under Section 9—304 or in proceeds for a 10 day period under Section 9—306;

(c) a purchase money security interest in farm equipment having a purchase price not in excess of $2500; but filing is required for a fixture under Section 9—313 or for a motor vehicle required to be licensed;

(d) a purchase money security interest in consumer goods; but filing is required for a fixture under Section 9—313 or for a motor vehicle required to be licensed;

(e) an assignment of accounts or contract rights which does not alone or in conjunction with other assignments to the same assignee transfer a significant part of the outstanding accounts or contract rights of the assignor;

(f) a security interest of a collecting bank (Section 4—208) or arising under the Article on Sales (see Section 9—113) or covered in subsection (3) of this section.

(2) If a secured party assigns a perfected security interest, no filing under this Article is required in order to continue the perfected status of the security interest against creditors of and transferees from the original debtor.

(3) The filing provisions of this Article do not apply to a security interest in property subject to a statute

(a) of the United States which provides for a national registration or filing of all security interests in such property; or

Note: *States to select either Alternative A or Alternative B.*

Alternative A—

(b) of this state which provides for central filing of, or which requires indication on a certificate of title of, such security interests in such property.

Alternative B—

(b) of this state which provides for central filing of security interests in such property, or in a motor vehicle which is not inventory held for sale for which a certificate of title is required under the statutes of this state if a notation of such a security interest can be indicated by a public official on a certificate or a duplicate thereof.

(4) A security interest in property covered by a statute described in subsection (3) can be perfected only by registration or filing under that statute or by indication of the security interest on a certificate of title or a duplicate thereof by a public official.

Section 9—303. When Security Interest Is Perfected; Continuity of Perfection.

(1) A security interest is perfected when it has attached and when all of the applicable steps required for perfection have been taken. Such steps are specified in Sections 9—302, 9—304, 9—305 and 9—306. If such steps are taken before the security interest attaches, it is perfected at the time when it attaches.

(2) If a security interest is originally perfected in any way permitted under this Article and is subsequently perfected in some other way under this Article, without an intermediate period when it was unperfected, the security interest shall be deemed to be perfected continuously for the purposes of this Article.

Section 9—304. Perfection of Security Interest in Instruments, Documents, and Goods Covered by Documents; Perfection by Permissive Filing; Temporary Perfection Without Filing or Transfer of Possession.

(1) A security interest in chattel paper or negotiable documents may be perfected by filing. A security interest in instruments (other than instruments which constitute part of chattel paper) can be perfected only by the secured party's taking possession, except as provided in subsections (4) and (5).

(2) During the period that goods are in the possession of the issuer of a negotiable document therefor, a security interest in the goods is perfected by perfecting a security interest in the document, and any security interest in the goods otherwise perfected during such period is subject thereto.

(3) A security interest in goods in the possession of a bailee other than one who has issued a negotiable document therefor is perfected by issuance of a document in the name of the secured party or by the bailee's receipt of notification of the secured party's interest or by filing as to the goods.

(4) A security interest in instruments or negotiable documents is perfected without filing or the taking of possession for a period of 21 days from the time it attaches to the extent that it arises for new value given under a written security agreement.

(5) A security interest remains perfected for a period of 21 days without filing where a secured party having a perfected security interest in an instrument, a negotiable document or goods in possession of a bailee other than one who has issued a negotiable document therefor

(a) makes available to the debtor the goods or documents representing the goods for the purpose of ultimate sale or exchange or for the purpose of loading, unloading, storing, shipping, transshipping, manufacturing, processing or otherwise dealing with them in a manner preliminary to their sale or exchange; or

(b) delivers the instrument to the debtor for the purpose of ultimate sale or exchange or of presentation, collection, renewal or registration of transfer.

(6) After the 21 day period in subsections (4) and (5) perfection depends upon compliance with applicable provisions of this Article.

Section 9—305. When Possession by Secured Party Perfects Security Interest Without Filing.

A security interest in letters of credit and advices of credit (subsection (2)(a) of Section 5—116), goods, instruments, negotiable documents or chattel paper may be perfected by the secured party's taking possession of the collateral. If such collateral other than goods covered by a negotiable document is held by a bailee, the secured party is deemed to have possession from the time the bailee receives notification of the secured party's interest. A security interest is perfected by possession from the time possession is taken without relation back and continues only so long as possession is retained, unless otherwise specified in this Article. The security interest may be otherwise perfected as provided in this Article before or after the period of possession by the secured party.

Section 9—306. "Proceeds"; Secured Party's Rights on Disposition of Collateral.

(1) "Proceeds" includes whatever is received when collateral or proceeds is sold, exchanged, collected or otherwise disposed of. The term also includes the account arising when the right to payment is earned under a contract right. Money, checks and the like are "cash proceeds". All other proceeds are "non-cash proceeds".

(2) Except where this Article otherwise provides, a security interest continues in collateral notwithstanding sale, exchange or other disposition thereof by the debtor unless his action was authorized by the secured party in the security agreement or otherwise, and also continues in any identifiable proceeds including collections received by the debtor.

(3) The security interest in proceeds is a continuously perfected security interest if the interest in the original collateral was perfected, but it ceases to be a perfected security interest and becomes unperfected ten days after receipt of the proceeds by the debtor unless

(a) a filed financing statement covering the original collateral also covers proceeds; or

(b) the security interest in the proceeds is perfected before the expiration of the ten day period.

(4) In the event of insolvency proceedings instituted by or against a debtor, a secured party with a perfected security interest in proceeds has a perfected security interest

(a) in identifiable non-cash proceeds;

(b) in identifiable cash proceeds in the form of money which is not commingled with other money or deposited in a bank account prior to the insolvency proceedings;

(c) in identifiable cash proceeds in the form of checks and the like which are not deposited in a bank account prior to the insolvency proceedings; and

(d) in all cash and bank accounts of the debtor, if other cash proceeds have been commingled or deposited in a bank account, but the perfected security interest under this paragraph (d) is

(i) subject to any right of set-off; and

(ii) limited to an amount not greater than the amount of any cash proceeds received by the debtor within ten days before the institution of the insolvency proceedings and commingled or deposited in a bank account prior to the insolvency proceedings less the amount of cash proceeds received by the debtor and paid over to the secured party during the ten day period.

(5) If a sale of goods results in an account or chattel paper which is transferred by the seller to a secured party, and if the goods are returned to or are repossessed by the seller or the secured party, the following rules determine priorities:

(a) If the goods were collateral at the time of sale for an indebtedness of the seller which is still unpaid, the original security interest attaches again to the goods and continues as a perfected security interest if it was perfected at the time when the goods were sold. If the security interest was originally perfected by a filing which is still effective, nothing further is required to continue the perfected status; in any other case, the secured party must take possession of the returned or repossessed goods or must file.

(b) An unpaid transferee of the chattel paper has a security interest in the goods against the transferor. Such security interest is prior to a security interest asserted under paragraph (a) to the extent that the transferee of the chattel paper was entitled to priority under Section 9—308.

(c) An unpaid transferee of the account has a security interest in the goods against the transferor. Such security interest is subordinate to a security interest asserted under paragraph (a).

(d) A security interest of an unpaid transferee asserted under paragraph (b) or (c) must be perfected for protection against creditors of the transferor and purchasers of the returned or repossessed goods.

Section 9—307. Protection of Buyers of Goods.

(1) A buyer in ordinary course of business (subsection (9) of Section 1—201) other than a person buying farm products from a person engaged in farming operations takes free of a security interest created by his seller even though the security interest is perfected and even though the buyer knows of its existence.

(2) In the case of consumer goods and in the case of farm equipment having an original purchase price not in excess of $2500 (other than fixtures, see Section 9—313), a buyer takes free of a security interest even though perfected if he buys without knowledge of the security interest, for value and for his own personal, family or household purposes or his own farming operations, unless prior to the purchase the secured party has filed a financing statement covering such goods.

Section 9—308. Purchase of Chattel Paper and Non-Negotiable Instruments.

A purchaser of chattel paper or a non-negotiable instrument who gives new value and takes possession of it in the ordinary course of his business and without knowledge that the specific paper or instrument is subject to a security interest has priority over a security interest which is perfected under Section 9—304 (permissive filing and temporary perfection). A purchaser of chattel paper who gives new value and takes possession of it in the ordinary course of his business has priority over a security interest in chattel paper which is claimed merely as proceeds of inventory subject to a security interest (Section 9—306), even though he knows that the specific paper is subject to the security interest.

Section 9—309. Protection of Purchasers of Instruments and Documents.

Nothing in this Article limits the rights of a holder in due course of a negotiable instrument (Section 3—302) or a holder to whom a negotiable document of title has been duly negotiated (Section 7—501) or a bona fide purchaser of a security (Section 8—301) and such holders or purchasers take priority over an earlier security interest even though perfected. Filing under this Article does not constitute notice of the security interest to such holders or purchasers.

Section 9—310. Priority of Certain Liens Arising by Operation of Law.

When a person in the ordinary course of his business furnishes services or materials with respect to goods subject to a security interest, a lien upon goods in the possession of such person given by statute or rule of law for such materials or services takes priority over a perfected security interest unless the lien is statutory and the statute expressly provides otherwise.

Section 9—311. Alienability of Debtor's Rights; Judicial Process.

The debtor's rights in collateral may be voluntarily or involuntarily transferred (by way of sale, creation of a security interest, attachment, levy, garnishment or other judicial process) notwithstanding a provision in the security agreement prohibiting any transfer or making the transfer constitute a default.

Section 9—312. Priorities Among Conflicting Security Interests in the Same Collateral.

(1) The rules of priority stated in the following sections shall govern where applicable: Section 4—208 with respect to the security interest of collecting banks in items being collected, accompanying documents and proceeds; Section 9—301 on certain priorities; Section 9—304 on goods covered by documents; Section 9—306 on proceeds and repossessions; Section 9—307 on buyers of goods; Section 9—308 on possessory against non-possessory interests in chattel paper or non-negotiable instruments; Section 9—309 on security interests in negotiable instruments, documents or securities; Section 9—310 on priorities between perfected security interests and liens by operation of law; Section 9—313 on security interests in fixtures as against interests in real estate; Section 9—314 on security interests in accessions as against interest in goods; Section 9—315 on conflicting security interests where goods lose their identity or become part of a product; and Section 9—316 on contractual subordination.

(2) A perfected security interest in crops for new value given to enable the debtor to produce the crops during the production season and given not more than three months before the crops become growing crops by planting or otherwise takes priority over an earlier perfected security interest to the extent that such earlier interest secures obligations due more than six months before the crops become growing crops by planting or otherwise, even though the person giving new value had knowledge of the earlier security interest.

(3) A purchase money security interest in inventory collateral has priority over a conflicting security interest in the same collateral if

(a) the purchase money security interest is perfected at the time the debtor receives possession of the collateral; and

(b) any secured party whose security interest is known to the holder of the purchase money security interest or who, prior to the date of the filing made by the holder of the purchase money security interest, had filed a financing statement covering the same items or type of inventory, has received notification of the purchase money security interest before the debtor receives possession of the collateral covered by the purchase money security interest; and

(c) such notification states that the person giving the notice has or expects to acquire a purchase money security interest in inventory of the debtor, describing such inventory by item or type.

(4) A purchase money security interest in collateral other than inventory has priority over a conflicting security interest in the same collateral if the purchase money security interest is perfected at the time the debtor receives possession of the collateral or within ten days thereafter.

(5) In all cases not governed by other rules stated in this section (including cases of purchase money security interests which do not qualify for the special priorities set forth in subsections (3) and (4) of this section), priority between conflicting security interests in the same collateral shall be determined as follows:

(a) in the order of filing if both are perfected by filing, regardless of which security interest attached first under Section 9—204(1) and whether it attached before or after filing;

(b) in the order of perfection unless both are perfected by filing, regardless of which security interest attached first under Section 9—204(1) and, in the case of a filed security interest, whether it attached before or after filing; and

(c) in the order of attachment under Section 9—204(1) so long as neither is perfected.

(6) For the purpose of the priority rules of the immediately preceding subsection, a continuously perfected security interest shall be treated at all times as if perfected by filing if it was originally so perfected and it shall be treated at all times as if perfected otherwise than by filing if it was originally perfected otherwise than by filing.

Section 9—313. Priority of Security Interests in Fixtures.

(1) The rules of this section do not apply to goods incorporated into a structure in the manner of lumber, bricks, tile, cement, glass, metal work and the like and no security interest in them exists under this Article unless the structure remains personal property under applicable law. The law of this state other than this Act determines whether and when other goods become fixtures. This Act does not prevent creation of an encumbrance upon fixtures or real estate pursuant to the law applicable to real estate.

(2) A security interest which attaches to goods before they become fixtures takes priority as to the goods over the claims of all persons who have an interest in the real estate except as stated in subsection (4).

(3) A security interest which attaches to goods after they become fixtures is valid against all persons subsequently acquiring interests in the real estate except as stated in subsection (4) but is invalid against any person with an interest in the real estate at the time the security interest attaches to the goods who has not in writing consented to the security interest or disclaimed an interest in the goods as fixtures.

(4) The security interests described in subsections (2) and (3) do not take priority over

(a) a subsequent purchaser for value of any interest in the real estate; or

(b) a creditor with a lien on the real estate subsequently obtained by judicial proceedings; or

(c) a creditor with a prior encumbrance of record on the real estate to the extent that he makes subsequent advances

if the subsequent purchase is made, the lien by judicial proceedings is obtained, or the subsequent advance under the prior encumbrance is made or contracted for without knowledge of the security interest and before it is perfected. A purchaser of the real estate at a foreclosure sale other than an encumbrancer purchasing at his own foreclosure sale is a subsequent purchaser within this section.

(5) When under subsections (2) or (3) and (4) a secured party has priority over the claims of all persons who have interests in the real estate, he may, on default, subject to the provisions of Part 5, remove his collateral from the real estate; but he must reimburse any encumbrancer or owner of the real estate who is not the debtor and who has not otherwise agreed for the cost of repair of any physical injury, but not for any diminution in value of the real estate caused by the absence of the goods removed or by any necessity for replacing them. A person entitled to reimbursement may refuse permission to remove until the secured party gives adequate security for the performance of this obligation.

Section 9—314. Accessions.

(1) A security interest in goods which attaches before they are installed in or affixed to other goods takes priority as to the goods installed or affixed (called

in this section "accessions") over the claims of all persons to the whole except as stated in subsection (3) and subject to Section 9—315(1).

(2) A security interest which attaches to goods after they become part of a whole is valid against all persons subsequently acquiring interests in the whole except as stated in subsection (3) but is invalid against any person with an interest in the whole at the time the security interest attaches to the goods who has not in writing consented to the security interest or disclaimed an interest in the goods as part of the whole.

(3) The security interests described in subsections (1) and (2) do not take priority over

    (a) a subsequent purchaser for value of any interest in the whole; or

    (b) a creditor with a lien on the whole subsequently obtained by judicial proceedings; or

    (c) a creditor with a prior perfected security interest in the whole to the extent that he makes subsequent advances

if the subsequent purchase is made, the lien by judicial proceedings obtained or the subsequent advance under the prior perfected security interest is made or contracted for without knowledge of the security interest and before it is perfected. A purchaser of the whole at a foreclosure sale other than the holder of a perfected security interest purchasing at his own foreclosure sale is a subsequent purchaser within this section.

(4) When under subsections (1) or (2) and (3) a secured party has an interest in accessions which has priority over the claims of all persons who have interests in the whole, he may, on default, subject to the provisions of Part 5, remove his collateral from the whole; but he must reimburse any encumbrancer or owner of the whole who is not the debtor and who has not otherwise agreed for the cost of repair of any physical injury but not for any diminution in value of the whole caused by the absence of the goods removed or by any necessity for replacing them. A person entitled to reimbursement may refuse permission to remove until the secured party gives adequate security for the performance of this obligation.

Section 9—315.   Priority When Goods Are Commingled or Processed.

(1) If a security interest in goods was perfected and subsequently the goods or a part thereof have become part of a product or mass, the security interest continues in the product or mass if

    (a) the goods are so manufactured, processed, assembled or commingled that their identity is lost in the product or mass; or

    (b) a financing statement covering the original goods also covers the product into which the goods have been manufactured, processed or assembled.

In a case to which paragraph (b) applies, no separate security interest in that part of the original goods which has been manufactured, processed or assembled into the product may be claimed under Section 9—314.

(2) When under subsection (1) more than one security interest attaches to the product or mass, they rank equally according to the ratio that the cost of the goods to which each interest originally attached bears to the cost of the total product or mass.

Section 9—316.   Priority Subject to Subordination.

Nothing in this Article prevents subordination by agreement by any person entitled to priority.

Section 9—317.   Secured Party Not Obligated on Contract of Debtor.

The mere existence of a security interest or authority given to the debtor to dispose of or use collateral does not impose contract or tort liability upon the secured party for the debtor's acts or omissions.

Section 9—318.   Defenses Against Assignee; Modification of Contract After Notification of Assignment; Term Prohibiting Assignment Ineffective; Identification and Proof of Assignment.

(1) Unless an account debtor has made an enforceable agreement not to assert defenses or claims arising out of a sale as provided in Section 9—206 the rights of an assignee are subject to

(a) all the terms of the contract between the account debtor and assignor and any defense or claim arising therefrom; and

(b) any other defense or claim of the account debtor against the assignor which accrues before the account debtor receives notification of the assignment.

(2) So far as the right to payment under an assigned contract right has not already become an account, and notwithstanding notification of the assignment, any modification of or substitution for the contract made in good faith and in accordance with reasonable commercial standards is effective against an assignee unless the account debtor has otherwise agreed, but the assignee acquires corresponding rights under the modified or substituted contract. The assignment may provide that such modification or substitution is a breach by the assignor.

(3) The account debtor is authorized to pay the assignor until the account debtor receives notification that the account has been assigned and that payment is to be made to the assignee. A notification which does not reasonably identify the rights assigned is ineffective. If requested by the account debtor, the assignee must seasonably furnish reasonable proof that the assignment has been made and unless he does so the account debtor may pay the assignor.

(4) A term in any contract between an account debtor and an assignor which prohibits assignment of an account or contract right to which they are parties is ineffective.

PART 4

FILING

Section 9—401. Place of Filing; Erroneous Filing; Removal of Collateral.

First Alternative Subsection (1)

(1) The proper place to file in order to perfect a security interest is as follows:

(a) when the collateral is goods which at the time the security interest attaches are or are to become fixtures, then in the office where a mortgage on the real estate concerned would be filed or recorded;

(b) in all other cases, in the office of the [Secretary of State].

Second Alternative Subsection (1)

(1) The proper place to file in order to perfect a security interest is as follows:

(a) when the collateral is equipment used in farming operations, or farm products, or accounts, contract rights or general intangibles arising from or relating to the sale of farm products by a farmer, or consumer goods, then in the office of the ...... in the county of the debtor's residence or if the debtor is not a resident of this state then in the office of the ...... in the county where the goods are kept, and in addition when the collateral in crops in the office of the ...... in the county where the land on which the crops are growing or to be grown is located;

(b) when the collateral is goods which at the time the security interest attaches are or are to become fixtures, then in the office where a mortgage on the real estate concerned would be filed or recorded;

(c) in all other cases, in the office of the [Secretary of State].

Third Alternative Subsection (1)

(1) The proper place to file in order to perfect a security interest is as follows:

(a) when the collateral is equipment used in farming operations, or farm products, or accounts, contract rights or general intangibles arising from or relating to the sale of farm products by a farmer, or consumer goods, then in the office of the ...... in the county of the debtor's residence or if the debtor is not a resident of this state then in the office of the ...... in the county where the goods are kept, and in addition when the collateral is crops in the office of the ...... in the county where the land on which the crops are growing or to be grown is located;

(b) when the collateral is goods which at the time the security interest attaches are or are to become fixtures, then in the office where a mortgage on the real estate concerned would be filed or recorded;

(c) in all other cases, in the office of the [Secretary of State] and in addition, if the debtor has a place of business in only one county of this state, also in the office of ...... of such county, or, if the debtor has no place of business in this state, but resides in the state, also in the office of ...... of the county in which he resides.

Note: *One of the three alternatives should be selected as subsection (1).*

(2) A filing which is made in good faith in an improper place or not in all of the places required by this section is nevertheless effective with regard to any collateral as to which the filing complied with the requirements of this Article and is also effective with regard to collateral covered by the financing statement against any person who has knowledge of the contents of such financing statement.

(3) A filing which is made in the proper place in this state continues effective even though the debtor's residence or place of business or the location of the collateral or its use, whichever controlled the original filing, is thereafter changed.

Alternative Subsection (3)

[(3) A filing which is made in the proper county continues effective for four months after a change to another county of the debtor's residence or place of business or the location of the collateral, whichever controlled the original filing. It becomes ineffective thereafter unless a copy of the financing statement signed by the secured party is filed in the new county within said period. The security interest may also be perfected in the new county after the expiration of the four-month period; in such case perfection dates from the time of perfection in the new county. A change in the use of the collateral does not impair the effectiveness of the original filing.]

(4) If collateral is brought into this state from another jurisdiction, the rules stated in Section 9—103 determine whether filing is necessary in this state.

Section 9—402.　Formal Requisites of Financing Statement; Amendments.

(1) A financing statement is sufficient if it is signed by the debtor and the secured party, gives an address of the secured party from which information concerning the security interest may be obtained, gives a mailing address of the debtor and contains a statement indicating the types, or describing the items, of collateral. A financing statement may b⌐ filed before a security agreement is made or a security interest otherwise attaches. When the financing statement covers crops growing or to be grown or goods which are or are to become fixtures, the statement must also contain a description of the real estate concerned. A copy of the security agreement is sufficient as a financing statement if it contains the above information and is signed by both parties.

(2) A financing statement which otherwise complies with subsection (1) is sufficient although it is signed only by the secured party when it is filed to perfect a security interest in

(a) collateral already subject to a security interest in another jurisdiction when it is brought into this state. Such a financing statement must state that the collateral was brought into this state under such circumstances.

(b) proceeds under Section 9—306 if the security interest in the original collateral was perfected. Such a financing statement must describe the original collateral.

(3) A form substantially as follows is sufficient to comply with subsection (1):

Name of debtor (or assignor) . . . .

. . . .

Address . . . .

. . . .

Name of secured party (or assignee)

. . . .

Address . . . .

. . . .

1. This financing statement covers the following types (or items) of property:

(Describe) . . . .

. . . .

2. (If collateral is crops) The above described crops are growing or are to be grown on:

(Describe Real Estate) . . . . . .

. . . .

3. (If collateral is goods which are or are to become fixtures) The above described goods are affixed or to be affixed to:

(Describe Real Estate) . . . . . .

. . . .

4. (If proceeds or products of collateral are claimed) Proceeds— Products of the collateral are also covered.

Signature of Debtor (or Assignor) . . . .

. . . .

Signature of Secured Party (or Assignee) . . . .

. . . .

(4) The term "financing statement" as used in this Article means the original financing statement and any amendments but if any amendment adds collateral, it is effective as to the added collateral only from the filing date of the amendment.

(5) A financing statement substantially complying with the requirements of this section is effective even though it contains minor errors which are not seriously misleading.

Section 9—403. What Constitutes Filing; Duration of Filing; Effect of Lapsed Filing; Duties of Filing Officer.

(1) Presentation for filing of a financing statement and tender of the filing fee or acceptance of the statement by the filing officer constitutes filing under this Article.

(2) A filed financing statement which states a maturity date of the obligation secured of five years or less is effective until such maturity date and thereafter for a period of sixty days. Any other filed financing statement is effective for a period of five years from the date of filing. The effectiveness of a filed financing statement lapses on the expiration of such sixty day period after a stated maturity date or on the expiration of such five year period, as the case may be, unless a continuation statement is filed prior to the lapse. Upon such lapse the security interest becomes unperfected. A filed financing statement which states that the obligation secured is payable on demand is effective for five years from the date of filing.

(3) A continuation statement may be filed by the secured party (i) within six months before and sixty days after a stated maturity date of five years or less, and (ii) otherwise within six months prior to the expiration of the five year period specified in subsection (2). Any such continuation statement must be signed by the secured party, identify the original statement by file number and state that the original statement is still effective. Upon timely filing of the continuation statement, the effectiveness of the original statement is continued for five years after the last date to which the filing was effective whereupon it lapses in the same manner as provided in subsection (2) unless another continuation statement is filed prior to such lapse. Succeeding continuation statements may be filed in the same manner

to continue the effectiveness of the original statement. Unless a statute on disposition of public records provides otherwise, the filing officer may remove a lapsed statement from the files and destroy it.

(4) A filing officer shall mark each statement with a consecutive file number and with the date and hour of filing and shall hold the statement for public inspection. In addition the filing officer shall index the statements according to the name of the debtor and shall note in the index the file number and the address of the debtor given in the statement.

(5) The uniform fee for filing, indexing and furnishing filing data for an original or a continuation statement shall be $ . . . .

Section 9—404. Termination Statement.

(1) Whenever there is no outstanding secured obligation and no commitment to make advances, incur obligations or otherwise give value, the secured party must on written demand by the debtor send the debtor a statement that he no longer claims a security interest under the financing statement, which shall be identified by file number. A termination statement signed by a person other than the secured party of record must include or be accompanied by the assignment or a statement by the secured party of record that he has assigned the security interest to the signer of the termination statement. The uniform fee for filing and indexing such an assignment or statement thereof shall be $ . . . . If the affected secured party fails to send such a termination statement within ten days after proper demand therefor, he shall be liable to the debtor for one hundred dollars, and in addition for any loss caused to the debtor by such failure.

(2) On presentation to the filing officer of such a termination statement he must note it in the index. The filing officer shall remove from the files, mark "terminated" and send or deliver to the secured party the financing statement and any continuation statement, statement of assignment or statement of release pertaining thereto.

(3) The uniform fee for filing and indexing a termination statement including sending or delivering the financing statement shall be $ . . . .

Section 9—405. Assignment of Security Interest; Duties of Filing Officer; Fees.

(1) A financing statement may disclose an assignment of a security interest in the collateral described in the statement by indication in the statement of the name and address of the assignee or by an assignment itself or a copy thereof on the face or back of the statement. Either the original secured party or the assignee may sign this statement as the secured party. On presentation to the filing officer of such a financing statement the filing officer shall mark the same as provided in Section 9—403(4). The uniform fee for filing, indexing and furnishing filing data for a financing statement so indicating an assignment shall be $ . . . .

(2) A secured party may assign of record all or a part of his rights under a financing statement by the filing of a separate written statement of assignment signed by the secured party of record and setting forth the name of the secured party of record and the debtor, the file number and the date of filing of the financing statement and the name and address of the assignee and containing a description of the collateral assigned. A copy of the assignment is sufficient as a separate statement if it complies with the preceding sentence. On presentation to the filing officer of such a separate statement, the filing officer shall mark such separate statement with the date and hour of the filing. He shall note the assignment on the index of the financing statement. The uniform fee for filing, indexing and furnishing filing data about such a separate statement of assignment shall be $ . . . .

(3) After the disclosure or filing of an assignment under this section, the assignee is the secured party of record.

Section 9—406. Release of Collateral; Duties of Filing Officer; Fees.

A secured party of record may by his signed statement release all or a part of any collateral described in a filed financing statement. The statement of release is sufficient if it contains a description of the collateral being released, the name and address of the debtor, the name and address of the secured party, and the file number of the financing statement. Upon presentation of such a statement to the filing officer, he shall mark the statement with the hour and date of filing and shall note the same upon the margin of the index of the filing of the financing statement. The uniform fee for filing and noting such a statement of release shall be $.........

[Section 9—407. Information from Filing Officer.

(1) If the person filing any financing statement, termination statement, statement of assignment, or statement of release, furnishes the filing officer a copy thereof, the filing officer shall upon request note upon the copy the file number and date and hour of the filing of the original and deliver or send the copy to such person.

(2) Upon request of any person, the filing officer shall issue his certificate showing whether there is on file on the date and hour stated therein, any presently effective financing statement naming a particular debtor and any statement of assignment thereof and if there is, giving the date and hour of filing of each such statement and the names and addresses of each secured party therein. The uniform fee for such a certificate shall be $........ plus $........ for each financing statement and for each statement of assignment reported therein. Upon request the filing officer shall furnish a copy of any filed financing statement or statement of assignment for a uniform fee of $........ per page.

Note: *This new section is proposed as an optional provision to require filing officers to furnish certificates. Local law and practices should be consulted with regard to the advisability of adoption.*

PART 5

DEFAULT

Section 9—501. Default; Procedure When Security Agreement Covers Both Real and Personal Property.

(1) When a debtor is in default under a security agreement, a secured party has the rights and remedies provided in this Part and, except as limited by subsection (3), those provided in the security agreement. He may reduce his claim to judgment, foreclose or otherwise enforce the security interest by any available judicial procedure. If the collateral is documents, the secured party may proceed either as to the documents or as to the goods covered thereby. A secured party in possession has the rights, remedies and duties provided in Section 9—207. The rights and remedies referred to in this subsection are cumulative.

(2) After default, the debtor has the rights and remedies provided in this Part, those provided in the security agreement and those provided in Section 9—207.

(3) To the extent that they give rights to the debtor and impose duties on the secured party, the rules stated in the subsections referred to below may not be waived or varied except as provided with respect to compulsory disposition of collateral (subsection (1) of Section 9—505) and with respect to redemption of collateral (Section 9—506) but the parties may by agreement determine the standards by which the fulfillment of these rights and duties is to be measured if such standards are not manifestly unreasonable:

(a) subsection (2) of Section 9—502 and subsection (2) of Section 9—504 insofar as they require accounting for surplus proceeds of collateral;

(b) subsection (3) of Section 9—504 and subsection (1) of Section 9—505 which deal with disposition of collateral;

(c) subsection (2) of Section 9—505 which deals with acceptance of collateral as discharge of obligation;

(d) Section 9—506 which deals with redemption of collateral; and

(e) subsection (1) of Section 9—507 which deals with the secured party's liability for failure to comply with this Part.

(4) If the security agreement covers both real and personal property, the secured party may proceed under this Part as to the personal property or he may proceed as to both the real and the personal property in accordance with his rights and remedies in respect of the real property in which case the provisions of this Part do not apply.

(5) When a secured party has reduced his claim to judgment, the lien of any levy which may be made upon his collateral by virtue of any execution based upon the judgment shall relate back to the date of the perfection of the security interest in such collateral. A judicial sale, pursuant to such execution, is a foreclosure of the security interest by judicial procedure within the meaning of this section, and the secured party may purchase at the sale and thereafter hold the collateral free of any other requirements of this Article.

Section 9—502. Collection Rights of Secured Party.

(1) When so agreed and in any event on default, the secured party is entitled to notify an account debtor or the obligor on an instrument to make payment to him whether or not the assignor was theretofore making collections on the collateral, and also to take control of any proceeds to which he is entitled under Section 9—306.

(2) A secured party who by agreement is entitled to charge back uncollected collateral or otherwise to full or limited recourse against the debtor and who undertakes to collect from the account debtors or obligors must proceed in a commercially reasonable manner and may deduct his reasonable expenses of realization from the collections. If the security agreement secures an indebtedness, the secured party must account to the debtor for any surplus, and unless otherwise agreed, the debtor is liable for any deficiency. But, if the underlying transaction was a sale of accounts, contract rights, or chattel paper, the debtor is entitled to any surplus or is liable for any deficiency only if the security agreement so provides.

Section 9—503. Secured Party's Right to Take Possession After Default.

Unless otherwise agreed a secured party has on default the right to take possession of the collateral. In taking possession a secured party may proceed without judicial process if this can be done without breach of the peace or may proceed by action. If the security agreement so provides, the secured party may require the debtor to assemble the collateral and make it available to the secured party at a place to be designated by the secured party which is reasonably convenient to both parties. Without removal a secured party may render equipment unusable, and may dispose of collateral on the debtor's premises under Section 9—504.

Section 9—504. Secured Party's Right to Dispose of Collateral After Default; Effect of Disposition.

(1) A secured party after default may sell, lease or otherwise dispose of any or all of the collateral in its then condition or following any commercially reasonable preparation or processing. Any sale of goods is subject to the Article on Sales (Article 2). The proceeds of disposition shall be applied in the order following to

(a) the reasonable expenses of retaking, holding, preparing for sale, selling and the like and, to the extent provided for in the agreement and not prohibited by law, the reasonable attorneys' fees and legal expenses incurred by the secured party;

(b) the satisfaction of indebtedness secured by the security interest under which the disposition is made;

(c) the satisfaction of indebtedness secured by any subordinate security interest in the collateral if written notification of demand therefor is received before distribution of the proceeds is completed. If requested by the secured party, the holder of a subordinate security interest must seasonably furnish reasonable proof of his interest, and unless he does so, the secured party need not comply with his demand.

(2) If the security interest secures an indebtedness, the secured party must account to the debtor for any surplus, and, unless otherwise agreed, the debtor is liable for any deficiency. But if the underlying transaction was a sale of accounts, contract rights, or chattel paper, the debtor is entitled to any surplus or is liable for any deficiency only if the security agreement so provides.

(3) Disposition of the collateral may be by public or private proceedings and may be made by way of one or more contracts. Sale or other disposition may be as a unit or in parcels and at any time and place and on any terms, but every aspect of the disposition including the method, manner, time, place and terms must be commercially reasonable. Unless collateral is perishable or threatens to decline speedily in value or is of a type customarily sold on a recognized market, reasonable notification of the time and place of any public sale or reasonable notification of the time after which any private sale or other intended disposition is to be made shall be sent by the secured party to the debtor, and except in the case of consumer goods to any other person who has a security interest in the collateral and who has duly

filed a financing statement indexed in the name of the debtor in this state or who is known by the secured party to have a security interest in the collateral. The secured party may buy at any public sale and if the collateral is of a type customarily sold in a recognized market or is of a type which is the subject of widely distributed standard price quotations, he may buy at private sale.

(4) When collateral is disposed of by a secured party after default, the disposition transfers to a purchaser for value all of the debtor's rights therein, discharges the security interest under which it is made and any security interest or lien subordinate thereto. The purchaser takes free of all such rights and interests even though the secured party fails to comply with the requirements of this Part or of any judicial proceedings

(a) in the case of a public sale, if the purchaser has no knowledge of any defects in the sale and if he does not buy in collusion with the secured party, other bidders or the person conducting the sale; or

(b) in any other case, if the purchaser acts in good faith.

(5) A person who is liable to a secured party under a guaranty, indorsement, repurchase agreement or the like and who receives a transfer of collateral from the secured party or is subrogated to his rights has thereafter the rights and duties of the secured party. Such a transfer of collateral is not a sale or disposition of the collateral under this Article.

Section 9—505. Compulsory Disposition of Collateral; Acceptance of the Collateral as Discharge of Obligation.

(1) If the debtor has paid sixty per cent of the cash price in the case of a purchase money security interest in consumer goods or sixty per cent of the loan in the case of another security interest in consumer goods, and has not signed after default a statement renouncing or modifying his rights under this Part, a secured party who has taken

possession of collateral must dispose of it under Section 9—504 and if he fails to do so within ninety days after he takes possession, the debtor at his option may recover in conversion or under Section 9—507(1) on secured party's liability.

(2) In any other case involving consumer goods or any other collateral a secured party in possession may, after default, propose to retain the collateral in satisfaction of the obligation. Written notice of such proposal shall be sent to the debtor and except in the case of consumer goods to any other secured party who has a security interest in the collateral and who has duly filed a financing statement indexed in the name of the debtor in this state or is known by the secured party in possession to have a security interest in it. If the debtor or other person entitled to receive notification objects in writing within thirty days from the receipt of the notification or if any other secured party objects in writing within thirty days after the secured party obtains possession, the secured party must dispose of the collateral under Section 9—504. In the absence of such written objection the secured party may retain the collateral in satisfaction of the debtor's obligation.

Section 9—506. Debtor's Right to Redeem Collateral.

At any time before the secured party has disposed of collateral or entered into a contract for its disposition under Section 9—504 or before the obligation has been discharged under Section 9—505(2) the debtor or any other secured party may unless otherwise agreed in writing after default redeem the collateral by tendering fulfillment of all obligations secured by the collateral as well as the expenses reasonably incurred by the secured party in retaking, holding and preparing the collateral for disposition, in arranging for the sale, and to the extent provided in the agreement and not prohibited by law, his reasonable attorney's fees and legal expenses.

Section 9—507. Secured Party's Liability for Failure to Comply with This Part.

(1) If it is established that the secured party is not proceeding in accordance with the provisions of this Part, disposition may be ordered or restrained on appropriate terms and conditions. If the disposition has occurred, the debtor or any person entitled to notification or whose security interest has been made known to the secured party prior to the disposition has a right to recover from the secured party any loss caused by a failure to comply with the provisions of this Part. If the collateral is consumer goods, the debtor has a right to recover in any event an amount not less than the credit service charge plus ten per cent of the principal amount of the debt or the time price differential plus ten per cent of the cash price.

(2) The fact that a better price could have been obtained by a sale at a different time or in a different method from that selected by the secured party is not of itself sufficient to establish that the sale was not made in a commercially reasonable manner. If the secured party either sells the collateral in the usual manner in any recognized market therefor or if he sells at the price current in such market at the time of his sale or if he has otherwise sold in conformity with reasonable commercial practices among dealers in the type of property sold, he has sold in a commercially reasonable manner. The principles stated in the two preceding sentences with respect to sales also apply as may be appropriate to other types of disposition. A disposition which has been approved in any judicial proceeding or by any bona fide creditors' committee or representative of creditors shall conclusively be deemed to be commercially reasonable, but this sentence does not indicate that any such approval must be obtained in any case nor does it indicate that any disposition not so approved is not commercially reasonable.

ARTICLE 10

EFFECTIVE DATE AND REPEALER

Section 10—101. Effective Date.

This Act shall become effective at midnight on December 31st following its enactment. It applies to transactions entered into and events occurring after that date.

Section 10—102. Specific Repealer; Provision for Transition.

(1) The following acts and all other acts and parts of acts inconsistent herewith are hereby repealed:

(Here should follow the acts to be specifically repealed including the following:

    Uniform Negotiable Instruments Act

    Uniform Warehouse Receipts Act

    Uniform Sales Act

    Uniform Bills of Lading Act

    Uniform Stock Transfer Act

    Uniform Conditional Sales Act

    Uniform Trust Receipts Act

Also any acts regulating:

    Bank collections

    Bulk sales

    Chattel mortgages

    Conditional sales

    Factor's lien acts

    Farm storage of grain and similar acts

    Assignment of accounts receivable)

(2) Transactions validly entered into before the effective date specified in Section 10—101 and the rights, duties and interests flowing from them remain valid thereafter and may be terminated, completed, consummated or enforced as required or permitted by any statute or other law amended or repealed by this Act as though such repeal or amendment had not occurred.

Note

Subsection (1) should be separately prepared for each state. The foregoing is a list of statutes to be checked.

Section 10—103. General Repealer.

Except as provided in the following section, all acts and parts of acts inconsistent with this Act are hereby repealed.

Section 10—104. Laws Not Repealed.

[(1)] The Article on Documents of Title (Article 7) does not repeal or modify any laws prescribing the form or contents of documents of title or the services or facilities to be afforded by bailees, or otherwise regulating bailees' businesses in respects not specifically dealt with herein; but the fact that such laws are violated does not affect the status of a document of title which otherwise complies with the definition of a document of title (Section 1—201).

[(2) This Act does not repeal ...., cited as the Uniform Act for the Simplification of Fiduciary Security Transfers, and if in any respect there is any inconsistency between that Act and the Article of this Act on investment securities (Article 8) the provisions of the former Act shall control.]

Note: *At * in subsection (2) insert the statutory reference to the Uniform Act for the Simplification of Fiduciary Security Transfers if such Act has previously been enacted. If it has not been enacted, omit subsection (2).*